Computer Fundamentals and Information Technology

COMPUTER FUNDAMENTALS AND INFORMATION TECHNOLOGY

By

RAMESH BANGIA
B.Sc. Dip. Comp. Sc. (IIT D)
Formerly: Incharge Computer Centre,
Hindustan Copper Limited, New Delhi
Ex. Managing Editor: Software Today

FIREWALL MEDIA
(An Imprint of Laxmi Publications Pvt. Ltd.)
An ISO 9001:2008 Company
BENGALURU • CHENNAI • COCHIN • GUWAHATI • HYDERABAD
JALANDHAR • KOLKATA • LUCKNOW • MUMBAI • RANCHI • NEW DELHI
BOSTON (USA) • ACCRA (GHANA) • NAIROBI (KENYA)

COMPUTER FUNDAMENTALS AND INFORMATION TECHNOLOGY

Printed and bound in India

Typeset at : Goswami Associates, Delhi.

First Edition : 2009, *Second Edition* : 2016

ISBN : 978-81-318-0296-0

Branches

✆ **Bengaluru**	080-26 75 69 30
✆ **Chennai**	044-24 34 47 26
✆ **Cochin**	0484-237 70 04, 405 13 03
✆ **Guwahati**	0361-254 36 69, 251 38 81
✆ **Hyderabad**	040-27 55 53 83, 27 55 53 93
✆ **Jalandhar**	0181-222 12 72
✆ **Kolkata**	033-22 27 43 84
✆ **Lucknow**	0522-220 99 16
✆ **Mumbai**	022-24 91 54 15, 24 92 78 69
✆ **Ranchi**	0651-220 44 64

PUBLISHED IN INDIA BY

FIREWALL MEDIA

(An Imprint of Laxmi Publications Pvt. Ltd.)

An ISO 9001:2008 Company

113, GOLDEN HOUSE, DARYAGANJ, NEW DELHI-110002, INDIA

Telephone : 91-11-4353 2500, 4353 2501

Fax : 91-11-2325 2572, 4353 2528

www.laxmipublications.com   info@laxmipublications.com

C—11783/016/04

Printed at : N.K. Book Binder, Delhi.

Contents

Part - I

Part - I

Introduction to Computer and Information Technology

1

BRIEF HISTORY OF DEVELOPMENT OF COMPUTERS

Would you not like to know how the present day computers were invented? Well, they were not like these from very beginning. These have been developed over the years. In the early days people started exchanging goods and in this process they felt the need of counting. This was done with the help of stones. Each stone represented a single unit. Stones could be counted before giving or taking the things.

Next, they started drawing lines on wall or on sand before selling or purchasing the goods. It was a simple but a lengthy process for large numbers. So even this was abolished later.

Then in 3000 B.C., Abacus was invented by the **Chinese**. Later it was modified by **Egyptians** and **Indians**. Let us see how this **Abacus** looks like.

Abacus

It is a rectangular wooden frame with rods and rounded moveable beads which are used for counting. It has **10 rods** with **7 beads** in each. Each rod has 2 sections, upper and lower. In lower section there are 5 beads representing a single unit. Upper section has 2 beads representing number 5 each. The beads move on the rods from one end to other end and the resultant number is represented by the beads at the centre.

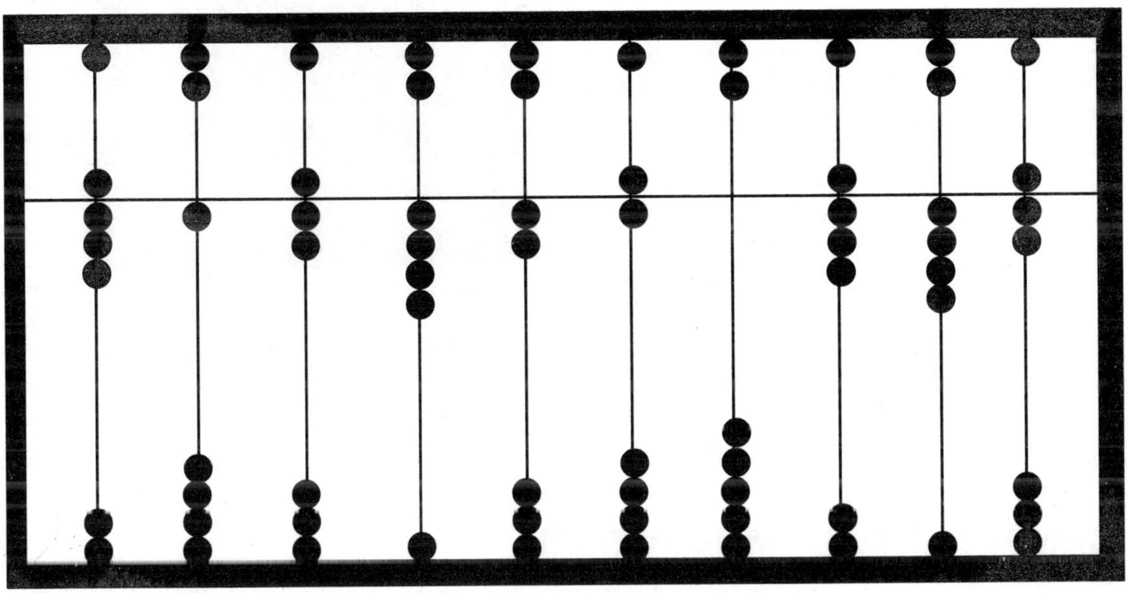

After this lots of developments took place. This is mentioned here year wise.

OTHER COMPUTER DEVELOPMENTS

1617- **John Napier** invented a machine which consisted of a set of numbered rods for doing multiplications. Each rod contained digits from 1 to 9.

1642- A famous French mathematician **Blaise Pascal** developed the first mechanical calculating machine. This machine had a number of teeth and wheels connected together by chains. Numbers were fed into the machine by dialing them on the wheels. It could add and do multiplications.

1671- Ad Gofried Leibrietzi – Modified or improved the Pascal's machine.

1792 – 1871 Charles Babbage, an English Mathematician, designed a machine, named **Difference Engine**. In 1833- 34, Babbage invented another machine with an automatic computing mechanism. He named it **Analytical Engine**. This machine could store the data in **Memory**, which became the base of Modern Computers. This is why he is known as the **Father of Computers.**

1880- **Herman Hollerith**, a mathematician, invented a Tabulating Machine by using punch cards for the census (calculation of population) in USA. The cards used to have holes for different answers. When these cards passed through this machine, the machine could detect holes on cards, recognize numbers and it could make required calculations.

1930-1939 During the IInd World War, Computers were utilized in military operations for decoding secret messages and creating designs for aircrafts. They were nicknamed **Z1** and **Z2** machines.

1940- IBM had made a computer and named it **Harvard Mark–I**. It worked electro mechanically without any manual efforts. It could perform three addition operations and one subtraction operation per second. As multiplication, it could perform one operation per second. It was a first computer and was also called **A**utomatic **S**equence **C**ontrolled **C**omputer (ASCC).

1946- **ENIAC** computer was developed in 1946. This was based on Mark 1, which was developed by **Howard Aitken** and **Grace Hopper** in 1930.

COMPUTER SYSTEM CONCEPTS

In broad terms it can be said that we feed into computers what is called raw data through the various input devices. The computer in turn processes it and gives the result through the various output devices. In fact a computer performs 4 operations to carry out the above activities.

Input/Output Operations

A computer can accept data (input) and supply information (output) to input/output devices.

Text Manipulation and Calculations

It can manipulate letters and other symbols used in words and sentences. It can also perform calculations on numbers.

Logic/Comparison Operations

A computer can perform logic operations, simple comparisons (comparing two data items) and then, depending upon the results, follows a predetermined course of action to complete its task.

Storage and Retrieval Operations

Data and program instructions can be stored internally in a computer. Stored program instructions can be stored internally in a computer. Stored programs or files may be quickly called for use.

Functional Components and Their Inter Connections

In all Computers have the same 6 groups of hardware components:

- Input Devices
- Output Devices
- Processor/Motherboard
- Storage Devices
- Adapters/peripherals
- Power supply

The above are discussed below. Some of them would be discussed in details later.

Input Devices

As per the name, these are used to input various form of data/information into the computer for processing purposes. These devices can be connected to the computer as your requirements. The most common one however, is the keyboard, which is a must.

Output Devices

These are used to show the result of the processing either on screen or in the printed form using the printer. Though monitor is a must, printer is optional. If you have to circulate the results in the printed form, then use printer, if only you have to see the results, see them on the screen only.

Processor/Motherboard

This is the main processing board. This is where the processing takes place. You must have heard about the speed of the computer, well this is the board which determines it. For example, a Pentium IV computer has a Pentium IV chip installed on the motherboard and thus the computer speed is that of Pentium IV.

Storage Devices

These are used to store the information or the data which is fed into the computer. Various types of devices are used according to the needs of the user. Most common among the one which is fixed is called the Hard Disk, which is a must for all the computers, since this is where the operating system of the computer is kept.

Among the removable ones are CD ROM, on which you can write data and remove it to read it in another computer or in the same computer at a later stage. But, to be able to write data on the CD-ROM, you need to have a CD Writer attached to your computer.

Adapters/Peripherals

You can attach as many peripherals to the computer as it can support. Among the various peripherals which you can add are Modem for accessing Internet maybe, Speakers for listening to music or even a

Tape back unit for backing up your data on the Tape. All of these need to have a driver which is put into the computer for accessing that particular drive or peripheral.

Power Supply

It is the integral part of the CPU. It is used to keep the various cards inside the CPU, cool. It has a fan in it which is used for this purpose.

COMPUTER SYSTEM CHARACTERISTICS

Speed

A computer is an electronic device in which electrical signals travel at the speed of light. So, a computer can perform operations at a high speed. It can add and subtract numbers, compare of letters to determine alphabetic sequence, move and copy numbers and letters. It can perform their hundreds of thousands of operations in a very short time. It never slows down and keep working at a uniform speed. Its speed is measured in microseconds (1 millionth second) and in even smaller units.

Computers provide the processing speed essential to our fast-paced society. The quick service we have come to expect - for bank withdrawals, telephone calls, and travel reservations, to name a few - is made possible by computers. Businesses depend on the speedy processing computers to handle high volume activities such as balancing ledgers and designing products.

The smallest unit of time in the human experience is, realistically, the second. Computer operations - for example, the execution of an instruction, such as multiplying pay-rate with numbers of hours worked - are measured in milliseconds, microsecond, nanoseconds and picoseconds (one thousandth, one millionth, one billionth, and one trillionth of a second respectively). Although all computers are fast, but there is a wide diversity of computer speeds. The execution of an instruction on a very slow computer may be measured in less than a millisecond. Most computer can execute an instruction measured in microseconds range, but still to be broken in the picosecond barrier.

A computer speed is generally expressed in megahertz (MHz), millions of machine cycles per second. Thus a PC (Personal Computer) listed at 100 MHz has a processor capable of handling 100 million machine cycles per second. Another measure of computer speed is MIPS (one million instructions per second). MIPS is often a more accurate measure than clock speed, because some computers can use each tick of the clock more efficiently than others. A third measure of speed is the megaflops (MFLOPS), which stands for one million floating point operations per second. It measures the ability of the computer to perform complex mathematical operations.

Accuracy

A computer is a 100% accurate machine. There are only two situations where a computer can give you wrong results. One is when the set of instructions given to the computer are wrong. The other is when the data fed to the computer is wrong. Errors do occur in computer based information systems, but precious few can be directly attributed to the computer system itself. The vast majority can be traced to a program logic error, a procedural error, or erroneous data. These are human errors.

High accuracy implies small error, but accuracy is contrasted with precision e.g. three places of decimals properly computed are less precise but more accurate than four places of decimals containing an error.

The accuracy of the results obtained from computer mainly depends on the method of programming and the way the results are interpreted.

Reliability

Computer output is generally very reliable, subject to the condition that the input data entered computer should be correct and the program of instructions should be reliable and correct. Incorrect input data and unreliable programs give us computer errors and wrong results. Hence, the phrase GARBAGE IN-GARBAGE OUT (GIGO).

Computers are extremely reliable. Where reliability is the measurement of the performance of a computer, measured against some predetermined standard for operation without the failure of it.

Reliability Of Computer = Serviceable Time/Serviceable Time + Down Time

where serviceable time is the total time during which a computer is in a state where it can operate normally, including time when the computer is idle, but not the time when it is unattended.

Down time is the time when a computer is inoperable due to a machine fault. Computer systems are particularly adept at repetitive tasks. They don't take sick leave and tea breaks, and they seldom complain anything below 99.9% serviceable time, the time when the computer system is in operation, is usually unacceptable. For some companies, any down time is unacceptable. These companies provide backup computers that take over automatically if the main computer fails.

Storage

A computer can store very large amount of data, information and instructions in its memory. All information is passed on to the memory is in the form of electrical signals. These electric signals are called BITS and all the information received by the computer is accepted by it. Each letter of the alphabet, number or symbol we use in represented by a group of eight bits called a BYTE. The size of the memory is measured in KILOBYTES. One kilobyte is equal to 1024 bytes and is written as 1k or 1Kb or 1Kbyte. A Megabyte (or MByte) is a million bytes.

Computer systems can store tremendous amounts of data, which can be located retrieved efficiently. A typical mainframe computer system will have many billions of characters stored and available for instant recall. High end PCs have access to about a billion characters of data.

Capability

Because computers can operate on data at such phenomenal speeds, they can produce results that would simply not be feasible otherwise. For example, computers can be used to provide management with up-to-the-minute figures on all aspects of its business. With this information, managers can make more meaningful decisions.

Similarly, computers enable companies to provide customers with instantaneous services, such as airline flight available and charge account status. The result is that these companies can offer far more customer services than would be possible without computer.

Deligence/Tirelessness

Computers output is very reliable, A computer never gets tired or board if it can do the same job again and again. Even if it has to do a million calculations, it will do the last one with the same speed and accuracy as the first one. Not only this, it can produce the data again and again on demand.

Intangible Benefits

There are many companies that utilize computers for intangible benefits such as flexibility, ability to accommodate growth and the psychological factor that may give them a competitive edge in attracting consumers to buy their products or services.

Reduced Cost

With the ever-increasing advances being made in the state of the art, the cost of computer equipment has dropped drastically over the years. Hardware costs have been decreasing at an estimated annual rate of

25%. Thus, companies that at one time could not justify the cost of acquiring their own computer system may now find it now only feasible to acquire a system, but cost-effective as well.

Automation

You can perform repetitive functions through the programs. Also, you can connect different stages through a program to be carried on automatically. Once the instructions have been given, a computer can carry on its job automatically till it is complete.

Versatility

A computer is capable of performing a large number of different jobs working logically step by step.

Memory Capability

Computer systems have the ability to recall of data because of secondary storage (a type of detachable memory) capability. Every piece of information can be recalled even after several years, he information recalled will be as accurate as on the day when it was fed to the computer.

No Feelings

Computers have no feelings and no instincts because they are machine. Computers cannot make such judgements on their own. Their judgement is based on the instructions given to them in the form of programs that are written by us. They are only as good as man makes and uses them.

CAPABILITIES AND LIMITATIONS

Despite being the most powerful machine available to us these days, the computer still has its own limitations. Some it does perform abnormally, due to some reasons or others which may be baffling to the users. To ensure that the computers work normally, we have to see that the following are taken care of:

Reliability of the Programs

The most common problems faced by computers come from the use of faulty software. These are the software which are usually called the Pirated software. One person buys the original software and makes copies of them for others to use. It is possible that while copying something or the other is missed and you would not know about it immediately. Most of the popular computer software are subjected to the vigorous tests before releasing in public. It can be possible that a particular eventuality is not taken care of and that occurs for some unknown reason. This can give problem.

Logic of the Program

Computer works on logic, if your logic is wrong, it will give bad results. It is like chess, where making a move you have to mentally sit on the opposite side and think of all the possible moves, before making your own move. Similarly, a program has to look into all the possible situations.

TYPES OF COMPUTERS

On the basis of the usage of data (i.e., discrete or continuous) computers can be classified as:

1. Analog computers
2. Digital Computers
3. Hybrid Computers

Analog Computers

Analog computers are in which numerical magnitudes are represented by physical quantities, such as electric current, voltage or resistance, mechanical movements etc. Analog computers accepts data and then process it to produce analog data.

Analog computer are machines designed to perform arithmetical functions upon numbers where the numbers are represented by physical quantity. For example, in mechanical analog computers the number are often represented by physical dimensions of the members forming the various functional units for instance by the angular rotation of the shaft or gear wheels.

In electrical analog machines voltages are used to represent the input variables.

Essentially an analog computer must be able to accept inputs which vary with respect to time, and directly apply these inputs to various devices within the computer which perform the computing operations of addition, subtraction, multiplication, division and integration. The output from the system may be in the form of a graph produced by a plotting pen or a trace on a cathode-ray tube. The computing units of analog computers are able to respond immediately to the changes which they detect in the input variable and the connection of these various units in a particular fashion can cause an analog computer to perform very complex arithmetical functions at high speed while the actual process under study is in operation.

The ability to operate in real time mode means that analog computers has many application in the scientific and industrial fields in simulating various physical systems or automatically controlling industrial processes. They are widely used for research into design problems. Analog computers are used in manufacturing units where temperatures, pressure or flow of liquids are to be monitored continuously. It also used at service station where gasoline pump contains an analog processor that connect fuel flow measurements into quantity and price values.

Drawbacks

1. Analog computers do not have the ability of digital computers to store data in large quantities.
2. They do not have the logical facilities afforded by programming digital machines.
3. Although the arithmetic functions performed by the computing units are more complex in analog machines than in the digital systems, the cost of the hardware required to provide a high degree of accuracy in an analog machine is often prohibitive.

Digital Computers

A digital computer operates on data in the form of digits, rather than the physical quantities used in analog computers. That is, its input must be discrete rather than continuous and may consist of combinations of numbers, characters and special symbols, written in appropriate programming language. Computers generate digital signals representing bit patterns, whereas standard telephone lines were designed to handle analog signals in the form of voices and other sound patterns to use telephone for data communication digital signals need to be converted to an analog format.

Originally digital computers were mechanical devices employing cogs, gears and levers, they now depend upon electronic technique enabling them to deal automatically with a wide range of problems at a very high speeds. Some of the earlier digital computing devices were developed from punched card machines and the program was set up by means of connections on a plugboard, machines of this category are generally referred to as calculators, rather than computers.

Modern digital computers are usually based on the binary notation, numbers and letters being coded into group of digits consisting only of 1 or 0. Each of these digits is represented in an electronic circuit or magnetic store by a component in an on or off state. For example, passing current or not passing current, magnetized or not magnetized. Data in this form is processed in the CPU of the computer by gates (switches) which obey the instructions of the program.

The individual operations performed by a digital computer are very simple arithmetic or logical processes involving the manipulation of the bits in words or characters of information. The great power of any digital computer rets in the ability to store large volumes of data and to perform these various functions at extremely high speed. Arithmetic and logical circuits for processing data in binary form are constructed from simple basic units designed to perform the operations of Boolean algebra AND, OR, NOT etc. These simple units are used as building blocks in constructing the complex logic and control circuits required.

Classification Of Digital Computers

Digital computer can be classified into two parts :

General Purpose Digital Computer

It is also known as all purpose digital computer. Theoretically it can be used for any type of application. e.g., computers that are used for payroll, graphs, analysis etc.

Special Purpose Digital Computers

A digital computer designed to solve problems of a restricted type. That is, special-purpose digital computer is designed to be especially efficient in a certain class of applications. For example, computers installed in washing machines.

Hybrid Computers

Hybrid computer is the outcome of the integration of analog computer components and digital computer components. This integration is obtained by digital-to-analog converter and analog to digital converter. A hybrid computer may use or produce analog data or digital data. It accepts a continuously varying input which is then converted into a set of discrete values for digital processing. Digital processing is considerably faster and more sophisticated than analog processing. The basic objective of hybrid computer is to obtain for the user the best properties of the two computing philosophies (i.e., digital and analog).

In analog computer data is handled in a continuous form and this permits true real time operation. Such systems can perform mathematical operations viz., integration with speed and ease, and have great potential for tackling on-line simulation exercises, model building and forecasting. On the other hand they are not as accurate as digital computers, and have a very limited form of memory and less developed logical processes than digital computers.

The digital computer has large memory capacity and can perform logical operation easily. Digital machine is more accurate than the analog machine and it can perform complex mathematical function but only through interactive routines. A hybrid computer can be obtained either by interconnecting a digital and analog computer via a hybrid interface or the analog unit is integrated as a part of the central processor of a digital computer which ultimately helps in getting input/output directly. The digital unit is able to exert control over the analog computer by means of instructions stored in the digital memory. These instructions can control the operation mode of the hardware units in the analog section, while the analog machine can interrupt the digital computer to initiate input/output operations. This type of system combines the properties of the true analog system with the accuracy, reliability, memory capacity and programming flexibility of the digital system.

Hybrid Machines are generally used in scientific applications or in controlling industrial processes, in both situations the user is able to exploit the machine's ability to process both discrete and continuous data using accurate digital subroutines where necessary and the analog machines for fast integration functions.

Classification of Computer by Size

Computers come in sizes from tiny to monstrous, in both appearance and power. The size of a computer that a person or an organization needs depends on the computing environments. Clearly, the National Weather service provided by Meteorological Department of India keeping watch on the weather fronts of many continents has requirements different from those of a two wheeler dealer's service department that is trying to keep track of its parts inventory. And the requirements of both of them are different from the needs of a salesperson using a small laptop computer to record client orders on a sales trip.

In general the classification of computers can be characterized by cost, size, storage capacity, number of users and processing speed. In many cases, there is a considerable amount of overlapping of these characteristics. So broadly, computers can be classified as

Super Computers

Mainframe Computers

Mini Computers

Workstations

Micro Computers or Personal Computers

Supercomputers, the biggest of all, have greater computing capacities than mainframe computers.

Mainframe computers have grater computing capacities than minicomputers and Minicomputers have greater computing capacities than microcomputers. Rapid advances in computer technology have blurred what used to be distinguishing characteristics (physical size, cost, memory capacity and so on).

Super Computers

The speed of a computer is limited by two things,

1. the switching time
2. the time taken by an electric pulse to go from one part of the computer to another.

The Switching time may be thought of as the time a transistor takes to go from a conducting state to nonconducting state or vice versa. Since the switching time is now only of one thousand millionth of a second, the time an electric pulse takes to travel from one part of the computer to another is becoming a more serious limitation. Nothing can travel faster than the speed of light and light can only travel one foot in a thousand millionth of a second. Thus it is not feasible to increase the speed of sequential computer (e.g. PCs, mainframe etc.) made with a single processor beyond a limit. The only alternative for achieving higher speed of computing is to use many processors to work in parallel. Also it is very important that everything is made as small as possible and the memory does not require too much space.

One of the problems with packing a very large numbers of silicon chips into a small space is that they use power and this means a lot of heat is generated in this space. An elaborate cooling system is a very important part of a supercomputer.

Drawbacks

Supercomputers are designed using multiprocessing to achieve much faster processing speed than mainframe, but they use this processing power to work on just one complex problem at a time instead of sharing processing time with many users, for example in meteorological department the fast processing speed of a supercomputer is used for a single purpose - forecasting the weather.

One of the problems of building computers of so much power is the tremendous amount of heat created by the machine. Every one of the major manufacturers of supercomputer, tackles this problem by cooling its machine with liquid coolants. Cray also designs some of their computers in a special curved shape that helps the machines to dissipate the heat generated by certain components.

Uses

Model Global Weather: Both long and short term weather forecasts require solution of large sets of non-linear partial differential equations. For short range forecasts these equations are to be solved in a very short time, based on measured values communicated to the forecasting centre, so that forecast are meaningful. Hundred of MFLOPS speed and large memory size have been found essential to solve such real time weather forecast.

Scientists build models of a computer processes and simulate the process in a supercomputer. One such process is nuclear fission. As a fissionable material approaches a critical mass, scientist want to know exactly what will happen during every millisecond of a nuclear chain reaction. A supercomputer is used to model the actions and reactions of literally millions of atoms as they interact.

There is a need of supercomputer to solve multivariate mathematical problems of real physical processes, occurring in disciplines such a aerodynamics, seismology, metrology and plasma physics. Oil companies use supercomputers for petroleum exploration by analyzing rock formation and samples. Military strategists use supercomputers to simulate defence scenarios. Cinematic specialists use them to produce sophisticated movie animations. Supercomputer has limited use and because of its price tag, limited market. Only a few dozen of these machines are operational in India, mostly at research centres of some government agencies.

The largest commercial users of supercomputers are in the entertainment/advertising industry.

Examples of Supercomputers

CRAY - 3 (Control Data Corporation)

Cyber 205 (ETA Systems Incorporation)

PRAM (INDIA)

Supercomputers are able to reach the large volume and speed performances for beyond the theoretical limits of mainframes by using parallel processing, pipeline processing and vector processing.

The speed at which computer operate, as measured by the number of basic operations performed per second, has undergone rapid and continual improvement. This has been mainly due to improvement in the technology of computing circuits and memory devices. It can be concluded that the computer speed has increased linearly by factor of about 100 per decade since 1930. It is widely believed that the rate of increase in computer speed due to technology improvements in diminishing, which suggests that significant increases in speed can come only from improved algorithms or heuristics. For example, we can see that the rate of increase of the speed of the basic electronic circuits used in supercomputer has been relatively slow. For instance the arithmetic processor of CRAY - 1 supercomputer built in 1978 took 12nsec to add two floating point numbers whereas that of CRAY - YMP built in 1988 took 6nsec. But from this we cannot conclude that there is no future for supercomputer.

Now supercomputers are moving towards the mainstream, for activities as varied as stock analysis, automobile design, special effects for movies and even sophisticated artwork. CRAY RESEARCH and ETA SYSTEMS, INC., firms located in the Minneapolis are two primary builders of supercomputer in the United States. Nippon Electric Co., Hitachi are Japanese Supercomputer builders. India is also present in the field of building supercomputer. India's first supercomputer built was named as PARAM.

Mainframe Computers

Next step down from supercomputers, in terms of speed and storage capacity are mainframes. Mainframes are large, relatively expensive machines that offer extensive problem-solving capabilities. It can have memory capacities measured in gigabytes and more. The largest mainframes can process well over 100 MIPS. Their operating systems usually handle multiple applications within a timesharing environment.

This provides many users with the ability to perform different processing tasks Data storage is primarily on hard disks, with tapes used as backup. Mainframe is a large computer, in particular one to which other computers can be connected so that they can share facilities the mainframe provides. e.g; a System/370 computing system to which personal computers are attached so that they can upload and download programs and data.

The term mainframe usually refers to hardware only : main storage, execution circuitry and peripheral units. Mainframe word-length may be 48, 60 or 64 bits. It has got a system memory (ie; RAM) of 64 to 256 MB, hard disk of capacity 1 -10 GB or more and processing speed of 30 - 100 Millions of Instructions per seconds. A substantial amount of peripherals can be attached to mainframe computer.

Mainframe computers are designed to handle tremendous amount of input, output and storage. Mainframe computers often act as host computers i.e., computers that serve as central receiving and switching computers in regional or national computer networks. Mainframe act as a database server, that is, the database is controlled by mainframe computer that can handle the input and output needs of all terminals connected to it.

Uses

Mainframe computers are used in research organizations, large industrial banks, airline and railway reservations where large data base is required. Insurance companies use mainframe to process millions of policies.

Mainframe can serve as the heart of a teleprocessing system with remote connections all over the world.

Examples of Mainframe

IBM 4300, IBM 308 X, IBM 3090

HP 9000 - 8705/400

VAX 8842

Minicomputers

The next step down from mainframe computers, in terms of speed and storage capacity are minicomputers. It is an intermediate - size computer that can perform the same kind of applications as a mainframe but has less storage capacity, processing power and speed than a mainframe.

It is functionally intermediate between a microcomputer and a mainframe. Minicomputers are floor-standing or desktop devices, frequently connected to a mainframe to perform subsidiary operations. They are priced for purchase by smaller businesses and are sufficiently compact to be located in a typical office environment. When Digital Equipment Corporation (DEC) began shipping its PDP series computer in the early 1960s the press dubbed these machines, minicomputers, because of their small size compared to other computers of the day.

Some minicomputers are uniprocessor systems whereas some are multiprocessor system. The processing speed lies in the range 10 30 MIPS. Memory capacity lies in the range of 8 - 256 MB and can easily range into gigabytes of temporary storage. Minicomputers have operating systems with multitasking and network capabilities enabling them to serve more than one user. It serves as a centralized storehouse for cluster of workstations or as a network server. For example, a team of architects working on different subsystem within the same building could be directly linked to the office minicomputer that maintains everyone's files and documentation. A mini computer can support more than 100 terminals. Generally, the processing speeds and related capabilities of minicomputers exceed those of microcomputers and more peripheral devices can be attached to them. Minicomputer also tend to have more sophisticated operating systems than microcomputers and can usually be programmed in a wider variety of programming languages.

Supermini

The term supermini has been coined to describe minis at the top of the size-price scale. It is a large minicomputer. Physically it is a 32-bit minicomputer which support more simultaneous users (one hundred or more) and more peripheral devices and large memories than previous minicomputer.

Advantages of Minicomputers

- Its affordability ie., cost effectiveness small businesses that were unable to purchase an expensive central computer in past have found that they can now afford to purchase minicomputers.
- It is commonly used as dedicated computers ie., used exclusively for one processing function. For example, for program development or payroll preparation.

The major minicomputer manufacturers include DEC, Data General, IBM and HewlettPackard.

Workstations

Between minicomputers and microcomputer in terms of processing power is a class of computers known as workstations. A workstation looks like a personal computer and is typically used by only one person, much as is a personal computer. Although workstations are still more powerful than the average personal computer, the difference is the capabilities of these types of machines.

Microcomputers And Personal Computers

The microcomputer is a scaled-down version of the mainframe. Microcomputer is a digital computer whose processing unit consists of one or more microprocessors, one or more input/output units and sufficient memory to execute instructions. The essential components of a microcomputer are often contained within a single enclosure. Microcomputers are usually desktop or portable devices with a display, a keyboard and tape disk and diskette storage, they are designed primarily for stand-alone operation but can be used as workstations in terminal emulation mode. Every microcomputer is capable of performing jobs once handled by only the largest computers. A typical microcomputer memory unit stores upto 64 MB of data. Processing speeds of microcomputer are measured in megahertz instead of MIPS. A microcomputer running at 90 MHz is faster than one running at 33 MHz and works at approximately 90 MIPS.

The terms microcomputer and personal computer are interchangeable however, PC-which stands for personal computer-has a more specific meaning. In 1981, IBM called its first microcomputer the IBM PC. Within a few years, many companies were copying the IBM design creating "clones" or "compatibles" that aimed at functioning just like the original. For this reason, the term PC has come to mean the family of computers that includes IBMs and compatibles.

Personal computer is a type of microcomputer primarily intended for stand-alone use by an individual. It is a desktop, floor - standing or portable microcomputer that usually consists of a system unit a display monitor, a keyboard, one or more diskette drives, internal hard disk storage, and an optional printer. PCs are designed primarily to give independent computing power to a single user and are inexpensively priced for purchase by individuals or small businesses. A few of the major personal computer manufacturers are APPLE, IBM, Compaq, Dell, AST and Hewlett-Packard.

Supermicros: The upper-end machines used by workers such as engineers, financial traders and graphics designers are small enough to fit on a desk top but approach the power of a mainframe.

Laptops

In recent years design changes have reduced the size of some microcomputers, making computer technology portable and affordable.

Laptop computers are roughly the size of a large notebook. Their power source - a battery- is completely self-contained yet can be recharged from an electrical outlet. Laptops, sometimes called notebook computers, can contains more than 500 MB of hard disk memory, 16+MB of RAM, floppy disk drives, keyboard, mouse and a colour monitor. Power adapters can be used to plug into any electrical outlet throughout the world. It can be connected with an additional battery or serial port, a network or fax equipment. Laptops are not as inexpensive as their size might suggests, many carry a price tag equivalent to full-size personal computer for business.

Palmtop Computer

Small enough to hold in one hand and operate with the other. Palmtops may have specialized keyboards or keypads for data entry applications or have small qwerty keyboards.

Notebook Computer

Portable computer that typically weighs less than six pounds (heavier than a pocket computer; lighter than a laptop).

GENERATION OF COMPUTERS

Computer generations can be derived on the basis of the various methods used in the making of the computer.

	Generations	*Based on*	*Period*
(i)	First Generation	**Electronic Valves**	1950
(ii)	Second Generation	**Transistors**	1960
(iii)	Third Generation	**Integrated Circuits**	1965
(iv)	Fourth Generation	**Microprocessors**	1975
(v)	Fifth Generation	**Large Scale Integrated Systems**	1980

First Generation Computers

J.P. Eckert and J.W. Muchly developed the first electronic computer known as ENIAC. The other computers which come into this category are NIVAC, EDVAC, UNIVAC etc.

Second Generation Computers

Second Generation Computers were based on transistor (transfer resistor) technology which replaced the vacuum tubes. Examples of second generation computers are: UNIVAC 1108, IBM 700, 1401, CDC-1604, 3600.

Third Generation Computers

The transistors used in second generation were then replaced with Integrated Circuits (ICs) or chip. Example: IBM –360, 370, ICL–1900.

Fourth Generation Computers

These computers were based upon the development of Large Scale Integration (LSI). Examples: INTEL 4004 Apple Series I and II, Spectrum 7.

Fifth Generation Computers

Fifth Generation Computers focused on connectivity. This method of connecting of computers is called Networking.

PERSONAL COMPUTERS

Personal Computers were introduced by International Business Machine (IBM) in 1981. IBM has brought out different versions/models with variations of floppy disks, hard disks, chips etc. making them faster and faster.

The various versions of IBM PC computers are:

Model	RAM Chip	Type of Chip	Floppy Drive 5¼"	Floppy Drive 3½"	Hard Disk
PC	640 K	8088	2	Nil	Nil
PC-XT	640 K	8088	1	Nil	20 MB
PC-AT/286	1028 K	80286	1	1	40 MB
PC-AT/386	4 MB	80386	1	1	120 MB
PC-AT/486	8 MB	80486	1	1	260 MB
PC-Pentium	16 MB	Pentium	Nil	1	720 MB
PC-PIII	32 MB	Pentium–III	Nil	1	4.3 GB
PC-PIV	128 MB	Pentium - IV	Nil	1	40 GB
PC-PV	512 MB	Pentium - V	Nil	1	80 GB

To understand the various terms used in the table, it is important to know the following terms:

1 byte	=	1 character (0 to 9 or a to z or a special character like $)
1 Kilobyte (KB)	=	1,000 Bytes approx.
1 Megabyte (MB)	=	1,000 Kilobytes approx.
1 Gigabyte (GB)	=	1,000 Megabytes approx.

NEWER PCs

Among the newer computers are the PCs with more than 1GB of memory, about 100 GB of Hard Disk, with all the new features of Internet connections like Wireless Internet, etc. High speed CD writer with DVD capabilities, etc..

Multiple Choice Questions

1. Herman Hollerith invented a tabulating Machine which used:
   (a) Punch cards (b) Memory
   (c) Teeth and wheels
2. Tabulating machine was invented in
   (a) 1940 (b) 1880
   (c) 1671
3. First generation computers was developed by
   (a) J.P.Eckert (b) J.W.Muchly
   (c) Both
4. Second generation computers were based on
   a) Transistors
   (b) Integrated (Circuits)
   (c) Electronic Valves
5. Pascal's machine was modified by
   (a) John Napier (b) Charles Babbage
   (c) Ad-Gofried Leibrietzi
6. John Napier's machine contained digits from
   (a) 1 – 9 (b) 0 – 9
   (c) 1 – 10
7. ENIAC computer was developed in
   (a) 1930 (b) 1946
   (c) 1940
8. Fifth generation computers were based on
   (a) Microprocessors
   (b) Integrated Circuits
   (c) Large Scale Integrated Systems
9. ENIAC computers was based on
   (a) Mark – 1 (b) Memory
   (c) Z2 machines
10. Personal Computers were introduced by
    (a) IBM
    (b) Apple Computers
    (c) Grace Hooper

Descriptive Type Questions

1. Who developed Abacus.
2. How does Abacus works?
3. What is the use of Rods and Beads in Abacus?
4. Write a short note on the followings:
   Napier Bones Pascal's Calculator
   Leirnitz's Machine
   Jacquard's Loom Difference Engine
   Lady Ada Lovelace
   Boolean Algebra Hollerith Machines
   Electro-Mechanical Computers
   EDSAC EDVAC
   UNIVAC
   LEO Analog Computer
   Hybrid Computers
   The ALTAIR 8800
5. What is a Digital Computer?
6. What are the drawbacks of Analog Computers?
7. Write down some basic features of Super Computers.
8. What are the drawbacks of Super Computers?
9. What are the uses of Super Computers?
10. What are the uses of Main Frame Computers?
11. What are the uses of Mini Computers?
12. What are Workstations?
13. What are the Characteristics of Computers.
14. What is a Lap Top?
15. Write Short notes on the following:
    First Generation Computers
    Second Generation Computers
    Third Generation Computers
    Speed
    Accuracy
    Rcliability
    Storage
    Capability
16. Classify the computers according to their size.

2 Computer Organization and Working

INTRODUCTION

Central Processing Unit is a computer's brain and is a place where data are manipulated. In a microcomputer, the entire CPU is contained on a tiny chip called a microprocessor. Every CPU has at least three parts:

1. Control Unit
2. Arithmetic-Logic Unit
3. Memory

The parts of the CPU are usually connected by an electronic component referred to as bus.

THE CONTROL UNIT

Just as the processor is the nucleus of a computer system, the control unit is the nucleus of the processor. The control unit contains circuitry that uses electrical signals to direct the entire computer system to carry out or execute stored program instructions. The instruction set, which is built into the circuitry of the control unit is a list of operations that CPU can perform e.g.; ADD, SUB, DIV, JUMP etc. The control unit does not execute instruction itself, but it tells others what to do.

The function of the control unit is to coordinate all the computer's activities, for this all the instructions and data are sent along wires or bus lines. The bus is the path (circuitry) that connects the CPU with internal and external components. Peripheral hardware is connected to CPU (i.e.; control unit) through the expansion bus.

The control unit has three primary functions:

1. To read and interpret program instructions
2. To direct the operation of internal processor components
3. To control the flow of programs and data in and out of RAM

A program must first be loaded to RAM before it can be executed. During execution, the first in a sequence of program instructions is moved from RAM to the control unit, where it is decoded and interpreted by the **decoder**. The control unit then directs other processor components to carry out the operations necessary to execute the instruction.

The control unit contains high-speed **working storage** areas called registers, which are temporary storage and can store no more than a few bytes. Registers handle instructions and data at a speed about 10 times faster than the register, called the **instruction register**, contains the instruction being executed. Other general-purpose registers store data needed for immediate processing and also store status information. For example, the **program register** (counter) contains the RAM address of the next instruction to be executed. Registers facilitate the movement of data and instructions between RAM, the control unit, and the arithmetic and logic unit. Registers are not a part of memory; rather they are special additional storage locations that offer the advantage of speed. They work under the direction of the control unit to accept, hold and transfer instructions or data and perform arithmetic or logical comparison at high speed.

Most computer use several types of registers. Inspite of variation in the number of registers in different computers. These are some registers which are common to all computers. These are:

1. An **accumulator**, which collects the result of computations. It also holds the initial data to be operated upon. In many computers there are more than one accumulator.
2. A **general-purpose register**, which is used for several functions e.g.; arithmetic operations.
3. A **program register**, which keeps track of where a given instruction or piece of data is stored in memory. Each storage location in memory is identified by an address.
4. A **decoder**, decoders and interprets the instruction given to computer through input.
5. A **memory address register** (MAR) contains the address of a word currently required.
6. A **memory buffer register** (MBR) is used for storing a word as it is read from memory or just prior to being written into memory.

When the computer runs a program it looks upto the commands contained in the program in the CPUs instruction set and execute them in order. CPUs that are made by different companies (viz., Intel, Cyrix, Motorola) have different instruction sets.

THE ARITHMETIC-LOGIC UNIT:

The arithmetic-logic unit (ALU) contains the electronic circuitry that executes all arithmetic and logical operations.

Arithmetic operations

The ALU unit can perform four kinds of arithmetic operations:

1. Addition,
2. Subtraction,
3. Multiplication, and
4. Division

All the arithmetic a computer performs is, essentially, addition. The computers can add two numbers to obtain a sum. Subtraction is actually negative addition, multiplication is repeated addition, and division is repeated negative addition. For example, a computer will use addition to find solutions of the following problems.

Subtraction	**Multiplication**	**Division**
9 – 3 = n	9 x 3 = n	9 / 3 = n
9 + (–3) = 6	9 + 9 + 9 = 27	9 + (-3) + (-3) + (-3) = 0

In the division computation the computer determines the answer (3) by counting the number of -3s that must be added before 0 is reached. Thus simple **addition** enables the computer to solve complex arithmetic problems. Repetitions of **arithmetic functions** (especially addition) takes very little time, because millions of instructions can be processed every second.

Logical Operations

The ALU unit can also perform logical operations. A logical operation is usually a comparison. So the ALU unit can compare letters, numbers, or special characters. The computer can then take action based on the result of the comparison. Logical operations can test for three conditions:

Equal-to Condition:

In a test for this condition, the ALU compares the values to determine if they are equal.

Less-than Condition:

To test for this condition, the computer compares values to determine if one is less than another.

Greater-than Condition:

In this type of comparison, the computer determines if one value is greater than another.

In fact, a logic unit can usually distinguish six logical relationships:

1. Equal to
2. Less than
3. Greater than
4. Less than or equal to
5. Greater than or equal to
6. Less than or greater than (it is same as not equal to)

The symbols that let you define the type of comparison you want the computer to perform are called **relational operators**. The most common relational operators are:

1. the equal sign (=)
2. the less-than symbol (<), and
3. the greater-than symbol (>)

As with arithmetic, the computer executes logical functions at ultrahigh speeds, performing **millions of instructions per second**, or **MIPS**.

MEMORY

The CPU contains the logic and circuitry to run the computer, but one thing it does not have built into it is room to store programs and data. The CPU does contain **registers** for data and instructions, but these are small areas that can hold only a few bytes at a time. Also the storage in registers are temporary in nature.

In addition to the registers, the CPU needs to have millions of bytes of space where it can store whole programs. The memory we are talking here consists of some chips either on motherboard or on a small circuit board attached to the motherboard. This built-in memory allows the CPU to store and retrieve data very quickly. This built in memory is called as **main memory** (also **primary storage unit**). It holds data and instructions between processing steps and supplies them to the control unit and arithmetic-logic unit during processing.

Primary storage media such as semiconductor storage chips are called **direct access** or **random access** memories (RAM). It means that an element of data or instructions (such as a byte or record) can be directly stored and retrieved by selecting and using any of the locations on the storage media. It also means that each storage position has a unique address and can be individually accessed in approximately the same length of time without having to search through other storage positions. For example, each memory cell on a microelectronics semiconductor RAM chip can be individually sensed or changed in the same length of time.

The **Primary Storage** (main memory) of most modern computers consists of microelectronics **semiconductor storage** circuits. Millions of semiconductor storage circuits can be etched on LSI circuit chips. Memory chips with capacities of 8MB to 512 MB are used in current computers.

Some of the major attractions of semiconductor storage are small size, great speed, shock and temperature resistance, and low cost due to mass production capabilities. One major disadvantage of semiconductor memory is its nature of **volatility**. i.e.; it tends to lose the contents stored when the computer the computer's power is shut off. So uninterrupted electric power must be supplied or the contents of memory will be lost. This implies that a standby electrical power (through battery packs or emergency generators) is required if data are to be saved. Another alternative is to permanently "burn in the data" in semiconductor devices so that they can't be erased by a loss of power.

Major trends and development in primary storage are shown in Figure 9.3. Each generation is related to memory capabilities. From the figure we an analyse that the major trend of primary storage is towards large capacities and use of smaller microelectronics circuits.

There are two types of built-in memory :

1. Non volatile memory and
2. Volatile memory.

Nonvolatile memory

In it the memory chip always retain the data they hold even when the computer is turned off, e.g., ROM

READ ONLY MEMORY (ROM)

Read-only-memory, as the name specifies there is no way of changing it, i.e., they are nonvolatile and in addition the data in them can not be changed. Putting data permanently into this kind of memory is called "burning in the data."

One of the main reason that a computer needs, ROM is that it helps in knowing what to do when the power is first turned on. It contains a set of startup instructions that check to see that the rest of memory is functioning properly and look for an operating system and hardware devices. So the ROM is used to store the system's startup programs (the BIOS, Basic Input/Output System program). In some portable computers application and even the operating system are stored in ROM. There are other types of ROM viz., PROM, EPROM, EEPROM which can be programmed after manufacture.

PROM (Programmable ROM)

Chips memory cell contains a 1. In order to store data or software on it, the contents of selected cells are changed to 0. For PROM chips this process is irreversible.

EPROM (Erasable PROM)

It is a user programmed semiconductor memory. Here the stored data can be erased by bathing the chips in ultraviolet light. The chip can then be reprogrammed i.e. selected memory cells can be set to zero value.

EPROM chips are found in nearly every PC. They supply the boot-up information to the PC. When an EPROM is in use in the microcomputer, it behaves like a ROM. In order to erase information and re-program that EPROM, it needs to be taken out of the microcomputer.

EEPROM (Electrical Erasable PROM)

Here individual cells can be reprogrammed by reversing the voltage used to create a 0.

EEPROMs are used where the application requires stable storage without power, but where the chip may have to be reprogrammed. EEPROMs (Microcontrollers) are useful in prolonging the use of machine tools. The device can sense the wear and automatically compensate by reprogramming its EEPROM so that frequent adjustments of the machine are not required. An important application of a ROM is to store stables which do not change, e.g., tables of trigonometric functions. Another application of ROM is for storing short programs for special applications, e.g., a program to control the sequencing of operations of a washing machine may be stored in a ROM and interpreted by the processing unit.

EEPROM is often called a Read Mostly Memory (RMM) since it is often used to store data for extended periods of time.

Volatile Memory

In it the memory chip losses its contents. When the computer's power is shut off.

RAM : Random-Access Storage

Memory that can be changed is called RAM. When people talk about computer memory in connection with microcomputers, the usually mean the volatile RAM memory. The purpose of RAM is to hold programs and data. Information can be read off a RAM chip and written to it. When a computer is switched off, any information stored in RAM is lost i.e.; memory is volatile. RAM is also called read/write memory or user memory. It is used to store user program and data.

Data, the raw material from which information is derived, are stored **temporarily** during processing in a section of the computer system called **primary storage**. Primary storage is also called **random-access memory (RAM)**. Whereas data are stored permanently on **secondary storage** devices such as magnetic tape and disk drives.

Unlike magnetic secondary storage devices, such as tape and disk, **RAM** (primary storage) has no moving parts. With no mechanical movement, data can be accessed from RAM at electronic speeds, or close to the speed of light.

Most of today's computers use **CMOS (Complimentary Metal-Oxide Semiconductor)** technology for RAM. But there is a major problem with semiconductor storage. When the electrical current is turned off or interrupted, the data are lost. Scientists are working to perfect a RAM technology that will retain its contents after the electrical interruption. Several "nonvolatile" technology have emerged, namely:

Bubble Memory

If the surface of a non-magnetic material is coated with a thin layer of magnetic material which is magnestised in a small magnetised in the opposite direction away from the surface. There bubbles can be moved around and used to represent the binary digits.

Bubble memories can not replace the main memory (CMOS) because they are too slow. However they can contain a great deal of information in a small space and may be used to replace the magnetic disk eventually, as they have the advantage of no moving parts. Bubble memory is highly reliable, it is not susceptible to environment fluctuations and it can operate on battery power for a considerable length of time.

These qualities make bubble memory well suited for use with industrial robots and in portable computers.

Flash Memory (Flash RAM)

It is a high-density non-volatile technology. These memory chips are non-volatile and are therefore a true replacement for disk storage. The contents of the flash memory can be altered by the computer, and the data can still be retained when the power is turned off. Access to data in flash memory is not as fast as a RAM, but is still many times faster than retrieving data using a disk drive (secondary storage). Because flash memory does not use any moving parts that draw power, it is used when power consumption must be kept to a minimum. This is particularly good for portable computers relying on batteries.

The first common application of flash memory will probably be replacing hard disks in laptop and notebook computers. Next, you will be able to plug your laptop's memory card into your PC to transfer programs and data between them easily.

Flash chips are currently being used in cellular phones and cockpit flight recorders and they are replacing disks in some handheld computers. Flash memory chips are being produced in credit-cardlike packages, which are smaller than a disk drive and require only half the power; that is whey they are being used in notebook computers and handheld personal digital assistants.

Holographic Memory

Engineers are currently developing a new storage medium called holographic memory. Holographic memory will be a 3-D optical medium capable of storing upto 6.5 terabytes of data in a cube the size of a sugar cube.

Charged-coupled Memories

Charged - coupled memory store data as electronic charges within a chip. It uses a large number of charge-coupled devices for data storage and retrieval; whereas charge-coupled devices are semiconductor devices arrayed so that the electric charge at the output of one provides the input stimulus to the next. It is suitable for applications where memory is accessed serially. Charge-coupled memories suffered the same fate as the bubble memory and are now just a footnote in computer history.

Wafer-Scale Integration

When dynamic or static RAM devices are made, hundreds are built at a time on one semiconductor wafer. After the processing of the wafer is completed, it is sliced up who are pushing wafer-scale integration think that they can build cheaper, large-capacity memories by placing an entire wafer into one memory device. They have access times of a few microseconds. If these devices can be built in quantity at low prices, they may replace disks in many applications.

Capacity of RAM

The capacity of RAM is stated in terms of the number of bytes it can store. Memory capacity is usually stated in terms of Kilobytes (KB), which is equivalent to 1024(2^{10}) bytes of storage, and in terms of megabytes (MB) which is 1,048,576 (2^{20}) bytes. Note that 1 KB is about 1000 and 1 MB is about 1000,000, thus the origin of the prefixes kilo (thousand) and mega (million). Occasionally you will see memory capacities of individual chips stated in terms of Kilobits (Kb) and megabits (Mb).

There are several types of memory that can be implemented in a given machine. Dynamic Random Access Memory (DRAM) is the most common low-cost and flexible RAM available. DRAM is now usually implemented using SIMM (Single In-line Modules) packs and SIMM slots. Static RAM (SRAM) is much faster, but also much more expensive. DRAM is usually used in the cache portion of the machine because of speed requirements.

Static Memory is made up of flip-flops and it stores a bit as a voltage.

Dynamic Memory is made up of MOS transistor gates and it stores a bit as a charge.

The advantage of dynamic memory is that a large number of transistor gates can be placed on a memory chip, thus it has high density and is faster than static memory. The disadvantage is that bit information stored gets leaked, so the information needs to be read and written again after every few msec. This is called refreshing the memory.

Function of RAM

RAM provides the processor with temporary storage for programs and data. All programs and data must be transferred to RAM from an input device or from secondary storage before programs can be executed or data can be processed. RAM space is always at a premium; therefore, after a program has been executed, the storage space it occupied is reallocated to another program awaiting execution.

The input message is interpreted and the processor initiates action to retrieve the appropriate program and data from secondary storage. This is a nondestructive read process, i.e; the program and data that are read, reside in both RAM (temporarily) and secondary storage (permanently). The data are manipulated according to program instructions and an information is received at output.

A program instruction or a piece of data is stored in a specific RAM location called an address. Addresses permit program instructions and data to be located, accessed and processed. The content of each address is constantly changing as different programs are executed and new data are processed.

Virtual Memory: Imaging RAM

For the execution of a program, all the data and programs needed should be resident in RAM. Therefore, RAM is a critical factor in determining the throughput of a computer. Once RAM is full, no more programs can be executed until a portion of RAM is made available.

Virtual memory is a system software addition to the operating system that effectively expands the capacity of RAM through the use of software and secondary storage. This allows more data and programs to be resident in RAM at any given time.

Cache Memory

A cache is similar to RAM except that it is extremely faster compared to normal memory. The cache speeds up processing storing frequently used data or instructions in its high-speed memory. Whenever the CPU requests information from RAM, the cache controller intercepts the request and searches its own memory for the requested information.

If the information is not there the CPU retrieves the required data from the memory (RAM) and also sends a copy back to the cache. The next time the CPU needs the same information, the cache finds that information and quickly sends it to the CPU leaving RAM out of the loop.

The small amount of data that a CPU needs at any time is placed in a very high-speed memory the cache. Also the computer system must be able to quickly move unnecessary data out of fast memory and replace it with new data. Cache memory can be created at many levels in the computer system. A cache can be created in the CPU itself, between the CPU and the main memory and in the hard disk.

A simpler way to store small amounts of data temporarily is to put it in a buffer. A buffer differs from a cache in that it must be read from randomly. Further as it does not use sophisticated methods of storing data it can not access its data as quickly as a cache can.

Math Coprocessor

When the computer has to do a lot of floating-point arithmetic (viz; in spreadsheet, drawing programs or CAD programs) the presence of a math coprocessor either built into the CPU (viz; 486 DX-2 or Pentium) or added on the motherboard (viz; in 286, 386 - in these 287 and 387 chip are acting as math coprocessor) can speed up processing considerably. So math coprocessor is a chip or part of a chip that is specially designed to handle complicated mathematical operations.

Flash Memory

A long-standing speed problem has been the rate of accessing data from a secondary storage device such as a disk, a rate significantly slower than internal computer speeds. To overcome this, flash memory (non-volatile RAM) can be used. Since data and instructions will be ever-closer to the microprocessor, conversion to flash memory chips would have a pivotal impact on a computer's processing speed.

RISC: More Is Not Always Better

An important aspect of computer system is the design of the instruction set for the processor; because it determines the way, machine language programs are constructed. Early computers had small and simple instruction sets; this was because of the high cost of hardware. With the invention of integrated circuits, computer instruction set tend to increase both in number and complexity. For example, the most common microprocessors found in small computers today viz; 80x86 and 680x0 families uses large (from 100 to 200) instruction sets.

A computer with a large number of instructions is classified as a complex instruction set computer (CISC).

CISC Characteristics

The main reason for provision of a complex instruction set is due to the requirement of the simplification of compilation, and the requirement in the improvement of the overall computer performance. The task of a compiler is to generate a sequence of machine instructions for each high level language statement. The task is simplified if there are machine instructions that implement the statements directly.

The essential goal of a CISC architecture is to attempt to provide a single machine instruction for each statement in a high level language.

Examples of CISC architecture are:

IBM 370 and VAX

Another characteristics of CISC architecture is the incorporation of variable-length instruction formats.

RISC Characteristics

A newer theory in the design of microprocessor holds that, if the instruction set is kept small and simple each instruction will execute much faster, allowing the processor to complete more instructions during a given period. This design results in a faster and less expensive processors. CPUs designed around this methodology are called reduced instruction set computers (RISC). The major characteristics of a RISC methodology are:

1. Relatively few instructions
2. Memory access limited to load and store instructions
3. All operations done within the registers of the CPU
4. Fixed length, easily decoded instruction format

RISC technology is used extensively in mid-size computers such as the IBM RS/6000 and high-end UNIX workstations such as those built by Hewlett Packard & Sun Microsystem.

RISC CPUs are also used extensively in printers and other intelligent devices that have their own internal CPUs.

RISC technology are designed and manufactured by the same companies that produce CISC technology.

In 1989, Intel introduced i860 RISC Chip of 64-bit, which contains more than 1 million transistors. Newer RISC chip include the Intel i960, the Motorola 88100. Sun Microsystems are also produced a RISC chip known as SPARC, which it uses in its UNIX workstations.

Parallel Processing

Computer manufacturers have relied on the single processor design architecture since the late 1940s. In this environment, the processor addresses the programming problem sequentially, from beginning to end, i.e., the processor gets an instruction from memory, acts on it, returns processed data to memory, and then repeats the process. The problem with the conventional computer is that the single electronic pathway, the bus line, acts like a narrow outlet which impedes smooth data flow. Because of this computers are restricted to handling one piece of data at a time, so they are not efficient for application, such as simulating the air flow around an entire aeroplane in flight.

Today designers are doing research on computers that will be able to break programming problem into pieces. Work on each of these pieces will then be executed simultaneously in separate processors, all of which are part of the same computer. The concept of using multiple processors in the same computer in known as parallel processing. By dividing the word load among several special-function processors, the system throughput can be increased. In parallel processing, one main processor (a host mainframe) examines the programming problem and determines what portions, if any, of the problem can be solved in pieces. Those pieces that can be addressed separately are routed to other processors and solved. The individual pieces are then reassembled in the main processor for further computation, output, or storage. The net result of parallel processing is better efficient output.

Computers using parallel processing are:

1. IBM 3090 which has two to four processors
2. Cray XMP4 has four processors

At the other end of the spectrum, dual processor version of PCs are available today. Unfortunately, the DOS operating system can't make use of the added power of an additional processors. Whereas some UNIX developers have developed software that takes advantage of the additional processor.

Data Representation in Memory

Binary Codes for Data

George Boole held that all logical conditions could be described as either true or false. Computer circuitry is an application of this theory. When electricity is present, circuits on paths through the computer's processing components may be either open or closed to the electrical pulses. Bit patterns or combinations of these ON/OFF bits, are how data and programs are processed and stored.

An "ON" or "OFF" electronic state is represented by a bit. The presence or absence of a bit is referred to as ON-BIT and OFF-BIT, respectively. In the binary numbering system and in written text, the ON-BIT is 1 and the OFF-BIT is a 0.

The vacuum tubes, transistors, and integrated circuits that characterize the generations of computers all enable them to distinguish between ON and OFF and, therefore, use binary logic. Physically, these states are achieved in a number of ways. For example, in primary memory the two electronic states are represented by the direction of the current flow. Another approach is to turn the circuit itself ON and OFF. In secondary memory the two states are made possible by the magnetic arrangement of the surface coating on magnetic tapes and disks.

This bits representation may be fine for computers to understand, but human beings are more comfortable with letters, decimal numbers and colours that we put to a computer system must be translated into 1s and 0s for processing and storage. The computer translates the bits back into letters, decimal numbers and colours on output. This translation is performed so that we can recognize and understand the output.

Encoding Schemes: Combining Bits to Form Bytes

All input, whether a keystroke from a keyboard or a scan from a scanner, is converted to zeros and ones. Keystrokes can be alphanumeric symbol or a control character which represent, special instruction for cursor movement, tabulation, carriage, return, and so on. A scanner converts a photograph into a computer-usable format by organizing the image into rows and columns of dots whose location and colour are represented in binary code.

Music is converted to bit combinations to indicate the pitch and duration of individual notes. Different combinations of bits represent textual, graphical, and audio data. Now the question arises that which particular set of bits is equivalent to which character. In theory we could make up our own definitions, declaring certain bit patterns to represent certain characters. Since we need to communicate with the computer and with each other, it is appropriate that we use a common scheme for data representation, i.e; there must be agreement on which groups of bits represent which characters. So bits are combined according to a standard encoding scheme for data representation, i.e; there must be agreement on which groups of bits represent which characters. So bits are combined according to a standard encoding scheme to represent letters (S, U, K, H and so on), numbers (5, 7, 9 etc.). In practice, several standard binary codes exist to represent textual data. Typically, computers use codes that assign either 7 or 8 bits per byte. Codes vary according to the type of computer system used.

Standard Codes for Data:

1. ASCII and
2. EBCDIC

ASCII (American National Standard Code for Information Interchange)

Most smaller computers use a 7-bit code called the ASCII (pronounced "as-kee"). ASCII was used originally by the communication industry for transmission over telegraph lines.

This code has been adopted as the standard for many computers, particularly PCs. With ASCII, users can transmit data from one computer to another, even if the machines have different internal coding systems. Even software also exists to convert data to an ASCII file for storage on disk.

The 7-bit ASCII code can represent upto 128 characters (2^7). Although the English language has considerably fewer than 128 printable characters, the extra bit configurations are needed to represent a variety of common and not-so-common special characters viz; - (hyphen); @ (at); ~ (tilde).

ASCII is a 7-bit code, but the microcomputer byte can store 8- bits. There are 256(2^8) possible bit configurations in an 8-bit byte. Hardware and software vendors use the extra 128 bit configurations to represent control characters or non character images to complement their hardware or software product.

For example, the IBM-PC version of extended ASCII contains the characters of many foreign languages [viz; Â (umlaut) and Ë (acute)] and a wide variety of graphic images that can be combined on a text screen to produce larger images.

EBCDIC (Extended Binary Coded Decimal Interchange Code)

Larger computers (viz; mainframe) use an 8-bit code called EBCDIC (pronounced "ed-shidik"). Whereas ASCII is used most commonly with PCs and data communication, EBCDIC is used primarily for internal data handling by larger computers.

8-bit code EBCDIC has 256 different combinations. These coding systems adequately cover all the written characters traditionally used in English and other Indo-European languages, however, they do not take into consideration other languages, such as Japanese and Chinese, that employ thousands of characters. A new 16-bit system called Unicode support 65,536 different binary combinations. Unicode is designed as a way for computers to process and store text in every written language.

Multiple Choice Questions

1. Full form of RAM is:
   (a) Random Access Memory
   (b) Read And Memory
   (c) Read Access Memory
2. Central Processing Unit has:
   (a) Control Unit
   (b) Arithmetic Logic Unit
   (c) Both
3. Two main memories of computer are RAM and:
   (a) RAC (b) ROM
   (c) RMA
4. Capacity of RAM is measure in:
   (a) bytes (b) litres
   (c) grams
5. Which of the following is not a memory?
   (a) Flash (b) Bubble
   (c)Triple

Descriptive Type Questions

1. Distinguish between RAM, ROM, PROM and EPROM. For a given computer, which type of memory would have the greater capacity to store data and programs: Cache or RAM? RAM or registers? registers or Cache?
2. What are the two types of computer memory, and how do they differ?
3. What is a RAM disk? How is it used? What is stored in RAM?
4. What types of internal storages, are you familiar with? Name the dominant internal storage technology of today? What technology, you think, may emerge in the future?
5. What purpose does the RAM serve when it is simply a volatile storage medium?
6. What do you mean by volatile memory? What can be done to overcome the problems of this kind of memory?
7. What do you mean by non-volatile memory? How is it used?
8. Why are semiconductor chips poplar as storage devices? Name two computers which have used this technology?
9. Which are the storage elements that may be found in CPU? How may these elements be used?
10. What operations are performed by the central processing unit? What is the role of registers in the CPU? Mention the set of important registers commonly found in every CPU and explain their functions.
11. List the two main components of a CPU, and explain what each one does?
12. What is a cache and how does it enhances the CPU's performance?
13. Which two functions are performed by the ALU?
14. What are the functions of a supervisory control unit?
15. What is the basic difference between CMOS (Complimentary Metal-Oxide Semi-conductor) technology and non-volatile technology, such as bubble memory?
16. What do you mean by parallel processing? List three potential benefits.
17. Which type of computer architecture has the smaller instruction set, RISC or CISC?
18. Which portion of the fundamental computer instruction designates the operations to be performed?
19. How is a microprocessor's processing speed measured?
20. How is unicode different from ASCII and EBCDIC?
21. How many Unicode and EBCDIC, bytes can be stored in a 32-bit word?
22. Differentiate between a bit, a byte, and a word.

23. How is 'storage capacity' of a computer measured? What do you mean by 'nibble'?
24. Convert 9MB to KB, Mb and Kb. Assume a byte contains 8-bits.
25. What is the difference between a millisecond, microsecond, nanosecond and picosecond?
26. What is the difference between a byte, KB, Kb, MB, Mb, GB and Gb?
27. Explain how the processor uses memory addresses to locate data and instructions.

Input Devices

3

INTRODUCTION

As was mentioned in the last chapter, computer processes data which is fed into it and gives results in the form you like. You can feed in this data for processing using a number of input mediums available and take the resultant output on various other medias available. In this chapter we will read about all these input and output devices through which we can input the data and take the processed output.

Since output is dependent on the data which is inputted, it must be ensured that the data is correct else the result will be wrong too. If by mistake you type the bank account 9634 instead of 9631 then the amount would be credited to a different person. So one must ensure that the data is accurate. As you will read later in the chapter, there are devices which allow you to feed the directly to the computer whereas there are others which allow you to feed the data off line, record it in some media and then feed this media into the computer.

In this chapter I have divided the devices into 2 sections, namely; **Input Devices** and **Output Devices.** Let us start with Input Devices and most important of them all, the keyboard.

KEYBOARDS

One look at it and you would be reminded of the old typewriter keypad. Well yes, the placing of alpha keys is exactly the same. This is called the QWERTY type of keyboard. This has been done specially keeping in mind the migration of people from typewriter to keyboard.

It is the most important part of the computer. I am yet to see a computer without it. It is there in each computer. There are some software available in the market which teach you how to master the keyboard, but the old asdf method of typing would be sufficient. If one does not have speed for typing, it is ok but, the placement of keys is very important before you sit down on computer.

Let us see how the various keys are placed on the keyboard.

Keyboard Keys

Most keyboard layouts are still a variation of the key layout of a typewriter, at least for the alphabetic, numerical and special character keys. Keyboards are available for various other languages than English too, but, for our purposes we would stick to the English one. There are mostly **101 keys** on the keyboard. The important keys are as follows:

Alpha Keys

Alphabet keys are marked from [A] to [Z]. As in typewriter, you can use [SHIFT] to make them capital, i.e., ABCDE, etc. So if you press a b c d e .... etc., with [SHIFT] key already pressed, you will get A B C D E .... etc. Similar results can be obtained by putting CAPS LOCK key ON. For typing capital A, you press [SHIFT] key and then while keeping [SHIFT] key pressed, press the "a" key. Otherwise for typing a, you don't need to press the [SHIFT] key, just press the a key.

Numeric Keys

The numeric keys (with the characters 0 to 9) are located on the computer's keyboard at two places. You can see them in the top row above the alpha keys (as in typewriter). A second set of these keys is provided on the right-hand side of the keyboard. The numeric keys in the top row can be used straightaway to type in numeric characters. By simultaneously holding down the Shift key (as in the typewriter), you can also type in special upper characters like ! % $ *, etc. However, to type numeric characters by using the keys on the right side, you will need to press the Num Lock key ON.

Function Keys

These keys are marked [F1] to [F12]. These keys are used for specific purposes as defined in the computer (a computer program is a set of instructions given to a computer to perform a specific task) which you may be using. For example, in BASIC programming (BASIC is a computer language used for writing programs) [F3] will load the program, [F1] will list the program after loading and [F2] will run the program.

Arrow Keys

On 101 keys keyboard these are placed at two places. The first is called the cursor pad which works independently. The other is the numeric-cum-cursor pad. It is similar to the one on the 84 key keyboard. When the Num Lock key is not in the ON position, pressing the key of the numeric keypad moves the cursor in the direction shown on each key. Otherwise, this portion is used to enter numbers.

Special Keys including Spacebar

There are several other keys which serve some definite purposes. Some of these keys are available on the typewriter too. The special keys are:

[SHIFT]	Shift Key	It is used for typing capital letters and special characters. In combination with both Control and Alternate keys, it is sometimes used to execute a particular command too.
[CTRL]	Control Key	On its own, this key does not have any purpose. However, combined with different keys, it performs some useful operations. For example, in WordStar software, Control if pressed alongwith B, will make the character Bold.
[←]	Backspace	It allows the cursor to go back by one character. Some types of computer programs allow the backspace to delete the last character. A cursor is usually a blinking line (_), on the screen, which shows where he character you type on your keyboard will appear.

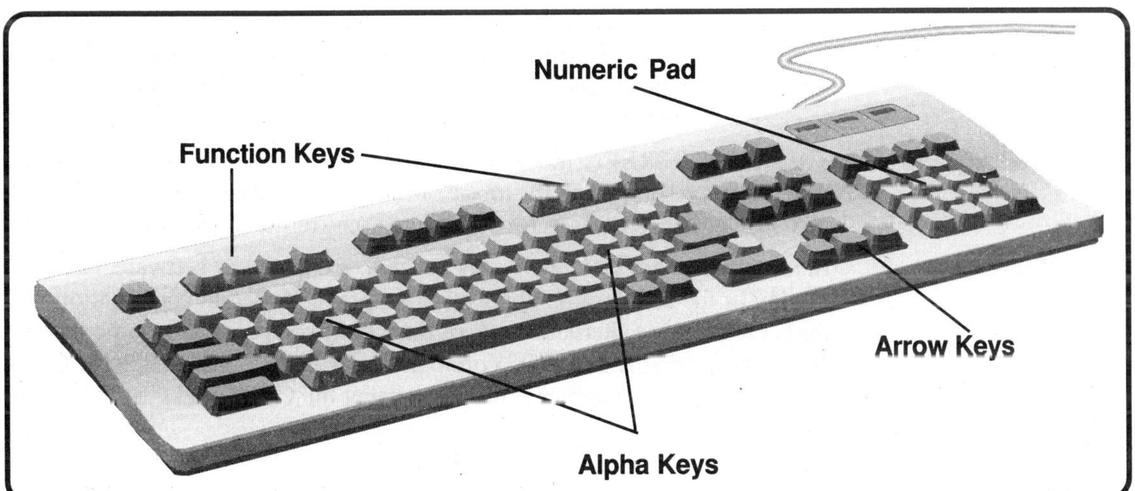

Spacebar
As in the typewriter, the Spacebar is used to leave space between words.

Enter Key
It informs the computer that the line of the matter, you are typing, has come to an end. After that you begin typing from a new line. It is also used, while programming, to tell the computer to execute certain commands which you give. Thus, while writing a computer program, you can also use this key to indicate the end of a given command.

Del Key
If, by mistake, you have typed in something which you did not want to, you can erase the wrong character by pressing the DEL (short for Delete) key.

The Numeric Pad

As mentioned earlier the numeric pad is used for entering the numeric data, from 0 to 9. But, there are other keys too, which are shown here.

NUM LOCK
As mentioned you need to put this ON for typing the numeric data. When you put on the computer system, this key is put on.

Arithmetic operators
The number pad includes keys for the four standard arithmetic operators, / (divide), * (multiply), - (subtract) and + (add).

Numbers/cursor keys
When the Num Lock key is off, the various keys here act differently. They act as they are mentioned on the keys. For example, there is Home on the 7 key, there is Up Arrow at the 8 key. So while the Num Lock key is off, you can use the numeric pad for other purposes.

INSERT/DELETE
These two keys are the zero and period of the number pad when it is in number mode; in cursor control mode, they duplicate the actions of the INSERT key and the DELETE keys.

ENTER
This is a second ENTER key that remains an ENTER KEY regardless of the number pad's mode.

Special-Purpose Keys

These keys are used for some special purposes. Each key has a special purpose attached to it and can be used for it:

Esc
The Escape key is typically enabled as an exit key by most software applications. It is used to cancel out of a command or to exit an application. It is also used in combination with other keys to create special key values and to indicate other actions. For example, in Windows the ESC key can be used to close a context menu.

Print Screen/SysRq
The PRINT SCREEN mode of this key got its name back in the MS-DOS days, when pressing it sent the image of the display to the printer. On a Window system, the image of monitor's display is sent to the Windows Clipboard.

Pause/Break
In its default mode (PAUSE), this key will, it enabled by software, pause the display or the action of an application program. If used in combination with the CTRL key, the alternate mode of this key interrupts or halts some software programs, primarily MS-DOS commands and applications. Using the CTRL and BREAK keys together is the same using the CTRL and C keys to break an action.

MOUSE

These days even the mouse has become very important part of computer. It has become integral part of computer since Windows has become the operating system for computers. It is in fact a pointing device. With this you can point at any place on the monitor and start the typing or clicking from that point. All Windows-based programs use mouse, making working with computers easier as you are not required to type commands.

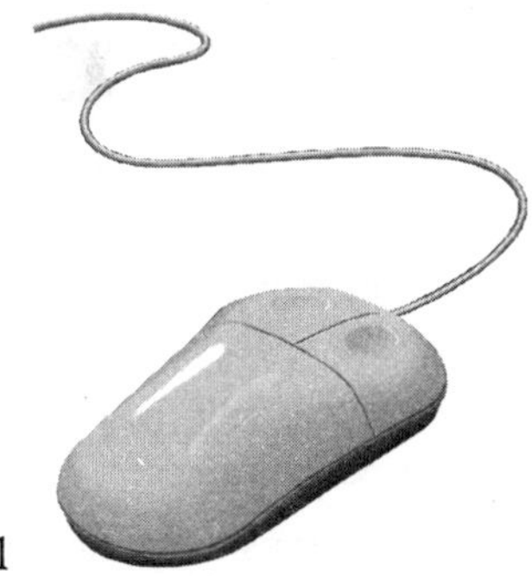

Types of Mouse

There are three basic types of Mouse

1. Mechanical Mouse
2. Optomechanical Mouse
3. Optical Mouse

Mechanical Mouse

A mechanical mouse has a rubber or metal ball on its underside that can roll in all directions. Mechanical sensors within the mouse detect the direction of the rolling ball and make a movement of the screen pointer accordingly.

Optomechanical Mouse

Optomechanical mouse is also similar to a mechanical mouse except that it uses optical sensors to detect the movement of the ball on the Mouse Pad.

Optical Mouse

Optical mouse uses a laser beam to detect the movement of mouse on specially designed Mouse Pad. We must move the mouse along a special mat with a grid so that optical mechanism has a frame of reference. This type of mouse has no mechanical moving parts. Optical mouse respond more quickly and precisely than any other mouse. These are expensive than the other two.

JOYSTICKS (OR PADDLE)

You must have seen a joystick with a video game at various video game parlours. Well the same joystick can be attached to the computer too. For playing game obviously. It consists of a small, vertical lever (called the stick) mounted on a base that is used to steer the screen cursor around. Some joysticks are mounted on a keyboard, others function as stand- alone units. The joystick can be moved left or right, forward or backward, springs are often used to return the joystick to its home center position.

OPTICAL RECOGNITION INPUT

There are two types of optical recognition input devices.

1. Optical Character Recognition (OCR) and
2. Optical Mark Reading (OMR)

Optical Character Recognition (OCR)

A special kind of devices called scanners use the principle of OCR to input the printed matter on the paper or any other object. This matter can be in the coded form (bar codes) or simple text/ graphics (pictures). Bar Code Readers and Scanners come into this category of devices. OCR is a technique which permits the direct reading of printed character. Optical character recognition readers or scanners typically examine each character as if it were made up of a collection of minute spots. Once the whole character has been scanned, the pattern detected is matched against a set of patterns stored in the computer. Whichever pattern it matches, or nearly matches is considered to be the character read. Patterns which can not be identified are rejected.

Optical Mark Recognition

It is an automatic optical sensing of marks recorded on a data medium. In this method special preprinted forms are designed with boxes which can be marked with a dark pencil or ink. These documents are applicable in areas where responses are one out of a small number of alternatives and the volume of data to be processed is large. Thus they are used for

1. Objective type answer papers in examinations (e.g., in UPSC) in which large number of candidates appear.
2. Market surveys, population surveys etc., where responses can be restricted to one or more out of a few possibilities.
3. Order forms containing a small choice of items.

These preprinted documents filled by user are passed under a light source and presence of mark is detected by measuring very accurately the infra-red light levels. A mark reader may be able to detect coloured marks. It can also be designed to be insensitive to certain colours. Now these particular colours could be safely used in the pre-printing of the documents without the risk of their being read as marks intended for recognition.

SCANNERS

Whereas a keyboard, mouse or trackball requires manual input of data, scanners allow input of printed data. A scanner reads text, photographs and graphics from paper which are then converted into bit patterns for processing, storage or output. Scanner is a device that examines a spatial pattern one part after another and generate analog or digital signals corresponding to the pattern. Scanners are often used in mark sensing, pattern recognition or character recognition.

Practically scanner uses light for examining the spatial patterns. In a scanner, as the image is scanned, it is converted into light and dark picture elements, or pixels, similar to newspaper photo. Colour scanners can assign a specific colour to a pixel. The pixel are then stored as bit patterns. This technique makes the images usable by word processing, desktop publishing, and graphic packages.

There are two types of scanners, Hand-held scanner and Flat-bed scanner

Hand-Held Scanner

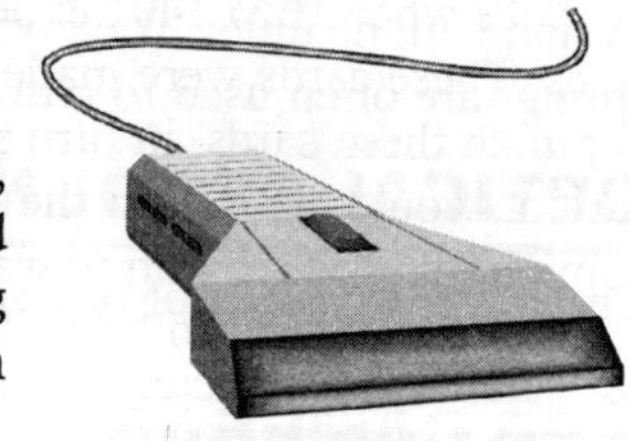

These devices read data on price tags, shipping labels, inventory part number, book ISBNs, and the like. Hand-held scanner, sometimes called wand scanners, use either contact or laser technology. It has a set of light emitting diodes. It is placed over the material to be scanned and slowly dragged from the top to the bottom.

The light emitted by the diodes are not reflected by black lines and are reflected by whole areas. The material is converted and stored in a bitmap. Typical applications are to store images and reproduce them in publications.

Flat-bed Scanner

It consists of a box with glass plate on top, which is used for placing the document to be scanned. The light beam is situated below the glass plate and is moved from left to right horizontally. After scanning one line the beam moves up little and scans the next line. The scanner can also store colour images.

BAR CODES

These represent alphanumeric data by varying the width and combination of adjacent vertical lines. These zebra strips can be sensed and read by a bar code reader, a photoelectric device that reads the code by means of reflected light. When a bar code is scanned, the light source is reflected off the spaces between the marked bars. This returned light is then converted into bit patterns. A decoder in the scanning system translates the bit patterns into meaningful letters and numbers. The bar code merely identifies the product to the store's computer; the code does not contain the price, which may vary. The price is stored in a file that can be accessed by the computer. This is because of the reason that it is easier to change the price once in the computer than to have to restamp the price on each book. The computer automatically tells the point-of-sale terminal what the price is; a printer prints the item description and price on a paper tape for the customer.

DIGITAL CAMERA

A digital camera can store many more pictures than an ordinary camera. Pictures taken using a digital camera are stored inside its memory and can be transferred to a computer by connecting the camera to it. A digital camera takes pictures by converting the light passing through the lens at the front into a digital image.

MICR

Its full form is Magnetic Ink Character Reader. This process is used by a special machine which reads coded numbers you see on your bank cheques. These days most cheques issued and used bear MICR numbers to speed up clearing of cheques. It is a technology related to the recording of information on document by means of magnetized ink characters and automatic recognition of such characters by means of machines. In this technology the magnetic ink contains particle of magnetizable material (viz., iron oxide), which can be energized to facilitate automatic reading of printed characters. Magnetic ink document reader helps in translating the information read into a coded format usually for direct insertion into an input area of a computer's core storage in an order according to the digits recorded in a specified field, i.e., account number, etc.

CARD READER

In 1960s when IBM 1401 & 360s were the main computers in the market, the input media was punched cards. These cards were made of thick brownish paper. A special machine called Card Punch was used to punch these cards, in turn making holes in the cards. When this card was fed into the computer, the current would pass from the holes and thus forming the characters which was punched on the card. Sometimes even the output was also taken on these cards. Since these cards could be used only once, the medium turned out to be quite costly affair.

WEB CAMERAS

It is fast becoming an integral part of the computer specially for those who use Internet quite often. With this you can take an instant picture of the object to whom you focus it. It is very useful specially for those who have to show their designs, products, etc., on the computer to the clients. The picture transfer is almost instant.

LIGHT PENS

A light pen is a small pen-shaped wand, which contains light sensors. The light pen is used to choose objects or commands on the screen either by pressing it against the surface of the screen or by pressing a small switch on its side. This sends a signal to the computer, which then works out the light pen's exact location on the screen. The advantage of a light pen is that pen is that unlike a touch screen it doesn't need a special screen on screen coating. Used like an ordinary writing pen, this electronic pen is used to enter data by writing on the screen. The data you write is displayed on the monitor.

TRACKBALL

Trackball is a pointing device that works like an upside-down mouse. You rest your thumb on the exposed ball and your fingers on the buttons. To move the cursor around the screen, you roll the ball with your thumb. Because you do not move the whole device, a trackball requires less space than a mouse. It is particularly used in notebook and laptop computers.

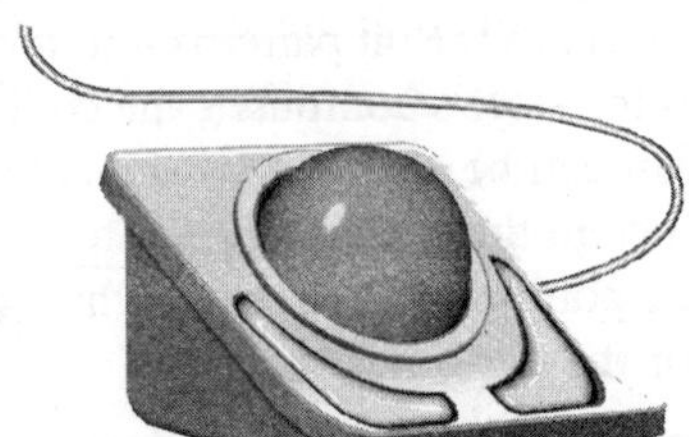

TOUCH SCREENS

Similar in use to the light pen is the touch-screen, which enables users to input instructions by merely touching on-screen prompts. The edges of the monitor of a touch-screen emit horizontal and vertical beams of light that criss-cross the screen. When a finger touches the screen, the interrupted light beams can pinpoint the location selected on the screen. Such screens are especially helpful when people are unfamiliar with computers. Information systems in shopping malls, airports, and amusement parks are now being developed using touch-sensitive screens as the only input hardware.

TOUCH PAD

A small, touch-sensitive pad is used as a pointing device on some portable computers. By moving a finger or other object along the pad, we can move the pointer on the display screen. The touch pad is related to the touch screen, but activated by different means. The touch pad uses pressure sensitive materials to record data at the point where the pad is touched. Many appliances around the home, such as microwave ovens, use touch pads for programming time or temperature.

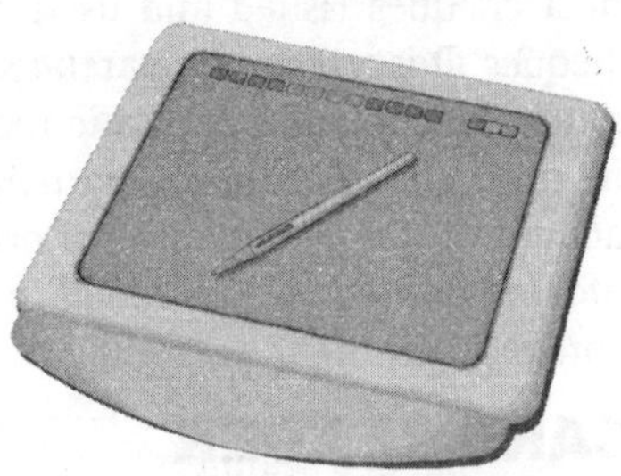

DIGITIZER

A digitizer, or graphics tablet, is similar to a light pen; however, instead of drawing on the screen, a separate tablet is used on which a special stylus is moved. Input tablets or digitizer tablet are typically found in CAD terminals or engineering workstations, etc. Digitizers are also called Digitizing Tablets, Graphics Tablets, Touch Tablets or simply Tablets.

VOICE INPUT

Speaking to a computer, known as voice input or speech recognition, is another form of source input. Voice recognizers accept the spoken word through a microphone and convert it into binary code (0s and 1s) that can be understood by the computer. Most voice recognizer systems are speaker dependent - that is, they must be separately trained for each individual users. Therefore, a database of words must be created for each person using the system. To create this database, each person using the system must repeat - a minimum of 20 times - each word to be interpreted by the system. This training is necessary because we seldom say a word the same way each time.

VOICE RECOGNIZERS

Voice recognizers are used in some graphic workstations as input devices to accept voice commands. The voice-system input can be used to initiate graphics operations or to enter data. These systems operate by matching an input against a predefined dictionary of words and phrases.

Multiple Choice Questions

1. For seeing the output, you use:
   (a) Monitor (b) Keyboard
   (c) Mouse
2. In programming, you use the following keys:
   (a) Arrow keys (b) Function keys
   (c) Alpha keys
3. Keyboard has ________ number of keys.
   (a) 100 (b) 88
   (c) 101
4. Mouse is a ________ device.
   (a) Input (b) Output
   (c) Both
5. A scanner scans
   (a) Pictures (b) Text
   (c) Both
6. With digital camera, you can store:
   (a) text (b) pictures
7. In MICR, C stands for:
   (a) Colour (b) Code
   (c) Character
8. Trackball has a
   (a) ball (b) track
   (c) football

Descriptive Type Questions

1. Describe the various type of keys on the keyboard.
2. Describe the various types of mouse available.
3. Describe the various types of optical recognition devices.
4. What is a trackball?
5. Describe the working of joystick.
6. What are OCRs? How do they work?
7. What is the difference between hand held and flat bed scanners?
8. What are bar codes?
9. What is digital camera used for?
10. Decribe the working of Light pens.
11. What is a trackball?
12. What is a touch screen?
13. What is a touch pad?
14. How would you enter data into computer by speaking?

4 Output Devices

INTRODUCTION

The success of business today can depend to a large extent on how meaningful and timely the information a computer can produce, i.e., the output. So the two most important requirements of computer output are that it is meaningful and convenient to use.

MONITORS AND DISPLAYS

There would be no What You See Is What You Get (WYSIWYG) on PCs, if there were no monitors or displays on which to see what you get. The PC must produce outputs that can be handled by the senses of humans and so far, technology is limited to sight and sound. Given a choice, most of us still prefer sight over sound. You can accomplish a lot on a PC without sound, but not much would get done without the ability to see what you are working on.

The two general categories of PC visual presentation are the monitor and the display. A monitor has a CRT (cathode ray tube) and look something like a traditional television set (without the controls, of course). On the other hand, a display is a flat-panel device that can be attached to a portable PC or hung on the wall. A monitor is largely desk or table-bound, but a display can get up and move about. A flat-panel display is really an adaptation of the monitor, but because it uses different technology, they are treated as two different components.

The PC Monitor

With personal computer technology advancing as fast as it is, it is hard to believe that any part of a PC could be considered an investment. However, the PC monitor is the only part of the personal computer that actually hold its value and has some durability. A good quality monitor will last for years through several generations of the PC systems.

Video Cards

In general, the video card processes the graphics data produced by software running on the PC and prepares it for use by the monitor for converting it from digital data to an analog signal. The video card also sends out the data needed by the monitor to refresh the image or renew it as it changes.

Video cards, graphics cards and accelerator cards are all names for the adapter card inside the PC that is responsible for generating the signals that tell the monitor what to display. The relationship between the video card and the monitor should be carefully matched. These two device must be compatible in terms of the signal used to communicate to the monitor, the type of connector used to connect them together, the video display standards they support and their speed.

Dumb Terminal

It has been named as such since it is really dumb. It has no memory or processing unit, just a keyboard and the monitor. It takes everything else from the computer which it is attached.

Smart Terminal

If you add microprocessor to dumb terminal, then it becomes a smart terminal. But, it still depends upon the main computer for programming and other jobs.

Intelligent Terminal

First we add microprocessor, now we add everything else. It is full-fledged computer in itself but connected to a large computer. It can be programmed and has processing power. Most of the work can be done at the terminal itself. Only for jobs that require large processing and storage facility, the main computer is used.

COMPUTER OUTPUT ON MICROFILM

If only this method was adopted was adopted by Government offices, their stores would have become non existent. In this each record is made into a small film image and thus the volume of data becomes very very small. Sometimes the reduction is to the tune of about 50 times. This means that an A 4 size paper is reduced to a film of about 1 square inch. This is done with the help of high speed cameras. Since the process is costly and takes time, it is usually taken up for large volumunus type of jobs.

MULTIMEDIA PROJECTOR

As the name suggests it is used for presentations of multimedia projects. Instead of displaying the presentation on small computer monitor screen it is displayed on large screen which is usually mounted on a wall. This way the projection can be seen by many instead of few. It is not only possible to enlarge the image but you can give audio effect too. Since multimedia presentaion has become the most common way of presentation, this device is quite in use.

SPEECH SYNTHESIZER

If one hand you have microphones which convert your text to the format which the computer understands, the reverse has also been made possible. This method converts data from the computer to the spoken words or sentences. You can then convert this into speech and broadcast it over the speakers. Take for example, you cannot speak but can listen, then this becomes a big boom. Whatever you have to say write it on computer terminal and convert it to speech which others can listen. Even those have problems with seeing the text can also listen to it.

PRINTERS

Once considered an expansive luxury for any PC, especially for home or small office systems, a printer is now virtually a necessity on any PC system. Technology has advanced to the point that good quality, color printers are available for less than Rs.8,000 and it is common for PC sale bundles to include one.

When software was still fairly unsophisticated and applications that produced output worth saving were few, the printer was a true luxury. Electronic spreadsheet and word processing applications allowed the user to prepare budgets, reports, letters and other documents prepared for the sole purpose of being physically shared. Even in today's networked environments, where documents can be shared and collaborated on electronically, the need to produce a printed paper copy of a document is still a necessity for a significant portion of documents produced on the PC. The printer has definitely become a necessity for today's PC user.

The printers can be divided into two distinct categories:

1. Impact Printers
2. Non-impact Printers

IMPACT PRINTERS

A printer in which printing is the result of mechanically striking the printing medium. An impact printer makes contact with the paper to produce an image. The impact may be produced by a print hammer character, like that of a typewriter key striking a ribbon against the paper or by a print hammer hitting paper and ribbon against a character.

An impact printer must be used if printing a multiple copy report so that the duplicate copies will receive the imprint. Impact printers are of following types:

DOT-MATRIX PRINTER

In it the individual characters are formed by a matrix of wires or styluses. Dot-matrix printers are also called serial printers. The images are formed by a print head that is composed of a series of little print hammers that look like the heads of pins. The print head usually has nine pins or 24 pines. The bottom 2 pins are used to form the descenders of lower case letters, viz., p, q, g and y. Many expensive dot-matrix printers do not provide descenders, but print quality is improved when they are used.

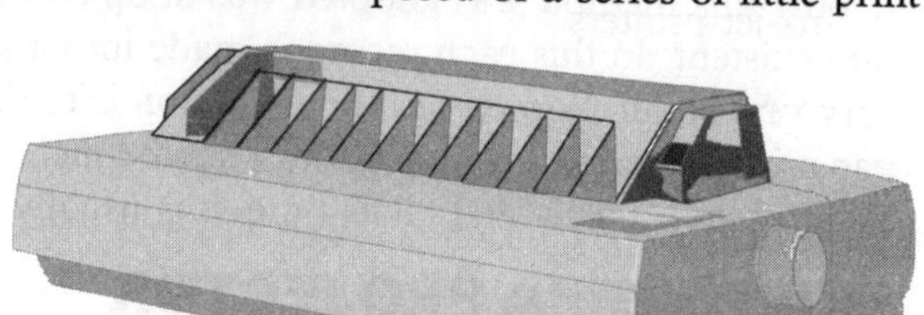

Features common to most dot-matrix printers include boldface, underline, subscript and superscript and compressed print (narrowed letters). Optional features include proportional spacing (using more or less space, depending on the width of the character) and italics. Dot matrix printers are very versatile since the character set can be changed by software or firmware such as a PROM for different styles, alphabets or graphic symbols. Dot-matrix printers are comparatively inexpensive and one of the fastest types of character-at-a-time printers available. The speed ranges from 50 cps to 400 cps (character per second).

Their abilities to use different type fonts, different line densities and different types of paper are also important.

DAISYWHEEL PRINTERS

A serial impact printer in which the printing element is a plastic hub that has a large number of flexible radial spokes, each spoke having one or more different raised printing characters, the wheel is rotated as it is moved horizontally step by step under computer control, and stops when a desired character is in a desired print position so a hammer can drive that character against an inked ribbon.

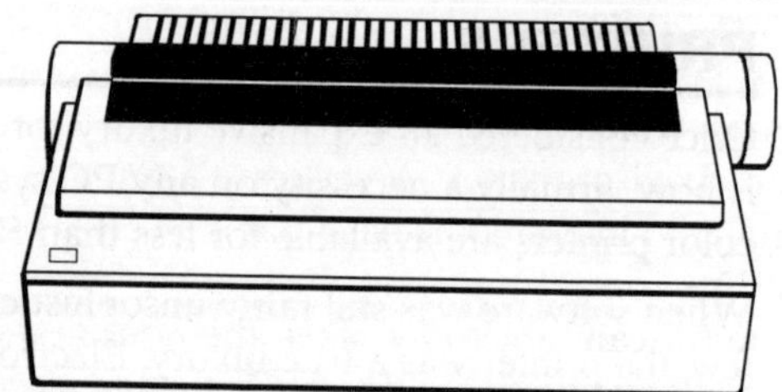

Daisy Wheel Printers are slower than dot-matrix printers, but they produce a high-resolution output. This high-resolution output is often called letter quality printing because it is suitable for business letters and memos. You can print in as may type fonts or foreign languages on a daisywheel printer as there are print wheels to fit your particular model of machine.

It is also called as a smart printer because of its bi-directional printing and built-in microprocessor control features.

LINE PRINTERS

It prints an entire line in a single operation without necessarily printing one character at a time. These are generally electro-mechanical devices which print complete lines of print, up to 160 characters in width, at speeds about 300 to 2000 lines per minute. Line printers are used primarily in the mini/mainframe processing environment.

Examples of line-at-a-time impact printers are:

1. Chain Printers
2. Band Printers and
3. Drum Printers

NON-IMPACT PRINTERS

Printers that do not strike characters against ribbon or paper when they print, are non-impact printers. Example of non-impact printers include

1. Ink-jet printers
2. Laser printers

These printers makes much less noise than impact printers.

If you are using a non-impact printer, do not try to print on multiple-part carbon forms: because no impact is being made on the paper you will end up with no copies.

INK-JET PRINTERS

It uses a technique of projecting droplets of ink at paper to form the required image. Ink-jet printer create an image directly on paper by spraying ink through as many as 64 tiny nozzles.

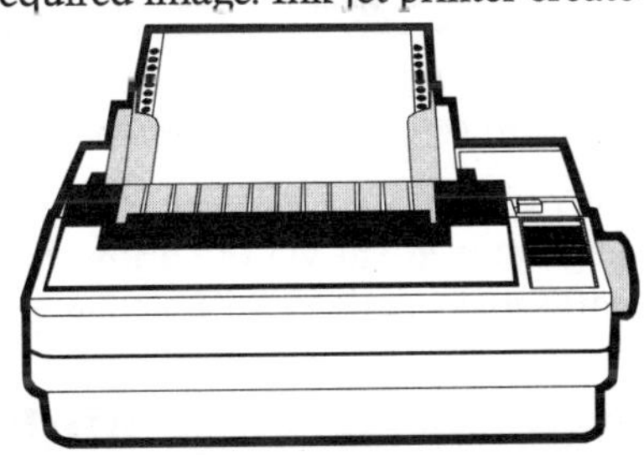

It provides a print resolution of around 360 dots per inch.

LASER PRINTERS

The physical properties of LASERs (Light Amplification by Stimulate Emission of Radiation) allows for the very precise positioning of narrow beam of light, transferring a high energy source to a very small area. This property is used to control printing, i.e., laser printers, to read information from bar codes and to read and write information in optical storage devices.

Laser printer is a non-impact printer that creates, by means of a laser beam directed on a photosensitive surface, a latent image which is then made visible by a toner and transferred and fixed on paper. A separate computer is built into the printer to interpret the data that it receives from the computer and to control the laser. Just as electron gun in a graphic monitor can target any pixel, the laser in a laser printer can aim at any point on a drum creating an electrical charge.

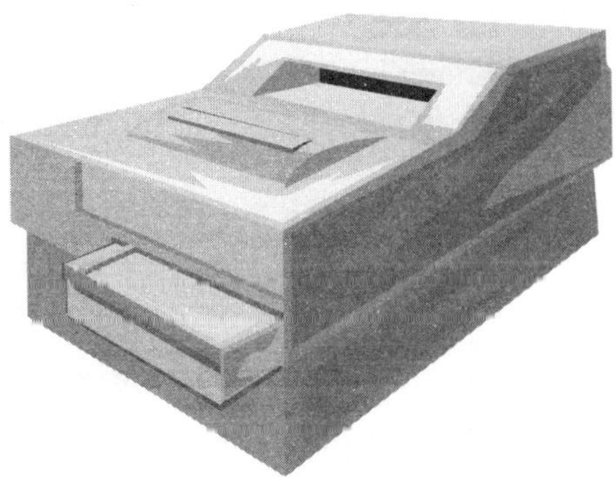

The resolution of laser printers is 600 DPI both horizontally and vertically; some high-end models have resolution of 1200 DPI.

GRAPHICS OUTPUT DEVICES

Business people have found that sophisticated and colourful graphics add an aura of professionalism to any report or presentation. This demand for presentation graphics has created a need for corresponding output devices. Computer-generated graphic images can be re-created on paper and transparency acetates with printers and plotters. Graphic images also can be captured on 35-mm slides, or they can be displayed on a monitor or projected onto a large screen.

The main popular graphic output device is the plotter, which can draw hard-copy graphics output in the form of maps, bar charts, engineering drawings and even two or three-dimensional illustration. Plotters often come with a set of four pens in four different colours. Most plotters also offer shading features.

PLOTTERS

It is an output unit that directly produces a hardcopy record of data on a removable medium, in the form of a two-dimensional graphic representation. Plotters are designed to produce large drawings or images such as construction plans for buildings or blueprints for mechanical objects.

There are two major types of pen plotters:

1. Flatbed plotters
2. Drum plotters

FLATBED PLOTTERS

It uses a bed or tray to hold paper in a fixed position. A movable pen is usually held by a single arm that can move the pen both horizontally and vertically. The computer instructs the flatbed plotter by directing the pen to x-y position on the page.

DRUM PLOTTERS

It has a single arm that can only move across the drum horizontally. The drum itself moves the paper forward or backward to enable the pen to draw in any vertical direction.

Any type of diagonal line is drawn by combining a horizontal movement of the pen arm with a vertical page movement via the drum. Drum plotters are used to produce continuous output, such as plotting earthquake activity, or for long graphic output, such as the structural view of a 'skyscraper'.

Multiple Choice Questions

1. With CD you can:
   (a) Read (b) Write
   (c) Both
2. Printer is an ________ device.
   (a) Input (b) Output
   (c) Both
3. Laser printer is an __________ device.
   (a) Input (b) Output
   (c) Both
4. Dumb terminals have terminals and
   (a) mouse (b) speakers
   (c) keyboard
5. Dot matrix printers uses ______ for printing
   (a) hammers (b) slugs
   (c) mouse

Descriptive Type Questions

1. Describe the various types of terminals available.
2. How are microfilms used for keeping data?
3. What is multimedia projector used for?
4. How is speech synthesizer used?
5. Decscribe the working of Dot Matrix Printer.
6. How do the daisywheel printers print?
7. Describe the working of Line printers.
8. What is an inkjet printer?
9. Describe the working of laser printer.
10. Describe the working of various type of plotters.

Storage Devices

5

INTRODUCTION

In this chapter we discuss the devices which act as both input and output devices and those which can be used for storing data.

Secondary Storage

Although the central processing unit has internal memory but this memory cannot store both an application program and data indefinitely for processing; Also internal memory is semiconductor memory - which is costly and volatile in nature - where the data are lost when the electricity is interrupted or computer is switched off. Another limitation of primary storage is that the storage requirements for programs and data on which it operate exceeds the capacity of primary storage in all computer system.

For example, the RAM capacity of a large mainframe computer would not come close to meeting the data and program storage needs of even a small company. So it is necessary to extend the storage capabilities of a computer by using devices external to main-memory.

An external storage is also called secondary storage (or auxiliary storage) because it ,provides a second, longer-term storage for programs and data needed frequently but not currently active. It usually consists of disk units electronically connected to the system. An input/output operations is required to access or retrieve information stored in secondary storage. Secondary storage is necessary because primary storage can be used only temporarily. Data is placed in primary storage only when it is needed for immediate processing; where as data which is not being currently processed reside in the secondary memory. Also data in secondary storage remains there until overwritten with new data or deleted and is accessed when needed.

Secondary storages are used to store system programs (viz; operating system, assembler, interpreter, compiler and so on), data files, software packages and so on. The arithmetic and logical operations can not be performed directly on the data stored in secondary storage this is because the reason that central processing unit can not read informations directly from the secondary storage. The programs and data (residing in secondary storage) if needed by the central processing unit for processing are first transferred from the secondary to the RAM (primary memory). Then the CPU reads it from the RAM and processes it.

The characteristics of secondary storage are:

Nonvolatile Storage: Secondary storages are nonvolatile storages i.e., the data and programs remain intact when the computer is turned off. So secondary storages do not need continuous supply of electricity as do the primary storages require.

Capacity: Secondary storage devices have larger capacity as compare to primary storage. For example, Secondary storage like hard disk are available in few gigabits (GB) as compare to primary storage, which are still available in their maximum capacity in few megabytes (MB).

Cost Effectiveness: Secondary storages are less expensive in terms of per bit of information stored as compared to primary storage this is because of the reason of adoption of magnetic and optical technology for storing data into secondary storage; whereas primary storage uses semiconductor (CMOS) technology for storing data in RAM.

Reusability: The data which is not processed currently is stored in secondary storage for future use. So secondary storage devices stores a program for future use; gets a backup of programs during execution and helps in storing of information in files. Also data in secondary storage remains there until overwritten with data or deleted. After deletion of data, that space, in secondary storage can be used to store fresh data or programs.

Reliability: Data in secondary storage is basically safe since secondary storage is physically reliable. Also it is more difficult for unscrupulous people to temper with data on disk than data stored on paper in a file cabinet.

Storage Media

Over the years manufacturers have developed a variety of devices and media for the permanent storage of data and the programs. Paper tape, punched cards, the data cell, and a variety of others have become obsolete. Two main technologies are used to store data today:

1. Magnetic Storage, and
2. Optical Storage

Although devices that store data typically employ one or the other, some combine both technologies. The primary types of magnetic storage are:

1. Floppy disks (diskettes)
2. Hard disks
3. Magnetic tapes

The primary types of optical storage are:

1. CD-ROM
2. WORM
3. Magneto-optical media

The most common storage devices use magnetic technology. When data and program files are constantly changing, magnetic storage media are most often used. Magnetic-disk-or-tape drive record data by magnetizing small areas on the storage media. These magnetized areas store the binary codes representing data or programs instructions. When the file is no longer needed, the storage hardware overwrites the binary code and records new information in its place.

The three most common storage devices floppy disk drives, hard disk drives and tape drives - all use similar techniques for reading and writing data, because all use the same medium. The surface of diskettes, hard disk and magnetic tapes are all coated with a magnetically sensitive material (usually iron oxide) which reacts to a magnetic field. As the read/write head passes over the disk's or tape surface, the direction of current in its electromagnetic aligns iron particles on the disk or tape in one of two polarities.

HARD DISK DRIVES

Hard disks have been there since the time of mainframe systems of 3rd generation computers. The only difference is that the disks at that time were removable and were of very small capacity. However, the basic technology used in the earliest hard disks has not changed all that much over the years, although the size and capacity of the drives has.

FLOPPY DISK DRIVES

Although manufacturers have been trying for years to replace the floppy disk, with a device that holds more data, the 3.5 inch floppy disk drive is still very common on most PCs sold today. The floppy disk has survived well beyond what anyone expected. It has changed in size over the years and is available in drives that fit inside the system case as well as outside. The floppy disk has come in a variety of sizes over its lifetime, but for about the past ten years the most popular size has been the 3.5 inch diskette.

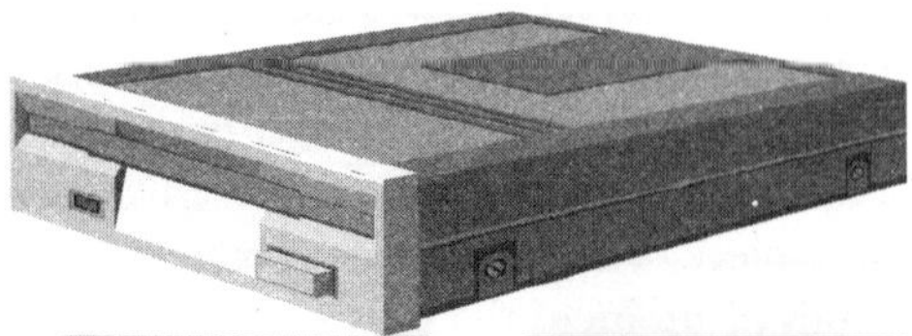

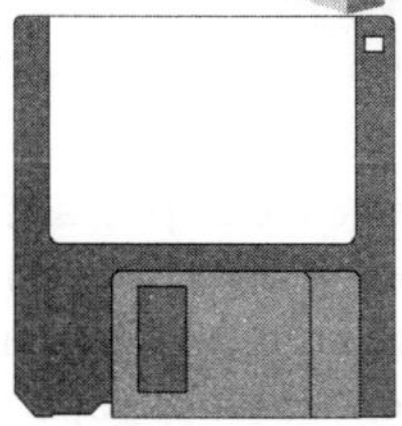

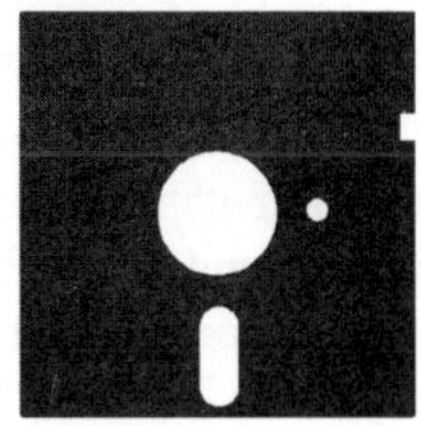

CD-ROMS AND DVDS

The CD-ROM and its comparatively huge storage capacity (over 600 floppy disks) has been very attractive to software and multimedia producers and soon virtually all software, including databases, books encyclopedias and other materials not available to the PC in the past suddenly became very available and accessible for the PC.

A CD-ROM drive is as common on PCs today as floppy drives were only a few years ago. In fact, some manufacturers now replace the floppy disk drive with a single CD-ROM on their latest PC models. The CD-ROM is by far the most common method of software distribution and data storage due to their combination of high capacity and easy, inexpensive manufacturing. A PC without a CD-ROM drive simply is not able to install the vast majority of PC software available on the market today. Some CD-ROM software even requires that your PC's drive meet a specific minimum requirement. For example, if you have an older CD-ROM drive, such as a 4X, in your system, it may need to be replaced before it can run some newer CD-ROM titles that require at least a 12X drive.

CD-ROM Technology

The CD-ROM uses compact disc (CD) technology, the same technology used to record the music on your favorite audio CDs. The physical media used for recording data, programs, music and multimedia on a CD-ROM is the same as that used to record music. In fact, the physical disc is the same for both.

Video CD (VCD)

The video CD (VCD) is used to store compressed video information using a standard also defined in the White Book. VCDs use MPEG (Motion Picture Experts Group) compression to store 74 minutes of full-motion video in the same space used by CD-DA audio. To play a video CD requires a CD-ROM drive or video CD player that is video CD-compatible. The compression algorithm used for VCD does not produce a high quality video; this format will likely give way to the DVD.

CD-Recordable

Each of the CD types covered to this point have been CD-ROMs or read-only discs, which means that except for during their manufacturing processes, data cannot be stored to them and they cannot be modified, other than to be destroyed. To take advantage of its large storage space, methods have been developed, along with special CD media that allow data to be written to a CD. A CD Recordable (CD-R) disc is manufactured essentially the same as a CD-ROM disc, with some slight variations. In place of the substrate is a layer of organic dye, over which is placed a reflective gold-colored metallic coating. Over this is the protective lacquer layer, just like a CD-ROM.

Two general types of CDs that can be modified in a special CD-R are:

CD MEDIA

Like other computer storage, such as discs and floppy disks, a CD stores data in digital form, which means that it actually stores only two values: 1s and 0s. However, where the hard disk and diskette stored data in magnetic form, data on a CD recorded in a physical recording technique. A CD starts out as a round piece of polycarbonate substrate about 4.75 inches in diameter and 1.2 millimeters (approximately) 1/20th of an inch) thick. A metal stamp, made from a master of a finished disc, is then used to stamp indentations into the substrate, a process called mastering. A CD-ROM produced this way is said to have been mastered.

The indentations are referred to as pits, and the flat, unpitted surfaces are referred to as lands. The substrate surface and its pits are then covered with a shiny, reflective silver or aluminum coating, which plays a very important part in reading and playing the contents of the CD. A clear plastic cover is then placed over the silver coating on which a paper or silk-screened label is applied. A disc manufactured in this way is called a single-session disc.

Reading the CD

When a CD is loaded into a player or CD-ROM drive, it spins and laser moves over the lands and pits, sensing thousands of them per second. When the laser hits a land, its light reflects off the metallic coating to a sensor. A pit on the CD surface does not reflect the laser back to the sensor. When it hits a pit, the light does not reflect back to the sensor. Whether the sensor sees a reflection or not is how it knows if the bit on the CD is a 1 or a 0. Unlike a floppy or hard disk, a CD is recorded on a single long (about three miles long, in fact) spiral rather than in discrete tracks. The spiral is wound onto the disc in a pattern that is the equivalent of about 16,000 tracks per inch on a hard disk drive.

The first sector on the CD is located at two minutes, no seconds and no hundredths of seconds (00:02:00) or 600 blocks. On a CD-ROM using 512-byte blocks a minute of data contains 18,000 blocks, which means that there are 300 in a second and 600 in the first two seconds. This also means that Logical Block 0 is at 00:02:00 as well.

ORGANISING AND ACCESSING STORED DATA

As a user of computer system, you just offer data as you are instructed to do; but in real sense data can not be dumped helter- skelter into a computer. System analyst has to decide how data from users will be received, organized and stored, and also in which manner data will be processed by the computer.

Organizing Data: To be processed by the computer, raw data is organized into a hierarchy. The six levels of the hierarchy of data organization are bit, character, field, record, file, and database. Each information system has a hierarchy of data organization, and each succeeding level in the hierarchy is the result of combining the elements of the preceding level. Bits - the first level - are handled automatically. The other five levels are important design considerations for any information processing activity.

Bits and Characters: A character is represented by a group of bits that are configured according to an encoding scheme, viz; ASCII (7-bits) or EBCDIC (8-bits). On the one side the bit is the basic unit of primary and secondary storage, and on the other side character is the basic unit for human perception. In terms of data storage, a character is usually the same as a byte. A character is a letter, digit, or special character.

Fields: A field contains a set of related characters. It is the lowest level logical unit in the data hierarchy. For example, a single character viz; S has little meaning out of context. But when characters are combined to form a name (e.g; SUKHVIR or SATYAPAL), they form a logical unit.

A field is best described by example: first name, middle name, last name, address.

These are all fields. An address is not one, but four fields: Street name, city, state and pincode. Whereas the field is the general reference, the specific content of a field is called the data item.

Records: A record is a collection of related fields. Thus on the publisher mailing list, author's name, address, city, pincode, and phone number constitute a record.

Files: A file is a collection of related records. The term file is also used to refer a named area on a secondary storage device that contains a program, textual material or even an image. All the author records for the publisher compose a file. Figure 12.3 shows how the publisher data might look.

Database: A database is a collection of interrelated files stored together with minimum redundancy. For example, if records are kept in a traditional file environment and an author moves, his or her address must be changed in all files that maintain address data. In a database author address data are stored only once and are made available to all department. Therefore, only one update is needed.

Data Manipulation and Retrieval:

Data management encompasses the storage, retrieval, and manipulation of data. Many existing information systems are designed using traditional approaches to develop new information systems. In traditional, or flat file, processing files a re stored, merged, and processed by a key field (a unique identifies for a record). For example, in an author file the key might be "author's number"

In addition to organizing the expected data, a plan must be made to access the data on files.

File Plan: Now that you have a general idea of how data is organized, we need to consider what way would be appropriate to place data on a storage medium - tape or disk.

Consider these application examples to see how an access decision might be made.

1. When a student, makes a request for issuing a book on his/her card, a librarian checks the validity of the student from his account and takes appropriate decision. The librarian needs immediate access to the student record in the student file.
2. Reports of airline flight attendant next month schedules are computer-produced monthly and delivered to the attendants' home- base mailboxes. The schedules are put together from information based on flight records, whose entire file can be accessed monthly at a convenience of the airline and the computer-use plan.

As you can see, the question of access seems to come down to whether a particular record is needed right a way, as it is in example. As we will see, this immediate need for a particular record means access must be direct. It follows that the organization must also be direct, or at least indexed, and that the storage medium must be magnetic disk.

File Organization: Based on the differences in the speed and method of access there are three major methods of storing files of data in secondary storage:

1. Sequential File Organization, in which records are organized in a particular order.
2. Direct File Organization, in which records are not organized in any special order.
3. Indexed Organization, in which records are organized sequentially, but indexes built into the file allow a record to be accessed either directly or sequentially.

Sequential File Organization: Sequential file processing means records are in order according to a primary key field. If a particular record in a sequential file is wanted then all t he prior records in the file must be read before reaching the desired records. Tape storage is limited to sequential file organization. Operationally, the magnetic tape is same as the one in home and automobile tape decks.

Sequential files, used for sequential processing, contain records ordered according to a key field. If the key field in an employee record is employee name, the records are ordered and processed alphabetically by last name. A sequential file is processed from start to finish. The entire file must be processed, even if only one record is to be updated.

An example of direct access: Assume there are 13 address (0 through 12) available in the file. Dividing the keynumber 327, which is SUKHVIR employee number, by the prime number 13 yields remainder 2. Thus, 2, is the address for key 327. However, for the key 678, dividing by 13 yields remainder 2, a synonym, since this address has already been used by the key 327, which also has a remainder of 2. Hence the address becomes the next location i.e; 3.

Note, incidentally, that keys (and therefore records) need not appear in any particular order.

Direct File Organization

Direct access, allows the computer to go directly to the desired record by using a primary key; the computer does not have to read all preceding records in the file as it does if the records are arranged sequentially. Direct access requires disk storage, in fact, a disk device is called a direct-access storage device (DSAD) because the computer can go directly to the desired record on the disk. An added advantage of direct access organization is the ability to read, change, and return a record to its same place on the disk, this is called updating in place.

Indexed File Organization

It is useful in applications where a file needs to be in sequential order but, in addition, access to individual records is needed. In indexed file organization records are stored in the file in sequential order, but the file also contains an index. The index is like a directory, with the keys to all records listed in order (ascending or descending). To access a record directly, the record key (primary key) must be located in the index; the address associated with the key is then used to locate the record on the disk. To access the entire file of records sequentially, begin with the first record and proceed through the rest of records.

MAGNETIC TAPE

Like your tape recorder's cassette, it has magnetic coated plastic material. It is very useful to store large volumes of data. While larger tape spools with magnetic tape units are used with mainframe computers, the small cassette tapes, similar to music cassettes are used with Personal Computers.

Physical Characteristics of a Magnetic tape

The tape is made of plastic material with iron oxide (ferrite) coating on one side of the tape, which is magnetically sensitive, and it is this surface that is used for the recording of data. The magnetized spots or bits are extremely small and not visible to the human eye.

One main advantage of tape is that large volumes of data can be condensed into a relatively small area. Typically magnetic tape is 1/2 inch wide and comes in reels which are 2400 to 3600 feet long and have a diameter of about 10 1/2 inch.

WINCHESTER DISKS

A magnetic disk drive which is similar in size to a floppy disk but overcomes speed and storage limitations by closer head alignment and denser recording. The movable read/write head floats above a rotating disk on a cushion of air produced by the rotating surface. When rotation stops, the air cushion is lost and the head comes to rest on the surface of the disk in a landing zone where no data is recorded. Winchester drives are sealed to prevent contamination that can cause head crash. A Winchester is a fixed disk system and is named after the 30-30 Winchester rifle, the original Winchester disk being 30 MB of data on 30 tracks. The disk is coated with a special lubricant which reduces the friction when the heads land.

Standard sizes are 5.25 inch and 8-inch. Storage capacities range around 40 MB to 760 MB. Mostly it is used with microcomputers. A Winchester hard disk contains several disk platters stacked on a single rotating spindle. Data are stored on all recording surfaces. The enclosure of Winchester disk keeps the disk-face surfaces free from contaminants such as dust and cigarette smoke. The rotational movement of a magnetic disk passes all data under or over read/write head, thereby making all data available for access on each revolution of the disk. A fixed disk will have at least one read/write head for each recording surface. The heads are mounted on access arm that moves over the spinning recording surfaces.

Winchester disks normally are permanently installed in the same physical unit as the processor and diskette drives. There are interchangeable hard disk also These interchangeable Winchester disks are inserted and removed in a manner that is similar to the way you insert and remove tapes on a VCR. Only a small percentage of PCs are configured to accept interchangeable Winchester disk.

Virtual Memory Operations Use Disk Drives as Extension of the Computers Memory.

ERASABLE DISKS: MAGNETO-OPTICAL DISKS

A hybrid disk, called magneto-optical (MO), combines the best features of magnetic and optical disk technologies. A magneto-optical disk has the high-volume capacity of an optical disk but can be written over as a magnetic disk. The disk surface is coated with plastic and embedded with magnetically sensitive metallic crystals.

To write data, laser beam melts a tiny spot on the plastic surface and a magnet aligns the crystal before the plastic cools. The crystal are placed in such a way that some reflect lights and others do not. Later on, when the data is read by a laser beam, only the crystals that reflect light are picked up.

Disadvantages

1. Magneto-optical disks are too expensive and do not offer anywhere near the kind of reliability that users have come to expect of magnetic media.
2. The access time in magneto-optical disks are relatively slow, about the same as a low-end, Winchester disk.
3. As optical disk technology matures to offer reliable, cost-effective, read/write operation, it eventually may dominate secondary storage in the future as magnetic disks and tape to today.

Multiple Choice Questions

1. Floppy disk popular these days is of size:
   (a) 3½″ (b) 5¼″
   (c) 5½″
2. CDs are of which shape:
   (a) round (b) square
   (c) rectangular
3. Hard disks has
   (a) cubicles (b) platters
   (c) keys

Descriptive Type Questions

1. How Magnetic Media Works?
2. What do you under by File Organization? Explain different types of File Organization.
3. What do you understand by Magnetic Tape? What are the Physical Characteristics of a Magnetic tape?

4. How Data is represented on a Magnetic Tape?
5. What is a Floppy disk? Define different types of Floppy disk.
6. What is a Floppy disk drive? Define different types of Floppy disk drive.
7. What do you understand by Winchester Disks?
8. What are the Physical Characteristics of Magnetic Disks?
9. What is CD-ROM? Define different types of CD-ROMs.
10. What do you understand by Erasable Disks? What are the drawbacks of Erasable Disks?

6

Computer Virus and Elimination

INTRODUCTION

Have you ever been bitten by a virus. Well the chances are that you have. So, would your computer say after some time. Computer virus though not very similar to the biological one, is probably more destructive. There are virus which can literally wash your hard disk clean. Let us try to understand how it gets generated and how it is treated.

Please ignore this chapter if you are not in a mood for lighter moments. Way back in 60s there was a film called Parakh, made by Mr. Bimal Roy. In this an old lady in her will had left some amount to be given to the best person of the village. So everybody of the village try to impress upon others to show his worthiness. The crux of story is that while trying to prove his worth, the Doctor of the village, introduces a certain type of medicine in the pond of the village. This results in people who are dependent on that water start falling ill and the doctor comes into the picture having the antidote of the same. No doubt his status in the eye of the villagers increases.

The main reason of my telling you this is that there is a saying that most of the Anti-virus software manufactures are the one who introduce the such viruses in the market and then sell their antidotes to make good money. How far is this true, well it is difficult to know but one thing is very clear, the computer virus is a man made thing. Man does make the virus and he makes the elimination possible too. But, in between the chances of losing data becomes very high. So keeping all this in mind one should be very careful about saving his computer from virus.

HISTORY OF VIRUS

The first computer virus for a personal computer was discovered (and created) around 1980. That means we've had about 21 years to get acquainted with them and used to their presence. Computer viruses are not a short-lived curiosity; they are today and will continue to be here for as long as anyone can foresee.

They are sufficiently widespread to be a real danger to most computers, requiring people using computers to have at least a basic knowledge of their workings if they want to avoid infections.

So the virus can be said to have the following properties.

1. A virus is a self-replicating program whose main purpose is to propagate itself to as many different places as possible.
2. A virus propagates itself by modifying another program to include itself.
3. A virus can only propagate itself by an (unknowing) act of a user of the system in which it exists.

How viruses actually work?

Virus are created using common programming tools, using knowledge that can be found in any computer book dealing with technical specifications on DOS/Windows.

Virus programming demands no special skills. Indeed, many viruses have shown such poor programming skills that it's a wonder they function at all. Yet virus programmers seem to have obtained the reputation of being master programmers.

How does a virus infect a computer?

The computes virus are of many types. There are some which would affect the boot sector of the computer, some would affect the executable files only, and so on. But, in most cases it is the data which is more likely to be affected since this is what you will have difficulty in creating. The software as such can be loaded again into the computer.

Then there are the partition and boot sector viruses. The partition sector/boot sector is the first part of any hard disk or floppy. It contains small programs, called the partition record/boot record, which is executed each time the computer is turned on. This program can, like normal files infected by the file infectors, be modified by a virus and thus infected. Viruses targeting the partition or boot sector are called partition-sector virus/boot-sector viruses.

Virus detection

For a virus to propagate, it needs to perform a number of specific actions, such as reading directory entries, opening files, writing to files, etc. Most of these actions are performed all the time by the system itself and other programs alike, although a few would not be performed under ordinary conditions.

Detection entails monitoring the system, to watch out for such dubious action. A dubious action could be opening (reading) a COM or EXE file in write mode, as one would not expect executable files to be modified.

All viruses cause some change to the system in which they infect. The change is almost always very easy to spot with normal DOS tools: **increase in file length** (use DOS command dir and a bit of arithmetic), **decrease in memory** (use chkdsk or mem), **change of time/date stamp** (use dir), etc.

For your to detect any change, it is of course required you have the initial state, file length, respectively mem-size before infection, to compare with which is not always possible. If you receive a disk from a friend or a commercial program, the size of the programs on the disk before any possible infection is not known. But even if you do not know if your system is virus free (has the initial state), it is possible to detect any further virus spread, when the virus changes the size of other, until now clean, files.

One of the most common virus protection schemes is called Stealth, Stealth is when a crafty virus uses interrupt hooking to run some of its own code that performs according to the virus's wishes. There are numerous ways to use and implement stealth and can, when performed right, be a very cunning way for the virus to hide itself. It is, however, not new thing.

One of the earliest viruses, Brain, used some stealth techniques. Brain redirected a request to read the boot sector (now infected) to the original boot sector and thus showed no infection. This would fool an antivirus program using a scan-string search and a checksum search.

Stealth is an active defence of the virus and requires that the virus have been run. As such it can easily be defeated using a know clean, uninfected, write protected disk to boot your computer.

Future of Viruses

As far as the computer goes there would always be viruses. So do not worry, take precautions. Have a good anti-virus program loaded into your computer all the time. There is something called Virus shield too, which would warn you when some virus infected is floppy is put in. But, remember nothing works better than precaution. Take care and enjoy.

Some popular viruses are listed below:

Scores Virus

These viruses are prevalent in Macintosh computers. Scores virus have a built-in time trigger that activates after two, four and seven days from the date when the disk becomes infected. The consequences are varied, ranging from printing problems and system crashes to malfunctioning of disk operations. This virus does not directly affect data files but detection of this virus requires detection of all files.

Brain Virus

This is one of the first viruses that come into existence. Also known as the Pakistani virus, it was, developed by Pakistani brothers to keep track of low cost software that were sold out of their outlet in Lahore. The virus pops up a screen saying, "Welcome to the Dungeon". This virus are known to destroy data and are highly contagious.

Lehigh Virus

This virus originated at the Lehigh University Computer Centre. The virus stays in the stack space of COMMAND.COM. When the PC is booted from an infected disk, the virus is spread through commands such as COPY, DIR, TYPE etc. On any other disk with COMMAND.COM the virus code gets copies to another disk and a counter is incremented on the parent. When the counter reaches a value of 4, all files of the disks gets erased. The boot sector gets ruined and the FAT is also corrupted.

Friday the 13th

The virus attacks only COMMAND.COM but also other executable files. When a Com or an EXE file is executed for the first time after booting the virus capture a specific interrupt and inserts its own code. After this whenever any EXE file is executed, the virus code is written to the end of the file, resulting in an enlargement in the size of the file by 1808 bytes. In COM files, the virus code is written to the beginning of the file. The enlargement in the size of the EXE and COM files causes the program to become too large to be loaded into the memory. Also, after a certain interval of time, delays are inserted, resulting in considerable slowing down of the program. The worst disaster occurs when the infected EXE or COM file is executed and when the system date is Friday the 13th; on that day, all the first get deleted.

Sunnuvale Slug

This does a variety of things like displaying a message "Greeting from Sunnyvale. Can you find me?" and sometimes modifies the COPY command resulting in deletion of files instead of copying.

Raindrops

This virus infects COM files. It intercepts the load and executes the function of MS-DOS. It checks whether the file is an EXE file or not. If the file is not an EXE file, the first three bytes of the file are replaced by a jump instruction at the end of the file where it gets attached after encryption. This result is dropping or showering of characters on the screen like raindrops and is also accompanied by appropriate sound effects.

Happy Birthday 30th

This virus gets activated on January 5th, if any of the infected program gets executed and would ask the user to type Happy Birth 30th. It might destroy all the data stored on a disk. The symptom of this virus are that the computer memory is reported as 6KB lesser than actual; e.g. it would show a memory of 634 KB instead of 640 KB.

Multiple Choice Questions

1. What is a computer virus?
   (a) a program (b) a device
   (c) a disk
2. Can a virus be cured?
   (a) no (b) yes

Descriptive Type Questions

1. What is a Computer Virus?
2. When was the first Computer Virus detected?
3. How does the Virus work?
4. How does the Virus effect the Computer?
5. How can you detect a Computer Virus?
6. Write a short note on following viruses:

Scores Virus	Brain Virus
Lchigh Virus	Friday the 13th
Sunnuvale Slug	Raindrops
Happy Birthday 30th	

Computer Software

7

DIFFERENCE BETWEEN HARDWARE AND SOFTWARE

There are two ways of looking at it. First is this that Hardware is something which we can see with our eyes and touch whereas Software is something which we don't see and works in the background and definitely we can't touch it. A very practical example of this can be given in the form of a VCR. In this case the VCR where the video cassette is put is the hardware whereas the video cassette which has the film in it can be called as Software. Without each other they have no value. You cannot run video cassette without a VCR and VCR is nothing but a machine in itself has no movie to run.

Similarly in computers Hardware and Software go neck-in-neck. They are totally dependent upon each other. This is why when you buy a software, it has the hardware requirements mentioned on it since without that much of hardware, it will not work. But, software is a very vast field. Lots and lots of software are available, which one would suit your requirements, you have to use according to your needs.

SOFTWARE

So far we have talked about one side of the computer system, i.e., the hardware, the machine itself. Now, we will talk about its usage. How this machine can be used with the help of various programs. This is called Software. There are various types of software. Some are needed for some particular type of operations and others for running the computer. The basic difference between Hardware and Software can be explained by simple term that Hardware is something which can be seen and touched whereas Software cannot be seen or touched. Software is essential for running the computer.

As mentioned it is needed to run the computer, but, what is it? It is nothing but a set of instructions that directs the computer to process information. These instructions are called programs. A set of programs is called Software. There are mainly two types of software—System software and Application software.

SYSTEM SOFTWARE

As the name implies it is needed to run the system. It also coordinates the operations of the various hardware components of the computer. It is needed to run the computer system. It also acts as an coordinator between the computer and its user.

Most of the system software are machine based so usually the manufacturer of the machine provides the software. There are two types of system software and they are:

(a) The Operating System; and

(b) The Language Translators

Operating System (OS)

It is a collection of programs that controls the overall operations of a computer. It helps the computer to supervise and manage its resources. Operating system calls the application program whenever needed, translates the programs and manages data needed to produce the output.

Language Translators

There are different type of translators available.

Assembler It is used to convert the program written in assembly language into machine language.

Compiler It translates a source program that is usually written in a high level language by a programmer into machine language, which the computer understands. It is capable of replacing source program with a series of machine-language instructions or with a subroutine. It is different for different languages. A compiler creates a unique object program, i.e., if a source program is compiled there is no need of that source program because output can be obtained by executing that object program.

Interpreter It translates each source program statement into a sequence of machine instructions and than executes these machine instructions before translating the next source language statement. Interpreters are also unique for each high level language. Basically, the function of the compiler and interpreter are the same; the only difference is that compiler provides a separate object program but the interpreter does not. At the time of using interpreter each and every time the source program is needed. Another difference is that interpreter translates the source program line wise, i.e., it would not execute the next line unless the first one has not error.

APPLICATION SOFTWARE

It is a set of programs designed for specific uses or applications such as word processing, graphics or spreadsheet analysis. In fact, most of the commercial software fall under this category. Application software can be custom-made but is usually purchased off the shelf.

Popular Software Packages

Word Processors

This is the software where you play with the text. You enter the text by typing and manipulate it to create a good looking letter, brochure, thesis, etc., and print them according to your needs.

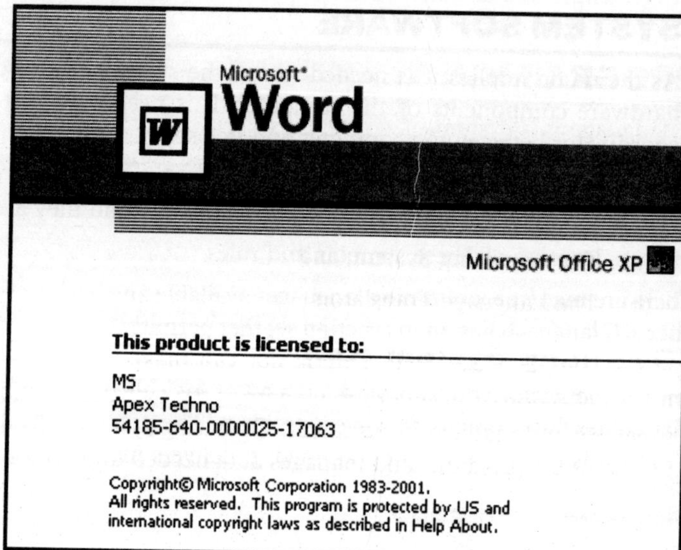

Spreadsheets

A spreadsheet is a matrix of rows and columns. These columns and rows are used for entering text and numbers, which can then be used for calculations. An ideal software for accounting purposes and is very widely used for creating balance sheet, etc.

Database System

These software are used to create and extract data from a database in the form needed by you. Most of the information needed by you can be totalled too. It also helps you in arranging the data in a particular format too.

Accounting Packages

Various accounting packages are available in the market which would take care of all your accounting needs from ledgers to reports. There are provisions for creating exclusive reports too.

DTP Packages

Without these packages, this book would not have been possible. It sort of acts as via media between computer and printing press. All the pre-press work can be done using these software. From designing a page with text and graphics to creating complicated art works, everything can be done using them.

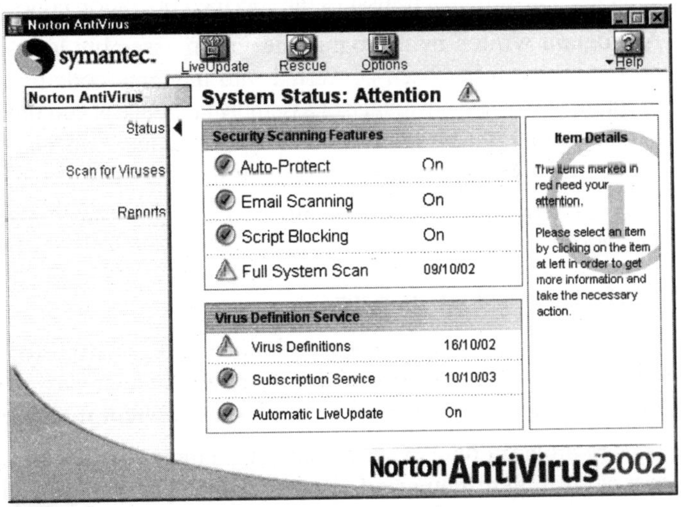

Graphic Packages

These are used for working with pictures and graphics instead of numbers and text. Computer-accessible data can readily be converted to graphic form on the screen as well as on paper using dot-matrix printers, ink-jet printers or plotters.

Anti Virus Software

Though viruses are mushrooming at a faster rate than virus vaccines, still there are few very good and reasonable anti-virus software to assist users to keep their computer system virus free.

PROGRAMMING LANGUAGES

A language is a system of communication. In order to communicate with each other, humans need languages like English, Hindi, etc. In the same manner, for communicating with the computer, we use computer language called programming language. A programming language consists of all the symbols, characters and usage rules that permit people to communicate with computers. Learning to program requires learning all these symbols and rules.

There are many programming languages available and each one has its symbols, character set and syntax but each language has an instruction set that permits those familiar operations to be performed. We know that the computer can neither think nor can make any decision on its own. It needs instructions to understand what to do. A program is a set of logically related instructions that are arranged in a sequence that guides the computer to solve a problem. The process of writing a program is called programming. If a system is not correctly programmed; it delivers incorrect information.

Machine Language

This is a sequence of instructions written in the form of binary numbers consisting of 1s and 0s to which the computer responds directly. A machine language would have two parts. The first part is the command or an operation that tells the computer what functions are to be performed. The second part of the instruction is the operand that tells the computer where to find or store the data on which the desired operation is to be performed.

The machine language is the only one that computer can understand directly. In the earlier computers programmers had to translate instructions directly into machine language from the computers understood. This task was very difficult and very few programmers could do this job. So, this language was very difficult to understand. But the main advantage of this language is that it is faster in execution as the computer directly starts executing it.

Assembly Language

To ease the burden of the programmer, mnemonic operation codes and symbolic addresses were developed during the early 1950s. The mnemonic refers to a memory aid. One of the first steps for improving the program preparation process was to substitute letter, symbols and mnemonics for the mnemonic machine-language operation codes. Today every computer has a mnemonic code, though the actual symbols vary among makes and models. Machine language is still used by the computer as it process data but assembly language software first translates the specified operation code symbol into its machine language equivalent.

A program written by a programmer in an assembly language is called a Source Program. After this source program has been converted into machine code by an assembler, it is referred to as an Object Program. The main advantage of assembly language is that the programs written in it are easy to understand as compared to the programs of machine language. And a big drawback is that they are machine-oriented, depending upon the model of processor being used.

Also, the programs written assembly language are slower to execute as compared to those in the machine language.

High Level Language

The development of mnemonic technique and macro-instruction led, to the development of high level languages that are often oriented towards a particular class of problem. Unlike assembly programs, high-level language programs may be used with different makes of computes with the little modifications.

Thus re-programming expense may be greatly reduced when new equipment is acquired. The time and cost of creating machine and assembly languages was quite high. And this was the prime motivation for the development of high level languages.

Some of the programming languages with their main characteristics have been described as follows:

LOGO	It allows you to draw pictures on the computer screen using a friendly little cursor called TURTLE. Most of the school going children are taught computers using this software.
FORTRAN	In early 90s, it was the most popular software used for carrying out scientific and mathematical computations. Since it is suitable for large amount of data, it is not used for business programming applications.
COBOL	If FORTRAN was for scientific purposes then this was for business purposes. It was capable of handling any type of data. COBOL programs are characterised by their easy readability due to their verbose syntax and good data organization and file handling.
BASIC	Probably the first computer language you would learn while learning programming. Its ease of use made it more popular with the users. But the main problem in BASIC is that most versions of this language do not support indexed files.

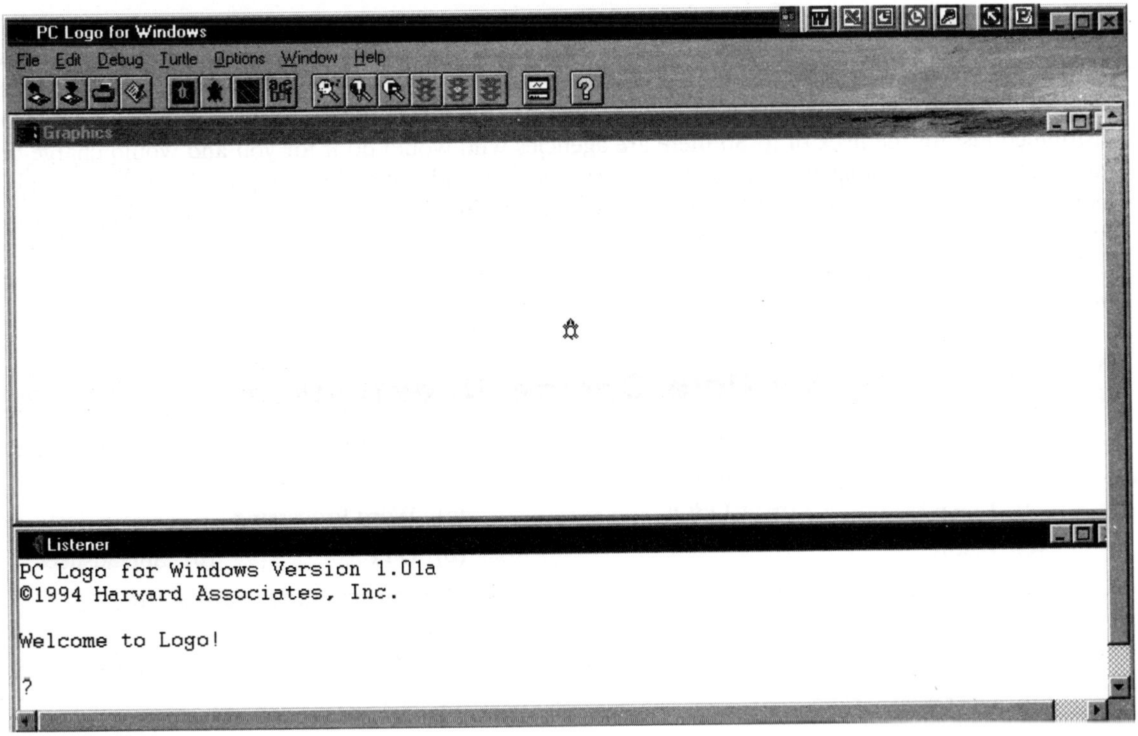

PROLOG It lays stress on the usage of logic to solve problems. PROLOG is basically known as a theorem-providing system, using a formal logic technique known as predicate calculus to prove the truth of propositions from a set of axioms.

PASCAL It is a general-purpose language that can be used for a wide range of numeric and non numeric applications. It is a well-structured and well organized programming language.

C It is a general-purpose structured programming language characterised by the ability to write very concise source programs. The compiler of C is commonly available for the computers of all sizes. The compilers are usually compact and they generate object programs that are small and highly efficient as compared to the programs written in any other language.

C++ It is an object-oriented programming language. It is based on the concept of Object-oriented programming. Most of the new software are developed using this language.

JAVA The language for the Internet. JAVA is an object-oriented programming language that was developed after C++. Java was designed to be small, simple and portable across platforms.

4GL Language The fourth generation of language has not been defined as that of the other generations. Fourth generations of languages are commonly referred to as 4GL. These are high level languages that requires significantly fewer instructions to accomplish a particular task than a third generation language does. Thus a programmer should be able to write a program faster in a 4GL than in a third generation language.

FREE DOMAIN SOFTWARE

As the name suggests, it is available free. Whatever maybe the reason behind it, the fact of the matter remains that it is free. Sometimes a researcher who has developed a new software, would like it to be distributed just for the heck of it. So there are agencies who would do it for you and would charge the minimum fee for handling and media. Now-a-days with the advent of Internet, the things have become more easier. You just download from the sites and start using the software without bothering about the copyright and even paying for it. Usually what happens is that when you have got used to using the software and want to know more about it, then they would charge for updation. So if are of the type who does not want to grow, then it is ok to use free software else be prepared to pay more.

Multiple Choice Questions

1. A computer language which is used for drawing pictures on the screen is:
   (a) LOGO (b) COBOL
   (c) BASIC
2. Computer program which controls the operations of computer is called:
   (a) Assembler
   (b) Operating System
   (c) Interpreter
3. A computer program used for Business applications is:
   (a) LOGO (b) COBOL
   (c) BASIC
4. A software package for creating printing artworks is called:
   (a) Word Processing
   (b) DTP (b) Spreadsheet
5. Computer understands the ________ language.
   (a) Machine (b) Assembly
   (c) High level language
6. Computer language used on Internet is
   (a) PASCAL (b) JAVA
   (c) BASIC

Descriptive Type Questions

1. What is the difference between Hardware and Software?
2. What are the different type of system software?
3. Describe the various language translators.
4. Which are the various popular software packages?
5. What are assembly and machine languages?
6. Describe briefly the following languages:

LOGO	FORTRAN
COBOL	BASIC
PROLOG	PASCAL
C	C++
JAVA	

8 Operating Systems

WHAT IS AN OPERATING SYSTEM?

When the computer is put on, the first thing that it needs is the operating system, i.e., the software needed for running the computer. Most of the time you would not see the working of the operating system. It mostly works in the background. Even after the computer is fully on and the operating system has handed over the computer to the user, it still keeps on working in the background.

An operating system consists of a set of instructions that coordinates all the activities of the hardware devices. It also enables application software to be executed. Some of the popular operating systems are DOS (Disk Operating System) and Microsoft Windows.

There are more too, but they are not very popular. You can say that an operating system is a Resource Allocator. Many computer resources are required to solve a problem CPU time, I/O devices, memory space, file storage space, etc. The operating system acts the manager of these resources and allocates them to specific programs and users as necessary for their tasks, thus maintains the efficiency of the computer.

OPERATING SYSTEM FUNCTIONS

The main functions of the operating systems are defined below::

Input/Output Operations: The Operating System is responsible for handling various types of inputs, e.g., input from keyboard, input from mouse, etc., and various types of outputs in the appropriate manner. For instance, if the input is coming from mouse, then it requires different type of handling as compared to input coming from keyboard. Similarly, if an output is targeted for printer, then it requires different type of handling as compared to output targeted for monitor.

Handling File System: This task involves the making of decisions regarding the storage of files, i.e., where and how a particular file is to be stored, maybe on floppy disk or hard disk.

Execution of Program: The Operating System is responsible for executing various programs whether user programs or system programs, i.e., special programs required for the machine functioning.

Allocation of Resources: This task aims at proper use of resources available. For example, if multiple files are to be printed then "who and in which order this task will take place?" will be decided by the operating system.

Detection of Errors: The Operating System is also responsible for detecting any type of error that occurs and then properly handling it.

Information and Resource Protection: The Operating System is responsible for ensuring that the information and resources available on machine and used in the current way. The Operating System foils the attempts to use them incorrectly.

These services ensure that your computer works smoothly.

The functions offered by different operating system differ form one operating system to another, but more or less they provide the same type of services.

OPERATING SYSTEM TYPES

As mentioned there are various type of operating systems available, but they may be from various vendors and may be for various type of computers. But, broadly they can be divided into the following types:

Single Program Operating System: This is single user operating system. At any point of time only one user program can be supported and executed.

Multiprogram Operating System: This type of system supports multiprogramming i.e. more than one user can be supported by it, therefore, more than one user programs are loaded and active in the main store at the same time.

Time Sharing Operating System: This operating system uses the time sharing technique. Each active user program is given a fair share of CPU time, if the time elapses or on I/O operation is requested, CPU shifts over to the next job waiting and the previous program is put to wait (in case time is over) or handed over to I/O manager (in case I/O request is made). The active programs are scheduled for execution using certain job scheduling techniques.

Real Time Operating System: In this type of operating system the jobs have to be finished within the deadlines. The performance of the system is measured by its ability to complete its jobs within the deadlines. If a work cannot be completed, this situation is called deadline overrun.

Microprocessing Operating System: This is capable of handling more than one processor as the work have to be executed on more than on processor. This operating system should be capable of loadsharing in case of identical processors os that the system's efficiency improves.

SOME POPULAR OPERATING SYSTEMS

Following are the few popular operating systems.

Disk Operating System

Microsoft Corporation developed it is early 1980s as a single user operating system for personal computers. PC-DOS and MS-DOS represent systems that became extremely popular. With the passage of time, DOS has undergone a number of changes and upgradations. The latest version is 6.22.

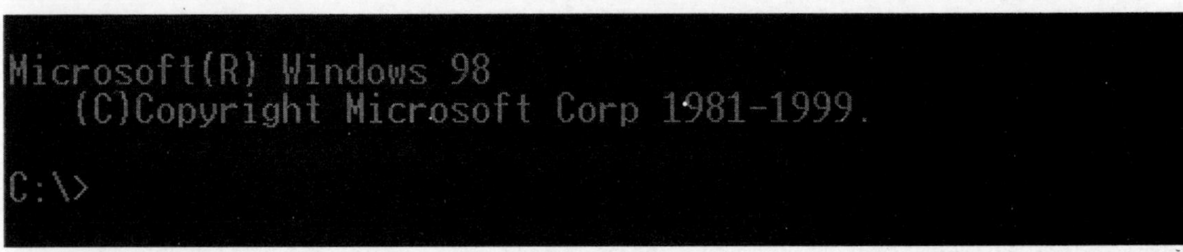

Microsoft Windows

Microsoft developed an operating system having a graphical user interface known as Windows. Three earlier versions of Microsoft Windows were Windows 3.0, Windows 3.1 and Windows 3.11. These, however, were not operating system, and instead, comprised the operating environments. An operating environment is a graphical user interface that works in combination with an OS to simplify its use.

Windows'95 was specially developed as a true multi-tasking operating system. It did not require DOS to run but still retained some features of DOS and Windows 3.x for downward compatibility. It has a graphical user interface that improved its working very considerably. It takes full advantage of 32 bit processors and supports an efficient system of multi-tasking. It also has the provision of Networking and e-mail.

An upgrade to the Windows'95 operating system was known as Windows 98. It is more efficient than Windows 95. Integrated with Internet, it also provides faster system start up and shut down, better file management and multimedia option, it also supports the Universal Serial Bus (USB) that enables users to add and remove devices more easily.

Microsoft Windows 2000 is also a complete multi-tasking operating system with Graphical User Interface (GUI). Two of its basic versions are Windows 2000 Server and Windows 2000 Professional. The latest in this series is the version Windows XP (Extra Professional).

UNIX

This multiuser operating system was developed as early as 1970. A powerful operating system, it is capable of handling a large number of transactions in a multi-user environment. It is also capable of working with mutliple CPUs. It is used most often as a Server in workstations. The only demerit of UNIX is that its commands are difficult to remember and use. It also lacks some of the system administrative features. UNIX has a command-like surface and that make it tough to use. Several versions of UNIX exist but they are different from each other.

OS/2

An operating system from IBM and not from Microsoft. It was designed to work with 32 bit microprocessors. It enables users to simultaneously run a number of programs. Like Windows it also has a Graphical User Interface (GUI). With intensive support available to it by IBM, it is extensively used on IBM systems. It can also run most of the Windows 3.x compatible programs.

LINUX

It surprises many to learn that, as an operating system, Linux emerged in an attempt to break the stranglehold of the Windows. It also has a Unix-like Graphical User Interface (GUI) and has been distributed free. Unlike other proprietary software, Linux is an open software that makes available its source code to the users. This operating system thus offers two major advantages:

1. Users can customize it to suit their specific needs.
2. It could be obtained free, thus representing a virtual body blow to the high price line of Windows.

Despite these advantages, Linux suffered from a major disadvantage. It specifically comprised the extremely limited availability of various application software packages that could be used under Linux. It will be clear from the fact that only a few companies like Corel Corporation and Red Hat software develop their products to run on Linux.

Multiple Choice Questions

1. An operating system is a must for the computer:
   (a) Yes (b) No
2. Most popular operating system for the PCs, now is:
   (a) DOS (b) Windows
   (c) Unix
3. Full name of DOS is:
   (a) Disk Operating System
   (b) Direct Operating System
   (c) Data Operating System

Descriptive Type Questions

1. What is an operating system?
2. Describe the various functions of the operating system.
3. Describe the various types of operating systems.
4. List out the various popular operating systems.

9 Application Software

INTRODUCING MICROSOFT OFFICE 2000

Microsoft Corporation which is the largest producer of software in the World, in the 90's introduced the concept of Office Suite. The idea behind was to provide all the possible software which a small office or home office would probably use. This concept was introduced first for Macintosh machines of Apple and was named Microsoft Office Suite. It was in 1990 that the first suite for Windows was introduced. Initially the software were stand-alone software but were sold as a bundle, as part of the marketing strategy. It was later on formed as an integrated package. The first in this line was Microsoft Office ver. 4.3 for Windows 3.1 followed by Microsoft Office 7.0 for Windows 95 and Microsoft Office 97 for Windows 95 and now Microsoft Office 2000 for Windows 98.

Microsoft Office is a powerful combination of software which allows to you to write letters, prepare a presentation, keep database records, prepare a spreadsheet, publish a newsletter and many more applications. Integration of the various constituents is very useful because this was you can write a letter in Word 2000 and have figures from the database Microsoft Access in it and a spreadsheet in a tabular form from Microsoft Excel. It is this integration which makes the Microsoft Office as the number 1 selling software in the World. Various constituents of the suite are:

MICROSOFT WORD 2000

A word processing software which allows you to write letters, edit them and print them after formatting it according to your needs. It has all the possible options of a word processer in the form of font style and size; indents; line spacing; margins; spell checking and grammar checkers to name a few.

MICROSOFT EXCEL 2000

This spreadsheet program allows you to manipulate and present your data in almost any way you choose. It allows you to work on a tabular pad consisting of columns and rows where you can perform all your mathematic, financial and statistical calculations. These calculations can be as simple as totalling a row or column of values or as complex as figuring the rate of return on an investment under varying circumstances. It also allows you to make a graphical representation of all your data in the form of 2- or 3-dimensional graph or pie chart.

MICROSOFT ACCESS 2000

A software to take care of most of your database requirements. It allows you to store and organize information in sets of tables, which can be displayed in the form of columns and rows to look like a table or an index card. What's more it allows you to perform calculations and find for you simple statistics like totals and averages. It allows you to sort the data in any form and extract the required information based on the key given by you.

MICROSOFT POWERPOINT 2000

Want to make a presentation in a hurry! This is an ideal program fo the same. Make sophisticated slide shows and professional looking electronic presentations. It also allows you to add charts, tables and pictures for make the presentation look alive.

MICROSOFT OUTLOOK 2000

It is an electronic tool for managing appointments, addresses, e-mail, and notes. With lots of stress being given to the e-mail these days, it is an ideal software for sending and receiving e-mail.

INTERNET EXPLORER 5.0

An ideal program for exploring the net. It is the Web Browsing program. It helps to connect to Web sites and surf the Web using hypertext links, and dowload files and programs from the net.

MICROSOFT FRONTPAGE 2000

A program which allows you to create you own Web site. With FrontPage 2000, the knowledge of HTML programming language is no longer required. FrontPage 2000 carries out the programming for you in the background, allowing you to concentrate on the other features in your Web pages such as design, feel and functionality.

MICROSOFT PUBLISHER 2000

It is Microsoft's answer to the various other publishing software available in the market like PageMaker. It allows you to create invitations, design business-cards, and letter-heads, make your own calenders, produce newsletter, etc.

MICROSOFT PHOTODRAW 2000

It is used to create and enhance drawings and photgraphs. It is the newest member of the Microsoft Office Suite. With this software, even with little capabilities in graphic designing, you can create good looking graphics.

MICROSOFT OFFICE BAR

With so many software and their options, does it not seem to an impossible task to master all of them. Well, No. Microsoft had this is mind when it decided on to have quite a number of similar commands for these software. Not only that their launch and opening has been integrated into a small toolbar called Microsoft Office Manager. When you install Office into your computer, this bar finds a place on your desktop. It is a rotating toolbar and can be moved anywhere on the screen and can be hidden if not needed.

Let us see what this toolbar has:

❶ ❷ ❸ ❹ ❺ ❻ ❼ ❽ ❾ ❿

❶ Close button	This button allows you to make toolbar icons smaller or bigger. You can even hide the toolbar using this button. You can also get information about Microsoft Office from this button.
❷ New Office Document	This button allows you to open a new office document from the dialog box which is produces after you click this button.
❸ Open Office Document	This button allows you to open an existing document from your computer.

❹	New Appointment	It allows you set a new appointment in Microsoft Outlook.
❺	New Task	This button allows you to set a new task in Microsoft Outlook.
❻	New Contract	This button allows you to make a new contract in Microsoft Outlook.
❼	New Journal Entry	This button allows you to make a new journal entry in Microsoft Outlook.
❽	New Note	This button allows you make a new note in Microsoft Outlook.
❾	Microsoft Word	This button opens Microsoft Word for you.
❿	Microsoft Excel	This button opens Microsoft Excel for you.

❶ ❷ ❸ ❹ ❺ ❻

❶	Microsoft PowerPoint	This button opens Microsoft PowePoint for you.
❷	Microsoft Outlook	This button opens Microsoft Outlook for you.
❸	Microsoft Access	This button opens Microsoft Access for you.
❹	Windows Explorer	This button opens the Windows Explorer for you.
❺	Control Panel	This button opens the Control Panel.
❻	Microsoft FrontPage	This button opens the Microsoft FrontPage for you.

This toolbar is available on the desktop as shown on the next page:

USING THE MOUSE

Since most of the activities in Microsoft Office are done using the mouse, it is very important to have the complete knowledge of working of mouse while using the constituents of Microsoft Office.

To click

Position the pointer on a menu, a button, or an icon and click the left mouse once.

To double-click

Position the pointer on an item and click the left mouse button twice in quick succession.

To select

1. Position the pointer on the first item to select.
2. Click and hold down the mouse button.
3. Move the mouse pointer across the items to select.
4. Release the mouse button.

To drag

1. Position the pointer on an item.

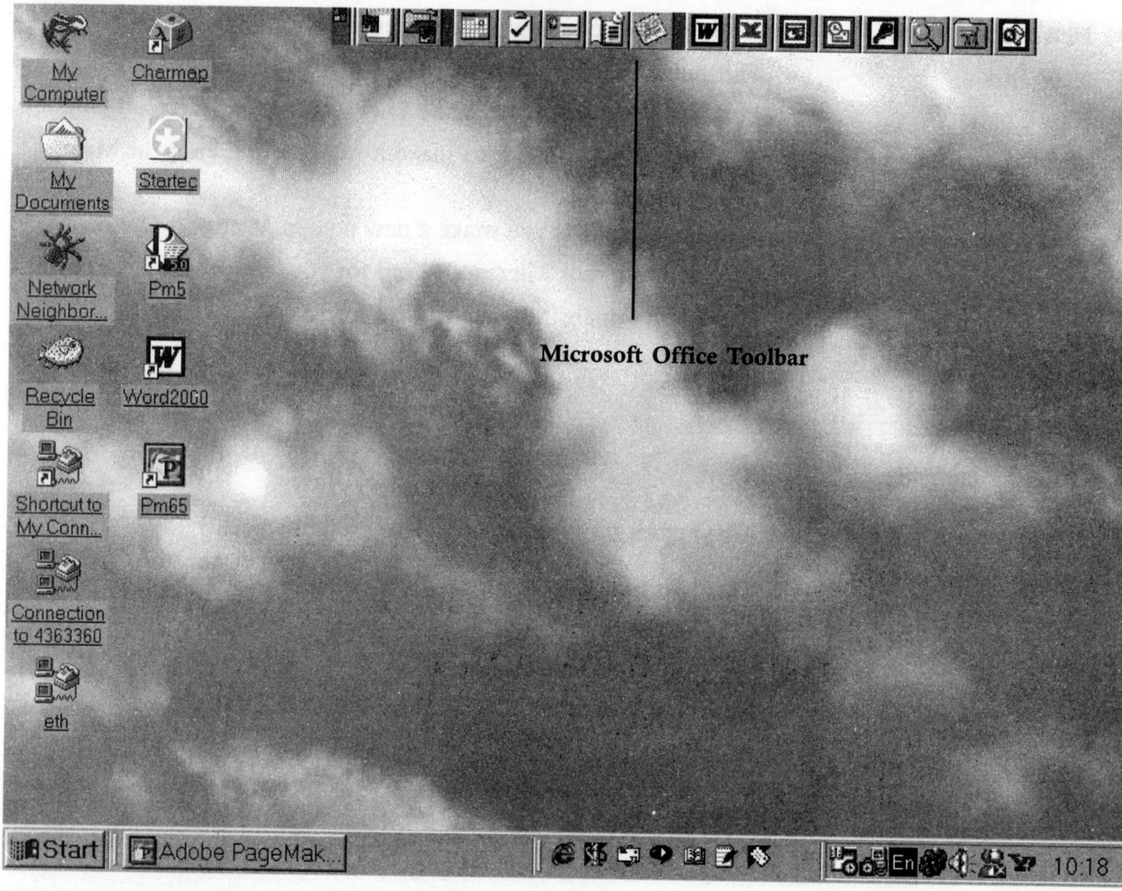

2. Click and hold down the left mouse button.
3. Move the mouse.
4. Release the mouse button.

To scroll

Drag the scroll button in the scroll bar up or down.

Or

Click a scroll arrow at either end of the scroll bar.

To choose from a menu

1. Click a menu name.
2. Click an item on a menu.

   Or

   If the item is followed by an arrow, position the mouse pointer on the item to open the submenu and then click an item on the submenu.

To move a window

Position the pointer on the window's titile bar and press and hold the mouse button as your drag the window.

To resize a window

Position the pointer on the window's corner and, when you see the diagonal pointer, drag to resize the window.

To minimize a window

Click the Minimize button.

To restore a minimized window

Click the button for the window on the taskbar.

To maximize a window

Click the Maximize button.

To switch windows

Click any visible part of the window

Or

Click the button for the window on the taskbar.

To close a window

Click the Close button on the window

Or

Right click the button for the window on the taskbar and choose Close from the shortcut menu.

COMMON KEYBOARD COMMANDS

Ctrl + N	Open a new document
Ctrl + O	Opens a existing document
Ctrl + S	Saves the current document
Ctrl + W	Close the current document
Ctrl + P	Prints the current document
Ctrl + C	Copies the highlighted matter to store it in clipboard
Ctrl + X	Cuts the highlighted matter to store it in clipboard
Ctrl + V	Pastes the matter available on the clipboard
F1	Call for help
Shift + F1	Use the What's This? Button
Ctrl + F6	Switch between open documents
Ctrl + Z	Undo an action
Ctrl + Y	Redo an action

Multiple Choice Questions

1. Word processing in MS Office is done by:
   (a) Microsoft Word
   (b) Microsoft Excel
   (c) Microsoft Access
2. A spreadsheet is created by:
   (a) Microsoft Word
   (b) Microsoft Excel
   (c) Microsoft Access
3. A database is created by:
   (a) Microsoft Word
   (b) Microsoft Excel
   (c) Microsoft Access
4. A presentation can be created using:
   (a) Microsoft Word
   (b) Microsoft PowerPoint
   (c) Microsoft Access

Descriptive Type Questions

1. What is Micorsoft Office?
2. Define the various constituents of Microsoft Office.
3. What are the various icons on the Microsoft Office bar?
4. How would you use the mouse for:

Clicking	Selecting
Dragging	Scrolling
Choosing a Menu	Moving a Window
Resizing a Window	Minimizing a Window
Restoring a Window	Maximizing a Window
Switching Window	Closing a Window

10 Number System

NUMBER SYSTEM

Symbols could be combined to represent specific quantities, but the order of their combination followed no consistent rules. None of the early symbolic systems included all the concepts necessary for straight forward mathematical computation. Separate symbols were needed for each possible digit value (included zero) and other symbols were needed to separate the whole part of the number from the fractional part.

Arithmetic Systems

To a computer, everything is a number. Numbers are numbers, letters are numbers and punctuation marks, symbols and even the computer's own instructions are numbers. Computers do not use the same number system as the one we use. In fact, people who program computers use several different number systems, in addition to the familiar base 10 (or decimal) scheme that we use all the time. The most important of these are the binary or base 2 system and the hexadecimal or base 16 system.

Number System

Any system for representing numeric values or quantities, e.g., the decimal system utilizes ten digits 0 to 9. These digits can be arranged in groups, the contribution of each digit being made according to the value of the digit and the significance of its position in the group. The decimal number system is used almost universally by humans.

Decimal System

The decimal system is important because it is universally used to represent quantities outside a digital system. This means that there be will situations where decimal values have to be converted to binary values before they are entered into digital system, e.g., computer. Likewise, there will be situations where the binary values at the outputs of a digital circuit have to be converted to decimal values for presentation to the outside world.

In addition to decimal and binary number system, two other number systems find wide spread applications in digital systems. The octal (base 8) and hexadecimal (base 16) number systems are used to provide a convenient and efficient means for representing large binary numbers. In digital system, three or four of these number systems may be in use at the same time, so that an understanding of the system operation requires the ability to convert from one number system to another. You would learn about these conversions later in the chapter.

Decimal Numbers

Decimal numbers are the numbers in everyday use and also known as Denary numbers or **numbers to base 10**, because 10 is the base of the decimal number system.

The system of writing numbers in which successive digit positions are represented by successive powers of radix 10 and in which lowest integral weight is 1.

For example, $187.3 = 1 \times 10^3 + 8 \times 10^2 + 7 \times 10^0 + 3 \times 10^{-1}$

This is called **expanded notation** for the integer. Decimal numbers system uses ten different digits 0, 1, 2, 3, 4, 5, 6, 7, 8, 9.

The base or radix of a number system is defined as the number of digits it uses to represent numbers in the system. Since the decimal number system uses ten digit so its radix is 10. The decimal number system is also called as base 10 number system.

In computers decimal numbers are usually represented by binary digits arranged in group of four, each group corresponding to a digit of a decimal number. The decimal system is a positional value system in which the value of the digit depends on its position. All positional number system have the highest numerical symbol having a value one less than the base or radix, e.g., in decimal system the base of it is 10 and its symbols vary from 0 to 9.

For Example:

Explain the weight of each digit of the number 18730.

$1 \times 10^4 = 10{,}000$

$8 \times 10^3 = 8{,}000$

$7 \times 10^2 = 700$

$3 \times 10^1 = 30$

$0 \times 10^0 = 0$

1 8 7 3 0

Most significant digit **Least significant digit**

The weight of each digit of a decimal number depends on its relative position within the number. In a positional representation system, the factor by which the value represented by a character in a digit place is multiplied to obtain its additive contribution in the representation of a number.

The weight of the 1st digit of the number from the R.H.S. = 1st digit X 10^0

The weight of second digit of the number from the R.H.S. = 2nd digit X 10^1

and so on.

Its general form that is weights/significance of the nth digit of the number from R.H.S.

= nth digit x 10^{n-1}

= nth digit x $(\text{radix})^{n-1}$

BINARY SYSTEM

The turning point in the history of number system occurred in 1666 A.D. when Leibniz generalized treatise on positional number system. Thirteen years later Leibniz defined the binary number system which today is so important that every beginner in computer science has to learn this number system.

Many of the electronic components of a computer are bistable in nature, i.e., they can be in either of two states ON or OFF. Reliable recording and reading on a magnetic surface is achieved when the surface is magnetized in either clockwise or anticlockwise directions.

Thus all data to be stored and processed in computers are transformed as strings of two symbols 0 and 1, which are also the symbols for digits of the binary number system. It is an example of positional numeration system.

Programmers usually use data and other information in the form of decimal digits, alphabets and special symbols. This information is converted to binary codes within the computer because a digital computer operates on binary bits only.

Binary number system has a base or radix of 2. Its two digits are denoted by 0 & 1 and are called **bits**. There is no digit in the binary number system to represent 2 or 3 etc. Therefore, using positional technique

2 is written as 10

3 is written as 11

4 is written as 100

and so on.

The weight of each binary bit of a binary number depends on its relative position within the number, i.e., the weight of a digit in any positional number system depends on its relative position within the number and the base of the number system in binary number system with base 2 the weight of nth bit of the number from R.H.S. = n^{th} bit x 2^{n-1}

CONVERSION BETWEEN NUMBER BASES

Conversion from Decimal to Binary

External to computer we use decimal numbers whereas internally we use binary representation, so we have to convert decimal numbers to binary. Also it is sometimes convenient to use a number in a base different from the base currently being used, i.e., to change the number from one base to another.

In a decimal number the value of the

1st digit from R.H.S. = $10^0 = 1$

2nd digit from R.H.S. = $10^1 = 10$

3rd digit from R.H.S. = $10^2 = 100$

Similarly in a binary number the value of the

1st digit from R.H.S. = $2^0 = 1$

2nd digit from R.H.S. = $2^1 = 2$

3rd digit from R.H.S. = $2^2 = 4$

.... and so on.

The process, often called the remainder method, is basically a series of repeated divisions by the number of the base to which you are converting (in our case base is 2). There are two points to remember:

Keep dividing until you reach a zero quotient

Use the remainder in reverse order.

Under the process of conversion we determine which multiples of 2 are present in a given decimal number. Consider the following examples.

Example

$(187)_{10}$ =

2	187		
2	93	1	Least significant bit. (L.S.B.)
2	46	1	
2	23	0	

2	11	1	
2	5	1	
2	2	1	
2	1	0	
	0	1	Most significant bit. (M.S.B.)

$(187)_{10} = (10111011)_2$

Another Example

$(330)_{10}$

2	330		
2	165	0	Least significant bit. (L.S.B.)
2	82	1	
2	41	0	
2	20	1	
2	10	0	
2	5	0	
2	2	1	
2	1	0	
	0	1	Most significant bit. (M.S.B.)

$(330)_{10} = (101001010)_2$

The binary equivalent of the decimal number is given by the sequence of remainders obtained during division. L.S.B. of the binary number is the 1st remainder obtained and M.S.B. is the last remainder.

Conversion from Binary to Decimal (to base 10 from base 2)

In this process we first mark the bit position and then we give the weight of each bit to the number depending on its position. The sum of the weight of all bits gives the equivalent decimal number. Also we know that the weight of nth bit of the number from R.H.S. in binary system = nth bit x 2^{n-1}. For example consider the following binary numbers.

Example: Convert $(10111011)_2$ to decimal.

Bit Position

	8	7	6	5	4	3	2	1
	1	0	1	1	1	0	1	1
Weight of each bit	2^7	2^6	2^5	2^4	2^3	2^2	2^1	2^0

Sum of weight of all bits

$= 1 \times 2^7 + 0 \times 2^6 + 1 \times 2^5 + 1 \times 2^4 + 1 \times 2^3 + 0 \times 2^2 + 1 \times 2^1 + 1 \times 2^0$

$= 128 + 0 + 32 + 16 + 8 + 0 + 2 + 1$

$= (187)_{10}$

Another Example: Convert $(101001010)_2$ to decimal

Bit Position

	9	8	7	6	5	4	3	2	1
	1	0	1	0	0	1	0	1	0
Weight of each bit	2^8	2^7	2^6	2^5	2^4	2^3	2^2	2^1	2^0

Therefore, decimal number = sum of weight of all bits

$= 1 \times 2^8 + 0 \times 2^7 + 1 \times 2^6 + 0 \times 2^5 + 0 \times 2^4 + 1 \times 2^3 + 0 \times 2^2 + 1 \times 2^1 + 0 \times 2^0$

$= 256 + 0 + 64 + 0 + 0 + 0 + 8 + 0 + 2 + 0$

$= (330)_{10}$

BINARY ADDITION

Only four cases can occur in adding the two binary digits (bits) in any position.

They are

0 + 0 = 0

0 + 1 = 1

1 + 0 = 1

1 + 1 = 10 = 0 + carry of 1 into next position

1 + 1 + = 11 = 1 +, carry of 1 into next position

The last case occurs when the two bits in a certain position are 1 and there is a carry from the previous position. When we add two binary numbers we write the numbers one below the other with their LSB, aligned, e.g.,

Full Adder				
X	Y	Z	SUM	CARRY
0	0	0	0	0
0	0	1	1	0
0	1	0	1	0
0	1	1	0	1
1	0	0	1	0
1	0	1	0	1
1	1	0	0	1
1	1	1	1	1

When we add, we start with least significant bit depending upon the values of x,y and z of the bits to be added we will have a sum and may have a carry to the next stage of addition. There are 8 possible combinations of x, y, and z.

Example Calculate the binary sum of 110010 and 101101.

Solution

```
 110010
 101101
-------
1011111
```

Example Calculate the sum of 1010, 1100, 1110, 101

Solution

```
 11
 111 : Carry
 1010
 1100
 1110
 101
--------
 101001
```

or

```
 1010
 1100
 10110
+01110
 100100
+000101
--------
 101001
```

Example Calculate the sum of 11011.01 and 10.1101

Solution First write the binary numbers such that they are vertically aligned and then add

```
11.1 : carry
11011.0100
10.1101
11110.0001
```

It is not necessary to consider the addition of more than two binary numbers at a time because in all digital systems the circuitry that actually performs the addition can handle only two numbers at a time. When more than two numbers are to be added the first two are added together and then their sum is added to the third number and so on.

Most modern computers perform operations, viz., subtraction, multiplication and division by actually using only binary addition as their basic operation.

SUBTRACTION OF 1'S BY 2'S AND 2'S COMPLEMENT METHOD

The subtraction in the decimal number system can be performed as:

Step 1 If the lower (sutrahend) digit is greater than the upper (minuend) digit, borrow from the next column to the left.

Step 2 Subtract the lower value from the upper value.

For example, first consider the decimal subtraction (187-139)

Step1 717

187 Minuend

-139 Subtrahend

Step 2 717

187

-139

8

Step 1 717

& Step 2 1~~87~~

-139

48 Difference

Note that there was only one borrowing; ten was added to 7 to make 17 and one was subtracted from 8 to make it 7.

Now consider the binary subtraction.

Binary subtraction also uses the two steps

0 - 0 = 0

1 - 0 = 1

1 - 1 = 0

0 - 1 = 1, with borrow of 1 from the next column.

Consider the following example.

Example Find the binary difference (1101 - 1010)

Solution 0

1101

1010

0011

Note that we borrowed 1 from the 3rd-column because the difference 0 - 1 in the 2nd column.

Example Find the binary difference (110000 - 100111)

Solution 0111

110000

100111

001001

Note that a difference 0 - 1 occurs in the 1st column, hence we borrow from the 5th column where the first nonzero digit to the left appears and the 3-intervening zeros become ones.

OCTAL SYSTEM

The Octal Number System

The **Octal** number system uses exactly eight symbols 0, 1, 2, 3, 4, 5, 6 and 7, i.e., it has a base or radix 8. Since $8 = 2^3$, therefore, each octal digit has a unique 3 bit binary representation. The use of octal as a shorthand for binary is common in printed output of main storage and in some cases in programming.

IBM XT and some earlier micro computers used octal numbers for Input/Output operations but now this number system has been superseded by the hexadecimal system as its base 16 corresponds to half cycle.

Base 10 (Decimal)	Base 2 (Binary)	Base 8 (Octal)
0	0000	0
1	0001	1
2	0010	2
3	0011	3
4	0100	4
5	0101	5
6	0110	6
7	0111	7
8	1000	10
9	1001	11
10	1010	12
11	1011	13
12	1100	14
13	1101	15
14	1110	16
15	1111	17

Note here that $(10)_8$ is pronounced as one zero and not ten. The weights assigned to the digit of an octal system are powers of 8.

HEXADECIMAL SYSTEM

The Hexadecimal Number System

Think about a situation, when you actually have to work with the computer in binary. It would be so time consuming to encode instructions and to decode output that it would hardly be worth the trouble. For this reason, it made sense to devise a method to represent all the ones and zeros that make up binary numbers in a form that is easier to read, write and understand.

The base 16 number system, which is also called hexadecimal or hex, uses 16 symbols to represent numbers. Since there are only ten different numerals in the decimal number system (0 through 9), hex uses letters instead of numerals to stand the values greater than nine, i.e., 0, 1, 2, 3, 4, 5, 6, 7, 8, 9, A, B, C, D, E and F. In hexadecimal system A, B, C, D, E and F represents 10, 11, 12, 13, 14 and 15. Hexadecimal numbers are more convenient for people to recognize and interpret than the long strings of binary numbers.

It is synonymous with Sexadecimal. Since $16 = 2^4$, each hexadecimal digit has a unique 4-bit representation. Therefore, since a byte is made up of eight bits, any byte can be represented by exactly two hex digits.

For example, consider binary number

$(00101101)_2 = (45)_{10}$

When you split this number into two groups of 4-bits, it becomes

0010 1101

2 D = $(2\ D)_{16}$

Subscript

When you write numbers in a number system other than base 10, it is customary to follow the number with another subscript number to show which number system you are using. So at all times use subscript to indicate the base used if there is any risk of confusion without them. The subscript itself is always in decimal. For example when we combine these two hexadecimal digits (i.e. 2 and D) to form one number (2 D) the number is followed by a subscript 16 to show that the number is a hex representation.

Another method for indicating that a number is represented in hex digits is to follow the last digit with the character "h" or "H" or less commonly use "X". For example 3DH or 2DX. Also note that "H" or "h" or "X" are not part of the number, it just shows that the number is represented with hexadecimal digit.

Advantages of Hexadecimal Notation

- It is more compact as compared to decimal, binary or octal
- Easy to convert to base 2 form and vice versa.
- In most computers, binary data occupy some multiple of 4-bits and hence, some multiple of a single hex digit.

BINARY CODED DECIMAL (BCD)

In this system when you convert a decimal number to a binary number, every decimal digit is shown as equivalent binary coded number. The most common method is to represent each digit by its eqivalent using 4 bits. For example, 478 can be represented as 0100 0111 1000, since 0100 represents 4, 0111 represents 0111 and 8 is represented by 1000. The main advantage of the BCD code is the relative ease of converting to and from decimal.

This ease of conversion is especially important from a hardware stand point because in a digital system it is the logic circuit that perform the conversion to and from decimal.

ASCII CODE

It is the most commonly used code in the computer industry. By ASCII, we mean American Standard Code for Information Interchange (ASCII). It is a 7 bit code (usually the 8th bit is inserted for parity) and so it has $2^7 = 128$ possible code groups. It is used for the transfer of alphanumeric information between a computer and input/output devices such as video terminals or printers. Out of 128 ASCII codes 94 are printable and 34 non printing character used for various control functions.

Multiple Choice Questions

1. Computer uses which number system.
   (a) Decimal (b) Binary
   (c) Octal
2. Hexadecimal system has a base of.
   (a) 2 (b) 8
   (c) 16
3. Decimal system uses the numbers from 0 to:
   (a) 8 (b) 9
   (c) 16
4. Decimal systems have the base:
   (a) 8 (b) 10
   (c) 16

5. A Binary system number can be represented as 0 and:
   (a) 1 (b) 8
   (c) 16
6. Binary system numbers are usually:
   (a) short (b) long
   (c) zeros
7. Octal number system uses numbers from 0 to:
   (a) 8 (b) 16
   (c) F
8. Hexadecimal number system uses numbers from 0 to:
   (a) 8 (b) 16
   (c) F

Descriptive Type Questions

1. Which are the various number systems in use?
2. What is the base of Decimal system?
3. What is the base of Binary system?
4. What is the drawback of Binary system?
5. How would you convert a Decimal number to its Binary counterpar?
6. How would you convert a Binary number to its Decimal counterpart?
7. What is an Octal system?
8. What is hexadecimal system?

Data Communication and Networks

11

INTRODUCTION

It is not that the Personal Computers are for personal use only. They can be used for sharing of information too with others having similar type of equipments. Logically it sometimes is feasible to have a number of PCs then having a bigger computer which can give the same thoughput as the number of PCs. But, overall it becomes a expensive proposition and sometimes is not feasible, specially for individuals and small businesses or small companies.

Another problem arises for those who are physically placed at a distance. They would need to send messages and receive messages, or use the same data at, or share program at, many different locations. One answer to this problem is to keep separate data files at each location, but this approach is very costly and potentially a dangerous solution. It is very expensive to maintain these redundant files of data and difficult to ensure the continuing accuracy of data at any one location. The solution of both, the need for more power and the ability to receive, send messages and share data, are found in data communication technology.

COMMUNICATING DATA

When you send data from one location to another using any electronic means, it is called Data communication. Linking one computer to another permits the power and resources of that computer to be tapped. It also makes possible the updating and sharing of data at different location. Computer that are located in the same room office building, can communicate data through a direct cable link. For example, in a multiuser system, a single processing unit is linked by several dumb terminals through direct cables. Since multi-user systems link inexpensive terminals instead of the more expensive personal computers used with other systems, multi-user systems provide cost savings for small companies purchasing a complete system or adding users to a system currently in operation. In general, multi-user systems are most appropriate for companies requiring a shared data base for extensive data input and output. Computer located far away from the processor use a special form of data communication – telecommunication or telegraph. For example, teller and point-of-sale terminals are spotted in location away from computers: airlines, car-rentals, railway reservation systems and hotel reservation systems have thousands of terminals located many miles from the processors. In these cases, the process of using communication facilities such as the telephone system and microwave relays to send data between computers is a form of data communication, sometimes referred to as telecommunication, or tele-processing.

Dr. George Stibitz was the first to link computer and computing devices and send data way back in 1940. He used telegraph lines to send data files from Dartmouth College in New Hampshire, USA to a Bell Laboratories calculator in New York City, USA. An early large-scale business application was the Sabre passenger reservation system, developed in late 1950s and early 1960s by American Airlines. Hundreds of terminals were linked to the central processing unit. Communication usage has grown steadily since then.

Now-a-days minis and larger machines are in constant communication with outlying terminals. With available attachments, computers can use telecommunications channels to link up with information retrieval services, banks and electronic bulletin boards. An electronic-mail message can be sent from one place to another and an answer can be returned by electronic mail as soon as it is received. This service eliminates the hassle of continually trying to return a call, or long mail delays.

DATA TRANSMISSION TECHNIQUES

Telephone lines are used for sending human voice. They were never planned to send Data. So to send data through telephone lines you have to convert the data into the format which can be read by telephone lines. These are called analog signals. For data communication between computers to take place over a telephone line, the digital pulses of the data to be transmitted must be converted to an analog signal before they are transmitted.

After its journey over the telephone lines, the analog signal must be re-converted to digital pulses so that it can be used by the receiving computer. The process of converting digital pulses to an analog signal is called modulation. And the process of re-converting an analog signal to digital pulses is called demodulation. The device that accomplishes modulation-demodulation process is called a modem.

There are 3 basic types of modems used in microcomputers.

Acoustic Coupler Modem

This is used to provide the necessary interface. The acoustic coupler is attached to a portable terminal and a standard telephone handset fits into rubber cups located on the coupler. The acoustic coupler modem sends data through the mouthpiece and receives data through the earpiece of the handset. The digital pulses produced by the terminal are converted into audible tones that are picked up by the handset receiver. The signals from these tones are then sent to the processor location where another modem converts them back to digital pulses.

External Direct-Connect Modem

It is external to the computer and connects directly to computer via RS-232 serial interface cable and to the telephone line via a modular phone jack. An external direct-connect modem may be equipped with microprocessors, storage chips and specialized communication chips. Such intelligent modem is programmed to automatically perform dialing, disconnecting functions, check the operating status using status lights and speakers, self test to verify the modem's ability to correctly transmit data, respond to commands from a communication program and change the speed at which data are transmitted.

Internal Direct-Connect Modem

It has all the needed communication circuitry on a plug-in board that fits into one of the expansion slots inside the computer. Internal direct connect modem also links directly to the telephone line via a modular phone jack.

These modems have many of the same special features as the external direct connect modems.

COMMUNICATION CHANNELS

It is actually the media through which data is transmitted from one place to another. There are 3 types of communication channels.

Wire Cable

These are the most popular and widely used channels to transmit data from one location to another. This is so because it is cheaper and easier to use. Wire cable includes telegraph lines, telephone lines and coaxial cables. An advantage of wire cable is that the technology used to transmit data over wire cables is standardized, thus reducing the compatibility problems.

A disadvantage of wire cable is that it is subject to electrical interference making it less reliable than other types of communication channels. Another disadvantage is that wire cable must transmit data in analog form. Therefore, digital data must be converted to an analog signal before they reach the wire cable. This conversion not only needs special hardware, i.e., modem but also slows down the transmission of digital data.

Various items used are:

Telephone Lines

Telephone lines may be used to transmit computer data using the modems. The lines themselves may be either leased or switched.

Leased Lines

A leased line is a telephone line that is leased for the express purpose of maintaining a communication channel between two computers. The line is not shared with any other users and is available at all times for data communication between the computers. A leased line is similar to a telephone connection that is always open. Both computers are always listening for a signal to start the communication. Leased lines are used in computer networks where computers or terminals in the network must be in constant contact with one another. For example, leased lines are used in a network employing point-of-sale terminals, as the terminals must be in constant contact with the main computer. Leased lines are often conditioned to limit the level of noise on the line. Conditioned leased lines are usually necessary to carry on high speed data communication. Security requirements often require that leased lines be shielded from outside interference and unauthorized snooping.

Switched Lines

A switched line can be used for either voice or data communication and is switched from user to user, as requirements dictate. When switched lines are used, one computer must establish contact with the other by dialing a telephone number. After the transmission has been completed, the connection between the computers is broken, just as if a telephone receiver were hung up.

Twisted Pair Cable

Twisted pair [YP] is a common scheme for using copper wire as telecommunication cable. Because copper is such a good conductor of electrons, copper wires do not constrain electromagnetic signals well. When two copper wires conduct electric signals in close proximity, a certain amount of electromagnetic interference occurs. This type of interference is called cross-talk. In addition, because of the electromagnetic range used, TP transmits and receives unwanted signals from other sources. Twisting the copper wires reduces cross-talk and signal emissions. Each intertwined strand conducts a current whose emitted waves are cancelled out by the other wire's emissions. Twisted pairs are formed by two insulated 22 to 26 gauge copper wires that are twisted about each other. When one or more twisted pairs are combined within a common jacket, they form a twisted pair cable.

The two types of TP cables are:

Unshielded Twisted Pair Cable

This type of cable is composed of a set of twisted pairs with a simple plastic encasement. You may be familiar with UTP because it is commonly used in telephone systems. It is widely available and has been largely standardized. The Electrical Industries Association (EIA) popularized a category labeling scheme for five different qualities of twisted pair cable.

Category 3 and Category 5 UTP are commonly used in computer networking. While Category 3 is suitable for most contemporary computer networks, Category 5 included some enhancements, such as more twists per foot and a higher grade insulator, to improve the transmission media performance. Category 5 installations also require compatible equipment and more exacting installation techniques. Due to its voice telecommunication heritage, computer network UTP is often installed in the same manner as most telephone installations. A user device contains a port which accommodates a modular RJ-45 (4-pair) or RJ-11 (2-pair) telephone connector. The cost of UTP is extremely low compared to other transmission media. It continues to be mass produced for telecommunications and has become a popular computer network medium.

Some network integrators use existing spare wires from telephone cables to significantly reduce the already low implementation costs. However, this practice is not recommended if the existing UTP cable is lower than Category 3, if the cable drops exceed 100 meters, or if significant crosstalk is already present between the voice wires. UTP installation equipment is also inexpensive, easy to use and widely available.

Installation techniques are so simple that the cable can be adequately installed with very little training. Because voice telecommunication connection techniques have been optimized for easy moves, adds and changes, UTP is easily managed and reconfigured. Using current and emerging techniques, UTP may support data transfer rates from 1 to 100 Mbps at distances up to 100 m. Ten Mbps is the most common transmission rate in use today. All copper wire suffers from rapid attenuation when used as a communication medium. UTP is no exception.

Current technology restricts the effective range of UTP to hundreds of meters.

The copper cable used in UTP is very susceptible to EMI. Although the twists greatly reduce crosstalk, a certain amount of interference exists between pairs of wires.

Also, signals on the pairs are easily influenced by outside emitters of electromagnetic waves. External devices can also be used to intercept signals that are emitted from the pairs, breaching the security of a network.

Shielded Twisted Pair Cable

Though most of the cable is unshielded, but some forms of Shielded Twisted Pair (STP) is also used at some places. STP is insulated cable which included bundled pairs wrapped in a foil shielding. Various transmission media specifications from Apple Computer and IBM use STP cable. STP is more difficult to install than UTP.

Like coaxial cable, an electric ground, created by special connectors and installation techniques, must be provided for the shield. However, STP is more difficult to install than coaxial cable. If you use standardized and pre-configured cables, it makes installation simple. Bulk STP is moderately expensive. It currently costs more than UTP but is less expensive than thick coaxial or fiber optic cable. With the reduction of outside interference, STP can use higher frequencies and more bandwidth-efficient signaling techniques.

It is capable of greater transmission speeds, up to 500 Mbps at 100 m, but has not been widely implemented at data rates higher than 155 Mbps. The most common transmission rate is 16 Mbps. The biggest difference between UTP and STP is the reduction of interference and EMI emissions provided by STP's shielding. However, STP still suffers from relatively low immunity from interference. STP suffers from attenuation at a rate similar to UTP. Current technology also restricts the effective range of STP to hundreds of meters.

Coaxial Cables

This type of cable come in protective cover which shields the cable from physical dangers as well as from electromagnetic interference. Within the cover, the various cables are shielded from interference with one another. Coaxial cables are used in communication networks that require many simultaneous communication links. Each coaxial cable can provide more than 5000 links. The initial installation of coaxial cable is relatively simple. However, current installation techniques usually use a single strand of cable, which may become difficult to manage and reconfigure.

Local drops may be connected to the base cable to make device connections easier. Using current technologies, coax supports data transfer rates between twisted pair and fiber optic cable, although the typical data rate in use today is 10 Mbps. Much greater data rates are available. However, these higher rates are only infrequently used in computer networking. It is important to note that coaxial cable's bandwidth potential increases with the diameter of the inner conductor.

The cost of coaxial cable increases with the diameter and composition of the conductor. The cost of thin coaxial cable is relatively low (less than STP or Category 5 UTP). Thick coaxial cable is moderately expensive (more than STP or Category 5 UTP). Both are more expansive than Category 3 UTP (all comparisons are made in reference to bulk cable with no connectors).

As a copper wire media, coaxial cable suffers from high attenuation, but at a much lower rate than either variety of twisted pair. Using current LAN technology, the effective range of coaxial cable is in the low thousands of meters. While copper wire generally is a poor resistor to EMI, the shielding provided by coaxial cable greatly reduces its effects.

There are two types of coaxial cables: baseband and broadband.

A baseband coaxial cable transmits a single signal at a time at very high speed, while a broadband coaxial cable can transmit many simultaneous signals using different frequencies. A baseband cable transmits a single stream of digital data at a very high communication rate (millions of bits per second) but must be amplified every 1000 feet or so. It is mainly used for local area networks. A baseband coaxial cable can carry only an analog signal, so it must be used in conjunction with a modem. It is more complex to use in a network.

Fiber Optics

They are very reliable communication channels and they transmit data in digital form. They use light impulses that travel through clear flexible tubing (tiny threads of glass or plastic). A single glass fiber is thinner than the size of a human hair and it can transmit all the characters in dozens of books of the same size of this one across the country in a single second. It would take about 21 hours to send the same information over a copper telephone line. Since thousands of these fibers can be fit in the same amount of space required for one wire cable, the future cost of broad band transmission capability should be within the reach of small organizations and individuals.

Fiber optics can transmit data at very high speed with no errors. Unlike wire cables, fiber optic cables are not subject to electrical interference. They do, however, require repeaters to read and boost the signal strength because light pulses will lose signal strength over long distances. Optical fibers support extremely high bandwidths because they are limited by the high-frequency photon properties of light rather than by lower frequency properties of electrical systems.

Current technologies allow data rates from 100 Mbps to over 2 Gbps, at distances from 2 to 25 km. The data rate of a given fiber optic system is dependent upon the fiber composition (glass or plastic), the mode and the wavelength of the light transmitted. The most common LAN installations include glass multi-mode fiber and 850 nm wavelength LEDs. This configuration can sustain a transmission rate of 100 Mbps at distances of approximately 20 km. Historically, bulk fiber and connectors have been relatively expensive compared to copper wire, but these costs are falling rapidly.

However, the extreme cost of installation far outpaces the cost of materials. The nature of fiber optic cable poses installation problems. Every fiber junction, splice, or connection must be made with extreme care to ensure that the light path is unobstructed. Installers must be careful not to excessively stretch or bend the fiber. Fiber optic cables have extremely low attenuation rates. The amount of attenuation varies depending upon the operating wavelength, but effective ranges are usually measured in kilometers. Therefore, fiber optic cable attenuates much less than any copper wire transmission medium. Due to the use of the light spectrum, fiber optic cables do not leak signals and are immune to electromagnetic interference and eavesdropping. Also, the light spectrum does not require electrical grounds, so fiber optic cables do not suffer from potential shifts to the electrical ground not do they produce sparks. These characteristics make fiber ideal for hazardous, high voltage, or eavesdropping sensitive environments.

Microwave

This is also a type of analog communication channel. Microwave signals are transmitted through the atmosphere rather than through wire cables, similar to the way radio and television signals are transmitted. Microwave signals must be transmitted in a straight line, they do not bend around corners or around the curve of the earth. Transmitter stations redirect and boost the signals. The data may be beamed to a communications satellite that acts as a reflector by accepting signals from one point on earth and returning the same signals to some other point on earth.

The satellite appears from the earth to be stationary target for the microwave signals because its precisely positioned 22,300 miles above the equator with an orbit speed that matches the earth's rotation. Dozens of satellites are now in orbit to handle international and domestic data, voice and video communications.

Compared to wire cable, microwave has a much lower error rate, making it more reliable. Also, because there are no physical links between the sending and receiving systems communication links can be made over large distance and rough terrains. The only disadvantage is the high cost of ground stations and satellites to support a microwave network.

BANDWIDTH CHANNELS

The bandwidth, or grade, of a communication channel determines the rate or speed that data can be transmitted over a channel. The term **bandwidth** is often shortened to **band**.

There are 3 bands for communication channels.

Narrow-band

The narrow-band channel is used where data volume is relatively low and which transmits data at a rate between 40 to 100 bits per second (bps). Telegraph lines are an example of narrow-band channels and their transmission rate is slow.

Voice-band

The voice-band channels are able to speed up the transmission rate between 110 to 9600 bits per second. Telephone lines are an example of voice-band channels. In many cases, a terminal operator at a remote location uses the regular dial-up telephone switching network, calls a number at the control processor location and enters the data. For large volumes of data, it is cheaper for an organization to acquire its own dedicated or leased line which can be used for both voice and data transmissions.

Broad-band

The broad-band channels are used where data volumes are large and which transmit data at rate upto several megabits per second. Microwaves, coaxial cables, fiber optics and communications satellites are examples of broad-band channels.

DATA TRANSMISSION

The 2 forms of data transmission are discussed below.

Analog Data Transmission

Here the transmission of data is in a continuous wave form. The telephone system, for instance, is designed for analog data transmission.

Waves are measured using one or more of the following 3 characteristics.

Amplitude

You can consider the amplitude of a wave as the signal strength compared to some reference value (measured in volts). Analog signals are based upon amplitude, or strength, shifts which vary constantly from positive to negative values. Amplitude is commonly expressed in volts when measuring electrical potential, amps when measuring electrical current, watts when measuring electrical power, and decibels when measuring the ratio between the power of two signals.

Frequency

The frequency of a wave is the time it takes for a wave to complete one cycle. In other words, if a signal takes one second to make a transition from high amplitude to low and back to high, the frequency of the wave is one second. Frequency is typically measured in hertz[Hz], or cycles per second.

Phase

The phase of a signal refers to the relative state of the wave when timing began. Two signals cross at a slightly different time. Signal phase is measured in degrees. As with digital signals, analog signals can be modulated on encoded to represent binary data.

Current State

The most common analog current state strategies use different signal amplitudes or frequencies to represent data. These are two type of analog signal encoding schemes:

Amplitude-shift keying (ASK)

Amplitude-shift keying encodes binary data by varying the signal's amplitude between two or more levels. For example, a binary 0 might be one volt and a binary 1 might be three volts.

Frequency-shift keying (FSK)

Frequency-shift keying encodes binary data by varying the signal's frequency between two or more values.

For example, a binary 0 would be one frequency or group of frequencies and a binary 1 would be some other frequency or group of frequencies.

Network devices, using current state analog signaling, periodically measure the signal's amplitude, frequency, or both simultaneously.

State Transition

Transitions from one analog phase to another can also encode data on an analog signal. This method of analog signaling is called Phase-Shift Keying (PSK). This encodes binary data by varying the phase of the signal to indicate a value. For example, a 180 degree phase shift could represent 1 and no shift could indicate 0. Network devices periodically measure the analog signal to determine if a phase change has occurred.

Digital Data Transmission

It is the transmission of data using distinct **ON** and **OFF** electrical states. Computer circuitry represents data as a pattern of **ON** or **OFF** electrical states. These two states are represented by a 1 or **ON** and 0 for **OFF**. Digital data communication is faster and more efficient than analog. All the data communication between the computers is in digital form as the computers understand and work only in digital forms.

However, telephone system, an analog data transmission system, is used for a great percentage of data communication because it is the largest and the most widely used communication system in the world. The modem, sometimes referred as interface element, is used to bridge the gap between digital and analog data transmission, or to allow the digital data to be transmitted/received over from the telephone lines.

BUFFERS AND PROTOCOLS

Before data are transmitted, a set of traffic rules and procedures, called protocol, must be established. The same protocol must be followed by all devices participating in the communication session. These rules may vary depending on the devices being used. Prearranged signals defining the protocol to be followed when transmitting and receiving data are sent between computers in an exchange called handshaking. Data communication between computers takes place independently of the CPU through the use of buffers at both the receiving and sending ends.

A buffer is a section of RAM which holds the data being transmitted or received. When the sending computer's buffer is almost empty, the CPU is interrupted and asked to refill the buffer. At the receiving end, the receiving buffer interrupts the CPU when it is full and the data are moved to their ultimate destination such as screen, printer or disk.

If the buffer size is large or the communication rate is slow, the buffer may be manipulated without interrupting the transmission of data. If the buffer size is smaller the communication rate is high, the sending and receiving modems use a protocol or prearranged sequence of signals, to interrupt the transmission while the buffer is filled or emptied. When the receiving computer's buffer is full, the receiving modem sends a signal to inform the sending computer to stop. When the buffer has been emptied, the receiving modem sends another signal to inform the sending computer to resume sending.

ERROR DETECTION

A number of methods have been used to detect errors while transmitting data. The most popular method for detecting errors is inserting a parity bit alongside the data bits for a character. When the receiving modem detects an incorrect parity bit, it can request the sending modem to retransmit the character.

SERIAL AND PARALLEL INTERFACE

A parallel interface is the one that uses eight wires to transmit all 8 bits in a byte at the same time. Therefore, parallel interfaces are faster and more expensive than serial interfaces. An interface connection is often called a port. The program instructions used by the computer to communicate with other devices is called driver program. In other words, most data are organized into 8 bit bytes. In some computers, data are further organized into multibyte words. Sometimes data are transmitted, a byte or a word at a time. This is done by using many wires, with one wire carrying each bit, which is known as parallel communication.

Unlike parallel interface, in a serial interface, the 8 bit bytes are lined up into a single stream for bits for transmission to a peripheral device. That is, a serial interface transmits only one bit at a time and hence it is slow. Parallel communication is used primarily for transferring data between devices at the same site. For example, communication between a computer and a printer is mot often parallel, so that an entire byte can be transferred in one operation. Communication between computers is almost always serial.

RATE OF DATA TRANSMISSION

The speed at which data travel over a communication channel is called the communication rate. It is also known as the transmission speed. The rate at which the data are transferred is the baud rate. Baud rate is the number of time per second that the signal being transmitted changes (modulation or demodulation).

Baud is often equated with bits per send (bps), however, this comparison is not entirely accurate because a signal does not always carry one bit.

Although higher speeds are possible, typical data transmission speeds are 300, 1200, 2400, 4800 and 9600 bps. Modems used with microcomputers typically use 300, 1200 or 2400 bps. Larger computer systems used for communication in business typically transmit data at speeds of 4800 bps or higher using high-speed modems.

METHODS OF DATA TRANSMISSION

There are 3 main methods of data transmission.

Asynchronous Transmission

Here one character is transmitted at a time. The transfer of data is controlled by start bits and stop bits. Each character is surrounded by bits that signal the beginning and end of the character. These characters allow the receiving terminal to synchronize itself with the receipt of data on a character-by-character basis. Asynchronous transmission is often used for low-speed transmission of data in conjunction with narrow-band and few slower speed (less than 1200 bps) voice band channels where the transmitting device operates manually or intermittently. It is least expensive of the two methods. Because the bit strings are relatively short, timing errors between the two device's clocks will not cause the receiving device to mistake the start of a frame.

This type of transmission is often used when characters are generated at random intervals, such as when a user types at a terminal. The start and stop bits not only indicate when a receiver should measure for the presence of bits, but also indicate the beginning and end of the data stream.

Synchronous Transmission

This transmission of data is a method in which blocks of characters are transmitted in timed sequences. Rather than using start and stop bits around each character, each block of characters is marked with synchronization characters. The receiving device accepts data until it detects a special ending character or a predetermined number of characters at which time the device knows the message has come to an end.

Synchronous transmission commonly uses the faster (greater than 1200 bps) voice-band and broad-band channels and is usually used when data-transfer requirements exceed several thousand bits per second. It is much faster than asynchronous transmission. Synchronous transmission is used in direct computer-to-computer communication for large computer systems because of the high data-transfer speeds required. The special characters used by asynchronous (start/stop bits) and synchronous (synchronization characters) transmission to alert the modem when data are being send and when the transmissions are finished are called message characters.

Synchronized transmissions resist timing errors much better than a synchronized transmission because both the transmitter and receiver use the same clock. To maintain framing when no data is being transmitted, synchronous transmission systems use fill bits. The sender can then maintain the integrity of the transmission timing. As with asynchronous transmission, synchronous transmission can perform error detection.

A method known as Cyclic Redundancy Check (CRC) is often used the CRC process subjects the block of data to an algorithm. The result of the computation (called the CRC) is appended to the block of data prior to transmission. On the receiving side, the same algorithm is used and the results are compared with the CRC field. Any difference is assumed to mean frame damage occurred during transmission. CRC is less vulnerable to multiple bit errors than asynchronous error-detection methods.

Isochronous Transmission

These methods use a constant fixed-frequency transmission clock to create set time slots. A clock signal is generated by a designated network device and is passed to all other devices on the network. Using the prescribed media access rules, the network devices monitor the network for free space within the slots and insert data as needed.

Multiple frames can be inserted into each slot until the slot is full. By using this method, a clock signal is not provided for every frame like asynchronous, or provided by the sender at the beginning of a string like synchronous. Rather the clock is provided at a constant rate by a single device for all other devices on the network.

COMMUNICATION CHANNEL CONFIGURATIONS

The two main communication channel configurations are as follows:

Point-to-point

In a point-to-point channel configuration, a device is connected directly to another devices by a dedicated communication channel. This communication channel configuration can be inefficient and costly if a terminal is not active enough to keep the line busy.

Multi-point

In the multi-point channel configuration, three or more devices, e.g., a terminal or computer, are connected to the same line. Compared to point-to-point configuration, multipoint channel configuration is more efficient and less costly because it reduces the amount of intercabling needed.

COMMUNICATION PROCESSORS

A number of communication processors are used by network designers to achieve their goals. They increase the efficiency of a communication channel. These processors are used for a number of purposes, some of which are as follows:

Multiplexing

It is the process of combining the transmission, character by character, from several devices into a single data stream that can be transmitted over a single communication channel. A multiplexer is a device that produces multiplexing. It is also used at the receiving end to separate the transmissions and send them back in their original order for processing. A multiplexer allows the communication channels to transmit much more data, at any one time, than what a single device can send. Multiplexers are more efficient and less expensive. The equipment that multiplexes and demultiplexes is sometimes called a multiplexer or mux.

The following methods are used by multiplexers to allow multiple devices to communicate concurrently.

Frequency-Division Multiplexing

It uses separate frequencies to establish multiple channels within a broadband medium. To do this, the mux creates special broadband carrier signals that operate on different frequencies. Data signals are added to the carrier signals and are removed, at the opposite end of the media segment, by another mux. FDM is used in broadband LANs to separate different direction traffic on the cable and to provide special services like dedicated connections between machines.

Time-Division Multiplexing

These systems divide a single channel into short time slots. Bits, blocks of bits, bytes, or frames can be placed into each time interval is not exceeded. Time division is a multiplexing technique that you can use on baseband systems. You can also use it on an individual channel of a broadband FDM system. Conventional TDM systems are sometimes called synchronous TDM because the time-divisions are fixed when the muxes are set up. The time slots are always of the same length and are assigned in the same order.

Statistical Time-Division Multiplexing

Conventional synchronous TDM systems waste bandwidth if many of the time slots are left unused. Statistical time-division multiplexing (StatTDM) solves this problem by dynamically allocating time slots to active devices on a first-come, first-served or priority basis. A control field identifies the owners of each slot's data so that the receiving mux can appropriately split out all the individual signals.

Concentration

Very often, it is required to connect more devices (or terminals) to a computer so that the communication channel can handle all at once. Concentration is the process of connecting and serving these devices. A concentrator is hardware that provides concentration. The data are stored in the buffer of concentrator for later transmission, when the number of devices transmitting exceeds the capacity of the communication channel. However, today's micro-processor equipped multiplexers perform much like concentrators. Compared to concentrators, multiplexers are less expensive.

Message Switching

The message switcher receives and analyzes data messages from points in the network, determines the destination and the proper routing and then forwards the messages to other network locations. If needed, a message can be stored till an outgoing line is available.

Front-end Processing

The front-end processor is a computer, which is usually located at a central computer site. It handles all the data communication control functions while the Central Processing Unit (CPU) of the front-end processor handles all the communication tasks. Its purpose is to relieve the main computer – called a host computer – of a number of the functions required to interact with and control the communications network. The two processors interact only when data need to be passed between them.

A typical front-end processor might control scores of communication channels of varying types and speeds coming from a number of diverse remote terminals. The functions of communication processors differ from one network to another and there may be an overlapping of functions. A message switching processor, for example, may also function as a remote concentrator; a front-end processor may perform message-switching function; and, in less complete networks, the host computer may perform most or all of the functions of the front-end processor.

TRANSMISSION MODES

Data transmission may occur in one of the following 3 modes.

Simplex Mode

In this mode, data can be transmitted in one direction. A device using the simplex mode of transmission can either send or receive data, but it cannot do both. Simplex mode (circuits) are seldom used because a return path is generally needed to send acknowledgment, control or error signals.

Half-duplex Mode

Here, data can be transmitted back and forth between two stations, but data can only go in one of the directions at any point of time. An example is a citizens band radio where the user must either talk or listen, but cannot do both at the same time.

Full-duplex Mode

The full-duplex mode allows a device to receive and send data simultaneously. A full-duplex mode is faster, since it avoids the delay that occurs in a half-duplex circuit each time the direction of transmission is changed.

COMMUNICATION PROCEDURES

All communication between computers are managed by data communication software. The precise procedures used depend on the particular software, but the following account outlines the general procedures.

Communication Between Two Microcomputers

A small business that uses microcomputers has accumulated information that it wants to send to a customer who also uses microcomputers.

The procedure used to send the information is as follows:

1. Both the business and the customer start the communication program, which gives them a menu of options.
2. Both the business and the customer choose the same options, including the number of start and stop bits, the type of parity checking, the communication rate, full-duplex or half-duplex transmission and so on.
3. The communication link is established. The users decide who will originate the telephone call and the originator enters the telephone number. The communication program then instructs the modem to detail the number and reports to the users if a connection has been made.
4. After the connection has been made, the users can have an on-line conversation. They can type messages back and forth to each other and can record their conversation.
5. When the business is ready to transfer the information, it sets its computer to send; the customer sets its computer to receive. The business starts, the transfer. The communication program takes over by reading the information from the disk and sending it through the communication link. The receiving computer stores the incoming information on a disk. The transfer proceeds without any further human attention.
6. When the transfer has been completed, the business and the customer say "goodbye" and terminate the connection.

Communication Between Microcomputer and Larger Computer

The procedure for communication between a microcomputer and a minicomputer or mainframe is similar. The only difference is that the larger computer have safeguards that limit access to files and facilities to authorized users. The most common safeguards are the user identification number and the user password. After the communication link has been established, the receiving computer asks for the user's identification number.

This number is assigned to the microcomputer user by the operators of the larger computer. When requested to do so, the microcomputer user types in the user identification number. The receiving computer checks that the identification number is valid. It then asks for the user's password.

A password is a confidential sequence of characters that allows access to the system.

An example of a password is:

S12$T11

The password is required for the user to obtain access to the larger computer. It also determines exactly which files and facilities the microcomputer user is allowed to read. If the typed password is valid, the microcomputer user is allowed access to the large system.

Going On-Line

Before you establish a communication link, you must adjust various settings to match those of the computer you want to connect with. Called communication parameters, these settings vary with different types of computers and programs. Fortunately, most communication programs let you store and retrieve the parameters that apply to various remote systems. When you connect to a remote system such as an on-line information service, you will probably be asked to reply to one or more on-screen questions.

Generally, you will need to provide some kind of identification, such as your name, an account number and a password. This brief dialogue between you and the remote system is often called a logon procedure. Some remote systems compare your identification with a list of paid subscribers. Obviously, if you are not on the list, you would not be able to access the service.

Other systems use the logon procedure as a security measure, protecting valuable records from tampering. In either case, the remote system maintains a record or log of every caller. Many communication programs support automated logon procedures. When you log on for the first time, the program "records" your entries for later use.

Subsequently, when you access the remote system, these entries are automatically supplied in response to prompts from the remote system. Many communication software packages let you dial, connect and log on to a remote system at the touch of a single function key. Once you have gone through the formalities, the remote system usually welcome you with a greeting and waits for your net command.

At this point, your communication software has turned your computer into a simple video terminal, allowing you to use the remote system's software as if you were connected directly to the system.

File Transfer

Transferring files to and from your disk drive is one of the most common communication applications. These files may be bulletins, electronic mail messages, airline information or even computer programs. In addition to matching communication parameters, file transfer requires that both systems in a communication link agree on a common protocol.

A protocol consists of the technical details that regulate data transmission between computers. Fortunately, you need only a rough idea of how a protocol works in order to use one. The simplest to understand is the text or ASCII protocol. This method sends a file as one uninterrupted stream of ASCII characters.

While this protocol offers transmission of maximum characters in the shortest possible time, it is also the one most likely to produce errors, especially over noisy telephone lines. To combat flaws in file transfer, most protocols offer error correction. Specific methods vary from protocol to protocol, but the basic error correction scheme is the same; breaking up a file into small blocks and then comparing the received blocks to those that were sent to make sure they are identical.

Each block includes an extra character mathematically derived from the ASCII values of the characters it contains. If the receiving computer comes up with a different value for that character after it receives a block, it assumes an error has occurred and requests that block again. While this procedure reduces throughput, error checking and correction virtually assure error free file transfer.

Common error correction programs now include more advanced session level protocols that check for errors throughout an entire communication session, not just during file transfer.

Choosing Parameters

Before loggin on, you must make sure that you and the remote system are using the same communication parameters – the various settings that regulate the means of communication. To clarify this point, baud rate, parity, stop bits and echo are further discussed. Baud rate refers to the rate or "speed" of data transfer. In common parlance, this means the number of bits per second (bps) sent or received.

Technically, baud rate refers to the rate of the phase-shifting method a modem uses to transmit information – which is not necessarily the same as the bps rate. However, most modem manufacturers use baud rate to describe bps and this corruption of the technical term is now commonplace. Since transmitting one character usually takes 10 bits, dividing the baud rate by 10 will give you a rough approximation of how many characters per second are being transferred. Which baud rate you use depends on the capabilities of your modem, as well as the equipment used by the remote system.

Most modems for personal computers transfer data at 300, 1200 or 2400 baud. Whatever baud rate your modem supports, it has to be seen that the rate for your modem and the remote system must be identical. Sometimes a remote system will have different phone access numbers for different baud rates. In general, you should communicate at the highest baud rate possible, since this reduces the amount of connect time you are charged for.

However, some commercial information systems charge premium rates for communication at higher baud rates. Even so, the time saved makes using higher baud rates more economical when transferring large files. Parity refers to a scheme using a single bit along with each character to test for accurate data transfer. The most popular configuration for PC communications uses seven bits for data and the eighth bit for even parity. Using even parity during data transfer means that the eight bit always makes the 1 and 0 bits within a character add up to an even number. If the receiving computer detects an odd number, it either requests re-transmission or ignores the character completely.

Sometimes, however, eight bits are used for data and an additional bit is used for parity, resulting in other common setting; eight bits and no parity. Other parity schemes, such as odd number, space and mark are also used, but they are rather uncommon in PC communications. Stop bits refer to the variable number of bits used to mark the end of each character transferred. Often, you may see parity, the number of data bits and the number of stop bits in one reference. "E-7-1" for example, means even parity, seven data bits and one stop bit.

One stop bit is used almost universally in personal computer communication and many communication programs automatically use this setting unless you specify otherwise. Echo refers to a remote system's practice of sending back the characters you transmit, giving you on-screen verification that the characters have been received.

Mainframe computers and commercial information services often use this procedure, while most PC link-ups omit echo. When you are on-line, it is easy to determine whether to turn the echo function on or off. If you see no characters on the screen as you type, turn echo on; if the characters you type appear in duplicate, turn echo off. Most communication programs let you adjust the echo setting while you are engaged in a communication session.

Logging Off

When you have finished a session with a remote system, you need to formally log off. Usually, the system displays a message on screen confirming that log off procedures have been properly completed. Standard log off commands include log out, Bye, Quit, Off and Exit. If you disconnect without formally logging off the system, the remote system may be fooled into believing that you are still connected. When you are using a commercial service that charges by the minute for connect time, this can be quite an expensive mistake. Therefore, it is a good idea to watch for the remote system's log off confirmation on screen.

APPLICATIONS OF DATA COMMUNICATION

The applications of data communication fall into one of 4 categories.

Electronic Mail

A business depends on the efficient exchange of information between different parts of the business and between the business and the outside world. Much of this exchange has been traditionally carried out through paper documents, delivered by secretary, mail or messenger service. With the growing use of personal computers, a more efficient alternative has emerged, i.e., electronic mail. Electronic mail is usually used to exchange messages and data files. Each user is assigned an electronic mailbox.

Using the appropriate command, the user can scan a list of messages in the mailbox, display the contents of a particular message, send a message to another user and so forth. To send a message, it is not necessary for the recipient to be present at the computer. The message resides in the mailbox until it is read. The sender may restrict delivery of the message to authorized readers by using a password. That is, the recipient must "sign" for the message by typing his or her identifying password. Many other features of standard mail delivery are implemented in electronic mail systems.

For example, mail can be forwarded, stored for delayed delivery and sent to anyone at a particular phone number. In addition, electronic mail systems implement many new features. An electronic mail system can deliver copies of a message to all individuals listed in a certain file. It also allows merging of standard data (from a data file) with a particular message. Now-a-days, several companies have started subscription to electronic mail services. These services are accessed through a modem and allow users to communicate with other subscribers to the service. The service may also accept a message and transmit it to its destination city. There the message is printed out and delivered with the next day's mail. This technique can be used to communicate with people who are not subscribers to the network.

Using External Databases

The most important applications of data communication is the ability to access external databases. There are literally thousands of databases containing information on almost every conceivable subject. Users can subscribe to many of these databases at a cost of the initial fee and a charge for the amount of time spent accessing the database. Users can locate information in an index or can just browse through the database as they would brows through books at a public library.

The types of information available through services vary greatly, as can be seen in the following examples. The Dow Jones News Services provide current news, current stock and commodity prices and securities research data. The stock prices are very nearly the same up-to-the-minute prices that are simultaneously crossing the tape at the major stock exchange. This allows users to use the service for the data on which they base trading decisions. A number of subscription services supply on-line transactions. For example, a number of banks now allow subscribers to bank through a communication link to a personal computer. Some services even allow users to pay bills in this way. Personal computers may also be used to execute stock trades through several on-line brokerage systems. Transaction-oriented services are in their infancy. In the years to come, they will certainly grow in number and sophistication. A number of multiple-listing real estate services offer on-line options.

This allows a broker to find all homes meeting particular criteria, price range, neighborhood, size and so on, to match client demands. Also in the real estate field, services supply on-line listings of currently available mortgage money, interest rates and restrictive terms. These services allow a prospective home buyer to shop the entire country to obtain the best mortgage terms.

Sharing Data Files

Probably no single data communication application is as important to a large business as is the link between its micro-computers and its mainframe computers. In the last few years, businesses have purchased millions of personal computers to increase their employees productivity. The initial applications of personal computers were stand alone activities, such as word processing and the use of spreadsheets.

To increase productivity further, businesses are taking the additional step of making data stored in mainframe computers available to microcomputer users. The savings including financial ones can be huge. With data communication and networking, the tasks of data collection, analysis, decision making, report writing and data distribution can be integrated into a single, efficient system. In effect, the entire office (or even the entire company) becomes one large communication network.

Bulletin Board Systems

A bulletin board is a communication system that allows users to call in and either leave or retrieve messages. It is similar to an electronic mail system, but there are no private mailboxes, only a single large mailbox. The messages may be directed to all users of the bulletin board or only to particular users. But all messages can be read by all users. Some computer equipment manufactures maintain bulletin boards that users may call to determine the status of company products, corrections to programs and the like. Users may report problems, ask for literature or place orders. Some computer user groups maintain bulletin boards for notifying members of meetings and other group activities. Other bulletin boards are maintained by individuals are meeting places for like-minded people.

COMMUNICATION PROCESSING

Communication processing is the collective term for all the activities that help to ensure the successful entry, transmission and delivery of information. Just as data processing involves taking raw data and adding value by changing the inherent information content, communication processing adds value to the raw message by ensuring that the message arrives at its destination in a timely manner, in the proper form, at the proper speed, in the proper language and without errors.

The basic responsibilities of communication processing can be divided into three major areas: editorial, conversion and arbitration. Editorial functions include formatting of the message, editing the data and controlling errors. Conversion functions include translating transmission speed and code. Arbitration functions involve network control and message routing. Communication processing can be performed in any intelligent device, using the storage and processing capabilities of that device. In the microcomputer based of LAN, most communication processing occurs within the micro-computer itself. Within a network, communication processing is implemented as protocols, the rules that govern the transmission of information.

The following are sample communication processing services:

- Accommodating different video display characteristics such as screen size, line strength and paging.
- Translating data into the standard network format and subsequently re-translating the data to meet the requirements of the receiving station.
- Controlling the sequence in which messages are sent.
- Assembling and transmitting messages on the basis of time interval, order received, receipt of particular character or other characteristics.
- Alerting users to error conditions and possible problems.

Packets

It is neither practical nor advantageous to transmit long messages as a single entity. Therefore, for the purpose of data transmission, particularly in local area networks, messages are broken down into segments, called packets. Each packet normally contains five parts.

- A start frame, identifying the beginning of the packet.
- A header, containing information for maintaining control of the packet and the network.
- An information field, containing a segment of the total text information or data to be communicated.
- An error control field, permitting the system to verify packet integrity.
- An end frame, signifying the end of the packet.

The control information contained in the header includes the source address, which identifies where the packet originated; the destination address, to which the segment is to be delivered; the packed sequence number, which helps insure that the packets can be reassembled in proper order; and a control block, which helps prevent duplication, loss or looping (in which a packet is routed back and forth in an endless circle) of the packet.

Additional information to insure proper operation of the network under various overload or impaired operating conditions also may be included. Overhead is the additional information that must be transmitted through the network in order to facilitate the proper transmission and delivery of messages. It is created by the system's need to maintain control of all transactions. A percentage of overall network capacity is dedicated to this control information. Overhead information exists on the network in two basic forms; data appended to each user packet, such as the control and error-checking fields named above. The amount of data appended to a basic message varies from one system to another and itself contained acknowledgment and control packets, which are transmitted from one device to another. These packets keep the system advised of the status of the components.

Communication Software

Most computer applications, including data communication, require both appropriate hardware and software. Specialized data communication software is required to set up a communication link between two computers and to transmit data. Data communication software performs a number of jobs. One is to send data at the proper speed; if the receiving and sending computers do not agree on the communication rate, the receiving computer will not be able to understand the communication. Another job is to monitor signals from the receiving computer that indicate any transmission errors. The communication program you choose plays a key role in data exchange between computers. If you are on the receiving end, communication software lets you decide whether you want to save data to disk, send it to a printer or simply let it scroll off the screen.

When you transmit data, most programs let you choose between sending it form a disk file or typing it directly from the keyboard. Software for communication also stores telephone numbers, modem commands and other critical settings. Usually, these parameters reside in a dialing directory, so you do not have to re-enter them each time you want to hook up with a remote system. A well-designed communication program makes it easy to select a remote system from the directory and begin connection procedures. Many communication programs direct modems to dial, hang up and answer incoming calls automatically. While it is modem that actually performs these tasks, the software provides the appropriate instructions. For example, when the program sends the modem a dial command and a phone number. The modem automatically goes off-hook (the same as lifting a telephone handset), waits for a dial tone and proceeds to generate click pulses or tones that dial the number.

Most modems provide an audible indication that dialing is in progress, followed by a signal that a connection has been made. You will hear the modem beeping out tones like fast fingers on a touch-tone phone. Then, if all goes well, you should hear the remote system's line ring and the remote modem "pick up" the call. The remote modem then generates a high-pitched answer tone, to which your modem responds with a burst of tones of its own. This opening interchange is called handshaking. Once two modems are locked on to each other, most communication programs display a 'Connect' message on screen. In the foregoing paragraphs, we listed the rudimentary features of a communication program but a typical one has many additional features. Some programs allow users to redial a number repeatedly (if the line is busy, for example) until a connection is made and others allow users to take remote control of the computer at the other end. That is, the program user can control the other computer from his own keyboard. This allows communication with no one in attendance at the other end. Some programs allow users to dial a sequence of numbers one after the other. These are sometimes used to generate recorded advertising calls.

MICRO-TO-MAINFRAME LINK

Micro-computers can also be connected to large systems in a micro-to-mainframe link to share data and computing power. As the number of micro-computers used in business increases, this connection is being seen more and more. Line micro-to-micro communication, micro-to-mainframe communication can be accomplished via modem and telephone lines or by hard wiring. However, the connection is not as simple because large systems use different formats for communication and they handle data differently internally. To complicate the problem, the communication and data formats used among the various large systems also differ. Specialized hardware designed for the particular type of computer being used is usually needed to make the data compatible.

For a micro-computer to communicate with a large system, three facts must be known:

1. Type of mainframe to be communicated with;
2. Mainframe's specific data format; and
3. Mainframe's specific communication protocols.

Communication Challenges

The use of data communication is not without its challenges. Data sent over communication channels are subject to various kinds of interference which may alter or destroy some of that data. In addition to ensuring the security of the data, privacy of the data must often be protected. However, unauthorized access to data files can be limited by the use of passwords and access codes. To prevent highly sensitive data from being accessed and used from the communication channels, the data are often encrypted, or scrambled, based on some code before they are sent. Then they are unscrambled using that same code after they are received.

SUPPLIERS OF DATA COMMUNICATION SERVICES

Various kind of Data Communication Carriers are:

Common Carriers

To handle large public telephone and telegraph networks, services of common carriers are availed. A common carrier is an organization that is licensed and regulated by the government to transmit the data communication property of others at regulated rates. There are thousands of licensed common carriers of data communication.

Specialized Common Carriers

In addition to these common carriers that offer a wide range of facilities, there are specialized common carriers whose public networks are often restricted to a more limited number of services. MCI communication corporation is an example of satellite using organizations.

Value Added Carriers

A value added carrier is an organization that leases communication channels from the common carriers (it may not have its own transmission facilities) and adds extra services over and above what the common carriers provide. For example, Tymnet and Telenet both have computer networks that receive customer data coming in over telephone lines. These data are temporarily stored and organized into 'packets' of characters. These packets are then routed and transmitted at high speed over the final data destination. At these offices, data in the packets are reassembled into the complete message for transmission to the final destination. The transmission cost of value-added network (VAN) is less than directly utilizing common carrier channels. Telenet and Tymnet are sometimes referred to as packet-switching networks.

MICRO-TO-MICRO LINK

Microcomputers are often connected for data communication in a micro-to-micro link so that microcomputer users with incompatible data formats can share data. For instance, data on an Apple IIc disk cannot be used by an IBM PC/XT drive because the data are not saved on the disk in a format that the IBM can read. However, that data, provided they are in a standard format such as ASCII, can be sent via modem and telephone line to the IBM, saved on the disk by the IBM and used in that format. The reverse, sending data from the IBM to the Apple computer, is also possible. If the two computers are located near each other, another option is to connect directly (hard wire) using a null modem cable. The null modem cable uses a different pin configuration from a modem cable and eliminates the need for a modem by directly matching the data transmit pin from one computer to the data receive pin on the other computer.

The advantages of hard wiring are:

- It allows incompatible computers to transfer data.
- It eliminates the need for modems at each computer.
- It allows data transfer to take place at speeds upto 9600 bps.

However, there are no error dedication capabilities with hard wiring. A small business that uses microcomputers has accumulated information that it wants to send to a customer who also uses microcomputers. The precise procedures used depend on the particular software, but the following account outlines the general procedures:

1. The business and the computer both start the communication program, which gives them a menu of options.
2. The business and computer both, choose the same options, including the number of start and stop bits, the type of parity checking, the communication rate, full-duplex or half-duplex transmission and so on.
3. The communication configuration is made. The users decide who will originate the telephone call and the originator enters the telephone number. The communication program then instructs the modem to dial the number and reports to the users if a connection has been established.
4. When the connection has been established, the users can have an on-line conversation. They can type messages back and forth to each other and can record or capture their conversation.
5. At the business end, if the computer is ready to transfer the information, it sets its computer to send; the customer set its computer to receive. The business starts the transfer. The communication program takes over by reading the information from the disk and sending it through the communication link. The receiving computer stores the incoming information on a disk. When

the transfer of a file has been completed, the business and customer sides computers saying "good-bye" and then terminate the connection.

INTRODUCTION TO NETWORKING

Networking is a concept, where 2 or more than 2 computers are joined together to share information. This can be in the form of data or programs. These computers can be within a walking distance or in the same building of the office or in the same city or even across the cities.

But, why is this needed. Have you ever found yourself rushing from one computer to another in your office or home, attending to several different jobs at various locations? Or do you often find yourself moving files that need printing form a PC that you happen to be working on the PC that is connected to the printer? All of these situations can be made easier by allowing the various machines to communicate with each other – by networking the PCs.

The distance between the computers is narrowed down by the telephone lines. The information from the computer is converted to the media understandable by the communication lines and then transferred from one place to another.

With networking you can not only share data and programs, but can also share the resources like printers, scanners, etc. In PC technology, such a collection of computers, all located within a few thousand feet of each other, is called Local Area Networking.

NETWORKING BASICS

Networking several computers together allows data to be transmitted form one machine to another in rapid and easily managed data streams. This sharing of data allows many of the resources that are located on a single machine to effectively become available to all other machines on the network.

These resources can be physically located on the machine, e.g., as files on the hard disk, or connected logically to the machine. An example of a logically connected resource would be a printer that is connected to a PC, but which is then available over the network to other machines on that network.

An alternative situation would be where access to the Internet is available to all the PCs on a network through a special communication device attached to the network. Access to all external and internal resources are thus made available to PC users on the network.

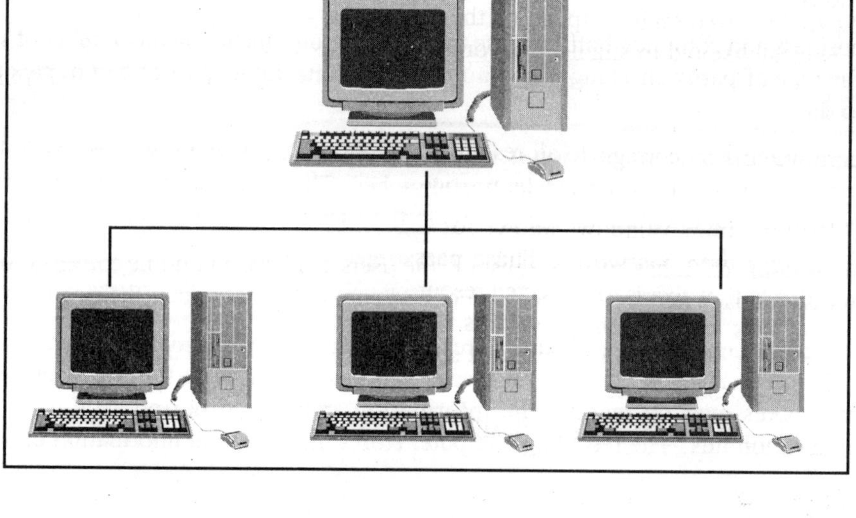

A network server provides network services to a user workstation (server) on the network. Services can range from sharing database and files, printers; communications or other network resources. Thus, the network servers are also called file servers, print servers, communication servers, etc. They can be dedicated to the task of providing network services.

They are then called dedicated network servers. Otherwise, they may be called non dedicated servers. A typical networking is shown on the last page.

Another factor which also favours the networking is the cost factor.

COST REDUCTION

If you have 2-3 computers attached in a single networking system, you may go in for a single printer which can be used by all of them. The same goes for other devices like Scanner, Plotter, etc. This results in lots of costs.

The main advantages of Networking can be clubbed as follows:

RESOURCE SHARING

There are two main types of networking systems. The type used for larger networks is known as the Client/Server model. This model involves using a powerful computer that runs a Network Operating System and acts as the 'server'. The Network Operating System then runs the server, supplying network services to the other 'client' computers.

These services might include the management of file transfers, running printing jobs, or even running applications across the network. For example, a word processing software package running on a PC is actually being 'served' form the server across the network, rather than being loaded onto the PC's local hard disk.

The problem with the Client/Server model is that it requires specialized hardware, software and to a large extent skilled networking techniques to configure and maintain the network. All of this can become expensive.

The second model, the Peer-to Peer system or resource Sharing is fortunately a lot easier to implement and maintain and it is this model that we will use in this book.

Resource Sharing is incorporated into Windows 98 and allows all network users access to all resources such as the hard drives, directories, printers or CD-ROM drives that are available on the network. It also allows access to external resources across the network via special intermediary devices.

Resource Sharing involved each computer on the network taking on equal an equal part in the networking process and is ideally suited to smaller networks.

SECURITY

Being able to have complete access to all resources on the network is not always desirable. It is often the case that certain resources may need to be restricted to certain users.

Resources Sharing within Windows allows for this and incorporates the ability to protect access to particular resources with passwords. These passwords can then be stored within the windows 98 configuration files so that access to protected resources is automatically assigned once the user has gained access to the network; the relevant passwords is therefore only entered once during the network login procedure. This function can also be disabled so that a password is required every single time the user attempts to access a protected resource.

Password access can also be configured to allow the user to read but not to change a particular resource or to allow full access, including the ability to write to a resource (which would be necessary for sending jobs to a printer).

Each individual resource can also be configured separately so that different passwords and access rights can be assigned for different resources

TYPES OF NETWORKING

The three basic types of networks are:

1. Local Area Networks or LAN
2. Metropolitan Area Network or MAN
3. Wide Area Network or WAN

Let us see them in details.

LOCAL AREA NETWORK

A local area network (LAN) is two or more computers directly linked within a small well-defined area such as a room, building, or group of closely placed buildings. A LAN may be made up of only microcomputers or any combination of microcomputers and large systems.

A LAN usually consists of the following:

1. Two or more computers
2. Peripheral devices such as printers and hard-disk drives
3. Software to control the operation of the computers or other devices connected to the LAN
4. Special cables, usually coaxial or fibre optic, to connect the computers and other devices
5. A plug-in board to handle the data transmissions.

Some computers require that all the computers be of a certain brand, while others allow a variety of brands to be connected. The number of computers in a LAN varies from smaller LANs that typically connect 2 to 25 computers, to large LANs that can connect as many as 10,000 computers.

The length of the cable connecting a computer to a LAN also varies depending on the LAN. Most LANs allow cables of about 1,000 feet, but some allow cables of several miles to be used. The data transfer speeds range from several thousand bits per second to around 10 million bits per second. The programs that control the LANs also vary in the features they offer. Some programs allow the user of more than on operating system; others allow only one. On some LANs file access is limited to one user at a time; on others, more than one user can access a file simultaneously.

Hardware for LAN

The following are the major hardware components/devices for establishing LAN:

1. Transmission Channel
2. Network Interface Unit or NIU
3. Servers
4. Workstations

Transmission Channel for LAN

Generally four types of channels are used for data transmission in a LAN. These are:

1. Twisted Pair Cables

2. Coaxial Cables
3. Fibre Optic Cables
4. Radio Waves

Interface for LAN

Network interface units connect each devices in the LAN network to shared transmission device. It contain the rules or logic to access the LAN. NIU is also used to implement LAN protocols and for device attachments. Its function depends on the type of topologies (to be told later in the this chapter), used in LAN.

Server and Workstations

One of the major benefits of implementation of LAN is sharing expensive resources such as storage devices, printers, etc. This is achieved through providing servers on the LAN. It is dedicated computer that controls one or more resources. This contains both hardware and software interface for LAN. Three major categories of services used in LANs are:

1. File Server
2. Printer Server
3. Modem Server

In networking, file server is used to share storage for files. Besides providing storage space for files in a LAN environment, it is used for taking periodical backup, and also to provide gateway to other servers with and between LANs. Similarly printer server is used to handle printing works of all workstation connected in the network. In LAN environment also modem is required to get connected to other network or simply to use a telephone. A modem server is used to share this expensive resource by all connected workstations in a network ring.

Software for LAN

LAN operating system is required to operate on the LAN system. It has basically two aspects:

1. Server Software
2. Workstation Software

LAN operating system facilitates :

1. Sharing of expensive resources, e.g., printer, storage space, etc.
2. Security for data
3. Connection to other network

There are various types of LAN operating system. Some popular LAN operating systems are :

- Novel Netware
- Ethernet
- Corvus
- ArcNet
- LAN Server
- Omni Net
- PC Net

— IBM PC LAN

— Etherlink Plus, etc.

WIDE AREA NETWORKS OR WAN

A wide area network is two or more computers that are geographically dispersed, linked by communication facilities such as telephone system or microwave relays. This type of network is usually limited to use by large corporations and government agencies because of the high cost involved in building and maintaining them. A WAN is a network that links separate geographical locations and this network can be a public system or any of the various packet switched services provided by the public telecommunication agencies.

The main difference between a WAN and LAN is under the complete control of the owner, whereas the WAN needs the involvement of another authority like telecom department. LANs are successful and capable of handling very high data transfer rates at low cost because of the small area covered. Besides LANs have a lower error rate than WANs.

Transmission Channel for WAN

Generally 3 types of channels are used for data transmission in a WAN. These are:

1. Radio Waves
2. Micro Waves
3. Communication Satellites

Hardware Requirements for WAN

There are mainly 4 hardware devices which are required to establish linkage between geographically separated computers. These are:

1. Bridges
2. Routers
3. Gateways
4. X.25 Standard Interface

These are explained below.

Bridges

These are used to connect two LANs that use the identical protocols over a wide area. The bridge acts as an address filter which picks up packets from one LAN that are intended for a destination on another LAN and passes these packets on the network. The amount of processing required at the bridge is minimal because all the devices use the same protocols. In case the distance between two LANs is very large then the user is required to employ two identical bridges at either end of the communication link.

Routers

It is a special type of device that can be used to connect networks that may not be similar. Such type of devices provide connectivity between two LANs and two WANs over large geographical distances. These devices operate at the Network Layer of the OSI model. These devices participate in a routing protocol to access the network topology, and on the basis of this information routers compute the best route from a sender to the receiver.

Gateways

These are used to connect two dissimilar LANs. The terms Gateways and Routers are used interchangeably, though there is discriminating difference between the two. A router operates at the network layer whereas a gateway operates on the application layer of the OSI model. A gateway is required to convert data packets from one protocol format to another before forwarding it, as it connects two dissimilar networks.

X.25 Standard Interface

X.25 is a protocol for interfacing to a Public Packet Switched Network. It is not a protocol used for implementing a network. Two systems that support X.25 can't necessarily be connected back-to-back. They can only be connected through a DCE in a Public Packet Switched. International Telegraph and Telephone Consultative Committee (ITTCC) developed X.25 as the standard interface between the Data Terminal Equipment (DTE) and Data Circuit Terminating Equipment (DCTE). This recommendation has been widely accepted as the industry standard for public packet switched networks.

TYPES OF WIDE AREA NETWORKS

There are mainly two types of WAN:

Public Networks

These are those networks which are installed and run by the telecommunication authorities and are made available to any organization or individual who go for their subscription.

Private Networks

The basic technique used in all forms of private WAN is to use private circuits to link the locations to be served by the network. Between these fixed points the owner of the network has complete freedom to use the circuits in any way they want. They can use the circuits to carry large quantities of data or for high speed transmissions. Private wide area networks can be built using whatever standard technology is available.

TOPOLOGY

There are ways in which you can connect the various computers for networking. This physical arrangement is called Topology. Different types of topologies are:

The Ring Topology

As the name suggests all the server/nodes are joined together to form a ring. There is no central server in this case. A ring may be unidirectional or bi-directional. A unidirectional ring moves data in one direction only; a bi-directional ring moves data in both directions, but only one direction at a time. In a unidirectional ring, if one computer breaks down, special software is required to keep the network functional. When one node malfunction in a bi-directional ring, a message can usually be sent in the opposite direction still allowing the node to communicate with all the other active nodes in the network.

Advantages of the Ring Network

1. **Short cable length:** the amount of cabling involved in a ring topology is comparable to that of a bus and is small relative to that of a star. This means that less connections will be needed, which will in turn increase network reliability.
2. **No wiring closet space required:** Since there is only one cable connecting each node to its immediate neighbours, it is not necessary to allocate space in the building for wiring closets.

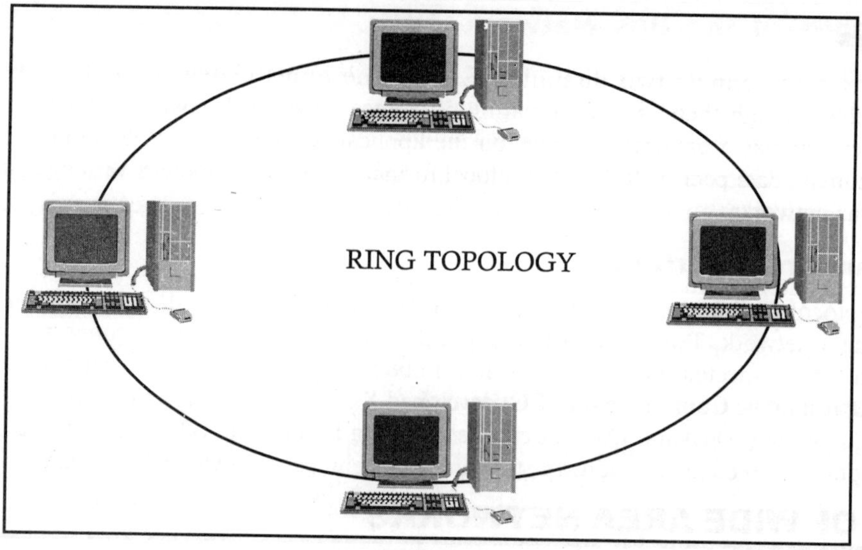

3. **Suitable for optical fibers:** Optical fibers offer the possibility of very high speed transmission. Because traffic on a ring travels in one direction, it is easy to use optical fibers as a medium of transmission. Also, since a ring is made up of nodes connected by short segments of transmission medium, there is a possibility of mixing the types used for different parts of the network. Thus, a manufacturing company's network could use copper cables in the office area and optical fibers in the factory areas, where electrical interference may be a problem.

Disadvantages of the Ring Network

1. **Node failure causes network failure:** the transmission of data on a ring goes through every connected node on the ring before returning to the sender. If one node fails to pass data through itself, the entire network has failed and no traffic can flow until the defective node has been removed from the ring.
2. **Difficult to diagnose faults:** The fact that failure of one node will affect all other has serious implications for fault diagnosis. It may be necessary to examine a series of adjacent nodes to determine the faulty one. This operation may also require diagnostic facilities to be built into each node.
3. **Network reconfiguration is difficult:** The all or nothing nature of the ring topology can cause problems when one decides to extend or modify the geographical scope of the network. It is not possible to shut down a small section of the ring while keeping the majority of it working normally.
4. **Topology affects the access protocol:** Each node on a ring has a responsibility to pass on data that it receives. This means that the access protocol must take this into account. Before a node can transmit its own data, it must ensure that the medium is available for use.

THE BUS TOPOLOGY

In this case all the server/nodes share a common bus of connecting cables. Every computer can communicate directly with every other computer or device in the network. Each node is given an address.

To access a particular, a user just needs to know its address. This topology is frequently used with local area networks. Going through a hierarchy of nodes is not necessary.

Advantages of the Bus Network

1. **Short cable length and simple wiring layout:** Because there is a single common data path connecting all nodes, the bus topology allows a very short cable length to be used. This decreases the installation cost and also leads to a simple, easy to maintain, wiring layout.
2. **Resilient architecture:** The bus architecture has an inherent simplicity that makes it very reliable from a hardware point of view. There is a single cable through which all data passes and to which all nodes are connected.
3. **East to extend:** Additional nodes can be connected to an existing bus network at any point along its length. More extensive additions can be achieved by adding extra segments connected by a type of signal amplifier known as a repeater.

Disadvantages of the Bus Network

1. **Fault diagnosis is difficult:** Although the simplicity of the bus topology means that there is very little that can go wrong, fault detention is not a simple matter. In most LANs based on a bus, control of the network is not centralized in any particular node. This means that detection of a fault may be performed from many points in the network.
2. **Fault isolation is difficult:** In the star topology, a defective node can easily be isolated from the network by removing its connection at the center. If a node is faulty on a bus, it must be rectified at the point where the node is connected to the network. Once the fault has been located the node can simply be removed. In the case where the fault is the network medium itself, an entire segment of the bus must be disconnected.
3. **Repeater configuration:** When a bus-type network has its backbone extended using repeaters, reconfiguration may be necessary. This may involve tailoring cable lengths, adjusting terminators, etc.
4. **Nodes must be intelligent:** Each node on the network is directly connected to the central bus. This means that some way of deciding who can use the network at any given time must be performed in each node. It tends to increase the cost of the nodes irrespective of whether this is performed in hardware of software

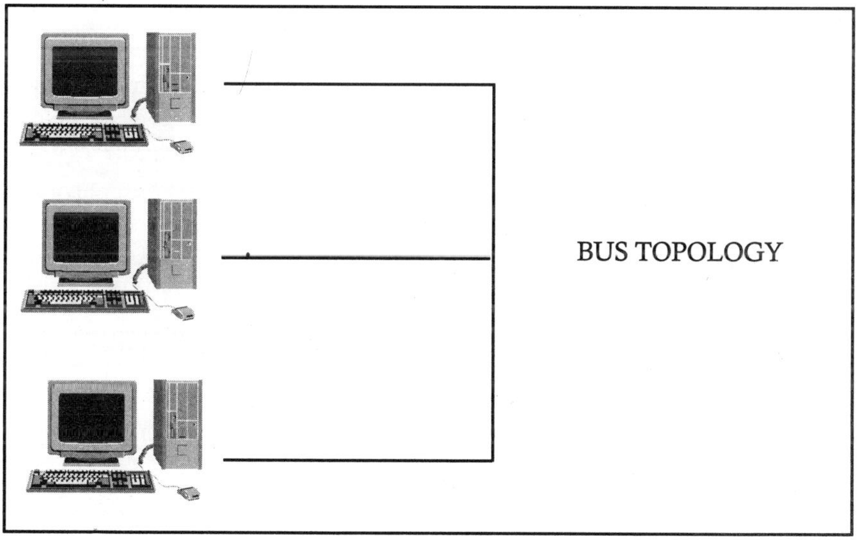

The Star Topology

In this case all the computers and the main server form a star like shape. All the computers are connected to a single main host. All communication first goes through the centralized computer allowing it to control the operation, work load, and resource allocation of the other computers in the network. For example, a bank with branch offices would typically use a star network to control and coordinate those branches. The advantage is relative simplicity, but a problem exists with the single-point vulnerability of the network. If the central computer breaks down, none of the other computers can communicate with each other.

Advantages of the Star Network

1. **Ease of service:** The star topology has a number of concentration points, i.e. at the central node or at intermediate wiring closets. These provide easy access for service of reconfiguration of the network.
2. **One device per connection:** Connection points in any network are inherently prone to failure. In the star topology, failure of a single connection typically involves disconnecting one node from an otherwise fully functional network.
3. **Centralized control/ problem diagnosis:** The fact that the central node is connected directly to every other node in the network means that faults are easily detected and isolated. It is a simple matter to disconnect failing nodes from the system.
4. **Simple access protocols:** Any given connection is a star network involves only the central node and one peripheral node. In this situation, contention for who has control of the medium for transmission purposes is easily solved. Thus in a star network, access protocols are very simple.

Disadvantages of the Star Network

1. **Long cable length:** Because each node is directly connected to the center, the star topology necessitates a large quantity of cable. While the cost of the cable is often small, congestion in cable ducts and maintenance and installation problems can increase costs considerably.
2. **Difficult to expand:** The addition of a new node to a star network involves a connection all the way to the central node. Expansion is usually catered for by providing large numbers of redundant cables during the initial wiring. However, problems can arise if a longer cable length is needed or an unanticipated concentration of nodes is required.

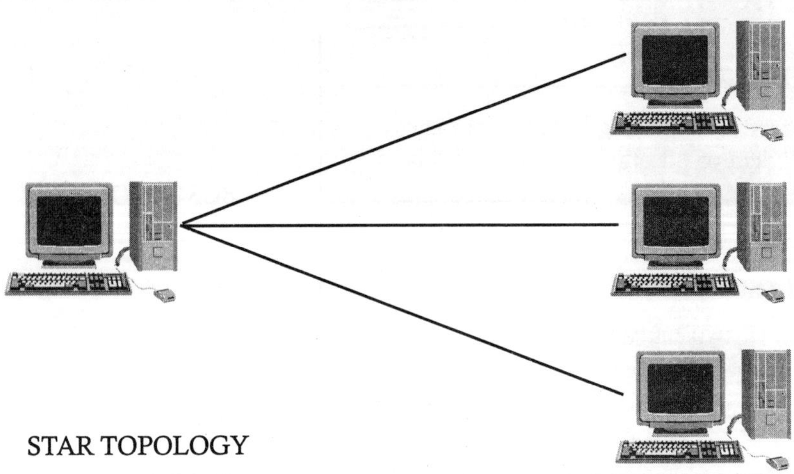

STAR TOPOLOGY

3. **Central node dependency:** If the central node in a star network fails, the entire network is rendered inoperable. This introduces heavy reliability and redundancy constraints on this node.

Mesh Topology

A network topology featuring a direct path between two nodes. The backbone of this topology looks like this, where most major cities have a direct connection to most major cities.

Advantages and Disadvantages of the Mesh Network

- **Units affected by media failure:** Mesh topologies resist media failure better than other topologies. Implementations that include more than two devices will always have multiple paths to send signals from one device to another. If one path fails, the transmission signals can be routed around the failed link. Theoretically, no units are affected by media failure. However, if all paths normally use the maximum capacity of each link, some performance degradation will occur are signals are routed around a failed link.
- **Ease of installation:** Mesh networks are relatively difficult to install because each device must be linked directly to all other devices. As the number of devices increases, the difficulty of installation increases geometrically.

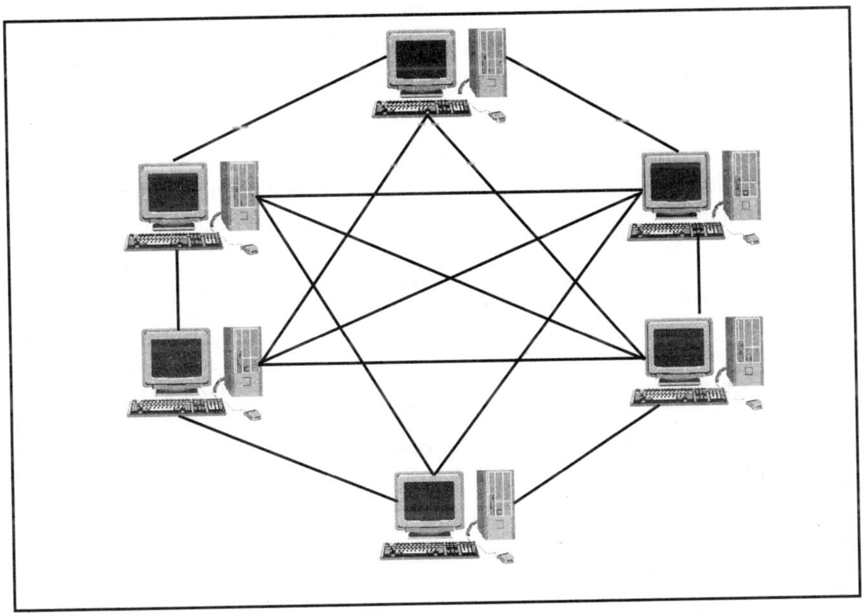

- **Ease of troubleshooting:** Mesh topologies are easy to troubleshoot because each medium link is independent of all others. You can easily identify faults and can isolate the affected link.
- **Ease of reconfiguration:** Mesh topologies are difficult to reconfigure for the same reasons that they are difficult to install.

Hybrid Topology

A combination of two or more network topologies. The resultant is a hybrid network. Although the backbone is mostly a mesh network, each local loop is a star network with the central office at each hub.

Advantages of the Hybrid Network

1. **Fault diagnoses and isolation:** The presence of concentration points in the network greatly eases

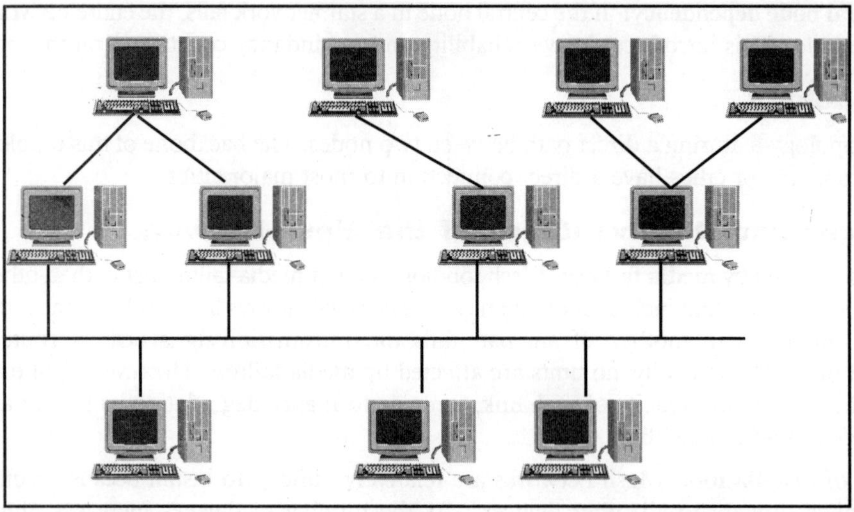

fault diagnosis. If a fault is detected on the network, the initial problems to find out which concentration point in the ring is to blame. The fact that this ring is quite small in relation to the total size of the network makes this problem more manageable. The offending concentration point can be isolated easily, leaving the network in a fully functional state while further fault diagnosis is carried out.

2. **Ease of expansion:** The modular construction of a star-ring network means that new sections may be easily added. When designing the network originally, each concentration can have extra, unused lobes which can be called upon later, if needed. The next growth step involved adding a new concentration point and wiring it into the ring.
3. **Cabling:** The concentration points in a star-ring are connected via a single cable. This simplifies wiring between areas in an installation and cuts down on the congestion of cable ducts. Also, the wiring practices involved are very similar to that of telephone system installation. These techniques are well understood by building engineers and lend themselves well to the prewiring of buildings.

Disadvantages of the Hybrid Network

1. **Intelligent concentration points required:** Depending on the implementation used, the concentration points may need to have built in intelligence/processing ability. This will be necessary if it is to assist in network fault diagnosis, node isolation or conversion from one form of transmission medium to another.
2. **Cabling:** The intercloset cabling in a star ring is critical to its operation. This may mean that redundant cabling in the form of one or more back up rings may be necessary to meet reliability requirements. The largest section of the network (i.e. between the concentration points and the nodes) is laid out in a star. This means that a considerable amount of cable may be required.

Tree Topology

From a purely topological viewpoint, this network resembles a interconnection of star networks. Individual peripheral nodes must transmit to and receive from one other node only, toward a central node. An advantage of a tree structure is that functional groupings can be created.

For example, one branch could contain all the general ledger terminals, another branch all the accounts receivable terminals, and so on. If one branch stops functioning, the other branches in a tree network are not affected. However, data movement through this network can be slow.

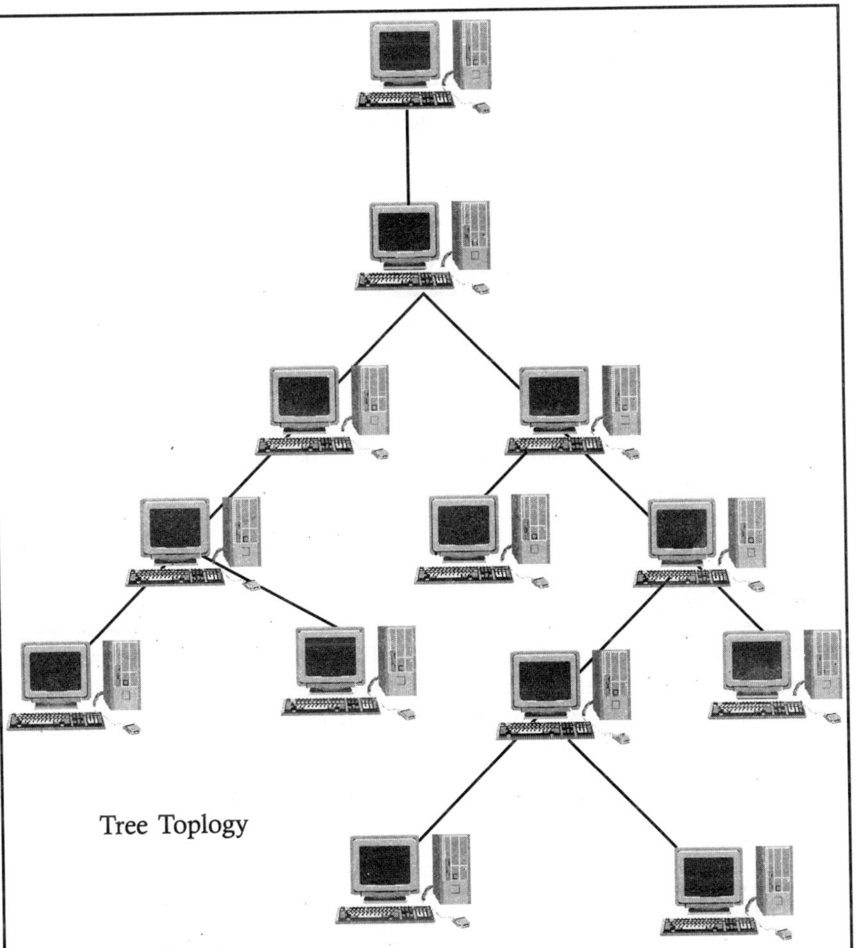

Tree Toplogy

Advantages of the Tree Network

1. **Easy to extend:** Because the tree is of its very nature, divided into subunits, it is easier to add new nodes or branches to it.
2. **Fault isolation:** It is possible to disconnect whole branches of the network from the main structure. This makes it easier to isolate a defective node.

Disadvantages of the Tree Network

1. **Dependant on the root:** If the "headend" device fails to operate, the entire network is rendered inoperable. In this respect, the tree suffers from the same reliability problems as the star.

APPLICATIONS OF NETWORKING

In business, government organizations, universities and many other organizations networks of all types of computers provide tremendous benefits. Four of the most compelling benefits are as follows:

SIMULTANEOUS ACCESS

In business computing, most office workers use the same software package. With a network, business can save a lot by purchasing special network versions of the most commonly used software rather than buying separate copies for each machine. When employees need to use the software, they simply load it from a shared storage device into their own desktop computer.

Since a single network copy of the software can serve the needs of large number of users simultaneously, all the employees also save the storage space that the software program would occupy on his computer's disk drive. The same is true of data that multiple employees need access to at the same time. Another major area of computer network advantage is access to remote databases.

SHARED PERIPHERAL DEVICES

The best incentive for small businesses from computers networking is sharing of peripheral devices, especially expensive ones such as laser printer and scanners.

EASIER BACKUP

In business, data can be extremely valuable, so making sure that employees backup their data is critical. One way to address this problem is to keep all valuable data on a shared storage device that employees access through a network. That way, one person can be charged with making regular backup of the data on the shared storage device.

ELECTRONIC MAIL

Computer networking has helped in increasing the speed of the message transfer tremendously. With the help of e-mail, messages can be transferred through computer network within a short span of time. User can send written message without worrying about whether the other user is currently using his/her computer or not. Over centralized networks, the message is delivered almost instantaneously. E-mail cross time zones, can reach many people with the same message, reduces the paper flood and does not interrupt meetings the way a ringing phone does.

VOICE MAIL

It releases workers from the tyranny of the telephone. In it, if the person being called does not answer, the called is given instructions to dictate a message to the system. The voice mail computer system stores the message in the recipient's Voice mailbox. Later when the recipient dials the mailbox, the system delivers the message. A voice mail system translates the word of a message into digital impulses, which it then stores on disk, just as any other data. Later this message is reconverted to audio form.

THE ETHERNET PROTOCOL

Ethernet is the most popular protocol used for LAN communications. In essence it uses a digital 'packet' that can contain any other digital information. Every computer that uses this protocol contains an Ethernet Network Interface Card (NIC) that has a unique address code embedded into a microchip on the NIC. This address is used by the protocol to identify each individual computer. This allows every electronic packet that is sent from one machine to another to contain the destination address for which the packet is intended.

Every computer on the network 'listens' for packets that contain its own address. When a packet is placed on a network, that packet is broadcast to and received by every other computer on the network but only the computer which corresponds to the destination address is allowed to claim that packet and receive the digital information contained within it. Only a single packet is allowed onto the network at any one time, but the process operates at such a high speed that effectively the packet is delivered to the destination within milliseconds, allowing the next packet access to the network almost immediately.

The Ethernet protocol also provides a means of preventing two computers from trying to place packets onto the network at the same time. When a NIC tries to place a packet onto the network, it first 'listens' to see if there is already a packet being transmitted to and from other machines, If so, then it is forced to wait for a random amount of time (milliseconds), before trying again. This continues until a 'gap' is found and then the packet can be successfully transmitted onto the network. The Ethernet protocol provides a means of delivering data from any PC on the network to any other on the same network at a theoretical rate of up to 10 Mega bits per second. Ethernet can also be used to connect remotely located PCs, but this requires special communications links to be set up over specialized equipment.

Fast Ethernet

It is a new standard of the Ethernet protocol, based on the existing 10 Mhz standard, but designed to operate at the much faster data rate of 100 Mhz. Mhz stands for megahertz or a million cycles per second and represents the operating frequency of the protocol. The terms 'Mhz' and 'Mega bits per second' are often used interchangeably, but this is only true where one cycle represents one bit (a bit being a unit of data). For many protocols, this direct relationship holds true, but it is not always the case and so the terms should be used with caution.

THE TCP/IP PROTOCOL

TCP/IP is actually two protocols. These two protocols are almost invariably use together, hence the term TCP/IP has come to be accepted as describing a single system. We will be using this assumption here. TCP/IP is the networks protocol that is used throughout the Internet. It was originally developed in American academic institutions as a means of communicating between university computer systems, first locally and then nationally across America and internationally between universities, that formed the basis of what is now know as the Internet.

It is the capability for being used over existing telephone systems that gives TCP/IP (and hence the Internet) its enormous potential for worldwide data communication. Ethernet is designed to run over relatively short distances at a very high data rate, but the physical limitations of the public phone systems mean that this high data rate cannot normally be sustained, except perhaps over the larger truck routes between countries and major cities. TCP/IP however is independent of the various data rates associated with different communication media and so can be used over both very slow and very high speed systems. Like Ethernet, the TCP/IP protocol uses an addressing system to determine the intended destinations for a data packet, but unlike Ethernet TCP/IP also includes a source address in the data packet. This system of addresses is used to route the data packet across the Internet, very much like the address on a envelope is used to route a letter across the various national postal systems.

However, unlike Ethernet, each packet is not broadcast cross the entire network, but is routed individually using the addressing system to a single destination. This system is known as 'packet switching'.

Packet Switching

When one computer communicates with another using the TCP/IP protocol, it breaks the information it needs to send into 'chunks' small enough for the TCP/IP packet to be handle and then attaches a destination address and a source address. The packet is then sent out across the Internet, containing all of the information it needs to navigate its way to a remote destination. It is a feature of the Internet that each individual packet can then take one of many different routes via the thousands of intermediate computer systems across the world to reach its final destination. Each computer along the way reads the destination address of he packet and routes it according to certain sets of rules to the next computer system on the Internet. This fragmenting of information and use of many alternative routes means that the receiving computer may well receive the packets in a different order to that in which they were sent. It must therefore have some means of making sure that it reads the incoming packets in the correct order.

The job of the 'TCP' part of TCP/IP is to ensure that each packet reaches its destination intact and that the packets are numbered effectively so that the receiving computer can put the incoming packets back into the correct order. It is the 'IP' part TCP/IP that looks after the addressing. Because TCP/IP packets contain a source address as well as a destination address, the receiving computer system also has a way or replying automatically to the sender by simply reading the source address and then generating another TCP/IP packet using this source address as the destination address for the new packet.

Another feature that is very useful part of the TCP/IP protocol is that because each packet is essentially self-sufficient in its journey across the Internet, many packets from different sources can share a single communication channel, allowing perhaps hundreds of thousands of channels to share a single cable at the same time.

BASIC ELEMENTS IN NETWORKING

All networks require the following three elements:

1. **Network Services**: At least two individuals who have something to share.
2. **Transmission Media**: A method or pathway for contacting each other.
3. **Protocols**: Rules so that two or more individuals can communicate.

NETWORK SERVICES

Network services are provided by numerous combinations of computer hardware and software. Depending upon the task, network services require data, input/output resources and processing power to accomplish their goals.

In the computer industry, the following 3 types of service providers and requestor are as follows:

Servers: Servers are only allowed to provide services.

Clients: Clients are only allowed to request services from others.

Peers: Peers may do both concurrently.

Computer networks are often classified as one of the following two types:

Peer-to-Peer Networks

This type of networks allow any entity to both request and provide network services. Peer-to-peer network software is designed so that peers perform the same or similar functions for each other.

Server-Centric Networks

This network involves strictly defined roles. By definition, a server-centric network places restrictions upon which entity may make requests or service them. Currently, the most popular personal computer networks are server-centric.

TRANSMISSION MEDIA

It is the pathway by which networked entities use to contact each other. Computer transmission media includes cable and wireless technologies that allow networked devices to contact each other. Transmission media cannot guarantee that other network devices will understand a message. It can, however, guarantee a message delivery path.

PROTOCOLS

A protocol can be one rule or a complete set of rules and standards that allow different devices to hold conversations. For example, human communication would be impossible without language, grammar and cultural rules. The following is an example of set of rules and standards in which network service requesters and service providers can communicate:

- How is the transmission media physically set up?
- How do network entities contact one another?
- How do network entities know how much data can be transmitted?
- How are network entities guaranteed that a message has been received correctly?
- How is a message passed to the intended recipient(s)?
- How are bits transmitted on the media?
- How do network entities, with disparate languages, communicate?
- How do network entities know when to transmit data?

When you formally agree that you will both use the same language in future communications, you have established a communication protocol.

VALUE ADDED NETWORKS

Another type of network is the value added network. This is an established data communication network that owns a leases communication facilities and computers to manage communication. The facilities may include microwave antennas and communication satellites. The owners design and maintain the value added network. They then rent the network simultaneously to many subscribers, who link their own equipment tot he facilities. Using value added network saves organizations the time and cost of designing and maintaining their own networks. The concept of value added common carriers was important in the development of computer networking.

A value added carrier leases communications facilities from conventional common carriers and uses these in conjunction with computers to build a network which offers new types of communications services and tariffs. These are called Value Added Networks (VANs). Graphnet offered services for delivery of documents, often in facsimile form. Telenet built a network for the interconnection of data processing machines, like the ARPA network although the software and hardware mechanisms eventually became substantially different from ARPANET. Telnet delivers packets of data between computers or terminals in a fraction of a second and charges by the packet. TYMNET offering similar services evolved from a private time sharing network to a value added common carrier. In 1971 the United States Office of Telecommunications Policy recommended a policy of first tier second tier common carriers.

The first tier carriers construct and own telecommunications links and lease channels to their customer. They typically own 50% to 100% of the channel miles in service and lease the remainder from another carrier. The second tier carriers are the value added carriers. They add equipment including multiplexers and computers, to channels leased from first tier carriers and sell services that they create in this way, including message delivery services, computer networks and possibly information retrieval services and computer timesharing devices. It seems likely that second markets will develop in may telecommunications areas. The second tier carrier may minimize investment in terminals by letting the customer provide these. Legislation in favour of second tier carriers has increased the diversity and competitiveness of the telecommunications industry in those countries where it has been passed.

In most countries, such legislation does not yet exist. Telecommunication systems use computer in different ways. Some use them for switching; some for sorting messages which are transmitted; some for processing the data transmitted. At one extreme the computer merely switches the circuits; at the other the circuits are merely linked into a data processing system. The term "computer utility" became used for describing public access to computer networks and in 1966 the United States Federal Communications Commission (FCC) initiated a lengthy inquiry to determine whether public computing services should be regulated. Hybrid communication services must be completely tariffed and regulated by the FCC. Common carriers may not offer data processing services (hybrid or otherwise) except through a separate corporation with separate facilities, officers and accounting. AT&T has been excluded from offering any such unregulated services under an earlier consent decree. Most countries do not have these legislative problems because the state telecommunications authority rigorously enforces its absolute monopoly over all telecommunications, no matter how bad its service may be.

Public Networks

During the mid 1970's the need for building a public data network was realized by the telecommunication administration of various countries, with two specified objectives. One was to provide better services to the computer community and the other was to earn revenue which was enormous. This is the revenue from the switches, concentrators, multiplexers polling equipment, line control equipment, etc., - the various devices used in the interconnection of machines.

Common carriers operate (this term includes the telecommunication administrations of countries with government-controlled telecommunications – the PTT's) the equipment for switching and routing telephone calls; it seemed natural that they should operate the new equipment for switching routing data. One computers were used for switching the desire grew to use them for other functions also. AT&T developed its plans for ACS (Advanced Communications Service) in which the nodes would not only switch data but provide a variety of functions which need processing and storage. The British Post Office created its Viewdata scheme (subsequently called Prestel) for operating public data bank accessible with television sets in homes or offices, initially via the telephone network.

Private Networks

Some networks are designed specifically for and used completely by individual organizations. They are called private networks. The communication equipment that forms the network is purchased or leased in the name of the organization. The first WAN to be designed and developed was the private network, ARPANET, a United States network. The objective was to make the interesting and unique computer facilities available in some computer centers accessible to a large community of users. It has grown from a four-site experimental network to a nationwide communication system interconnecting more than fifty universities and research centers. A few computer networks link computer centers in multiple locations. To operate these multicorporate networks, a separate service organization is usually set up and that organization will take care of creating and operating the network. A leading example is the SWIFT electronic fund transfer network that passes financial transactions between banks. SWIFT (Society for Worldwide Interbank Financial Transactions) is a non-profit organization set up and wholly owned by the banks connected to it. The objective of this network is to replace mail, cable and telex and work for 24 hours a day and 7 days a week. It handles over a million transactions per day. It is used to send money, messages and bank statements at high speed between banks and the transaction time is drastically reduced.

SWIFT connects about 3000 financial institutions in more than 600 countries. Citibank Corp. in New York, was the first one to opt for the system and over 40 banks in India have joined the network. The computer based terminals of these banks are hooked with SWIFT's access center in Bombay, which is maintained by CMC Ltd. From here, messages are relayed to the overseas communication center of VSNL and then transmitted to SWIFT's international receiving centers based in London or Singapore, depending on the location of the receiver, through VSNL's GPSS services. The software needed for the operations has been supplied by SWIFT terminal services, a wholly owned subsidiary of SWIFT and the hardware is being supplied by Tata Unisys, Digital Equipment (India) Ltd. The participating banks finance the system and a tariff structure has been built based on the message, connection charge and annual charge.

COMMON NETWORK SERVICES

The following common network services are available:

File Services

The network file services improve the efficient storage and retrieval of computer data, they are one of the primary services offered on computer networks. The following file service functions are :

- File transfer – Rapidly move files from place to place.
- File storage and data migration – Use storage hardware efficiently.
- File update synchronization – Manage multiple copies of the same file.
- File archiving – Back up critical data

File Transfer

Before computer networks were widely implemented, users physically moved storage media from computer to computer. This inefficient practice has been called "sneaker-net" (because users hand carried data from machine to machine). Organizationally, it is relatively expensive and time consuming to employ people to move computer storage media. The network file service file transfer refers to any service that saves, retrieves, or moves files for a network client. This service allows you to handle data much more efficiently. The major advantage of Computer Networks is, file transfers can be performed with relative ease regardless of file size, distance and often even the local operating systems. This service increases the organization's efficiently, as well as it also provided access to data and information that were previously inaccessible. File services may also coordinate access rights because of the increased information access that the file transfer service provides. An organization may allow network transfer of sensitive information, but only by authorized individuals. During file transfer, network file services often use passwords to control access to systems and files. They use data encryption schemes to encode data so that it can only been read by appropriate individuals.

File Storage and Data Migration

The rapidly increasing amount of computerized data has caused the development of numerous online, nearline and offline storage devices. Hard disk drive, tape jukebox and removable storage is an example of online storage, nearline storage and offline storage respectively. Computers store data on a variety of magnetic and optic disks, diskettes and tapes. Each storage medium exhibits characteristics that make it suitable for a specific use. Because the efficient use of each storage device requires continuous management of multiple devices, network application are well suited to control data storage activities on different storage systems. In addition, if you are working with high end equipment, such as magnetic tape banks or optical libraries, you can use the network's economy of scale to justify the equipment purchase, operation and maintenance. Using file storage and data migration functions, all networked computers can take advantage of the data storage device that is appropriate for their access time, reliability and longevity needs. As data ages and becomes less used, it can be moved from expensive online hard disk drives to less expensive and longer life offline storage media. Moving data from one storage media or location to another is call data migration. Through data migration, you can set up file services to move files based on age, user, size or various other criteria.

File Update Synchronization

File update synchronization is a service that compares the time and date corresponding files were saved and determines which is most current. It may also keep track of who has a specific file and if intermediary changes have been made. Using this information, it automatically updates all file locations with latest version. For examples, mobile computers are not always connected or available to the network. If you are a mobile computer user and you want access to a file that is on a network file server, you would normally save a copy of the file to your computer' shared drive. However, someone else may access and change the original file in the meantime. If that person does make changes, your copy now contains out of date information. Somehow you need to recognize when changes have occurred and take the appropriate action.

File Archiving

Many organizations create duplicate copies of important data on magnetic tape or some other offline storage media in case of emergency. This practice is called file archiving or file backup. The original file can be kept in addition to the backup copy, or it can be removed from online storage media so that the offline media contains the only copy. When file storage devices are interconnected on a network, file archiving becomes much easier. Computer operators use the network to traverse great distances, saving the organization time and money.

Print Services

These are network applications that control and manage access to printers and fax equipment. Print services accept print job request, interpret print job formats and printer configurations, manage print queues and interact with networkable printers and fax equipment for network clients.

The following are print service functions:

- Provide multiple access from limited interfaces – Reduce the number of printers your organization needs.
- Eliminate distance constraints – place printers wherever is most convenient.
- Handle simultaneous requests – Queue print jobs to reduce the time your computer spends sending a print job.
- Share specialized equipment – share specialized printers efficiently.
- Network fax service – Computerize the transmission and reception of fax images.

Providing Multiple Access from Limited Interfaces

Reducing the total number of printers can save your organization a substantial amount of money having fewer printers reduces the number of devices to buy, maintain and manage.

Most modern printer provide multiple ports or interfaces. However, the number of interfaces is finite and relatively small. Typically, only two or three computers may be directly connected to each printer. On the other hand, a network connection requires only one interface. Through this interface, many computers may send data to the printer.

Therefore, print services allow numerous clients to be serviced by a single printer. Managing access to printers, or other devices with limited interfaces, is a major use of modern computer networks.

Eliminating Distance Constraints

Printer ports are often based on cable interface specification that limit the distance between the printer and attached computers. Network cable systems and devices allow longer distances for cable specifications. Organizations can use the network to place printers in strategic locations throughout a building or campus.

Handling Simultaneous Request (Queuing)

Print servers can often handle simultaneous request for print services. When two users try to send data to a printer at the same time, both applications compete for the printer's limited ability to accept and store print request. Queuing solves this bottleneck problem. A print queue is the part of the print server which captures and stores computer print jobs. Depending upon each implementation's specific features, print queues can hold, prioritize, and manage print jobs. When printing with network printing services, your application sends print requests and data to what it believes is a printer. These requests are actually routed to a print queue. The print requests remain in the queue until the desired printer is available. Print queuing increases the efficiency of network print services by organizing the interaction between printers and their clients. In addition, because multiple clients may send data simultaneously to the print queue at full network speeds, each may complete print request rapidly and return to other tasks.

Sharing Specialized Equipment

Some printer are designed for specific use, such as high speed output, large format paper, or color printing. Specialized equipment may be expensive or may not be frequently used by end users. The economies of scale produced by networking each device with numerous clients can reduce the effective cost per user and optimize printer use.

Network Fax Service

Network fax allows users to send and receive faxes using special network hardware and software. This service is becoming increasingly popular because it reduces the time and paper handling normally involved in traditional fax transmissions. Traditional fax machines use computer modem, scanner and printer technologies to send a digital document image to remote locations. Network fax systems use the same computer technologies and computer networks to better integrate fax service with the rest of the network's print and message services.

Message Services

Message services include storing, accessing and delivering text, binary, graphic, digitized video and audio data. Message services are similar to file services. However, unlike file services, message services deal actively with the communication interactions between computer users, user applications, network applications, or documents. Instead of simply storing data files, message services transport data from point to point.

The following are the message services functions:

- Electronic Mail
- Integrated electronic mail and voice mail
- Object oriented applications
- Workgroup applications

Electronic Mail

A business depends on the efficient exchange of information between different parts of the business and between the business and the outside word. Much of this exchange has been traditionally carried out through paper documents, delivered by secretary, mail or messenger service. With the growing use of personal computers, a more efficient alternative has emerged, i.e., electronic mail. Electronic mail is usually used to exchange messages and data files. Each user is assigned an electronic mailbox

Using the appropriate command, the user can scan a list of messages in the mailbox, display the contents of a particular message, send a message to another user and so forth. To send a message, it is not necessary for the recipient to be present at the computer. The message resides in the mailbox until it is read. The sender may restrict delivery of the message to authorized readers by using a password. That is, the recipient must "sign" for the message by typing his or her identifying password. Many other features of standard mail delivery are implemented in electronic mail systems. For example, mail can be forwarded, stored for delayed delivery and sent to anyone at a particular phone number. In addition, electronic mail systems implement many new features. An electronic mail system can deliver copies of a message to all individuals listed in a certain file. It also allow merging of standard data (from a data file) with a particular message. Now-a-days, several companies have started subscription to electronic mail services. These services are accessed through a modem and allow users to communicate with other subscribers to the service. The service may also accept a message and transmit it to its destination city. There the message is printed out and delivered with the next day's mail. This technique can be used to communicate with people who are not subscribers to the network.

Integrated Electronic Mail and Voice Mail

Message services that integrate E-Mail and voice mail are also being developed. Voice mail is a service offered by specialized computer hardware and software that answers telephone calls and records audio messaged. Because voice mail systems are simply specialized computers, thy can be incorporated into computer networks. Computer network and voice mail vendors are currently developing ways to make voice mail system cooperate on computer networks. Eventually, user could retrieve messages from whatever type of device is convenient.

Object Oriented Applications

Object oriented application are computer programs that combine smaller applications to accomplish complex tasks. Message services often facilitate communications between objects on a computer network. Messaging application accomplish this by acting as the object's agent, so every object does not meet to contact every other object. The object simply communicates with an agent from the local messaging service. The agent then become responsible for communicating the message to the destination object.

Workgroup Applications

Message service have also been used to create a new class of applications called workgroup applications. The following are common types of workgroup applications:

Workflow management

Workflow management application intelligently forms, route notices and documents among network clients. These service providers are designed to handle multiuser distributed business processes. For example, assume that you want to convert a payroll process using workflow management. The old manual process required that employees fill out a paper based time card. The time card was then signed by a manager and sent to the payroll department. Upon receipt payroll employees entered the information from the time card, calculated the employee's pay and benefits and generated a check. At each point along the path, an auditor verified that the steps were completed correctly and that errors did not occur. In addition, all of these steps had to take place hurriedly to meet employee expectations and government regulations. Message services are ultimately responsible for making workflow routing and delivery decisions. Workflow management can improve this process by intelligently routing electronic forms to each individual. The form can contain data provided previously by other users that is customized to represent the formats required by each individual. In addition, data can now be moved, stored, manipulated, verified and presented to each user much faster than similar manual processes.

Linked object documents

The computer industry is moving towards the linked object model for creating compound documents. Linked object documents, similar to object oriented applications, incorporate independent data objects into larger structures. For example, a single electronic document could contain text, spreadsheets, graphics, voice and video elements which are linked to other files, objects, or parts. Although this technology is still in development, network message services may act as agents on behalf of the data objects that comprise linked object documents. Conceptually each object includes the intelligent required to pass messages between a document element and its originating application of file. A single document serves as the integrator of the various pieces.

Application Services

Application services are network services that run software for network clients. They are different from file services because they allow computers to share processing power, not just share data. The two other aspects normally associated with application services are:

Specialization of Servers

The greatest benefit of application serves is that they can employ specialized equipment to increase speed, data integrity and security. However, how much processing should be handled by a server and how much is left to the client? Application servers have more computing power than user workstations and they often use special operating systems that have been optimized to perform a specific operation. For example, a personal computer user wants to perform a complex mathematical calculation to create a graph. Using a personal computer (PC), the calculation would take an extremely long time. To accomplish the task more rapidly, the PC sends out the math portion of the calculation to be processed by a mainframe computer. The mainframe quickly processes the request and sends back the results. The PC is only required to collect the resulting data set and generate the graph. What would normally take a very long time can now be accomplished much more rapidly.

Scalability and Growth

Network application services can also provide organizations with relatively inexpensive upgrade paths. If more computing power is required, only the network application server is upgraded. For example, assume that you use an extremely complex modeling application and that the application server software currently runs on a minicomputer. As your company grows, the minicomputer becomes overworked and response time gets worse and worse. To improve response times you simply move the application software to a faster computer, or add another server. You can improve the processing power of your computer while leaving other client and server computer totally unaffected.

Database Services

Network database services provide server based database storage and retrieval that allow network clients to control data manipulation and presentation. A special term has been created to describe database applications that allow clients to request data from these specialized servers: client server databases. Client server database applications divide and optimize the tasks involved in requesting and providing data. Depending upon the design goal, the client is given a portion of the tasks involved in formulating the request and processing the response, while database servers typically evaluate incoming requests and return data.

Network database provide the following services:

- Optimize the computers which store, search and retrieve database records.
- Control where data is stored geographically
- Organize data logically between organizational departments.
- Provide data security.

- Reduce database client access time.

The following aspects of network database services are:

Coordinating Distributed Data

Large organizations often segregate tasks and information between multiple departments. When data access is shared, concerns arise about who controls what data and where it should be stored. Network database services employ a tactic called distributed data to achieve seamless data sharing. They divide control over the pieces of the database among the various departments' computer systems. The database management system is responsible for making the database appear as one logical unit while coordinating changes that occur on various computer systems.

Replication

Data from local databases may typically be retrieved much more rapidly than from remote databases. Therefore, users prefer to work on local data. However, when more than two copies of a database exist, organizations run the risk of making decisions based upon out-of-data or incorrect information. Replication creates and synchronizes multiple copies of a database over the network. Presently, the leading database software uses two different methods to perform replication. One method uses a master database, which is the repository of all additions and changes. The database management system is responsible for making sure that the changes recorded in the master are sent to all copies of the database. The second method gives several local databases responsibility for recording adds and changes. In addition, the local portion of the management system must then coordinate adds and changes with all the other copies.

DESIGNING THE NETWORK

So far we have theoretically learned about the networking and how the computers are connected to each other in different type of networkings. In this chapter you will read about the various types of cables used in connecting the computers. We would also look at the various type of conduits and wall boxes used in networking.

First thing first, let us understand about the type of cables that are used for networking.

ETHERNET CABLES

Ethernet cables use RJ-45 plugs. If you have never seen an RJ-45 plug, it looks like a modular phone plug with eight connectors instead of the 4 connectors that phone wires use. The recipe for making cables is:

1. Category 5 Unshielded Twisted Pair (UTP) cable, available at computer stores and electrical supply houses.
2. RJ-45 ends, which are also available at computer and electrical supply houses.
3. An RJ-45 Terminating Tool. This is a tool that enables you to put the RJ-45 ends of the UTP cable. Typically, good terminating tools will work for both 8-wire and 4-wire plugs. They are expensive but they are worth it if you are working on lots of cables.
4. Inexpensive cable continuity tester.

Start with the cable. Strip the outer insulation back about an inch, very carefully, you do not want to damage the wires inside. Notice that you have 4 pairs of wire inside, one is white/orange and orange, one is white/green and green, one is white/blue and blue, and one is white brown and brown.

Separate the wires so that they line up in the following order from left to right.

1. white/orange

2. orange
3. white/green
4. blue
5. white/blue
6. green
7. white/brown
8. brown

Trim the ends so that they are of the same length. This can be done with wire cutters if you have got them, or you can use the cutter edge on your terminating tool.

Now comes the tricky part, insert all 8 wires into the RJ-45 end so that they are inserted as far as possible. Then push the cable jacket up under the notch in the end.

Carefully insert the end in the terminating tool to its full depth and squeeze the terminating tool tight. This will crimp the end onto the cable and connect the pins on the RJ-45 jack to the wires in the cable.

Now do the other end.

You have just made a cable to the 568B cabling spec, the most common wiring used for networking.

If you have followed the instructions, you should be able to plug the cable you have made into a cable continuity tester and see that pin 1 at one end connects to pin 1 at the other end, all the way to pin 8. Do not get discouraged if your first able does not work. Like anything else, this takes practice.

Crossover Cables

If you have got Ethernet hubs or switches to interconnect, it is necessary in many cases to use a specially made cable a crossover cable. Essentially, it looks like a standard 10BASE-T patch cable except that it is wired differently. Most 10BASE-T and 100BASE-T patch cords are straight-through, which means that the colours are lined up the same at both ends.

In a crossover cable, the difference is that the wire on pin 1 at each end must connect to pin 2 at the other end, and pin 3 on each end must terminate at pin 6 at the other end. So the wiring scheme is as follows:

Pin #	*End 1 colour*	*End 2 colour*
1	white/orange	orange
2	orange	white/orange
3	white/green	green
4	blue	blue
5	white/blue	white/blue
6	green	white/green
7	white/brown	white/brown
8	brown	brown

This works because Ethernet only uses pins 1, 2, 3, and 6. A crossover cable connects pin 1 at one end to pin 2 at the other, and pin 3 to 6. It is useful and it is easy to make.

THINNET CABLES

It uses a special kind of coax cable. It is referred to by the coax cabling standards as type RG58 C/U. The main characteristics of this cable are an impedance rating of 50 ohms and an outside diameter of 4.95mm. Various cable manufacturers refer to this cable generically as Thinnet, Thin Ethernet of Cheapernet coax and the specific characteristics may very slightly from vendor to vendor.

Most will guarantee the cable to conform to the Ethernet standard which is technically referred to as the IEEE 802.3 standard.

Advantages & Disadvantages of Thinnet Cables

Advantages:

- Inexpensive

Disadvantages:

- 10MHz Ethernet only
- More vulnerable to network failure

TWISTED PAIR (UTP)

It is made up of copper. Data cabling systems are now based around the Twisted Pair model. This type of cables are available as two types, referred to as Category 3 (Cat3) UTP and Category 5 (Cat5) UTP where the 'UTP' standing for Unshielded Twisted Pair. Both types consist of eight copper cores arranged as four pairs twisted together and surrounded by a protective sheath.

The twisting of the pairs is carefully controlled during the manufacturing process to give the high speed data carrying capacities associated with this kind of cable. The Cat 3 cable is rated to carry up to 10MHz and the Cat 5 to 100 MHz. As most new installations need to be 'future proofed' for new data technologies, the Cat 5 cable is generally the most popular and as such is more widely available at little additional cost.

Advantages & Disadvantages of Twisted Cables

Twisted Pair 'Star' System

Advantages:

- More compliant to International Standards
- 10 MHz and 100 MHz Ethernet capability
- Less vulnerable to network failure

Disadvantages:

- Requires a distribution hub
- More cabling required

TWISTED PAIR (STP)

It is also available as Shielded Twisted Pair or STP. This type of cable contains an additional metal shield around the four pairs and is used in installations where protection from excessive electrical noise is required, e.g., in heavy engineering establishments. In most cases this type of additional protection is unnecessary.

INSTALLING CONDUITS & WALL BOXES

If your working environment does not already contain an easily accessible cable ducting system you may choose to use wall mounted conduits and wall boxes when installing your cabling system. It is well worth considering this, even though it will require extra expense and work, as this will protect your cabling system from damage. This is especially important for the Thinnet system.

However, the multiple cables associated with the Twisted Pair system are also likely to require containment to prevent tangles of additional cables from cluttering up your working environment. It is worth nothing here that both types of network topology can be accommodated by similar conduit systems, with just a few minor differences between the two.

Conduits

Plastic conduits with adhesive backings can be used and these are available from most builders, merchants as either 16 mm by 16 mm or 16 mm by 25 mm. The smaller is suitable for Thinnet installations and the later for Twisted Pair. The larger dimensions may be necessary for the Twisted Pair arrangement as multiple cables may be routed through the conduits as opposed to the single cable need for the coax bus.

Wall Boxes

The wall boxes consist of two parts: the backbox (which attaches to the wall) and the faceplate (which fits onto the front of the backbox). The backbox should be the standard 87 mm by 87mm type used for many kinds of wall outlets. Thinnet installations should use backboxes that are 44mm deep, whereas the Twisted Pair connectors can be accommodated in backboxes 37 mm deep.

Faceplates

These are of a specialized type depending on which type of network system is being installed. Faceplates are available either as 'fixed' where the connector adapter is fixed directly into the faceplate or 'modular' where the adapter is retained in a small mounting plate which then snaps into the faceplate. The modular arrangement allows different types of adapters to be combined at a single outlet, e.g., to combine a network outlet module with a telephone outlet module.

Installing the conduit system is simply a matter of deciding the best routers for your cabling system and then cutting your conduits to the appropriate lengths and fixing to the wall or to whatever surfaces are available. The conduits should be routed to your chosen wallbox locations, which are ideally positioned at about 30mm from the floor. If you have a raised floor or a ceiling void that is easily accessible, then you might consider laying your cables loose in these and then routing your conduits directly up or down to the wallboxes, drilling suitable holes in the floor or ceiling.

In all cases, be careful to avoid running your data cabling parallel to any existing power or lighting cables within about 50cm. Crossing the paths of these existing power cables can be safely done provided the data cable crosses the power cable at right angles. Running active data cables in parallel to cables can lead to induced currents, with a consequent degrading or failure of your network performance.

It is not recommended that you attach conduits to furniture, as it is likely that these will be moved at some point, thereby causing potential damage to the cabling system.

THINNET CABLES INSTALLATION DESIGN

A coax network installation simply requires that the Thinnet coax cable runs from the PC to the next using the bus topology model. The cable is typically installed in a conduit that runs around the walls of a room or office suite, with outlet wall points strategically located. At the outlets, the coax cable is routed out of a wall box to a PC and then back again to the wall box via the two wallbox adapter connectors on the wallbox faceplate. This arrangement maintains the bus topology.

It is technically feasible for the coax cabling to run loose from one PC to the next without the need for installing conduits or wall boxes. If you prefer to adopt this method, care must be taken not to damage or disturb the loose cables during the life of the network. The coax cable connects to each PC via a specialized adapter called a 'T Piece' adapter which taps into the coax bus in a 'T' junction arrangement. This T junction arrangement is used at every PC, leaving the cable ends effectively loose at each end of the bus. These ends must be terminated using a specialized adapter which contains a 50 Ohm resistor. The termination adapters can either be fitted to the rear of the end faceplate adapters, or to the end T Pieces.

Distance Rules

The Thinnet system is defined by an Ethernet cabling standard that requires that certain distance and configuration rules are applied when designing and installing the cabling structure. These rules are as follows:

- A single coax bus is referred to as a segment. Each segment must not exceed 180 meters in length, including the combined lengths of all the coax cables to and from the individual PCs.
- The distance between each T piece adapter on the bus must not be less than 0.5 meter.
- There must be on more than 30 PCs attached to a single segment.

Other Considerations

When designing and installing a coax cabling system, care must be taken to ensure that the cable does not bend excessively or kink at all. The ability of any coax cable to perform to its specifications will be severely affected by excessive bending and especially by kinking. A maximum bend radius is usually quoted for a particular type of coax cable and for Thinnet cable this is usually about 20 mm.

CABLING

Having designed the physical layout of your Thinnet system and installed any conduits and wallboxes, you are now ready to install, terminate and test the cabling.

What You Will Need

You will nee the following before you begin:

- One Thinnet faceplate for each wallbox outlet. These will contain two Thinnet 'barrel' adapters.
- Thinnet coax cable sufficient to connect all of your PCs together in their planned physically locations. Allow approximately one meter of additional coax cable per wallbox outlet to allow an excess for the termination procedure. Don't forget to include enough cable for the 'flyleads' from the wallbox to the PC and back.
- Two Thinnet Terminator adapters; one for each end of the coax bus.
- One Thinnet T Piece adapter for each PC that you will be connecting to the network.
- Six Thinnet connectors for each PC on the network. That's four for connecting into and out of the Wallbox BNC adapters and two for connecting to the T Piece adapters. If you are not using wallbox outlets then you will only need two Thinnet connectors for each PC, to connect to the T Piece adapter. Whichever way you decide to cable your system, it will probably be wise to purchase some spare Thinnet connectors, as mistakes during the termination procedure are quite likely before you get the hang of it!
- A BNC Crimp Tool, suitable for crimping the Thinnet connectors.
- A pair of cable cutters or pliers for cutting the cable.
- A sharp knife, for cutting and trimming the coax sleeving.
- A small hand-held Multimeter, for testing the continuity and resistance of the finished cabling system.

As an alternative to the sharp knife, a Coax Wire Stripper tool is available that cuts the coax cable sleeving automatically in exactly the right places and to the correct depth.

If you are going to be doing many Thinnet terminations, then the slightly tricky setting up procedure for this tool may well be worth the effort!

Laying the Cable

Once you have acquired the necessary components for the cable installations, begin by laying the coax loosely into the conduits, allowing approximately 50cm of cable to loop out of the walboxes. Once the cable is in the conduits, you can fit the conduit coverings as you will not need further access except for at the far ends of the cable bus, where the cable should be left loose inside the conduit ready to be terminated.

Terminating the Cable

The cable should now be terminated so that it will connect to the backs of the wallbox faceplate adapters.

First cut the loop as it emerges form the wallbox in the centre using the pliers, leaving two loose cable ends of approximately 25cm. If you are using the automatic Coax Wire Stripper tool then prepare the cable ends according to the tooling instructions for RG58 coax cable type.

If you are not using the Coax Wife Stripper tool, then prepare the cable ends as follows;

1. Cut the cable back to allow enough length from the wallbox to enable you to manipulate the cable for termination, but not so long that the remaining cable length after termination will not fit comfortably inside the wallbox without excessive bending or kinking. This would normally to be about between 10-15 cms from where the cable enters the wallbox from the conduit.
2. If you have been supplied with plastic or rubber cable support pieces, then thread this over the cable now. Then thread the crimp sleeve along the cable. Do this now as it may be difficult to thread it over after removing the outer cable sleeving.
3. Trim the outer jacket to 17mm from the end of the cable using the knife. Be careful not to damage the metal braiding directly underneath the outer sleeving. This can usually be accomplished by cutting lightly around the outer sleeving and then by working the sleeving off, tearing the remaining plastic in the process.
4. Gently loosen the braiding so that it can be folded back over the cable, exposing the second plastic sleeving. You can ease this process by passing a sharp point forwards through the braiding to loosen the weave. If there is a metal foil around the second plastic sleeving, then gently run a blade around the foil just forward from where the braiding folds back and remove.
5. Trim the inner sleeving back to 5 mm from the end of the cable, again taking care not to damage the copper core beneath. This will expose either a solid copper core, or a series of copper filaments, depending on the brand of cable that you have used. If you have copper filaments, twist them gently together. This is a very important step as it will ensure that stray filaments are not left loose to cause a short circuit after inserting this section into the central pin.
6. Insert the central core into the pin and crimp using the smaller indentations in the crimping tool. If you find that the twisted core will not fit into the pin, then gently untwist the filaments, carefully remove two or three filaments with the cable cutters, re-twist and insert back into the pin.
7. Push the connector body over the pin and cable assembly so that the pin produces a distinct 'click' as it locates correctly within the connector body. Try gently pulling the pin and cable assembly back out of the connector body. If you can do this easily then the pin has not located properly, possibly due to the core bending slightly behind the pin. If this is the case then re-insert and then

firmly pull the pin from the front of the connector body using a pair of nose pliers, being careful not to damage the pin. You could use a piece of cloth between the pin and the jaws of the pliers to do this. Improper location of the pin is a common cause of poor network performance.

8. Fold the braiding filaments back over the connector body so that they lie neatly and evenly around the outside of the knurled collar at the back of the connector body. If necessary, trim the filaments back so that they sit against the collar and end a few millimeters from the main connector body.
9. Slide the crimp sleeve forwards and over the braiding until it butts against the back of the connector body. The braiding will now be trapped between the knurled collar and the crimp sleeve. Now crimp the crimp sleeve the larger identification on the crimp tool (ensure that the crimp sleeve stays butted against the back of the connector body during the crimp operation).

Any cable support can now be slide forward over the crimp sleeve to complete the termination process. Having completed the first termination, repeat the process for all the wallbox rear connections and for the far ends of the cable bus.

When all of the terminations are complete, add the Terminator Adapters to both ends of the cable and plug in all of the terminated wallbox connectors into the rear of the Thinnet faceplates. Ensure that the connected faceplates will mount comfortably onto the wallboxes without undue bending or kinking of the coax cable behind the faceplates, but do not screw into place yet, leaving the faceplates loose for the time being.

Coax Flyleads

Now cut two lengths of coax cable for each PC, sufficient to reach from the wallbox to the back of the PC and allowing for any routing around furniture, etc. Remember that these cable lengths are the most vulnerable to potential damage from users and route them so that the possibilities of damage are minimized. Do not, of course, run cables across walkways, etc, where they will present a 'trip' hazard.

For each PC, connect both flyleads to the 'straight through' part of the T Piece adapter and then connect the other ends of the flyleads into Thinnet faceplate at the wallbox. You should now have a complete coax bus, with Thinnet Terminator adapters at each end and the coax cable bus running in and out of the wallboxes from one T Piece adapter to the next.

Testing the Coax Bus

Testing the coax bus is a relatively simple matter of checking the electrical continuity of the bus circuit using a small Multimeter. This is best done by checking the T Piece adapters for the combined electrical effect of the presence of both Terminator Adapters at either end of the coax bus. Any breaks or shorts in the circuit will then show up as an incorrect reading.

Firstly, ensure that your bus is complete, with all wallbox, T Piece and Terminator adapter connections in place. Set up your Multimeter to read up to 50 Ohms. Then read the resistance between the exposed central pin and the connector body of any of the T Piece adapters on the bus.

If this reading is between 20 and 30 Ohms, then congratulations! – your coax bus cabling system is complete and functional. It should ideally ready about 25 Ohms, this being the combined result of the two 50 Ohm resistors within the Terminator adapters, arranged 'in series'.

If not, then there is either a shorted or broken circuit somewhere along the length of the bus. If the resistance reading is close to zero Ohms, this indicates a short; if the reading is close to infinity, this would indicate a break in the circuit.

Test for the location of a fault as follows:

1. Start at left-hand end of the bus. Remove the Terminator adapter and using the Multimeter set up

as before, check for a reading of approximately 50 Ohms resistance between the central pin and the body of the Terminator adapter. If this is correct, then reconnect the Terminator adapter and move to the first wallbox along the bus. Otherwise you will need to replace the Terminator adapter.

2. Disconnect the left-hand connector from the rear of the wallbox faceplate and check the resistance across this connector. If the left-hand connector produces the correct reading, then this section of the bus so far is functional and the problem must therefore lie further along the bus. If not, then the fault lies between the left-hand Terminator adapter and this connector. As the fault is unlikely to be within the cable itself, then one of the two connectors between here and the left-hand Terminator adapter is likely to be t he cause of the fault. As there is no way to test exactly which of the two is causing the problem, you will need to reterminate the one and test and then the other if this does not solve the problem.
3. Having established that the bus is functional to this point and that any further faults must lie further along the bus reconnect the left-hand connector to the rear of the wallbox faceplate. Then disconnect the right-hand connector from the rear of the wallbox faceplate and test both sides in the same way as before. If the reading to the left-hand side is now incorrect then the fault lies along the flylead section external to the faceplate. You can then isolate which particular section is responsible by testing to the left at the T Piece.

You can see that this is a process of moving along the bus to each wallbox in turn, then breaking the bus and testing backwards to check for continuity to the left-hand Terminator adapter at each point, correcting any errors that appear as you go. Continue this process until both sides of the bus produce the correct resistance, or until you reach the right-hand Terminator adapter. Finally, test this for 50 Ohms resistance. When you are satisfied that any faults have been corrected, reconnecting he entire bus will produce a combined resistance of 25 Ohms at the T Piece.

TWISTED PAIR INSTALLATION – DESIGN

A twisted pair network is based around a central distribution hub. The function of the Ethernet hub is to receive incoming Ethernet packets from a PC and then to broadcast these unchanged to all other PCs on the network. The hub is often referred to as a repeater hub, because of the process of receiving ethernet packets and then replaying or 'repeating' them to several other PCs.

All of the network PCs are connected to the hub via individual twisted pair cables to ports on the hub device. The main advantage of this arrangement is that a fault in any single cable or PC interface on the network can be detected at the hub and automatically isolated from the rest of the network. This ability to 'intelligently' isolate faults is a common feature of most Ethernet hubs.

There are various types of Ethernet hubs available but for the moment we will simply treat the hub as a device with several ports. The cabling simply consists of running individual twisted pair cables from each PC to a port on the hub. This can either be done directly, or by running the cabling through a conduit system to strategically located wallboxes and then via a 'flylead' to the PC.

The connection to both the PC interface and to the hub is via a standard connector commonly known as the RJ45 Modular plug. The adapter socket used at the wallbox is similar to the one used at the ports on the hub and is commonly known as an RJ45 Outlet Module, or a Cat 5 Outlet Module to denote compliance to the more modern 100Mhz standards. In designing the twisted pair cabling system we will assume compliance to the Cat 5 standard, and Unshielded Twisted Pair (UTP) cabling.

Distance Rules

When designing a Twisted Pair cabling system, certain distance limitations must be considered. These limitations are due to electrical standards requirements that must be met when the ethernet hubs are designed, and simply state that the end-to-end distance between hub and the PC interface must not exceed 100 meters. This is further modified to take account of the use of flyleads and wallbox interfaces, etc., such that in this instance the total length of the flylead must not exceed 5 metres, with the remaining 95 metres allowed for the main cable.

TWISTED PAIR INSTALLATION – CABLING

Having designed the physical layout of your Twisted Pair system and installed any conduits and wallboxes you are now ready to install terminate and test the cabling.

What You Will Need

You will need the following before you begin:

- One Cat 5 RJ45 faceplate for each wallbox outlet. These will contain one or two Cat 5 RJ45 Outlet Modules in either a fixed or modular arrangement.
- Two or three 'stuffer caps', for punching down the twisted pair cores at the punch down blocks on the Outlet Modules.
- Cat 5 UTP cable sufficient to connect the hub to all of the PCs in their planned physical locations. Allow approximately 50cm of additional cable per RJ45 outlet to provide an excess for the termination procedure. Don't forget to include enough cable for the 'fluload' from the walbox to the PC.
- Three RJ45 Modular Plugs for each PC on the network. That's two for the flylead and one for connecting to the Ethernet hub. If you are not using wallbox outlets then you will only need two RJ45 plugs to connect the hub directly to the PC. It will probably by wise to purchase some spare RJ45 Modular Plugs, as mistakes during the termination procedure are quite likely!
- An RJ45 Termination Tool.
- A pair of small cable cutters or pliers for cutting the cable.
- A sharp knife, for cutting and trimming the UTP sleeving.
- A small hand-held Multimeter, for testing the continuity of the finished cabling system.

Hub Location

The hub can be located in any convenient position that has access to a power point. It is common for the hub to be kept somewhere secure to avoid any accidental disconnection or tampering.

If the total span of the network exceeds 100 metres, then it would be sensible to locate the hub somewhere near the middle of the system to prevent the cabling distance rules being broken.

Laying the Cable

Once you have acquired the necessary components for the cable installation, being by laying the UTP cable loosely into the conduit. Allow approximately 25cm of cable to extend out of the wallboxes for termination and enough cable to reach to the hub location at the other end. Once the cable is in the conduits, you can fit the conduit coverings as you should not need further access to the cable within.

Terminating the Cable

The UTP cable contains 8 copper cores, arranged in four pairs an colour coded according to an international standard. This color coding is used to ensure correct termination at the RJ45 Modular Plug and at the rear of the RJ45 Outlet Module.

As you lay each cable between the hub and the wallbox outlet, mark the cable at both ends with a sequential numbering system using tape, or a market pen. This will allow you to identify which cable goes to which wallbox.

Terminating the Outlet Module

Terminating the UTP cable onto the cat 5 Outlet Module is done by 'punching down' the cable cores into 'punchdown blocks' on the Outlet Module. Terminate the UTP cable (to the RJ45 Outlet Module) at the wallbox as follows:

1. Cut back the UTP cable to about 15cm from the point where it enters the wallbox cavity, using the cable cutters.
2. Trim the outer jacket to 50mm form the end of the cable using the knife. Be very careful not to damage the insulation of the individual cores directly underneath the outer sleeving.

   As you lay each cable between the hub and the wallbox outlet, mark the cable at both ends with a sequential numbering system using tape, or a market pen. This will allow you to identify which cable goes to which wallbox.

   This can usually be accomplished by cutting lightly to a depth of about 1 mm around the outer sleeving and then by working the sleeving off, tearing the remaining plastic in the process.

   You will find that the cores the color and arranged in pairs as follows:

- Green/White and White/Green
- Orange/White and White/Orange
- Blue/White and White/Blue
- Brown/White and White/Brown

   You will also find that the 'punchdown block' on the Outlet Module is color coded in a similar way.

   Beware: There are many different types of RJ 45 Outlet Module available, but all with identical functions. The main difference is that some require a specialized and relatively expensive 'punchdown' tool, while others supply some form of stuffer cap.

3. Arrange the twisted pairs so that the green and down pairs lie to the left and the blue and orange pairs lie to the fight at 90 degrees to the cable. The cable is then placed in the gap between the two punchdown blocks, so that the twisted pairs lie in the gap between the punchdown blocks and the front section of the module.
4. Untwisted each pair a couple of turns and guide each individual core into its respective slot according to the color coding. Take care not to untwist the pairs by more than about 15mm from the termination slot. Untwisting a pair by more than this can affect network performance at high speeds.
5. The stuffer cap is then pushed over the top of the punchdown block and forced down until the cores appear at the limit of the slots in the stuffer cap. If you are feeling strong, placing the Outlet Module on a hard surface and pushing down firmly with the thumb should provide enough 'punchdown' force. Otherwise, tap lightly down with a track hammer, or use a pair of slip pliers. If you cannot obtain Stuffer Caps, then an 'Insertion Tool' will serve the same purpose.
6. Excess cores in the gap between the punchdown blocks can then be removed by carefully running a sharp blade along the inside ledge on the punchdown block, taking care not to damage the cable.

Terminating the Modular Plug

Terminating UTP cable with an RJ45 Modular Plug requires the use of a specialized termination tool.

You will need to terminate the cables that will connect to the hub, as well as the flyleads that will connect the wallbox outlet to the PC. If you are using ready-made flyleads then the latter will not be necessary.

Terminate the Modular Plugs as follows:

1. If you have been provided with a Strain Relief boot for your plug, then feed this onto the cable first.
2. Trim the outer jacket to 20mm from the end of the cable using the knife. Be very careful not to damage the insulation of the individual cores directly underneath the outer sleeving.
3. Untwist the pairs and arrange the cores. Arrange the cores so that they lie as flat as possible and in as straight a line as possible.
4. Use a sharp blade or the cable cutters to accurately trim the cores at a right angle to the cable to 13mm from the cable sleeving.
5. Check the order of the color coding. Then, hold the RJ45 Modular Plug in your right hand so that the metal contacts are facing towards you and the rear of the plug is to the left and hold the cable in your left hand so that the White/Green core is at the top. (If you are left handed, reverse this). Slide the cores into the rear of the Modular Plug. If the cores are all lying flat and straight, you should find that they are guided smoothly into their separate channels. Push the cores in firmly so that they butt fully against the end of the plug.
6. With the cable fully butted into the plug, insert the plug into the termination tool and crimp to complete the termination. You can then slide any strain relief components along the cable and onto the back of the plug.

Testing the Twisted Pair Cabling

In order to test the twisted pair cabling system, we need to check electrical continuity between the pins on the Modular Plugs at either end of the link between the hub and the PC. As these plugs are likely to be at some distance from each other, testing across the length of the link will be difficult with a normal hand held Multimeter. The solution to this problem is to make a simple 'loop back' plug.

This plug will be fitted into the Outlet Module and will connect the appropriate pairs of connection links together at the Outlet Module. This link completes the circuit at the Outlet Module, allowing us to test for continuity across the appropriate contacts at the hub-end Modular Plug.

Make up the 'loop back' plugs as follows:

1. Terminate a length of UTP cable with a Modular Plug as before and then cut the cable at about 5cm from the back of the plug. You will find it easier to do it this way, rather than to try and terminate a short length.
2. Remove about 3 cm of the cable sleeving from the end of the cable, being careful as before not to damage the core insulation underneath. Separate the twisted pairs.
3. Then, one at a time untwist each pair, strip the insulation from the core to expose the copper and then twist the bare copper cores firmly back together so that Green/White connects to White/Green and so on. Cover each exposed contact with some tape to prevent shorting.

With this loop back plug, you can then test each link one at a time by inserting the loop back plug into the Outlet Module and testing for continuity using the Multimeter across the contacts at the hub-end Modular Plug that corresponds to the outlet.

Using the standard numbering system where, with the cable down and the metal contacts on the Modular Plug facing you, the left end pin is No. 1 and the right end pin is No. 8 test for continuity across the following contacts:

- i&2 – Green pair
- 3&6 – Orange pair
- 4&5 – Blue pair
- 7&8 – Brown pair

ETHERNET HUBS

Ethernet hubs are available in a wide variety of formats. The types suitable for twisted pair Ethernet operation and known as 10BaseT or 100BaseT hubs, depending on the Ethernet speed. The 'I0 or 'I00' refers to the operating frequency (10Mhz or 100Mhz); the 'Base' refers to baseband which is the type of signalling used and the 'T' refers to twisted pair.

10BaseT hubs are available as either rack mounted (which are designed to fit standard networking equipment racks) or desktop (which are designed to sit freely on a desktop or shelf). Rack mounted hubs are mainly used in large scale networks, whereas desktop hubs are more suitable for the small office environment.

Desktop hubs contain either four or (more usually) eight Ethernet ports.

Thc simplcst cight port hubs are the perfectly adequate for our needs.

Other features that you may find arc hubs that arc SNMP compatible or that integrate other types of Ethernet ports for connection to other types of Ethernet media (e.g., Fibre optics). SNMP stands for Simple Network Management Protocol an advanced system that allows for a standardized form of network management.

Stackable Hubs

One feature that is available for Ethernet hubs and may be useful is the ability to stack hubs together. This allows for the number of ports available to the network to be increased by connecting further hubs to the existing hub in a 'stacking' arrangement. This facility therefore allows for each expansion of the initial network configuration as the need arises.

Multiple Choice Questions

1. STP is
   (a) shielded twisted pair
   (b) short twisted pair
   (c) small twisted pair.
2. The three bands of communication channels are: Narrow band, Voice band and:
   (a) sand band (b) broad band
   (c) tin band.
3. The three transmission modes are simplex mode, half-duplex mode and:
   (a) half made
   (b) small duplex made
   (c) full-duplex mode
4. LAN is.
   (a) local area networks
   (b) low area networks
   (c) line area networks
5. WAN is:
   (a) wrong area networks
   (b) wide area networks
   (c) whole area networks.

Descriptive Type Questions

1. How is the data communicated?
2. Which are the common data transmitting techniques?
3. Describe the various type of modems?
4. Describe the various communication channels?
5. Describe the following in context of communications:

Wire Cables	Telephone lines
Leased lines	Switched lines
Twisted pair cables	Coaxial cables
Fiber optics	Microwave

6. Which are the famous bandwidth channels?
7. Describe the following:

Narrow-band	Voice-band
Broad-band	

8. Describe the following terms in context of data transmission.

Amplitude	Frequency
Phase	Current State
State Transition	

9. What are Buffers and Protocols?
10. How is the error detected?
11. What do you mean by Serial and Parallel Interface?
12. How do you compare rate of data transmission?
13. What are the various data transmission methods?
14. Describe the following data transmissions:
    Asynchronous Transmission
    Synchronous Transmission
    Isochronous Transmission

'. How would you configure the communication channel?

. Describe the terms:
   Point-to-Point
   Multi-Point

Describe the various communication processes?

18. Describe the following terms:
    Multiplexing
    Frequency-Division Multiplexing
    Time-Division Multiplexing
    Statistical Time-Division Multiplexing
    Concentration
    Message Switching
    Front-end Processing
19. Describe the various Transmission Modes?
20. Describe the following modes:
    Simplex Mode
    Half-duplex Mode
    Full-duplex Mode
21. Describe the communication between Two Microcomputers.
22. Describe the communication between Microcomputer and Larger Computer.
23. Describe the various applications of Data Communication.
24. Define the terms:
    Electronic Mail
    Sharing Data Files
    Bulletin Board Systems
    External Databases
25. Describe what do you understand by Communication Processing.
26. What do you understand by Micro-to-Mainframe Link?
27. Describe the various suppliers of Data Communication Services.
28. What do you understand by Micro-to-Micro Link?
29. What is Networking?
30. What are the Networking Basics?
31. What do you understand by Resource Sharing?
32. Define different types of Networking?
33. What are the hardware requirements are required for Networking?
34. Define different types of Transmission Channel for LAN.

35. Write short notes on the following"
    Server
    Workstations
    LAN
    WAN
    Bridges
    Routers
    Gateways
    Private Networks
    Electronic Mail
    Voice Mail
    Packet Switching
    Transmission Media
    Protocols
    Fast Ethernet
    Transmission Media
    Public Network
    Private Network
    Sharing Specialized Equipment
    Network Fax Service
    Message Services
36. What kind of software are required for LAN?
37. Define different types of Transmission Channel for WAN.
38. Define different types of Transmission Channel for WAN.
39. What kind of software are required for WAN?
40. What are the different kinds of Wide Area Network?
41. What do you understand by Topology? Define different types of topologies?
42. What are the advantages and disadvantages of the following:

Ring Network	Bus Network
Star Network	Mesh Network
Hybrid Network	Tree Network

43. What are the uses of Networking?
44. What is Ethernet Protocol?
45. What is TCP/IP Protocol?
46. What are the Basic Elements in Networking?
47. What do you understand by Value Added Networks?
48. What do you understand by Common Network Services?
49. What do you understand by File Storage and Data Migration?
50. What do you understand by File Update Synchronization?
51. What is Print Services?
52. What is Application Services? What are the three aspects are associated with application services?
53. What do you understand by Database Services?
54. What are Ethernet Cables?
55. Describe the various colours of the cables.
56. What are crossover cables?
57. What are Thinnet cables?
58. Describe the various advantages and disadvantages of Thinnet Cables.
59. What are the Twisted Cables?
60. What are the advantages and disadvantages of twisted cables?
61. What are Twisted Pair of Cables?
62. Describe the complete process of installing Conduits and Wall Boxes.
63. Write a short note on Thinnet Cable installation.
64. What all you need for setting up cables for Networking?
65. Describe the complete process of terminating the cables.
66. How would you test the coaxial bus?
67. Write note on Twisted Pair Installation.
68. How would you set the Ethernet Hubs?

Part - II

Part - II

12 Disk Operating System (DOS)

INTRODUCTION

DOS translates the commands that we enter through the keyboard into signals that can be interpreted by the computer. The CPU (Central Processing Unit) processes the raw data as per the commands we feed (Input) into the computer and returns the results (gives the Output).

The results are displayed on the Monitor in our language. The results can also be printed on a printer. Directed by the instruction that we type, the DOS operates and controls the operating system. With DOS we can do the following:

- Create new files
- Delete old files
- Rename existing files
- List all the files in the hard disk or floppy
- Enhance the storage capacity of the disk
- Format new floppy or hard disk for usuage
- Reorganize the storage files on the disk
- Make back up files on the hard disk or to the floppy diks
- Scan for viruses

TYPE OF DOS COMMANDS

There are 2 types of DOS commands, mainly, Internal and External commands.

Internel Commands

These commands can be given from the DOS prompt, irrespective of the fact the command is there in the DOS directory or not. These can be said to be the in-built commands of DOS. For example, the following commands are internal commands:

Chdir It changes the current directory, shortname is CD.

Cls It clears the screen.

Copy It is used for copying files, read more about it later in the chapter.

Copy cont It is used to create a quick batch file.

Ctty This command is used to redirect the keyboard and screen to the serial port.

External Commands

These commands are such they have to be present in the hard disk to be used. Some of external commands are given below:

Append It lets programs open data files as if they were in the current directory.

Assign It is used to reassign drives when programs work only with specific drives.

Attrib It changes file attributes, which are settings in every DOS file.

Backup/Restore It lets you backup your hard disk onto as many floppies as required. Restore command can be used to use backedup files.

Chkdsk It checks disk status, memory status, files and flags unidentifiable files.

Comp It compares two files for identical content and reports up to 10 mismatches.

FILE STRUCTURE IN DOS

All the data in the computer is stored in terms of Files. Each file is unique and is identified by name, date and time of creation, number of bytes, etc. The name of the file usually in the form of 8 + 3 digits (also called 8.3 rule) which is recognised by DOS. The 8 digits are reserved for the first name and the next 3 for the extension, which signifies the type of the file.

A typical filename in DOS can be represented as:

```
MSM.COM
```

where

MSM is the first name

. is always there

COM represents the last name or popularly called extension

STORAGE OF FILES

Files are stored in the hard disk just as we store packets in godown. A hard disk is divided into various subdirectories like rooms in a house. When you start your PC, the first directory that you see is the root directory. The root directory can be compared to a house. Within a subdirectory, you can have another subdirectory and files. You can create and delete these directories yourself. Related files are kept in the same directory.

Seeing the File

If you want to see the files or subdirectories available in a particular directory, you use the DIR command. Simple DIR command produces the display shown on the next page.

All the files in this directory will be listed along with the information like name, extension, number of bytes, data and time of creation. At the end, the total number of files in the directory is given along with the total number of bytes used. The total number of bytes remaining free in the hard disk is also given.

```
USER     DEF            11  12-17-02 11:14a USER.DEF
AUTOEXEC 001            26  12-06-02 12:38p AUTOEXEC.001
PR_ADDC  DBF           872  12-13-02  7:23p pr_addc.DBF
PR_ADDC  CDX         9,216  12-13-02  7:23p pr_addc.CDX
MTNL_G~1 DBF           360  12-13-02  7:23p mtnl_groupc.DBF
OUT      TXT           132  12-18-02  3:59p out.txt
C&CGOLD        <DIR>        01-26-03 12:52a c&cgold
        26 file(s)        281,630 bytes
        13 dir(s)          189.29 MB free

C:\>
```

Another way of using the DIR command is DIR/P.

```
 Directory of C:\

USERS    TXT            90  01-05-02  5:46p USERS.TXT
FRUNLOG  TXT         1,012  04-20-99  9:59a FRUNLOG.TXT
AUTOEXEC BAT            35  12-11-02  1:23p AUTOEXEC.BAT
CONFIG   SYS            10  11-14-02  9:05a CONFIG.SYS
WINDOWS        <DIR>        04-20-99  9:46a WINDOWS
PROGRA~1       <DIR>        11-13-01 11:31a Program Files
SETUPXLG TXT         1,104  06-01-02  2:31p SETUPXLG.TXT
INFERNO  LOG            67  08 17 01  8:20p inferno.log
PM65           <DIR>        08-18-01 10:53a PM65
KPCMS          <DIR>        08-18-01 10:54a KPCMS
ACROBAT3       <DIR>        08-18-01 10:54a Acrobat3
PSFONTS        <DIR>        08-18-01 10:54a psfonts
SCANDISK LOG         2,393  02-21-03 10:50a SCANDISK.LOG
ADOBEAPP       <DIR>        08-18-01  8:58p ADOBEAPP
WINZIP         <DIR>        08-18-01 11:34a WinZip
WINDOW~1 BMK            63  08-21-01  6:30p WINDOWSWinHlp32.BMK
NCDTREE        <DIR>        09-12-01  7:58p NCDTREE
LOGFILE  TXT           108  09-30-01 12:36a LOGFILE.TXT
TRACE    LOG             0  11-06-01  2:07p TRACE.LOG
Press any key to continue . . .
```

The /P added to DIR, stands for pagewise. Suppose there are a large number of files and subdirectories within a directory. Now when you use DIR command, you will find that most of the file names scroll past the screen and only the last few entries are displayed. This may result in your not seeing the required file which may appear in the first lot. For this you should be able to stop and continue at will, the scrolling of the listing to look for a particular file. The following command gives you that option.

Once the screen has been filled up, the listing on the screen will stop with this message at the bottom:

```
Press any key to continue . . .
```

When you do press any key, the monitor will again display the next screen and stop. You can repeat this till all the files in the directory have been displayed.

Another option is DIR/W.

```
C:\>dir/w/p

 Volume in drive C has no label
 Volume Serial Number is 2919-10EC
 Directory of C:\

USERS.TXT        FRUNLOG.TXT      AUTOEXEC.BAT     CONFIG.SYS       [WINDOWS]
[PROGRA~1]       SETUPXLG.TXT     INFERNO.LOG      [PM65]           [KPCMS]
[ACROBAT3]       [PSFONTS]        SCANDISK.LOG     [ADOBEAPP]       [WINZIP]
WINDOW~1.BMK     [NCDTREE]        LOGFILE.TXT      TRACE.LOG        WINZIP.LOG
STUB.LOG         [MYDOCU~1]       ADOBEWEB.LOG     NETLOG.TXT       COMMAND.COM
FRONTPG.LOG      [SCANJET]        AILOG.TXT        [SIERRA]         TMP.INI
CONFIG.000       AUTOEXEC.000     USER.DEF         AUTOEXEC.001     PR_ADDC.DBF
PR_ADDC.CDX      MTNL_G~1.DBF     OUT.TXT          [C&CGOLD]
        26 file(s)          281,630 bytes
        13 dir(s)            189.27 MB free
```

The /W stands for widthwise display. This command is used when you want to see only the names of the files and are not interested in any detail. This results in the appearance of file names on the screen in groups of 3-4. Usually, all the files are listed together on the screen. If however, the files still don't fit together on the screen, you can give the command DIR/W/P. Then the following will be displayed:

CREATING AND CHANGING DIRECTORY

To create a new directory, you have to assign a name to it. This should, as far as possible, signify the type of data or programs you are going to store into it. The command is given as following:

MD LAXMI

This will create a new directory by the name of LAXMI. In the beginning, it is blank. Your cursor will remain at the position of its start.

Supposing you want to enter this or any other directory, then the command will be:

Change Directory

This command can be given as following:

```
C:\>CD LAXMI
C:\>LAXMI>
```

This means that you have entered the directory called LAXMI. However, if you are in any other directory and want to enter the LAXMI directory from there, the command becomes:

```
C:>CD\
```

The backslash (\) means that you are entering a different directory. Actually (\) means more than that. If you type CD\ at the DOS prompt of any subdirectory, your cursor reaches the root directory. This is a

```
C:\>cd windows

C:\WINDOWS>
```

Computer Room Activity

Creating Multiple Directories

Supposing you have to keep your notes of the various subjects in separate directories. So you will create directories with various names of the subjects. For this you have to do the following:

```
C:\md doe
C:\cd doe
C:\doe>md it_tools
C:\doe>md bus_sys
C:\doe>md web
C:\doe>md c
C:\doe>dir
.             <DIR>      04-23-03     5:09p
..            <DIR>      04-23-03     5:08p
IT_TOOLS      <DIR>      04-23-03     5:09p     it_tools
BUS_SYS       <DIR>      04-23-03     5:09p     bus_sys
WEB           <DIR>      04-23-03     5:09p     web
C             <DIR>      04-23-03     5:09p     c
              0 file(s)      0 bytes
              6 dir(s)       982.89 MB free
C:\doe>_
```

Now you have all the 4 directories in the single main directory called doe. Do this on your computer in the lab and show it to your teacher.

quick way to go to the root directory, skipping several levels of subdirectories. If you write only CD then it will show the current directory.

Remove Directory

Sometimes, it is possible that you have finished using a software and do not want to keep it or have finished with a project and taken the backup too and don't want to burden your hard disk by keeping it. In this case you would like to remove the directory all together. This would help in having more space for working. This command has to be given from outside the directory which you want to remove. So, if you are in the directory, go out from it and then give the remove directory command. You can use either RD or RMDIR. The command is given as:

```
RD LAXMI
```

Before, you do this, however, you must make sure that you have removed all the files in the directory by using the DEL command. If you have not done so, this command will give you the message that the directory is not empty and cannot be deleted.

DOS COMMANDS

Now you will be introduced to various DOS commands, mainly copy, delete, rename, etc.

Copying a File

It is used to copy file or files from one directory to another or to shift to another drive. The command given is:

```
Copy laxmi.doc a:laxmi.doc
```

Here the file laxmi.doc would be copied to drive A with the same name, i.e., laxmi.doc. If you want to change the name, that is also possible. Then after the a: type the new name.

Another way of using the copy command is by using the wild card option, i.e., *. This is how it is used:

```
Copy *.doc a:
```

The above command will copy all files ending with doc to the floppy drive a. Let us use * at both the places, for example:

```
Copy *.* a:
```

This will copy all files irrespective their names or extensions to drive a.

You can, if you want, copy files starting with an alphabet. For example:

```
Copy l*.doc a:
```

will copy all doc files starting with l.

Computer Room Activity

Copying Files

Supposing you have to copy all your doe document files into floppy disk. For this you have to do the following:

```
C:\copy doe*.doc A:
6 files copied
C:\
```

This will copy all the doe files with doc extension to drive A, if the space is there in drive A.

Xcopy

This command is an extended command of copy. Here you can copy any number of files from any place in the hard disk to another place. The command is written as:

```
Xcopy source:path  target:path switches
```

where you have to define the path of the source files and similarly define the path of the target. Various switches used here are listed below:

Switch	*Action*
/A	Copies only those files matching the source specification that also have their archieve bit set.
/D:date	Copies file sthat were modified on or after the specified data.

/E	Creates subdirectories on the target location, even if there are no files in them.
/M	Resets the archive bit in a file after making the copy.
/P	Issues a prompt asking you to confirm the copy of each source file.
/S	Copies files matching the source specification that are found in sub directories nested below the source subdirectory.
/V	Performs a verification check against the image of the file in memory.
/W	Causes XCOPY to pause before making copies allowing you an opportunity to change disks in the source drive if necessary.

For example,

```
Xcopy c:\laxmi\*.doc a:
```

This command will copy all the doc files from the laxmi subdirectory to the drive a.

Backup

There are times when you need to backup files to another drive to save the disk space area. The command is used as:

```
MSBACKUP file(s) /switches
```

where file(s) are the files which have to be backedup. Following switch options are available:

Switch	*Action*
/BW	Starts MSBACKUP in black-and-white for monitors that have trouble displaying the screen colours.
/TD	Backups up all files named in the specification file that have changed since the last full backup.
/TF	Backs up all files named in the specification.
/TI	Backs up all files named in the specification file that have changed since the last full backup.

Deleting a File

By deleting the name of a file, you remove it completely, including its contents. So be very sure that you are not going to need the file again before giving the delete command. You can delete a file by giving its full name. For example, when you give the following command:

```
DEL LAXMI.DOC
```

This would delete the file called laxmi.doc.

Date and Time

These commands are used to display system time and date. By simply typing Date and Time, you can see the system date and time. What's more you can change them too, by retyping the Date and Time in the same format as displayed. Date is usually displayed in the format of Day and mm-dd-yyyy, where dd, mm and yy have the usual notations. Time is shown in terms of hours, minutes, seconds, etc. You can opt to display the time in 12-hour or 24-hour format.

```
C:\>time
Current time is  1:44:33.97p
Enter new time: _
```

```
C:\>date
Current date is Mon 04-21-2003
Enter new date (mm-dd-yy):
```

Prompt

If you do not like the usual C:\ format, you can change it various other options available under DOS. The various switch options are:

Switch	Action
PROMPT	This option is used to get the default setting.
String	Specifies the text that you want to display as your system prompt.
$$	$(dollar sign)
$_	Carriage return/linefeed.
$B	| (bar or pipe symbol)
$D	Current date
$e	Escape code (you cannot use E instead)
$G	> (greater than symbol)
$H	Backspace (erases the preceding character)
$L	< (less than symbol)
$N	Current drive
$P	Current drive name and path name
$Q	= (equal sign)
$T	Current time
$V	System DOS version number

```
D:\>prompt $D

Mon 04-21-2003
```

Renaming a File

Sometimes, you may not like the name that you gave to a file. You may want to give it a new name without distributing the contents of the file. For this, you use the Rename command as following:

```
REN LAXMI.DOC GOLDEN.DOC
```

This will result in changing the name of the file from laxmi.doc to golden.doc. Remember to put a space in between the two file names.

Restore

Once you backup the file, you must restore them too. The command for this is:

```
Restore source drive: target drive: /switches
```

where source drive has the files which have been backed up. Various switch options are:

Switch	*Action*
/A:mm-dd-yy	Restores only those files that were modified on or after the specified date, where mm is the month, dd is the day and yy is the year.
/B:mm-dd-yy	Restores only those files that were modified on or before the specified date, namely mm-dd-yy.
/D	Displays file name(s) on the backup disk but does not restore them.
/E:hh-mm-ss	Restores those files modified at or earlier than the specified time, where hh is the hour (in 24 hour format), mm is the minutes after the hour, and ss is the seconds.
/L:hh: mm: ss:	Restores only those files that were modified at or after the specified time.
/M	Restores files that were modified since the last backup was made.
/N	Restores files that were deleted since the last backup.
/P	Prompts to confirm the restoration of files that were changed since the last backup or marked as read-only files.
/S	Restores files in sub directories nested below the specified target subdirectory.

Changing the Attrib

Each file in DOS has various attributes attached to it. These attributes decide the fate of the file. Among them are read-only, hide, etc. So you can change the attribute of a file using the command called Attib, and the options attached to it. The command is:

```
Attrib modes path /switches
```

where path is the path of the file whose attributes you want to change. Various switches in use are:

Switch	*Action*
+A	Changes file setting to archived.
–A	Changes file settings to not archived.
+H	Changes specified file(s) to hidden, which means the file(s) will not be visible to most DOS operations.
–H	Makes hidden files visible again.
+R	Changes specified file(s) to read-only which means the file(s) cannot be overwritten or erased.
–R	Changes specified file(s) to read write which means, the file may be overwritten or erased.
+S	Marks specified file(s) as DOS system file(s).
–S	Removes DOS system-file setting.
/S	Used with the file names that contain wildcard character or subdirectory names without file names. This option will include matching files in sub directories nested below the current subdirectory.

Type

This command is used to see the contents of a text file. The command is:

```
Type filename
```

where filename is the name of the file whose contents you have to see. Since this shows the plain listing of the files, it is adviced that you use this command mainly for plain text files and not for formatted document files.

You can use | More to see all the contents of the file.

```
C:\>type out.txt
Num cars in race = 4
Num cars in race = 4
Num cars in race = 4
Num cars in race = 4
Num cars in race = 4
Num cars in race = 4
```

This is not the end of the DOS commands, there are more. The commands given here are just to give you an idea of the type of commands available under DOS. You can get the complete list of commands of DOS by typing

```
?
```

at the DOS prompt.

Multiple Choice Questions

1. Which command is used to shift the command from one directory to another?
   (a) CD (b) MD
   (c) RD
2. Which command would you use to create a new directory?
   (a) CD (b) MD
   (c) RD
3. The main directory of the hard disk is:
   (a) Main directory (b) Root directory
   (c) Final directory
4. Which command will always transfer to the root directory?
   (a) CD\ (b) CD/
   (c) CD
5. For listing the files widthwise, we give the command as?
   (a) DIR/P (b) DIR/W
   (c) DIR

Descriptive Type Questions

1. Describe the rename command.
2. What is the command to rename all files in a directory?
3. Which are the different options of the DIR command?
4. What is the root directory?
5. How is it possible to see the system date?

Windows 95/98

13

HISTORY OF MICROSOFT WINDOWS

Windows is nothing but graphics-based operating environment from Microsoft. It provides a desktop environment similar to the Macintosh, in which each active application is displayed in a resizable, moveable window on the screen. Initially Windows ran on DOS platform, but now-a-days it runs on its own platform.

Windows 1.x, Windows 286 (2.x) and Windows 386 were first attempts. Windows 3.0 had its own enhanced user interface and ability to manage extended memory, upto 16MB with built-in DOS extender.

Windows 3.1 (1992) was faster and supported multimedia, true type fonts, drag and drop, among other features. It was the last of the Windows versions based to work on DOS platform. From this point onward Microsoft introduced Windows 95 which was independent of DOS and had its booting capabilities.

Windows for Workgroups for introduced in 1993. It was the first version of Windows which truly supported networking. This was later enhanced to Windows NT, which was introduced in 1993.

WINDOWS 95

An operating system with a graphical user interface for 80386, was released by Microsoft Corporation in 1995.It was intended to replace Windows 3.11 and MS DOS. Windows 95 was a complete operating system rather than a shell that required MS-DOS as did the earlier versions of Windows. For compatability Windows could run all the DOS programs. Various other features of Windows 95 are listed below:

32-bit File Sysem

It had an installable 32-bit file system, thus ensured faster disk performance than the 16-bit file system used by Windows 3.1 and DOS.

Convenional Memory

Windows 95 provided DOS program with more conventional memory space by implementing device drivers such as SmartDrive, Mouse drivers, Share.exe, CD-ROM and SCSI device drivers as 32-bit drives handled by Windows 95.

DOS Applications

It ran all DOS applications and Windows 3.x applications.

GUI

A new GUI (Graphical user interface) with substantial improvements over Windows 3.x.

Laptop Docking

Supported PCMCIA cards for laptop computers and the use of laptop docking stations. That is, without rebooting the operating system, it would acknowledge what you plugged in and automatically reconfigure the system accordingly.

Long File Names

It supported long file names replacing the earlier used eight-letter file names used by DOS. Thus with Windows 95 files could have names up to 255 characters long.

Microsoft Exchange

It included a new mail system called Microsoft Exchange for managing all the types of messages such as e-mail, Internet communications, Faxes and Documents.

Multitaksing

This meant it could run multiple applications simultaneously more smoothly than Windows 3.1 did.

Multi-Users

It supported multiple users, each with their own settings such as desktop icons, shared resources, user rights etc.

Networking

Like Windows for workgroups, Windows 95 too included built-in peer-to-peer networking, with a more efficient 32-bit network drivers as well as support for the increasingly popular TCP/IP protocol for accessing Unix-based systems such as the Internet.

OLE

It incorporated Object Linking and Embedding (OLE) version 2.0. This means users could easily create comprehensive documents combining information from several different application programs. This made it easy to incorporate graphs, charts, music, video, clipart, etc into your word-processing documents.

Plug and Play

It supported the new Plug and Play standard for hardware, developed by PC makers. Plug and Play lets you simply plug a new board such as a video or network card into your computer without having to set switches or make other settings. Windows 95 will automatically recognize what you plugged and adjust the settings to make it work.

Program Manager

A more intuitive interface, doing away with the confusing Program Manager/File Manager design and incorporating a single integrated arrangement that allowed you to place document icons and folders on the Windows desktop and work with them from there.

Registry

The software and hardware settings are consolidated in a central location called the Registry.

Self Operating System

Unlike Windows 3.x, Windows 95 was not working on top of MS-DOS, but on DOS 7 that was designed to work hand-in-hand with this new version of Windows. The new DOS7/Windows 95 combination was finally a full-fledged graphical operating system and not a graphical operating environment working on top of DOS.

WINDOWS 98

This version of Windows was released in 1998. It integrated all the needs of Internet, allowing users to to access remote files in the same way as they would access file on their hard disks. Hardware wise it could handle, AGP ports, TV tuner, DVD drives, multiple modems, multiple monitors, and various IEEE ports. Various features of Windows 98 are listed below:

32-bit Data Link

The Data Link Control (DLC) protocol is used primarily to access IBM Mainframe and IBM AS/400 computers. The 32-bit DLC protocol software built-in to Windows 98 enables a network administrator to add support for 32-bit and 16-bit DLC programs.

ActiveMovie

ActiveMovie is a new media streaming architecture for Windows that delivers high-quality video playback while exposing an extensible set of interface upon which multimedia applications and tools can be built.

Backup Program

Windows 98 backup program now supports SCSI tape devices and has general enhancements so that backing up your data is simpler and faster.

Conversion Utility

For added flexibility, Windows 98 includes a graphical FAT32 conversion utility, which can quickly and safely convert a hard drive from the original version of FAT and FAT32.

Disk Defragmenter Optimization Wizard

Windows 98 uses the process of disk defragmentation to increase the speed with which your applications run. Thus the wizard creates a log file, which identifies your most commonly used programs. Once this log file has been created, it can be used by the disk defragmenter to store the files associated with those programs. By storing all of the files associated with a given application in the same location on your hard disk, this wizard optimizes the speed with which your application runs.

Display Enhancements

Now you can dynamically change your screen resolution and color depth without having to reboot Windows as in earlier versions.

Dr. Watson

This is a tool for capturing information about the system at the time of a program or system malfunction. Dr. Waton reports which program corrupted records the relevant details, such as state of the system and can display it and / or save it on disk for later perusal.

FAT 32

FAT32 is an improved version of the FAT (File Allocation Table) file system that allows disks over two gigabytes to be formatted as a single drive. FAT32 also uses smaller clusters than FAT drives, resulting in a more efficient use of space on large disks.

Intel MMX Processors Support

Provides support so that third parties can build software that exploits the Intel Pentium Multimedia Extensions (MMX) for fast audio and video support on the inter Pentium Processors.

Internet Browsing Functionality

With Windows 98 (via Internet Explorer 4) surfing the Web has become easier due to advanced browsing capabilities such as AutoComplete, enhanced Web searching, improved Favorites list, navigation history on the Forward/Back buttons and improved printing.

Internet Communication

Windows 98 also contains rich tools for online communication including Outlook Express, Microsoft NetMeeting Personal Web Server and the Web Publishing Wizard.

Multilink Channel Aggregation

That means you can connect multiple modems together (assuming you have multiple dial-up phone line available) to get higher transfer speeds to the Internet, other dial-up services or remote computers.

Multiple Display support

Multiple Display Support allows you to use multiple monitors and/or multiple graphics adapters on a single PC. This can be beneficial for doing work such as: desktop publishing, Web development, video editing and for playing computer games.

New Generation of Hardware

Since Windows 95 came out, lots of new types of hardware has come up, e.g. Universal Serial Bus (USB), Accelerated Graphics Port (AGP), Advanced Configuration and Power interface (ACPI) and Digital Video Disc (DVD) and some new video conferencing devices. Windows 98 has drivers, controls and software programs for these new hardware devices.

Point-to-Point Tunneling Protocol (PPTP)

The Point-to-Point Tunneling Protocol (PPTP) provides a way to use public data networks, such as the Internet, to create virtual private networks connecting client PCs with servers.

System File Checker Utility

Along the same lines as the Windows System Update, which works on-line. This new utility works off-line when you are not connected to the Internet to verify if your Windows 98 system files (*.dll, *.com, *.vxd, *.drv, *.ocx, *.inf, *.hlp and so on) are altered, dead or missing.

Windows Scripting

Windows 98 supports direct script execution from the user interface or the command line (a script as a series of commands that can be automatically executed). This support is provided via the Windows Scripting Host (WSH) and allows administrators and / or users to save time by automating many user interface actions such as creating a shortcut, connecting to a network server, disconnecting form a network server, etc.

Windows System Update

This feature ensures you have the latest system software such as drivers and system files that are available. You can access the Microsoft Web-based service over the Internet.

Window Tune-Up Wizard

A new program in the System Tools group keeps the operating system and hard disk in peak condition by defragmenting the hard disk, removing unnecessary startup commands, deleting unnecessary temp, setup and Internet files and checking a hard disk for errors. This result in faster program execution and more disk space.

STARTING MICROSOFT WINDOWS

As we learned in the earlier part of the chapter, Windows 98 is an operating system, it does not need to be started. It starts when the computer is put on. The first software which takes over the computer is Windows 98. The first thing that you see on the screen is the desktop, which is like the platform from where every application is launched and you would return to it after completing the application.

DESKTOP

As you might have noticed that there are various icons on the desktop. These are nothing but the graphical representations of the applications, programs, documents, etc. I will explain later in the chapter, how these icons can be created. By clicking with mouse onto an icon, once or twice, as you may set in the Windows setup, you can run the program or application.

On the desktop, there are few icons which are a must for all the desktops being used by Windows and there are few which are optional and are created by the users according to their likings. Among the permanent ones are: My Computer, Recycle Bin, My Documents, Network Neighborhood, etc.

I will explain about them a little later. First about icons.

ICONS

Icon is a graphic presentation of a window element. Icons are of four types which are as follows:

Disk Drive Icons

These type of Icons represents the Drives of the computer. For example: Drive3½ Floppy A:, Hard Disk drive, CD Drive, etc.

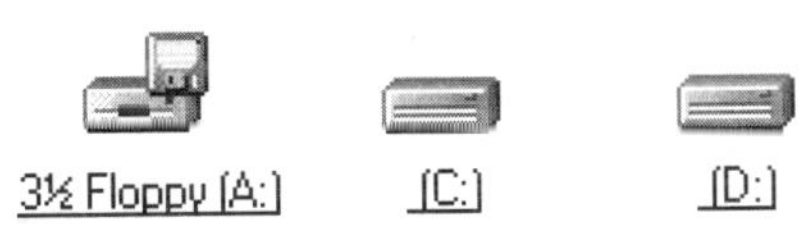

Application Icons

Application Icons means the software package which are used to run various programs. For Example: MS-Office, MS-Word, MS-Excel, MS- Access, PageMaker, CorelDraw etc.

Shortcut Icons

Shortcut Icons are created by using the option from Desktop/New/Shortcut.

Document Icons

You can create a graphical representation of any document.

Computer Room Activity

Booting of the System

Boot the computer from the very beginning and see the desktop and icons on the screen.

USE OF START BUTTON

There are lot of things which can be done from the Start button. For others you have to use either My Computer or Windows Explorer. I would talk about them a little later but let us concentrate on Start button first. At the bottom most left corner of the desktop is the Start button. By pressing it you can launch the following options (your computer may different options, but quite a number of them are same):

Windows Update Microsoft from time to time announces the update of the software. Using this option you can upgrade your Windows version after connecting to the Microsoft website.

WinZip A very useful program for compressing the files.

Kundli for Windows An astrological software, not available with Windows but put in for use by yours truly.

TRUCHHIPLAYSTATION Another one of my programs.

New Office Document This helps you in creating a new office document, which can be a document of MS Word, a spreadsheet of MS Excel, etc.

Open Office Document Similar to above, you can open an existing document.

Programs It opens a list of various folders and their programs to choose from to run them.

Favorites It gives you access to various channels, links and software updates.

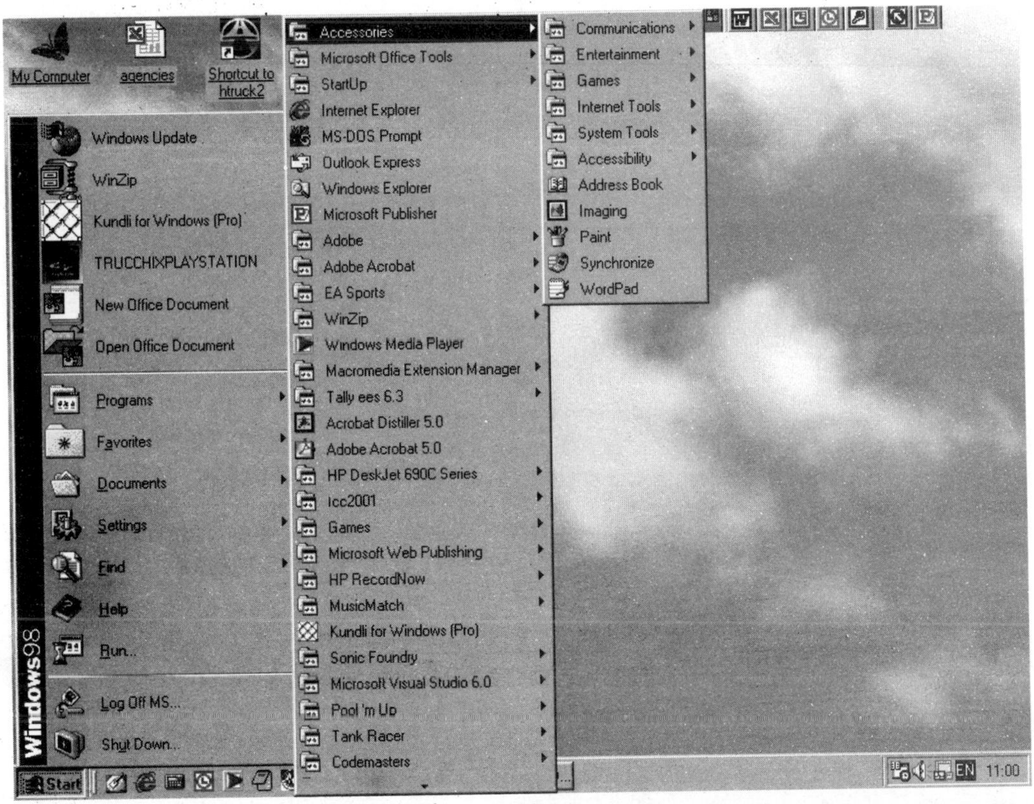

Documents It gives you access to the last 15 documents opened.

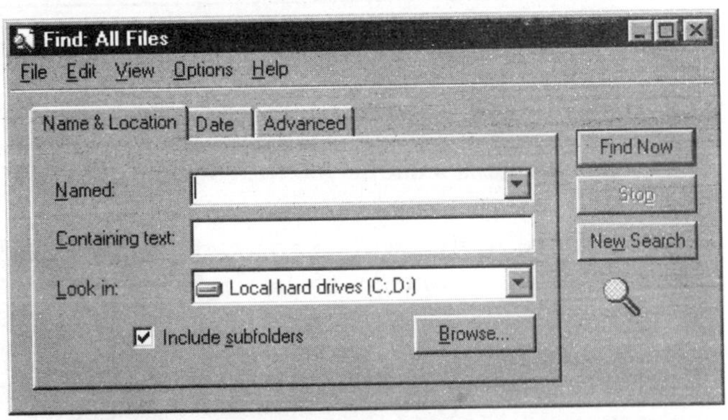

Settings It provides access to Control Panel, Printers, Taskbar and Start Menu, Folder Menu, Active Desktop and Windows update controls.

Find Using this you can search for a file, folder, device or a computer. You can also search the Internet and look for personal contact information.

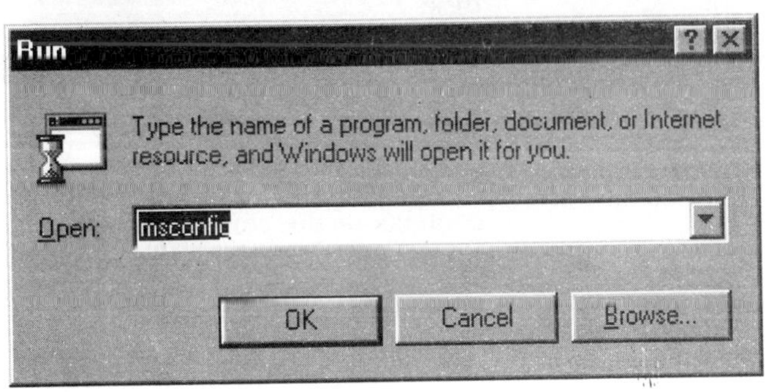

Help It opens the extensive Windows Help system and gives you access to the Troubleshooting

Run Allows you to run a particular program using a dialog box.

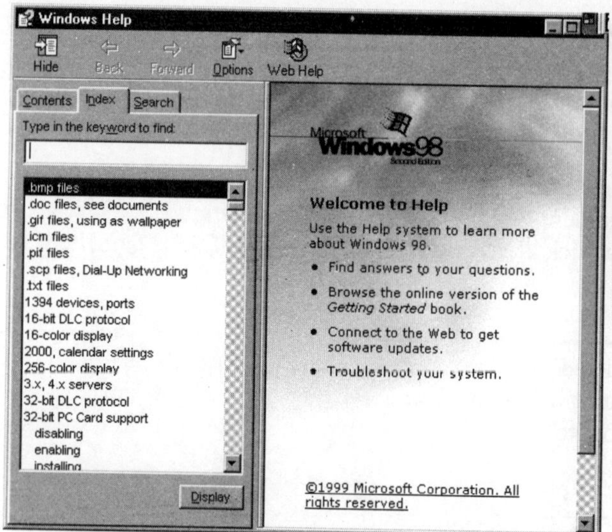

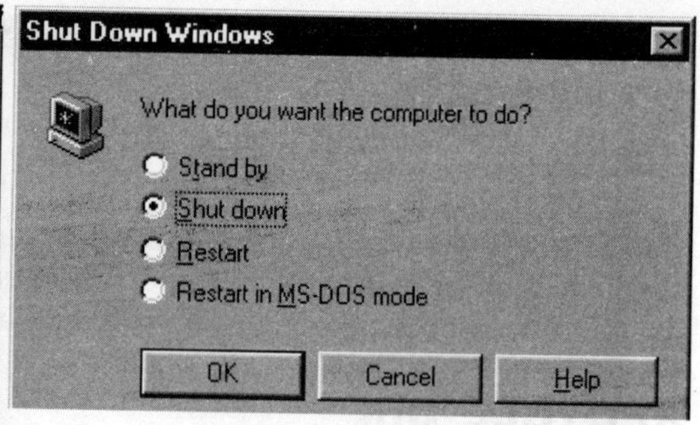

Log Off It logs off the system quickly so that you can log back on with a different user profile or so that another user can log on.

Shut Down.. It prepares the computer to shut down or to be restarted.

Computer Room Activity

Using the Help

Click at Help from the Start button and see the topics covered under it.

Now we talk about the various parts of the desktop, starting with My Computer.

MY COMPUTER

As the name suggests it shows you the contents of your computer. This has the following icons for the followings:

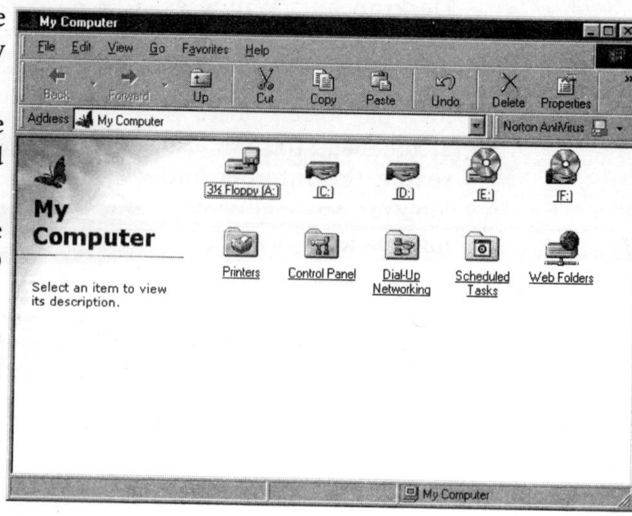

Drive A: It will show the contents of the floppy drive.

Drive C: It will show the contents of the hard disk.

Drive D: It will show the contents of drive D (CD drive).

Control Panel It will show the contents of the control panel.

Printers It will show the number of printers installed.

Scheduled Tasks	It will show you the tasks which you have scheduled to be performed at a particular time.
Dial-up Networking	It will dial the network for you.
Web Folders	It will show you the various web folders.

Clicking the icon of drive C will show you the icons in the drive. Clicking at the various folders you can see the files under them. If you click at any document file, it would launch the program associated with it and open the document in it. Similarly if you click at an application, the application is launched.

RECYCLE BIN

It is like a dust bin of the computer. All the deleted files are transferred here. You can in fact open this folder to see the files present in it. If you want at any stage to retrace any file, you can do it, if it is present in the Recycle Bin. However, if you choose to empty the recycle bin and delete the files altogether, then you cannot restore any of the file.

Computer Room Activity

Using the Recycle Bin

Delete an icon from desktop. Now, go to the Recycle Bin and restore it.

MY DOCUMENTS

This folder contains all your files which you have created and saved in it. Irrespective of the program, you can click the files to open them. The relative program will be launched automatically.

NETWORK NEIGHBORHOOD

It opens a viewer that presents system information about your computer's place in a network. So far we have talked about shortcuts or icons on the desktop. But, we have not told you how they are created.

EXPLORING THE TASKBAR

It is the bottom key line on the desktop. Starting with the right most corner, we see the following:

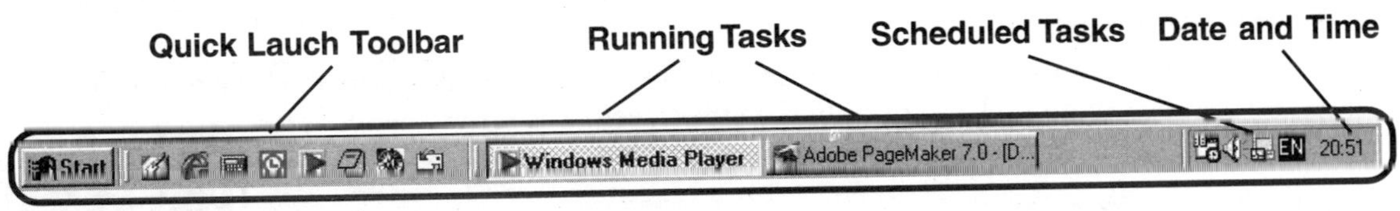

Date and Time	It shows you the date and time of the system.
Task Scheduler	It shows the tasks which you have scheduled for running at different times.
Quick Launch Toolbar	Various icons here are the ones used for launching different programs. You have an option to put these icons here for the programs which you often use.

Running Tasks When you have a program running in your system, its name will be reflected here on this taskbar to show that this program is open.

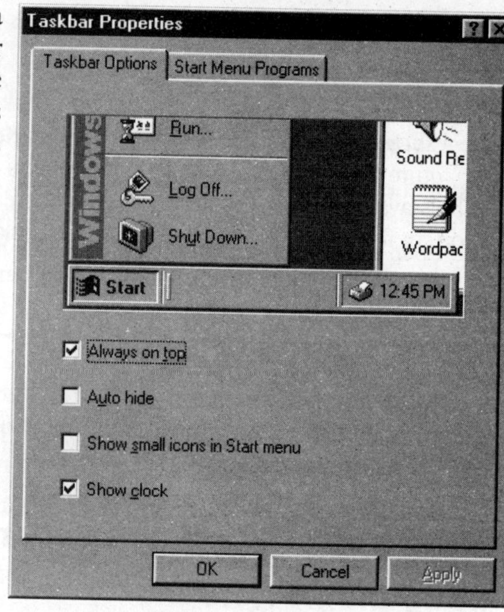

You can change the various options of the taskbar using the option dialog box from Start button, Settings, Taskbar and Start menu. This dialog box is shown here. It has 2 panels: Taskbar options and Start Menu Programs. Select the panel and make the changes you would like to make.

RUNNING AN APPLICATION

An application can be run under Windows by various methods. They are:

By Icon

Clicking at the icon of the application at the desktop.

From Windows Explorer

Click at the file/icon of the application in Windows Explorer.

From Start Menu

Click at Program and then the program name from its sub-menu. For example, for running Paintbrush, you will have to go to Programs, Accessories and then Paint.

WORKING ON WINDOWS

So far you have seen how the various sections of Windows work. Now we see how you can control the working of the Windows or for that any of the Windows dialog box.

Minimizing the Windows

You can work on more than one application at the same time under windows. For this you have to minimize one application, which is done by using Minimize button, as shown here. Once you are though with the other application you can minimize that and come back to this application.

Restoring the Windows

If you have minimized an application, then there must be some button to restore it. Using this button you can restore the application back to its position on the screen. The restore button is in the centre here.

Maximizing the Windows

Using this button, you can make the full use of Windows screen.

Closing of Windows

Using this button you can close the running application. However, if the running application is not saved, then it will be pointed out to you.

CREATING SHORTCUTS

This is what I had promised in the beginning. Supposing you have a program loaded into the computer and you have to often use it. So you would like to have a shortcut for it. For example, I use Character Map, quite often to use the special characters and symbols available in the system. So, I have created a shortcut for this and it is available on the desktop.

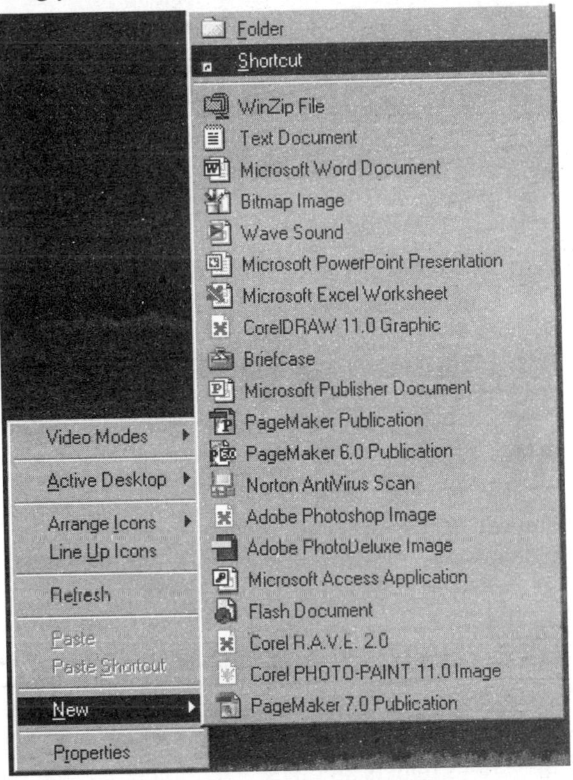

Let us learn how this character map icon can be created on the desktop. For this you follow the steps here.

1. Minimize all your opened programs.
2. Click at the right button of the mouse on the desktop to get a menu.
3. Click at New to get the new menu. Click at Shortcut to create one.
4. This will give rise to a dialog box. Side by side, you will notice that it has created a new folder with New Shortcut as the name.
5. Click at the browse button to locate the file associated with the new shortcut. It is located in Windows directory by the name of CHARMAP.EXE. Once selected it will be filled up in the File name column. Click it to open it. This will lead us back to the main dialog box of Create Shortcut.

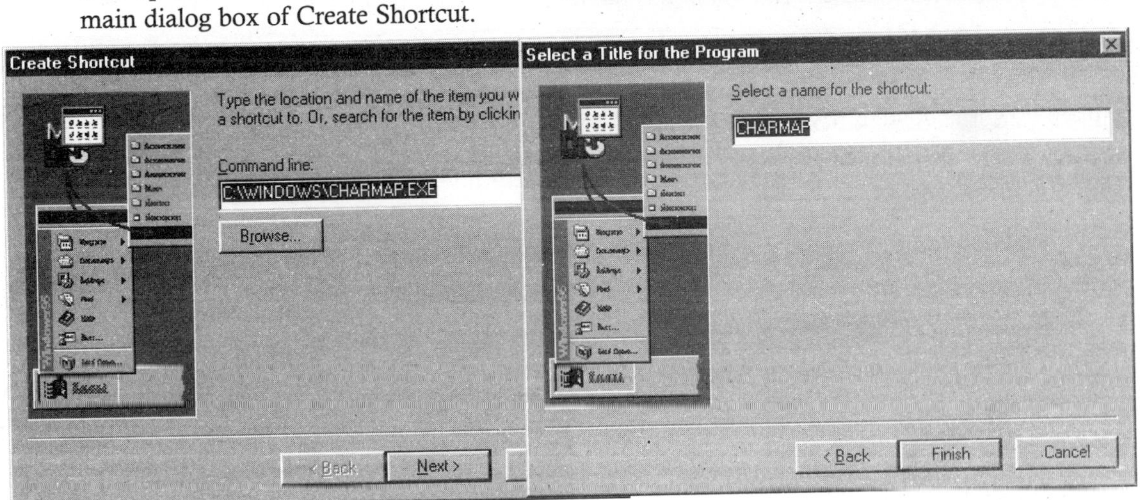

6. You will now see that the command line has been filled up with the exact location of the file which is to be Run for launching of this shortcut from the desktop.
7. Click at Next to get the next dialog box. This will ask you fill up the name you want to give to the shortcut. Here we have given it as CHARMAP.

8. Clicking at Finish will end the procedure to create the shortcut. Oncc done, it will create a new shortcut named CHARMAP on the desktop. You can now use it to launch Character Map.

WINDOWS EXPLORER

It offers you the easiest way of viewing folders, files and other resources located on your machine. The default Explorer is a two-pane window. When you click on an item in the left window pane, the right pane displays the contents.

You can choose different viewing options from the View menu, the two options, small icons and details are shown on the next page. For moving files from one folder to another, you can open more than one window of the Windows Explorer and then drag & drop.

CREATING AND RENAMING OF FILES AND FOLDERS

A folder is like a directory where all the relative files are kept. For example, all your files pertaining to a book would be in one folder. If you look at the picture shown earlier of Windows Explorer, it contains the various folders and files. Each folder has the files related to that folder.

Creating a Folder

For creation of a new folder, you will have to go to either My Computer or Windows Explorer. Let me explain how it is done in My Computer.

For that follow the following steps.

1. Start My Computer from the desktop.
2. Right click the mouse to get the following menu.
3. Click at New and then Folder to get a new blank folder on the screen.
4. By clicking at its name you can type the name you want for the folder.
5. After typing press Enter to have the folder.

Copying of a File

For copying also you can use either My Computer or Windows Explorer. Let me explain how it is done in My Computer.

For that follow the following steps.

1. Start My Computer from the desktop.
2. Right click the mouse to get the menu.

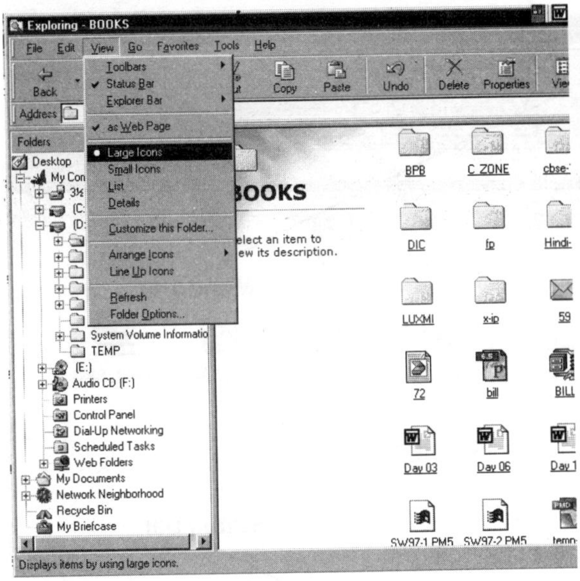

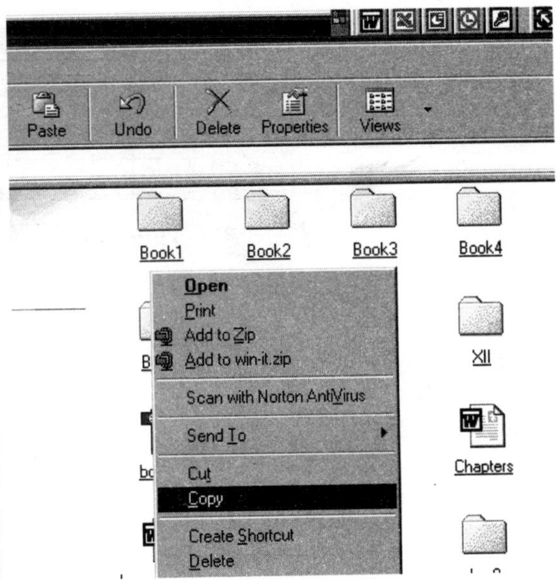

3. Click at Copy and then the Folder where you want this file to be copied.
4. Rcclick the right mouse.
5. Select Paste this timc
6. The copied file will be pasted here.

Renaming the Files/Folder

After giving the files their names, you can change them if you like. For this we have the Rename command. Follow the following procedure to rename a file.

1. Select the file which you want to rename by single clicking it.
2. From the File menu, click at Rename.
3. Retype the new name for the file.

Similarly you can change the name of the folder.

Computer Room Activity

Creating Folders

As the method of creating folders mentioned above, create folders with the names of CLASS IX, CLASS X, CLASS XI and CLASS XII.

Renaming Folders

Rename a folder with a different name and show it to your teacher.

BASIC COMPONENTS OF A WINDOW

A window here is taken here as the name of the dialog box, as mentioned earlier in the chapter. Let me explain the various components of a dialog box/window.

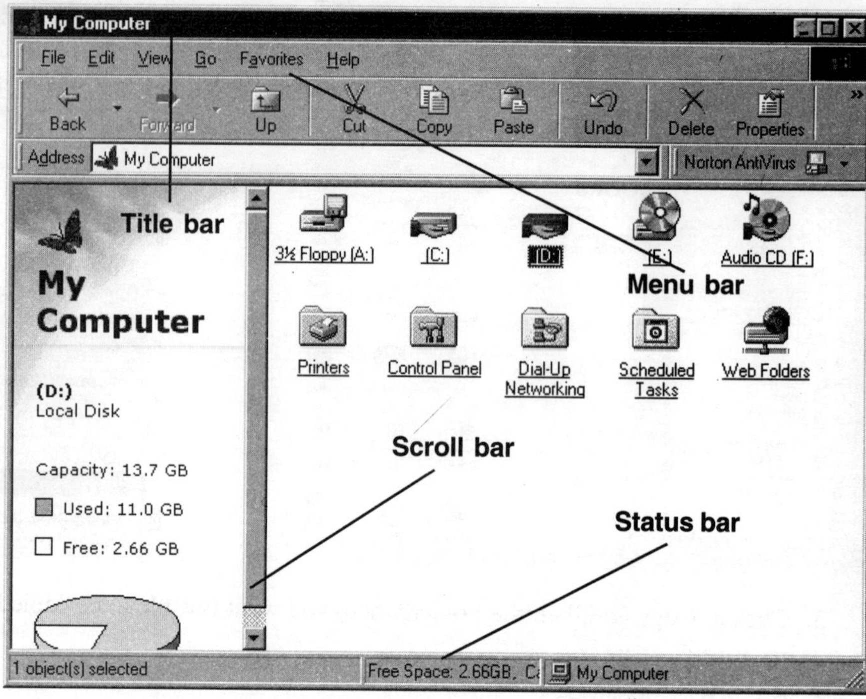

Title bar

This bar is displayed at the top of the window. It displays the name of the program and name of the currently active document.

Menu bar

This bar is just below the Title bar. When you select a key word on the Menu bar, a list falls down.

Some of the items will be grey in colour, which shows that they cannot be used at this stage. Select one of the available item to perform some operation.

Scroll bar

There are two types of scroll bars: the horizontal and the vertical scroll bar. When there is insufficient space available, these scroll bar appears automatically. We can scroll either by clicking on the arrow marks or by dragging the little bar with the help of the mouse.

Status bar

This bar displays the information about the active document or the task that the user is currently working on.

WINDOWS ACCESSORIES

Accessories play a major part in Windows. They are so called additional programs which are there alongwith the main program called Windows. These are small small program which you would need while working under Windows. As you read about them, do not worry, how and when would be needing them. They would be used when the demand arises.

ACCESSING ACCESSORIES

Accessories can be accessed from Start Menu and Programs. They can also be accessed from the Windows Explorer. Mostly Start Menu is used.

As you can see there are various heads in Accessories, each giving rise to a different sub menus, which have been clubbed together to form a group of activities of similar types. It is possible that your computer may have a different set of accessories than mine because of configuration of your system.

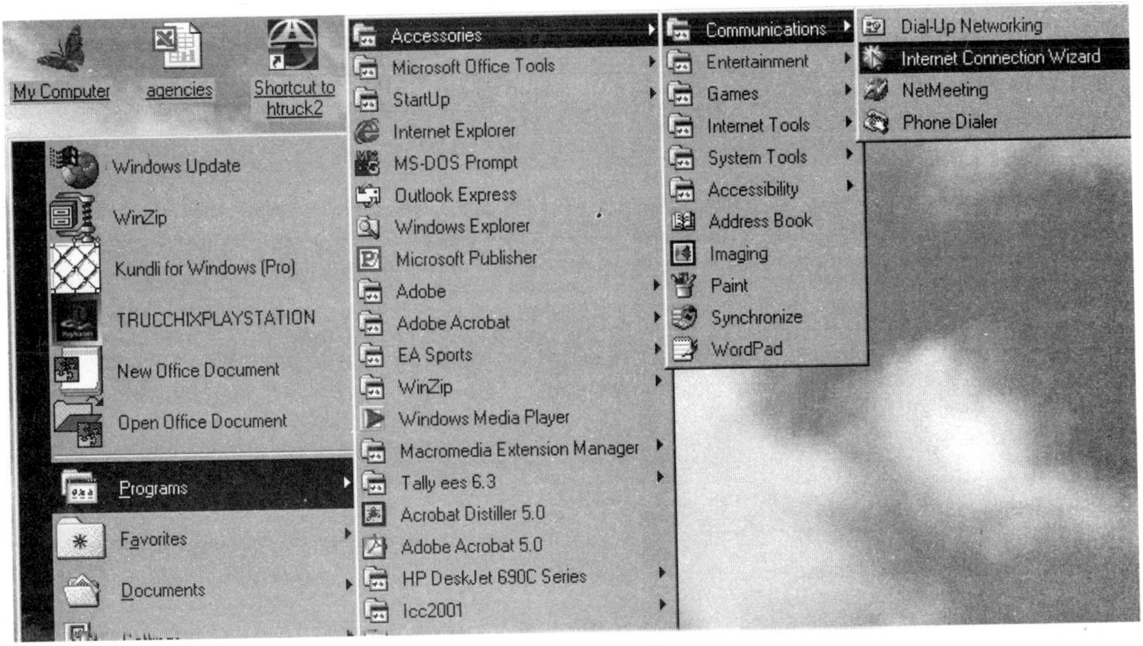

ACCESSIBILITY

It has two options, mainly Accessibility Wizard and Magnifier. Let us see each one of these individually.

Accessibility Wizard

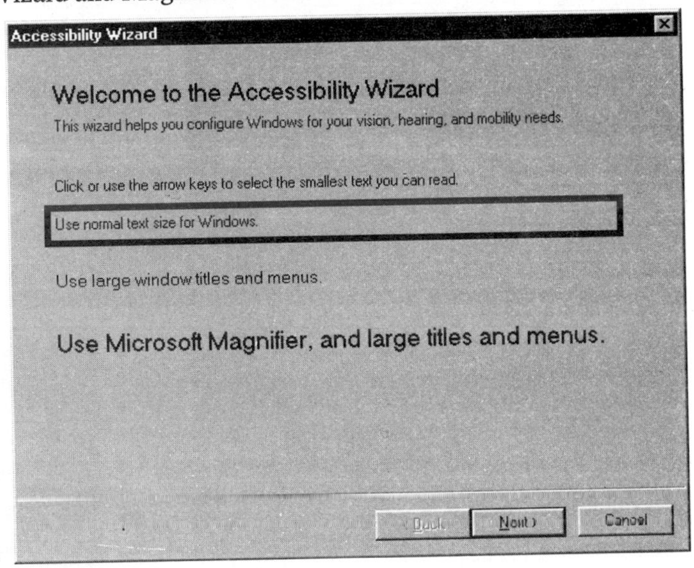

This gives you the option to select to see the various items on the screen, the way you like. Pressing Next in the following screen would lead to various other screens, which would access you capabilities of seeing and hearing and then set the Windows according to your needs. In one of the screens it asks whether you are:

Blind

Deaf

Have difficulty in using the keyboard or mouse, etc.

This is indeed very helpful for people who are handicapped like this.

Magnifier

This option is mainly for those who have difficulty in seeing the things on the screen. This option enlarges them for the benefit of users. You can even select the level of magnification. By using mouse you can see the magnified icons.

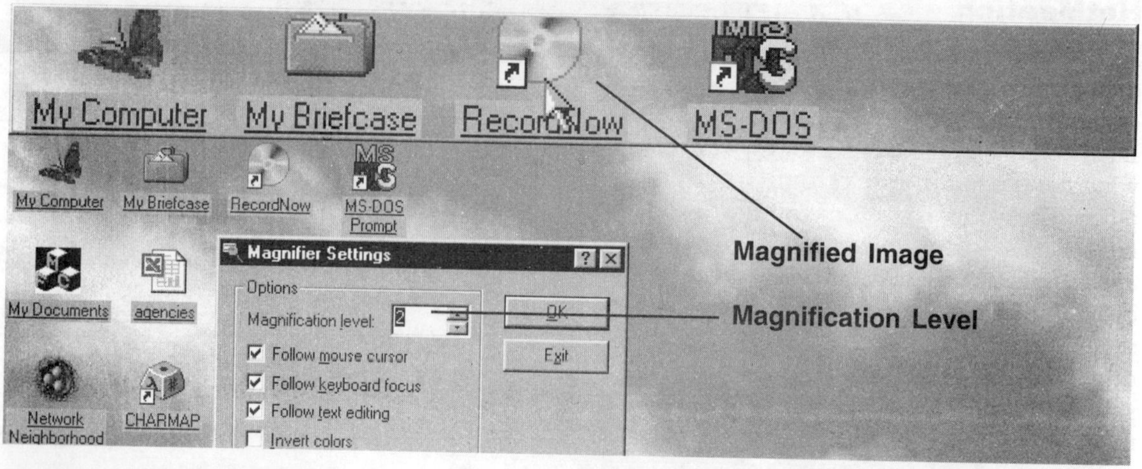

COMMUNICATIONS

Dial-up Networking

As you must be knowing that for connecting to Internet you need Modem and a telephone connection. That telephone connection is configured from here. It is like a Wizard which would guide you to establish connection between a modem, a telephone and your computer. You can even set up your networking also through this.

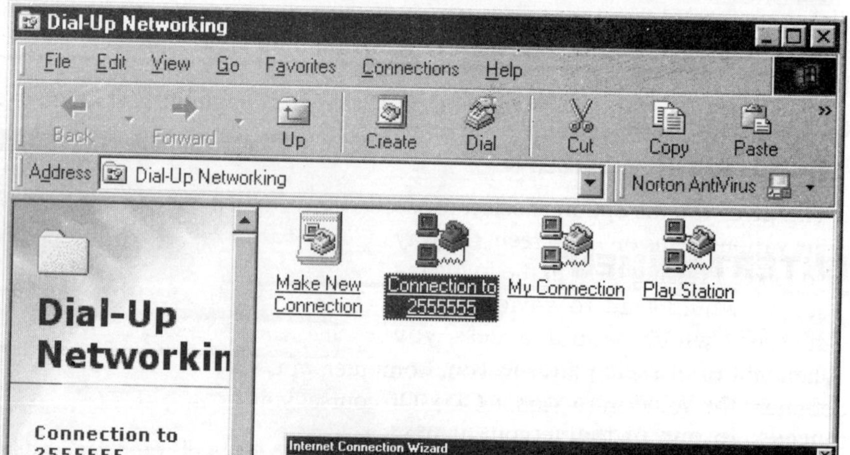

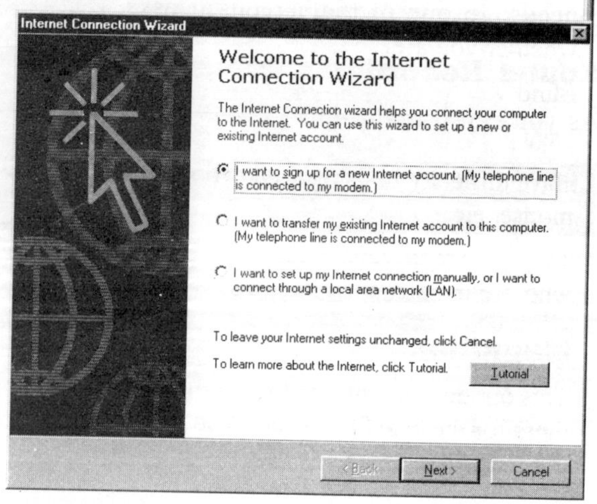

Internet Connectivity Wizard

Well if you have modem attached to your computer, then the next logical step would be setup the computer for Internet. This wizard will guide in the whole process of setting up.

NetMeeting

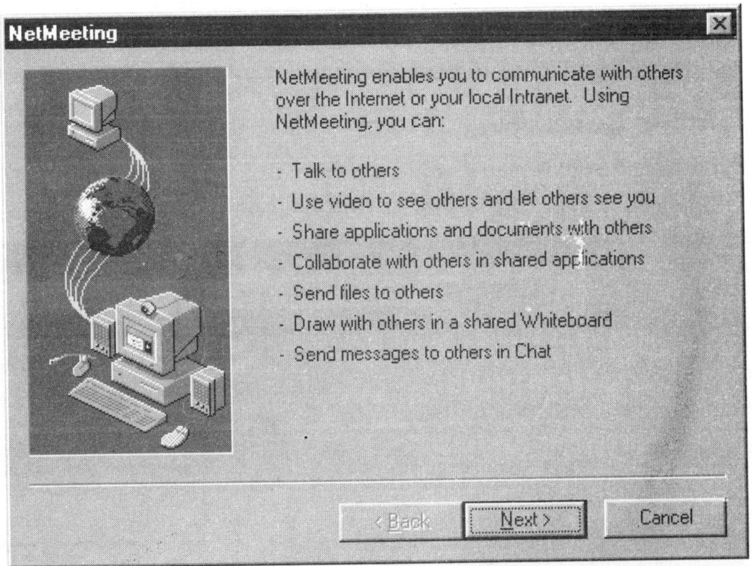

It enables you to setup the communication channel to communicate with others on the Internet. Among the other things which you can do are: Talk to others; Use video to see others and let others see you; Share applications and documents with others; Collaborate with others in shared applications; Send files to others; Draw with others in a shared Whiteboard; Send messages to others in Chat.

This is again a Wizard, for which you can set up your own options.

Phone Dialer

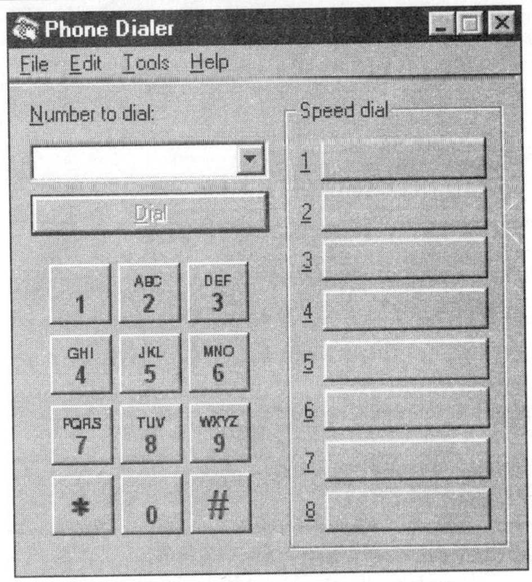

If you have modem attached to your computer, then you can dial your friends from the computer itself. Just dial their numbers and talk to them. It is all possible from this Phone Dialer.

Of course, you can store numbers which you use often and then dial them with a single digit.

ENTERTAINMENT

CD Player

When you have a CD player in your computer, you would definitely like to listen to Audio CDs. Of course, you need to have speakers attached to your computer.

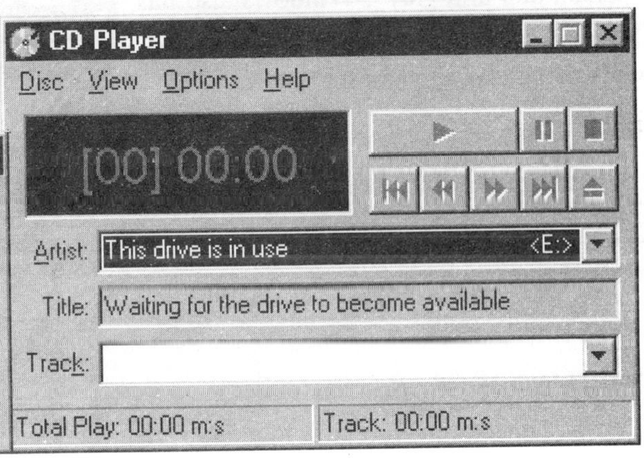

Sound Recorder

As you can listen to music, there must be a

method to record your voice or music too. This will help you do the same. Of course, you must have the multimedia kit attached to your computer.

Volume Control

If you want a sophisticated volume control to listen to your music, then this option is for you. You can your adjustment here according to your likings.

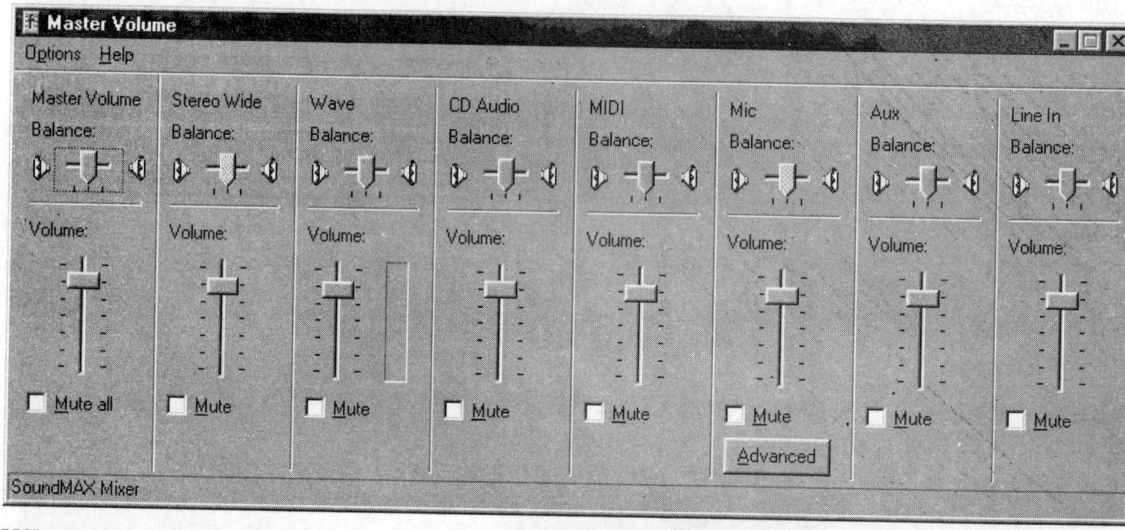

Windows Media Player

When you can listen to Audio CDs, then why not see the Video CDs too. Well, for that you have this media player. From here you can see movies of all types, even the animated ones too.

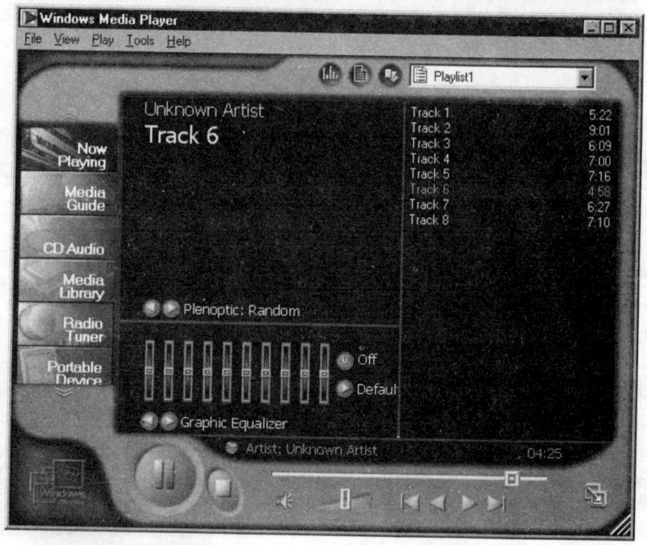

GAMES

As they say "All work and no play will make a person dull and gray", Windows also has taken for your needs for games.

It has the following games:

Free Cell

It is a card game which needs lots of skill and time.

Hearts

Another card game.

Minesweeper

Another game where you have to guess which mine will blast and which will not.

Solitaire

This game was discovered way back in 18th century and has been played by most of the persons who are alone and have nothing to do. This computer version is equally good.

INTERNET TOOLS

This category of tools are for those who use internet quite often. These tools would be very helpful to them.

Personal Web Server

Microsoft Personal Web Server (PWS) is a desktop Web server. If you are connected to an intranet, or a corporate network, you can share documents with your coworkers from your own computer. Use PWS to develop and publish your personal home page. You can also test your Web site before you upload it to an Internet service provider.

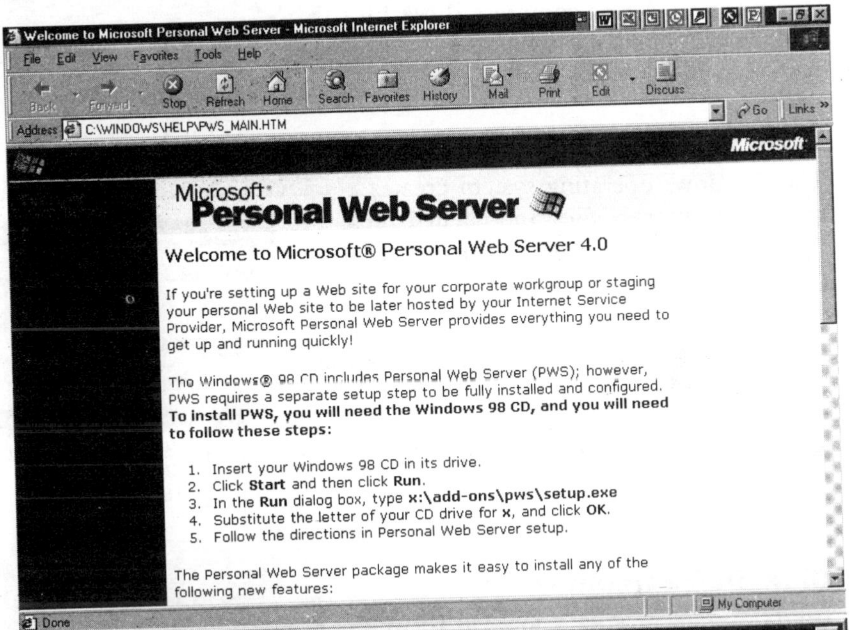

Web Publishing Wizard

This wizard helps you publish your Web pages, support files, and other Web content files on a Web server. The Web server can be located on your local area network (LAN), or it can be maintained by your Internet service provider (ISP).

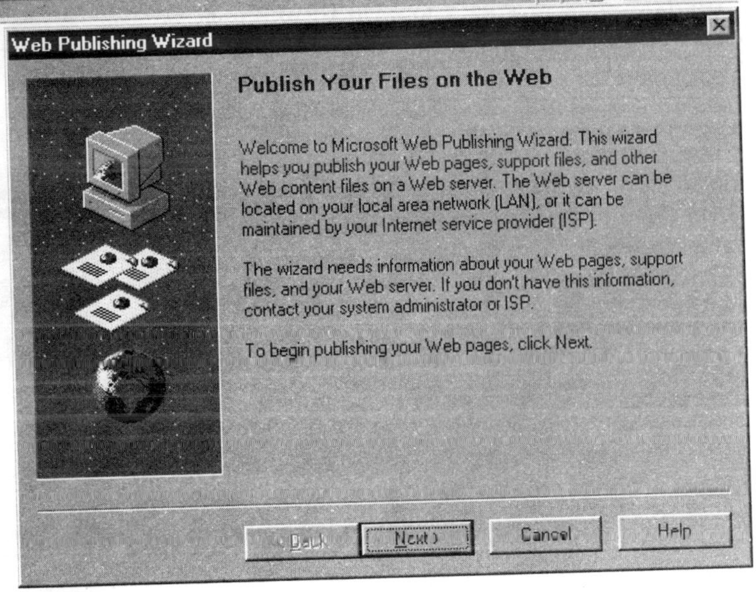

SYSTEM TOOLS

This category of accessories are there to enhance the working of the computer with different tools which not only speed up the computer but also keeps the system clean of any unwanted elements.

Compression Agent

It works with DriveSpace3 to control and change the degree of compression used on your files. For example, you could improve performance on file save operations by telling DriveSpace to use No Compression. Then you can have Compression Agent compress these files when your computer is not in use.

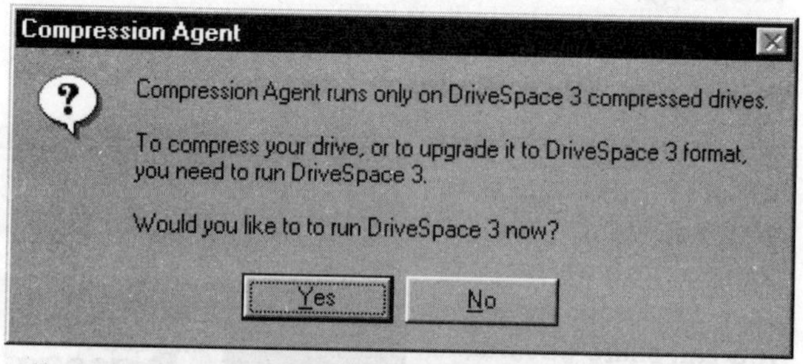

Disk Cleanup

The Windows operating system creates a mass of temporary files and cached files—all designed to speed up the performance of the graphical interface.

These files do a pretty good job but, often do not get deleted when they should be. This results in a lot of files cluttered up on your hard drive. When you run Disk Cleanup, it checks for files that can be safely deleted and then presents a list of such files.

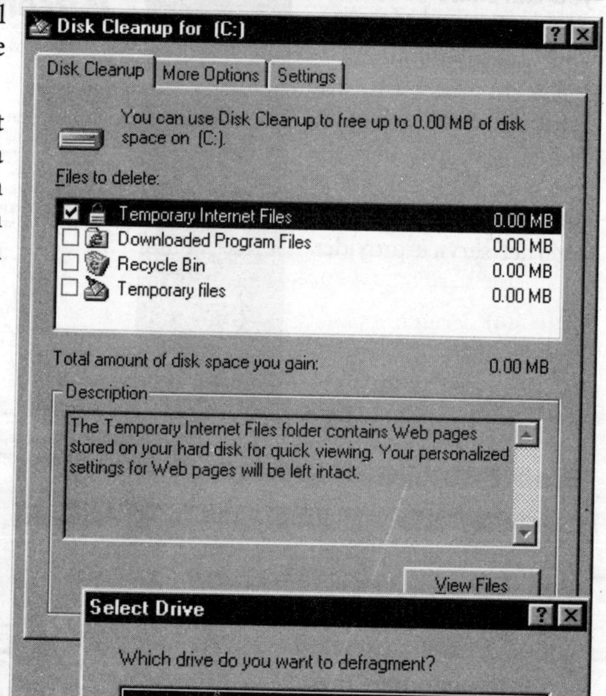

Disk Defragmenter

While writing files on a hard disk, Windows keeps the files at random and keeps track of its position using FAT. This results in having the files placed in hard disk, quite staggered.

This command, which was there even in DOS, does the job of housekeeping and puts the files on one side and the blank space in the hard disk on the other side. This results in speeding up the activity of the hard disk.

It is advised that once you run Disk Defragmenter, you must run Disk Cleanup after it.

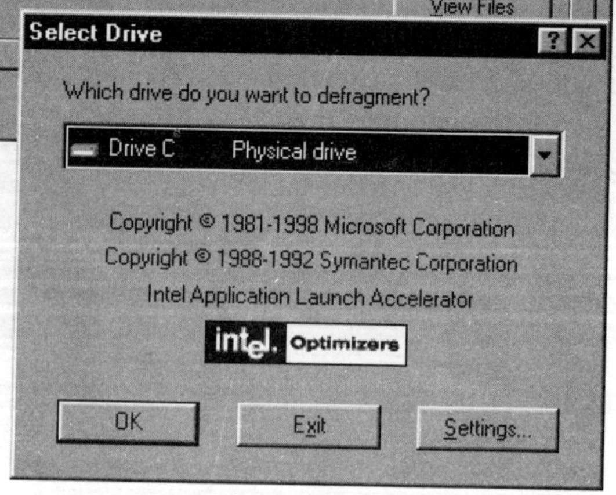

Multiple Choice Questions

1. Help menu is available at which button:
   (a) Taskbar (b) Start
   (b) End
2. Various applications and documents are represented on the Windows desktop by:
   (a) Symbols (b) Labels
   (c) Icons
3. Network Neighborhood is a permanent icon on the desktop:
   (a) True (b) False
4. Various programs can be accessed from the _______ button.
   (a) Start (b) End
   (c) Taskbar
5. How many recent documents are shown in the documents window:
   (a) 14 (b) 15
   (c) 16
6. For searching various files, folders, etc., on the hard disk, you use
   (a) Search (b) Find
   (c) Locate
7. You can also run applications from the _____ dialog box.
   (a) Start (b) End
   (c) Run
8. For accessing your networks you will use the icon
   (a) Recycle Bin (b) My Computer
   (c) Network Neighborhood
9. You keep your personal files/folders in
   (a) My Folder
   (b) My Documents
   (c) My Files
10. Title bar is part of
    (a) Taskbar
    (b) Windows dialog box
    (c) Desktop
11. Which accessory allows you to see the items in bigger size in Windows?
    (a) Mirror (b) Bigger
    (c) Magnifier
12. For setting up your modem to access for using Internet, you would use which accessory?
    (a) Dial up networking
    (b) Monitor (c) CDPlayer
13. Among the 2 types of calculators, one is standard and the other one is?
    (a) Ordinary (b) Scientific
    (c) Physical
14. Which accessory would you use to schedule your tasks?
    (a) Disk Cleanup
    (b) Disk Defragmenter
    (c) Task Scheduler

Descriptive Type Questions

1. How would you start Windows 98?
2. Describe the various items on the desktop of Windows 98.
3. What type of icons are there on the desktop?
4. What all is available on the Start button?
5. What all is there in My Computer?
6. What is Recycle Bin used for?
7. What is the significance of Network Neighborhood?
8. Describe the various features of Taskbar.
9. How would you change the features of Taskbar?
10. How can you run an application in Windows?

11. What do you understand by:
    Minimizing the Windows
    Maximizing the Windows
    Restoring the Windows
    Closing the Windows
12. What is the function of Windows Explorer?
13. How would you do the following using Windows Explorer?
    Rename a file
    Copy a file
    Create a folder
    Delete a file
    Move a file
14. Describe the various components of a Windows dialog box.
15. What is the purpose of Disk clean up?

14 Advanced Features of Windows

HARDWARE

In the versions Window XP onwards, Windows automatically detects the new hardware attached to the machine and asks for its installation, which can be done using the process given below:

Adding a new Hardware

The Add Hardware Wizard enables you to add new hardware or troubleshoot any hardware-related problems.

To open the Add Hardware Wizard

1. Click Start
2. Click Control Panel
3. Double-click Add Hardware.
4. Opens the Add Hardware Wizard, as shown here.

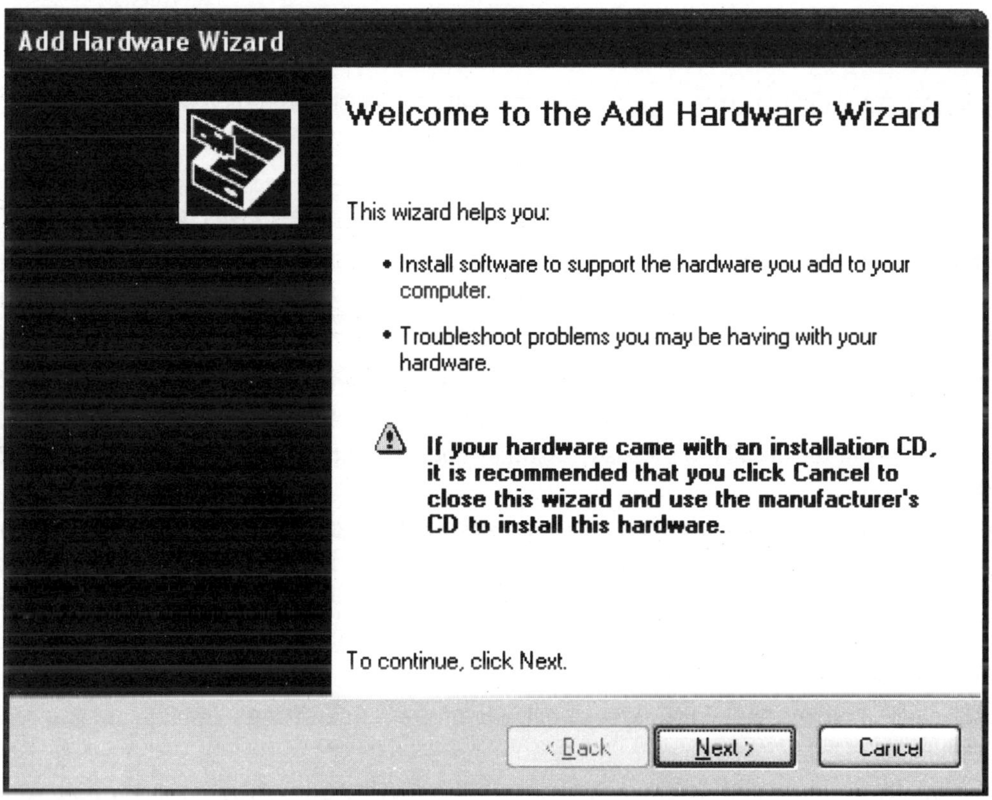

Adding a non-Plug and Play Device

You must be logged on as an administrator or a member of the Administrators group in order to complete this procedure. If your computer is connected to a network, network policy settings might also prevent you from completing this procedure.

1. Attach the non-Plug and Play device to your computer.
2. Open Add Hardware in Control Panel.
3. In the Add Hardware Wizard, click Next.
4. Click Add a new hardware device, and then click Next.
5. Do one of the following:
   - Click Search for and install the hardware automatically (Recommended) if you want Windows to try to detect the new non-Plug and Play device you want to install.
   - Click Install the hardware that I manually select from a list (Advanced) if you know the type and model of the device you are installing and you want to select it from a list of devices.
6. Click Next, and then follow the instructions on your screen.

Installing a non-Plug and Play device may require you to restart your computer. You may want to print this Help topic before restarting your computer, because you will not be able to open Help during startup.

To install a Smart Card Reader on a computer

Depending on the type of reader you have purchased, attach your reader to an available serial or USB port or insert the PC card reader into an available PCMCIA slot.

If you connected a serial port reader, restart the computer to detect it and then log on.

Do one of the following:

- If the device driver for the smart card reader is available as part of Windows XP, the installation of the driver takes place without any prompting by the user. This may take a few minutes.
- If the device driver for the smart card reader is not available as part of Windows XP, the Add Hardware Wizard starts. Follow the directions for installing the device driver software.

Important

- Smart card readers generally come with setup instructions from the manufacturer. If your reader comes with instructions, you should use those. If not, then use these general procedures.

You can confirm that the installation was successful by confirming that the reader appears in the Device Manager tree.

If the smart card reader is not installed automatically or the Add Hardware Wizard does not start automatically, then your smart card reader may not be compliant with Plug and Play specifications. You should contact the smart card reader manufacturer for the device driver and the instructions on how to install and configure the device.

To install an Unsupported Modem

You must be logged on as an administrator or a member of the Administrators group in order to complete this procedure.

If your computer is connected to a network, network policy settings might also prevent you from completing this procedure.

1. Open Phone and Modem Options in Control Panel.

2. If you are prompted for location information, specify the dialing information for your location, and then click OK.
3. On the Modems tab, click Add.
4. In the Install New Modem Wizard, select the Don't detect my modem; I will select it from a list check box, and then click Next.

Follow the remaining instructions provided by the Install New Modem Wizard.

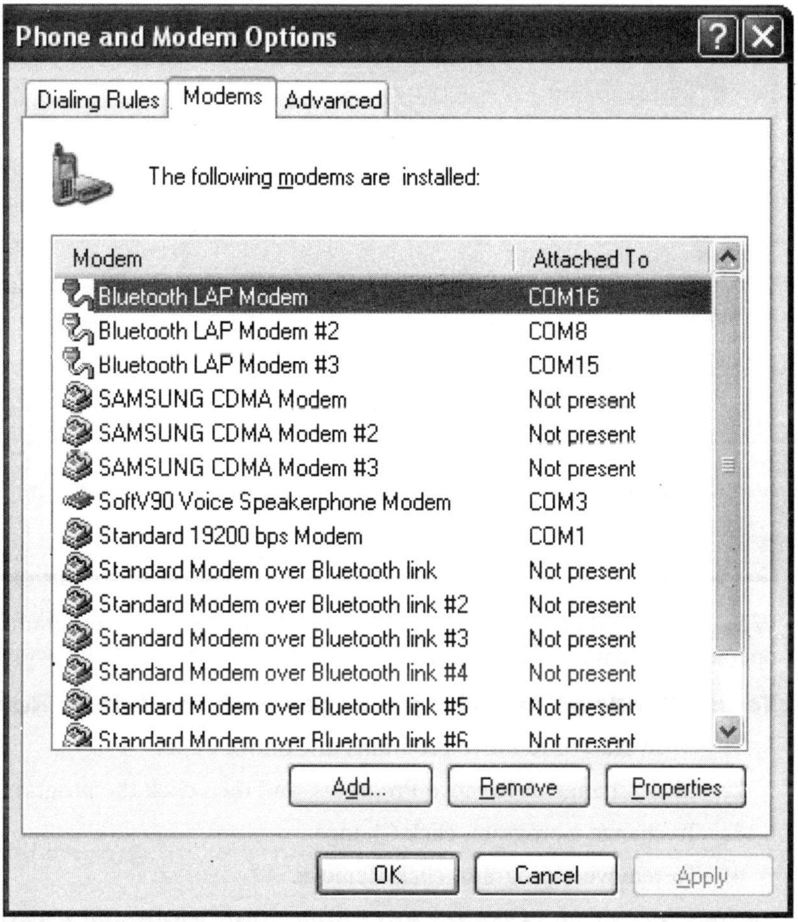

If possible, get the latest installation disk or modem inf file designed for Windows XP from the manufacturer. This can usually be downloaded from the manufacturer's Web pages. If Windows XP installation files are unavailable, you can try using an installation disk or .inf file for Windows 95, Windows 98, Windows NT, Windows 2000, or Windows Millennium Edition. It may work correctly in Windows XP as well.

If no installation file is available for the modem, the manufacturer's instructions that came with the modem may specify a compatible modem. Otherwise, click **(Standard Modem Types)** in **Manufacturers**, and try choosing the standard modem with the speed that matches your modem.

If a cable is not provided with an external modem, refer to the manufacturer's instructions for cable requirements.

Most, but not all, off-the-shelf cables will work. Some cables do not have all the pins connected. Do not use the 9-to-25 pin converters that come with most mouse hardware, because some of them do not carry modem signals.

SOFTWARE

To add a program from a CD or floppy disk

1. Open Add or Remove Programs in Control Panel.
2. Click Add New Programs, and then click CD or Floppy.
3. Follow the instructions on your screen.

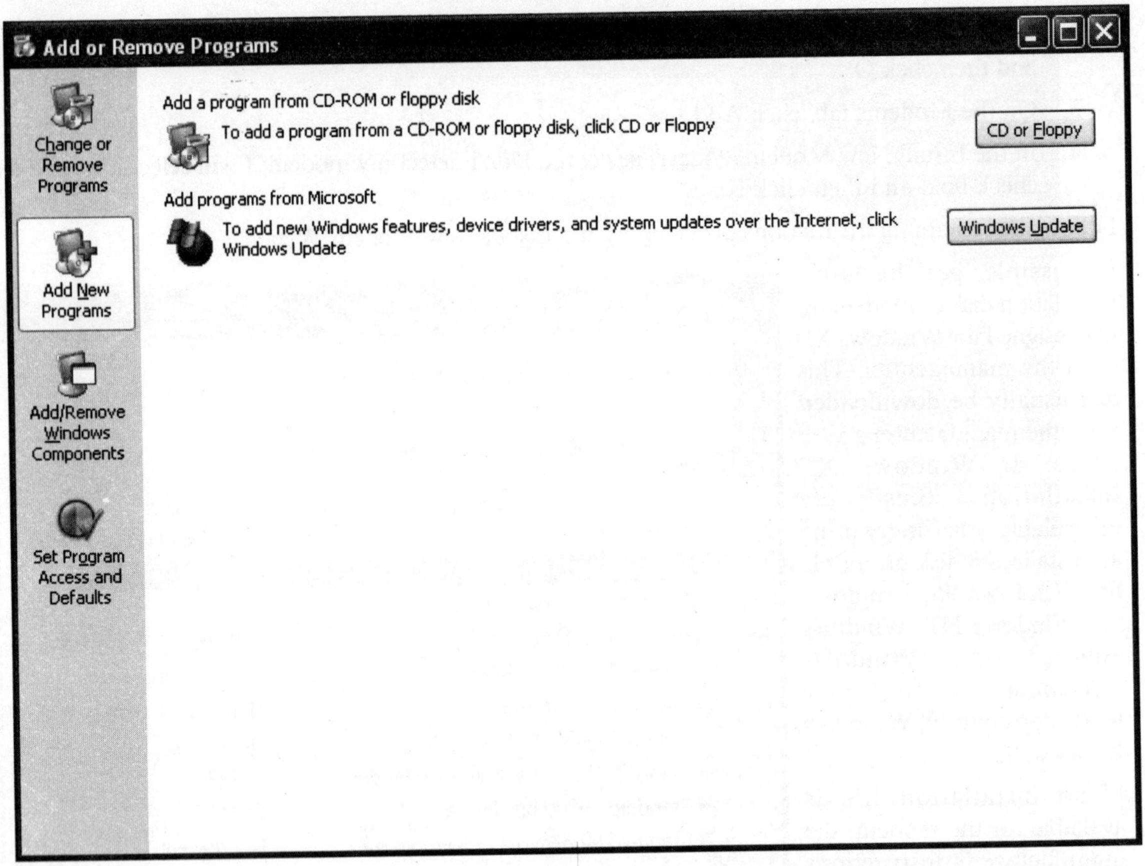

When using Add or Remove Programs, you can only install programs that were written for Windows operating systems.

To use Windows Installer packages with the Add or Remove Programs utility

1. Open Add or Remove Programs in Control Panel.
2. Click Change or Remove Programs, and then click the program you want to change or remove.
3. To change a program, click Change.
4. To remove a program, click Remove.

To use Windows Installer packages with Windows Explorer

1. Open Windows Explorer.
2. Right-click the Windows Installer package (.msi file), and then click Install, Repair, or Uninstall.

USING SCANNER

To install a Scanner or Digital Camera

1. Plug your camera or scanner into your computer.
2. If your camera is Plug and Play, the Scanner and Camera Wizard starts.

   -or-

   Double-click Add Device.

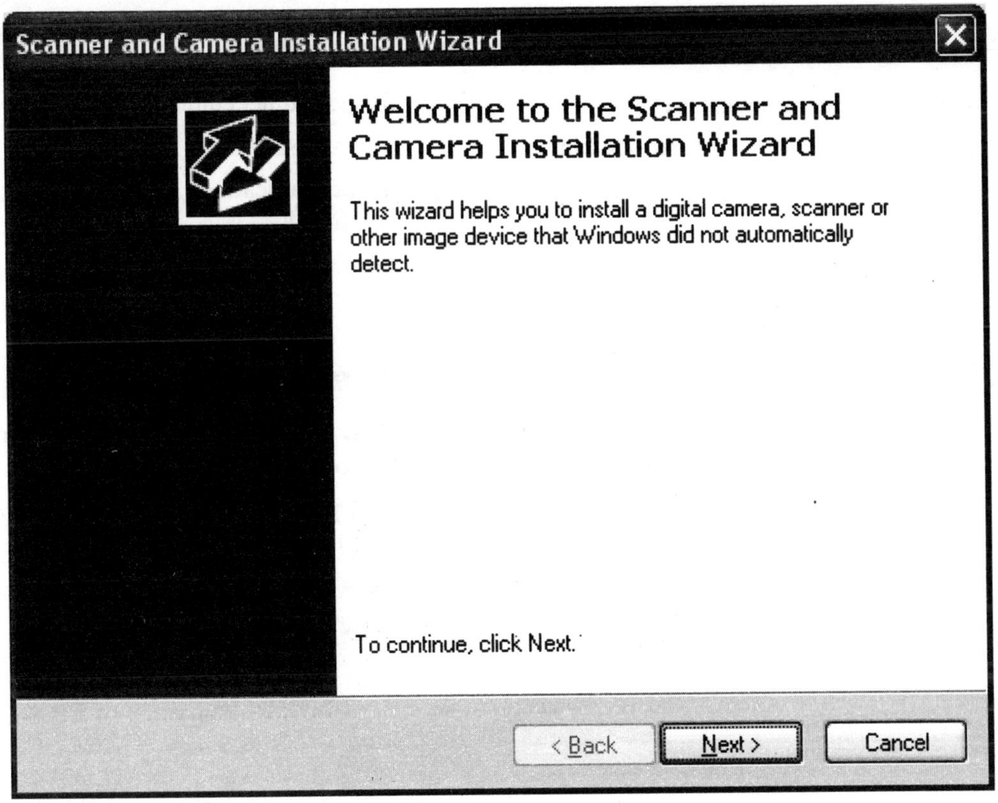

3. Follow the instructions on your screen.

Notes

- To open Scanners and Cameras, click Start, click Control Panel, and then double-click Scanners and Cameras.
- If you have a Plug and Play camera, Windows detects it and installs it automatically.
- If your camera or scanner is not Plug and Play, follow the installation instructions that came with the device.
- If your camera or scanner is not listed in the Scanner and Camera Installation Wizard, try to install it using Device Manager. For more information, click Related Topics.
- After you install your scanner or camera, you can test it. For more information, click Related Topics.

To test a scanner or digital camera

1. Right-click the scanner or camera you want to test, and then click Properties.
2. On the General tab, depending on which device you are testing, click Test Scanner or Test Camera.

Notes

- To open Scanners and Cameras, click Start, click Control Panel, and then double-click Scanners and Cameras.
- A message will tell you if the scanner or camera completed the test successfully.
- You must have a camera or scanner installed and connected to your computer to view properties.

Multiple Choice Questions

1. Add Hardware command is in:
   (a) control panel (b) recycle bin
   (c) desktop
2. Modem is the short form of:
   (a) modecule education
   (b) moduler emulation
   (c) most deman
3. To add a scanner you use scanners and command
   (a) printers (b) modems
   (c) cameras

Descriptive Type Questions

1. How would you add a new hardware?
2. How is a non-Plug and Play device added?
3. How would you add a Smart Card Reader?
4. How would you install an Unsupported Modem?
5. How would you add a new program from CD or Floppy Disk?
6. Can you use Windows Installer to Add or Remove Remove program?
7. How would you install scanner?
8. How would you test a scanner?

System Tools

15

SYSTEM TOOLS

This category of accessories are there to enhance the working of the computer with different tools which not only speed up the computer but also keeps the system clean of any unwanted elements.

Compression Agent

It works with DriveSpace3 to control and change the degree of compression used on your files. For example, you could improve performance on file save operations by telling DriveSpace to use No Compression. Then you can have Compression Agent compress these files when your computer is not in use.

Disk Cleanup

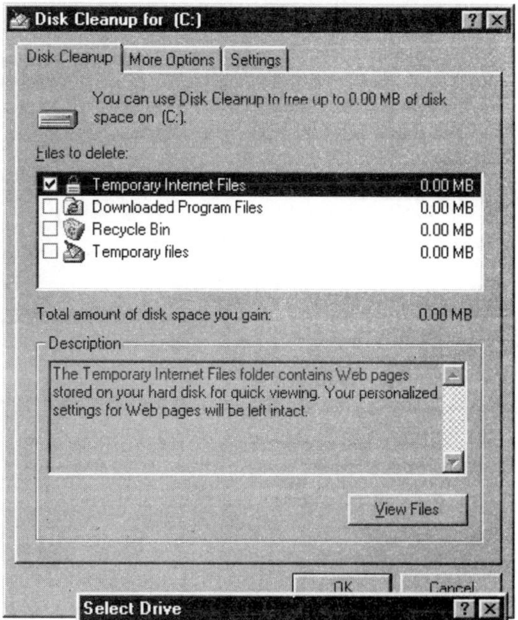

The Windows operating system creates a mass of temporary files and cached files—all designed to speed up the performance of the graphical interface.

These files do a pretty good job but, often do not get deleted when they should be. This results in a lot of files cluttered up on your hard drive. When you run Disk Cleanup, it checks for files that can be safely deleted and then presents a list of such files.

Disk Defragmenter

While writing files on a hard disk, Windows keeps the files at random and keeps track of its position using FAT. This results in having the files placed in hard disk, quite staggered.

This command, which was there even in DOS, does the job of housekeeping and puts the files on one side and the blank space in the hard disk on the other side. This results in speeding up the activity of the hard disk.

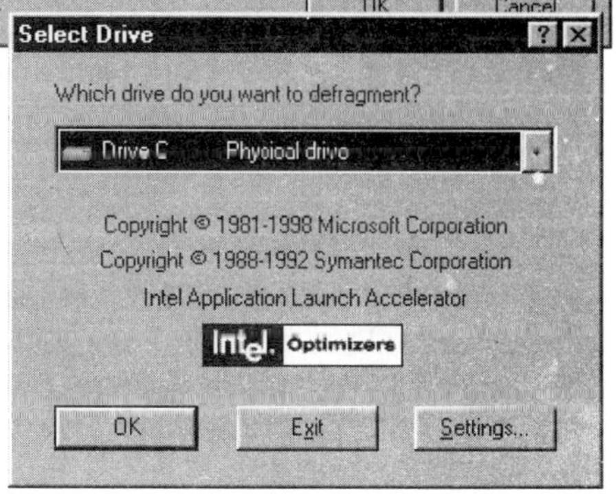

It is advised that once you run Disk Defragmenter, you must run Disk Cleanup after it.

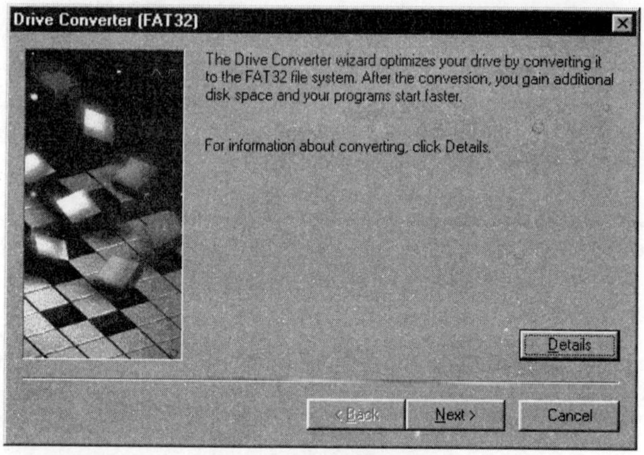

Drive Converter (FAT32)

Once you run this your hard disk will be converted to FAT 32 file system.

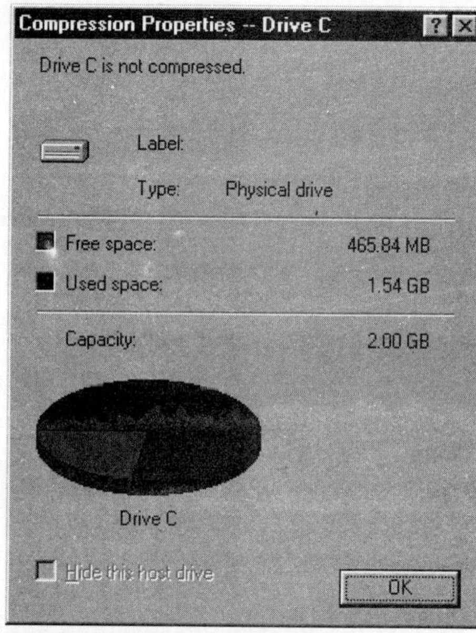

Drive Space

If at any stage of time you want to see how much of the space of the hard disk is used up, you can see by using this command.

This also shows you the free space available on the hard disk.

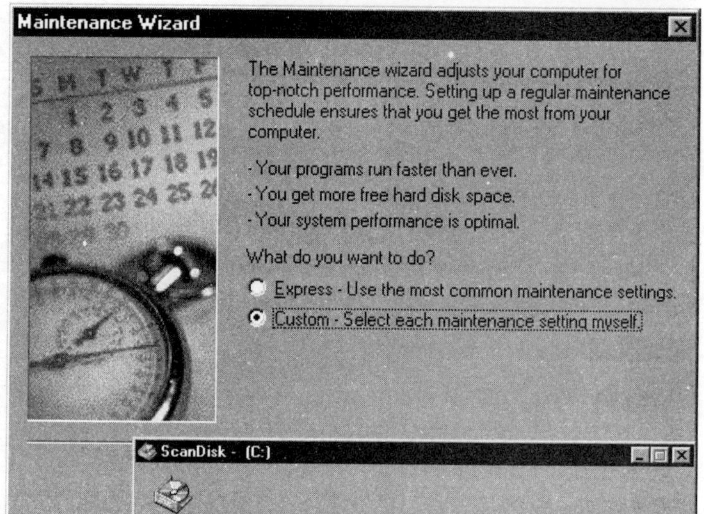

Maintenance Wizard

For maintaining your hard, you need to run Scan Disk, Disk Defragmenter and Disk Cleanup at regular intervals. But, how many times would you run it. You will always forget to use one program or the other or may not use them at all. So, Windows has a solution for the same.

Through this maintenance wizard you can set a time for doing the same. It will automatically run all the 3 programs for you.

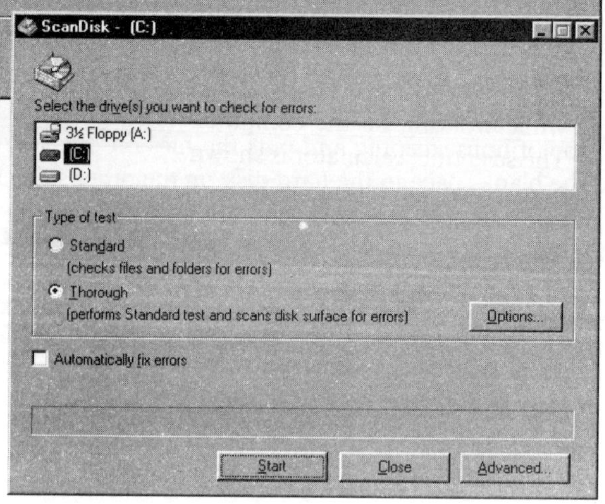

Scan Disk

As mentioned above in maintenance wizard, this command alongwith the other commands is used to keep the utilization of hard disk to the optimum. You can even choose to fix the errors automatically.

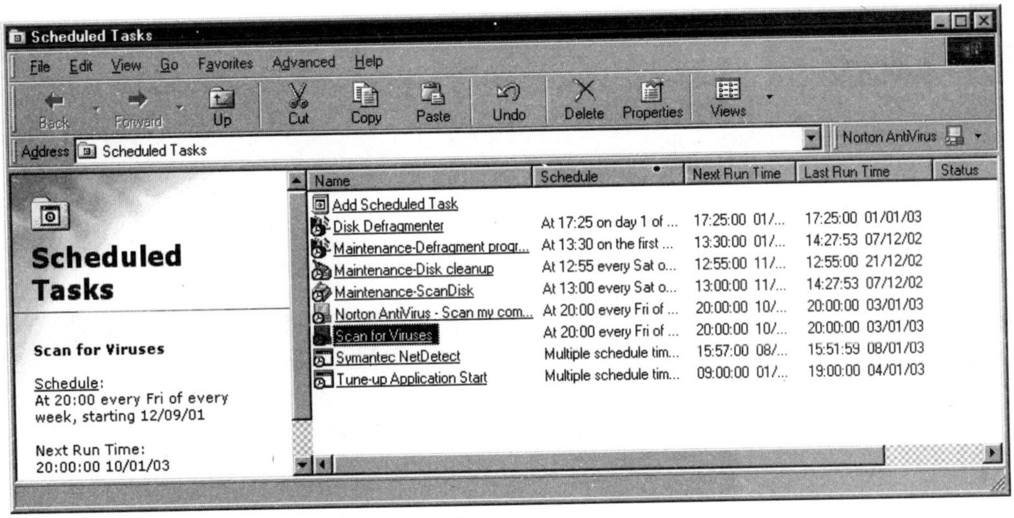

Scheduled Tasks

As in the case of maintenance wizard, you have to define a time when you have to run it. Similarly, you can have other programs also scheduled to be run at particular times. This command will tell what all is lined up.

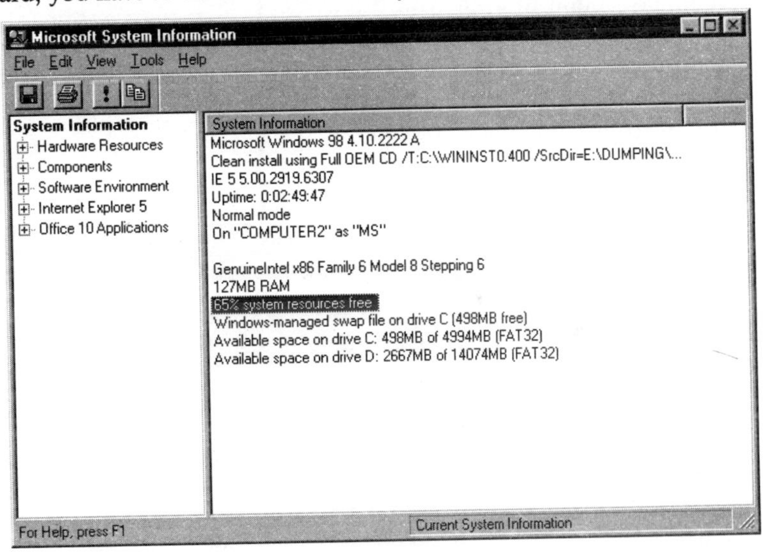

System Information

This command is mainly used by the people who are supposed to correct your computer. It gives the specific information about your computer when he is troubleshooting your configuration. It quickly finds the data that is needed to resolve your system problem.

while working on the computer. The scientific calculator is shown here.

Multiple Choice Questions

1. Compression agent is used to compress:
   (a) Hard disk (b) Printers
   (c) CD ROM

2. Disk clean up would clean
   (a) CD ROM (b) Hard disk
   (c) Printer

Descriptive Type Questions

1. Describe the various system tools?

16 Communication

Introduction

Following form the part of the Communication of the Windows Accessories.

Hyper Terminal

You can use HyperTerminal to send and receive files, or to connect to computer bulletin boards and other information programs. You can also use HyperTerminal and a modem to connect to a remote computer, even if the remote computer is not running Windows.

Internet Connection Wizard

Definitely bound to a hit with the users, specially who are planning to have their internet connection set up. This wizard will guide you through the complete setup and have the connection made for you.

NetMeeting

This option allows you to communicate with others over the Internet or your local intranet. Using this you can Talk to others; Use video to see others and let others see you; Share applications and documents with others; Collaborate with others in shared applications; Send files to others; Draw with others in a shared whiteboard and Send messages to others in chat.

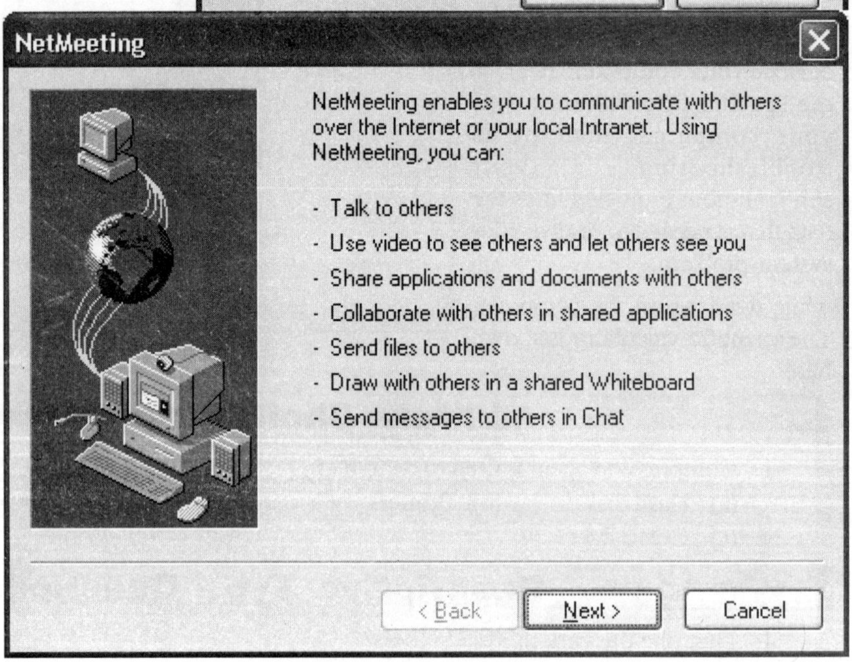

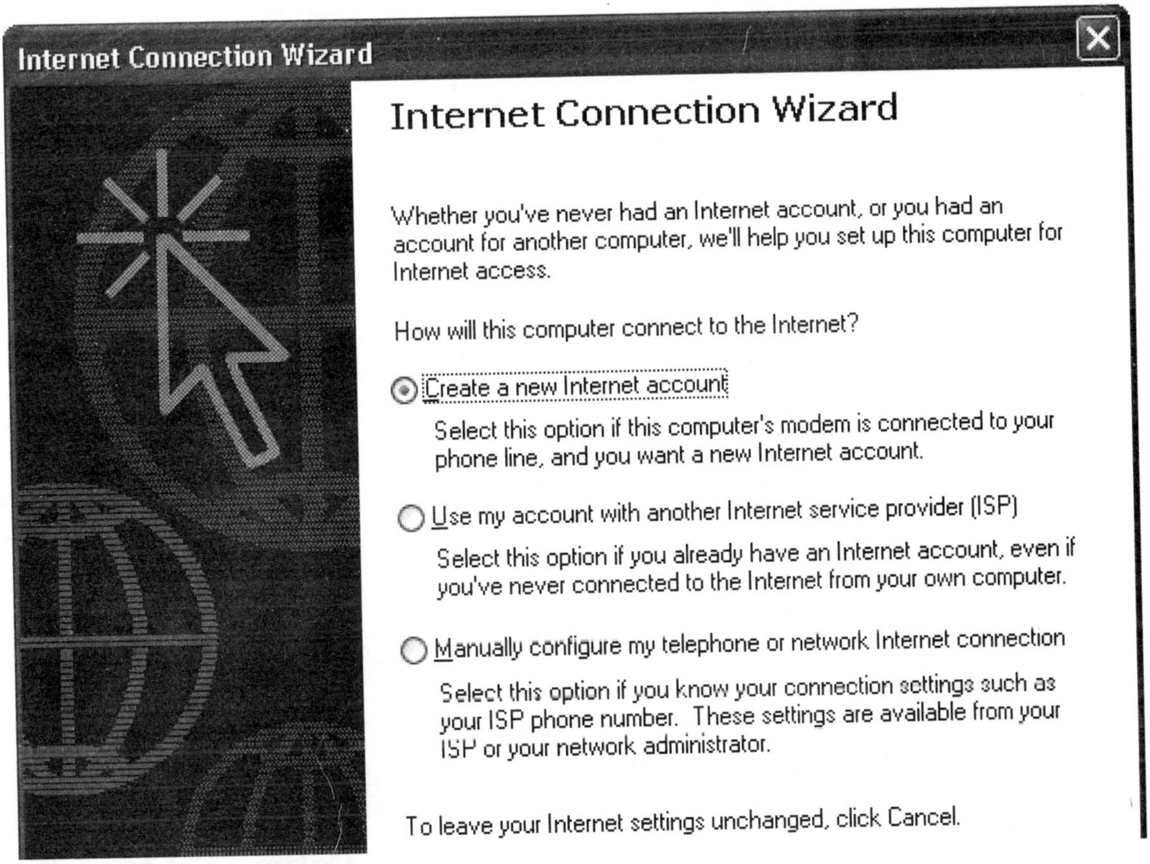

Network Connections

This command shows you the type of networking connections your computer has.

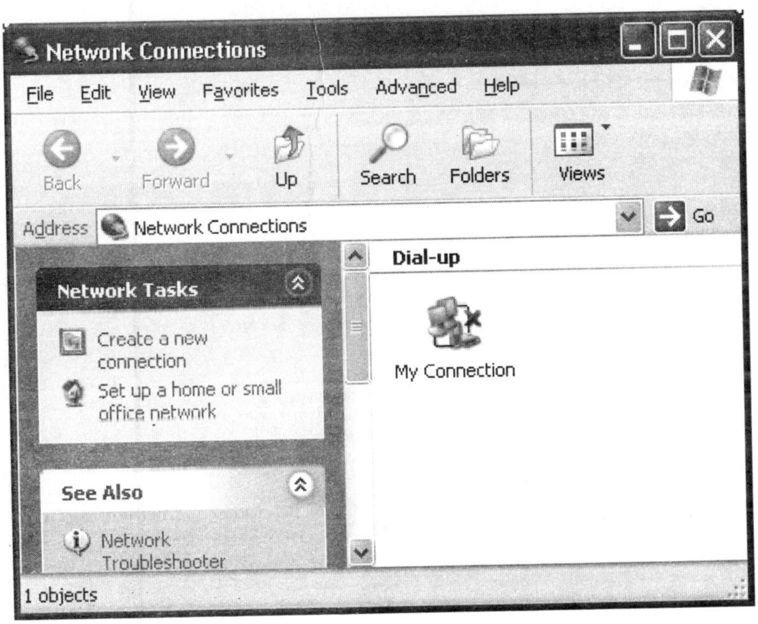

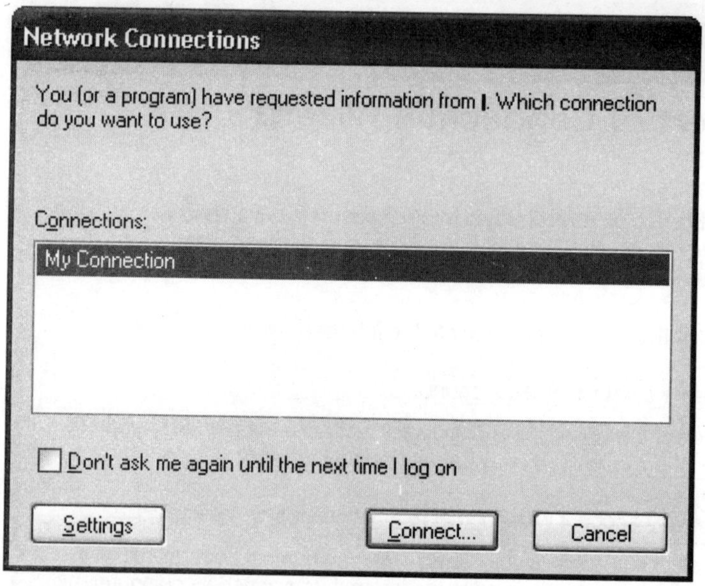

Network Connection Wizard

Like Internet Connection Wizard, this wizard will guide you through various aspects of setting up networking on your own.

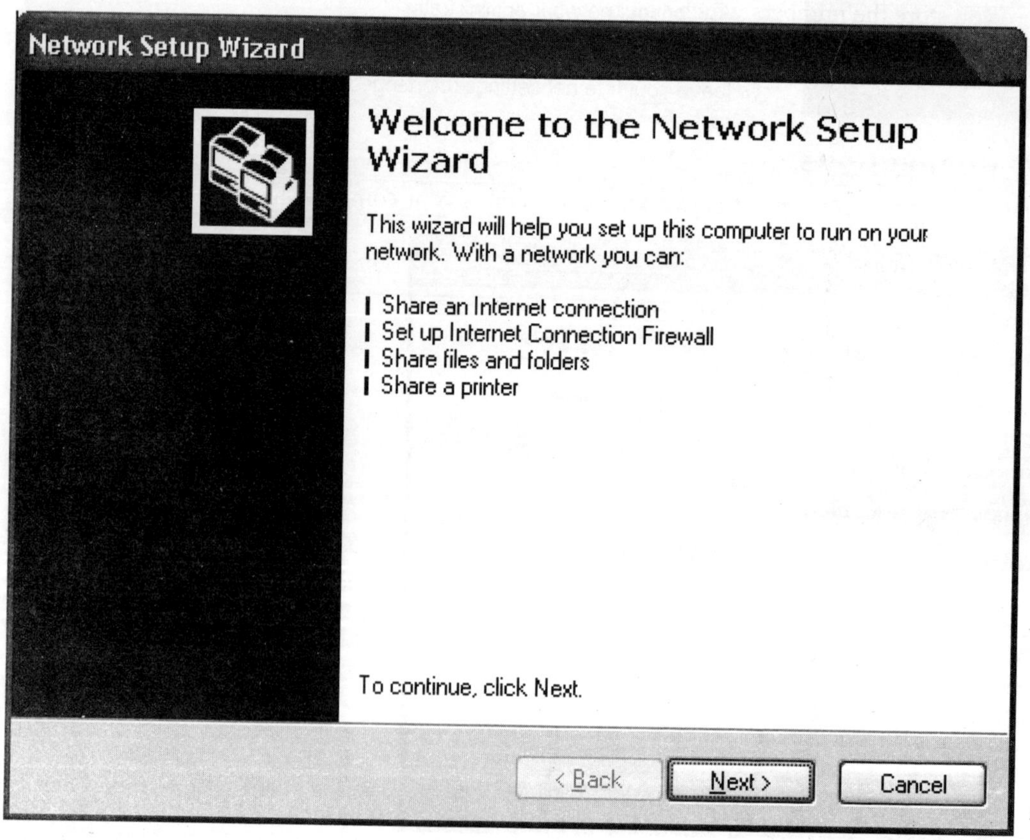

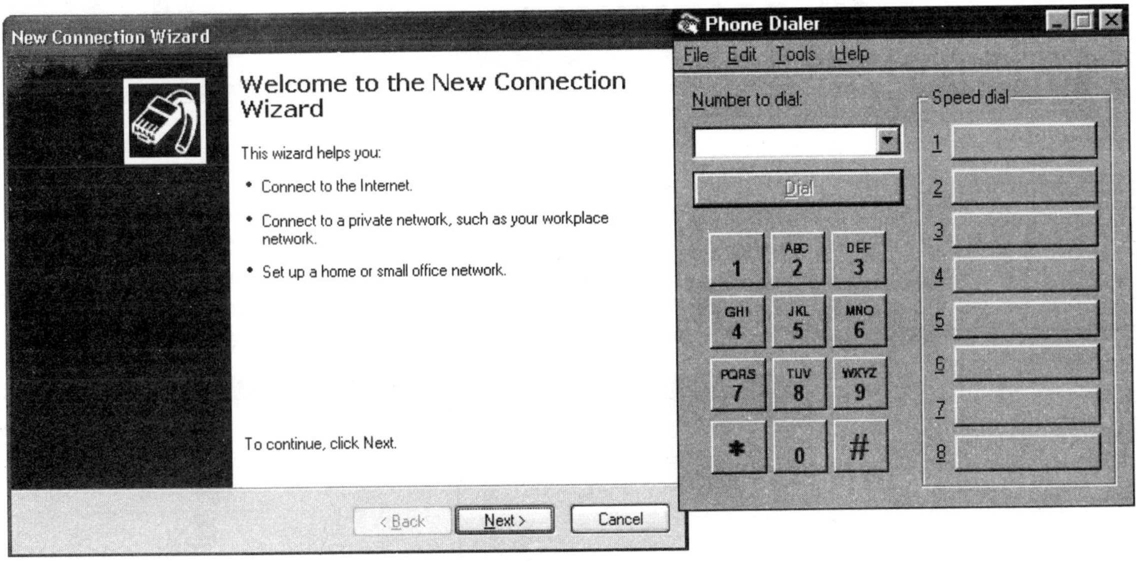

New Connection Wizard

Another wizard which will guide you to set your internet or networking connection.

Phone Dialer

As you must have seen on various phones, various numbers are stored in the phone for speed dialling. Similarly here you store the numbers which you have to dial occasionally, so that they can be dialled by just pressing a single digit number.

Multiple Choice Questions

1. Communication is part of Windows _____:
   (a) Accessories (b) Control Panel
   (c) Recycle Bin
2. For dialing from the computer you use:
   (a) Calculator (b) Phone Dialer
   (c) Dialer

Descriptive Type Questions

1. What does Hyper Terminal do?
2. Describe the various screens of Internet Connection Wizard.
3. What purpose does NetMeeting have?
4. What does Network Connections do?
5. Describe the various screens of Network Connection Wizard.
6. Describe the various screens of New Connection Wizard.
7. What does Phone Dialer do?

Multiple Users Features of Windows

17

ACCESSIBILITY

The Accessibility Wizard guides you through the process of customizing your computer with tools designed to help meet your vision, hearing, or mobility needs. Accessibility options (such as StickyKeys, ShowSounds, and Mousekeys) help users with disabilities to make full use of the computer. Some of the options, such as MouseKeys, may be of interest to all users. Once the Accessibility tools are set up, they can be accessed through Control Panel and the Accessibility menu.

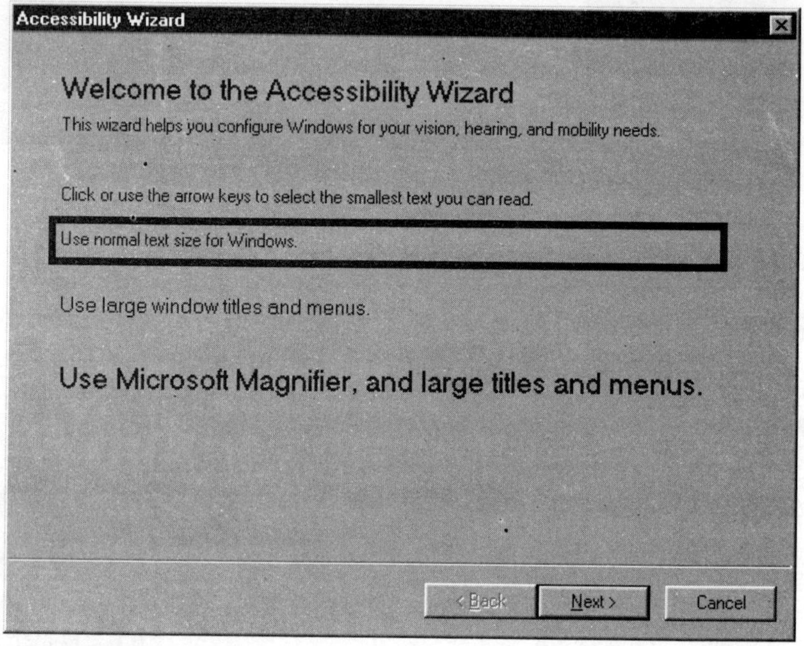

- To open the Accessibility Wizard, click Start, point to All Programs, point to Accessories, point to Accessibility, and then click Accessibility Wizard.
- The accessibility tools that ship with Windows are intended to provide a minimum level of functionality for users with special needs. Most users with disabilities will need utility programs with more advanced functionality for daily use.

SHARING INFORMATION BETWEEN PROGRAMS

Sharing Files and Folders

You can share the files and folders stored on your computer, on a network, and on the Web. The method you choose depends on whom you want to share files with, and what computer they will use to access the files.

When you share files or folders, they are not as protected as they are when you do not share them. People with access to your computer or your network might be able to read, copy, or change files that are in a shared folder. You should always be aware that the files and folders that you share are available to other people and be sure to monitor your shared files and folders on a regular basis.

- If your computer is not joined to a domain, you can use the Network Setup Wizard to automatically turn file and printer sharing on or off. To start the Network Setup Wizard, click Start, click Control Panel, and then double-click Network Setup Wizard.

If you both use the same computer

You can put the files you want to share in the Shared Documents folder. Files stored in the Shared Documents folder or its subfolders are always available to other users on your computer.

To share files and folders on your computer

Moving or copying a file or folder to Shared Documents makes it available to anyone who has a user account on your computer.

1. Open My Documents.
2. Click the file or folder that you want to share.
3. Drag the file or folder to Shared Documents in Other Places.

Notes

- To open My Documents, click Start, and then click My Documents.
- If you are connected to a network ·domain, the Shared Documents, Shared Pictures, and Shared Music folders are not available.
- If the file or folder you want to share is not located in My Documents or one of its subfolders, use Search to find it. To open Search, click Start, and then click Search.

If both computers are on the same network

You can share a folder or drive on your computer with others on the network. You can also control whether the files in the shared folder can be modified by other users.

If your computer is connected to a network domain, use this procedure:

Using Shared Folders

1. Open Computer Management (Local).
2. In the console tree, click Shares.
3. Where?
   - Computer Management
   - System Tools
   - Shared Folders
   - Shares
4. On the Action menu, click New File Share.
5. Follow the steps in Create Shared Folder.

You will be prompted to select a folder or drive, type a new share name and description of the shared resource, and set permissions. After you provide this information, click Finish.

Using Windows Explorer

1. Open Windows Explorer, and then locate the shared folder or drive to which you want to add a new share name.
2. If you are logged on to a domain, do the following:
3. Right-click the shared folder or drive, and then click Sharing and Security.
4. Click Share this folder.
5. Set any other options that you want, and then click OK.

If you are not logged on to a domain or if you are running Windows XP Home Edition, do the following:

1. Right-click the shared folder or drive, and then click Properties.
2. On the Sharing tab, click Share this folder on the network.
3. Set any other options that you want, and then click OK.

Using a command line

1. Open Command Prompt.
2. Type:

net share sharename=drive:path

Value	Description
net share	Creates, deletes, or displays shared resources.
sharename=drive:path	The network name of the shared resource and the absolute path of its location.

If your computer is connected to a workgroup

To share a drive or folder on the network

1. Open Windows Explorer, and then locate the drive or folder you want to share.
2. Right-click the drive or folder, and then click Sharing and Security.
   - If you are sharing a drive, on the Sharing tab, click If you understand the risk but still want to share the root of the drive, click here.
   - If you are sharing a folder, go to the next step.
3. Do one of the following:
   - If the Share this folder on the network check box is available, select the check box.
   - If the Share this folder on the network check box is not available, this computer is not on a network. If you would like to set up a home or small office network, click the Network Setup Wizard link and follow the instructions to turn on file sharing. Once file sharing is enabled, begin this procedure again.

Remember

- To open Windows Explorer, click Start, point to All Programs, point to Accessories, and then click Windows Explorer.
- When you share a drive or folder, anyone who has user access to the network can read the contents of that drive or folder. If you want to remove the drive or folder from the network, follow steps 1 and 2 above to get to the Sharing tab. On the Sharing tab, in Network sharing and security, clear the Share this folder on the network check box.
- To allow complete access to the contents of your shared drive or folder, follow steps 1 and 2 above to get to the Sharing tab. On the Sharing tab, in Network sharing and security, select the Allow network users to change my files check box.
- To change the name of your folder on the network, in the Share name text box, type a new name for your folder. This will not change the name of the folder on your computer.
- If you are logged on as a guest (a guest account provides access to the computer for any user who does not have a user account on the computer), you cannot create a shared folder.

- The Sharing option is not available for the Documents and Settings, Program Files, and WINDOWS system folders. In addition, you cannot share folders in other user's profiles.

If you want to share your files online

You can publish pictures and documents on the Web using the Web Publishing Wizard. The files will be stored in a private, online folder that you manage.

To publish a file or folder to the Web

1. Open My Computer.
2. Double-click a drive or folder.
3. Click the file or folder you want to publish to the Web.
4. Under File and Folder Tasks:

   click Publish this folder to the Web

   -or-

   click Publish this file to the Web.
5. Follow the instructions in the Web Publishing Wizard.

If you don't want others to access your files

You can prevent other users from accessing your folders and the files they contain. When your computer is connected to a domain, this is called setting permissions for your file or folder. When your computer is connected to a workgroup, this is called making your folders private.

If your computer is connected to a network domain, use this procedure:

To set, view, change, or remove file and folder permissions

1. Open Windows Explorer, and then locate the file or folder for which you want to set permissions.
2. Right-click the file or folder, click Properties, and then click the Security tab.
3. Do one of the following:
   - To set permissions for a group or user that does not appear in the Group or user names box, click Add. Type the name of the group or user you want to set permissions for and then click OK.
   - To change or remove permissions from an existing group or user, click the name of the group or user.
4. Do one of the following:
   - To allow or deny a permission, in the Permissions for User or Group box, select the Allow or Deny check box.
   - To remove the group or user from the Group or user names box, click Remove.

If your computer is connected to a workgroup, use this procedure:

To make your folders private

1. Open My Computer.
2. Double-click the drive where Windows is installed (usually drive (C:), unless you have more than one drive on your computer).
3. If the contents of the drive are hidden, under System Tasks, click Show the contents of this drive.
4. Double-click the Documents and Settings folder.

5. Double-click your user folder.
6. Right-click any folder in your user profile, and then click Properties.
7. On the Sharing tab, select the Make this folder private so that only I have access to it check box.

UNDERSTANDING OLE

Object Embedding/Linking is a way to transfer and share information between applications by pasting information created in one application into a document created in another application, such as a spreadsheet or word processing file.

Information created in another program that has been pasted inside your document. When information is embedded, you can edit the information in the new document using toolbars and menus from the original program.

To edit the embedded information, double-click it and the toolbars and menus from the program used to create the information appear. Embedded information is not linked to the original source. If you change information in one place, it is not updated in the other.

EMBEDDING/LINKING USING CUT AND PASTE

To embed information in another document using Cut and Paste.

1. Select the information you want to embed in another document.
2. On the Edit menu, click Copy.
3. Click the location in the document where you want to insert the information.
4. On the Edit menu, click Paste Special, and then click OK.

Remember

- In Paste Special, select the option that will allow you to edit the embedded information with the toolbars and menus you need. For example, if you embed an Excel worksheet into a Word document, in Paste Special, select Microsoft Excel Worksheet Object.
- Not all programs support embedding. If embedding isn't supported, your information will be copied to the document, but you will not be able to edit it using the toolbars and menus from the original program.
- You can embed information in documents that were created in different programs.
- If you want the embedded information to be updated when it is changed in the original document, you may be able to link the information instead of embedding it.

EMBED/LINK USING INSERT OBJECT

1. Select the information or object you want to link to another document.
2. On the Edit menu, click Copy.
3. Click the location in the document where you want to place the linked object.
4. On the Edit menu, click Paste Special.
5. Click Paste Link, and then click OK.

Remember

- Some programs do not support linking. If linking isn't available, Paste Special will not be available on the Edit menu.

- You can link information between documents that were created in different programs.

MANAGE EMBEDED/LINKED OBJECT

Cutting information from one document and pasting it into another is a good way of reusing information. When you paste information into a document, the information that you paste becomes part of the second document. If you make changes to the information in the original document, those changes will not be reflected in the second document. For Windows-based programs that support drag-and-drop functions, you can use linking or embedding to transfer information from one document to another document, even if that document is in a different program.

Linking means inserting information that retains a connection to the information stored in the original file. Linking keeps the inserted information up to date by refreshing it when there is a change to the original document.

Embedding means inserting information (such as text or a graphic) into a document in a different program. The embedded information, or object, becomes part of the new document. Changes you make to the original document will not be reflected in the new document. To edit an embedded object, double-click it; the program in which the object was created opens. In order to edit an embedded object, the program in which the object was created (or another program capable of editing the object) must be installed on your computer. When you finish editing the object and return to your document, the document reflects all of the changes you've made.

Use linking when you want the information to be updated dynamically as the data in the source file changes. Use embedding when you want to edit the information separately from the source file or if you think the source file will not be available.

Multiple Choice Questions

1. You can share files and _____ in windows.
   (a) Folders (b) Program
   (c) Both
2. OLE is:
   (a) object line embeded
   (b) object linking embeded
   (c) over linking embeded

Descriptive Type Questions

1. What does Accessibility Wizard do?
2. How would you share the information between files and folders?
3. What is OLE?
4. How would you embed/link an object using Cut and Paste?
5. How would you embed/link an object using Insert Object?
6. How would you manage an embedded/linked object?

18 Linux Operating System

INTRODUCTION

Bill Gates is no doubt the richest man in the World. He made his money by selling commercial software, specially operating software like MS-DOS and Windows. Compare this with the Linux which is nothing short of a phenomenon. It is an operating software which has no financial strings attached to it. It can be just downloaded freely from the net. Imagine if the producers of this software too would have insisted on selling it commercially they would have been in league with Bill Gates. But, they choose not to do so.

It is not that since Linux is available cheaply it would be cheap in performance too. In fact, it lacks no punch as far as its competitors in operating system from Microsoft, Apple, Novell and IBM. It is also handling more demanding applications, it is also a serious contender against rival Unix-derivative operating systems such as Solaris, HP-UX and SCO-Unix for larger businesses.

HISTORY OF LINUX

Linux was created as an offshoot of Unix. It has more similarities to UNIX than to any other operating systems. As an operating system, Unix continues to be widely used in commercial environment, as well as in the educational world, although it is also often found running on today's client-server intranet networks too. While versions of Unix have long been available for PCs, they never had the grace or power of the operating systems available for minicomputers, mainframes and today's servers.

In addition, the early commercial versions of Unix were costly, sometimes costing more than the PC hardware they were destined to run on. This lack of accessibility ultimately gave birth to Linux as a means to make a Unix-like operating system available on a widespread basis. Richard Stallmand and the Free Software Foundation (FSF) began work on this alternative operative system in the mid-1980s. By the end of that decade, they had developed functional alternatives to every major Unix component except the kernel. Linux Torvalds at the University of Helsinki in Finland developed the original Linux kernel in 1991.

The combined work became the Linux as you know today. Torvalds originally intended to develop Linux as a hobby. Early versions of Linux didn't have consumers in mind; instead, they provided the barest bones of functionality to allow Unix programmers the apparent joy or programming the kernel. As the core of the operating system, the kernel keeps everything running smoothly – without a stale, powerful kernel, you don't have an operating system. But as programmers integrated the work of the FSF with the Torvalds kernel, the base software for a complete operating system emerged. It became clear to those involved that Linux was evolving the state where it could respectably be called an operating system.

In March 1992, version 1.0 of the kernel came into being, marking the first official release of Linux. At this point, Linux ran most of the common Unix tools from compilers to networking software to X Windows. Linux continues to evolve as the pre-eminent Unix-clone operating system for PCs. Hardware support is now broad, including the most popular and common peripherals; performance is strong, giving many PCs power comparable to that of mind range workstations such as Sun Microsystems' SPARC systems.

Linux is even now ported to the PowerPC and Compaq Alpha platforms, among others. Although technically today's Linux is not Unix because it fails it fails to quality for the brand name, Linux is functionally equivalent to Unix in almost every important way.

LINUX AS AN OPERATING SYSTEM

Linux is used in two ways: specifically to refer to the kernel itself-the heart of any version of Linux-and more generally to refer to any collection that run on the kernel, usually referred to as a distribution. The kernel's job is to provide the basic environment in which applications can run, including the basic interfaces with hardware and the systems for managing tasks and currently running programs. In the specific sense, there is only one current version of Linux at any one time the current revision of the kernel. Torvalds keeps the kernel as the domain in the world of Linux development, leaving all the applications and services that sit on top of the kernel to any of the thousands of other Linux developers in the world.

In the general meaning of the term Linux, referring to cohesive collections of applications that run on top of the Linux kernel, there are numerous versions of Linux. Each distribution has its own unique characteristics, including different installation methods, different collections of features and different upgrade paths. But since all distributions are fundamentally Linux, in almost every case an application that works with a current version of one distribution will work with a current version of another distribution. The interesting thing about this dichotomous use of the term "Linux" is that it exactly parallels the same confused usage of the term "operating system".

For consumers, an operating system has come to mean a large collection of applications centered around a kernel. This is what Windows 95, 98, Me, NT and 2000 are. This is what the Macintosh OS is. In a purist, technical sense, an operating system is a much smaller core kernel that provides those basic system functions needed to develop any application. In both ways, Linux is an operating system. One of the features of the Linux kernel that sets it apart from other consumer operating systems designed to run on desktop PCs is that it is both multitasking and multiuser.

A MULTITASKING OPERATING SYSTEM

You are probably familiar with the term multitasking, even if you are not really sure what it means. When desktop computing graduated from Windows 3.1 to Windows 95, the multitasking capabilities of the then-new Windows 95 were among its biggest claims to fame. To say that a system can multitask is to say that it can appear to be running more than one application, or process, at a time. For example, the system can print a document, copy a file and dial into the Internet while the user is comfortably typing in a word processing program.

Even with these background tasks happening, the foreground word processor should not freeze up or be unusable. This is the wonder of multitasking: It allows a computer with a single processor to appear to be performing multiple tasks simultaneously. Of course, a single CPU an execute only a single instruction at a time – that is, only one action can be taking place at any one time. Multitasking creates the appearances of simultaneous activity by switching rapidly between tasks as the demands of those processes dictate. When multitasking words well, a user running a word processor while several other things happen will not be aware of the extra work the computer is doing.

All processes will seem to be running smoothly and the computer will be responsive. Historically, Unix systems have been much better than Windows at multitasking; Unix is able to run large numbers of simultaneous applications in a way that made it an ideal fit for large corporate servers and high-powered work stations.

Today, only Windows 2000 and its predecessor Widows NT 4.0 can really claim to offer a similar robust multitasking implementation. Even Windows 95/98/Me, despite all of this fanfare, has trouble effectively handling large numbers of simultaneous processes. To take thing further, Linux, like Windows NT and Windows 2000, offers support for computer with multiple processors, such as dual-Pentium III systems.

These systems can in fact perform two actions at exactly the same time. Combining multitasking with multiple processors greatly increase the number of simultaneous applications a computer can run smoothly.

A MULTIUSER OPERATING SYSTEM

Even more important than being a multitasking operating system, Linux-like all versions of Unix and Unix clones – is a multiuser operating system. All consumer versions of Windows and the Mac OS are single-user systems. In other words, only one user can be logged in and running applications at any one time in these operating systems. By comparison, Linux allows multiple simultaneous users, fully leveraging the multitasking capabilities of the operating system. The great advantage of this is that Linux can be developed as an applications server. From their desktop computers or terminals, users can log into a Linux server across a LAN and actually run applications on the server instead of on their desktop PCs.

LINUX APPLICATIONS

As an operating system, Linux can be used to develop almost any type of application. Among the applications available for Linux are the following:

Text and Word Processing Applications

In addition to commercial word processing software such as WordPerfect, StarOffice and Applixware, Linux offers powerful tools for editing text files and processing text in an automated fashion.

Programming Languages

A wide variety of programming and scripting languages and tools are available for Linux and all Unix operating systems. This abundance of programming tools makes it easy to develop new applications that can run not only on Linux but also on most Unix and Unix-like operating systems.

X Windows

X Windows is Unix's answer to the graphical user interface (GUI). X Windows is a highly flexible and configurable GUI environment that runs on Linux as well as on most Unix systems. Numerous applications that run in X Windows help to make Linux an easy-to-use operating system.

Internal tools

In addition to supporting well-known software such as Netscape and Mosaic, Linux provides a wide range of Internet software, including character-based and graphical mail-reading applications, the full range of software needed to create Internet serves (Web servers, mail servers and news servers), plus complete network support to connect to the Internet via a local network or modem.

Databases

Like all Unix platforms, Linux provides a robust platform for running client-server database applications. From its earliest days, powerful, free databases such as mSQL and PostgreSQL have been available for

Linux. As Linux has grown in popularity, especially in corporate information systems, the number of commercial relational database servers for Linux has grown. Today, Oracle, Sybase and Informix all offer relational database products for Linux.

DOS and Windows compatibility software

Linux can be made to run DOS software with a high degree of stability and compatibility and offers several approaches to running Windows software. In fact, the entire text of this book was written using Microsoft Word for Windows on a computer running Linux. This provides strong evidence of Linux's ability to work well in a Windows environment. In addition, emulators are available for other popular computer systems, including the Macintosh and Atari ST computer lines.

LINUX AS FREE SOFTWARE

Given all the capabilities promised by Linux, you might think that the operating system is expensive. On the contrary, the Linux kernel and most of the applications written for Linux are available for free on the Internet, often with no restriction on the copying and redistribution of the software. To begin with, the Linux kernel is distributed under the GNU General Public License (GPL). This special software licence, developed by Stallman's Free Software Foundation, promotes the open distribution and more importantly open development of software.

Unlike the software licenses common with most commercial software, the GNU license allows anyone to redistribute software, even for a fee, so long as in the redistribution, the terms of the GNU license are still in force. In other words, anyone can take GNU software, alter it if they wish and redistribute it, but they can't stop someone who buys GNU-licensed software from them from turning around and redistribution it again. Most of Linux is available under the GNU General Public License.

This makes it possible for many different vendors to produce both free and commercially available Linux distributions. This approach to free software is not the same as public domain software. With GNU products, the software developers retain the copyright to the software and may choose in the future to stop distributing that software under the GNU license. What is special about the GNU license is that it encourages iterative development of applications by many people, each making changes that they consider important or necessary and then redistributing the software. This process is enabled by the fact that all GNU-licensed software must be distributed with its complete source code.

Unlike commercial software, where the original code is unavailable and hence unalterable, GNU software not only makes it possible to alter and customize software but actually encourages interested and capable users to do so. In fact, this model has been so successful in the development of Linux and applications for Linux that Netscape has adopted it for its Web browser product lines. Using basic BNU principles, Netscape makes its Web browser freely available and allows anyone to license the source code for its Web browser or to redistribute them.

COMMERCIAL APPLICATIONS FOR LINUX

There are commercial applications for Linux as well as commercial distributions of Linux. In these cases, most products are licensed under terms more restrictive than the GNU standards of the Linux world.

But even if a distribution of Linux includes commercial components that cannot be redistributed freely, this doesn't change the underlying GNU license that applies to the Linux kernel and those core applications found in all Linux distributions. If the original license of an application in the GNU General Public License, then the license of the redistributed copy of the software is likewise the GNU General Public License.

LINUX FEATURES

Version 7.1 of Red Hat Linux offers several new features not found in earlier versions and still not found in all distributions of Linux. These features include the following:

The 2.4 Linux kernel

The evolution of the Linux kernel over the past year is impressive. While every revision to the Linux kernel is small, the development of the kernel over the past year has resulted in new features for the desktop, for servers and for smaller devices such as handlheld computers.

These new features include the following:

Integrated PC hardware support

While USB support is growing version 2.4 also promises improved performance for PCMCIA (PC Card) and Plug-and-Play ISA devices, by integrating their drivers directly into the kernel.

A diversity of platforms

With the new kernel, you can now run Linux on a wide variety of non-Intel platforms, including Alpha, Sparc, MIPS, PowerPC and ARM-based computers. The new kernel even supports the IBM s/390 mainframe computer.

Support for Smaller Devices

The new kernel is designed for use in compact devices such as handheld computers and other portable network devices.

Few Limits

The new kernel now supports a large amount of RAM (64GB), virtually unlimited multitasking and the ability to create a single volume over multiple disks for very large files.

New Configuration Tools

Linux has always had a strong of both command-line and graphical tools for configuring and administering a Red Hat Linux-based system. Starting with version 5, these were expanded to include a user information tool to set user information such as name and phone number, a user password tool that makes it easy to change users' passwords and a file system tool that allows the mounting and unmounting of file systems from a graphical interface.

Red Hat Linux also offers a tool for configuring the free version of X Windows, XFree86 called Xconfigurator. Xconfigurator has always been easier to use than the configuration program included with XFree86. In Red Hat Linux, Xconfigurator offers additional improvements such as automatic ditection of video cards and their features.

Red Hat Linux now includes new tools for configuring printers and firewalls, known as printconf and gnome-lokkit. Printconf allows you to set up printers locally or remotely through a standard graphical user interface. Gnome-lokkit allows you to configure a firewall to protect your computer and network from intruders, configuring firewall rules based on simple questions that determine your communication needs.

Altogether, these improvements make Red Hat Linux easy to manage for most usrs and help bring to the Linux word the types of graphical management tools found in rival systems such as Windows 2000.

Improved X window systems

Red Hat Linux 7.1 includes XFree86 version .0.3 the latest version of the Linux X Window System. This creates a more stable platform and improved 3-D graphics for the two major desktop environments, GNOME and KDE both of which are also included in Red Hat Linux 7.11. GNOME and KDE are desktop environments for X Windows designed to make application development easier and to provide a more consistent, professional quality desktop environment for Linux users.

Improved Performance Features

Red Hat Linux 7.1 offers several new or improved features that can be used to leverage high-end hardware to improve the performance and stability of Red Hat Linux systems. These features include better implementation of symmetric multiprocessing (SMP), which allows Red Hat Linux to leverage the performance gain offered by multiprocessor systems. In addition, Red Hat Linux 7.1 includes an improved version of Disk Druid, which detects errors as you set up partitions during installation.

BASIC LINUX ELEMENTS

Various Linux elements are given below:

File System

File, files and files. In LINUX everything is s file. Whether it is a file or directory. Even all hardware devices, such as input output devices, storage devices, etc., are all treated as files. The LINUX file system is organized in an hierarchy which starts with the root directory, as is done in the DOS. The root is represented by a forward slash (/). Under the root directory are several system directories and the home directory.

Kernel

It is the core of LINUX system and is loaded into the memory as soon as the system starts. This in fact, manages main memory, files and peripheral devices. Maintaining the time and date, launching applications and allocating system resources are also its functions.

Shell

It is different from the DOS Shell. It is a program which interprets commands given by the user. The command can be either typed in through the command line or contained in a file called 'shell script'. Commands in 'shell script' files are interpreted by the shell.

LINUX DIRECTORIES

Different from DOS and Windows, which use backslash (/) as separator for directories, LINUX uses forward slash (/). A subdirectory booksdir of the directory user, will be shown as /user/booksdir. The slash (/) before the user represents the root directory. Some of the prominent directories are mentioned below:

/bin It contains executable program files (binary files). Here, you can find the files for the LINUX commands.

/dev It contains the special device files. Printer may be a file known as prn in this directory, the hard disk may be hda file and its first partition would be hda().

/etc It contains all the system-wide configuration information as text files.

/kernel It contains all the kernel specific code. Kernel is the heart of the LINUX system. It is responsible for resource allocation, security and low-level hardware interfaces.

/lib It contains the library files. Library files contain the reusable functions and routines for the programmer to use.

/mnt It is the directory where the storage devices other than hard disks are mounted. This directory contains the subdirectories "floppy" and "cdrom" which when these devices are mounted show the contents of the floppy disk or CD-ROM respectively.

/tmp It contains all the temporary files, which will eventually be deleted from the system. Similar to the C:\windows\temp directory in Windows 98.

/usr It contains the home directories of the users, source text for the online manual (man) pages, games and other directories. There is one home directory for each user.

FILE HANDLING IN LINUX

Through DOS we are familiar with pathname. In LINUX too, each directory or file has a pathname. Here it is referred to from the beginning of the root directory. For example, the directory user is referred to as /user; book is referred to as /user/book, where user is the parent directory of book directory.

A pathname can be of two types

- Absolute Pathname
- Relative Pathname

Absolute Pathname

It tells you the complete path of a directory starting from the root, as explained above. For example, absolute pathname of "ittools" directory is /usr/books/laxmi/doe/ittools.

Relative Pathname

It gives location of a directory, relative to the current working directory. For example, suppose your current working directory is /usr/books/laxmi/doe/ittools. Then the relative pathname to the "ittools" directory is ittools. Relative pathnames do not start with a "/".

If you do not start a pathname with "/", LINUX assumes that you are using relative pathname.

WHAT IS A DISTRIBUTION?

The concept of a distribution can be little hard to understand in a world of commercial operating sytems such as Windows 98 and 2000, Mac OS, and even commercial Unix systems such as Solaris and HP-UX. After all, in all these cases, the name of the operationg ystem denotes a very specific product.

For instance, Windows 98 defines the complete set of Windows utilities, application, driver, or utility that Microsoft ships. There is no room for variation. Any application, driver, or utility that users add to their systems is not considered part of Windows 98, and Windows 98 does not technically exist as a product with less than its complete set of software and tools.

In the Linux world, however, this definition becomes blurred. While strictly speaking, Linux is just the kernel (the heart of the operating system), the term Linux can refer to everything from the kernel to any collection of Linux-based applications put together with a kernel to produce a functioning system running Linux. The lack of a clear set of applications, utilities, drivers, and a kernel that together can clearly be identified exists because Linus has opened the door to different flavours of Linux that meet different needs. These flavours are the distributors. Distributors can be built on different versions of the kernel, can include different sets of applications, utilities, tools, and driver modules, and can offer different installation and upgrade programs to ease management of the system. It might seem that this type of flexibility would come chaos. This is a logical deduction. After all, how is it possible to have potentially infinite varieties of Linux and yet have some level of reasonable assurance that Linux applications can be installed and run on any of these systems?

Luckily, this system tends to work. In all the diversity that is Linux is an undelying thread of similarity that provides the compatibility need to develop applications that can be used on most Linux systems. At the heart of most Linux distributors is a common set of basic programs, utilites, and libraries that application developers can reasonably expect to find on any Linus system. In addition, most Linux distributions now adhere to such standards as the Linux File System Hierarchy Standard (FHS). Therefore, large scale commercial applications such as Netscape or Corel WordPerfect can be developed for Linux and be expected to work on the majority of Linux systems. Even if a component, such as a program or library, upon which an application depends is missing, it can be downloaded from one of the large Linux software repositories on the Internet to enable the application to work.

AN OVERVIEW OF MAJOR DISTRIBUTIONS

The majority of Linux distributions are freely available. They can be downloaded from Linux software archives such as the Metalab FTP site or the TSX-11 Linux Repository at MIT. Of course, the average Linux distributions can be quite large, ranging from a few dozen megabytes to several gigabytes in size and most users will not want to spend valuable online time and bandwidth downloading a complete Linux distribution.

To alleviate this solution, numerous Linux distributions are available on CD-ROM from the organizations that produce the distributions or form third-part sources that bundle one or more distributions into CD-ROM sets the include additional Linux software and documentation.

The Major Distributions

There are numerous Linux distributions. In recent years, through, six distributions have emerged as the most common: Red Hat, Slackware, Caldera, S.U.S.E., Debian and Corel. Generally, these distributions have some of the longest histories in the Linux community and together they control the lion's share of the market. In addition, all six distributions are freely available, which has made them the basis for other distributions and for commercial packages that include a Linux distribution. After these six, there is a second tier of Linux distributions that includes some long-standing distributions such as Yggdrasil and newer distributions such as Turbolinux and easyLinux.

Red Hat

By most counts, Red Hat Linux from Red Hat Software (www.redhat.com) has emerged as the favourite Linux distribution for most users. This distribution is the target, or base, distribution for many commercial Linux software developers and is the benchmark against which many Linux distributions are measured.

Red Hat has gained fame particularly for its tools for installing and upgrading the operating system and for its well-designed system for installing, uninstalling and tracking software application packages. Red Hat Linux has also won numerous awards, including Network Magazine's Product of the Year awarded in 2000. In 1998, Red Hat Linux came in first in a survey of InfoWord's Web site visitors that asked readers to indicate their choice for Product of the Year (receiving 27 percent of the vote, well ahead of the number two package, OS/2 Warp 4, which had just over 8 percent). Red Hat Linux has also been used in project that have prove the commercial viability of Linux, including animation work for the movie Titanic. Red Hat Linux is available in a free version that can be downloaded from popular Linux archives on the Internet and in a reasonably priced $40 commercial version that includes a manual, a CD-ROM and several commercial applications to supplement its collection of free software. Red Hat Linux 7.1 is also available in Deluxe Workstation and Professional Server editions.

Red Hat Linux 7.1 is the current version of the distribution and is the distribution included with this book. In addition to the Red Hat Linux 7.1 distribution included on the CD-ROM, you can always download the latest version from the Red Hat FTP server at ftp.redhat.com or from the libiblio Linux Archive at ibiblio.org/pub/Linux/distributions/redhat. If neither of these site is easily accessible, there are a number of "mirror" sites with a copy of the distribution listed at http//www.redhat.com/download/mirro.html.

Slackware

Before red Hat Linux came to fame, Slackware was the distribution to beat. Slackware is still a popular distribution; but as of this writing, its future is in some doubt due to some recent industry consolidation. Patrick Volkerding, the head of the Slackware project, is currently looking for another sponsor for his developers. For the latest developments on Slackware and for more information including download sites and sales, refer to their home page (www.slackware.com).

The version of Slackware available at the time of this writing is Slackware 7.1. The distribution offers the full range of expected utilities, tools and application including X Windows, development tools such as the GNU Compiler, PPP support, full Java support and the Java SDK (Developer's Kit) for Linux. Like most Linux distributions, Slackware offers the Apache Web server for using Linux to set up an internet or Internet Web site, as well as several freely a available Web browser.

As of this writing, Slackware can be downloaded from a number of different FTP and HTTP sites as listed on http:///www.slackware.com/getslack/.

Caldera OpenLinux

Caldera caused a stir in both the Linux and the broader computer markets by trumpting the call of supportable commercial Linux. Now the call has been roundly taken up by other Linux vendors, most notably Red Hat. The idea is to offer tested, stable and supported versions of Linux that appeal to the corporate market and to application developers who want a secure target distribution of Linux to develop for.

To some extent, this strategy has worked. Corel's WorkPerfect 6 for Linux was initially targeted for Caldera's Network Desktop distribution. Previous version of StarOffice for Linux were aimed at Caldera distributions and the Linux version of Netscape's FastTrack Web server package has been ported by Caldera any is available as part of the eDesktop and eServer packages.

Currently, the Caldera OpenLinux distribution comes in two editions: eDesktop 2.4 for workstation and eServers. It can be purchased or downloaded form the Web. Both distributions include the following features:

A non-commercial license of StarOffice for Linux.

NetWare support

A license of Dreamweaver-DOS for DOS compatibility

Webmin, a powerful, customizable Linux administration system that opens up in a Web browser.

An integrated version of Partition Magic to help users configure their hard drives before installing Linux.

S.u.S.E. Linux

S.u.S.E. Linux is a popular Linux distribution available primarily in Europe and is offered in both English and German versions. The version of S.u.S.E. available at the time of this writing 7.1, is unique in several ways when compare against the other major distributions. S.u.S.E. offers the following:

KDE 2.0, the latest version of the XFree86 X Windows server (some distributions are one version behind)

System administration tools called YaST and YaST2, which are useful for configuring everything from dial-up Internet connections to scanners and network cards.

SaX2, a custom utility for configuring X Windows.

A copy of the latest version of STarOffice.

Like Caldera and Red Hat, there are two editions of S.u.S.E. 7.1 that are currently available. The boxed version of S.u.S.E. Linux 7.1 Personal Edition includes over 700 programs and separate application and configuration manuals. The boxed version of S.u.S.E. Linux 7.1 Professional Edition includes over 2500 applications on seven CD-ROMs and one DVD, which may make this the most comprehensive Linux distribution available today.

S.u.S.E. Linux supports versions for non-Intel platforms as well, including Digital Alpha, the PowerPC and the IBM S / 390 Enterprise Server.

DEBIAN/GNU

As one of the six major Linux players, debian/GNU (www.debian.org) is the odd man out, because it is not "owned" by any specific company. Red Ht is developed by Red Hat Software and Slckware has a home at Walnut Creek; however Debian/GNU Linux is produced by a term of volunteers in much the same way that Linux development itself takes place. Debian offers more than 3950 software packages using its own package management system, which is designed to offer similar functionality to that offered by the Red Hat distribution. As of this writing, the current version of Debian/GNU Linux is 2.2r3.

The Debian distribution is unique in some ways. Their Web site highlights a commitment to giving back any code they generate to the free software world. They publicise their bugs, making bug reports easy to find and they won't include applications in their distribution that don't match Debian's definition as free software (which includes free redistribution rights, available source code, and allowances for modifications and derived work).

Corel

The newest major distribution in Corel Linux. It was developed as the first Linux distribution explicitly targeted as a replacement for Microsoft Windows on the desktop. Corel Linux Second Edition includes these features:

The Corel control Center, a system administration tool based on the KDE Control Center

A four-step installation process

Tools such as User Manager and Print Wizard that are explicitly based on equivalent Microsoft Windows tools

SmartMove, which allows you to import profiles and settings from existing Microsoft Windows computers.

Corel Linux is built on the Debian distribution. In other words, they add features to debian Linux and well it as their own distribution. This is explicitly allowed under the terms of the General Public License.

Other Distributions

Other English-language distributions of Linux that are worth noting include LinuxPro, LinuxWare, Turbolinux and Yggdrasil among others. In addition, there are several non-English distributions, particularly in French and German.

LINUX DISTRIBUTORS AND THEIR WEB SITES

Following is the list of above said and other distributors and their web site addresses for getting the software information.

Best Linux	http://www.bestlinux.net/
Black Cat Linux	http://www.blackcatlinux.net/
Blue Linux	http://www.bluelinux.net/
Caldera OpenLinux	http://www.calderasystemslinux.net/
Conectiva Linux	http://www.conectivalinux.net/
Corel Linux	http://www.corellinux.net/
Debian/GNU Linux	http://www.debian.org/
DLX Linux	http://www.wu-wien.ac.at/usr/h93/h9301726/dlx.html
EasyLinux	http://www.easylinux.net/
ESware Linux	http://www.esware.com/
Eurielec Linux	http://www.eurielec.etsit.upm.es/linux/
Gelecek Linux	http://www.gelecek.com.tr/
Icepak Linux	http://www.icepack-linux.com/
Laser5 Linux	http://www.laser5.co.jp/
Linux Mandrake	http://www.linux-mandrake.com/
Linux PPC	http://www.linuxppc.org/
LinuxWare	http://www.trans-am.com/linux.htm
MkLinux	http://www.mklinux.org/
MNIS Linux	http://www.mnix.fr/
Red Hat Linux	http://www.redhat.com/
Slackware Linux	http://www.slackware.net/
Stampede Linux	http://www.stampede.org/
S.u.S.E. Linux	http://www.suse.com/
TurboLinux	http://www.turbolinux.net/
Vine Linux	http://www.vinelinux.net/

LINUX FILES

Following is the list of web sites from where you can download Linux and Linux files.

BLINUX's FTP Site	ftp://leb.net/pub/blinux/
Caldera's FTP Site	ftp://ftp.caldera.com/pub/
Debian's's FTP Site	ftp://ftp.debian.org/
Freshmeat.net	http://ww.freshmeat.edu/
Georgia Tech's Linux Archive	ftp://ftp.cc.gatech.edu/pub/linux/
Linux Applications	http://linuxapps.com/
Linux Kernel Archieves	ftp://ftp.kernel.org/
Linux Software Map	http://www.execpc.com/lsm/
Red Hat's FTP Site	ftp://redhat.com/pub/
Tucows Linux	http://linux.tucows.com/
UNC's Linux Archive	http://ww.ibiblio.org/pub/Linux/
Woven Goods for Linux's Software Page	http://www.fokus.gmd.de/linux/linux-softw.html

INSTALLING LINUX

Before installing any software, you must check whether your computer hardware is going to support it or not. So before we read about the actual installing, we must know what all is needed both in terms of Hardware and Software for installing Linux.

Hardware Requirements

For an ideal Linux based PC your computer must have the following:

- An IBM Compatible PC with minimum 80386. 80486 is better.
- Any processor from Intel, Sparc, Alpha or AMD
- Minimum 128 MB RAM
- Minimum 2 GB free hard disk space
- Input devices such as keyboard, mouse, etc.
- Controller cards such as SCSI, IDE, etc.
- A Network card such as ISA, PCI or USB etc.
- Sound card compatible to LINUX

Software Requirements

- A partitioning program such as fdisk or disk druid supplied by Red Hat.
- Linux Software package.

STEPS BEFORE INSTALLATION

First you must create an installation disk.

Creating an installation disk

For this do the following:

1. Copy the file **boot.img** from the Red Hat CD-ROM disk to a floppy disk. This file can be found

in the /images directory of the CD. The file can be created using either the DOS rewrite command (in a DOS/Windows system) or the Linux dd command (in an existing LINUX or UNIX system). For example, to create an installation diskette using the dd command, do the following:

(a) Insert and amount the CD-ROM and then insert a blank floppy into the floppy drive of your computer.

(b) Now give the following command

```
# dd if = mnt/cdrom/images/boot.img of = /dev/fd0 bs = 1440k
```

and then press Enter

The above command will copy form the input file ("if) mnt/cdrom/boot.img onto the output file ("of") /dev/fd0. It is assumed that floppy drive is accessible from /dev/fd0. To create an installation diskette using the rewrite program, give the following command. (it is assumed that CD-ROM is accessible as drive D):

```
D:>cd images dousutils\rawrite enter
```

For the source file enter "D:\boot.img" and for destination enter "A:".

The bootable installation disk is now ready and you can use it to install your LINUX system.

Red Hat LINUX can also be installed by booting using any of the following methods using :

- a floppy diskette
- CD-ROM
- hard drive partition to hold the installation software
- DOS command line
- a network using HTTP or FTP protocols.
- an NFS (Network File System) mounted hard drive.

2. This is the most important step, partitioning. For this you must have some knowledge of the hardware. For this you have to look into the followings:
   - Disk space, required now and maybe in future
   - Requirement of any other operating system
   - Installation of applications software, now and in future
   - Data back up needs
   - Number of users
3. Refer to the step above, where if you have opted for one or more operating system besides Linux, then then step becomes compulsory. All you have to do is to select a boot loader. It is a software that is responsible for booting LINUX along with any other operating system. It can be either LILO (LINUX Loader) or GRUB (Grand Unified Boot loader). Here you must know whether the version of operating system is compatible with the current version of Linux.
4. Now insert the floppy disk (the installation diskette you have created if you are using floppy to boot your system) into a floppy drive and power-on your system. After a few moments, the Red Hat installation program screen will appear.
5. Follow the steps as directed on the screen.

HARD DRIVE PARTITIONING

I have mentioned about hard disk partitioning above in step 2. Here I give you an optimum partition of a hard disk.

/swap directory	About double the main directory size. For example, a system having 128 MB memory should get 256 MB swap space.
/directory (root)	About 60% of the available space. That is about 1200 MB in a 2 GB hard disk.
/bin directory	About 20% of the available space. This is about 400 MB in a 2 GB hard disk.
/user directory	Remaining space

The size of /user should be the largest one. This is because all the users' directories and files, installed application softwares, web pages, log files etc. will be stored here only. You can have a perfectly running LINUX system on a single partitioned hard disk also. Partitioning the hard disk however, has the following advantages:

(a) Reduces the time required to perform file system checks.

(b) Mounting of one or more of your partitions as read only.

(c) Protects filesystem. If a filesystem gets destroyed due to some reason, you will probably lose only the files on a single partition. All other partitions will remain unaffected.

(d) Allows you to have multiple operating systems.

BOOTING A LINUX SYSTEM

The booting process may differ from system to system and depending upon the type of hardware platforms being used. Generally, it involves checking of the basic subsystems of your computer, such as amount and validity of RAM, CPU time and speed, presence of floppy, CD-ROM or hard drive, keyboard and other attributes and peripherals. The booting process will fail, if there is hardware failure or if there is mismatch in the configuration. Next, comes the software part which is there in the BIOS of the bootable disk or CD, whichever may be mentioned in the bootable process of the BIOS. Then it will look for the boot code in the Master Boot Record (MBR) of the first hard disk. This area of the disk (MBR) contains the boot sector which loads the boot loader (viz. LILO, GRUB or BootMagic).

Once the operating system of Linux is loaded, Kernel takes over and performs the following operations:

- Initializes the RAM disk image.
- Performs timing tests
- Parse for any boot time kernel arguments.
- Recognise, set-up and initialise the CPU.
- Set up kernel memory and process handling.
- Open a console for displaying kernel boot messages.
- Initialize configured system devices.
- Start memory handling
- Set up and mount the file system
- Start the init command

The entire sequence of events that take place when the LINUX kernel is loaded can be found in the file usr/src/linux/init/main.c. If all goes well, you will see a "login" prompt. You can now login using your username and password.

LINUX AS A FILE SERVER

Perhaps the most fundamental need on a small network is a file server. File servers supply common places to store data, thus allowing shared files to be accessed by all users who need them and providing centeralized locations for backing up files (thereby eliminating and need for daily backups on each workstations on a network).

On a Windows or Novel network, this is generally done in one or two ways:

Using dedicated file servers

Using peer-to-peer networks

Dedicated File Servers

A dedicated file server is a system that is not used as a workstation but is set up as a central file server for the network. Users at different workstations or computers on the network can access directories on the file servers as if these were directories or disk drives on their own computes. Dedicated file serves offer the advantage or centralising the management of shared data and the backup process, but they cost more than peer-to-peer networks. They also offer the benefit of being able to set up network access control policies for confidential, core or shared data to ensure that unauthorised users don't have easy access to the information.

Linux is ideally suited to run as a low-cost file server for a small network. Linux can act as a file server to Unix/Linux, Windows and Novel networks making it an easily developed universal file server for a network containing different types of computers and workstations. In addition, the stability and the true multitasking capabilities of Linux make it a better choice than some other well-known options (such as Windows 95/98/Me) when a robust file-server solution is needed.

PEER-TO-PEER FILE SHARING

In a peer-to-peer network, there is no central file server. Instead, each user decides which directories and drives on their PC should be shared on the network and what level of access control to impose. In this way, each workstation or computer on the network becomes a small file server.

While there is flexibility in this approach, allowing users to decide what data to share and with whom, there are also drawbacks. These include no centralized management of file sharing and access control policies, no centralized location for the backing up of critical data and a performance impact on a user's desktop when several other individuals on the network are accessing shared files on that user's PC. Linux can act as a reasonable peer-to-peer file server because of its ability to share with multiple types of networks. In addition, the true multitasking abilities of Linux mitigate much of the impact on performance when multiple users access files on a PC being used for other work.

Ultimately, though the low cost of setting up a Linux-based dedicated file server for a small network makes the dedicated file server approach more attractive because of the management and centralized backup benefits it provides.

LINUX AS A PRINT SERVER

In addition to file servers, print servers are another component of the network. Generally, dedicated file server also plays the role of offering print services to the network, serving double duty. It is not uncommon to find print services provided in both a centralised, dedicated fashion and the peer-to-peer method on the same network. Some users who use a printer heavily may warrant their own printers at their desks, while others who use the printers less frequently may share a printer located n a common area.

Often, a user with a dedicated printer shares it on the network so that other users can print documents for that user's attention directly to the dedicated printer rather than to the common shared printer. Linux, of course, can work in both environments. Linux supports a healthy range of printers, including most PostScript and HP-compatible PCL printers. In addition, its printer-sharing option include the ability to share printers on Unix/Linux, Windows and Novel networks.

LINUX AS A DATABASE SERVER

Like most Unit platforms, Linux has long had a wide selection of free database packages available for it, including PostgreSQL and mSQL.

- Starting in 1998, though, major commercial database vendors gave Linux a boost in the database market by announcing and releasing Linux vesions of their products. For example:
- Red Hat has just released as of this writing the Red Hat Database, which integrated PostgreSQL7.1.2, optimized for Red Hat Linux 7.1. This database is targeted at mid-size businesses and independent corporate business units as an alternative to the large corporate database systems that seem to dominate the market.
- Oracle released in early 2001 its 9i suite of database/application server tools, optimized for the Linux 2.4 kernel. This promises to move a number of heavier business databases from higher-end Unix system to Linux.
- Sysbase Builder supports the SQL. Anywhere database Studio application on Linux. They have documented examples where the total cost of this package is about half the cost of the equivalent Window sNT/2000-style solution.
- IBM has released its flagship DB2 Universal Database for Linux, which encourages users to move their databases from higher-end Unix as well as Windows NT/2000 systems.
- Where Linux once provided only an alternative for file servers and Web servers in an organization, Linux can now be deployed as a robust, scalable database platform for an organizing using standard, widely-used relational database system.

As we mention late, combining a Linux-powered database with a Linux-powered Web server allows Linux to serve as a complete intranet server solution.

LINUX AS AN INTRANET SERVER

If you follow the computing trends today, you have probably heard a lot about intranets: internal corporate network that use Internet technology such as TCP/IP, Web browsers and Internet-standard e mail to share information and applications within an organisation. Many articles that discuss intranets and the hardware and software used to deploy them depict intranets as expensive endeavours suited only to large corporations and organizations. This couldn't be further form the truth.

Even in small offices, an intranet can provide a convenient way to publish information to be read by all employees through a Web browser. With a little forethought, you can eliminate some of the paperwork in your office by introducing electronic, online, Web-based forms for everything from leave requests to expense report submissions. In addition, if you have small database scattered across your organisation, each used on a daily basis by different users, an intranet can provide a common means by which occasional users of the data can access the information in a database without needing full accesses to the database tools used to create, maintain and update the data. By integrating the database with an intranet Web server, simple Web-based forms can be used to query the database.

Linux, which offers a wealth of powerful and flexible Web server as well as fully functional relational database systems, can allow the creation of an intranet server without the cost involved in deploying Windows Nt/2000, a commercial database such as Oracle and an expensive Web database integration tool. There are even some free tools for Linux that make it relatively easy to produce intranet programs and applications that make use f your corporate databases.

LINUX AS AN APPLICATIONS SERVER

Linux is by nature designed to act as both a file/print/intranet server and a full fledged applications servers. With an applications server, applications actually run on the server and are only displayed on a terminal or workstation, using the X Windows protocol or a terminal connection such as Telnet.

In contrast, on many typical Windows networks the applications run on the desktop and the data is stored on the server and accessed there. For some types of applications and in some situations, centralizing the running of applications can bring both performance and management benefits. If you are running a Windows or Novell network, a Linux system can act as an application server for several purposes:

Running character-based programs such as powerful Unix/Linux mail software.

Running a custom-designed, character-based database interface to centralised Linux database.

Accessing custom in-house applications, such as a corporate telephone book, designed to run in a Unix/Linux shell.

If you install an X server on a Windows desktop, you can even deliver centrally managed X Windows applications to the desktop while running the applications on a Linux applications server. Where budgets are low, Linux can create full-fledged GUI networks without the hardware or software expense of running Windows 95/98/Me or NT/2000. For instance, I have deployed a 10-desktop network running Linux exclusively. The desktops are all 486-class machines with 8MB of RAM. It would be exceptionally difficult to run Windows plus Microsoft Office on them and the cost for the necessary software licenses would run over US$300 per desktop. But with Linux on their older hardware, these systems can act as simple X terminals, displaying applications that run on a single applications server. In this case, the applications server is a Pentium 2000MHz system with just 98 MB or RAM. With the development and free release of several Linux office suites, software licensing costs are essentially down to zero.

A network like this can provide performance to the user that feels like a low end Pentium system with 32MB of RAM running Windows 95/98/Me. All of the management of software, user accounts, backups and system maintenance can be done centrally on one or two servers. Of course, this type of solution takes a fundamental strategic decision: not to use popular Windows-based productivity applications. But where cost is of the essence of the availability of modern hardware is limited, Linux makes a strong candidate for an organisation-wide computing platform.

LINUX AS A ROUTER

The concept of a router is simple: Where two or more networks need to be connected, a router is the device that makes it possible to communicate between the networks. Routers come in all shapes and sizes from software-based routers running on Windows NT/2000 servers to hardware routers form well-known vendors such as Cisco. Routers can connect to networks in different ways, using technology ranging from regular modems to Ethernet cards to ISDN connections. Let's consider an example: an office with a small network that is connected the Internet by a high-speed connection such as DSL or a cable modem. That is, a small company has a single high-speed connection to the Internet but has a network of two or more computers that would like to share the connection.

A router for this situation offers a single Ethernet connection to the local network and corresponding high-speed connection to the Internet. All computers on the network send all packets to the router. The router decides if the packet is destined for another location on the local network or for an outside address (in other words, somewhere on the Internet). All local packets are sent by the router back out in on the Ethernet connection to the local network. If a packet is destined for the outside world, it is sent through the high-speed connection. Since it is always connected, network packets do not have to wait for a modem connection to get to the Internet. Similar routing situation include connecting two separate Ethernet networks through a router that has two or more Ethernet connections. The basic configuration of other high-speed networks such as Fast Ethernet (100Mbps), Gigabit Ethernet (1000Mbps), or Asynchronous Transfer Mode (155Mbps and up) 9s similar.

Linux has all the features needed to act as a router:

Support for multiple Ethernet cards

Support for regular modems and high-speed connections such as DSL and cable modems.

Support for IP forwarding (the means by which packets can be received, analyzed and routed by the Linux-based router)

In fact, for small Ethernet to-Ethernet interconnectivity or Ethernet-to-high-speed-connection Internet routing, a Linux-based solution can be far less expensive than dedicated hardware routers and once it is properly configured can be very secure and reliable.

LINUX AS A WORKSTATION

A final use of Linux in a small office environment is as the actual desktop operating system. If the application base available in Linux is suitable to the work of the office, then Linux-based desktops provide the following advantages:

Stability and performance

Full remote management by the network administrator

Full network backup capabilities

Lower cost of ownership in comparison with Windows-based desktops.

Where money is available, high-powered Linux workstations can offer speed rivalling that of the more expensive Windows speed Systems. Linux also offers peer-to-peer networking that is more robust and offers better performance than is seen on many systems, especially those running Windows 95/98/Me. Also, as mentioned in the previous section, Linux can enable low-end or old hardware that can't run the latest Windows software to become full-fledged X terminals, providing performance on obsolete desktop hardware that feels like that of a low end Pentium system.

WHAT IS X WINDOWS?

Put in its simplest terms, X Windows is a complete graphics interface for Unix and by extension, for Linux. But this doesn't say it all. X Windows is a highly configurable environment that provides a broad range of flexible options for both the user and the application developers producing software to run under X Windows.The core X Windows concept is the client-server framework. What this means in practical terms is that X Windows provides an environment that is not bound to a single processor.

Applications can run on different servers and machines on a network and applications can display to X Windows terminals and workstation elsewhere on the network.This separation between where an application runs and where it is displayed is a concept missing in the Windows and Macintosh environments, which tie the application to the display. The benefit of this separation is that in a networking environment, it is possible to have sophisticated graphics desktops displaying applications that are running on well-maintained, powerful and easy-to-manage central application servers. In fact, this very capability is what gives Unix/Linux and X Windows such a good reputation among professional system administrators of large networks.

Another concept introduced in the X Windows environment is the separation of windowing form the interface. On an X windows system, two applications must run to provide a complete GUI. The first is the X server, which sets up the graphics displays (i.e, resolution, refresh rate and color depth), displays the windows and tracks mouse movements, keystrokes and multiple windows. But an X server does not provide menus, windows borders,· or mechanism for moving, switching, minimizing or maximizing windows. There is no fancy color background no sophisticated window borders or menu controls, and no other features that make a complete GUI. All these features are provided by a second application called a window manager. The features of the window frames the control buttons and the control menus as well as a Taskbar and a virtual desktop system. The window manager provides all of these. The window manager talks to the X server in a standard predefined way as does the X server to the X applications. This means that different window manages with different interface features can all talk in this standard way to the X server. Likewise, the variety of X server that are available, which offer support for different graphics cards, monitors, and other performance features, can also talk in a standardised way to application.

MICROSOFT WINDOWS VS. X WINDOWS

Given some of the descriptions of X Windows you have seen, it would be natural to assume that Microsoft Windows and X Windows are pretty much the same thing. The reality though, is that they are fundamentally different beasts. For example, Microsoft Windows is a complete operating system, with everything from a kernel to a shell to a windowing environment and more. X Windows is just one piece of that operating system puzzle the windowing environment. Another contrast is in the interface: The Microsoft Windows interface is fairly rigid while the X Windows interface has an amazingly flexible and customizable design.

Similarities

So, what is similar about X Windows and Microsoft's current operating system? The main similarities are that they both provide graphical interfaces and make it possible to work with multiple windows. On top of this, they allow the user to interact with information using more than a keyboard and plain characters. Users can utilize a mouse as well as a keyboard, and can create interfaces that combine menus, forms, windows, and dialog boxes.

Differences

There are numerous differences between the two windowing systems. The main differences are in the following areas:

Flexibility of the interface

Fine tuned control over the interface configuration

Client server technology

Flexible Interface

The flexiblity of the X Windows interface is one of the joys of this environment for many users. As discussed already, the separation of the user interface layer from the basic windowing layer makes it possible to create multiple interfaces for X Windows through the creation of different window managers. Multiple interfaces do not simply provide subtle differences in appearance, as some customization tools for the Microsoft Windows interface offer, rather, they allow complete redesigns of the user interface from a window manager to window manager.

Fine Tuned Control

Another advantage of the X Windows environment is that if offers fine tuned control over all aspects of the windowing environment and the interface. By setting any of dozens of settings, it is possible to control all aspects of the environment, from the background and foreground window colours to cursor colour, default font, and default window size. Users can also define modes of interaction. For instance, it is possible to use the mouse pointer to make a window automatically jump to the foreground or to change cursor focus to a background window. In additon, these and other features can be defined on a per-applicaiton basis, creating different settings for each application so that each application lauches in the most convenient way possible. It is also possible to define which windows and applications open each time the X environment starts, as well as have the sytgem make logical choices about which window manager to use when starting X Windows.

Client Server Environment

As mentioned previously, the X Windows world works on a client server model in which applications are clients to an X server that drives the physical display. This has made X Windows well adapted to network environments, allowing applications to urn on one machine on the network while displaying their output on another. Microsoft Windows lacked this ability until recently and now has it only in a limited and expensive fashion through its Terminal Server services on high-end mulitiuser Windows NT and 2000 system. In the Linux, Unix, and X worlds, even the lowliest system is capable of playing either the client role or the server role in this X windows client server model.

LINUX FOR POWERPC PROCESSORS

The LinuxPPC project is managed and developed by PowerPC Linux. It offers a stable and complete distribution that runs a wide range of Power Macintosh computers. Supported applications and features include the following:

- PCI bus systems
- SCSI and IDE hard disk drives
- Multimedia support
- Web browsers such as Netscape
- X Windows and a wide range of window managers
- Java JDK 1.2.2

A project is also under way to develop an emulator of the Mac OS to run inside Linux on the PowerPC just as Wine is an attempt to develop a Windows emulator for Linux on the Intel x86 CPU.

Windows NT

19

INTRODUCTION TO WINDOWS NT

Windows NT is the latest version of Microsoft's enterprise server operating system. The Windows NT family is the successor to the Windows 2000 Server family, which in turn built upon Windows NT Server. Windows NT introduces many new features and offers significant improvements to many features found in earlier Windows NT operating systems.

Before you can begin using Windows NT, though, you need to understand the family of products that carry the Server name and how they differ from one another. You also have to understand their common memory and processor architecture and some of the basic technologies that Windows NT is built upon.

Windows NT Features

When Microsoft introduced Windows 2000 Server, they created a family or series, of server operating systems. That family continues in Windows NT and consists of four separate products:

- Windows NT – Standard Edition
- Windows NT – Web Edition
- Windows NT – Enterprise Edition
- Windows NT – Datacenter Edition

Microsoft has also announced a 64-bit version of Windows NT, which will be available on server computers utilizing Intel's Itanium processor or compatible processors from other companies. 64-bit editions of both Windows NT – Standard Edition and Windows NT – Enterprise Edition will be available. Each of the three Windows NT editions has specific capabilities designed to meet specific business needs and they build upon one another. In other words, Windows Enterprise Server can do everything the standard edition can do and more.

Windows NT – Standard Edition

The standard edition of Windows NT provides all of the basic functionality a server operating system needs. The standard edition is intended to support small – to medium – sized businesses as a file server, application server platform or domain controller.

Syntax A file server stores files, like Microsoft Office documents and enables users to access these files over a network. An application server runs application server software, such as a Web server or database server. A domain controller is a special type of server that centralizes security and user accounts for a business.

Windows NT has the following limitations:

- A maximum of four microprocessors may be used.
- No more than 4GB of memory is allowed. Of that 4GB, the operating system always reserves 2GB for its own use, allowing applications on the server to share the remaining 2GB.

Windows NT – Web Edition

Specially designed for use as a Web server, Windows Web Server provides a subset of the overall Windows NT functionality. The Web Server edition is optimized for Microsoft's Internet Information Services (IIS) Web server platform. The Web Server edition does not support some advanced services, including:

- Advanced network security features like Internet Authorization Server
- Fax services
- Terminal services

As the name implies, Windows Web Server is ideal for servers used as Internet or intranet Web servers.

Windows NT – Enterprise Edition

Windows Enterprise Server builds upon the Windows NT standard edition. It provides all of the same features and capabilities as the standard edition and adds the following:

- Support for up to eight microprocessors in a server
- Expanded memory support that reserves only 1GB of memory for the operating system, allowing applications on the server to share the remaining 3GB.
- The ability to create clusters of two servers.

Some software applications are specifically designed to take advantage of these additional features. For example, Microsoft SQL Server 2000 is available in an "Enterprise Edition" that enables you to create clustered SQL Servers. The Enterprise Edition cannot be installed on the standard edition of Windows NT because cluster support isn't included in that edition.

Enterprise Server is targeted toward medium to large businesses that need to run extremely powerful servers, use clustering or run especially powerful application server software.

Windows NT – Datacenter Edition

Windows' Datacenter Server edition is the most powerful version of the operating system. Like the Enterprise Server edition, Datacenter Server builds upon the standard Windows NT edition and adds the following features and capabilities:

- Support for up to 32 processors in a single server
- Support for up to 64GB of memory
- Support for clusters of up to four servers

Microsoft designed Datacenter Server to be the most stable, reliable and powerful version of Windows NT. As such, it is also one of the most expensive. Also, Datacenter Server is the only version of Windows NT that you cannot purchase and install yourself.

Datacenter Server is targeted to large businesses that need the most powerful servers possible and who also require extremely reliable servers that rarely crash and rarely need to be rebooted (aside from scheduled maintenance operations).

HARDWARE REQUIREMENTS

Windows NT can be installed on any PC with minimum of following features:

RAM: minimum of 16MB.

Hard disk: minimum of 2GB

All other features like mouse, keyboard, monitor, etc.

PLANNING NETWORKS

One of the primary purposes of any operating system is to help manage the mass-storage devices in your computer, and Windows NT is no exception. It provides powerful and flexible features that enable you to get the most from the hard drives installed in your computer.

Disks, Partitions and Drives

Windows NT is designed to automatically recognize all of the hard disks installed in your computer and it refers to each one as a disk. The first hard drive is referred to as disk 0, the second as disk 1 and so forth. All new disks are referred to as basic disks, which means they can contain a limited number of partitions and cannot be used for special features like fault tolerance. Once partitions have been created on a disk, they are assigned drive letters by the operating system. These drive letters represent logical drives. Drive letters A and B are reserved for the first two floppy disk drives in your computer; the first hard drive partition is usually lettered C, the next one D and so on. CD-ROMs and other types of drives also receive drive letters. Drive letters are the primary way of accessing the contents of a drive. All of the folders and files on a drive are referenced by their location on a specific drive letter.

Disk Management

Windows NT includes a special application to help you manage the disks and drives on your computer. The application is located within the Computer Management application, which is located in the Administrative Tool s folder on the Start menu. After launching Computer Management, select the Disk Management item to see the disks and drives attached to your computer.

You can use Disk Management to accomplish several important tasks:

- To create a new partition, right-click the empty area of a hard disk and select Create Partition from the pop-up menu.
- To change the drive letter assigned to a CD-ROM or partition, right-click it and select Drive Letters from the pop-up menu.
- To convert a basic disk to a dynamic disk, which supports more partitions as well as special features like fault tolerance, right-click the disk and select Convert to Dynamic Disk from the pop-up menu.
- To remove a partition, right-click it and select Delete from the pop-up menu.

Fault Tolerance

Unfortunately, hard drives can sometimes break. When they do, all of the information on that hard drive is often lost. Modem hard drives can be enormous and when one breaks, you can lose an enormous amount of data. Windows NT helps prevent such losses by providing two levels of software-based fault tolerance: mirroring and RAID 5.

Mirroring

Mirroring allows two identically sized partitions, located on separate disks, to automatically duplicate one another. Both partitions become a mirror set, which means they always contain the same content and appear to the operating system as if they were a single partition. Mirror sets use only one drive letter.

If one of the disks in a mirror set fails, the other one continues operating and no data is lost. Disk Management gives you the tools necessary to work with mirror sets:

- To create a mirror set, select an empty, unformatted area of a dynamic disk. Hold down the Ctrl key and select another unformatted partition of the same size. Right-click one of the disks and choose New Volume from the pop-up menu. On the New Volume dialog box, choose Mirror Volume.
- To break a mirror set, right-click one of its partitions and choose Break Mirror from the pop-up menu. The first partition retains the drive letter that was assigned to the mirror; the other partition becomes a normal logical drive, although it will contain the same content as the first.
- If one of the drives in a mirror set fails, replace the affected disk. Break the mirror, and then re-create the mirror using the new disk.

RAID 5

RAID is an acronym that stands for Redundant Array of Inexpensive Devices. That's a fancy way of saying disks are fairly inexpensive, and using several of them together (the array) can help improve fault tolerance. Each of the several different RAID "levels" has different features. Mirror sets, in fact, are also referred to as RAID 1 on some operating systems.

On Windows NT, RAID 5 arrays consist of at least three partitions of equal size. You create a RAID 5 array in much the same way that you create mirror sets: Select all of the areas you want to include in the volume, right-click one and select New Volume from the pop-up menu. On the New Volume dialog box, select RAID 5 Volume.

In a RAID 5 array, the operating system saves data to all of the array partitions at once, dividing saved information between them. The operating system also calculates checksum data, which is derived by performing a mathematical operation on the saved data. This checksum data allows the operating system to re-create missing data and the checksum data is also spread across the partitions in the array.

If one disk in a RAID 5 array fails, the checksum data from the remaining drives is used to recreate the data that was stored on the failed disk. Until the failed disk is replaced, the checksum data is used to recalculate the missing data, as if the disk had never failed. Once the disk is replaced, the checksum data is used to rebuild the data on the new disk. If two or more disks in the array fail, then all of the data on the array is lost.

The greatest disadvantage to RAID 5 arrays is that some of your available disk space is sacrificed to store the checksum information. In any RAID 5 array, your total disk space equals the space available on all but one of the disks in the array. For example, in an array with five 10GB disks, you have a total of 40GB of available space. The other 10GB is used to store checksum data. Most administrators feel the tradeoff of disk space for fault tolerance is a good one and you'll find that most servers use RAID 5 arrays.

File Systems

Once you've configured the disks and partitions in your computer, including any fault tolerance features you choose to use, you need to select a file system. File systems are used to organize the data on a drive into files and folders. Windows NT supports several different file systems, each with different features:

- FAT16. The FAT16 file system is compatible with older operating systems like MS-DOS and Windows 95. FAT16 is an inefficient file system and causes wasted space on modern, large hard drives. Use FAT16 only if the file system needs to be accessed by older operating systems.
- FAT32. The FAT32 file system is more efficient than FAT16 and is compatible with Windows 98 and Windows Me (as well as later versions of Windows 95). FAT32 does not provide the ability to assign security permissions to files and folders, does not support encryption or compression and is less efficient than NTFS.

- NTFS. The NTFS file system is the best file system to use with Windows NT. It is very efficient, supports compression, encryption and security permissions and is compatible with Windows 2000 and Windows NT 4.0 Service Pack 4 and higher. You should use the NTFS file system unless you have a specific reason not to.

Windows NT enables you to format almost any type of disk, including removable disks like floppy disks, with these file systems. The one exception is CD-ROM and DVD-ROM discs, which are always formatted with their own special file systems.

Once you've selected a file system for a partition, you need to format the partition with the file system. Formatting is a process that organizes the partition and allows the operating system to begin saving data to it. Use Disk Management to format partitions by right-clicking the partition, selecting Format from the pop-up menu and then selecting the appropriate file system from the dialog box.

Disk Optimization

Windows NT offers additional capabilities to improve the performance of the disks in your computer. Most hard drives have pretty standard capabilities for transferring data to the operating system, so once you've installed top-of-the-line drives in your computer, you have to look at optimization methods to improve the performance of those drives.

Using Disks Carefully

Carefully planning how the disks in your computer are used can help improve disk performance. The key is to not overburden and any one disk with too much work. For example, suppose your computer contains four hard drives. You could use one hard drive for the operating system files and another hard drive for user data files. The remaining two drives might be saved for future expansion. That scenario sounds goods, but the user data drive would be doing an awful lot of work if you have a lot of data on it.

A better solution is to use one drive for the operating system files and make a RAID 5 array from the remaining three drives. You'll achieve much better performance because all three drives can share the load of the user data, rather than dumping all of the work on one drive.

Many administrators insist on at least five drives in every server. The first two drives are configured as a mirror and used to store the operating system files. The mirror ensures that the operating systems is protected from the failure of a single drive. The remaining drives are made into a RAID 5 array, which provides great performance and fault tolerance.

SERVER SECURITY

Windows NT can play different roles on a network, depending on your security requirements:

- As a standalone server, Windows NT maintains its own user accounts and groups. These accounts determine who can use the server. Standalone servers don't share security information with each other. If a user wants to use two different standalone servers, he must have a user account and password on each.
- As a domain controller, Windows NT maintains user accounts and groups that can be shared with other servers. This collection of users and groups is called a domain and enables users to access multiple servers with a single user account and password. In Windows NT, domains are handled by Active Directory, which you'll learn more about in the next session.
- As a member server, Windows NT maintains its own user accounts, just like a standalone server. Member servers can also use the user and group accounts in an Active Directory domain. This capability means member servers can grant access to users with a domain account or users with a local server account.

Windows NT's flexible security architecture makes it suitable for a wide range of computing environments. For example, small companies with only one or two servers can use standalone servers, which require very little administrative effort to maintain. Larger organizations can have an Active Directory domain, which provides central control of user accounts and makes it easier to work with a large number of servers. Larger organizations usually have a mix of domain controllers, which store the domain's user accounts, and member servers, which often contain resources that users access with their domain user accounts. Very large organizations may have several different domains, allowing different divisions of the company to maintain their own user accounts, while still sharing resources and servers with each other.

Local Users and Groups

The key to server security is users and groups. A user or user account, represents a real person who needs to use the resources on a server. In addition to granting access to the server, users and groups are also used to control exactly what people can do once they gain access to the server. As you will learn in Session 6, access to the files and folders on a server is controlled by specifying which users and groups are permitted to access each file or folder.

Users

User accounts are configured with several pieces of information:

- A user name or user ID, which uniquely represents and identifies the account- for example, "JohnL," "DJones," or "RhondaHinz." User names are often an abbreviation of the user's full name, which makes it easier for the user to remember.
- A proper name, which is the user's full name. While Windows NT doesn't actually care about the user's full name, it's a useful piece of information that can help administrators easily identify user accounts.
- A password, which is a series of numbers, symbols, and letters. Passwords are intended to be a secret that only the user and the server know. When a user provides the correct password, the server is assured that the user is who they claim to be.
- Account properties, which define special information about the user. For example, account properties may indicate whether or not a user is allowed to access a server only during business hours. Account properties may also be used to temporarily lock users out, preventing them from accessing the server even if they have the correct password.

Managing users

Windows NT enables you to create user accounts using the Computer Management application (assuming you are logged on to the server with a user account that has the authority to create user accounts). The application is located in the Administrative Tools folder, which can be accessed from the Start menu. Once the application is opened, just expand the Local Users and Groups folder.

The Computer Management application has a Graphical User Interface (GUI) that makes it very easy to manage user accounts and groups. Generally, you can modify a user account just by right – clicking it with your mouse and selecting the appropriate task from the pop-up menu. For example, to create a new user, right – click the Users folder and select New User from the pop-up menu. Fill in the new user's user name, password and other information, and you're finished!

Use the Computer Management application to create new user accounts, modify old ones or delete user accounts that are no longer used. Some common tasks that you might perform using the Computer Management application include

- Changing users' passwords when they forget them
- Locking and unlocking user accounts to control access to the server
- Creating new user accounts and deleting old ones

Built - in users

Windows NT also includes two built-in user accounts with special capabilities:

- Administrator. The "super user" of the server. Administrator can do anything on the server and cannot be locked out. You supply the password for the Administrator account when you install Windows NT. You cannot delete the Administrator account, but you can rename the account and change the account password.
- Guest. Intended for users who want to access the server but don't have user accounts on the server. When you install Windows NT, the Guest account has a blank password and is disabled, preventing it from being used. You can rename the Guest account and change its password. Because the Guest account usually does not have a password, anyone can use it to access your server. To prevent anyone from accessing your server without authorization, leave the Guest account disabled unless you have a specific reason not to.

Groups

Most of the time, you do not want to permit individual users to access the files, folders and other resources on a server. Instead, you can permit several users to access those resources. Groups are designed to help you organize your users, making it easier to grant access to several users in one step.

What groups should you create?

Groups often reflect the organization of your company. For example, you might create groups to represent each department in your company: accounting, human resources, operations and so forth. Those groups can then contain the user accounts that represent the members of those departments.

Try to create groups that represent the groups of people you will assign permissions to. If a couple of people need access to a particular file, create a user group. Add the appropriate user accounts to the group, and grant the group access to the file. It's usually easier to assign permissions on a file or folder to a group even if the group contains only one user. That way, if you ever delete the user account (either on purpose or by accident), the group will still have permission to the file or folder. You can just add other user accounts to the group as necessary to permit users to access the files or folders.

Managing groups

Groups are managed with the Computer Management application. The Local Users and Groups folder expands to reveal a Groups folder, which you can select to see the groups that have been created. As shown in Figure groups can contain as many users as necessary. Individual user accounts can be placed in more than one group and those users gain the capabilities of all the groups they belong to. Groups cannot, however, include other groups; they can contain only user accounts.

To create a new group, just right-click the Groups folder and select New Group from the pop-up menu. Fill in the group's name and use the buttons to add and remove user accounts from the group's membership list.

Built-in groups

Windows NT includes several built-in groups that have special capabilities. Any user account placed into one of these built-in groups automatically has the special capabilities associated with that group. The built-in groups include

- Administrators. Members of this group can perform any action on the server. The built-in Administrator account is automatically a member of this group.
- Server Operators. Members of this group can perform tasks such as shutting the server down, controlling access to files and folders and so forth.
- Print Operators. Members of this group can manage the printers that may be attached to a server. They can control who is allowed to use a printer, delete print jobs and add new printers to the server.
- Backup Operators. Members of this group are allowed to read any file or folder on the server, for the purpose of copying those files and folders to backup tapes. This capability enables Backup Operators members to partially bypass the normal security on a file, so that they can make a safe copy of the file in case it is accidentally modified or deleted.

The built-in groups should never be renamed or deleted. If you don't want anyone to have the special capabilities of a particular group, simply remove all of the user accounts from the group. The groups themselves don't have passwords, so they cannot be broken in to by hackers.

Local Account Policies

Windows NT enables you to customize the behavior of your user accounts by configuring special account policies. You work with policies by using the Local Security Policy application, which is in the Administrative Tools folder on the Start menu. After you launch the Local Security Policy application, expand the Account Policies folder.

Password policies

Password policies control how your users' passwords are treated. You can modify the policy settings by simply double-clicking the policy and filling in the appropriate information. The most commonly used password policies are

- Enforce password history. This policy tells Windows NT to remember the passwords your users have used in the past. Users are not permitted to reuse old passwords. Instead, they have to use new passwords whenever they change their passwords. You can configure how many old passwords are remembered.
- Maximum password age. You can configure the maximum number of days that users can keep their passwords. Once that number of days has passed, users are required to change their passwords.
- Minimum password age. You can configure the number of days users must wait before changing their passwords again.
- Minimum password length. Short passwords are easy for hackers to guess. You can help make passwords more secure by requiring that they be at least a certain length. Common minimum lengths are between six and ten characters, with longer passwords being harder for hackers to guess than shorter passwords. Of course, longer passwords are also harder to remember, so don't make the minimum password length longer than ten characters. Of course, users are always welcome to use passwords that are longer than the minimum.

Well-planned password policies ensure that your users' passwords are hard to guess and are changed frequently, the two key factors that help prevent hackers from guessing users, passwords and breaking into your servers

Account Lockout policies

If a hacker is trying to break into your system by guessing a user's password, she will often try several times Windows NT keeps track of how many times an invalid password is used with a user account and can be configured to lock out the user account to prevent any further attempts at password guessing. This configuring is performed using the Account Lockout policies in the Local Security Policy application.

Just like Password policies, the Account Lockout policies can be modified by double-clicking the appropriate policy and filling in the required information.

The important Account Lockout policies are

- Account lockout threshold. This policy determines how many times Windows NT enables someone to try to access a user account with the wrong password After the threshold has been passed. The account is locked out. For example, by setting this policy to 3, you can be assured that user accounts are locked out after the third wrong password is tried. Don't set this policy too low or users may find their accounts locked out just because they mistyped their passwords. On the other hand, setting this policy too high allows a hacker several attempts to guess the password. A good setting for this policy is between three and five attempts.
- Account lockout duration. This policy determines how long an account remains locked out. You can specify a value in hours or you can specify zero to leave the account permanently locked out. Once an account is locked out, you can use the Computer Management application to unlock it. Simply right-click the account select Properties from the pop – up menu and clear the Account Is Locked Out check box to unlock the account.

Security Auditing

You may need to keep track of who is using your server and what they're doing on it. Windows NT maintains a Security Event Log, which you can view with the Event Viewer application. The Event Viewer can be found in the Computer Management application. Once the application loads, select the Security folder to see any security events, as shown in Figure.

By default, Windows NT does not automatically report on common security events. However, you can use the Local Security Policy application to configure Audit policies, which allows Windows NT to add entries to the Security Event Log for specific events. The Audit policies include:

- Audit logon events. This policy tells Windows NT to create Security Event Log entries whenever someone attempts to access the server.
- Audit account management. This policy audits the creation, modification, or deletion of user and group accounts.
- Audit object access. This policy allows Windows NT to audit file and folder access, helping to keep track of what files and folders are being accessed by users.
- Audit policy change. This policy audits any changes to the local security policies, so you can see if another user has changed the policies you have defined.

The Audit policies can be configured to audit only successes, only failures or both. Successes occur when a user is permitted to perform an event, such as logging on with the correct password. Failures occur when a user is denied an event, such as attempting to log on with the incorrect password.

MANAGING FILE SHARING AND FILE SECURITY

As its name implies, Windows NT is a network server operating system. That means your servers primarily are used by users who connect to the server via a network, rather than by users who log on to the server itself. As a network operating system, Windows NT provides powerful, flexible features that enable you to determine who may access your files and what they can do with them.

FILE SECURITY

The basis of Windows NT's file security system is the NTFS file system because only the NTFS file system supports file-level security. On any volume formatted with NTFS, every single file and folder includes an Access Control List or ACL. The ACL is basically a list of users and groups who ate permitted to access the file or folder and a list of the actions those users may perform.

Managing permissions

File and folder permissions are managed from within Windows Explorer. Simply right – click any file or folder (or a group of files and folders) and select Properties from the pop-up menu.

The Security tab enables you to specify the users or groups that should have access to the file or folder. On the tab, you can do the following:

- You can select users and groups from the local users and groups on your computer. However, keep in mind that domain controllers don't have local users and groups.
- If your computer is a member of a domain, you can also select users and groups from the domain. On a domain controller, this option is your only one.
- You can select more than one user or group and assign different permissions to each.

Permission types

Once you select the users and groups you want, you need to assign their actual permissions to the file or folder. There are several basic permissions:

- Full Control. Allows the user to perform any action on the file. Full Control includes all of the other possible permissions.
- Modify. Allows the user to change the contents of the file or delete it. However, the user cannot change the permissions on the file. This permission includes Read, Read & Execute, and Write permissions.
- Read. Permits the user to examine the file but not change or delete it.
- Read & Execute. Allows the user to load the file into memory (in the case of an executable file) and run it. This permission is appropriate for applications.
- Write. Allows the user to change the contents of the file.
- List Folder Contents. This permission applies only to folders and never to files. This permission allows a user to see what other files and folders are in a particular folder.

Assigning permissions

Each of these permissions can be assigned in one of three states:

- Allow. Gives the permission to the user.
- None. Doesn't assign any permission to the user. However, users may gain permission through membership in another group (more in this in a bit).
- Deny. Prevents the user from gaining the permission through any means.

Imagine that you work for World Metro Bank and have a user named Linda. Linda belongs to a group named Accounting. If you allow the Accounting group Read permission to a file, Linda gains Read permission through her membership in the, group – she doesn't need explicit permission on the file. You can deny Linda Read permission on the file, which prevents her from accessing the file even though the

Ownership and permissions

The creator of a file is considered to be its owner and the owner of a file always has Full Control over the file, even if he isn't specifically listed on the Security tab. In addition to the permissions I described earlier, you can assign two special permissions to files:

- Take Ownership. This permission gives users the right to become the owners of a file. By default, the Administrators group always has Take Ownership permission over all files on the computer.
- Change Permissions. This permission gives users the ability to change the list of groups and users who can access a file and to change the permissions on a file.

Both of these special permissions are included in the Full Control permission I described previously.

Understanding inheritance

Windows NT supports inheritance in file and folder permissions. Inheritance means that a file or folder doesn't have to have permissions applied to it. Instead, the file or folder picks up the permissions from the folder it is contained in.

For example, suppose you create a folder named Documents and apply security permissions to it. By default, any other subfolders you create within Documents, as well as any files contained within Documents or those subfolders, have the exact same permissions as the Documents folder itself. You can assign different permissions to subfolders and those permissions combine with the ones on the parent. The actual permissions on any file or folder are a combination of its own explicit permissions and the ones inherited from its parent folder.

You might not always want inheritance to work, though. To continue the example, suppose you create a subfolder named Private under the Documents folder. You might want the permissions on Private to be completely different from those on Documents. Also, you might not want any future changes to the permissions on Documents to "fall through" to the Private folder through inheritance.

To block inheritance, modify the Security properties on the folder (like Private) that should have different permissions. Click the Advanced button on the Security tab to display the Advanced Security Settings dialog box.

Uncheck the, "Inherit from parent the permission entries that apply to child objects" check box. Windows NT prompts you to copy the parent's permissions or remove them completely.

- If you want use the parent folder's permissions as a starting point, select Copy. Then, modify the permissions to meet your needs.
- If you want to start with a clean slate, select Remove. Then, assign the appropriate permissions.

Inheritance can be very tricky to figure out. Windows NT helps by always showing you the current combined permissions on a file or folder in the Security tab. Permissions gained through inheritance are grayed out, indicating that you cannot modify them directly. This behavior enables you to easily identify permissions applied directly to the file or folder and permissions that were inherited from the parent folder.

Sharing Files

Once you've secured your files and folders by using file permissions, you can make them available to the other users on your network. You start by sharing one or more folders on your server. Sharing makes the folder and its contents available to network users.

To share a folder, right-click it and select Properties from the pop-up menu. Then click on the Sharing tab and select the "Share this folder as" radio button.

You must provide a share name, which is the name users will use to access the folder. The share name may be different from the folder name or it may be the same, depending on your needs.

Once a folder has been shared, users can access it by using a UNC path. UNC stands for Universal Naming Convention and a UNC path is a standardized way of accessing shared resources on a network. UNCs begin with two backslash characters, followed by the name of the server hosting the shared resource. The server name is then followed by a single backslash and the name of the shared folder. So, if a server named Server01 is hosting a shared folder name Documents, the UNC would be \\Server01\Documents.

Accessing Shared Folders

Windows desktop operating systems, such as Windows 98, Windows Me, windows 2000 Professional and Windows XP, make it easy to use UNCs to access shared resources. For example, you can select Run from the Start menu, type a UNC and click OK. The designated shared folder appears in an Explorer window, enabling you to work with the files in the shared folder.

Mapping drive letters

Many users find it difficult to remember UNCs, especially when they have to remember a lot of them. On the other hand, most users are comfortable working with drive letters, since the hard drives on their computers already use drive letters (such as C:\ and D:\). Windows operating systems enable users to map a UNC to a drive letter. Mapping assigns a drive letter to a specific UNC, enabling the user Go to open the UNC just as if it were a hard drive or CD-ROM on her computer.

To map a drive letter to a UNC on Windows XP Professional:

1. Open the Start menu.
2. Right-click My Computer and select Map Network Drive from the pop-up menu.
3. On the Map Network Drive dialog box, type the UNC the drive letter should map to and select the drive letter you want to use.
4. If you want the drive letter to automatically remap to the same UNC ever time you log on, check the "Reconnect at logon" checkbox.
5. Click OK.

Share Security

Shared folders can have their own permissions, called share permissions. Remember, files on a FAT16 or FAT32 volume cannot have file permissions. If you want to share files on a FAT16 or FAT32 volume, then share permissions offer the only means of limiting user access to the files.

When you create a new shared folder, it starts out with the special Everyone group having Read permission on the share. You can modify the share permissions by clicking the Permissions button on the Sharing tab.

Shared folders have only three types of permissions:

- Full Control. Allows users to take any action with the shared files.
- Change. Allows users to modify the shared files.
- Read. Allows users to read the shared files. This is the default permission assigned to new file shares.

When a shared folder is sharing files that are located on an NTFS volume, the share permissions and file permissions combine. The most restrictive combination of the share and file permissions take effect. For example, suppose you have a file named Private.doc, located in a shared folder named Documents.

Private.doc has NTFS file permissions assigned, granting Read permissions to the Domain Users user group. The Documents shared folder has the default share permissions, granting Full Control to the special Everyone group. The effective permissions on the file or the permissions that users will encounter, is the most restrictive combination of the two. In this example, the Domain Users group will have Read permissions, despite the more lenient permissions on the shared folder.

Other special groups include:

- System. Represents the operating system itself.
- Interactive Users. Represents any user logged on to the server's console.
- Network Users. Represents any user accessing the server from across the network.

Best Practices for File Security

With so many options for file and share security, it's easy for things to get out of control. World Metro Bank has chosen to follow the industry best practices regarding file security:

- Always assign permissions to domain local groups (or to local groups if you're not in a domain).
- Place users into domain global groups.
- Place domain global groups into domain local groups (or local groups) to assign permissions to the users in the global groups.
- Only use share permissions when you need to control access to files on a FAT16 or FAT32 partition.
- When sharing files on an NTFS partition, only use NTFS file permissions. Combining file and share permissions makes it difficult to troubleshoot any security problems you may encounter.
- Allow inheritance to work whenever possible. Try to organize your folders so that you don't have to block inheritance. Blocking inheritance can lead to tricky situations when it comes time to troubleshoot access problems.
- If you do need to assign different permissions to a file or folder, block inheritance before doing so. If you don't, the file or folder will still inherit permissions from its parent folder and combine those with the permissions you apply directly. This situation makes it very difficult to troubleshoot the file permissions if a user has trouble accessing the file or folder.

Multiple Choice Questions

1. Windows version of linux is:

   (a) L Windows (b) X Windows

   (c) M Windows

2. Linux components have:

   (a) kernel (b) shell

   (c) both

Descriptive Type Questions

1. Describe the various features of Windows NT.
2. Describe the various editions of the software.
3. What are the hardware requirements for Windows NT?
4. How would you make the disk partitions for Windows NT?
5. How would you optimize the disk for Windows NT?
6. Describe the various policies regarding the security.
7. How would you manage file sharing in the software?
8. How would you manage permissions?
9. Describe the terms:

   Password policy — Security auditing

   Raid 5 — Mirroring

   Fault Tolerance — Ownership and permissions

   Accessing Shared Folders — Mapping drive letters

   Share security

Part - III

20 Word Processing & Microsoft Word

INTRODUCTION TO WORD PROCESSING

Word processor is a computer program for processing of words, very similar to a food processor (*mixie*) which processes food. Most of the word processors would start from a blank screen assumed to be a blank page with a blinking starting point known as **Cursor**. For all practical purposes it is like a typewriter, but it is much more than that.

You can type the text (even enter graphics) in the word processor, save it under a name to recall it again and again. Spell check it for errors, format it to look good, and then if needed print it too.

This makes it much easier for writing the text since you can make as many mistakes as you like since you can correct them by just pressing a key. This way you save a lot of paper and make the document look more neat and clean.

SOME IMPORTANT TERMS OF WORD PROCESSING

Before we go any further and study word processing, let us understand few basic terms of word processing:

Text — It is the matter which you type.

Document — It is whole text matter which you create, like a letter, or a chapter, etc.

Fonts — In typewriting you have just one type of handwriting. In word processing you can have your text written in many writings, these are called Fonts. Each font has its own way to writing the alphabets (A to Z) and even numerals (0 to 9).

Cursor — It is as said before, the blinking point which tells you where to start typing or what your current position is.

Arrow keys — These keys are on the arrow pads of your keyboard and are shown as: Up-arrow (↑), Down-arrow (↓), Left-arrow (←) and Right-arrow (→).

Space bar — It plays a very important role in word processing. The space between the words is given by this.

Tabs — These are used to set the text into tabular form.

Backspace — This is another important keyboard key which is used to delete the wrongly typed character in your text. You can even use the Del key for this.

THINGS WHICH CAN BE DONE BY WORD PROCESSING

Let us now see what are the things which can be done by Word Processing and cannot be done on the typewriter.

Alignment — You can set your text in any alignment, e.g., Left, Right or Centre. You can even do box setting, i.e., aligned from both sides.

Deleting Mistakes	You can delete word, line, paragraph in a stroke and the rest of the matter will get adjusted automatically.
Line Spacing	You can set line spacing according to your liking from one to nine.
MailMerging	A very important feature of any word processing. This helps you in sending the same text to the different people, all in original format.
Moving the Cursor	You can move your cursor from word to word or from paragraph to paragraph, if needed.
Naming a Document	As mentioned earlier, you can name a document and recall it anytime from hard disk for editing, updating, correcting and even printing.
Overwriting Mistakes	You can overwrite your mistakes on the screen itself. No more messing of eraser and spoiling of paper.
Page Breaks	You can set a page break at any place within the text so that while printing it will jump to next page.
Page Numbers	You can set page numbers according to your liking.
Search and Replace	You can search for a particular word in the whole document and replace it with another one. You can even replace all the occurrence of the same word.
Spell Checking	Probably the most important part of any word processing. Each word processor comes with a dictionary built inside it. You can check your text with it see whether any word has been wrongly typed.

IMPORTANT WORD PROCESSING PROGRAMS

Most of the big time software producers have a word processing program of their own. But, it depends on the operating system which you are using. If you are working under DOS, then there is nothing to beat WordStar. It has been very popular word processing software till more and more users started working under Windows. Then, the preference shifted to Word for Windows. So here we will discuss Word for Windows.

STARTING WORD

You can start Word by one of the following methods:

From Start Button

Click at Start button to access the various commands. Click on Programs to get the various programs. From here click at the program called Microsoft Word to run Word for Windows, as shown here.

From Icon of Word

You can choose to have an icon of Word on your desktop. This icon can be created by using the feature of Creating Shortcut.

MICROSOFT WORD SCREEN

Once started Word give rise to a blank slate for typing your text. This screen has various items on it. One must know them before actually starting typing and using the commands.

Close button	This would close Word for Windows session.

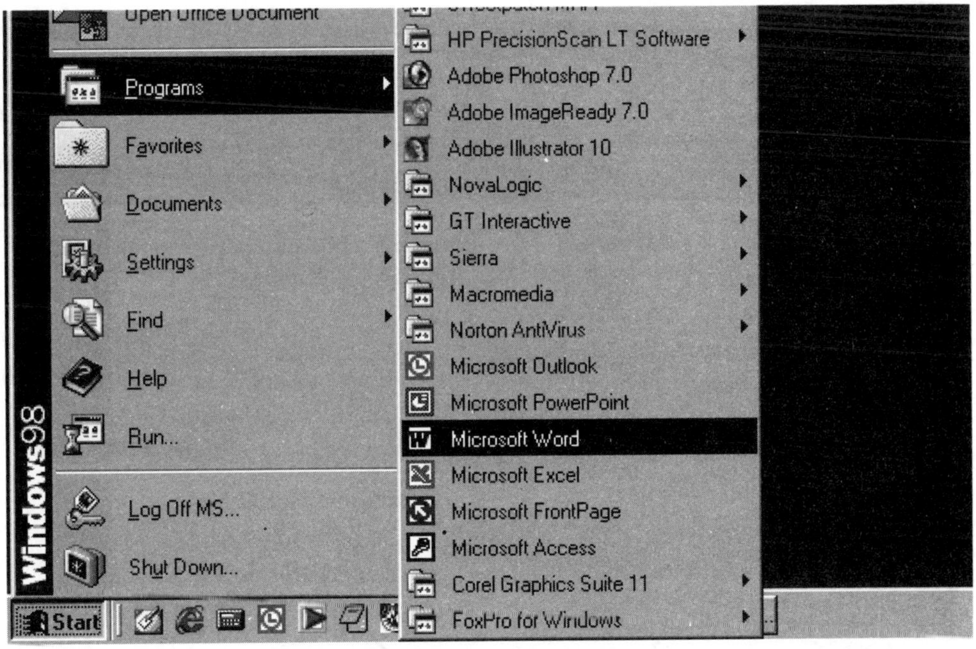

Drawing toolbar	One of the various toolbars which can be made available on the screen. This particular one is used for making drawings in the document.
Formatting bar	This bar is used to format the text. For example you can set font, font size, alignment, etc., using this bar.
Horizontal scroll bar	Sometimes the width of the text is such that it cannot be displayed on the whole screen. This bar is then used to see the text on the left or right.
Menu bar	Like in other programs Word for Windows also has various commands which can be accessed by clicking at the menu options under these menu heads.
Minimize button	While working, you can minimize your word document to reach desktop for working with another program, maybe.
Restore button	You have the option of working between two different views of the document by toggling this switch.
Ruler	Using this ruler you can see how much of the line you have consumed by typing.
Standard toolbar	There are a number of toolbars which allow you to select various tools for working in Word for Windows. This one is the standard which has all the icons of various file options, etc.
Starting point	This is the starting point of your text on the document. This is the point from where you would start typing.
Status bar	This bar will always show you your current position as far as the

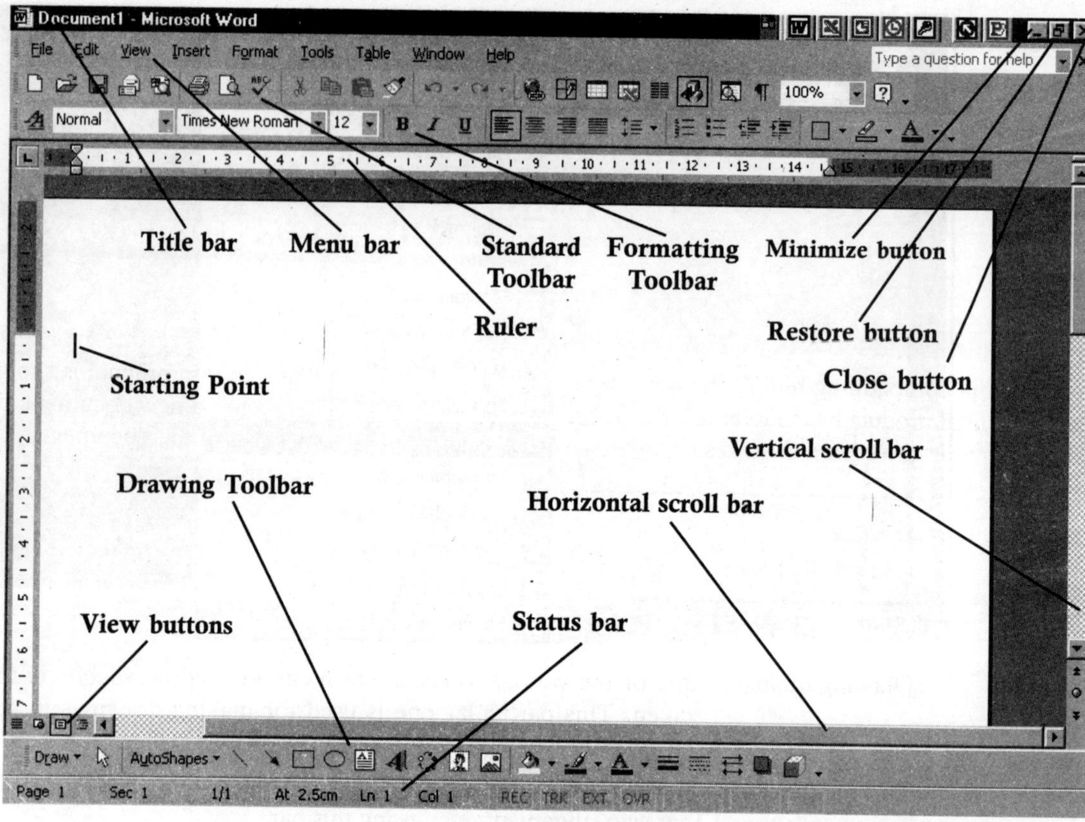

text goes. It will tell you your current position with respect to page number, line number, etc.

Title bar — Another permanent feature of Word for Windows which shows you the name of the file on which you are working and at the end has the various buttons like Close, Restore and Minimize.

Vertical scroll bar — For a larger text in the document, you can scroll the vertical bar to see the text at various positions.

View buttons — Word for Windows allows you to work in various views of the document. Using these buttons you can go from one view to another.

It is not these options are a must. You can choose to have different ones according to your style of working. Instead of Drawing toolbar, you may choose to have another toolbar.

CREATING A DOCUMENT

The best way to learn about a software is to run it. It is like jumping into the swimming pool to learn swimming. So we will create a document of our own in Word 2000 and learn the various commands side by side.

We have earlier learnt how to start Word 2000. Now we have to start a new document in it. After you have opened Word 2000 click at **New** from the **File menu** as shown on the next page.

Supposing we have to create a document in the form of a letter written to the General Manager of Unit

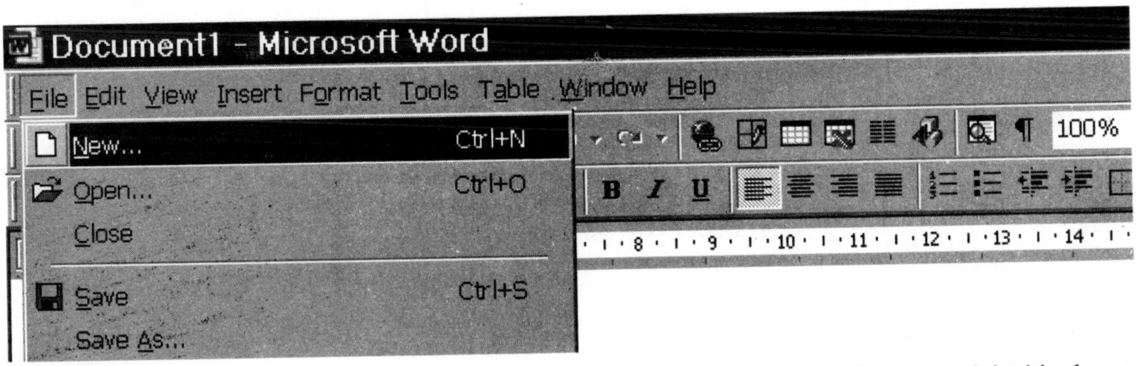

Trust of India complaining him of the non receipt of dividend warrant. This letter in original is shown below. The final product has to look like the one shown. Now that you have opened a new document, do not worry about any typing mistakes or any formatting, just type the text as it is of the document.

15th September, 2000

To,

The General Manager
Unit Trust of India
Gulab Bhawan
New Delhi - 110 002

Ref: Non-receipt of Dividend Warrant againt Folio no. 4000245497

Sir,

I am holder of the 100 units under the above folio number. For the last so many years I have been receiving the dividend againt it during the month of July itself. But, this year so far I have not received any intimtion. In fact, I have received dividend for my other units in July itself.

I hope that you would try to search for my dividend warrant and send the same to me at the earliest.

In case it is lost in post, please send me the replacement.

Hoping for an early action,

Thanking you,

Yours faithfully,

Shekhar Suman
T-391 Ahata Kidara
Delhi - 110 006

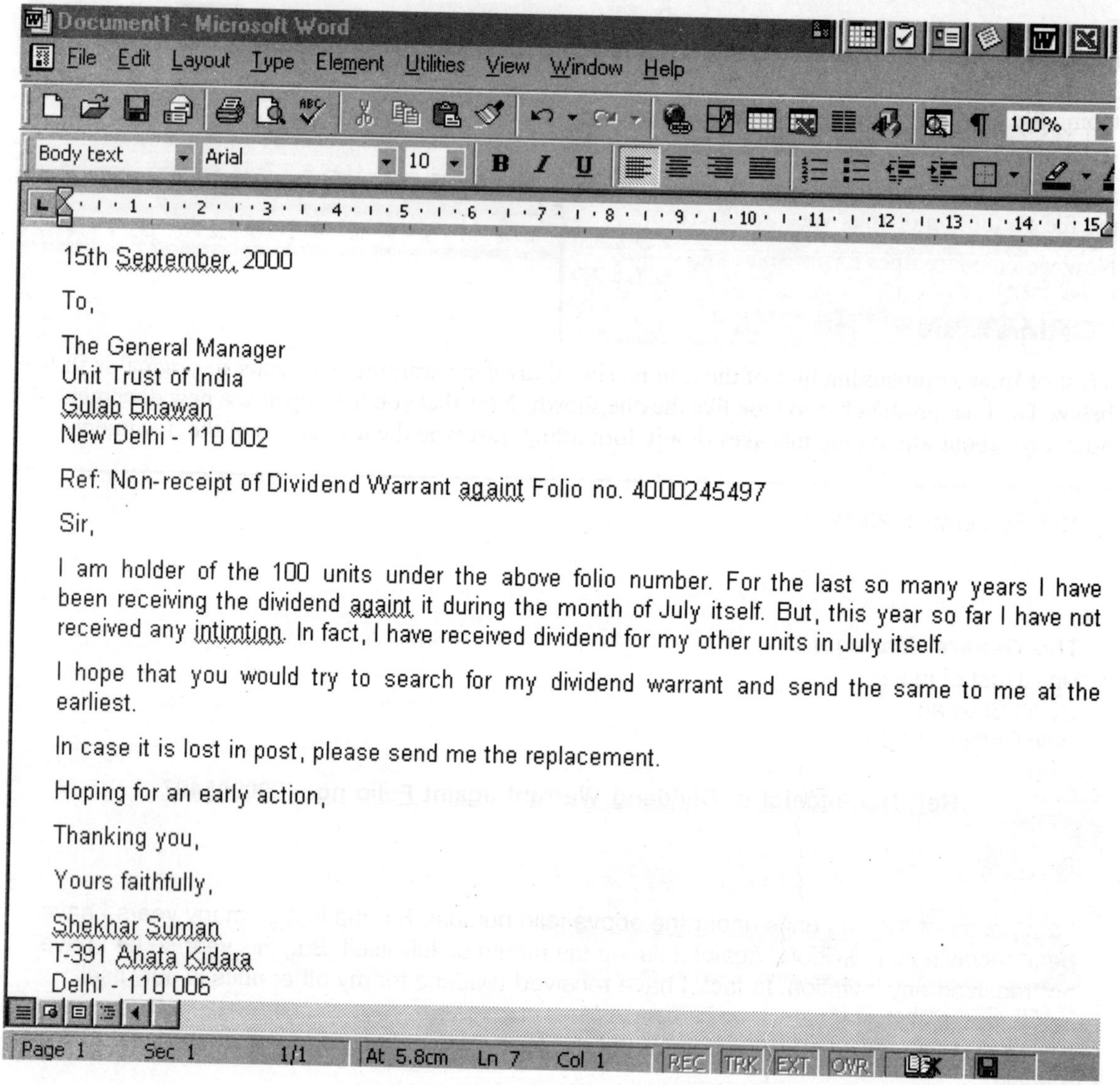

15th September, 2000

To,

The General Manager
Unit Trust of India
Gulab Bhawan
New Delhi - 110 002

Ref: Non-receipt of Dividend Warrant againt Folio no. 4000245497

Sir,

I am holder of the 100 units under the above folio number. For the last so many years I have been receiving the dividend againt it during the month of July itself. But, this year so far I have not received any intimtion. In fact, I have received dividend for my other units in July itself.

I hope that you would try to search for my dividend warrant and send the same to me at the earliest.

In case it is lost in post, please send me the replacement.

Hoping for an early action,

Thanking you,

Yours faithfully,

Shekhar Suman
T-391 Ahata Kidara
Delhi - 110 006

After typing, your screen will look like as shown above.

As you must have noticed there are few red and green wavy lines. The red lines, show that the word is incorrectly typed as per the dictionary available with the system and the word/words under whom the green line is, show that the words are grammatically wrong. This is the opinion of the software, you may beg to differ from it. Since most of the proper names like Shekhar Suman, are shown as wrong.

This is just the raw text which has been typed. Now we have to do the formatting. But, before that, lest the file gets tangled in power failure or something, we must save the file.

SAVING THE FILE

It is the process by which you give the name to the file and save under that name. Since our letter pertains to non receipt of dividend from Unit Trust of India, we will call our file as **Unit**.

For saving, just select the **Save** option under **File** menu. You will get the dialog box, as shown here. Just type the name **Unit** in the space provided for typing the filename and click **Save**.

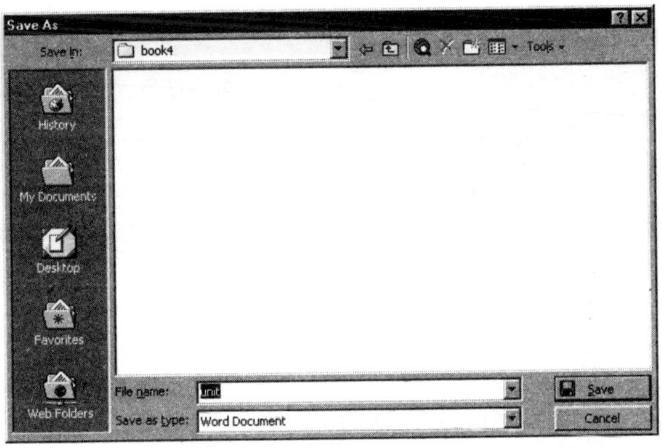

Your file will be saved under this name and automatically the title bar will show the name of the file on the top of the Word 2000 screen.

Now we come to other formatting tools.

FORMATTING THE TEXT

Let us now start our formatting from the top. The first line containing address has nothing to be done.

The second line containing **To**, has to be *italized.*

For this do the following:

1. Click the mouse button at the left of T of To.
2. Now drag the mouse, still having it pressed to the right so that the next character o also gets highlighted. At this stage both T and o are highlighted.
3. Now leave the mouse with To highlighted.
4. With the mouse, click at I in the formatting toolbar to make To as *To.*
5. See how To looks in the figure below.

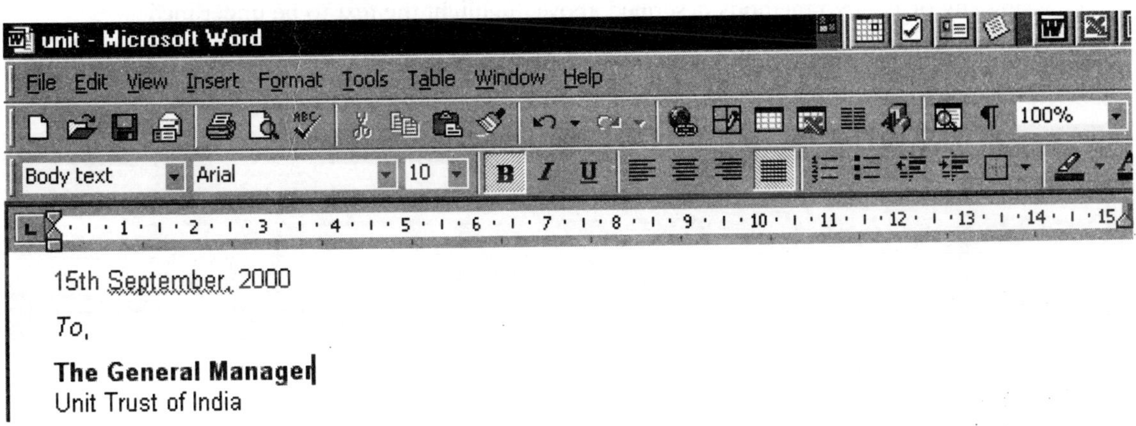

Now we come to the line having **The General Manager**. This line has to be made bold. This is how we do it.

1. Click the mouse button at the left of T of The General Manager.
2. Since we had highlighted the matter using mouse in the case of To, we will use a different approach here. Press Shift key and start pressing right arrow key ⇨. You will see that as the right arrow key is pressed the matter on the right gets highlighted. So highlight the matter till the point you want it to highlight. In this case highlight till r of Manager.
3. Now leave the shift key.

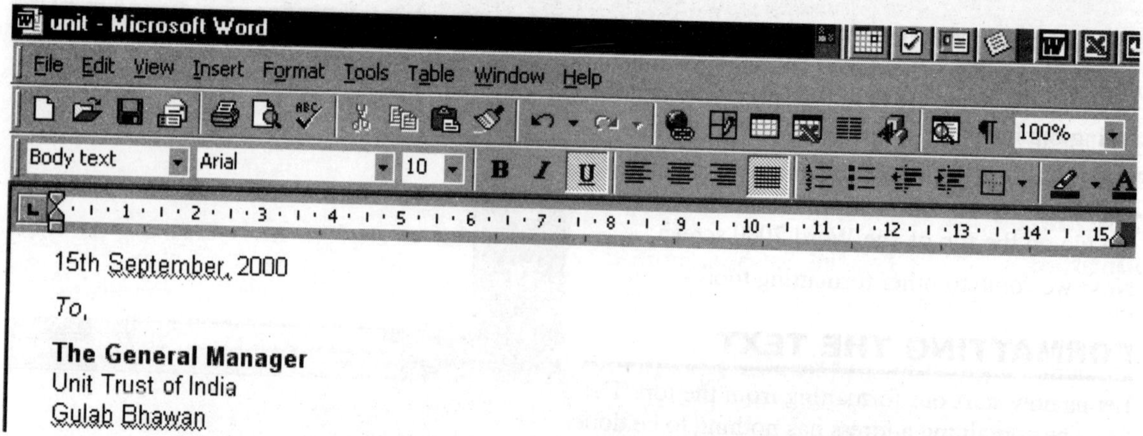

4. With the mouse, click at B in the formatting toolbar to make the highlighted text as **Bold**.
5. In the figure above, see how the text looks now with the The General Manager in Bold.

Next in the line is the address, whose last line New Delhi - 110 002 has to be underlined. Word 2000 allows you the option of underlining the word with one or more lines.

This option is available under **Font**. But for the time being, we will stick to single underline.

For this do the following:

1. Click the mouse button at the left of N of New Delhi - 110 002.
2. Using any of the two methods described above, highlight the text to be underlined.
3. With the mouse, click at U in the formatting toolbar to make the highlighted text **Underlined**.
4. You can see the text underlined below.

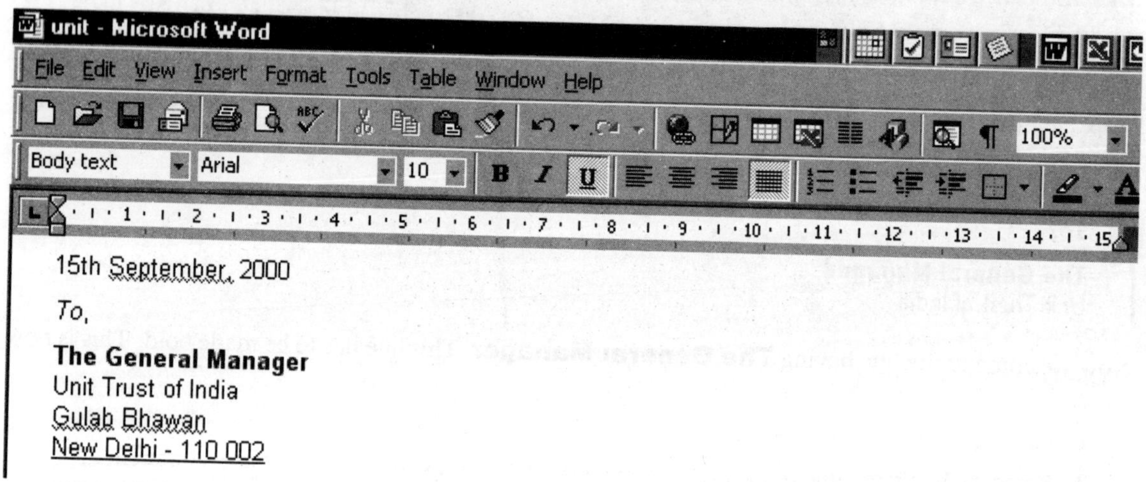

Coming down now you see the line containing the folio number. This line has to be underlined and centralized. I am not describing here the method to underline this line since it is similar to the one followed by you in the above case. I am sure you can do it yourself. Let us now concentrate on alignment. Let us see how it is done in Word 2000.

ALIGNMENT OF TEXT

Word 2000 gives you the option of placing the text in four different alignments. These are:

Left aligned This line is left aligned.

Right aligned This line is right aligned.

Centralized This line is centrally aligned.

Justified This line has been justified.

You will not notice much of a difference here in left aligned text and justified text. This is so because the matter is small. Just notice the whole text of this book, it is justified, i.e., it aligns to the left and right both. Whereas this **particular paragraph is left aligned** and see the difference for yourself.

All the four alignments are there on the formatting toolbar. You can choose any one of them. (If you do not have all 4 of them, click at **Add and Remove button** on the right of the toolbar to add the missing alignment to the formatting toolbar).

Coming back to our text. We have to centrally align the line containing the folio number.

For that do the following:

1. Click the mouse button at the left of R of Reference: Non-receipt of Dividend Warrant againt Folio no. 4000245497.
2. Click at the icon which shows the centralized alignment.
3. Notice here that you do not have to highlight the text for alignment. This is so since the whole matter of the paragraph has to be aligned to the same alignment.

   It is not possible to align one word to one alignment and another word to another alignment.
4. You can see the text underlined and centralized aligned in the figure below.

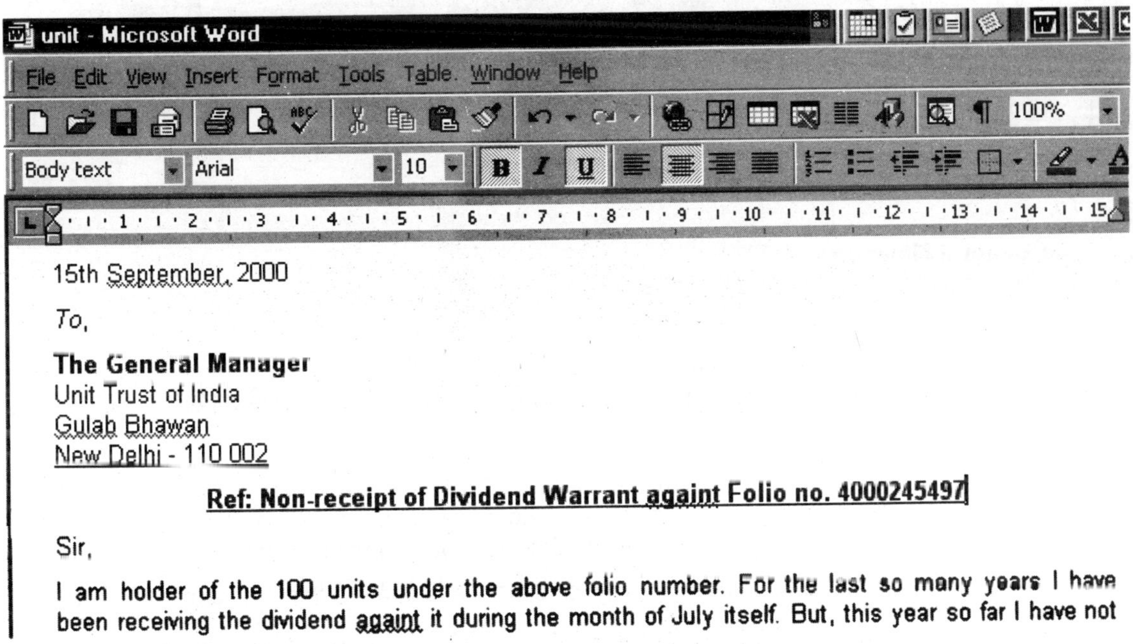

Now that the next lines have nothing much to be done, expect that Shekar Suman has to be made bold. This I presume you will be able to do without any difficulty.

It is time to save the document again so as to make sure that the changes made by you are stored in the hard disk.

Next, let us try to put some fancy things on the text. First among them is font.

APPLYING FONTS

It is upto you to select the same font for the whole text or have different fonts for different paragraphs.

Let us see how it is done.

1. Click at any place in the text with the mouse.
2. Click at Select All in the Edit menu or simply press Ctrl and then A. This will highlight the whole text in the document.
3. Now you can select the font of your liking in the whole text. You can also change the size of the font too.
4. Select Arial for font and size 10 for the whole text in the Formatting toolbar.
5. This will make the whole text 10 points and will have Arial as the font.
6. The previous changes made by you in terms of **Bold**, *Italics* will remain intact and will not be disturbed by doing this.
7. Now if you want you can change the font of particular items like address, etc., to make it more decorative.

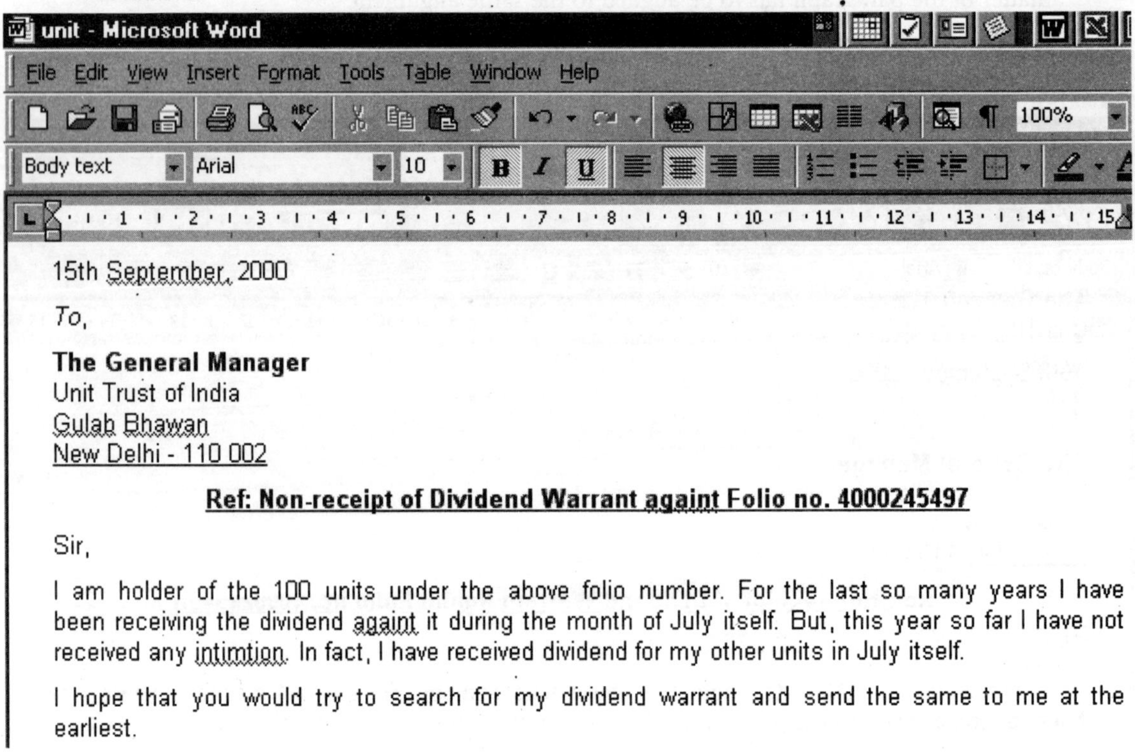

15th September, 2000

To,

The General Manager
Unit Trust of India
Gulab Bhawan
New Delhi - 110 002

Ref: Non-receipt of Dividend Warrant againt Folio no. 4000245497

Sir,

I am holder of the 100 units under the above folio number. For the last so many years I have been receiving the dividend againt it during the month of July itself. But, this year so far I have not received any intimtion. In fact, I have received dividend for my other units in July itself.

I hope that you would try to search for my dividend warrant and send the same to me at the earliest.

Now that our letter is ready, we can just print it, but before that we must check the spelling in the document so as no typological errors remain in the document.

SPELL CHECKING

As was mentioned earlier, Word 2000 points out the spelling errors by underling the word/words with red wavy line. Since our document is just one page long. It is not difficult to pin point the errors. I am quite sure you must have noticed them by now.

There are two methods of correcting these errors. One method is to correct these errors one by one, picking them up. Secondly, you spell check the whole document. Let us do both on our document. Looking from top to bottom of the text in the document file **Unit**, you will see few of the words underlined by **wavy red line**. Few of them are the proper words and thus cannot be corrected.

Words like Gulab is basically a *Hindi* word, so it cannot be in the dictionary of Word 2000 and that is why it has been shown as an error. Similar is the case with Bhawan which is again an *Indian* word and is not there in the dictionary and need not to be corrected. For this follow the following procedure:

1. Click with the mouse at any place within the word to be corrected, in this case againt. An alphabet s is missing in this.
2. Now right click the mouse button.
3. A pop-menu will pop-up as shown below.
4. Among the various options are:

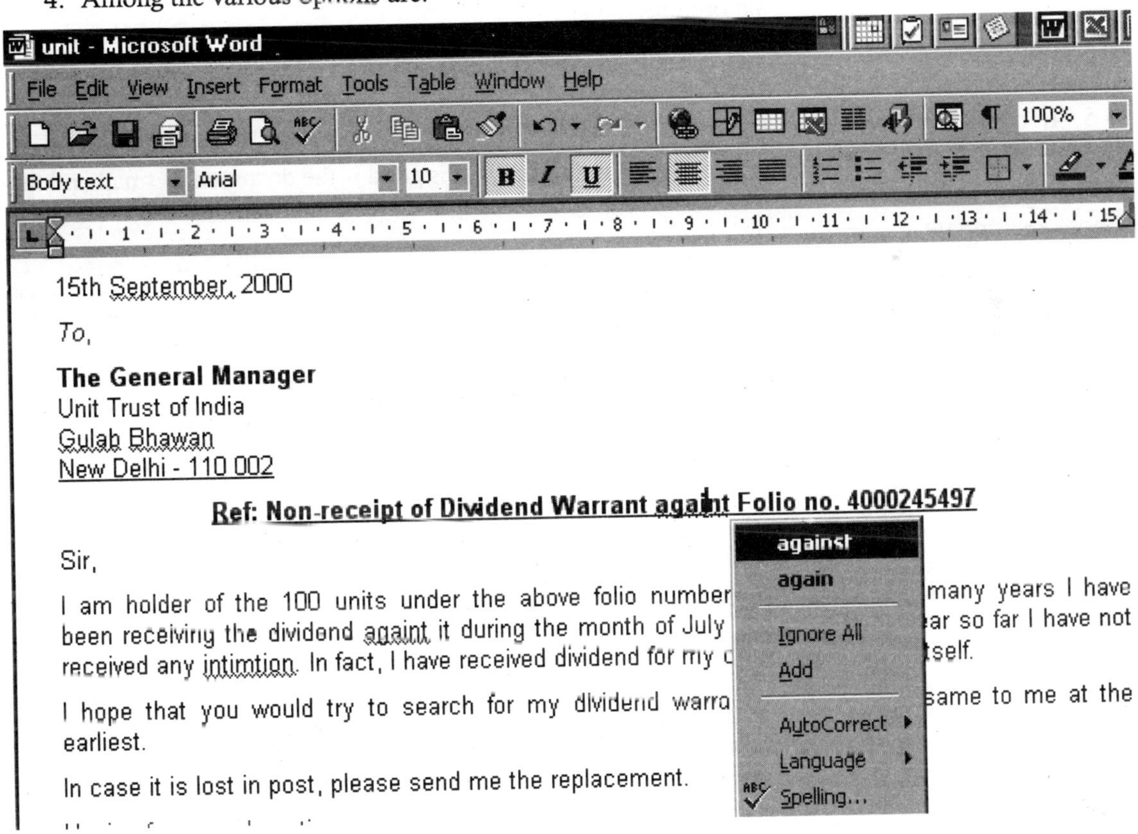

Alternative words	Word 2000 displays few words which are similar to the word in question with a hope that these may had been word in your mind while typing this word wrongly. You can choose any one of them, which you feel is the right word by just clicking and selecting that and leaving the mouse. The word will stand corrected with the new word and will replace the wrong word.
Ignore All	It is like over ruling the dictionary and saying that whatever you have typed is right and would like the dictionary to ignore this not only at this place but also at all other places within the document.
Add	You feel that this word is right and would like this word to be added to the dictionary so that it is not shown as an error in the future.
AutoCorrect	You will learn about AutoCorrect in the later chapter. But, only thing to understand here is that it is a list of mostly misplaced word which can be corrected without referring to the dictionary. For example, you may have the bad habit of typing *the* as *teh*. You can add this to AutoCorrect to correct *teh* to *the* always without even telling you.
Language	You feel that this particular word which has been pointed as wrong by the current dictionary would be available in other language dictionary. So mention here the name of the other dictionary where this word could be found. If you do not have a second dictionary loaded, just ignore this.
Spelling	By clicking at this, you can start the spell checking of the whole document from this point onward.

5. In our case we will accept against as the correct substitute for the wrong word againt.

Similarly you can correct the other words too. But, this method is good if the document is small and the errors are less. On the other hand, if you have a long document, then the other method of spell checking is more appropriate.

Now we come to the second way of spell checking which is checking the whole document. In this case place the cursor at the beginning of the text in the document. In our case we will place the cursor at the left of **1** of **15th September**.

From here do either of the following to start the spell checking.

1. Select Spelling and Grammar from the Tools menu.

   Or

2. Press F7

   Or

3. Click at Spell Checking button on the Standard toolbar.

This will initiate the spell checking process and will start the spell checking of the document with each word of the document being searched with the similar word with the words available in the dictionary. If not found it will point out as shown below.

Consider the case shown on the next page, the error has been pointed out in the word September, which is not a spelling error, this is a grammatical error. The suggestion given here is that you put only **September** and not **September,** i.e., comma (,) after September is not required. Now the choice is

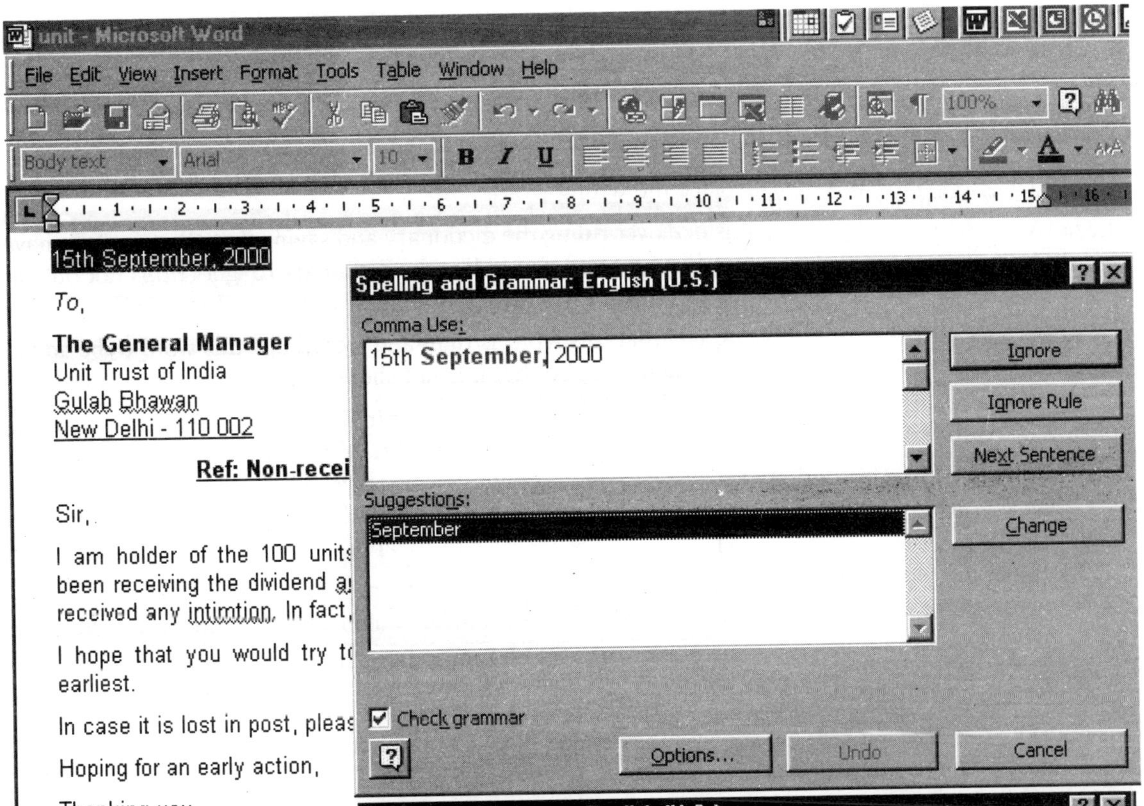

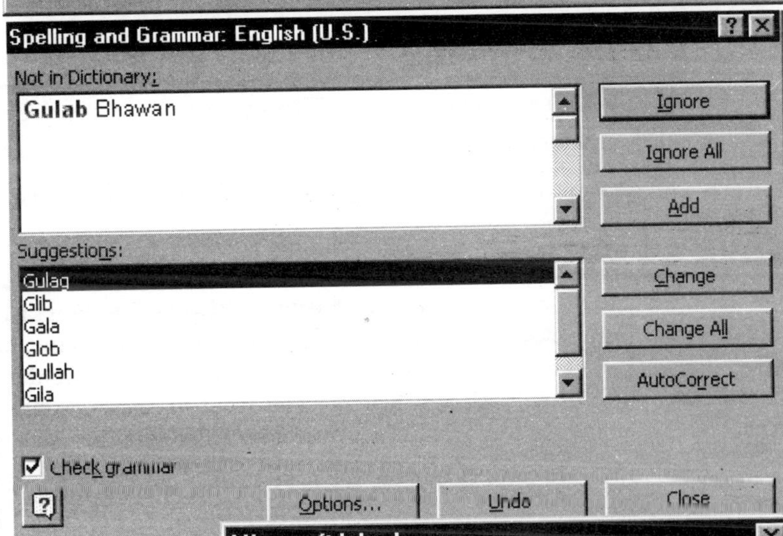

yours to **Ignore** this or just accept the suggestion as it is and make it September. I suggest we let it remain as it is. For this click at **Ignore** and see what happens.

Now it selects *Gulab* of **Gulab Bhawan**. As was mentioned before it is a proper *Hindi* word, so it cannot be corrected. **Ignore** to proceed further. Other words in the document are also corrected till you reach the end of the document and it stops checking the spelling of the document. In between it will correct the words **againt** by **against** and **intimtion** by **intimation**.

After this there is no other word to correct and the spell checking ends with a dialog box, saying that the spelling checking is complete.

Remember, you can spell check a portion of the text or a word by just highlighting it and then clicking at **Spell Checking Icon**. Then there is another option called **Thesaurus**.

CONSULTING THESAURUS

Thesaurus is there to help you find **Synonym**, words with similar meanings and **Antonym**, words with opposite meanings. Using the thesaurus not only helps your vocabulary, but gives you alternatives to using the same word over and over again throughout your text.

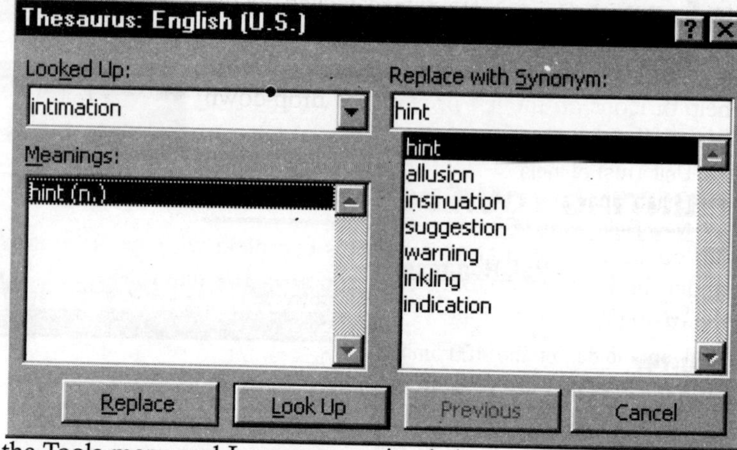

Let us try to use this option in our text. We would like to see the alternatives to the word **intimation**. For this we do the following:

1. Select the word intimation in the paragraph.
2. Now select Thesaurus from the Tools menu and Language or simply by pressing Shift + F7.
3. You will get the dialog box as shown here.
4. The options given here are shown in the dialog box. You can opt to change it anyone of them or let the word remain as it is.

CLOSING OF THE FILE

You can choose **Close** command from **File** menu to close the document file. Or you can do so by clicking at ☒ button on the extreme right top of the word document.

But don't forget to save the file before closing else the software will ask you to do so.

SAVE AS OPTION

Let us understand the difference between **Save** and **Save As**. You save your document file as you save any other file. **Save As** option allows you to save with another name, maybe another format at another drive/directory. It is not that the system will not allow you to save the file with the same name under **Save As** option. It will ask you whether you want to overwrite the file which exists. This is just a precautionary option so that you do not overwrite a file with the same name accidentally.

Now suppose that you have closed the file after saving, the next option obviously is open this file.

OPEN FILE

Opening of the file can be done by 2 methods if you are already working under Word 2000.

From File menu

There is an **Open** command under the **File** menu. Click at it to open the Open dialog box as shown next.

From Open Icon

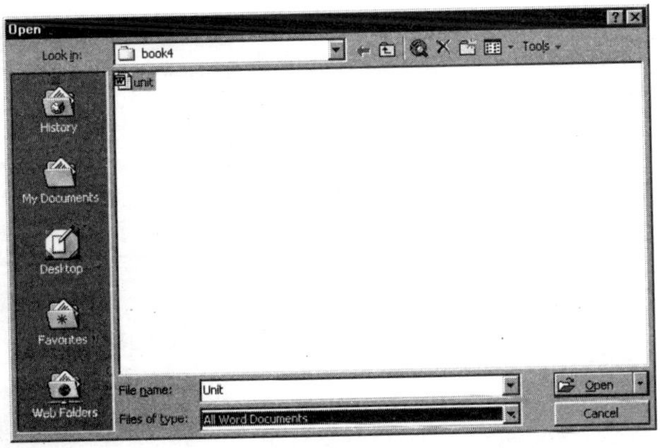

You can get the same Open dialog box by clicking at Open icon on the **Standard** toolbar.

In both cases you will get the dialog box shown on the next page. From here you can click the file you want to open. If it is not there on the screen, try to locate it in different directories with the help of icons on the left or from the drop-down list of directories.

PRINTING YOUR DOCUMENT

No document preparation process is complete without printing it. For this we have the **Print** option under the **File** menu. Once clicked it gives rise to a dialog box as shown below. The various options on the dialog box are as follows:

Printer — Select the printer to which you want to send the printing. From the drop-down list, you can select one of the many printers which you may have installed under Windows.

Properties — Clicking at it would lead to a dialog box having the properties of the selected printer. If some adjustments are to be made in the properties of the selected printer, they can be done here.

Print to file — Sometimes it is possible that you may like to print the document to the printer which is not installed in your computer. In this case you will select this option and create a print file for that particular printer and copy the file and then print on that printer where it is installed.

Print range — You may like to print few selective pages instead of printing the whole document. So either click **All**, for printing all pages of the document or **Pages**, for defining the pages you want to print. You can even print the current page, i.e., page on the screen.

Copies — Word 2000 allows you to print multiple copies of the pages in the document. You can mention here the number of copies you want. What's more you can have the copies collated for you, if you select the **collate** option.

Print what — Various options available here are Document, Document properties, Comments, Styles, AutoText entries, Key assignments. But, most of the time you would be printing with Document option.

Print — You have the option of printing all pages or all **odd pages** or all **even pages**.

Zoom — Pages per sheet allows you to print 1 to 16 pages of the document on one sheet. Scaling allows you to scale your document to the various sizes of the paper.

Options — This will lead to the print options, already described under **Options** and select the option of your choice.

Once you are sure that you have selected all the options required by you, just click Ok to for document to start printing. However, do not forget to have the Printer ON before giving the final print command.

Your final document should look like the one shown on the next page.

I suggest you write this letter in your computer and go through the whole process. Print it and show it to your teacher.

I had mentioned about selecting the word and character while formatting, but there are other options too for selecting.

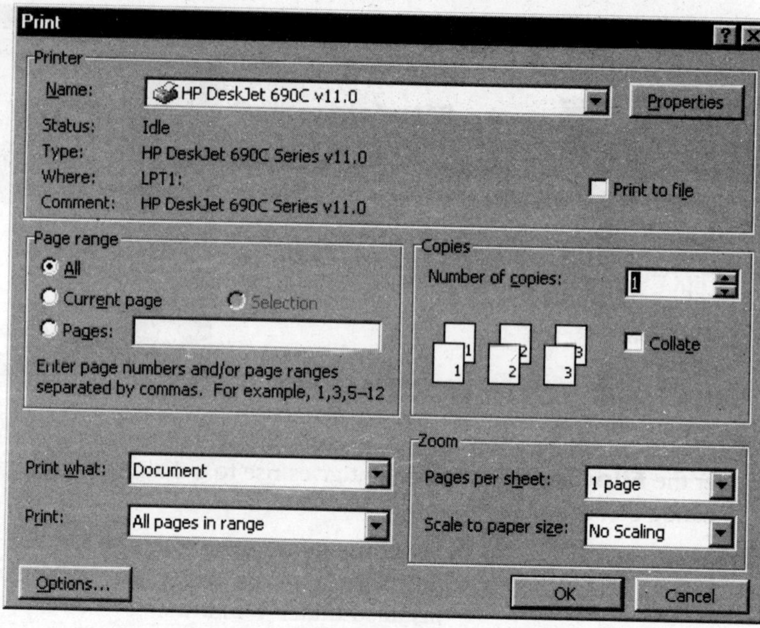

SELECTING THE TEXT

For any text to be formatted, it has to be selected. There are various ways of selecting the text.

Selecting from keyboard

For selecting, place the cursor at the left of the word to be selected and then do the following:

Press shift + right arrow	To select one character to the right
Press shift + right arrow	To select one character to the left
Press shift + up arrow	To select one line up
Press shift + down arrow	To select one line down
Press shift + end	To select to the end of the line
Press shift + home	To select to the beginning of the line
Press shift + ctrl + end	To select till end of the document
Press shift + ctrl + home	To select from the beginning of the document
Press ctrl + a	To the complete text

Selecting the text with the mouse

For this do the following:

1. Position the cursor to the left of the first character to select.
2. Hold down the left mouse button and drag it to where you want to stop.
3. Release the mouse.

Selecting with mouse clicks

1. Double click to select a word.

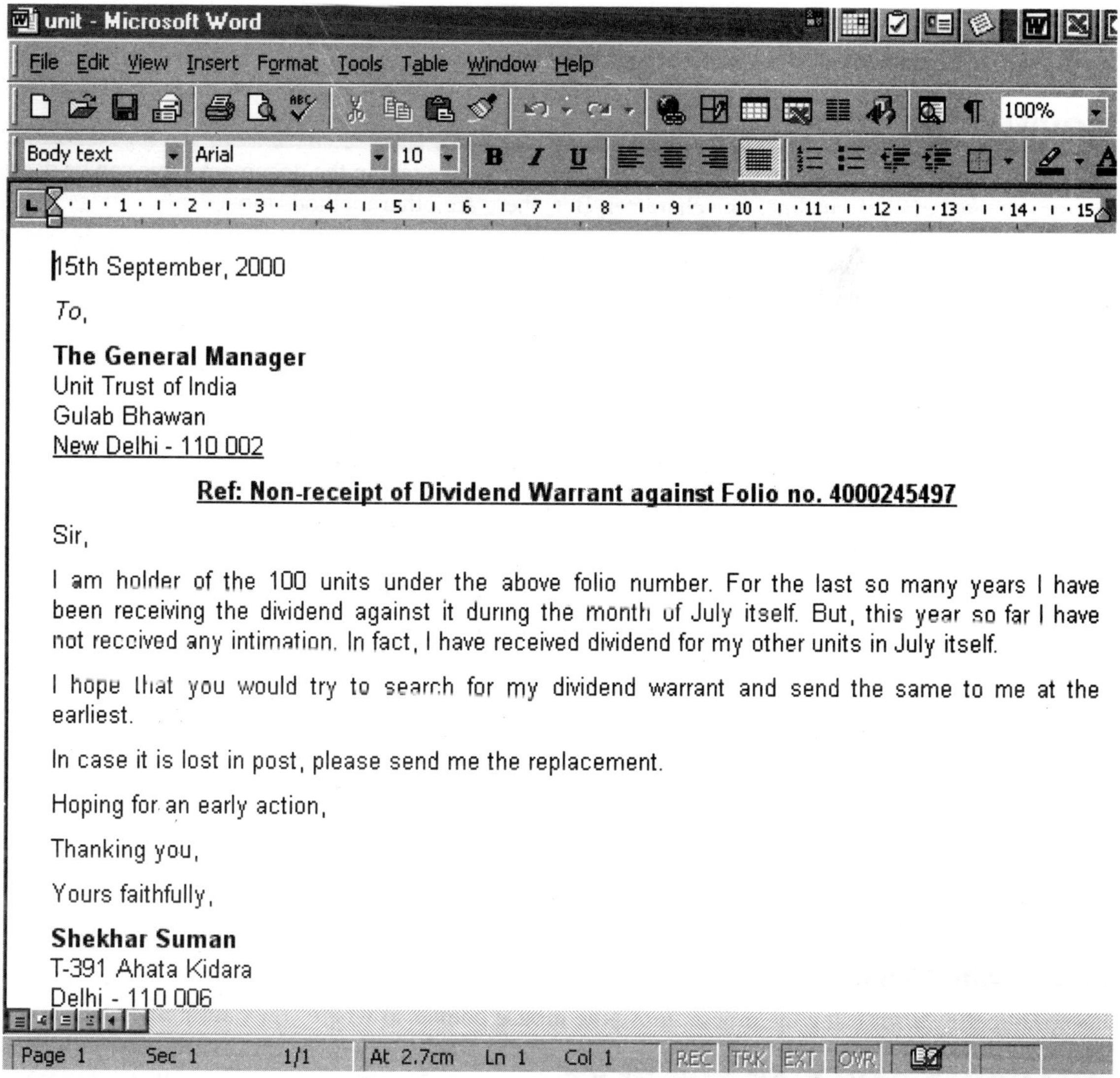

15th September, 2000

To,

The General Manager
Unit Trust of India
Gulab Bhawan
New Delhi - 110 002

Ref: Non-receipt of Dividend Warrant against Folio no. 4000245497

Sir,

I am holder of the 100 units under the above folio number. For the last so many years I have been receiving the dividend against it during the month of July itself. But, this year so far I have not received any intimation. In fact, I have received dividend for my other units in July itself.

I hope that you would try to search for my dividend warrant and send the same to me at the earliest.

In case it is lost in post, please send me the replacement.

Hoping for an early action,

Thanking you,

Yours faithfully,

Shekhar Suman
T-391 Ahata Kidara
Delhi - 110 006

Computer Room Activity

Creating a Document

Open Word and create a document asking permission from the Principal of the school make use of the library in the summer vocation. Also perform the following operations on it:

Spell checking

Formatting like Bold, Italics, etc.

Align the various lines of text differently.

After doing all this take a print of the same and show it to your teacher.

2. Triple click to select the full paragraph.
3. Ctrl + click in a sentence to select the full sentence.

MOVING THE TEXT

There are times when you would be needing to move around the text in the document. This can be done by using arrow keys but one line, one character. But, there are other methods too.

From the keyboard

Right arrow	One character to the right
Left arrow	One character to the left
Up arrow	One line up
Down arrow	One line down
Ctrl + right arrow	One word to the right
Ctrl + left arrow	One word to the left
Ctrl + up arrow	To the beginning of the current paragraph
Ctrl + down arrow	To the beginning of the next paragraph
End	To the end of the current line
Ctrl + end	To the end of the document
Home	To the start of the current line
Ctrl + home	To the start of the document
Page up	Up one screen
Page down	Down one screen
Ctrl + page up	To the first character on the current screen
Ctrl + page down	To the last character on the current screen

Moving with Mouse

To position the cursor using the mouse, move the mouse pointer to where you want it and click.

CHANGING STYLE OF THE TEXT

By style in Word, we mean the appearance of the text. The various formats supported by Word are:

Bold

Italics

Underline

These are the main styles and we had earlier used them in our letter. But, if you go deep into the working of the software, you would see that it allow you to convert the character to:

Strikethrough

Double strikethrough

Superscript

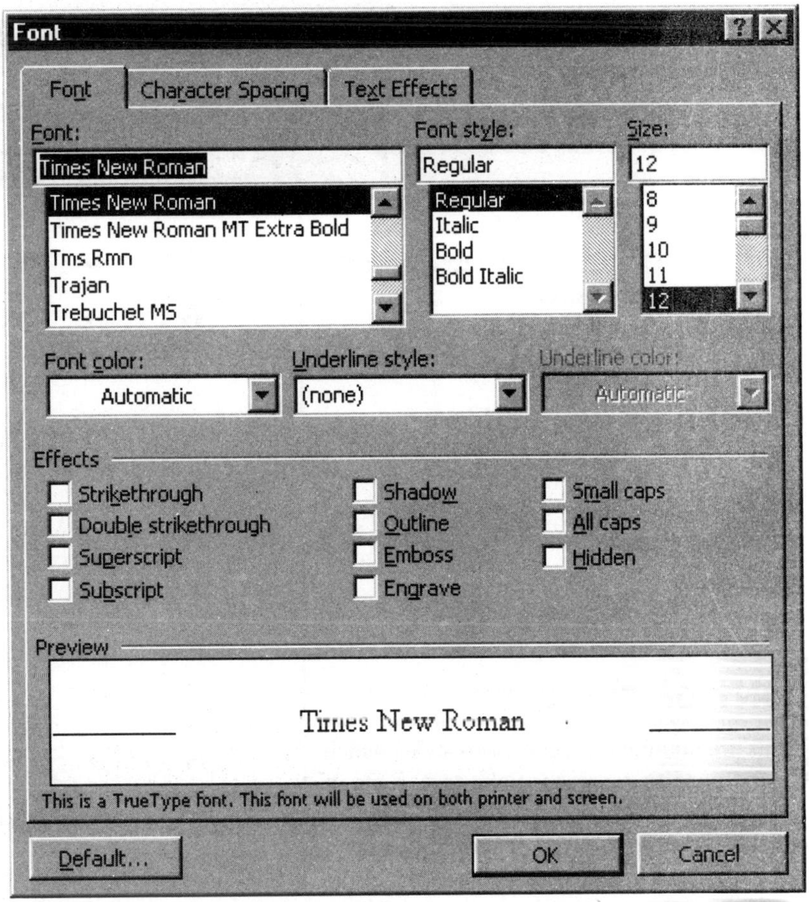

Subscript

Shadow

Outline

Emboss

Engrave

Small Caps

All Caps

Hidden

The first 3 are there on the Standard toolbar only. They can be used by just clicking at them. For example, if you have to make a word, Bold, then select the word and click at B in the Standard toolbar, it will be made Bold. Similarly, you can make the characters italics and underlined.

Bold

Italics

Undeline

The above example shows how they appear after changing the styles. For the other styles you have to do the following:

1. Select the text whose style you have to change.
2. Click at Format menu and select Font from it.
3. In the dialog box, select the option you want to use.
4. You text would be changed accordingly.
5. Various options of the text are shown above.

SIZE OF TEXT

The size of the text, pertains to the thickness of the text. As the size increases, the width of the character also increases. In fact, the proportionate height of the character also increases. You can change the size of the text from 2 places in Word.

From the Formatting Bar

1. Select the text whose size you want to change.
2. Click at font size in the formatting bar to have Word display various sizes
3. Select the size which you want.

From the Font Dialog Box

1. Select the text whose size you want to change.
2. Click at Format and select Font.
3. From the Font dialog box, select the size you want to have.
4. Click Ok to have your text changed to the required size.

The following examples would show how the font size make the differencc:

A	12 point
A	20 point
A	40 point

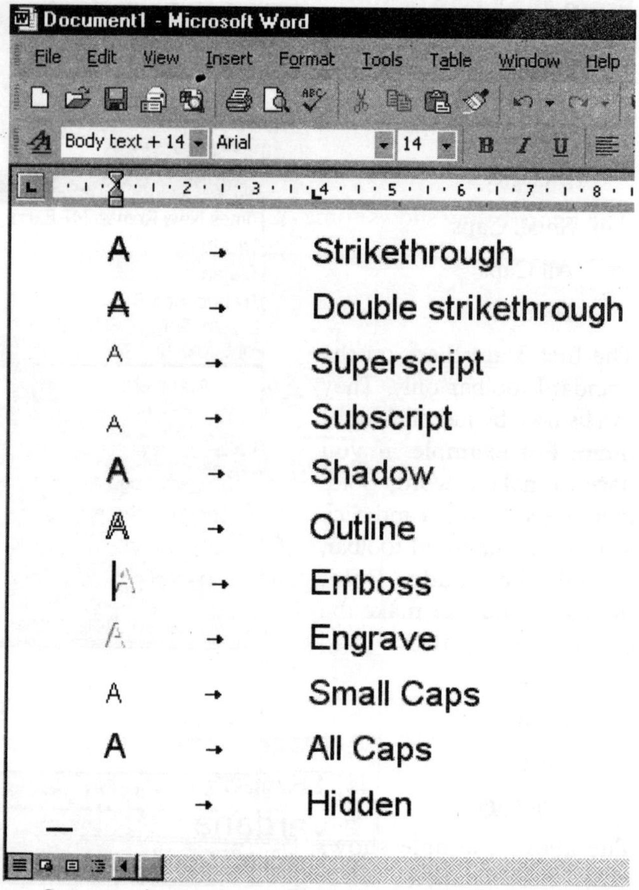

FONT OF THE TEXT

Fonts are nothing but the various styles which can be used to represent your text. Lots of fonts are available from fancy ones to ornamental types. Microsoft Word on its own does not have fonts, but, it takes the fonts available under the Windows. As usual there are 2 ways of selecting the font for the text.

From Formatting Toolbar

1. Select the text whose font you want to change.
2. Click at font in the formatting bar to have Word display various fonts.
3. Select the font which you want.

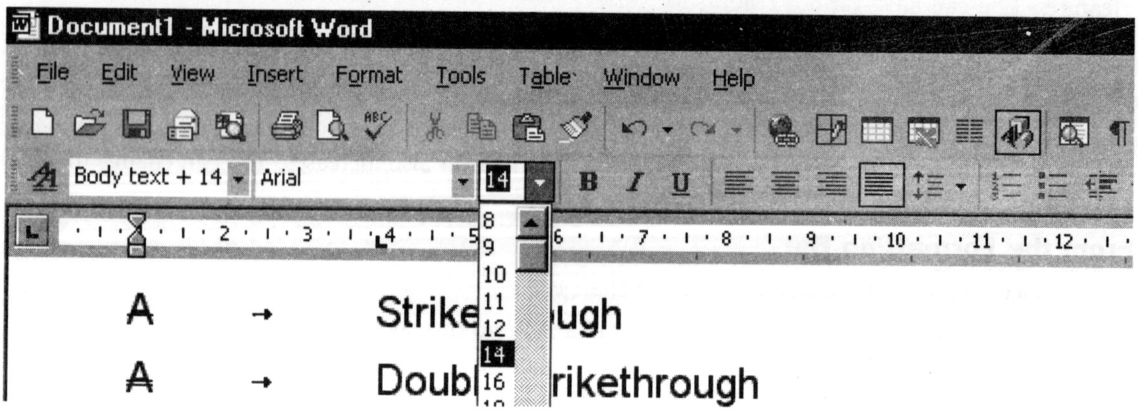

From the Font Dialog Box

1. Select the text whose font you want to change.
2. Click at Format and select Font.
3. From the Font dialog box, select the font you want to have.
4. Click Ok to have your text changed to the required font.

The figure below shows some of the fonts available.

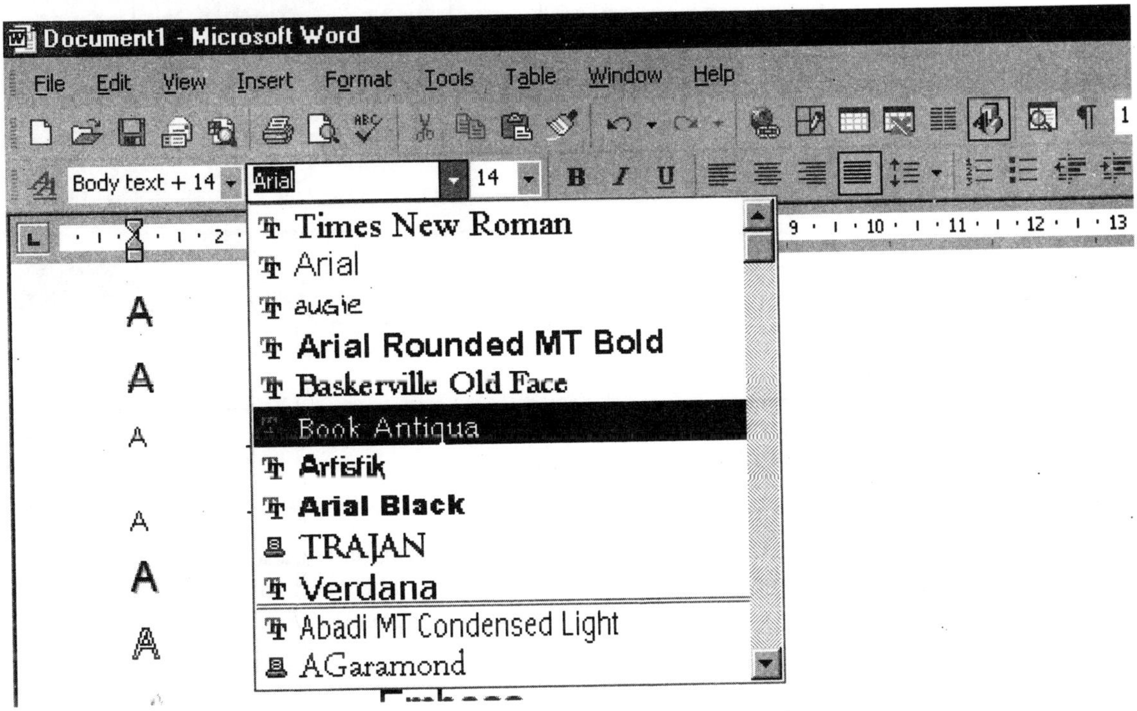

COLOUR OF THE TEXT

You can if you want can change the colour of the text too. Since of the printers now-a-days have the colour capabilities, you can print your letters in colours too. Microsoft Word supports the full colour features. You can have various colours for various portions of the text in your document.

For changing the colour of the text, do the following:

1. Select the text whose colour you want to change.
2. Click at A on thc formatting toolbar.
3. A colour template would be shown to you.
4. Select the colour which you want.
5. Your text would be changed to that colour.
6. If you click at More Colors, another dialog box would give you more options of colours to choose from.
7. Both the dialog boxes are shown on the next page.

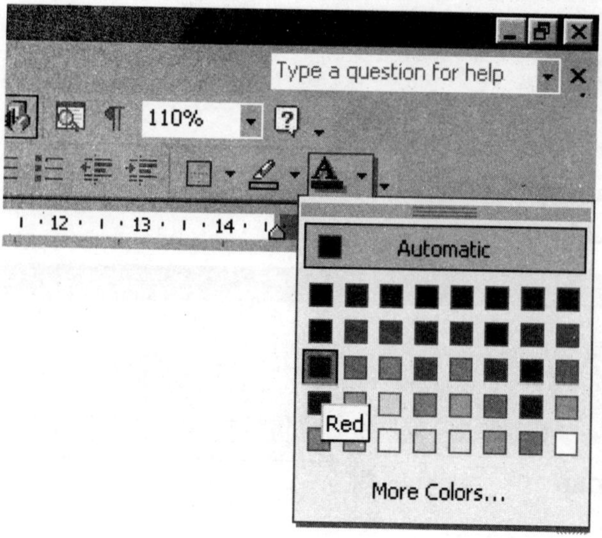

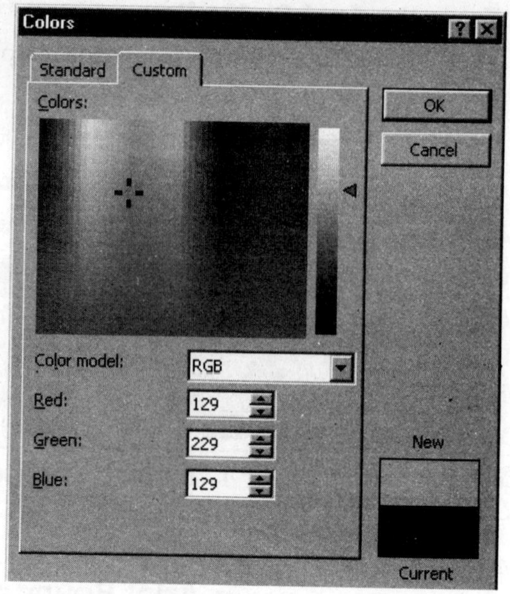

EDITING TOOLS

Many editing functions are performed on selected text, such as cut, copy, move, and delete. There are various tools provided by Word to help you edit text:

Cut, Copy

Cutting and copying items places them on the Clipboard and you can paste these items anywhere in the document, wherever required. These items can be text, graphics, tables and any other object which is there in the word document. Cut and Copy can be performed using mouse and key strokes.

Paste

It is the command used to paste whatever is available on the Clipboard to paste it in the document. This is also done by the use of mouse and key strokes.

Move

It is an action associated with the mouse. However, if you cut and paste from one place to another, it can also be called move.

Insert Mode

It is the feature that adjusts spacing when you add new text to the document.

Overtype Mode

This option replaces the existing text with your new text.

Delete

It is an action you should reserve for text you want to permanently remove. Deleted text is not placed in the Clipboard. You can delete text with either mouse or key strokes.

Undo and Redo

Using these commands you can reverse the tasks performed earlier.

All these commands are available on the toolbars as icons too.

You can find them in the Edit menu too.

For either cutting or copying, you have to highlight the part of the text on which you want to perform this operation. All these commands have their keyboard strokes associated with them too.

They are:

Cut	Ctrl + X
Copy	Ctrl + C
Paste	Ctrl + V
Move	Ctrl + X and then Ctrl + V
Delete	Backspace or Delete
Undo	Ctrl + Z
Redo	Ctrl + Y

INSERTING GRAPHICS

It is not that Word is only for text. You can have graphics into it. You can in fact enter graphics into it. This graphics could have been created in other software which is capable of creating graphics. However, Word has its own set of Clip Arts too, which can be used to enhance your word document.

To add a graphic to the word document do the following:

1. Place the cursor where you want to insert the graphic.
2. Click at Picture in the Insert menu. From the sub-menu select From File to open the Insert Picture dialog box.
3. If necessary, select the folder where the graphic is stored from the Look In drop-down list.
4. The Files of Type drop-down list is automatically set to display All Pictures, but you can select the specific type of graphic file you want to appear in the list.

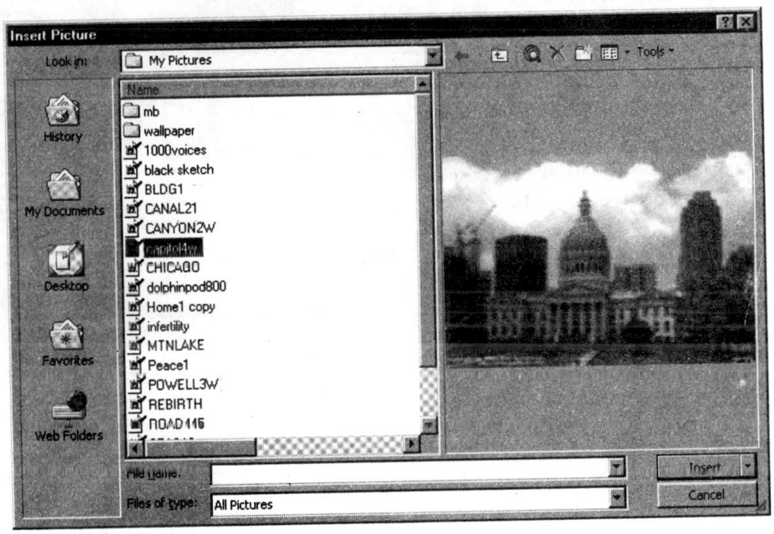

5. Select the name of the file you want to use from the listed files, enter the name in the File Name text box, or highlight the file. Click the down arrow next to Views on the toolbar and then select Preview to see a preview of the selected file.
6. Click any of the following options from the Insert drop-down list:
   - Insert. Inserts the picture at your cursor position in the document.
   - Link to File. By default, Word embeds pictures in the document, which adds to the size of the file. Choose this option to reduce the size of the file by linking to it. One benefit of linking is that the graphic in the document updates immediately if any changes are made to the original file.
   - Insert and Link. Inserts the picture into the document and links to the source file so the picture is immediately updated if the original graphic is changed.
7. Choose Insert to add the graphics image to your document.

Insert Clip Art

Word comes with a library of Clip Art, which is comprised of drawings and pictures you use to add visual appeal and interest to your documents. Adding clip art to the documents is easy and it can be the added element that draws attention to your document versus someone else's in a competitive market.

Add Clip Art to a Document

1. Place your cursor where you want to put the clip art picture or drawing in your document.
2. Open the Insert menu and choose Picture, then choose Clip Art from the submenu to open the Insert Clip Art dialog box.

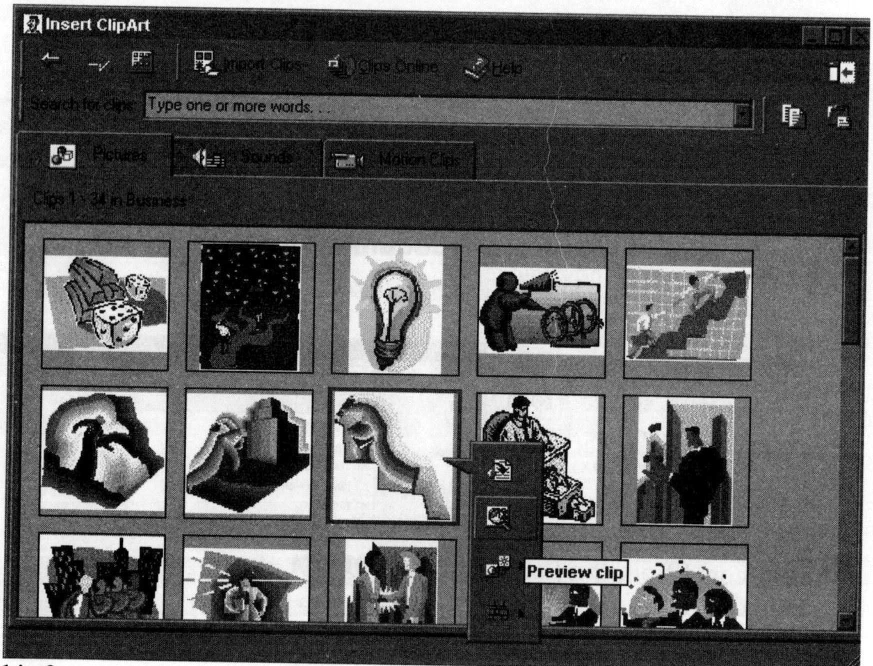

3. The Pictures tab is displayed, showing a set of clip art categories.
4. Click a category picture to display the clips in that category. When you point to one of the clips, the graphic format and categories of that clip appear as a pop-up.
5. Click once on the clip to see a menu.
6. Choose Insert Clip to insert the clip in your document.

Computer Room Activity

Inserting graphics in the Document

In the document created earlier, add graphics in the form of a picture available in the hard disk or any clip art from the Word.

Take the print out and see how the picture looks with the text.

Wrap Text around Graphics

A graphic causes a break in your text. The text immediately after the graphic does not start until the next line after the picture, leaving whitespace to the left or right of the graphic. It also leaves space on the top and bottom of the graphic. This is called text wrap and is Word's default setting for wrapping text around a picture.

Set Text Wrap Options

1. Select the image.
2. Open the Format menu and select Picture, choose Format Picture on the Picture toolbar, or right-click the graphic and select Format Picture from the pop-up menu.
3. When the Format Picture dialog box appears, select the Layout tab.
4. Under Wrapping Style, select a style of text wrap—In Line with Text, Square, Tight, Behind Text, or In Front of Text—depending on how close you want the text to wrap around the picture.
5. Choose Advanced to set text wrapping specifics in the Advanced Layout dialog box.
6. Select the Text Wrapping tab. Under Wrap Text, select the sides on which you want the text to wrap—Both Sides, Left Only, Right Only, or Largest Only.

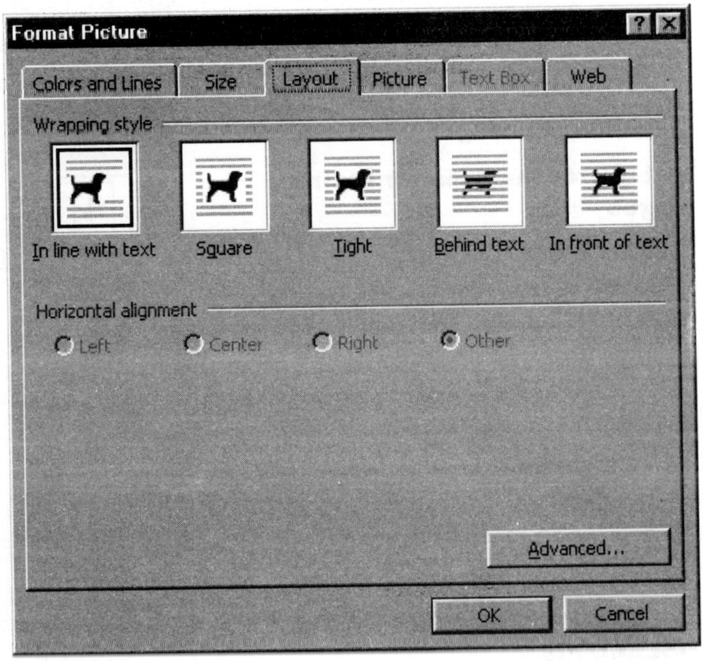

7. To set the distance between the edge of the picture and the beginning of the text wrapping around it, enter the distance in the **Top**, **Bottom**, **Left**, and **Right** boxes under Distance from Text.
8. Choose Ok to close the Advanced Layout dialog box.
9. Choose Ok to close the Format Picture dialog box.

The picture would be adjusted in the text as your needs.

Computer Room Activity

Wrapping Text around the Picture

As per the instructions given in the last para, wrap the picture around the text and see the result. Use all the options and see which one gives the best result.

PAGE SETUP

You can change the page layout of the document. Set the margins according to your likings. For all this you have the command called Pageset in File menu.

Change Page Margins

1. On the File menu, click Page Setup, and then click the Margins tab.
2. Under Margins, select the options you want.
3. To change the default margins, click Default after you select new margin settings. The new default settings are saved in the template on which the document is based.
4. Each new document based on that template automatically uses the new margin settings.

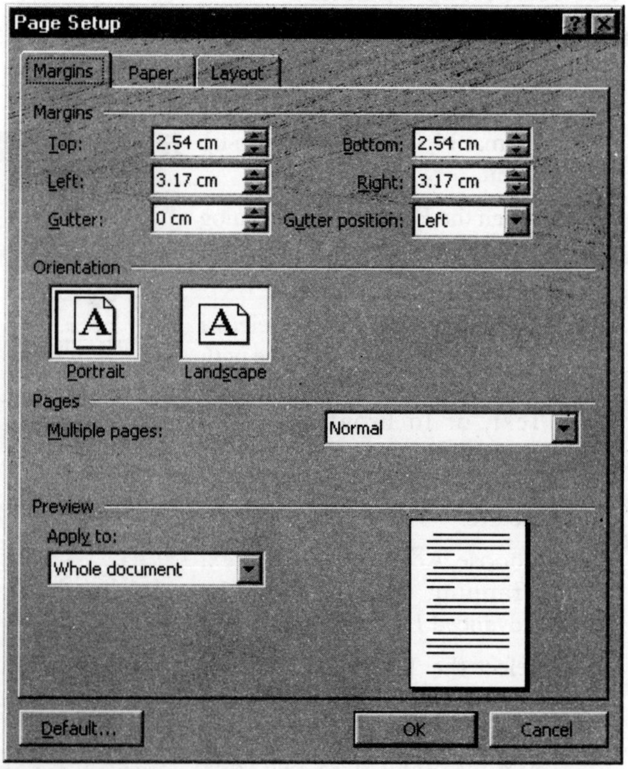

Set mirror margins for facing pages

Margins of the left page are a mirror image of those on the right page. That is, the inside margins are the same width, and the outside margins are the same width.

1. On the File menu, click Page Setup, and then click the Margins tab.
2. In the Multiple pages list, select Mirror margins.
3. In the Inside and Outside boxes, enter values for the mirror margins.

Set gutter Margins for Bound Documents

A gutter margin setting adds extra space to the side or top margin of a document you plan to bind. A gutter margin ensures that text isn't obscured by the binding.

1. On the File menu, click Page Setup, and then click the Margins tab.
2. In the Gutter box, enter a value for the gutter margin.
3. In the Gutter position box, click Left or Top.

4. To change the margins for part of a document, select the text, and then set the margins you want. In the Apply to box, click Selected text.
5. Microsoft Word automatically inserts section breaks before and after the text with the new margin settings. If your document is already divided into sections, you can click in a section or select multiple sections, and then change the margins.

Change the Orientation of Text

You can change the text orientation in drawing objects, such as text boxes (text box: A movable, resizable container for text or graphics. Use text boxes to position several blocks of text on a page or to give text a different orientation from other text in the document.), shapes, and callouts, or in table cells so that the text is displayed vertically or horizontally.

1. Click the drawing object or table cell that contains the text you want to change.
2. On the Format menu, click Text Direction.
3. Click the orientation you want.

Select a paper source

1. On the File menu, click Print.
2. Click Properties.
3. Click the Paper tab.
4. In the Paper source box, click the paper source you want.

Select paper size

1. On the File menu, click Page Setup, and then click the Paper tab.
2. Click a paper size.

Computer Room Activity

Setting the Page Size in the Document

You can change the page setup of the document created earlier. Change the page setup to have the following options:

Top Margin 1 inch

Bottom Margin 1 inch

Gutter Margin 1.5 inch

Left Margin 1 inch

Right Margin 1 inch

Page Width 6 inch

Page height 8 inch

Orientation Portrait

Header DOE O Level

Footer IT Tools and Applications

See the preview of the page in the Print Preview.

3. To change the paper size for part of a document, select the pages and then change the paper size as usual. In the Apply to box, click Selected text. Microsoft Word automatically inserts section breaks before and after the pages with the new paper size. If your document is already divided into sections, you can click in a section or select multiple sections, and then change the paper size.

FIND AND REPLACE

Supposing you had a document which contained the name of the city as **Calcutta**. Now since the name of the city has been changed to **Kolkatta**, naturally, you would like to change the name of the city too. For this you have the option of Find and Replace in Word. This option will find the particular word required by you and then replace with another word, as suggested by you. This option can be used separately too as Find and Replace.

You can use Find and Replace to do the following:

Text strings

Either strings of text embedded in words, or discrete words or whole phrases.

Text strings with formatting

Strings of text that are formatted a particular way, such as Bold.

Formatting

Font formatting options, such as underlining and bold, that are not necessarily associated with words or text.

Styles

Find all instances of a named style or replace one named style with another.

Special characters

Tab markers, forced line breaks, non-breaking spaces, non-breaking hyphens, whitespace, and so on.

Let us first see how the command Find works.

FIND

This command will find for you the exact text which is mentioned in its box and will stop for further action. Normally the finding of the text starts from the position where the cursor is. If you have selected some text, the finding will be restricted to that block of text only.

So if you have to select the entire text, then it is advised to put the cursor at the beginning of the text in the document.

To start the Find command, do any of the following:

1. Open the Edit menu and select Find.

   Or

2. Press Ctrl + F.

   Or

3. Click the Find icon, which is part of Standard toolbar. If it is not there you can add it on your toolbar from the Add and Remove buttons.

Find and Replace dialog box, as shown next will appear in each of the above cases.

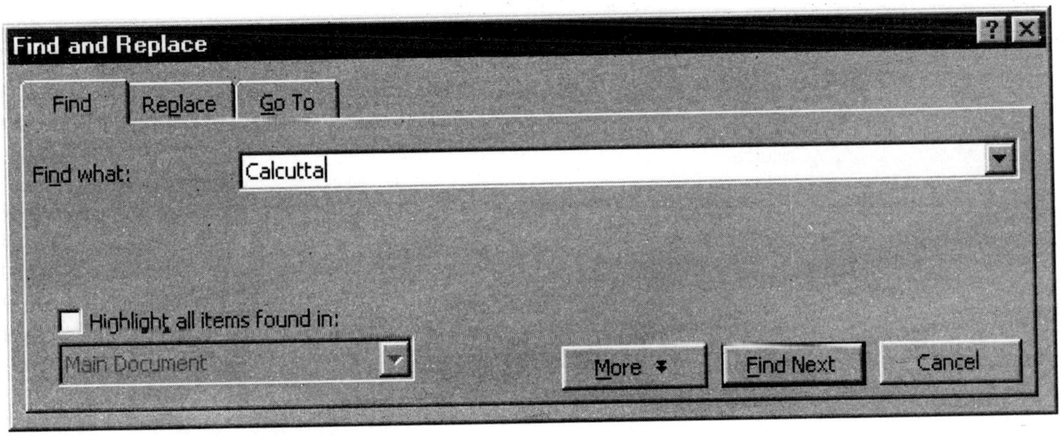

This is how you will use the Find command.

1. Type the text that you are seeking in the Find What? text box. This word or phrase is also referred to as the search string.
2. Choose the More button (if necessary) to specify search options.
3. Choose Find Next. Find looks through the document for text that matches your search strings. When it finds matching text, Word highlights the text in the document and stops. The Find and Replace dialog box remains on screen.
4. Choose Find Next if you want to continue the search for another instance of the search string. Click Cancel or press Esc to close the dialog box and return to the document. The text in the document is still highlighted.

When Word finishes the entire document, or if it could not find the search string in the document, a dialog box displays a message to that effect. Choose Ok to continue working in the document.

REPLACE TEXT

Next step after finding the required text is to replace it with some other text. For this we would call the command called Replace. To get the replace command do the following.

1. Open the Edit menu and select Replace.

   Or

2. Press Ctrl + H.

   Or

3. Click the Find icon, which is part of Standard toolbar. If it is not there you can add it on your toolbar from the Add and Remove buttons.

Now on the Find and Replace dialog box click at the Replace panel and do the following:

1. Type the text you want to replace in the Find What text box (in this case, *Calcutta*). You can leave this field blank if you have to search for a formatting only. However, you have to search for something.
2. Type the text you want to replace it with in the Replace With text box (in this case, *Kolkatta*). If you search for text and leave this field blank, you are in effect telling Word to delete all instances of the search strings, because they would be replaced by a blank.

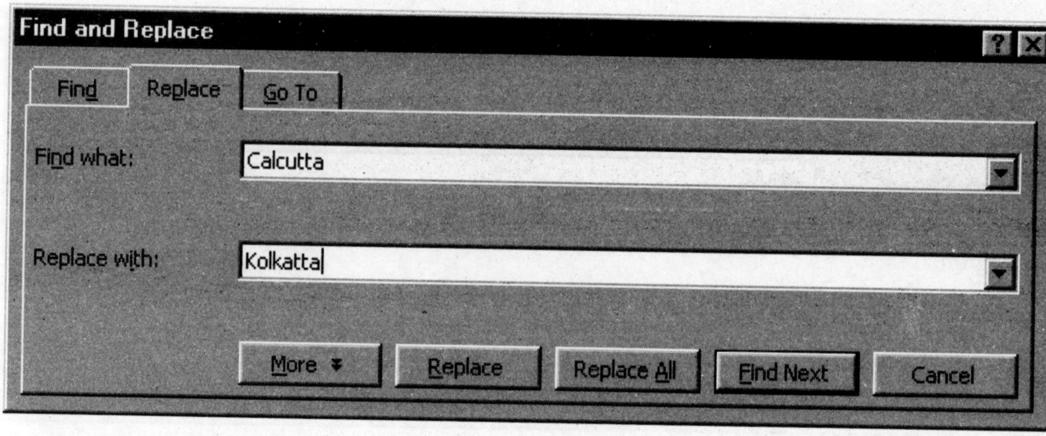

3. Choose the More button (if necessary) to specify search options.
4. Choose Find Next to locate and highlight the first occurrence of text that matches your search string.
5. Then do one of the following:
   - Choose **Replace** to replace the text matching the search string with the replacement text and then locate the next occurrence of the search string in your document.
   - Choose **Find Next** to leave the text matching the search string unchanged and to locate the next occurrence of the search string.
   - Choose **Replace All** to replace text in the entire document that matches the search string with the replacement text.
6. Choose Cancel. Alternatively, press Esc to close the Find and Replace dialog box and return to the your document.

When Word has finished searching through the document and has replaced all occurrences of the search text or can't find any further occurrences, a message box appears. Click Ok to return to your document.

Computer Room Activity

Finding and Replacing the Text

In the document created earlier, change from summer vocation to winter vocation. See how many changes have been made. Take a print out and see the changes made.

WORKING WITH PARAGRAPHS

Text in the document is typed in terms of paragraphs. A paragraph can have a number of lines. What we would learn now is how to leave some space between the paragraphs, lines of the paragraphs and their alignments.

For most of these we would be using the dialog box called Paragraph, which is available under Format menu and is shown on the next page. Various options which you can choose or change are given below:

General

This has the following options:

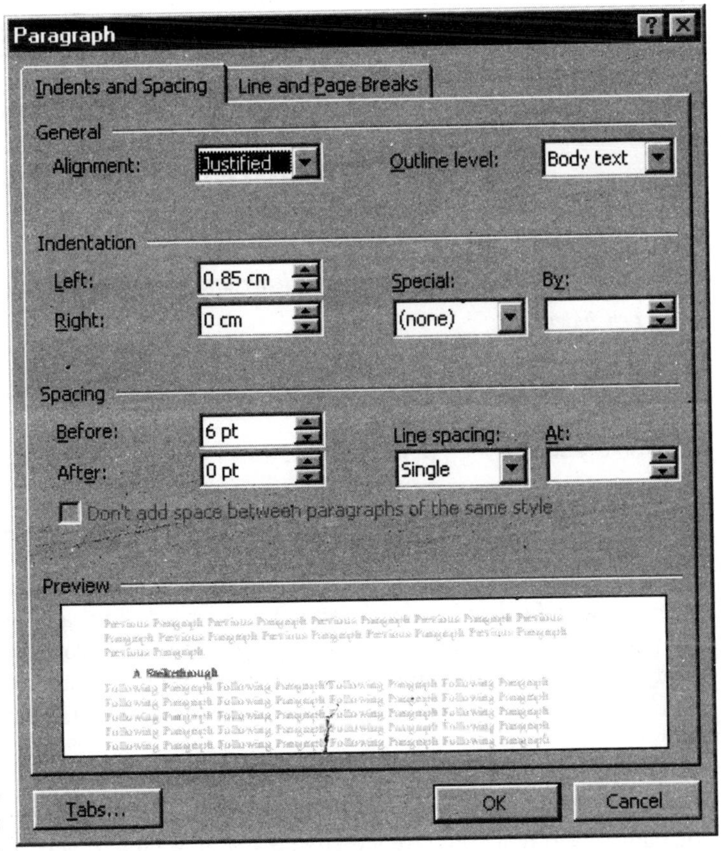

Alignment

As discussed above the various paragraph alignments are available here too for changing.

Outline Level

You can set here the various levels of text alignments.

Indentation

From here you can set the various options of paragraph spacing.

Left

Set here the margin from where the paragraph would be starting. If you set here 1", then the paragraph would start, leaving 1" space on the left.

Right

Similar to above, you can set here the space for the right margin.

Special

From here you can select whether you want to have the above margins applied to the first line or whole paragraph.

By

Within the above indentation/margins you can even have further indentation by setting margins here.

Spacing

Here you set the space which can be given after and before the paragraph.

Before

Set here the space which you want to give before the paragraph.

After

Set here the space which you want to give after the paragraph.

Line spacing

You have the option of selecting Single line, Double line, Exactly, etc. Select the type of space you want between the lines.

At

You can set here the width between the lines in terms of inches or other measure.

Preview

Whatever operation you perform above would be shown here in the form of preview in this window. So before applying a particular option you can see how it would look when applied.

Computer Room Activity

Setting Paragraph Options

Choose one of the paragraph from your letter and apply the following paragraph options to it:

Left indent	*1.5 inch*
Right indent	*1.5 inch*
First line indent	*.5 inch*
Line spacing	*2 lines*

After applying these options, see the paragraph in Print Preview.

WORKING WITH TABLES

When you put the data in tabular form, it looks good. You can also show data in tabular form to highlight that particular data. Tabs were used in the earlier word processing software for this, but, now you have a full fledged table menu in the new Microsoft Word. Though you will still use Tabs to reach the next cell of the table but the working of the whole tables is much easier.

Creating a Table

A table can be created by two methods. You can create the table structure before you enter any text, or you can convert text you have already created to a table. There is an easy way to create the structure for a simple table and a way to create a more complex table.

To create the structure for a simple table

1. Position the insertion point at the location for the table.
2. Click the Insert Table button on the Standard toolbar.
3. Drag across, the number of columns and down, the number of rows you want

   An unformatted table appears

   or you can follow the following alternate method.

1. Position cursor at the location for the table.
2. From the Table menu, choose Insert and Table.
3. In the Insert Table dialog box, specify the columns and rows, in this case we have chosen a table of 3 x 3.
4. Click Ok.

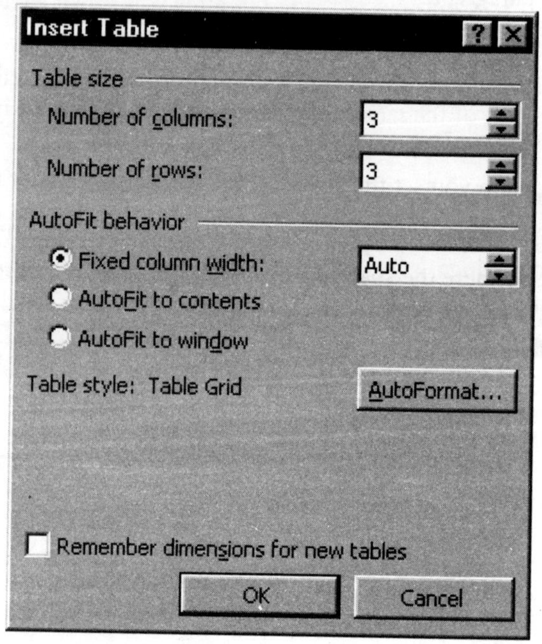

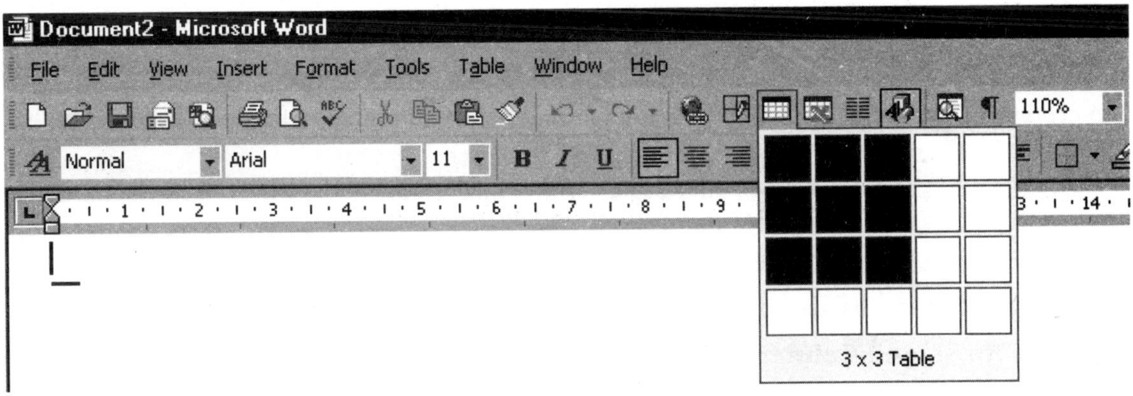

At this stage you should not bother about the other features of the dialog box. Now that the table in available you would like to enter the data into it.

ENTERING DATA IN A TABLE

Data can be typed directly into the cells or it can be moved or copied from other cells.

To Enter Data in a Table

1. Click in a cell with the mouse and type the data required to be typed. As you type, the cursor wraps within the cell and the entire row will become taller if it needs to accommodate multiple lines of text.
2. Press Tab to move to the cell to the right, and type text in the next cell.
3. Continue pressing tab after you finish each cell.
4. When you finish entering text in the last cell of the table, press Tab to create a new row, if required.

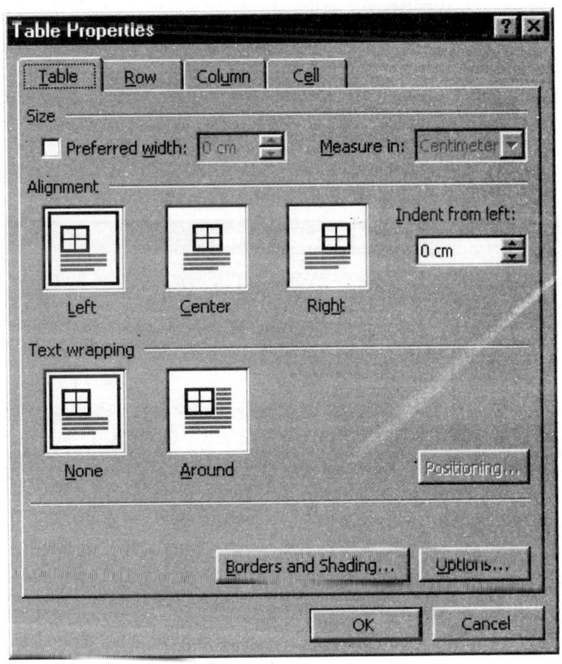

Aligning Data in a Table

For aligning of the data, you can use either of the following:

To Align Data Vertically or Horizontally Within Cells

1. Select the cells you want to align.
2. Click the Table Properties in the Table menu.
3. A dialog box will appear.
4. From here select the Table panel and the alignment wanted by you.

Changing Direction of Text

1. Select the cells you want to change.

2. Click the Change Text Direction tool on the Tables and Border toolbar.
3. The text would change the direction as required by you.

Another thing which we can do to our table is to decorate a bit by turning the headings as **bold**. For this do the following:

1. Click at the heading with the pointed small arrow which comes to the screen when you move the cursor to the left of the text within the cell.
2. The whole cell will be highlighted.
3. Click at B in the Standard toolbar to make the text Bold.

Inserting Rows and Columns

You can add rows and columns to any portion of your table on all the sides using the following options.

To insert a row

1. Click in a cell at the location for the new blank row.
2. From the Table menu, choose Insert and then choose Rows Below from the Insert submenu.

Using this option we will add a new row to our table in the document.

To insert a column

1. Position the mouse pointer at the top of the column at the location for the new column. A large down-arrow appears.
2. Click while the down-arrow is visible to select the column.
3. From the Table menu, choose Insert and then select one of the Columns options from the Insert submenu.

To insert multiple columns or rows, select the number of existing columns or rows corresponding to the

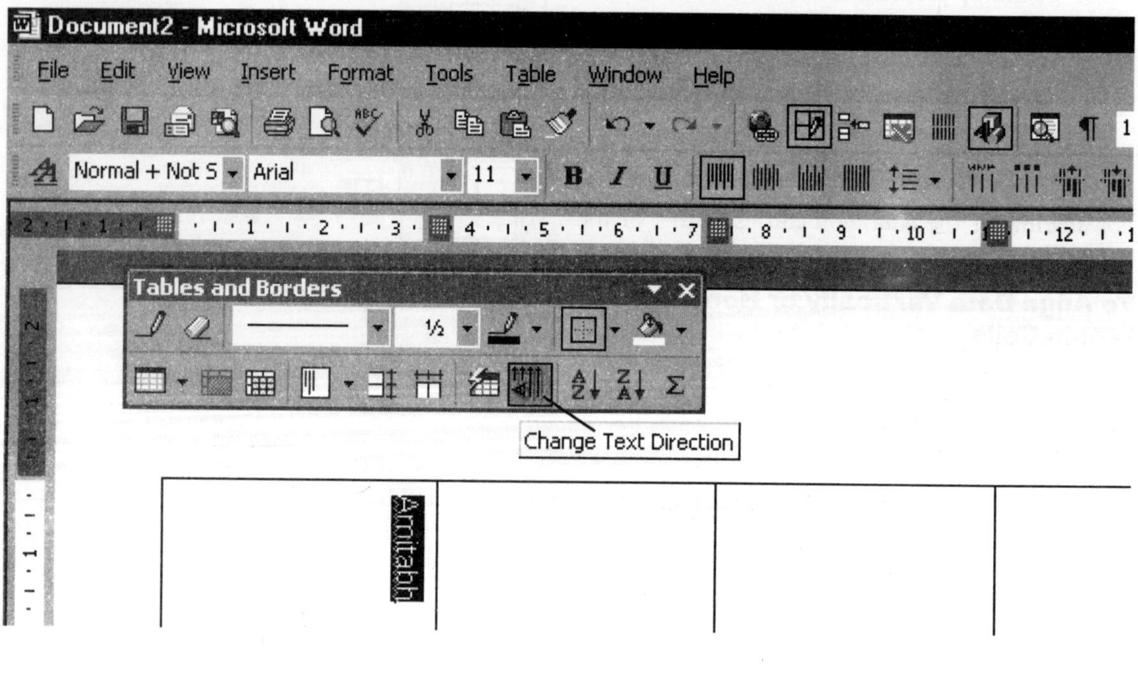

number that you want to insert before you choose an option from the insert submenu. If there are not enough existing columns or rows where you want to do the insertion, do multiple Insert operations.

Computer Room Activity

Creating a Table

Create a table with the following data, table is of 4 x 4 nature:

Player	*Innings*	*Run scored*	*Average*
Sachin	*8*	*600*	*75.00*
Ganguly	*7*	*420*	*60.00*
Dravid	*7*	*560*	*80.00*

Create this table and see the preview.

MAIL MERGE

MailMerge is one of the very important application of any word processing software. Word has indeed made it very easy to operate. In MailMerge you have the variable data coming from a data source which can be either a database file, spreadsheet, or even a text file with fields marked in it. Then you have the document file whose text remains the same for all the subsequent merged files changing only the data which has been received from the source. So in fact you create multiple documents having the same text but having different fields depending upon the source.

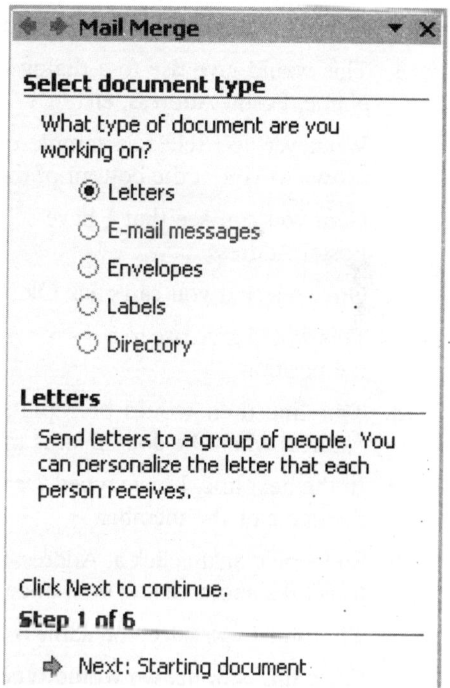

Well, one can think of various usages of the MailMerge. The most important being sending the same letter to various parties. Sending the same invitation to various guests. Sending payment reminders to various creditors. Calling all the directors to the same board meeting. In all these cases, the text would remain more or less the same but the name and address of the receiver would change. You can even change the salutation too, for example, Dear Mr. so and so, picking the name from the data source.

MailMerge in Word is done in steps. Creating document (text), data source and then merging them before printing. Let us see how it is done. For your information, here I am creating a appreciation letter for the various members of the victories Indian Cricket Team. So, lets start.

1. Start Word.
2. On the Tools menu, point to Letters and Mailing and then click Mail Merge Wizard to open the Mail Merge task pane showing Step 1 to 6 in the wizard.
3. In the task pane, click the Letters option, and then click Next: Starting document at the bottom of the pane, to reach the step 2, as shown on next page.
4. In the task pane, click the Use the current document option, then click Next: Select recipients at the bottom of the pane. Step 3 to 6 in the wizard appears, as shown on next pages.

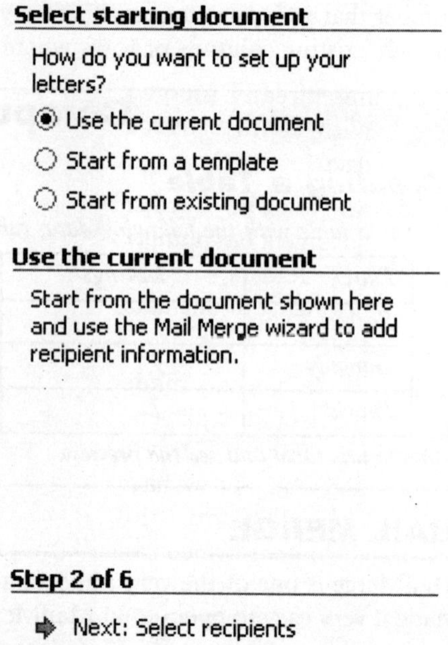

5. In the task pane, click the Type a new list to type a new list of the recipients and click at Create to get a New Address dialog box, shown on next to next page.
6. Here type your first entry with all the details known to you. You can leave the fields blank too, if not required. After entering the first entry, you can click at New Entry to get the next blank form for filling. Once done click at Close to get Save dialog box, to name your data source.
7. Here you are shown the data that you have entered into the Mail Merge Recipients which you can edit, if you want to by clicking at the required field.
8. When pressed Ok, you are returned to Mail Merge with Step no. 4 displayed by Word, as shown on the next page.
9. In this step you have to type your document. Here as mentioned earlier, we will type the letter of congratulations to the members of Indian Cricket Team.
10. This letter is also shown on the next page.
11. In the first line, you would like to print the name and address of the member of the team to whom you would like to send the letter.
12. For this at the cursor click at Address Block in the Task Pane.
13. This would give rise to a dialog box, which gives you the option of having Name, Company's Name, Postal Address, etc.

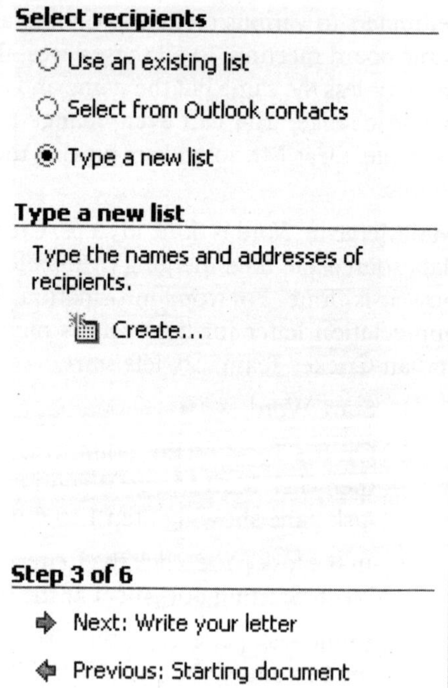

14. Whatever you select, a sample of the same, would be shown to you at the bottom of the dialog box.
15. Here you can see that I have selected only Name and Postal Address.
16. Once selected you can click Ok.
17. This would give rise to a << <<Address Block>> >> at the position.
18. This line then would be replaced by the Name and Address when the document is merged.
19. In the next line, I have typed Dear and after this I want the name of the member.
20. So I would again click at Address Block in the Task Pane to get the above dialog box, once again.
21. This time I will select the name only and not the address.
22. Once this is done, we would type the complete letter.
23. So now that the matter of Step 4 is complete, we will click at Next in Task Pane to go to the next step.

24. The Step 5 would ask you to preview the letter, which Word has already merged with your source data.
25. So now your document has number of letters, each belonging to one data source.
26. Since we had made the data for 3 players, i.e., Sachin, Dravid and Ganguly, we have 3 letters in the document, which can be reviewed by moving the cursor up and down.

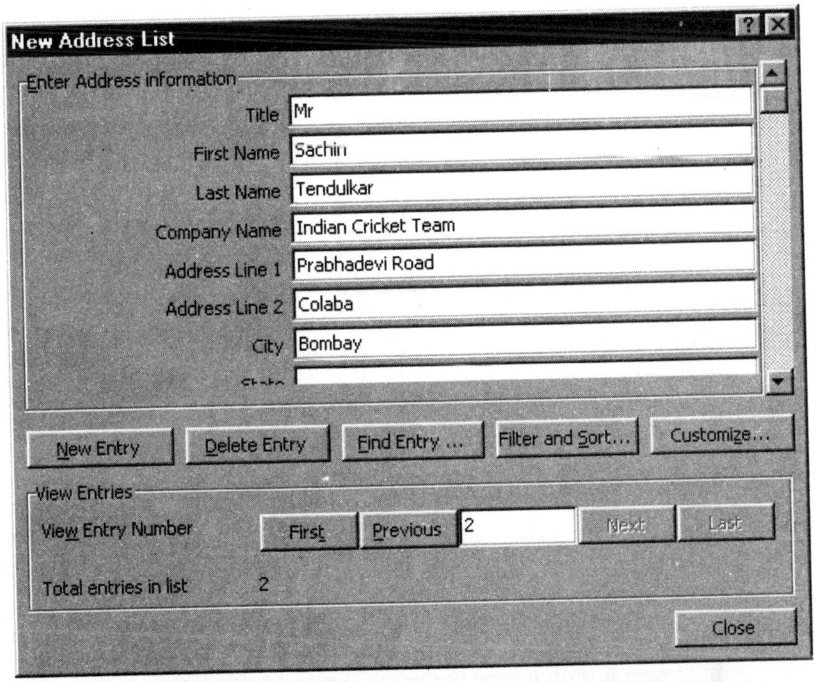

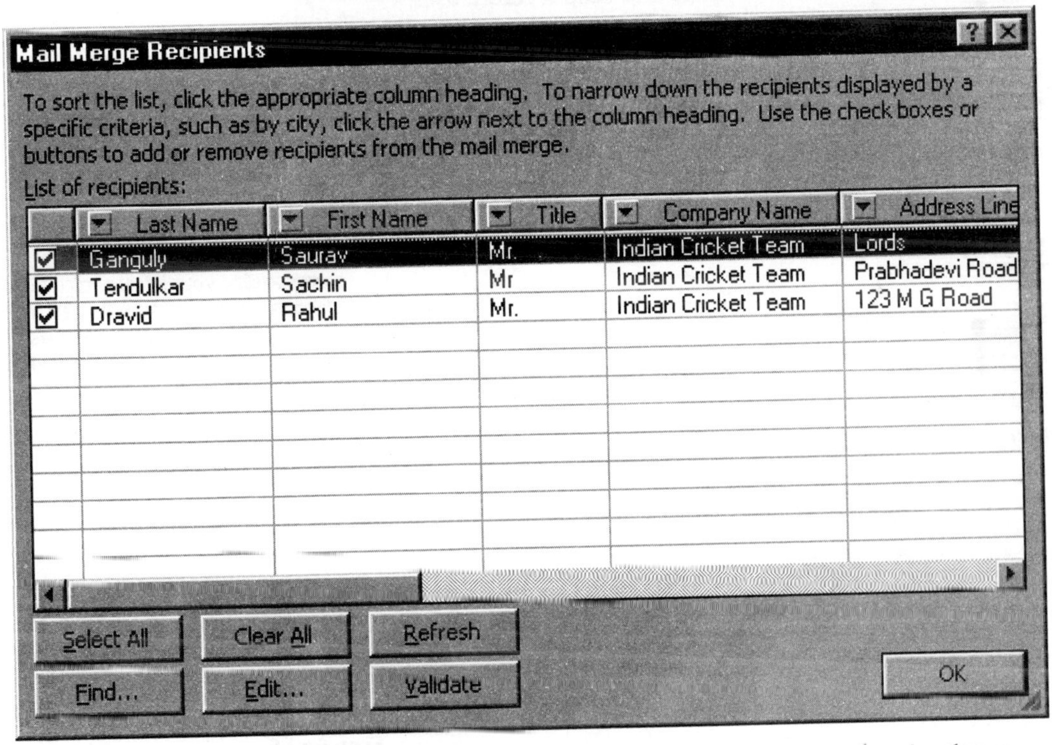

27. If you feel that there is something wrong, you can go back step by step and make changes.
28. The merged letter looks like the one shown next.

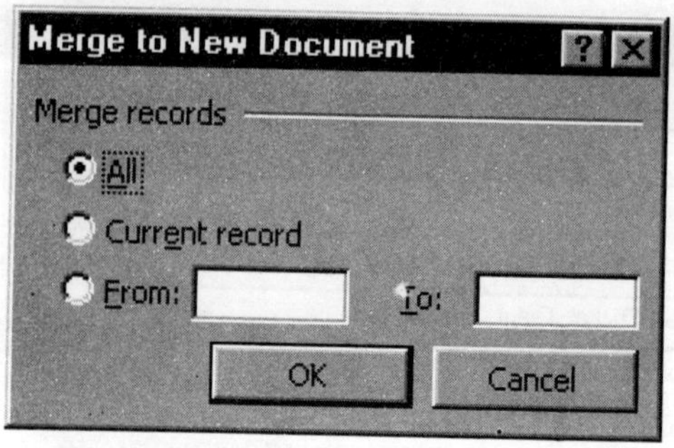

29. If you think the letter is Ok, click at Next to go to the next step.
30. In Step 6 you are told that Word is ready for the mail merge, if you are.
31. You have the choice of either printing or editing the letters individually.
32. You also have the choice of merging all the records or some selected ones.
33. Remember, this new file has not been saved, so you must save it with a new name and keep it future use.

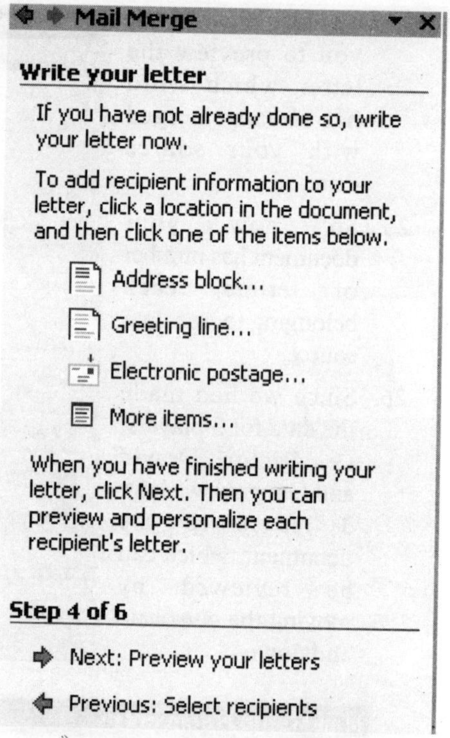

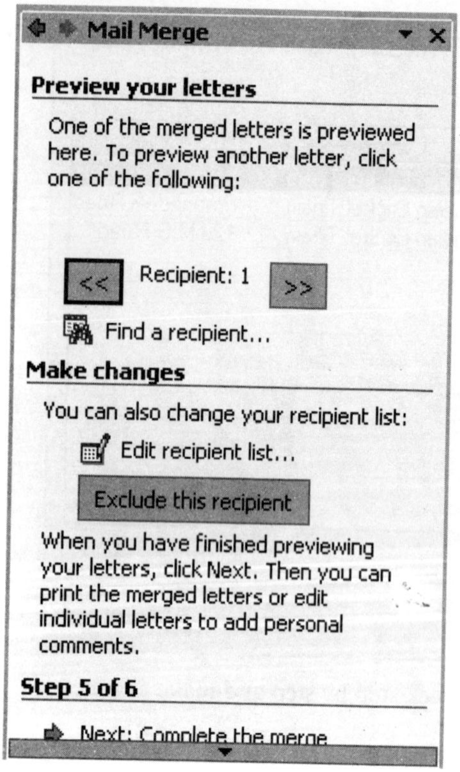

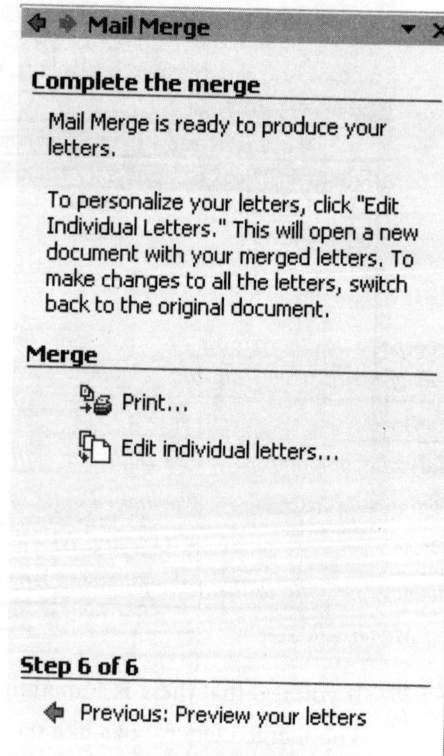

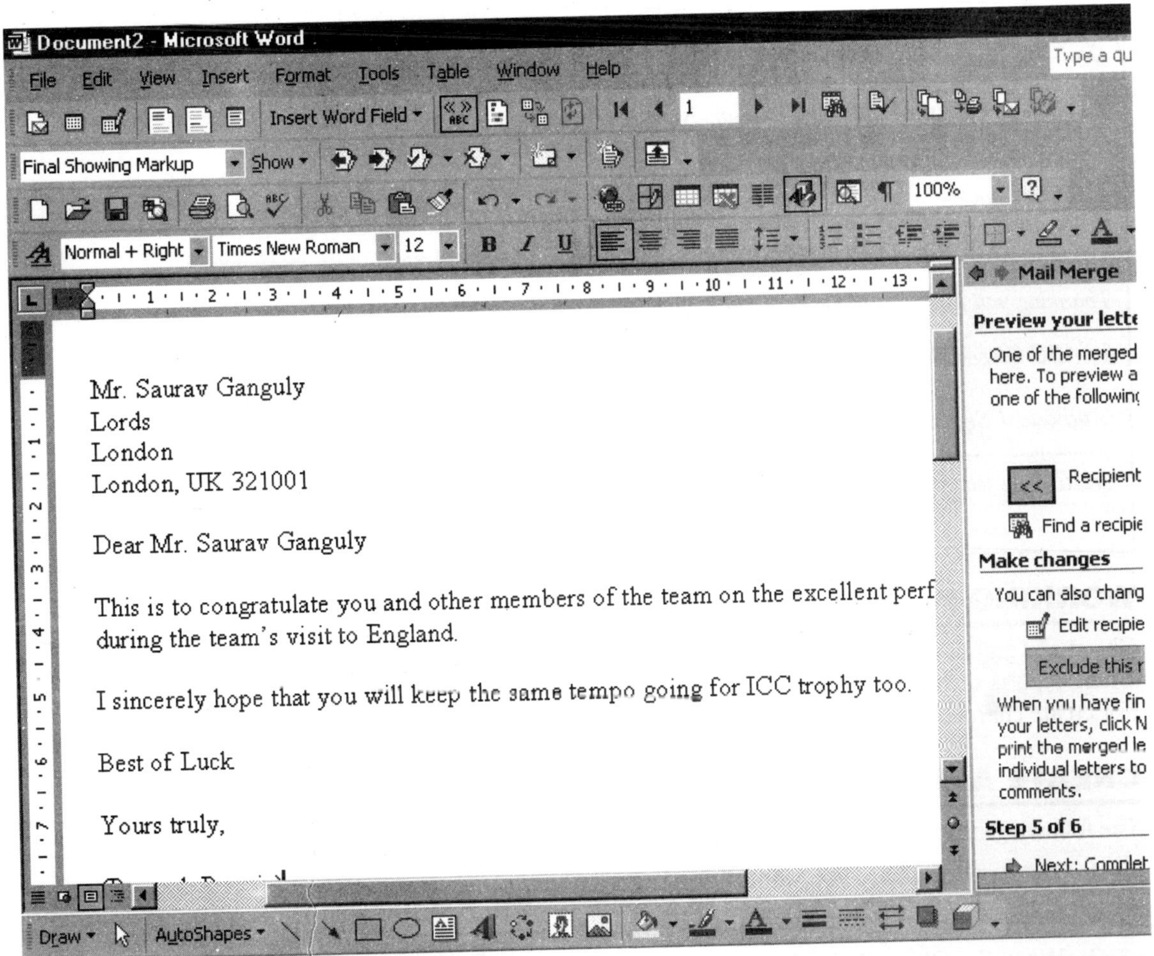

Computer Room Activity

Mail Merging Documents

A company has the following amount to be taken from the parties since the date given. You have to send a letter to all of them, using MailMerge option, mentioning the amount due from the date given:

Party	*Address*	*Bill No.*	*Amount due*	*Due Since*
Satyam Computers	*134 Budhwar Peth, Pune*	*1134*	*34,624.75*	*31.3.2000*
Reliance Industries	*Nariman Point, Mumbai*	*2496*	*1,24,653.97*	*1.7.2001*
DCM	*K G Marg, New Delhi*	*4576*	*6,78,775.22*	*31.12.2002*

You have to write to them the following letter.

31st March, 2003

<Party>
<Address>

contd...

Dear Sir,

As per our records the following amount is pending with you, since <Due Since>.

<Bill No.>
<Amount due>

You are requested to look into this matter seriously and clear the outstanding immediately.

Thanking you and hoping for an early reply.

for ABC Corporation

(Authorized Signatory)

Create these letters and print them to see how the MailMerge works in Word.

WORKING WITH CHARTS

Charts and graphs are another options of presenting your data in the form of pie charts and column graphs. Often, reports such as a annual report contain charts illustrating data such as sales and profits. Word does not create charts but uses a program called **Microsoft Graph**, which is installed by default.

CREATE A GRAPH

The following steps show you how to insert a chart using Microsoft Graph into your Word 2000 document.

1. Place cursor where you want the chart to appear.
2. Open the Insert menu and select Object.
3. When the Object dialog box appears, click the Create New tab.
4. From the Object Type box, select Microsoft Graph 2000 Chart.
5. Choose Ok.
6. A column chart and a Datasheet window appears. The Datasheet contains sample data that you replace to create your own graph. The chart is transformed automatically as you add your data and select formatting options, until it becomes the chart you want.

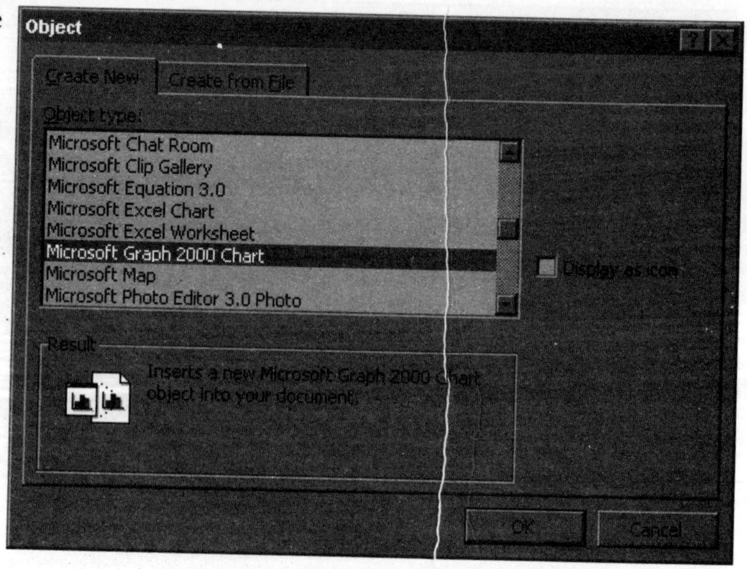

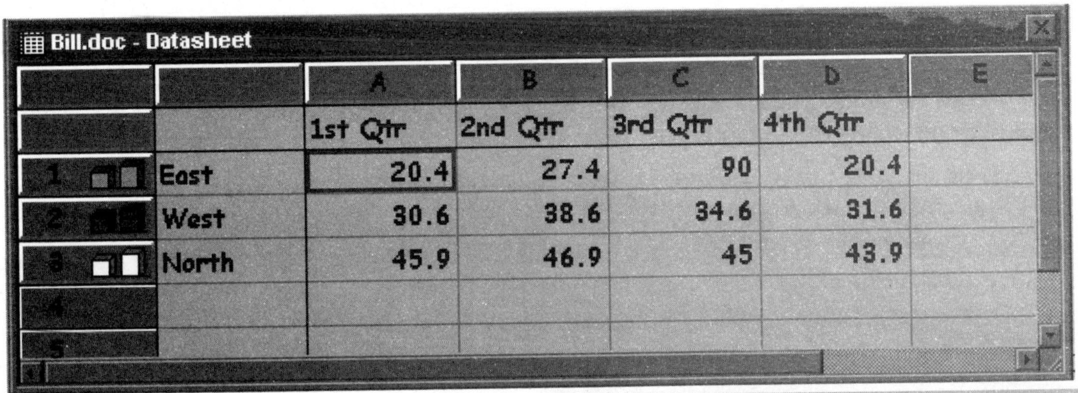

7. To replace the sample data, click in the cell in the Datasheet where you want to put new data and then type your own data there. Press Enter to accept the data and move down one row; press Tab to move one cell to the right and Shift+Tab to move one cell to the left (the arrow keys also help you navigate in the Datasheet). Choose View Datasheet on the Standard toolbar to close the Datasheet.

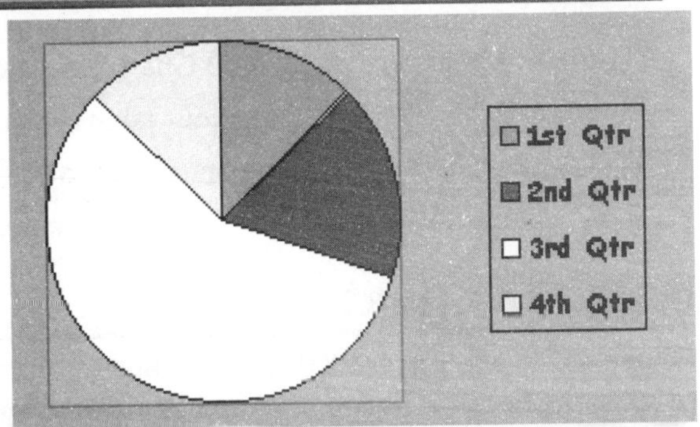

8. Click the down arrow next to the Chart Type button on the Standard toolbar to select a chart from the types shown. Then click the picture of the type of chart you want to create.

9. Click outside the border around the graph to return to the Word document (double-click on the chart to return to the Microsoft Graph 2000 program).

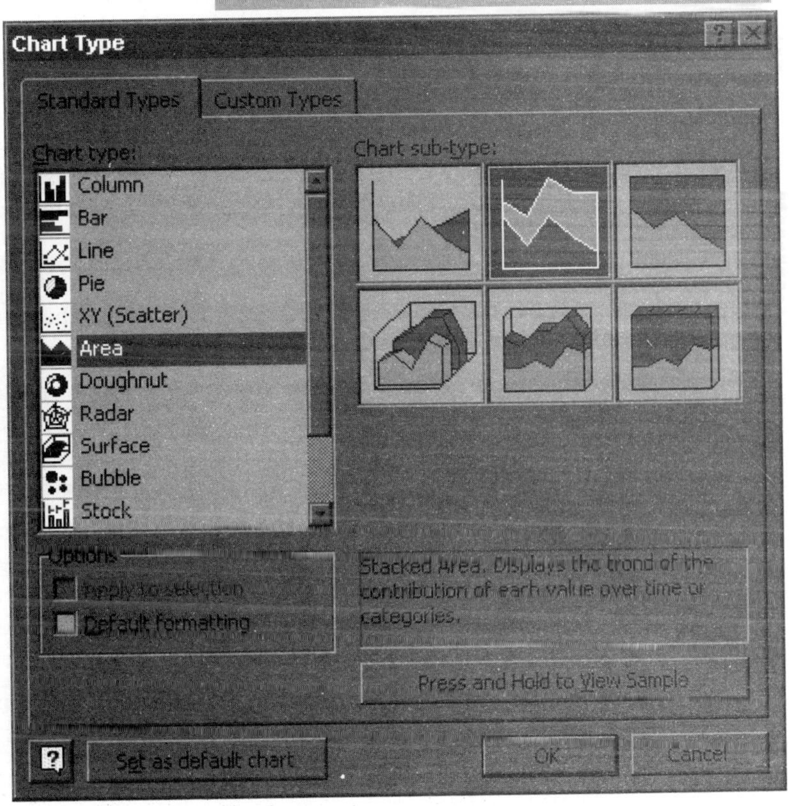

The sample data that appears in the Datasheet when you start a new chart is always the same. It serves as an aid that helps you enter the data in the right places. Be sure to delete any of the sample data that remains after you have entered you own information.

CREATE A CHART FROM A TABLE

Data that exists in a table (such as sales and profit data) can act as the data for your chart. If you have the data you need for a chart in a Word table, there is no need to enter the data again in the Datasheet. Instead, start the chart with the following steps.

1. Create the table in Word. Put text labels in the cells in the top row and in the left column. Put numbers in the other cells.
2. Select all the cells in the table (click in the table to put your insertion point there and then open the Table menu, choose Select, and then select Table from the submenu), unless your table includes a row and a column of totals. In that case, select all the cells except those total rows or columns.
3. Open the Insert menu and select Object and then select the Create New tab in the Object dialog box.
4. Select Microsoft Graph 2000 Chart from the Object Type box.
5. Choose Ok. The data from your table appears in the Datasheet.
6. Choose Chart Type on the Standard toolbar and then select a chart type.
7. Click outside the graph area to return to your Word document.

MODIFY A CHART

Once a Microsoft Graph 2000 chart is embedded in your document, double-click the middle of the chart to activate Microsoft Graph 2000 and modify the chart. To help you in modifying the chart, tips pop up when you point to the various components of the chart. This helps you in identifying the item you want to change. You can modify the chart when your are in Microsoft Graph 2000 in a number of ways, from changing the data to altering its appearance.

The following list gives you some suggestions on how you can modify your chart.

- To edit the data, open the Datasheet by choosing View Datasheet on the Standard toolbar. Replace data by clicking in the cell and typing the new value or label. Press Enter or move the insertion point to the next cell to accept the change.
- To change the chart type, open the Chart menu and select Chart Type to open the Chart Type dialog box. From the Chart Type list, select the type of chart you want. Then make a selection from the Chart Sub-Type options and choose Ok.
- To change the colour of bars, lines or areas, double-click on the item to open the Format Data Series dialog box. For pie chart slices, click once on the pie and then double-click the slice you want to change to open the Format Data Point dialog box. Set the line style and colour on the appropriate options. Then choose Ok to apply them to the chart.
- To change the number format (how the numbers appear) of the chart values, double-click the numbers on the value axis (Y-axis) to open the Format Axis dialog box and then select the Number tab. Choose a number format (such as currency or percentage) from the Category box. The options vary with each category, so you may have to specify number of decimal places, symbols, appearance of negative numbers, use of a thousand separator, data and time formats, and so on. Choose Ok.
- To set the interval between the numbers or specify the minimum or maximum values, double-click the numbers on the value axis (Y-axis) to open the Format Axis dialog box and then select the Scale tab. Change the Major Unit number to specify the interval between numbers, which also

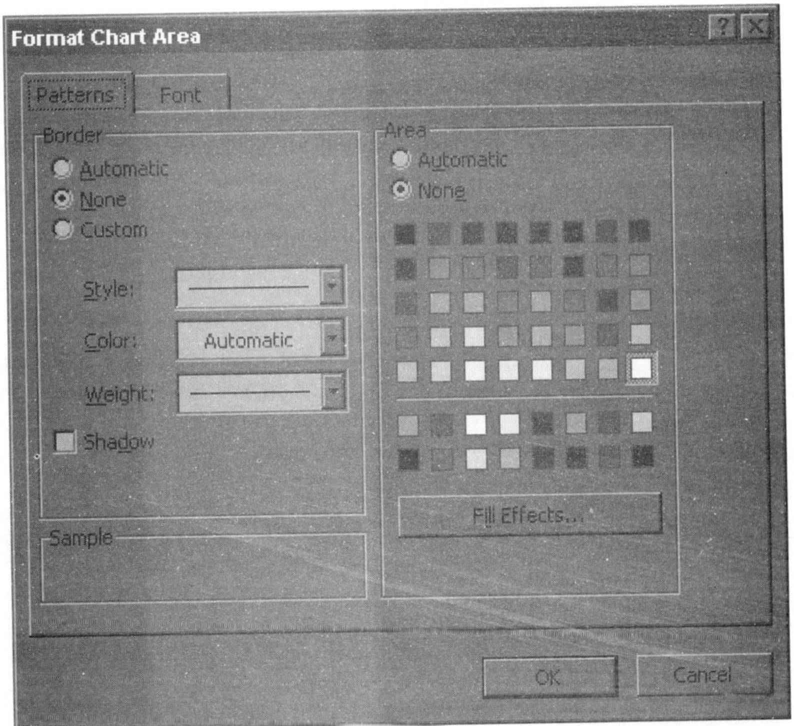

sets the spacing between the gridlines (lines that act as a reference to help you evaluate data in relation to the axes). Enter values in the Minimum and Maximum boxes to change those values. Choose Ok.

- To add titles to the value and category axes, click open the Chart menu and select Chart Options on the menu to open the Chart Options dialog box. Select the Titles tab and enter the title text in the Category (X) Axis or Value (Y) Axis box. Click in the Chart Title box and enter a title for the entire chart. Click Ok.

When you complete your modifications, click outside the graph border to return to your Word document. Move the graph by pointing in the middle of it and dragging it to a new position on the page. Change the size of the chart by selecting it and then dragging one of the handles (small hollow boxes surrounding the chart) toward or away from the center of the graph. After you click outside the graph, it acts like any graphic inserted into a word document.

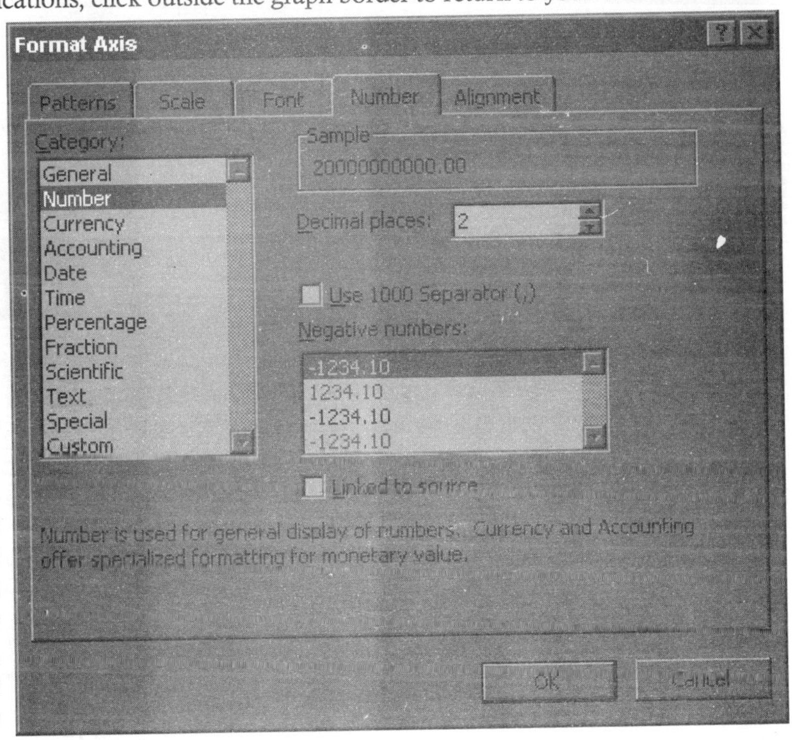

Now that you have seen how Word 2000 handles all the graphics, Tables, Charts and other graphics, we will revert back to the text in the next chapter and see how Word 2000 handles the text of larger volumes, such as Books, Project Reports, etc., where you have more than one document file and the whole thing is divided into various sections.

WORKING WITH WIZARDS

Wizards are there in any software to guide and create for you in a flash the document/output which you are trying to create using the software. These are there for like having fast food instead of having a good sit down dinner. Here everything is ready made and you have to just fill in the data and the document is ready for you. I will start with Resume Wizard, which I am sure that at some stage of your life you must be needing it.

RESUME WIZARD

When you are looking for a job, the first thing you need a resume of yours or better known as Bio-data in this part of the World. Word 2000 helps you in preparing a professional looking, neat and organized resume in no time. The following steps you have to take to create a resume using the Wizard.

1. Click the File menu and select New.
2. When the New dialog box appears, select the "Other Documents" tab.
3. Click the Resume Wizard icon to select it and then choose Ok. The Resume Wizard dialog box appears.
4. Choose Next. The wizard offers you 3 styles of resumes —Professional, Contemporary, or Elegant. A preview of each style appears beneath the option. Click the style you want to use.
5. Choose Next. The Resume Wizard lets you select the type of resume you are preparing. Use Entry-Level Resume if you are entering the job market or have limited experience, Chronological Resume to list your experiences in chronological order, Functional Resume to show your administrative level experience in several areas, or Professional Resume to highlight your education and accreditation.

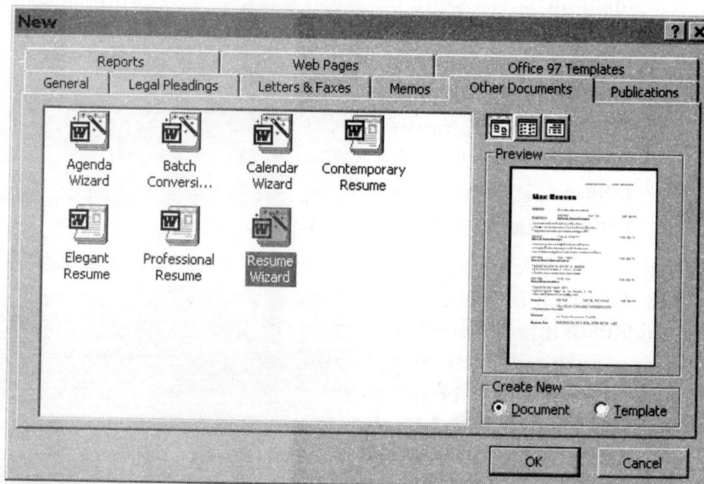

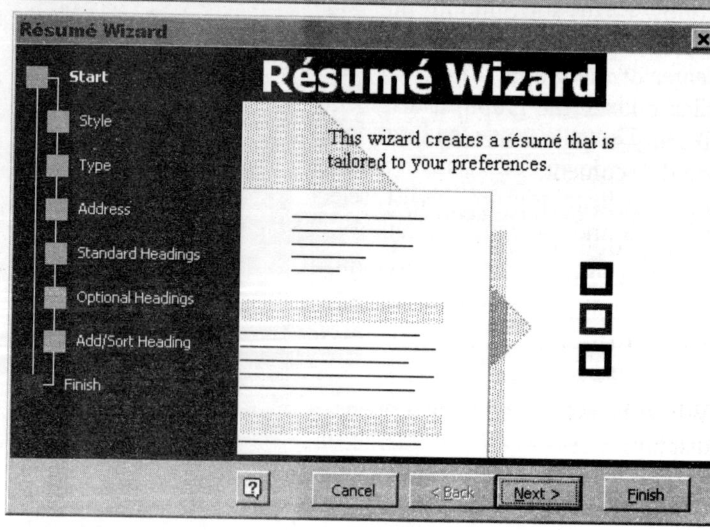

6. Choose Next. On the screen enter your contact information in the Name, Address, Phone, Fax, and Email fields. Be sure to include are codes with the phone numbers.
7. Choose Next. The Resume Wizard list a series of headings that can appear on the resume style you choose. Click the ones you want included on your resume to check those boxes and remove the check marks from the headings you don't want to use.
8. Choose Next. Another set of heading choices appears. These can be included, but you probably won't use them unless they are relevant to the objective of the resume. Click to check the headings you want to use.
9. Choose Next. The resume headings you selected are listed on this screen. If you want to add another heading, type the heading in the text box and then choose Add. To set the order of appearance in your resume, select a heading by clicking on it and then choose Move Up or Move Down to move the heading up or down in the list. To remove a heading from the list, select it and then choose Remove.
10. Choose Next. You have filled in all the information needed for the resume, so choose Finish.

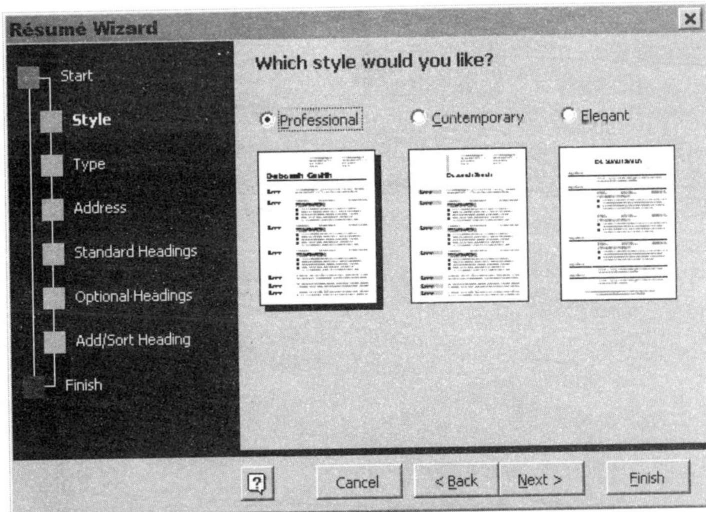

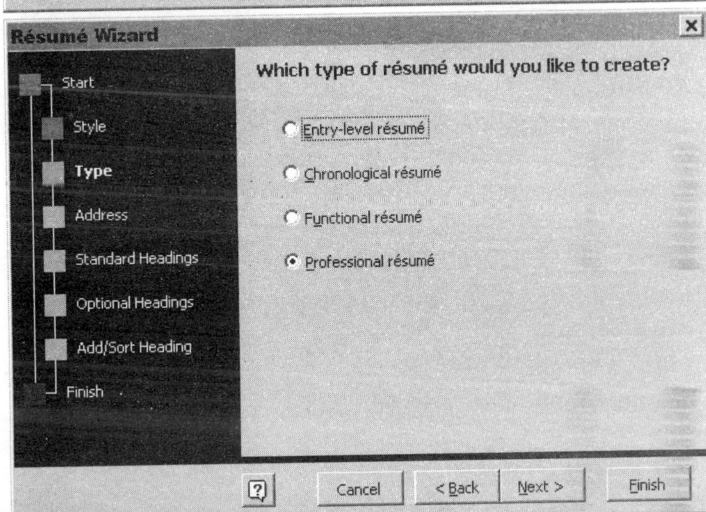

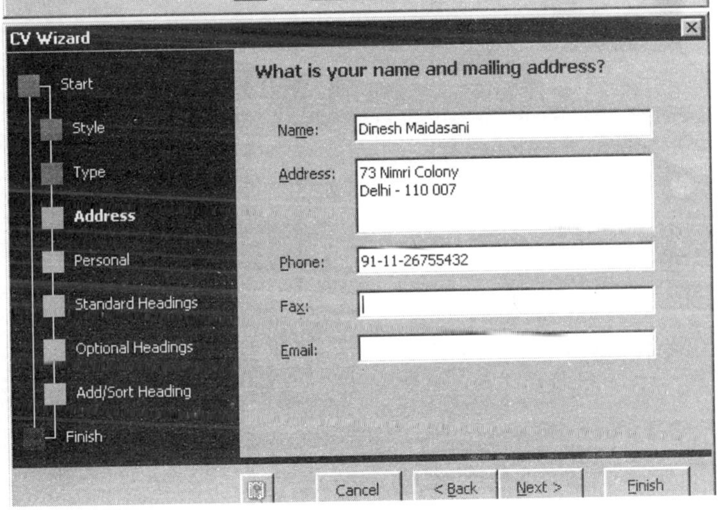

When the resume document opens, it displays a series of fields marked in gray and enclosed by brackets ([ ]). Close these fields and enter the necessary information to complete the resume document. Then you save and print the resume as you would any document. On the las few pages you have seen the various screen of the wizard and the finally the resume. As seen from the above resume there is an Office Assistant which offers help in the following options that you might need in finishing your resume.

The final resume can be seen below.

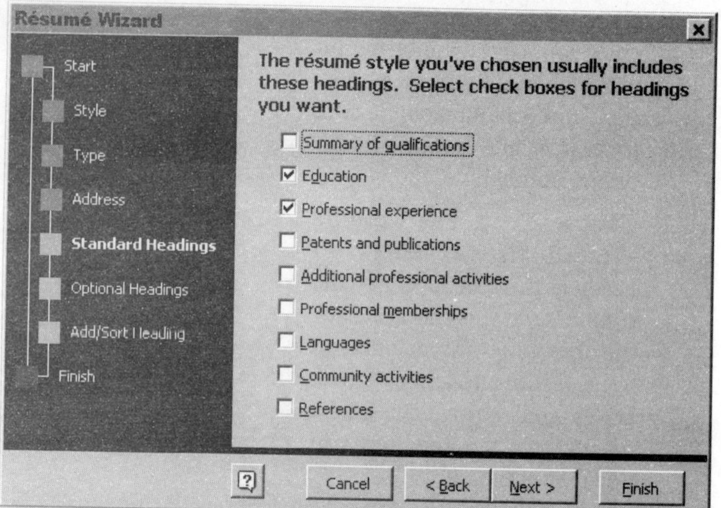

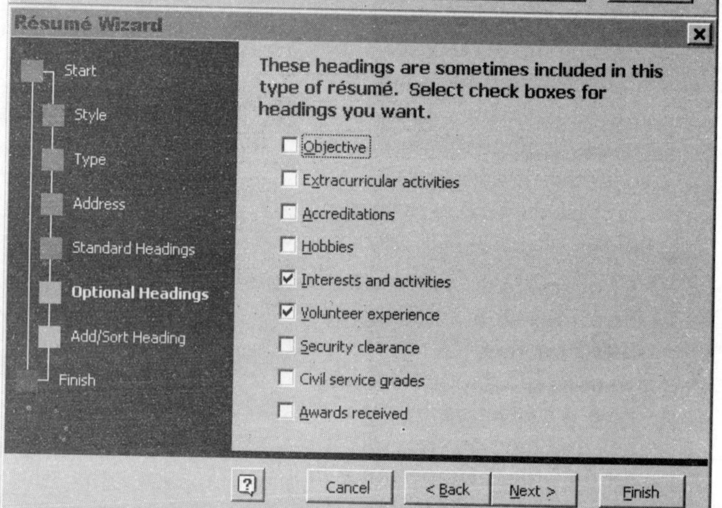

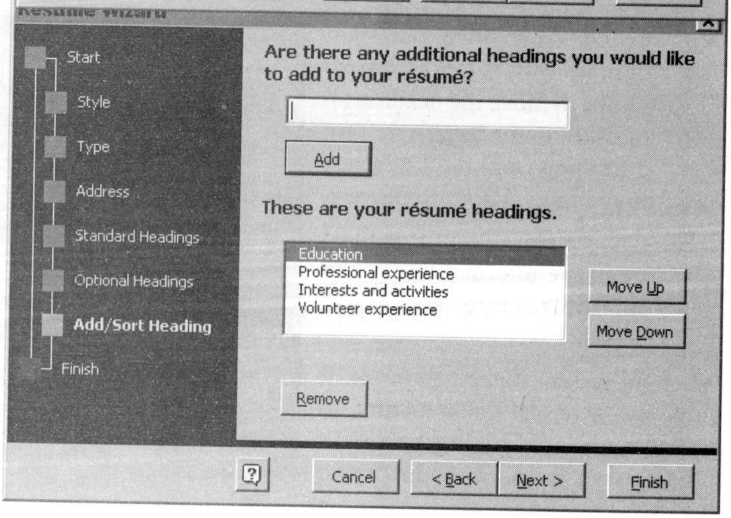

TEMPLATES

Every Microsoft Word document is based on a template. A template determines the basic structure for a document and contains document settings such as AutoText entries, fonts, key assignments, macros, menus, page layout, special formatting, and styles. The two basic types of templates are global templates and document templates.

Global templates, including the Normal template, contain settings that are available to all documents.

Document templates, such as the memo or fax templates in the **New** dialog box, contain settings that are available only to documents based on that template. For example, if you create a memo using the memo template, the memo can use the settings from both the memo template as well as the settings in any global template.

Word provides a variety of document templates, and you can create your own document templates.

Working with Global Templates

When you work on a document, you can typically use only the settings stored in the template attached to the

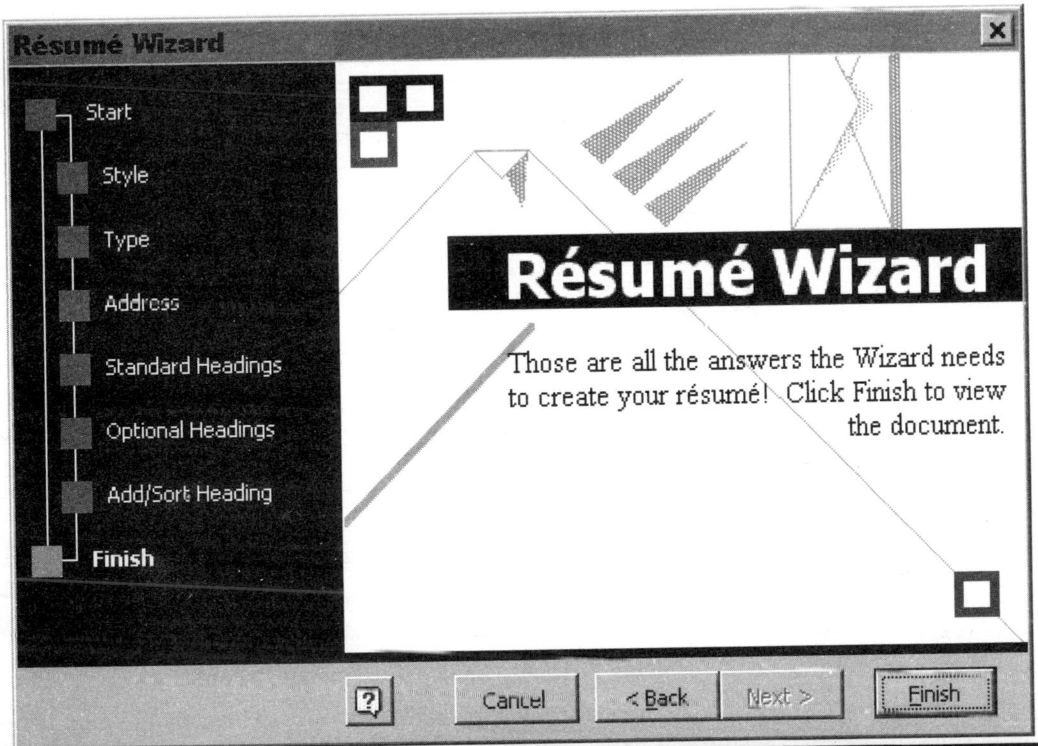
Résumé Wizard
Start
Style
Type
Address
Standard Headings
Optional Headings
Add/Sort Heading
Finish
Résumé Wizard
Those are all the answers the Wizard needs to create your résumé! Click Finish to view the document.
Cancel
< Back
Next >
Finish

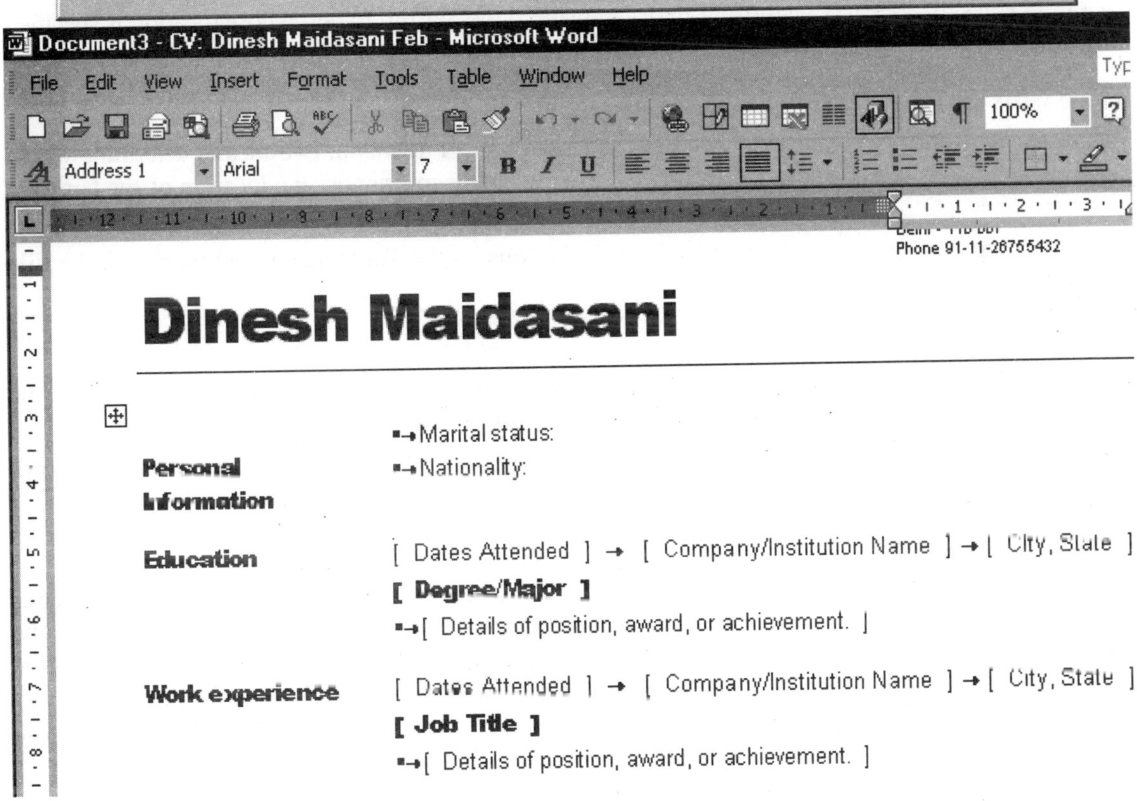
Document3 - CV: Dinesh Maidasani Feb - Microsoft Word
File Edit View Insert Format Tools Table Window Help
Address 1
Arial
7
100%
Phone 91-11-26755432
Dinesh Maidasani
Marital status:
Nationality:
Personal Information
Education
[Dates Attended] → [Company/Institution Name] → [City, State]
[Degree/Major]
[Details of position, award, or achievement.]
Work experience
[Dates Attended] → [Company/Institution Name] → [City, State]
[Job Title]
[Details of position, award, or achievement.]

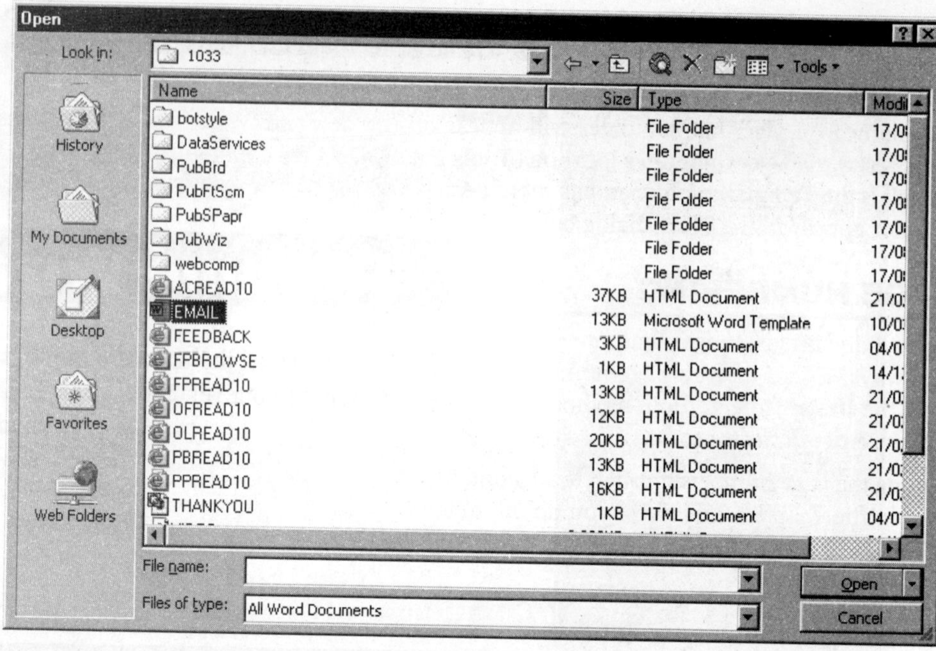

document or in the Normal template. To use any such items that are stored in another template, you can load the other template as a global template.

After you load a template, items stored in that template are available to any document during the remainder of the Word session. When you're finished with the items, be sure to unload the template to conserve system resources.

Add-ins and templates that you load are unloaded when you close Word. To load an add-in or template each time you start Word, copy the add-in or template to the Startup folder, whose location is specified on the **File Locations** tab (**Tools** menu, **Options** command).

Locating templates

When you or someone in your workgroup clicks **New** on the **File** menu, two factors determine which document templates are available and which tab each template appears on: the location of the template and your file location settings for **User templates** and **Workgroup templates**.

To check your template file location settings, click **Options** on the **Tools** menu, and then click the **File Locations** tab.

Workgroup templates

It is recommended that your system administrator store templates that you share on a network in the **Workgroup templates** file location specified on the **File Locations** tab.

To keep custom templates from being inadvertently altered by others, the administrator should mark them as read-only or store them on a server with limited permissions.

User templates

Save your custom templates in the **Templates** folder. (In Microsoft Windows 95 or 98, the **Templates** folder is located by default in either the C:*Windows_folder*\Application Data\Microsoft folder or the C:*Windows_folder*\Profiles*User_name*\Application Data\Microsoft folder. In Microsoft Windows the **Templates** folder is located by default in the C:*Windows_folder*\Profiles*User_name* folder.)

Template files that you save in the **Templates** folder appear in the **New** dialog box (**File** menu). Any document (.doc) file that you save in the **Templates** folder also acts as a template.

Templates you save in the **Templates** folder appear on the **General** tab. If you want to create custom tabs for your templates in the **New** dialog box, create a new subfolder in the **Templates** folder and save your templates in that subfolder.

The name you give that subfolder will appear on the new tab. When you're saving a template, Word switches to the **User templates** location (**Tools** menu, **Options** command, **File Locations** tab), which by default is the **Templates** folder and its subfolders. If you save a template in a different location, the template will not appear in the **New** dialog box.

PAGE NUMBERING

Printed documents longer than one page should have page numbers. You can set up page numbering in two ways. Either insert a page number code while editing headers and footers, or insert page numbers from the **Insert** menu. Both methods insert a page number code in you documents' header or footer, but there are two differences.

Putting the page numbers through header and footer, we will learn that when we learn Header and Footer, later in the chapter. Otherwise you do the following:

1. Click the Insert menu and select Page Numbers to open the Page Numbers dialog box, as shown here.

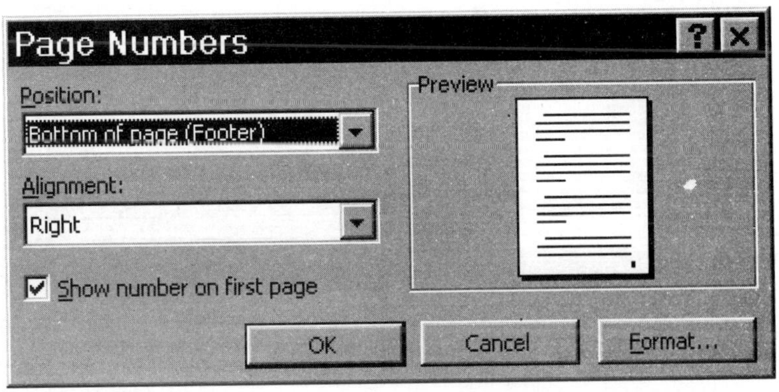

2. From the Position drop-down list, select the position on the page where you want your page numbers to appear. The options are:

   Top of the Page (Header)

   Bottom of the Page (Footer)

3. From the alignment drop-down list, select Left, Center, or Right to specify the horizontal position of the page number in relation to the right or left margins.
4. If you want the page number to appear on the first page, Show number on first page to place check mark there. Deselecting this option creates a separate header or footer for the first page.
5. Click Ok.

When you insert a page number, Word automatically switches you to Print Layout view so you can scroll to the portion of the page where the page number appears to check its appearance.

HEADER AND FOOTER

As you must be knowing that **Header** appears on the top of the page and **Footer** appears on the bottom of the page. Word 2000 allows you to put both of them on the document pages.

Headers and footers can vary within a document. Choices include:

1. The same header and footer on every page.
2. A different header and footer for the first page only

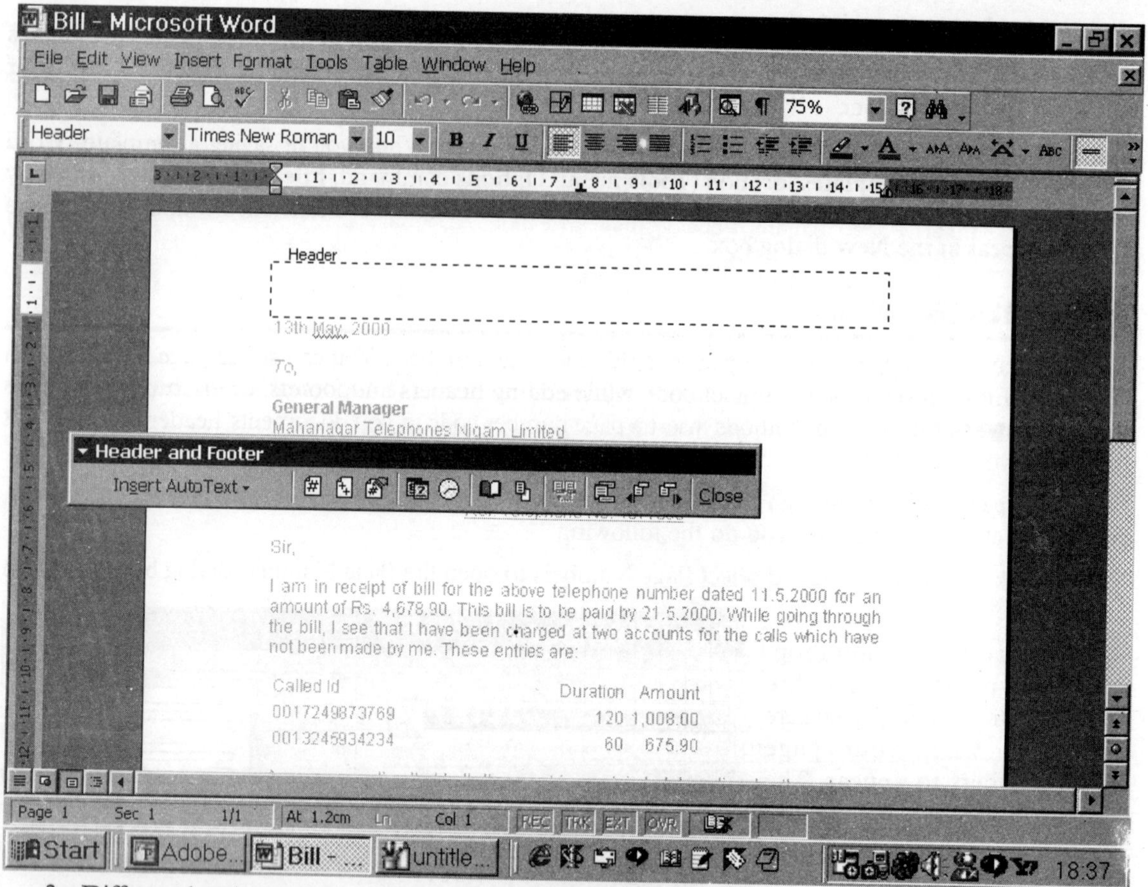

3. Different headers and footers for odd numbered pages than those on even numbered pages.
4. Different headers and footers for each section of the document.

Adding a Header or Footer in Your Document

1. Click the View menu and select Header and Footer. The document appears in the Print Layout view with the header area indicated by a nonprinting dashed line box, as shown here. Regular document text is gray, and the header and footer toolbar is displayed.
2. Type the header or footer text. Edit and format the text as you would anywhere else in the document. Both the header and the footer have two tabs set to help you align your text a centre tab at the center of the page and a right tab at the right margin.
3. Use the toolbar buttons, as shown on next page, to add page numbers, total page numbers, date, time, etc.
4. Choose Close on the Header and Footer toolbar to return to the document.

INSERT A SYMBOL

The symbols will depend upon the fonts that you are using in your computer. Some of the popular fonts with symbols are: *Symbol*, *Wingdings*, *Zaph Dingbats*, *Monotype Sorts*, etc. You can insert symbols from these fonts into your document.

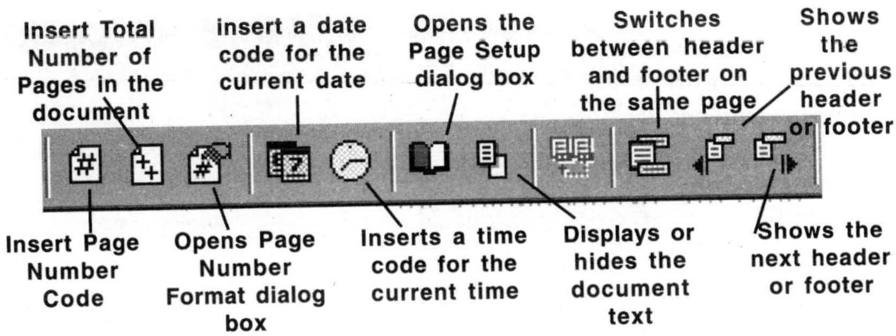

1. Place cursor where you want the symbol to appear.
2. Open the **Insert** menu and choose **Symbol** to open the **Symbol** dialog box. Click the **Symbols** tab if it is not already on top.
3. From the **Font** drop-down list, select the symbol set you want to use. Choose (normal text) to see the list for the current font, which includes letters with diacritical marks, currency symbols, the paragraph symbol, the registered mark, the trademark symbol, the copyright symbol, and so on. Using various fonts you can even get mathematical symbols, arrows, pointing hands, snowflakes, bullets, and more.

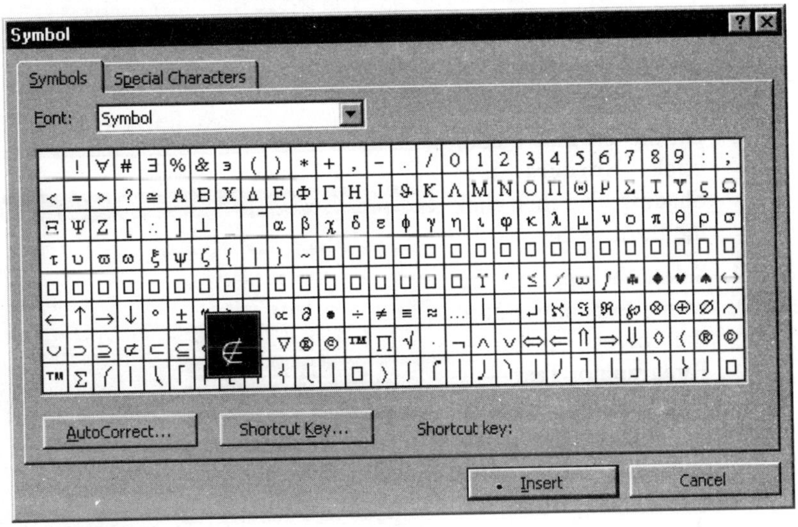

4. Look through the grid of symbols for the one you want. Click a symbol square to see an enlarged view of the symbol.
5. To insert the selected symbol in your document, choose **Insert** or double-click the symbol.
6. Choose **Close** to close the dialog box after you inset one or more symbols. Choose **Cancel** to close the dialog box without inserting a symbol.

BORDERS AND SHADING

You can add a border to any or all sides of each page in a document, to pages in a section, to the first page only, or to all pages except the first. You can add page borders in many line styles and colors, as well as a variety of graphical borders.

You can set apart paragraphs or selected text from the rest of a document by adding borders. You can also highlight text by applying shading. You can add borders to a table or individual table cell, and you can use shading to fill in the background of a table. You can also use the Table AutoFormat command to quickly give a table a polished look with a variety of borders, fonts, and shading.

You can add borders to drawing objects (including text boxes and AutoShapes) or to pictures, and you can enhance your drawing objects by adding a gradient (shaded), patterned, textured, or picture fill.

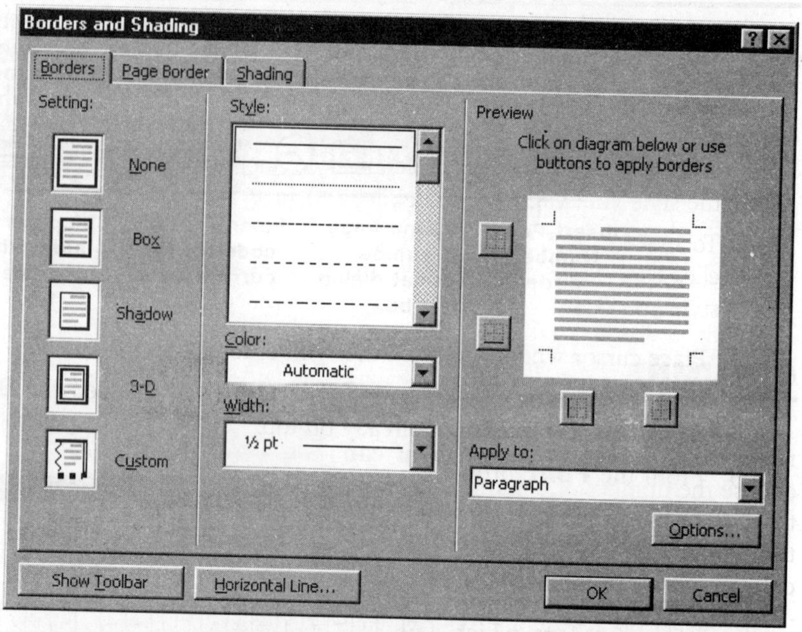

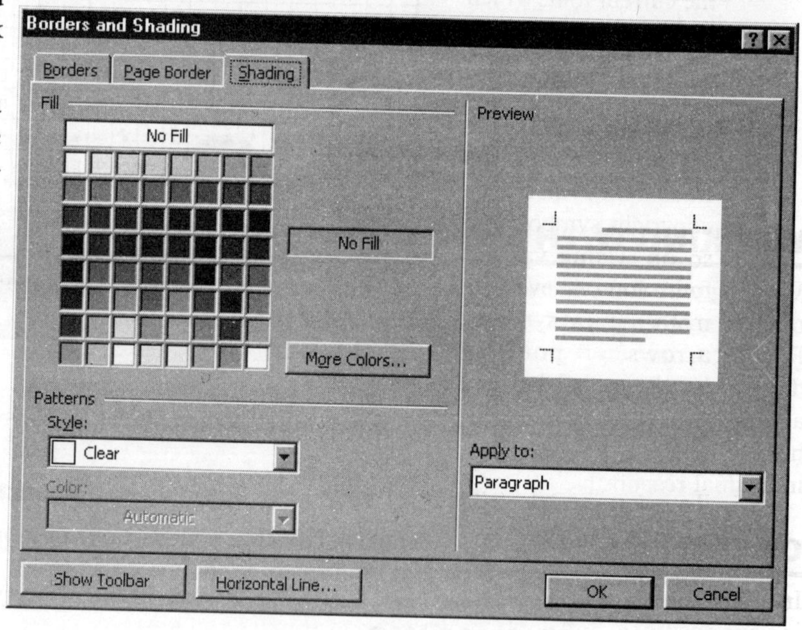

Add a Border to Text

Do one of the following:

1. To add a border to a paragraph, click anywhere in the paragraph.
2. To add a border only to specific text, select the text.
3. On the **Format** menu, click **Borders and Shading**, and then click the **Borders** tab.
4. Select the options you want, and make sure the correct option — **Paragraph** or **Text** — is selected under **Apply to**. For Help on an option, click the question mark and then click the option.
5. To specify that only particular sides get borders, click **Custom** under **Setting**. Under **Preview**, click the diagram's sides, or use the buttons to apply and remove borders.
6. To specify the exact position of the border relative to the text, click **Paragraph** under **Apply to**, click **Options**, and then select the options you want.

Add a Border or a Line to a Drawing Object

1. Select the drawing object you want to change.
2. Click **Drawing** to display the **Drawing** toolbar.

3. To add a color to the line or border, click the arrow next to **Line Color**, and then click the color you want. If you don't see the color you want, click **More Line Colors**. Click a color on the **Standard** tab, or click the **Custom** tab to mix your own color, and then click **OK**.
4. To give a line or border a different style, such as a heavier weight, click **Line Style**, and then click the style you want — or, click **More Lines**, and then click a style.
5. To make a dashed line or border, click **Dash Style** , and then click the style you want.

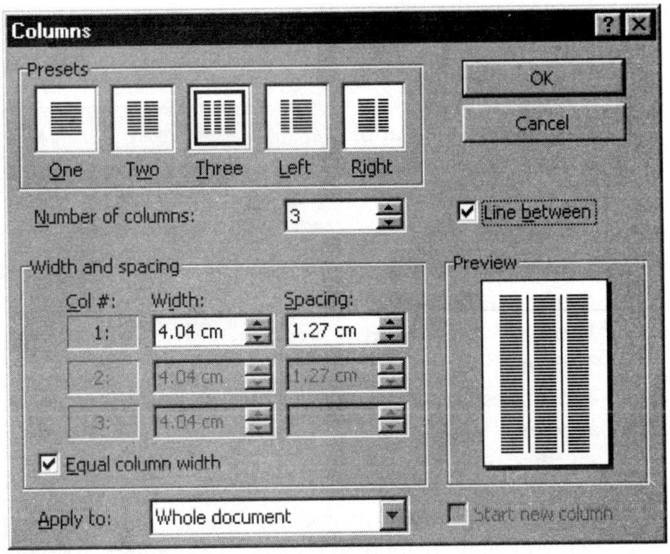

COLUMNS

This command is used to make your text run into different columns. You can choose the number of columns you want to have in your text. You can make your text look like a newspaper having 5 coloumns.

1. Select the text which you want to divide into columns.
2. Select Columns from Format menu to get Columns dialog box as shown here.
3. Choose the option and click Ok.

WORKING WITH LONGER DOCUMENTS

Working with long documents is cumbersome, particularly when several files created by several users need to be combined into one seamless report. For example, documents and reports such as Books, Annual Reports, Company Policies, are often the combined efforts of a team of people representing several departments. Each of these people create a separate file for their contribution to the report from which a final product is generated. When the files are bound into one large report, the need for page numbers, headers and footers, a table of contents, an index, and consistent formatting becomes apparent to the individual responsible for the final, printed version. Some of the features are covered here.

CREATE A TABLE OF CONTENTS

In all the books, in the beginning of the book, you will find a table of contents. It lists all the main topics in your document and notes on which page number each topic starts. Word helps you generate a table of contents for your document automatically. The easiest method for doing this is to assign one of Word's built-in heading styles (Heading 1 to Heading 9) to the headings you want to include in the table of contents. If you are not using Word's heading styles, you must assign a table of contents level to the styles you are using or mark text for inclusion in the table of contents.

Create a Table

1. Apply the built-in heading styles Heading 1 to Heading 9 to the headings in your document that you want to include in the table of contents.

2. Place the cursor in the document where you want the table of contents to appear. You may want to add a section or page break before your document text so the table of contents is on a separate page. You may also want to add a title for your page, such as "Table of Contents".

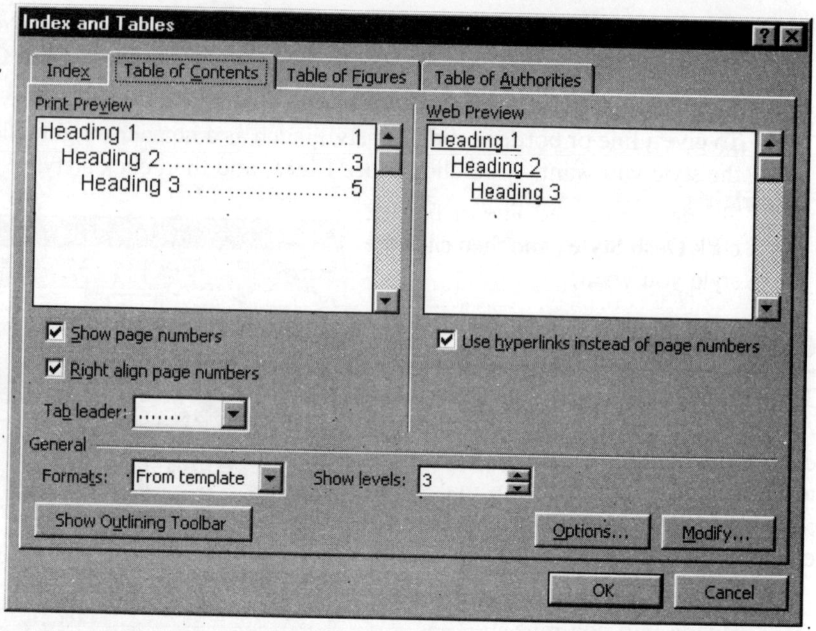

3. Click the **Insert** menu and select **Index and Tables**. The Index and Tables dialog box appears.
4. Select the **Table of Contents** tab if it is not already displayed.
5. From the **Formats** drop-down list, select the format that you want to apply to the table of contents. As you click a format, a sample appears in the **Print Preview** window and in the **Web Preview** window.

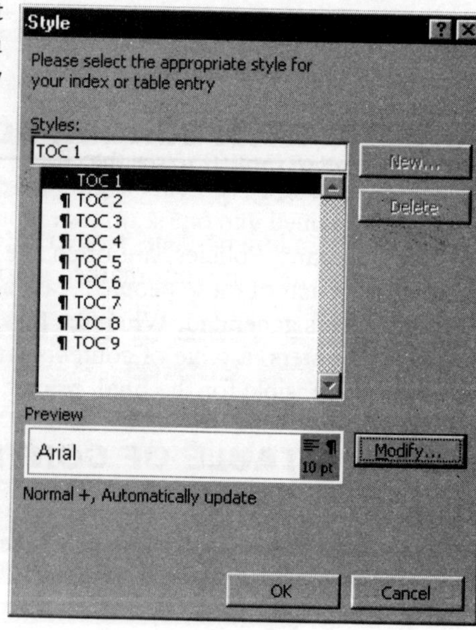

6. If you want the page numbers to appear for each topic, click **Show Page Numbers** to enable that option. Click **Right Align Page Numbers** if you want the page numbers lined up on the right margin.
7. In the **Show Levels** box, enter the number of headings levels you want to appear in the table of contents, or use the up and down arrows to select the number.
8. From the **Tab Leader** drop-down list, select the repeat character (leader) you want to appear between the heading and the page number (it can be dots, dashes or underscores). Select **None** if you do not want any leaders.
9. If you want to change the format, choose **Modify** to open the Style dialog box. From the Styles box, select the heading level you want to change in the table of contents and then choose Modify to open the **Modify Style** dialog box. Choose **Format** to select the type of format you want to specify and then select the formatting options you desire. Choose Ok to return to the Style dialog box, and then choose **Apply**.
10. Choose Ok. Word generates the table of contents for your document.

MARKING TEXT FOR TABLE OF CONTENTS

Table of contents entries can be marked by field codes, marking each entry as you type. Use this method if you have items you want to include in the table of contents, but those items do not have styles associated with them. You can use this method in combination with creating tables of contents using styles.

Marking Entries of a Table of Contents

1. Place cursor immediately before the text you want to include in the contents.
2. Click the **Insert** menu and select **Field**. The Field dialog box appears.
3. From the Categories list, select **Index and Tables**.
4. From the Field Names list, select **TC**.
5. Following the TC in the **Field Codes** box, enter the text that you want to appear in the table of contents. The text should be enclosed in double quotes.
6. Choose Ok. A field code is inserted in the document text but is hidden. Choose **Show/Hide** on the Standard toolbar to see the code.

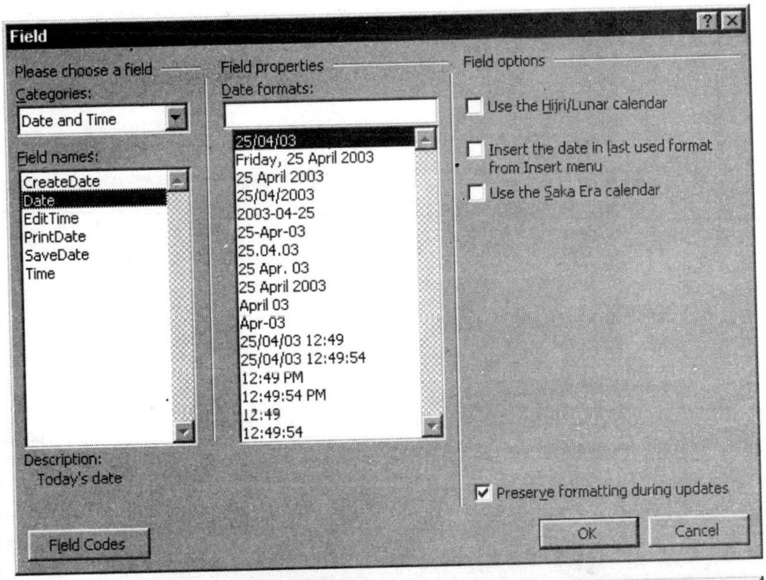

Perform the following steps to generate a table of contents from your marked entries.

Generate a Table of Contents from Marked Entries

1. Place the insertion point where you want the table of contents to appear.
2. Click the **Insert** menu and select **Index and Tables**. The Index and Tables dialog box appears
3. Select the **Table of Contents** tab if it is not already selected.
4. Choose **Options** to open the **Table of Contents Options** dialog box. Click **Table Entry Fields**. Choose Ok to return to the Index and Tables dialog box.

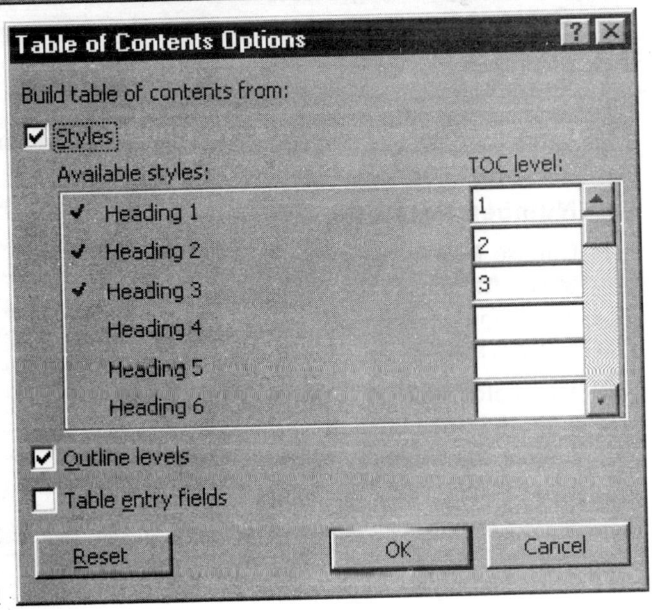

5. Choose Ok to generate the table of contents.

CREATE AN INDEX

An index usually appears at the end of the book. It contains references to the text which appears in the book alongwith the page number where it appears. It can have multiple entries, e.g., a word can appear at different places in the document at various pages.

To create a topic and page reference in your index, you must mark the words or phrases you want to appear in the index. Doing this provides Word a way to know what and where indexed references appear in your document.

Marking Index Entries

1. Select the text that you want for the index entry.
2. Click the **Insert** menu and select **Index and Tables** to open the Index and Tables dialog box.
3. Select the **Index** tab.
4. Choose **Mark Entry**. The Mark Index Entry box appears.
5. The selected text appears in the **Main Entry** box. Edit that text or enter new text if the selected text is not exactly what you want to display in the index.
6. Under **Options**, select **Current Page** as the page number you want cited in the index. If you want to add formatting to the page numbers as they appear in the index, click **Bold** or *Italics* under **Page Number Format**.
7. Choose **Mark** to mark the entry. Choose **Mark All** to mark the first occurrence in each paragraph of your document that exactly matches the text and case of the entry.
8. The dialog box remains open so you may make additional index entries. To make another entry click in the document to make it active, then select the text in the document or click immediately after it, click back in the **Mark Index Entry** dialog box to make it active, and repeat steps 5 to 7.

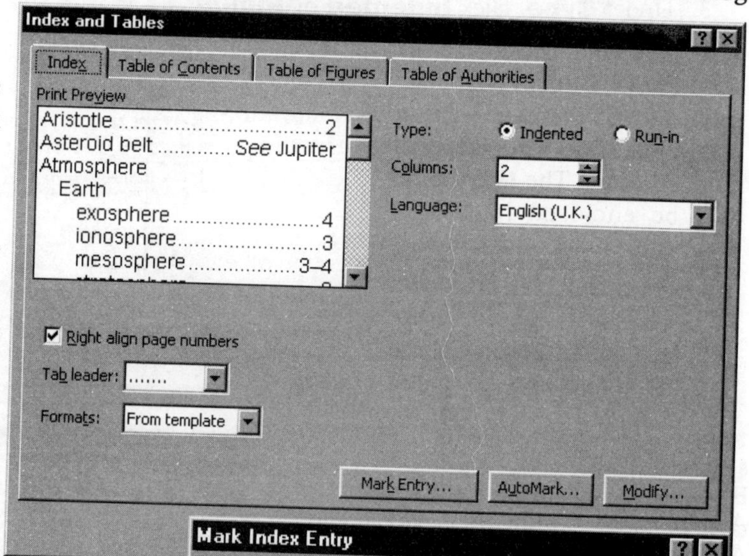

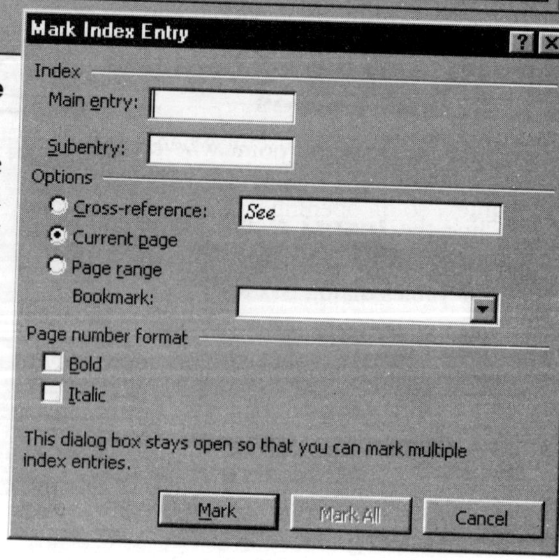

9. Repeat step 7 for each index entry you want to make in this session. Choose **Close** to close the Mark Index Entry dialog box.

Word marks each index entry by inserting a field immediately after the entry text in your document. If the field is not visible, choose **Show/Hide** on the **Standard** toolbar.

After you have all the index entries marked in your document., you are ready to generate the index. You may want to insert a section or page break at the end of the document where you want the index to start so it begins on a new page.

GENERATE AN INDEX

1. Put cursor at the location in your document where you want the index to appear.
2. Click the **Insert** menu and select **Index and Tables**. When the Index and Tables dialog box appears, select the **Index** tab.
3. Under **Type**, click **Indented** or **Run-In**. An indented index lists the subentries as indented paragraphs under the main topic. A run-in index lists all the subentries in a single paragraph, separated by semicolons. When you choose a type, a sample appears in the Print Preview window.
4. To choose from the predefined index formats available in Word, select one from the **Formats** list. When you do, the **Print Preview** changes to show you an example of that format.
5. Because the index can be lengthy but the lines are short, you may want to set it up to run in columns. Enter the number of columns you want in the **Columns** box.
6. Page numbers in an index generally follow immediately after the topics. If you would rather have your numbers appear on the right side of the line, click **Right Align Page Numbers**. Choose a character from the **Tab Leader** drop-down list, if you want to join the entry text with the page number by a tap leader.
7. Choose Ok to generate the index.

USING BOOKMARKS

A bookmark is a location in your document or a selection of text that you name for reference purposes. After you place a bookmark, you can return to the same location again and again by selecting the bookmark when you use Word's **Go To** feature (pressing **Ctrl+G** or **F5**). Bookmarks are especially useful when you are modifying or editing a large document. Create a bookmark when you close the document so on opening it again, you can find where you left. Bookmarks are also useful as reference points for cross-references, index entries, and macros.

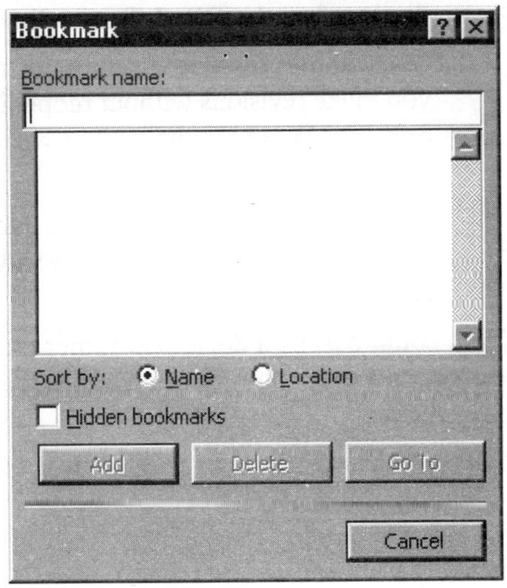

Add a Bookmark

1. Place cursor where you want to insert the bookmark.
2. Click the **Insert** menu and select **Bookmark** to open the Bookmark dialog box.
3. Type a name for the bookmark in the **Bookmark Name** box (do not enter any spaces in the name) or

select one from the list. If you select the name of an existing bookmark, it will move the bookmark location to the current position of your cursor.

4. Choose **Add**.

Deleting Bookmark

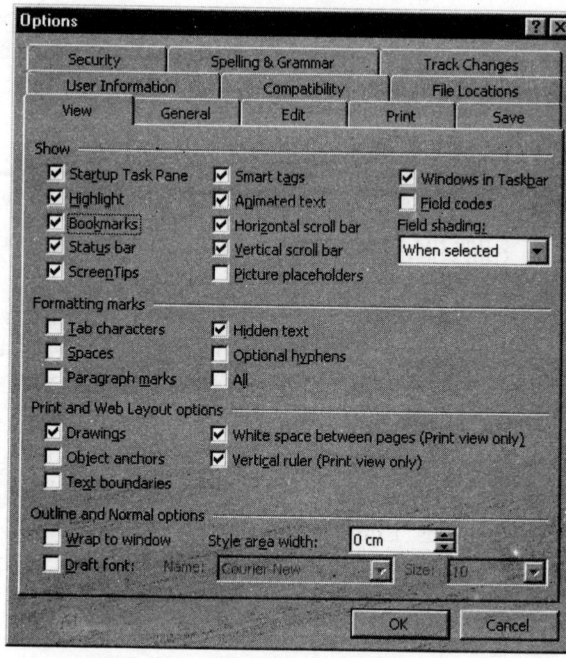

1. Click the **Insert** menu and select **Bookmark**.
2. Select the name of the bookmark you want to remove.
3. Choose **Delete**.
4. Choose **Close**.

Displaying Bookmarks

Bookmarks are not visible in the document. They can be made to appear as square brackets ([]). To see the bookmarks in your document, do the following:

1. Click the **Tools** menu and select **Options**.
2. Select the **View** tab.
3. Under **Show**, click **Bookmarks**.
4. Choose Ok.

COUNT WORDS

You can count the number of words in your document using the option called Word Count.

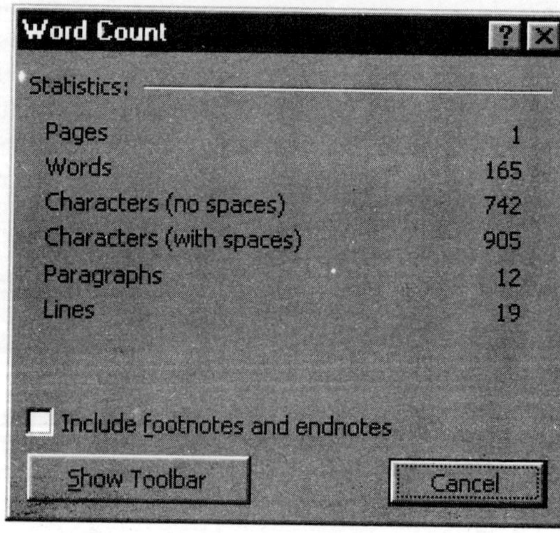

1. On the **Tools** menu, click **Word Count**. The results of everything Microsoft Word counts are displayed in the **Word Count** dialog box.
2. Click **Show Toolbar** if you want to recount as you make revisions without reopening the dialog box. The **Word Count** toolbar will open in your document.
3. If you want to include footnotes and endnotes in the count, select the **Include footnotes and endnotes** check box

If you count part of a document rather than the whole, Word counts the footnotes or endnotes that refer to the selected text.

Word recounts when you select or clear the check box.

Multiple Choice Questions

1. In word processing, you manipulate ______
   (a) numbers (b) text
2. You can set Left, Right and ______ alignment in word processing.
   (a) Center (b) Justify
   (c) Both
3. Can you spell check you text in word processing?
   (a) Yes (b) No
4. Can you locate a word in word processing?
   (a) No (b) Yes
5. Blinking point which shows your position in the text is called:
   (a) Cursor (b) Blinker
   (c) Position
6. Spacebar is used for :
   (a) giving space (b) deleting space
7. You can start Microsoft Word by using ______ button.
   (a) New (b) Start
   (c) Program
8. For creating a document, you use ______ command at File menu.
   (a) New (b) Open
   (c) Document
9. For saving a document, you need to have ______ for it.
   (a) Name (b) Surname
10. For opening an existing document, you need to give ______ command.
    (a) New (b) Open
    (c) Close
11. You can select the text by:
    (a) Keyboard (b) Mouse
    (c) Both
12. You click at B to make the text
    (a) Bold (b) Italics
    (c) Underline
13. Can you emboss you text?
    (a) Yes (b) No
14. You can change the size of the text from:
    (a) Formatting bar (b) Font dialog box
    (c) Both
15. You click at I to make the text
    (a) Bold (b) Italics
    (c) Underline
16. You can change the font of the text from
    (a) Formatting bar (b) Font dialog box
    (c) Box
17. Colour of the text can be changed:
    (a) Yes (b) No
18. You click at U to make the text
    (a) Bold (b) Italics
    (c) Underline
19. Word supports alignments like Left, Right, Center and ______
    (a) Justify (b) Up
    (c) Down
20. You can change the line and para spacing from ______ dialog box.
    (a) Font (b) Paragraph
    (c) Open

Descriptive Type Questions

1. What is word processing?
2. What are the various features of word processing?
3. Define the following terms:

Text	Document
Fonts	Cursor
Arrow keys	Space bar
Tabs	Backspace

4. Describe the various methods of starting Microsoft Word.
5. Describe the various items on the screen of Word.
6. How would you create a new document?
7. Describe the process of saving a document.
8. How would you set the timing for AutoSave?

9. If you do not save before closing, what will happen?
10. Describe the process of opening an existing document.
11. Describe the various methods of selection of text.
12. Describe the process of making the text, Bold, Italics and Underline.
13. Describe the various options of Font dialog box.
14. How would you change size & font of the text?
15. Describe the process of changing the colour of the text.
16. What is an alignment? Describe the various alignments supported by Word.
17. Describe the various options of Paragraph dialog box.
18. How would you allot page numbers to various pages in your document?
19. How is spell checking ?
20. What are various options of spell checking dialog box?

Spreadsheets & Microsoft Excel

21

INTRODUCTION

Excel for Windows is a spreadsheet program. A spreadsheet is a graphical representation of rows and columns. Data can be fed into these rows and columns and mathematical and other operations performed on it. An opening screen of Excel is shown here.

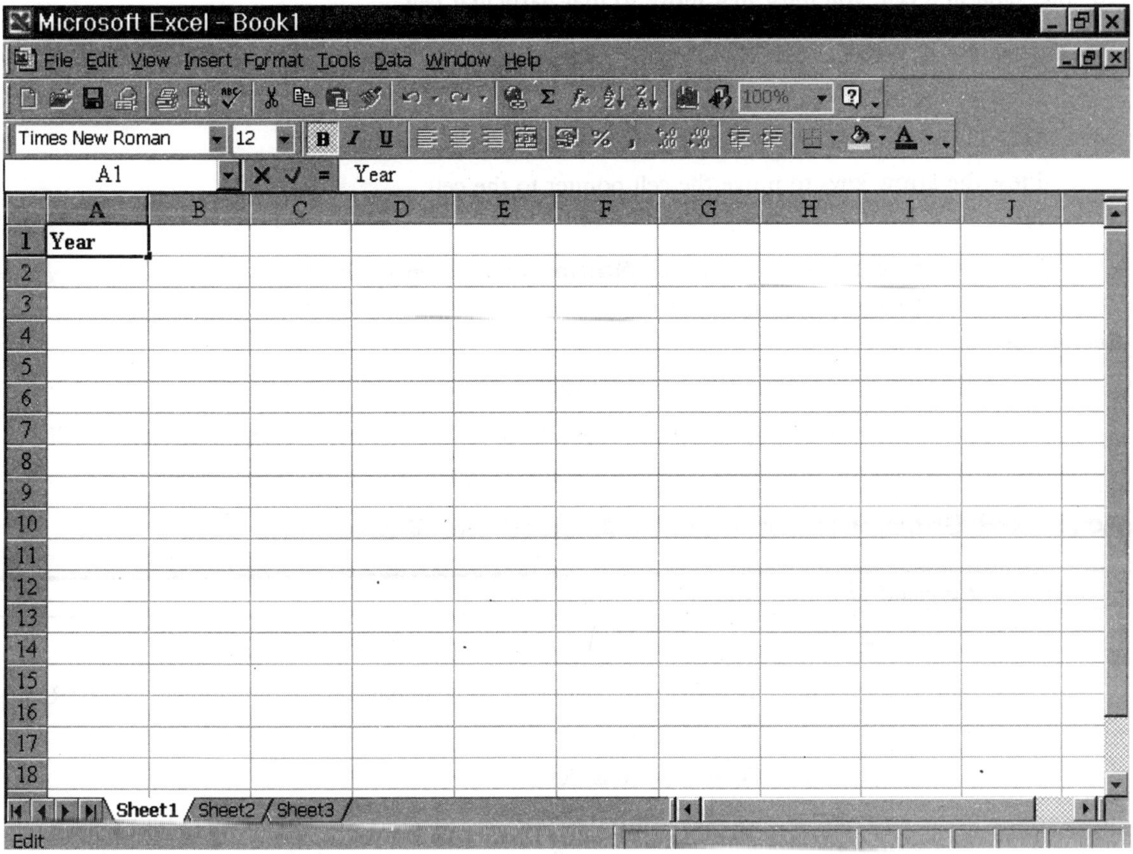

Naming Convention

It is not I have named rows from 1 onwards and columns A onwards on my own but they are so numbered by the software itself. These are the standard way of expressing these columns and rows.

If we have to name a large number of cells or columns, for that too we have the convention which asks us to call them with starting cell address and last cell address with colon in between. For example, see the addressed cells here.

Another convention is of the sheets in the worksheet.

SHEETS

These are like pages in a book. Initially there are 16 worksheets in a file. But, you can add more. However, there may be only 6 of them visible on the screen. These sheets are independent but you can transfer data from one sheet to another.

These sheets are very helpful. For example, for a salary spreadsheet, one sheet may belong to one month and there may be a sheet for the total of the year.

MOVING WITHIN A SHEET

To enter data in a cell, you must first move to that particular cell.

To Move to a Cell

1. Click in the cell.

   Or

   Press the arrow keys to move the cell pointer to the cell.

   Or

   Select the current cell address in the **Name** box and replace it with the address of the cell to which you want to move.

Remember

1. The cell surrounded by the cell pointer is called the active cell.
2. You can use the scroll bars to scroll through the document without changing the active cell.
3. To move within the worksheet, you can use the keyboard shortcuts, given below:

Keyboard Shortcuts for Moving Around the Worksheet

Keyboard Shortcut	*Result*
Arrow key	Moves to the adjacent cell (Up, Down, Left or Right)
Ctrl+Arrow Key	Moves to the edge of the current data region (Up, Down, Left or Right)
Tab	Moves right one cell
Shift + Tab	Moves left one cell
Enter	Moves down one cell
Shift + Enter	Moves up one cell
Home	Moves to the first cell of the row
Ctrl + Home	Moves to cell A1
Ctrl + End	Moves to last cell of last row with data
Page Down	Moves down one screen
Page Up	Moves up one screen

Alt + Page Down	Moves one screen to the right
Alt + Page Up	Moves one screen to the left
Ctrl + Page Down	Moves to the next sheet in the workbook
Ctrl + Page Up	Moves to the previous sheet in the workbook

ENTERING DATA

You can enter text, a number, or a formula into each cell in a worksheet. You enter text to create a label, such as a column heading. You can enter a number to provide information with which you can do calculations.

To Type Data in a Cell

1. Select the cell.
2. Type text, a number, or a formula. A flashing insertion point will appear at the end of whatever you type. You will notice that whatever you type will appear not only in the active cell but also in the Formula bar.
3. Press Enter key to move to the next cell. The cell below will become the new active cell.

Remember

1. You don't have to press Enter after you type the contents of a cell. You can simply press right arrow key to move to the next cell.
2. Excel right aligns the numbers in the cell but left aligns the text.

EDITING THE DATA

The easiest way to change the text or number in a cell is to click the cell and then type right over the contents. But if you have a formula or extensive text in the cell, you might prefer to edit the existing contents to avoid retyping the whole entry.

To edit data in a cell

1. Click the cell and then type over its contents

   Or

   Double click the cell to position an insertion point with the cell contents.
2. Edit the contents as though you were editing text in Word.
3. Press Enter to enter the revised text in the cell.

This is if you have just one cell to edit, But, if you have more than one cell to edit. Then you need to select the various cells.

SELECTING CELLS

You can select a number of consecutive cells called a range by one of the following methods:

1. Click and drag over the selection.
2. Click in one cell, and then hold down the Shift key and click in the opposite corner of the selection.

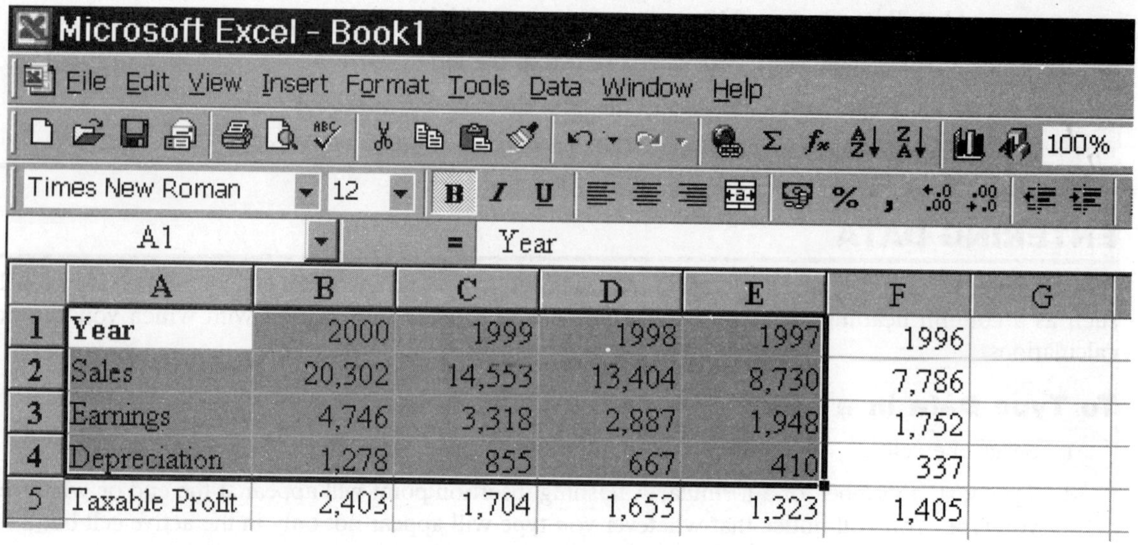

3. Click on the Select All button, the gray rectangle where the column and row heading meet, to select the entire worksheet.
4. Click in a column or row heading to select the whole column or row.

MOVING DATA

1. Select a range of cells. The cells will be highlighted.
2. Click on the Cut button. Moving dashes (called a marquee) will appear around your selection.
3. In this case the data does not disappear like text does in a word processor.
4. Click in the cell that will be upper left corner of the new location of the range. The cell will be selected.

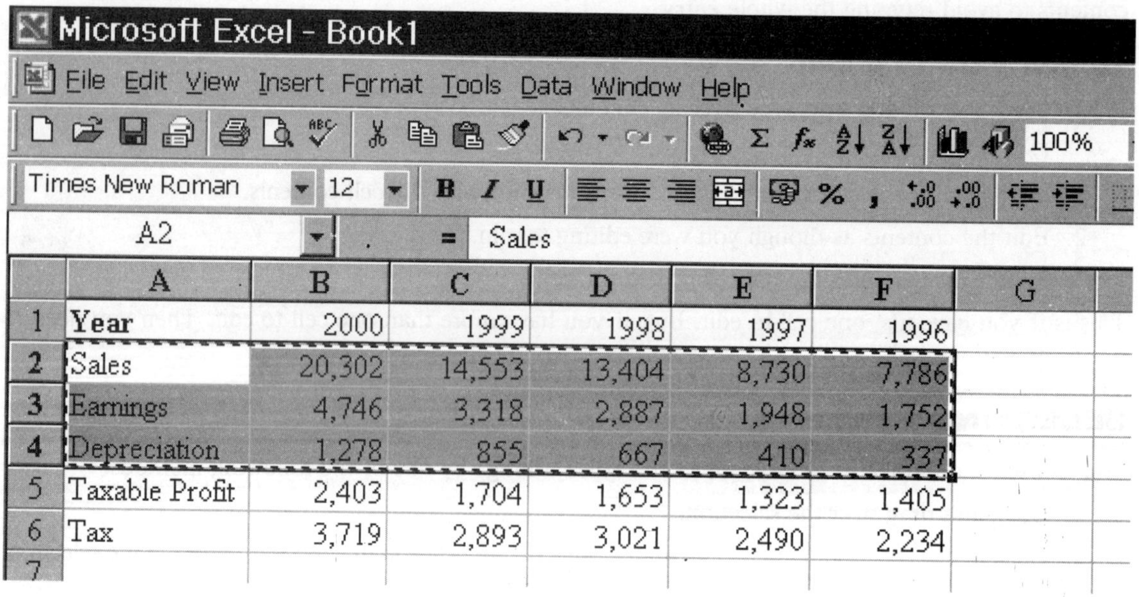

5. Click on the Paste button. The data will be pasted in the new location.

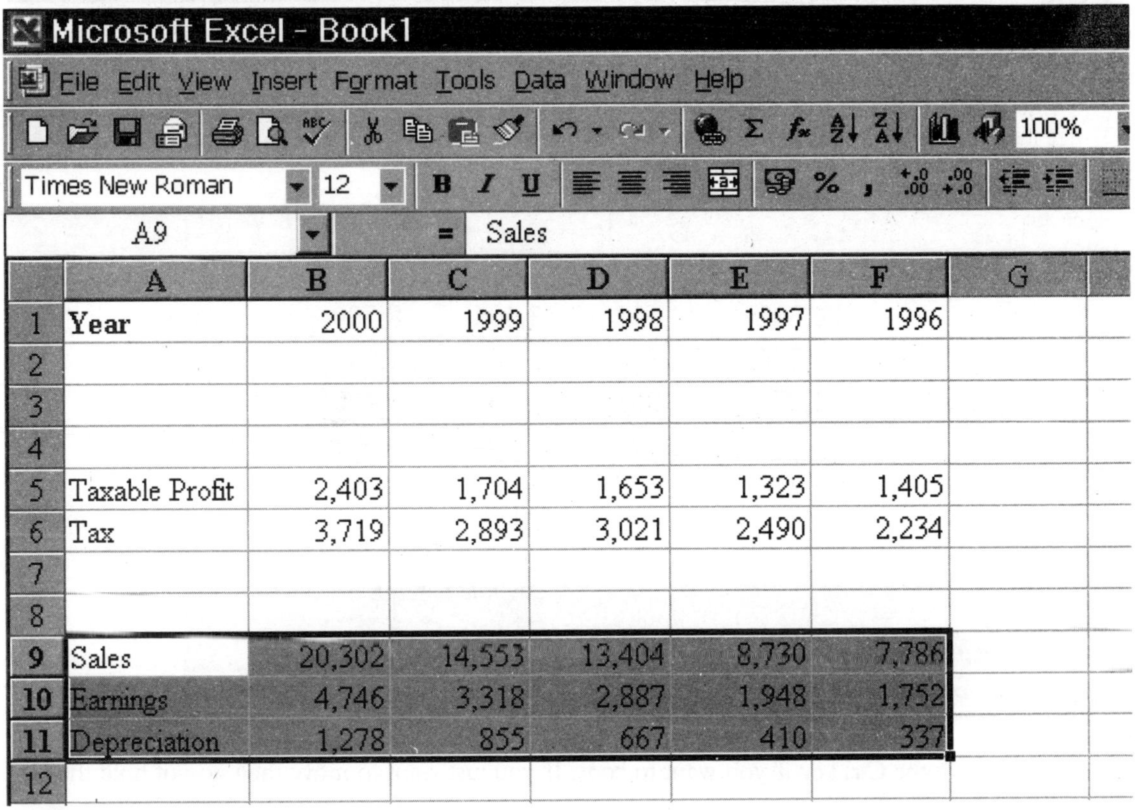

COPYING DATA

Copying puts selected data in a new location. Unlike moved data, copied data also remains in the original location.

1. Select a range of cell. The cells will be highlighted.
2. Click the Copy button.
3. A marquee (running dashes) will appear around your selection.
4. Click in the cell at the top left of the range where you want to place a copy.
5. Click on Paste button.
6. The selected range will appear in both the original location and new location.
7. If you want you can paste the selection at another location too.

The next figure show the result of highlighting, copying of the cells range and copying them at a new location.

DRAG AND DROP METHOD

This method makes the best use of mouse. You can move and copy using the mouse in a shorter way.

1. Select the cells you want to move or copy. The cells will be highlighted.

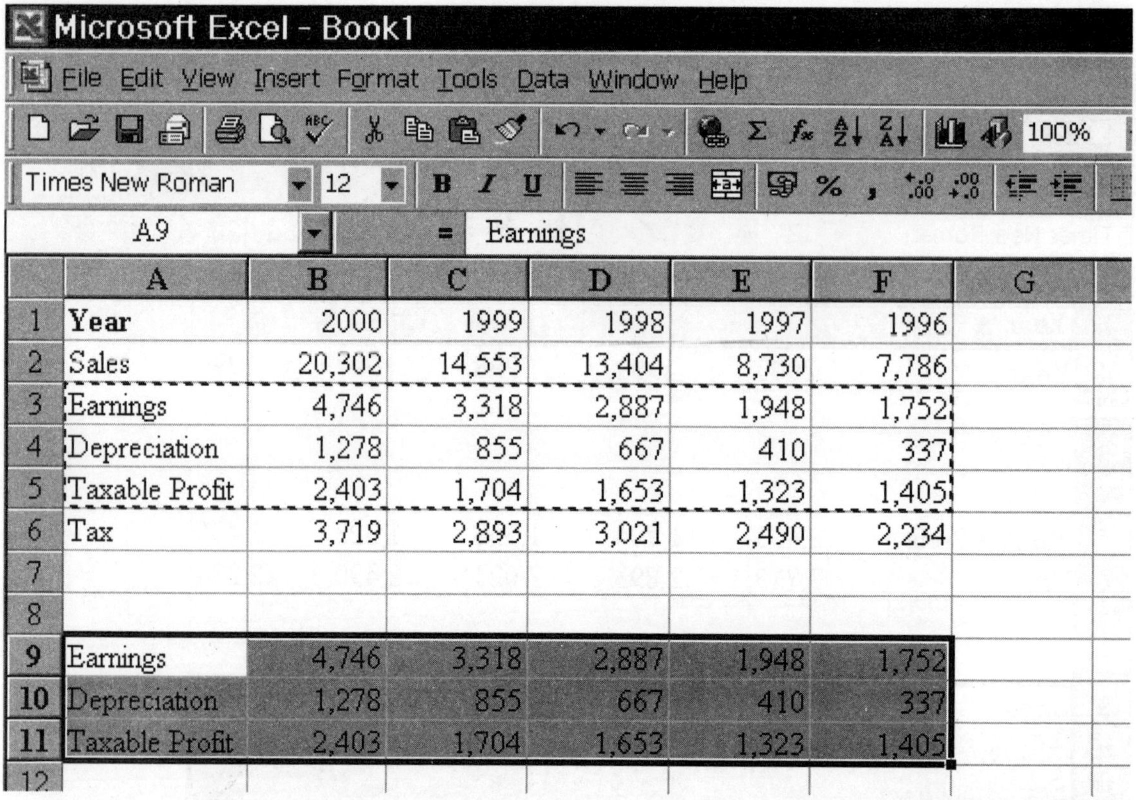

	A	B	C	D	E	F	G
1	**Year**	2000	1999	1998	1997	1996	
2	Sales	20,302	14,553	13,404	8,730	7,786	
3	Earnings	4,746	3,318	2,887	1,948	1,752	
4	Depreciation	1,278	855	667	410	337	
5	Taxable Profit	2,403	1,704	1,653	1,323	1,405	
6	Tax	3,719	2,893	3,021	2,490	2,234	
7							
8							
9	Earnings	4,746	3,318	2,887	1,948	1,752	
10	Depreciation	1,278	855	667	410	337	
11	Taxable Profit	2,403	1,704	1,653	1,323	1,405	
12							

2. Hold down the Ctrl key if you want to copy. If you just want to move then do not hold the Ctrl key.
3. Position the mouse pointer over the border of the selected area. The mouse pointer will become an arrow.
4. Press and hold mouse button as you drag the cells to a new location. The cell location you are dragging over will appear in a box below the mouse arrow.
5. Release the mouse button.
6. The cells will be dropped in the new location. This is much quicker than using buttons or menus.

INSERTING ROWS AND COLUMNS

You can insert rows and columns at any time, and Excel adjusts all formulas to accommodate the new rows or columns. If you insert a row, it will appear **above** the selected cell; if you insert a column, it will appear to the **left** of the selected cell.

To insert a row or a column

1. Click any cell of the row or column in which you had like to insert the new blank row or column.
2. From the Insert menu, choose Rows to insert a row or choose Columns to insert a column, as shown next.
3. A new Row in this case will be inserted, as shown next.

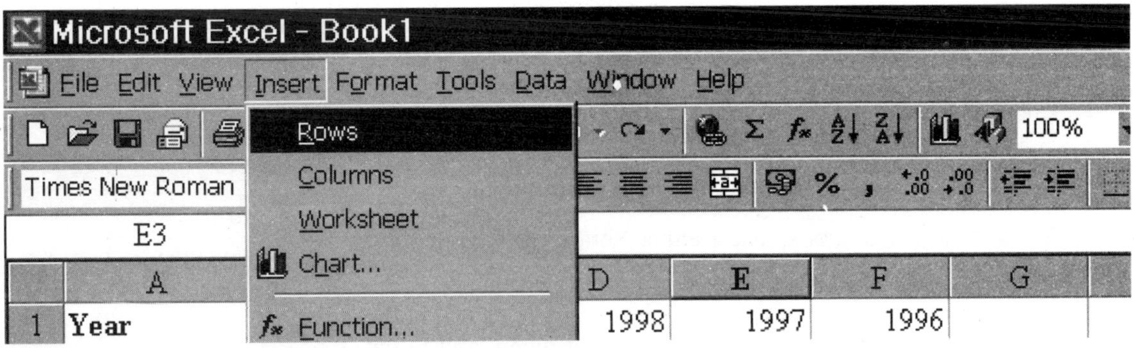

INSERTING AND DELETING CELLS

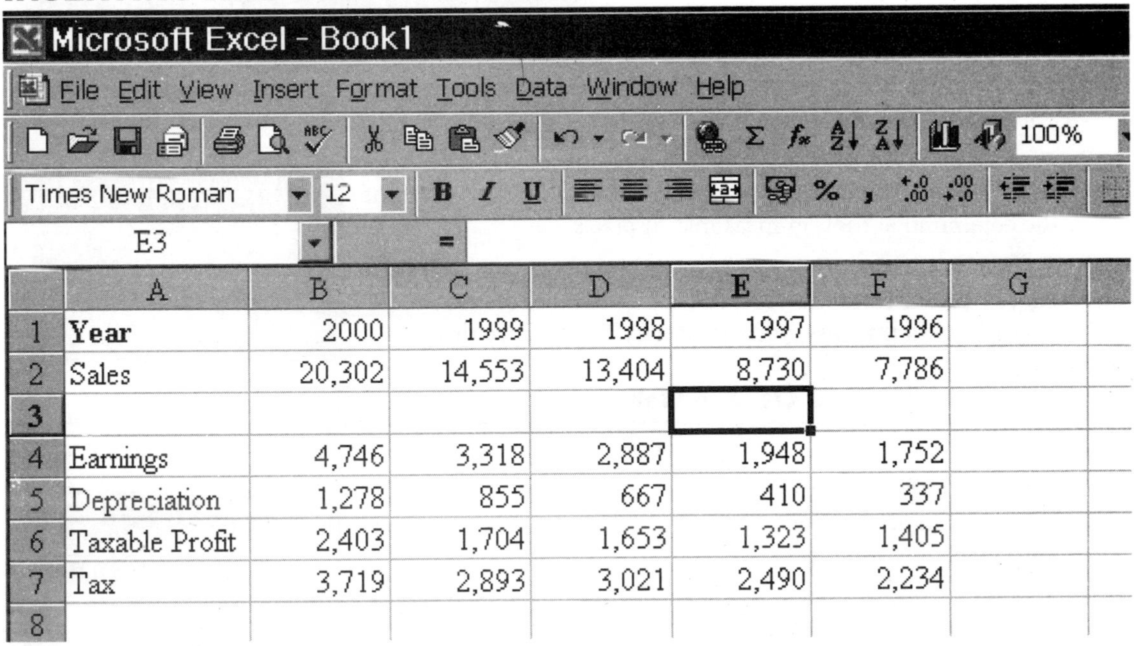

	A	B	C	D	E	F	G
1	Year	2000	1999	1998	1997	1996	
2	Sales	20,302	14,553	13,404	8,730	7,786	
3							
4	Earnings	4,746	3,318	2,887	1,948	1,752	
5	Depreciation	1,278	855	667	410	337	
6	Taxable Profit	2,403	1,704	1,653	1,323	1,405	
7	Tax	3,719	2,893	3,021	2,490	2,234	
8							

When you tell Excel to insert or delete a cell within a range of data, Excel needs to know how to move the data that is in adjacent cells. You specify your preferences in the Insert or Delete dialog box.

To Insert a Cell

1. Click the destination for the new, blank cell.
2. Choose Cells from the Insert menu.

   Or

   Right-click the cell and choose Insert from the shortcut menu.
3. In the Insert dialog box, select either Shift Cells Right or Shift Cells Down.
4. The new cell appears.

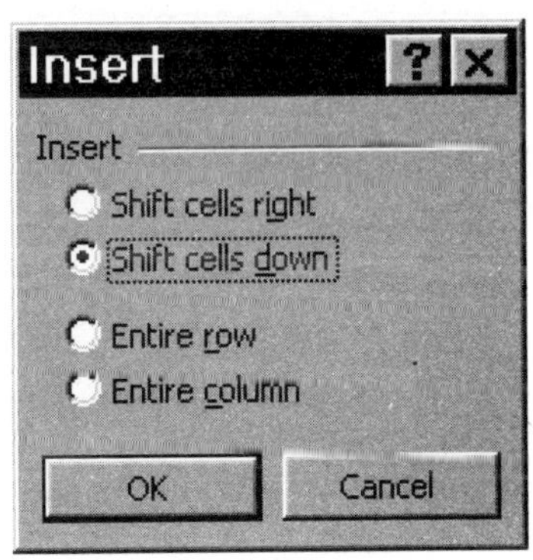

To Delete a Cell

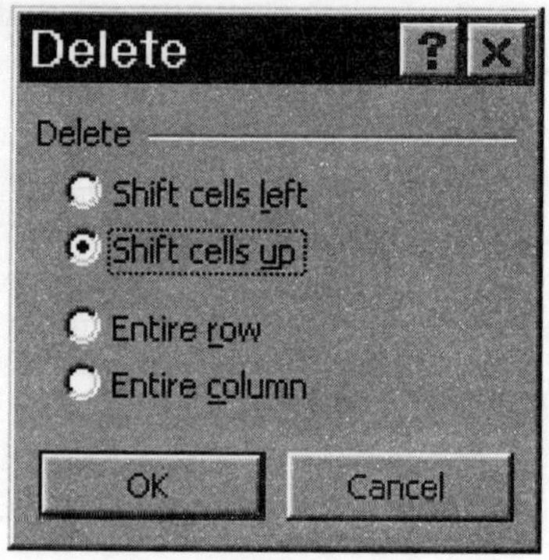

1. Click the cell you want to delete.
2. Choose Delete from the Edit menu.

   Or

   Right-click the cell and choose Delete from the shortcut menu.
3. In the Delete dialog box, select either Shift Cells Left or Shift Cells Up.
4. To delete an entire row or column, select at least one cell in the row or column, choose Delete from the Edit menu, and in the Delete dialog box, choose either Entire Row or Entire Column.

CHANGING WIDTH OF A COLUMN

1. Position the mouse pointer on the right edge of the gray column heading button for the column you want to widen.
2. When the mouse pointer changes to a double arrow, drag right or left. While you are dragging, you will see the new width of the column in a ToolTip measured in pixels.
3. You can also select Column from the Format menu and then choose Width from the submenu to open the Column Width dialog box. In this case, you can specify the exact setting.

CHANGING HEIGHT OF A ROW

1. Position the mouse pointer on the bottom edge of the gray row heading button for the row whose height you want to change.
2. When the mouse pointer changes to a double arrows, drag up and down.
3. You can also select Row from the Format menu and then choose Height from the submenu to open the Row Height dialog box. In this case, you can specify the exact setting.

FORMATTING TEXT

You can use formatting to improve the appearance of your worksheet and to make it easier to locate the information you need.

To format selected text

1. Select the cell or cells containing the text to format.
2. Choose formatting options by clicking the text formatting buttons on the Formatting toolbar.

   Or

1. Select the cell or cells containing the text to format.
2. From the Format menu, choose Cells, or right-click and choose Format Cells from the shortcut menu.

3. In the Format Cells dialog box, change the options on the Alignment and Font tabs.
4. Click Ok.

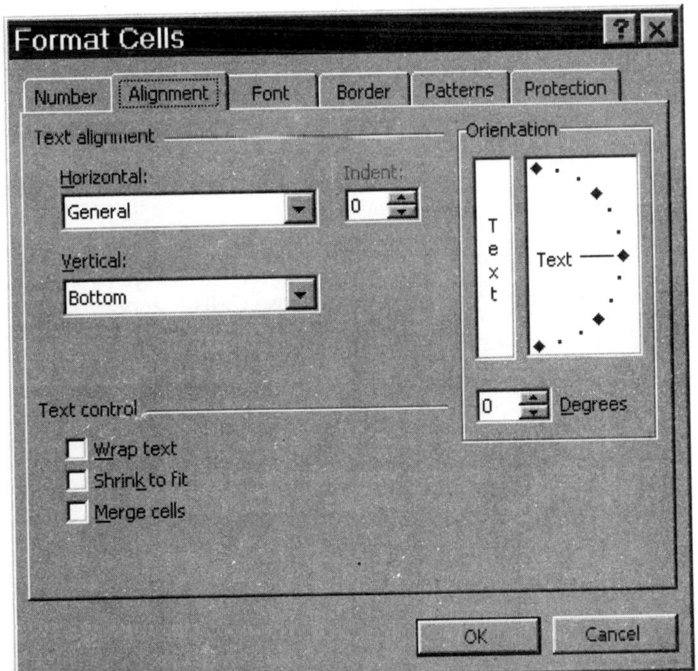

AUTOFORMAT

The fastest and easiest way to make a worksheet presentable is to give an AutoFormat command. **AutoFormat** supplies a complete look for a range of data by changing the font, text alignment, number formatting, borders, patterns, colours, column widths, and row heights. Excel provides a selection of AutoFormats, each with a unique look.

To choose an AutoFormat

1. Click any cell in the range to format.

   Or

   Select the range to format.
2. From the Format menu, choose AutoFormat.
3. In the AutoFormat dialog box, select an AutoFormat from the display.
4. Click Ok.

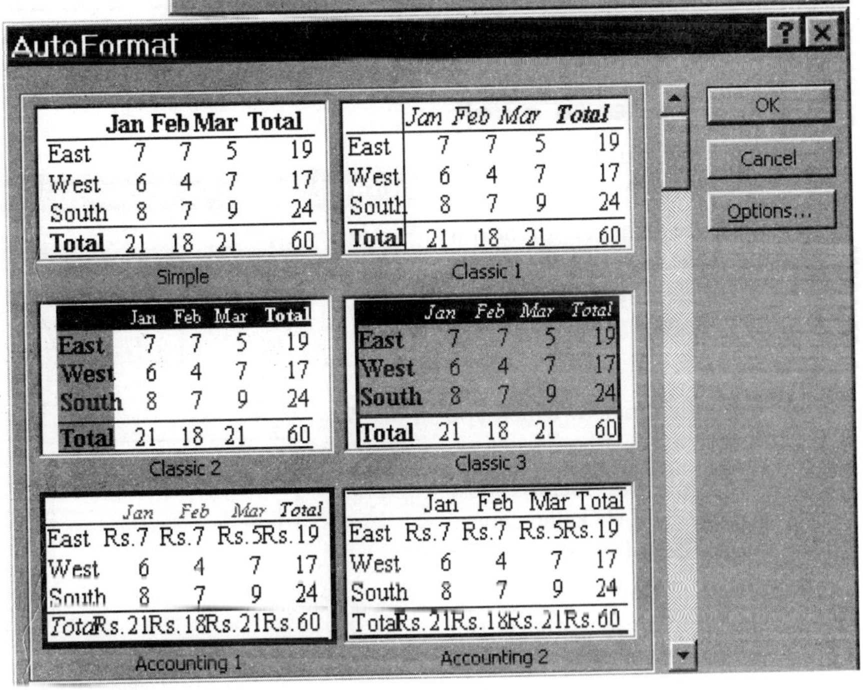

FORMATTING NUMBERS

Excel makes available to you a variety of number formatting options, some from the Formatting toolbar and others from the Format Cells dialog box.

To format numbers

1. Select the numbers to format.
2. Click the appropriate number formatting button on the Formatting toolbar.

Or

1. Select the numbers to format.
2. From the Format menu, choose Cells.
3. On the Number tab of the Format Cells dialog box, choose a category and other options.
4. Click Ok.

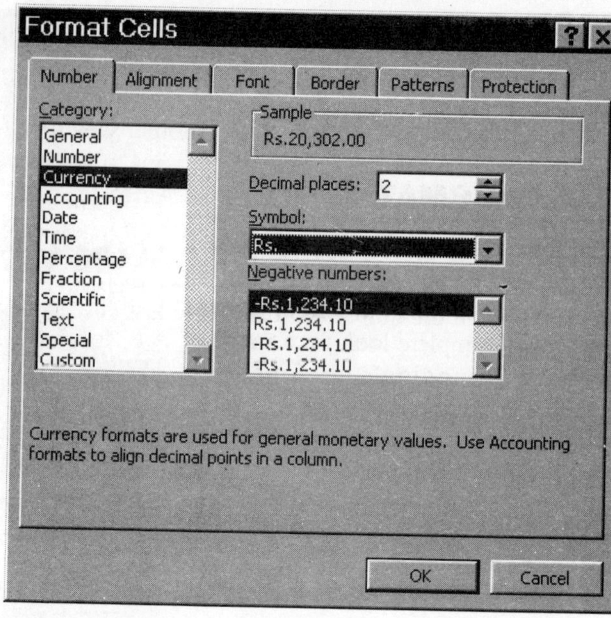

ADDING BORDER TO A RANGE

A border is a line at the edge of a cell. You can use borders to divide the information on the sheet into logical regions. Borders appear on the screen and will print when you print the sheet.

To add a border to a cell

1. Select the range to which you want to apply a border.
2. Click the arrow button next to the Borders button to see the full range of border you want for the range

Or

1. Select the range to which you want to apply a border.
2. From the Format menu, choose Cells, or right-click and choose Format Cells from the shortcut menu.
3. On the Border tab of the Format Cells dialog box, choose a border, a border style, and a colour.
4. Click Ok and the border is added to the range.

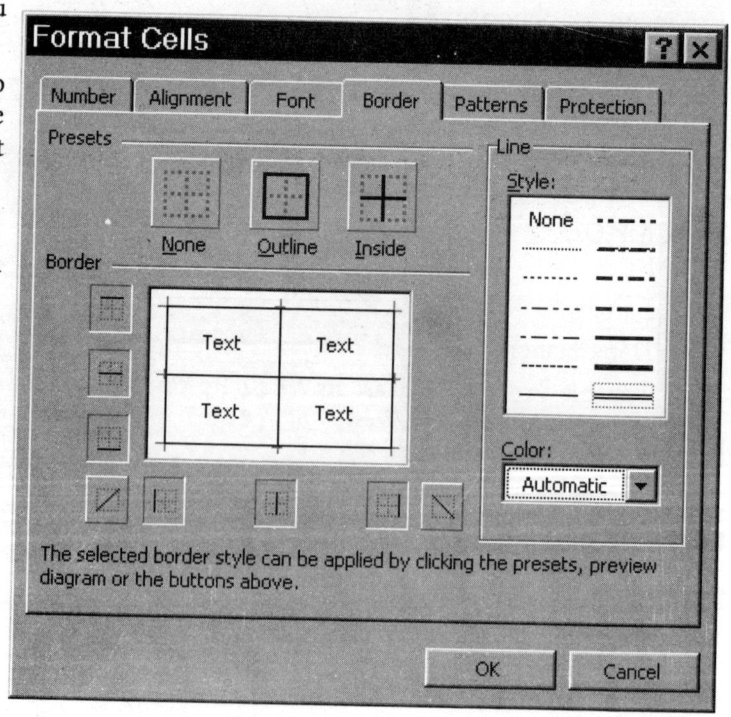

FORMULAE

They establish relationships between two or more cells. If you want to add the values in cells **C6** and **C7** and put the result in cell **C8**, move to the cell **C8** and type **=C6+C7** and press **Enter**. The result is displayed immediately in cell **C8**. Another way to achieve the same result is to move to cell **C8** and type **+**, point to cell **C6**, type **+**, then point to **C7**, and press **Enter**. The easiest way to achieve this operation is to point to **C8**, pick up the AutoSum button Σ on the toolbar.

SUMMING OF A ROW OR COLUMN

1. Click in the empty cell below the last entry in the column or to the right of the last entry in the row.
2. Click the AutoSum button on the Standard toolbar.
3. Press Enter to enter the formula that has automatically appeared in the cell.

Remember

1. Excel looks for the range of numbers to sum above the cell you have selected for the total. If it does not find a range of numbers or if it finds text, it looks to the left for a range of numbers.
2. Excel will not skip over an empty cell when it is looking for a range of cells to sum.
3. To quickly enter sums below multiple adjacent columns, select the empty cells at the bottoms of all the columns before clicking the AutoSum button. Excel will insert a sum in each selected cell.

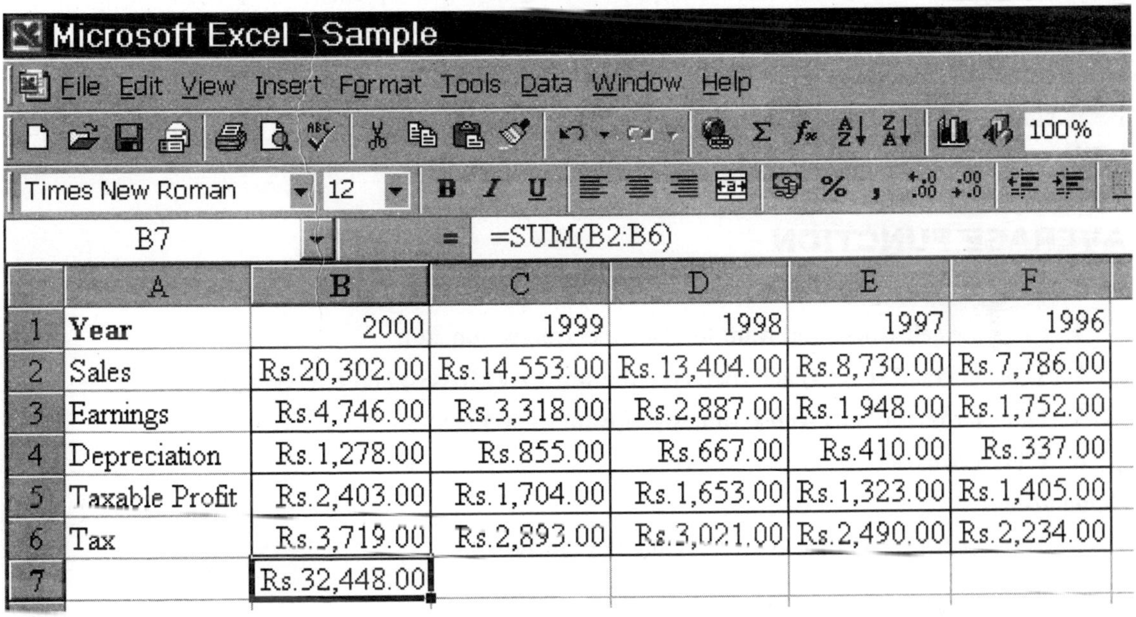

	A	B	C	D	E	F
1	**Year**	2000	1999	1998	1997	1996
2	Sales	Rs.20,302.00	Rs.14,553.00	Rs.13,404.00	Rs.8,730.00	Rs.7,786.00
3	Earnings	Rs.4,746.00	Rs.3,318.00	Rs.2,887.00	Rs.1,948.00	Rs.1,752.00
4	Depreciation	Rs.1,278.00	Rs.855.00	Rs.667.00	Rs.410.00	Rs.337.00
5	Taxable Profit	Rs.2,403.00	Rs.1,704.00	Rs.1,653.00	Rs.1,323.00	Rs.1,405.00
6	Tax	Rs.3,719.00	Rs.2,893.00	Rs.3,021.00	Rs.2,490.00	Rs.2,234.00
7		Rs.32,448.00				

SUM FUNCTION

The **Sum** function is perhaps the most commonly used of the Excel functions that carry out mathematical, statistical, financial, date, time, and other calculations.

1. Click the destination cell for the formula.

2. Type an equal sign to start the formula and then type the word SUM and a left parenthesis.
3. Drag down the column of numbers to sum.
4. Press Enter.

Remember

1. You do not need to type the close (right) parenthesis before you press Enter—Excel will do it for you.
2. Use this technique instead of AutoSum to sum ranges of cells that contain blanks.

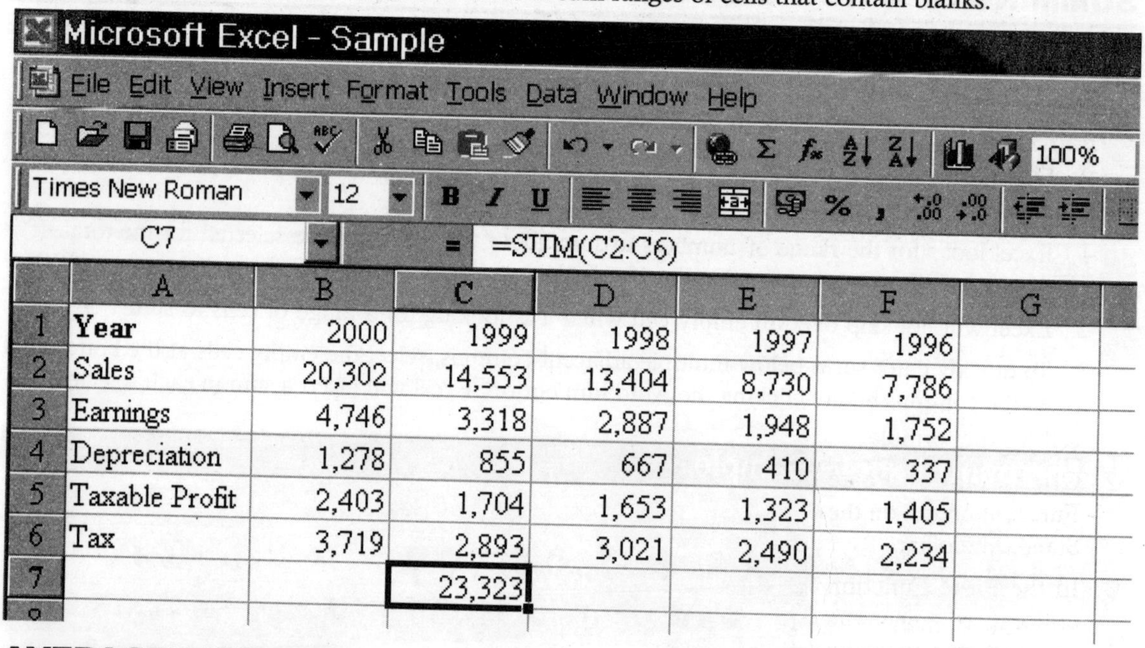

	A	B	C	D	E	F	G
1	**Year**	2000	1999	1998	1997	1996	
2	Sales	20,302	14,553	13,404	8,730	7,786	
3	Earnings	4,746	3,318	2,887	1,948	1,752	
4	Depreciation	1,278	855	667	410	337	
5	Taxable Profit	2,403	1,704	1,653	1,323	1,405	
6	Tax	3,719	2,893	3,021	2,490	2,234	
7			23,323				

AVERAGE FUNCTION

You can use the Average function to calculate the average of values in cells.

1. Click the cell where you want to place the average function.
2. Type an equal sign (=) and then type the word AVERAGE and a left parenthesis.
3. Drag across the cells whose values you want to average.
4. Press Enter.

Remember

1. Blank cells in the range are not counted in the average.

USING FUNCTION WIZARD

Sum and Average are just two of the most commonly used functions whereas there are lots of them in Excel 2000. You can use them to get the desired results in a flash. To get them click the **Paste Function** button on the Standard toolbar as your are building the formula. The Paste Function wizard takes you through the steps of building a formula.

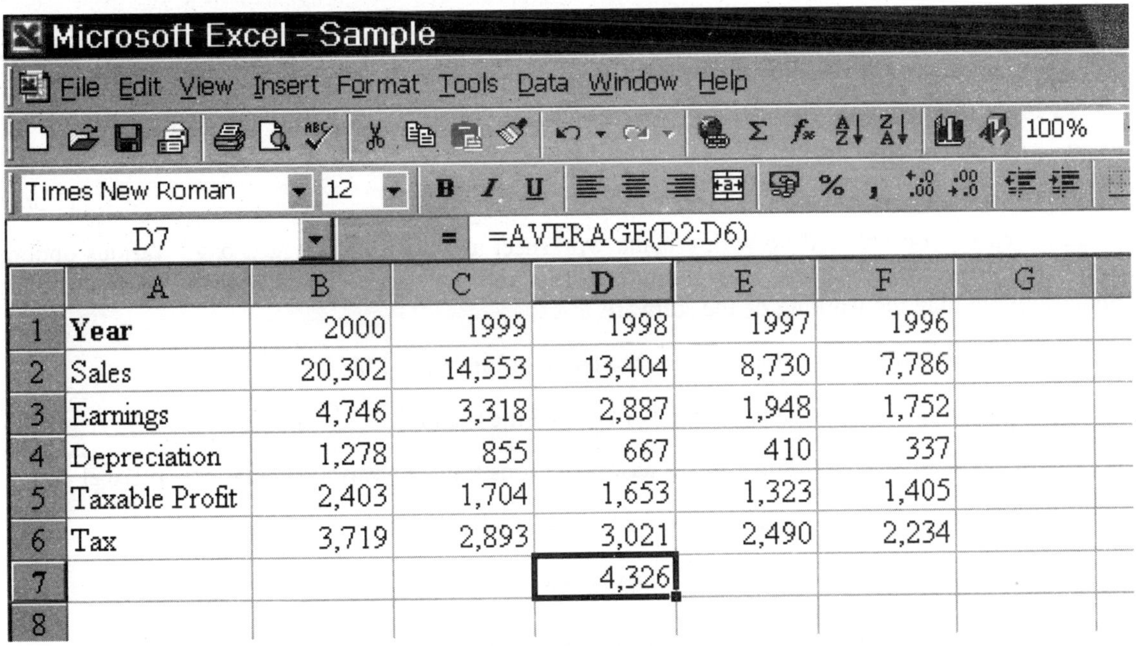

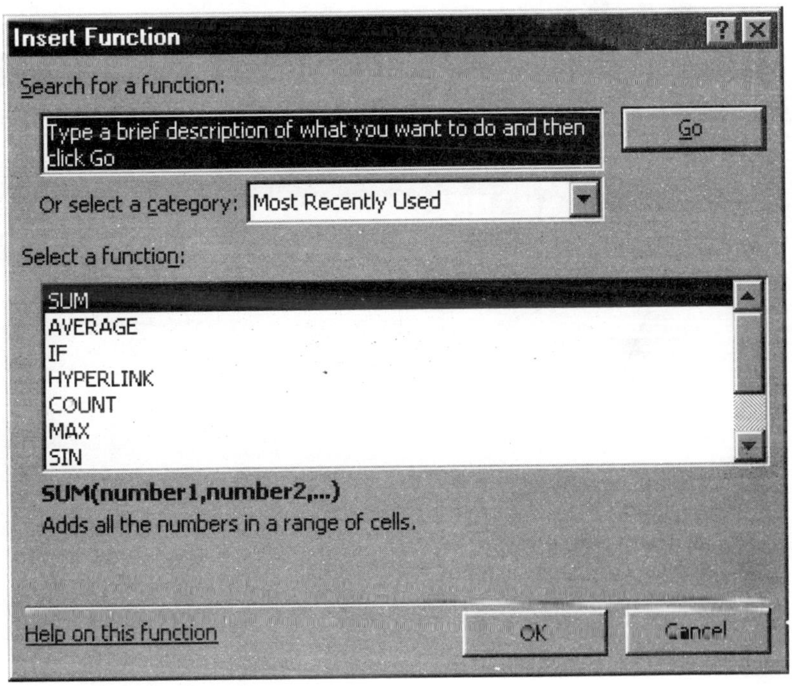

1. Click the destination cell for the formula.
2. Click the Paste Function button on the Standard toolbar.
3. In the Paste Function dialog box, select the category and then the function.
4. Click Ok.
5. Use the Paste Function Wizard to guide you in completing the formula.
6. Click Ok when you have finished.
7. The following screen has been created using the same function AVERAGE over the selected cells as used in the AVERAGE function.

UNDERSTANDING MICROSOFT EXCEL FOR WINDOWS

Before we understand how the software works, we must learn about the various tools and commands that are available in the software, only then we can use them. First thing first, let us start the software.

STARTING MICROSOFT EXCEL 2000

You can start Microsoft Excel by 3 methods.

1. From Start button
2. From Microsoft Office Bar
3. From Windows Explorer

In all the cases, you will end up with a blank worksheet as shown on the next page. Various options available on the worksheet are also pointed on this and next page. These tools are very useful in understanding fully the working of the software.

1	Excel toolbar	This contains the name of the opened file
2	Menu toolbar	This toolbar contains all the menus
3	Standard bar	This toolbar has the various tools for various operations in Excel
4	Font bar	It shows the font of the current cell
5	Selected Cell	It show the current cell

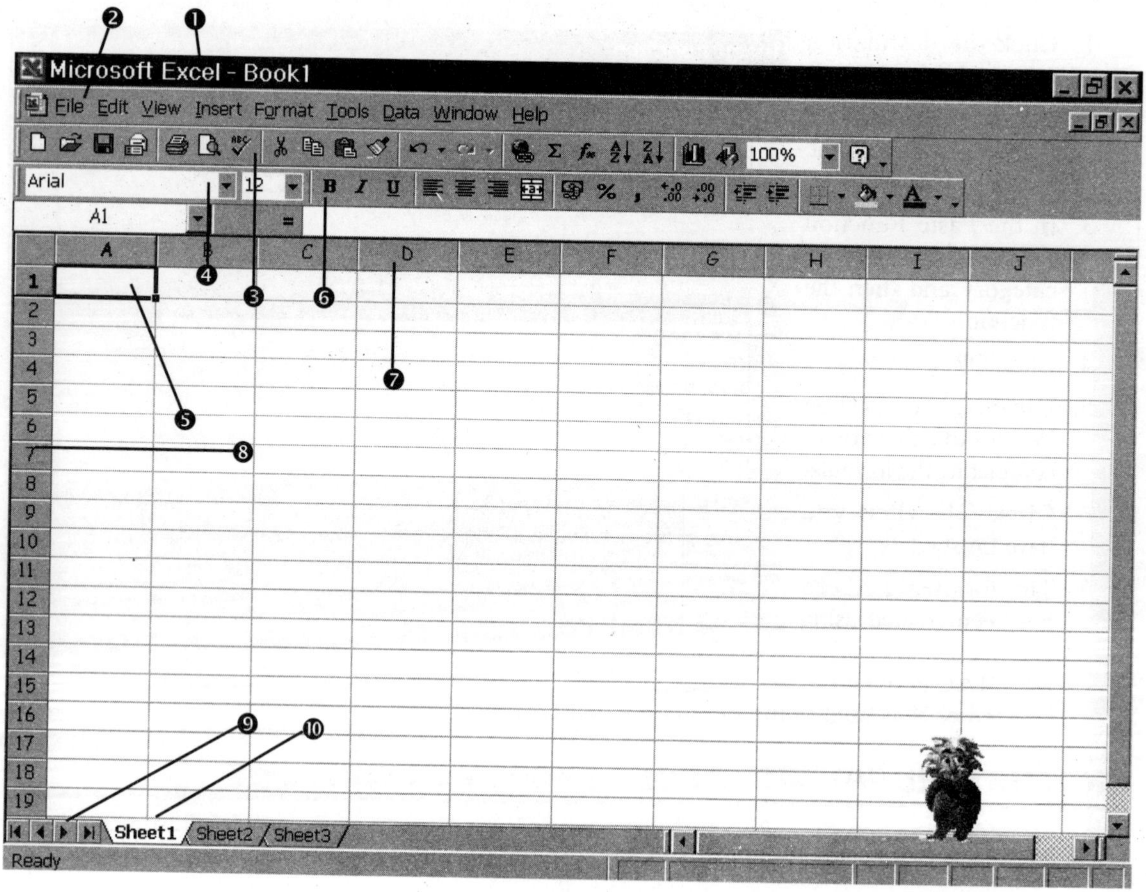

6	Formatting bar	This toolbar has the various options of formatting
7	Columns	A to J are shown here but there are more
8	Rows	1 to 19 are shown here but there are more
9	Scroll buttons	These are used to move around the worksheet
10	Sheet selecter	You can select the various sheets from here

With reference to the net figure, the following have the meaning.

1	Close button	This button closes the software
2	Toggle button	This button allows you to toggle between maximum and minimum of screen
3	Minimum button	This button makes Excel into an icon (minimum)
4	Cell block	This block will always show you the cell number on which you are working
5	Formula bar	This bar shows you the formula being applied
6	Horizontal button	Button for moving the screen horizontally
7	Office assistant	Click it to get the help

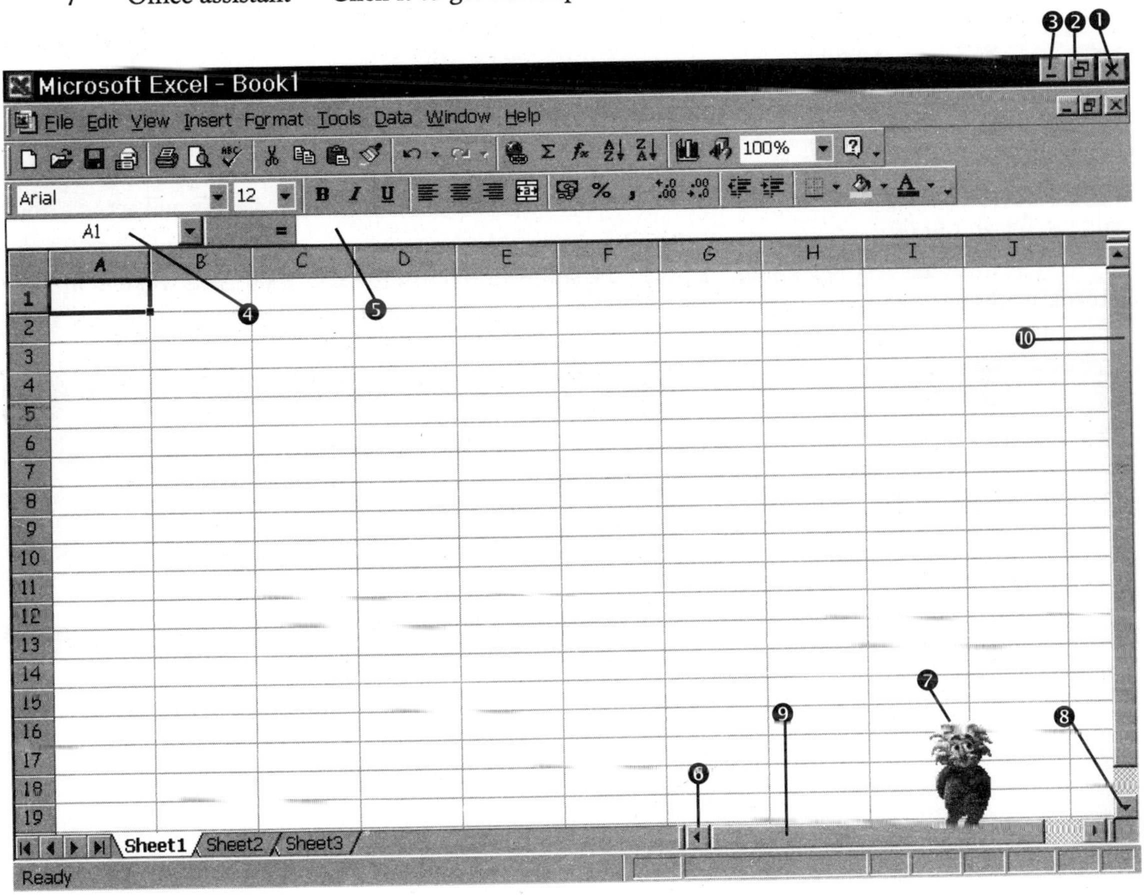

8	Horizontal bar	Horizontal scrollbar
9	Vertical button	For moving the screen vertically
10	Vertical bar	Vertical scrollbar

CREATING A WORKSHEET IN EXCEL FOR WINDOWS

We have learnt quite a number of commands and naturally would like to use them in a worksheet. So let us create a worksheet and use these commands side-by-side to see how they work out.

Supposing we have the financial highlights of a company as given below:

Year	Total Income (A)	Interest Paid (B)	Profit (C)	Tax (D)	Profit After Tax (E)
1992	4,500	To be	To be	To be	To be
1993	5,500	Calculated	Calculated	Calculated	Calculated
1994	7,000	as 15%	as Income	as 12% of	as Profit
1995	8,000	of the	minus	the Profit	minus Tax
1996	9,000	Total	Interest		(C) - (D)
1997	12,000	Income	(A) - (B)		
1998	15,000				
1999	20,000				

As you can see that there are quite a number of fields which have to be calculated. This will act as a good exercise for you to do.

Let us start from the very beginning, i.e., start the software Microsoft Excel 2000. You will end up with a blank worksheet, ready for you to take action, with the first cell **A1**, totally at your command to do something, as shown in the figure below.

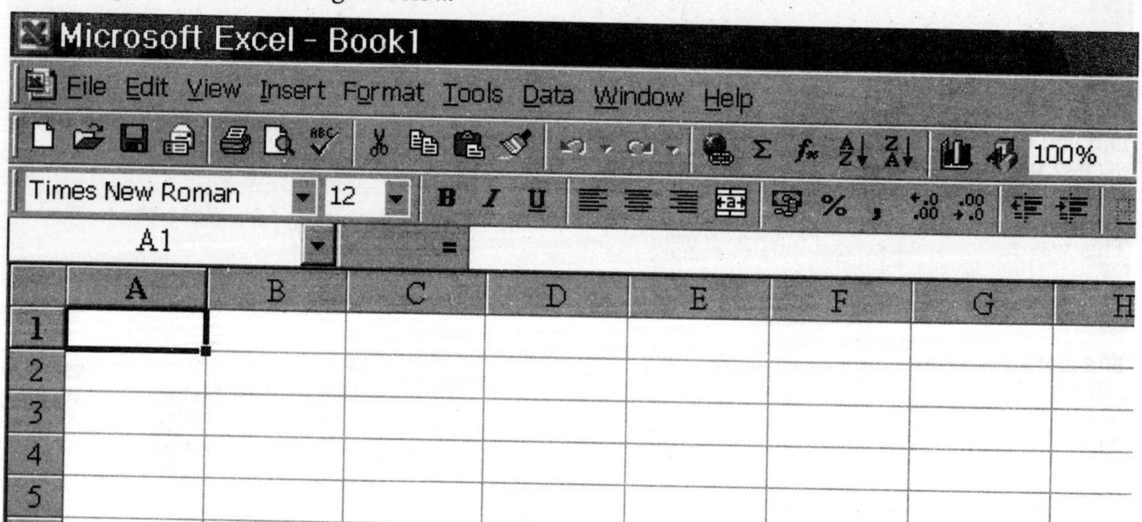

So what we have to do here. We have to type “Year”. So just type the word Year and press **Enter**. You will see the word being shown in the formula bar too. This will also take you to the cell **A2**. But, for typing the next heading, you have to go to the cell **B1**. So use the arrow keys right and up to reach **B1**.

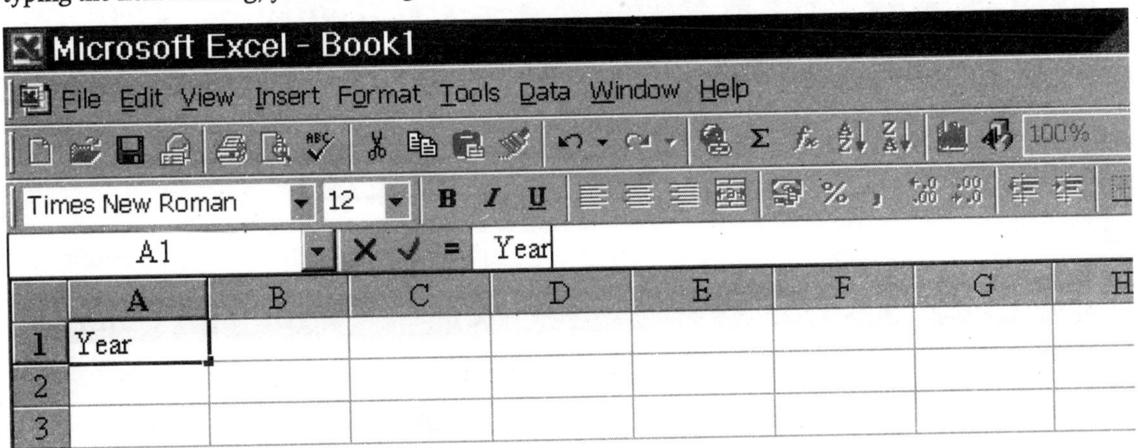

Next we have to type “Total Income”. (Please note that for the sake of convenience I had shown this heading in 2 lines, but, if permitted we will type it in one line. Also (A), (B), etc., in the table are just symbolic and are not to be typed).

So for type the next heading, “Total Income” in the cell **B1**, as shown next.

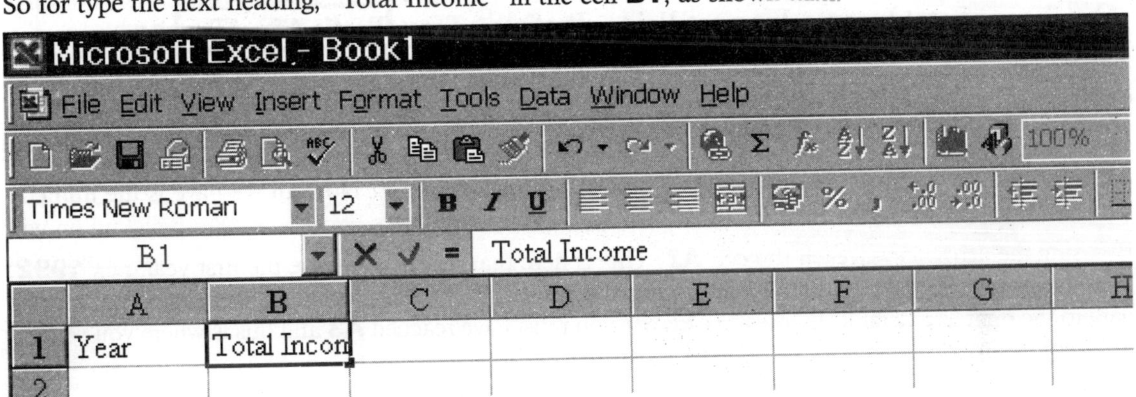

Did you notice anything wrong here? Well, the cell is not big enough to carry your heading. So what will we do? We will increase the width of the column **B**, by using one of the methods mentioned earlier in the chapter.

This way now we will type the complete headings, i.e., all of them, as shown next.

But, since these are headings, and are to be highlighted. We will make them **Bold** and put them in the centre of the cells. This way they will look good.

Highlight all the cells by just clicking at cell **A1** and then while pressing **Shift** key click mouse in the cell **F1**, the whole row gets highlighted.

Now click at B in the formatting bar to make the whole text as Bold.

With the text in the cells remaining highlighted, click at 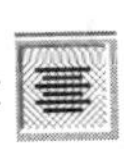 in the formatting bar. This will make the text in the cells centralized in all the cells. This is shown in the figure shown next.

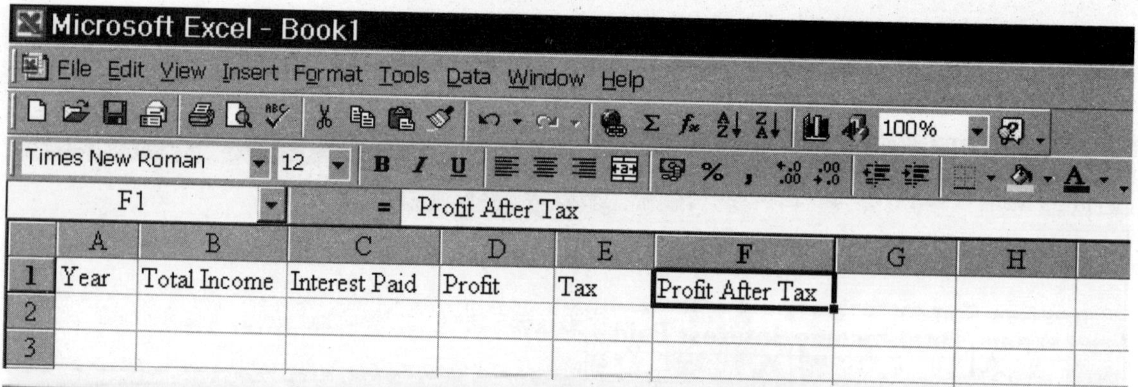

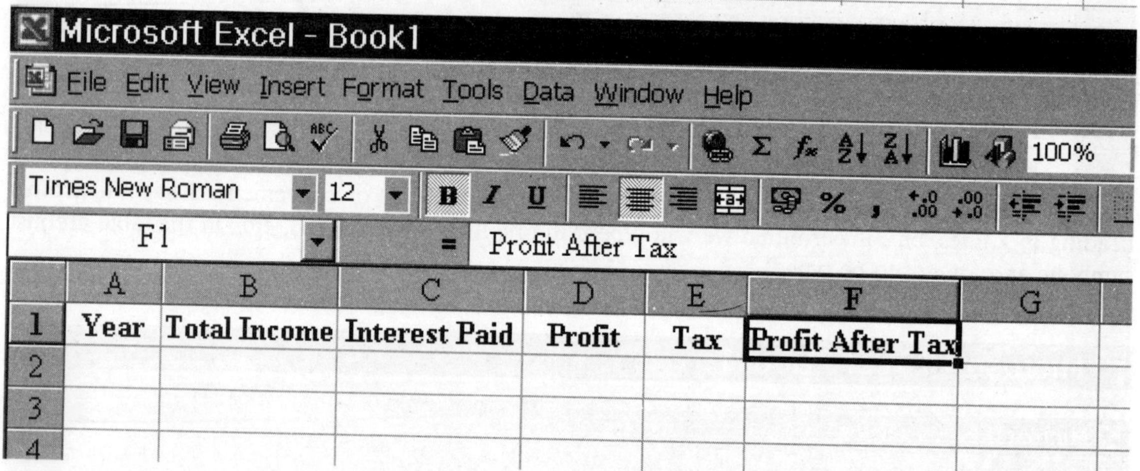

So now we have the headings ready. It was not very difficult, was it? Now all we have is the numeric data. Let us type them too. First of all we will type the various years.

By using the arrow keys, reach the cell **A2**. This is here that we have to type the first year, i.e., **1992**. Type it and press **Enter** to see the data getting aligned to the right. Remember, Excel aligns the numeric data to the right as a default. By pressing **Enter** you must have reached **A3** and this is where you wanted to be for typing the next year, i.e., **1993**.

So now type one year and press **Enter** to reach the next cell for typing the next year, till you reach the last year, i.e., **1999**. At this stage your worksheet will look like the one shown on the next page.

Next step is also easy. You have to just type the numbers in the cells **B2** to **B9**. All these figures are available with you. Just type one figure and press **Enter** to reach the next cell and so on till you reach the last cell in the column. After doing this your worksheet will look like the one shown next on the next page.

It would not be a bad idea to save this worksheet at this stage. For god forbid, if something happens, like power cut or so. So just press **Ctrl+S** to give the save command, as you would give in any other software. Now all you have to do it to give it a name and decide where you want to save this worksheet. Let us give the name **Finance** to it.

Now we come to the interesting part of this worksheet. So far we have typed whatever was available. Now we have to generate the figures. The column **C** is of Interest Paid which is to be calculated by using the formula.

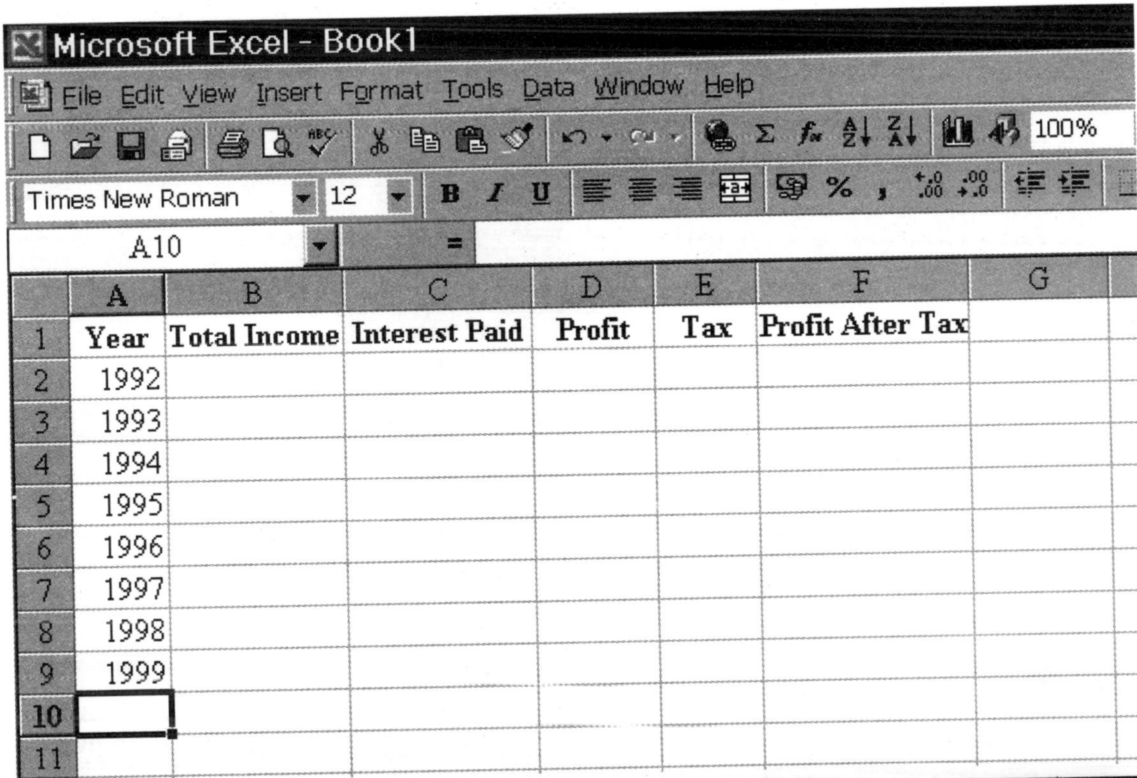
Microsoft Excel - Book1
File Edit View Insert Format Tools Data Window Help
Times New Roman 12
A10 =
Year Total Income Interest Paid Profit Tax Profit After Tax
1992
1993
1994
1995
1996
1997
1998
1999

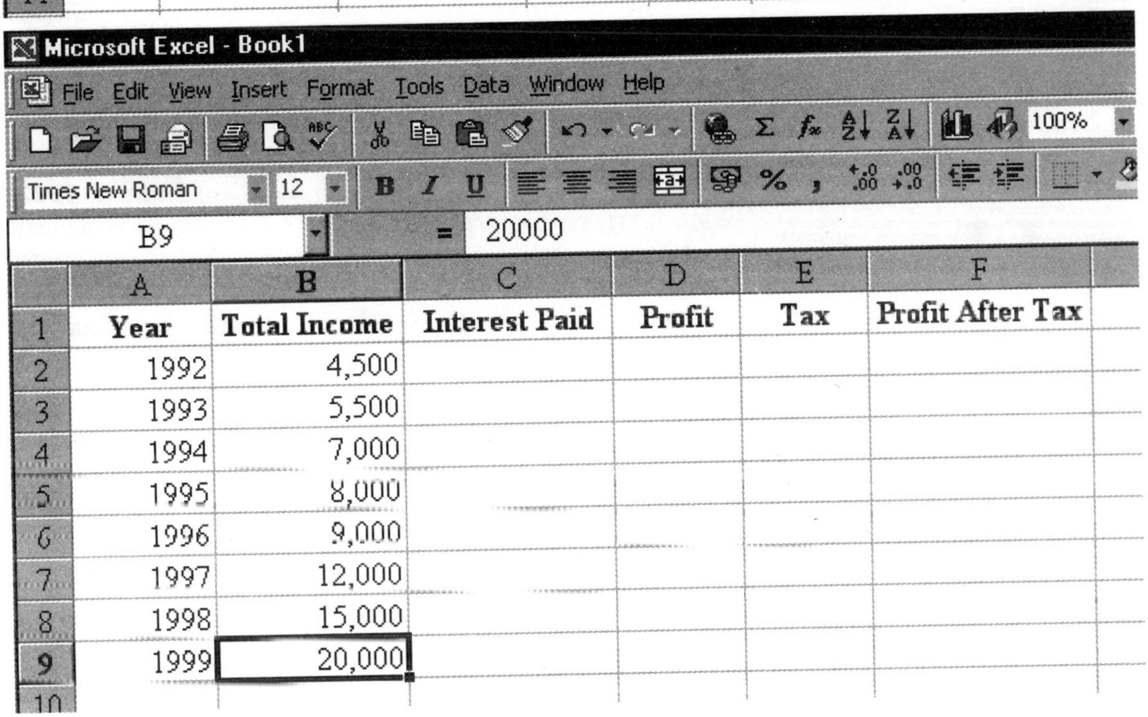
Microsoft Excel - Book1
File Edit View Insert Format Tools Data Window Help
Times New Roman 12
B9 = 20000
Year Total Income Interest Paid Profit Tax Profit After Tax
1992 4,500
1993 5,500
1994 7,000
1995 8,000
1996 9,000
1997 12,000
1998 15,000
1999 20,000

$$\text{Interest Paid} = \frac{\text{Total Income} \times 15}{100}$$

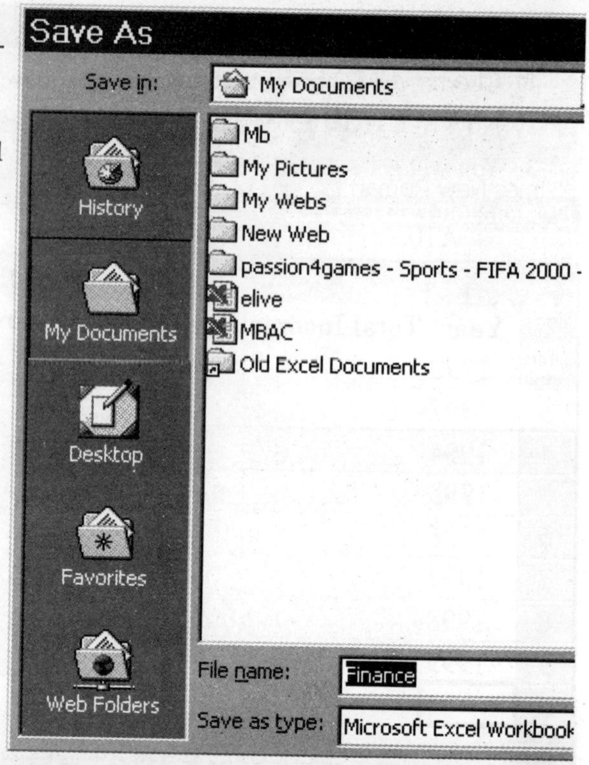

Transformed to the computer language it will become:

Interest Paid = (Total Income × 15)/100

If we put this in Cell **C2**, it will become:

C2 = SUM(B2*15/100)

Try putting this in thc cell **C2** and see the result. It will be as shown below. It has given a figure of 675. Calculate the amount manually to see whether the result is Ok or not. It is correct, isn't it? Now we have to apply this formula to all the cells from **C3** to **C9**. Do you have to put the formula for each cell or there is a method in Excel which allows you to copy the formula in each of the cell.

Well, fortunately there is. So this is how you will do it.

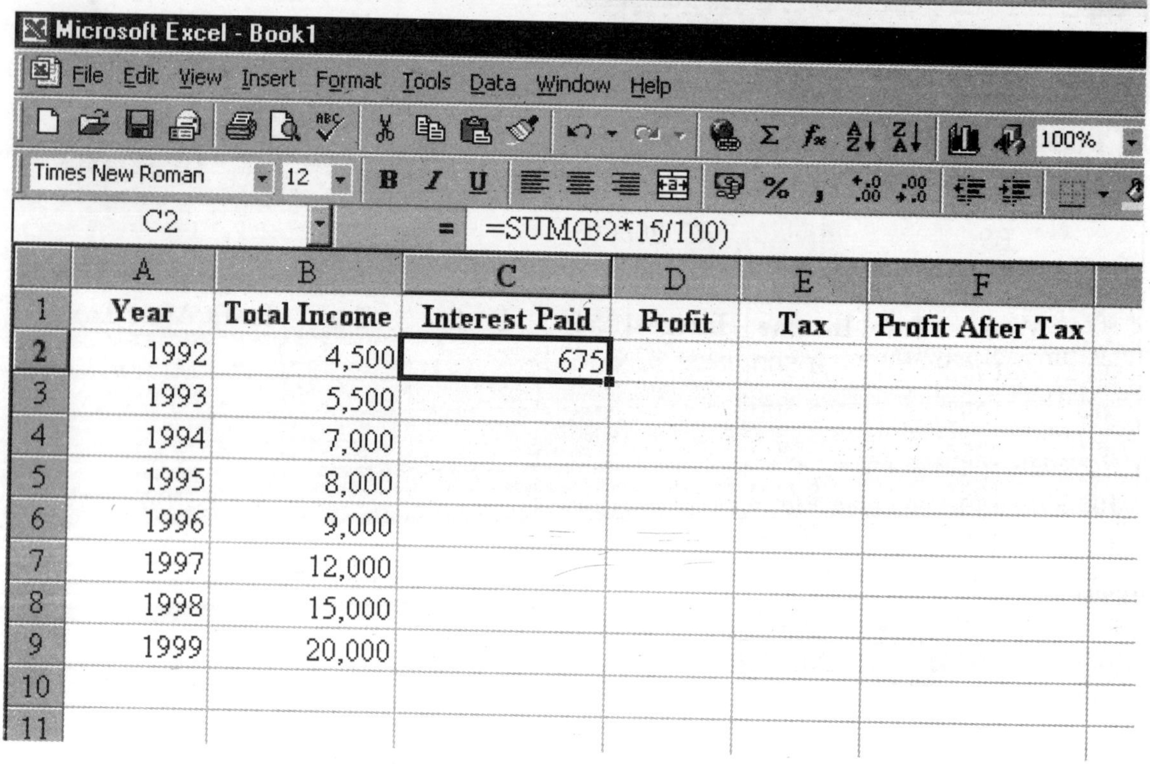

COPYING FORMULA

1. Click at cell C2 to have the formula displayed in the formula bar.
2. Now with your mouse having clicked at cell C2, press the right button of the mouse.
3. You will get a dialog box, as shown below, which has various commands at your disposal.

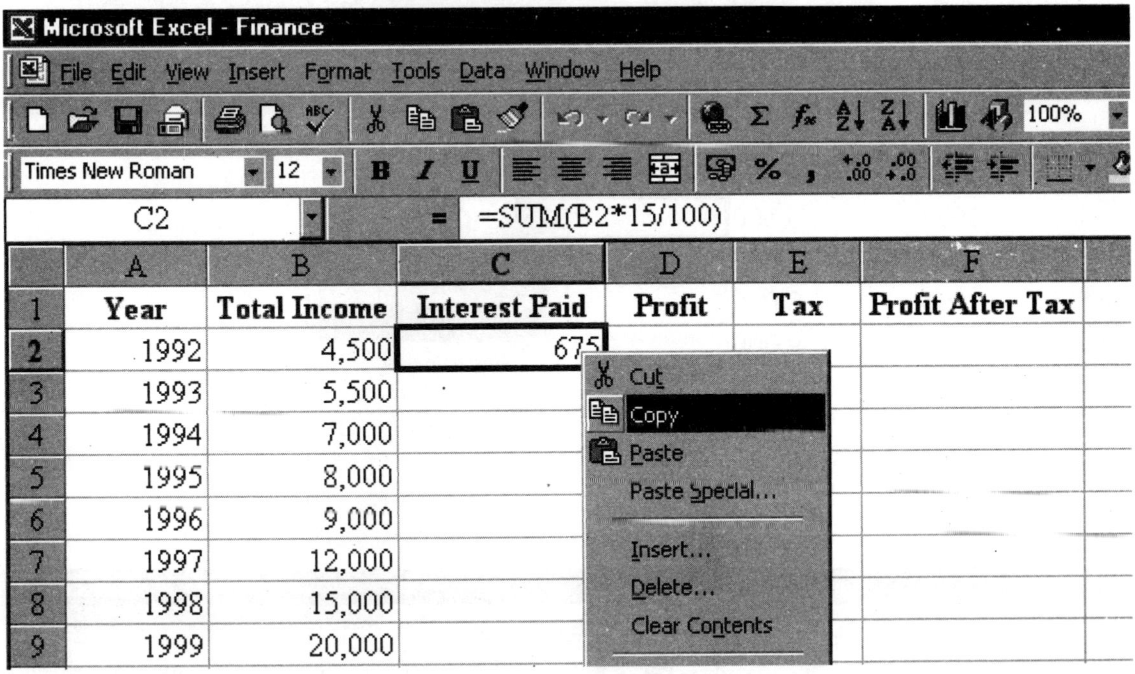

4. Choose copy, as shown here, to copy the formula.
5. Next step now is to paste the formula in their respective cells.
6. Now click at cell C3 with the mouse (left button).
7. Click the right button again to get the dialog box.
8. This time click at Paste instead, as shown on the next page.
9. Immediately you will get the figure in cell C3.

   This calculation has been based on B3 (see the formula bar) and not B2 which had been copied in our formula. Is it not great? Excel has changed the cell address for you. This is called relative addressing and is a very useful feature of Excel
10. Similar pasting in the cells from C4 to C9 can also be done.
11. Once done your worksheet should look like the one shown next.

Remember

1. You can take out the dotted lines blinking around the cell C2 by pressing the Esc key.

One look at the worksheet and you will notice that something is wrong. Some figures have no decimals and some have one. This does not look good. So what will you do? You will make them uniform. This is how:

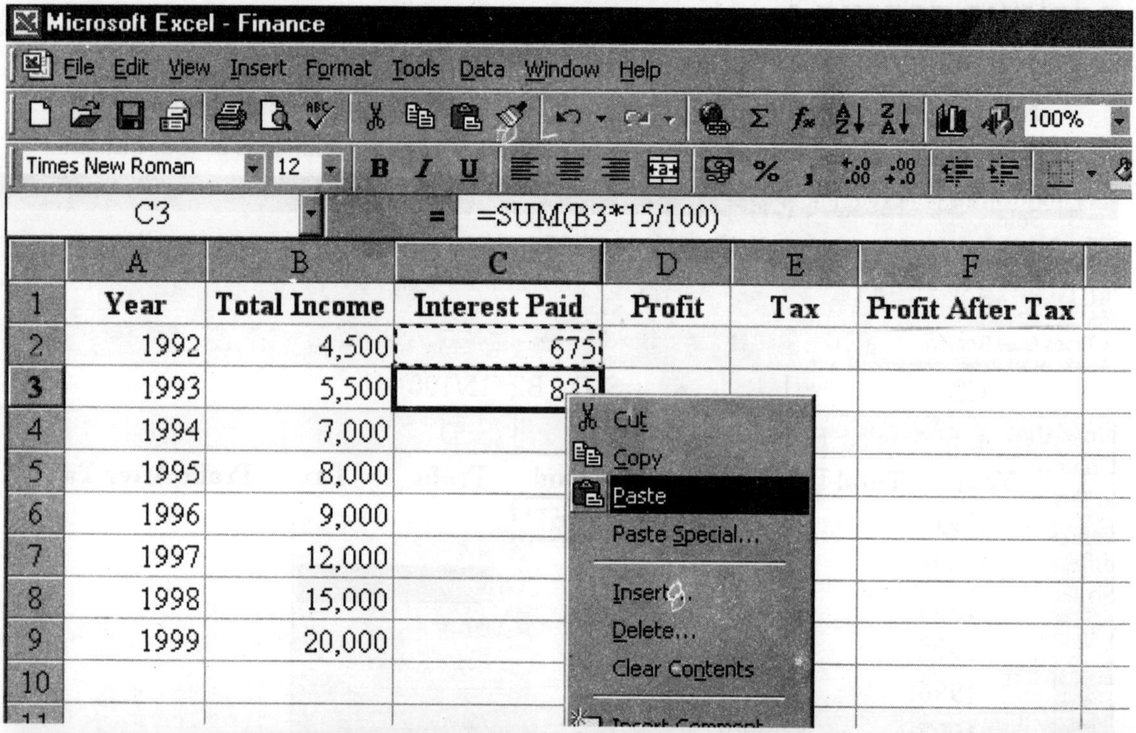
Microsoft Excel - Finance
File Edit View Insert Format Tools Data Window Help
Times New Roman 12
C3 = =SUM(B3*15/100)
A B C D E F
Year Total Income Interest Paid Profit Tax Profit After Tax
1992 4,500 675
1993 5,500 825
1994 7,000
1995 8,000
1996 9,000
1997 12,000
1998 15,000
1999 20,000
Cut
Copy
Paste
Paste Special...
Insert...
Delete...
Clear Contents

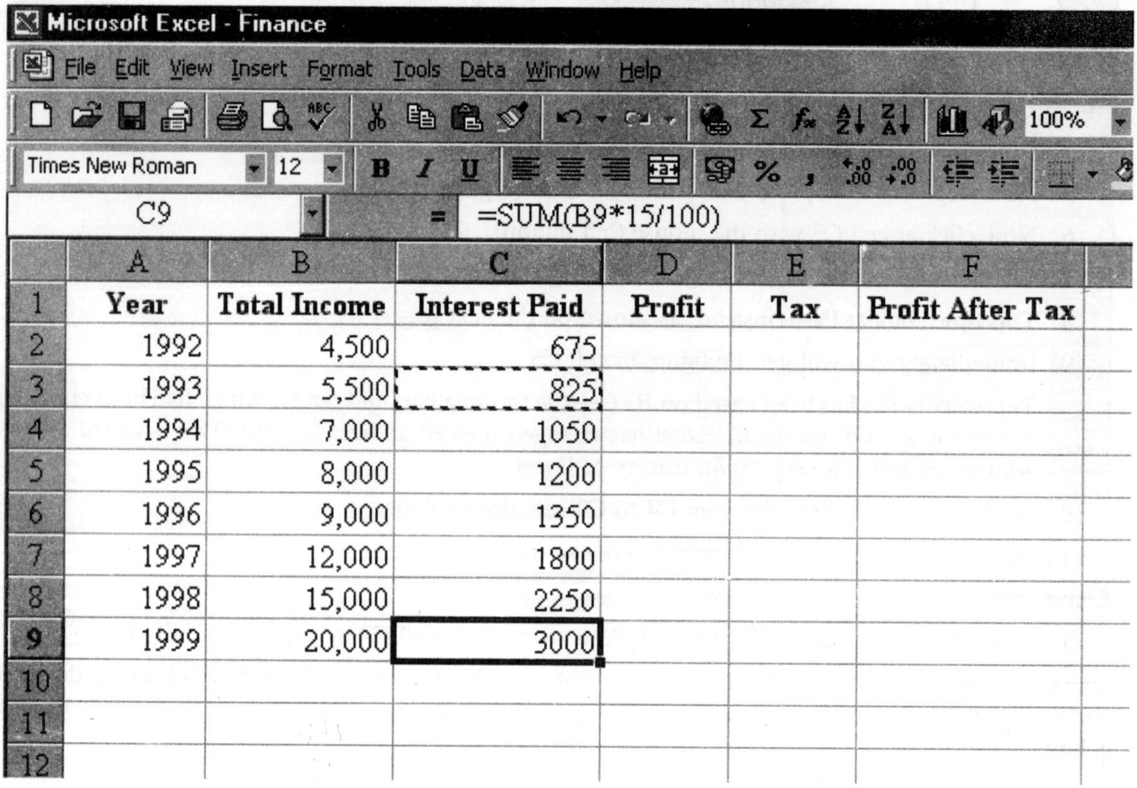
Microsoft Excel - Finance
File Edit View Insert Format Tools Data Window Help
Times New Roman 12
C9 = =SUM(B9*15/100)
A B C D E F
Year Total Income Interest Paid Profit Tax Profit After Tax
1992 4,500 675
1993 5,500 825
1994 7,000 1050
1995 8,000 1200
1996 9,000 1350
1997 12,000 1800
1998 15,000 2250
1999 20,000 3000

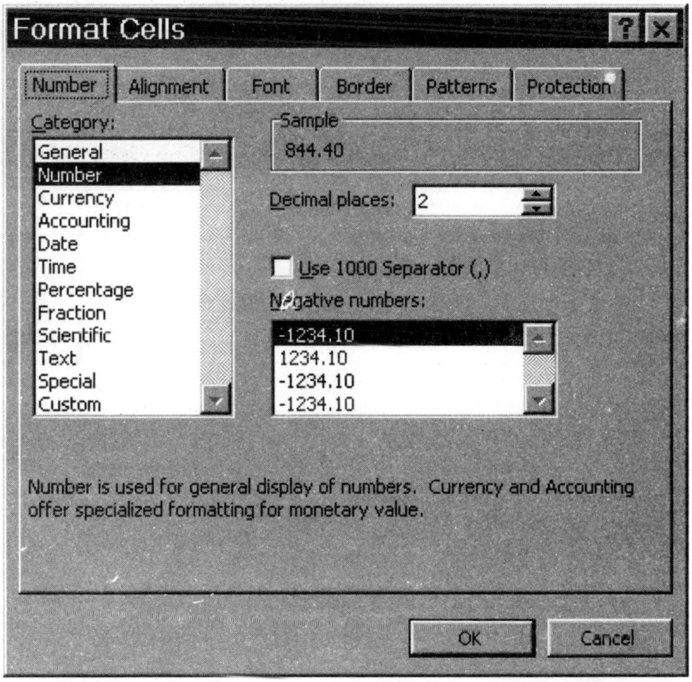

1. Highlight all the cells from C2 to C9.
2. From the Format menu, call the command Cells, which gives rise to a dialog box, as shown on the here.
3. Select the Number panel and then number Category and select the Decimal places as 2 and click Ok.
4. All your cells now have 2 places of decimals, as shown below.

Now that we have all the figures of Column **C** ready, we can proceed ahead to the next column, i.e., **D**. This column has "Profit", which is nothing but the difference of "Income" and "Interest". So let us calculate that.

Click at cell **D2** and put the formula

=SUM(B2 – C2)

This will give you the figure for **D2**. Calculate it manually to make sure that the formula is right.

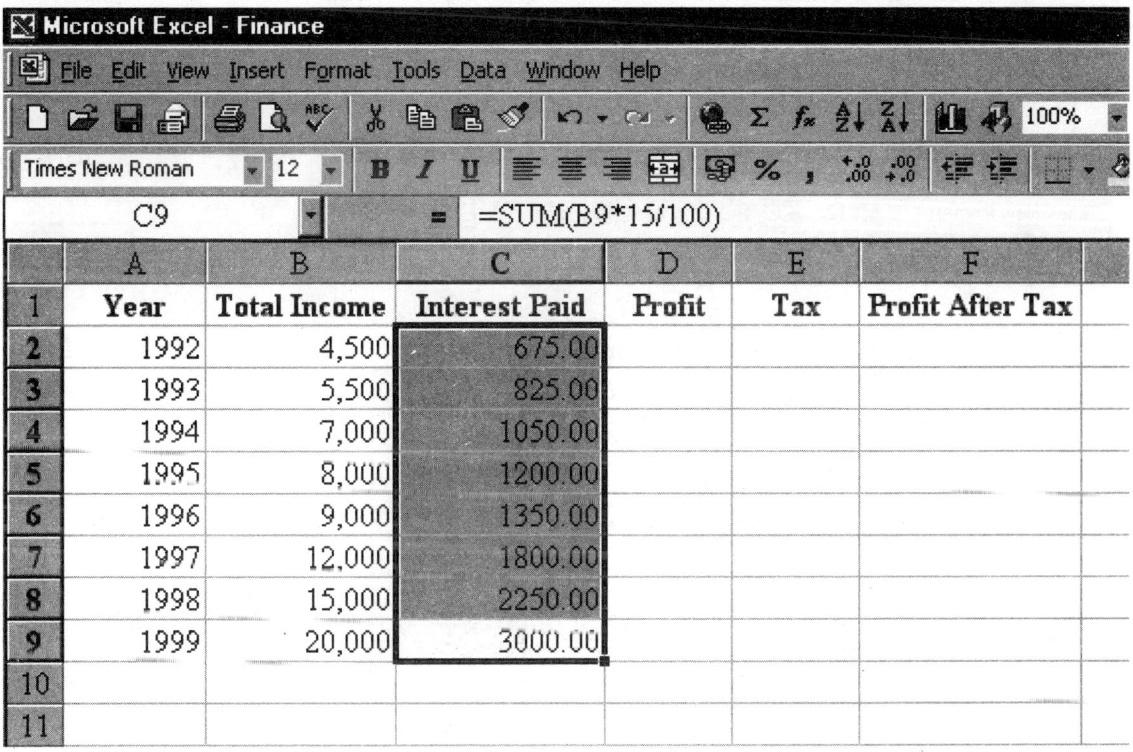

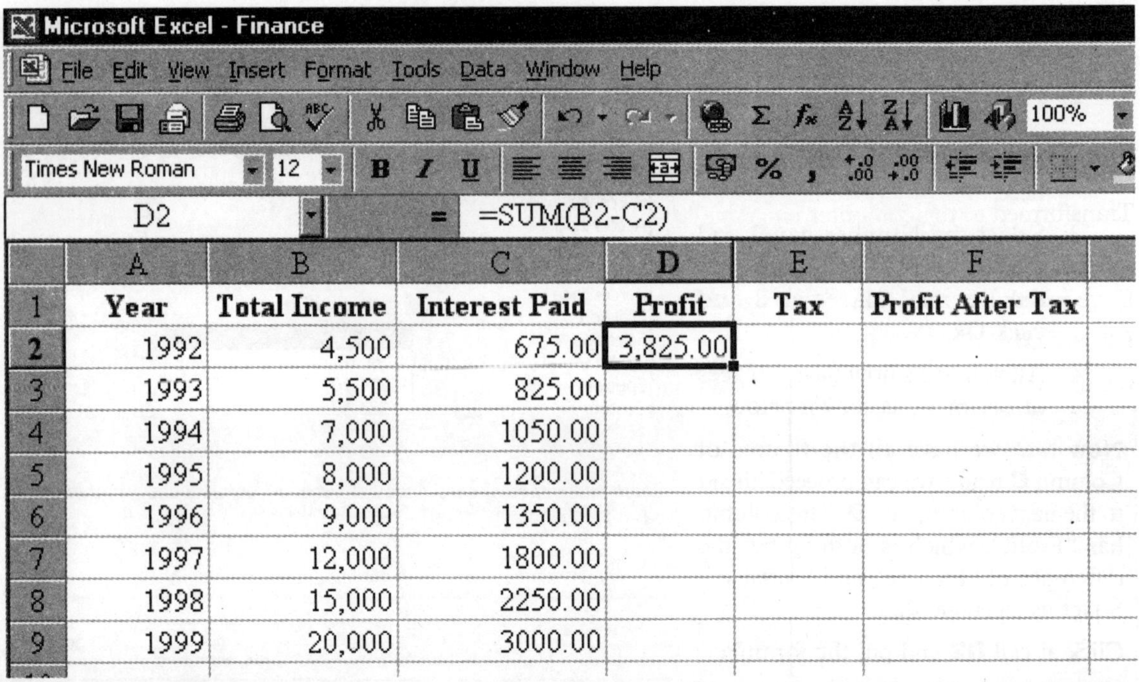

	A	B	C	D	E	F
1	Year	Total Income	Interest Paid	Profit	Tax	Profit After Tax
2	1992	4,500	675.00	3,825.00		
3	1993	5,500	825.00			
4	1994	7,000	1050.00			
5	1995	8,000	1200.00			
6	1996	9,000	1350.00			
7	1997	12,000	1800.00			
8	1998	15,000	2250.00			
9	1999	20,000	3000.00			

Now, as we had done in the earlier case of Interest Paid, we will copy the formula and paste it in other cell, as shown below. One by one you would be able to calculate all the figures of Profit and would be able to fill up the whole column **D**. After you have done so, your worksheet would look like the one shown above. These figures have been corrected to 2 places of decimals as was done in the earlier case.

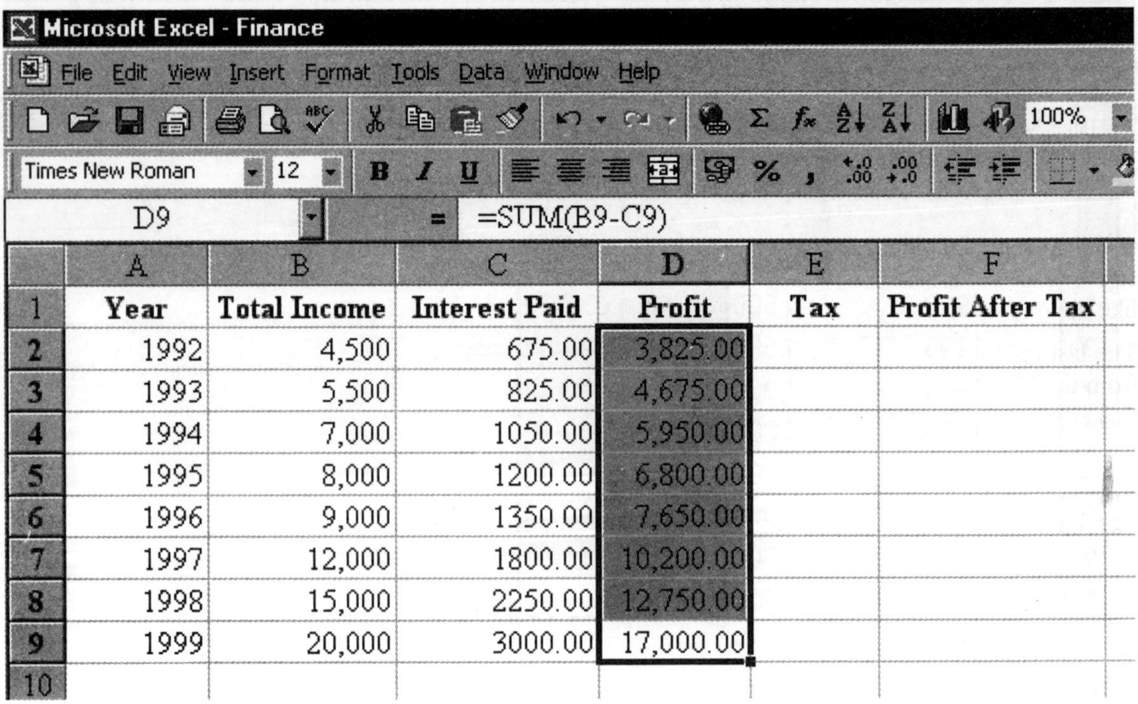

	A	B	C	D	E	F
1	Year	Total Income	Interest Paid	Profit	Tax	Profit After Tax
2	1992	4,500	675.00	3,825.00		
3	1993	5,500	825.00	4,675.00		
4	1994	7,000	1050.00	5,950.00		
5	1995	8,000	1200.00	6,800.00		
6	1996	9,000	1350.00	7,650.00		
7	1997	12,000	1800.00	10,200.00		
8	1998	15,000	2250.00	12,750.00		
9	1999	20,000	3000.00	17,000.00		
10						

Next in line is the column called Tax. This is as said earlier, 12% of the Profit. So this can be calculated as below:

$$\text{Tax} = \frac{\text{Profit} \times 12}{100}$$

Transformed to the computer language it will become:

Tax= (Profit x 12)/100

If we put this in Cell **E2**, it will become:

E2 = SUM(D2*12/100)

Let us apply this formula in **E2** and see what happens. It gives you the result as 459. Copying this formula

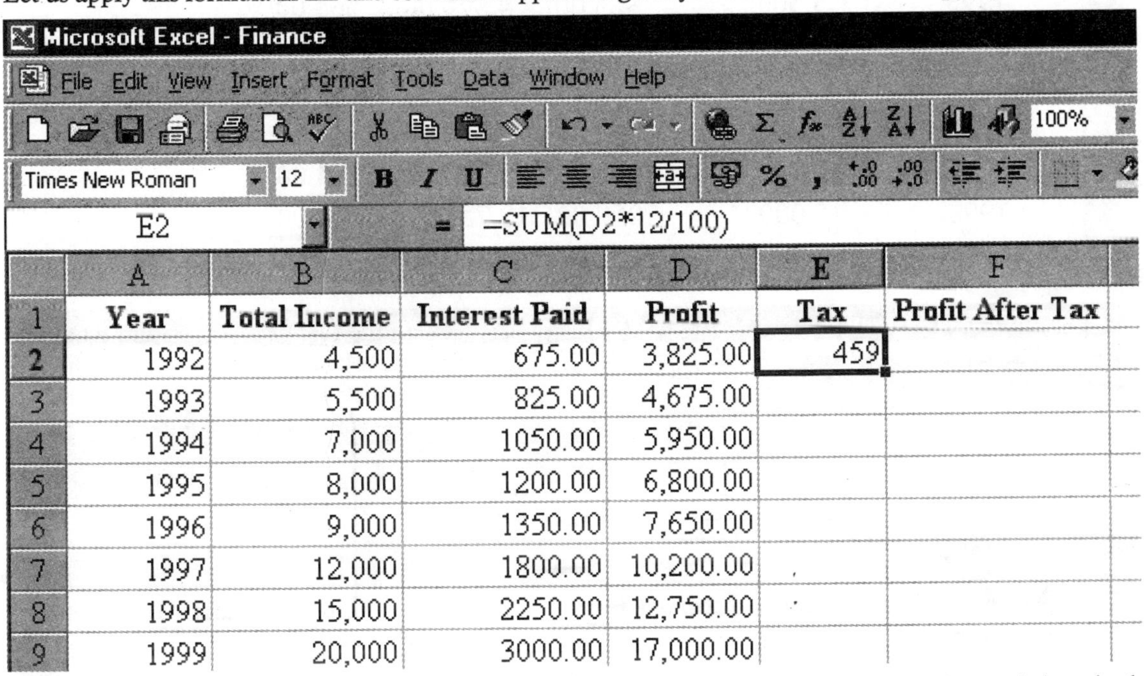

	A	B	C	D	E	F
1	Year	Total Income	Interest Paid	Profit	Tax	Profit After Tax
2	1992	4,500	675.00	3,825.00	459	
3	1993	5,500	825.00	4,675.00		
4	1994	7,000	1050.00	5,950.00		
5	1995	8,000	1200.00	6,800.00		
6	1996	9,000	1350.00	7,650.00		
7	1997	12,000	1800.00	10,200.00		
8	1998	15,000	2250.00	12,750.00		
9	1999	20,000	3000.00	17,000.00		

to the other cells, i.e., from **E3** to **E9**, you can fill up the whole column and make the worksheet look like the one shown on the next page.

The last column in this case is the "Profit After Tax", which can be calculated after subtracting "Tax" from the "Profit". This calculation I am not showing here, since I assume that you should be able to do this easily. However, your resultant worksheet should look like the one shown next.

You think the worksheet is complete. No. You still have to do the column totals without which the whole worksheet looks incomplete.

For this follow the following steps.

1. Click at cell B10 to get the total of figures from B2 to B9.
2. Now click at Σ symbol in the Standard toolbar.
3. It will search for the numeric cells above and put the formula for the same and highlight the cells it has selected.

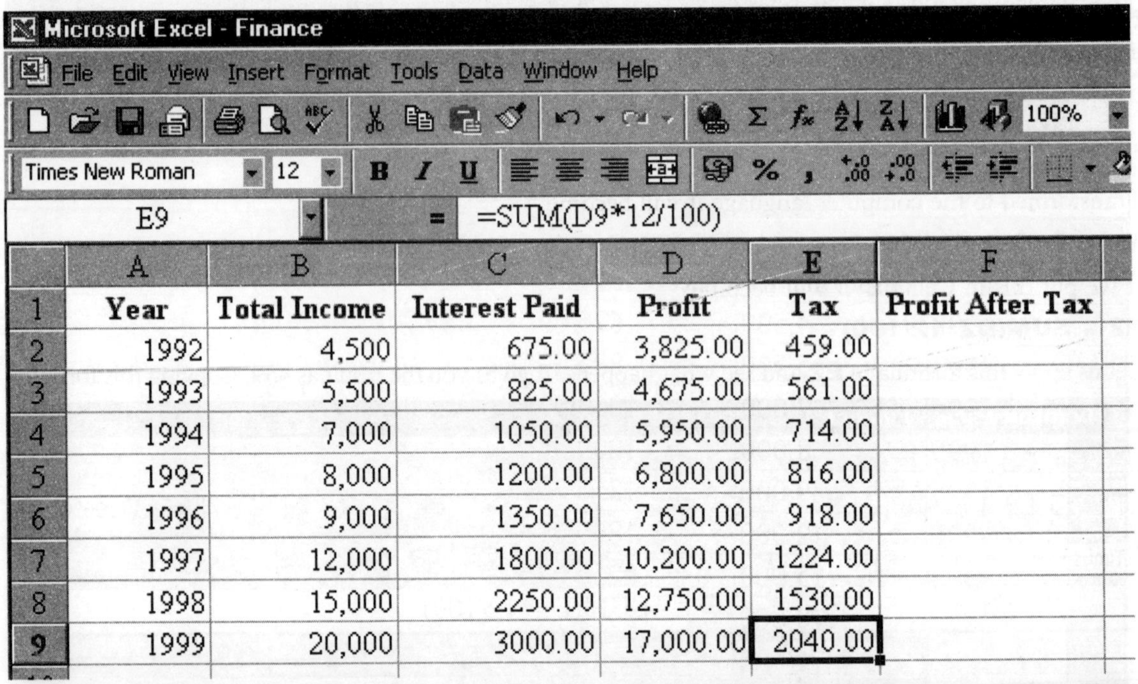

	A	B	C	D	E	F
1	Year	Total Income	Interest Paid	Profit	Tax	Profit After Tax
2	1992	4,500	675.00	3,825.00	459.00	
3	1993	5,500	825.00	4,675.00	561.00	
4	1994	7,000	1050.00	5,950.00	714.00	
5	1995	8,000	1200.00	6,800.00	816.00	
6	1996	9,000	1350.00	7,650.00	918.00	
7	1997	12,000	1800.00	10,200.00	1224.00	
8	1998	15,000	2250.00	12,750.00	1530.00	
9	1999	20,000	3000.00	17,000.00	2040.00	

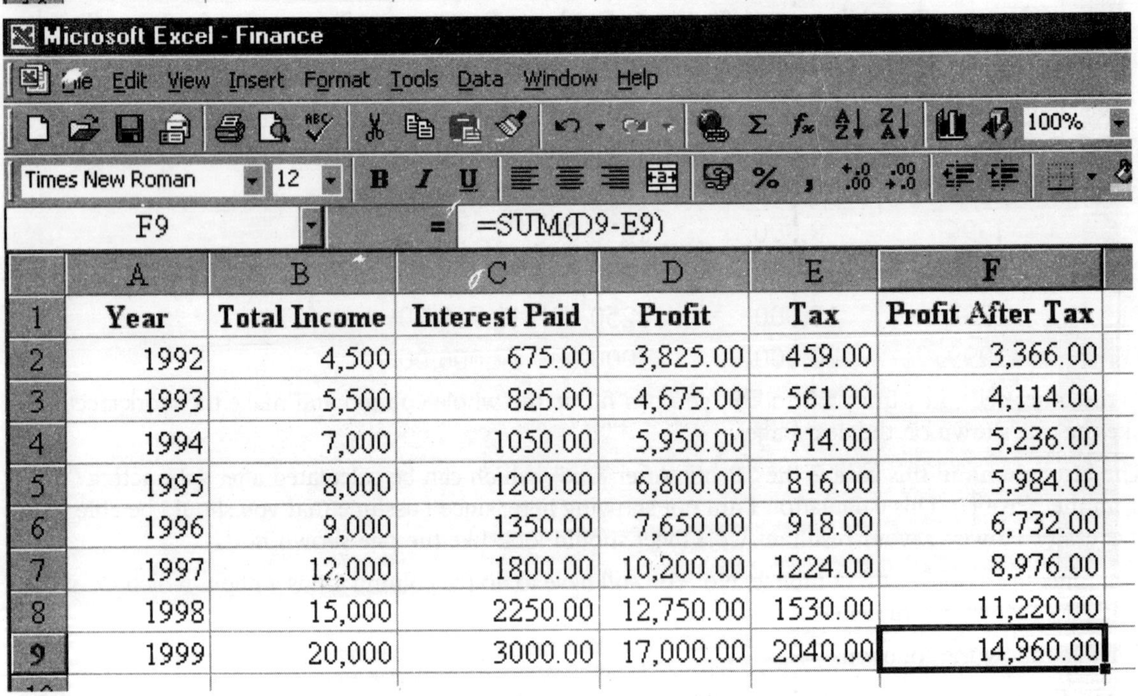

	A	B	C	D	E	F
1	Year	Total Income	Interest Paid	Profit	Tax	Profit After Tax
2	1992	4,500	675.00	3,825.00	459.00	3,366.00
3	1993	5,500	825.00	4,675.00	561.00	4,114.00
4	1994	7,000	1050.00	5,950.00	714.00	5,236.00
5	1995	8,000	1200.00	6,800.00	816.00	5,984.00
6	1996	9,000	1350.00	7,650.00	918.00	6,732.00
7	1997	12,000	1800.00	10,200.00	1224.00	8,976.00
8	1998	15,000	2250.00	12,750.00	1530.00	11,220.00
9	1999	20,000	3000.00	17,000.00	2040.00	14,960.00

4. It will wait for your Ok in the form of Enter to put the result.
5. Press Enter to get the total in the cell B10, as shown on the next page.

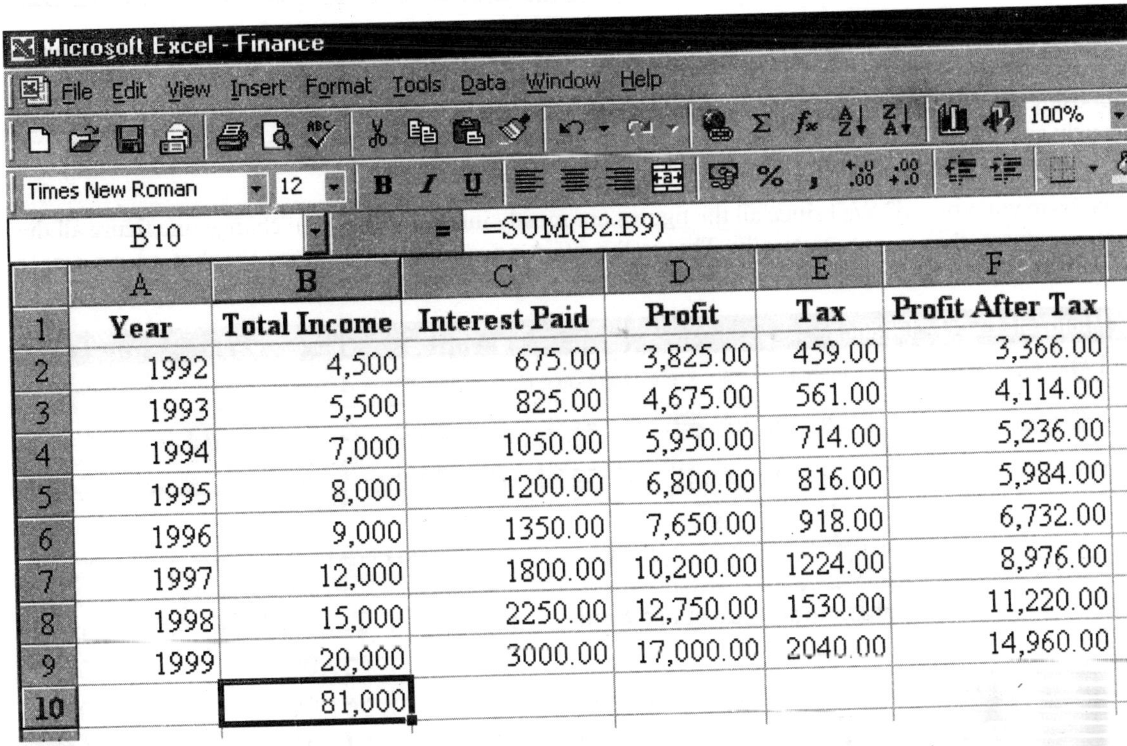

	A	B	C	D	E	F
1	Year	Total Income	Interest Paid	Profit	Tax	Profit After Tax
2	1992	4,500	675.00	3,825.00	459.00	3,366.00
3	1993	5,500	825.00	4,675.00	561.00	4,114.00
4	1994	7,000	1050.00	5,950.00	714.00	5,236.00
5	1995	8,000	1200.00	6,800.00	816.00	5,984.00
6	1996	9,000	1350.00	7,650.00	918.00	6,732.00
7	1997	12,000	1800.00	10,200.00	1224.00	8,976.00
8	1998	15,000	2250.00	12,750.00	1530.00	11,220.00
9	1999	20,000	3000.00	17,000.00	2040.00	14,960.00
10		81,000				

Similarly all the other columns can be summed up showing the result as shown below.

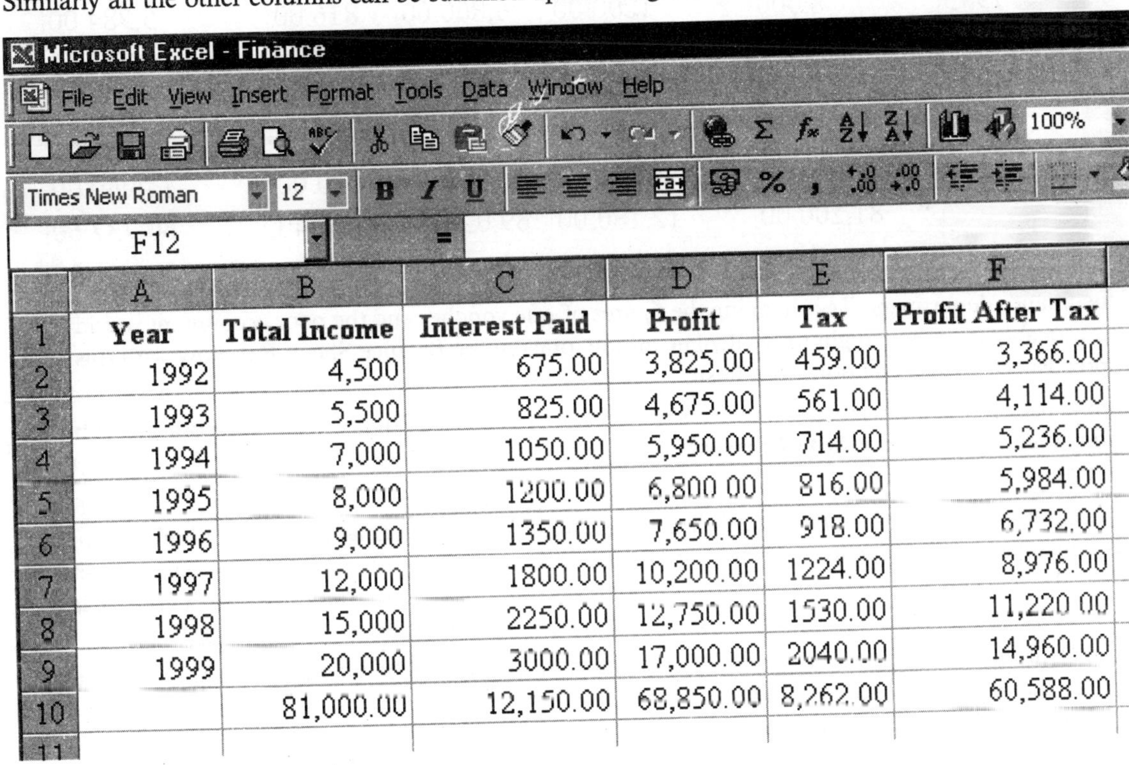

	A	B	C	D	E	F
1	Year	Total Income	Interest Paid	Profit	Tax	Profit After Tax
2	1992	4,500	675.00	3,825.00	459.00	3,366.00
3	1993	5,500	825.00	4,675.00	561.00	4,114.00
4	1994	7,000	1050.00	5,950.00	714.00	5,236.00
5	1995	8,000	1200.00	6,800.00	816.00	5,984.00
6	1996	9,000	1350.00	7,650.00	918.00	6,732.00
7	1997	12,000	1800.00	10,200.00	1224.00	8,976.00
8	1998	15,000	2250.00	12,750.00	1530.00	11,220.00
9	1999	20,000	3000.00	17,000.00	2040.00	14,960.00
10		81,000.00	12,150.00	68,850.00	8,262.00	60,588.00
11						

Now you can say that your worksheet is complete. But, supposing we want to make any change. This is done delibrately to show you the main advantage of Excel software.

Supposing, we change the figure of the year 1996 from 9,000 to 9,200, which we can assume that it was wrongly given to us or was a typing mistake. It is shown on next page. Try changing this figure in the cell **B6** and see the resultant effect.

What have you noticed? Well since all the figures are mostly inter-linked, if you change one figure all the relative figures change automatically. This is the main advantage of Excel or for that an electronic spreadsheet.

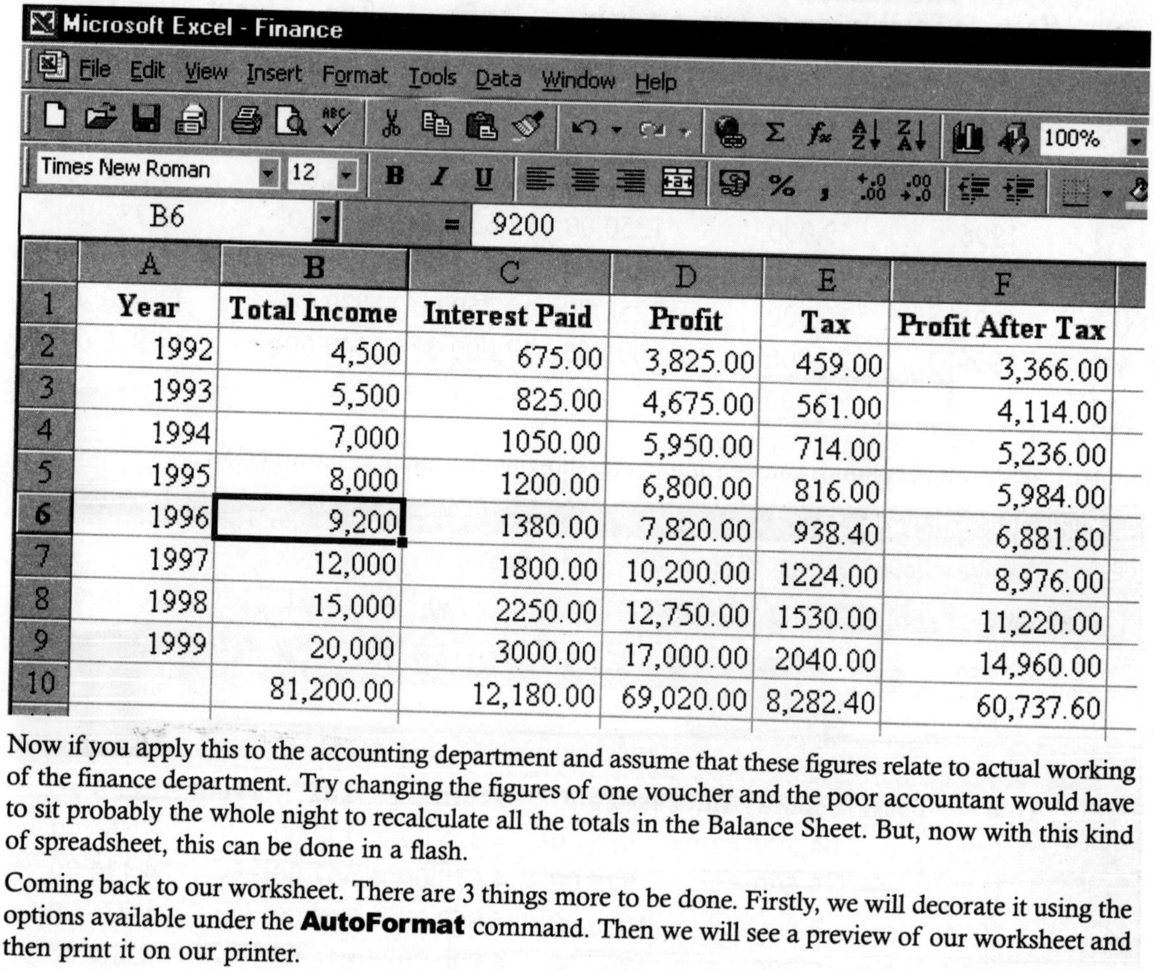

	A	B	C	D	E	F
1	Year	Total Income	Interest Paid	Profit	Tax	Profit After Tax
2	1992	4,500	675.00	3,825.00	459.00	3,366.00
3	1993	5,500	825.00	4,675.00	561.00	4,114.00
4	1994	7,000	1050.00	5,950.00	714.00	5,236.00
5	1995	8,000	1200.00	6,800.00	816.00	5,984.00
6	1996	9,200	1380.00	7,820.00	938.40	6,881.60
7	1997	12,000	1800.00	10,200.00	1224.00	8,976.00
8	1998	15,000	2250.00	12,750.00	1530.00	11,220.00
9	1999	20,000	3000.00	17,000.00	2040.00	14,960.00
10		81,200.00	12,180.00	69,020.00	8,282.40	60,737.60

Now if you apply this to the accounting department and assume that these figures relate to actual working of the finance department. Try changing the figures of one voucher and the poor accountant would have to sit probably the whole night to recalculate all the totals in the Balance Sheet. But, now with this kind of spreadsheet, this can be done in a flash.

Coming back to our worksheet. There are 3 things more to be done. Firstly, we will decorate it using the options available under the **AutoFormat** command. Then we will see a preview of our worksheet and then print it on our printer.

For decorating with the AutoFormat. Call the command from the Format menu, after highlighting the cells which you want to include in this AutoFormat and you will see the dialog box, which was shown earlier. As you can see, there are various options available under this. Ranging from Simple, Classic, Accounting to 3-D ones. For our worksheet we are going to choose the one called Classic 2.

Just click at this and it would be applied. I am quite sure you would be interested to know the result of this. See the worksheet shown above for the result. I am quite sure that you are impressed with your work. You can make it look more impressive using the features of Borders, Patterns, etc.

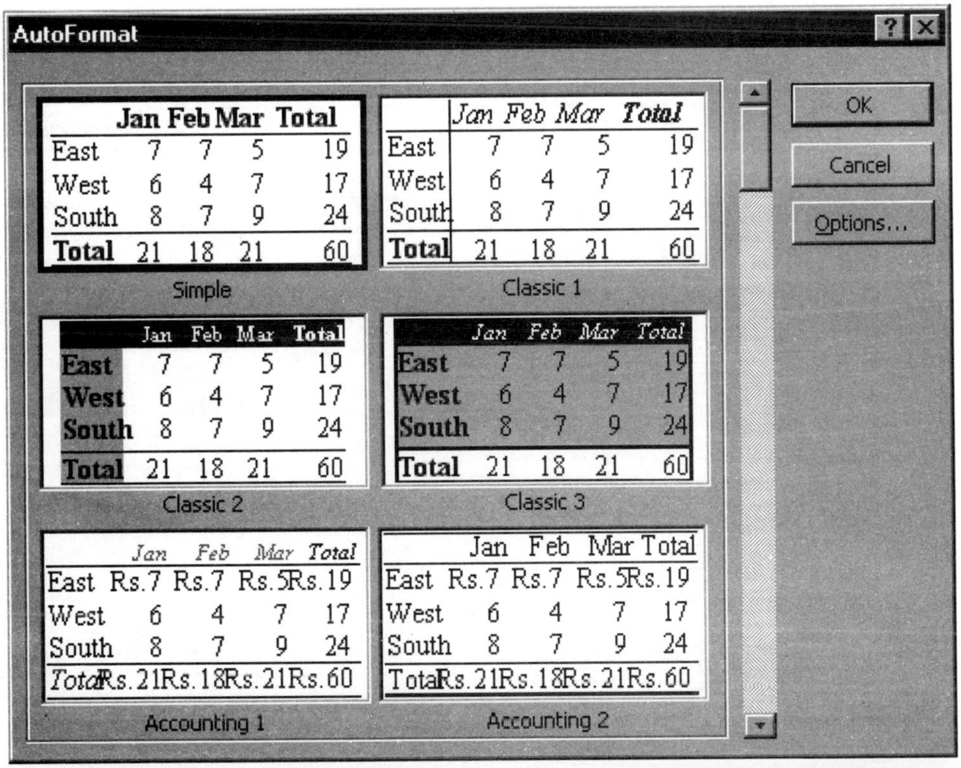

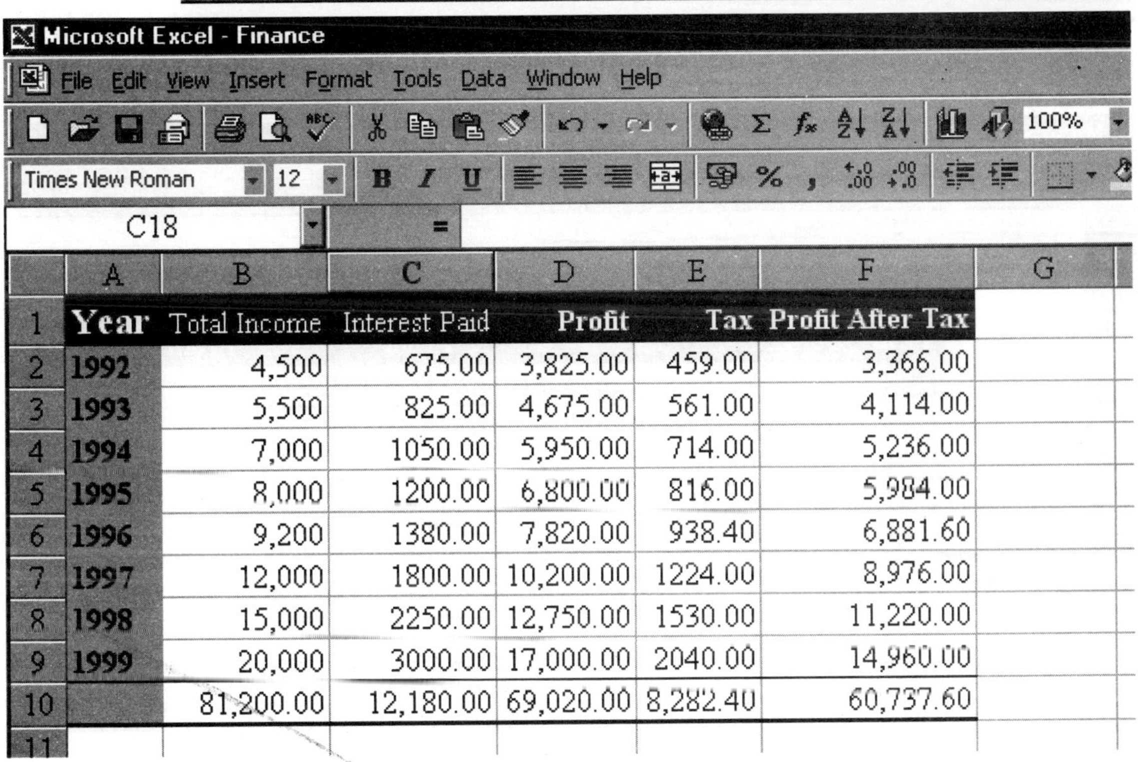

	A	B	C	D	E	F	G
1	Year	Total Income	Interest Paid	Profit	Tax	Profit After Tax	
2	1992	4,500	675.00	3,825.00	459.00	3,366.00	
3	1993	5,500	825.00	4,675.00	561.00	4,114.00	
4	1994	7,000	1050.00	5,950.00	714.00	5,236.00	
5	1995	8,000	1200.00	6,800.00	816.00	5,984.00	
6	1996	9,200	1380.00	7,820.00	938.40	6,881.60	
7	1997	12,000	1800.00	10,200.00	1224.00	8,976.00	
8	1998	15,000	2250.00	12,750.00	1530.00	11,220.00	
9	1999	20,000	3000.00	17,000.00	2040.00	14,960.00	
10		81,200.00	12,180.00	69,020.00	8,282.40	60,737.60	
11							

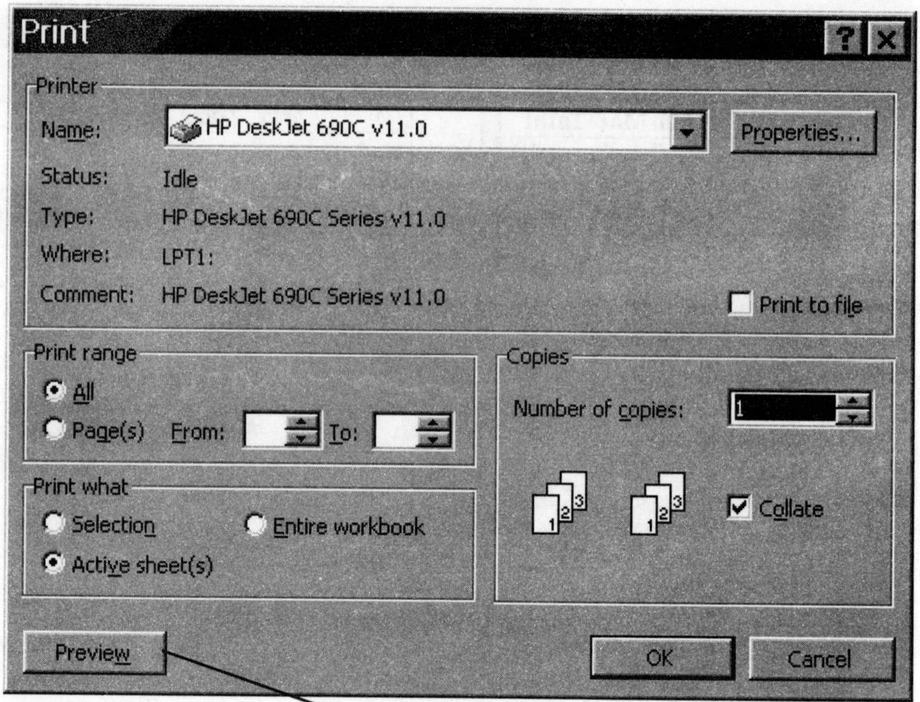

Preview button

Now that you have to print it on your printer to see the final result. But, before that we would like to see its **Preview**. This command is part of the **Print** command which is available under the **File** menu.

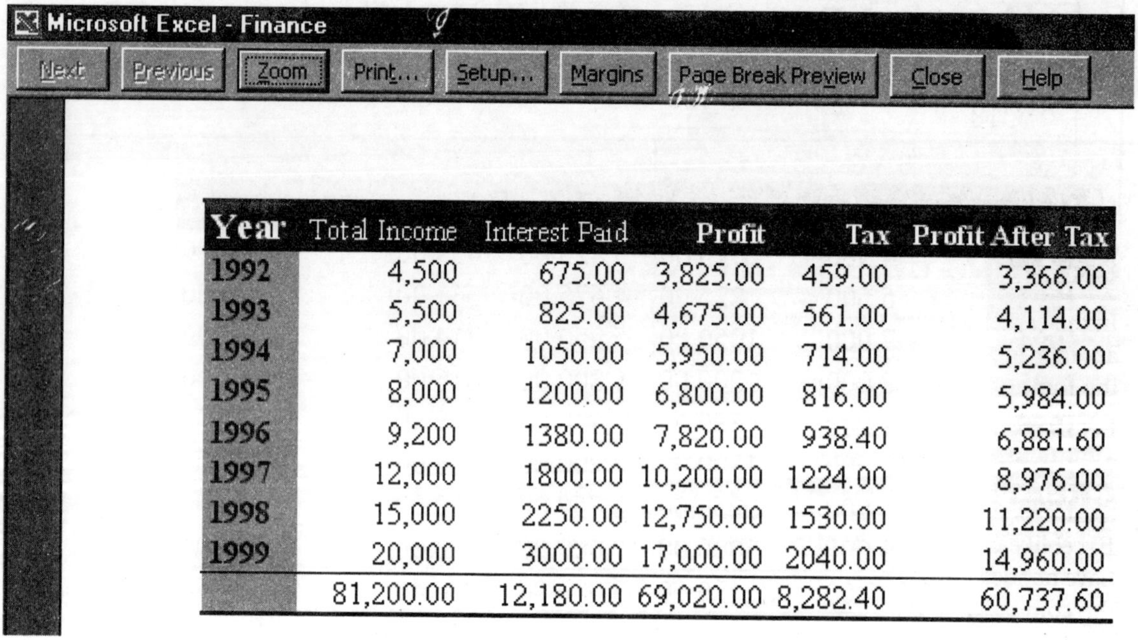

Year	Total Income	Interest Paid	Profit	Tax	Profit After Tax
1992	4,500	675.00	3,825.00	459.00	3,366.00
1993	5,500	825.00	4,675.00	561.00	4,114.00
1994	7,000	1050.00	5,950.00	714.00	5,236.00
1995	8,000	1200.00	6,800.00	816.00	5,984.00
1996	9,200	1380.00	7,820.00	938.40	6,881.60
1997	12,000	1800.00	10,200.00	1224.00	8,976.00
1998	15,000	2250.00	12,750.00	1530.00	11,220.00
1999	20,000	3000.00	17,000.00	2040.00	14,960.00
	81,200.00	12,180.00	69,020.00	8,282.40	60,737.60

There are various other options in the print dialog box, shown on the next page, alongwith the print preview of the worksheet.

Printer You have to specify the various options of your printer. It is usually the printer installed in your Windows.

Print range You specify whether you want to print the whole file or few selected pages.

Print what You can choose to print a selected portion of the worksheet, or a full worksheet or even few selected worksheet.

Preview As said earlier, this gives you the preview of the worksheet which you can see before printing.

Copies You can print number of copies of the worksheet and even collate the various pages of the worksheet.

Computer Room Activity

Creating a Spreadsheet

Create a spreadsheet with the following data, which is similar to the above example:

Year	*Profit After Tax (A)*	*Depriciation (B)*	*Gross (C)*	*Transferred to Reserves (D)*	*Nett Profit (E)*
1992	*3,3094.84*	*To be*	*To be*	*To be*	*To be*
1993	*3,999.60*	*calculated*	*Calculated*	*Calculated*	*Calculated*
1994	*5,278.32*	*as 33% of*	*as Profit*	*as 15% of*	*as Gross*
1995	*5,801.76*	*the Profit*	*After Tax*	*Gross*	*minus*
1996	*6,624.00*	*After*	*Minus*		*Transferred*
1997	*9,892.80*	*Tax*	*Depriciation*		*to Reserves*
1998	*10,915.92*		*(A) - (B)*		*(C) - (D)*
1999	*15,111.36*				

Create this spreadsheet and see its preview on the screen.

CREATING CHARTS IN EXCEL

In the earlier chapter we had created a worksheet and decorated it using the AutoFormat mode. There is another method of presenting this worksheet and that is by converting it into graphics and specially in the form of **Charts** in Excel.

Let us use the same worksheet to make charts of the same.

CREATING GRAPHS

Excel like other software of Microsoft Office, makes use of the software called Microsoft Graph. If you have no idea about the Charts, let Excel guide you through the various steps are creating Charts by using the command called **Chart Wizard**.

For this you do the following:

1. Select the entire worksheet area which you want to include in your chart.

   In our case we would select the whole worksheet from A1 to F10, which includes the totals.

2. Select Chart from the Insert menu.

3. The Wizard Chart Step 1 of 4 menu will be given to you to select the type of chart you want for your worksheet.

   For our worksheet we have selected Column Chart type, as can be seen in the first of the four Chart Wizard dialog box.

   Press Next to reach Wizard Chart Step 2 of 4.

4. In this chart you can opt for different ways of representing your chart, i.e., row wise or column wise.

   For our worksheet we have selected columns.

5. Press Next to reach the next step.

6. Chart Wizard Step 3 of 4 gives you the option of naming the chart and the Y and X-axis. In our case we have named the worksheet as Finance. Press Next to reach the next step.

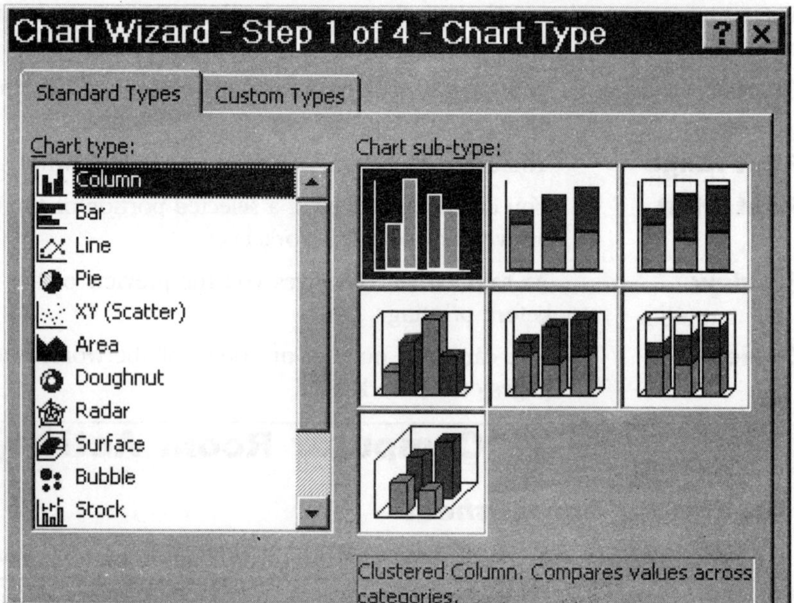

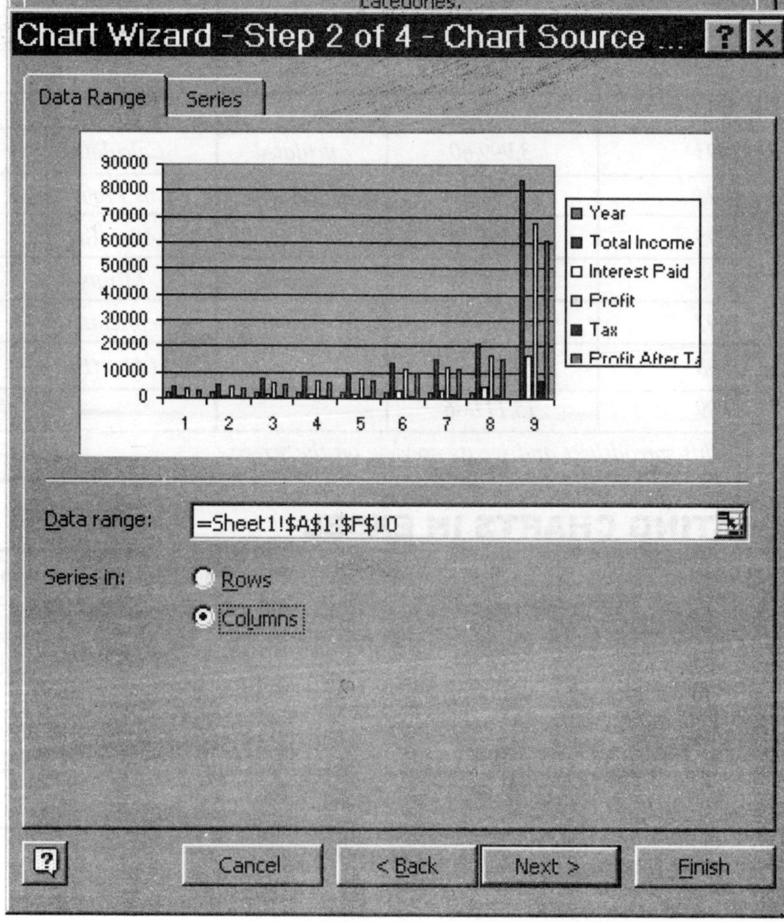

7. Chart Wizard Step 4 of 4 gives you the option of placing this chart in the worksheet as an object or in the form of a new cell.
8. Once this is over, you can press Finish to end the Chart Wizard routine.
9. A new chart will be placed in your worksheet with the Chart toolbar present for making the changes which you may require to do to your chart.
10. The final Chart is shown below.

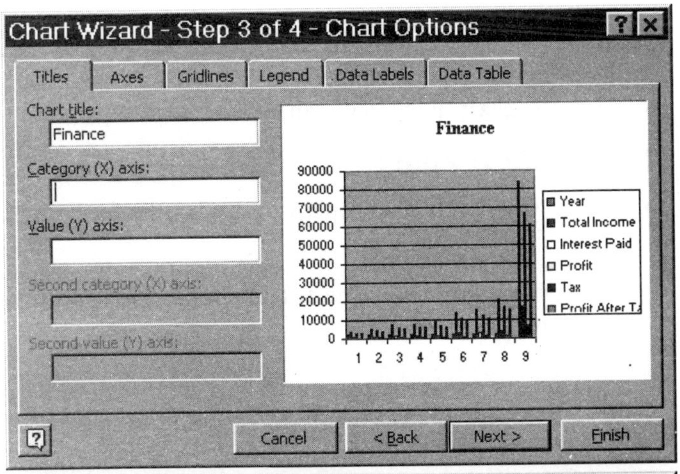

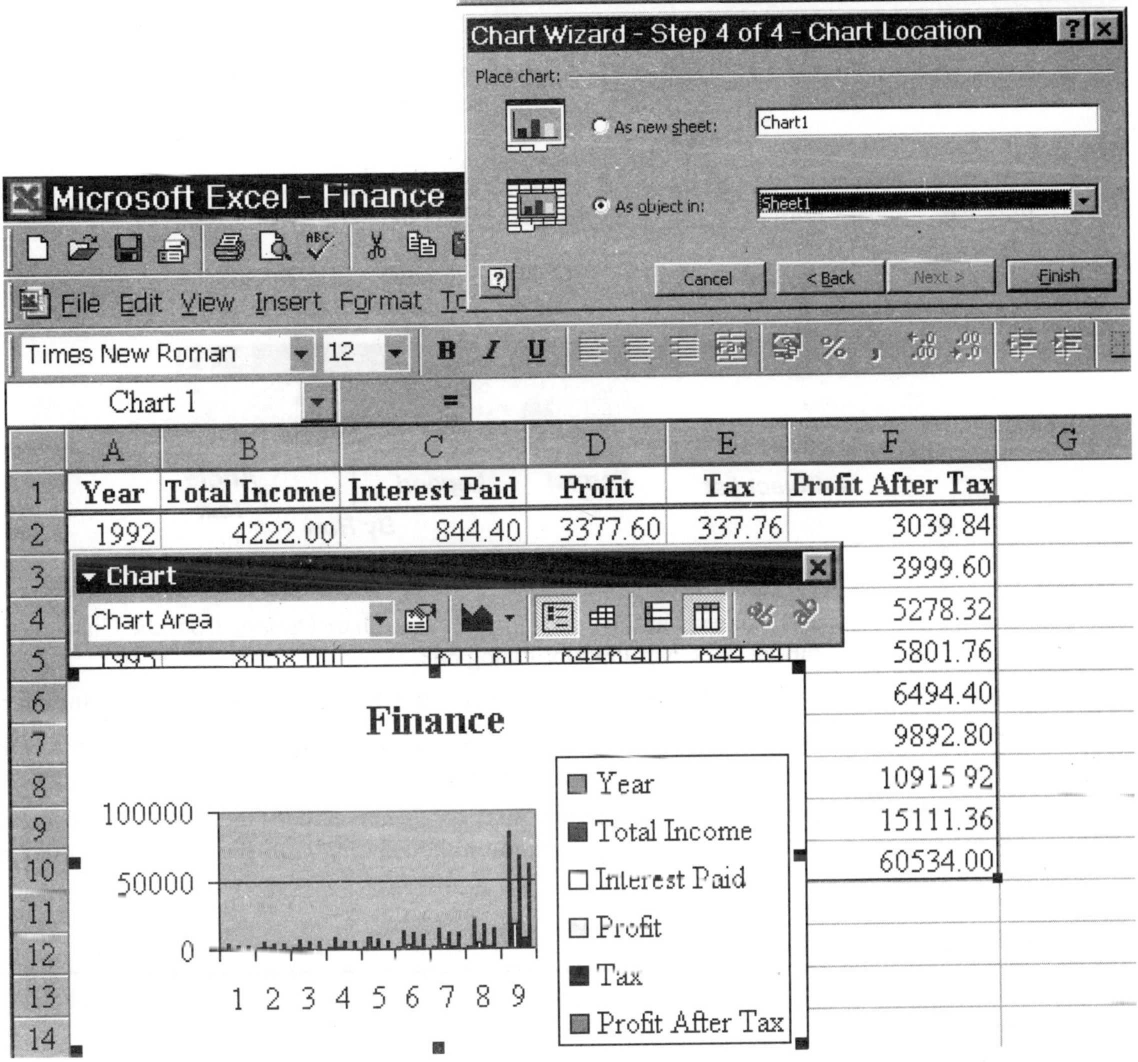

MODIFYING CHART

If you move the pointer slowly over areas of a chart, you can see ToolTips identifying the items that make up the chart. Each item can be formatted separately.

To modify a chart

1. Double click a chart object to display the formatting dialog box appropriate for that object.

   Or

   Right-click a chart object, and choose the appropriate formatting dialog box from the shortcut menu.

   Or

   Click a chart object, and click the Chart toolbar's Format button to display the appropriate formatting dialog box

   Or

   Click a chart object, and choose Selected Chart Area from the Format menu to display the appropriate dialog box.

   Or

   Choose the object you want to modify from the Chart Objects list on the Chart toolbar, and click the Chart toolbar's Format button to display the dialog box.

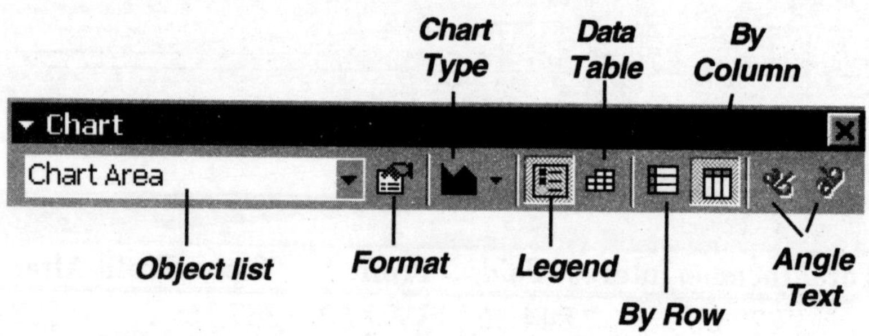

Remember

1. To modify several chart elements at the same time, choose Chart Options from the Chart menu and use the various tabs in the Chart Options dialog box.
2. Drag the chart to move it on the sheet, or drag the handles of the chart window to resize the chart.
3. Format the most general elements of the chart first (such as the chart area), and then format individual elements within that area (such as axis labels).
4. Don't be afraid to experiment with options you don't completely understand; you can easily undo almost any change by using the Undo command on the Edit menu or the Undo button on the Standard toolbar.

ADDING DATA TO A CHART

Once a chart has been created, you might want to extend it to include more data. For this do the following:

1. Select the chart.

2. From the Chart menu, choose Source Data.
3. In the Source Data dialog box, add more rows using the Series tab or extend the data range to include more columns using the Data Range tab.
4. Click Ok. The new row or column is added to the Chart.

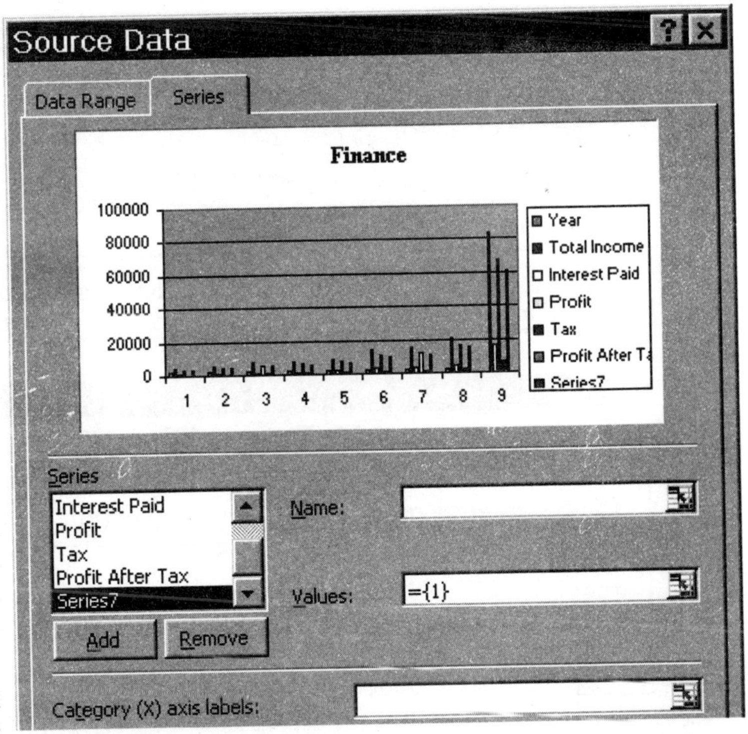

ADD A DATA TABLE TO A CHART

You can add a table of the data that is represented by the chart and add a trendline that shows the general trend, such as growth or decline, that emerges in the data.

1. Click the Data Table button on the Chart toolbar. The Data Table appears below the chart, as shown on the next page.

ADD A TRENDLINE

1. Click a data series for which you want to add a trendline.
2. From the Chart menu, choose Add Trendline.
3. In the Add Trendline dialog box, define the kind of trendline you want and set the options.
4. Click Ok.
5. The trendline is added, as seen in the figure on the next to next page.

CREATING A PIVOT TABLE REPORT

PivotTable reports can help you look at data in different ways. Once the reports are created, you can swap rows with columns for different views.

1. Click in the selected data area.
2. From the Data menu, choose PivotTable to start the PivotTable Wizard.
3. In the PivotTable and PivotChart Wizard Step 1 of 3, you have to define the type of data you have, and what type of report you want to create, whether Table or Chart.
4. Press Next to reach the step 2. Here you have to define the range for which you want to have this report.
5. Press Next to reach the Step 3 of the Wizard. It asks you whether you want to have the report in the existing worksheet or on a new worksheet.

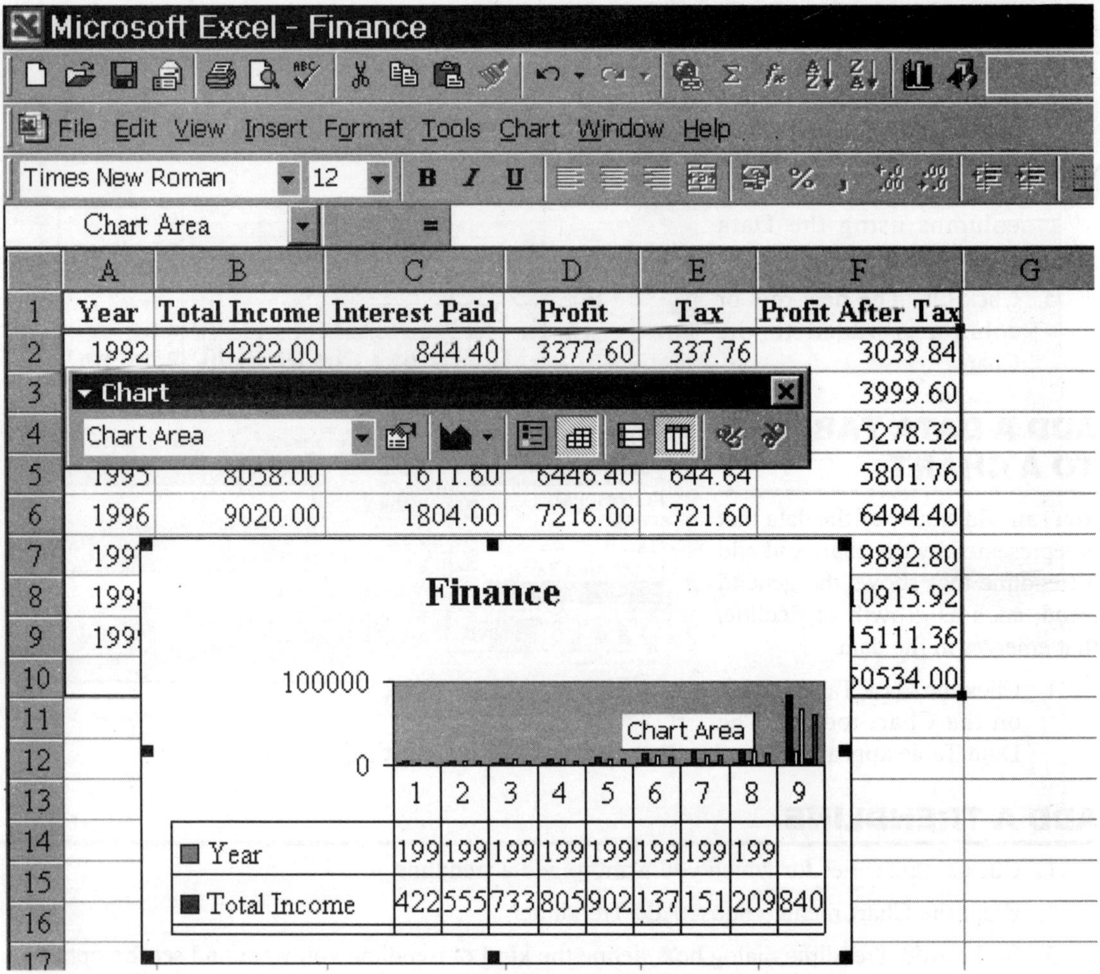

Select the one you want and press Finish to end the Wizard.

6. You will be given a worksheet view as shown on the next page. Position the table items to create the view you want. The rows and columns items are listed below the button area on the PivotTable toolbar.
7. Click the Format Report button on the PivotTable toolbar.
8. Choose a format from the AutoFormat dialog box.
9. Click Ok.
8. All the figures of the wizard are shown on next few pages.

MODIFYING THE CHART TYPE

Excel provides many chart types to help you display data in a way that will best communicate its meaning.

To modify the Chart Type

1. Click the chart.

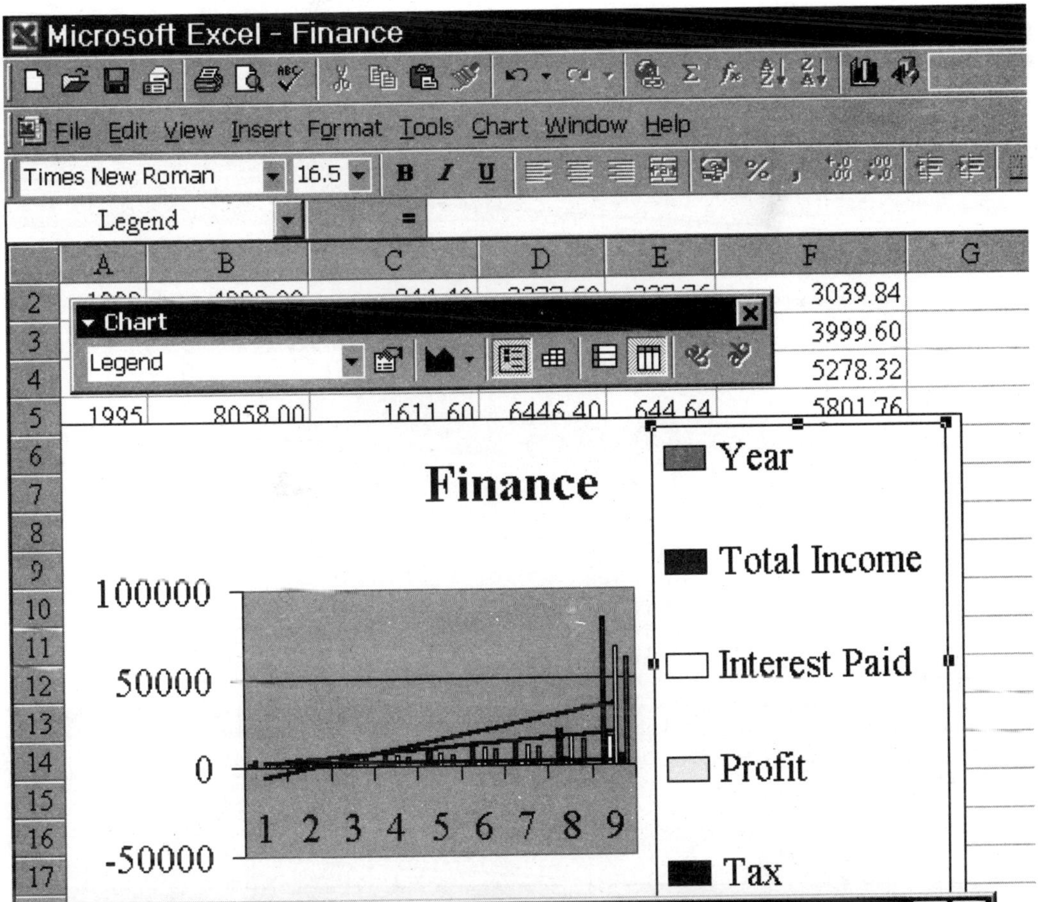
Microsoft Excel - Finance
File Edit View Insert Format Tools Chart Window Help
Times New Roman
16.5
Legend
Chart
Legend
Finance
100000
50000
0
-50000
1 2 3 4 5 6 7 8 9
Year
Total Income
Interest Paid
Profit
Tax
3039.84
3999.60
5278.32

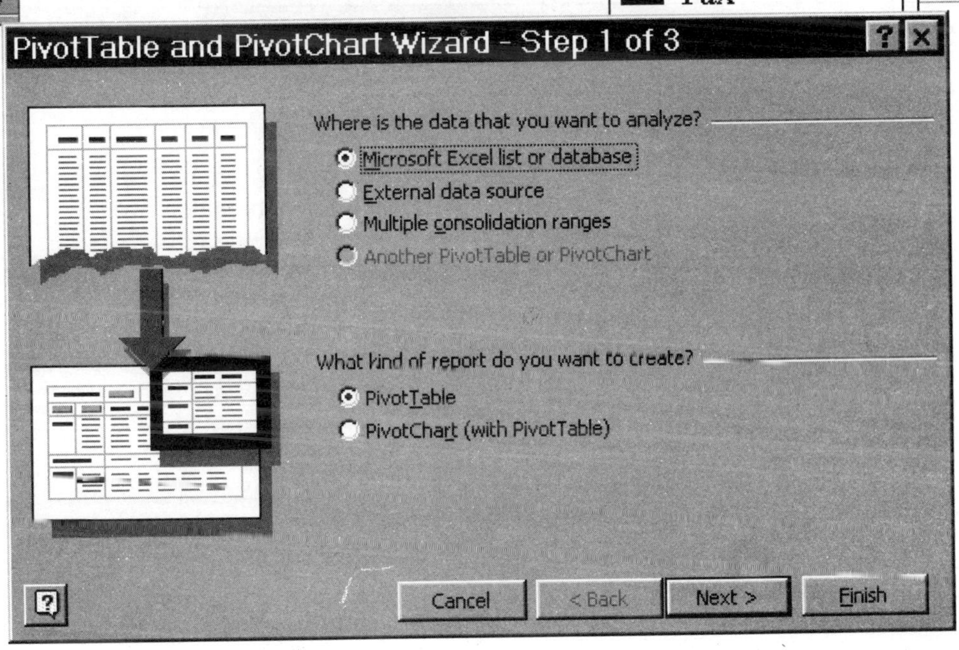
PivotTable and PivotChart Wizard - Step 1 of 3
Where is the data that you want to analyze?
Microsoft Excel list or database
External data source
Multiple consolidation ranges
Another PivotTable or PivotChart
What kind of report do you want to create?
PivotTable
PivotChart (with PivotTable)
Cancel
< Back
Next >
Finish

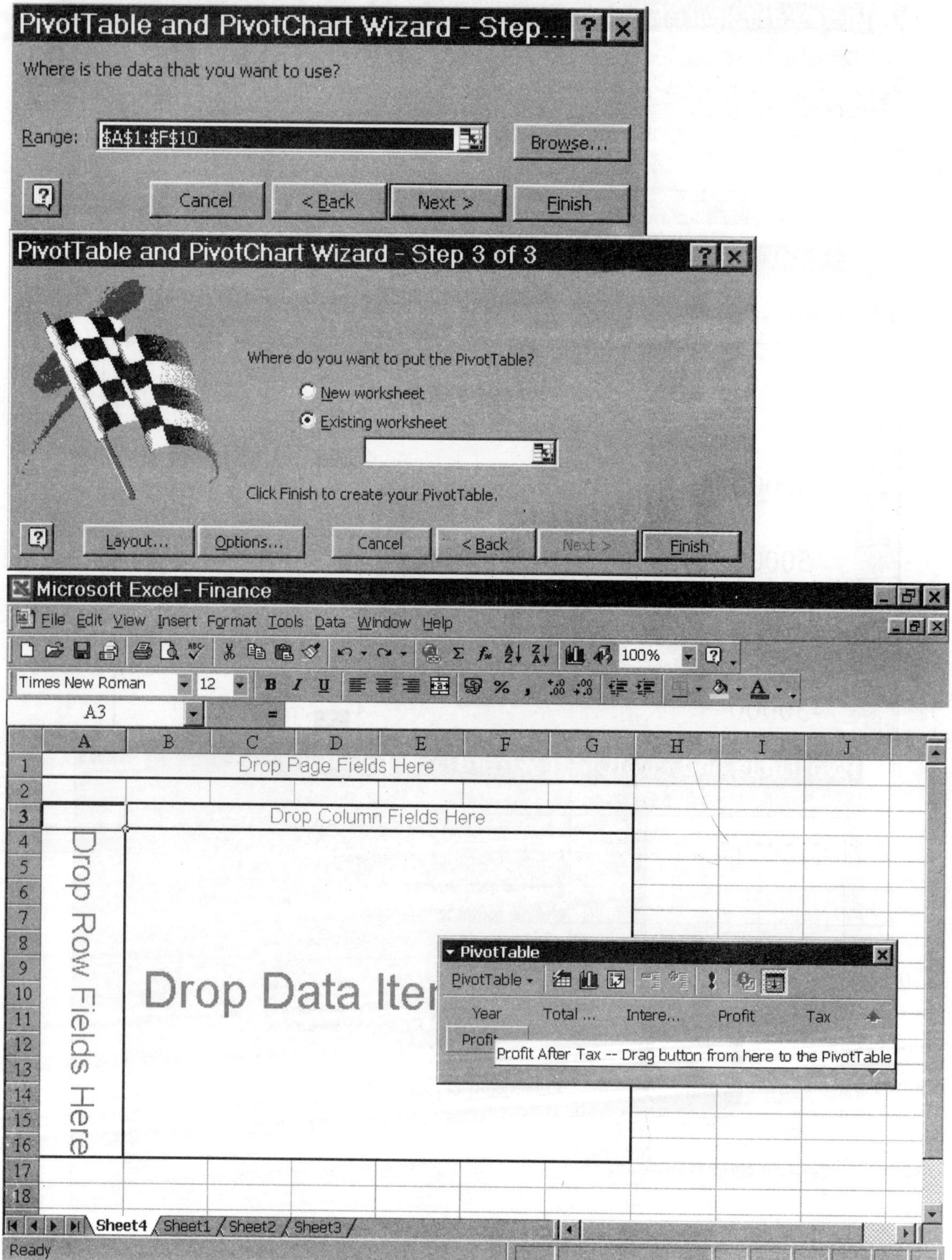
PivotTable and PivotChart Wizard - Step...
Where is the data that you want to use?
Range: $A$1:$F$10
Browse...
Cancel
< Back
Next >
Finish
PivotTable and PivotChart Wizard - Step 3 of 3
Where do you want to put the PivotTable?
New worksheet
Existing worksheet
Click Finish to create your PivotTable.
Layout...
Options...
Cancel
< Back
Next >
Finish
Microsoft Excel - Finance
File Edit View Insert Format Tools Data Window Help
100%
Times New Roman
12
A3
Drop Page Fields Here
Drop Column Fields Here
Drop Row Fields Here
Drop Data Iter
PivotTable
PivotTable
Year
Total ...
Intere...
Profit
Tax
Profit After Tax -- Drag button from here to the PivotTable
Sheet4
Sheet1
Sheet2
Sheet3
Ready

2. From the Chart menu choose Chart Type.
3. Select a type in the Chart Type dialog box.
4. Click Ok.

   Or

1. Click the chart.
2. Select a type from the Chart Type list on the Chart toolbar.

The Chart type changes.

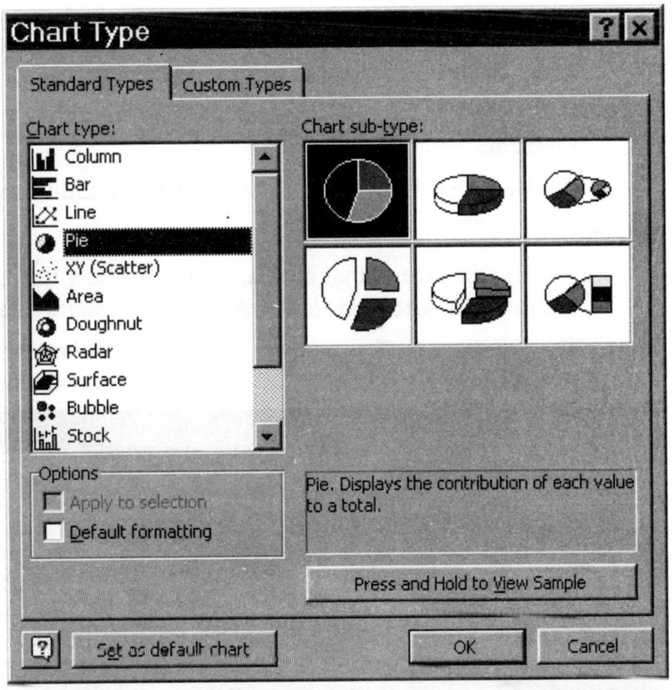

Computer Room Activity

Creating Spreadsheet and Chart

A company showed the following results in its 4 quarters. On the basis of this data, create a spreadsheet and then draw chart of the data:

	1st Qrt.	*2nd Qtr.*	*3rd Qtr.*	*4th Qtr.*
North	*55,000*	*66,000*	*77,000*	*88,000*
South	*40,000*	*50,000*	*60,000*	*70,000*
East	*35,000*	*40,000*	*45,000*	*50,000*
West	*60,000*	*70,000*	*80,000*	*90,000*
Total				

After creating the chart, see the preview on the screen.

MORE EXCEL COMMANDS

Now I will take you through the various other commands which you may not use in your regular routine working but are quite useful and can be used whenever required.

AUDITING A WORKBOOK

To avoid bogus results from incorrect formulas, you can have Excel identify the cells that have supplied data for a formula. That way, you can easily see whether all the cells you wanted have been included in the calculation.

To Trace the Precedents for a Formula:

1. Select the cell or cells that contain the formulas.
2. From the Tools menu, choose Auditing, and then choose Trace Precedents from the Auditing submenu.
3. Choose Trace Precedents again to view an additional level of precedents, if one exists.

Remember

1. To clear the arrows that have appeared to show the cells that are included in the formula, choose Remove All Arrows from the Auditing submenu menu.
2. The Auditing toolbar contains Trace Precedents and Remove All Arrows buttons. To view the Auditing toolbar, choose Show Auditing Toolbar from the Auditing submenu.

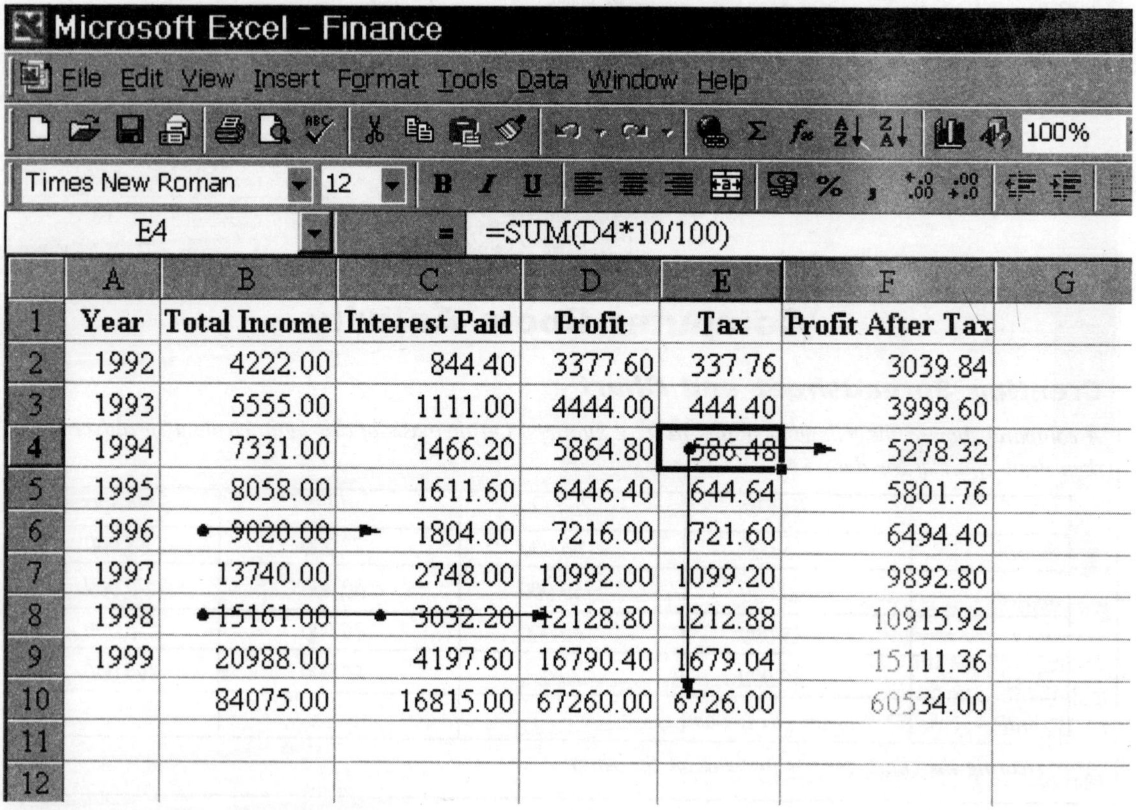

	A	B	C	D	E	F	G
1	Year	Total Income	Interest Paid	Profit	Tax	Profit After Tax	
2	1992	4222.00	844.40	3377.60	337.76	3039.84	
3	1993	5555.00	1111.00	4444.00	444.40	3999.60	
4	1994	7331.00	1466.20	5864.80	586.48	5278.32	
5	1995	8058.00	1611.60	6446.40	644.64	5801.76	
6	1996	9020.00	1804.00	7216.00	721.60	6494.40	
7	1997	13740.00	2748.00	10992.00	1099.20	9892.80	
8	1998	15161.00	3032.20	12128.80	1212.88	10915.92	
9	1999	20988.00	4197.60	16790.40	1679.04	15111.36	
10		84075.00	16815.00	67260.00	6726.00	60534.00	
11							
12							

COMMENTS INSERTING

A comment is an annotation that you attach to a cell to provide information about the cell's contents. This capability enables several people to review the same worksheet and attach their comments.

To insert a comment:

1. Select the cell to which you want to attach a comment.
2. From the Insert menu, choose Comment.
3. In the yellow text box that opens and displays your name, type the text for the comment.

4. Click in another cell to close the text box.

Remember

1. A comment is indicated by a comment marker (a small red triangle) at the upper right corner of the cell. To view the comment, pass the cursor over the cell.
2. To remove a comment, right-click in the cell, and choose Delete Comment from the shortcut menu.

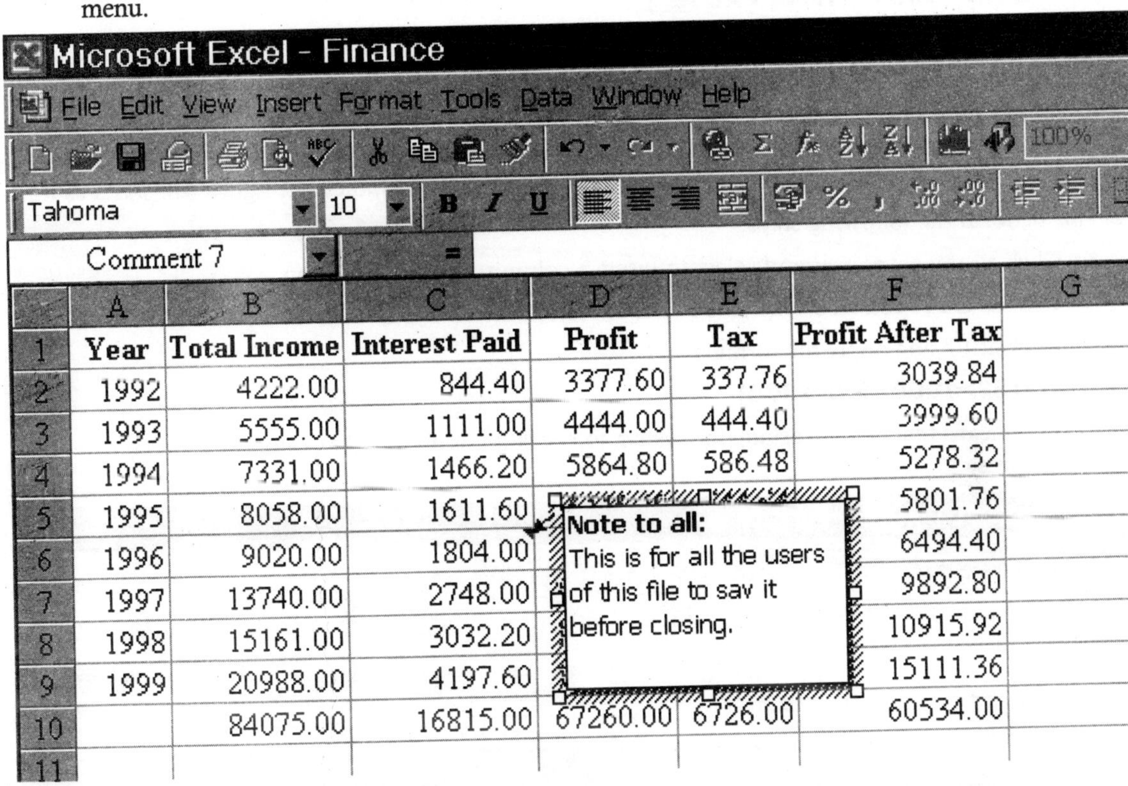

	A	B	C	D	E	F	G
1	Year	Total Income	Interest Paid	Profit	Tax	Profit After Tax	
2	1992	4222.00	844.40	3377.60	337.76	3039.84	
3	1993	5555.00	1111.00	4444.00	444.40	3999.60	
4	1994	7331.00	1466.20	5864.80	586.48	5278.32	
5	1995	8058.00	1611.60			5801.76	
6	1996	9020.00	1804.00			6494.40	
7	1997	13740.00	2748.00			9892.80	
8	1998	15161.00	3032.20			10915.92	
9	1999	20988.00	4197.60			15111.36	
10		84075.00	16815.00	67260.00	6726.00	60534.00	
11							

FORMULAS THAT MAKE DECISIONS

There will be a time when you want Excel to carry out one task under certain circumstances and another task if those circumstances don't apply. If you are familiar with any programming language, it is the case of IF, WHEN or IF, THEN. You have a similar IF function in Excel.

How the IF function works

In its simplest form, the IF function tests the value of a cell and does one thing if the test is positive (**TRUE**) and another if the test is negative (**FALSE**). It requires three arguments: the test data, the action to perform if the test is TRUE and the action to perform if the test is FALSE. You supply the arguments one after the other within the function's parentheses, separating them with commas (no spaces are to be given). The text which you want to appear as it is, i.e., TRUE or FALSE should be given under quotes, reference of cells like **C5**, etc., should be as it is.

Apply this formula in cell **B6** and see the result:

1. Select cell B6, type the following in place of formula and press Enter:

= IF(B2=0, TRUE, FALSE)

Excel checks whether the value in cell B2 is zero (the test), and because it isn't zero, it ignores TRUE (the action to perform if the test is TRUE) and displays FALSE (the action to perform if the test is FALSE) in cell B6.

2. Double-click cell B6, change formula to

   = IF(B2>1000, TRUE, FALSE")

   and press Enter. The entry in cell B6 instantly changes from FALSE to TRUE because the value in cell B2 is greater than one thousand; that is, the test is TRUE.

Now this was very simple. Isn't it. However, you can also build tests that involve other functions. Suppose that in our Finance worksheet, we say that the Tax has to be a minimum of 1000, which means that if the Tax is less than 1000 it has to be put as 1000 and if it more that 1000, then the figure will stand as it is. For this perform the following steps.

1. Click at any entry in E and select to insert a column from Insert Menu.
2. Use the Cut, Paste and Format buttons to restore the entries now in E2:E9 to F2:F9.
3. Click at F2 and apply the formula

   =IF(E2>1000, E2, 1000)

   This means that you are asking the system to check if it is above 1000, One of the two possibilities will arise:

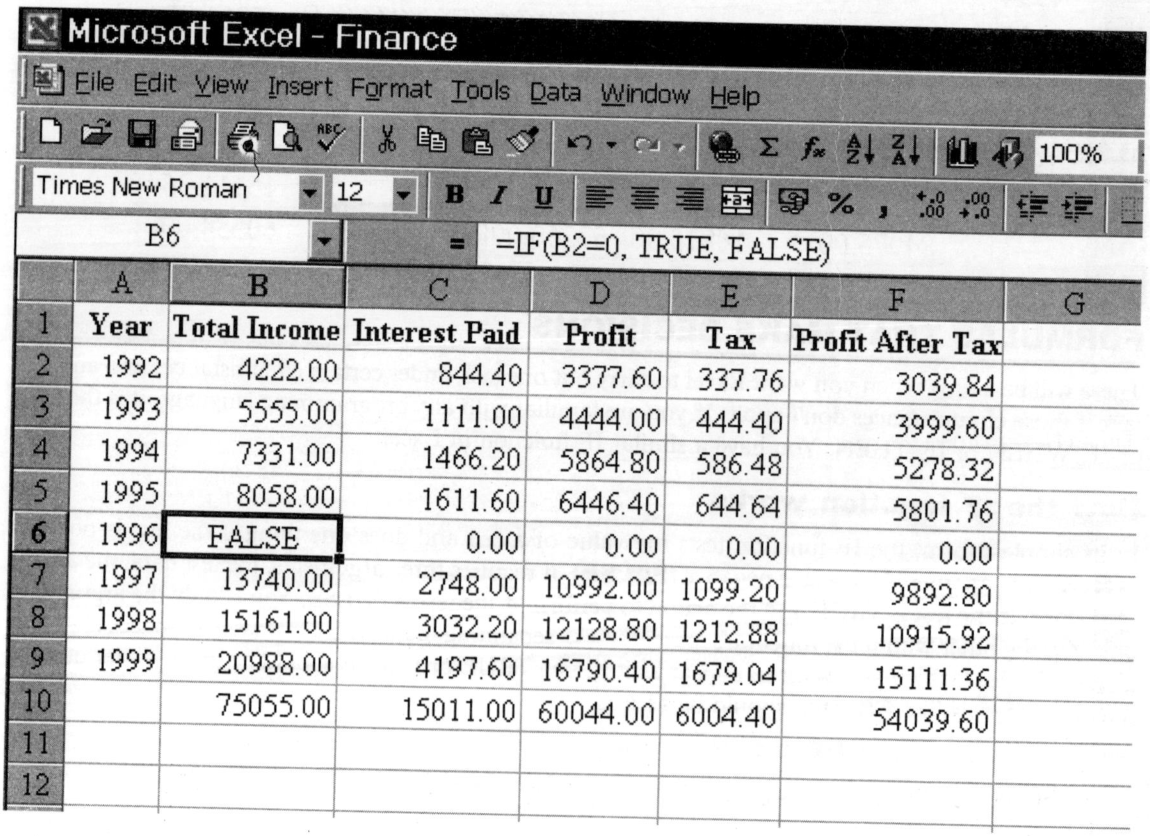

	A	B	C	D	E	F	G
1	Year	Total Income	Interest Paid	Profit	Tax	Profit After Tax	
2	1992	4222.00	844.40	3377.60	337.76	3039.84	
3	1993	5555.00	1111.00	4444.00	444.40	3999.60	
4	1994	7331.00	1466.20	5864.80	586.48	5278.32	
5	1995	8058.00	1611.60	6446.40	644.64	5801.76	
6	1996	FALSE	0.00	0.00	0.00	0.00	
7	1997	13740.00	2748.00	10992.00	1099.20	9892.80	
8	1998	15161.00	3032.20	12128.80	1212.88	10915.92	
9	1999	20988.00	4197.60	16790.40	1679.04	15111.36	
10		75055.00	15011.00	60044.00	6004.40	54039.60	
11							
12							

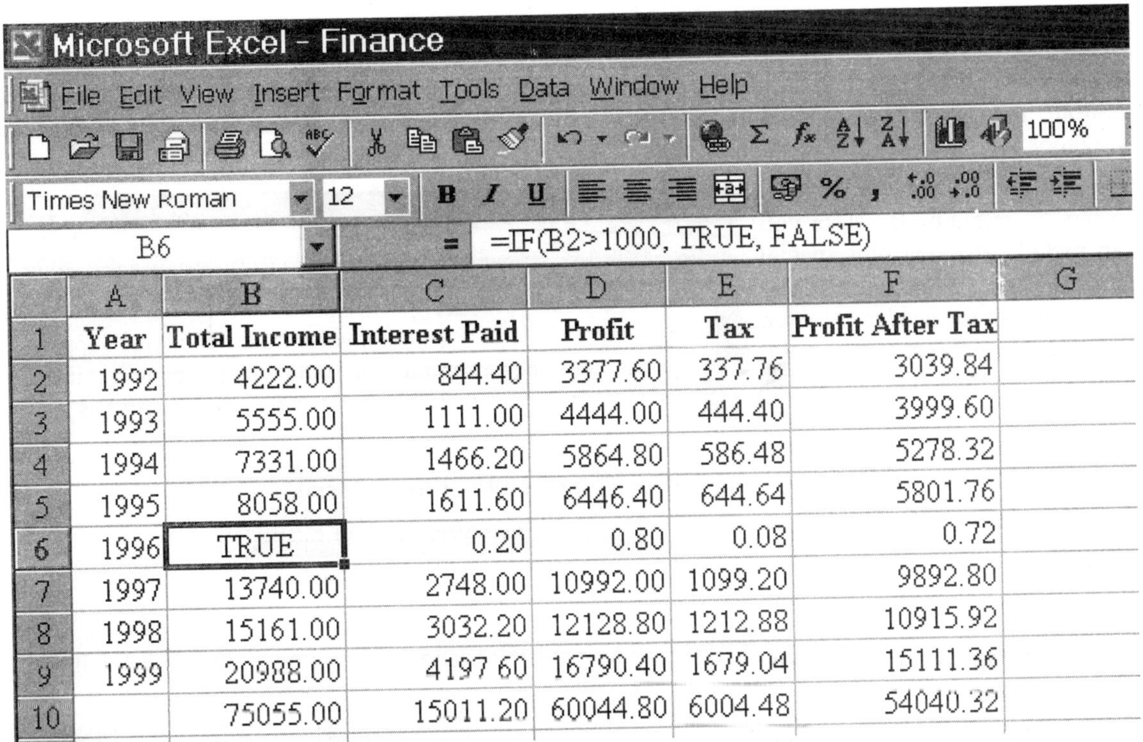

	A	B	C	D	E	F
1	Year	Total Income	Interest Paid	Profit	Tax	Profit After Tax
2	1992	4222.00	844.40	3377.60	337.76	3039.84
3	1993	5555.00	1111.00	4444.00	444.40	3999.60
4	1994	7331.00	1466.20	5864.80	586.48	5278.32
5	1995	8058.00	1611.60	6446.40	644.64	5801.76
6	1996	TRUE	0.20	0.80	0.08	0.72
7	1997	13740.00	2748.00	10992.00	1099.20	9892.80
8	1998	15161.00	3032.20	12128.80	1212.88	10915.92
9	1999	20988.00	4197 60	16790.40	1679.04	15111.36
10		75055.00	15011.20	60044.80	6004.48	54040.32

TRUE This means that the figure in cell is more than 1000, then the column will be replaced by the figure in **E2**, which means that it is not changed.

FALSE This means that the figure in the cell **E2** is less than 1000, then the second condition will be met, i.e., figure in cell **F2** will be replaced with the figure of 1000.

Repeat this for all the other cells of column **F**. The easiest way out to repeat the formula in each column.

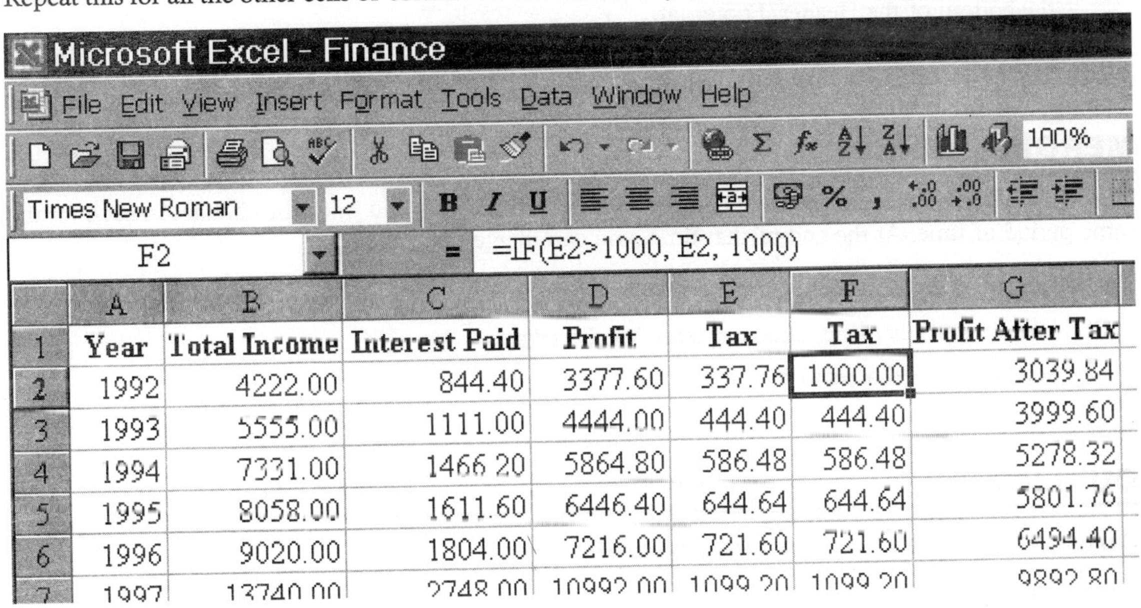

	A	B	C	D	E	F	G
1	Year	Total Income	Interest Paid	Profit	Tax	Tax	Profit After Tax
2	1992	4222.00	844.40	3377.60	337.76	1000.00	3039.84
3	1993	5555.00	1111.00	4444.00	444.40	444.40	3999.60
4	1994	7331.00	1466 20	5864.80	586.48	586.48	5278.32
5	1995	8058.00	1611.60	6446.40	644.64	644.64	5801.76
6	1996	9020.00	1804.00	7216.00	721.60	721.60	6494.40
7	1997	13740.00	2748.00	10992.00	1099.20	1099.20	9892.80

HEADERS AND FOOTERS

Excel lets you add headers and footers to print information at the top and bottom of every page of the printout. The information can include any text, as well as page numbers, the current date and time, the workbook file name, and the worksheet tab name.

You can choose the headers and footers suggested by Excel, or you can include any text plus special commands to control the appearance of the header or footer. For example, you can apply, bold, italic, or underline to the header or footer text. You can also left-align, center, or right-align your text in a header or footer.

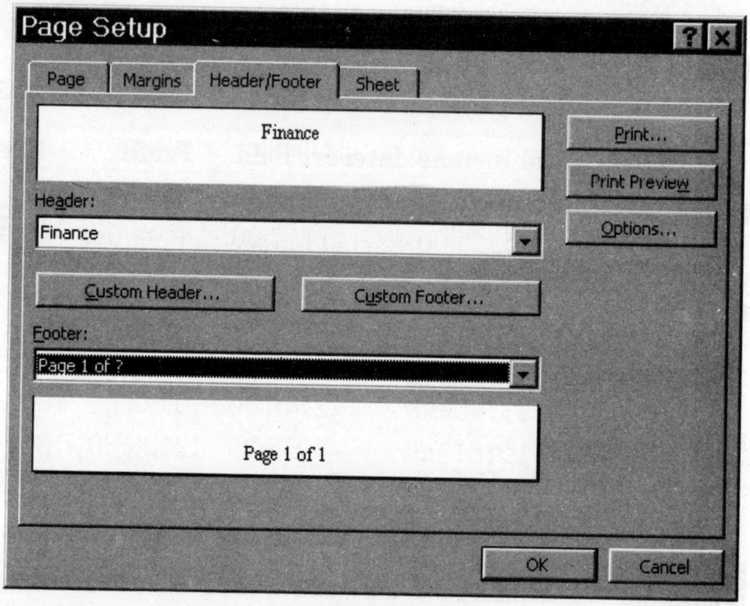

To add headers and footers, follow these steps:

1. Open the View menu and choose Header and Footer. The Page Setup dialog box appears.
2. To select a header, click the Header drop-down arrow, Excel displays a list of suggested header information. Scroll through the list and click the header you want. The sample header appears at the top of the Header/Footer tab.
3. To select a footer, click the Footer drop-down arrow, Excel displays a list of suggested footer information. Scroll through the list and click on a footer you want. The sample footer appears at the bottom of the Header/Footer tab.
4. Click Ok to close the Page Setup dialog box and return to your worksheet. Or click the Print button to display the Print dialog box, and click Ok to print your worksheet.

MERGING WORKBOOKS

Sharing work is to maintain multiple copies of a shared workbook and track the changes in each for the same period of time. At the end of that time, you can merge the copies.

To merge workbooks:

1. From the Tools menu, choose Merge Workbooks.
2. Select the workbooks to merge into the current one.
3. Click Ok.

OUTLINES

Outline a Worksheet Automatically

1. Select a single cell to outline or the entire worksheet

2. Select a range of cells to outline
3. Click Data menu, Group and Outline command, and click at Auto Outline.

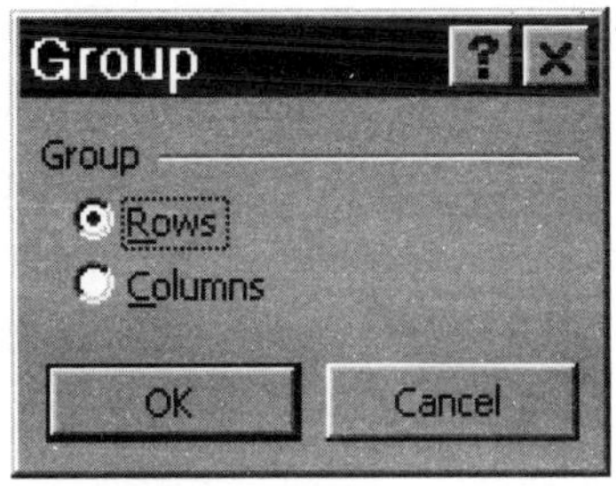

An outline created with outline symbols to the left of the row heading and/or above column headings.

Clear Entire Outline

1. Select any cell in outline
2. Click at Data menu, Group and Outline command, and Clear Outline.

Show or Hide Outline Symbols

1. Click at Tools menu, Hide Details command

Group Rows or Columns in an Outline

1. Select rows or columns to group
2. Click Data menu, Group and Outline, Group...

If Group dialog box appears

1. Select Rows or Columns
2. Click Ok

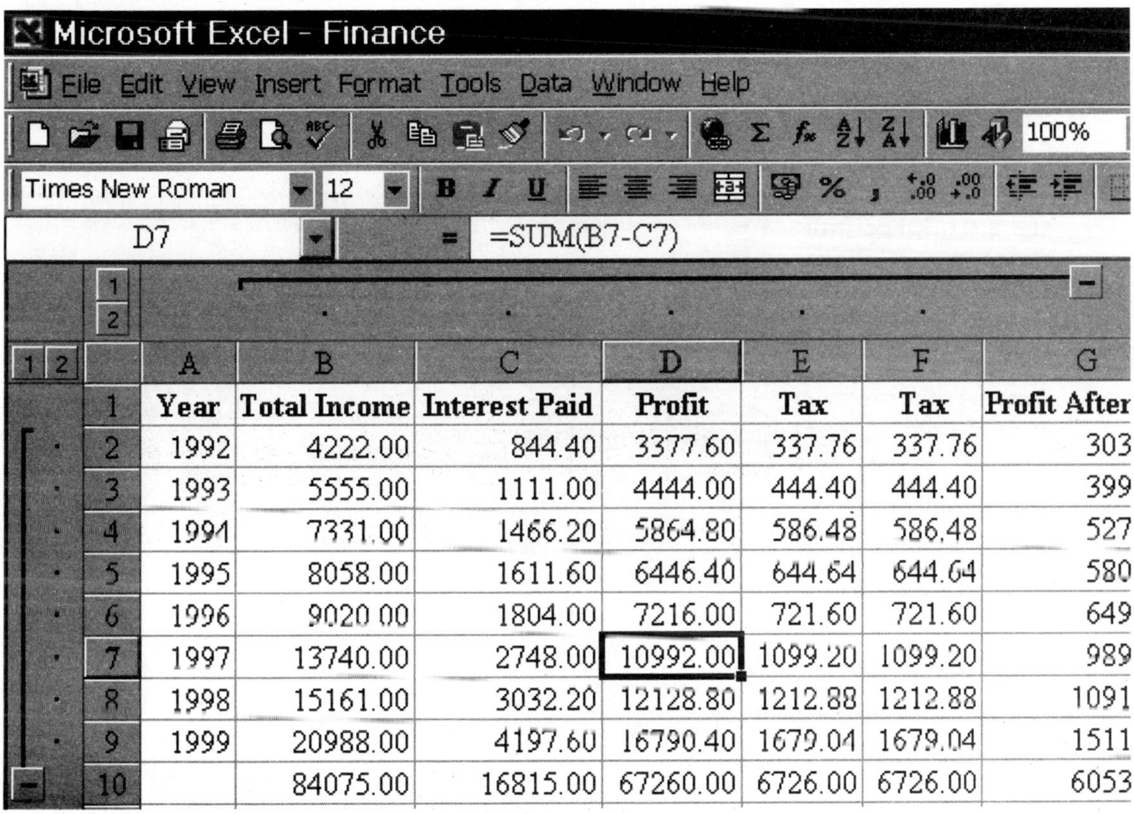

Ungroup Rows or Columns in an Outline

1. Select group in outline to ungroup
2. Click Data menu, Group and Outline command, Ungroup...

If Ungrouped dialog box appears

1. Select Rows or Columns
2. Click Ok

Remove Group from Outline

1. Select group in outline to remove
2. Click Data menu, Group and Outline, Clear Outline

Set Outline Options

1. Click Data menu, Group and Outline, Settings...
2. Select or deselect Direction options.

PRINTING COLUMN AND ROW LABELS ON EVERY PAGE

Excel provides a way for you to select labels and titles that are located on the top edge and left side of a large worksheet, and print them on every page of the printout. This option is useful when a worksheet is too wide to print on a single page. If you don't use this option, the extra columns or rows will be printed on subsequent pages without any descriptive labels.

Do the following for this:

1. Open the File menu and choose Page Setup. The Page Setup dialog box appears.
2. Click the Sheet tab to display the Sheet options.
3. To repeat column labels and a worksheet title, click the Collapse Dialog button to the right of the Rows to repeat at top text box.
4. Drag over the rows you want to print on every page. A dashed line border surrounds the selected area, and absolute cell references with dollar signs appear in the Rows to repeat at top text box.
5. Click the Collapse Dialog button to return to the Page Setup dialog box.

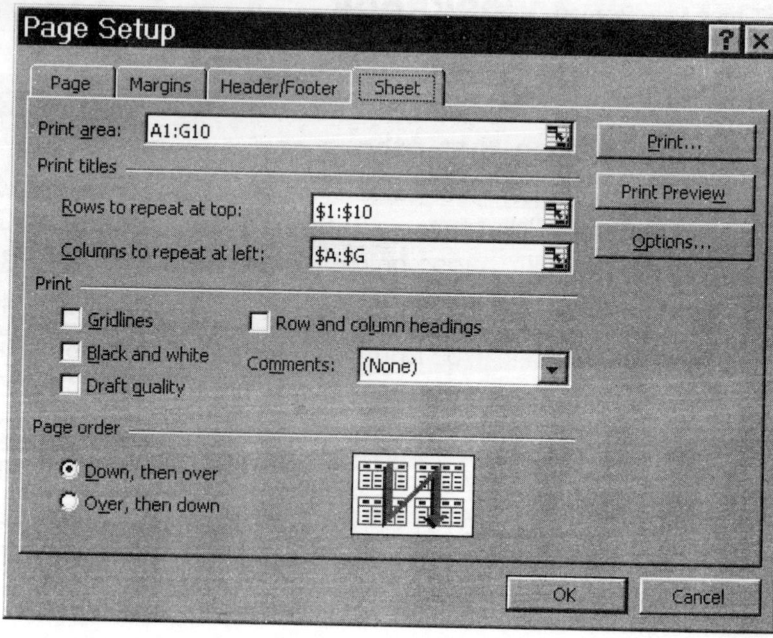

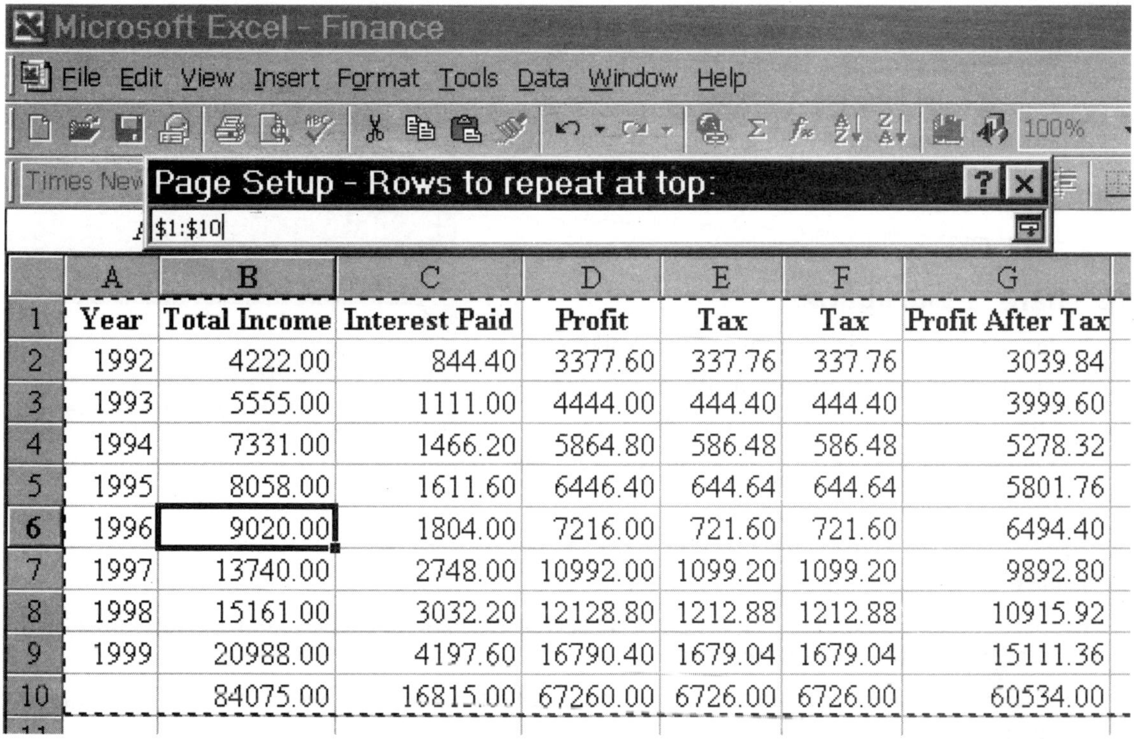

	A	B	C	D	E	F	G
1	Year	Total Income	Interest Paid	Profit	Tax	Tax	Profit After Tax
2	1992	4222.00	844.40	3377.60	337.76	337.76	3039.84
3	1993	5555.00	1111.00	4444.00	444.40	444.40	3999.60
4	1994	7331.00	1466.20	5864.80	586.48	586.48	5278.32
5	1995	8058.00	1611.60	6446.40	644.64	644.64	5801.76
6	1996	9020.00	1804.00	7216.00	721.60	721.60	6494.40
7	1997	13740.00	2748.00	10992.00	1099.20	1099.20	9892.80
8	1998	15161.00	3032.20	12128.80	1212.88	1212.88	10915.92
9	1999	20988.00	4197.60	16790.40	1679.04	1679.04	15111.36
10		84075.00	16815.00	67260.00	6726.00	6726.00	60534.00

6. To repeat row labels that appear on the left of the worksheet, click the Collapse Dialog button to the right of the Columns to repeat at left text box. Excel reduces the Page Setup dialog box. Then click Ok.

PROTECTING A WORKBOOK

You can allow others to work on portions of your workbook or all of your workbook, but it's good idea to set up cell formatting options in advance so that they do not make changes inadvertently.

To unlock cells so that others can edit the cell contents:

1. Select the cells that will be editable and choose Cells from the Format menu or right-click and choose Format Cells from the shortcut menu.
2. On the Protection tab in the Format Cells dialog box, clear the Locked check box.
3. Click Ok.

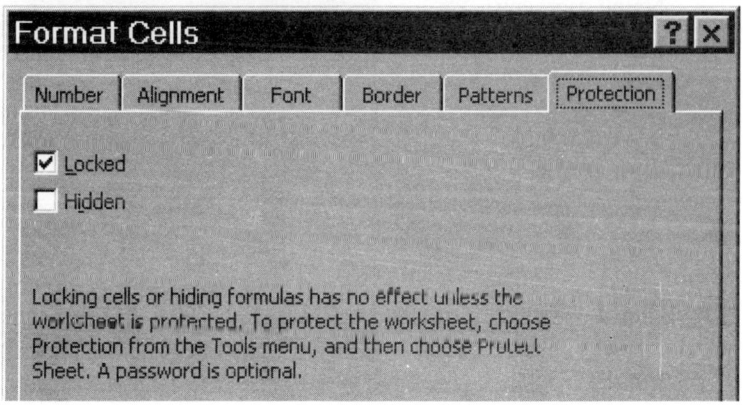

Remember

1. To hide formulas, check Hidden on the Protection tab in the Format Cells dialog box.

To protect a workbook:

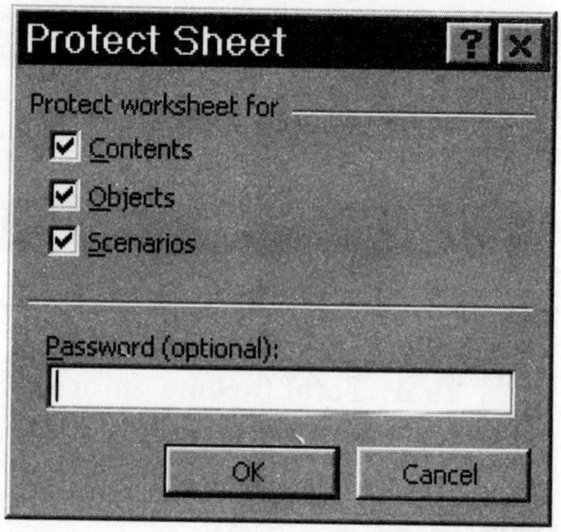

1. From the Tools menu, choose Protection, and choose Protect Sheet from the submenu.
2. In the Protect Sheet dialog box, you can assign a password so that you are the only one who can remove the protection.
3. Click Ok.

To share a workbook:

1. From the Tools menu, choose Share Workbook.
2. On the Editing tab in the Chart Workbook dialog box, enable changes by more than one user.
3. On the Advanced tab, specify when you want the changes updated and how you want conflicts handled.
4. Click Ok.

Remember

1. To return the workbook to its unshared state, choose Share Workbook from the Tools menus and clear the Allow Changes check box.
2. You can protect and share in one step by choosing Protect and Share Workbook from the Protection submenu.

RANGES, NAMING

When you assign a name to a range, you can use the range name in formulas rather than the range address. Range names make it easier to refer to data and easier to understand formulas.

To name a range:

1. Select the range that you want to name.
2. From the Insert menu, choose Name, and then choose Define from the Name submenu.
3. Enter the name in the Define Name dialog box.
4. Click Ok.

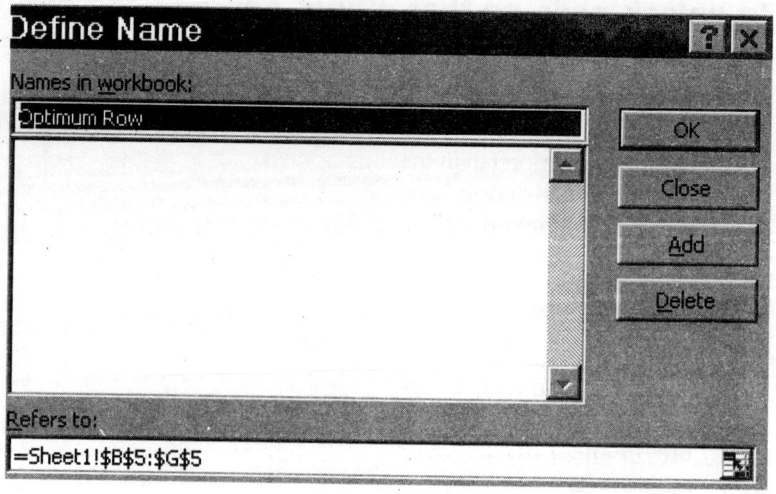

Remember

1. To use the name in a formula, choose Paste from the Name submenu.
2. You can assign a name to an individual cell or to a range of cells.

REFERENCES

By default, Excel uses relative references in its formulae. Relative references refer to cells by their position in relation to the cell containing the formula. So when you copy the formula in cell **F5** to cell **F6**, Excel changes the reference from **E5** to **E6**.

Absolute references

When you don't want a reference to be copied as a relative reference, you need to use an absolute reference. Absolute references refer to cells by their fixed position in the worksheet. To make a reference absolute, you add dollar signs before its column letter and now number.

For example, you would enter it as **$C$4:$C$9**. You could then copy formula that contained this reference anywhere on the worksheet and it would always refer to the range **C4:C9**.

Mixed references

References can also be partially relative and partially absolute. For example, **$C3** has an absolute column reference and a relative row reference and **C$3** has a relative column reference and an absolute row reference.

SEEKING GOALS

Use goal seeking to force a particular result in a calculation by changing one of the calculation's components. For example, if you know the percentage growth you are looking for, you can use Goal Seeking to determine the changes that would be necessary to produce that result.

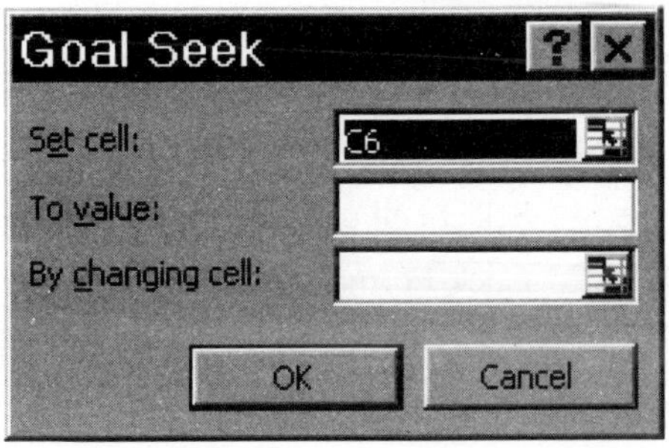

To seek a goal:

1. From the Tools menu, choose Goal Seek.
2. In the Goal Seek dialog box, specify the cell whose value you want to set (this should be a cell whose value is usually calculated through a formula), the value you want that cell to have, and the cell whose value can vary to make the result come out to the value you want.
3. Click Ok.
4. If a solution is possible, the Goal Seek Status dialog will tell you, and the variable cell you specified will change.
5. Click Ok to accept the change or click Cancel to reject it.

SHEETS NAMING

You can replace the default sheet names (Sheet1, Sheet2, and so on) with useful informative names (for example, Finance, Personnel, Manufacturing, Secretarial, etc).

To Name a Sheet:

1. Double click the tab of the sheet you want to rename.
2. Type the new name over the current name in the sheet tab.

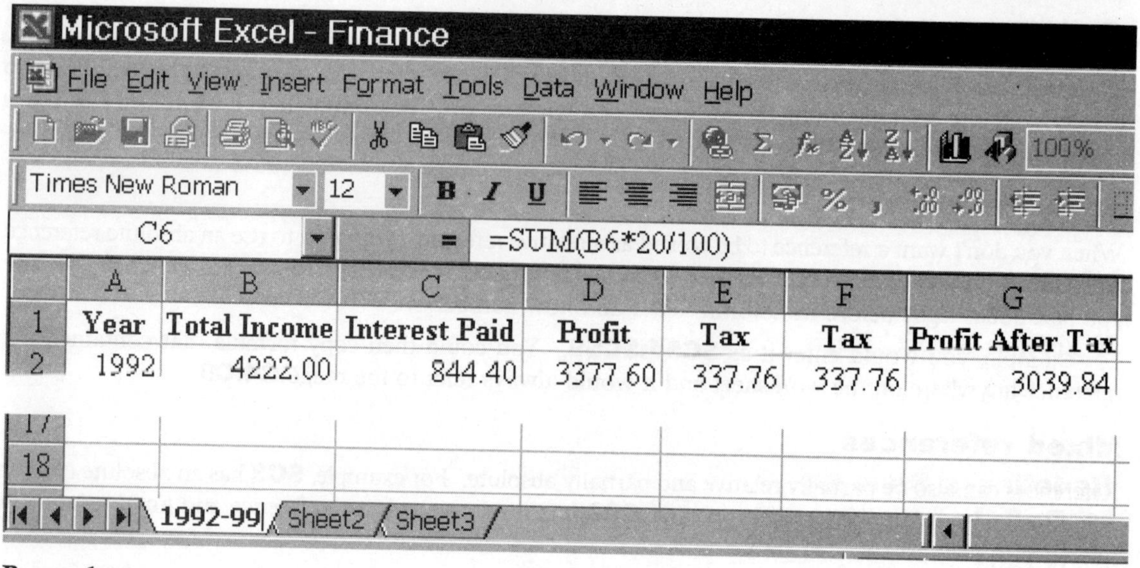

Remember

1. You can also choose Sheet and then Rename from the Format menu to select the sheet name in the tab of the current sheet, ready to be typed over.
2. Sheet names can be up to 31 characters long and can include spaces.

STYLES

Create a Style by Example

1. Select cell containing desired formats
2. Click Format menu, Style...
3. Type a name for style in Style Name: The style's formats in Style includes box.

Exclude formats of selected cell from style:

1. Deselect Style Includes (by example) options: Number, Font, Alignment, Border, Patterns, Protection
2. Click Ok.

Create a Style by Defining It

1. Click Format menu, Style...
2. Type a name for style in Style Name.

Exclude formats of selected cell from style:

1. Deselect Style Includes options:
2. Click Modify...
3. Click tab of format category to include
4. Select options for selected tab

Redefine a Style by example

1. Select cell containing formats to assign to style
2. Click Format menu, Style...
3. Type (do not select) name of style to redefine in Style name.
4. Click Add...

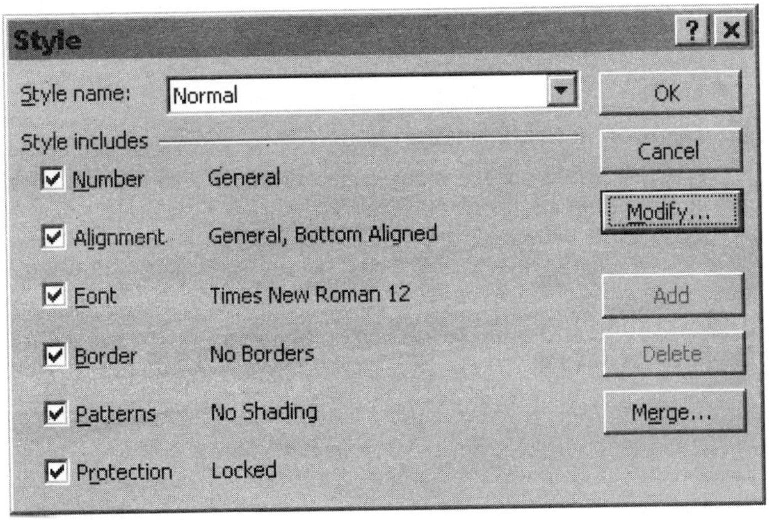

If Redefine prompt appears

1. Click Yes
2. Click Ok

Redefine a Style by Defining It

1. Click Format menu, Style...
2. Select name of style to redefine in Style Name

Exclude format categories from style:

1. Deselect Style Includes options:

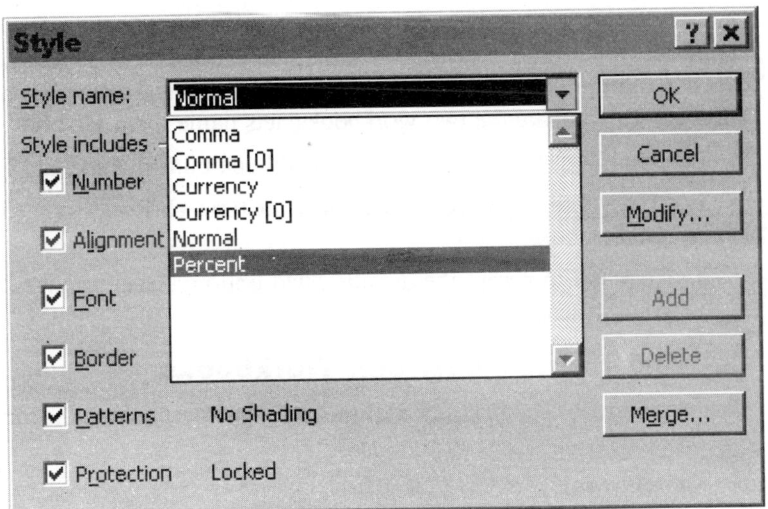

Change formats:

1. Click Modify...
2. Click tab of format category to change
3. Select options for selected tab.
4. Repeat steps for each format category to change
5. Click Ok

Apply a Style

Add the Style box to the Formatting toolbar if you use styles often. Then select or define styles quickly without opening menus.

1. Select cell(s) to which to apply style
2. Click Format menu, Style...
3. Select style name in Style Name
4. Click Ok

Copy Styles from Another Workbook

1. Open source and destination workbooks

2. Select destination workbook
3. Click Format menu, Style...
4. Click Merge...
5. Select name of source workbook in Merge Styles From: list
6. Click Ok

If merge styles message appears

1. Click Yes to replace styles in destination workbook that have the same name.

   Or
2. Click No to retain styles that have the samc names in destination workbook.
3. Click Ok

Delete a Style

1. Click Format menu, Style...
2. Select name of style to delete in Style Name

   Normal style cannot be deleted.
3. Click Delete
4. Click Ok

WORKING WITH WORKBOOKS

You can transfer data between two workbooks or compare the information in one workbook with that in another. To compare the two workbooks, lets name them **Book1** and **Book2**.

1. Open Book1 and click at New Workbook button. Excel displays a new workbook called Book2.
2. To see both the workbooks at the same time, choose Arrange from the Windows menu to display a dialog box.
3. Click Ok to accept the default Tiled option. Excel arranges Book2 and Book1 side by side on your screen.

Copying Entries Between Workbooks

The procedure for copying information between workbooks is the same as for copying between sheets in one workbook.

Do the following:

1. Activate Book1 by clicking its title bar.
2. Select a range and click the Copy button.
3. Click A1 cell of Book2 and click the Paste button. The data will be pasted in Book2.
4. Press Ctrl + Home to move to cell A1 and see the full result.

Moving Sheets Between Workbooks

A sheet can be easily moved within a workbook or from one workbook to another. For example, you can move a worksheet from Book1 to Book2.

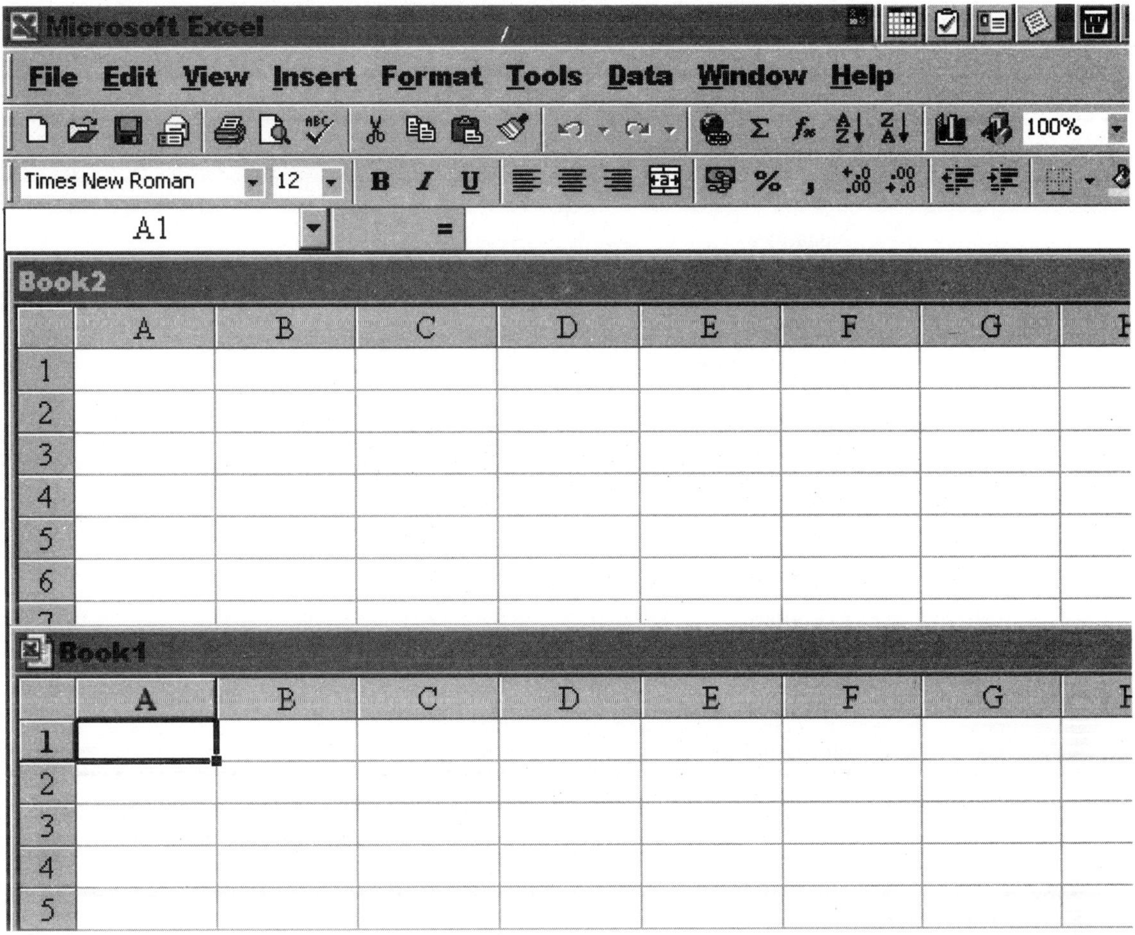

Do the following:

1. Activate the Book1 window.
2. Activate the Books2 Window.
3. Point to the Sheet1 tab and hold down the left mouse button. The pointer is now an arrow with a sheet attached to it.
4. Drag the sheet pointer until it sits between Sheet2 of the Book1 workbook. Excel indicates with an arrowhead where it will place the selected sheet.
5. Release the mouse button.

FUNCTIONS IN EXCEL

They establish relationships between two or more cells. If you want to add the values in cells A3 and A4 and put the result in cell A5, move to the cell A5 and type =A3+A4 and press Enter. The result is displayed immediately in cell A5. Another way to achieve the same result is to move to cell A5 and type +, point to cell A3, type +, then point to A4, and press Enter. The easiest way to achieve this operation is to point to A5, pick up the AutoSum button Σ on the toolbar.

The following symbols have their specific meaning in the formulae which are used in Excel.

Symbol	*Description*
:	Reference operator
,	Argument operator
–	Negation
%	Percentage sign
^	Exponent
*	Multiplication
/	Division
+	Addition
–	Subtraction
&	Text concatenation
>	Greater than
<	Less than
>=	Greater than or equal to
<=	Less than or equal to
<>	Not equal to

While working with the formulae you would come across the various errors too, which could happen due to wrong use of formula or wrong typing. The following are the common type of errors.

Error Type	*Description*
# # # #	the column is not wide enough to display the number so either widen the column, or reduce the font size or change the numeric format.
# DIV/0!	Dividing by zero is invalid
# N/A	Data is not available. It happens usually when you refer to a function or value where data is not available
# NAME?	The formula references a name that is unknown to Excel
# NUM !	The formula is using an invalid number
# REF !	A cell reference is not available may be because you deleted that cell or moved another cell onto it.
# VALUE !	The formula contains an invalid operator or argument, for example, adding a text value to a numeric value

USING AUTOSUM

It is the easiest to use formula and is available at the Standard toolbar. This is how it is used.

1. Click in the empty cell below the last entry in the column or to the right of the last entry in the row.
2. Click the AutoSum button on the Standard toolbar.
3. Press Enter to enter the formula that has automatically appeared in the cell.

Points to Remember

1. Excel looks for the range of numbers to sum above the cell you have selected for the total. If it does not find a range of numbers or if it finds text, it looks to the left for a range of numbers.
2. Excel will not skip over an empty cell when it is looking for a range of cells to sum.
3. To quickly enter sums below multiple adjacent columns, select the empty cells at the bottoms of all the columns before clicking the AutoSum button. Excel will insert a sum in each selected cell.

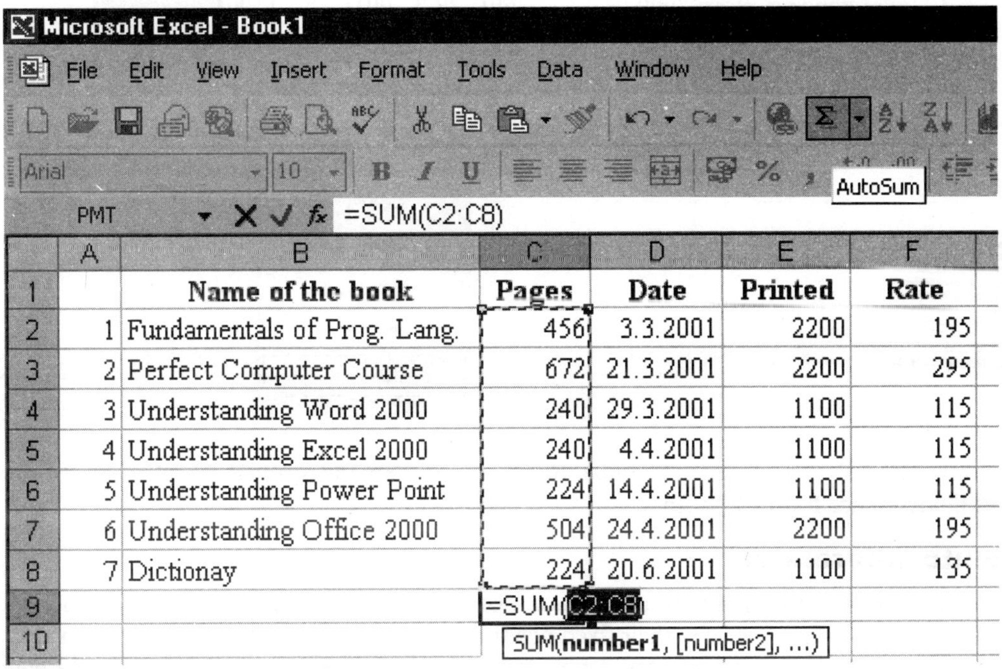

USING AUTOCALCULATE

It is very useful when you just want to total a number of columns but have the total in a particular field. The result will be displayed in Excel status bar and not in any cell. You can just view the sum. Perform the following steps to see the result.

1. Select the range whose total you want.
2. Right click at Status bar of the worksheet.
3. From the sub menu that appears, click at Sum.
4. The sum total would be displayed on the Status bar alongwith the sub menu, as shown below.

REFERENCES

By default, Excel uses relative references in its formulae. Relative references refer to cells by their position

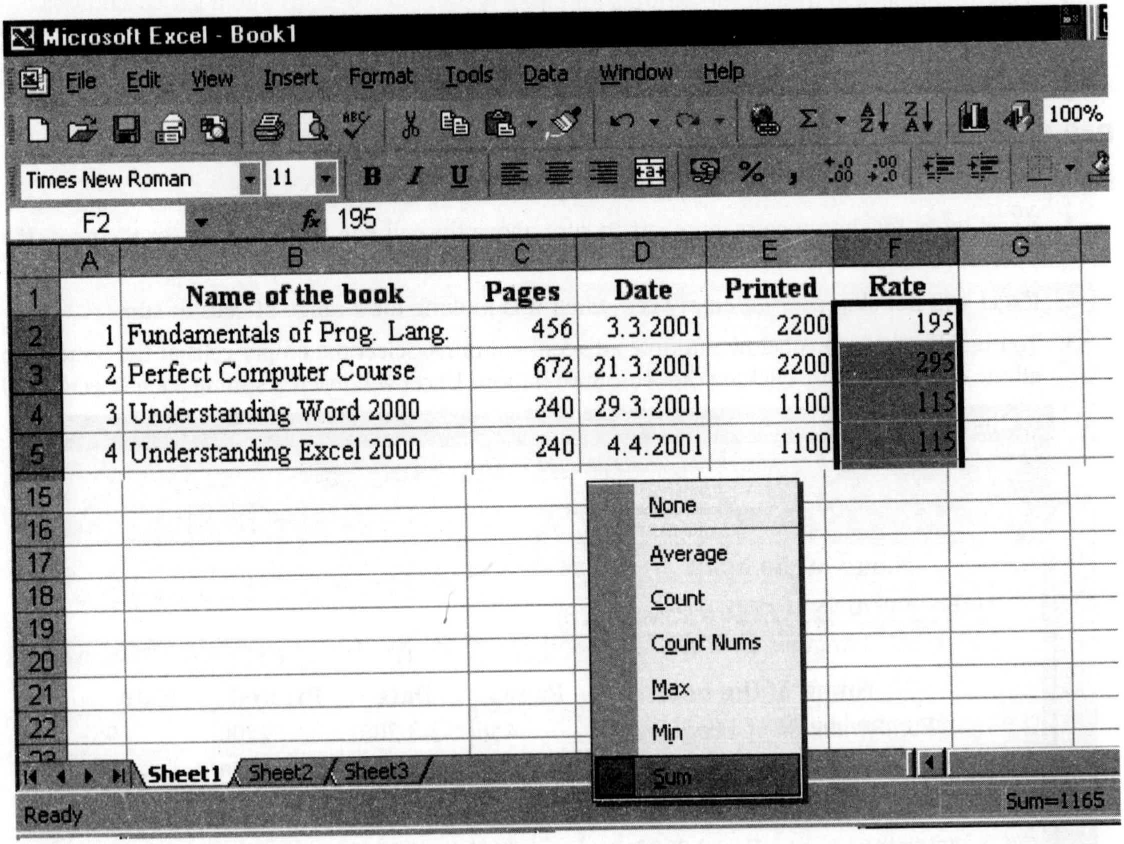

in relation to the cell containing the formula. So when you copy the formula in cell F5 to cell F6, Excel changes the reference from E5 to E6.

Absolute references

When you don't want a reference to be copied as a relative reference, you need to use an absolute reference. Absolute references refer to cells by their fixed position in the worksheet. To make a reference absolute, you add dollar signs before its column letter and now number. For example, you would enter it as $C$4:$C$9. You could then copy formula that contained this reference anywhere on the worksheet and it would always refer to the range C4:C9.

Mixed references

References can also be partially relative and partially absolute. For example, $C3 has an absolute column reference and a relative row reference and C$3 has a relative column reference and an absolute row reference.

SUM FUNCTION

The Sum function is perhaps the most commonly used of the Excel functions that carry out mathematical, statistical, financial, date, time, and other calculations.

1. Click the destination cell for the formula.

2. Type an equal sign to start the formula and then type the word SUM and a left parenthesis.
3. Drag down the column of numbers to sum, as shown below.
4. Press Enter.

Points to Remember

1. You do not need to type the close (right) parenthesis before you press Enter—Excel will do it for you.
2. Use this technique instead of AutoSum to sum ranges of cells that contain blanks.

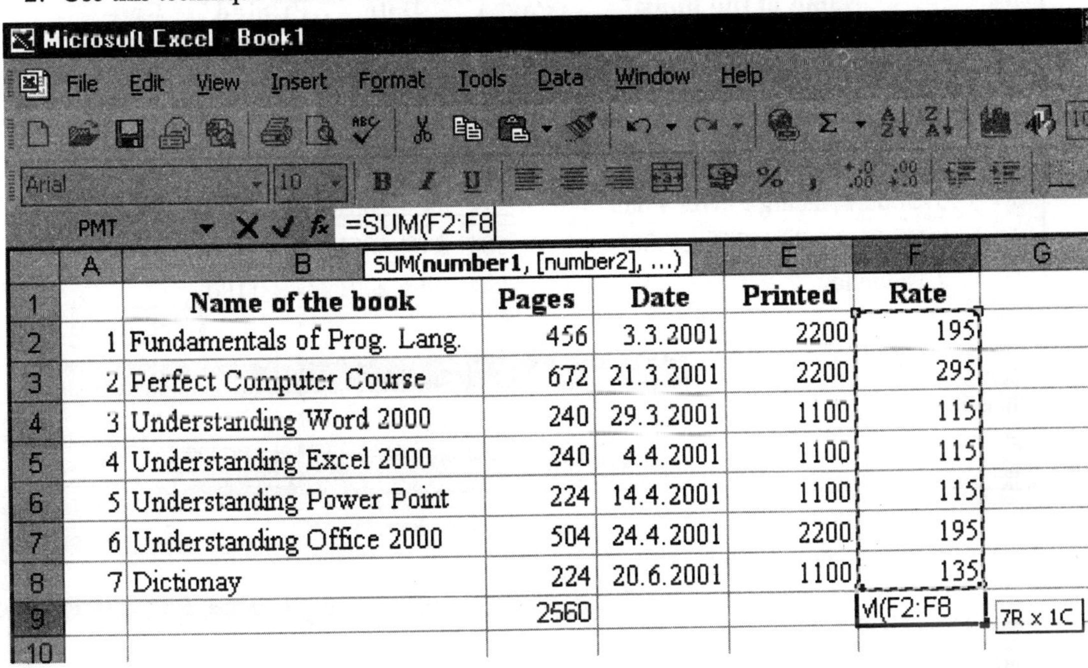

	A	B	C	D	E	F
1		Name of the book	Pages	Date	Printed	Rate
2	1	Fundamentals of Prog. Lang.	456	3.3.2001	2200	195
3	2	Perfect Computer Course	672	21.3.2001	2200	295
4	3	Understanding Word 2000	240	29.3.2001	1100	115
5	4	Understanding Excel 2000	240	4.4.2001	1100	115
6	5	Understanding Power Point	224	14.4.2001	1100	115
7	6	Understanding Office 2000	504	24.4.2001	2200	195
8	7	Dictionay	224	20.6.2001	1100	135
9			2560			M(F2:F8
10						

AVERAGE FUNCTION

You can use the Average function to calculate the average of values in cells.

1. Click the cell where you want to place the average function.
2. Type an equal sign (=) and then type the word AVERAGE and a left parenthesis.
3. Drag across the cells whose values you want to average.
4. Press Enter.
5. Blank cells are not counted in average.

FUNCTION WIZARD

Sum and Average are just two of the most commonly used functions whereas there are lots of them in Excel. You can use them to get the desired results in a flash. To get them click the Paste Function button on the Standard toolbar as your are building the formula. The Paste Function wizard takes you through the steps of building a formula.

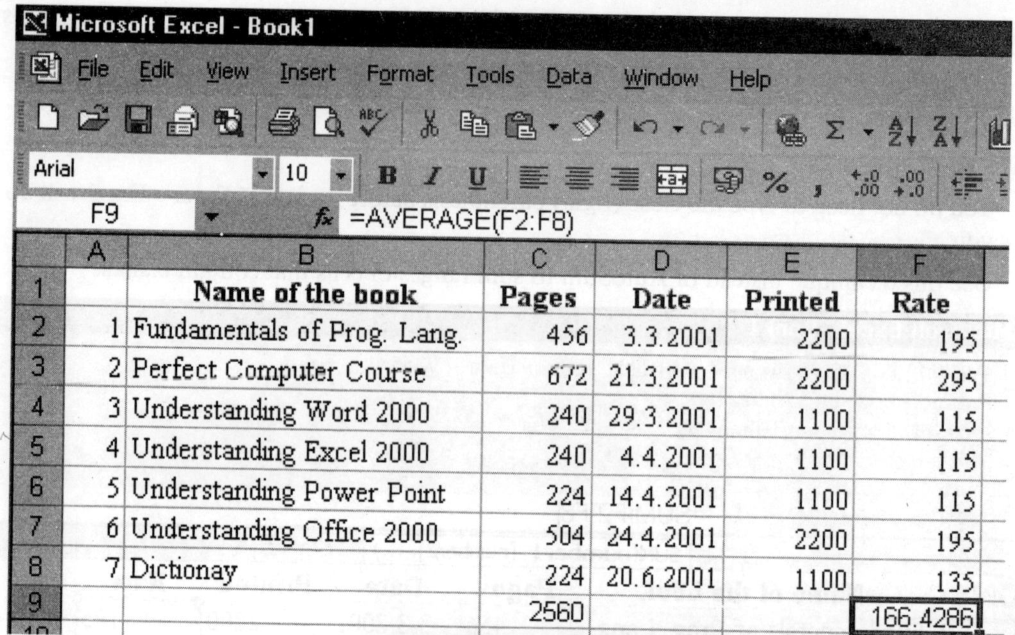

1. Click the destination cell for the formula.
2. Click the Paste Function button on the Standard toolbar.
3. In the Paste Function dialog box, select the category and then the function.
4. Click Ok.
5. Use the Paste Function Wizard to guide you in completing the formula.
6. Click Ok when you have finished.

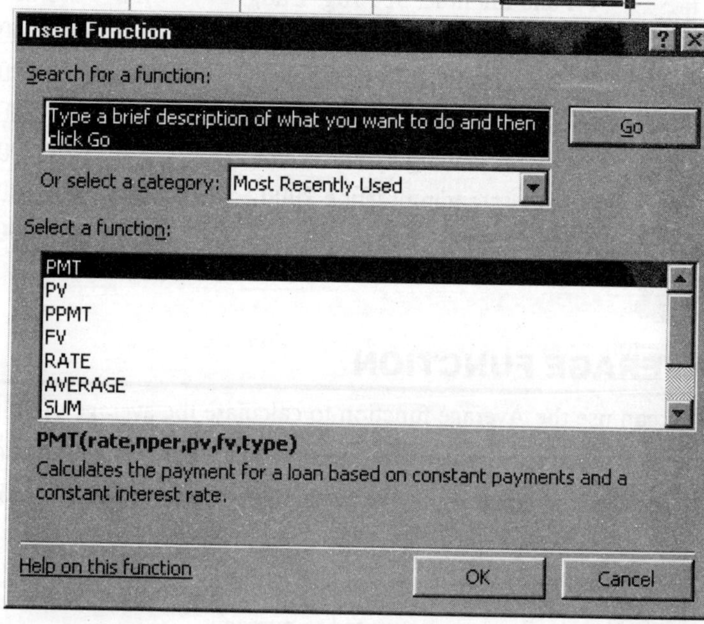

WORKSHEET FITTING ON A PAGE

If your worksheet is too large to print on one page even after you change the orientation and margins, you might consider using the Fit to option. This option shrinks the worksheet to make it fit on the specified number of pages. You can specify the document's width and height.

Follow these steps to scale a worksheet to fit on a page:

1. Open the File menu and choose Page Setup. The Page Setup dialog box appears.

2. Click the Page tab to display the Page options.
3. In the Fit to XX page wide by XX tall text boxes, enter the number of pages in which you want Excel to fit your data.
4. Click Ok to close the Page Setup dialog box and return to your worksheet. Or click the Print button in the Page Setup dialog box to display the Print dialog box, and then click Ok to print your worksheet.

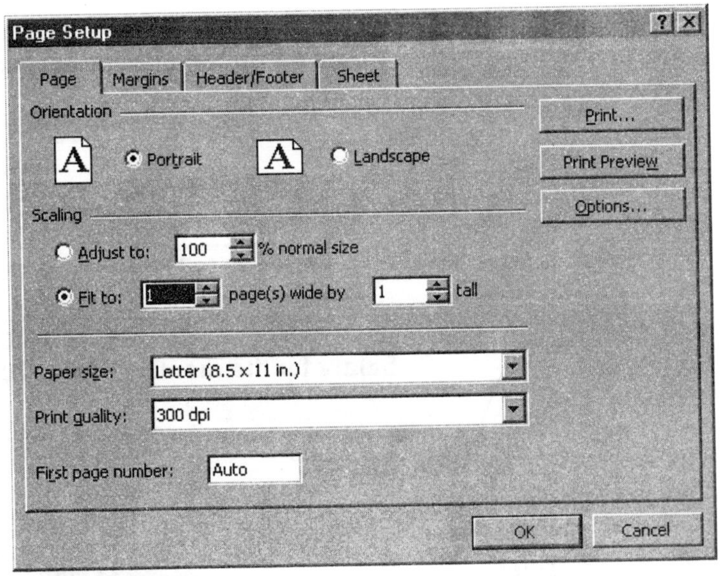

CONSOLIDATION OF WORKSHEETS

This command as the name sounds is used to consolidate the data of more than one worksheet in a single worksheet. The common data of various worksheets can be combined to create the worksheet to reflect the result of the consolidation.

This consolidation can be effected with the help of various statistical functions like Sum, Count, Avcrage, Max, Min and StdDev. This is vary useful when you have the data availble in the monthly format and you would like to combine the data in a single worksheet to create a total consolidate data for the year.

In a similar example, I have taken the salaries and deductions of 3 moths i.e., April, 2002; May 2002 and June 2002. I have tried to consolidate the data in a new worksheet.

Let us see how this is done.

The following data has been taken for consolidation. This data is various sheets of the same file.

	A	B	C	D	E	F
1		**Salary for the month of April, 2002**				
2						
3	**No.**	**Name**	**Salary**	**Deduction**	**Nett. Payable**	
4	1	Sachin Tendulkar	10,000	2,000	8,000	
5	2	Saurav Ganguly	12,000	1,000	11,000	
6	3	Rahul Dravid	11,000	1,500	9,500	
7		**Total**	**33,000**	**4,500**	**28,500**	

1. Open a blank sheet and type the heading for consolidation, for example, the consolidation results for the month of April, May and June, 2002.
2. Make cell A4 the active cell.
3. From from the Data menu choose the Consolidate command.
4. This gives rise to Consolidate dialog box, as shown on next page.

	A	B	C	D	E	F
1		Salary for the month of May, 2002				
2						
3	No.	Name	Salary	Deduction	Nett. Payable	
4	1	Sachin Tendulkar	10,000	1,000	9,000	
5	2	Saurav Ganguly	12,000	2,000	10,000	
6	3	Rahul Dravid	11,000	1,500	9,500	
7		Total	33,000	4,500	28,500	

	A	B	C	D	E	F
1		Salary for the month of June, 2002				
2						
3	No.	Name	Salary	Deduction	Nett. Payable	
4	1	Sachin Tendulkar	10,000	500	9,500	
5	2	Saurav Ganguly	12,000	700	11,300	
6	3	Rahul Dravid	11,000	0	11,000	
7		Total	33,000	1,200	31,800	

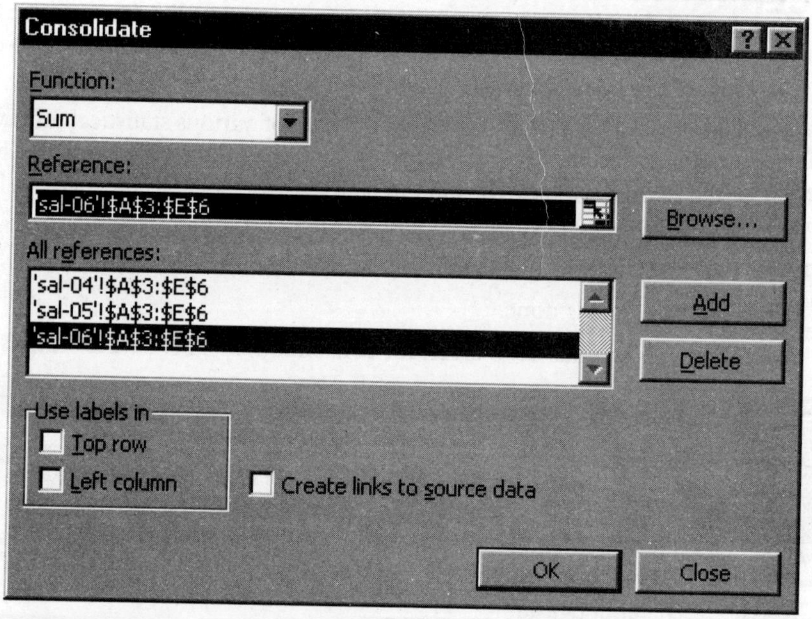

5. Here the Sum function is there by default. You can choose to have another function like Average, if you want to have average of the fields. In all cases the corresponding cells of each of the ranges that you specify in the next step would take effect.
6. Click the Reference box and then indicate the first reference by choosing the sal-04 tab and selecting the range of cells to be consolidated. In this case they are from A3 to E6. See how it is reflected in the Reference.
7. After choosing the range, click at Add to register it in the All references box.
8. Similarly do it for all the months and their ranges and have them stored in the All Reference column.
9. If you are using labels, make sure to point them out. In our case they are at the top of all the columns, so we will select the option Top row.
10. Click Ok to have the data consolidated in the worksheet.

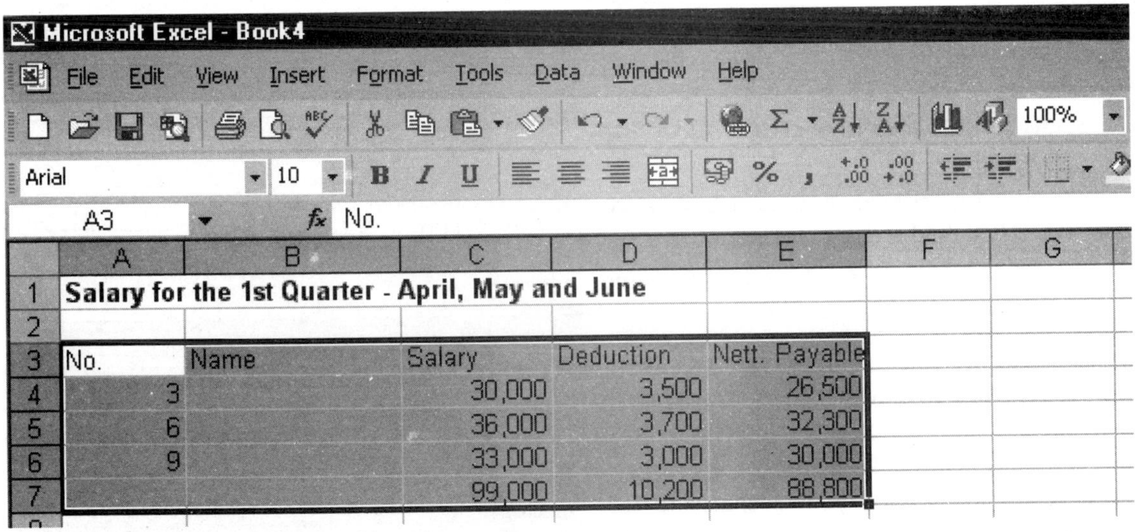

	A	B	C	D	E
1	Salary for the 1st Quarter - April, May and June				
2					
3	No.	Name	Salary	Deduction	Nett. Payable
4	3		30,000	3,500	26,500
5	6		36,000	3,700	32,300
6	9		33,000	3,000	30,000
7			99,000	10,200	88,800

11. The consolidated data is shown above.

SCENARIOS MANAGER

Human mind is made of What-if situations. The same what-if can be applied to your worksheet to see if the results of the selection displays the good or bad results.

Each time you change the data, the previous solution is lost. To address this limitation, the Scenario Manager helps you keep track of multiple what-if models. Using the Scenarios manager, you can create new forecasting scenarios, view existing scenario, run scenario management commands and display consolidated scenario reports. Let us start with creating a worksheet and then apply the scenario to it.

On the next page a worksheet is shown which has been taken as an example for creating a scenario. Here the figures are very simple and calculated. If you want you can use the constant figures too. Next we perform the following steps to create and view the scenario.

1. Click at Scenarios in the Tools menu.

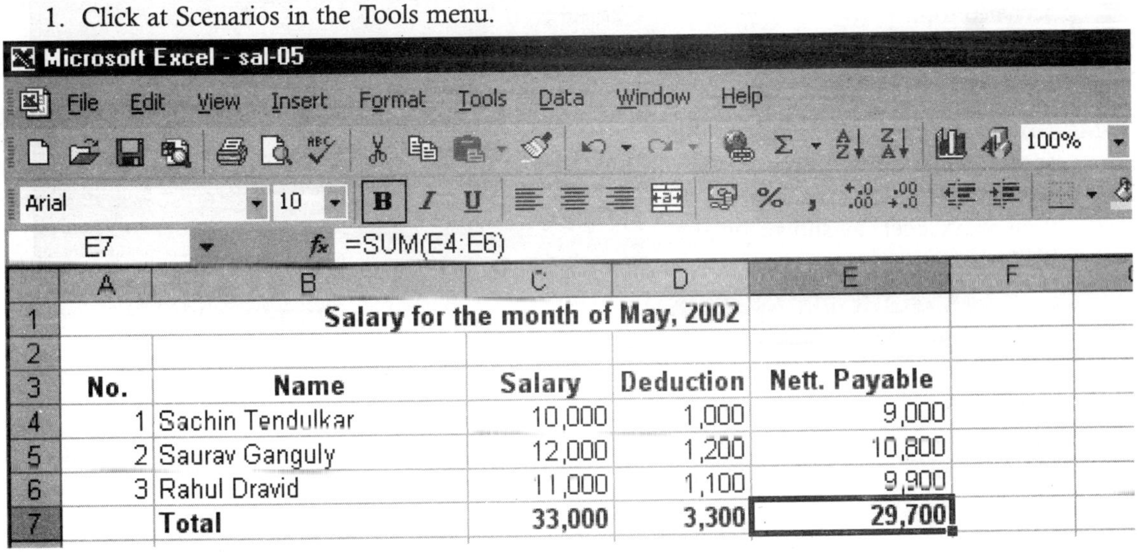

	A	B	C	D	E
1		Salary for the month of May, 2002			
2					
3	No.	Name	Salary	Deduction	Nett. Payable
4	1	Sachin Tendulkar	10,000	1,000	9,000
5	2	Saurav Ganguly	12,000	1,200	10,800
6	3	Rahul Dravid	11,000	1,100	9,900
7		Total	33,000	3,300	29,700

2. A Scenario manager dialog box would appear on the screen, as shown on the next page.
3. As the dialog box says, click at Add to add a scenario.
4. This gives rise to another dialog box, which is called Add scenario.
5. In this dialog box, you have to firstly name the screnario.
6. I have named it as Good.
7. You can type the cell names or choose them by clicking at those cells. I have chosen cells from E4 to E7.
8. Click OK to add your scenario to the Scenario Manager. You'll see the Scenario Values dialog box, which asks you for your model's variables. The default values are the numbers that were already in the cells.
9. Type the various values which you want to see in the scenario.
10. Click Add to create a second scenario. If you do not want another set, just click at Ok.
11. This will return you to the scenario manager with your scenario added to it.
12. As mentioned you can add another scenario to it.
13. Now we will see how this scenario works. For this click at Show.
14. Excel substitutes the values in the scenario for the variables in your worksheet and displays the results in your worksheet, as shown on the next page.

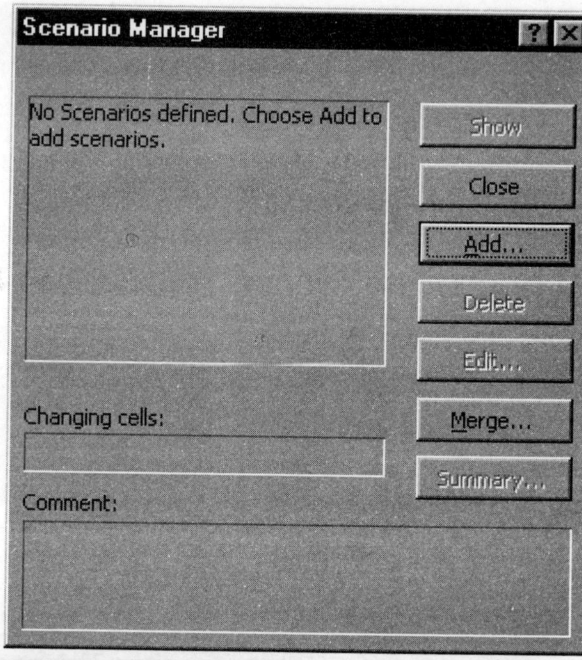

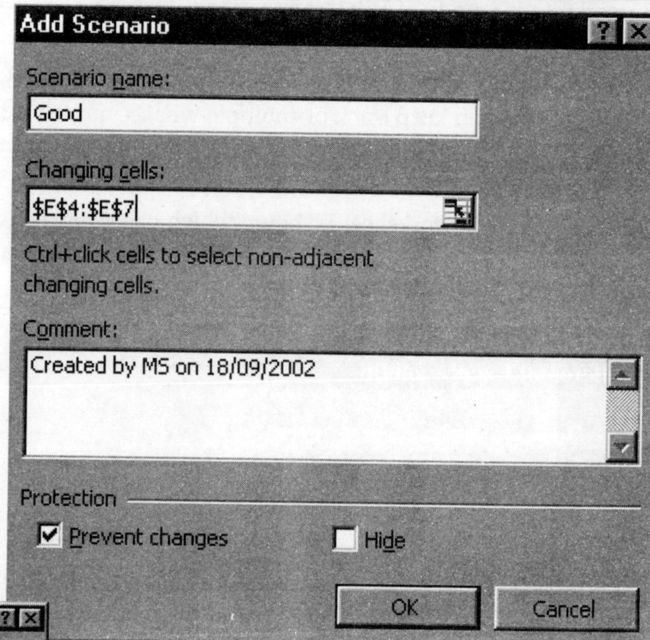

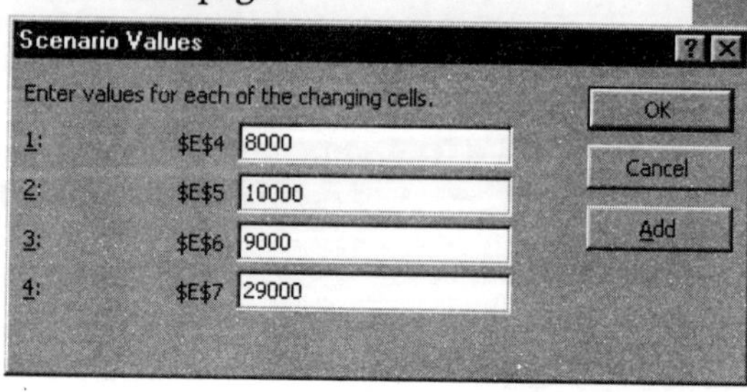

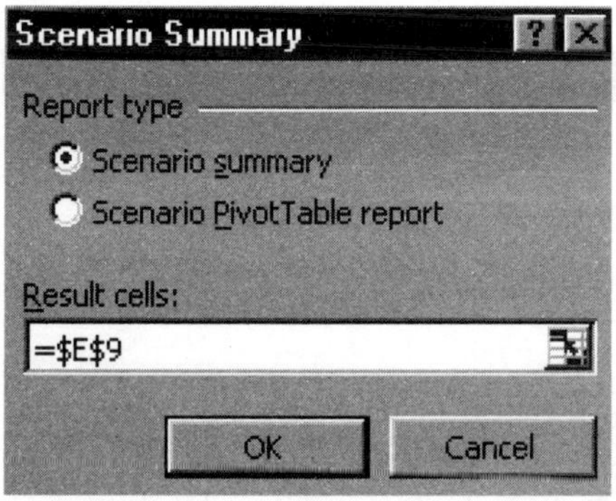

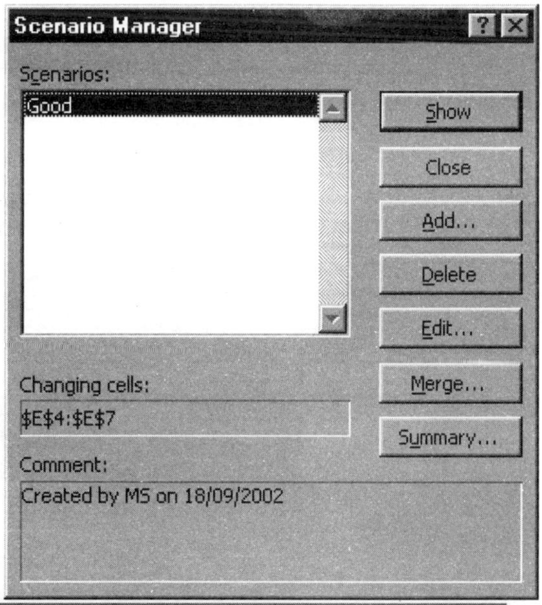

15. Next step is of having the Scenario Reports.
16. For this you choose the button called Summary from the Scenario Manager dialog box.
17. For this you will have to click at a cell where the summary would be placed.

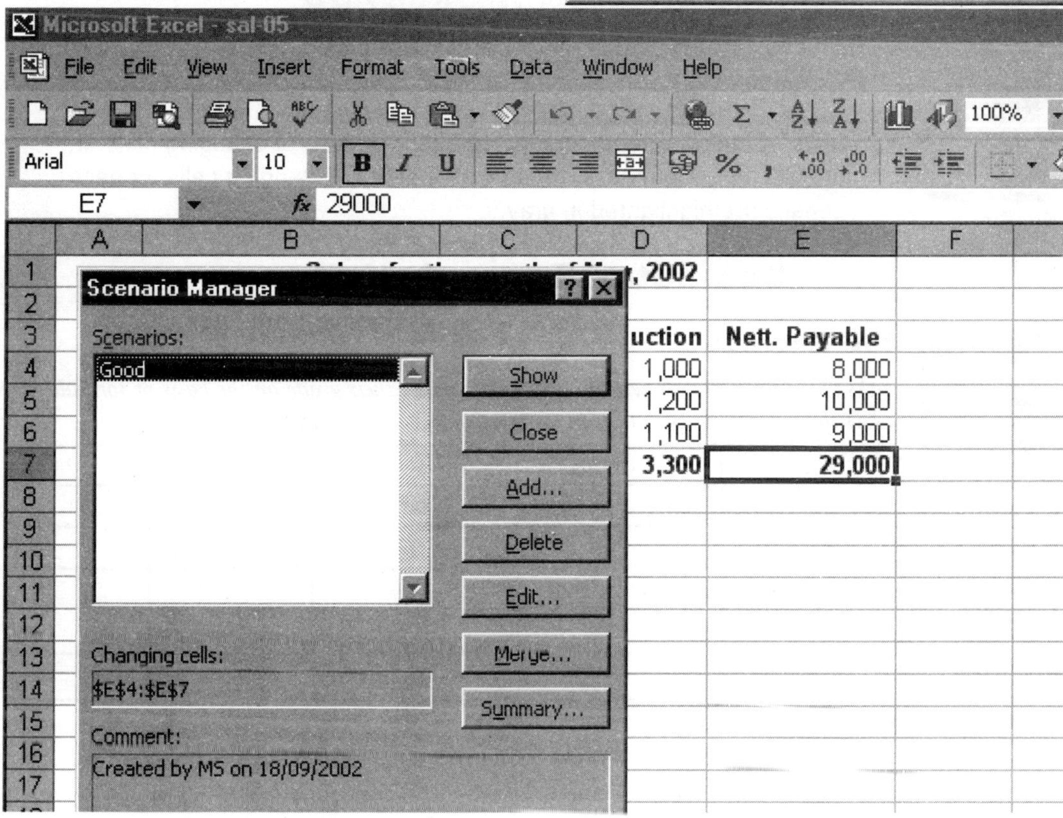

18. You also have to define whether you want the summary or the PivtoTable report. Click any one of the two.
19. I have taken here Scenario summary and have given E9 as the cell for showing the results.

20. The net results will be shown as below.

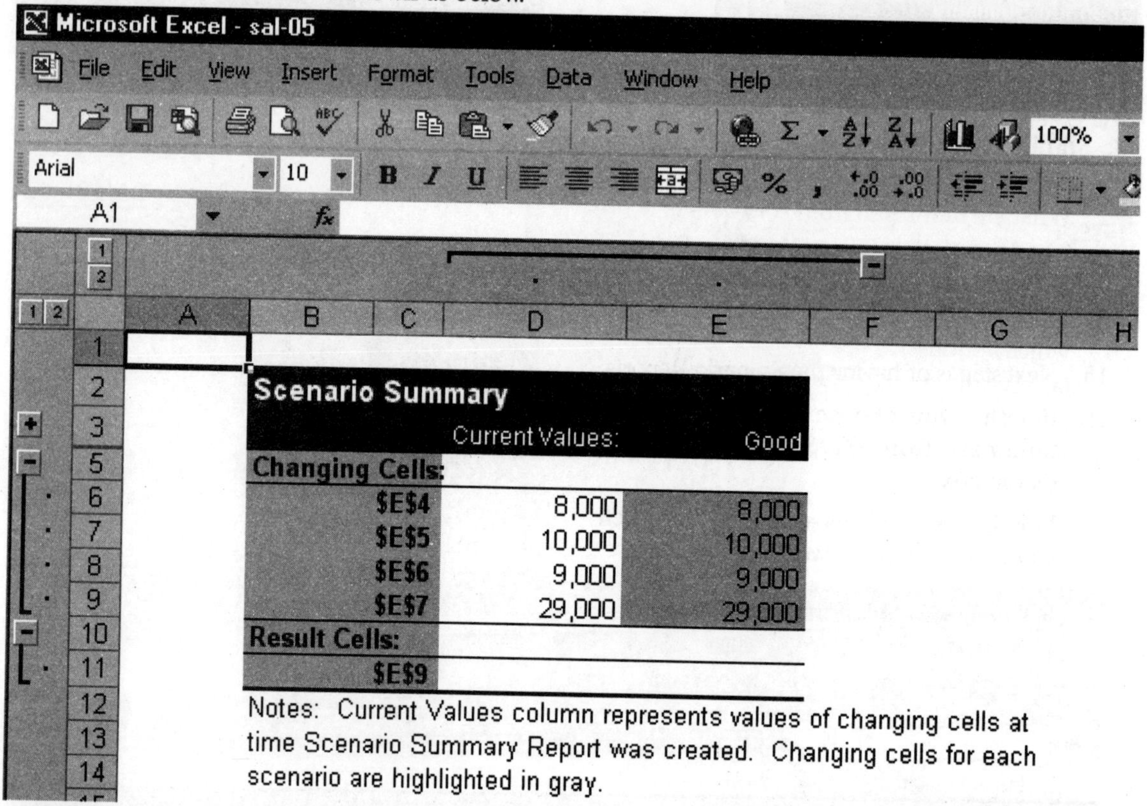

Computer Room Activity

Calculating the Average

Following are the marks obtained by the students of a class, calculate their grade on the basis of formula given below and also calculate the average marks taken by the students in that subject:

Student	*English*	*Maths*	*Hindi*	*Total*	*Grade*
Sachin	*60*	*75*	*55*		
Rahul	*65*	*70*	*50*		
Sauvav	*60*	*65*	*55*		
Yuvraj	*50*	*75*	*70*		
Average					

Formula for calculating the Grade is.

If total marks > 250	*Grade: E*
If total marks <250 and > 200	*Grade A*
If total marks <200 and > 150	*Grade B*
If total makrs <150	*Fail*

Create the spreadsheet, calculate Total, calculate Grade and then calculate the avearage in each subject.

Multiple Choice Questions

1. For opening and closing of the file in Excel you can use which bar.
   (a) Formatting (b) Standard
   (c) Title
2. What are numbered from A to Z, etc?
   (a) Rows (b) Cells
   (c) Columns
3. You can move around the worksheet using which buttons?
   (a) Scroll (b) Logic
   (c) Start
4. For making the text bold in the cell, you use B in which bar.
   (a) Standard (b) Formatting
   (c) Title
5. For getting the short menu on the screen, you click which button of the mouse.
   (a) Right button (b) Left button
   (c) Centre button
6. Charts are created using which option.
   (a) Chart Wizard (b) Pivto Table
   (c) Pie Chart
7. For editing the chart, you __________ the chart itself.
   (a) Click (b) Delete
   (c) Double click
8. In Excel formula starts with __________.
   (a) = sign (b) + sign
   (c) - sign
9. In Excel worksheets are given _____ extension.
   (a) .xls (b) .doc
   (c) .bmp
10. In Microsoft Excel, you use _______ for calcualtions.
    (a) Formula (b) Row
    (c) Cell
11. Formula which can be used directly from the Standard toolbar is
    (a) AutoSum (b) Auto
    (c) Sum
12. The result of AutoCalculate is shown at ___ bar.
    (a) Standard (b) Formatting
    (c) Status

Descriptive Type Questions

1. Describe various methods of starting Excel?
2. Describe the various components of the Excel worksheet window.
3. Describe the method of copying formula.
4. Describe the process of saving a worksheet.
5. Describe how would you insert a chart in the worksheet.
6. Describe the working of the Chart Wizard.
7. Describe the process of modifying chart.
8. How would you add data to the chart?
9. Describe the process of creating a Pivot Table.
10. How would you audit a worksheet? Explain.
11. Describe the process of inserting a comment in the worksheet.
12. Describe how the logical functions work in worksheet.
13. Describe how would you put Headers and Footers in a worksheet.
14. How would you merge two worksheets?
15. Describe the method of putting Outlines to worksheets.

22

Microsoft Power Point

INTRODUCTION

Microsoft Office has a powerful presentation program called PowerPoint. It helps in creating charts, graphs, slides, handouts, overheads, and various other formats of presentations which any office would require. You can also create a slide show of the presentations you create. You can even have these presentation put on the Web too. There are some ready made presentations for you to adopt to your likings. This way you can create a presentation very fast.

It is important to know that PowerPoint deals with various terms which you would probably not find them with other software. So I just explain them before going further to start the software.

Slides

These are the heart of every presentation you create in PowerPoint; they can be presented as overheads, as 35 mm slides, or electronically on-screen. Slides can contain text, graphics, charts and even sound and video.

Handouts

These are printed copies of your presentation. You can have two, three or six slides per handout per page and you can add additional elements, such as text or graphics. For example, you might want each page of the handout to include your company logo.

Outlines

These contain text of your slide presentation. You can enter text for your slides directly on the slides or in the outline.

Placeholders

These let you quickly add the type of element you are likely to put in a particular portion of the slide. When you pick a layout for your presentation, placeholders for such elements as text, graphics and charts are included.

Speaker's Notes

These provide the presenter with a page that corresponds to each slide and contains a small image of the slide along with additional notes.

Freehand Drawing

As you give electronic presentation on your computer screen, you can now use the freehand drawing tool to add temporary annotations to your slides. If you are good at it, you can even draw on your own.

Objects

These are the individual elements that make up presentations. Text elements—such as titles, bulleted lists, graphics and charts—are individual objects and can be moved, sized & rotated other objects in a presentation.

But, first thing first, let us start PowerPoint and proceed to learn.

STARTING POWERPOINT

You can start PowerPoint by one of the following methods:

Using the Start Menu

1. Click on Start button. The start menu will appear.
2. Click at Programs.
3. Click on Microsoft PowerPoint.

Using Shortcut

You can use this feature if the icon of the software has been created and is put on the desktop.

1. First, locate the Microsoft PowerPoint shortcut icon.
2. When you find it, position the mouse over the icon and click it to open the software.

Using Microsoft Office Bar

You can use Office toolbar too for starting the software.

1. Click at the Microsoft PowerPoint icon on the office toolbar.

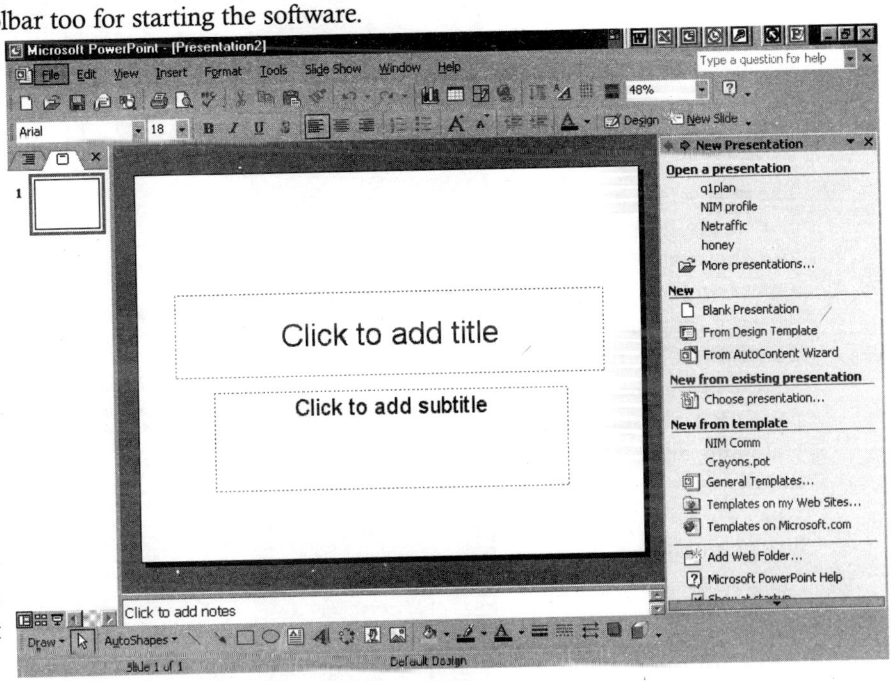

In all these cases you will end up with having the PowerPoint opening desktop on the screen, which is shown here.

There are various ways of creating a presentation in PowerPoint and the most popular and easy way to create one using AutoContent Wizard.

PRESENTATION BY AUTOCONTENT WIZARD

The Wizard would create for you a complete presentation, just add few graphics and text here and there, your presentation is complete. To create a presentation using AutoContent, do the following:

1. Select New from the File menu.
2. Select AutoContent from the General Panel or Click at From AutoContent Wizard in the Task Pane, as shown above.

3. The first screen of the AutoContent Wizard appears on the screen.

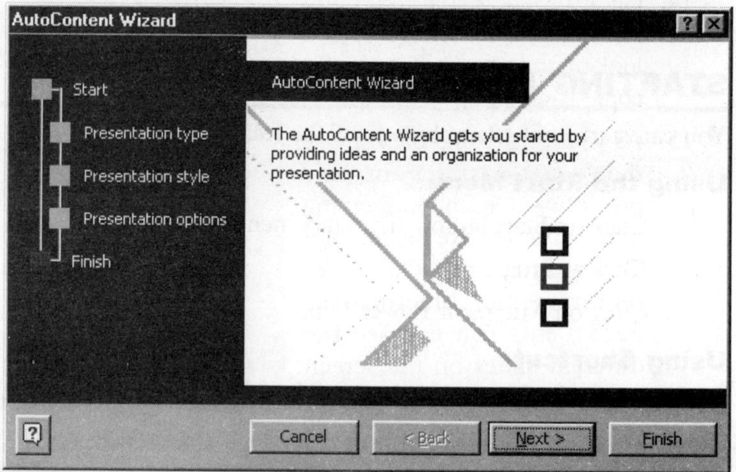

4. Click Next
5. The next screen of the Wizard allows you to choose a type of presentation you want. I have chosen here the Selling a Product or Service from the Sales/Marketing heading.
6. Click Next.
7. The next screen allows you to select the type of output you want. I have selected here the On-screen presentation.

   Various other options are also there which are shown here on the screen.

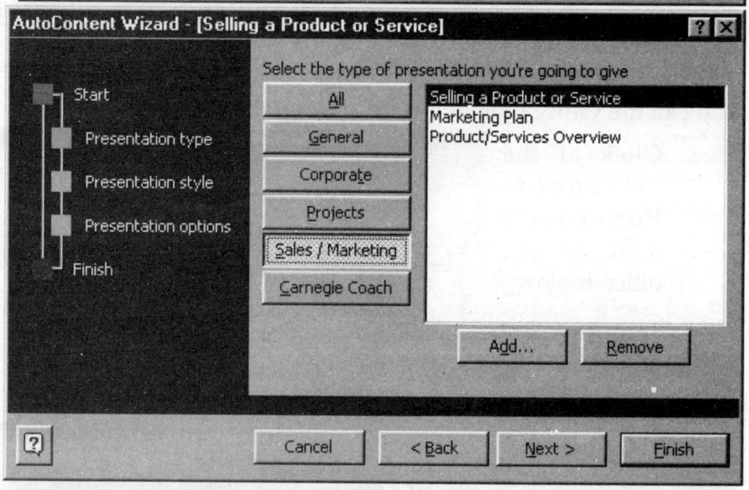

8. Click Next.
9. The next screen asks you to give title of the presentation and the text you want to appear on the footer page. I have put them as Selling of Toothpaste and New Toothpaste in the market. I have also chosen for the Date and Slide number to the displayed. Of course, you can have your own header and footer.

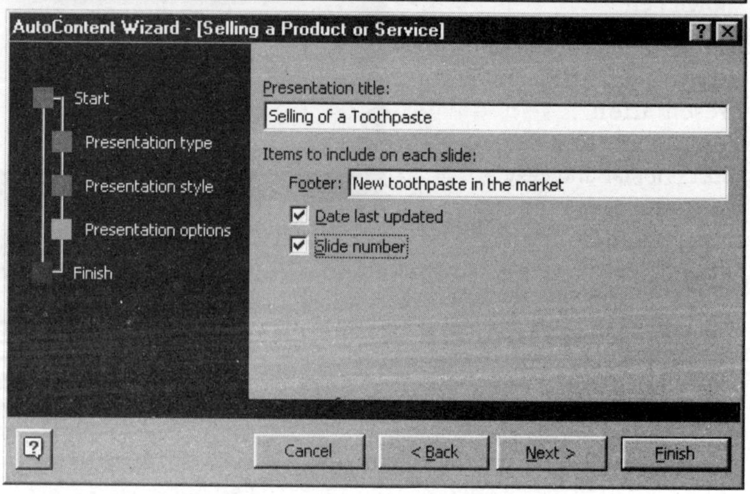

10. Click Next.
11. Click at Finish to end the AutoContent Wizard session.
12. The presentation you have chosen can be seen on the screen.
13. As you can see from the presentation, the left hand side of the screen contains text of the presentation and on the right hand side you can see the presentation.

14. Click at Slide Show to see full screen presentation as it would look on the screen. Press Esc to come back.
15. As you can see that there are as many as 8 slides in this presentation, each representing different head, like Selling of a Toothpaste, Customer requirements, Meeting the needs, etc. You can see the different slides on the screen when you move the vertical bar on the right hand side of the presentation.

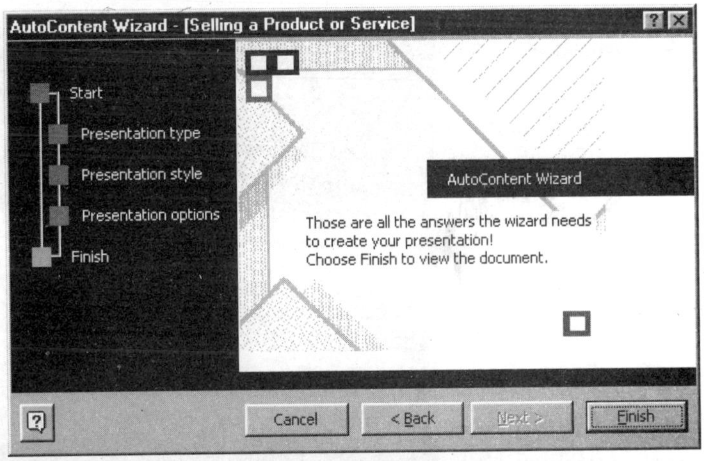

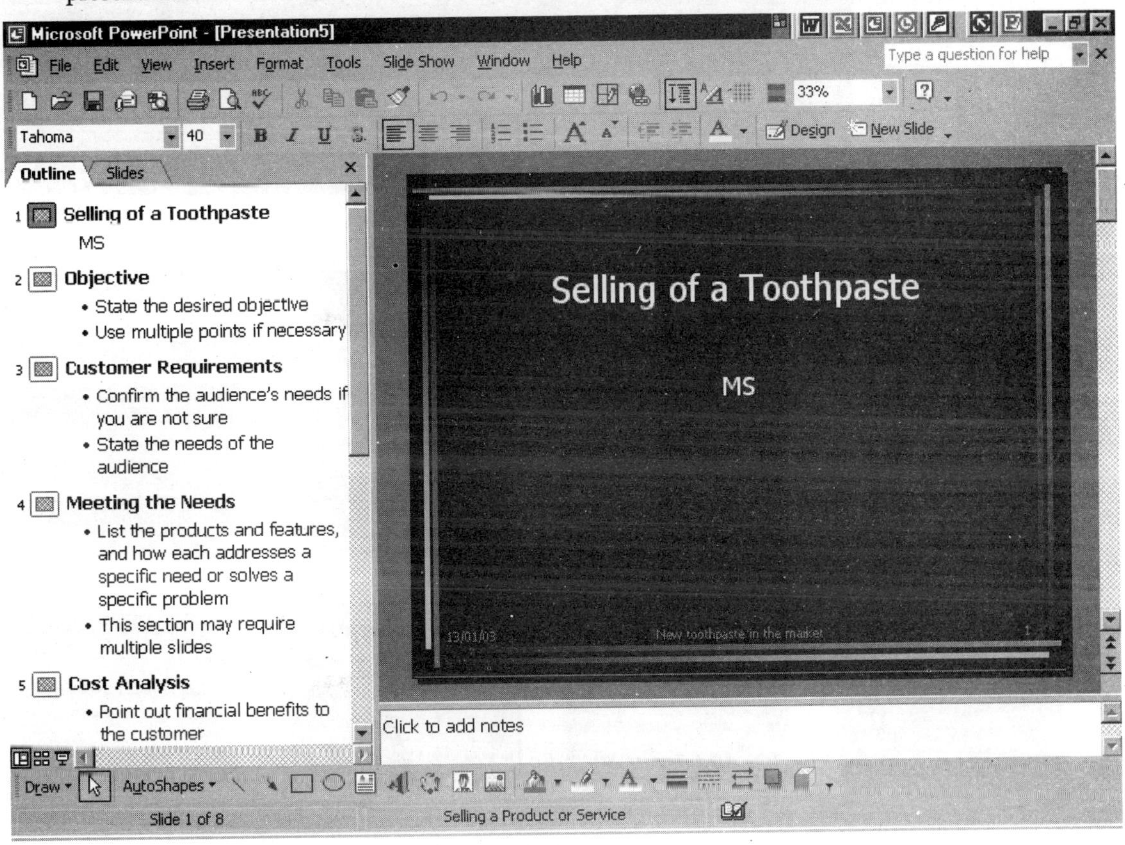

16. Here I have shown the slide numbers 4 and 7.
17. By choosing the Slide Sorter view you can see all the slides on the screen but in very small form. Slide sorter view of our presentation is also shown.

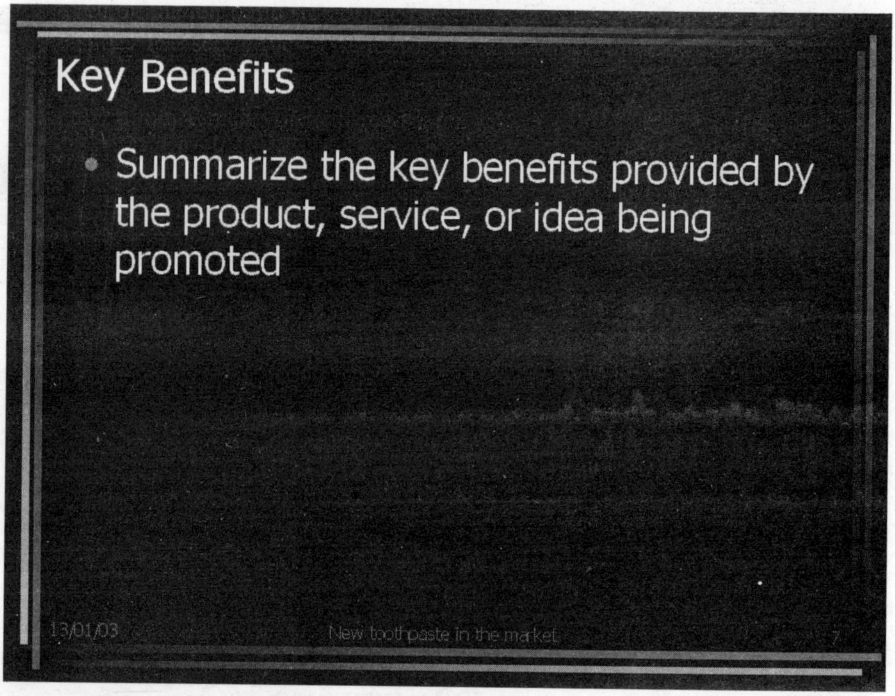

Points to Remember

1. Footer appear at the bottom of each page on the presentation.
2. You can skip the intermediatory steps by clicking at Finish in the first dialog box of the Wizard.
3. Each presentation is given a look which is preset. You can change this according to your liking.

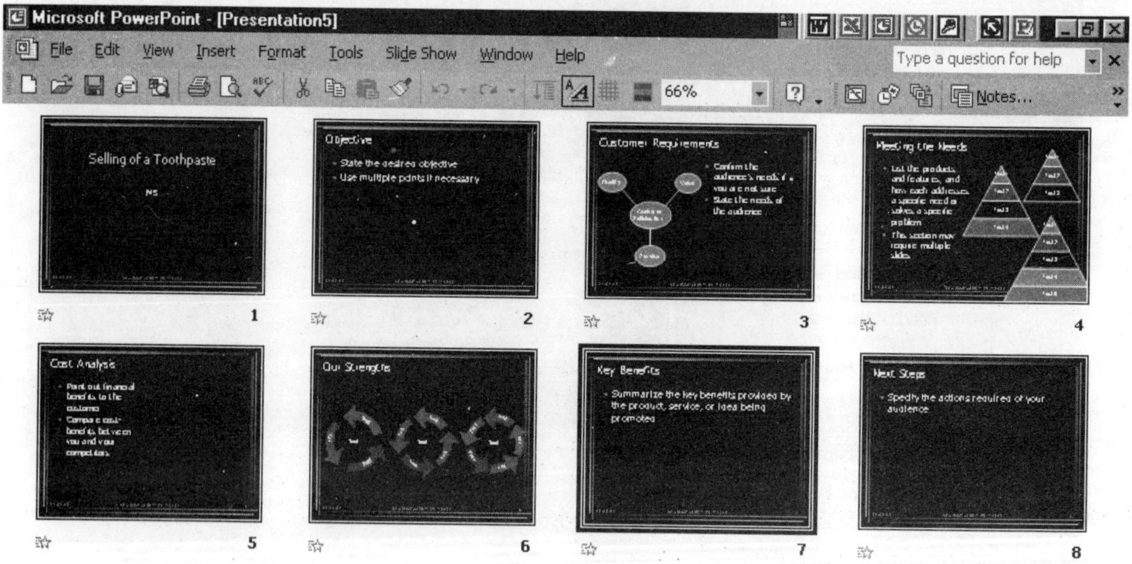

4. Two level of text is given on the left hand side of the presentation. The one with the serial number is the heading of the slide. The second level of text is the text which appears as the part of the presentation.
5. You can change this text about which you will read later.

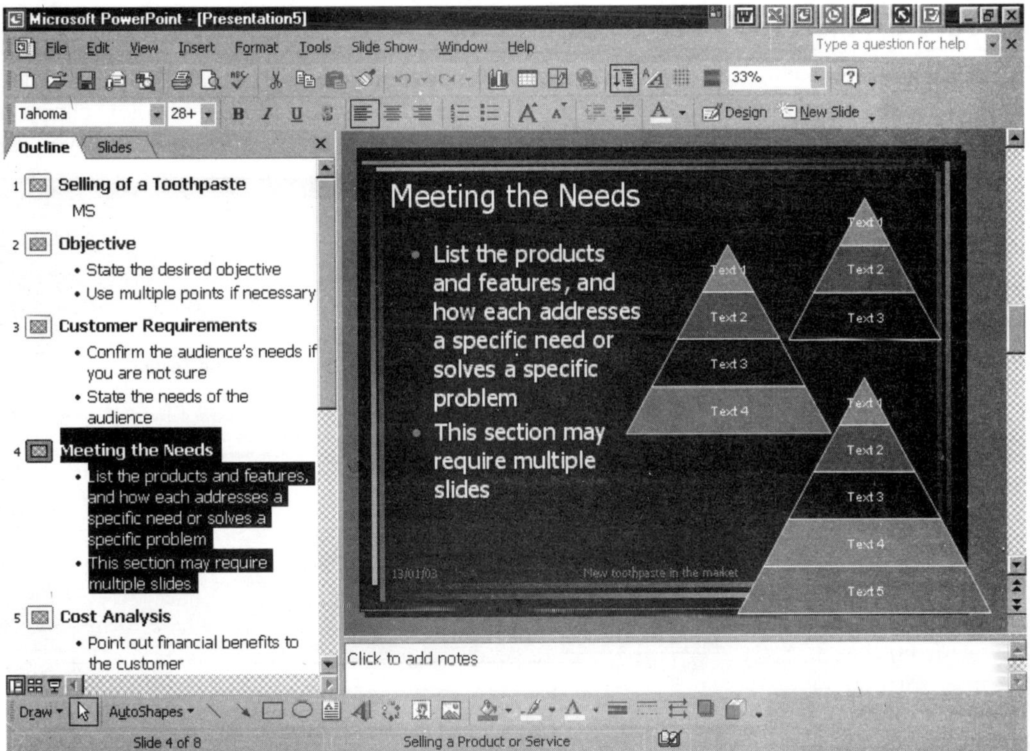
Microsoft PowerPoint - [Presentation5]
File Edit View Insert Format Tools Slide Show Window Help
Type a question for help
33%
Tahoma 28+
Design New Slide
Outline Slides
1 Selling of a Toothpaste
MS
2 Objective
• State the desired objective
• Use multiple points if necessary
3 Customer Requirements
• Confirm the audience's needs if you are not sure
• State the needs of the audience
4 Meeting the Needs
• List the products and features, and how each addresses a specific need or solves a specific problem
• This section may require multiple slides
5 Cost Analysis
• Point out financial benefits to the customer
Meeting the Needs
• List the products and features, and how each addresses a specific need or solves a specific problem
• This section may require multiple slides
Text 1
Text 2
Text 3
Text 4
Text 5
Click to add notes
Draw AutoShapes
Slide 4 of 8
Selling a Product or Service

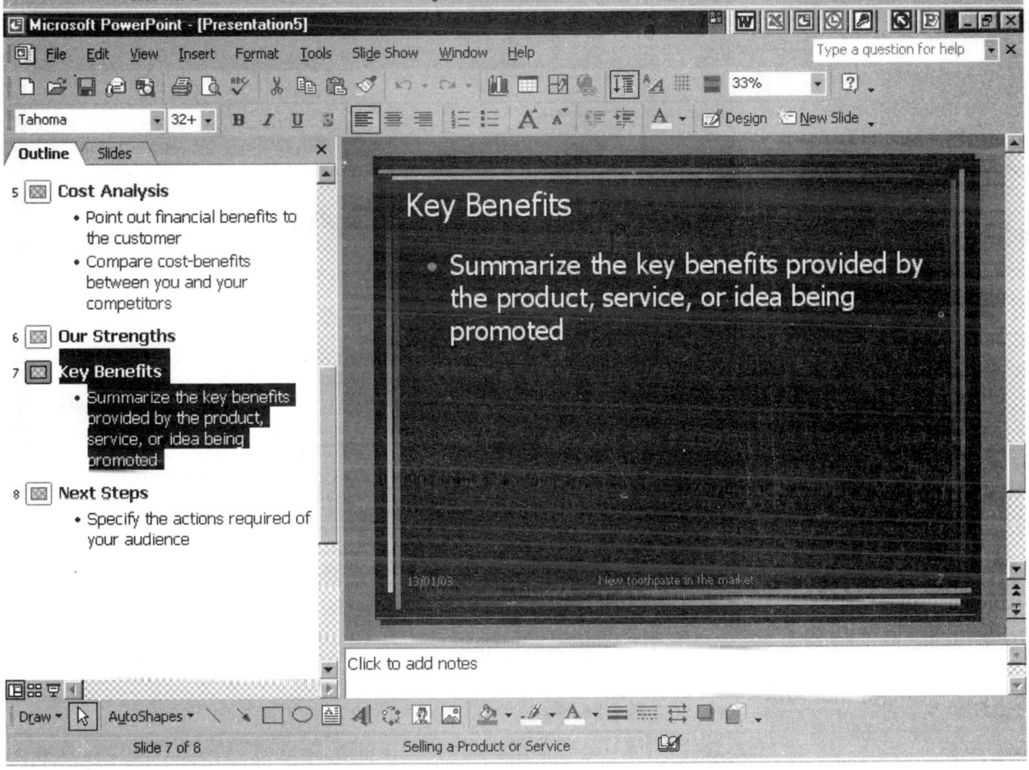
Microsoft PowerPoint - [Presentation5]
File Edit View Insert Format Tools Slide Show Window Help
Type a question for help
33%
Tahoma 32+
Design New Slide
Outline Slides
5 Cost Analysis
• Point out financial benefits to the customer
• Compare cost-benefits between you and your competitors
6 Our Strengths
7 Key Benefits
• Summarize the key benefits provided by the product, service, or idea being promoted
8 Next Steps
• Specify the actions required of your audience
Key Benefits
• Summarize the key benefits provided by the product, service, or idea being promoted
Click to add notes
Draw AutoShapes
Slide 7 of 8
Selling a Product or Service

CREATING PRESENTATION FROM TEMPLATE

As I had mentioned earlier that the software has available presentations, these are called Templates. These can be used for creating your own. Templates can provide either the graphic design and color scheme of a presentation (design template) or suggest content and structure, using a set of slides whose text you can edit.

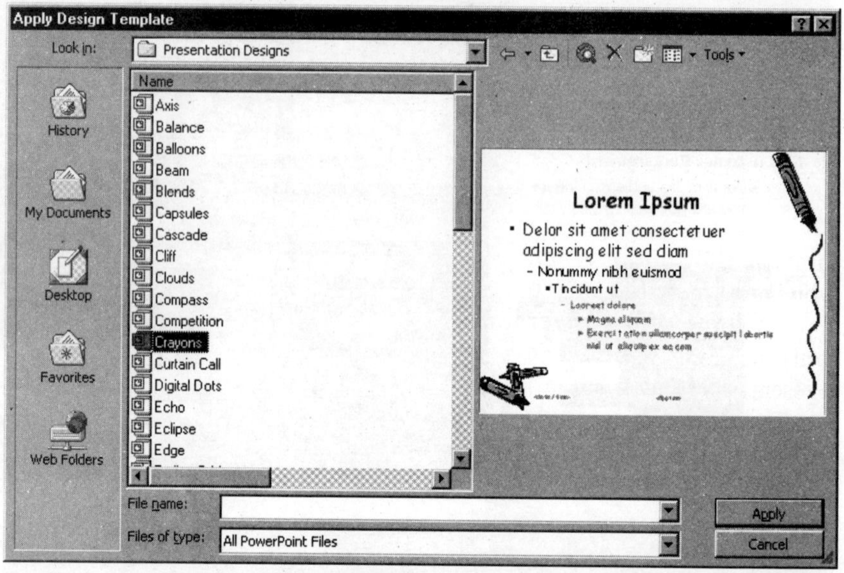

1. Select New from the File menu.
2. Select Design Templates option on the New Presentation dialog box or select From Design Templates from the Task Pane.
3. I have chosen here the option of Crayons from the various options available under Presentation Templates.
4. You would be given a choice to choose the type of slide. Here you can type the title of your choice and then add the subtitle of your choice.
5. I have type some text as shown.
6. From Insert menu, click at New Slide.
7. A new blank slide will appear.
8. This way you can keep adding slides and make your own presentation.
9. You can see its Slide Show, which you will learn later.

CREATING A NEW PRESENTATION

Another method of creating presentation is by using the option of New presentation using the Blank

presentation option. When you start a new presentation, PowerPoint offers several options in the New Presentation dialog box or in the Task Pane. You can select an option of text and graphics to make show on the screen.

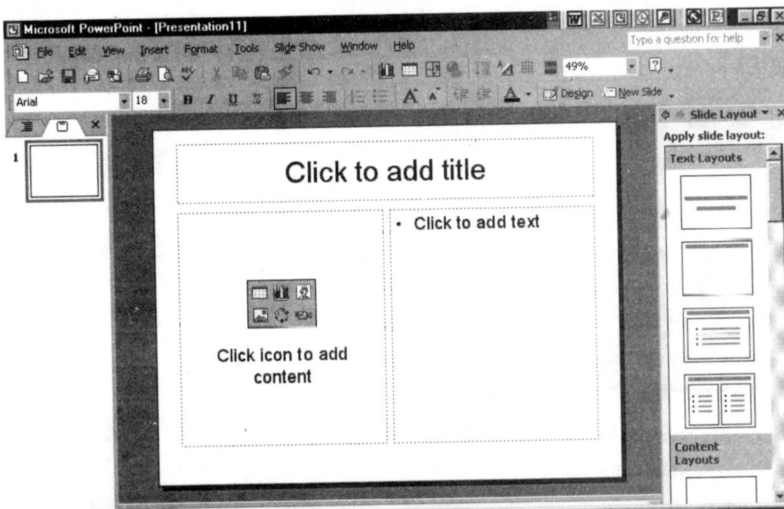

1. Select New from the File menu.
2. Select Blank presentation option from the General Panel or from the Task Pane.
3. A new slide option dialog box, is given to you on screen. Select the type of slide you want and click Ok. In this case I have chosen the one with text & clip art and it is shown on the small window on the screen.

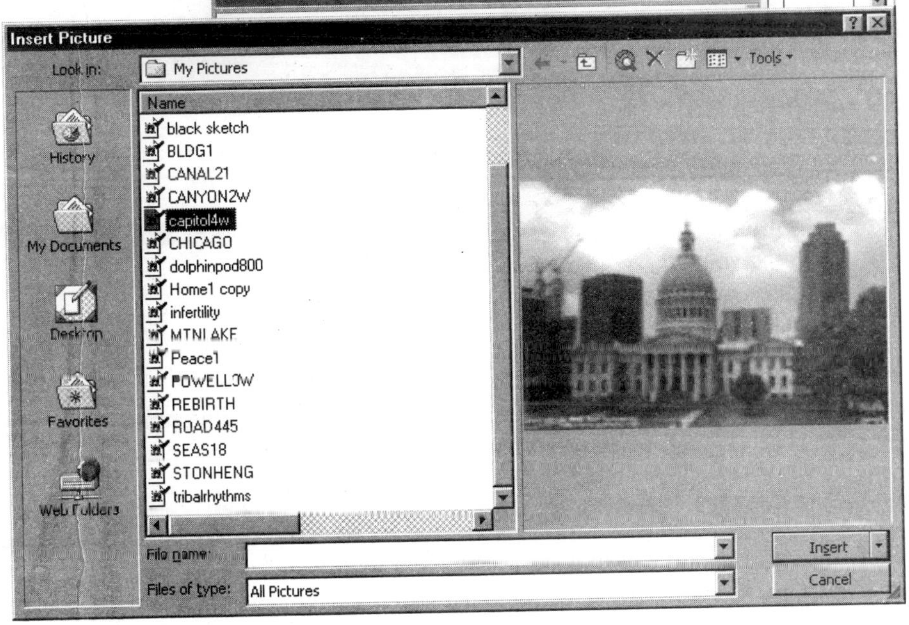

4. Add the text for the title.
5. In the second box type the text which you want to type.
6. The graphic icon allows you to add graphics of various types, i.e., Table, Chart, Clip Art, Picture, Diagram and Media Clip.
7. I have chosen to add a Picture here and have chosen the picture of Capitol Hill.
8. See how it looks when inserted in the slide on the next page.
9. On the otherhand you can choose a different option of text, graphics and even the type of slide too.

SAVING PRESENTATIONS

You can save the presentation you are working on by choosing Save Options from File menu or by clicking the Save button on the Standard toolbar. If you are Saving the presentation for the first time, Save As dialog box appears where you have to enter the file name.

Speed up Saving a Presentation

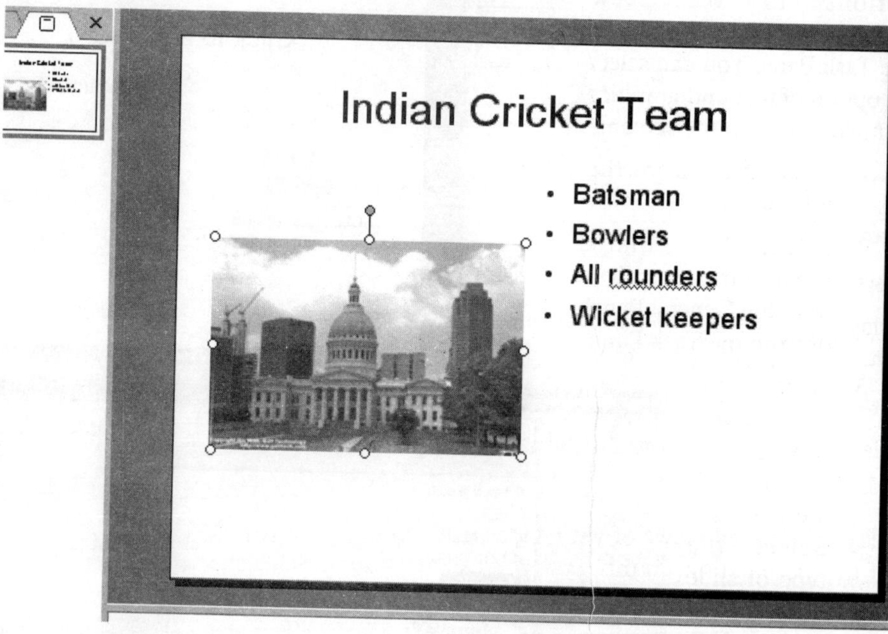

1. On the Tools menu, click at Options to get the options dialog box.
2. Click on the Save panel.
3. To Save only the changes to a presentation, select the Allow fast saves check box and then continue to Save as you work on the presentation.
4. To save a complete presentation, clear the Allow fast save check box when you finish working on the presentation and then save it. A full save occurs when this check box is clear.

If you select the Allow fast, PowerPoint saves only the changes to a presentation. Saving only the changes takes less time than a full save, in which PowerPoint saves the complete revised presentation.

POWERPOINT VIEWS

There are different ways of looking at the presentations. These are called the views. I had mentioned about some views earlier. There are as many as 5 different views in which you can see your presentation.

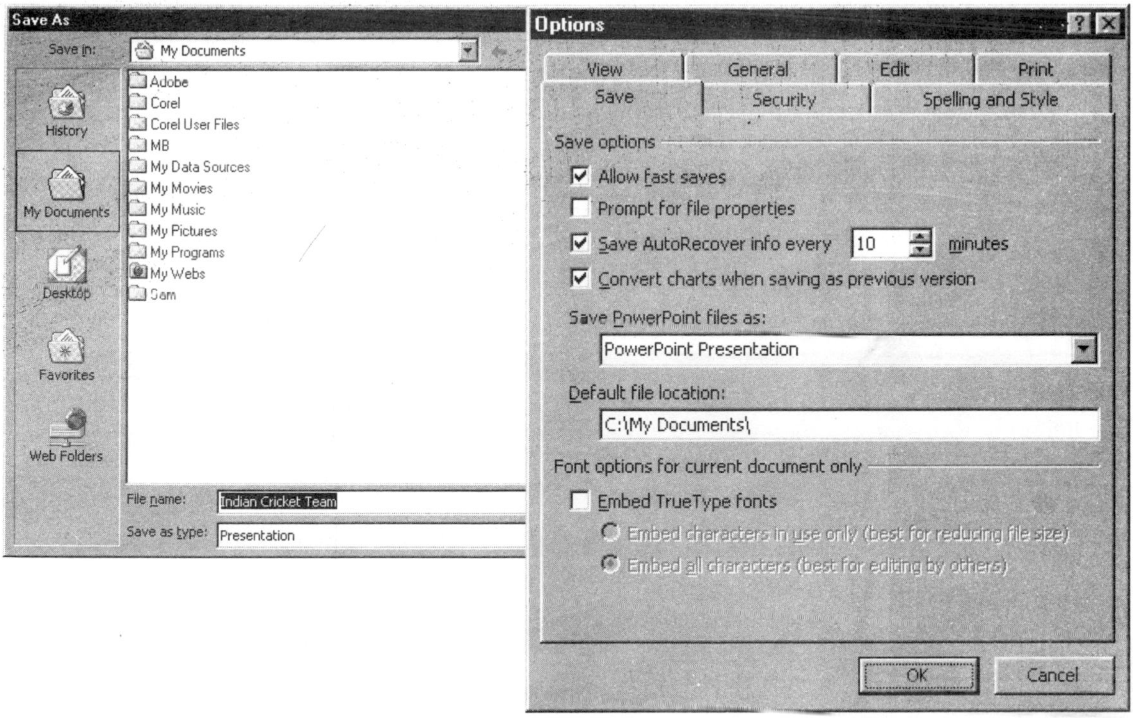

They are:

Outline view

It displays only the text of the presentation in the outline form, allowing you to work easily with the content.

Normal view

It displays 3 panes that show the outline, the slide, and an area which you can enter speaker's notes.

Slide Sorter view

It displays thumbnail views of your slides so that you can reorganize the slides and change the overall look of the presentation. In this view you can also add and edit the transition effects for the slide show.

Slide Show view

It displays the presentation one slide at a time in sequence as an automatic slide show.

Notes Page view

It is available only from the view menu, lets you enter and edit speaker's notes for the presenter.

Points to Remember

1. Each view shows a different aspect of the same presentation.
2. You can switch from one view to another at any time.
3. Right-click in Slide Sorter view or click the button at lower left corner of the current slide to display the Slide Show shortcut menu.

ENTERING THE TEXT

Let us create another presentation which has more of text. Here, we will add the text as per the following:

1. Create a new presentation which has only text in the slide.
2. Type the name Adobe Corporation in the title bar.
3. In the next box, type the name of the famous software of the company called PageMaker.
4. Pressing enter would lead you to another sub heading.
5. Type here the next heading, Photoshop.
6. Similarly press enter and type Type Manager.

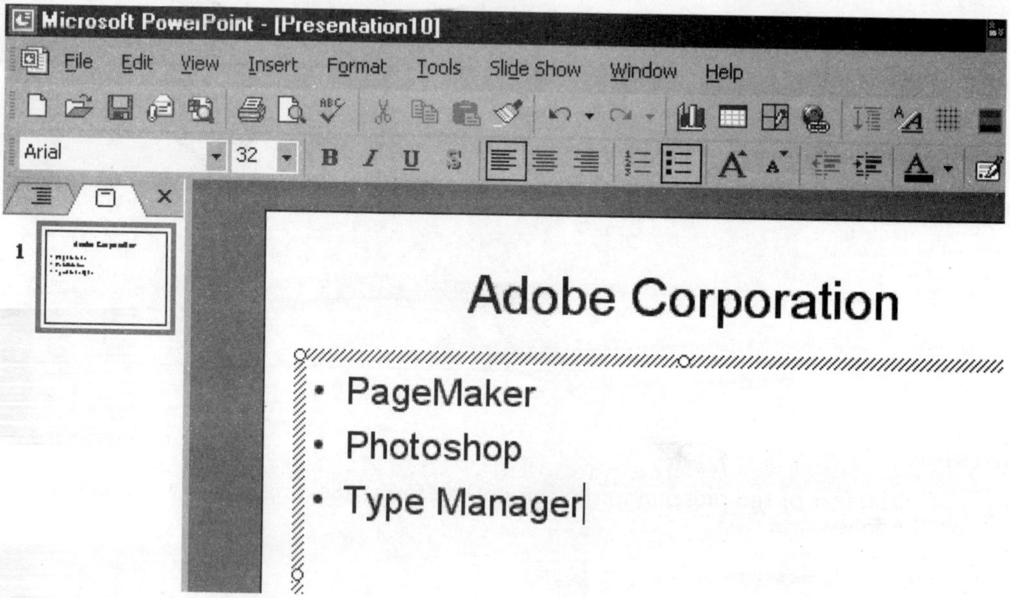

7. At this stage your presentation would like the one shown on the next page.
8. Now we come to adding text in between the main headings, i.e., sub-headings.
9. Place your cursor at the end of the first heading, i..e., after PageMaker and press Enter. A new heading with 2 will appear. Just press Tab to get the bulleted text format. Type here the first line of your tabbed matter, which is Version 6.5.
10. Press enter again to get the new line and type version 7.0.
11. At this stage your presentation will look like, the one shown on the next page.
12. You can thus type the date in the steps required by you.
13. Next obvious step would be change the data, read on.

CHANGING DISPLAY

You can hide the text of the bulleted text or the sub-heading and let only the headings remain visible. For this do the following:

1. Highlight the text you want to hide.

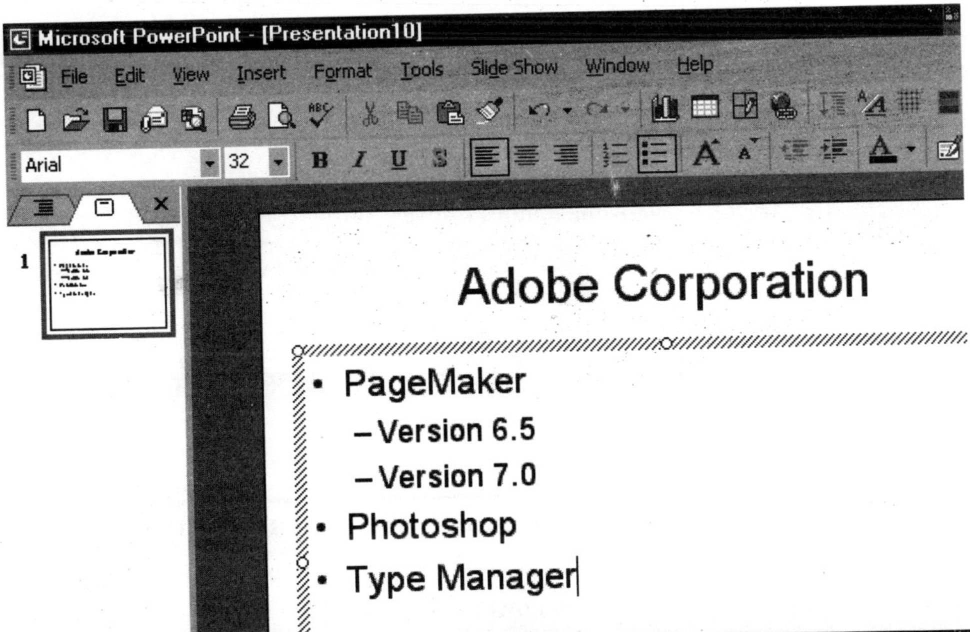

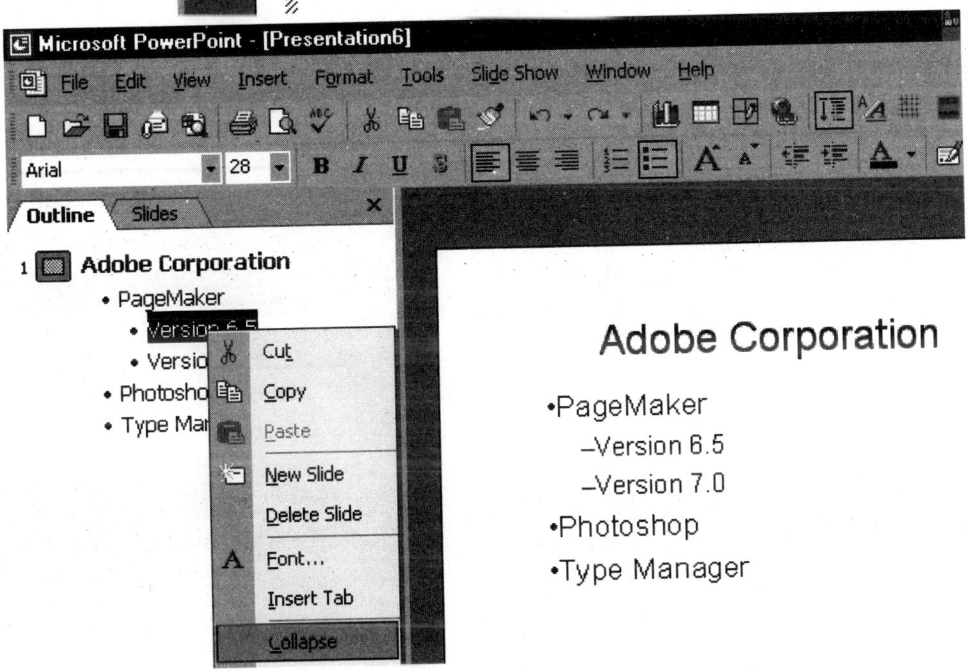

2. With text highlighted, click at right mouse button to get another submenu.
3. Select Collapse from here.
3. The text will be hidden and only the heading will remain in view, as shown on next to next page.
4. The heading which has text hidden underneath it is indicated by the text being shown as underlined.
5. When you press the Expand button after highlighting the heading which has text underneath it, the text will be expanded.

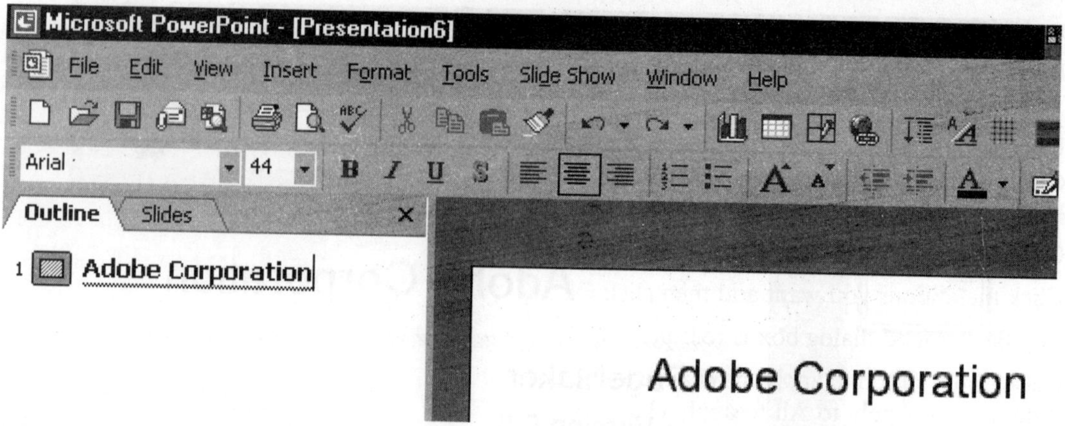

MOVING THE TEXT

You can move up or down a particular heading for reorganizing. For this do the following:

1. Highlight the text you want to move.
2. With text highlighted drag the text up or down.
3. Leave the mouse button at the place where you feel like placing the text.
4. The text will be moved there.

CHANGING THE COLOUR

The colour schemes are always used to suit the atmosphere. So it depends where the presentation is going to be. Depending upon that the colour of the presentations are selected.

To Change the Colours

1. Select Background from Format menu.

   Or

   Right click outside the placeholder areas in Slide or Normal view and choose slide colour scheme from the shortcut menu
2. Background dialog box appears, as shown here.
3. Under Background fill, click the down arrow.
4. To change to a colour in the colour scheme, click one of the eight colours below Automatic.
5. To change to a colour which is not there, click at More colours.
6. Click the colour you want on the standard tab or click the custom tab to mix your own colour and then click Ok.
7. Click Apply button to apply the changed colour to the current slide or click Apply to All, to apply the change to all slides in the presentation.

Working with Shaded Background

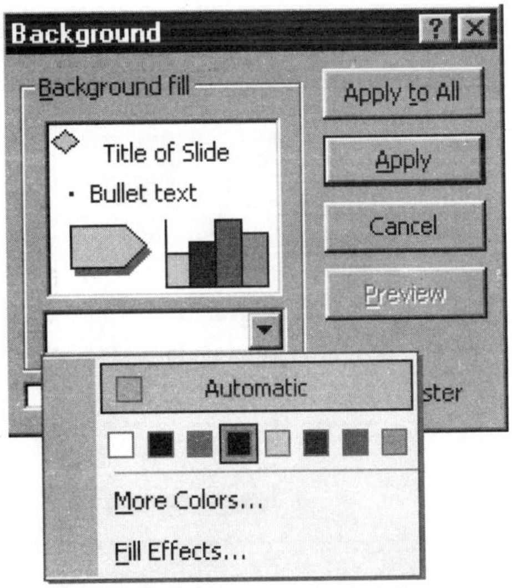

1. From the Format menu, choose background option. The background dialog box is displayed.
2. Under Background fill, click the down arrow and then click Fill Effects.
3. The Fill Effects dialog box is displayed. Click the Gradient tab.
4. Click the options you want and then click Ok.
5. The Background dialog box is redisplayed.
6. Click Apply button to apply the change to the Current slide or click Apply to All to apply change to all the slides.

To change a patterned slide background

1. From the Format menu, choose background option. The background dialog box is displayed.
2. Under Background fill, click the down arrow and then click Fill Effects.
3. The Fill Effects dialog box is displayed. Click the Pattern tab.
4. Click the option you want and then click Ok.
5. The Background dialog box is redisplayed.
6. Click Apply button to apply the change to the current slide or click Apply to All to apply change to all the slides.

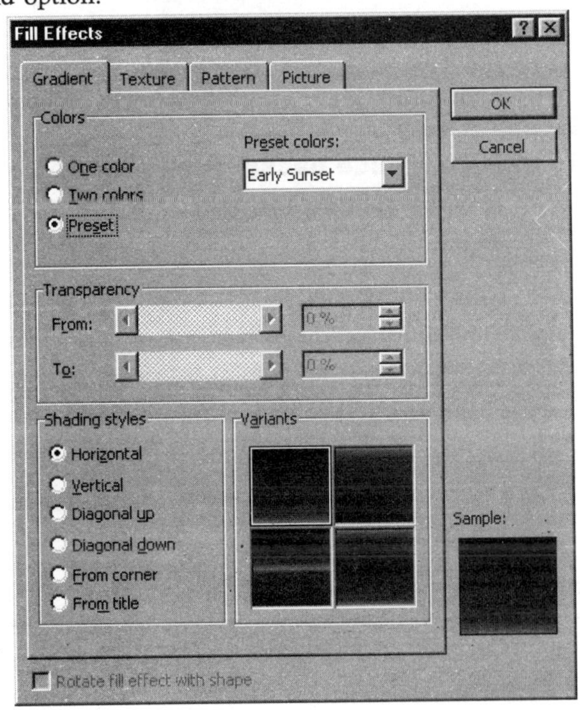

To change a textured slide background

1. From the Format menu, choose background option.
2. The background dialog box is displayed.
3. Under Background fill, click the down arrow and then click Fill Effects.
4. The Fill Effects dialog box is displayed. Click the Texture tab.
5. Click the texture you want and then click Ok.
6. The Background dialog box is redisplayed.
7. Click Apply button to apply the change to the current slide or click Apply to All to apply change to all the slides.

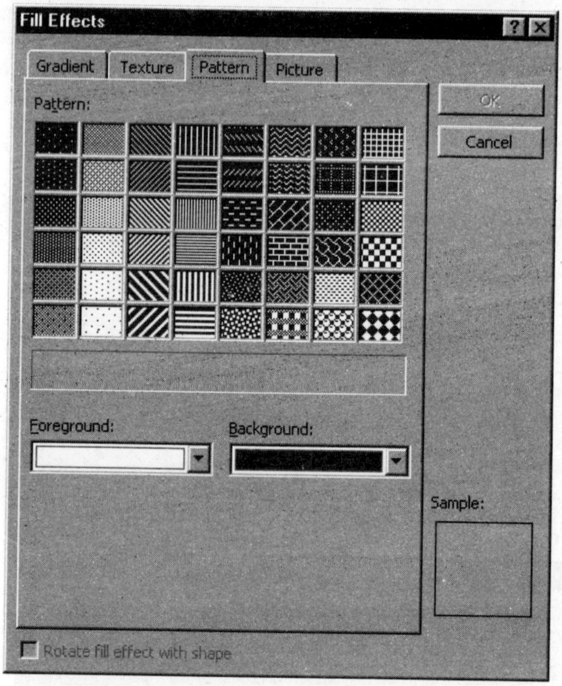

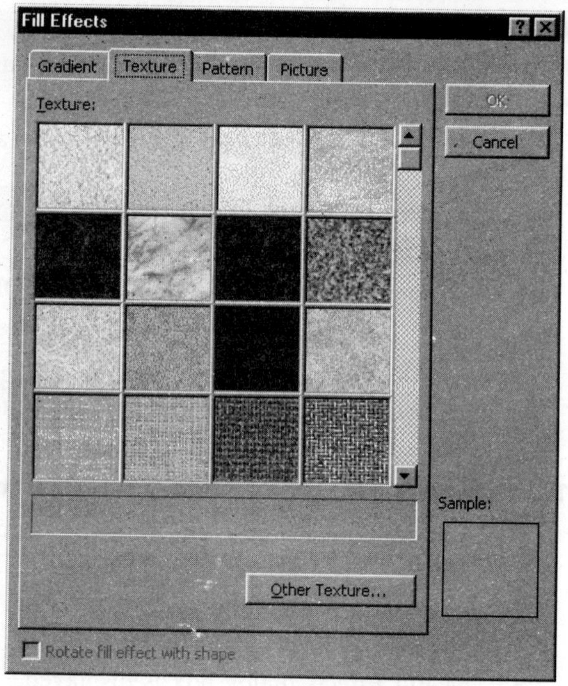

To change a slide background picture

1. From the Format menu, choose background option.
2. The background dialog box is displayed.
3. Under Background fill, click the down arrow and then click Fill Effects.
4. The Fill Effects dialog box is displayed. Click the Picture tab.
5. Click the Select Picture and find the folder that contains the picture you want. Double click the file name and then click Ok.
6. The Background dialog box is redisplayed.
7. Click Apply button to apply the change to the current slide or click Apply to All to apply change to all the slides.

FORMATTING PARAGRAPHS

In PowerPoint a paragraph can be formatted for the followings:

- Alignment
- Tab and Indents
- Line spacing
- Space before the after the paragraph

Let us see how each one of them is used.

Alignment

We all know about the alignment. We also know that there are 4 main alignments like Left, Right, Centre

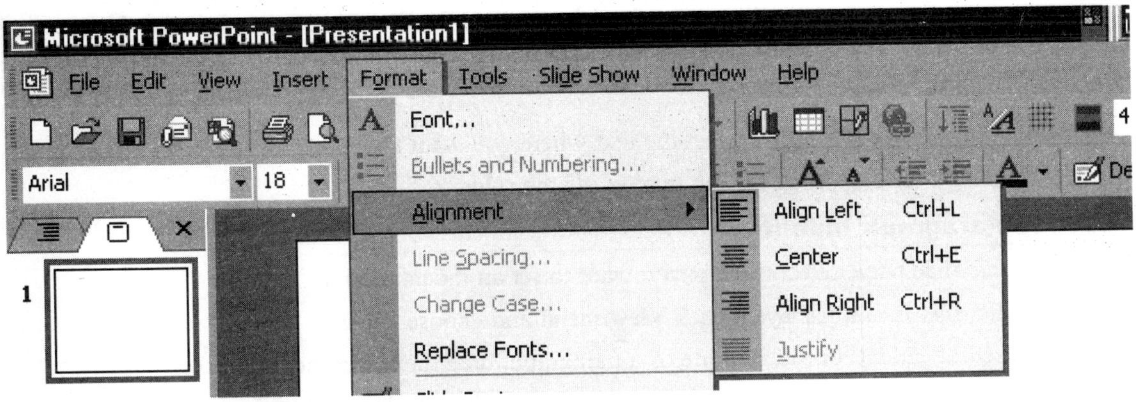

and Justify. PowerPoint supports all of them. As you would do in any of the word processing software, here also you just highlight the text of the para and click at Alignment in the Format menu.

Tabs

You would usually set tabs for making the text in the tabular manner. The tab is a small marker and tells the text where you want to stop. PowerPoint gives you the option of choosing four different tab stops: left, right, center and decimal tabs. In PowerPoint tabs are set in the following manner.

1. Choose the type of tab you want by clicking in the tab selection box at the left of the horizontal ruler until the tab type appears.
2. Move the pointer ruler bar and click the point at which you want to add the tab.

   Different types of tab types

Tab Type	*Description*
Left tab	The text left align at the tab
Right tab	The text right align at the tab
Center tab	The text is center align at the tab
Decimal tab	The decimal point where the numbering is aligned

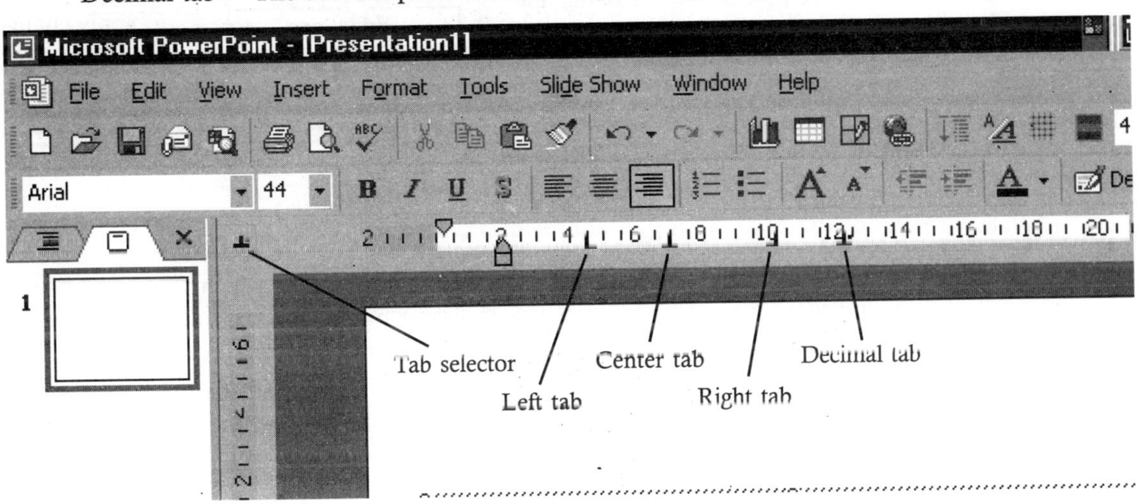

You can also change the alignment of text by opening the Format menu and choose Alignment. A small pop-up box of different alignment choices appears.

Clearing Tabs

1. Select the slide pane, then select the text where you want to set or clear tab stops.
2. To clear a tab stop, drag the tab marker off the ruler.

Setting Paragraph Indents

1. In this slide pane, select the text you want to set an indentation for.
2. If the ruler is not displayed, click View menu and choose Ruler.
3. To set the indent for the first line of a paragraph, drag the upper indent marker.
4. To set the left indent for other lines in a paragraph, drag the lower indent marker. The rectangular part of the lower indent marker also moves with it.
5. To maintain the relationship between the first line and the rest of the paragraph, move both markers by dragging the rectangular part of the lower market.

Line spacing

You may not need this for setting the line space but PowerPoint provides you with the option of changing the line space, in case it is required. For this do the following:

1. In the Slide pane, click anywhere in the paragraph you want to add space between lines.
2. Click the Format menu and choose Line Spacing. The Line Spacing dialog box appears as shown here.
3. In the Line spacing section, click up-arrow or down-arrow to increase of decrease the number of lines you want separating text lines.
4. In the Before Paragraph area, you do the same thing.
5. In the Slide pane, click anywhere in the paragraph if you want to add space after.
6. In the spinner box, click up-arrow or down-arrow for adding space after the paragraph.

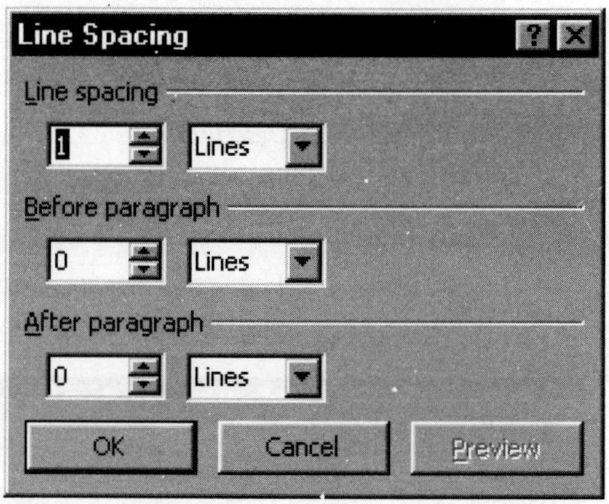

7. After you make changes in the dialog box click OK.

Spell Checking Text

If you think you can spell a document in Word only, you are wrong. You can check spelling of the text which you have typed in PowerPoint too. Here also you have the dictionary which takes care of your spelling needs. Like in any word processor, spellings are checked with the dictionary and the wrong ones are pointed out.

The spelling checker moves through your presentation one slide at a time and then checks the Notes Pages (if any) before closing the Spelling dialog box. You can stop using the spelling checker at any time by clicking the Close button in the Spelling dialog box.

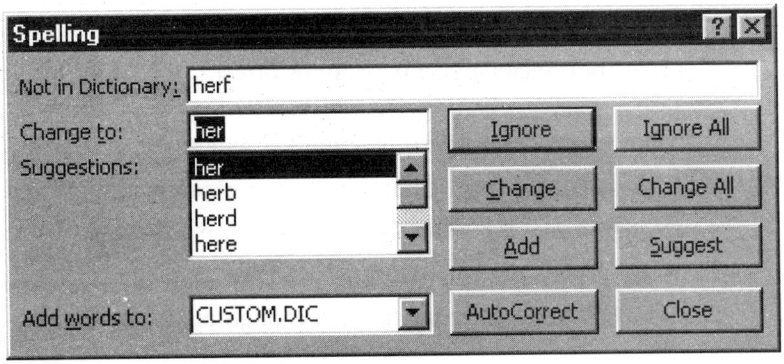

1. Place the cursor at the beginning of the text in the first slide and click Tools menu and then choose Spelling...

   Or

   Click the Spelling button on the Standard toolbar to display the Spelling dialog box. The spelling checker highlights the first unrecognised word in the presentation file and displays the word in the Not in Dictionary box.
2. Click the appropriate command button, from the following lists:

Ignore	Ignores this word and moves on
Ignore all	Ignores this word every time you find it.
Change	Changes the original word by replacing it with the word in the Change to: box.
Change all	Changes every occurrence of this word to the word in the Change to: box.
Add	Adds this word to the dictionary so the speller does not stop here any more.
Suggest	Searches the dictionary and displays possible replacement words (you choose the one that is correct).

3. The spelling checker takes the indicated action and then highlights the next unrecognized word.
4. Repeat step 2 until the spelling checker displays a message saying that the entire presentation has been checked.
5. Click OK.

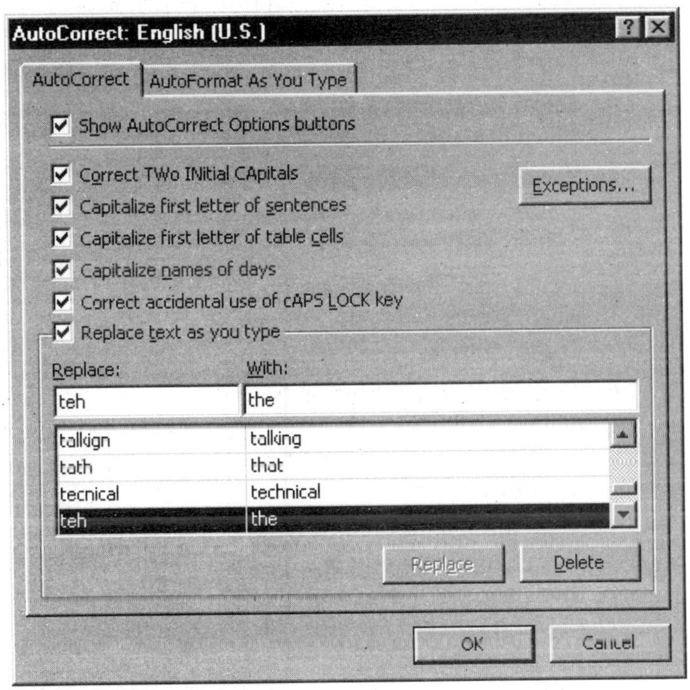

USING AUTOCORRECT

This is another feature which is there in the Word processing. It takes care of all your typing mistakes if know them in advance. For example, as shown here, if you have the bad habit of typing teh instead of the, then say that to the computer and it will take of this error every time it occurs. So Autocorrect will take care of all your commonly made errors.

I suggest you just sit with the dialog box and go through it and then add the most common mistakes you make.

For this do the following:

1. Click Tools menu and choose AutoCorrect... the AutoCorrect dialog box appears.
2. In the Replace: text box, enter the characters or words you want to type in order to have AutoCorrect change them to a word or a phrase.
3. In the With: text box, enter the word or phrase you want to appear after you enter the word.
4. Configure the way AutoCorrect works by selecting and deselecting the options.
5. To delete any autocorrections if select the characters in the Replace: box and click delete.
6. Click OK when you have finished configuring the dialog box.

WORKING WITH CHARTS

In a presentation, chart gives the best representation of the numeric figures. In all the constituents of the Microsoft Office, Charts play an important role and they make use of the software called Microsoft Graph which can be accessed by any of the software of the Office.

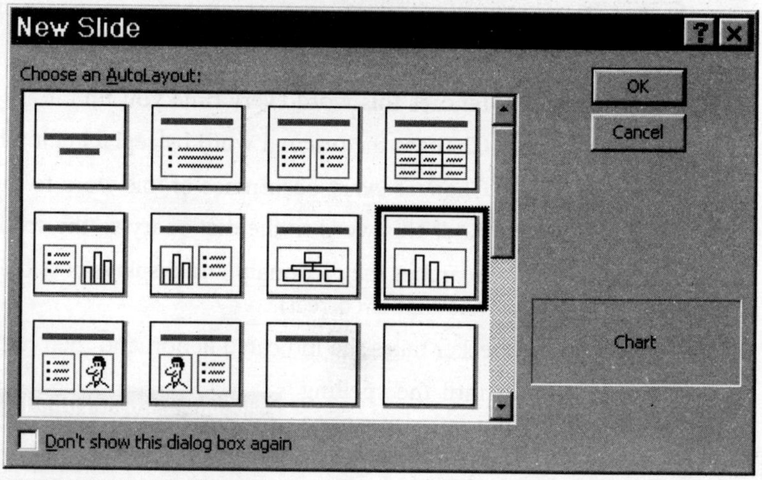

Let us see how charts are used in presentations.

For this you have to select a presentation with a chart.

1. Click at New from the File menu.
2. You would be given a New Slide dialog box.
3. Select here one of slide which has a chart in on it.
4. Pressing Enter will lead to a blank presentation with a chart, as shown here.
5. Double click at the place where it asks you to do so to add chart.
6. This will give you a dummy data table and its representation as a chart, as shown below.
7. Since this data is dummy, you change it with your own data. All the cells of the datasheet can be changed including the headings.

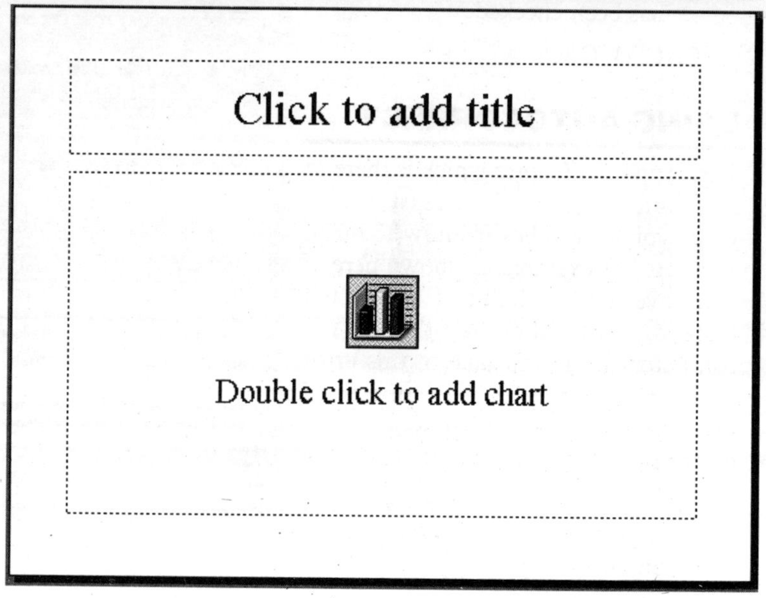

8. On typing one data you can either press right arrow to reach the cell on the right or press Enter to reach cell below.
9. Once you have filled up your data, your datasheet would look like the one shown below.

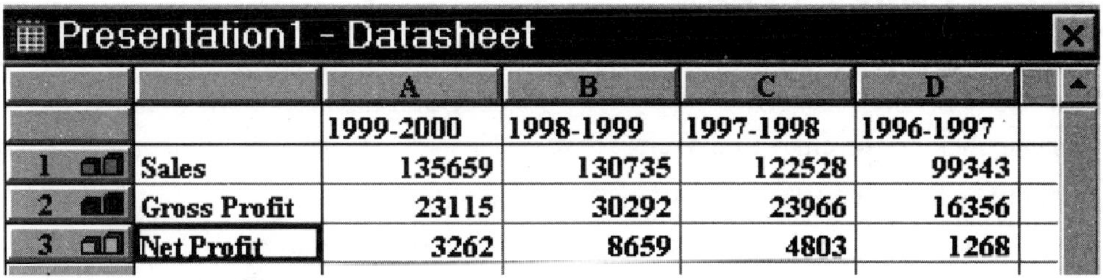
Presentation1 - Datasheet

		A	B	C	D
		1999-2000	1998-1999	1997-1998	1996-1997
1	Sales	135659	130735	122528	99343
2	Gross Profit	23115	30292	23966	16356
3	Net Profit	3262	8659	4803	1268

10. Graphical representation of the data would look like the one shown below.

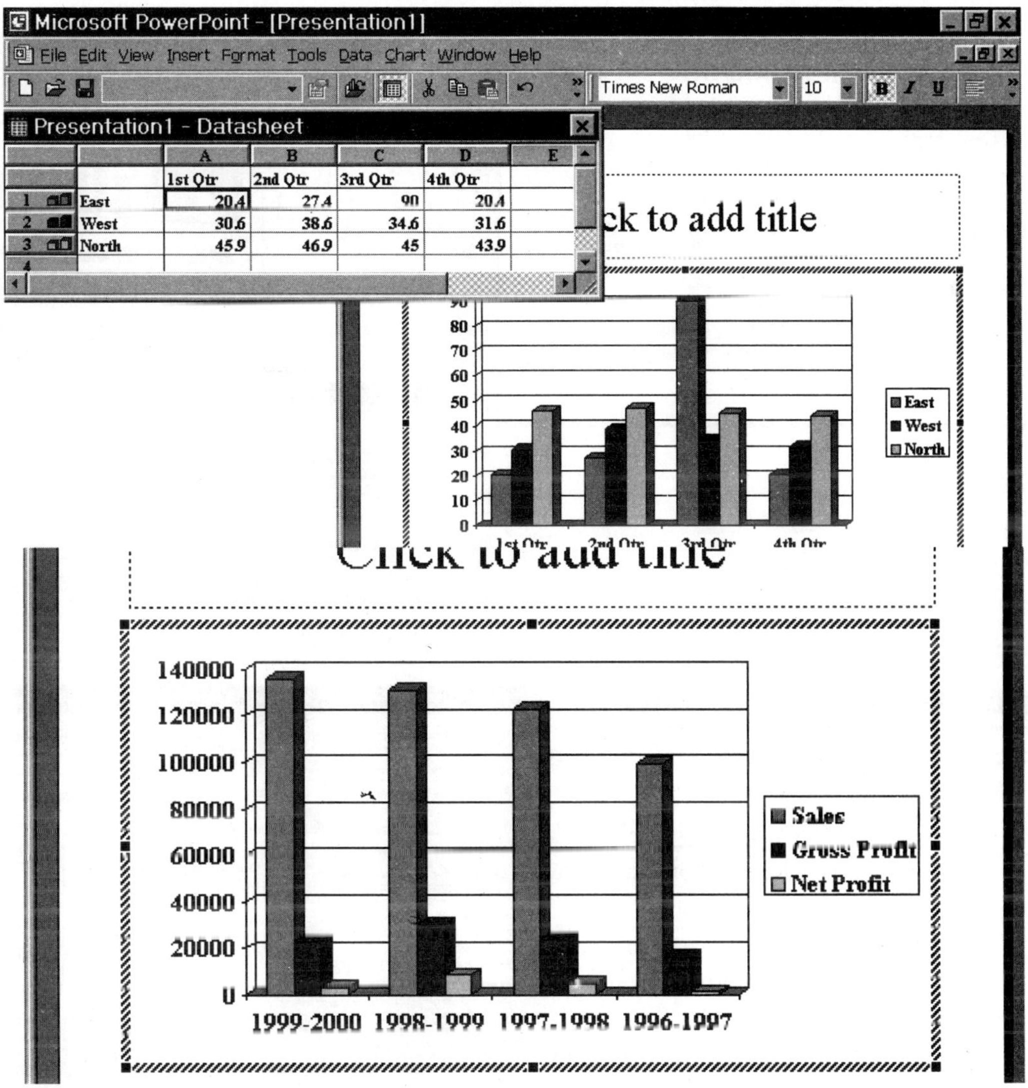

There are various other operations which can be performed on this chart as you would do any other chart using the chart software.

CHANGING CHART TYPE

It is not necessary for you accept the chart type which the software has given to you. You can always change it according to your liking. For this do the following:

1. Double click on the chart to make it active.
2. From the Chart menu, select Chart Type.
3. The Chart Type dialog box as shown next will be given to you.
4. Select any of the category you want and from the category too select the option you like most.
5. Here in this case I have selected the one with cylindrical shape.

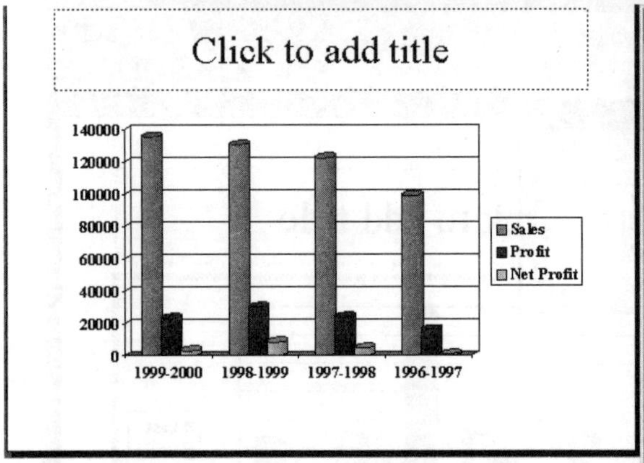

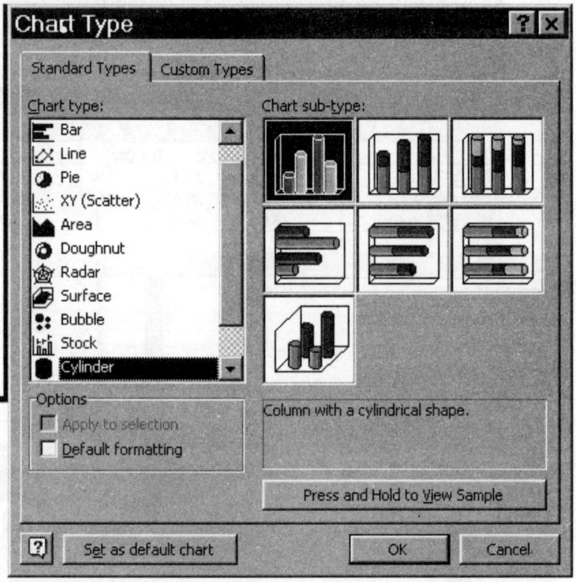

6. On pressing Ok you will get the chart shown on the next page.

CHANGING CHART OPTIONS

You can change the various options of the chart by using the Chart Options.

1. Highlight the chart by double clicking it.
2. You will get the Chart Option dialog box as shown here.
3. Among the various options of the Tiles, Axes, Gridlines, Legend, Data Labels, Data Table.
4. The first among these is Tiles, the settings of this are shown here.

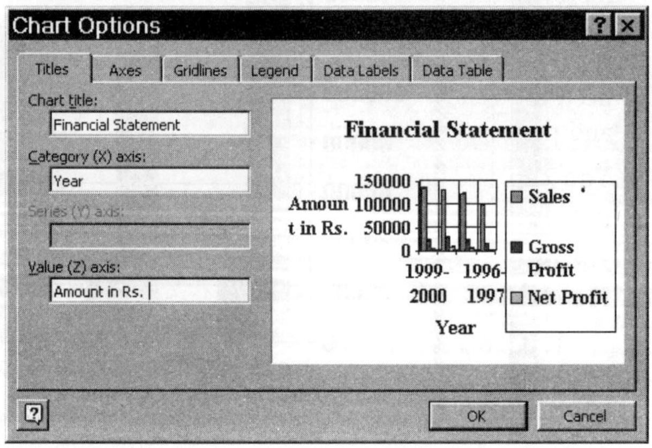

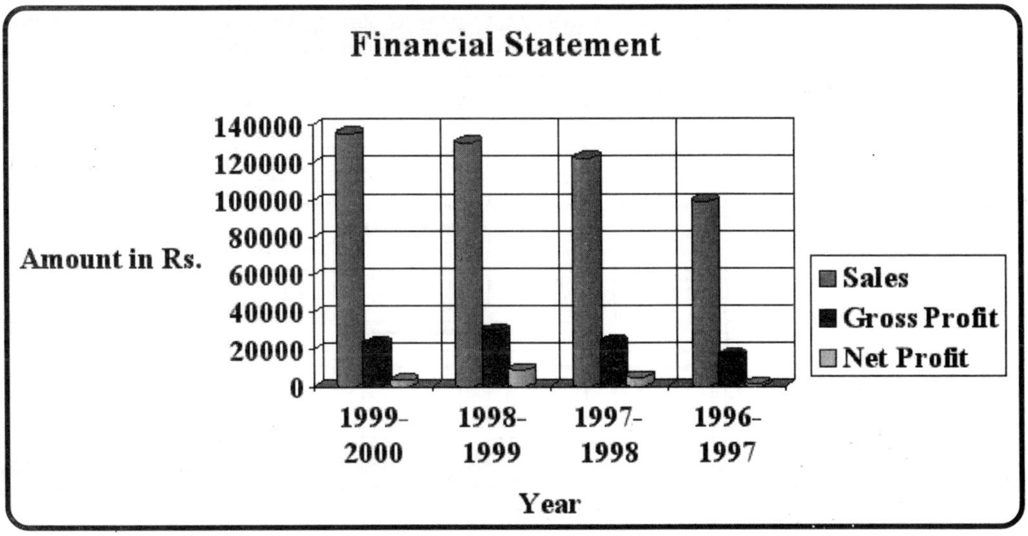

5. Similarly you can do the settings of the other ones. In case of any doubt just leave them as it is.
6. On completion press Enter to get the chart shown on the next page.

You can change the various other options of the chart.

CHANGING ELEMENTS

A chart is supposed to have different elements like Legend, Axis, etc. You can change them by just clicking at that particular option. Like for example clicking at Axis would give you the following dialog box and you can change the various settings from here.

By clicking at the column you can get the Format Walls dialog box to register your changes.

This way you can select the various dialog boxes and make the necessary changes.

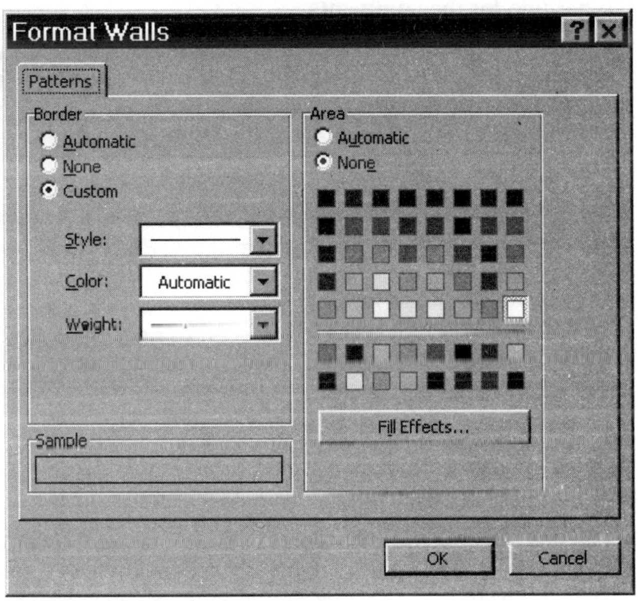

ORGANIZATION CHARTS

An organizational chart is a graphical representation of the personnel structure for a corporation, committee, or any other collaborative team. They are useful when you need to visually portray the team members and their respective relationships.

You can add organization charts in your presentation slide by two methods.

Adding Organization Chart by New Slide

1. Click at New slide.
2. Select a slide having an organization layout.

3. Click Ok to have the chart inserted in your slide.

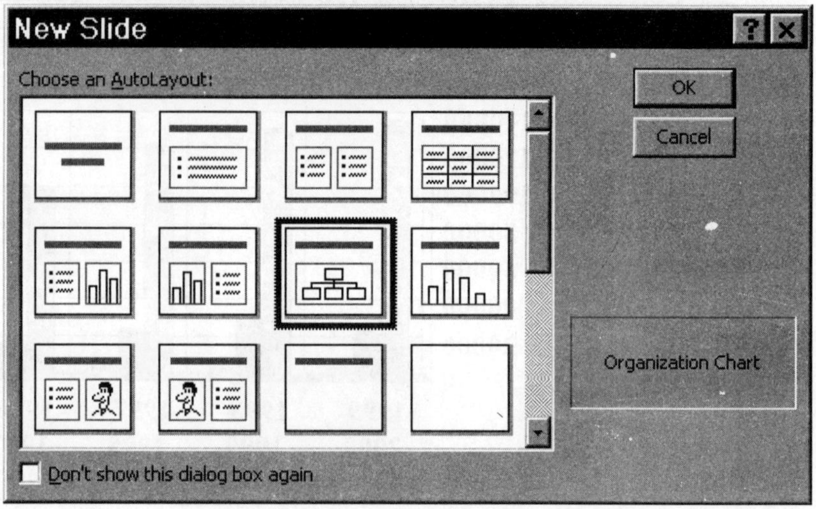

Adding Organization Chart from Insert Menu

1. Select a blank presentation.
2. Select Organization chart from Picture submenu in Insert Menu.
3. This leads to the starting of a software called Microsoft Organization Chart.
4. Notice the various boxes where you have to fill up the text later and also add the title of the chart where mentioned.

As organization chart is composed of boxes connected to one another by lines. Each box represents an individual in the organization. The lines that connect a box to other boxes illustrate the relationship of the individuals. There are 4 types of individual relationships: Manager, Co-worker, Subordinate, and Assistant.

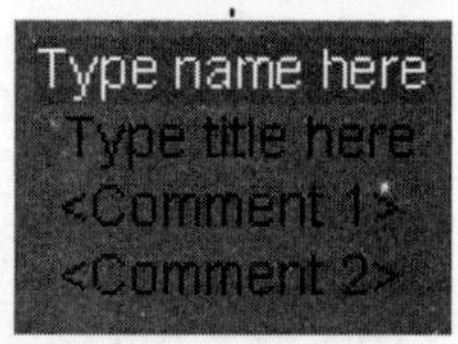

Entering Information

When a box is selected for typing the information, it will give you 4 lines for inserting the information. It has one line for the title, one for the name and the other two for the comments.

To enter the information, do the following:

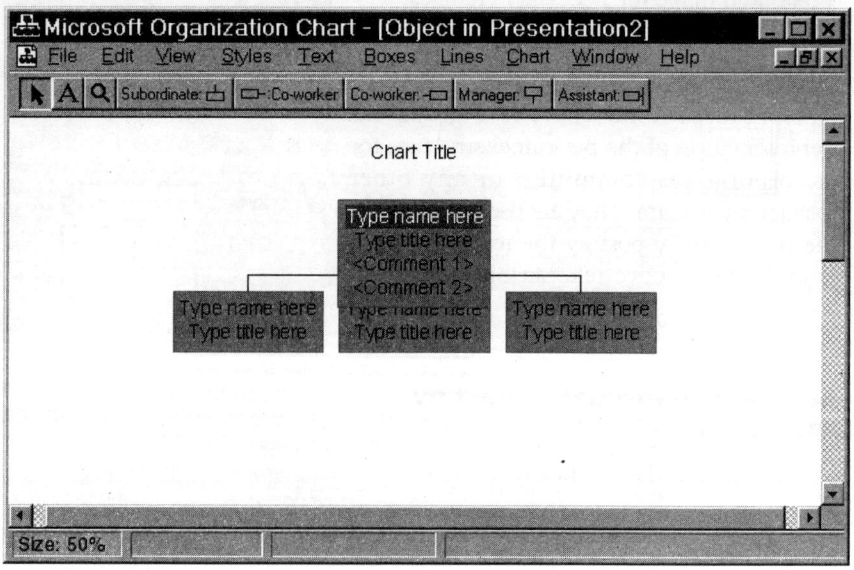

1. Click once on the box to select it.
2. Click a second time on the box. This box should expand to display all the fields available for text entry, as shown here.
3. Press the Tab key until the field you want to enter the information is selected.

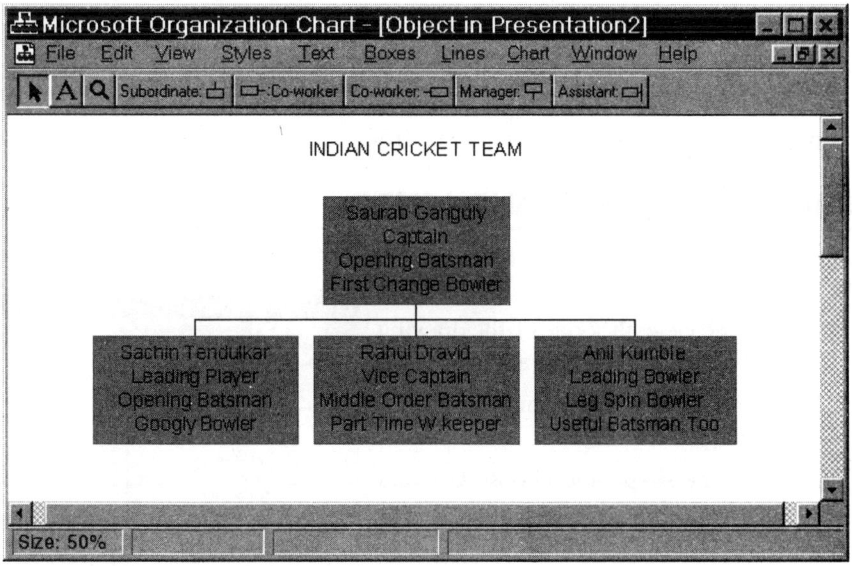

4. Type the information.
5. Press the Tab key to move to the next field.
6. Repeat steps 4 and 5 as necessary.
7. Click outside the box to deselect it.
8. I have typed the information as shown on the next page.
9. You can differ with me and create your own team.

ADDING PICTURE TO THE BACKGROUND

A picture can be inserted into any slide. This can be in the form of a logo of a company or any other picture. This picture can be a ready made graphic or a clip art. For this do the following:

1. Select Slide Master from Master command in the View menu.
2. You will get the dialog box as shown below.
3. From the Insert menu, select to insert Picture and Clip Art or any other picture which you may want to use.

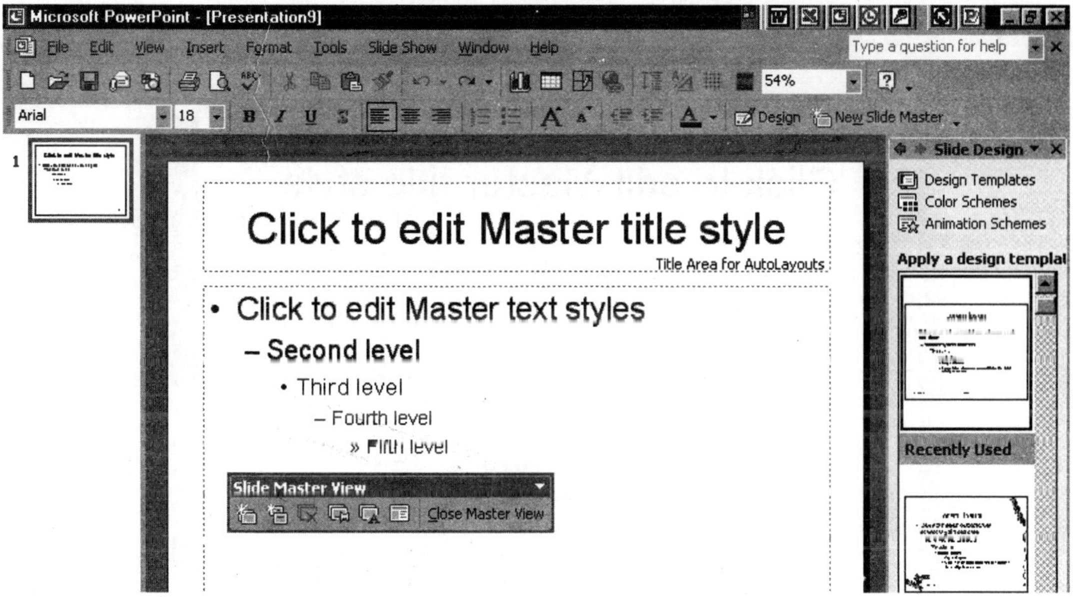

4. From the clip art menu, select the clip art.
5. The picture will be placed in the centre of the slide. You can increase or decrease its size and place it anywhere on the slide to be reflected at the slides in the presentation.
6. You can copy and paste a graphic from another program onto the slide master.

DRAWING SHAPES AND LINES

Using the drawing tools available with PowerPoint you can draw the various figures like squares, circles, etc.

1. In Slide view, click one of the drawing tools or menus on the drawing toolbar.
2. Drag with the mouse pointer to create the shape.
3. Click the shape and choose Colours and Lines from the Format menu.
4. In the Colours and Lines dialog box, choose a fill colour, line colour, and line style. Click Ok.
5. To type text inside the shape, click the shape and then begin typing.
6. To delete a line or shape, click it so that the handles appear, and press Del.
7. To keep a shape regular, i.e., drawing a square instead of a rectangle and

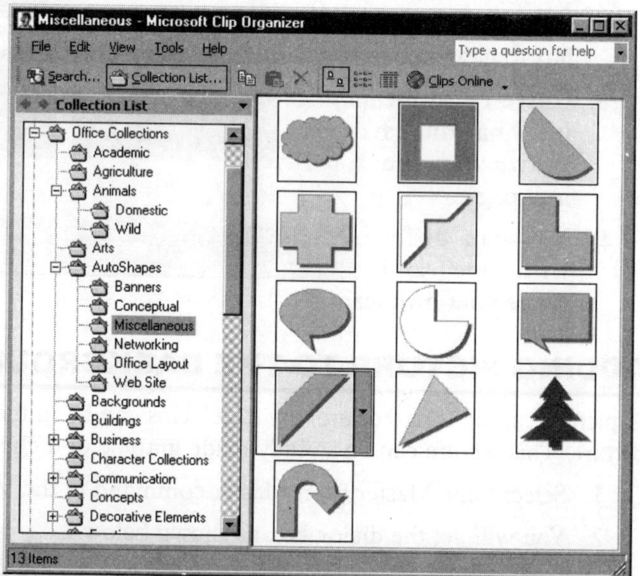

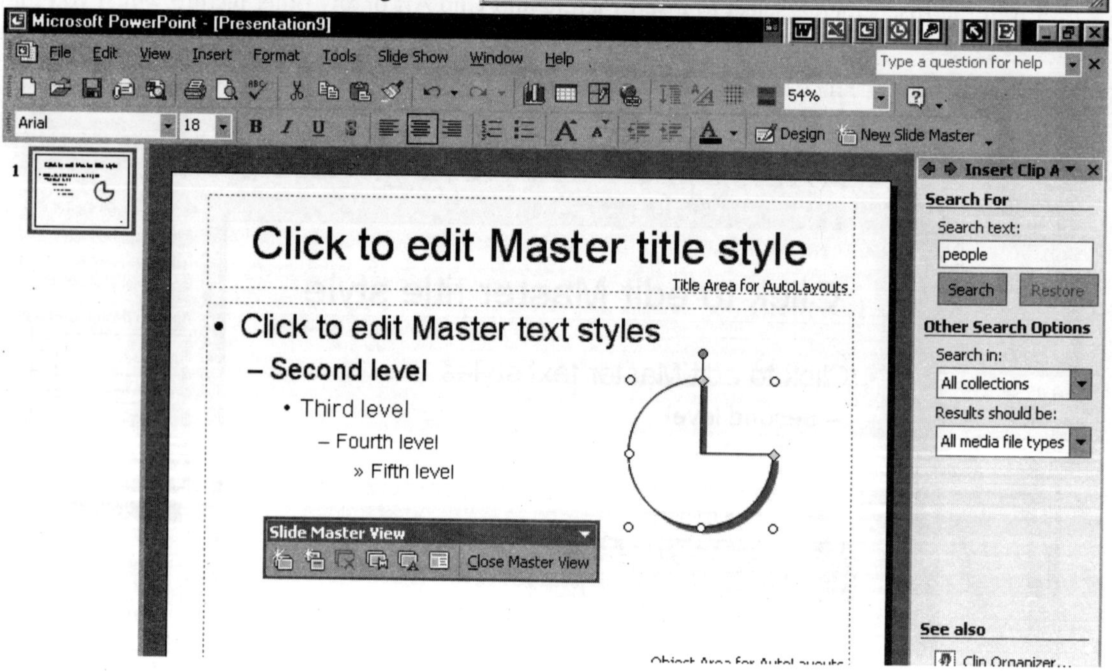

drawing a circle instead of an oval, etc., hold down the Shift key while dragging through the area to create the shape.

ADDING TEXT BOX

Supposing on a slide you want to add some text in the form of some message or an afterthought. You can always do so by adding a text block on the slide.

1. Select Text Box from the Insert menu.
2. Click in the slide where you want the text box to appear.
3. Type the text. The box expands to surround the text. Press Enter to create a new line of text within the box.
4. For precise control over the parameters of the text box (fill and line colour, word wrapping, internal margins, position, and so on), double-click one of the sides of the object to format the object.
5. In the Format Text Box dialog box, select the formatting you want.
6. Click Ok.

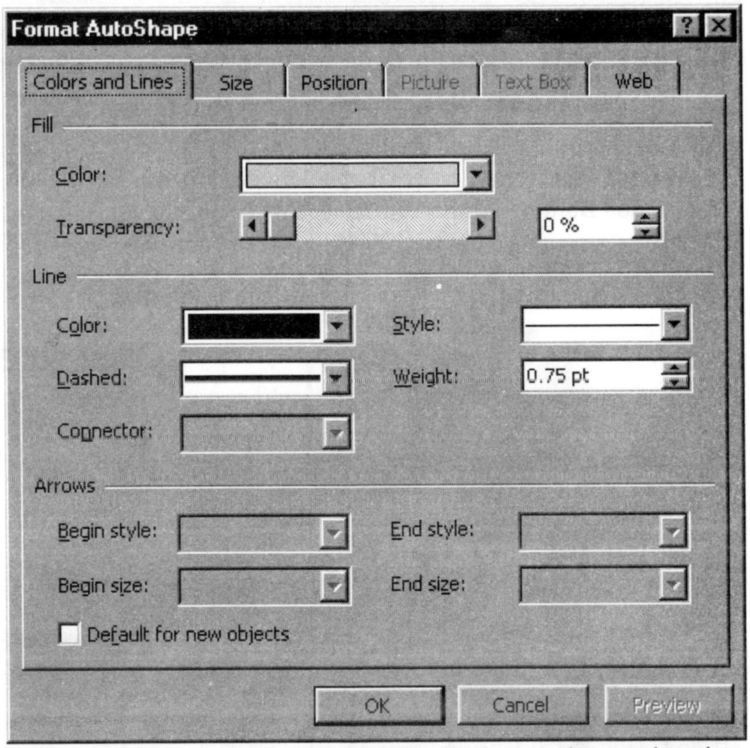

Remember

1. Change the location of the text box by clicking one of the sides (not at a handle) and dragging the box to the new location.
2. You can also add text to any other shape by clicking in the shape and typing.

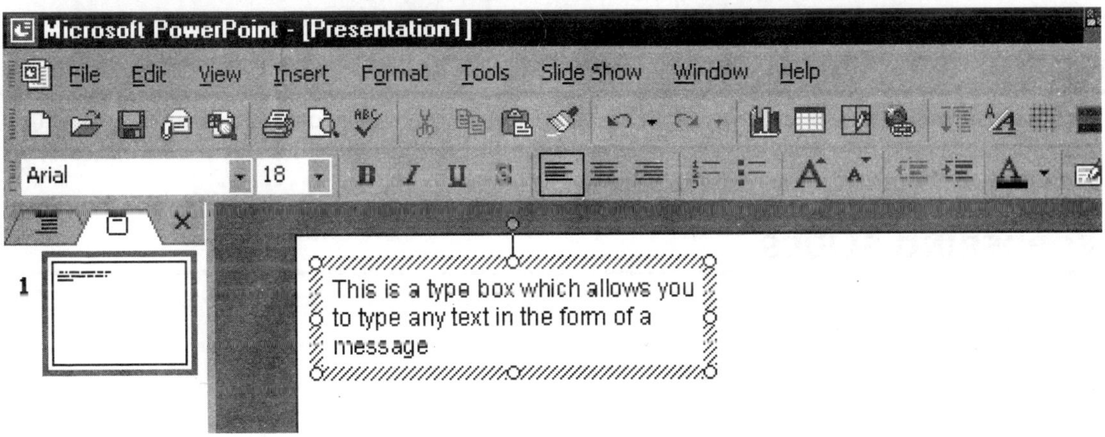

3. After you have entered the text, you can change the shape of the text box by dragging the side handles.
4. To delete a text box, click one of the sides so that the insertion point inside disappears and press Del.
5. To keep a shape you are drawing regular, hold down the Shift key as your drag to draw the shape.

ADDING PREDEFINED SHAPES

Autoshapes are the shapes given to you by the software are much more better looking than the usual ones drawn by you. Make the best use of them to highlight the text or that matter anything in your presentation.

1. AutoShapes button is available on the drawing toolbar.
2. Clicking on it will lead to the various other options on the menu, as shown on the next page. It has Lines, Connectors, Basic Shapes, Block Arrows, Flowchart, Stars and Banners, Callouts, and Action Buttons. More AutoShapes will lead you to more shapes.
3. Select one of the menu and then the shape.
4. The shape would be selected for pasting to the slide.

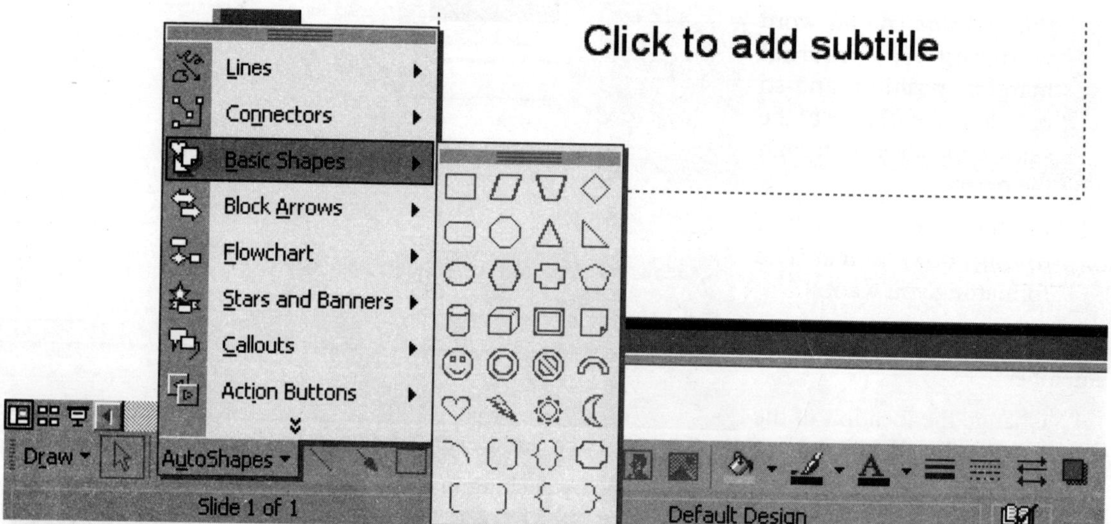

ADDING FROM WORDART

If you have through the chapter on Microsoft Word thoroughly you would have see the working of WordArt. In a very similar way, as you would enter the WordArt in your document in Word, here too you can enter a WordArt in your presentation.

REORDERING SLIDES

As you see from the view, each slide is numbered. These number belong to their order of display. This order can be changed at any point of time in the presentation.

To Change the Order of the Slides:

1. Click with the mouse the slide whose position you want to change.

2. Pressing the mouse button drag the slide to a new position.
3. A vertical line appears to indicate where the slide will drop when you release the mouse button. In the figure on the next page, the slide 6 is being moved to a between position number 3 and 4.
4. Releasing the mouse button will drop the slide at the right place.
5. In the figure on the next page (bottom), you will see that the slide 6 has been placed between the number 3 and 4. The numbering of all the slides has been changed subsequently.

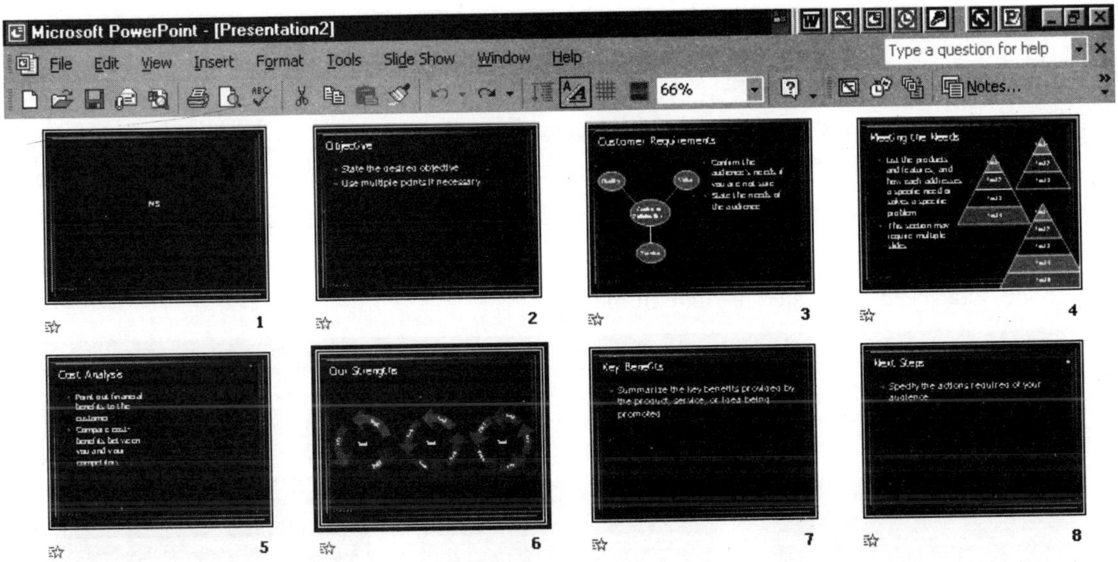

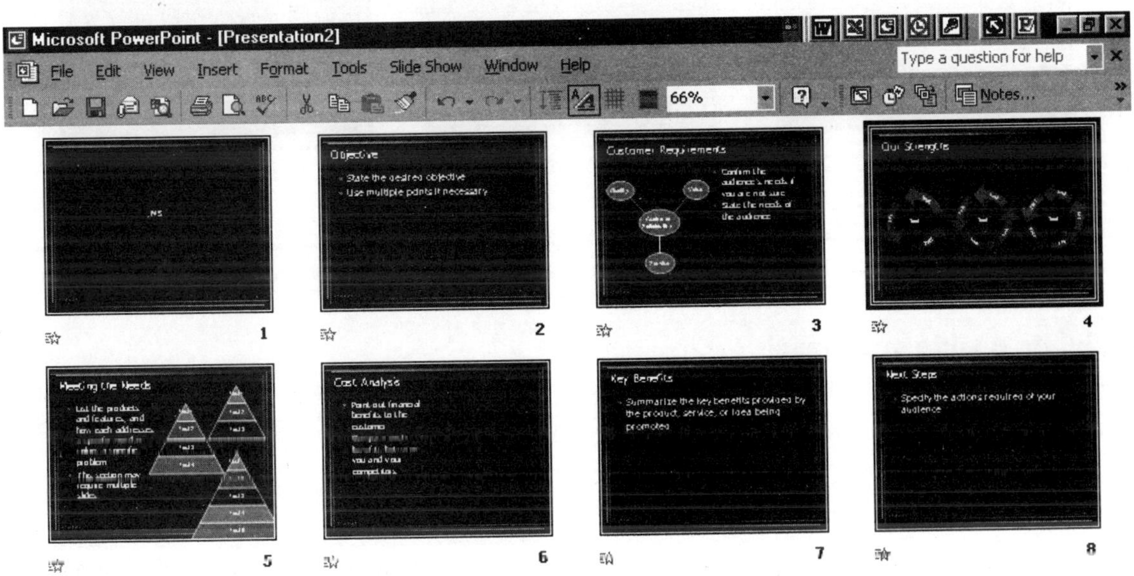

Points to Remember

1. You can select several slides to move by drawing a selection box around the group of slides and then dragging the group to the new position.

2. You can also select several slides by holding down the Shift key and selecting the first and last slides in the series.
3. To gather slides from different parts of a presentation, hold down the Ctrl key as you click each slide. Drag any one slide in the group to a new point in the presentation. All the selected slides will appear in sequence and in the same relative order at new position.

DUPLICATING SLIDES

You can duplicate selected slides in Slide Sorter view and see the effect on the flow of slides immediately.

To Duplicate a slide or slides:

1. Select the slide or slides you want to duplicate.
2. Select Slide number 2 .
3. Press Ctrl + D or click at Duplicate in the Edit menu to duplicate the slide.
4. See the result next.
5. Slide 2 has been duplicated as Slide number 3.

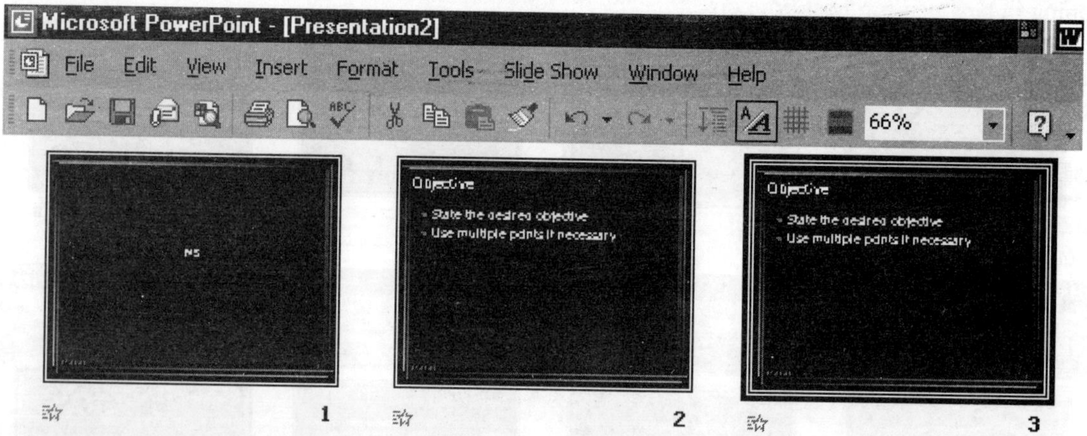

DELETING SLIDES

You can delete the selected slides in Slide Sorter view and see that the numbering of other slides change immediately.

To delete a slide or slides:

1. Select the slide or slides you want to delete.
2. Supposing we want to delete these new 3 numbered slides.
3. Press Del or Ctrl + X to delete the slides.
4. See the result of the deletion on the next page.
5. Notice the line after the slide number 2 indicating that the slides have been deleted from here.

Remember

1. You can also choose Duplicate or Delete Slide from the Edit menu.

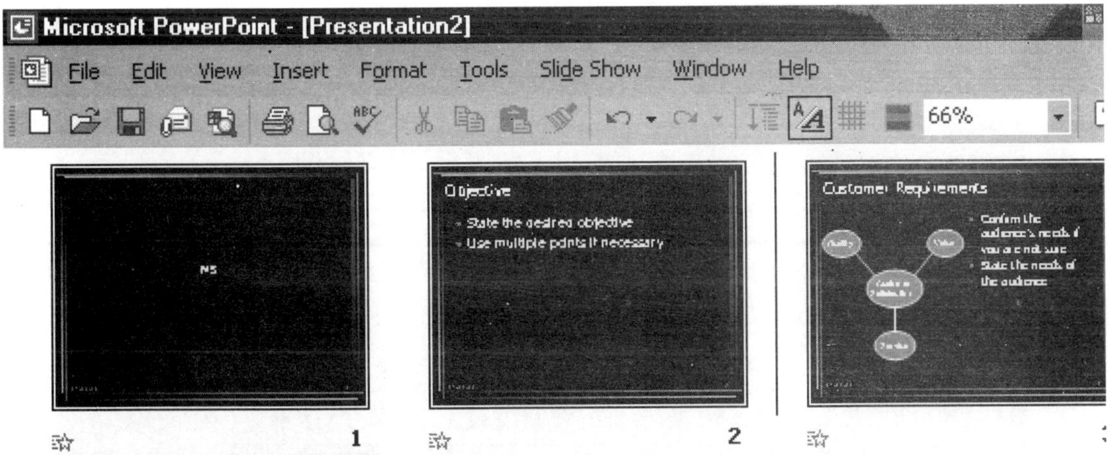

MAKING SLIDE SHOWS

This effect shows all the hard work you have put in making the slides. It shows one slide after another, stopping in between for a set time on either the monitor of your screen or on the projector which may have been attached to your computer. It is also possible to add animated effects on the slides and show them in a sophisticated manner. It is also possible to add audio, video, narration, music, etc., to your slides.

ADDING AUDIO

You can add sounds to the transition effects and to the preset animation. You can also add audio to your presentation by inserting files from the Clip Art Gallery or from other folders available to you.

To Add an Audio File

1. Select the slide where you want to put this audio and display it in the Slide view.

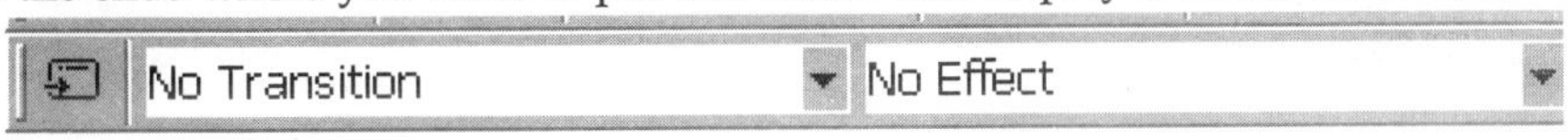

2. Select Sound from File in the Movies and Sounds command from the Insert menu.
3. Click Ok to add the sound effect, and select a file.
4. Answer Yes to have the sound play automatically or No to have it play when you click it.

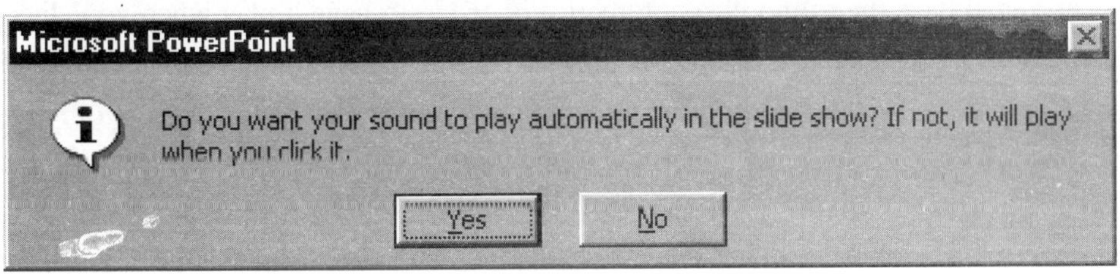

5. The sound icon appears in the middle of the slide. You can move it as you would any object.
6. If you right-click the sound icon, you can choose Play Sound or Edit Sound Object from the shortcut menu.
7. The sound icon as it appears on the slide is shown next.

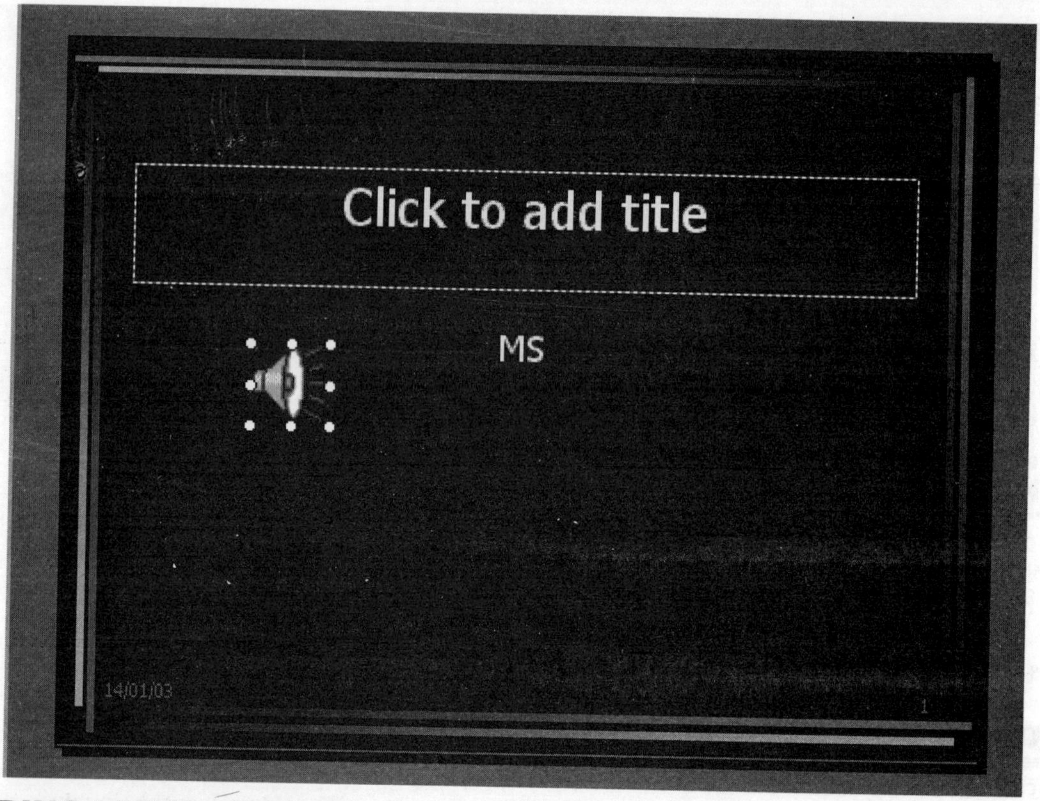

ADDING VIDEO EFFECT

Like sound, you can add video effects too. The steps are quite similar to the ones used in the case of Audio.

To Add an Video File

1. Select the slide where you want to put this video and display it in the Slide view.
2. Select Movies from File in the Movies and Sounds command from the Insert menu.
3. Click Ok to add the video effect.
4. Answer Yes to have the sound play automatically or No to have it play when you click it.
5. The video icon appears in the middle of the slide. You can move it as you would any object.
6. If you right-click the video icon, you can choose Play Video or Edit Video Object from the shortcut menu.

ADDING EFFECTS

These effects can be of the form of wipes, splits, dissolves, etc., which you usually see in the film show. For this you have to work in the Slide Sorter view.

To Add a Transition View

1. Choose the slide on which you want to put this effect.

2. Click on the arrow next to the transition effect as shown here.
3. This will lead to the Slide Transition dialog box as shown here.
4. In this dialog box, choose a transition effect from the drop-down list, a speed (slow, medium, or fast) and the advance option (on mouse click or after a period of time).
5. Click Apply to All to apply this transition effect to all slides, or click Apply to apply it only to the selected slide.
6. To apply the same transition effect to multiple slides, hold down the Shift key while you click the slides and then choose a transition effect.

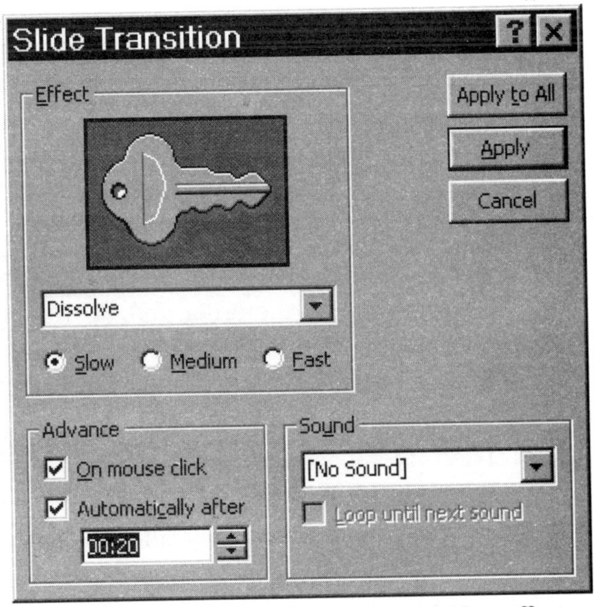

7. To preview the transition effect in Slide Sorter view, click the transition icon that appears below each slide that has a transition effect.
8. A small icon can be seen on all the slides in the Slide Sorter view.

ADDING ANIMATION

You can add animation to the slides which are going to displayed. This helps in presenting a slide with special effects. You can choose from the various animations available.

To Select an Animation

1. In the Slide Sorter view click at the slide to which you want to add the animation effect.
2. Once it has been applied, you can see the small icon being put under the slide to show that this slide has an animation effect.
3. You can see the preview of this animation effect by clicking at the preview button.
4. If you want you can apply different effects on various slides and see the whole presentation having the different effects.

Remember

1. You can also apply effects using the buttons on the Animation Effects toolbar. Choose Toolbars from the View menu and then choose Animation Effects from the pop-out menu.
2. To apply the same present animation effect to multiple slides, hold down the Shift key and click the slides and then choose an effect.
3. To preview the animation effect in Slide Sorter view, click the animation icon that appears below each slide that has an animation effect.

CREATING YOUR OWN ANIMATION

It is possible to have your own animation which can give you more control over the display of the presentation. This can be applied to both text and objects. These can be created only in Slide view.

To Create a Custom Animation

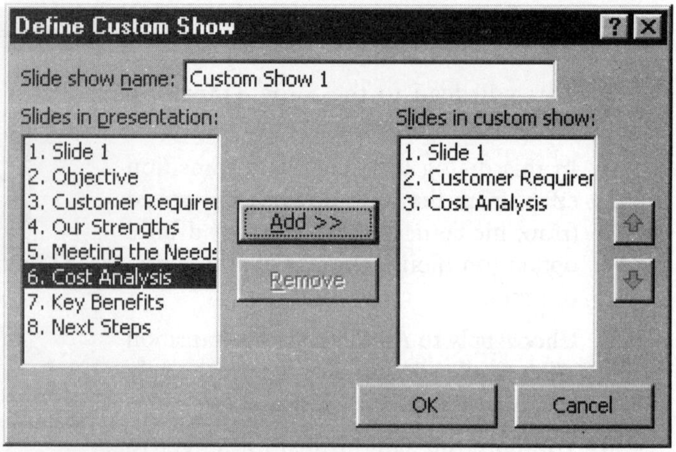

1. Select the slide where you want to put this animation and display it in the Slide view.
2. Select Custom Animation from the Animation Effects toolbar.
3. In the Custom Animation dialog box, check the items you want to animate and set the order and timing.
4. Click at Effects panel to select the effects from the drop-down list.
5. Select the options here according to your liking or choose the ones selected in the dialog box shown here.
6. You can also preview an animation by clicking the Animation Preview button on the Animation Effects toolbar.

ADDING ACTION BUTTONS

These buttons allow you to play sound, video at your choice when displaying the presentation.

To Add an Action Button:

1. Select the slide to which you want to add this button. This can be done in any view except Slide Sorter view.
2. Select Action buttons from the Slide Show menu.
3. Select a button of your choice.
4. Position the button in your slide at any place of your liking.

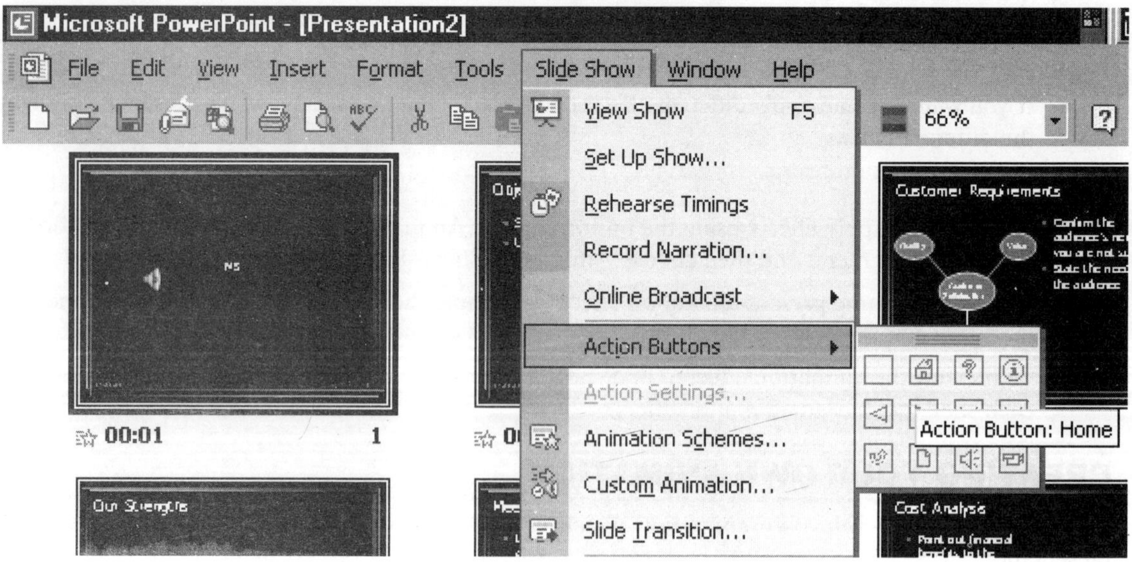

5. On clicking the button PowerPoint will give rise to a new dialog box called Action settings.
6. Make the necessary settings and click Ok.
7. You action button is now properly placed in the slide.
8. You can add actions to other objects simply by selecting them and then choosing Action settings from the Slide Show menu.

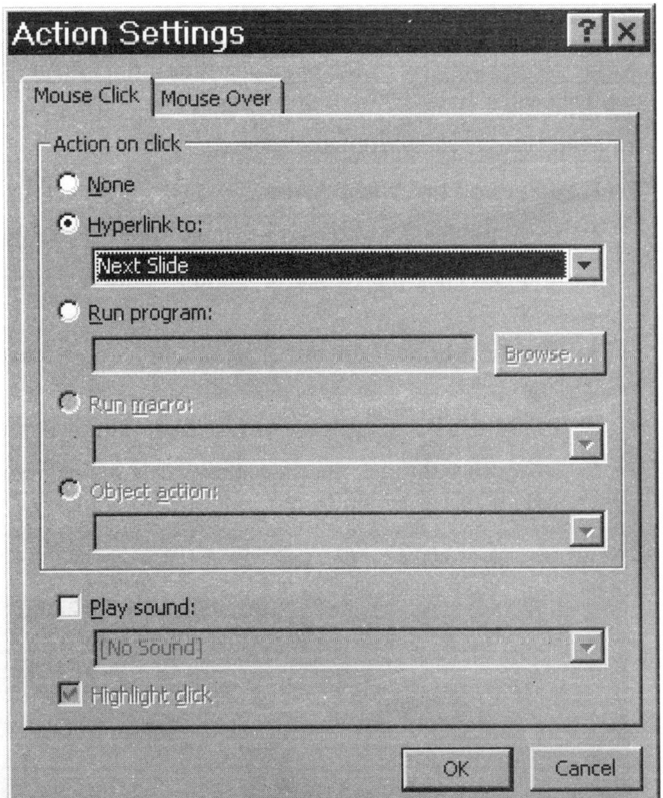

SETTING THE SHOW

Now comes the most important part of the software where you are going to setup the whole show of presentation to run without your help. You can choose to hide few slides for not displaying.

To Set Up the Slide Show:

1. From the Slide Show menu, choose Set Up Show.
2. In the dialog box, as shown on the next page, choose the type of show, which slides to show or hide, and the method to advance slides.
3. Click Ok.
4. Click the Projector Wizard button in the Set Up Show dialog box for help connecting your computer to a projector.
5. Choose Custom Shows from the Slide Show menu to add slides from this presentation to a custom show.
6. Even though a slide is hidden, you can display it by clicking a hyperlink or an action pointing to it.

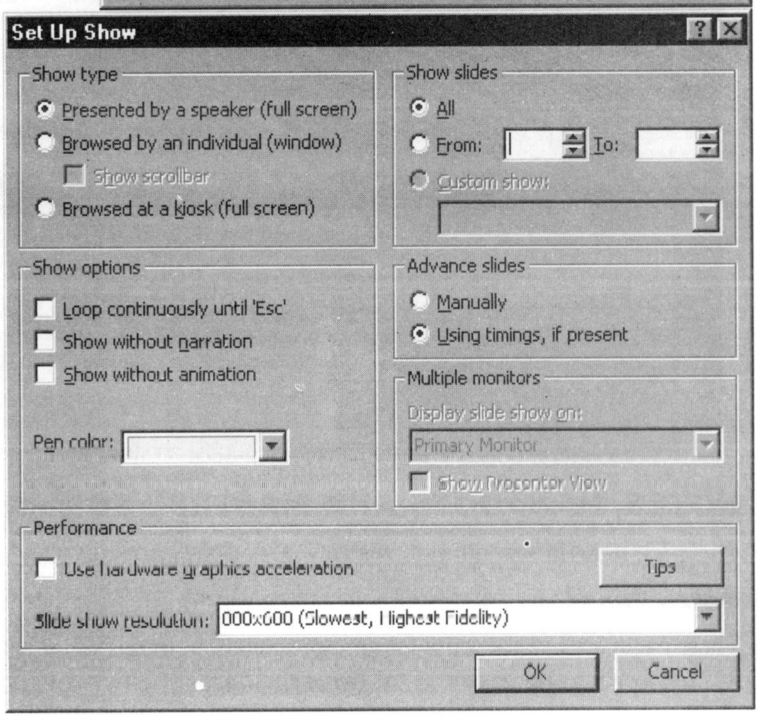

REHEARSING THE SHOW

As we see the preview of the page before printing. PowerPoint also allows you to do the same. For this you have what is called the Rehearsing of the Show.

You can run the show from any view.

To Rehearse the Slide Show:

1. From the Slide Show menu, choose Rehearse Timings.
2. You can click the Rehearse Timings button on the Slide Sorter toolbar too in the Slide Sorter view.
3. The show begins with the timer set at the top left hand corner of the screen, as shown on the next page.
4. To use these timings, choose Use Slide Timings in the Set Up Show dialog box.
5. To advance through the slide show, click anywhere on the slide. You can also right-click anywhere and choose as action from the shortcut menu.

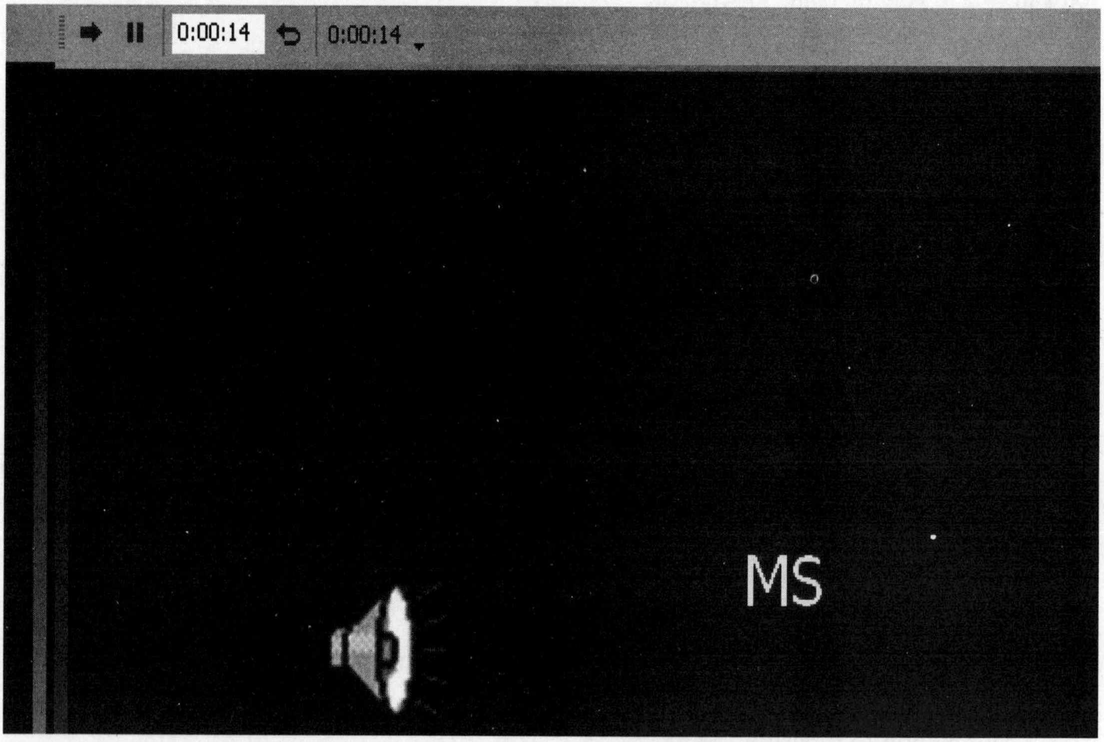

NOTES, HANDOUTS AND MASTERS FOR PRESENTATION

There are three important tools for your presentation. These tools are:

Notes Pages

These pages are like the script for your presentation. In this script you have an image of slides along with the words you want to deliver for the specific slide.

Handouts

These printed pages are the hard copies of the presentation slides which you can distribute to y or audience.

Master

These are control elements of a slide like the title master which controls appearance of the title on all the slides.

Using Notes Pages

Notes Pages act like a cheat sheet for your presentation. You would write the text you want to read without letting the audience know that you are reading during the course of a presentation for each slide.

Creating Notes

PowerPoint offers two ways for preparing Notes Pages. These notes can be prepared while working on slides or after you have finished with all the slides.

To create notes using Notes Pages, do this:

1. Click the View menu and choose Notes Pages.
2. In the Notes Page View, you see the entire Notes page as it will print. There is a picture of the slide at the top and a text place holder at the bottom. Click the place holder to begin entering the text for your Note.

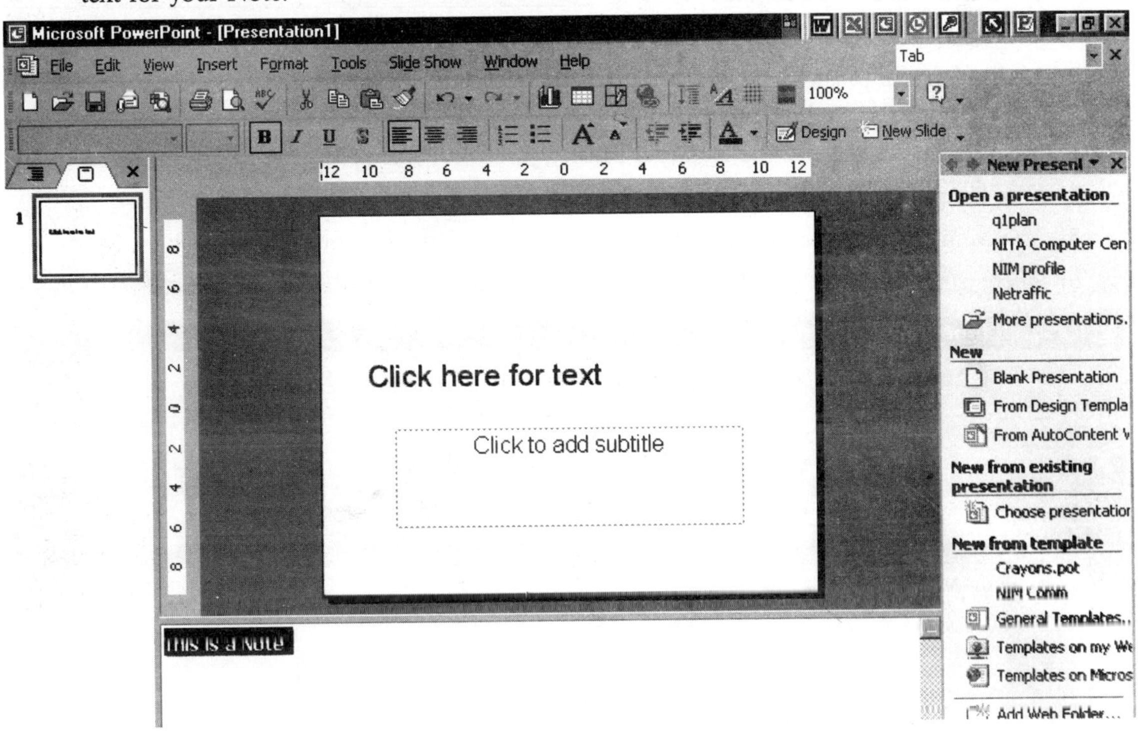

Printing Handouts

You can print your entire presentation in the form of handouts. These handouts are used to distribute among the audience in advance. You can also print specific slides, notes pages or outline pages.

For this do the following:

1. Open the presentation you want to print.
2. Click the File menu and Print. The Print dialog box appears.
3. In the Print what: box, click the item you want to print.
4. If you select Handouts, you can then select a number of slides per page and whether the order should be horizontal or vertical,
5. Select any other options you want to apply.
6. After applying the option in the handouts section, click OK.

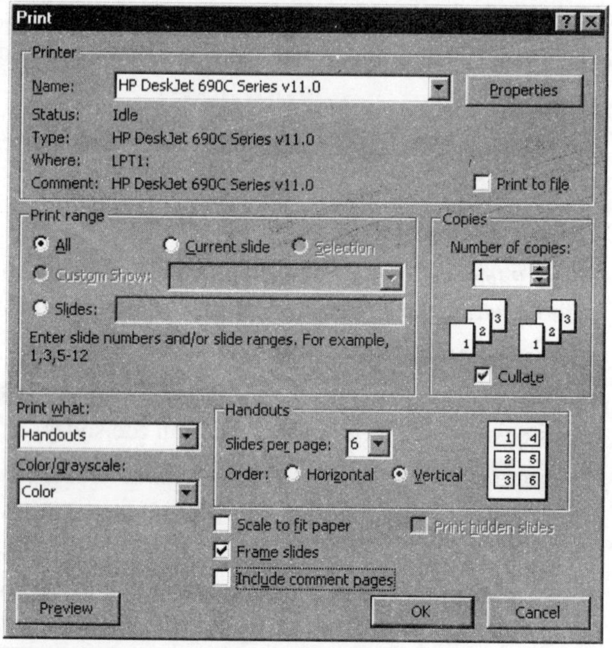

Handouts Master

The Handouts Master can be used to modify your Handout format. For this do the following:

1. Click the View menu, highlight Master and choose Handout Master. The Handout Master appears.
2. In the Handout Master view, you can select the two slide per page, three slides per page or the six slides per page formats by clicking on the Handout Master toolbar as shown.
3. To apply any changes to the Handout Master, just follow the procedure as for the Notes master.
4. Save the presentation file to save any changes you make to the Handout Master.
5. You cannot change the position of the slide images on the Handout Master.
6. There is no notes text placeholder on the Handout Master.

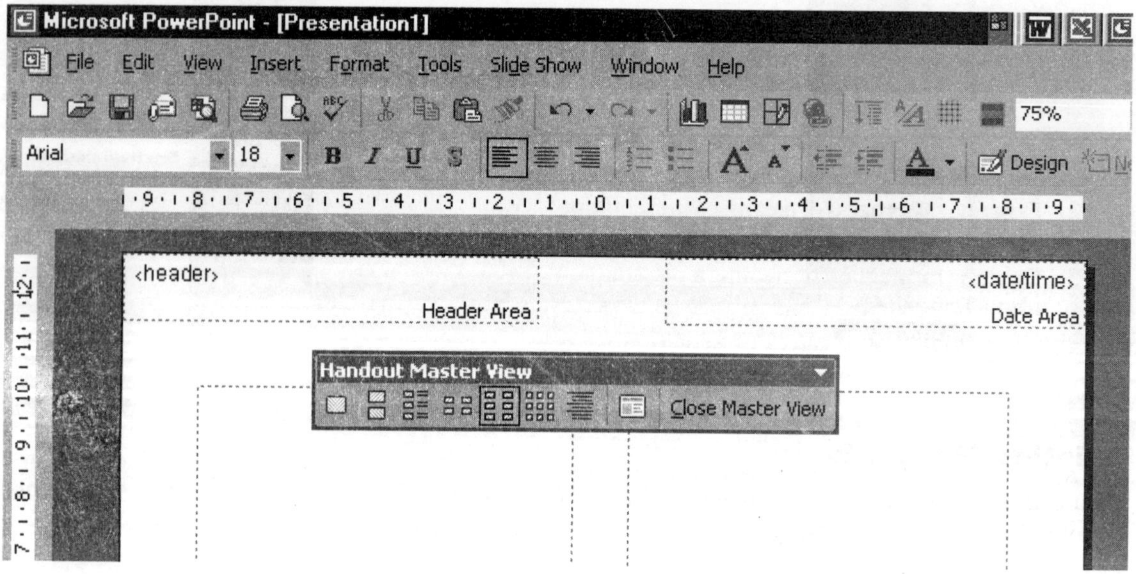

Computer Room Activity

Creating a Presentation

Prepare a presentation of your class highlighting the following:

Winner of most disciplined class in the school

Maximum number of first class in last smester

Five students representing the school cricket team

Two students representing the school hockey team

Winner of cleanest class in the school

After you have prepared the presentation, add notes and then run the slide show.

Multiple Choice Questions

1. PowerPoint is used for:
   (a) Word processing (b) Spreadsheets
   (c) Presentations
2. Overhead projections can be created using PoerPoint:
   (a) Yes (b) No
3. AutoContent Wizard creates a
   (a) Document (b) Presentation
   (c) Spreadsheet
4. There is no need to use templates in PowerPoint:
   (a) True (b) False
5. You can view your presentation through various views :
   (a) Yes (b) No
6. You can move your text in the slide, up and down:
   (a) Yes (b) No
7. A slide with background picture can be created in PowerPoint:
   (a) Yes (b) No
8. You can even have textured patterns in the background of a slide:
   (a) Yes (b) No
9. You can add organization format in the form of a :
   (a) Table (b) Chart
   (c) Graphic
10. You can use a picture as a background for a slide:
    (a) Yes (b) No

Descriptive Type Questions

1. How would you start PowerPoint?
2. Describe the process of creating a presentation using AutoContent Wizard.
3. Describe the method of creating a presentation using Tempaltes.
4. How would you create a presentation using the various slide options?
5. Describe the various views of looking at presentations in PowerPoint.
6. Describe the process of entering text into slides
7. What is the function of Collapse?
8. Describe the various type of backgrounds which you can have in your slides.
9. How would you change the alignment of the text of the slides?
10. How would you make sure that there is no misspelled word in your text.
11. How would you set the various options of AutoCorrect?
12. Describe the process of adding an audio clip to the slide.
13. How is a video clip added to the slide?
14. What is a Note Page?
15. What is a Handout?

Part - IV

23 Introduction to Visual FoxPro

INTRODUCTION

Visual FoxPro is an extension of the database software which has been in use from dBASE version I to IV, Foxbase+ and so on with FoxPro for DOS and now this version for Windows.

STARTING VISUAL FOXPRO

As you would do in the case of any windows based software, you start this software too either from the Start menu, Programs or in case you have the icon, you start with it. Other way of starting could be from Windows Explorer where you click/double-click at the file named VFP.EXE.

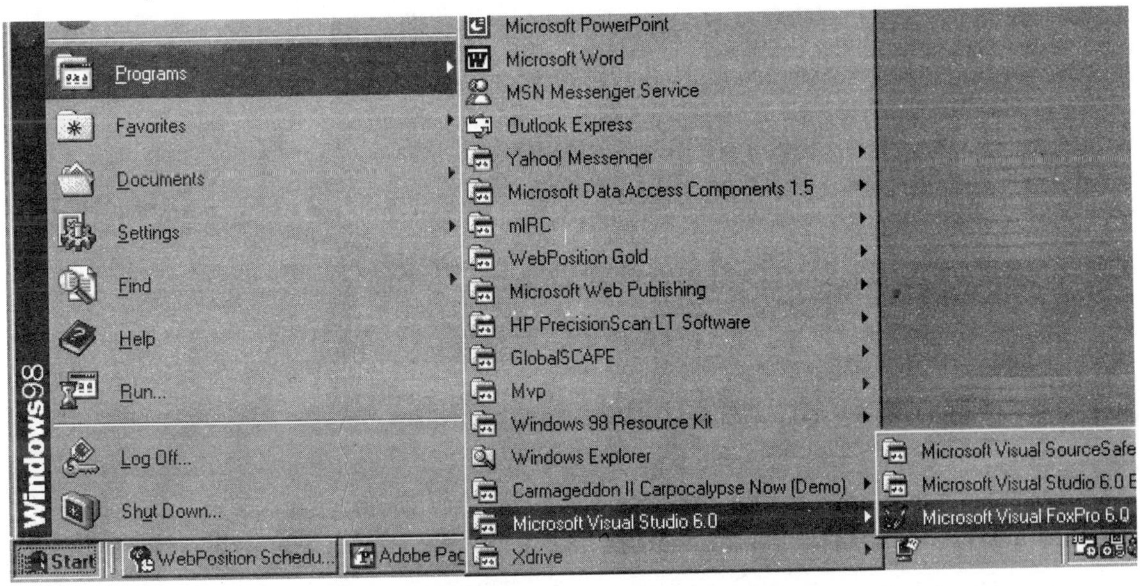

In all cases you would end up having a blank slate for operation, as shown on the next page. As you can see there is also a small Command window on the screen. This is used to write code. For all those who have graduated from DOS based software and quite keen to give commands by writing them. They can do so here.

THE MENU SYSTEM

This bar is there on the screen of most of the windows based software. It is here that you have all the menu options. Under each menu option you have the various commands which can be used to do most of the operations in the software.

You can access these menus either by mouse or by pressing the Alt key and then pressing the letter

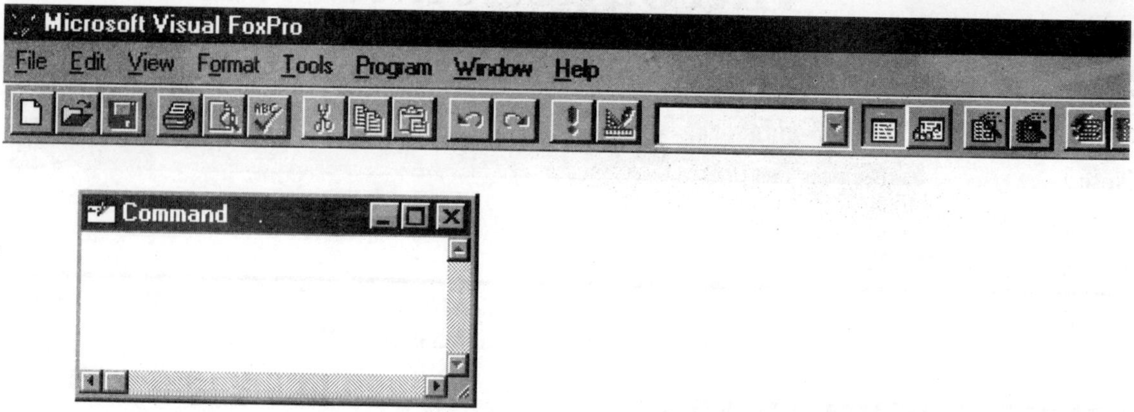

underneath the menu. For example Alt+F would open the file menu. Once it is opened, then you can use the arrow keys to move up and down. At a given time, some menu options might appear dimmed, which means that you cannot execute that option now.

To choose a menu item, highlight it and press Enter. A mouse click works just as well. You can even press the underlined letter in the option, if it has one. Notice that in the pop-up menus, you do not press the Alt key with the underlined letter. Some menu options have special key combinations, called shortcut keys, that enable you to jump to that option directly without going through the menu pads. FoxPro displays these shortcut keys along the right side of the pop-up menus. The shortcut key for file, open, for example is Ctrl+O. This means that you can press Ctrl+O any time while you are in Visual FoxPro with the System menu active to open an existing file.

FEATURES OF THE FOXPRO SCREEN

Each software has its own way of representing the various options on the screen. Now that you have seen how the opening screen looks like. Let me show you what these features are:

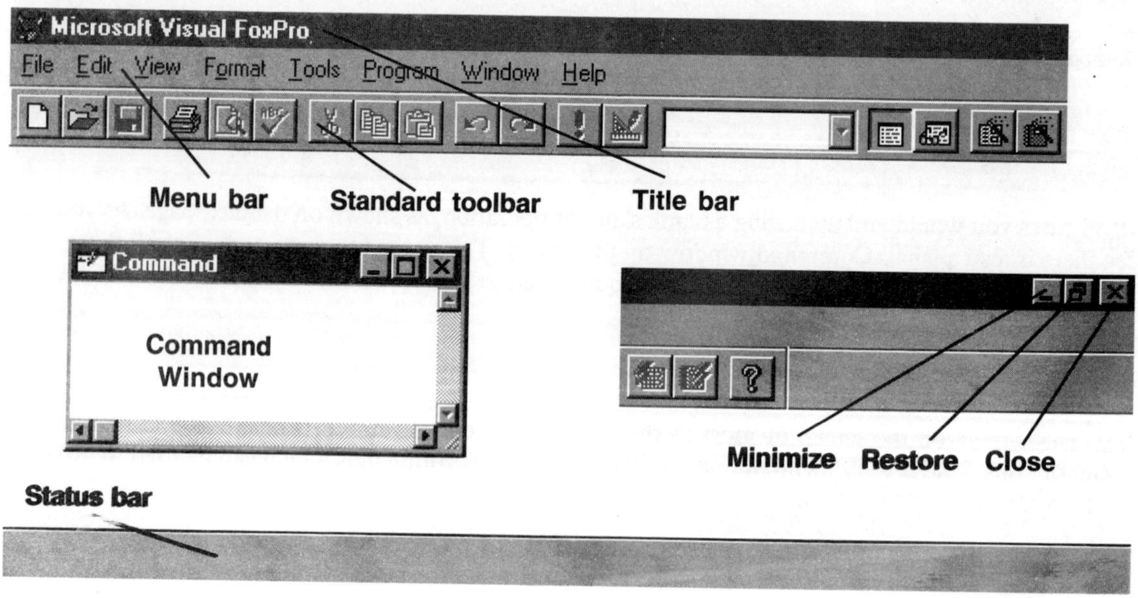

Minimize	It reduces FoxPro to an icon.
Maximize/Restore	It maximize the size of the main FoxPro window. When maximized, a window has no border. It can also be used to restore the window to preceding size after minimization or maximization.
Close	It closes FoxPro.
Command Window	It is normally placed at the bottom right corner of the screen and is used for typing commands.
Title Bar	It is at the top of the screen and displays the name of the program, i.e., Microsoft Visual FoxPro.
Status bar	It displays various kinds of information related to the window that is currently opened.
Standard Toolbar	It contains buttons for performing the most common actions in Visual FoxPro.

You will use them all later in the book.

FILE TYPES

With each software you work on files. Depending upon the software, the files have extensions. In fact from the extension of the files, you can guess from which software it has been created. For example, DOC files are usually the document files and are created using word processing programs. In FoxPro you work on various files. When you opt for creating a new file from the File menu, you come across a dialog box, as shown here.

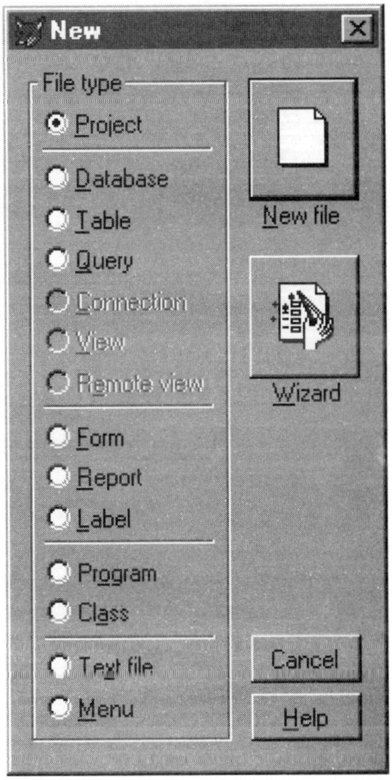

Various options of the dialog box are:

Project	In Visual FoxPro you work on projects which are in turn a combined effort of various files which are executable. It organizes various files to form a single project with extension .pjx.
Database	It is a collection of various data files which have something in common.
Table	It is used to hold the raw data of the database. Your data is entered into the tables. It is then organized into rows and columns.
Query	A query is there to extract information from the table. These can be used to select, change, add or delete records in your database.
Form	You can create forms for entering data for the database. This helps in displaying the data in structural manner and can be entered easily.
Report	These present the data you select in a printed format. Reports can be based on tables to show all the data from the given table, or they can be based on queries to show only information that meets certain criteria.

Label — It enables you to use table data to create mailing labels.

Program — It is a plain text file used to hold Visual FoxPro programming code.

Class — It is used in object oriented programming to hold a class.

Text file — It has a plain text file.

Menu — The file holds the specifications of the menu system for a custom application.

Besides these you have buttons for Connection, View and Remote view. These can be created only when you are using the software. A connection file lets you name and save the specifications used to connect to a server on the network. View and Remote view files let you create updatable queries based on local and remote tables.

THE TOOLBARS

For any software toolbar contains the various tools which help you work fast. They are like the tools which a doctor uses for operation. FoxPro has several toolbars, each of which is customized for the current task. This arrangement eliminates the confusion (and space problems) of having all buttons available at all times. You can experiment with the toolbars in FoxPro 6 by selecting View, which opens the Toolbar dialog box, shown earlier. From this dialog you can select specific toolbars or customize your own selection. You should only keep open the toolbars that you will need because the screen and workspace can become quite cluttered with a lot of toolbars on the screen.

The most important one of the toolbars is the one called Standard toolbar. It has the following commands. These commands are otherwise available under the various menu options too.

Button	*Name*	*Description*
	New	Opens the New File dialog box to create a new file.
	Open	Opens the Open File dialog box to open an existing file.
	Save	Saves changes made to the current file. By default, the button uses the file's original filename, except for a new file that has no name, in which case it prompts for a filename.
	Print	Prints the active file, Command window contents, or Clipboard contents.
	Print Preview	Uses a preview window to show what Print would output.
	Spelling	Activates the spell checker.
	Cut	Cuts the current selected text or object and places it on the Clipboard.
	Copy	Copies the current selected text or object and places it on the Clipboard.
	Paste	Copies the current contests of the Clipboard and pastes it at the current insertion point location.

	Undo	Undoes the last action or command, with some limitation.
	Redo	Repeats the last command or action.
	Run	Appears enabled if Visual FoxPro has an executable file open, such as a screen or program.
	Modify form	Switches the currently executing form back into designer mode.
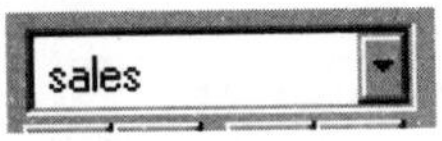	Database	Lists the names of all open databases in a drop-down list. The current database appears in the text box. You can switch to a different database by selecting it from the list.
	Command Window	Opens or a pop the View window back into view and makes it the active window.
	View Window	Opens or pops the View window back into view and makes it the active window.
	Form Wizard	Launches the Form Wizard.
	Report Wizard	Launches the Report Wizard.
	AutoForm Wizard	Creates a form from the current table.
	AutoReport Wizard	Creates a report from the current table.
	Help	Displays Visual FoxPro's Help Contents screen.

VISUAL DESIGNER

As mentioned earlier, we work with Tables, Queries, etc., in FoxPro. There are 2 easy way of creating them. One of them is Visual Designer and the other is Wizard. Personally I prefer Wizards. They ask you minimum questions and give you the maximum results. Visual Designer on the other hand lets you design above mentioned files yourself or customize those you have created using the Wizards. Designer are comparatively difficult to use.

WIZARDS

As we have see in quite a number of software, Wizards are the best way to start if you are not very much familiar with the working of the software. Wizards not only create the required files for you but also guide you to the working of the software.

There are as many as 22 wizards in Visual Fox Pro. They are:

Application	Cross-Tab	Database
Documenting	Form	Graph
Import	Label	Local View

Mail Merge
Oracle Upsizing
Remote View
Setup
Web Publishing
One to Many Form
PivotTable
Report
Table
One to Many Report
Query
SQL Server Upsizing
WWW Search Page

These can be accessed from the Tools menu, as shown here.

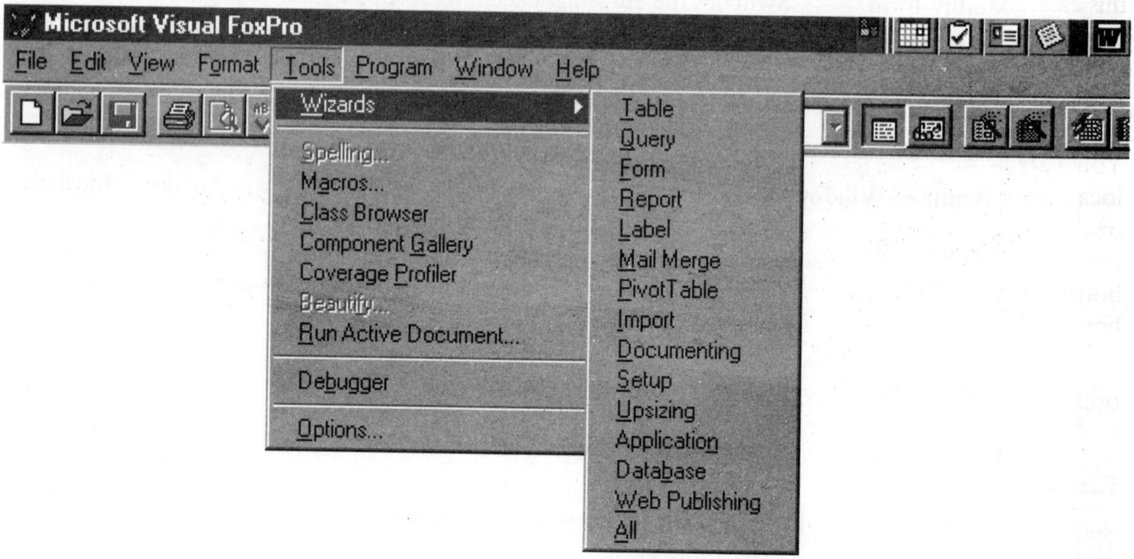

Let us create a project using Application Wizard and understand how this Wizard can help us in building up an application of our choice.

APPLICATION WIZARD AND BUILDER

As expected you would click at Application in the Wizards list selected from the Tools menu. Once clicked it would lead us to the first screen as shown here. You give here the name of the project which you want to run. The associated file would be shown to you. You should initially opt for creation of the project directory too. The wizard will put the application components into the project file, open the Project Manager for this new project, and show you the help file entry for the Developing Applications Using the Application Framework.

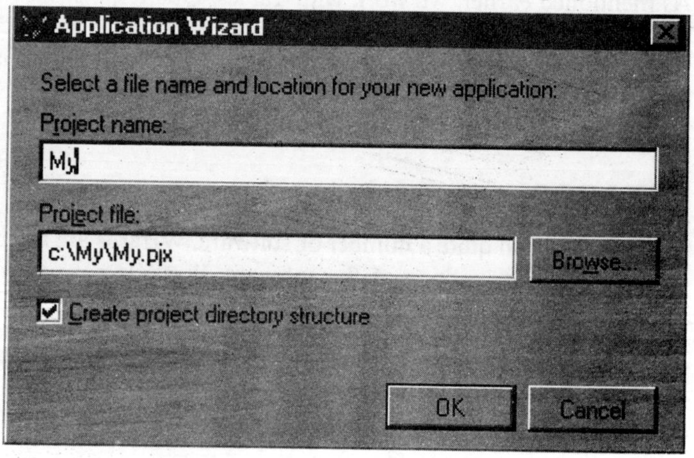

The directory structure will make it easy for your to keep track of the components of your application. Now comes the part of the Application Builder. First of its screen is now shown to you. It has 6 panels, you are given the first panel to work on, i.e., General.

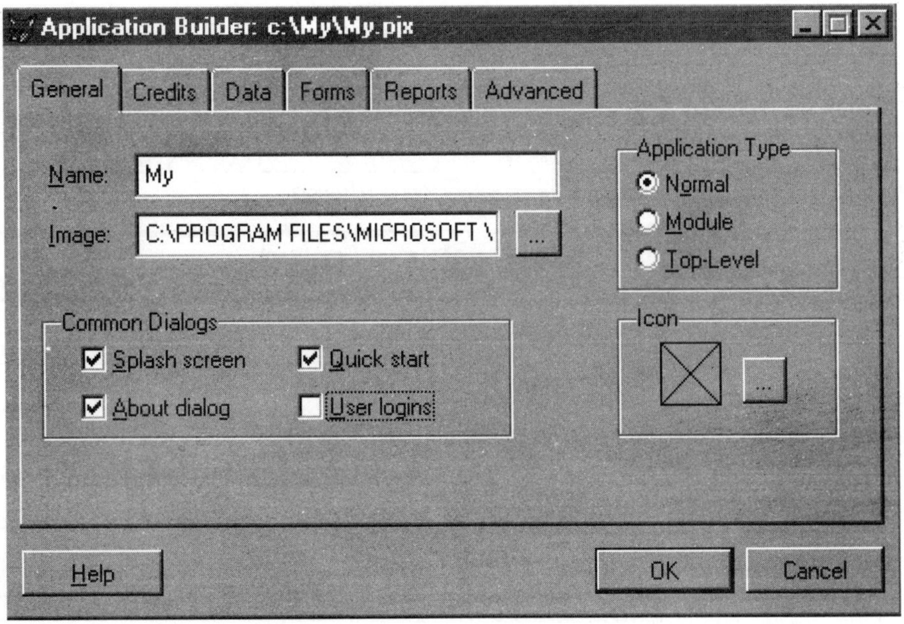

As you can see from the dialog box on the screen, you have to give the name of the project which you are working on, in this case, My. In the Image dialog box, you have to give the name of the file to be used as image. You can type the location of the file or browse by clicking at the button next to the box.

There are other options too on the screen, which are:

Common Dialogs

Splash Screen	If clicked it will create a splash screen that is displayed during the loading process of the application. If left unclicked, it will skip the splash screen.
About dialog	If clicked it includes an About dialog on the help menu. If unchecked it excludes About dialog.
Quick Start	It is a menu form which enables the user to access the forms and reports without using the menu system. If clicked this box includes a quick start form and if unclicked it excludes the quick start form.
User Logins	If clicked this box requires users to log the application using a user name and password. If unclicked it skips this option.

Application Type

Normal	If clicked then the application will run in the Visual FoxPro desktop. The main Visual FoxPro screen will contain the forms for the application.
Module	If clicked then the application will be a module that is called from some other application.
Top-Level	If clicked then the application runs outside of the Visual FoxPro screen as a top-level application under Windows.

Now click at Credit to get the next screen. Credit screen, as shown on the next page, has the following dialog boxes, which you have to fill up according to your requirements.

Next is the Data panel.

As you can see, I have chosen the option of Books from the database. You can choose from the various databases available to you. For this click at first of the 2 boxes on the top right corner of the box. When

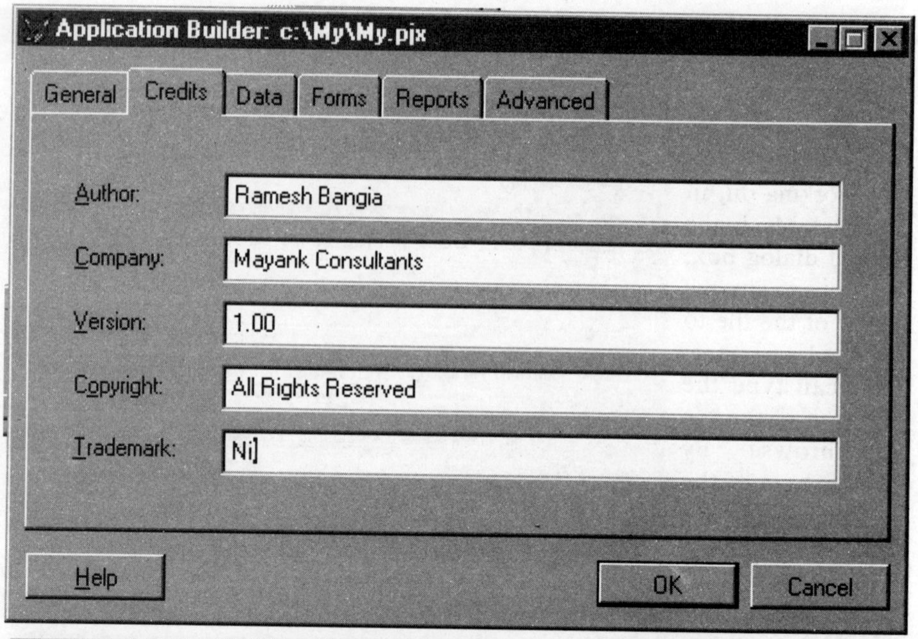

clicked it will give rise to the various screens of the database wizard and would allow you to create a new database. In this case I have chosen, as said before, Books. The various screen that this Wizard will present to you are shown on the next pages and also allows you to save this database.

Coming back to Data panel, it has the following options:

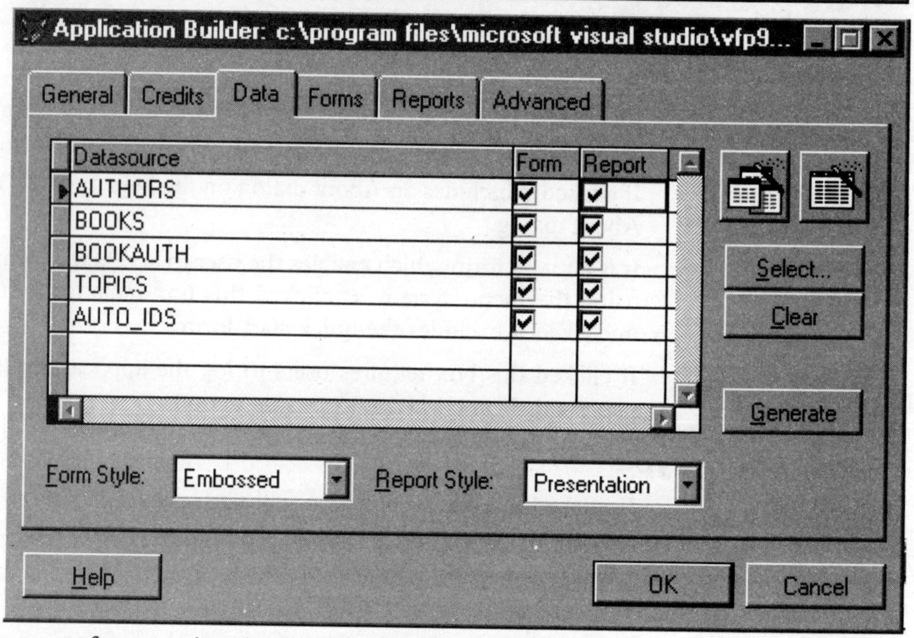

Datasource As mentioned I had chosen Books, so this will show the various datafields of the Book database. It will generally include all the tables of the database.

Form If clicked against any of the table name, it will create a form for the same using the Form Wizard.

Report As above, it will create a report format using the Report wizard.

Form Style The various styles to choose from are: Standard, Chiseled, Shadowed, Boxed, Embossed, Fancy, Stone, Flax, and Colorful. This would effect the way the forms created would look.

Report Style Various styles for report are: Presentation, Ledger, Executive, Banded, and Casual. Choose the one which you want for your report generated here.

Select If clicked it produces the File Open dialog box to enable you to search for tables or databases on the disk drive and include them in the list of tables.

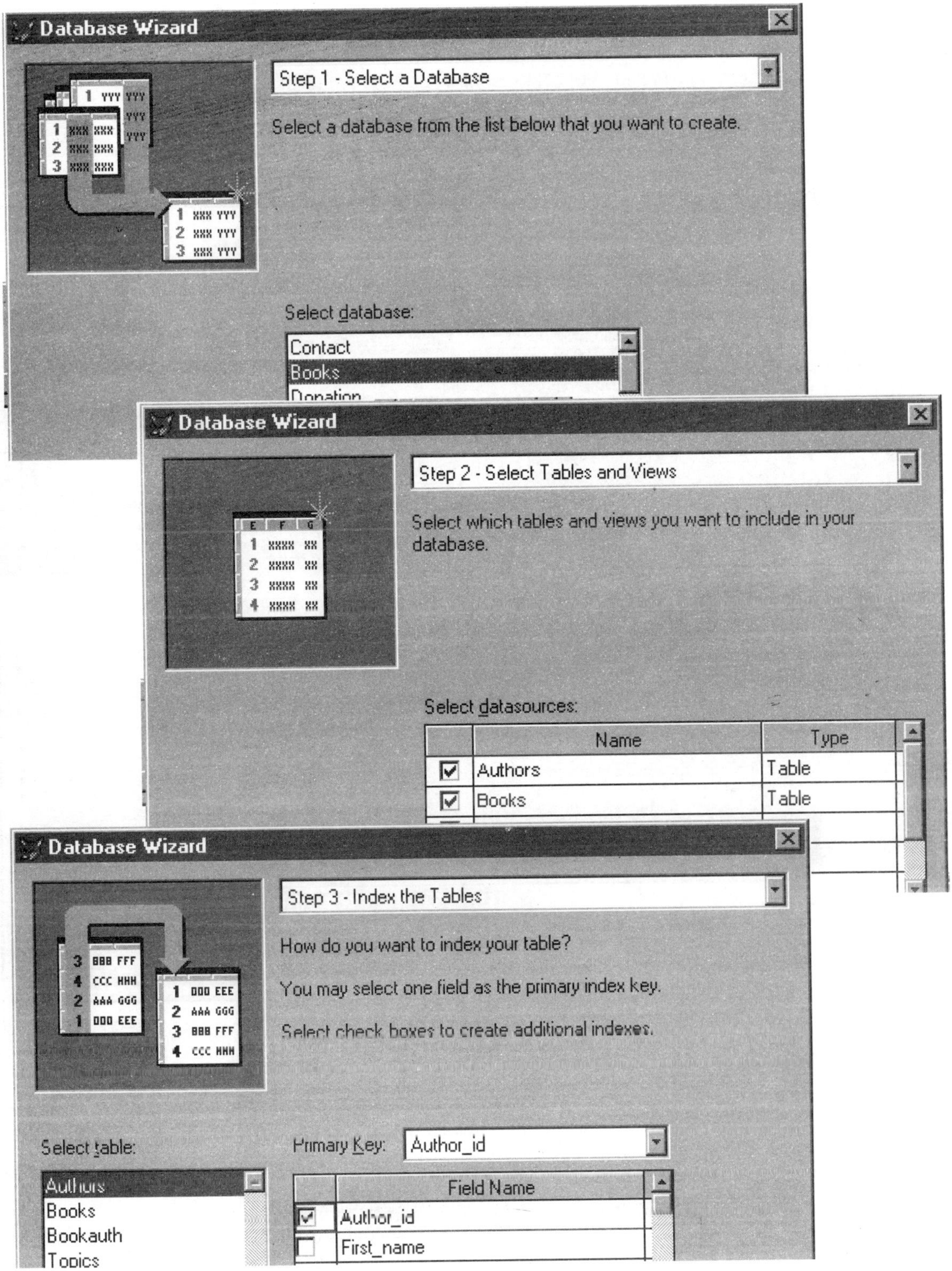
Database Wizard
Step 1 - Select a Database
Select a database from the list below that you want to create.
Select database:
Contact
Books
Donation
Database Wizard
Step 2 - Select Tables and Views
Select which tables and views you want to include in your database.
Select datasources:
Name
Type
Authors
Table
Books
Table
Database Wizard
Step 3 - Index the Tables
How do you want to index your table?
You may select one field as the primary index key.
Select check boxes to create additional indexes.
Select table:
Authors
Books
Bookauth
Topics
Primary Key:
Author_id
Field Name
Author_id
First_name

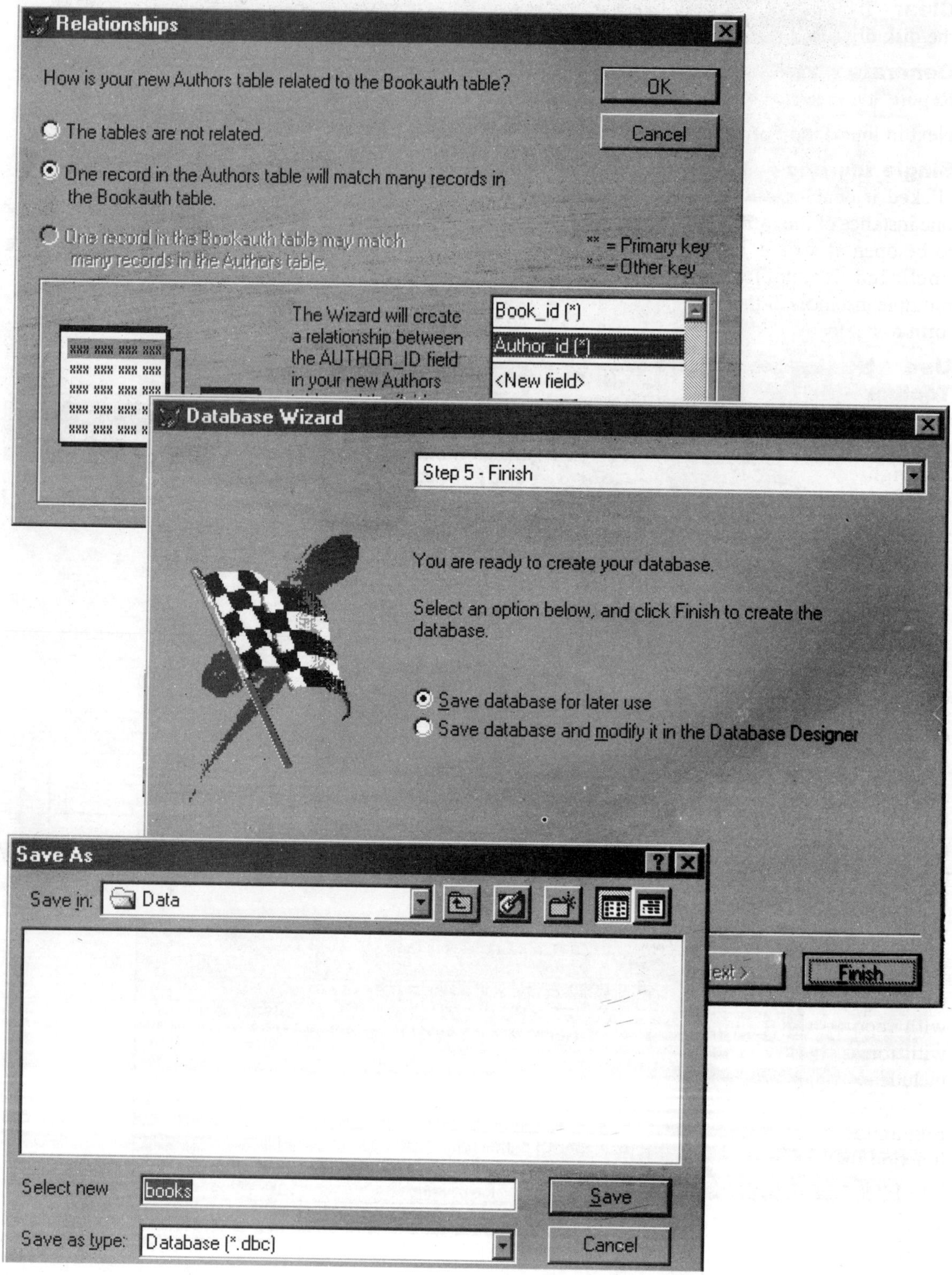
Relationships
How is your new Authors table related to the Bookauth table?
OK
Cancel
The tables are not related.
One record in the Authors table will match many records in the Bookauth table.
One record in the Bookauth table may match many records in the Authors table.
** = Primary key
* = Other key
The Wizard will create a relationship between the AUTHOR_ID field in your new Authors
Book_id (*)
Author_id (*)
<New field>
Database Wizard
Step 5 - Finish
You are ready to create your database.
Select an option below, and click Finish to create the database.
Save database for later use
Save database and modify it in the Database Designer
Finish
Save As
Save in:
Data
Select new
books
Save
Save as type:
Database (*.dbc)
Cancel

Clear It clears out the list of tables from the screen to allow you to search for tables or databases on the disk drive and include them in the list of tables.

Generate It generates a form or report for the selected table in the grid using the Form Style and/or Report Style selected with the combo boxes.

Next in line is the Forms panel, it has the following options:

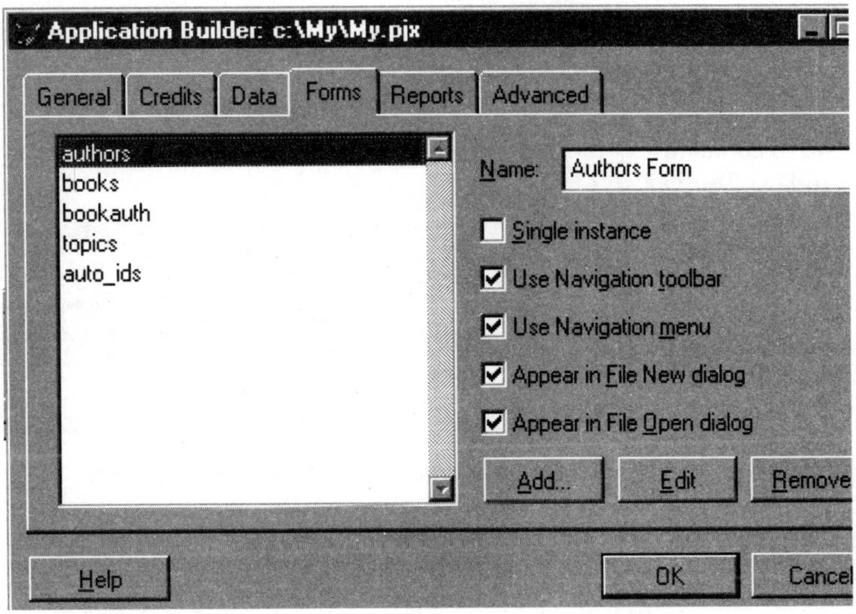

Single Instance If clicked it enables only one instance of the form to be open at a time, if unclicked it enables multiple instances of the form to be open.

Use Navigation Toolbar If clicked it will include a navigation toolbar for the highlighted form, if unclicked it omits the navigation toolbar.

Use Navigation Menu If clicked it includes a navigation menu for the highlighted form, if unclicked it omits the navigation menu.

Appear in File New Dialog If clicked it causes the form's name to appear in the application's New dialog.

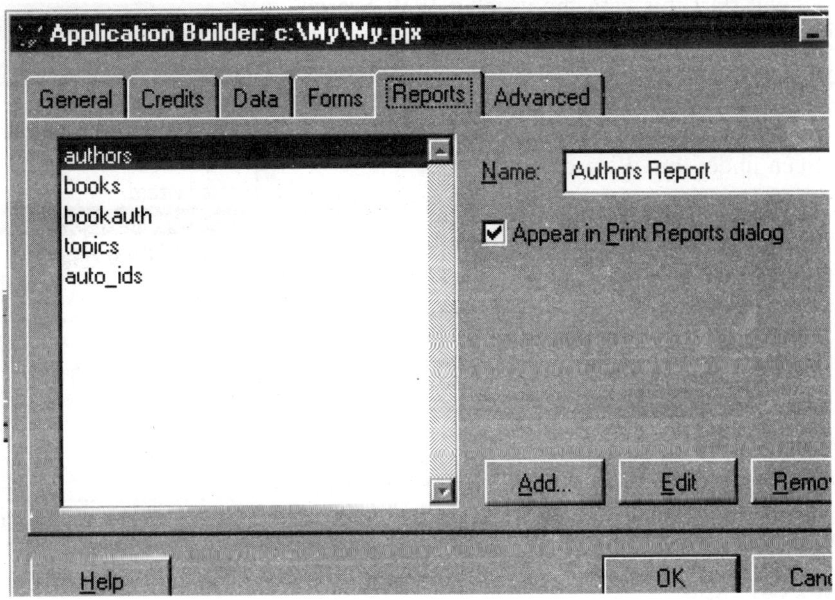

Appear in File Open Dialog If clicked it causes the form's name to appear in the application's Open dialog.

The next panel is Reports.

It is similar to the Forms panel except that it deals with reports rather than with forms. It is used to include existing reports in the application. The Add, Edit and Remove buttons function the same way as they on the Forms panel.

The last is Advanced panel.

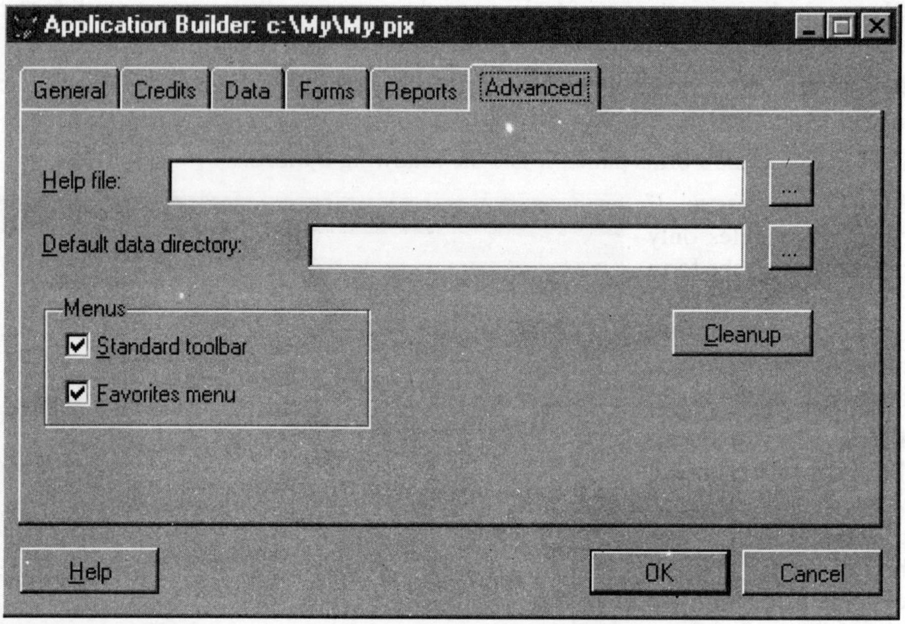

Here the Default Data Directory text box enables you to provide a path to the data that the application will use. The button alongwith allows you to browse for the directory you want. The menus: Standard Toolbar and Favorites Menu allow options to be included in their respective components. The Cleanup button runs a routing to reconcile any changes you have made in the Application Builder with the project file.

WWW SEARCH PAGE WIZARD

Next we will study the WWW Search Page Wizard. This allows you to create a Visual FoxPro based search page for the Web. For this you are required to have an Internet server set up to use the search page which is created. This will create 3 files with extensions, .HTM, .HTX and .IDC. You will need to copy these files into the WWW root directory for your Internet server application.

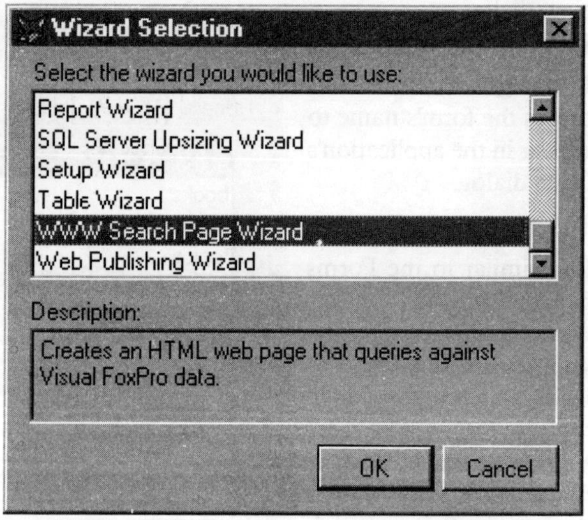

We will start this with the usual WWW Search Page from Tools menu and Wizards submenu. If you want you can select All to have the following dialog box and then select the one wanted by you. On the following pages, you will see the various screen under this Wizard.

The first one is just a welcome page. Next you have to choose the Search table from the table. The 3rd one asks you to set options. The 4th one sets up the Search page. The 5th one selects the fields. The 6th one allows set up background image. The 7th one is just the Finish one.

Once created you have to save the search page under a name.

Now you have to apply the search to get the page. For this you run the Visual FoxPro server application which is available under the Server subdirectory of Inetwzi and Tools directory. The file is named as

```
server.app
```

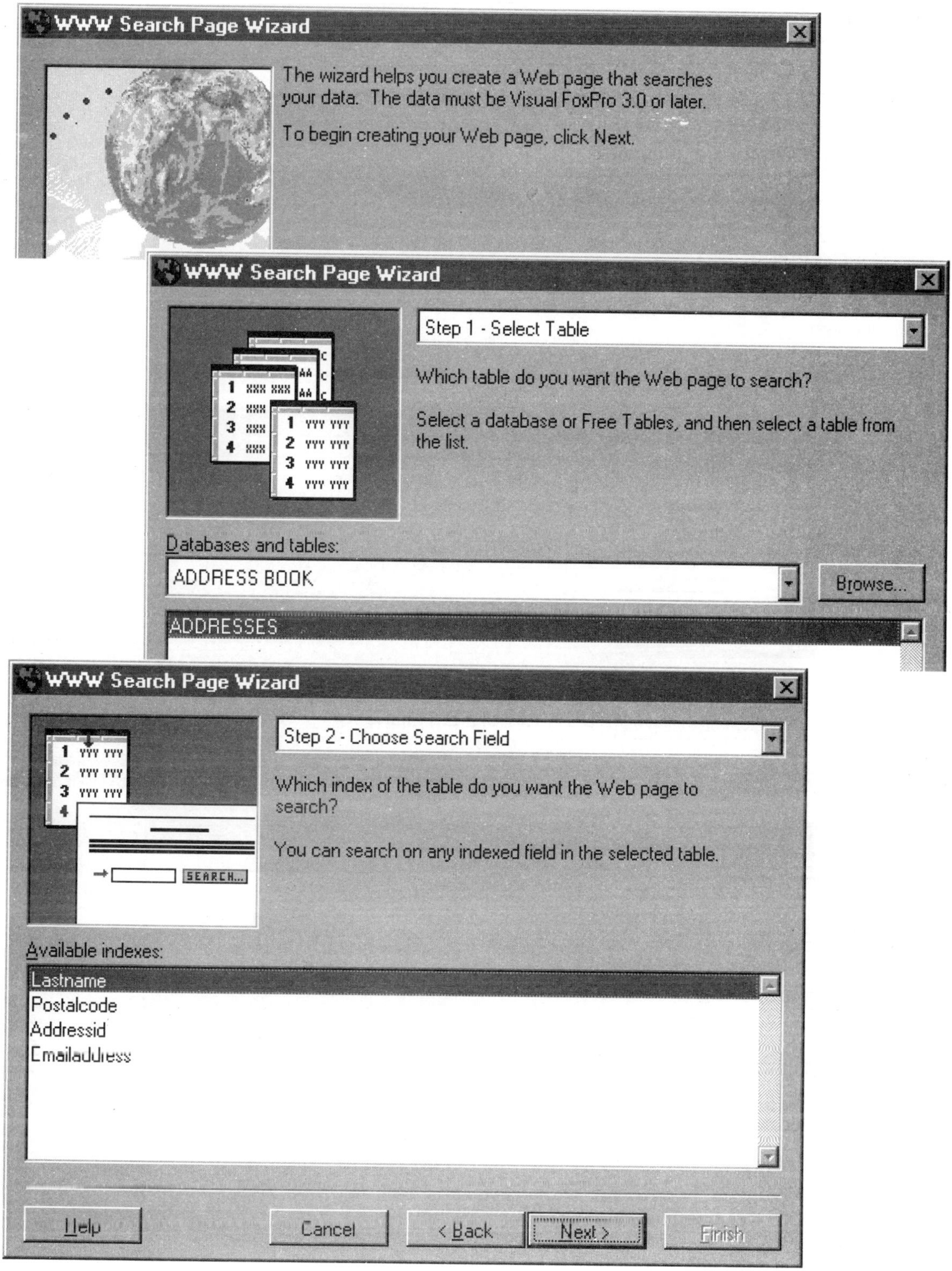
WWW Search Page Wizard
The wizard helps you create a Web page that searches your data. The data must be Visual FoxPro 3.0 or later.
To begin creating your Web page, click Next.
WWW Search Page Wizard
Step 1 - Select Table
Which table do you want the Web page to search?
Select a database or Free Tables, and then select a table from the list.
Databases and tables:
ADDRESS BOOK
Browse...
ADDRESSES
WWW Search Page Wizard
Step 2 - Choose Search Field
Which index of the table do you want the Web page to search?
You can search on any indexed field in the selected table.
Available indexes:
Lastname
Postalcode
Addressid
Emailaddress
Help
Cancel
< Back
Next >
Finish

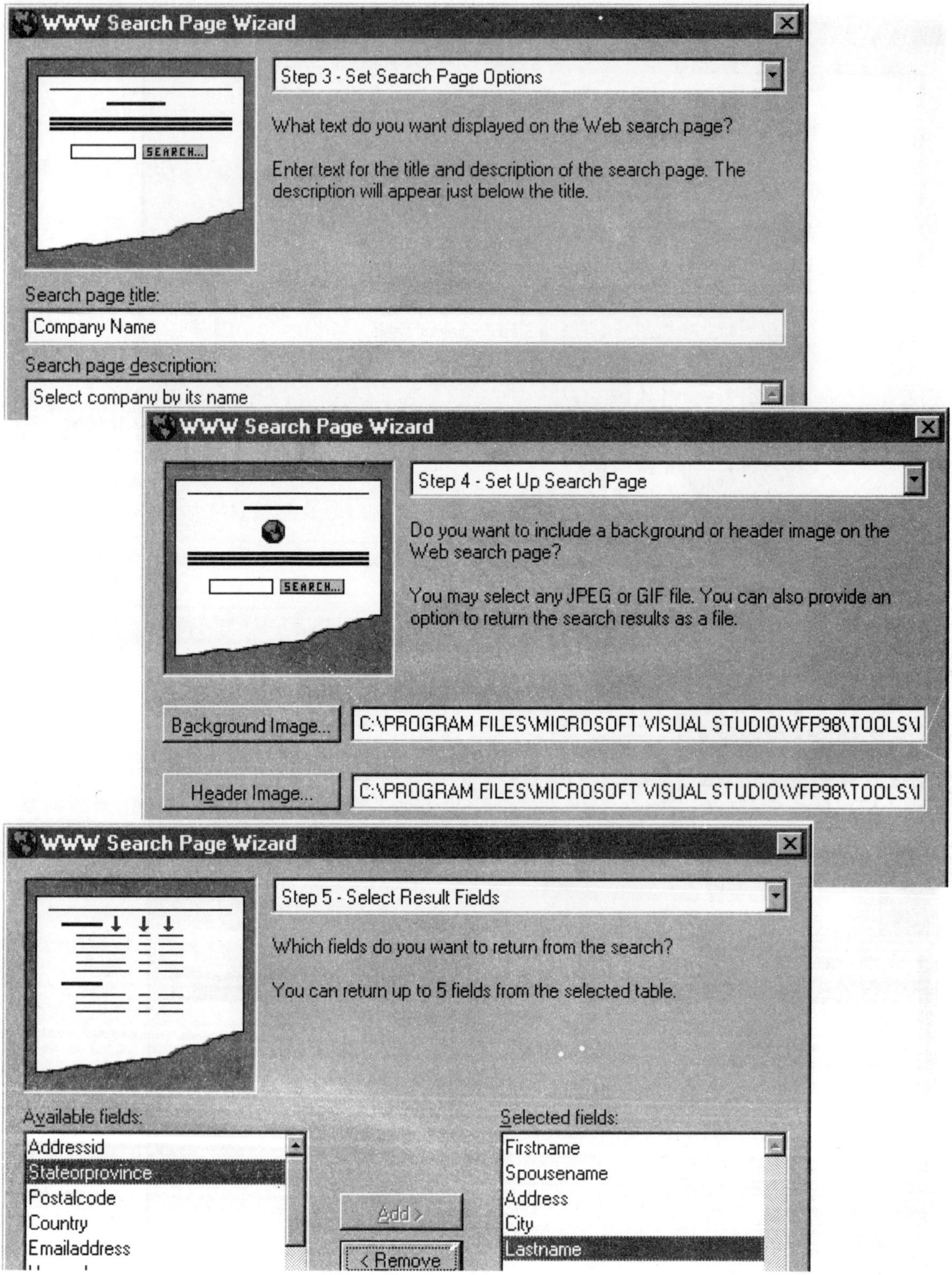
WWW Search Page Wizard
Step 3 - Set Search Page Options
What text do you want displayed on the Web search page?
Enter text for the title and description of the search page. The description will appear just below the title.
Search page title:
Company Name
Search page description:
Select company by its name
WWW Search Page Wizard
Step 4 - Set Up Search Page
Do you want to include a background or header image on the Web search page?
You may select any JPEG or GIF file. You can also provide an option to return the search results as a file.
Background Image...
C:\PROGRAM FILES\MICROSOFT VISUAL STUDIO\VFP98\TOOLS\I
Header Image...
C:\PROGRAM FILES\MICROSOFT VISUAL STUDIO\VFP98\TOOLS\I
WWW Search Page Wizard
Step 5 - Select Result Fields
Which fields do you want to return from the search?
You can return up to 5 fields from the selected table.
Available fields:
Addressid
Stateorprovince
Postalcode
Country
Emailaddress
Add >
< Remove
Selected fields:
Firstname
Spousename
Address
City
Lastname

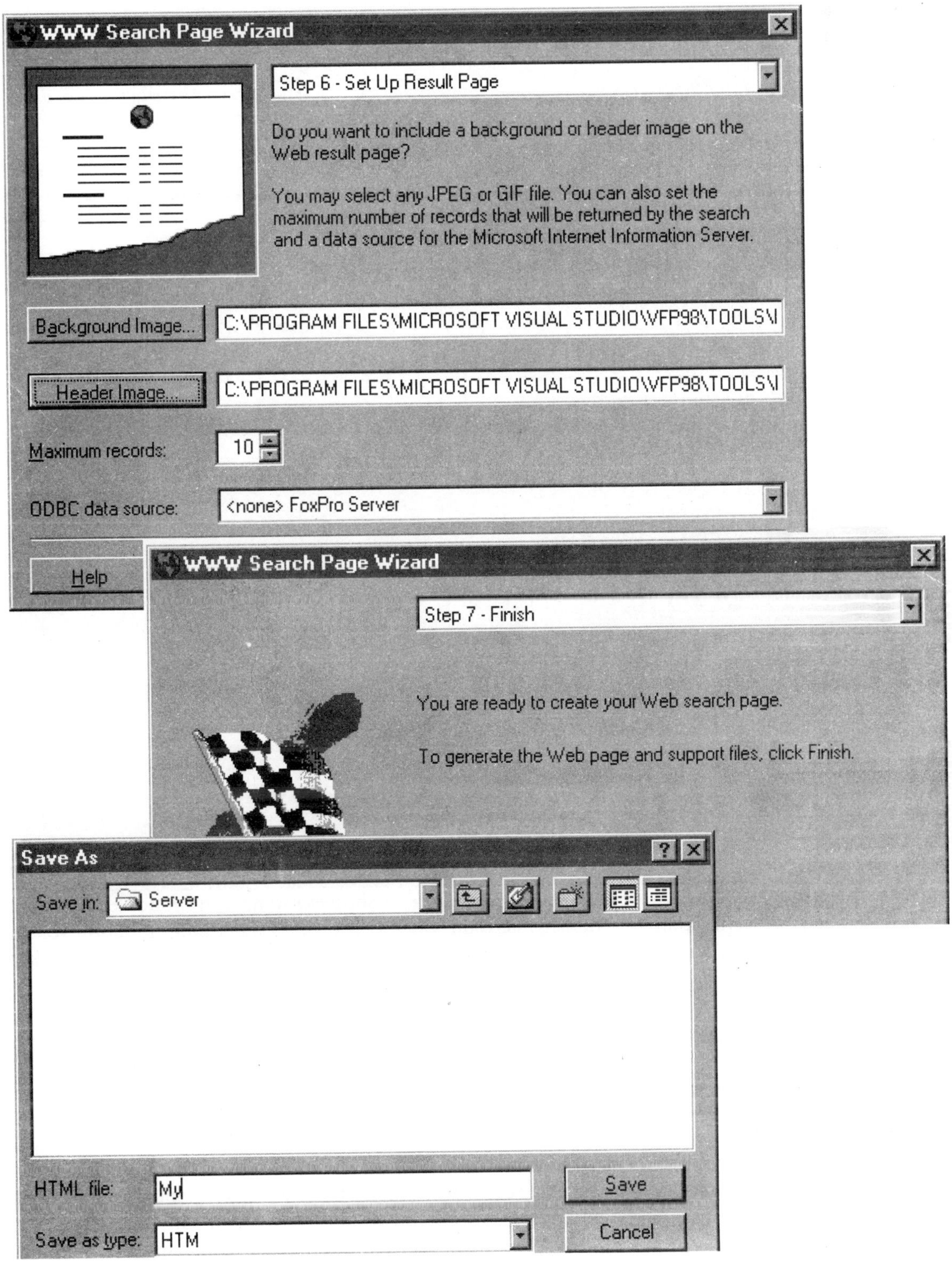
WWW Search Page Wizard
Step 6 - Set Up Result Page
Do you want to include a background or header image on the Web result page?
You may select any JPEG or GIF file. You can also set the maximum number of records that will be returned by the search and a data source for the Microsoft Internet Information Server.
Background Image...
C:\PROGRAM FILES\MICROSOFT VISUAL STUDIO\VFP98\TOOLS\I
Header Image...
C:\PROGRAM FILES\MICROSOFT VISUAL STUDIO\VFP98\TOOLS\I
Maximum records:
10
ODBC data source:
<none> FoxPro Server
Help
WWW Search Page Wizard
Step 7 - Finish
You are ready to create your Web search page.
To generate the Web page and support files, click Finish.
Save As
Save in:
Server
HTML file:
My
Save
Save as type:
HTM
Cancel

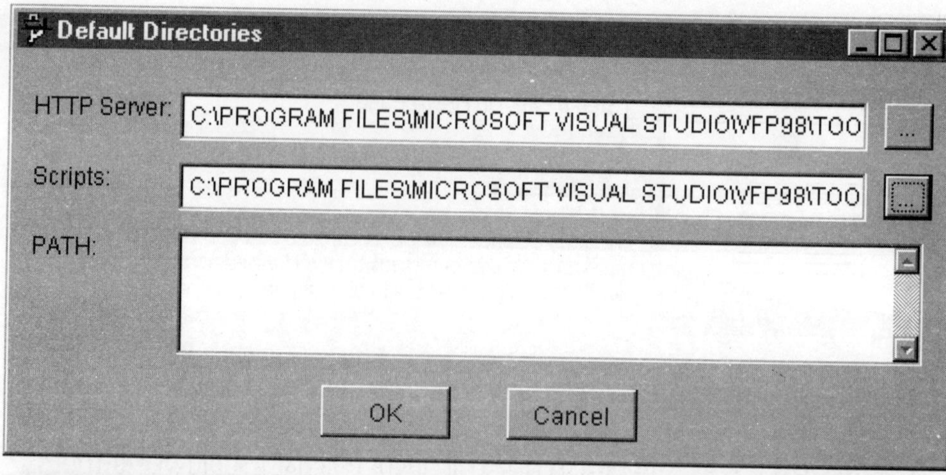

When you run this you get the dialog box as shown here. In this dialog box, you must specify the path to the WWW root directory in the HTTP Server text. The Scripts text box is used to enter the path to the WWW server's scripts directory. When clicked Ok it gives the box as shown above.

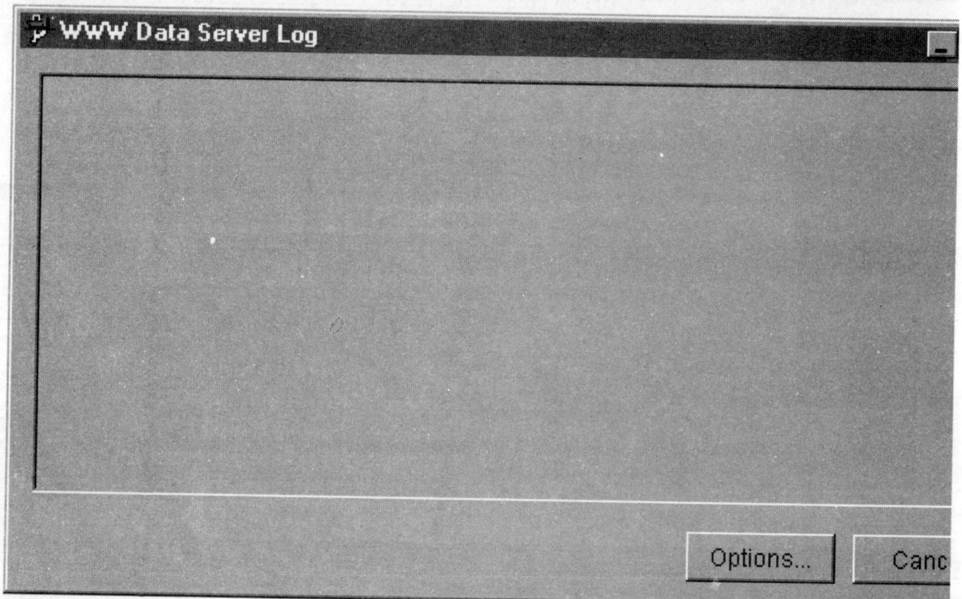

This box looks blank at this stage but will be filled up when you use the search page. To use your search page, you must have an Internet server running. You can then use your favorite Internet browser to navigate your file. Well look on the next page to see the output. Another interesting wizard is of Web publishing. It allows you to publish your data on the World Wide Web. It does not create a search page, as done in the above case but simply publishes the data.

So now you realize the importance of the Wizards in a software like this. It has in one routine created a project for you which can be used as your test project and the data can be filled in this to see the results.

THE COMMAND AND VIEW WINDOWS

Microsoft had been very smart. It knew that most of the users of Visual FoxPro would be those who will migrate from DOS version of dBASE or FoxPro. So it knew of the users who very happy typing the commands instead of clicking them by mouse. So it made a smart windows called Command Windows where you can alternatively type the command as would do in the DOS based software. It is just a convenient provided by Microsoft for those DOS users. However, if you feel confident of clicking the

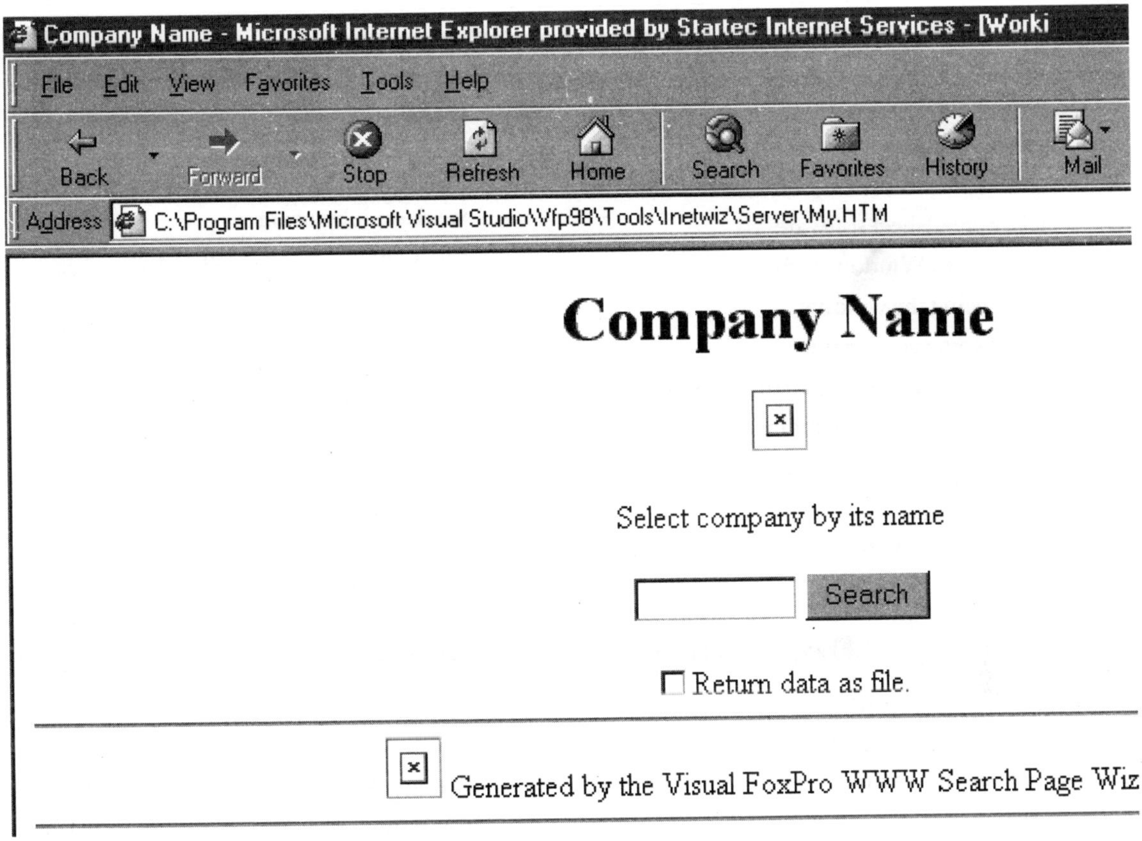

commands with mouse, you may not even this window. What's more you can even hide it you feel that it is disturbing your view.

View windows gives you a quick way of opening, setting up and displaying the data in tables. It also lets you control table properties and open multiple tables at the same time and relate them.

OTHER FEATURES OF VISUAL FOXPRO INTERFACE

While working with FoxPro you would come across various features of the software which are very useful for working. Some of them are listed here.

Status Bar: It displays information regarding the activities taking place on the screen. It does give you the short description of the menu command being used.

Alert Message: Nobody is perfect. It is possible that you will give some command at some stage which is not acceptable to the software, in that case it will give you the Alert message, very politely saying that it is possible to accept such command.

Escape Key: If you are stuck up in FoxPro, then Escape key is your way out. While in command mode it cancels the program. While in program mode, it stops the program.

System Message: It gives you the message regarding the use of the system at that particular time but does not stop the operation as such.

Multiple Choice Questions

1. Visual FoxPro is a :
   (a) Database software
   (b) Word Processing software
   (c) Spreadsheet software
2. Command Window is for :
   (a) Seeing the window
   (b) Typing commands
   (c) Giving command to the operator
3. In Visual FoxPro the main aim is to create :
   (a) Tables (b) Forms
   (c) Projects
4. How many wizards are there in Visual FoxPro:
   (a) 20 (b) 22
   (c) 21
5. You can extract information from table and work on it by using :
   (a) Query (b) Table
   (c) Form
6. You can create tables, forms, etc., using :
   (a) Visual Designer
   (b) Label Designer
   (c) Menus
7. Application Wizard is used for developing the :
   (a) Project (b) Application
   (c) Table

Descriptive Type Questions

1. What is Visual FoxPro?
2. How would you start Visual FoxPro?
3. What all the various features of FoxPro screen?
4. Which kind of files are used in Visual FoxPro?
5. Which are the various tools used in Visual FoxPro?
6. What is Visual Designer?
7. How are Wizards used?
8. What are Application Wizard and Builder?
9. How would you use WWW Search Page Wizard?
10. Describe the other features of Visual FoxPro Interface.

24 Working with Tables

CREATING A NEW TABLE

As we learned in the last chapter, the best way of creating anything in Visual FoxPro is through Wizard. So we will also create one using Wizard called Table Wizard and then later on we will create a table using Table Designer. But, before this we must understand what a Table is. Those of you who have used databases earlier are familiar with the word. But, in general, it can be said that a table is a compilation of data kept in records having various fields which are common to all records.

Let us create a table using the Wizard.

TABLE WIZARD

You can access the Wizards from the Tools menu. Here you select Table wizard for creation. The various steps here are:

Step1 asks you to select either Personal and Business. Based upon this it will show you the various tables it has in store for you. Select one and the respective fields of the same.

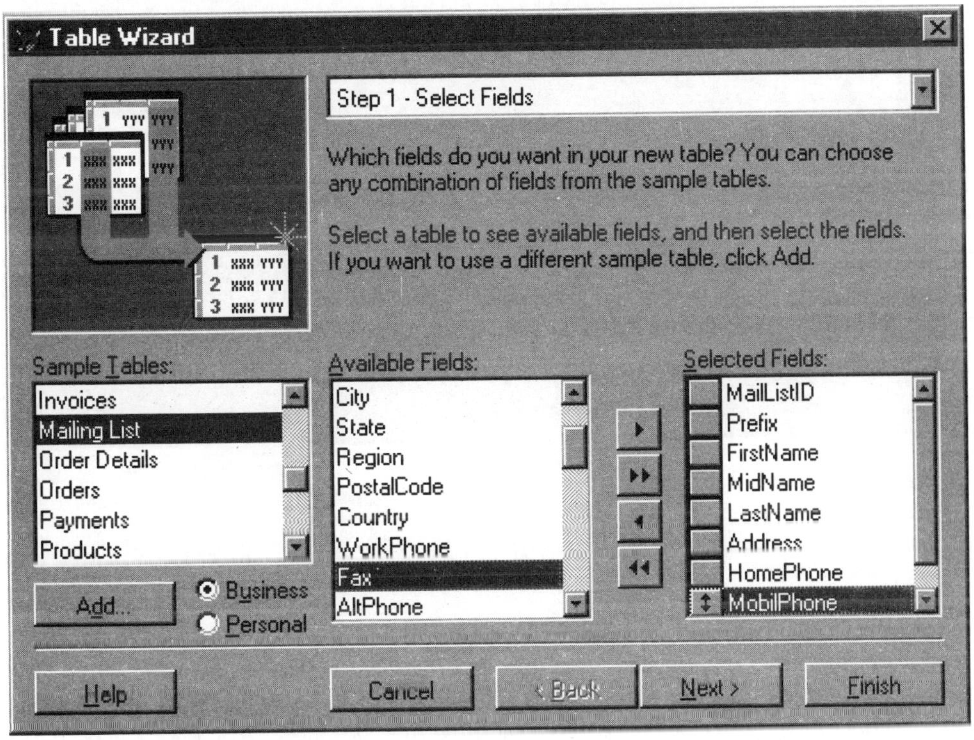

Step1a asks you whether you want this table to be stand alone or as an add on to another database.

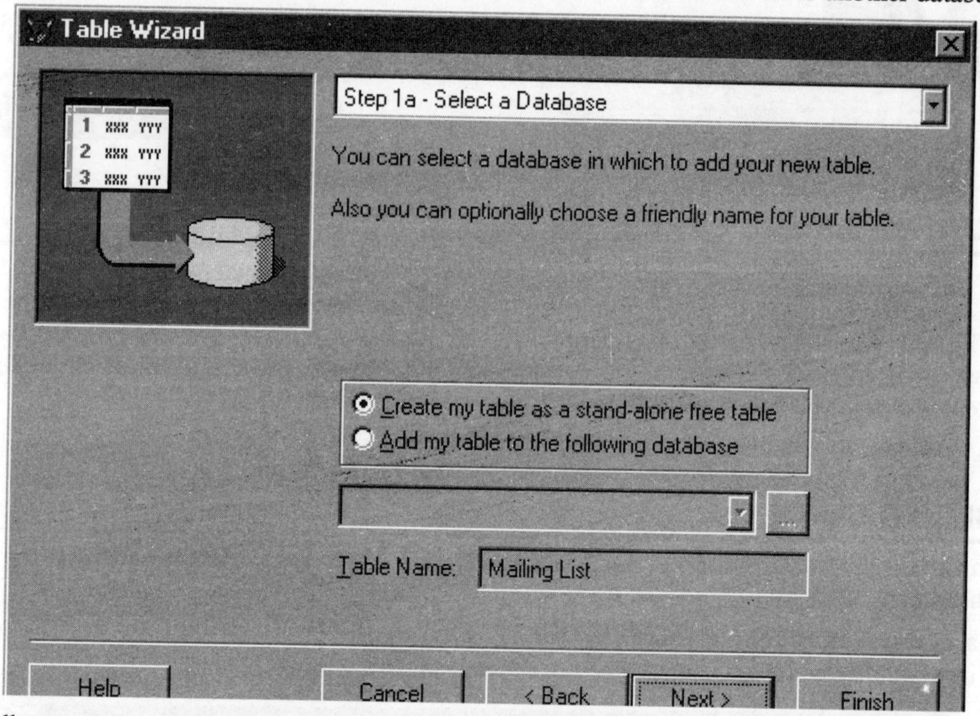

Step2 allows you to modify any of the above mentioned fields.

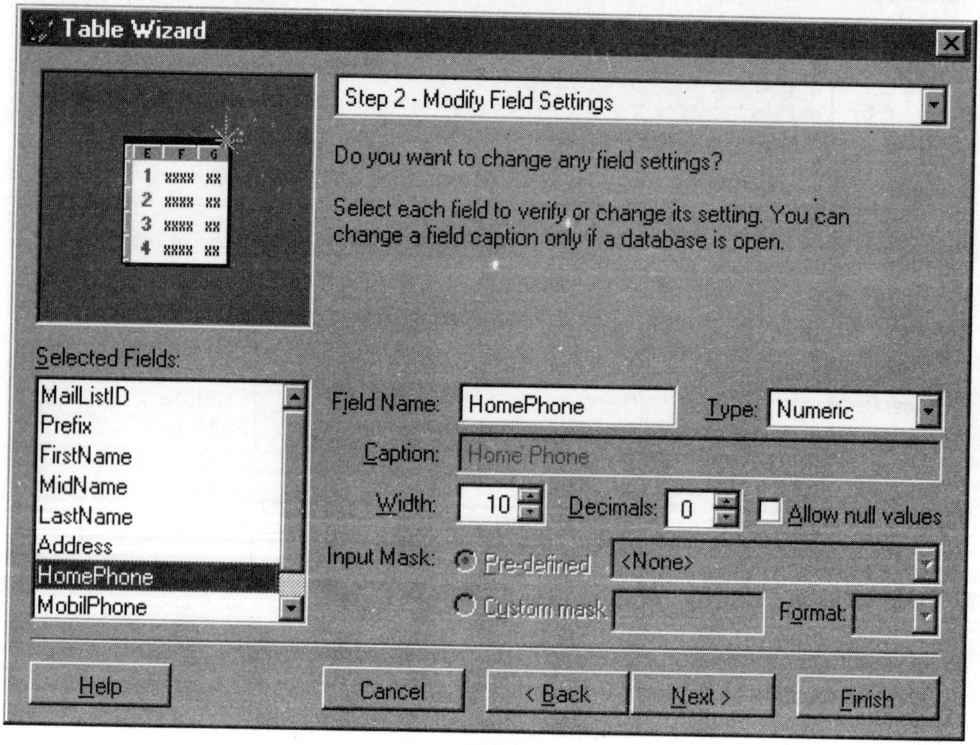

Step3 allows you to index the Table in particular fields.

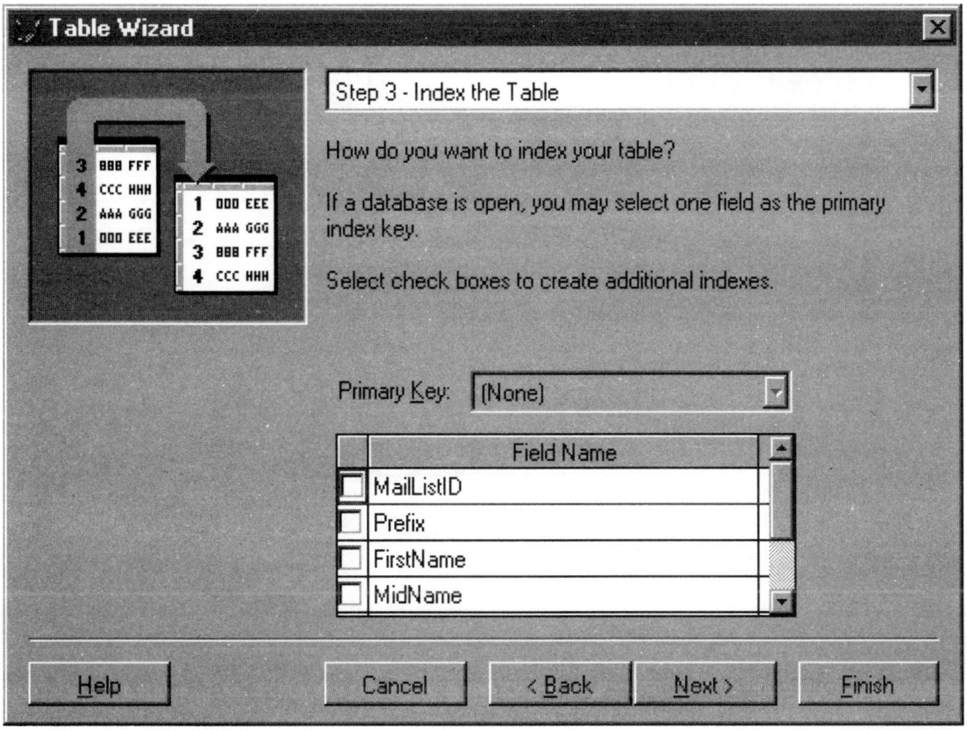

Step4 finishes the table and asks you to save with a name.

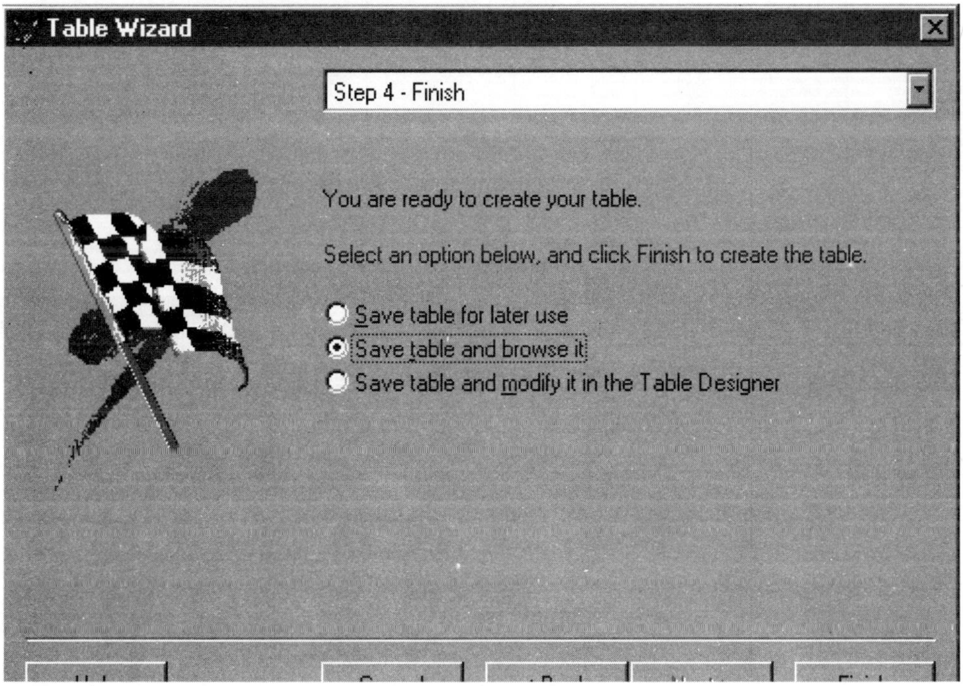

I have saved it with a name m_list and the format for this has been displayed in the next screen.

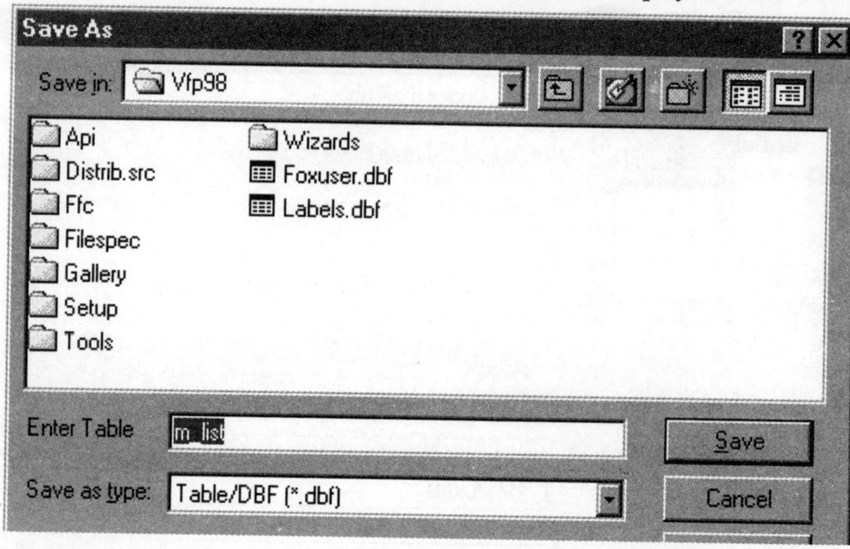

With this our table is ready for the data to be filled in.

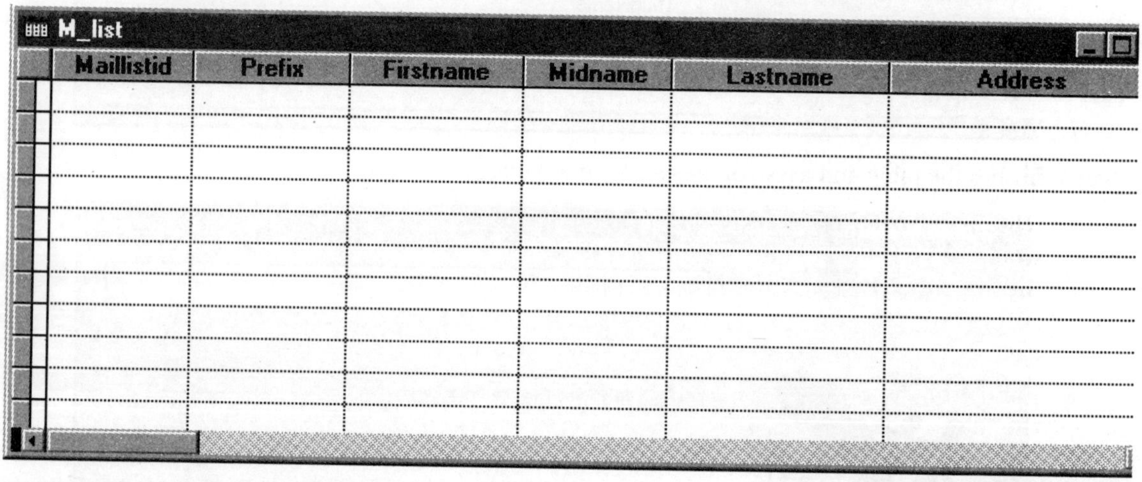

USING TABLE DESIGNER

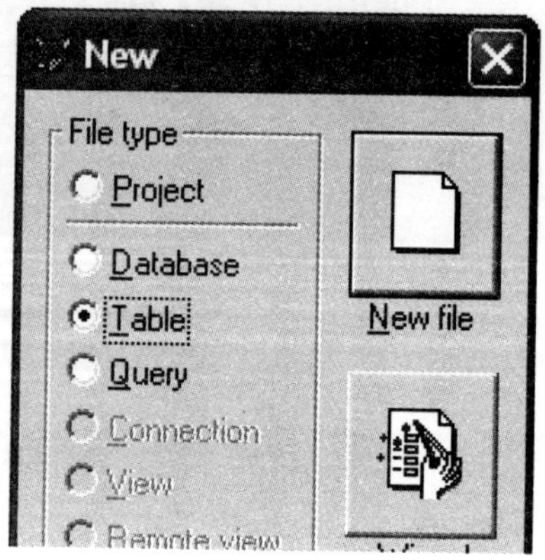

This is the method where you have to have the complete information about the various fields before proceeding further for creation of a table. As usual we will start with the New from the File menu and then follow the following steps:

1. In the dialog box, given here, select the Table option by clicking at the box next to it and then clicking at New File.
2. You would be asked to allot a name to the table or by default you would be given a name with table1, etc.
3. When you click at Save, you are given a dialog box with options

to select the various fields which you are going to have in your table.

4. You would be given a Table Designer dialog box, in which you will type out the fields which you want to have in your table.
5. You can press Tab key to reach one field to another.
6. When you have made all the required entries of the fields, click Ok.
7. You would be given another dialog box, in which you would be given the option of filling up the data.
8. For filling up the data, the fields are defined and space is left for filling.

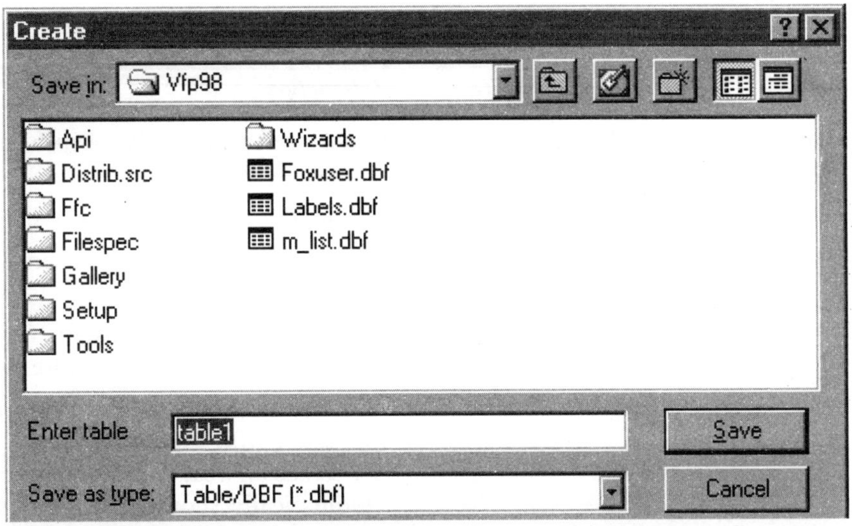

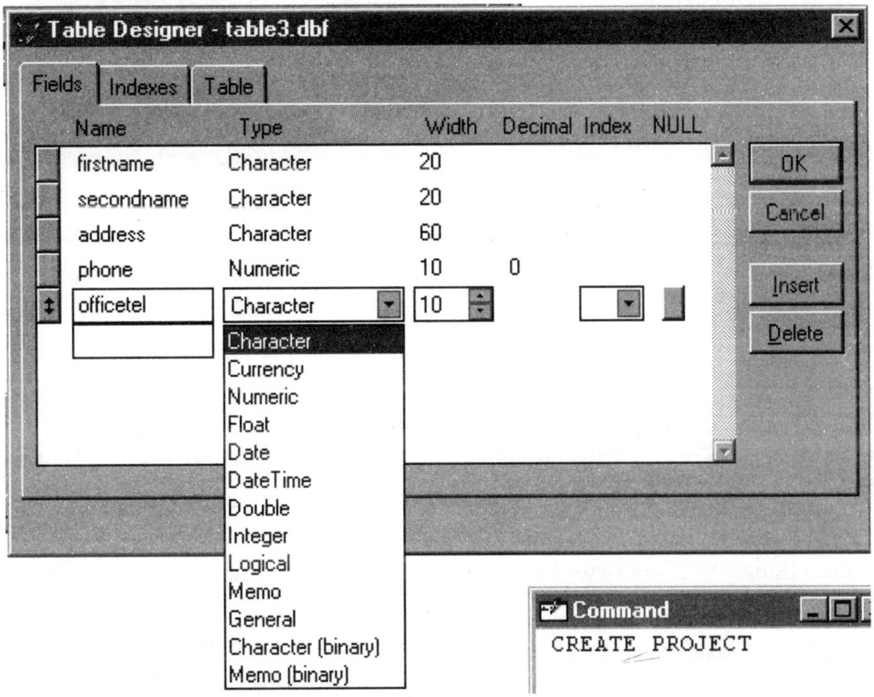

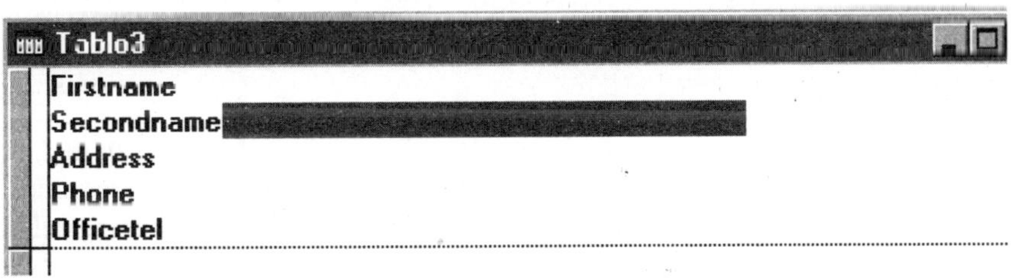

Before going further let me tell you about the various type of fields which you can have in your table.

Type	*Permitted Size*	*Description*
Character	1 to 254 bytes	It can take up any character such as letters, numbers, symbols or spaces.
Currency	8 bytes	It is used to store money values.
Numeric	8 bytes	It is used to store mainly numbers. If defined it will not accept any letter or alphabet.
Float	8 bytes	This field is specially useful for scientific and statistics calculations since it stores more significant digits internally.
Date	8 bytes	Here the date is stored in American format, i.e., MM/DD/YY where MM stands for month, DD stands for Date, and YY stands for Year. When you select date type, Visual FoxPro automatically shows the standard width for 8 characters including the slashes.
DateTime	8 bytes	It is a combination of date and time. The format for this is yyyy/mm/dd/hh/mm/ss. You can store date, time or both, as there is not Time field type.
Double	8 bytes	This field is used mainly for precise scientific and engineering applications.
Integer	4 bytes	It is used for non-decimal numeric values.
Logical	1 byte	This field will help in performing the logical part, i.e., T for true or F for false. You can even have Y/N.
Memo	4 bytes in table	It is similar to character field but is used when you have very long data to be filled in. The actual size of memo fields depends on the amount of data entered into them.
General	4 bytes in table	It is usually used for storing graphics.
Character (binary)	1 byte per character	Here the character is stored in the binary format and not converted to its ASCII character as would be done otherwise.
Memo (binary)	4 bytes in table	Similar to above here also the data is stored in binary.

MODIFYING TABLE STRUCTURES

It is always possible that you would be needing to modify your table. You may need to add a field, change it size, or even delete a field.

Adding Fields

Adding new fields to an existing table is one of the safes changes you can make. In fact, problems occur only if you attempt to use the same field name twice. Even in that situation, FoxPro responds automatically. FoxPro will not enable you to exit the name column if it is a duplicate of an existing field name. Rather, FoxPro displays an information box with the message Invalid or duplicate field name and enables you to edit it.

Deleting Fields

At some point, one or more fields in a table might become obsolete. Rather than waste space, you might decide to remove them from the table. To delete a field, simply display the table in the Table Designer dialog box, highlight the obsolete field, and click the Delete button. You delete a field and save the structure, it is gone forever, including any indexes that reference the deleted field. Make a backup copy of your .DBF before deleting a field.

Renaming Fields

Renaming fields might require only rewriting the .DBF header with the new field name. To change a field name, simply open the Table Designer dialog box, highlight the name, edit the name, and then save the structure. As long as an open index does not reference the field, FoxPro renames the field when you save the structure.

Correcting Mistakes

If you need to correctt a mistake, use the mouse or the insertion point to the field parameter you wish to correct and use Backspace or Del key to make the desired correction. To insert a new character between existing characters, place the insertion point at the desired location and then type the correction.

The following keys can be used for editing in Visual FoxPro.

Key	Actions
Left Arrow	Move insertion point left one character
Right Arrow	Move insertion point right one character
Up Arrow	Move insetion point up one line or one field
Down Arrow	Move insertion point down one line or one field
Ins	Toggle insert mode on/off
Del	Delete character at cursor
Backspace	Delete character to the left of the cursor
Esc	Abort operation
Tab	Move insertion point right one field
Shift + Tab	Move insertion point left one field
Ctrl + W	Save changes and exit

USING TABLES

Tables are integral part of the databases. They can be used for various purposes like modifying the data in it, generating queries based on the data in them. You can print the data in it or even create totals of the fields in it. You can even Find a particular data and Replace it with another.

You can Add, Delete records in the tables. You can even Modify the structure of the table at a later stage, if you find any field short for the data to be entered. It is not that you will always add the records in the end of the table, you can even add records in between the two records.

OPENING A TABLE

As you would open any file in any software, you would open a table in Visual FoxPro. Follow the following steps for it.

1. Choose Open from the File menu.
2. Open dialog box appears.
3. In the file types, click at Table (*.dbf)
4. You would be shown only the table files.
5. Click at the one to be opened by you.

WORKING ON A TABLE

Data is the main thing as far as the table is concerned. You can work on a table by working on the data within it. There are ways of adding and editing data. Some of them are discussed here.

Appending Data

There are two ways of adding records, one is adding to the last, which is called Appending. Second is adding in between the two records which is called Adding. This adding can be done using the commands Browse or Edit. Let us first see how you can add a new record.

Adding a Single Record

Just follow the following steps to do this:

1. Choose Browse command from the View menu.
2. Click on Append New Record in the Table menu. In doing so you will add a new blank record at the end of the Browse/Edit window in which the data for the new record can be entered.

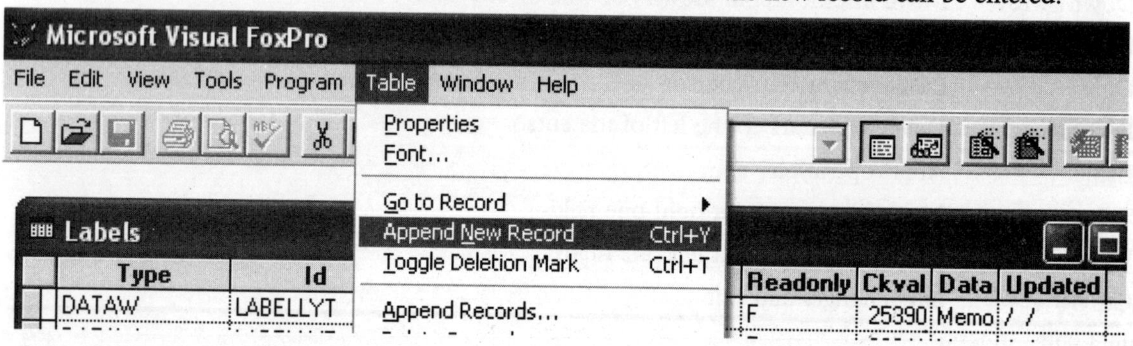

Adding Multiple Records

To add multiple records, do this:

1. As earlier choose the browse mode.
2. Click on Append Mode in the View menu to add series of records to the table. When you select this option, a new blank record is added to the end of the table.
3. Type the desired data. As soon as you add data to this record, Visual FoxPro adds another record to the end of the table. In this way you can continue to add data as long as you remain in Append mode.

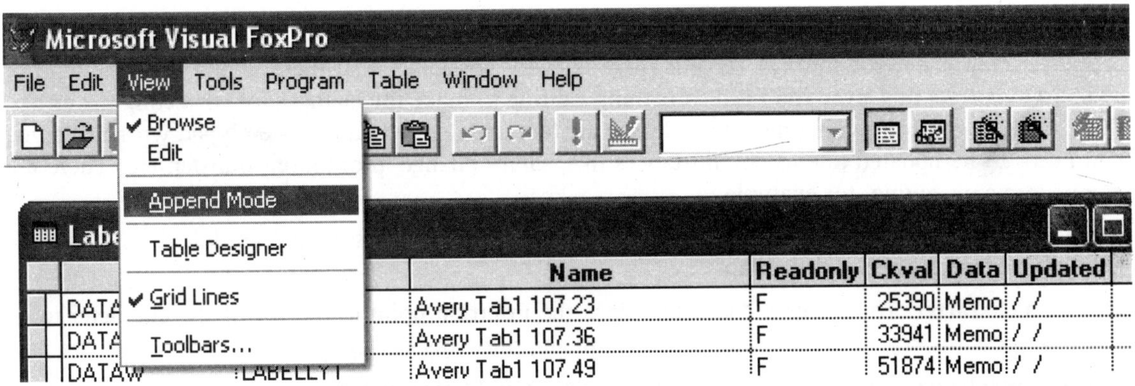

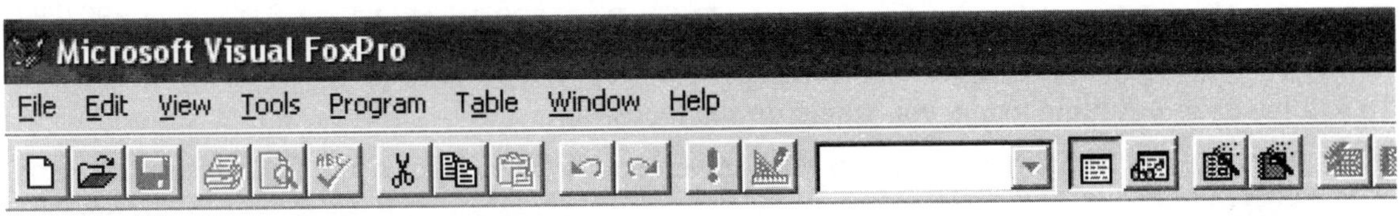

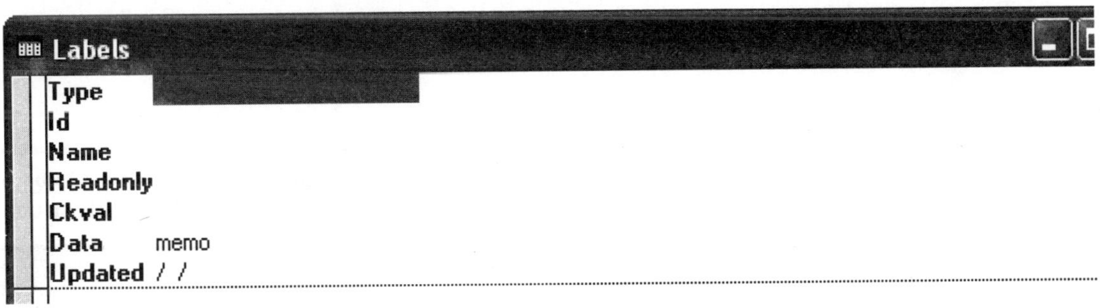

SWITCHING FROM BROWSE TO EDIT MODE

Using the View menu, you can switch from browse mode to Edit mode, as shown above. For some of you, Edit mode may be better choice than Browse mode. You can do editing in both the modes mentioned above, i.e., Browse and Edit. In Browse mode, records are listed in a horizontal format with one record per line. In Edit mode, because the records are displayed in a vertical format with one field per line, you can see more of the fields without scrolling the window. This feature makes Edit mode preferable for data entry in tables with many fields.

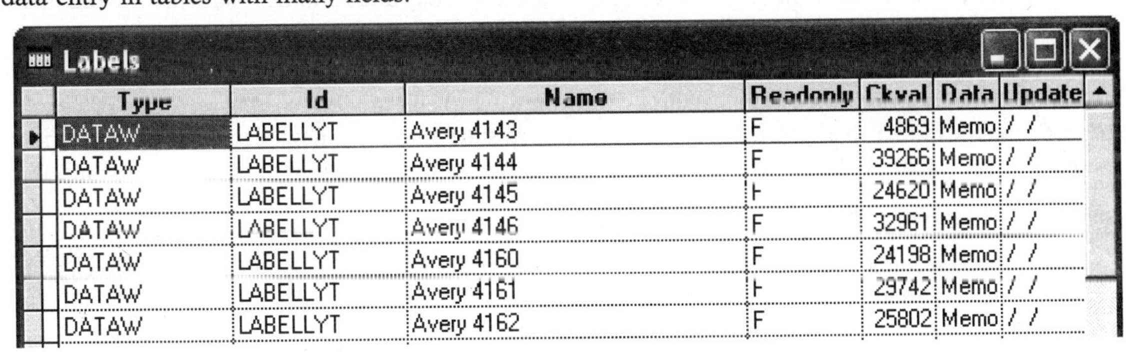

Editing Data

Whenever data is entered into the records there is every possibility that there would be some kind of error. So to correct this error you need something Editing to make the changes for correcting the errors. This change may have become necessary due to the fact that some data has been typed wrong or some data needs to be updated due to circumstances like, salary change, promotion, transfer, etc. There are various terms of editing, for example,

Insert Data: To insert data click the mouse button to the place of an insertion point where you want the new data to appear, then type the data.

Replace a character: To replace a character, place the insertion point to the left of the character to be replaced, press Ins key, type the replacement character, press Ins key again.

Replace the selected data: Select the data to be replaced and type the new data.

Delete the selected data: Select the data then press Del or Backspace key to delete the data and retype the entry.

To edit the data in Editing mode, you would do the following:

1. Move to the field whose data you wish to replace (double click on the field or use the arrow keys).
2. Type the new data.
3. Press Enter key.

APPENDING RECORDS

You create tables to add records to them. In fact, FoxPro is so sure that you want to populate a table with records as soon as possible that it prompts you to add records immediately on closing the table structure. Of course, this time might not always be the best time to add records. You can add records to a table in several ways. Different ways are discussed here:

Through BROWSE or EDIT Screens

Once you have the database open on the screen. You can give the following commands in the command window and append the record.

```
USE table3
APPEND
```

These commands open an edit window, add a blank record, and place the cursor in the first field. After you enter data in the fields of the first record, FoxPro automatically adds another blank record and places the cursor in it. This process continues until you close the window.

You also can open the Edit window directly with the EDIT command or open a Browse window with BROWSE. In these windows, FoxPro assumes that you want to edit or view existing records. You cannot simply move the cursor to a record beyond the last one to start entering a new record. Rather, you must press Ctrl+Y or open the table pull-down menu and choose Append New Record.

Adding Records Programmatically

You can append records to a table form within a program in several ways depending on the source of the records. The code that follows enables users to add a new table record and update the fields directly.

```
*Code appends record to table and updates fields directly
SELECT <table>
APPEND BLANK
*Call a previously created form that allows the user
*to enter fields
DO FILLForm
```

Appending Data from Other Tables

Suppose that you want to append records to the current table from a another table. You could read through one record at a time, store the fields in memory variables, and then append these values to a record in the second table.

MOVING THROUGH A TABLE

In both modes, Edit and Browse, you move record to record. This can be very cumbersome, specially if you have a table with large number of records. So Visual Fox Pro provides options wherein you can go to particular record quickly. First among them is the command called GoTo.

GO TO COMMAND

As mentioned you can go to a particular record using this command. There are various options of the command, among which are:

Top:	Positions the pointer on the first record in the table.
Bottom	Positions the pointer on the last record in the table.
Next	Positions the pointer on the record immediately after the current record.
Previous:	Position the pointer on the record immediately before the current record.
Record #	Displays a Go to Record dialog box, in which you specify a record number.
Locate:	Displays the Locate Record dialog box, in which you can find an indexed or unindexed field or locate more than one record in a table.

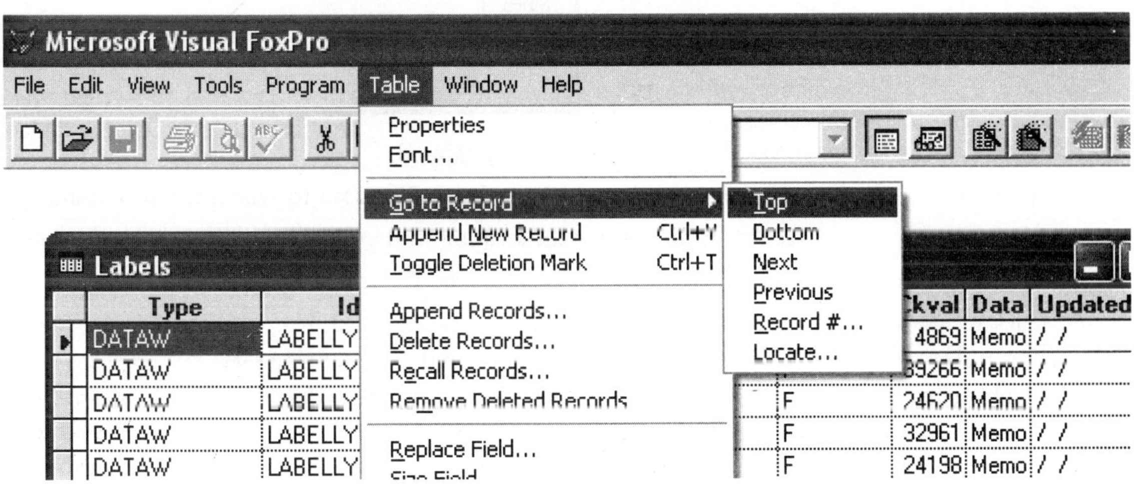

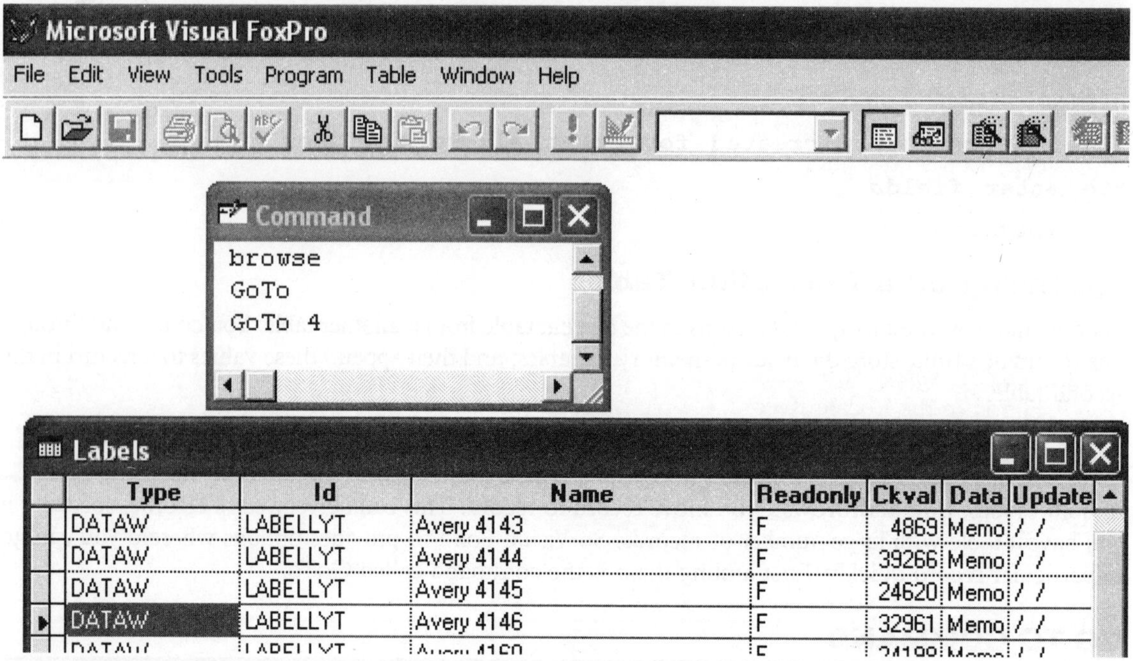

Of these Locate is probably the most commonly used one. Here is how it is used.

1. From the View menu choose to have the Browse mode.
2. Open the Table menu and click at Go To and then Locate.
3. You will get the dialog box, as shown here.

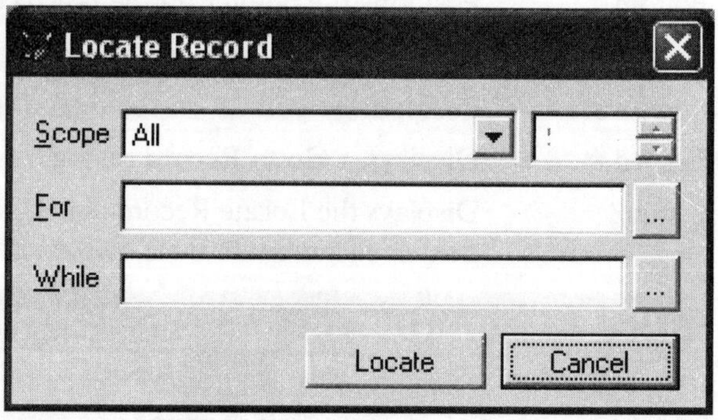

4. In the scrope option specify the record or choose any one of the following options which have the following meanings:

   All — It is used to specify and Locate all records

   Next — Use this option and then enter a number, which specifies a group of records starting with, wherever the pointer is currently located.

   Record — Use this and type this number of specific record to search for the condition.

   Rest — All records from the current location to the end of the file will be searched.

5. Selecting either the For or the While option displays the Expression Builder.
6. Click on the For option. The Expression dialog box is displayed; it is indicated by the Locate Record For: <expL> clause window in the upper portion of the dialog box.
7. Double click on name field from the Fields box.
8. Now select = operator from a pull down menu by clicking on Logical box.

9. Give a space and type the actual text which you want to locate.
10. Here I have used Avery 4145 and do not forget to have the expession within quotes.
11. Click on the Ok button to finish the entry. The Locate Record dialog box will reappear with the For option now selected.
12. Finally, select the Locate button in the Locate Record dialog box to start the search process.
13. When Visual FoxPro finds the matched record, it displays the same.
14. To find the next occurence of the same search click at the Command Window and type continue.

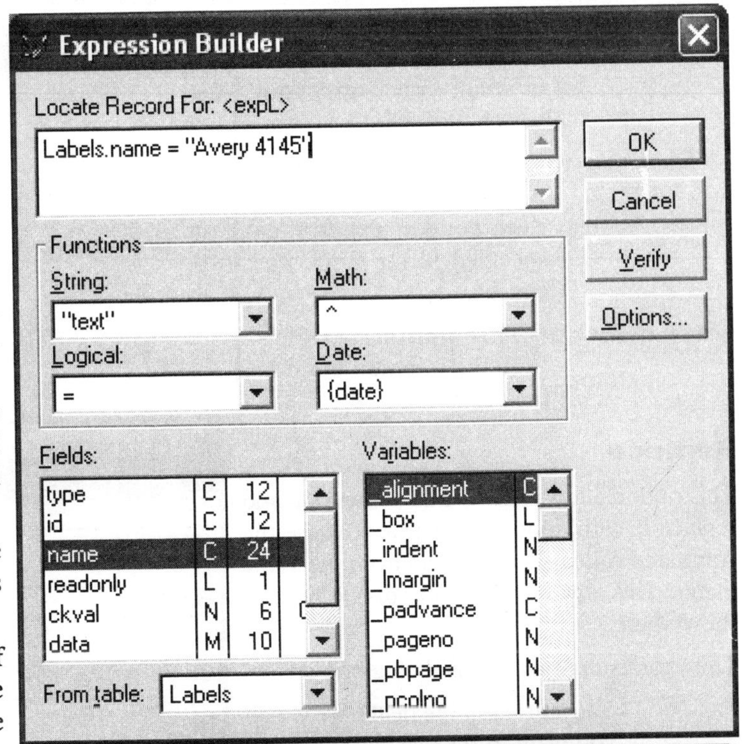

15. Now it starts the search again. Again if the match is found, it will be displayed.
16. If no match is found, you will get the mesage, End of Locate scope, at the Status bar.

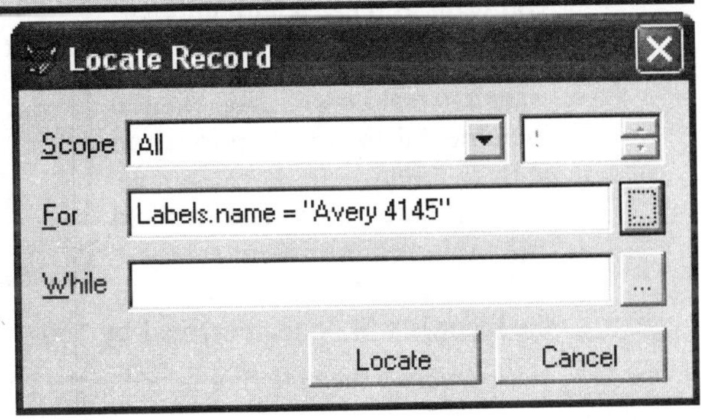

Next option of working with data in the records is the option of Finding something and Replacing it with another.

FIND AND REPLACE

Those of you who are familiar with Word Processing know how useful is this combination of Find and Replace command. You can find anything and replace it with another. Even Visual FoxPro has the same option which can be applied to the data in the records. Let us first see the command Find.

Find

This command can be called from Edit menu. This will give you a dialog box as shown on the next page. This dialog box has the following options:

Match case	This option finds the word specified in the Look for text: box with the exact combination of uppercase and lowercase letters.
Wrap around	This option searches from the position of the insertion point to the end of the file and then from the beginning of the file back to the insertion point, so that you can search

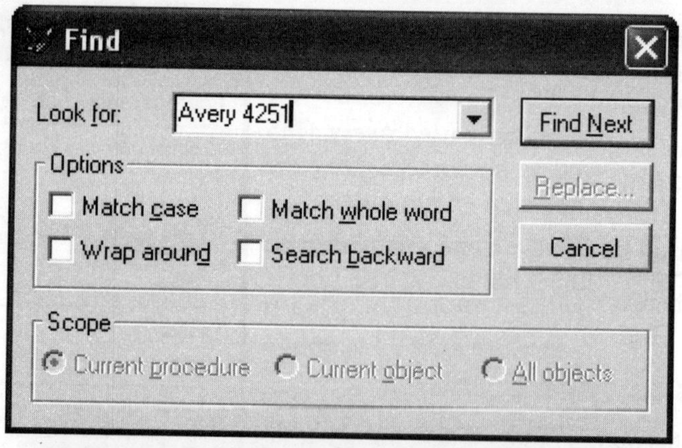

the entire table, regardless of where the insertion point is when you begin your search of the Find.

Match whole word — This option finds only occurrences of the word that appear exactly as specified in the Look For text box.

Search backward — This option searches from the insertion point to the beginning of the file.

Replace

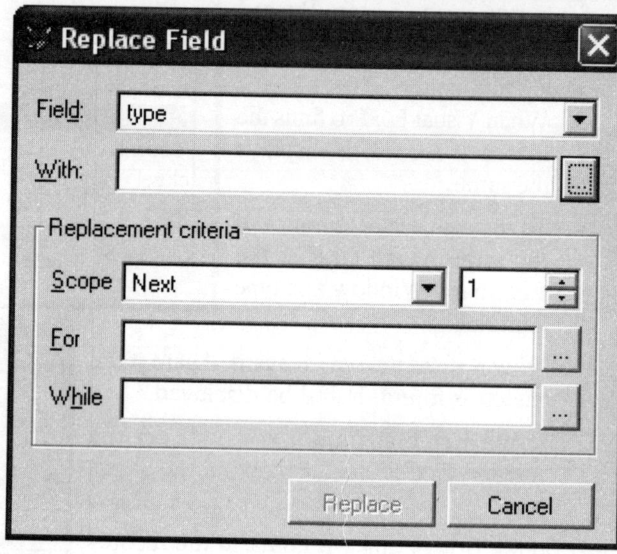

This option allows you to find something and replace it with another. For this you use the command called Replace Field from the Table menu. This also gives you the dialog box, as shown here.

The various options in this dialog box are:

Field — You can select the field here which you want to replace with another.

With — Here you select the field which you want it to replace with. You can add incremental or other options too with the field here. For example, you can have salary field in Field and replace it with field salary + 100, which means that all salary in the records will be incremented by 100.

Scope — Here you have the option of selecting the Next record or All records or even records by number.

For/While — You can select here the options of replacing for a certain criteria.

Deleting Record

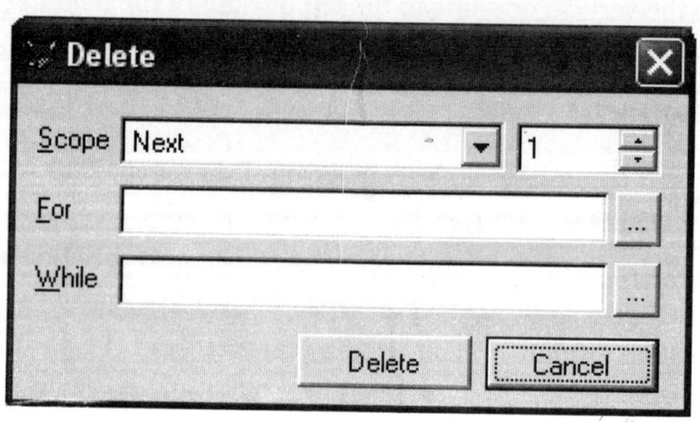

You can get rid of the records not needed by you. There is no option of recalling them back after deleting them. So make doubly sure that the records are not needed again before deleting them. Like most of the database programs, in Visual FoxPro too, the deletion is done in 2 two steps. In the first step the software marks the records for deletion without outrighting deleting them. In this case these records are not taken into account as far as totalling of fields are concerned. So when you are taking the total of salaries of all employees in the table, the salaries of the records which are marked for deletion is counted. In fact, till this stage you can recall these marked records, by using the command called Recall Records.

In the second step, the records are actually removed. For this you choose the option of Remove Deleted Records from the Table menu.

ALTERING THE SCREEN DISPLAY

There are various ways you can change the display of various options on the screen. First among them is Grid.

Grid Off/On

This option hides vertical lines that normally appear between columns. This option is a toggle switch; so selecting it will alternately hide and display the vertical lines. From View menu, select Grid lines. Selecting Grid lines hides both vertical and horizontal lines. You can reselect it to display the lines using same commands again.

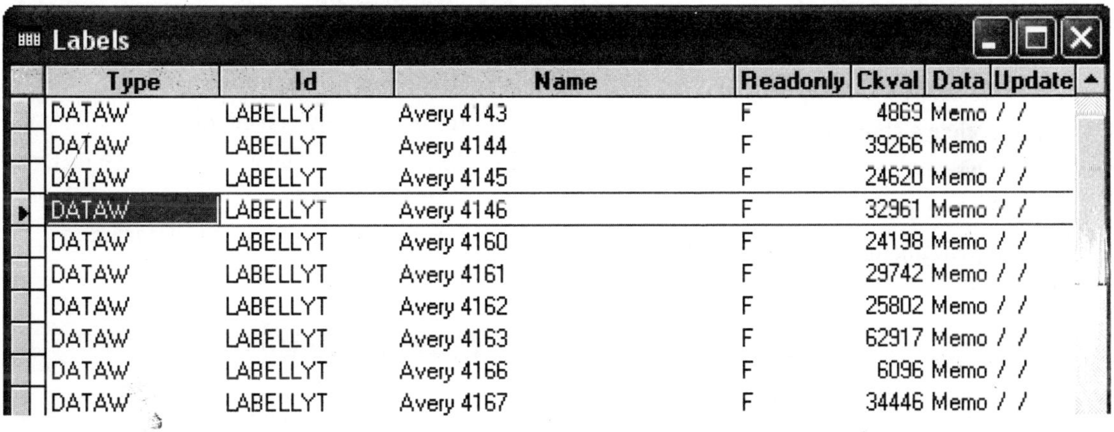

Type	Id	Name	Readonly	Ckval	Data	Update
DATAW	LABELLYT	Avery 4143	F	4869	Memo	/ /
DATAW	LABELLYT	Avery 4144	F	39266	Memo	/ /
DATAW	LABELLYT	Avery 4145	F	24620	Memo	/ /
DATAW	LABELLYT	Avery 4146	F	32961	Memo	/ /
DATAW	LABELLYT	Avery 4160	F	24198	Memo	/ /
DATAW	LABELLYT	Avery 4161	F	29742	Memo	/ /
DATAW	LABELLYT	Avery 4162	F	25802	Memo	/ /
DATAW	LABELLYT	Avery 4163	F	62917	Memo	/ /
DATAW	LABELLYT	Avery 4166	F	6096	Memo	/ /
DATAW	LABELLYT	Avery 4167	F	34446	Memo	/ /

Resizing Fields

If you feel that your screen is not able to show all the fields you want to see on the screen. For this you place the mouse pointer to the grid line to the right of the field's name, you want to resize. Note that the mouse pointer becomes a cross with arrowheads pointing left and right. Drag the gridlines (border) in or out until the columns is in the size you want. Using the mouse, resizing a field is very simple. Just click on the vertical grid line to the left or right of the field to be resized and drag the mouse to resize the field. Release the left mouse button when the field is of the desired size.

Moving Fields

By Moving Field you can move a field in a record of a table to a new location. Press tab key to the desired field. Select the Move Field in Table menu option and press left or right arrow keys to relocate the field and press Enter key. For interchanging the fields using mouse, move the pointer to the grid line to the right of the field's name. Hold down the left button and drag to left or right.

Multiple Choice Questions

1. Table wizard is in :
   (a) Tools menu (b) File menu
   (c) Edit menu
2. A Table is saved with an extension :
   (a) .dcf (b) .dbf
   (c) .ddd
3. Logical field can take up value T or :
   (a) S (b) F
   (c) U
4. Can you use the same field name twice :
   (a) Yes (b) No
5. A field can be renamed :
   (a) Yes (b) No
6. In Edit mode a Del key would :
   (a) Delete a character
   (b) Delete a record
   (c) Delete a field
7. In Appending the records are added in :
   (a) Between (b) First
   (c) Last
8. Append command is in the :
   (a) File menu (b) View menu
   (c) Edit menu
9. You can append records in current table from an existing table :
   (a) Yes (b) No
10. Find command is under :
    (a) File menu (b) Edit menu
    (c) Tool menu
11. Grid lines are :
    (a) Vertical lines between columns
    (b) Lines between rows
    (c) Lines between characters
12. You can resize fields on the screen using the mouse and then :
    (a) pushing (b) dragging
    (c) pulling

Descriptive Type Questions

1. What is a table?
2. How will you create a table using Table Wizard?
3. How would you create a table using Table Designer?
4. How would you modify the structure of the table?
5. How would you add, delete and rename the fields of the table?
6. How would you append records in the table?
7. How would you add records through program?
8. What is the function of GoTo command?
9. How is Find command used?
10. What is the function of Replace command?
11. How would you alter the screen display?
12. How would you use the option of Grid?

Working with Queries

25

INTRODUCING QUERY

So far I have talked about creations. Its time I talk about taking the results out of Visual FoxPro. This is mostly done by Query which is the short name of question. Here query means asking question to the software and getting the result from it. The questions are based on the database which is in use.

For example, in a school database, you can ask the following questions:

— How many students are there who live in Noida

— How many students have their height more than 170 cms

— How many students have taken up computer as additional subject

This way you can think of the various questions and get the result from system using the queries as mentioned above. The best part of queries is that they can be saved and run whenever required.

As usual we will first learn to create query using the Wizards.

CREATING QUERY WITH WIZARD

You can call the query wizard from the Tools menu and Wizards submenu. But before that you have to open the database based on which you want to create the queries. The query wizard dialog box shown on the next page gives you the choice of creating queries of various types. Since our query is of simple type, we would click at the Query Wizard and go ahead.

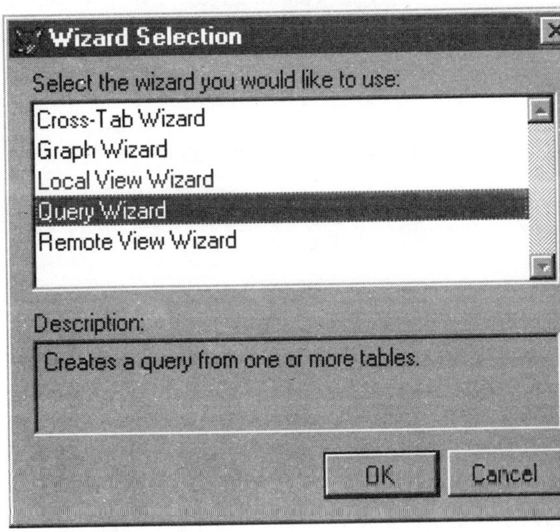

The following screens will appear.

Step1 will ask you about the fields from the database to be used.

Step2 is reserved for some other option.

Step3 will ask you about the filler records.

Step4 will ask you about the sequence in which to sort the records.

Step4a will ask you whether you want to limit your records to first or last records.

Step5 will finish the query wizard and ask you to save the query

Save the query with a name as shown in the Save As dialog box.

This way you create a query and save it under a given name. You can now run it anytime you need.

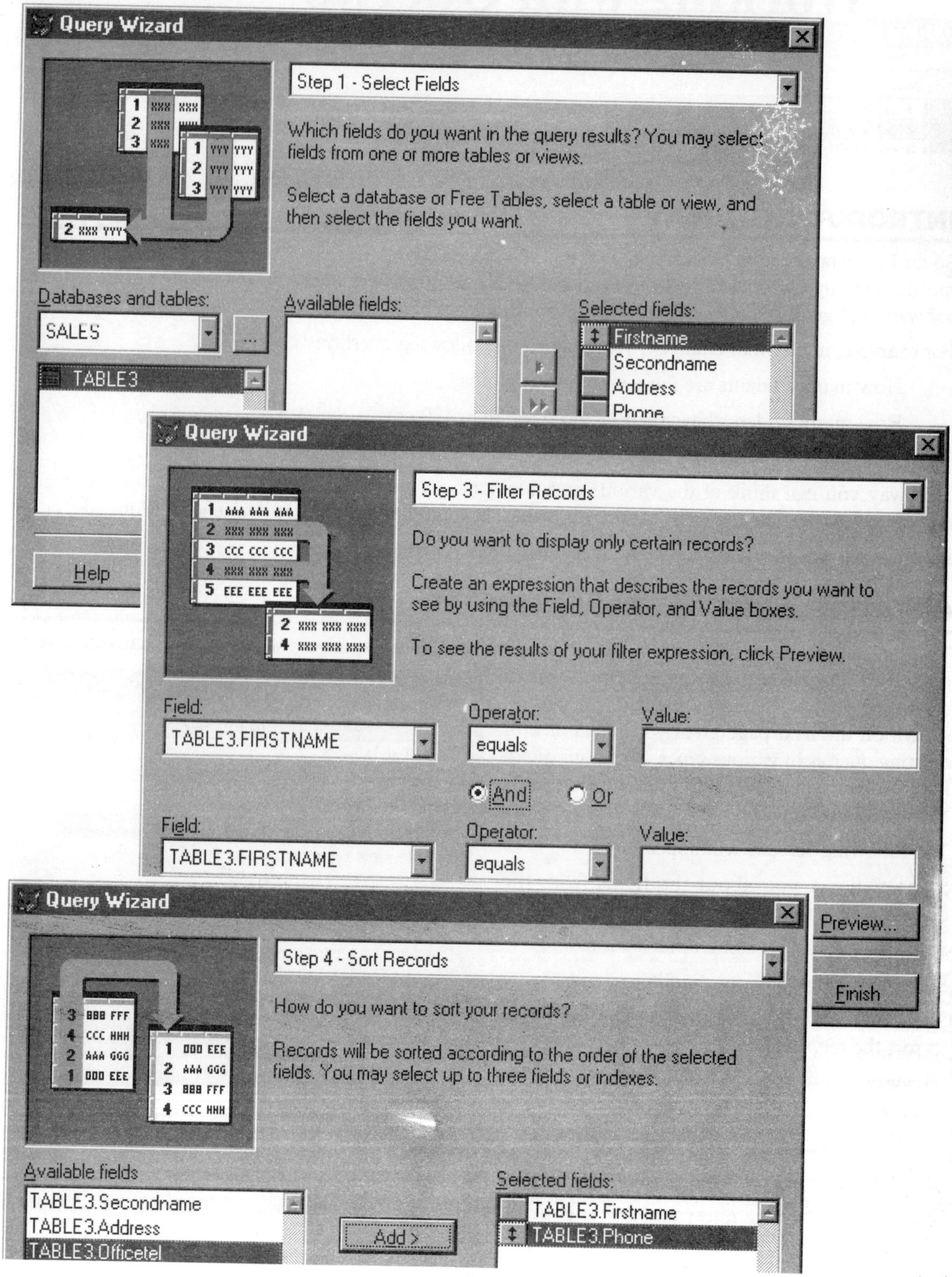
Query Wizard
Step 1 - Select Fields
Which fields do you want in the query results? You may select fields from one or more tables or views.
Select a database or Free Tables, select a table or view, and then select the fields you want.
Databases and tables:
SALES
TABLE3
Available fields:
Selected fields:
Firstname
Secondname
Address
Phone
Help
Query Wizard
Step 3 - Filter Records
Do you want to display only certain records?
Create an expression that describes the records you want to see by using the Field, Operator, and Value boxes.
To see the results of your filter expression, click Preview.
Field:
TABLE3.FIRSTNAME
Operator:
equals
Value:
And
Or
Field:
TABLE3.FIRSTNAME
Operator:
equals
Value:
Preview...
Finish
Query Wizard
Step 4 - Sort Records
How do you want to sort your records?
Records will be sorted according to the order of the selected fields. You may select up to three fields or indexes.
Available fields
TABLE3.Secondname
TABLE3.Address
TABLE3.Officetel
Add >
Selected fields:
TABLE3.Firstname
TABLE3.Phone

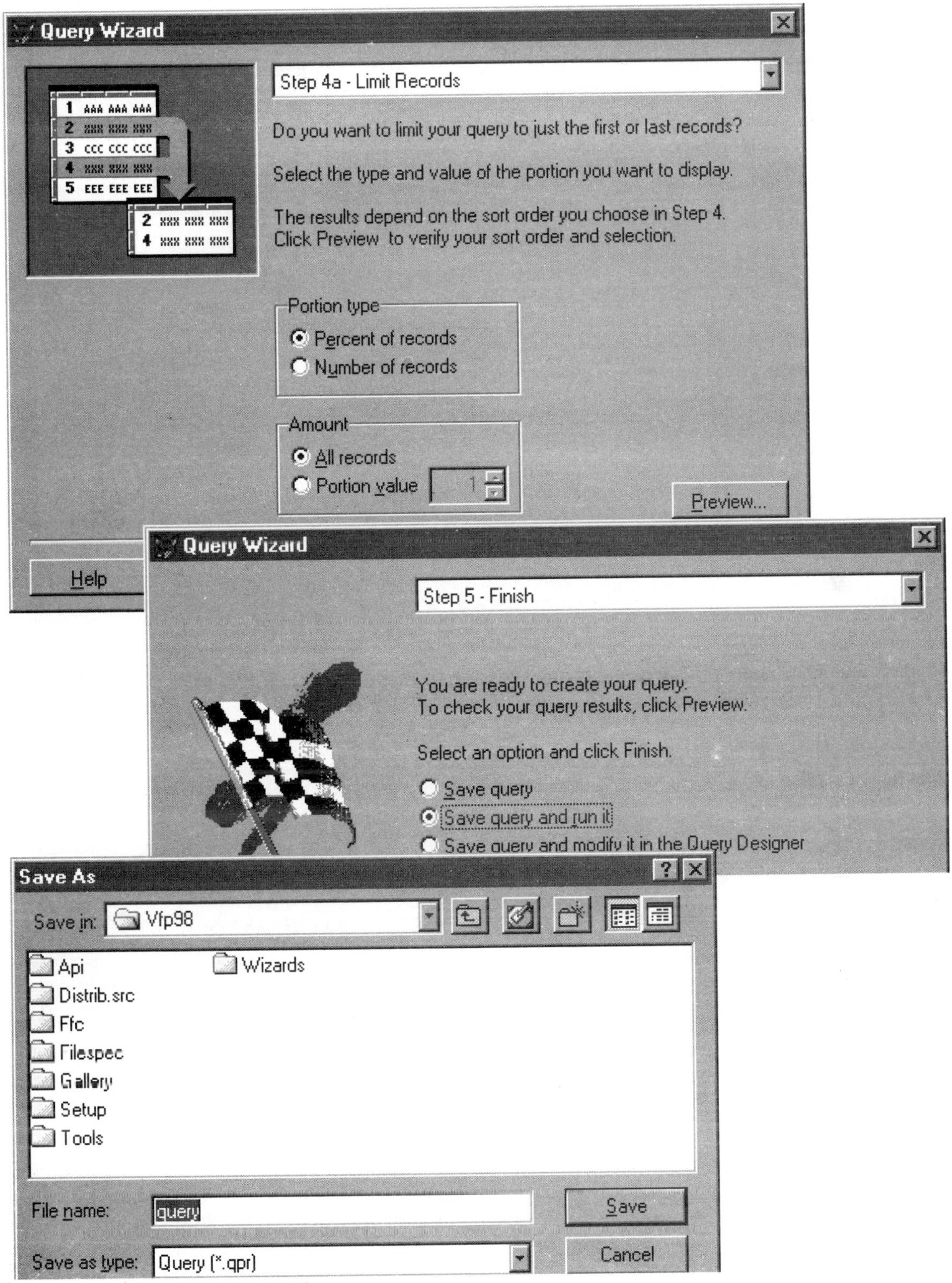
Query Wizard
Step 4a - Limit Records
Do you want to limit your query to just the first or last records?
Select the type and value of the portion you want to display.
The results depend on the sort order you choose in Step 4.
Click Preview to verify your sort order and selection.
Portion type
Percent of records
Number of records
Amount
All records
Portion value
Preview...
Help
Query Wizard
Step 5 - Finish
You are ready to create your query.
To check your query results, click Preview.
Select an option and click Finish.
Save query
Save query and run it
Save query and modify it in the Query Designer
Save As
Save in:
Vfp98
Api
Distrib.src
Ffc
Filespec
Gallery
Setup
Tools
Wizards
File name:
query
Save
Save as type:
Query (*.qpr)
Cancel

CREATING QUERY WITH QUERY DESIGNER

For this first select New from the file menu to get the dialog box shown here.

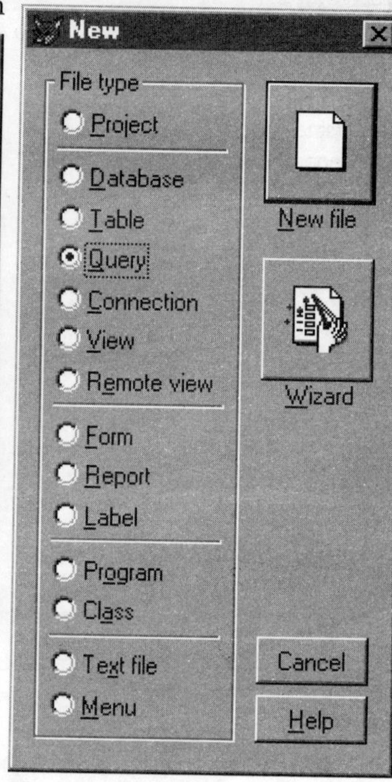

Select Query and click at New File. You would be asked to add a table or view to the query with the dialog box. In this case I have added the table called Table3.

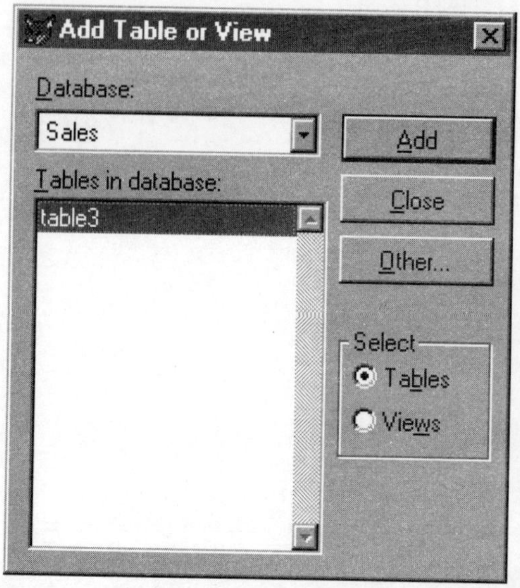

You are then given the dialog box which is called Query Designer. This is shown next. With this you are shown a toolbox which has the following options:

Add Table	Delete Table
Add Join	Hide/Show the SQL Window
Maximize the Table view	Query Destination

Besides these you have the various panels on the bottom. You can select anyone of them and respond to the query of them.

Fields in the Query

Now that you have the fields in the table available to you on the screen, you can add these fields by using the Add button. You can also use Add All in case you are planning to use all the fields.

To move a field, you do the following:

1. Drag the field from the Available list to the Selected list.
2. Click the field name in the table field list in the table view of Query Designer, and drag it to the selected list.
3. Double click the field name in the table field list in the table view of Query Designer.
4. Hold down the Ctrl key, click on multiple fields, and choose the Add button.
5. Drag or double-click the asterisk in the table field list in the table view to include all the table's fields.

Join Panel

It enables you to customize the join condition. You can select the type of join from the Type drop-down list, open the drop-down list for either field, and select fields to define the join relations. You can also change the connection criteria and reverse the logic by clicking the Not button. Join supports 5 criteria:

Equal	Like	Exactly Like

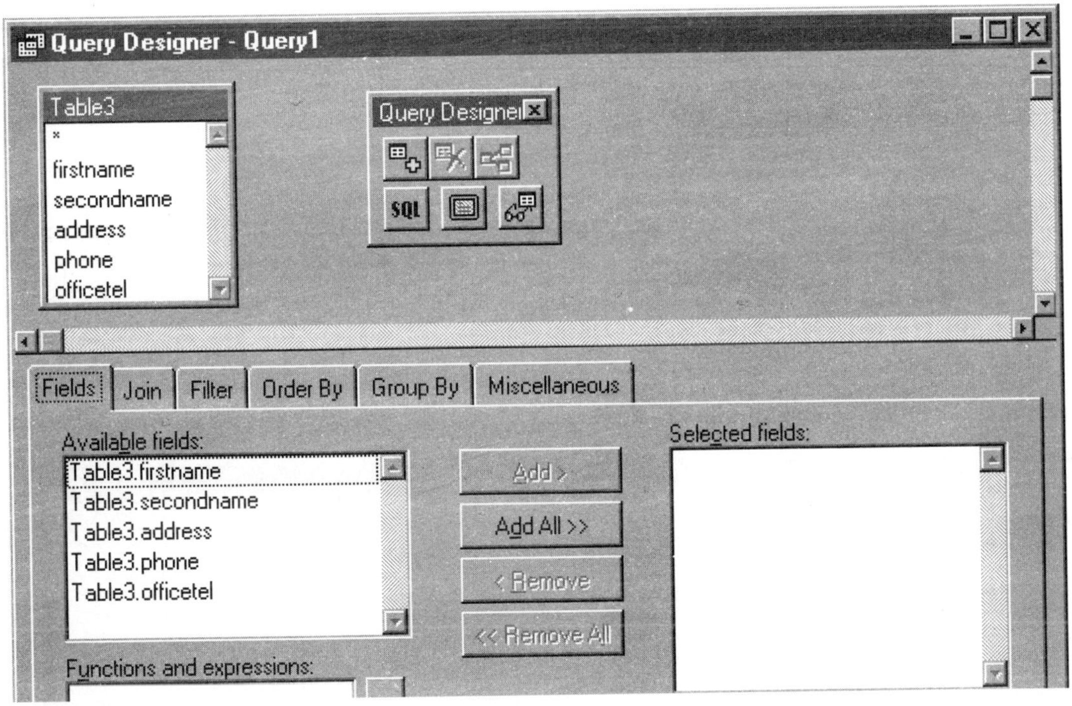

More Than Less Than

This dialog box enables you to select the type of join and describes each condition. The four types of joins are:

1. Inner join, which includes only the records from both tables that match the join condition.
2. Left outer join, which includes all records from the table on the left and records that match the join condition from the table on the right.

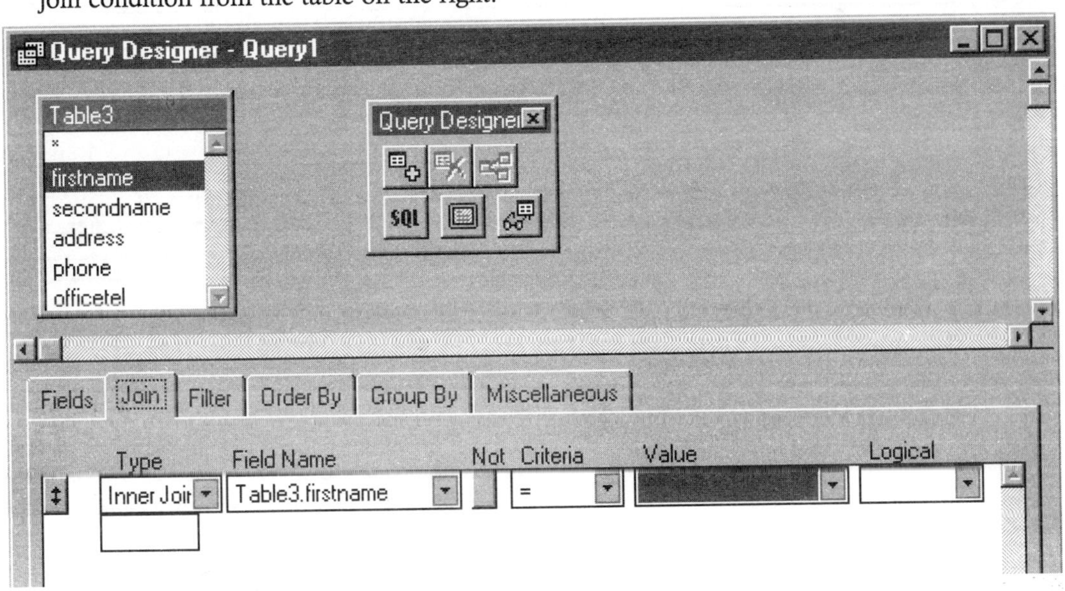

3. Right outer join, which includes all records from the table on the right and those records that match the join condition from the table on the left.
4. Full outer join, which includes all records from both tables and combines those that match the join condition into one record in the result set.

Filter Conditions

This allows you to put conditions on the fields. For example, you would like to field to have a maximum or a minimum value.

You may set a particular value for the field too. Clicking at criteria leads to Expression builder dialog box in which you can create any valid FoxPro expression.

So when you run this qucry thc result will shown according to their value and the criteria chosen by you.

You can run this query even from the database which is a combination of various tables stored together.

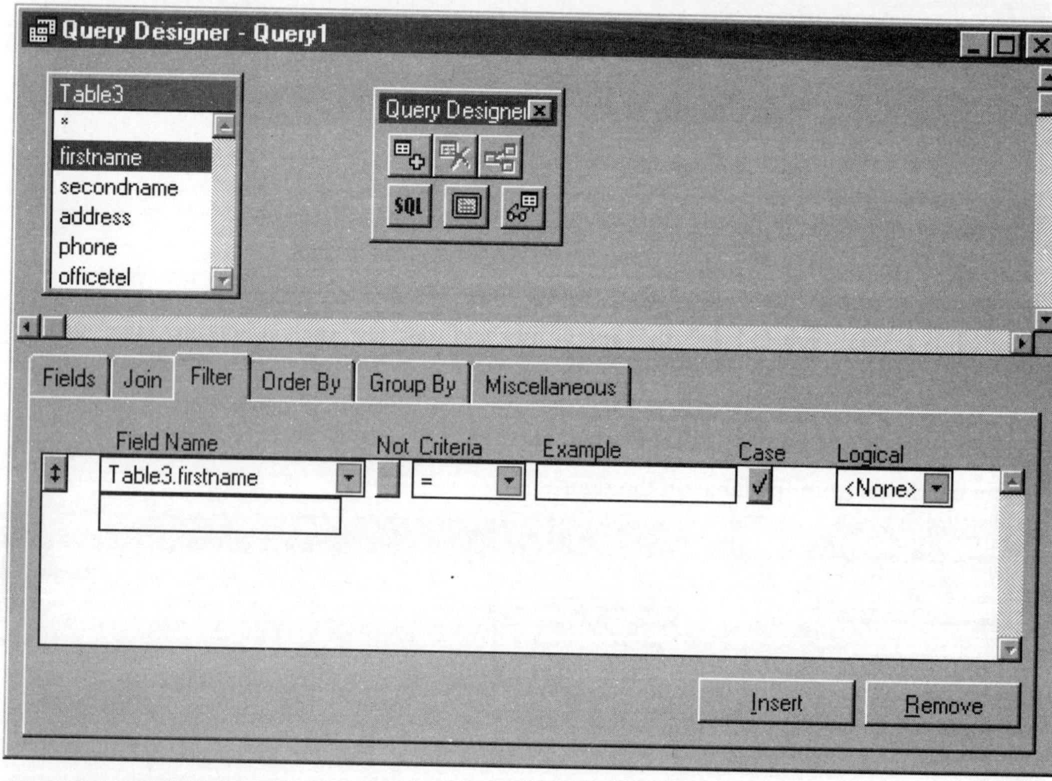

Order By Conditions

This option displays two list boxes that contain fields. The left box contains only the Selected fields. To begin the sort with the supplier's company name, click it and then click Add. As with adding fields, this action moves the selected field to the right list box.

Notice that a small arrow appears next to the field name in the Ordering Criteria list. This arrow indicates that the current sort order for this field is ascending. You can make it descending by selecting it and then clicking at the arrow.

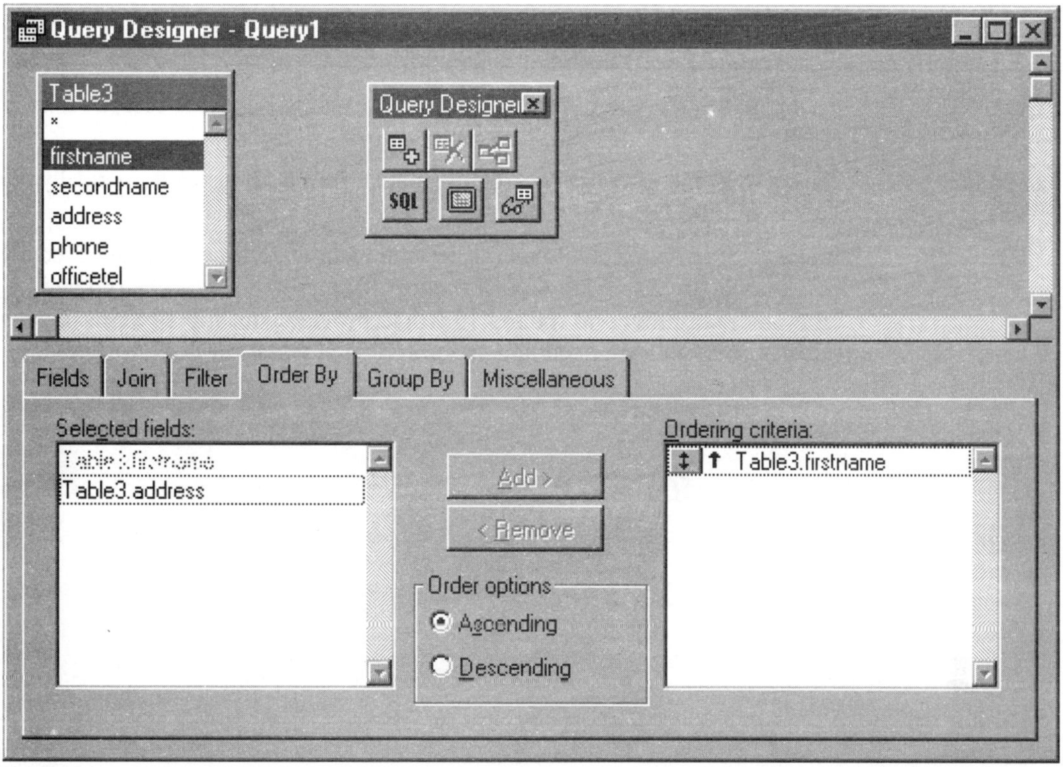

Group By Conditions

This allows you to group various fields into a group. So that when you take the total of the fields it does not give the total of individual fields but gives the total of the whole group as a single identity.

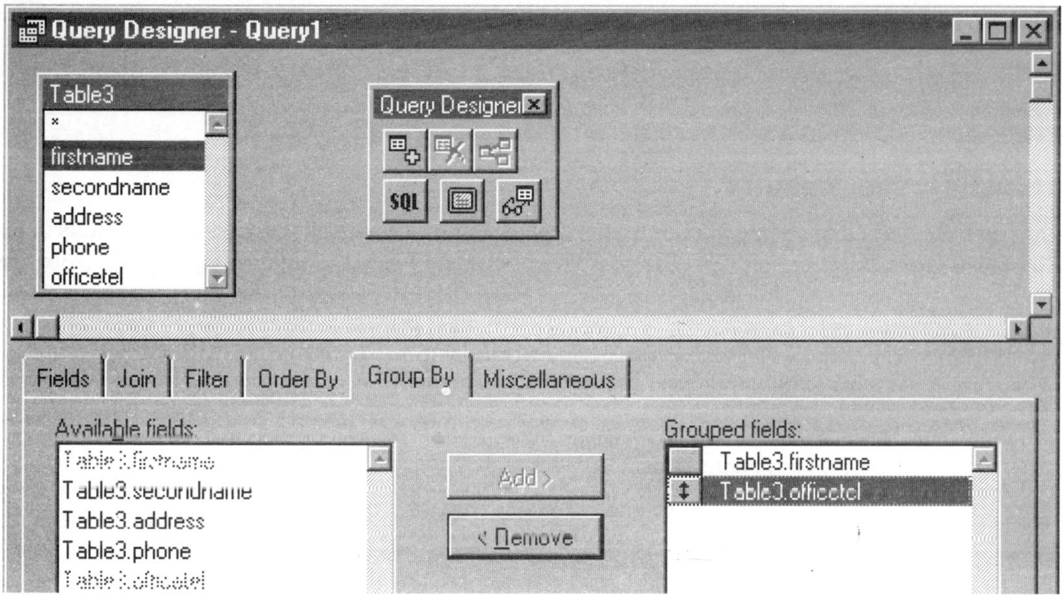

Miscellaneous Conditions

This option provides for additional record-selection criteria:

No Duplicates — This condition enables you to show or to exclude duplicate records from your selection.

Cross-Tabulate — This outputs the result set into a cross-tabular format. It also automatically selects the Group and Order By fields.

Top — It enables you to select all records, several records, or a percentage of records to be returned. If you want to show the top 10 sales items, a query ordered by the units sold and limited to the top 10 would provide your top 10 items. Changing the order option from ascending to descending provides the bottom 10 sales items.

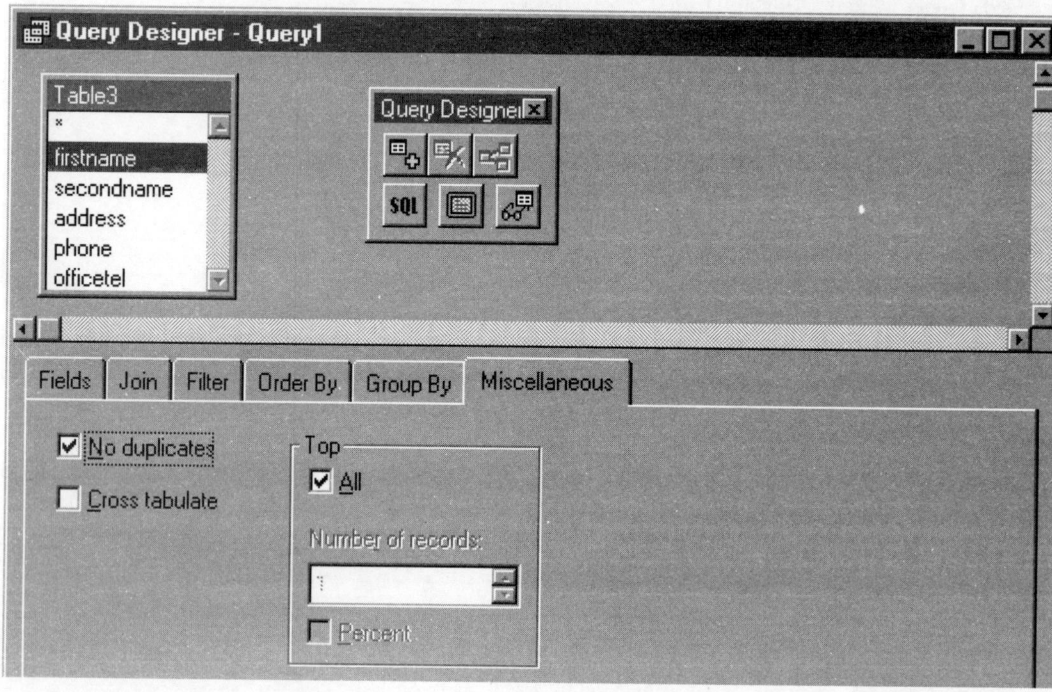

Outputting the Results

So far you have studied to see the queries on the screen. But, this is not all you can see the results on other too by changing the destination. To change it you open the Query Destination dialog box from Query toolbar.

As you can see there are various options on the screen. These are:

Browse — View query results in a Browse window only

Cursor — Create a temporary table or cursor with query results

Table — Crate a permanent table

Graph — Use query results to produce a graph with Microsoft Graph

Screen — Displays results to the screen only

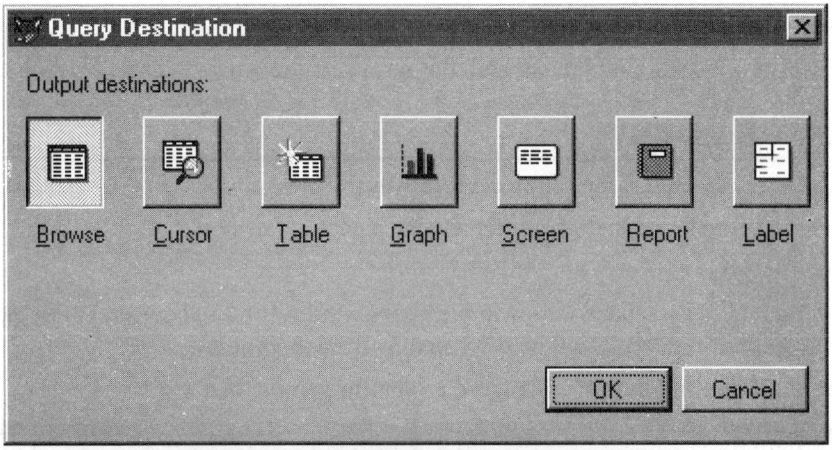

Report — Uses query results as a data source for a report

Label — Uses query results as a data source for labels

A few of them are discussed here.

Output to the Screen

This is used since the query results after writing on the screen fade away. So you must create a more permanent copy by selecting To Print or To Text File. Later on these can be used for sending to the printer.

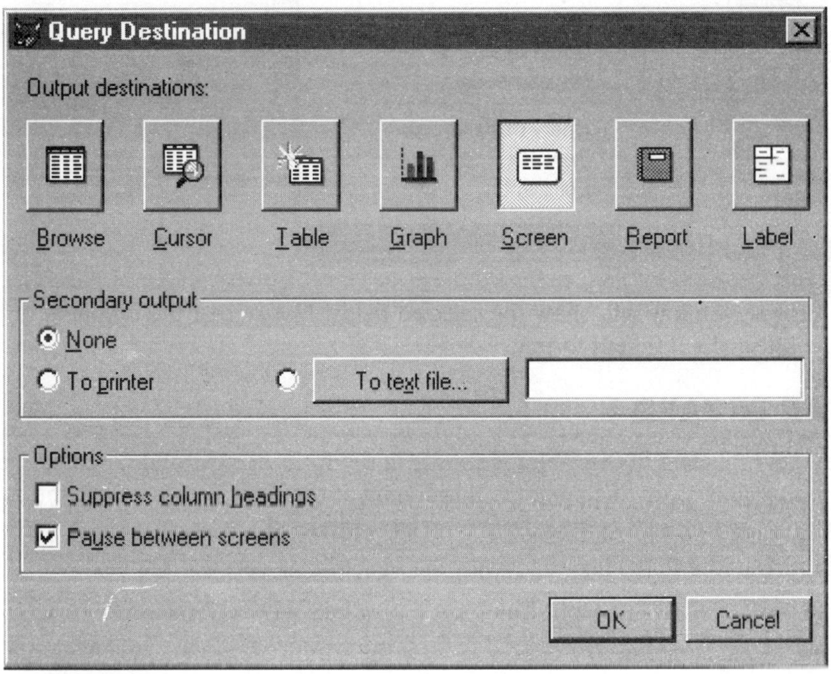

Output to a Report

Using this open you can club the results of the query with an existing report available under Open Report. By clicking Page Preview you can see the results before printing.

Output to a Label

Similar to the report option, here you can club the results of the query with an existing label format.

RUNNING THE QUERY

You can run the query in one of the following four ways:

1. You can select the Run Query from the Query menu.
2. You can also press Ctrl + Q keys together to run the query.
3. You can right click on table window in the query window and select Run Query option from the menu. By default the result will be displayed in Browse window.
4. You can click on ! mark on the Standard toolbar to run the query.

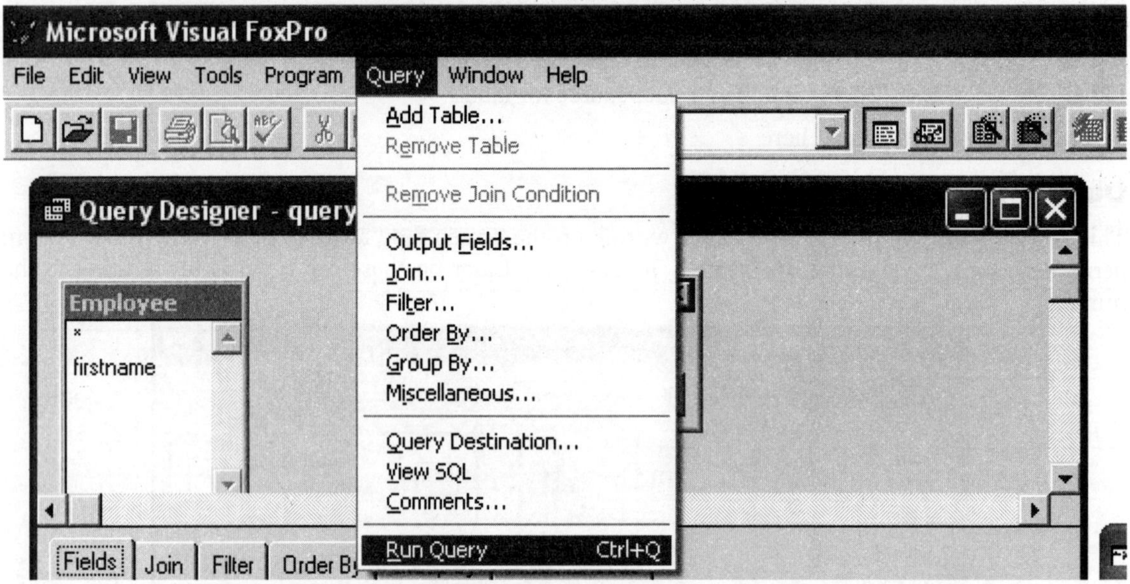

The resulting Browse window will show the selected fields. Notice that the output is in Browse mode, unless you have selected a different format.

CROSS TAB WIZARD

As we all know that the data in the tables is shown in the form of rows and columns. This wizard is a powerful tool which allows you to change the positioning of the data. You can show the data in rows and columns as per your needs. Let us see how it is created and used.

Let us now first create the following table, with the structure as you will see next.

1. Click on New in the File menu. The New dialog box will be displayed.
2. Click on Table and choose the option of New file button to create a new table file. This will give rise to another dialog box know as Create dialog box.
3. Type Table3.dbf in the enter table list box and then click Save button.
4. Table Designer dialog box appears; create the structure as shown here.

5. Click on OK button to save the structure of table3.dbf file.
6. A message box is displayed "Input data records now?".
7. Click on Yes. Visual FoxPro opens the table3 table in Append mode so you can begin adding records.
8. After adding these records press Ctrl + W keys together to save these records.
9. From the View menu choose Browse "Table3.dbf" to see the table records.
10. Again from View menu, choose Browse. Now records are displayed in browse mode.

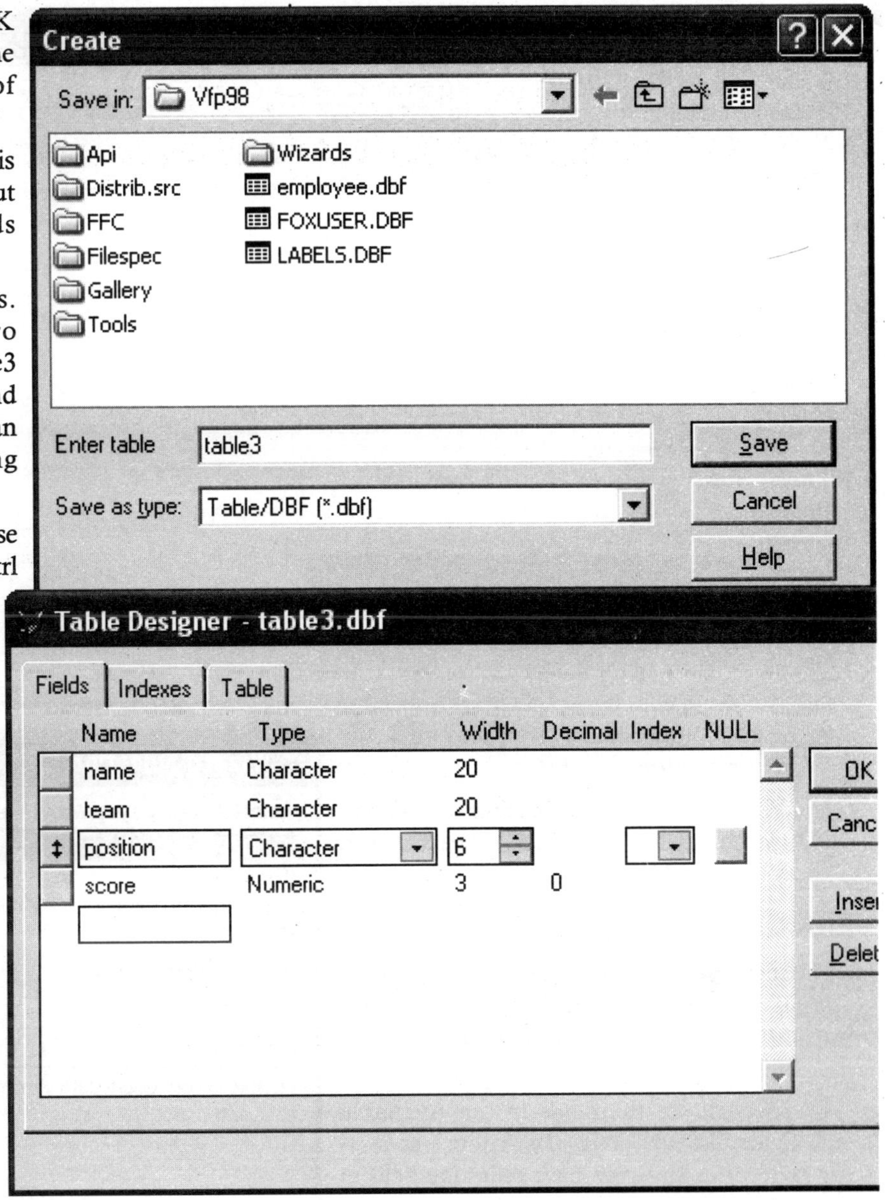

Now we will create a cross-tab of the table.

Creating a Cross-Tabs

This can be done if the following method:

1. From the Wizards submenu on the Tools menu choose Query.
2. In the Wizard Selection dialog box, choose Cross-Tab Wizard.

   Or

   From the File menu select New…option.

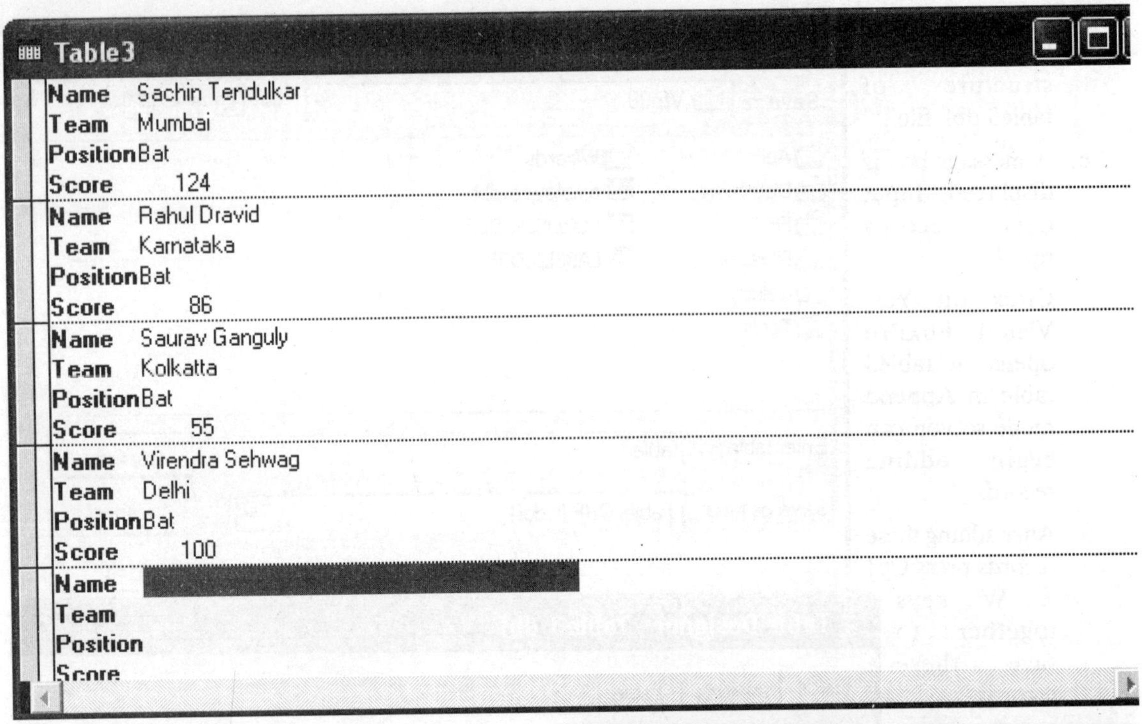

2. Select Query radio button and click the Wizard button.
3. When Visual FoxPro displays the Wizard selection dialog box, which appears as seen in figure, select Cross-Tab Wizard.

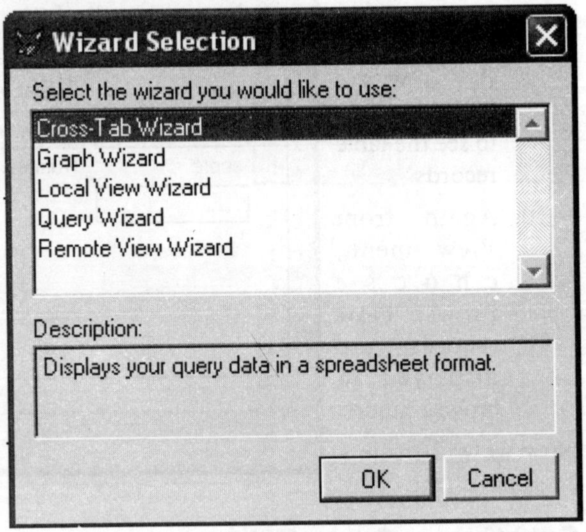

Selecting Fields

1. Click on … button of Databases and tables: it will open a dialog box. Choose your table, in this case Table3 and click OK button.
2. You can see the fields in the Available fields: list box. You must choose at least one field, since we have only one field in our Table3 table, so click (>>) button to move all the fields into the selected fields: box.
3. Click Next> button to move to next step.
4. The next step lets you lay out the Cross-Tab by clicking and dragging fields – one for the column headings, one for the row headings and one that is used as the basis of the calculations in the cells.
5. Your Cross-Tab query results will display a column for each unique value that exists for the table field that you drag to the Data box.
6. Click on Next> button to move to next step.

7. You can add a column that contains summary information add subtotals by selecting the appropriate radio button from the summary and subtotals areas. The totals will appear in the rightmost column of your Cross-Tab Query result.

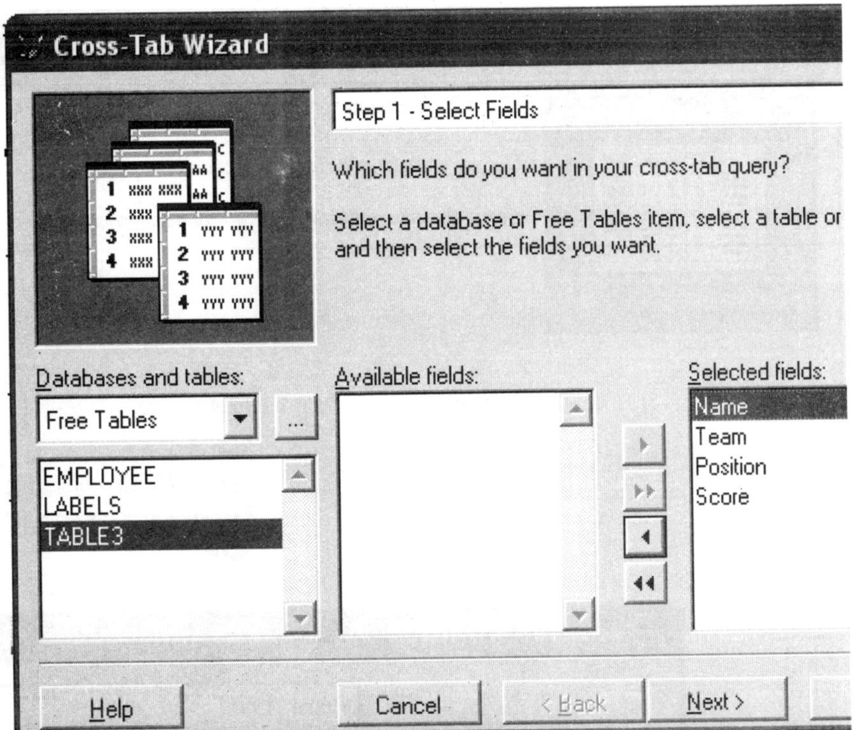

8. Quick on Next> button to move to the next step.
9. The next step lets you create the query and is similar to the Finish step of other wizards. Use the radio button to save the query for later use, to save and run the query or to save the query and modify it in the Query Designer. You can also click on Preview button to view the result of the query in a preview window.

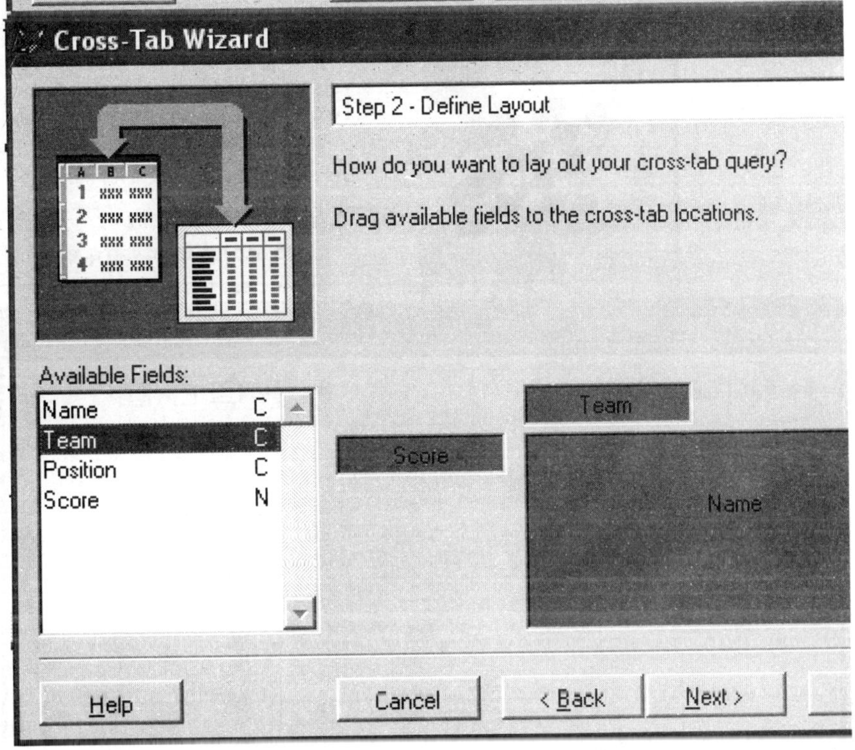

10. Now press the Esc key to close the Browse window.
11. Click on Save and run cross-tab query radio button to save the query and run it.

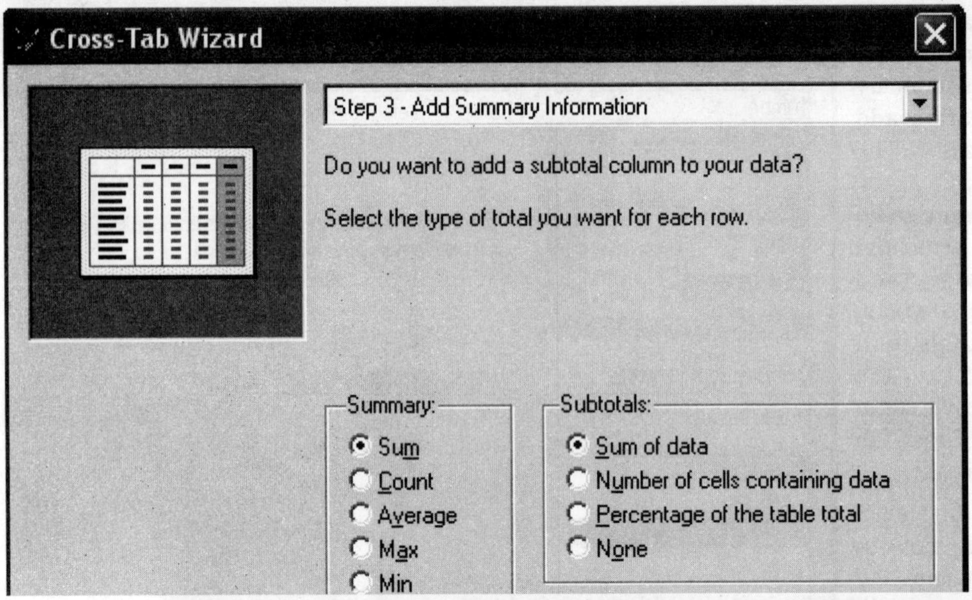
Cross-Tab Wizard
Step 3 - Add Summary Information
Do you want to add a subtotal column to your data?
Select the type of total you want for each row.
Summary:
Sum
Count
Average
Max
Min
Subtotals:
Sum of data
Number of cells containing data
Percentage of the table total
None

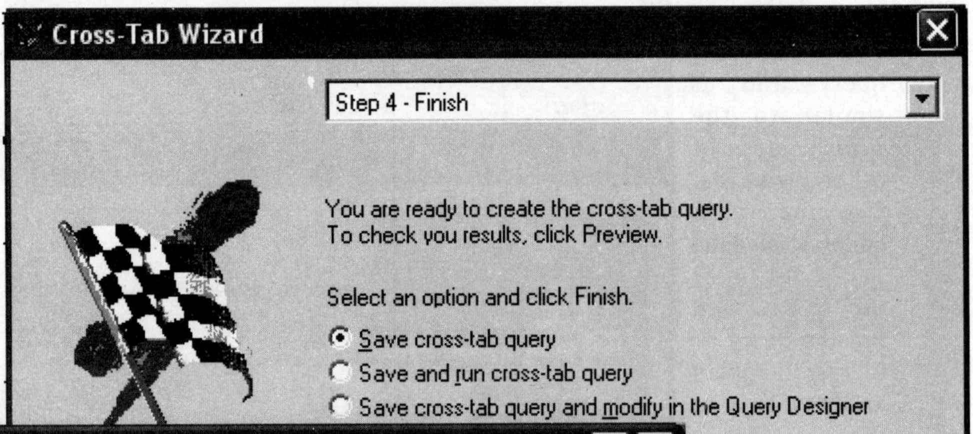
Cross-Tab Wizard
Step 4 - Finish
You are ready to create the cross-tab query.
To check you results, click Preview.
Select an option and click Finish.
Save cross-tab query
Save and run cross-tab query
Save cross-tab query and modify in the Query Designer

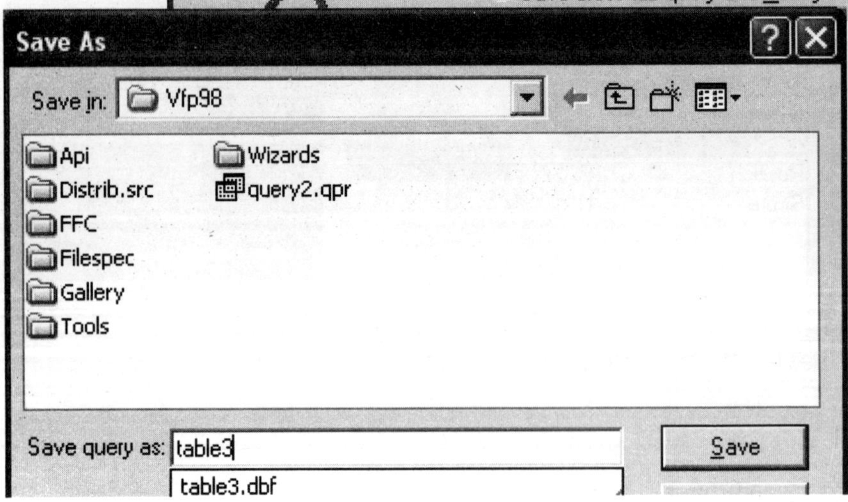
Save As
Save in: Vfp98
Api
Distrib.src
FFC
Filespec
Gallery
Tools
Wizards
query2.qpr
Save query as: table3
table3.dbf
Save

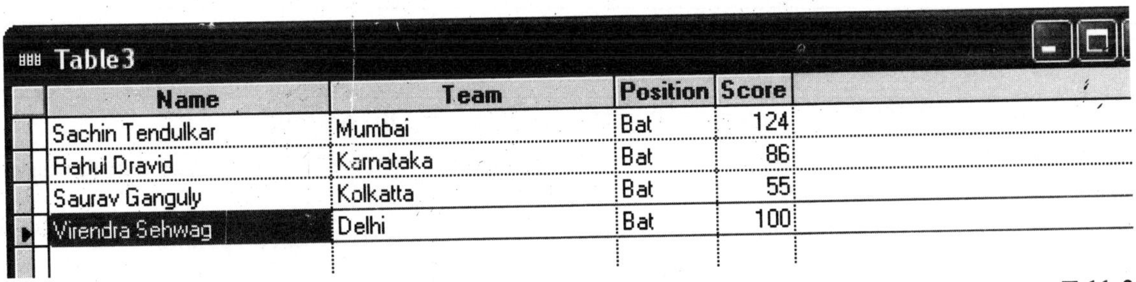

12. Click on Finish button. It will display a Save dialog box. Type the name of the query as Table3 and click on the save button.
13. Browse the table and see the difference.

USING THE QUERY

There are various options which can be used in the query. Some of them are listed here.

Using OR Condition (OR/IN Comparators)

You can create queries with multiple condition using OR and AND logical operators. Use the following simple procedure to display data.

1. Click on Field Name drop down list and select Table3.name in the drop down list.
2. Click in the Not Criteria drop down list and select Like.
3. Click in the Example text box and type Virendra Schwag.
4. Click in the Logical drop down list and select OR.
5. Click on the empty Field Name box to open the Field Name drop down list and select Table3.name.
6. Select Like from the Not Criteria drop down list.
7. Type Sacchin Tendulkar in the Example box.

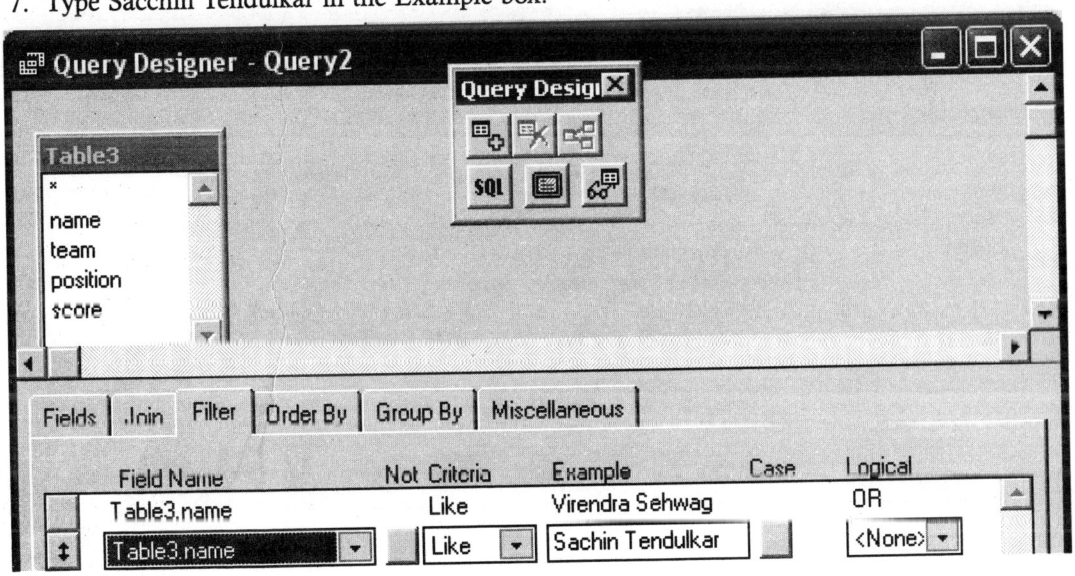

8. Click on the Run ! button to run the query.
9. Press Esc key to close the Browse window.

You can accomplish the previous query in a simpler way by using In comparator.

1. Remove the second selection criteria line, by clicking on Remove button. Notice that the third selection criteria line disappears.
2. Change the Like comparator in the first selection criteria line to an In comparator.
3. Place the cursor to the space immediately after 'g' of Virendra Sehwag in the Example text area and type Sachin Tendulkar.
4. From the Logical drop down list select <None>.
5. Select Run Query button and your result should be same as the previous one using the OR comparator.
6. Press Esc key to close the Browse window.
7. Click on the Remove button to remove existing selection criteria line.

Using more than (>) or less than (<) Comparators

Visual FoxPro allows you to compare using > (more than) or < (less than) comparators, while performing query. For example, suppose you want to extract all the records with score more than 90 from table3.dbf.

1. From Field Name drop down list, choose table3.dbf.
2. Choose > from the Comparison in the criteria drop down list.
3. In the Example text box, type 90.
4. Click on the Run (!) button from the Standard toolbar to run the query. Visual FoxPro will show all the records matching the criteria in Browse window.
5. Press Esc key to return to the Query Designer window.
6. Click on Remove button to remove the existing selection criteria line.

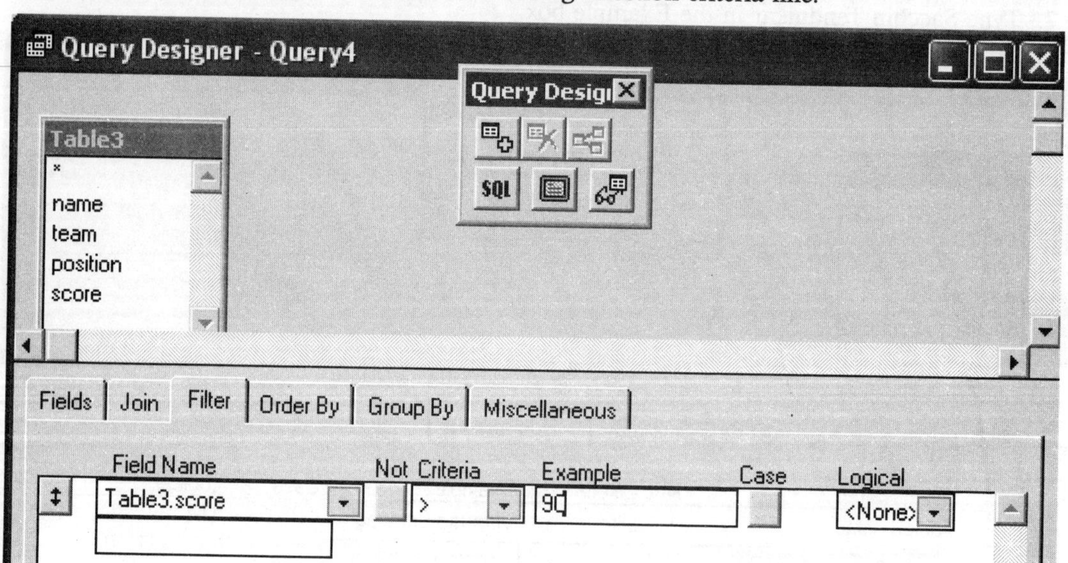

Using AND Condition

You can also create conditions that need to satisfy more than one criterion. Suppose that you are interested only in the records of employees whose team is Delhi and score should be less than 110. This can be done using AND condition, as detailed in the following;

1. Click on the Field Name drop down list, select Team.
2. Click on the Field Name drop down list, select Like.
3. Click in the Example text box and type Delhi.
4. From the Logical drop down list box select AND condition.
5. Now to specify second condition, click on the Field Name drop down list below table3 and select Score from the pull down list.
6. Click in the Criteria drop down list, Select < (less than) comparator.
7. Click in the Example text box and type 110.
8. Click on the Run ! button to run the query.
9. This will give you the only records which meets both the options.

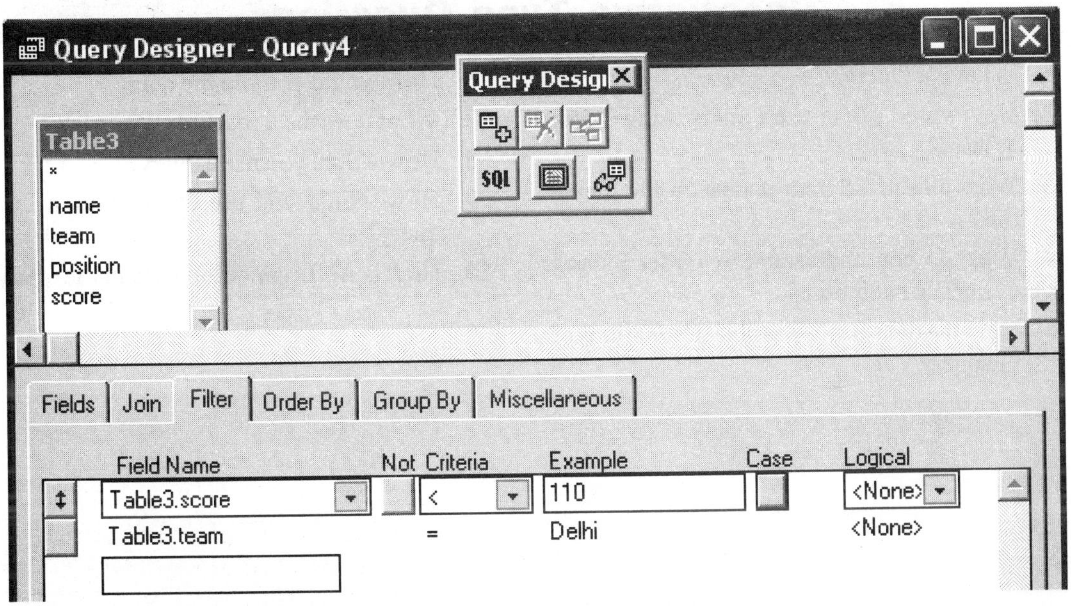

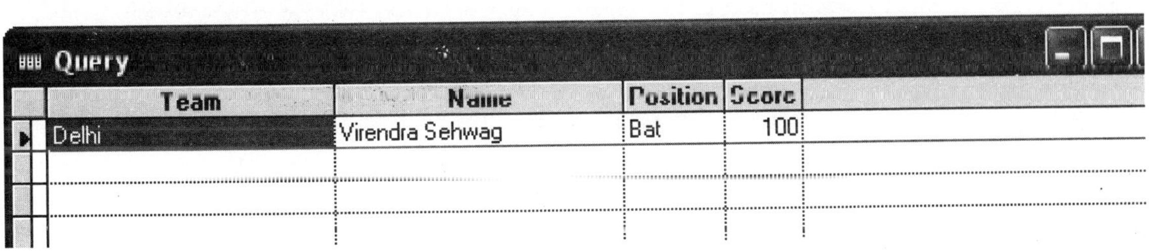

Multiple Choice Questions

1. Query works on :
   (a) Table (b) Forms
   (c) Reports
2. You can run Query from :
   (a) File menu (b) Query menu
   (c) Edit menu
3. Query can have multiple conditions using Or and :
   (a) OR (b) TO
   (c) AND
4. FoxPro expression can be created using :
   (a) Query Builder
   (b) Expression Builder
   (c) Design Builder
5. Inner join, which includes only the records from two tables that fulfill the condition of:
   (a) Match (b) Do not match
   (c) Nil
6. __________ includes all records from both tables and combines those that match the join condition into one record in the result set.
   (a) Right outer join (b) Left outer join
   (c) Full outer join

Descriptive Type Questions

1. What is a Query?
2. How would you create a query using Query Wizard?
3. What all the different panels on the dialog box?
4. What do you understand by Order By and Group By conditions?
5. Describe the various possible destinations of the query.
6. How would you run the query?
7. What does the Cross Tab Wizard do?
8. How would you use a query?
9. How would you use OR condition in the query?
10. How is AND condition used in the query?

26 Working with Forms

Generally, a form is used to fill in the data which forms part of a table. Each application in Visual FoxPro has atleast one form. Some may have more than one. Creating a Form is very easy. Since it is related to a table, you must have the table opened before you proceed further for creating of a form. The best way to create form as usual is the Wizard method.

CREATING A FORM USING WIZARD

From the Tools menu, select Wizards and Form to get a dialog box. This asks you whether you want to create a one to many form wizard or just form wizard. We would simply use a form wizard. This would lead to various screens of the wizards.

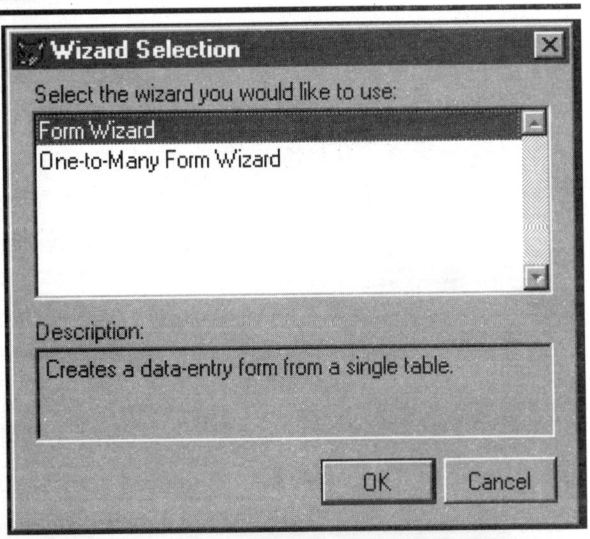

Step1 asks you to select fields which you want to use in the form from the table.

Choosing Fields

In the Available fields: list box, click Add All (>>) button (the one with two right pointing arrows) to select all the fields. The selected fields are now listed in the Selected fields: list box. Scroll through the list. Your screen should be as shown in the following figure.

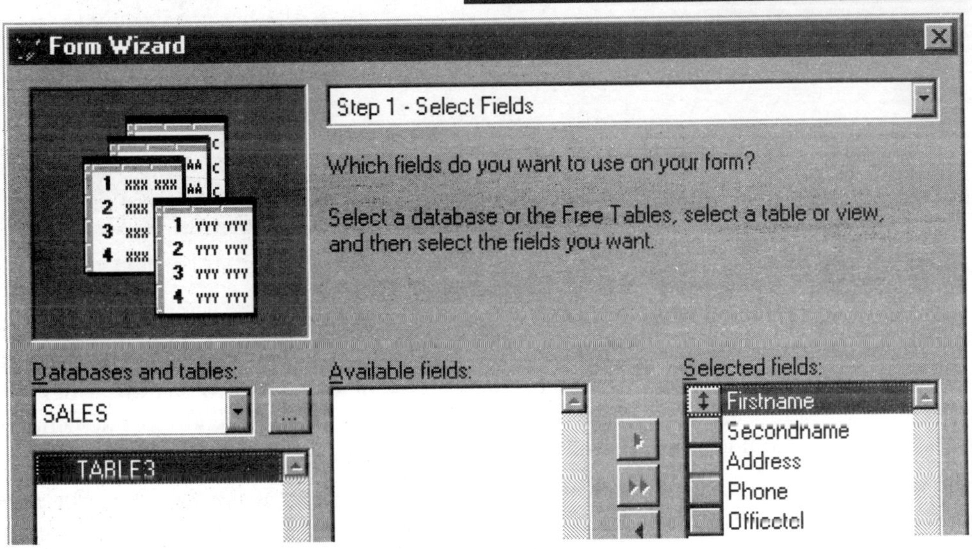

Choosing a Style

Next you have to select the style which you want to use on your form. Here you are given different styles to choose from: Standard, Chiseled, Shadowed, Boxed or Embossed.

The other options on the screen are: Standard colored area; Chiseled with three-dimensional lower border, Shadowed with the area having a shadowed line below and to the right; Boxed which is quite different because it puts both the prompt and the edit area into a box and changes the font to a bold typeface and finally Embossed, which has a classy three-dimensional look.

The magnifying glass view at the top of the screen will change with each selection to show you an example of the style you have just selected.

Button type options are: verify that text buttons is selected. In this screen, you also choose which style navigation buttons you prefer or whether you would like to use scrolling grid to navigate through your table.

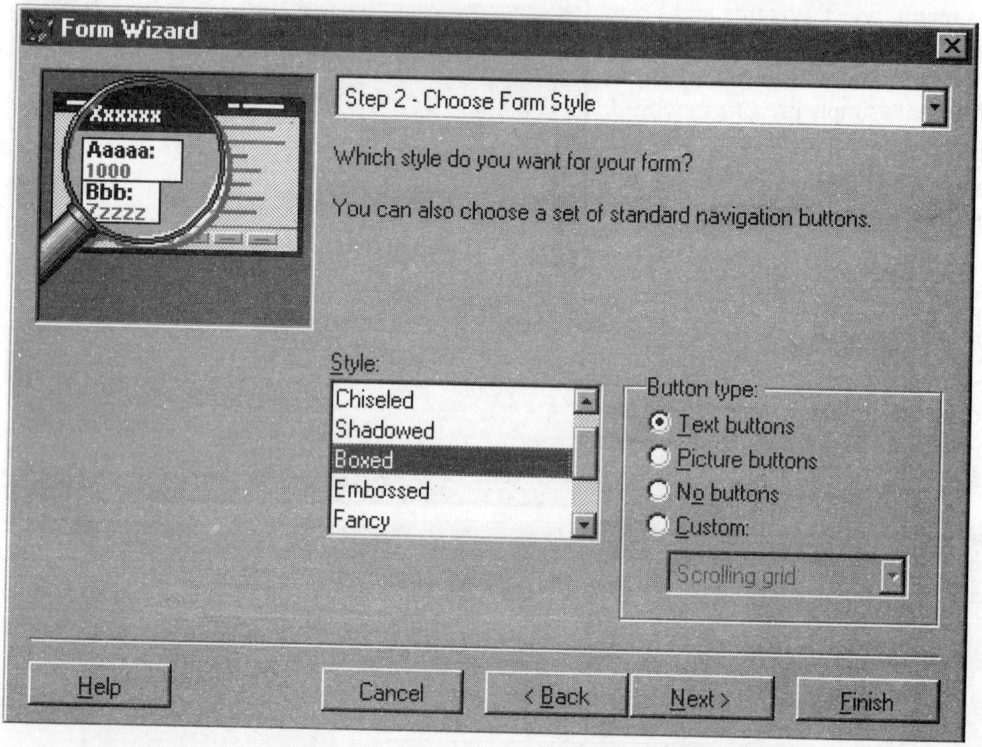

Choosing Sort Order

Next you are prompted to specify the Sort order to the table's records. You can add up to three fields on which to sort by clicking each desired field in the Available fields: list box. From the lists of fields, double click on Name field to move this field from Available field: list box to the Sort order or records list. Use the radio buttons to specify whether each field is to be sorted in Ascending or descending order. Note that Ascending radio button is selected by default.

Specifying Sort Order can make it easier to find records when you are using the form. For example, it would be easier to look up on Employee if the form for Employee Table were sorted in alphabetical order by Name.

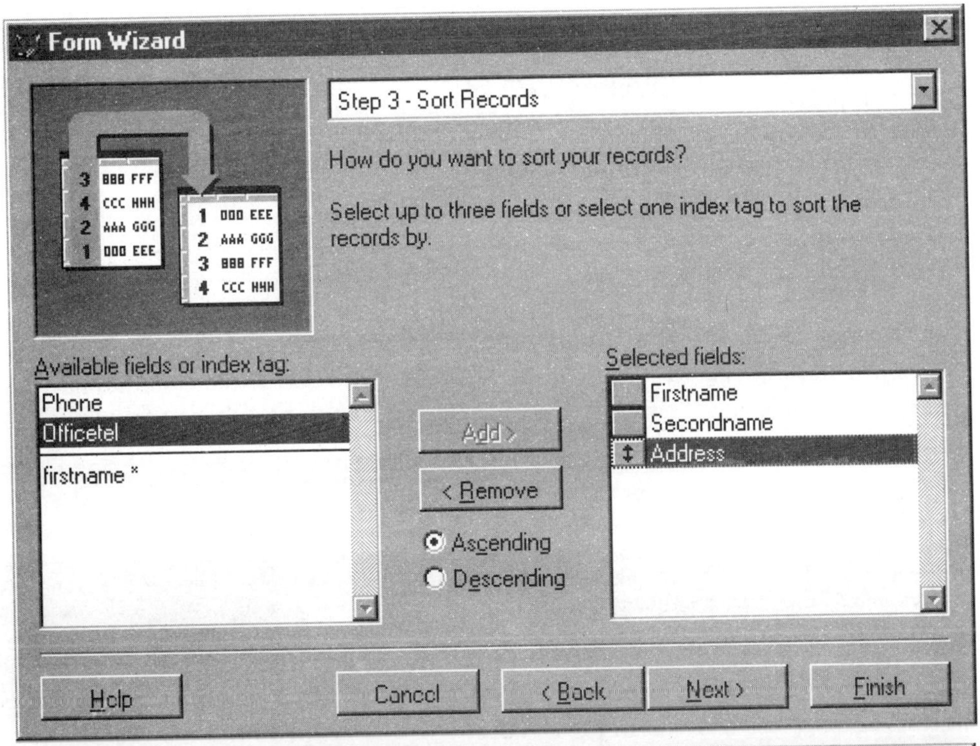
Form Wizard
Step 3 - Sort Records
How do you want to sort your records?
Select up to three fields or select one index tag to sort the records by.
Available fields or index tag:
Phone
Officetel
firstname *
Add >
< Remove
Ascending
Descending
Selected fields:
Firstname
Secondname
Address
Help
Cancel
< Back
Next >
Finish

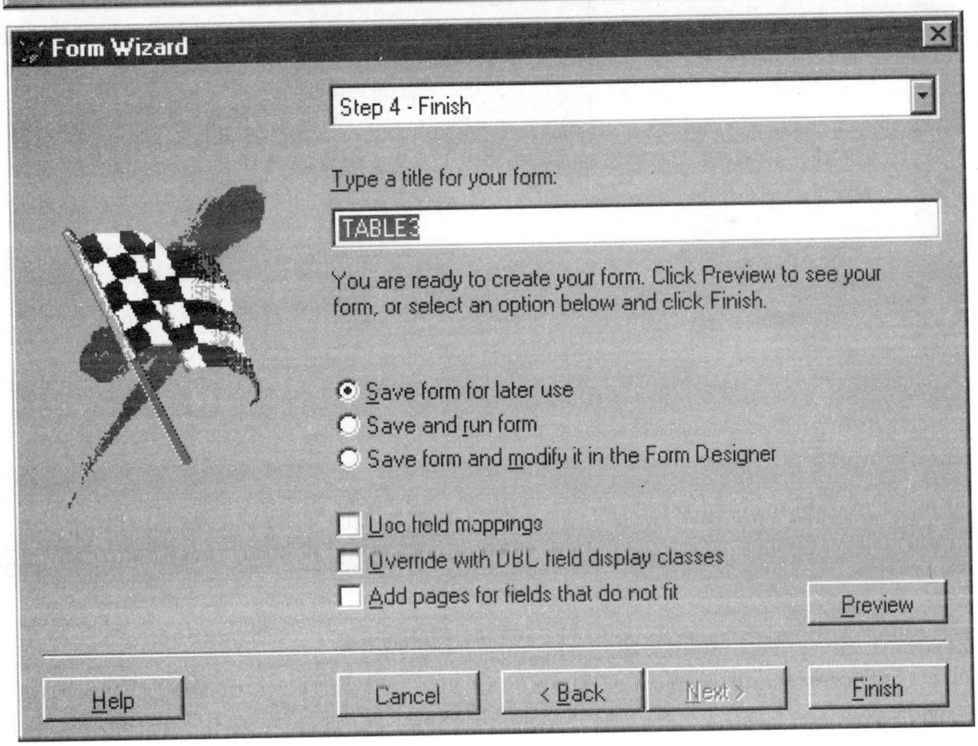
Form Wizard
Step 4 - Finish
Type a title for your form:
TABLE3
You are ready to create your form. Click Preview to see your form, or select an option below and click Finish.
Save form for later use
Save and run form
Save form and modify it in the Form Designer
Use field mappings
Override with DBC field display classes
Add pages for fields that do not fit
Preview
Help
Cancel
< Back
Next >
Finish

Generating the Form

Once you press Finish, the system asks you to save the form with a name.

This name should preferable be linked with the table. It will be saved with extension .SCX.

The form would be created as shown below.

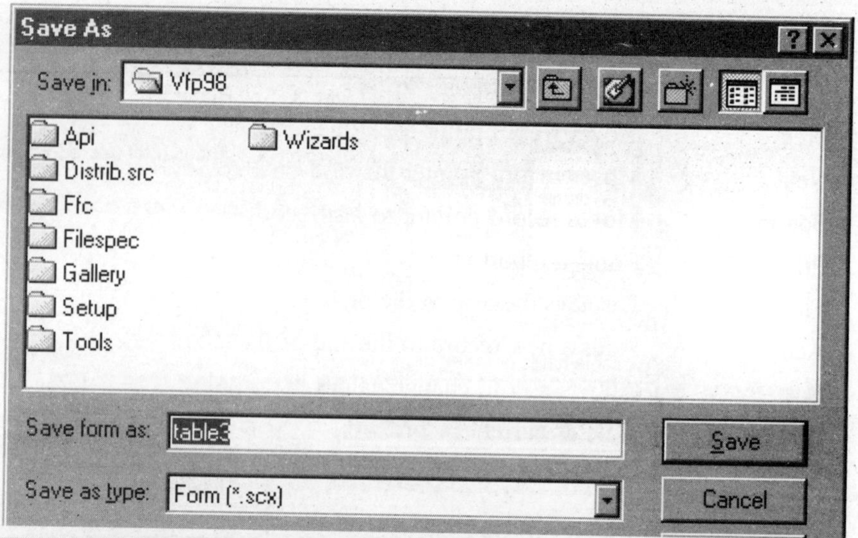

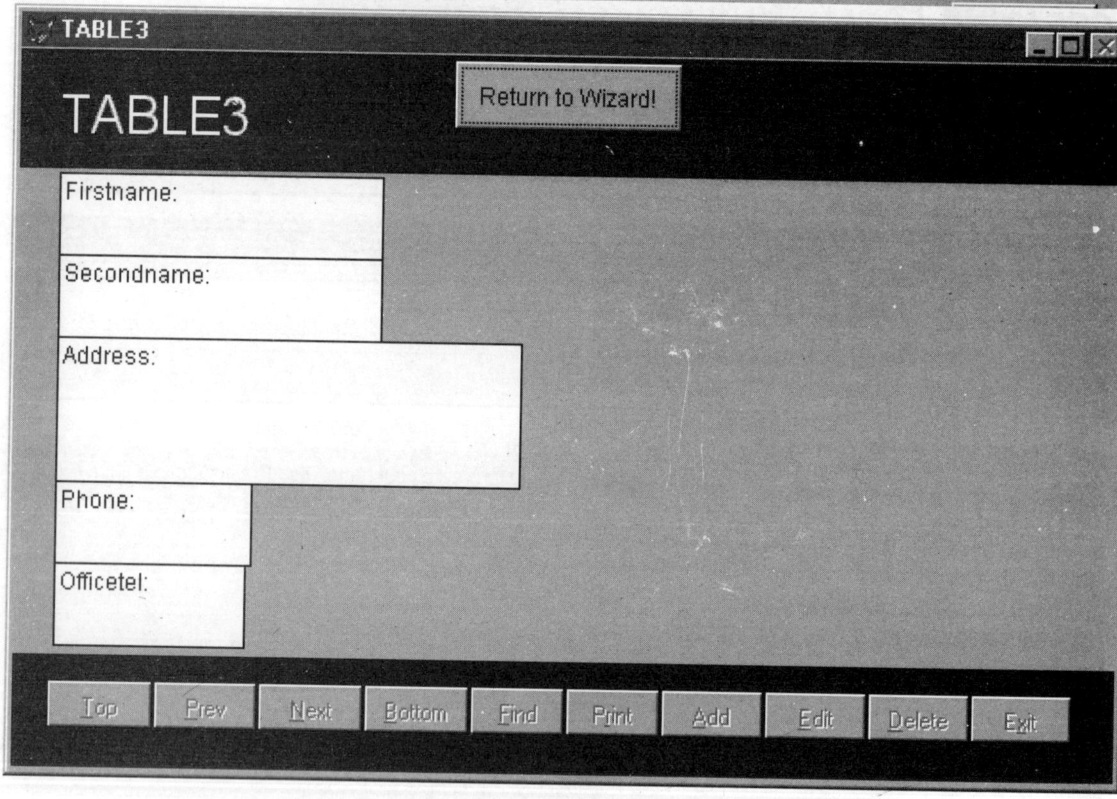

USING THE FORM'S CONTROL PANEL

The set of buttons at the bottom of the form are also called its Control panel. These buttons make it easy to work with the form.

These buttons are explained in the following table.

Button	*Description*
Top	Moves record point to first record
Prev	Moves record point back one record
Next	Moves record pointer forward one record
Bottom	Moves record pointer to last record
Print	Prints a report
Find	Displays the Search dialog box.
Add	Adds a new record to the end of the table.
Edit	Allows user to change values in current record.
Delete	Deletes current record
Exit	Closes form.

CREATING FORM USING FORM DESIGNER

Another method of creating Form is through the Form Designer which can be accessed by clicking New from the File menu. This would lead to the common dialog box from where you click at the Form and New File. Remember, you table must be open at this stage.

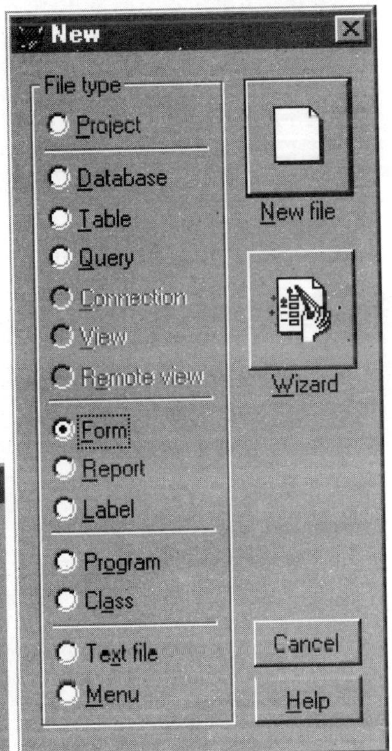

This would open up the Form Designer dialog box. Also it will give you the Form designer toolbox. On the toolbox click the one which opens the Data Environment form. This form, as shown here, has all the fields of the table.

Pick these fields one by one and place them on the form where you want to place them. Each field will make two boxes. One for the data and the other for the heading of the field. You may have to make some adjustments before reaching the final form.

A rough layout of the form is shown on the next page.

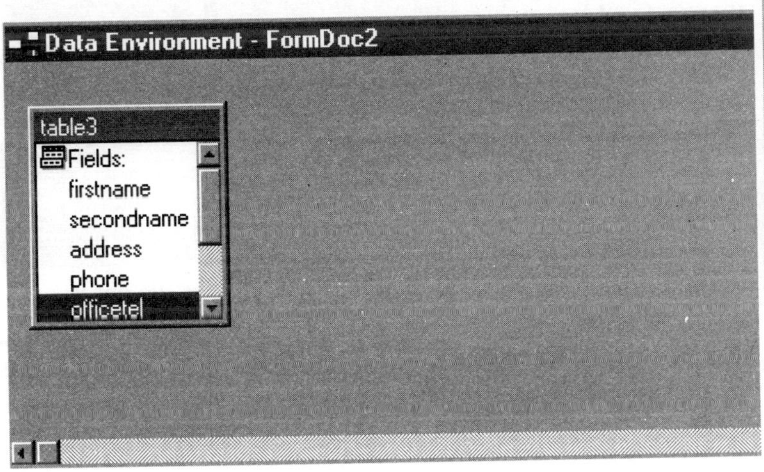

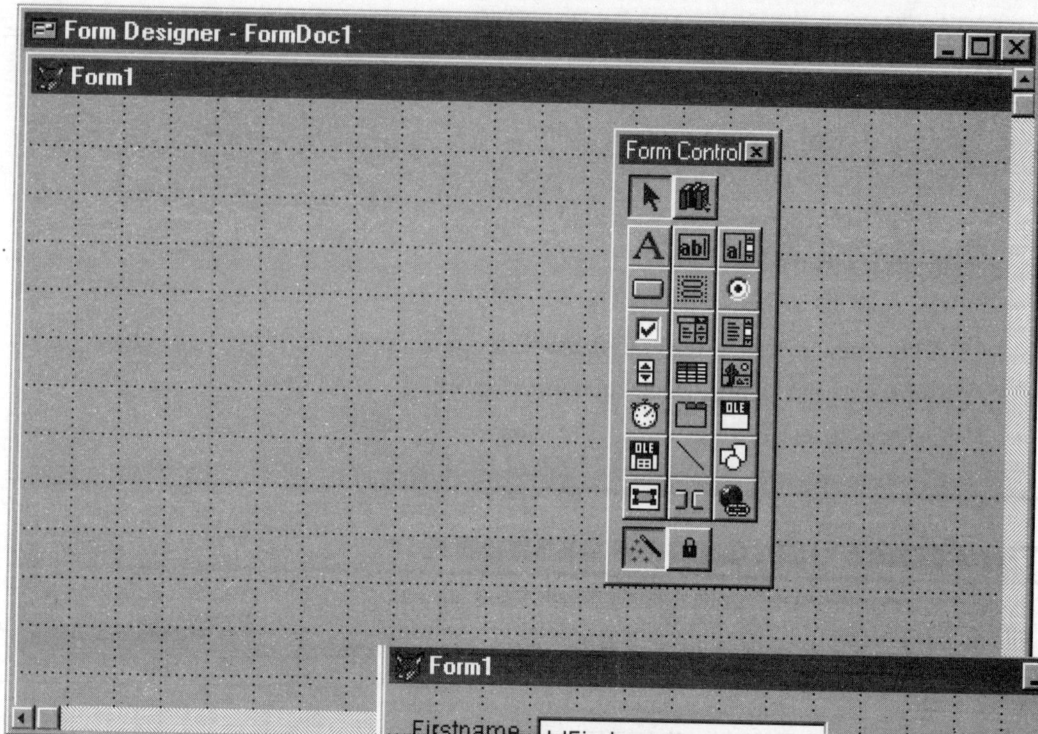

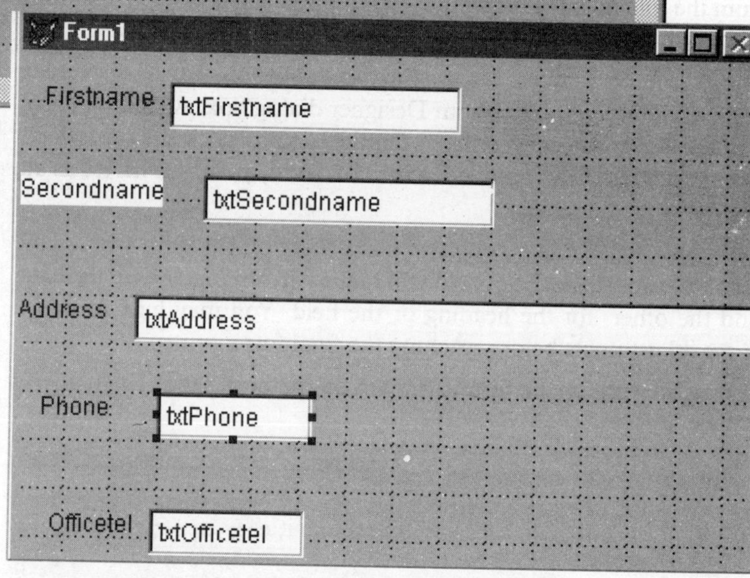

As you must have noticed that a Form Designer form has a properties dialog box alongwith it. This has various panels. The panels are:

All

It has all PEM setting for the object specified, including user-defined properties and objects.

Data

This shows only those properties related to the data for the control.

Methods

This shows all methods and events, including user-defined methods.

Layout

This shows all the native Visual FoxPro properties related to the physical apperance of the obect.

Other

This shows all the native Visual FoxPro properties that do not fit logically into the Data or Layout categories.

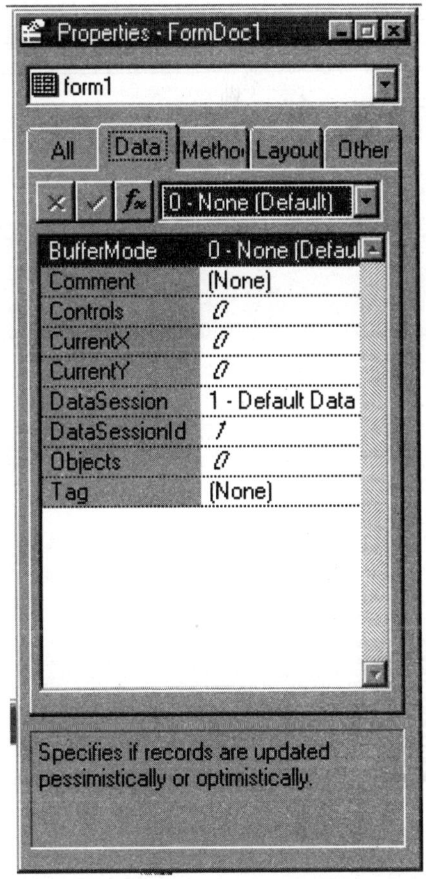

AUTOFORMS

You can create AutoFom by clicking at the AutoForm button on the Standard toobar. Rest everything is done by the software and in a flash you will see the form on the screen.

The form shows the field names and a text box to let you enter data in every field.

For memo fields, it includes a scrollable text box. If the memo field is too large to fit in the box, the scroll bar is activated so you can view it completely.

The form also includes buttons that make it easy to perform such basic operations as viewing, editing, and adding data.

RUNNING A FORM

Now that you have created a form, using it is quite easy. Just type the following command in the command window, or include it in your code:

```
DO FORM FROM1
```

This way you can run the form.

The other way of running is to double the form icon in the Open dialog box.

You can also Run Form from the Form menu. Form generated for Table3 is shown on the next page.

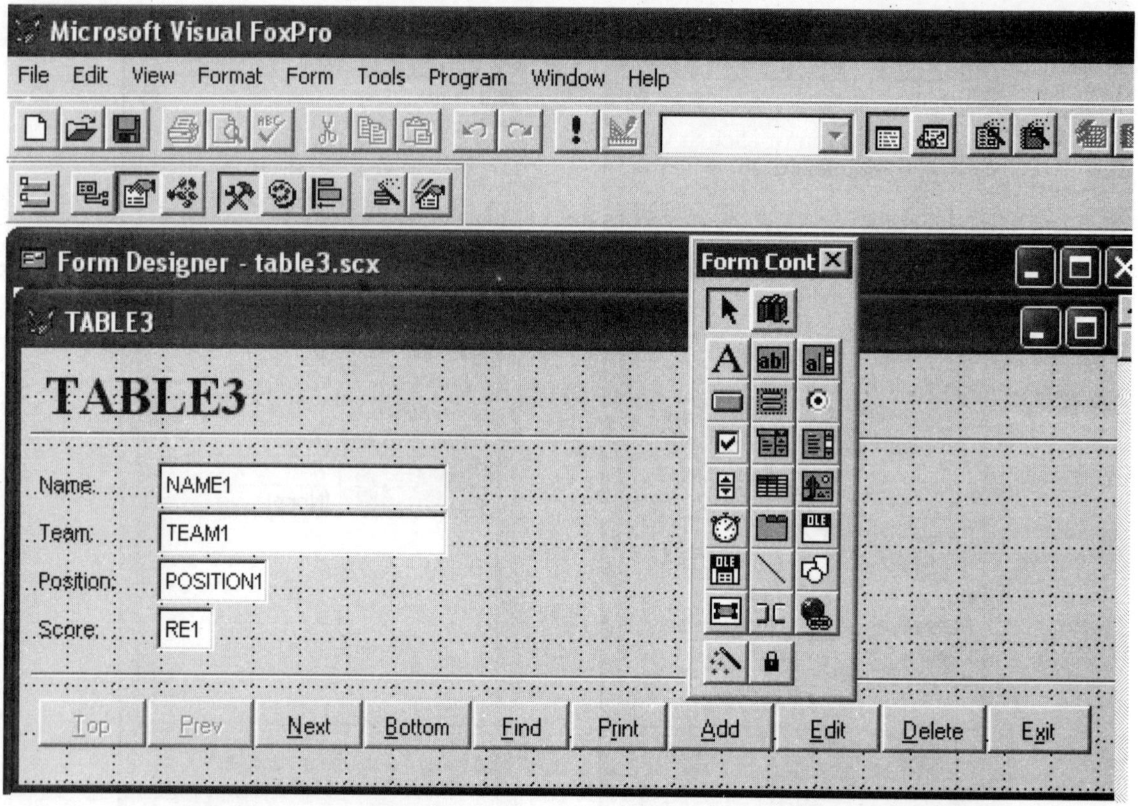

USING FORMS

You can use the form as you would do any other similar form. Mostly using the arrow and tab keys. Tab would allow you to go to the next field and arrow keys would allow you to move from one field to another. You can click on Next record to display next record. Click on Previous record to see the last record. Click on Exit to close the form.

What's more you can change form's design any time. You can resize, move, and delete field objects. But, remember, if you change and omit a field, all the data in that field would be lost and there is no way of retrieving that data.

USING BUILDERS

You can use various builders to build forms too. A builder is like a wizard which enables you to quickly and easily define some of the basic behaviours and formats of a form and its controls.

The following builders can be made using the Form Designer.

AutoFormat Builder

Command Group Builder

Form Builder

List Box Builder

Text Box Builder

ComboBox Builder

Edit Box Builder

Grid Builder

Option Group Builder

For creating any builder right-click at object with the mouse and the respective builder dialog box would come up.

This dialog box would have panels which would ask for various data to be filled up. Fill up the required data in the suggested location or click at the desired button and press Ok.

The various screens of the Text Box Builder are shown here and on the next page.

You can similarly create various other builders.

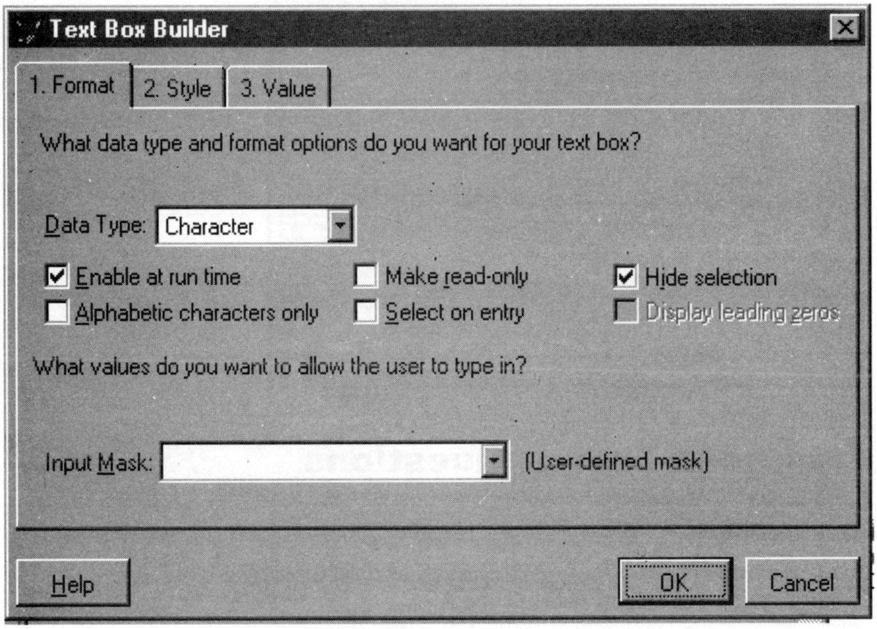

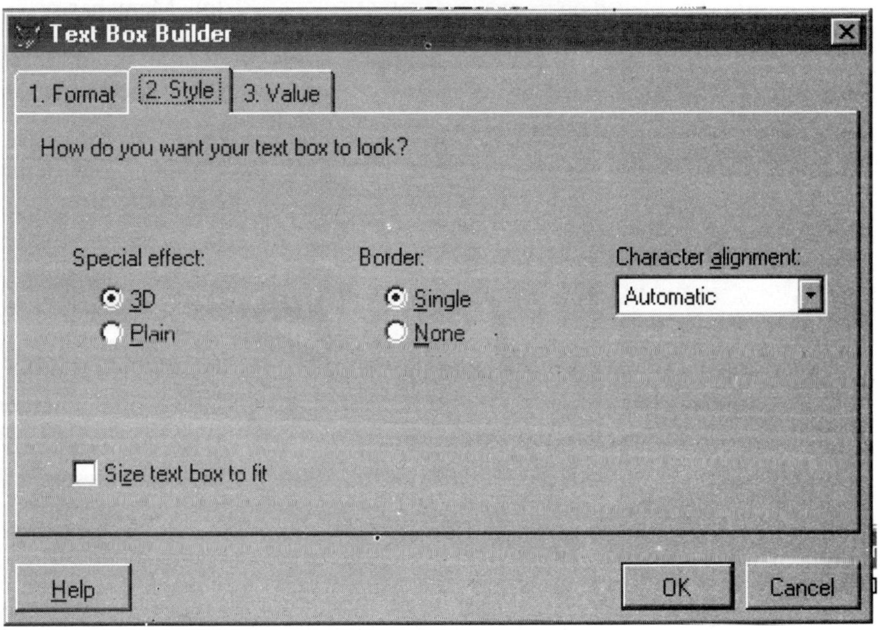

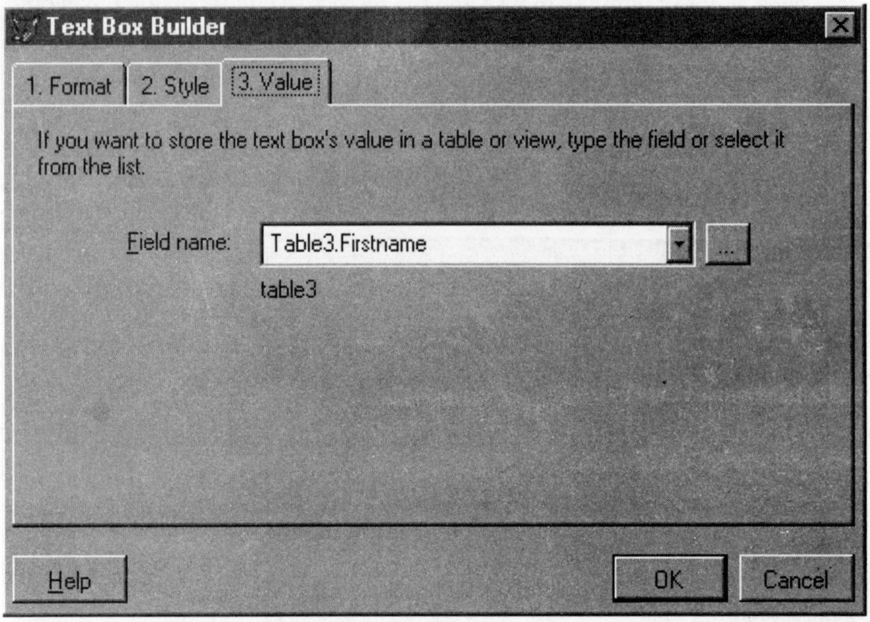

Multiple Choice Questions

1. Forms are saved with extension:
   (a) .scx (b) .dbf
   (c) .frm
2. A form is displayed on :
   (a) Printer (b) Screen
   (c) Hard disk
3. You can run a form using the :
   (a) Form menu (b) File menu
   (c) Edit menu
4. AutoForm button is on :
   (a) Standard toolbar
   (b) Title bar
   (c) Menu bar
5. Form takes field from :
   (a) Report (b) Table
   (c) Wizard
6. Bottom is one of the buttons on the control bar of the form.
   (a) Yes (b) No

Descriptive Type Questions

1. How would you create a form using the Form Wizard?
2. How would you use the Form's control panel?
3. What is AutoForms?
4. How would you run the Form?
5. How would you use the builders?
6. Describe the process of creating a form using the Form Designer.

Working with Reports

27

INTRODUCTION

Reports are the ways of presenting your table in any required form. It should be in such a way that it looks more presentable and is accurate. If possible the numeric fields should be totalled as grand total or group totals as the case maybe.

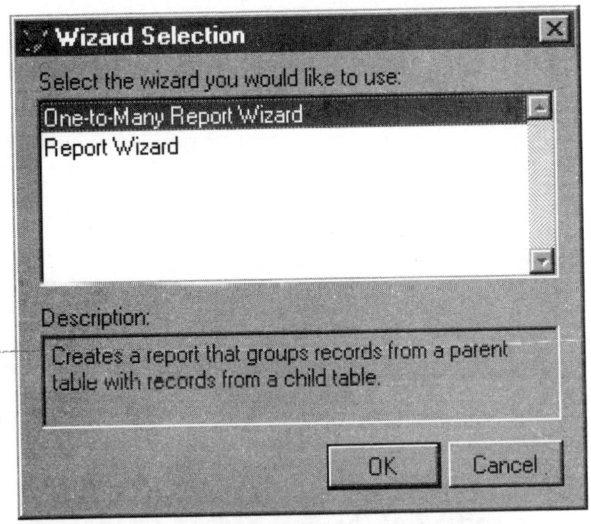

As usual we would first go through the Wizard method of creating the Report. It can be accessed from Tools menu and Wizard submenu. A number of wizard steps will appear on the screen from which you have to select the various options before moving further.

Once you have filled in the required information, press Next to go to the next screen.

Step 1 will ask you to select the table and fields.

Step 2 will ask you to group records.

In Step 2, both the screens of Grouping and Summing options are also shown.

Step 3 will ask you select the report style.

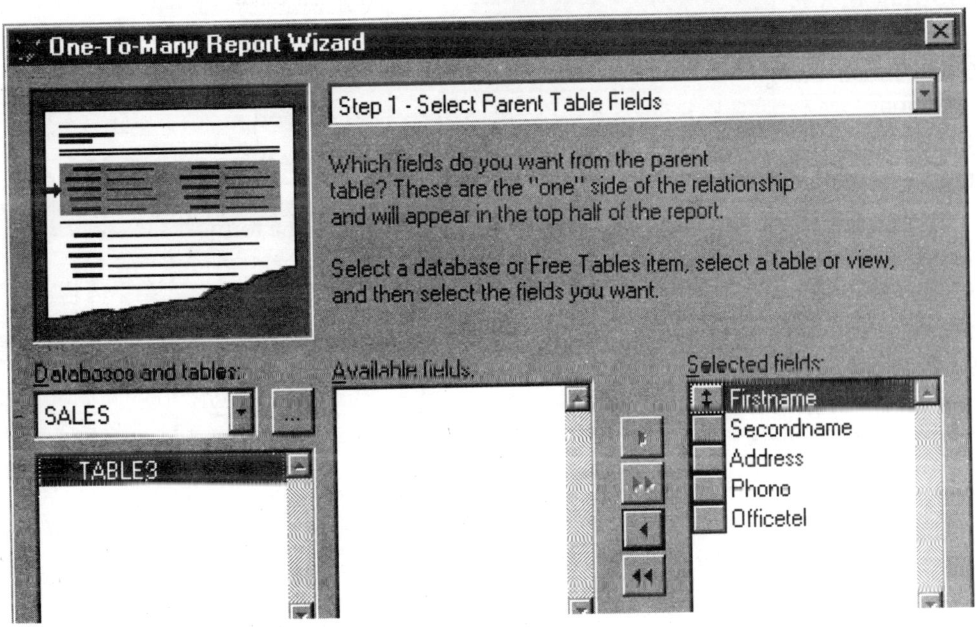

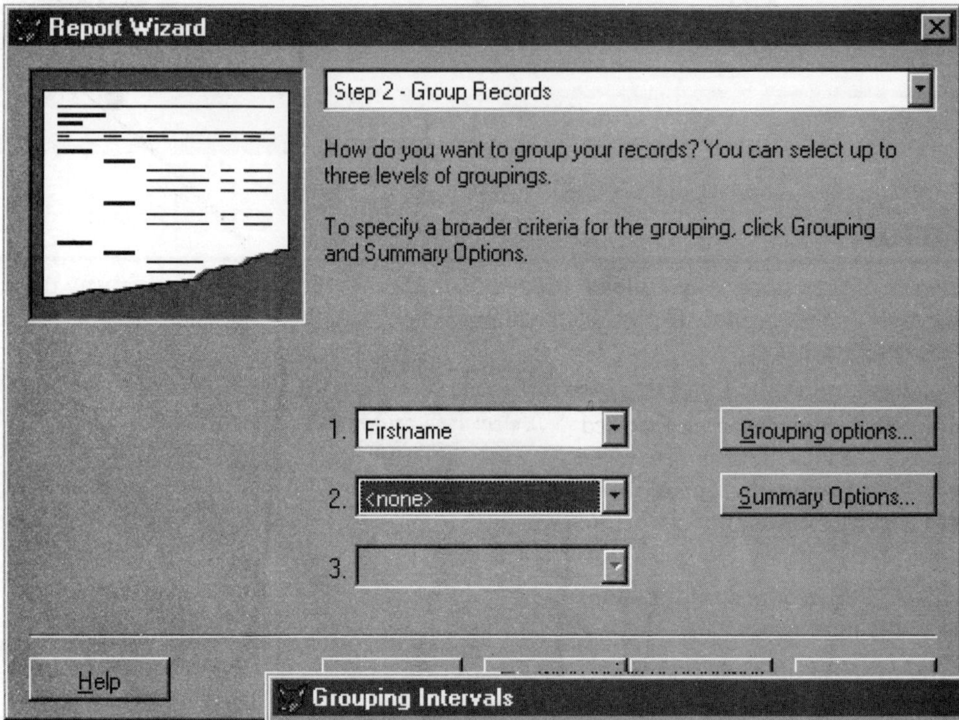

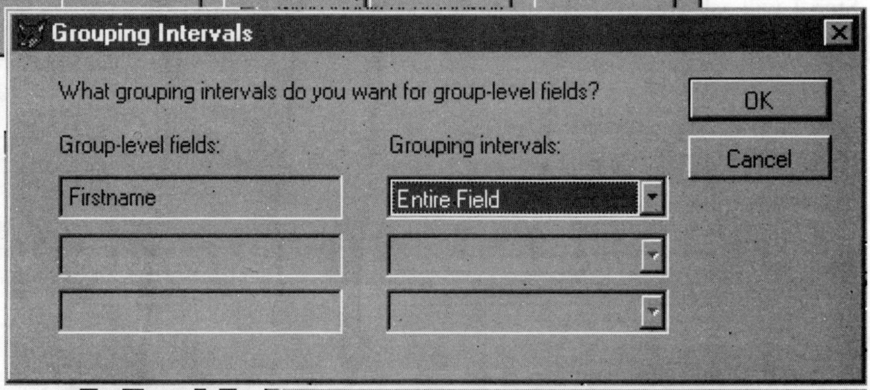

Step 4 will ask you to define the report layout.

Step 5 will ask you about sorting of the records.

Step 6 will finish the report creation.

After Step 6 you will be asked to save the report with a name.

In the Save As box, type the name of the report.

All these options are shown here and on next few pages.

In the end you will get the final report format where you have to just fill up the type of headings needed by you and the report is ready for you.

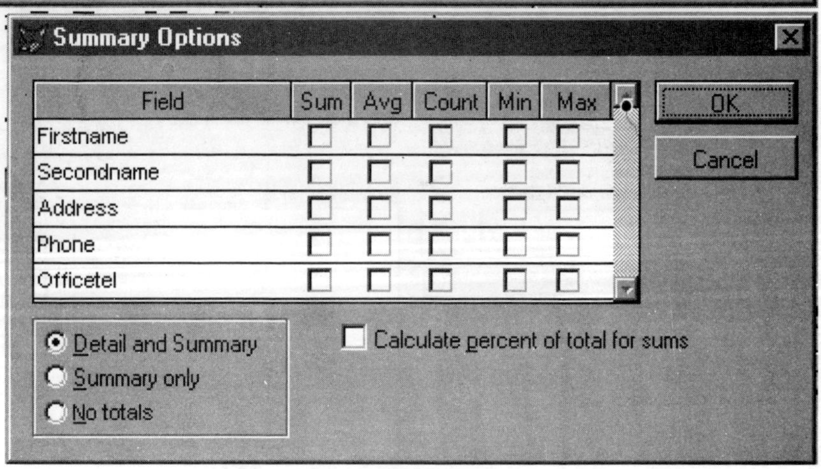

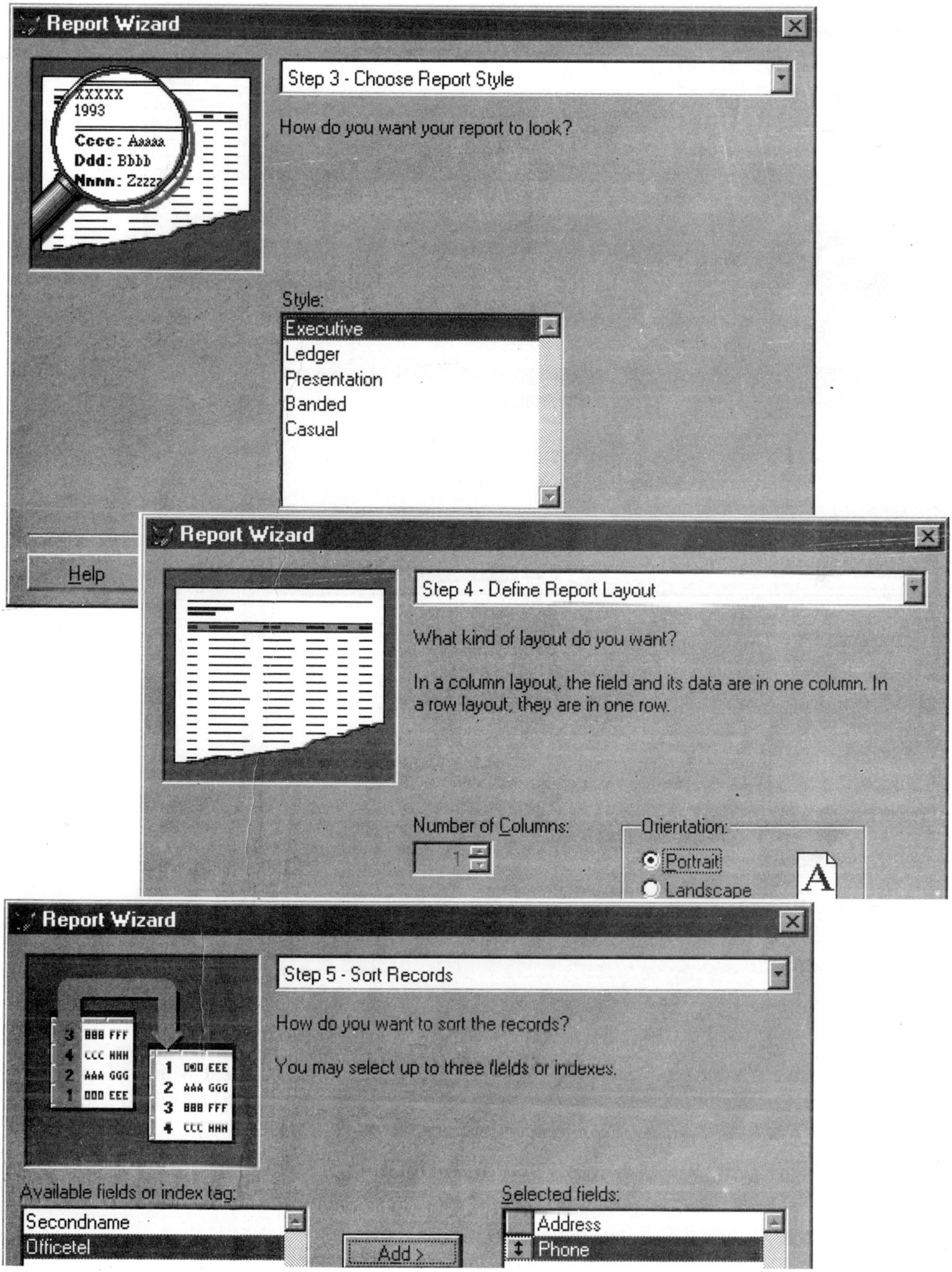
Report Wizard
Step 3 - Choose Report Style
How do you want your report to look?
XXXXX
1993
Cccc: Aaaaa
Ddd: Bbbb
Nnnn: Zzzz
Style:
Executive
Ledger
Presentation
Banded
Casual
Help
Report Wizard
Step 4 - Define Report Layout
What kind of layout do you want?
In a column layout, the field and its data are in one column. In a row layout, they are in one row.
Number of Columns:
1
Orientation:
Portrait
Landscape
A
Report Wizard
Step 5 - Sort Records
How do you want to sort the records?
You may select up to three fields or indexes.
3 BBB FFF
4 CCC HHH
2 AAA GGG
1 DDD EEE
1 DDD EEE
2 AAA GGG
3 BBB FFF
4 CCC HHH
Available fields or index tag:
Secondname
Officetel
Add >
Selected fields:
Address
Phone

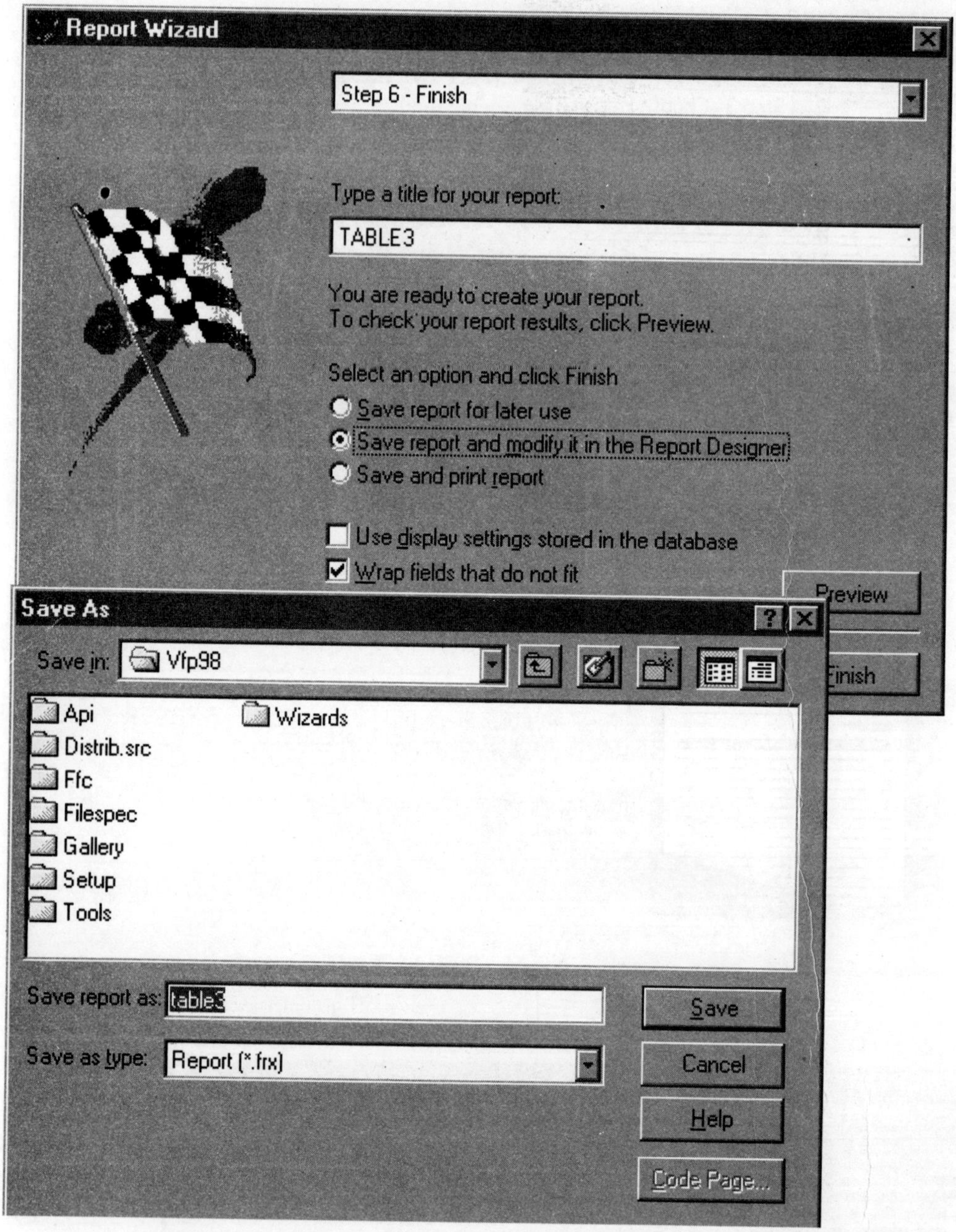

By double clicking at the fields you can get the Report Expression of that field which allows you to change the format from any of the format which you may select from the dialog box which it leads once you click at the ellipses.

Calculations button would lead to a dialog box which allows you to take average, etc. of the field.

Print when button when clicked leads to another dialog box.

This box allows you to use the various options, as shown above.

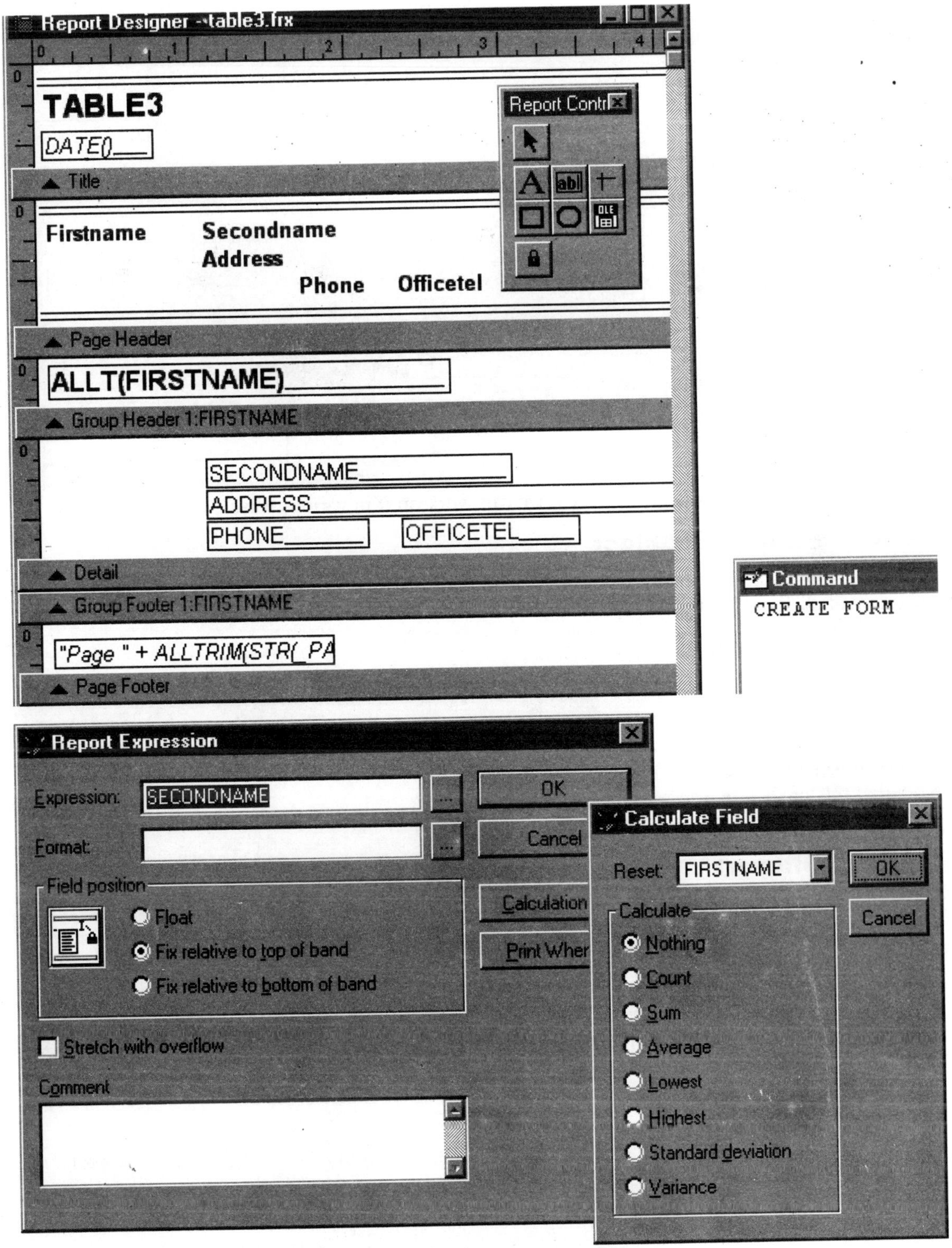
Report Designer - table3.frx
TABLE3
DATE()
Title
Firstname
Secondname
Address
Phone
Officetel
Page Header
ALLT(FIRSTNAME)
Group Header 1:FIRSTNAME
SECONDNAME
ADDRESS
PHONE
OFFICETEL
Detail
Group Footer 1:FIRSTNAME
"Page " + ALLTRIM(STR(_PA
Page Footer
Report Contr
Command
CREATE FORM
Report Expression
Expression:
SECONDNAME
OK
Format:
Cancel
Field position
Float
Fix relative to top of band
Fix relative to bottom of band
Calculation
Print Wher
Stretch with overflow
Comment
Calculate Field
Reset:
FIRSTNAME
OK
Cancel
Calculate
Nothing
Count
Sum
Average
Lowest
Highest
Standard deviation
Variance

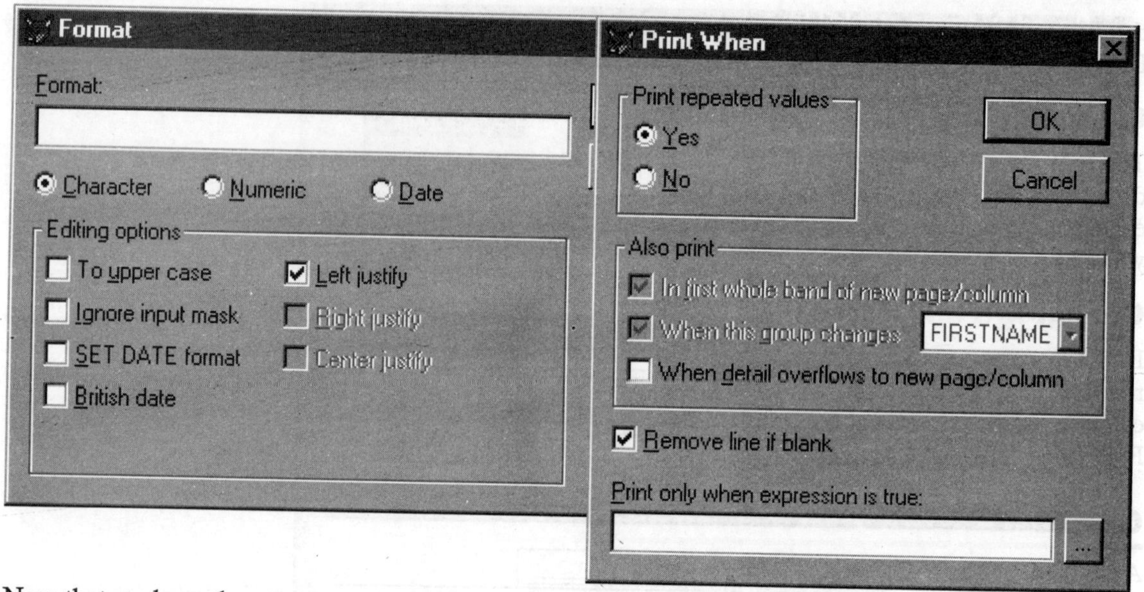

Now that we have the report canvas ready, we can work on it in various ways.

Selecting a Report Object

To select an object, make sure the Select Objects button is selected in the Reports Controls toolbar. Then point to and click on the desired type of object.

Deleting a Report Object

To delete an object, select the object on the report canvas and then press the Delete key or choose Edit, Cut. Note that this procedure also works for multiple selected items.

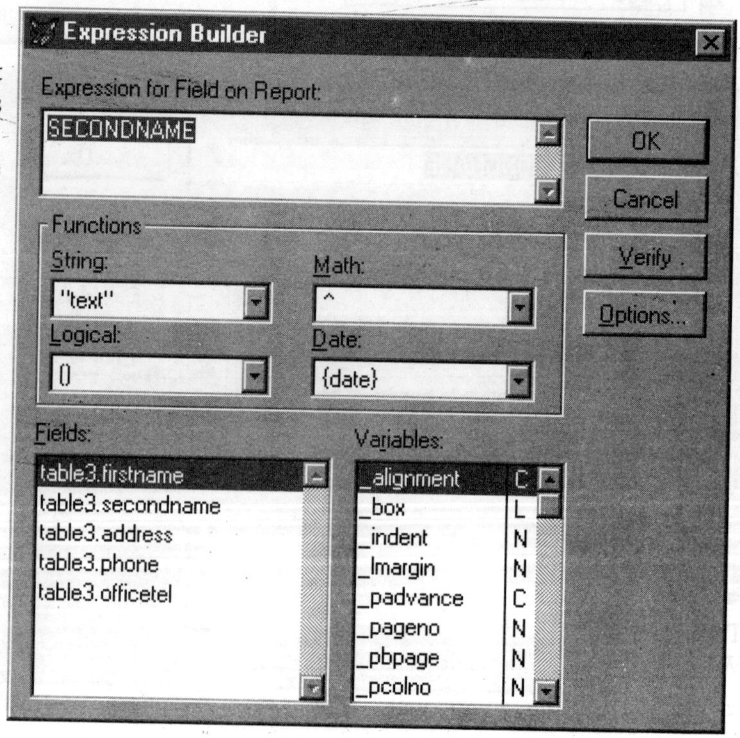

Copying a Report Object

To duplicate an object, select the object on the report canvas, choose Edit, Copy and then choose Edit, Paste. When you do so, a copy of the object appears near its original location. You can click the object and using the arrow keys or mouse, move it to a desired location.

Working with Fields

To add a field to the report canvas, select the textbox/field control from the Report Controls toolbar. When you click on the report canvas to add the control, the Report Expression dialog box appears, where you can specify several key properties, as follows:

Changing Field Expressions

The Expression text box includes the expression, field name, or function call that will evaluate to the data you want to show. You can type a field or expression into the box yourself, or you can use the ellipsis at the right to bring forward the Expression Builder, which includes a number of tools for helping you add data to your report, including a list of available fields.

Changing Field Formats

In the Format field of the Report Expression dialog box, you can enter formatting guidelines for the resulting text or numeric data. Clicking the ellipsis for this property accesses the Format dialog box. You can use this dialog box to quickly format the data you are showing on your report and then return to the Report Expression dialog box.

CREATING REPORT USING REPORT DESIGNER

As in the case of Table and Forms, you can create report too using the Designer. But, here you will have to mention everything yourself. For this do the following:

1. Open an existing table, in this case table3.dbf.
2. Type BROWSE in the command window to see the details of the records.
3. Press Esc to close the browse window.
4. Now type Create Report in the command window to have the Report Designer window on the screen.
5. Since the name has not been specified, it is giving the name as Report1.

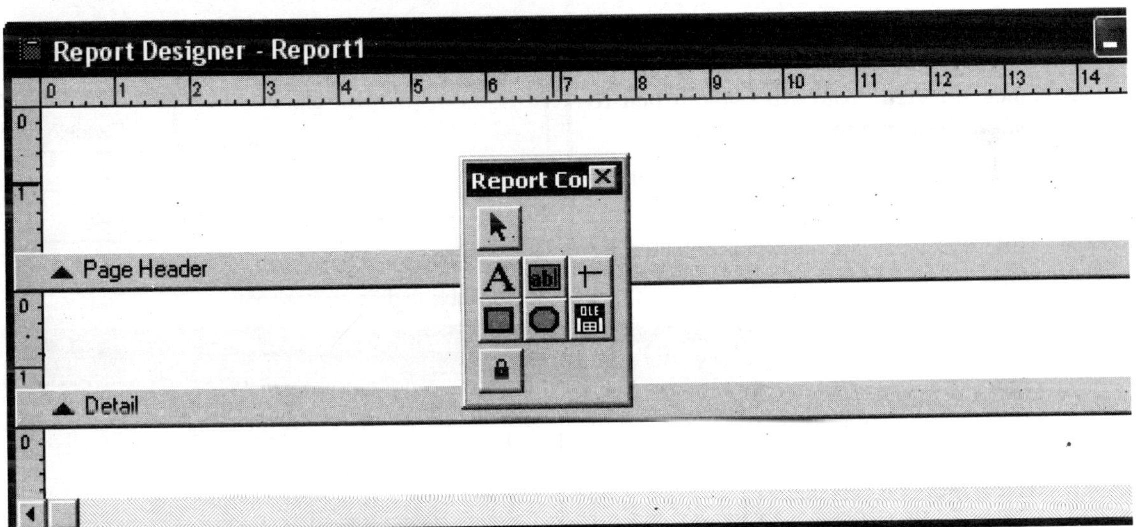

This screen as you can see is divided into 3 parts, Page Header, Detail and Page Footer (it is hidden here). We will fill up all 3 of them one by one. But, first let us see what each one of them should have.

In the Page Header, you will define the header of the report, or simply called the Report Heading. It should contain the name of the company, report name, various column heads, etc. Details will be used as the body of the report. Page Footer is similar to Page Header with the difference that it appears at the bottom instead of top. You can include it to have totalss, date, time, page number, etc.

GENERATING A QUICK REPORT

This is another method of creating a report quickly. Visual FoxPro does everything and creates the report for you, whether you like it or not. This is how it is done.

1. With the table open click at Report button on the toolbar.
2. You will get the Report Designer window on the screen.
3. From the Report menu, click at Quick Report.

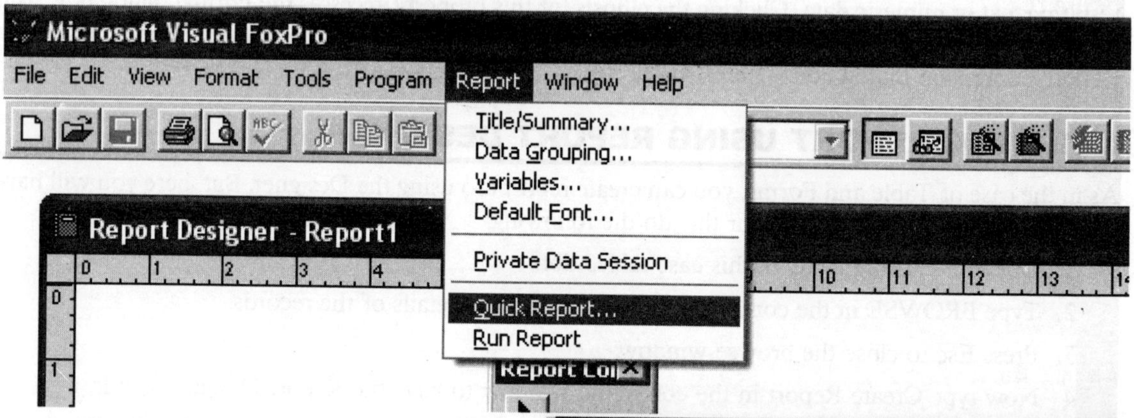

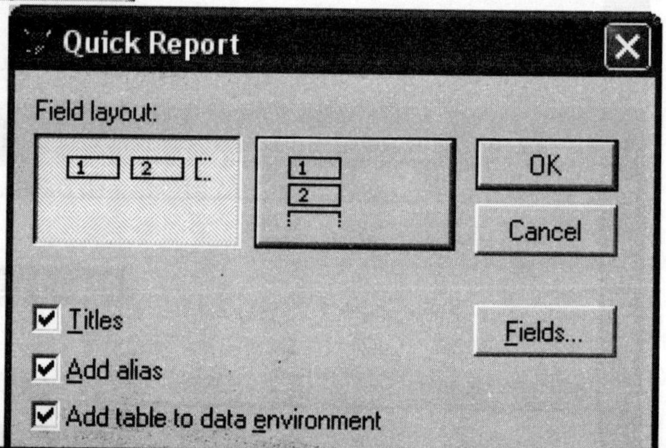

4. The first dialog box asks you to select the field layout.
5. If you click at Fields you get the Field Picker dialog box for selecting the fields.
6. Once selected, you will be returned to Quick report menu.
7. Click Ok to have the quick report on the screen.
8. This report has all the fields selected by you.
9. If you want you can see the Print Preview of the report.
10. If found ok you can print it too on your printer which must be attached and should be On to receive the report.
11. Preview of the report is shown on the next page.

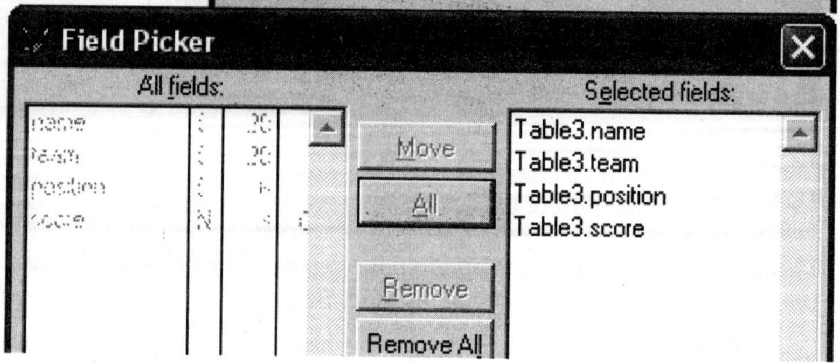

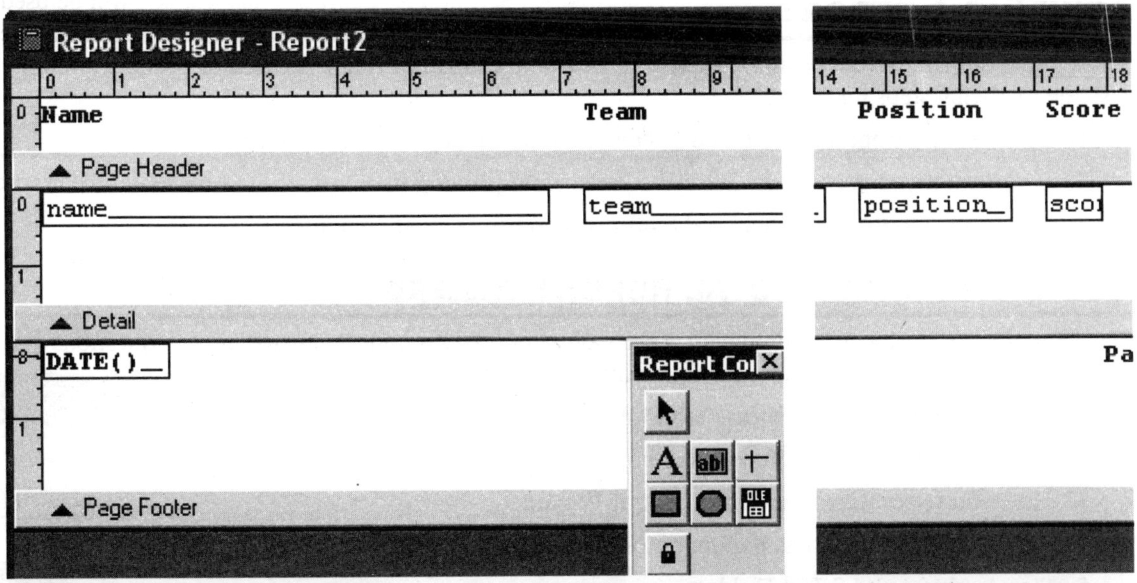

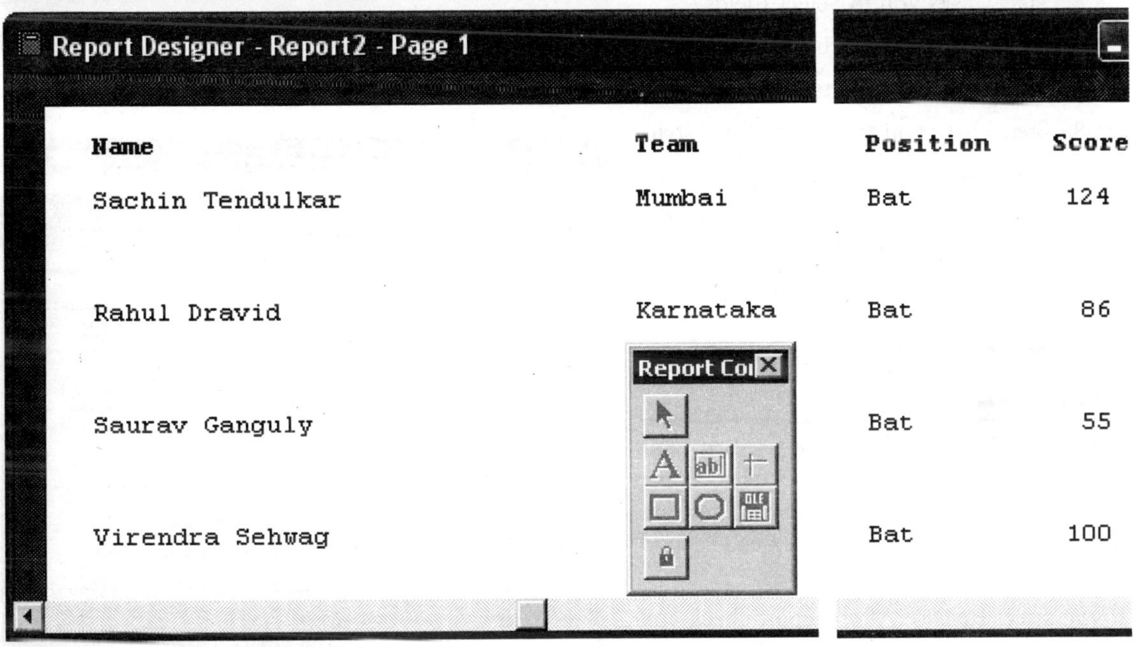

SAVING THE REPORT

Report is saved in Visual FoxPro with an extension .FRX. You can give a name of your choice to the report file. To save the report do the following:

1. Click on Save/Save As on the File menu.
2. Type the name.
3. Specify the desired drive and/or directory in which you wish to save the report.
4. Click on Save.

PRINTING A REPORT

I have printed the report in the above case. But, let us me explain the main method of printing a report. Use the following steps for it.

1. Choose Print from the File menu when you have the report on the screen.
2. If you want you can see the Print Preview before printing it.
3. The report would be printed on the printer attached to your computer.

USING THE GROUP/TOTAL REPORT WIZARD

This is another wizard which would help you create a summary report. By answering few questions you can get the required report. Follow the following steps to do this:

1. Open the table file, in this case table3.dbf.
2. Click at New to get the New dialog box.
3. Here you select Report and then click at Wizard.
4. The Wizard selection has the option of Group/Total Report Wizard. Select this.
5. Step 1 asks you to Select Fields.
6. Step 2 asks for selecting of Grouping of Records.
7. Step 3 asks for selecting the records for sorting.
8. Step 4 asks you to choose report style.
9. Step 5 finishes the wizard.
10. Click on Preview in step 5 to see the report.
11. The report can be printed too.

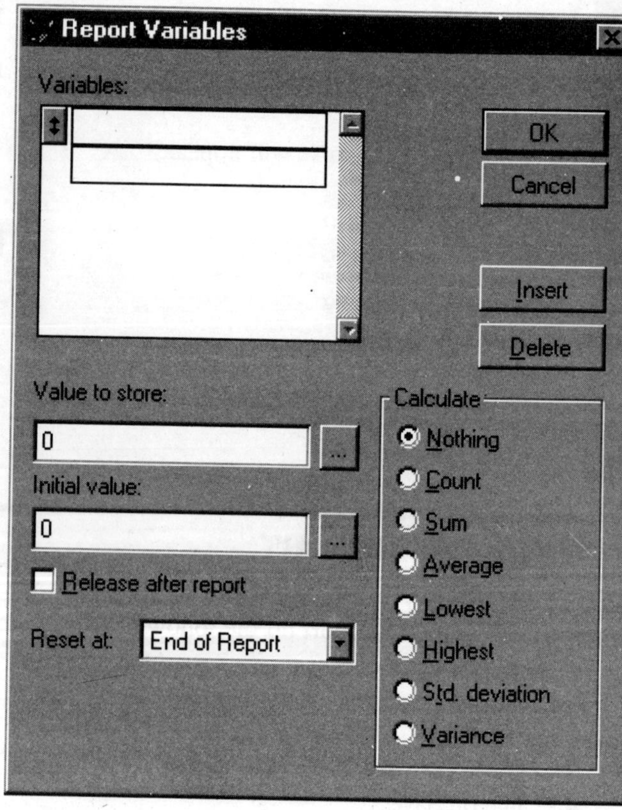

WORKING WITH REPORT VARIABLES

You can define variable to be used in your reports by selecting Report, Variables, as per dialog box, shown on the next page. These are used to keep running tallies that extend beyond the scope of the field calculations.

If you select Release After Report check box in the dialog box, the Report variables are scoped privately, which means that any user-defined function you call can access them. If you do not check this box, the variables will remain in memory as public variables. It is unlikely you would ever need to retain the variables in such a global scope.

WORKING WITH GRAPHICS AND PICTURES

Add text and shape objects is useful, but when your really want to decorate your report, attract attention to a particular piece of information, or just include a company logo, you can turn to a full-fledged graphics.

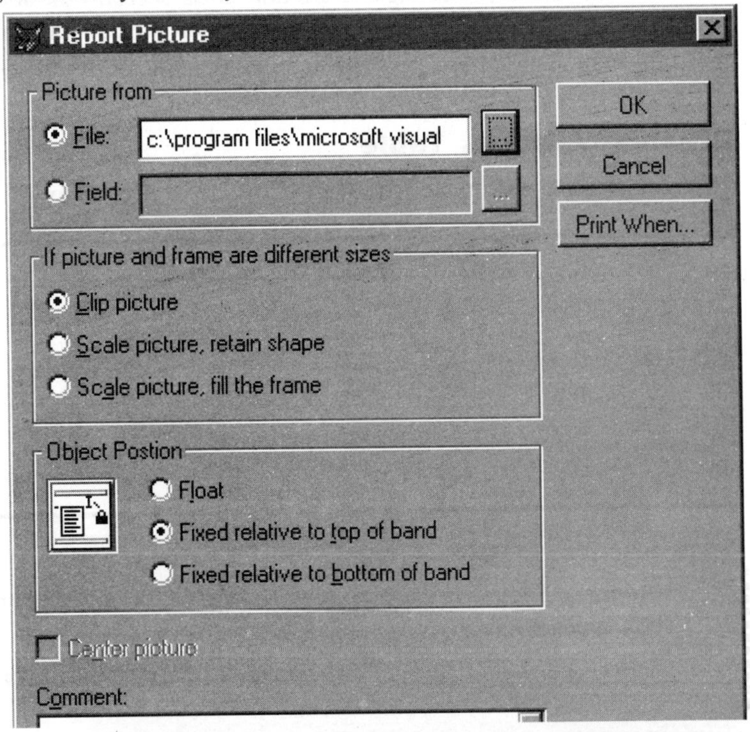

You can add graphics to a report from the general field of a Visual FoxPro table or from a file or from a file on disk.

You can add a picture to a report in the following manner:

1. Select the Pictures icon on the Report Controls toolbar.
2. Click at the staring point for the graphics and drag until the frame reaches the desired size for the picture. When you release the mouse, Report Picture dialog box appears.
3. Set the options to tell where to find the picture and how to size it relative to the band it is in.
4. Click Ok. The picture will appear in the report.

WORKING WITH SHAPES

You can easily add a shape or a line of text to a report. Just select it and drop it, as you would any of the controls. But you can also determine the behaviours of shapes and text on a report.

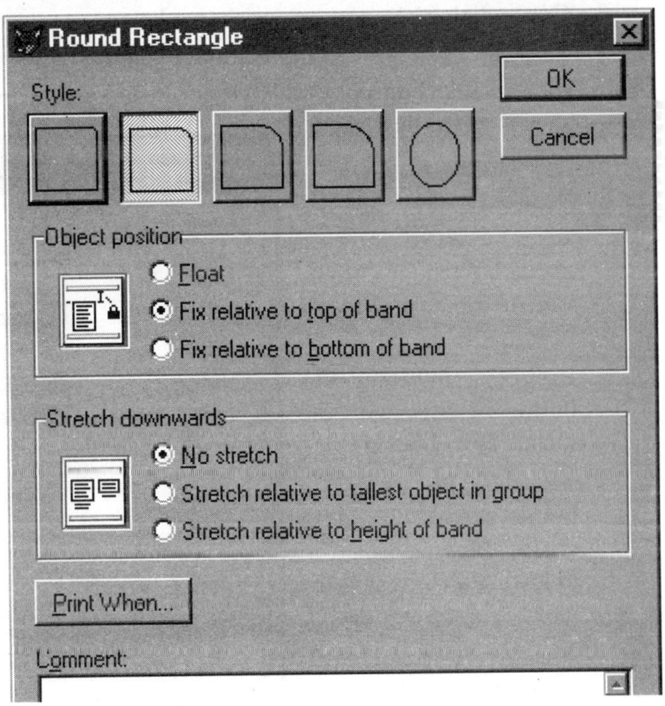

Double click on the object in a report, and the dialog box appears. In this case I have taken the rounded rectangles option. As you can see there are 5 different options to choose from.

Click at one of them and you have the same in the report.

MAILING LABELS

FoxPro is very useful for creating and printing labels, specially the address labels. Because of its capabilities of arranging the data in different orders you can sort the data in different fields and print the labels, town wise, pin wise, name wise, etc. What's more you can design the size of your labels according to your choice. Let us create and print some labels.

Creating Address Table

Let us create one table, table1.dbf with structure as given below:

Name	*Type*	*Width*
Code	N	4
Name	C	20
Address	C	20
City	C	8
Pin	N	6

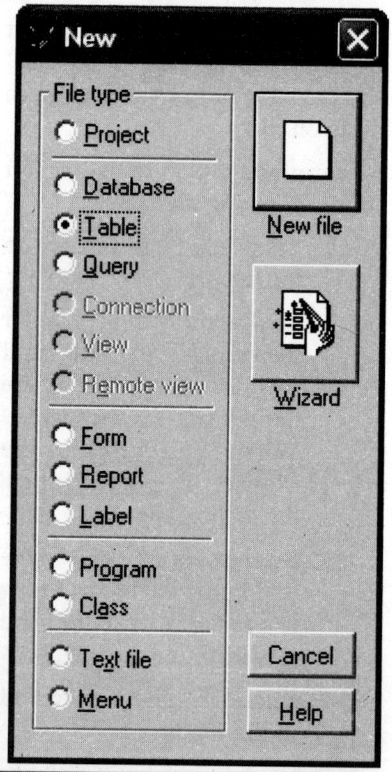

Let us now create the table.

1. From the File menu choose New .... Option. A new dialog box appears.
2. Select Table button and click on New File option at the top of the dialog box.
3. Create dialog box appears, as shown below.
4. Type the file name as table1 in the Enter table text box and click on Save button. A table Designer dialog box appears as shown on the next page.
5. Now fill the structure.
6. Click on OK button. Visual FoxPro shows a dialog box and ask if you want to input data records now.
7. Press Y to select Yes button or click with the mouse on yes button.

   Visual FoxPro displays a blank record for data entry. Now enter the following records into the table.

   After you have entered all the eight records, Visual

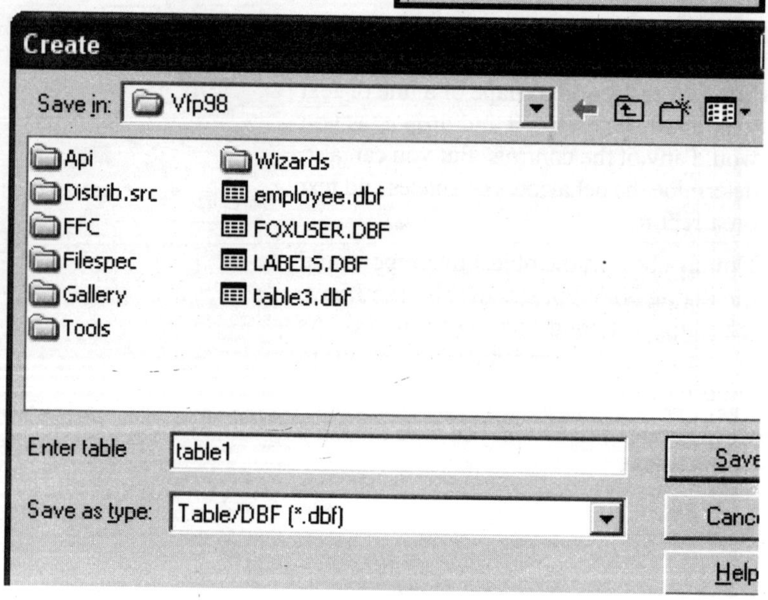

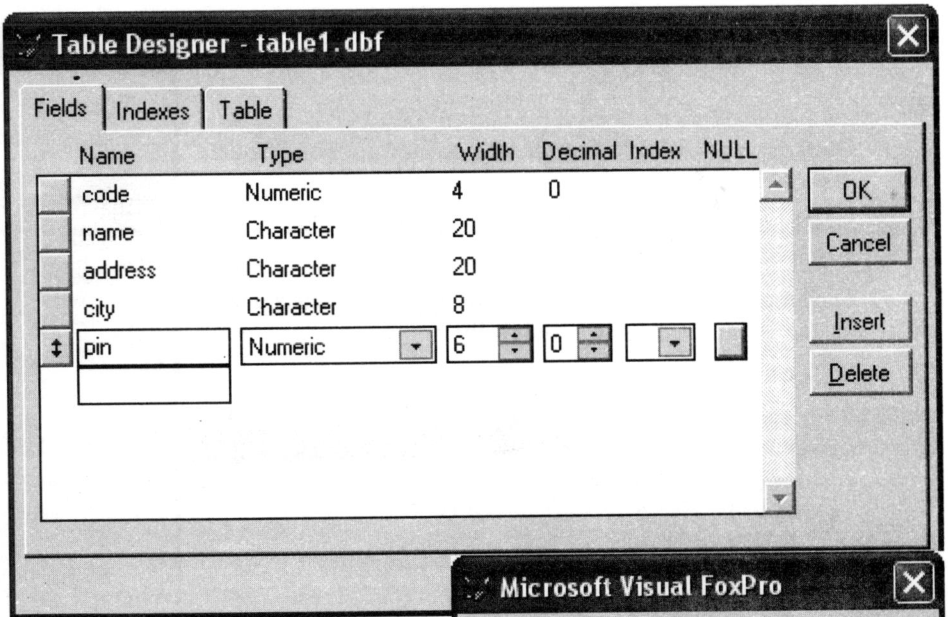

FoxPro displays the next empty record on the screen. Press Ctrl + W to save the data entered.

If you want you can view the data by choosing Browse from the View menu.

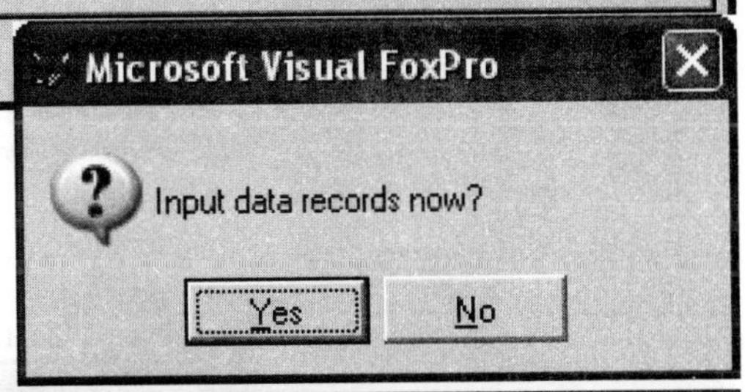

10. Press Esc key to close the Browse mode.

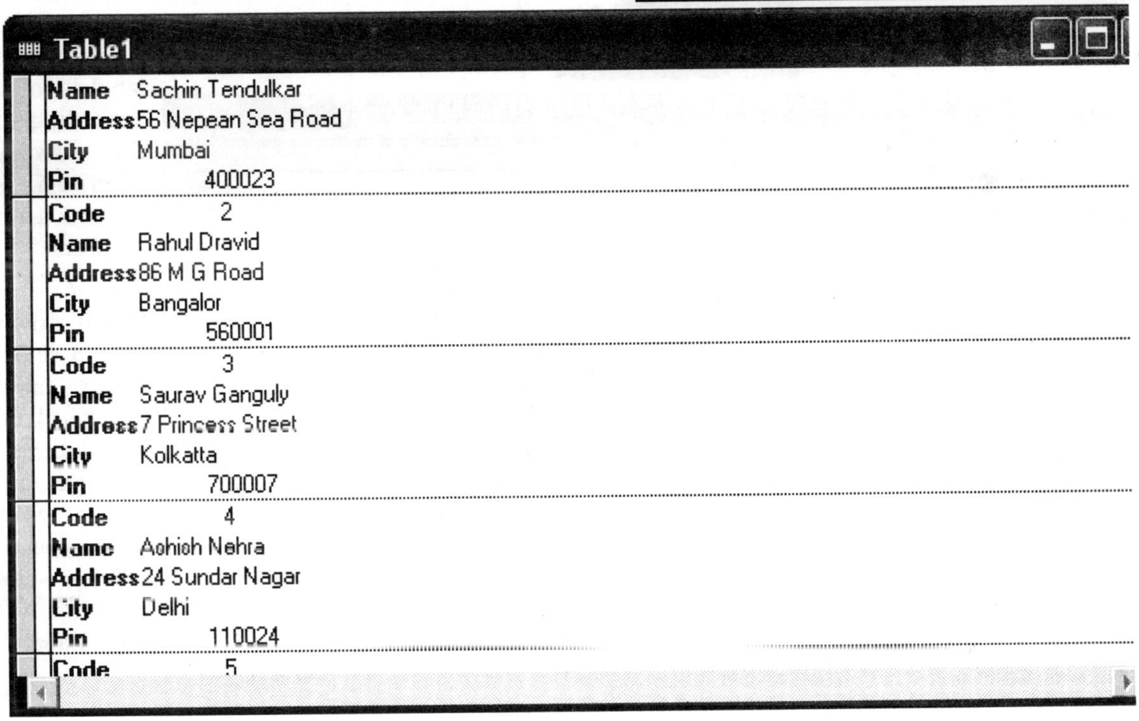

Label Wizard

Now, we come to the other part, i.e., creating labels using Label Wizard.

1. Open the New dialog box by clicking on New icon on Standard toolbar.
2. Select Label and click on Wizard to open the Label Wizard dialog box.
3. The Step 1 – Select Tables dialog box appears to select a table for the label. Let us select table1.dbf
4. Click on the Next button.

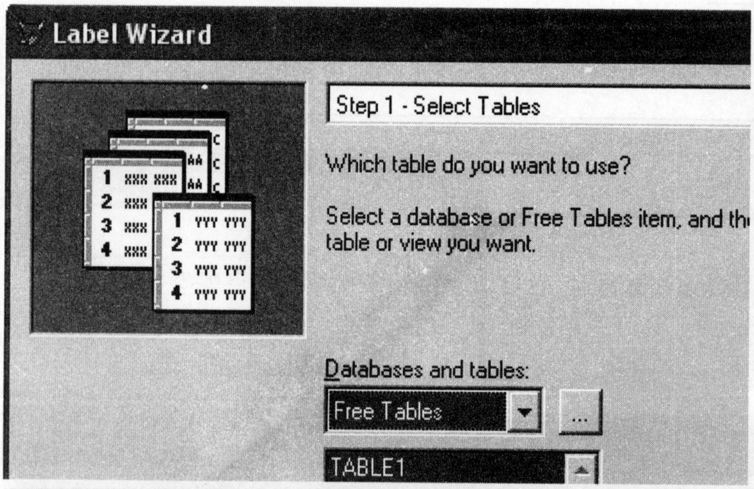

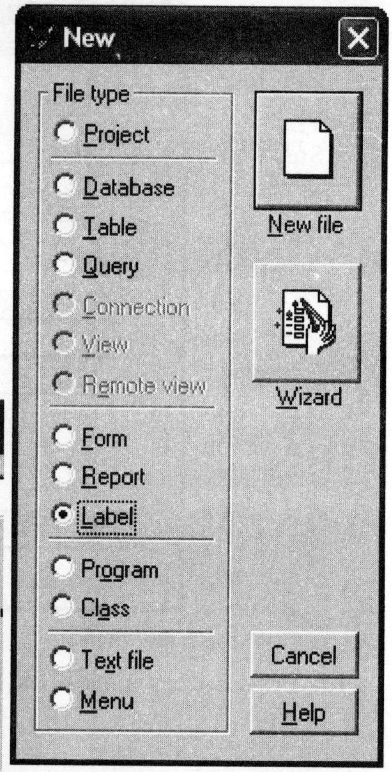

5. The Step 2 – Choose Label Type dialog box appears with listing of various label layouts according to the Avery company's product numbers.
6. Scroll down to and select Avery label number 4166 and columns 1. You can create your own type of label by clicking at New Label.

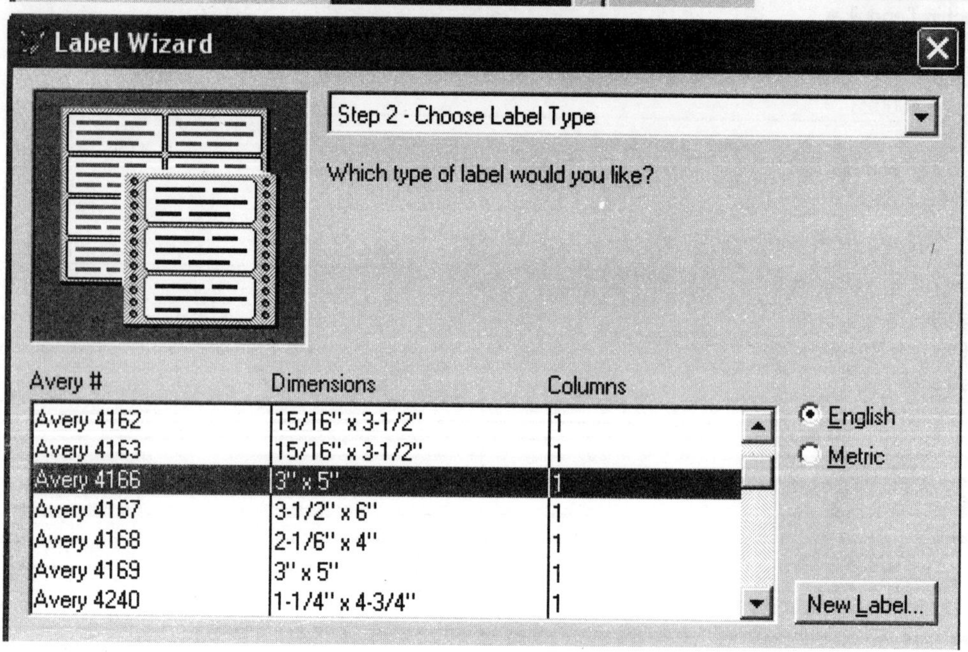

7. Click on Next > button.
8. The Label Step – 3 Define Layout window opens.
9. In the Step – 3 Define Layout dialog box, add the Fields in the order you want them to appear on the Label. You can use the punctuation, space and newline buttons to format the label. Use the Text box to add text.

   Here I have moved all the fields with comma (,) in between and a space.

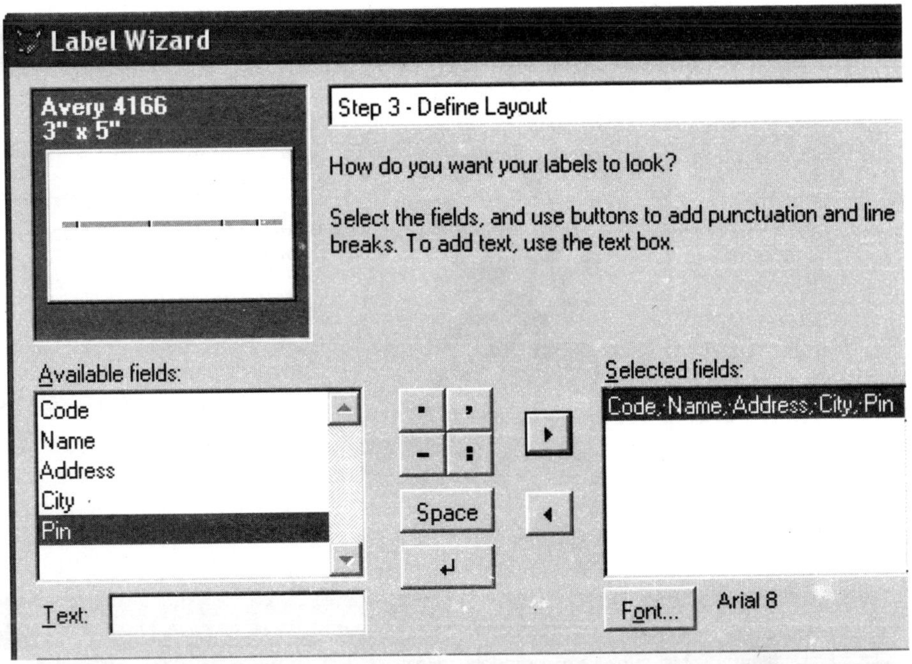

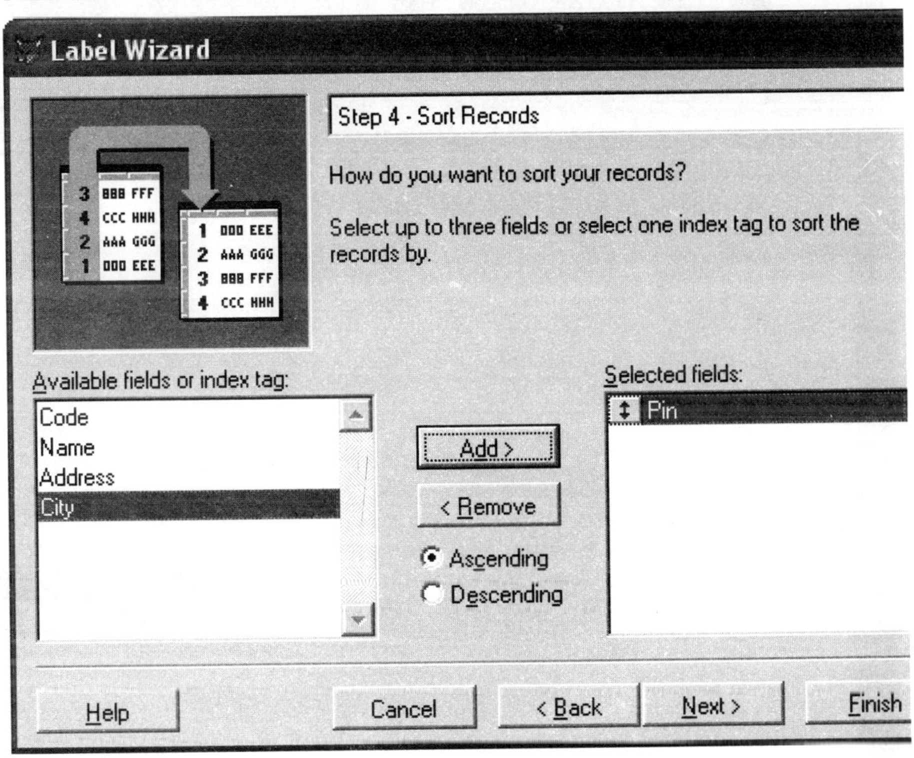

10. Click on Next button to move to Step 4 – Sort records dialog box.

Here you can select the fields or index tag in the order that you would like to sort the records. Now let us sort the records pin wise. Double click on pin field to move it to Selected Fields. Note that by default Ascending radio button is selected.

11. Click on Next button to move to Step 5 – Finish dialog box. You can choose Preview to verify your choices before finishing. Preview of the labels to be printed is shown below.

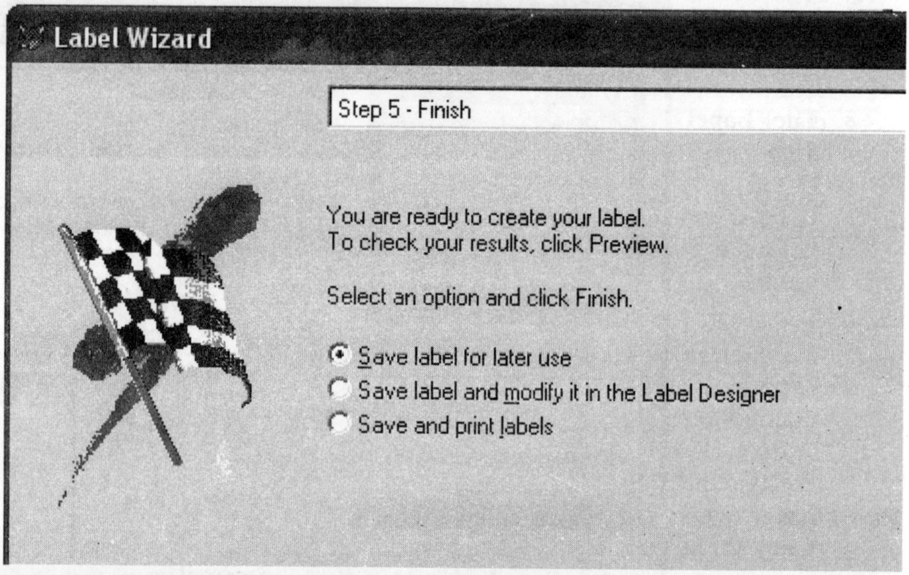

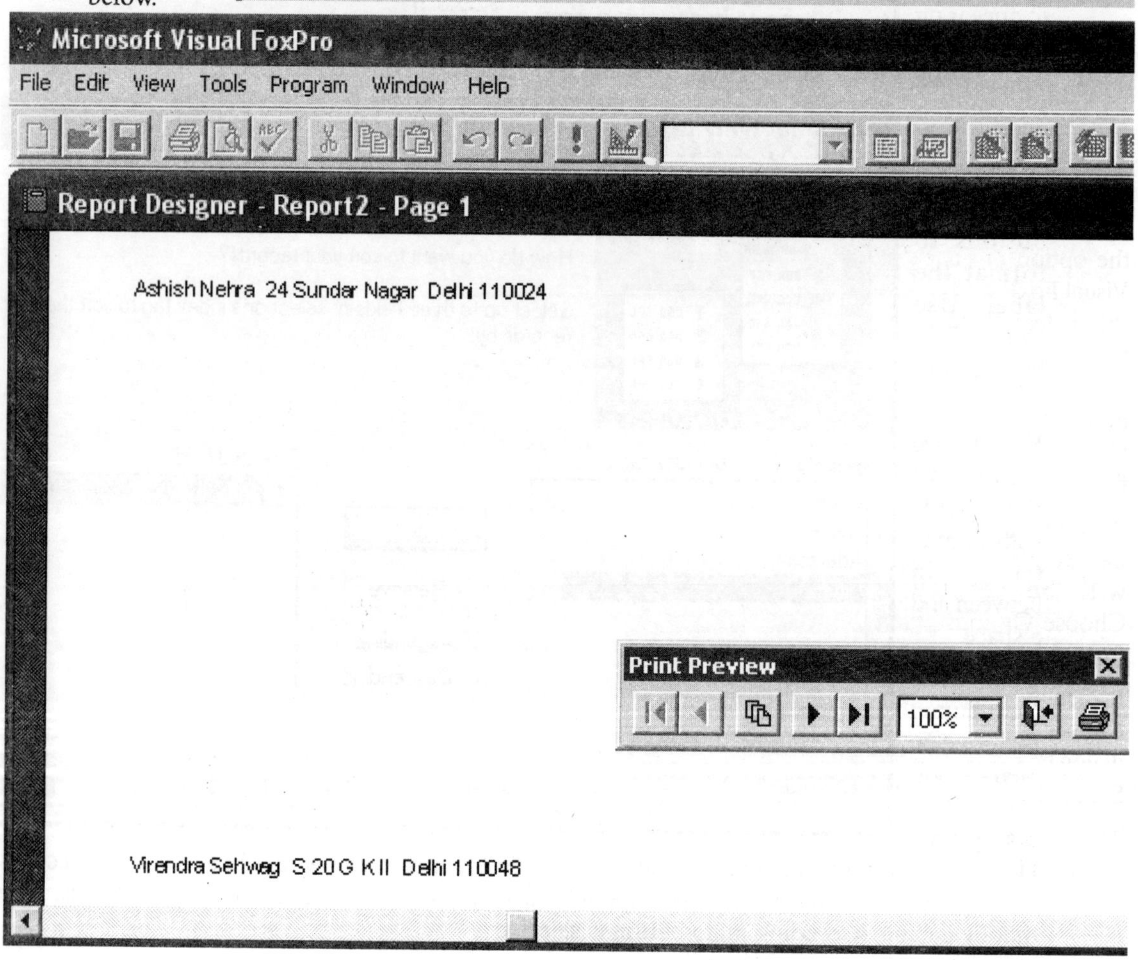

12. Press Esc key to close the Preview window and return to Finish dialog box.
13. Click on Finish button. The Save As dialog box appears. Type the name as table1 in the Save Label and click on Save button.
14. Label file is saved as table1.lbl.

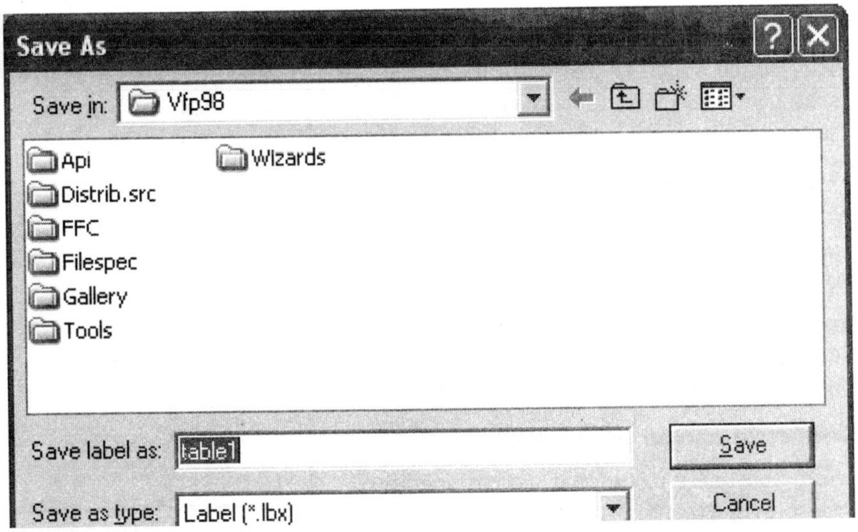

Printing Mailing Label

Now that we have created the labels, naturally we would like to print them too.

1. Open the required label file, in this case table1.lbl.
2. Insert the appropriate mailing labels stationery in the printer's paper tray.
3. Click on the Print button from the Standard toolbar.

Printing Selective Records

If you want you can select and print a selective number of records in the form of labels. For this we have the option of Scope in Visual FoxPro. To get to this select Print from the File menu. It displays a print dialog box, as shown here. Choose Options button from here.

A new dialog box named Print Options will be displayed. Choose Options again from this dialog box.

It displays Report and Label Print Option dialog box. Click on the Scope drop down list.

The Scope dialog box contains four options.

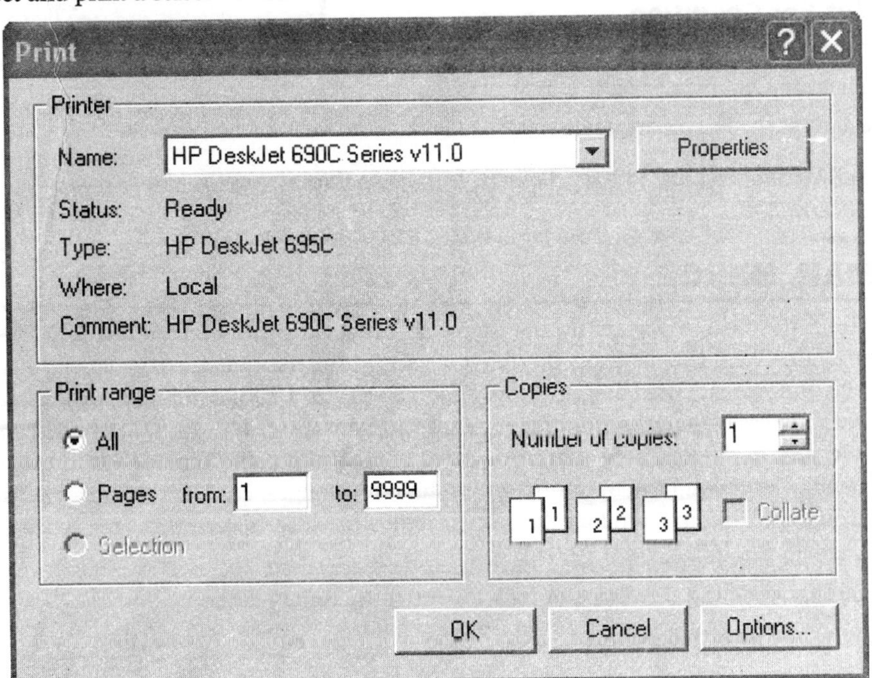

All which specifies all records.

Next, which specifies any number of records, starting with the current record (as selected in the mailing-label report's underlying table or query).

Record, which specifies a single record by its record number.

Rest, which specifies every record from the current record to the end of the table or query.

Now that we know what is there in the dialog box, let us see how we can achive the desired result by choosing the various options.

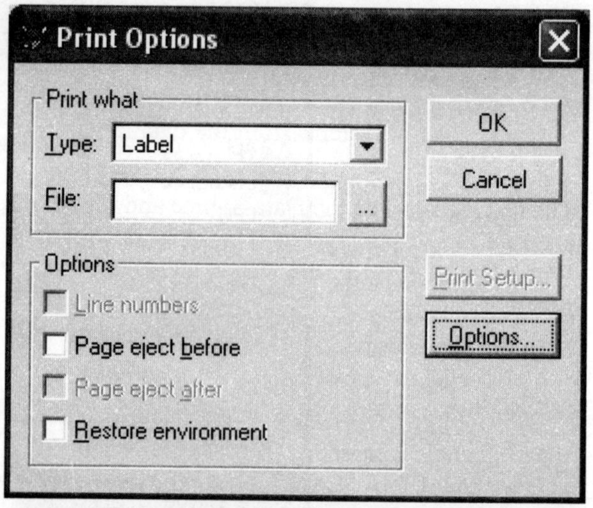

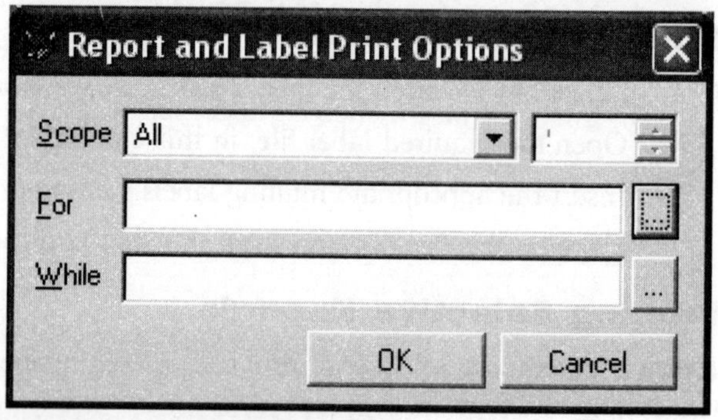

Generate range of labels

Select table query record that starts desired range; choose File, Print in type drop-down list. Select Labels. Click on button to the right of File box and double-click on desired label-layout file name; click on Options; click on Scope; click on Next or Rest. If you clicked on Next, type desired number of records. Click on OK.

Generate single label

In Scope dialog box, click on Record; type desired record number. Click on OK.

Set For Condition

In Print Options dialog box, click on For; use Expression Builder to build For condition expression. Click on OK.

Set While Condition

In Print Options dialog box, click on While; use Expression Builder to build While condition expression. Click on OK.

MAIL MERGE

This is the most important feature of a word processing program. But, what is it doing here in a database program. Well, the data source which is used in the mail merge is generated here, that is why it is used here. But, what is mail merge. Simply you can merge a mail letter with various name and addressess and create copies of letters with different name and addresses but the content of the letter remains the same. It is very useful specially when you have to mail the same type of letter to various people, like your clients whom you have to inform about the rate changes, creditors whom you have to send the payment reminders, Principal sending the similar letters to all staff members, etc. There can be many usuage.

In the example given below, I have used the same letter of Best Wishes to most of our cricket team members wishing them best of luck for the forthcoming series against the New Zealand.

Let us see how this is done.

Mail Merge uses two files:

1. a data file that contains a listing of data items (or fields) arranged in some specific order.
2. a master file that contains the standard text as well as the data variables which are replaced with specific data items from the data file during the merge operation. This file may be available in a Word processor say MS-Word.

The first file is called the Data Source and the second one is called the Main Document. This data source is created in Visual FoxPro. The Main document can be created in any word processing program, MS Word, WordPerfect or any other. This letter can be created in advance before starting the actual Mail Merge procedure from Visual FoxPro. If the letter is short, then you can do it at the same time too.

Mail merge is done in the following steps:

1. Create a data source
2. Create the main document
3. Insert data fields into the main document
4. Merge one record to see that everything is ok.
5. Merge the data source document and the main document.
6. Finally print the merged documents.

Mail Merge Process

To do this follow the following steps very carefully. The following steps are performed using the Wizard.

1. Click the Tools menu and choose Wizard and select Mail Merge.
2. The first Step dialog box appears, as shown here. Click on button to select table. Note that it displays your table and the fields in the Available fields.
3. Select first field and click on > to move to the selected fields. Similarly select other fields one by one. If you want to select all of them then click >> in the beginning itself.
4. Click on Next button to go to the next step.

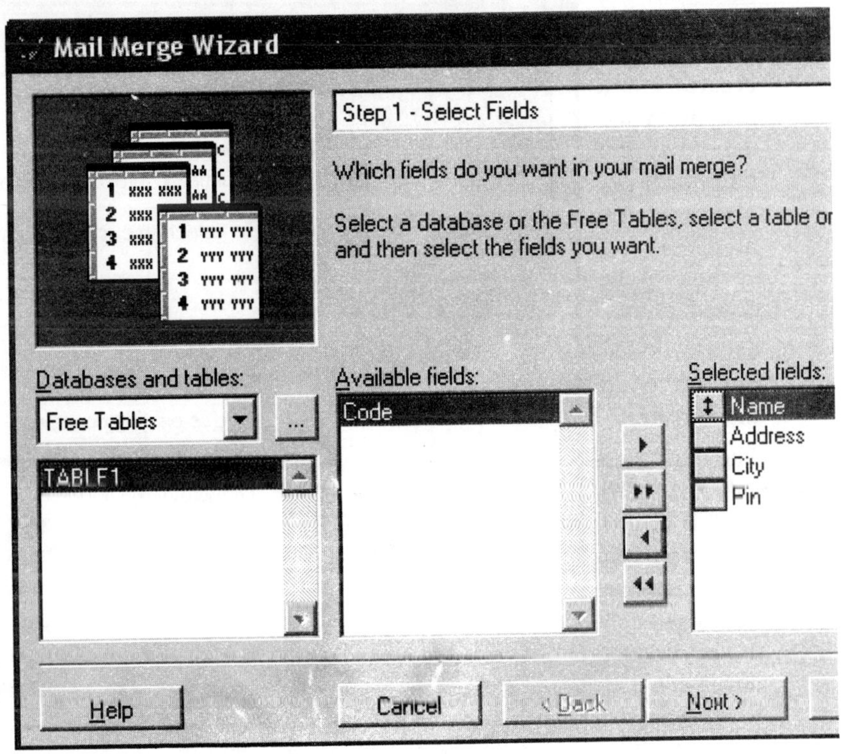

5. The second Step asks you to Choose Word Processor. Since here we have to create a document for merging, so your computer must have a word processor installed in your computer. Mostly Microsoft Word is used. If you are using any other word processing software, then it must have the capacity to create a comma-delimited text file, which is a plain text file having commas at the desired places.

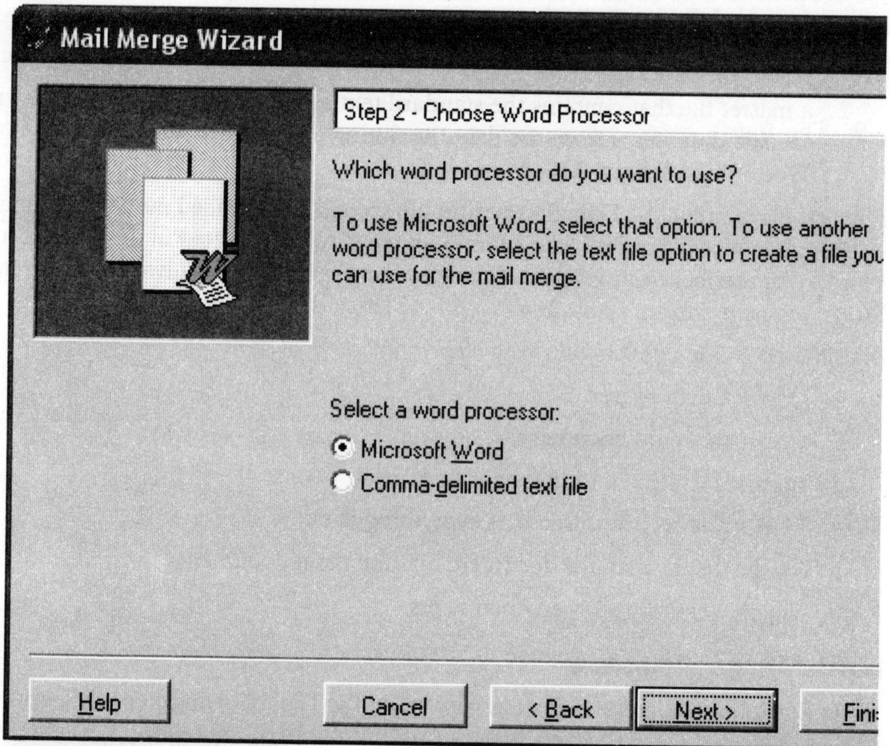

6. Click on Next button to go the next step.
7. The third Step asks you to Select Document Type, Create a new document or Use existing document. Let us choose to Create a new word processing document radio button.

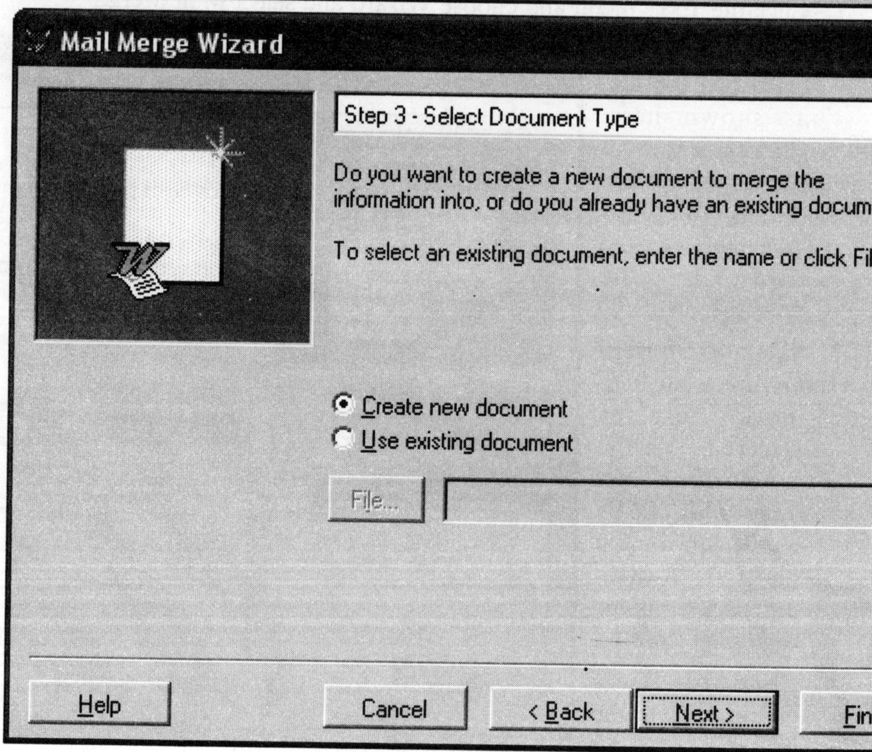

8. Click on Next button to go the next step.
9. The fourth Step aks you to Choose Document Style, which allows you to select one of the Microsoft Word image document types. Here, select a document type: as a Form letter.
10. Click on Next button to go the next step.
11. The fifth and last Step asks you to Finish.

    If you have chosen to create a Microsoft Word document, the wizard will open the document in Microsoft Word.

    If you have chosen to create a text file, the Wizard will prompt you to save. Since we have chosen Microsoft document, clicking on Finish button open a MS-Word blank doucemnt.

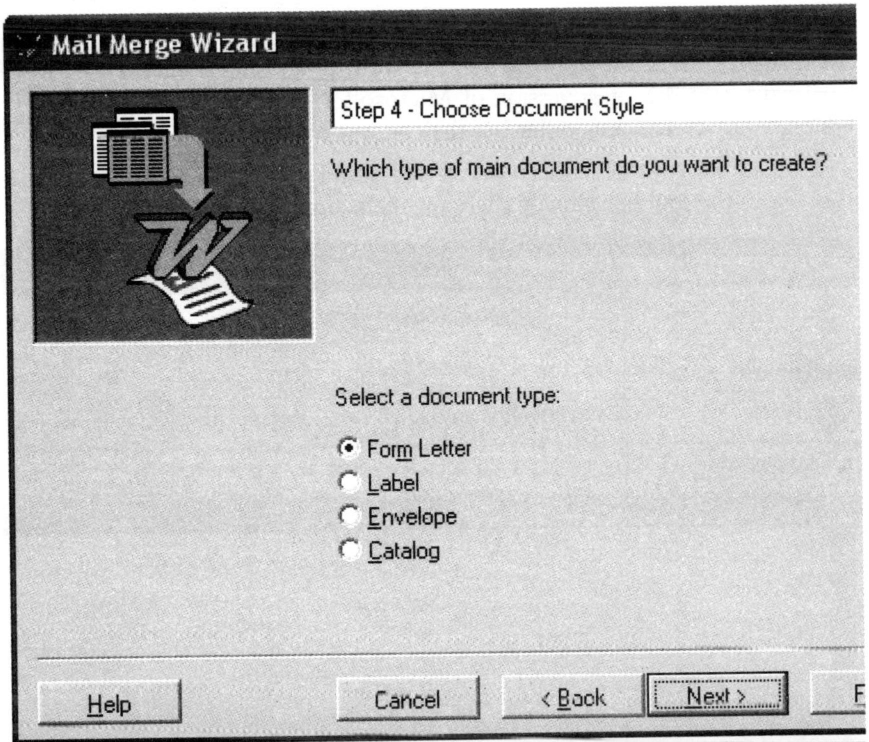

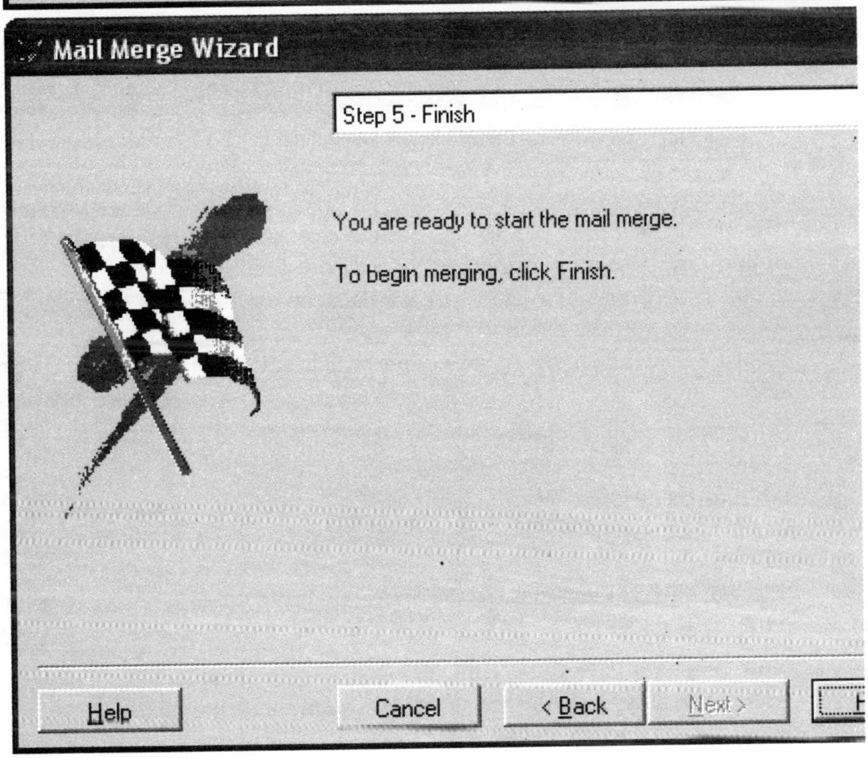

Now the control shifts to the Word Processor, i.e., Microsoft Word.

The following steps are performed in the word processing program, i.e., Microsoft Word. Please note that I have used the latest version of Microsoft Word which is Word 2002. If you are using the other version, your screens may differ but the concept remains the same.

1. Since the control has been transferred from FoxPro, the Word shows the MailMerge Wizard option with the tool bar already there for the actions, as seen below.

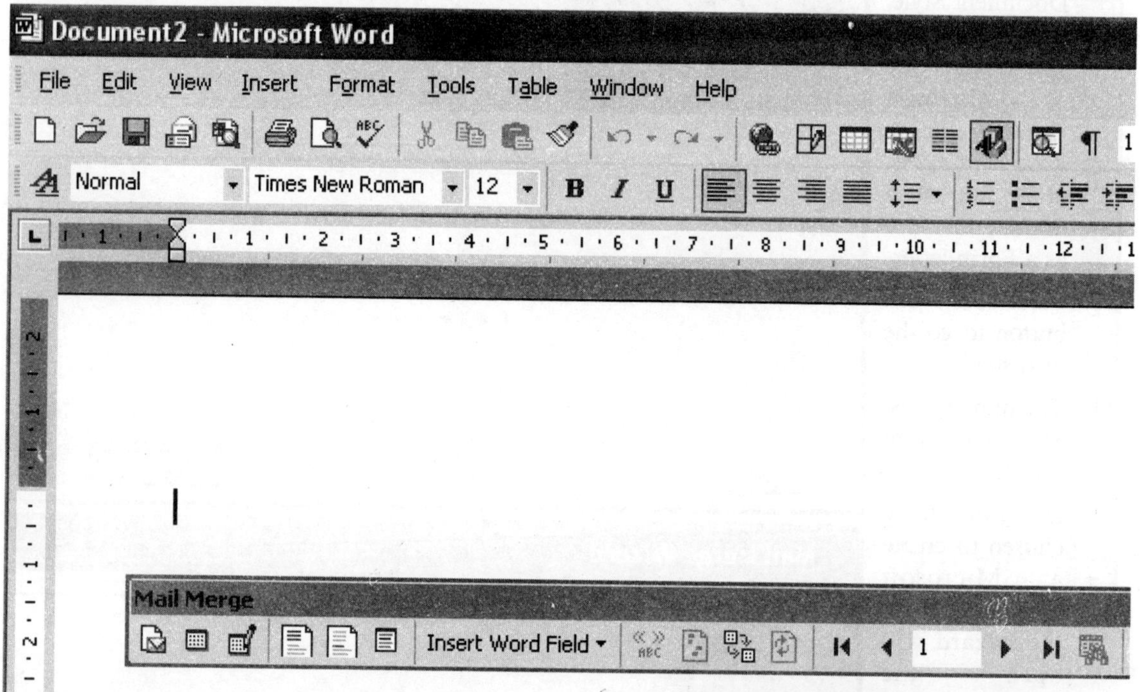

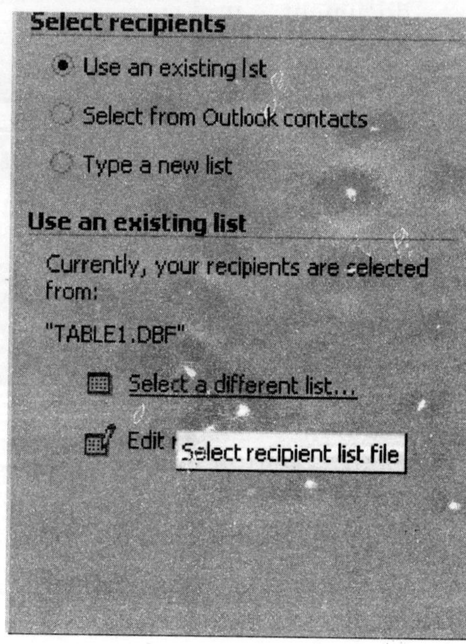

2. The next step it asks you to select the recipients. The options are: Use an existing list, Select from Outlook contracts or Type a new list. If you are using an existing list, it gives you the list of the table already in use, in this case TABLE1.DBF or any other which you may select.

3. Since you have the table to be used is already selected, click at Next to go to the option of Write your letter.

4. Now here you have the complete Word document at your disposal, type out the text which you want to merge using the data source called Table1.dbf.

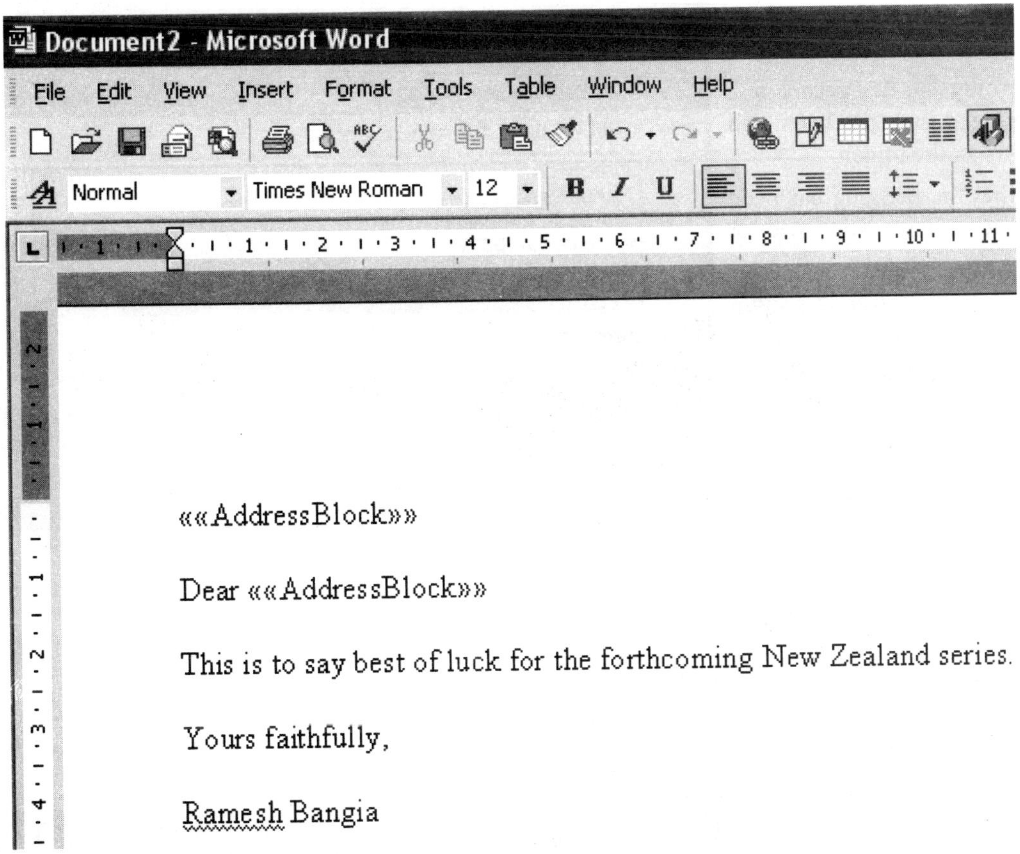

5. See above the text which I have typed. Now wait, where did I get the Address Block from. See you must be very sure in the beginning itself where you want what. So in the beginning of the letter, I want to put the name and address of the player from the source. So what do I do, I click at the option called Addresss block. It gives rise to another dialog box called Insert Address Block, which is shown on the next page.

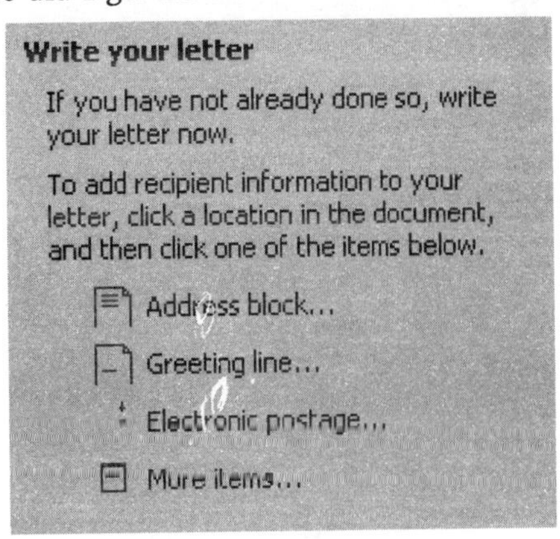

6. In the Insert Address Block select the option of Insert Company Name and Insert Postal Address and Ok it.
7. You will see the << <<Address Block>> >> in your document which means that here the actual address will be merged.
8. Next I have typed Dear and then again I have used Address Block.
9. This will again give rise to the dialog box. But this time I will select only the Company Naame and not its postal address. Since I want to address the person and not the address.
10. The next text is simple to understand.

11. Click on Next to get the option of previewing your lettter.
12. Here only the first record will be merged with the letter and shown on the screen.
13. See that the merging has been done according to your needs or not.
14. The merged letter is shown below.
15. The next step is to merge the whole file.
16. Before merging it will ask you whether you want to merge All or Current or you can choose a range.

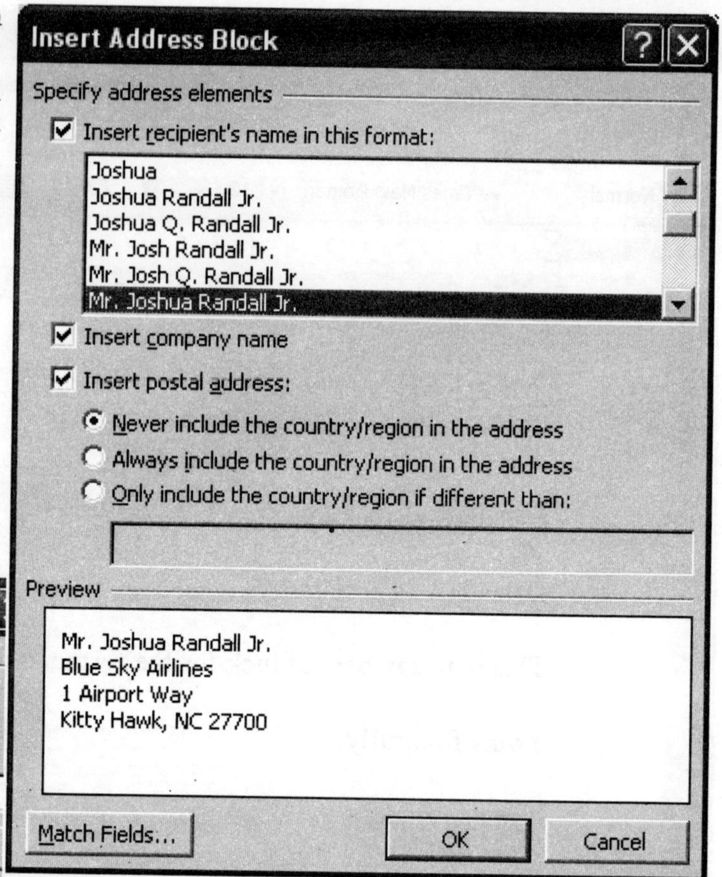

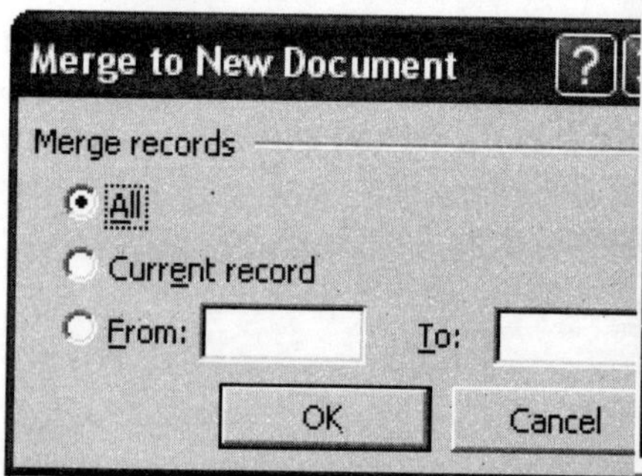

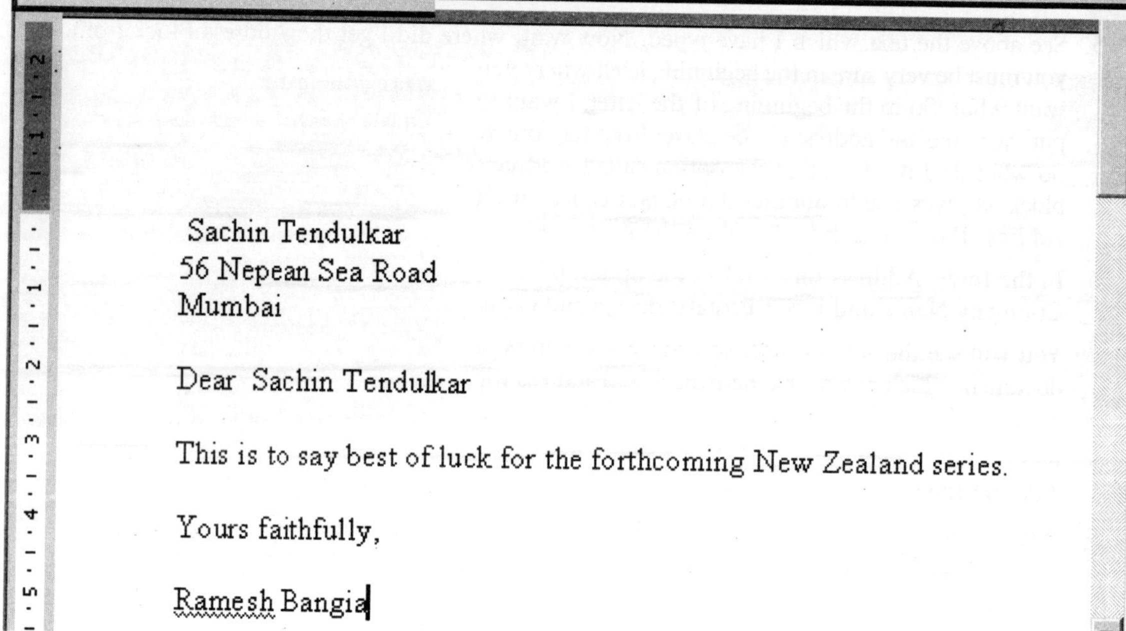

17. Well choose All and see that the whole range of letters created using the name and addresses from the file called table1.dbf.
18. If you want you can save the merged letter file.

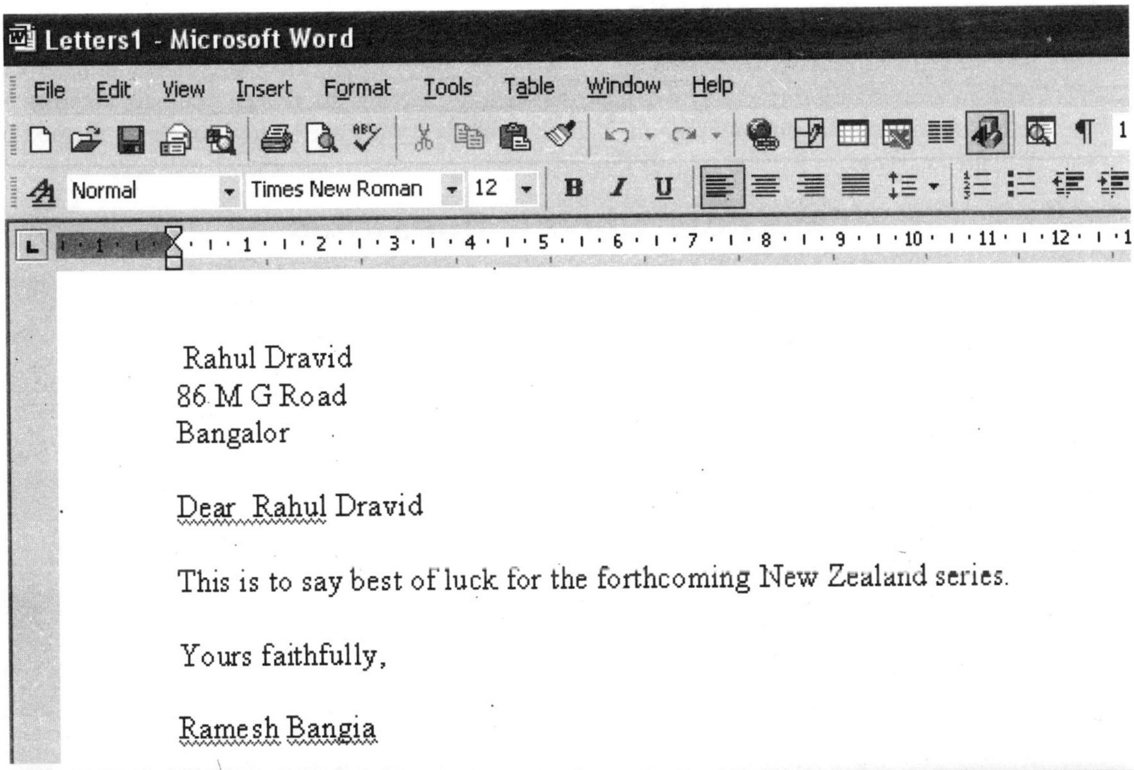

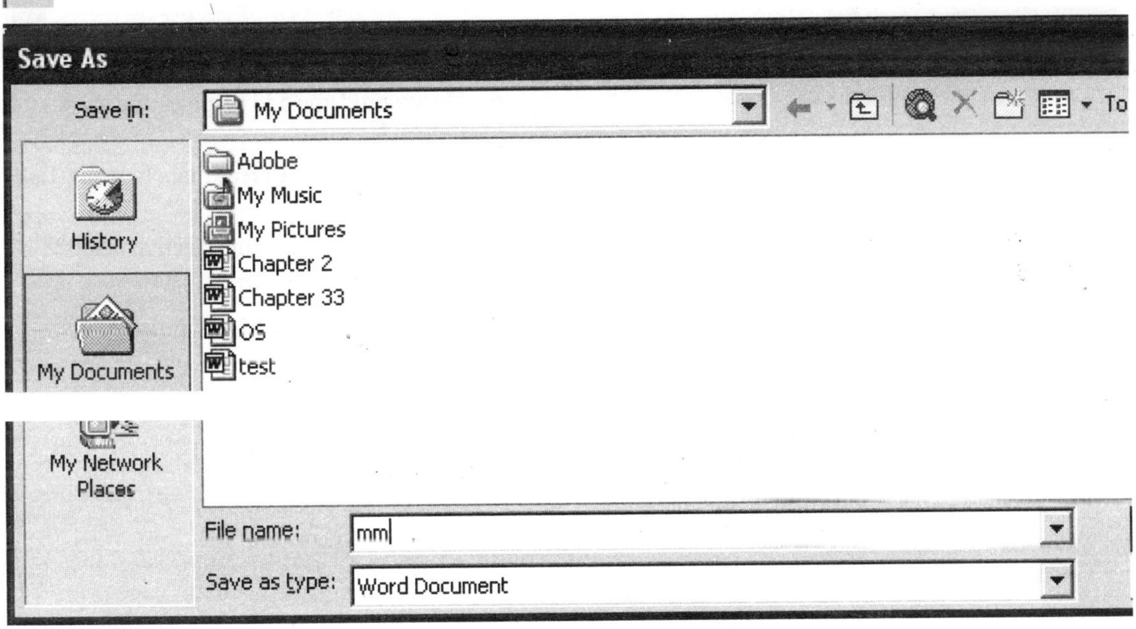

Printing Merged Letters

If you want to print the letters, make sure that the printer is switched on and is in ready mode. Then click at the Print command in the File menu or click at the Print button on the Standard toolbar.

Closing Merged Document File

1. Click the File menu and choose Close.
2. When a message appears asking whether you want to save this document, you have a choice to save it or click the No button to ignore it. In that case you will have to go through the method of mail merge again.

Multiple Choice Questions

1. In Visual FoxPro you can create a report easily using :
   (a) Quick Report (b) Report Wizard
   (c) Both
2. A summary report can be created using :
   (a) Group/Total Report Wizard
   (b) Summary Report Wizard
   (c) Sumamry Wizard
3. You can add graphics to the report :
   (a) Yes (b) No
4. MailMerge takes support of a :
   (a) Word Processing Program
   (b) Spreadsheet Program
   (c) Desktop Publishing Program
5. You can add shapes to the report :
   (a) Yes (b) No
6. You can create mailing labels in Visual FoxPro using :
   (a) Label Wizard (b) Mail Wizard
   (c) Label Maker
7. Report file in Visual FoxPro is saved with extension :
   (a) .scf (b) .scx
   (c) .frx

Descriptive Type Questions

1. What is a Report?
2. How would you create a report using Report Designer?
3. How would you create a report using Quick Report method?
4. How would you save and print a report?
5. What is Group/Total Report Wizard and how it is used?
6. How would you add graphics and shapes into reports?
7. How would you create labels using Label Wizard?
8. How would you print selective labels?
9. What is Mail Merge?
10. Describe the Mail Merge process.

28 Working with Command Window

INTRODUCTION

I remember that when I was a child, the most popular proverb was that you can do the same thing in two ways depending upon the option which you like. Since your interest would be more in the method which you feel convenient with, your result in this case would be of better quality.

So far I have talked about the way of using Visual FoxPro which would be used by someone who is using the software for the first time and specially those who have started using the computer after the evolution of Windows operating systems. But, what about those, who have graduated from Disk Operating System and have used the earlier version of FoxPro and are quite happy to write commands instead of clicking them with mouse. For them we have the concept of Command Window. This window is for those who want to write the command. It is very similar to the command prompt which was there in the DOS version of the software. Just type the command press Enter and you have the result on the screen.

In this chapter we will see how the commands can be given from the Command Window. Let us start from the very basic, i.e., creating a table and then we will use various commands on this table.

CREATING A NEW TABLE

For this the simple command is CREATE. You can use this giving the name of the file you want to create. So the command would become:

```
CREATE STUDENT
```

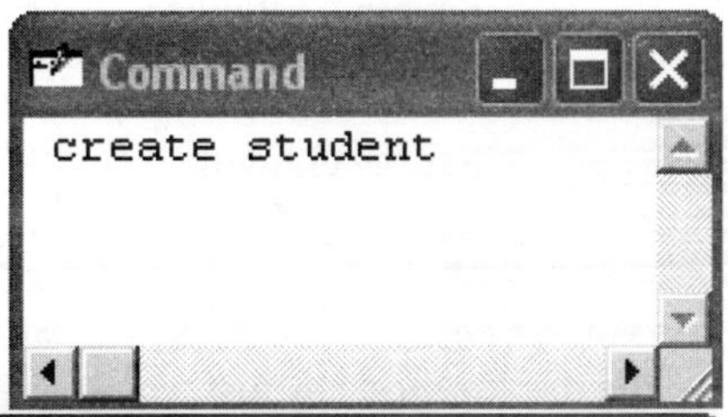

I have type in caps, but you can do otherwise too. This would give rise to a blank table creation dialog box, as shown here. Now that this is the blank structure of the table. You will have to fill it up with the type of data which you are going to have in this.

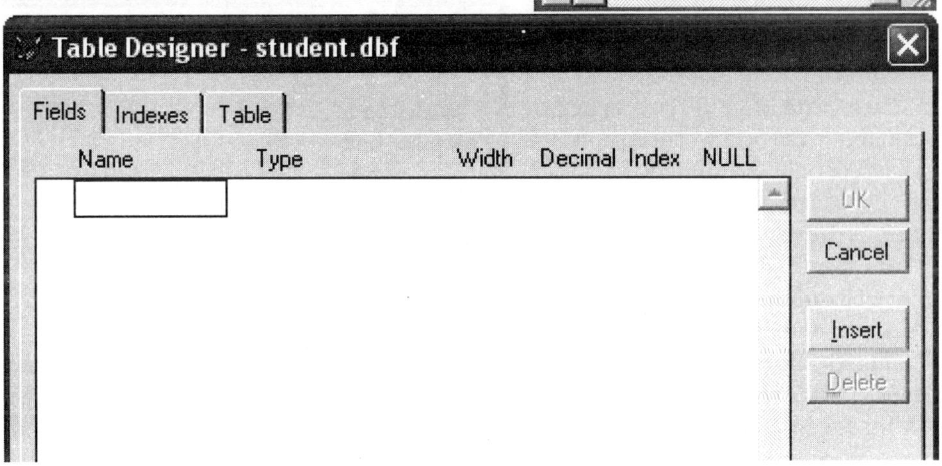

I am taking here the data of a student, with his student code named as std_code of 4 numeric, name of 20 characters, city as 10 characters, then the various marks of 3 numeric values each of English,

Hindi, Maths and Science, termed as marks_eng, marks_hnd, marks_mth and marks_sc, respectively. Once you fill up the structure, your Table Designer dialog box would look like the one shown here.

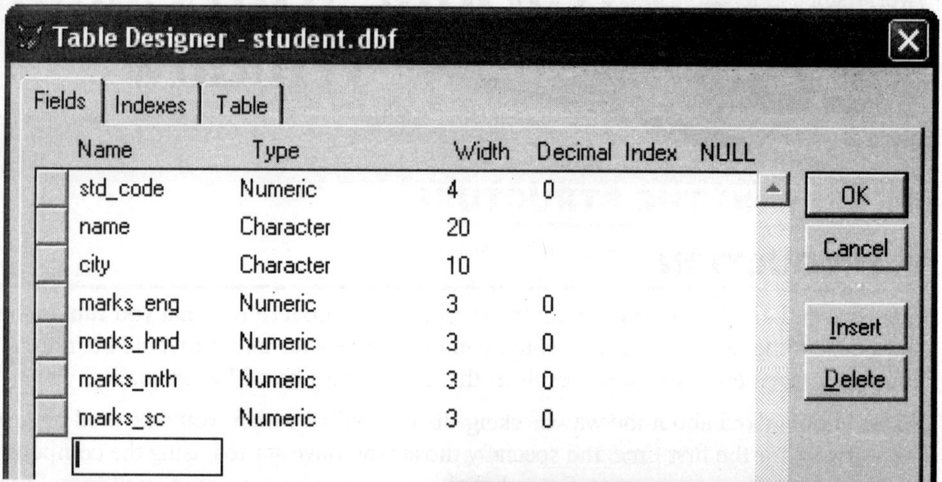

Now that you have the structure ready, what next, just fill up the data. So when you press Ok, the system asks you whether you want to enter the data now or would you do it later.

Say Yes to enter the data and fill up the following data. This is just a dummy data so you enter it and follow it up with Ctrl + W to save the data.

std_code	*name*	*city*	*marks_eng*	*marks_hnd*	*marks_mth*	*marks_sc*
1	Sachin Tendulkar	Mumbai	55	45	60	70
2	Rahul Dravid	Bangalore	60	44	65	65
3	Saurav Ganguly	Kokatta	55	60	50	45
4	Ashish Nehra	Delhi	70	66	55	44

As you see here I have entered the data in the display mode by just typing one entry after the another in the space provided for.

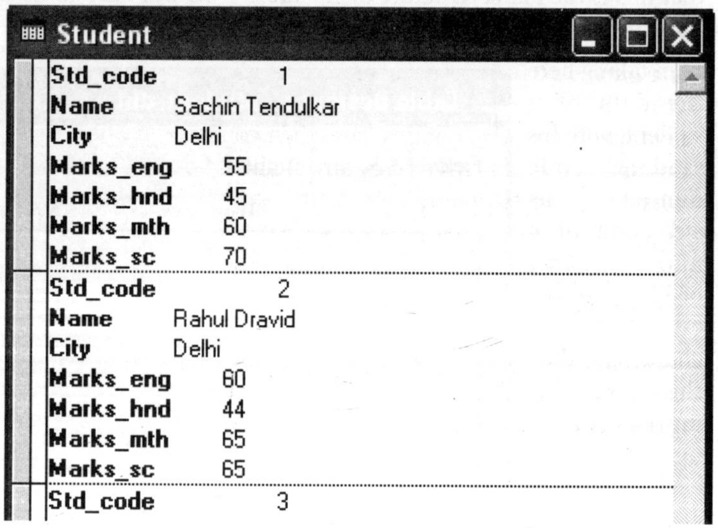

Please note that if you type an alphabet in the field which is supposed to accept only the numeric data then it will not be accepted. However, if you write a numeric data in a character filed it will be accepted since character field is actually there to accept alphanumeric. So keep this in mind while typing. As you can see here, I have wrongly typed City as Delhi for first two records. Do not worry since I am going to change them later, when I will come for correcting data. Once you have entered the data and saved with Ctrl + W, type browse in the command window and you will have the total data there on the screen in the form you would probably wanted to see.

Supposing after looking at the displayed data, you think that you should have made the name field more than 20, let us say 25. So what will you do. For this we have the command called Modify Structure.

MODIFYING THE STRUCTURE

The command for this is very simple, MODIFY STRUCTURE. Give this in the command window and you have the structure of the file in front of you. Now using the arrow keys or mouse change the field you want to change. Here I have changed the std_code from 4 to 5.

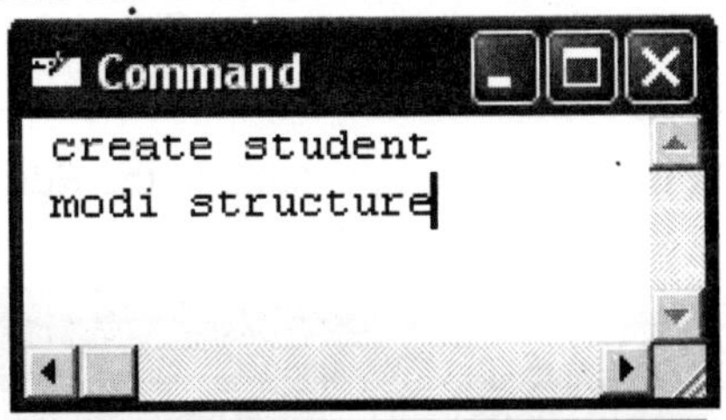

The immediate response from the system would be in the form of a dialog box, which asks you whether you want this change to be permanent. Say Yes, and the structure would be changed.

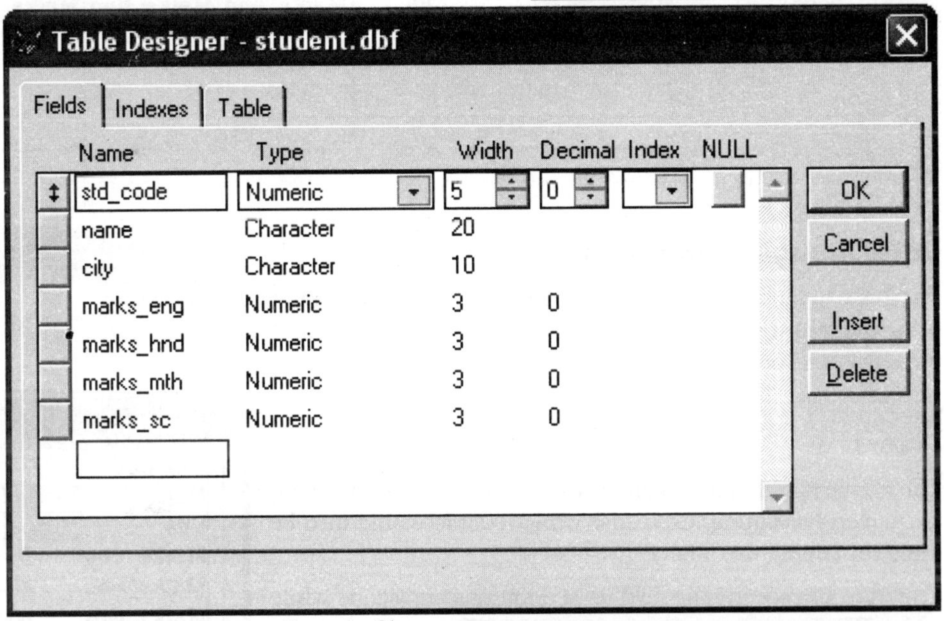

It is not that you can make changes only in the fields, you can even add a new field or delete a field.

Adding a new field would be easy since, you have to just click at Insert and a new field row would be available for you.

Deleting a field is a bit tricky. If you delete a field which already contains data, then you have it. Since this data cannot be retrieved by any method. So make sure what you have to do and then do it.

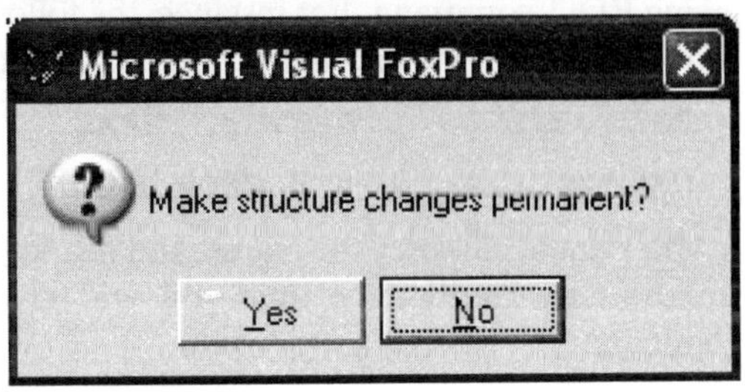

Now we come to editing of the data.

EDITING DATA

Editing of the data can be done using one the following commands:

APPEND	Append to add records in the .
EDIT	Edit or Change to display the table in Edit mode.

BROWSE Browse to display the table in Browse mode.

REPLACE Replace to change the contents in more than one record.

Let us study them one by one.

Append Command

Using this command you can enter more data then what it has. This command will add data at the end of the existing data in the form of new records. For this, you can use Command window. Assuming that the table is open, type the following commands in the Command window:

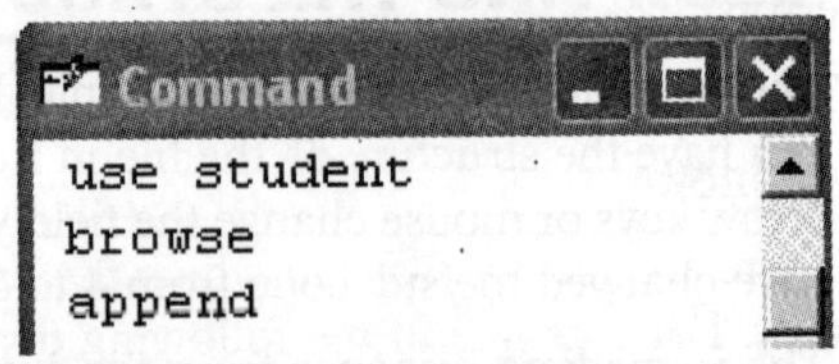

APPEND

You will be given the table in the Edit mode and would be ready to accept more data.

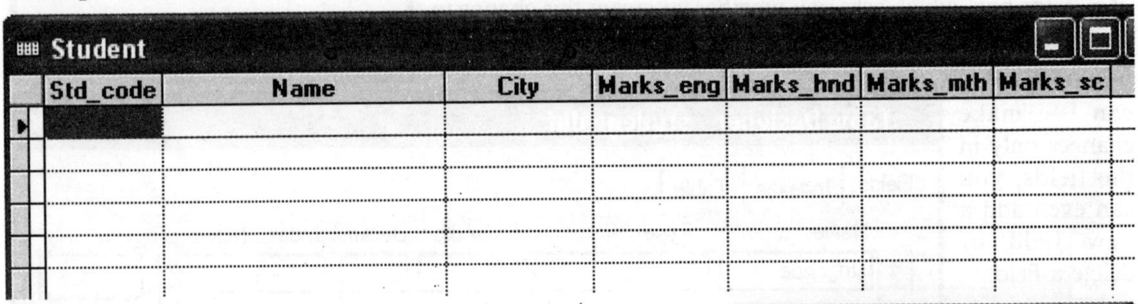

Edit/Change Command

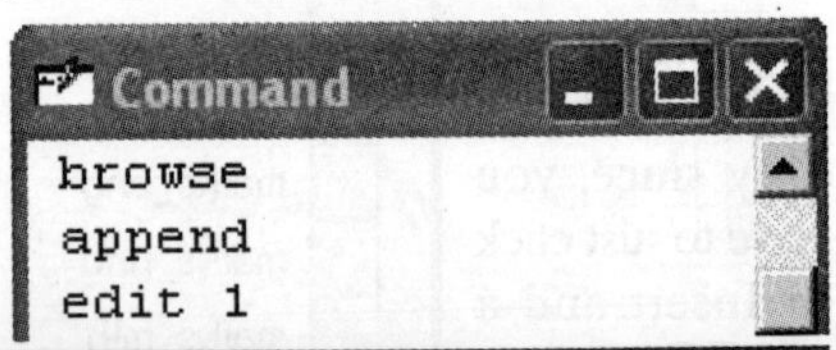

For this you must know which record to edit, since you would be using the record number for editing. If you simple type Edit, then the current record would be shown on the screen.

For example:

```
EDIT 1
```

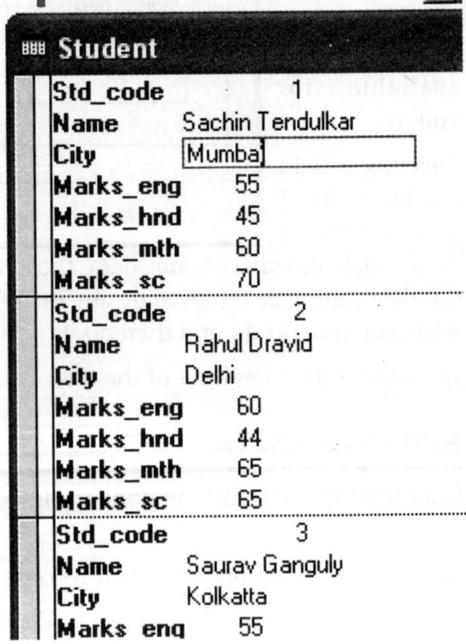

The above command will show you the record number 1 on the screen for editing. Of course other records would also be there for editing them later.

You may also specify the field list, conditions and scope while giving EDIT command. For instance, the following commands show only Std_code and name field for editing:

```
EDIT FIELDS STD-CODE, NAME
CHANGE FIELDS STD_CODE,NAME
```

If you want to edit only the Name, and Marks_hnd of the table for the City Delhi only, then you will give the following command:

```
EDIT FIELDS NAME, MARKS_HND FOR CITY =
"DELHI"
```

Browse Command

Browse is a powerful command in Visual FoxPro. It enables you to scroll through table horizontally as well as vertically. In addition, the Browse command shows records in a tabular format, displaying one record in one row. At the same time, fieldnames are placed at the top of the columns a headers. Browse command displays as many fields and records as will fit on one screen at a time. You can position the cursor at the data item you want to make changes to. You can also use Browse command for locating errors, like spelling mistakes in the table.

The command is very simple, just type BROWSE with table already opened:

```
BROWSE
```

There are various ways in which the browse command can be used. One of them is to browse few fields only. For example in the following display, I have browsed only the name and marks. See below:

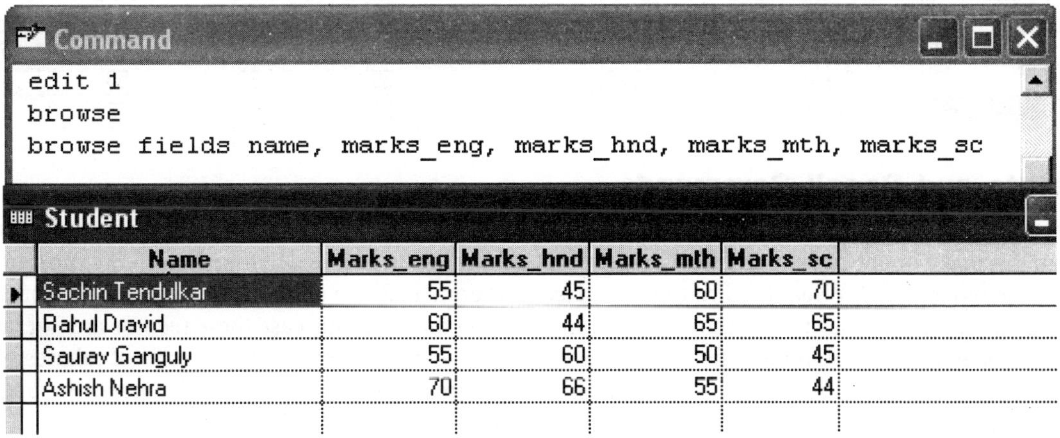

Name	Marks_eng	Marks_hnd	Marks_mth	Marks_sc
Sachin Tendulkar	55	45	60	70
Rahul Dravid	60	44	65	65
Saurav Ganguly	55	60	50	45
Ashish Nehra	70	66	55	44

You can see only the Name and the various marks. You may use the option NOEDIT or NOMODIFY with Browse command that disables any changes in the table. Thereafter, you cannot change data in any of the records. This option will also not allow you to add or delete any record accidently.

Enter the following command in the Command window:

```
BROWSE FIELDS NAME, CITY NOEDIT
```

You will now see the two fields in Browse window, but you will not be able to edit or change any of the fields. If you want to make changes, give the following command again:

```
BROWSE FIELDS NAME, CITY EDIT
```

Now you can edit the fields

Replace Command

Replace is a very powerful command and can replace any field data with another depending upon the command given. But, make sure that the command is given is right, since once replaced data cannot be called back.

The syntax of the Replace command is:

```
REPLACE[SCOPE] FIELDNAME WITH FIELD-REPLACEMENT FOR CONDITION
```

The scope parameter is optional and is used to determine the number of records that replace command will look at. The fieldname is that field for which the change will be made. Field-replacement is the expression with which the field will be replaced.

In the following example, I have changed all City values to Delhi. See the result.

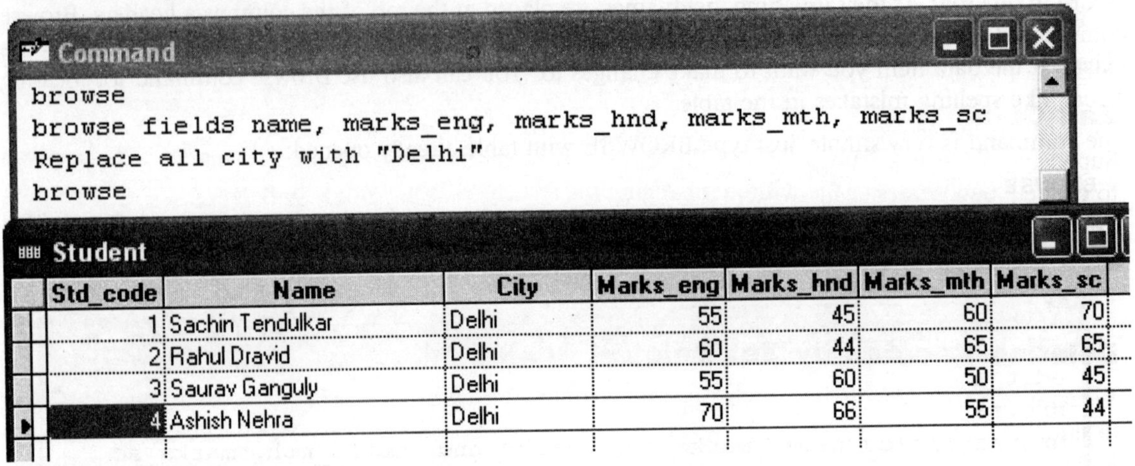

Std_code	Name	City	Marks_eng	Marks_hnd	Marks_mth	Marks_sc
1	Sachin Tendulkar	Delhi	55	45	60	70
2	Rahul Dravid	Delhi	60	44	65	65
3	Saurav Ganguly	Delhi	55	60	50	45
4	Ashish Nehra	Delhi	70	66	55	44

Delete and Recall Commands

You can get rid of the records not needed by you. There is no option of recalling them back after deleting them. So make doubly sure that the records are not needed again before deleting them. Like most of the database programs, in Visual FoxPro too, the deletion is done in 2 two steps. In the first step the software marks the records for deletion without outrighting deleting them. In this case these records are not taken into account as far as totalling of fields are concerned. So when you are taking the total of salaries of all employees in the table, the salaries of the records which are marked for deletion is counted. In fact, till this stage you can recall these marked records, by using the command called Recall.

In the second step, the records are actually removed. Let us see how it is done.

In the Edit or Browse mode mark the record for deletion by clicking in the far left column. With the command window, you can mark the record for deletion by using the record number. For example,

```
DELETE RECORD RECORD_NUMBER
```

In the other case, you go to that particular record which you want to delete by giving the command.

```
GOTO RECORD_NUMBER
```

Now you give the command as:

```
DELETE
```

Delete command puts a physical marker to the record, which you want to delete, but it does not actually remove the record form the file. They will remain in the table and they can be brought back with the Recall command at any time. In other words, the records with physical mark can be reclaimed.

The command for Recall is very simple:

```
RECALL RECORD N
```

Where n is the record number you want to recall. Once you have recalled the record then the physical marker from the record will be removed.

Next we come to the process of deleting the record permanently using the Pack command.

Pack Command

Pack Command permanently deletes the records marked for deletion from the table. The command can be given as:

```
PACK
```

There is another command in this category called Zap, read about it next.

Zap Command

Supposing you have created a student file as mentioned earlier for the 1st semester marks. Now you want to create a new semester file without changing the structure. What you will do is give the command as Zap and all the records with their data would be lost expect for the structure. The command for this is given as:

```
ZAP
```

Deleting Records by Set Deleted Command

Visual FoxPro, by default can use the records even though marked for deletion. Since records marked for deletion are still in the table, operations such as Sum, Total, Count, etc., can still use the marked records for such calculations. You can handle this problem in many ways. One method is to use Pack command before you use any other command. But this method is time consuming specially when you are working with a large table. If you delete records frequently and use these commands frequently, you will have to pack marked records table many times.

Another way to handle this problem is to use Set Deleted command. This command would hide records marked for deletion for doing some other operations on the table and thus, make them unavailable for most of the table operations. As an example, enter the following command:

```
GO TOP
DELETE NEXT 3
LIST STD_CODE, NAME
```

You will see first three records are marked for deletion with * mark at record 1, 2 and 3. Now if you enter the command Set deleted on, it will not include any records that are marked for deletion. If you enter the command Set Deleted Off and type List Std_code, Name again the records marked for deletion will be visible with the asterisk marking. Use Recall command to unmark records which were marked for deletion earlier. To do so, enter:

```
GO TOP
RECALL NEXT 3
LIST EMP_CODE, NAME
```

Records 1, 2 and 3 will now be unmarked for deletion.

Erase Command

This command is used to erase a file from the disk. The syntax of ERASE command is:

```
ERASE FILENAME \? [RECYCLE]
```

Filename specifies the file to be erased, including the path drive or directory if the file is on a different from the current drive or directory. Filename can contain wildcard characters such as * and ? For example, you can erase backup file with Erase *.back command. ? displays the delete box containing names of the files. From this, you can choose a file to erase. Recycle specifies that the file is not immediately deleted from disk and is placed in the Windows operating system's Recycle bin.

ADDITIONAL COMMANDS OF VISUAL FOXPRO

Following are some more commands which will be very useful to learn.

Run Command

Using this command you can run any DOS based command. Of course after running the command you can come back to Visual FoxPro. The result of a DOS Command appears in a separate Visual FoxPro Run command window. The command is stopped automatically when the command has finished its action.

Set Default Command

Visual FoxPro uses its default drive and directory for creating files, unless you specify the path separately. However, you can specify the default drive and/or directory by using the command Set Default To. For example:

```
SET DEFAULT TO C:
```

You can specify the full pathname of a directory by using:

```
SET DEFAULT TO C:\VISUALFOX
```

Display and List Command

Both these commands are used to see the records in the table. Of course, you can see the selected part of the table too.

Display command shows the contents of the current directory or file on the screen, unless you specify the number of records to be displayed whereas List displays the contents on the screen. Both Display and List commands display records on the screen behind any open Visual FoxPro window. If any window is opened you might move them to see the records.

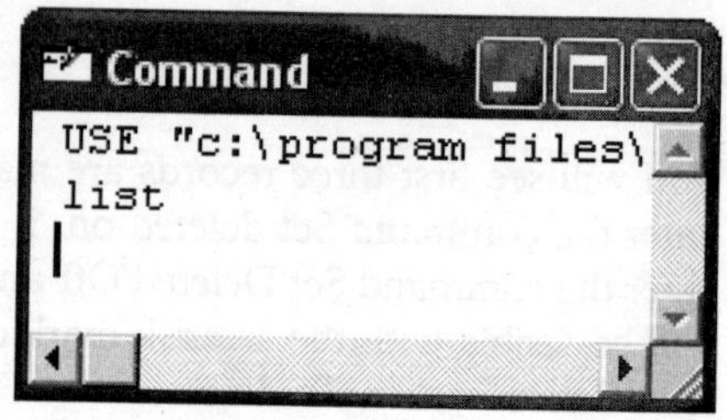

To view the contents of the records in the file student.dbf enter the following command from the Command window:

```
LIST
```

The records of the file student.dbf will be displayed as shown on the next page.

However, you can limit the display to certain fields by including the required field names after List. For example,

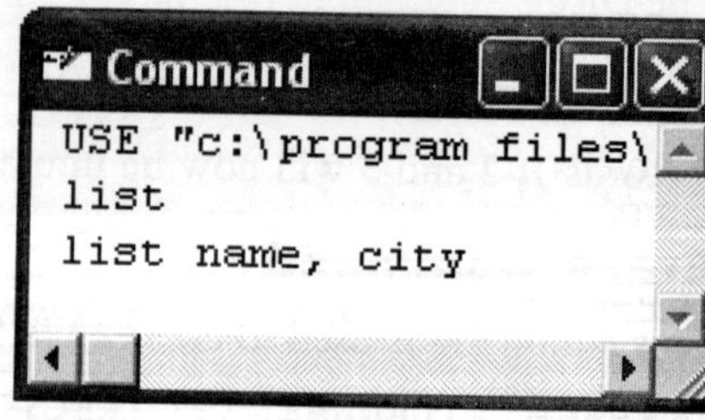


```
LIST NAME, CITY
```

This display a list of 2 fields namely Name and City as seen in second figure on the next page. To change the order of the fields, type the following in the Command window.

```
LIST NAME, STD_CODE
```

Thus, using this method of writing commands, you can display the records with the required fields. You can also use To Print at the end of List command to send the listing to the printer as well as to the screen. If you do not want record numbers to be displayed, add off option with the List command. For example:

```
                    Record#                        STD_CODE NAME
                    CITY                                                        MAF
MARKS_HND                          MARKS_MTH                    MARKS_SC
                          1                             1 Sachin Tendulkar
                    Delhi
       45                              60                              70
                          2                             2 Rahul Dravid
                    Delhi
       44                              65                              65
                          3                             3 Saurav Ganguly
                    Delhi
       60                              50                              45
                          4                             4 Ashish Nehra
                    Delhi
       66                              55                              44
```

```
Record#  NAME                                                          CITY

      1  Sachin Tendulkar                                              Delh

      2  Rahul Dravid                                                  Delh

      3  Saurav Ganguly                                                Delh

      4  Ashish Nehra                                                  Delh
```

```
LIST TO PRINT OFF
```

The Display command is different from the List command. By default, it allows you to view the current record only. The record you marked last is the current record. Visual FoxPro keeps track of the record where the cursor was. Visual FoxPro uses a pointer which remains move or close the Table. Whenever, a table is in use (open) it always points to one record at a time. When you open the file with Use Visual FoxPro command, it points to the first (top) record. The command for this is very simple, just type:

```
DISPLAY
```

You will find the Display command showing the contents of the first record, as shown on the next page, and status bar showing Rec: 1/4. It suggests that there are a total of 4 records in the table file in use and Visual FoxPro is pointing to the first record.

How about seeing all the records. To view more than one record with DISPLAY command, you must add an option clause such as All or Next. Let us type Display Next 4 in the Command window. Since

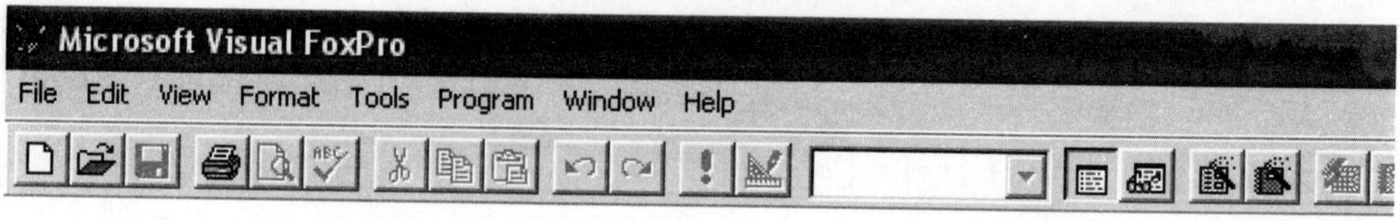

Record#	STD_CODE	NAME	CITY	MARKS_HND	MARKS_MTH	MARKS_SC	MAF
1	1	Sachin Tendulkar	Delhi	45	60	70	

Student (c:\program files\microsoft visu Record: 1/4 Exclusive

the record pointer was referring to 1st record, Visual FoxPro displays 3 more records starting from record number 1 because there are only 4 records in total. You can use another option All with Display command to view all the records of the table.

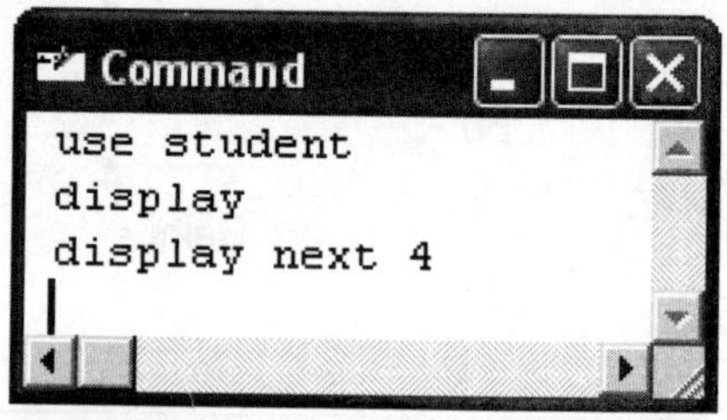

Record#	STD_CODE	NAME	CITY	MARKS_HND	MARKS_MTH	MARKS_SC	MAF
1	1	Sachin Tendulkar	Delhi	45	60	70	
2	2	Rahul Dravid	Delhi	44	65	65	
3	3	Saurav Ganguly	Delhi	60	50	45	
4	4	Ashish Nehra	Delhi	66	55	44	

Options with List Command

Let us now see the various options which can be used with the List command. On the next page, you will see the options which I have used. They are:

```
LIST FOR NAME = "SACHIN TENDULKAR"
LIST FOR MARKS_MATH > 50
LIST FOR MARKS_ENG = 50
```

```
Record#                          STD_CODE NAME
CITY                                                              MAF
MARKS_HND                   MARKS_MTH                    MARKS_SC
                1                           1 Sachin Tendulkar
Delhi
45                          60                                   70
```

```
Record#                          STD_CODE NAME
CITY                                                              MAF
MARKS_HND                   MARKS_MTH                    MARKS_SC
                1                           1 Sachin Tendulkar
Delhi
45                          60                                   70
                2                           2 Rahul Dravid
Delhi
44                          65                                   65
                4                           4 Ashish Nehra
Delhi
66                          55                                   44
```

```
                3                           3 Saurav Ganguly
Delhi
60                          50                                   45
```

All the 3 results are shown above.

A Relational operators such as <, =, >=, <=, etc., allow you to compare two (or more) values or expressions. Typical relational operators are:

Operator	*Description*
=	Equal to
>	Greater than
<	less than
<> or # or !=	not equal to
>=	greater than or equal to

<=	less than or equal to
$	substring (contained within)
= =	equal to and equal in length (exact match)

You can also use the logical operator And, Or and Not to combine two or more conditions (logical expressions) to obtain a compound logical value. (The query that contains an expression that results in either true or false is a logical expression).

Operation	*Meaning*
And	Both operands of the expression must be true for the entire expression to be evaluated as true.
Or	Either operands of the expression must be true for the entire expression to be evaluated as true.
Not or !	The expression that follows must be untrue for the entire expression to be evaluated as true.
()	Used for grouping.

Options with Display Command

Like List you can use Display command to search for specific information such as:

```
DISPLAY FIELDS STD_CODE, NAME FOR CITY = "DELHI"
```

This command will display the code and name only for those cases where the city is Delhi. In the following example, I have use the command as:

```
DISPLAY FIELDS NAME, CITY, MARKS_ENG FOR MARKS_ENG > 50
```

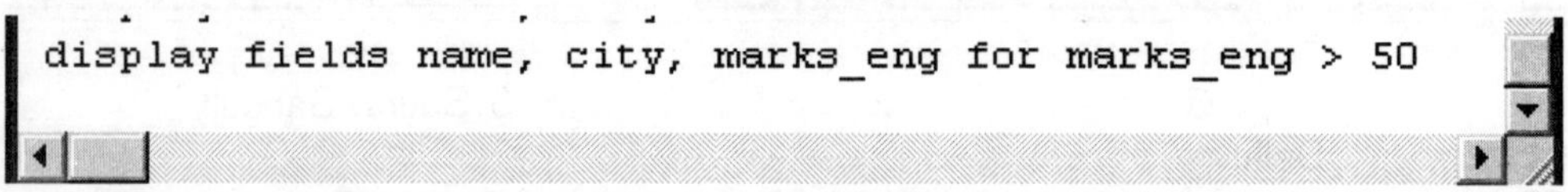

The displayed result is:

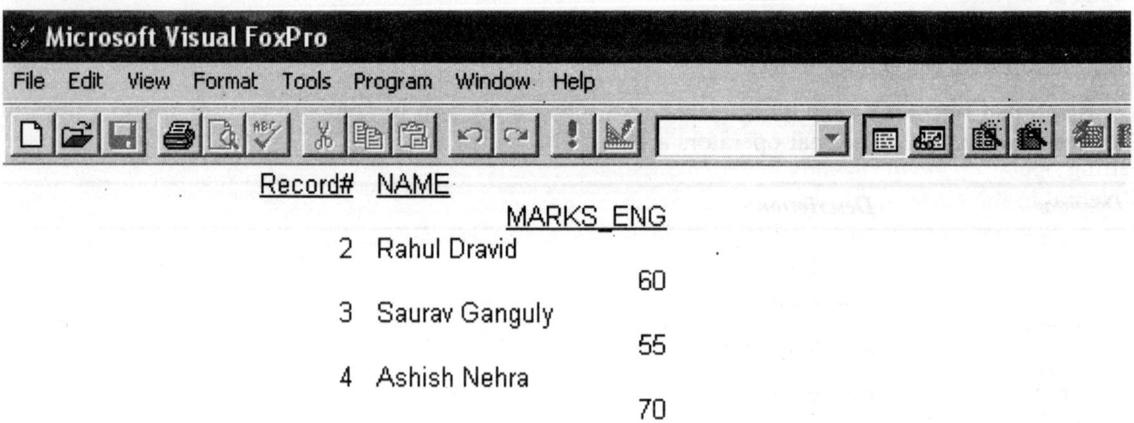

Query with Locate For Command

The Locate command is used for finding the position of a record in a table as per the required criterion. The criterion can be applied for one or more than one fields. Locate command does not show the record on the screen. It gives you only the record number(s) in the status bar, if a match is found. You can then use Display command to see the searched record or records on the screen.

In the following example I have used the command as:

```
LOCATE FOR NAME = "RAHUL DRAVID"
```

Visual FoxPro has found the record and waits for your next command, which I have given as Display. See the result.

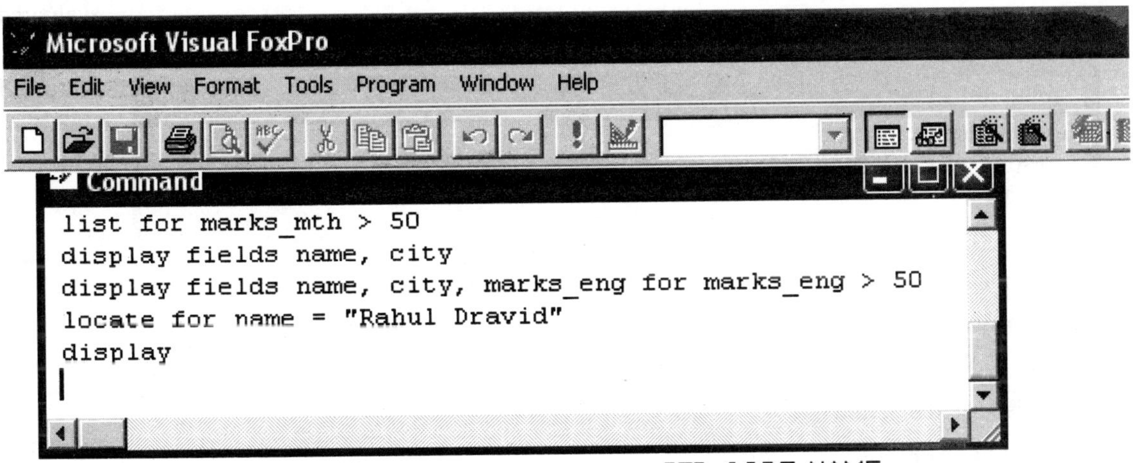

Record# STD_CODE NAME MAF
CITY
MARKS_HND MARKS_MTH MARKS_SC
2 2 Rahul Dravid
Delhi
44 65 65

Word Embedded in Text

Suppose you want to search for records whose Name field contains Nehra. The command Locate for Name = 'Nehra' will not be able to find any record because the word Nehra is embedded in the middle of the Name field. To retrieve this record, we need to give a command that asks similar to "Display all records that have the word Nehra embedded in the name field." Visual FoxPro can do so by means of the string operator ($) which finds the embedded word in the text. So, to locate such a record containing 'Nehra' in the Name field type the command:

```
LOCATE FOR 'NEHRA' $ NAME
```

The following is displayed

```
RECORD = 4
```

Then type the following command to display record 4.

```
DISPLAY
```

The record would be displayed as shown on next page.

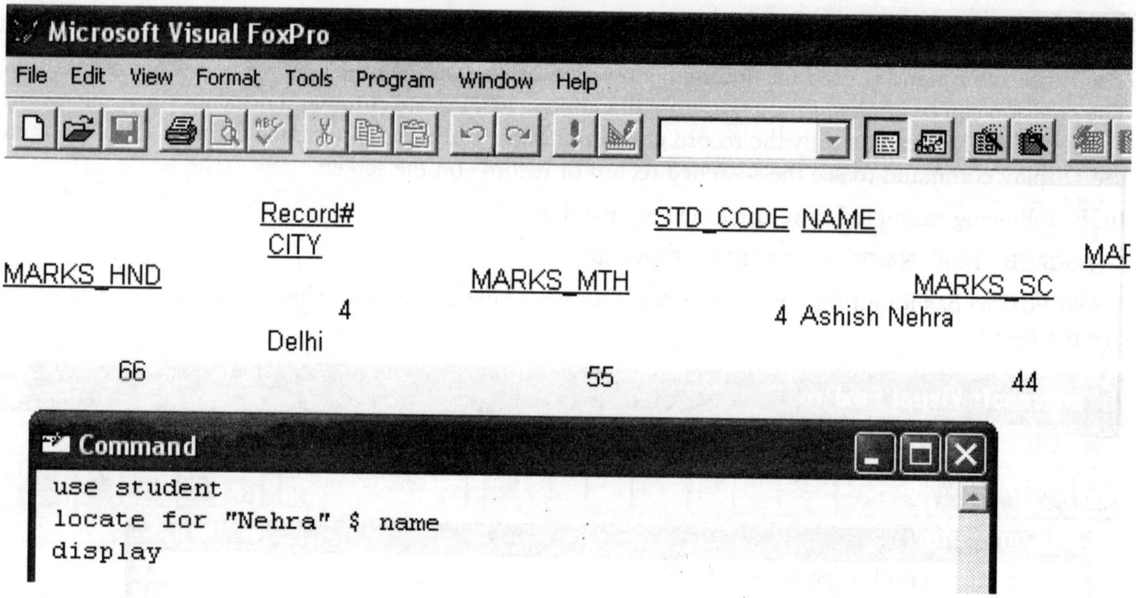

Then type the following command to locate the next occurrence of 'Nehra'

```
RECORD = 6
```

Type Display Enter repeatedly till you get message: End of Locate Scope in the status bar.

You can also use the command

```
LIST FOR 'NEHRA' $ NAME
```

This command will list and show all the records with 'Nehra' embedded in the Name field.

Multiple Conditions in Single Command

Another approach would be to ask for the desired record more specifically, that is using a logical operator. The various logical operators were defined earlier. Let us use the AND Operator. Now enter the command:

```
LOCATE FOR NAME = 'SACHIN TENDULKAR' AND CITY = 'DELHI'
```

The two statements connected with the operator And must be true to get the record. That is, the Name must be "Sachin Tendulkar" and the City must be "Delhi". The result after the first search will be:

```
RECORD = 1
```

Now use display command to view the record. So type:

```
DISPLAY
```

The result is shown on the next page. On using the command continue, you get the following message in the status bar.

```
END OF LOCATE SCOPE
```

There is so because there is no other record which satisfies the two conditions at the same time. The AND operator gives a result only when both the search conditions are true otherwise it does not give any output. If you require a listing of all employee records where name is either Sachin or Nehra embedded in the field Name, then type the following command:

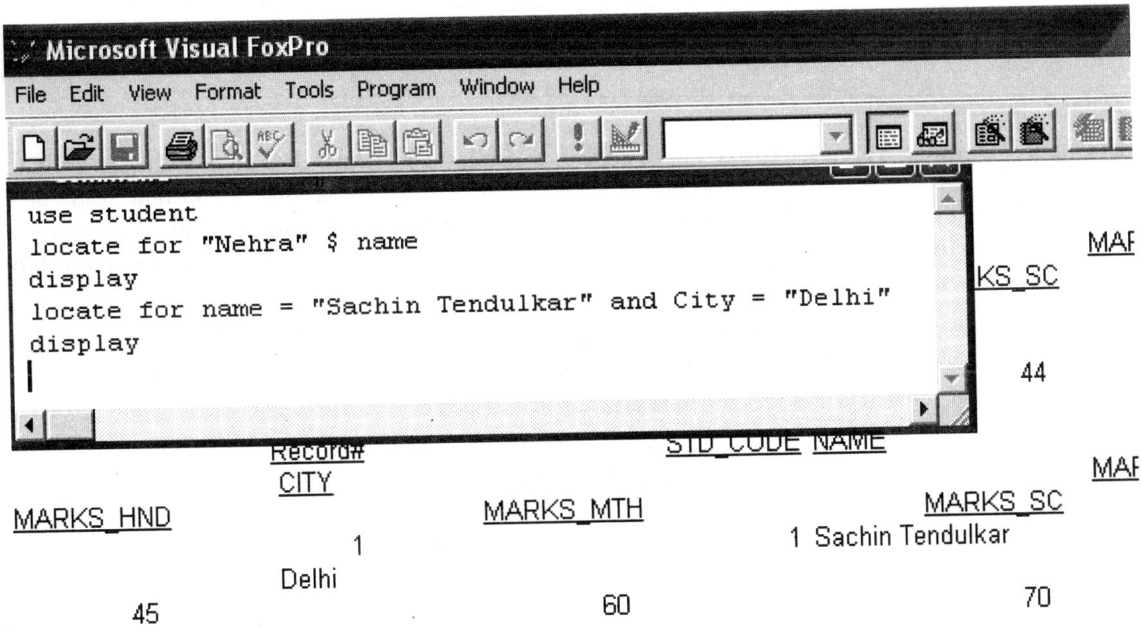


```
LOCATE FOR 'NEHRA' $ NAME OR 'SACHIN' $ NAME
```

Type Display Enter, Continue Enter repeatedly until you get the message: End of Locate scope. You can also use List For command to give similar result by using Locate, Continue command:

```
LIST FOR 'NEHRA' $ NAME OR 'SACHIN' $ NAME
```

The result will be seen in figure.

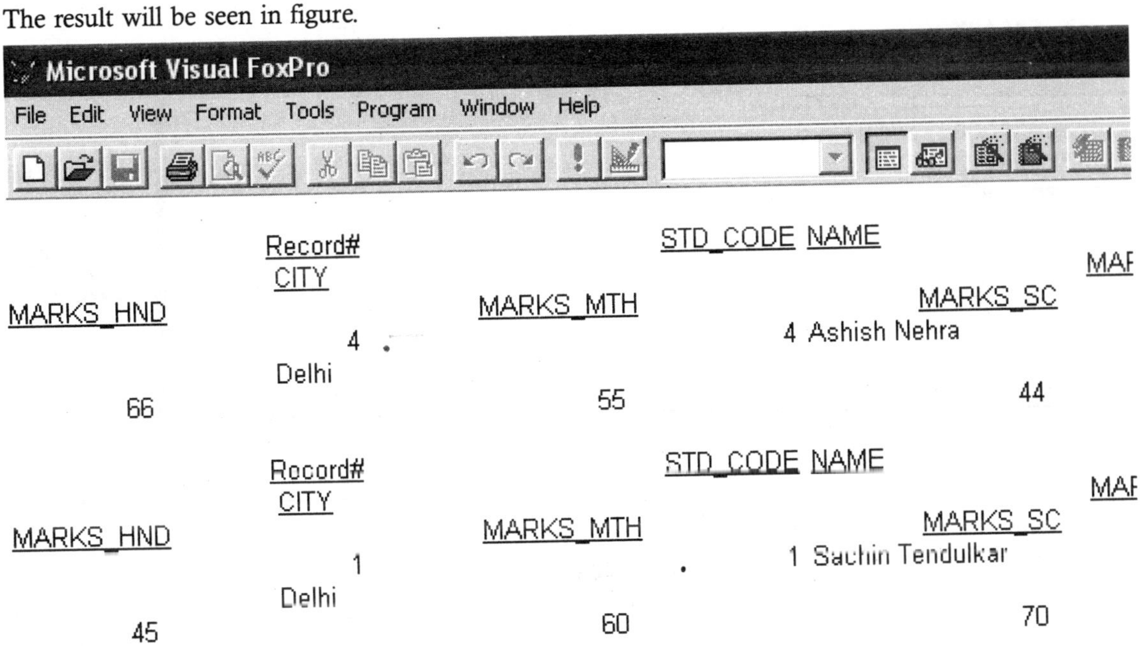

Note that by using And Operator in the above command would not display any output. It is so because there is no record which contains both Nehra and Sachin in the fieldname.

The ? Command

The ? and ?? commands are used to ask Visual FoxPro to display a particular data item on the screen. You can use ?/?? to display any type of information, such as a field, memory variable, a constant, result of a Visual FoxPro function, etc., or even combination of these. The difference between ? and ?? command is that the ? command issues a carriage return before printing the expression list, so it is positioned one line below the previous item displayed.

Memory variable can be created in one of the two ways: either using the Store command or with the assignment (=) statement. With either methods, you name the variable and assign a value to it in the same command.

The format for store command is:

```
STORE <EXPRESSION> TO <VARIABLE_NAME>
```

Or

```
VARIABLE_NAME = EXPRESSION
```

For example, type the following command in the Command window:

```
STORE "SACHIN" TO FNAME
STORE 5000 TO SALARY
? "ENTER NAME:"
?? FNAME
? "ENTER SALARY:"
?? SALARY
```

```
store "sachin" to FName
Store 5000 to Salary
? "Enter Name: "
?? FName
? "Enter Salary
? "Enter Salary:"
?? Salary
```

```
Enter Name: sachin
Enter Salary:      5000
```

If you type ? or ?? commands preceded by a Set print On command, then the output is printed by a printer. For example, type the following in the Command window:

```
SET PRINT ON
? "ENTER NAME:"
```

```
?? FNAME
? "ENTER SALARY:"
?? SALARY
SET PRINT OFF
```

USING EXPRESSION BUILDER

Expression is a concept. Using it you can create building blocks, like constants, fields, variables and functions and can use increasingly complex logical expressions that use the Boolean operators, like And, OR and NOT. Expressions are used in Visual FoxPro to communicate specifications and instructions for many commands and functions.

An expression can include several components. These are:

Field names

Variables

Constants (or literals)

Functions

Operators

You can either type directly in the Expression box of Expression Builder or select them using the Expression Builder controls as follows;

- Use the four drop-down controls at the top of the Expression to select functions and operators of different data types.
- Use the fields list to select Field names.
- Use the variables list to select variables. The Expression box shows the expression you have constructed with your selections. You can also type the expression or parts of it directly into this box. You can click the Verify button to check whether the Expression box holds a valid expression – i.e. one that does not contain any errors in syntax.

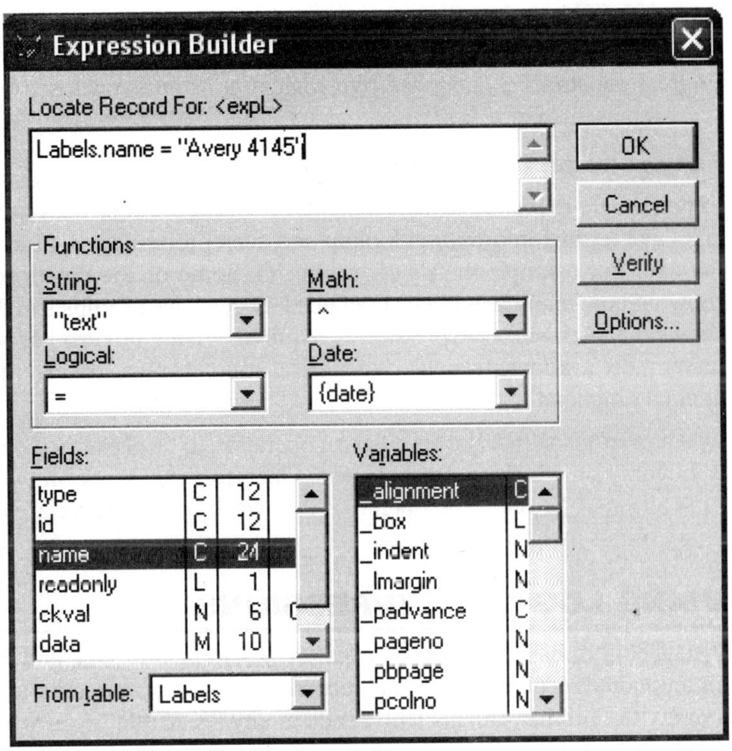

Fieldname

They are the names of fields of your table as std_code, name, city, etc. By default the names of all the fields in a table can be selected from the Fields list in the Expression Builder.

Variables

A variable is a named space in the Random Access Memory (RAM) of your computer where Visual FoxPro stores values. The name is given to the variable when you assign it a value. For example, Name = "Sachin". A variable is one of the Visual FoxPro's expressions and an important building block for the programming language. There are mainly two type of variables.

System Variables are built in, always beginning with the underscore character and always have the same meaning. For example, _PAGENO represents the current page of a rcport and it can be included in an expression added to the report Designer.

Memory variables are created by the user and are used in advanced expressions, used in Visual FoxPro programming.

Constant

It remains fixed throughout the use. Its value does not change. Constants may be letters, numbers or data that are used with their literal meaning. For example, if you wanted an expression to actually include the Word name: before each student's name, you would use the constant "Name" as part of that expression. Constant, that is used in an expression must include the following delimiters to indicate their data type:

Character constants Character constants must be enclosed in double quotation marks (" "), single quotation mar (' ') or square brackets ([ ]). For example, you could use "Hello" or 'Hello' or [Hello] in an expression to make an expression include the actual word Hello.

Date and DateTime constants These constant must be enclosed in curly brackets ({ }). For example, {12/23/99}

Number constant It is used without any delimiter. Simply use the number itself.

Logical constants There are two logical constants, enclosed by dots - .T. represents True and .F. represents False.

Functions and Operators

Functions are the fundamental elements of Visual FoxPro. They are, small programs that perform certain tasks like testing, information lookup and even processing. A function is identified by the parentheses at the end. For example the function upper(). Some of the functions have commas in their parentheses, showing how many arguments then need. Some have examples in their prarentheses such as expc, which shows that a character expression is required. Visual FoxPro has more than 300 in-built functions with many more available through commercial sources, plus you can make your own. These are called user-defined functions.

Operator in Visual FoxPro specifies an operation to be performed on operands to give a value. An operand is an entity on which an operator acts. Operators that work on two operand are called binary operators such as +, -, *, /, etc. The operators that work on one value are called unary operators. For example, unary minus assigns the negative value to a number as in –2.5.

USING LOGICAL EXPRESSIONS

Visual FoxPro has mainly two logical expressions, i.e., True and False. They are generally used to find an individual records or to isolate records that meet certain criteria. For example, if you wanted to make a query to find the students who reside in city "Kolkotta", you would have to use the expression City = "Kolkotta". Visual FoxPro looks at each record to see letters Kolkotta. If they are, the expression City = "Kolkotta" is evaluated as True. If not, the expression is evaluated as False.

LOGICAL FUNCTIONS

Some functions also return .T. true or .F. i.e., False although they are generally used in programming. Common examples of Logical functions are EOF(), i.e., End of File and BOF(), i.e., Beginning of File. Let us see thcm in details.

EOF()

End of File means the logical end of the file, i.e., the system has reached the last record of the file. The normal format of the function is simply EOF(). The function EOF() returns a logical True (.T.) value when the record pointer is at the end of a file and is then moved forward by one more record. The SKIP command can move the record pointer forward one record at a time. The syntax for this is:

```
EOF ((<NUMERIC EXPRESSION>/<CHARACTER EXPRESSION>))
```

Type the following in the Command window:

```
USE STUDENT
GO BOTTOM
SKIP 1
?EOF()
GOTO TOP
? STD_CODE, NAME
SKIP 1
```

As you can see from the figure below, in the first case, i.e., when ?EOF() was given the system response was .T. and when ? std_code, name was given, it responded by giving the std_code and name of the first record.

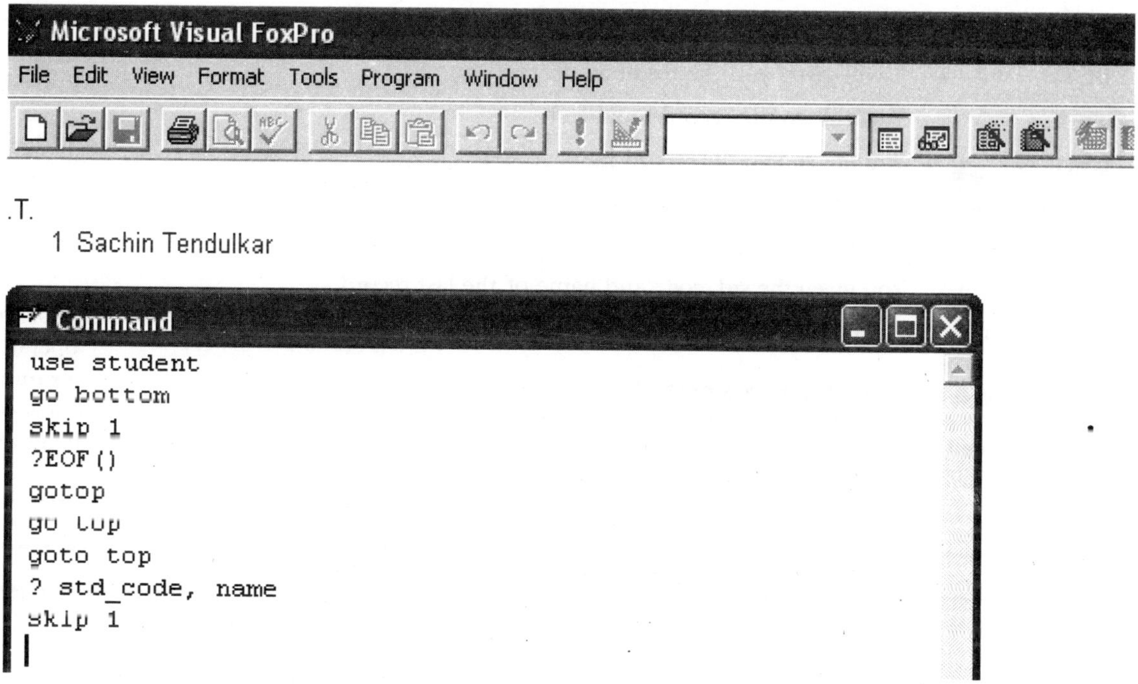

Now we come to Beginning of the File.

BOF()

It gives a logical value of .T. when an attempt has been made to push the record pointer above the first record in the file. Otherwise, it returns a logical value of .F. If the record pointer is positioned at the first record of a table, the Skip 1 command sets BOF() to True. The syntax for this is:

```
BOF ((<NUMERIC EXPRESSION>/ <CHARACTER EXPRESSION>))
```

Type the following the command window:

```
USE STUDENT
GOTO TOP
?RECNO ()
? BOF()
.F.
SKIP 1
? RECNO()
? BOF()
GO BOTTOM
? STD_CODE NAME
```

The above expressions can be explained as follows:

Use Student	The file student is put into memory.
GOTO top	Your control is transferred to the first record.
?Recno ()	You are shown the record number on the screen, i.e., 1.
? BOF()	It will given you the result as .F.
Skip 1	You will go the record number 1
? REcno()	You are shown the record number as 1.
? BOF()	You are shown the result as .T.
Go Bottom	You reach the last record
? std_code name	You given the std_code and name of the last record.

Now we come to the mathematical expressions, operators.

MATHEMATICAL OPERATORS

You learn about mathematical operators in probably the Nursery class but keep talking about them at every stage. Each software takes care of them. The are used for addition, subtraction, etc., on numerical type of data. The arithmetic operators are:

Operation	*Symbol*
Unary minus	

Exponentiation (raising to a power)	^ or **
Division	/
Multiplication	*
Subtraction	-
Addition	+

RELATIONAL OPERATORS

Relational operators determine the relation among different operands. In other words, relational operators are used to test the relation between two expressions or values. It may be used for comparing numerical variables. The values your compare can be constant or variables. Visual FoxPro provides six relational operators for comparing number and characters. Any comparison of values result in logical value of True or False. If the compression is True, the relational expression results into the .T. and .F. if the comparison is False. The $ symbol is used to search for a substring. The == operator which (means is identical to) is not the same as = (which means is equal to).

LOGICAL OPERATORS

Logical operators combine the results of one or more expression and it is called a logical expression. The logical operators are And, Or Not and () are explained in an earlier table.

STRING OPERATORS

These operators are used to combine two or more character strings, known as Concatenation. The Plus (+) sign is used to combine strings including blanks. The minus (-) sign is used to concatenate strings eliminating embedded blanks between them. For example,

```
? TRIM(FNAME)+ " " + TRIM(MNAME)
```

would now display Sachin Tendulkar, if FNAME has Sachin and MNAME has Tendulkar. The minus(–) sign is used to eliminate the blanks. It is generally used as a shortcut. The command:

```
? FNAME-MNAME
```

is similar to

```
? TRIM(FNAME)+ TRIM(MNAME)
```

Order of Precedence

I remember the class IX of mine where I was first taught about order of precedence. That was the time when we were studying so called Algebra and this was required since we did not know what would be solved first + or –. The confusion was solved when our teacher gave us him Guru Mantra and this was called BODMAS rule. This can be explained as follows:

B Bracket

O Overhead line

D Divide

M Multiply

A Add

S Subtract

Another interesting thing which I want to share with you is the expression:

2 + 3 * 4 + 5

If you solve this on a very ordinary calculator the result would be 25. And if you do this on a scientific calculator then the result would be 17. Guess which one is true. Apply the above BODMAS rule and you will understand what I am talking about. The result 17 is true since 3 * 4 would be solved first and then all additions will take place.

Similarly in Visual FoxPro we have the following order of precedence.

1. Expression enclosed in parenthesis, starting with the innermost set of parenthesis and bound to the rules of precedence within each set.
2. Functions
3. Mathematical operations, in the following order.
   a. Exponentiation
   b. Multiplication and division, form left to right
   c. Modules calculations
   d. Addition and subtraction from left to right.
4. Character string concatenation
5. Relational operators, from left to right
6. Logical operators, in the following order:
   a. Not
   b. And
   c. Or

SORTING AND INDEXING

The major difference between the two is that in the case of sort, a new file is created with the sorted records while in the case of indexing, the table remains the same but each record is marked for indexing. Sorting and indexing of the files can be done from the command window as shown below.

Sort

Sorting means grouping records in a particular order say ascending or descending based on a key field of the records. Ascending order means that the names in records of a table will be arranged beginning with the letter A at the top and Z at the bottom. On a numeric field, the smallest number comes first and on a date field, the record with the earliest date comes first. The descending order is just the reverse of it. This means, that names in a table will be arranged with the letter Z at the top and A at the bottom. This is particularly useful for date fields, where you often want the most recent date to come first.

A practical example of sorting of words is the arrangement of numbers and words in a dictionary where thousands of words are arranged in ascending order. Telephone dictionary is another familiar example where names of subscribers are arranged in alphabetical order. Sorting helps us in locating required records such as names of subscribers quickly. The different users of a table may need records in different sequences.

Sorting a Table

Visual FoxPro creates a new table using the sort command and stores the sorted records. From the command window, the format for the Sort command is

```
SORT TO <NEW FILE> ON <FIELD /A/D/C>, <FIELDS...>
```

The option /A specifies an ascending order for the field name. This order for the field name. This order places character field in alphabetical order (A to Z) numeric fields in numerical order (0 to 9) and date fields in chronological order (earliest to latest).

The option /D specifies a descending order, i.e., character fields are sorted in descending order (Z to A) numeric fields from highest to lowest (largest number to lowest numbers) and Date fields in reverse chronological order (from latest to earliest).

If you include /C option after the name of a character field, then uppercase and lowercase letters are treated equally in the sorting order. Otherwise upper case letter Z comes earlier to lower case letter a. you can thus use (/AC or /DC) after the name of a character field to ignore the distinction of upper case and lower case letters in either order i.e. Ascending or Descending..

Let us sort on marks_hnd field in student.dbf table using the Sort command. We will save the sorted data to a file called std2.dbf. The command will be given as:

```
USE STUDENT
SORT TO MARKS_HND TO STD2
USE
USE STD2
BROWSE
```

The result is shown below.

Std2

Std_code	Name	City	Marks_eng	Marks_hnd	Marks_mth	Marks_sc
2	Rahul Dravid	Delhi	60	44	65	65
1	Sachin Tendulkar	Delhi	55	45	60	70
3	Saurav Ganguly	Delhi	55	60	50	45
4	Ashish Nehra	Delhi	70	66	55	44

The records are sorted in the sequence of marks_hnd in ascending order i.e., from 44 to 66.

If the similar command is given to sort the records in the ascending order of name, then the command set would be :

```
USE STUDENT
SORT ON NAME TO STD1
USE
USE STD1
BROWSE
```

You will get result as shown in the figure on the next page.

Std1

Std_code	Name	City	Marks_eng	Marks_hnd	Marks_mth	Marks_sc
4	Ashish Nehra	Delhi	70	66	55	44
2	Rahul Dravid	Delhi	60	44	65	65
1	Sachin Tendulkar	Delhi	55	45	60	70
3	Saurav Ganguly	Delhi	55	60	50	45

Using FOR Clause to Sort Selected Records

You can create a sorted file to include only the selected records by giving specific command which would include suitable Scope and Condition. To produce such a sorted file that should contain only specific records from the table, you will use the "FOR" scope with the Sort command. The syntax for the Sort command when used in this manner is:

```
SORT TO <NEW FILE> ON <FIELD LIST> FOR <LOGICAL EXPRESSION>
```

For example, if you need to include records for students who belong to Delhi and put them in alphabetic order of name too then you give the following command at Command window:

```
USE STUDENT
SORT TO STD3 ON NAME FOR CITY = "DELHI"
USE
USE STD3
BROWSE
```

The following figures show both the results before and after sorting.

Student

Std_code	Name	City	Marks_eng	Marks_hnd	Marks_mth	Marks_sc
1	Sachin Tendulkar	Mumbai	55	45	60	70
2	Rahul Dravid	Delhi	60	44	65	65
3	Saurav Ganguly	Kolkotta	55	60	50	45
4	Ashish Nehra	Delhi	70	66	55	44

Std3

Std_code	Name	City	Marks_eng	Marks_hnd	Marks_mth	Marks_sc
4	Ashish Nehra	Delhi	70	66	55	44
2	Rahul Dravid	Delhi	60	44	65	65

Sorting Table on Multiple Fields

It is possible that you may need to sort a table on two fields instead of one. One will be the major field and the other would be minor field. The general format for the command is:

```
SORT TO NEWFILE ON FIELD1 [/A/C/D], FIELD2 [/A/C/D],........ LAST FIELD
[/A/C/D]
```

The above mentioned table Student can be sorted on City and Name to give the following result:

Std4

Std_code	Name	City	Marks_eng	Marks_hnd	Marks_mth	Marks_sc
4	Ashish Nehra	Delhi	70	66	55	44
2	Rahul Dravid	Delhi	60	44	65	65
3	Saurav Ganguly	Kolkotta	55	60	50	45
1	Sachin Tendulkar	Mumbai	55	45	60	70

INDEXING A FILE

I had talked about Indexing while defining Sort. It is a process of arranging the records. In indexing, original record numbers do not change. However, here the records are indexed in the alphabetic order of name. To get a better understanding of an index file, consider the index at the back of this book. If you wish to find information on a specific subject, just refer to the page number given along with the subject and you would find the detail of the subject on that page. Visual FoxPro supports two type of index files: These are:

a. Single Index files

b. Compound index files

Let us see them in details.

Single Index Files

The index file here is kept with the extension .IDX. This index can be kept up to date by opening the index everytime you do some editing, i.e., adding, altering, etc., you will have to open this index file too. In other words, if you keep the index files open (active), they automatically get updated regardless of the operation you perform. This type of index files can be two types:

Compact: These files are faster to access and occupy less disk space due to reduced size.

Non-compact: Here the files are slower to access and are use more space.

The command for Compact type is:

```
INDEX ON <EXPR> TO <.IDX FILE> COMPACT
```

For non compact one you will use the command:

```
INDEX ON <EXPR> TO <.IDX FILE>
```

Compound Index Files

These are identified by the .CDX extension. Unlike the IDX files, each of which can hold only one Index, compound index files can hold multiple indexes in a single file, which are identified by names called tags. The exact number of tags you can include in a .CDX index file is limited only by the available main memory of the machine you are using. Here also you have two types: Structural and Independent. Let us see what they mean.

Structural: It is opened automatically whenever you open the table. A structural compound index is automatically given the same name as the table file with the extension .CDX. To create a structural compound index file the syntax is:

```
INDEX ON <EXPR> TAG <TAGNAME>
```

When Visual FoxPro opens a table, it looks for a structural compound index file (a compound index file having the same name as the table with the extension .CDX). If such a file is found, Visual FoxPro opens it and updates it automatically as and when changes are made in the table.

Independent: Compound Indexes other than Structural Compound Index are called independent compound indexes. These can have any name with extension .CDX. however, these files cannot be given the same name as the table. To create an independent compound index file the syntax is:

```
INDEX ON <EXPR> TAG <TAGNAME> OF <.CDX FILE>
```

For most of the database applications, a structural compound index file serves well. However, if you have a group of indexes that you use only once in a year or so as to produce reports, keep them as a separate, independent index file. Then you can specifically use that file and reindex it once in a year before producing the reports.

Deleting Tags

When you put tag in an index file, there must be a way to delete them too. You can delete one or more tags from a compound index file by using the Delete Tag compound. If a tag is in a non-structural index file, you must open the index file before you execute the Delete tag command. The syntax is:

```
DELETE TAG <TAG NAME> OF <.CDX INDEX NAME>
```

you can also delete more than one tag at a time by specifying a list of tag names rather than a single tag in the Delete Tag command. The syntax is:

```
DELETE TAG <TAGNAME1> {OF <.CDX FILE1> [, <TAGNAME2>] [OF <.CDX FILE2]
```

you can also delete all the tags from compound index by adding keyword All to Delete Tag command.

```
DELETE TAG ALL [OF <.CDX FILE>]
```

Note the use of [OF <.cdx file>] clause implies reference to an independent compound index file.

CREATING INDEX

Index command is used to create an Index file or tag for the current table. Records in a table that has an index file are displayed and accessed in the order specified by the index expression. The physical order of the records in the table is not changed by an index file. The Index command in Visual FoxPro arranges records more efficiently from the command level.

The general format for index command is:

```
INDEX ON <FIELD EXPR> TO <.IDX FILE> \ TAG <TAG NAME> [OF <CDX FILE>]
[FOR <CONDITION>] [COMPACT] [ASCENDING/DESCENDING] [UNIQUE] [ADDITIVE]
```

The above command creates an index file for the table that is open in the current work area. The index command arranges records in an apparent order based on the field expression, but actual order of the records in the table file does not change. You can create an .idx index file by including file To <idx file> clause. The index file is given the default extension .Idx.

```
TAG <TAG NAME> [OF <CDX FILE>]
```

You can also create a compound index file by including Tag <tag name>. A tag of a compound index file (.cdx) contains multiple index tags within one file. If you do not specify a filename Visual FoxPro makes this a tag of the structural compound index file, which has the same name as the table file and is automatically opened whenever the table file is opened.

The optional For clause makes the index include only those records for which the logical expression is true. The compact option directs Visual FoxPro to create compact Idx index files. The compact option reduces the size of the index files and make them more efficient. The **Ascending** and **Descending** options allow you to tell Visual FoxPro whether to index the file according to ascending or descending values of the particular field. However, ascending option is the default. The **Unique** option makes the index file include the records with the first occurrence of a given value for the field expression only. This option will eliminate the duplicate data records from the index file. The **Additive** option allows previously opened index files to remain open while you create a new index file. We shall now use the index command to index Employee.dbf file on Name field.

For this, we just need to open student.dbf file and enter the following command:

```
INDEX ON NAME TO NAMES
```

The index command creates an index file (Names.idx) on name field and displays the following message:

```
4 RECORDS INDEXED
```

At this stage if you give the command as List you will find the screen as shown below.

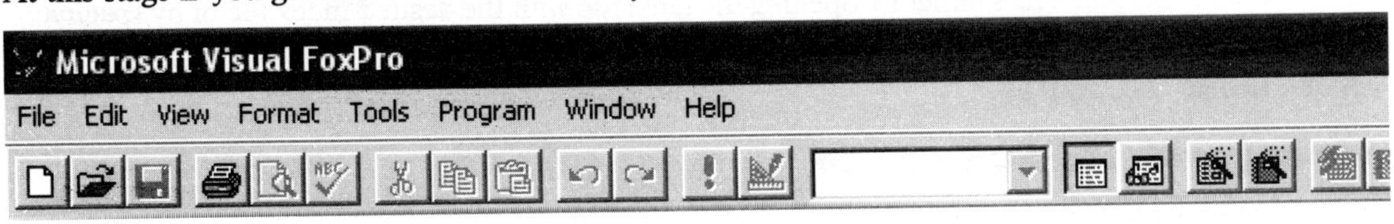

Record#	STD_CODE	NAME	CITY	MARKS_HND	MARKS_MTH	MARKS_SC	MAF
4	4	Ashish Nehra	Delhi	66	55	44	
2	2	Rahul Dravid	Delhi	44	65	65	
1	1	Sachin Tendulkar	Mumbai	45	60	70	
3	3	Saurav Ganguly	Kolkotta	60	50	45	

You see that there is no change in the order of the records. Each of the record is at the same place where it was.

We can also index records on another field say marks_eng. I am doing this deliberately since this field is numeric while name was character. Enter the following command in the Command window:

```
INDEX ON MARKS_ENG TO ENG
```

It displays message in status bar as:

```
4 RECORDS INDEXED
```

now type the command :

```
LIST STD_CODE, NAME, MARKS_ENG
```

Visual FoxPro displays the records in the ascending order of marks_eng.

Student

Std_code	Name	City	Marks_eng	Marks_hnd	Marks_mth	Marks_sc
1	Sachin Tendulkar	Mumbai	55	45	60	70
3	Saurav Ganguly	Kolkotta	55	60	50	45
2	Rahul Dravid	Delhi	60	44	65	65
4	Ashish Nehra	Delhi	70	66	55	44

Thus, you have two index files for student.dbf. One which contains sorted name, i.e., (names.idx) and other which contains sorted marks-eng, i.e., (eng.idx). At one time you can use only one of them. However you can select other index files either by opening the table file with the desired index file or by specifying the index filename with Set index command. For example,

```
SET INDEX TO NAMES
```

Indexing with the FOR clause

You can limit the number of records in a table and stored in the index file by using the For clause along with the Index on command. You can also do so by using the <for...> expression window of the Index On dialog box. If used from the command window, the syntax for the index command is as follows:

```
INDEX ON EXPRESSION TO FILENAME FOR CONDITION
```

Where the condition used with For is any expression that evaluates to a logical true or false. This is a powerful Visual FoxPro option that can, in effect, filter the table of the unwanted records but placing the records in order at the same time. The set filter command alongwith a simple use of the index command would also accomplish the same result. Assuming that an updated index already exists, then using for with index on is faster method is compared to using set filter.

Indexing a File and Adding Records using Append

Suppose you want to display data from the student table in order of name, enter the following command:

```
USE STUDENT INDEX NAMES
```

You can now add new records with the append command. Visual FoxPro adds a blank record at the end of a file and then you can enter data in the newly added record. After adding the new record to the table, press Ctrl + W to save it. If we type List or Browse command to view the records, then all the records including newly added record will be listed alphabetically by name. Thus there is no need to carry out indexing procedure again.

Indexing on Multiple Fields

You may index file on more than one fields similar to the case of sorting. But, you cannot directly index on multiple fields if the fields are not of the same type. For example, you can not index by Name and other fields in student.dbf table, because name is a character field whereas marks-eng is a numeric field. However, you can index student.dbf on City and the Name fields because both are character fields. Visual FoxPro will first index the file on City field and for records with the same city, it will rearrange them in alphabetic order.

Indexing on Multiple Fields of Different Types

I had talked about the multiple field indexing in the last step. But, what we can do is to change the type of the field using the string function called STR. Thus, in order to sort records on marks_eng and name fields, first you need to convert the field marks_eng which is numeric to string type using, STR() function. The STR() function converts the contents of a numeric field into a string of characters. For example:

```
INDEX ON STR(MARKS_ENG) + NAME TO MULNED
LIST NAME, MARKS_ENG
```

See that the records are in the order of name since there is no duplicate field of the name, if it had been then the one record with less marks in eng would have been given the priority.

Opening Tables and Index Files

You may open a table file with one or more index files simultaneously by adding the word "Index" and filenames after the <Use fielname> portion of the command. However only one index file is active at a time. The syntax for the use command, when taken with the index option would be:

```
USE FILENAME INDEX INDEXNAME1 [,INDEXNAME2]
```

For example, you could open the student table file simultaneously attaching the names and marks_eng index files with the following command:

```
USE EMPLOYEE INDEX NAMES, MARKS_ENG
```

INDEXING COMMANDS

For an index to control the order of the records, it must be active. You can easily tell which indexes are in use at any time by using the list status or list display commands.

Set index

An index that has just been created in active. But by using the Set index command, you can activate any of the indexes.

Set order

To activate an index file use the set order command. With set order, you use numbers such as, set order to 2. The number 2 here indicates the order in which the index file was originally opened.

Reindex

Reindex command recreates all the open index (.idx and .cdx) files. It rebuilds all open index files in the current work area. If any changes have been made to the table while the index file was closed, you can update it with the Reindex command. Index files must be reindexed specially if they were not closed properly, i.e., when PC is turned off or reset without using the Exit. Index files also need to be reindexed if they are not open when the records are appended or edited in the table.

Close Index

When you decide not to use any index file, use close index command to close the index files but keeping associated table files open.

SETTING A FILTER CONDITION

Specifying, or setting a filter condition is an efficient way of selecting a group of records from a table. For example, by using filter, you can display all records where city is Delhi or those records with marks_eng more than 50. After you set a filter, you need not worry about adding the criterion to each command. Records that do not meet your criterion are filtered out indefinitely, until you remove the filter. You can create a filter from the Command window by entering:

```
SET FILTER TO <LOGICAL EXPRESSION>
```

After you use a filter, it remains in effect until you change it or remove it. Before you can view the entire table again, you must remove the filter. If you want to remove the filter just enter Set filter to command without any logical expression. You can also create filter conditions in a special dialog box called the Expression Builder. You can use this dialog box when you need to provide an expression or condition to complete a command. To create a filter condition, do this:

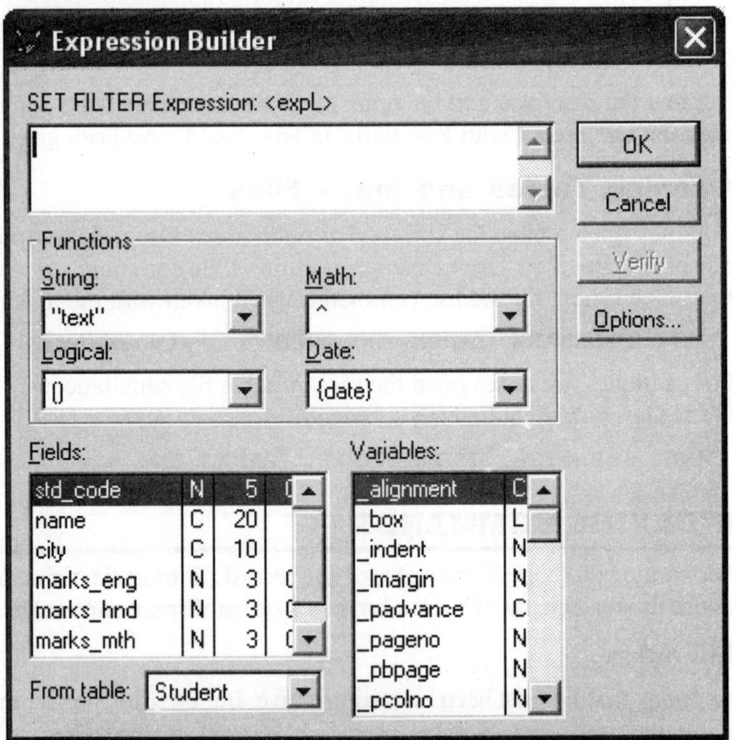

1. Open the table in the Browse window and click table menu. Choose Properties to open the Work Area Properties dialog box.
2. Click on the Data filter button.
3. Double-click on the field to be affected.
4. Type the remainder of the expression; or choose an operator from the Logical drop-down list, choose the type of string from the String drop-down list and type the condition.
5. To verify that the expression is valid, click on Verify.
6. Click OK button to return to the Work Area Properties dialog box.

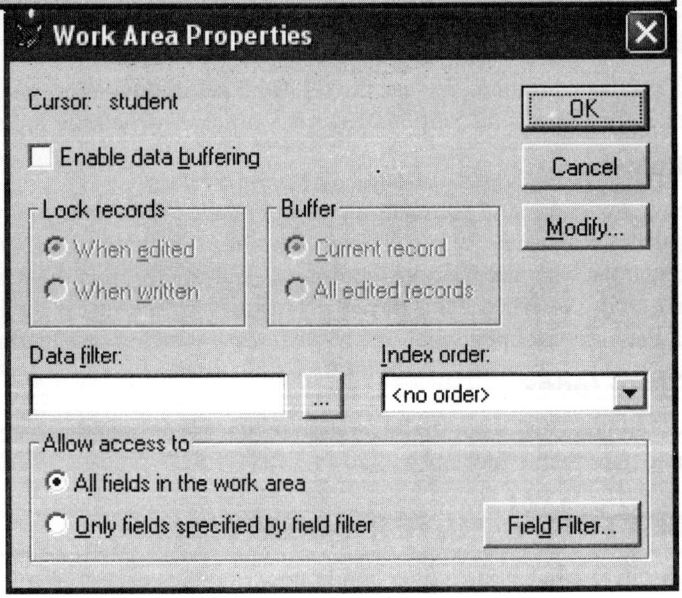

A mathematical operator is a symbol or sequence of symbols, such as +, * and = that tell the program to perform an operation to calculate a result. A function is a preprogrammed calculation that is performed by the program on request.

Changing a Filter Condition

To change an existing filter condition do this:

1. Open the Expression builder dialog box again.
2. In the Fields list box, double-click on the desired field.
3. Type the new expression; or choose the desired parameters from the Functions drop-down lists and type the new condition.
4. Click OK.

Removing a Filter Condition

You can remove a filter condition to display all the records in a table. To remove a filter condition do the following:

1. Select Table menu and choose Properties option. The Work Area Properties box will be displayed.
2. Click all fields in the work area radio button below the Allow access to box.
3. Click Field Filter... button. A Field Picker dialog box appears.
4. Select Remove All button to move the selected fields back to All fields: box.
5. Click OK twice.

MACRO(S)

The macro is just like an ordinary memory variable, but has an ampersand (&) in front of it namely, &Name, &Fld etc. When Visual FoxPro encounters a macro in a command file, it replaces that macro with the contents of the memory variable. For example, if you have a memory variable, called Fld and you have the word Pin_Code stored to that name, every time the &Fld macro is encountered in the program, Visual FoxPro automatically substitutes the word Pin_Code. A memo field can store any type of data namely, keyboard symbols, graphics or special symbols. Memo fields can also store data such as scanned image, digitized sound, binary objects, executable programs and any other data as well. You treat the data in a Memo field like variable length database character fields. The only limitation in using Memo fields is the amount of disk space available in your computer. Data stored in Memo fields do not form part of the database and are not stored in the file with extension .Dbf. FoxPro stores them in a separate file with the same name as original database file but with an extension of .FPPT.

Creating Table with Memo Field

You will now create a table self.dbf with the structure as shown here.

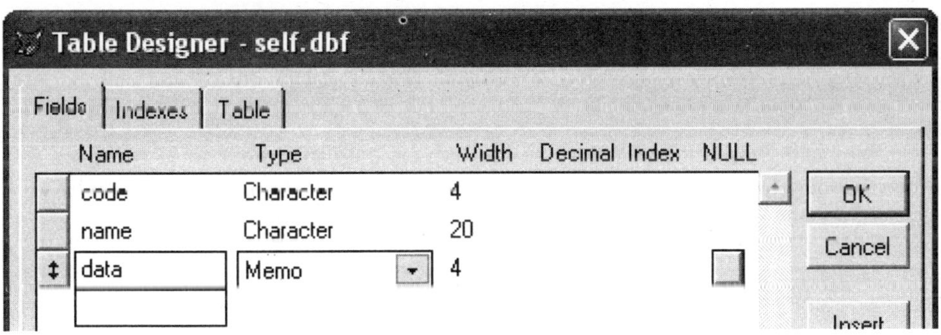

After defining the structure of self.dbf when you see the message "Input data records now?" select Yes and Visual FoxPro displays a blank record for data entry, as shown below.

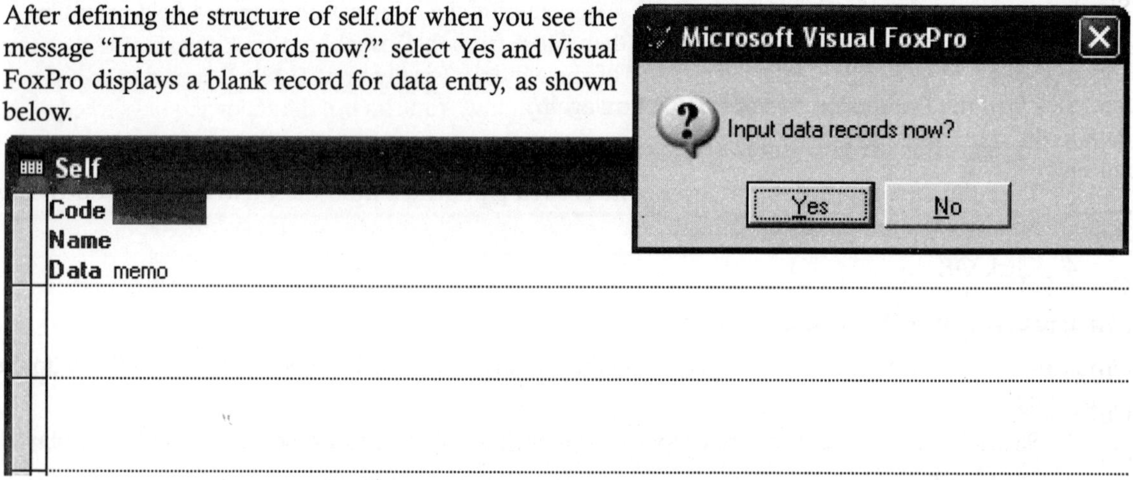

You can enter the following records in the table:

1. A101 Amitabh An excellent actor, has acted in more than 100 films to date. In more than 17 films, his name was Vijay. It was assumed that if his name is Vijay in the film, the film would be a success. Now, he is enjoying his second innings in the film industry.
2. S101 Shah Rukh Coming from Delhi and making a modest start, this actor has had an excellent run in the film industry in the last decade. He is still the number one choice of most of the producers, specially Chopra and Johars. They cannot think of making a film without him.

In the code field type the code of the first entry i.e., A101. Next enter Amitabh in the Name field. So far so good. Now comes the main part.

Entering Data into Memo Fields

Now we come the memo field and to enter data into it, double click the memo field with mouse. You would be shown a Visual FoxPro editor. Enter your complete text into it. This word editor works with Word wrap facility, so you do not have to enter the Enter key after every line. See how the data looks in the editor, below.

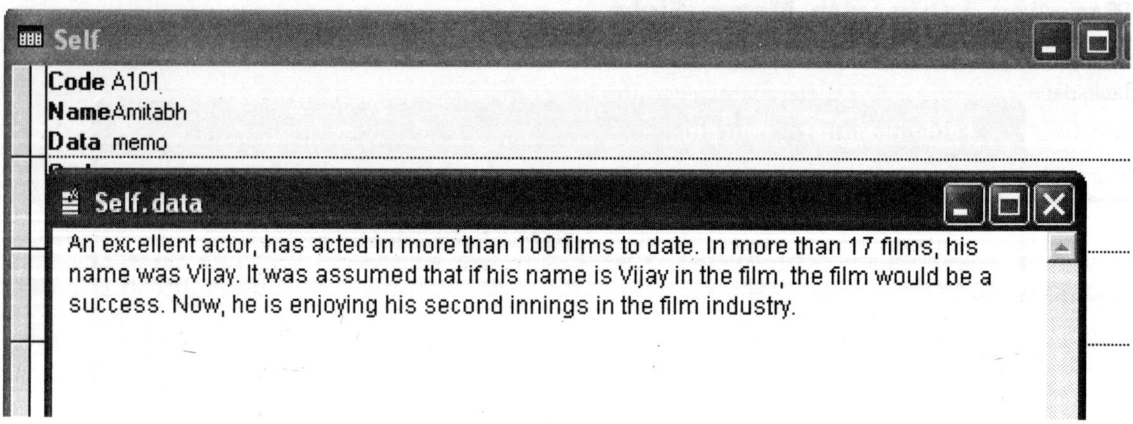

Similarly enter the data for the second record. After entering the information in memo field press Ctrl + W to save text in memo file or select File, and then Close from the Visual FoxPro. You can also click the Close (x) button, located on the top left corner of the window. Finally press Ctrl + W to save the records and click on close (x) button to return to Command Window. You can use the following keys to edit the data in the memo field. Most of you who are familiar with working of word processing would find them similar.

Key	*Description*
Ctrl + PgDn	Activate the Memo Editor when the cursor is in the memo field
Ctrl + Home	Move cursor to the top-left corner of the window
Ctrl + End	Move the cursor to the bottom-right corner of the window
Ctrl + left arrow	Move cursor left one word
Ctrl + right arrow	Move cursor right one word
Ctrl + W	Save changes and exit
Ctrl + A	Select all text within the window
Ctrl + U	Undo
Ctrl + R	Redo
Ctrl + X	Cut
Ctrl + C	Copy
Ctrl + V	Paste
Ctrl + F	Find
Ctrl + G	Find again
Ctrl + E	Replace and find again
Up arrow	Move cursor up one line
Down arrow	Move cursor down one line
Left arrow	Move cursor left one character
Right arrow	Move cursor right one character
Ins	Turn Insert mode on/off
Del	Delete character at cursor
Backspace	Delete character to the left of the cursor
Esc	Close memo field after prompting you to save changes
Shift + Arrow	Select a block text

Viewing Information in Memo Field

Once that you have added data to the memo field, you would like to see it too. Visual FoxPro does not display contents of memo field. Instead it displays the word Memo under the Detail field. To see the contents of Memo field, type the following command at the Command window and watch the output at the screen.

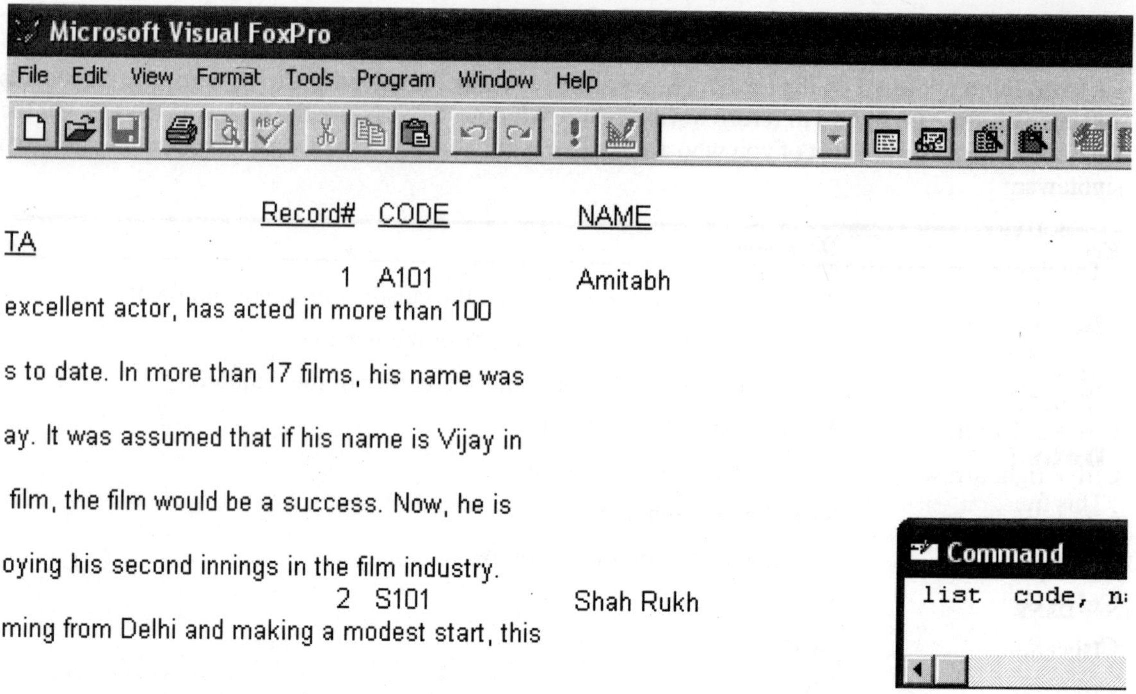


```
LIST CODE, NAME, DATA
```

When you use list command, it uses 50 characters (default) to display the contents of a Memo field. However you can use the Set Memowidth command to control the width of Memo field when displaying contents using list or display command. This may result in more convenient display of information contained in the Memo field. Type the following commands in Command window and watch the screen:

```
SET MEMOWIDTH TO 50 LIST NAME, DATA
```

See if you can find some difference.

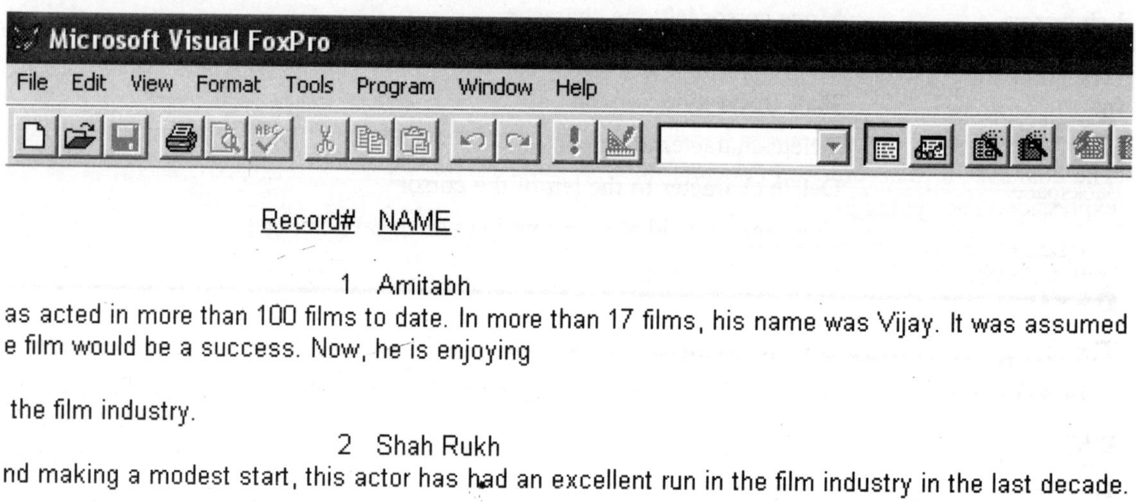

Modifying Memo Field

Modify memo command opens editing window for changing Memo fields in the current table. This command also allows you to view a Memo field's contents or make and save changes in it. If a record has more than one Memo field, then you can open a window for each Memo field. In the above case if you want to edit the memo field, just type:

```
MODIFY MEMO DATA
```

The data in the data field would be on screen for you to edit.

Date and Time Functions

Visual FoxPro offers several data and time functions. The following sub sections describe these with examples.

Date ()

This function reads the computer's system date and then supplies a date-type value representing it. The display will be in the default format mm/dd/yy or in some other as specified by the Set Date command. The syntax is:

```
DATE ()
```

The command ? DATE() would result in the current system date.

CDOW()

The character day of week function converts the date expression into the day of the week expressed in the text form, i.e., Sunday through Saturday. The syntax is:

```
CDOW(DATE)
```

The command cdow(Date) would give you the day of the week, i.e., Friday.

CMONTH()

The character month of year function converts the date expression into the month of the year expressed as a name. The syntax is:

```
CMONTH(DATE)
```

The command ?CMONTH(DTE) would result in the current month, i.e., September.

CTOD()

The character to date function converts the date expressed as a text string into a standard date type expression. The syntax is:

```
CTOD(CHARACTER_STRING)
```

DAY()

The day of month function converts the date expression into the day of the month. The syntax is:

```
DAY(DATE)
```

DMY()

This function returns a date expression in European Day Month Year format for the given date. It always returns the Month with a full spelling. The syntax is:

DOW()

The day of week function converts the dates expression into the day of the week expressed as a number. For example since 03/05/03, was the Wednesday and Wednesday is the fourth day of the week, so DOW({03/05/03}) returns 4. The syntax is:

```
DOW(DATE_EXPRESSION)
```

DTOC()

This function returns a character string containing the date corresponding to a date expression. The syntax is:

```
DTOC(DATE_EXPRESSION, 1)
```

DTOS()

This function returns an eight-digit character string in the format YYYYMMDD for a given date expression. The syntax is:

```
DTOS(DATE_EXPRESSION)
```

GOMONTH()

This function returns the date which is a certain number of months after or before a date expression. The syntax is:

```
GOMONTH(DATE_EXPRESSION, NUMBER_OF_MONTHS)
```

MDY()

This function returns a Month Day Year Character string for a given date expression. It always returns the month with a full spelling. The syntax is:

```
MDY(DATE_EXPTRESSION)
```

MONTH()

The month function converts the date expression into the month of the year expressed as a number. The syntax is:

```
MONTH(DATE)
```

Seconds()

This function returns the system time in seconds, thousandths format, with a resolution of 1 millisecond. The syntax is:

```
SECONDS()
```

SYS(1)

This function returns the current system date as a Julian day number expressed as a character string. The syntax is:

```
SYS(1)
```

SYS(2)

This function returns the number of seconds elapsed since midnight as a character string. The syntax is:

```
SYS(2)
```

SYS(10)

This function converts the numeric day number of a character string. The syntax is:

```
SYS(10, NUMBER)
```

SYS(11)

This function converts a date expression or a character string in date format to a Julian day number returned as a character string. The syntax is:

```
SYS(11, DATE_EXPRESSION/CHARACTER_EXPRESSION)
```

TIME()

The Time() function is eight characters long and is presented in the HH:MM:SS format. HH stands for hours, MM stands for minutes, SS stands for seconds. The time function gives you access to the system time. You can use this function to store the system time to a memory variable or table field. The syntax is:

```
TIME()
```

Year(0)

The year function converts thc date expression into a year expression. The syntax is:

```
YEAR(DATE)
```

CONCEPT OF MULTIPLE TABLES

So far, you have worked only with single-table database, which are sufficient for some simple business applications. Visual FoxPro is a relational database manager and hence gives you the choice one or more than one table at a time. It also enables you to define relationships between two or more table.

Relating Files

Earlier, you found that the current table in use is automatically closed as soon as you open a new file. However, using visual FoxPro relational power, you can create a relation to connect or join records from different tables and thus you can access their information at the same time. In a relation, one table is called the parent table and the other is called as child table. The parent table controls the child so that when you move the record pointer (select a record) in the parent table, Visual FoxPro automatically moves the record pointer to the first corresponding record in the child table. If a matching record cannot be traced in the child table, then record pointer moves to the end of the last record in a child file. Visual FoxPro is quite flexible in the ways in which it lets you draw relationships between tables.

You will read morc about these relative databases in a later chapter.

Multiple Choice Questions

1. Command Window is used for :
   (a) Writing commands
   (b) Getting to windows
   (c) Going to DOS
2. Append command adds the data to the :
   (a) Beginning (b) Last
   (c) Middle
3. Run command is used to run :
   (a) Windows commands
   (b) FoxPro commands
   (c) DOS commands
4. Locate command is used to :
   (a) finding the position of the record
   (b) finding the data (c) finding the field
5. ? command is used to display :
   (a) table (b) data items
   (c) form
6. FoxPro has two logical expressions True and:
   (a) Bad (b) False
   (c) No
7. String operators are used to combine two or more character strings, known as :
   (a) Combination (b) Strings
   (c) Concotation
8. An indexed file can be activated using :
   (a) Set order (b) Set index
   (c) Set sort
9. Macros have this character in the beginning :
   (a) * (b) &
   (c) %
10. List command displays on :
    (a) Printer (b) Screen
    (c) Plotter

Descriptive Type Questions

1. What is command window used for?
2. What is sorting and how it is done?
3. Explain Order of Precedence.
4. What is indexing? How does it differ from Sorting?
5. Describe the following with respect to indexing: Set Index, Set order, Reindex and Close Index.
6. Describe the working of following commands:

Append	Change
Browse	Replace
Delete	Recall
Pack	Zap
Erase	Run
Set Default	Display
List	?

7. Write short notes on the following functions:

DATE()	CDOW()
CMONTH()	CTOD()
DAY()	DMY()
DOW()	DTOC()
DTOS()	GOMONTH?()
MDY()	MONTH()
SECONDS()	SYS(1)
SYS(2)	SYS(10)
SYS(11)	TIME()
YEAR(0)	

Relational Database Concepts of Visual FoxPro

29

INTRODUCTION

You look at Relational Database in this way that if you create a relation between two databases then you can work not with one database but with two databases at a time. Simply putting, if you have databases of students. One having the marks, the other having name, roll number, etc., then you can work on these databases independently or together too, if you create a common field, which maybe rollno. In a Relational Database, data is organized in the form of rows and columns similar to a table. The tables are referred to as relations in a relational data model. Rows of the table are referred to as tuples and the columns of a table are referred to as attributes.

Table in a relational database is similar to the traditional file system with its records, fields and files. The table's rows, called tuples, contain records and columns, called attributes, contain fields. Each tuple or row, has values for the attributes. The attribute describes some feature or property of the objects.

Advantages of Relational Database

a. You can use it with a PC with small memory too.

b. Relational database is very effective for small databases.

c. Relational database is much easier to use because it enables a computer system to accommodate a variety of enquiries in an efficient manner.

d. Relational database is only concerned with data and not with the structures, which improves the performance. The processing time and storage space is comparatively large in relational database but the user is not required to know the intricacies of the structure design, thus making relational database easy to use and learn.

e. Other traditional databases use pointers to implement record relationship. But, in relational databases record relationship is implemented using primary key or composite key field(s). Hence it is very simple and represents the logical relationship among the data items rather than physical relationship (like hierarchical and network model).

f. Relational model is very useful for representing most of the real world object and the relationship among them.

Relationships among Tables

As mentioned above, you have to have a primary keyfield which establishes the relation between the two tables. This key should be present in the tables involved. As mentioned above in the case of students tables, the roll number of the student becomes the keyfield. The type of relationship that can be established are:

One to One

This is the simplest one. Like above each student has a unique roll number which is there is all the relative tables.

One to Many

In this type of relationship, one record in one table has many corresponding records in the other table. This is why it is called One to Many. One-to-many relationship is the most common relationship used in a relational database. For example, one department has many workers.

Many to Many

In many to many relationship, a record in one table has many corresponding records in a second table and for every record in the second table, there are many corresponding records in the previous table. For example Many students would take Many tests.

CREATING A NEW DATABASE IN VISUAL FOXPRO

We have earlier learned about creating tables. The method of creating a database is very similar. Of course we would be using Wizard or Database Designer, as we had done in the case of tables.

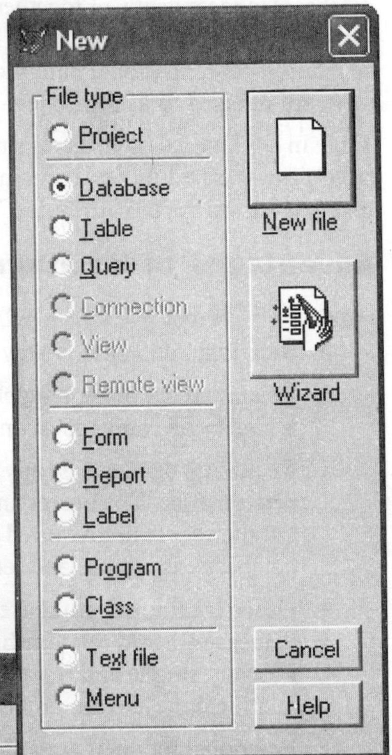

1. Click File menu and choose New... In the New dialog box that appears select the Database radio button and click New File button.
2. Alternatively, you can create a new Database by giving the Create Database command in the Command Window.
3. In the Create dialog box that appears select the directory of your choice and provide a name for the new Database file. We have provided the name "student". Click Save.
4. You will not note that a Database Designer window opens up. If the toolbar is not visible, select it from Toolbars dialog box. This dialog box appears when you click Toolbars... From the View menu. There are different buttons in the Database Designer toolbar. Click the "Add Table button" and add tables "student.dbf" and "table1.dbf" into the database. You will note in figure that one can also create new table or remove existing tables using the Database Designer toolbar.

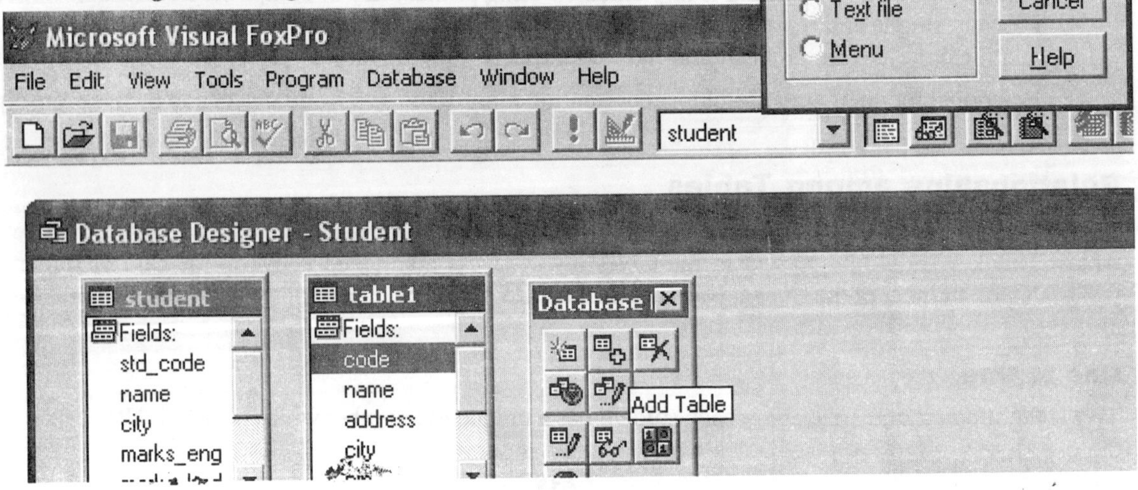

5. Press Ctrl + W keys, when finished.

You have thus created a relational database “student” with the two tables “student.dbf” and “table1.dbf”.

ENTERING AND VIEWING DATA USING THE FORM WIZARD

Earlier we had created form for a single table, now we would create a form from two tables which are there in a relation. The One-to-Many Form wizard creates a form from two related tables. One table is considered as the parent table and other as the child table. The fields of child table appear in a grid below the fields of parent table. To do this, we do the following:

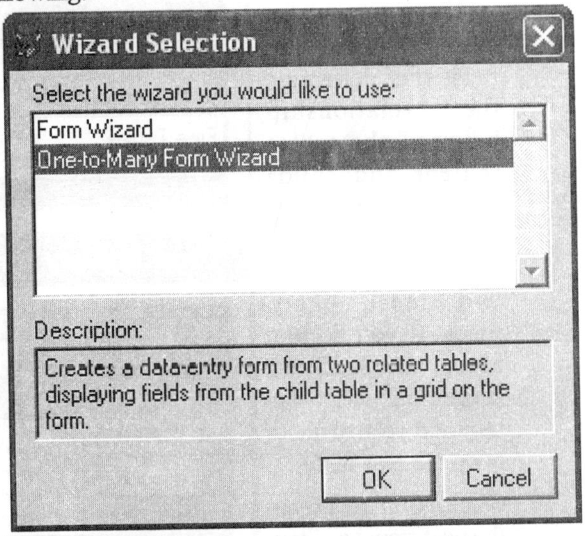

1. Click Tools menu, highlight Wizard and choose Form.
2. The Wizard Selection dialog box will appear. Choose One-To-Many Form Wizard and then click OK.
3. In the dialog box that appears the Databases and Tables: area will show the current Database which is “student” in our case. If you want a table other than this, click on the small button to the right of Databases and Tables: area. The Open dialog box will get opened and you can open the required table using this dialog box. In our case, we have chosen “student.dbf” table. Therefore, this table forms our parent table.

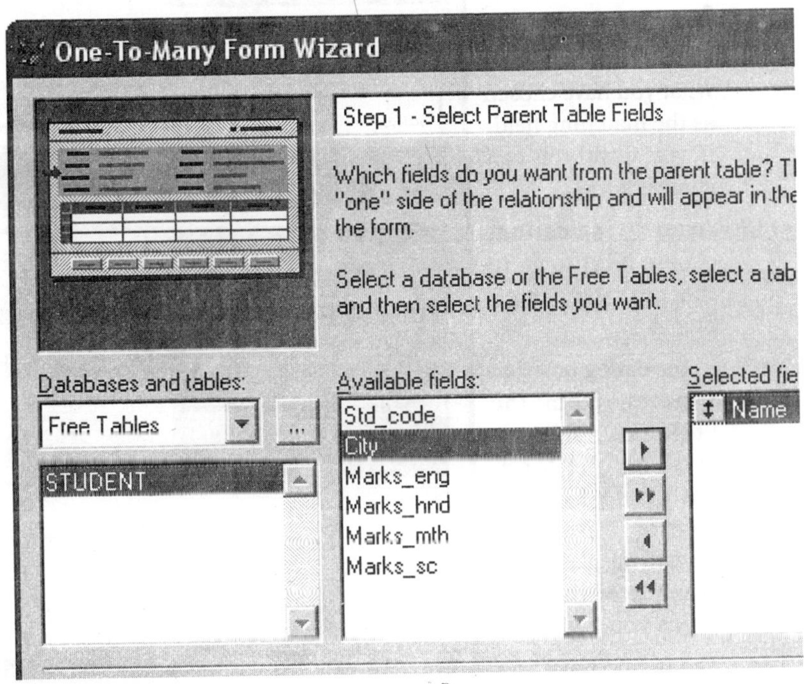

4. From the Available Fields, select the field which you want in your form, then click > button. To select all the fields present in the Available Fields: area click the >> button. I have selected here the filed called Name.
5. To remove a field from the Selected Fields: area click the < button. To remove all the fields, click the << button.
6. Click Next to go to next Step, i.e., Step 2.
7. Similarly, select the fields from the “child”

table in the dialog box that appears. In our case, we have chosen the "table1.dbf" table to be the child table.

8. Click Next.
9. In the dialog box that appears you can accept or select the fields that determine the relationship between the tables (parent and child) from the fields list. Visual FoxPro will itself show you the two most likely fields. If you do not accept the FoxPro's suggestion, select the required related field from the two tables.
10. Click Next to go to the next step, i.e., Step 3.
11. Here it shows that what you have chosen as the matching field. If you want you can change it too.
12. After selecting, choose Next to go to the next step, i.e., Step 4.
13. In the dialog box that appears, from the Style box, select a Style for the form. The wizard displays a picture in the magnifying glass as an example of the style which you highlight.
14. The Button type: area

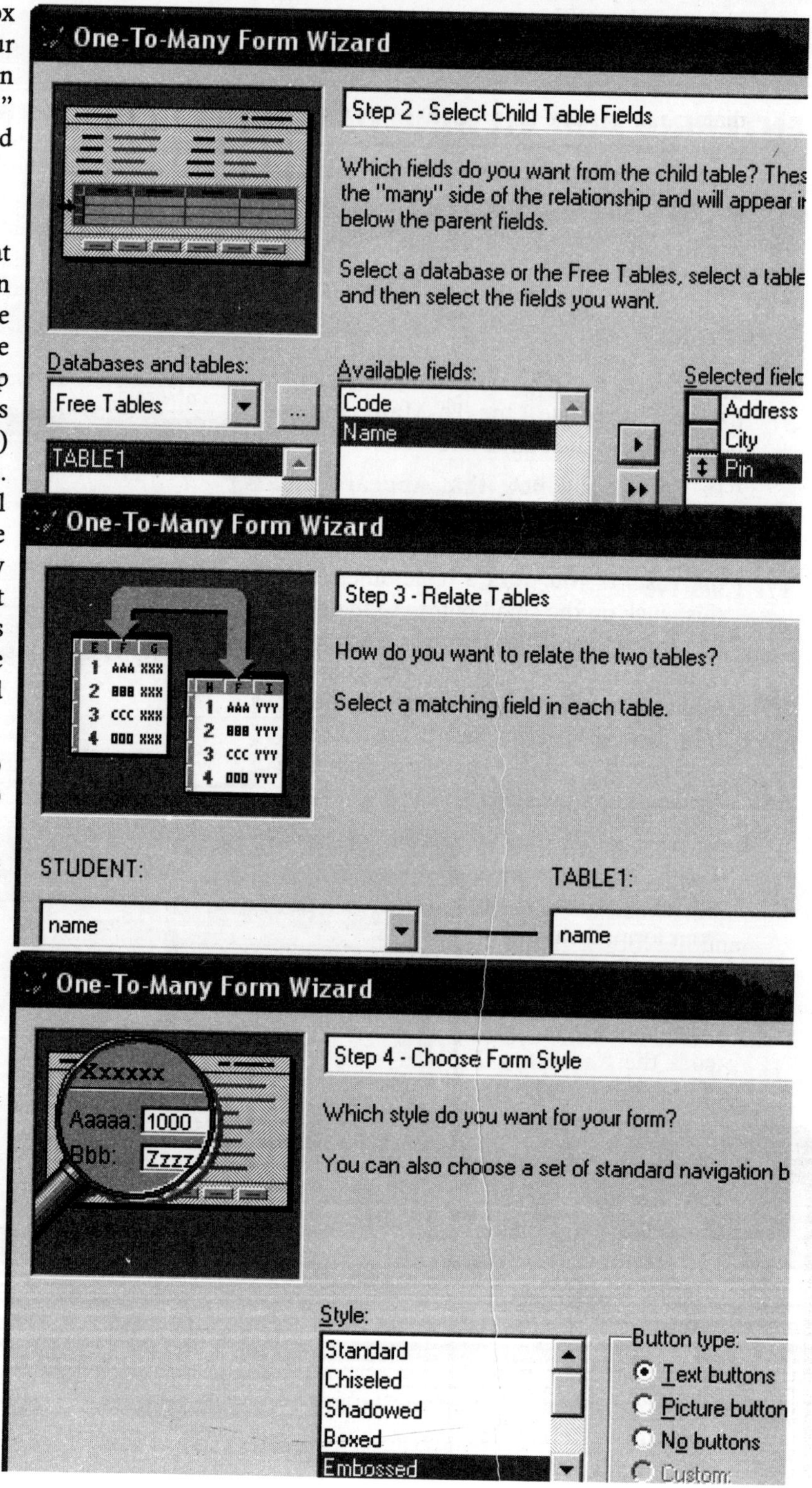

specifies the form's navigation buttons. You will note that this dialog box is same as that of the "form Wizard" you studied in earlier chapter.

15. Click Next to go to the next step, i.e., Step 5.
16. In the next dialog box that appears, select the fields based on which you want to sort the records in the parent table. Here I have chosen Name.

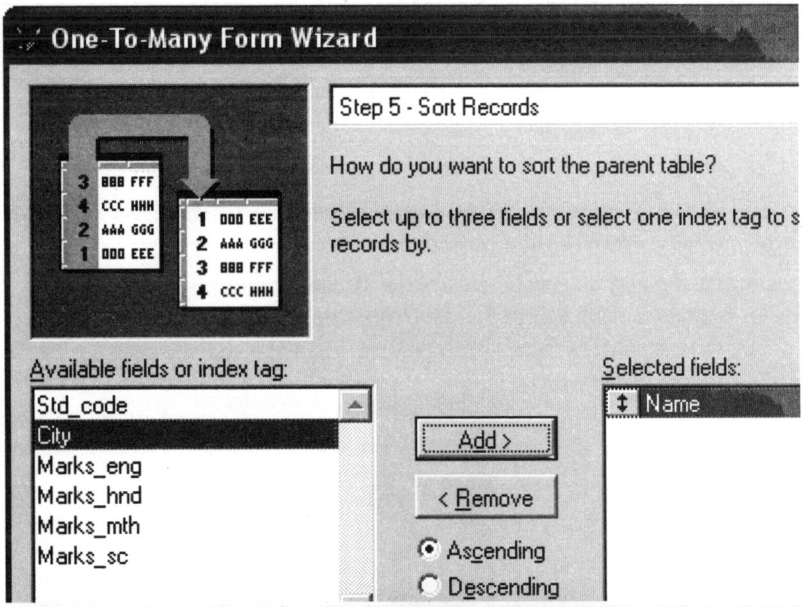

17. Click Next.
18. In the dialog box, click the Preview button to view the form before you exit the One-To-Many Form Wizard. Otherwise, select any of the listed options and click Finish. We have selected "Save and run form". In the Save As dialog box we provided the name "student" and the form appeared as shown here.

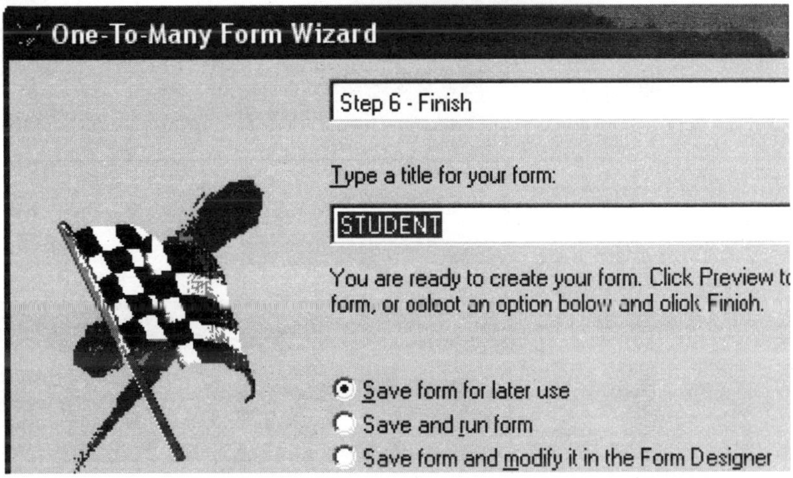

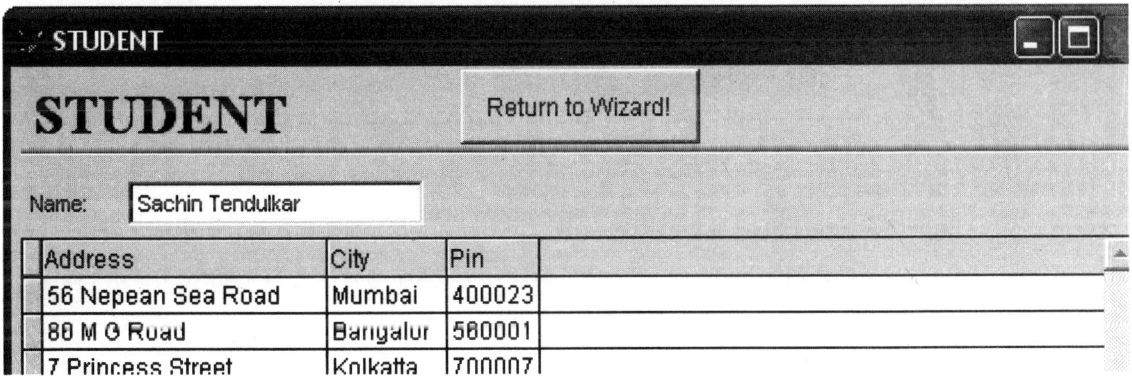

QUERY WIZARD TO WORK WITH RELATIONAL DATABASES

Similar to Form, you can create Query too using Query Wizard to work with fields from more than one table of a relational database. For this do this.

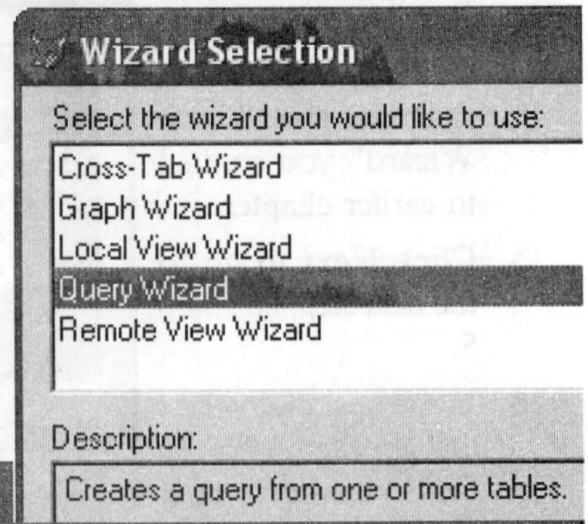

1. Click Tools menu, highlight Wizards and choose Query.
2. In the Wizard Selection dialog box that appears select Query Wizard and click OK.
3. In the first screen of the Query Wizard dialog box that appears first select fields from one table. Move the required fields from the Available Fields to the selected fields.
4. Click Next to go to the next step, i.e., Step 2.
5. Here since I have not asked to choose the next table, there is not Step 2.
6. In the dialog box that appears, select related fields from the fields lists to determine the relationship between the two tables.
7. Click Next.
8. From the dialog box that appears, you have to choose whether you want to include only related rows from both tables or all rows from either table. By default, only related records are included.
9. Click Next.

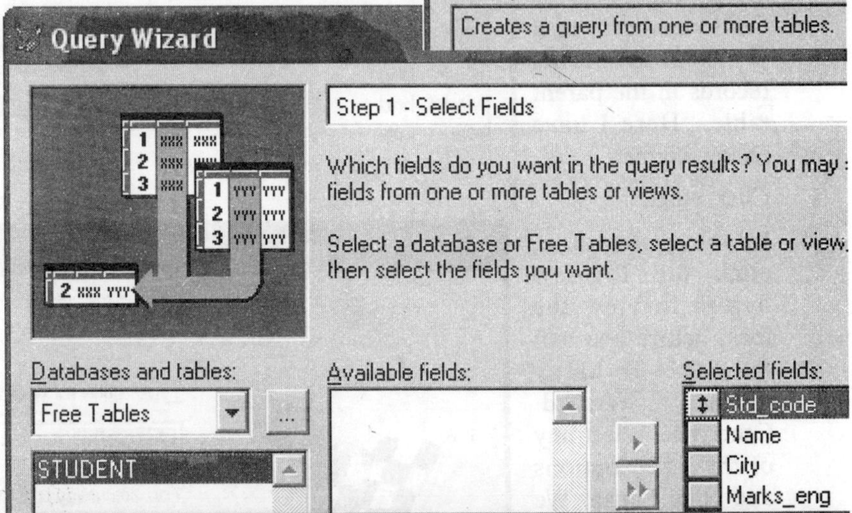

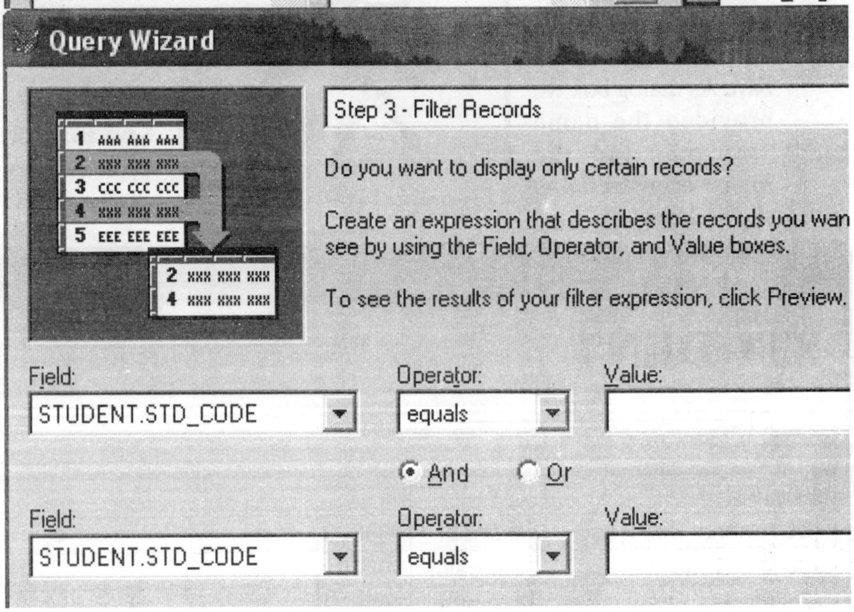

10. The next step is to determine the order in which your query results will be sorted. Select a field from the Available fields and click the Add> button to move it to the Selected fields.

    Select Ascending to sort the results in ascending order, or Descending to sort them in descending to sort them in descending order.

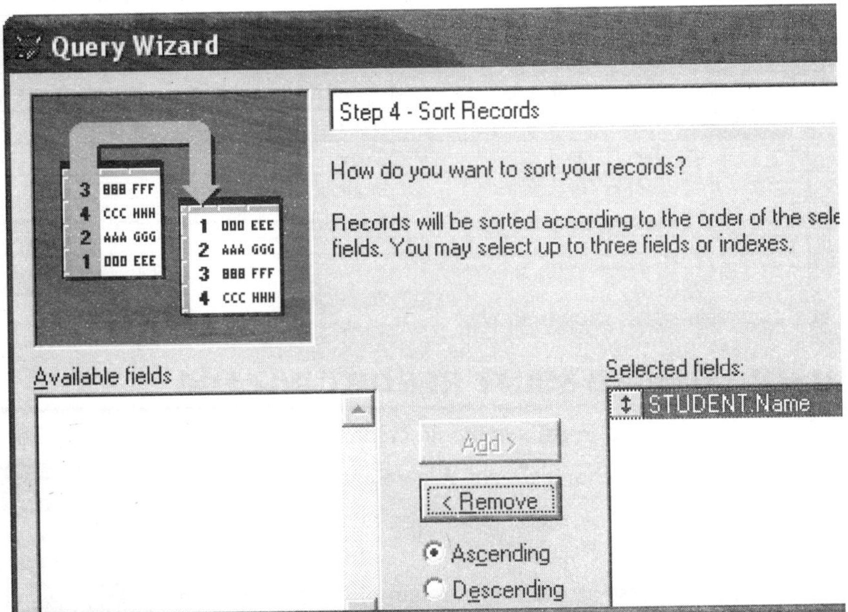

11. Click next.
12. In the dialog box that appears, mention whether you want all the records of only a portion of the records (in percentage). I have chosen to view all the records.

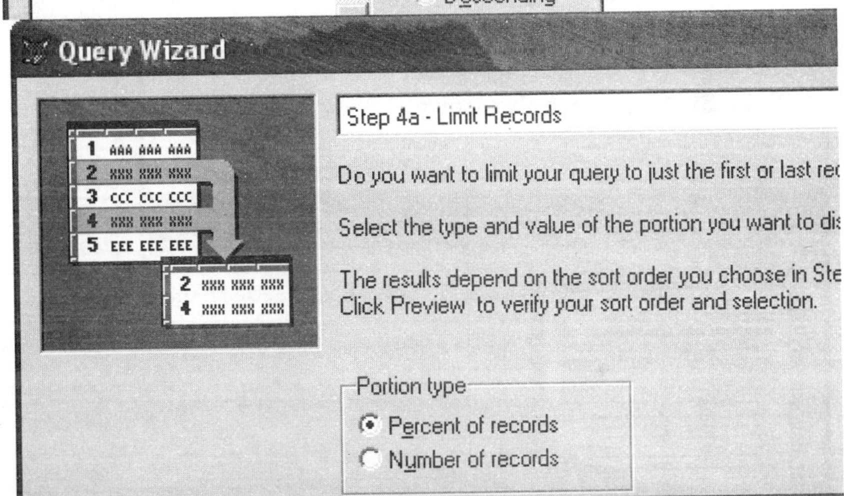

13. Select an option of your choice from the dialog box that appears and click Finish button. I have selected the "Save query" option.

    Click the Preview... button to view the output without existing the wizard.

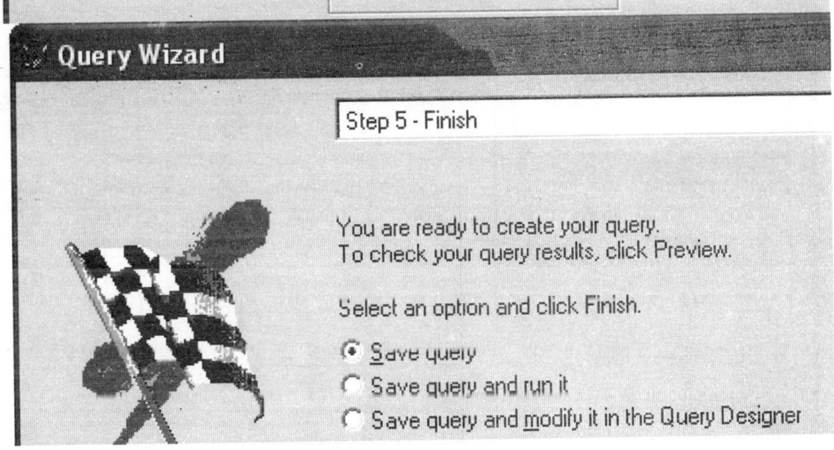

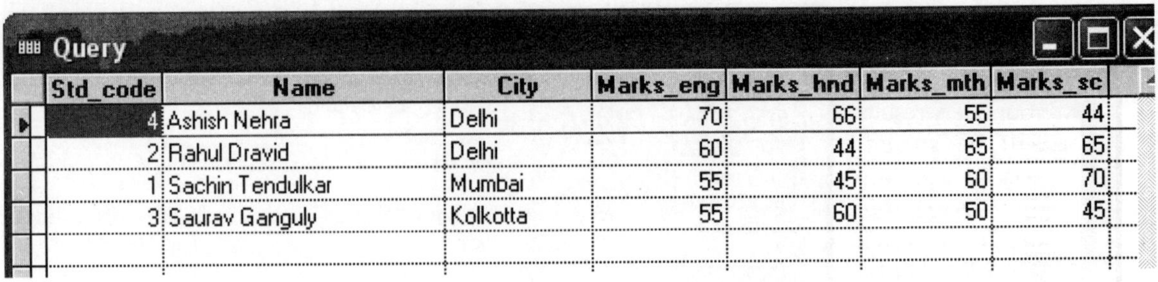
Query

Std_code	Name	City	Marks_eng	Marks_hnd	Marks_mth	Marks_sc
4	Ashish Nehra	Delhi	70	66	55	44
2	Rahul Dravid	Delhi	60	44	65	65
1	Sachin Tendulkar	Mumbai	55	45	60	70
3	Saurav Ganguly	Kolkotta	55	60	50	45

The query output is shown above.

USING ONE-TO-MANY REPORT WIZARD

Similar to Query and Form, we would create a one-to-many report too. For this do the following:

1. Click Tools menu, highlight Wizard and choose Report.
2. In the Wizard Selection dialog box that appears choose One-To-Many Report Wizard.
3. Since the rest of the steps are simple to follow, I am not writing details about them, but, just showing the figures.
4. Lastly the report is also shown.

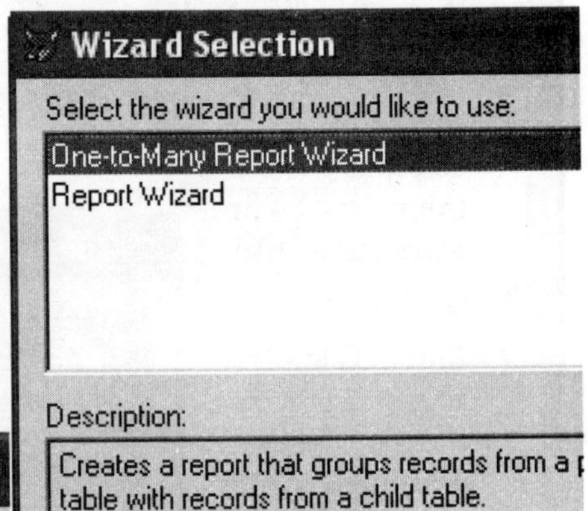

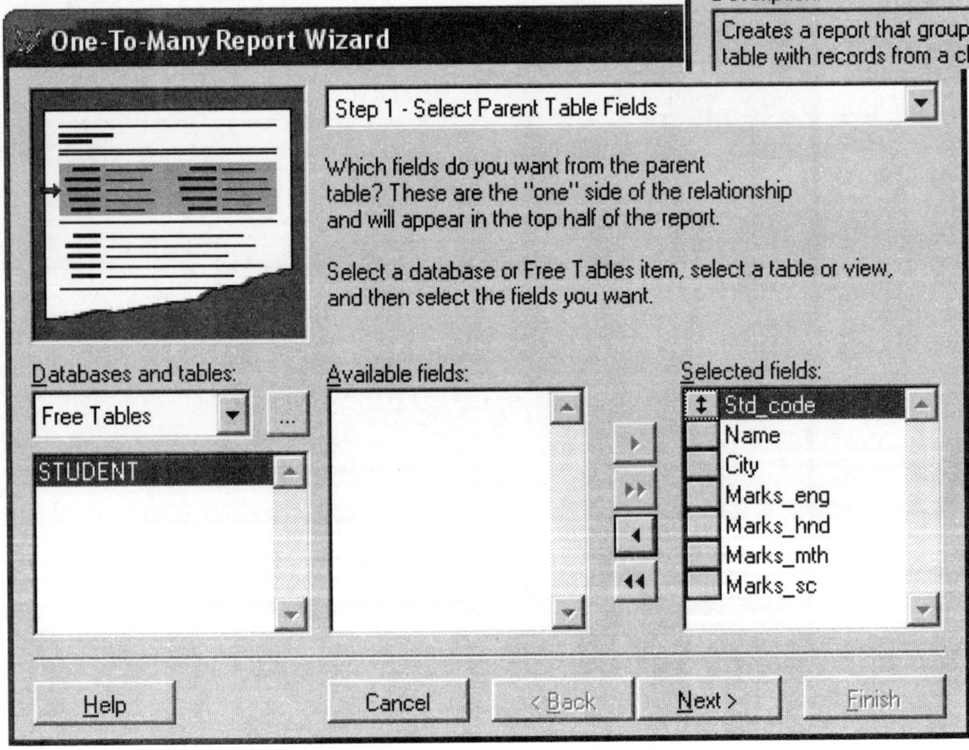

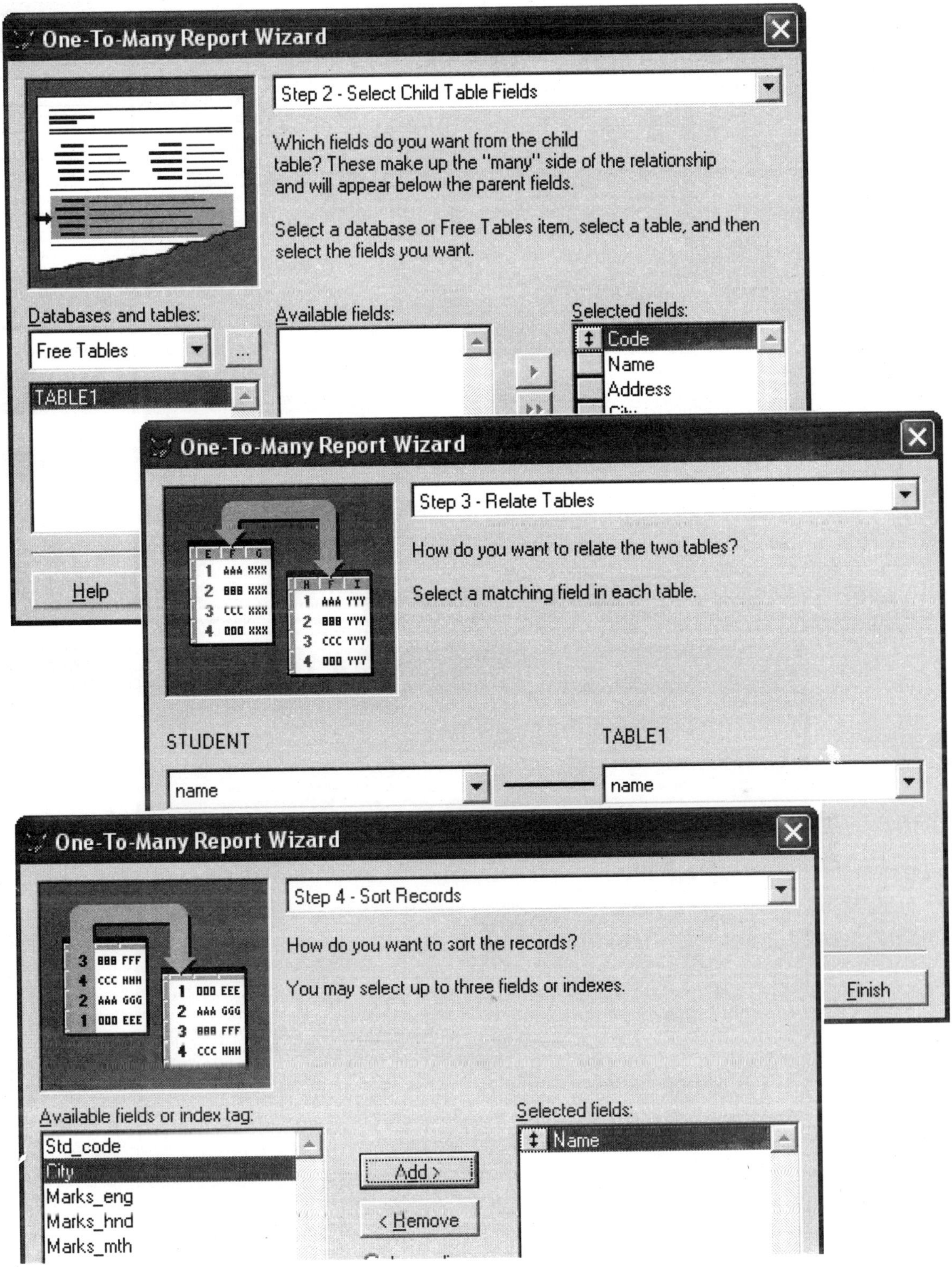
One-To-Many Report Wizard
Step 2 - Select Child Table Fields
Which fields do you want from the child table? These make up the "many" side of the relationship and will appear below the parent fields.
Select a database or Free Tables item, select a table, and then select the fields you want.
Databases and tables:
Free Tables
TABLE1
Available fields:
Selected fields:
Code
Name
Address
Help
One-To-Many Report Wizard
Step 3 - Relate Tables
How do you want to relate the two tables?
Select a matching field in each table.
STUDENT
TABLE1
name
name
Finish
One-To-Many Report Wizard
Step 4 - Sort Records
How do you want to sort the records?
You may select up to three fields or indexes.
Available fields or index tag:
Std_code
City
Marks_eng
Marks_hnd
Marks_mth
Add >
< Remove
Selected fields:
Name

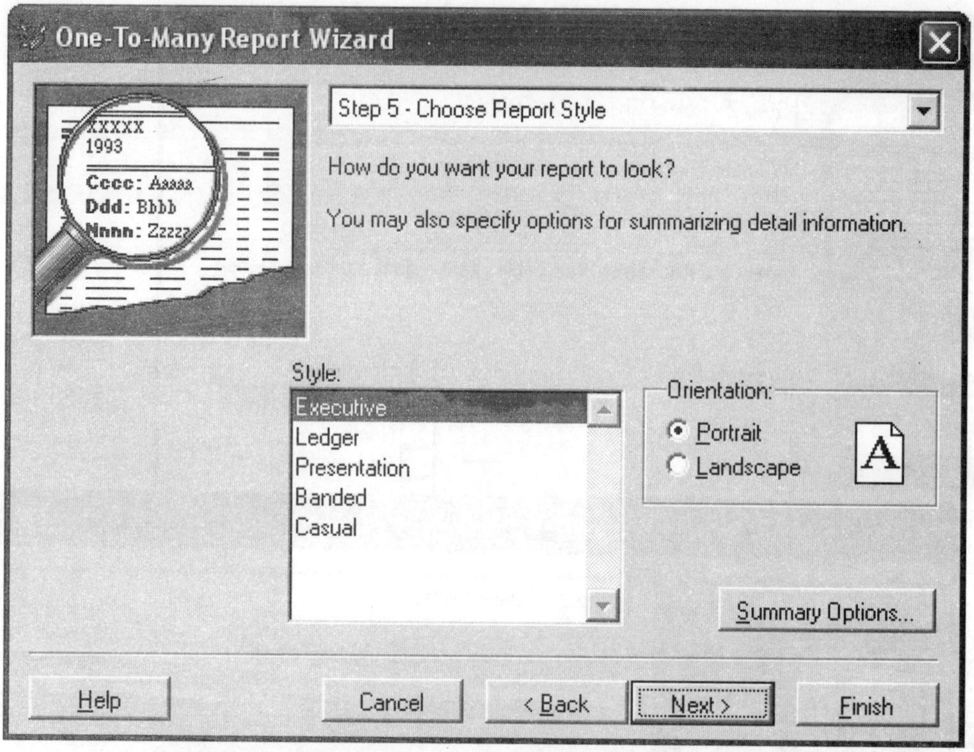
One-To-Many Report Wizard
Step 5 - Choose Report Style
How do you want your report to look?
You may also specify options for summarizing detail information.
Style:
Executive
Ledger
Presentation
Banded
Casual
Orientation:
Portrait
Landscape
Summary Options...
Help
Cancel
< Back
Next >
Finish

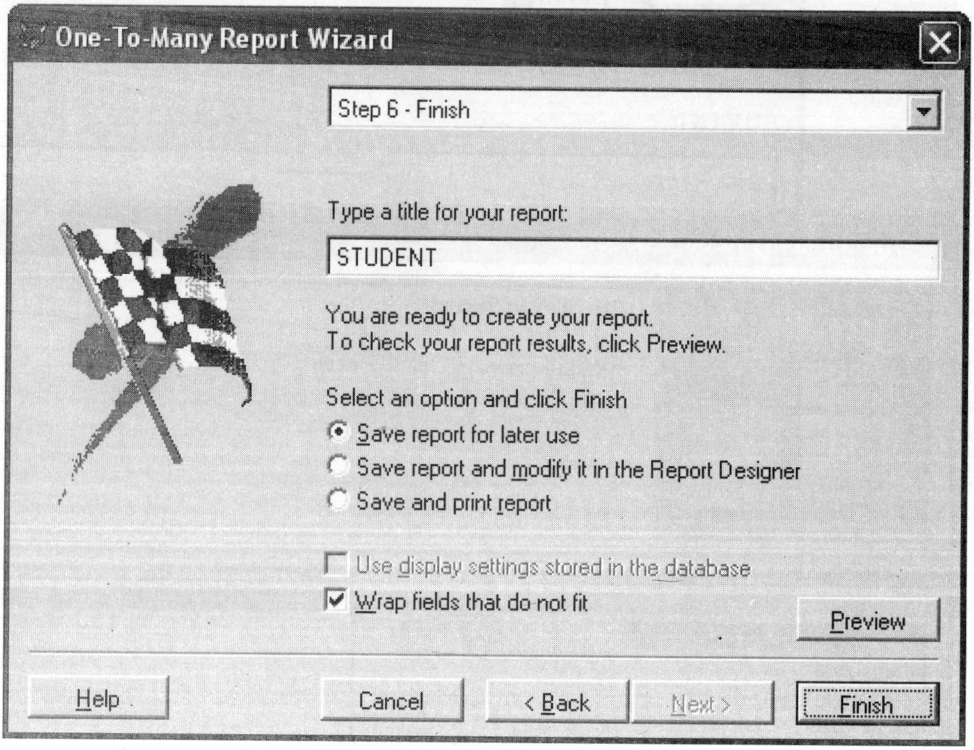
One-To-Many Report Wizard
Step 6 - Finish
Type a title for your report:
STUDENT
You are ready to create your report.
To check your report results, click Preview.
Select an option and click Finish
Save report for later use
Save report and modify it in the Report Designer
Save and print report
Use display settings stored in the database
Wrap fields that do not fit
Preview
Help
Cancel
< Back
Next >
Finish

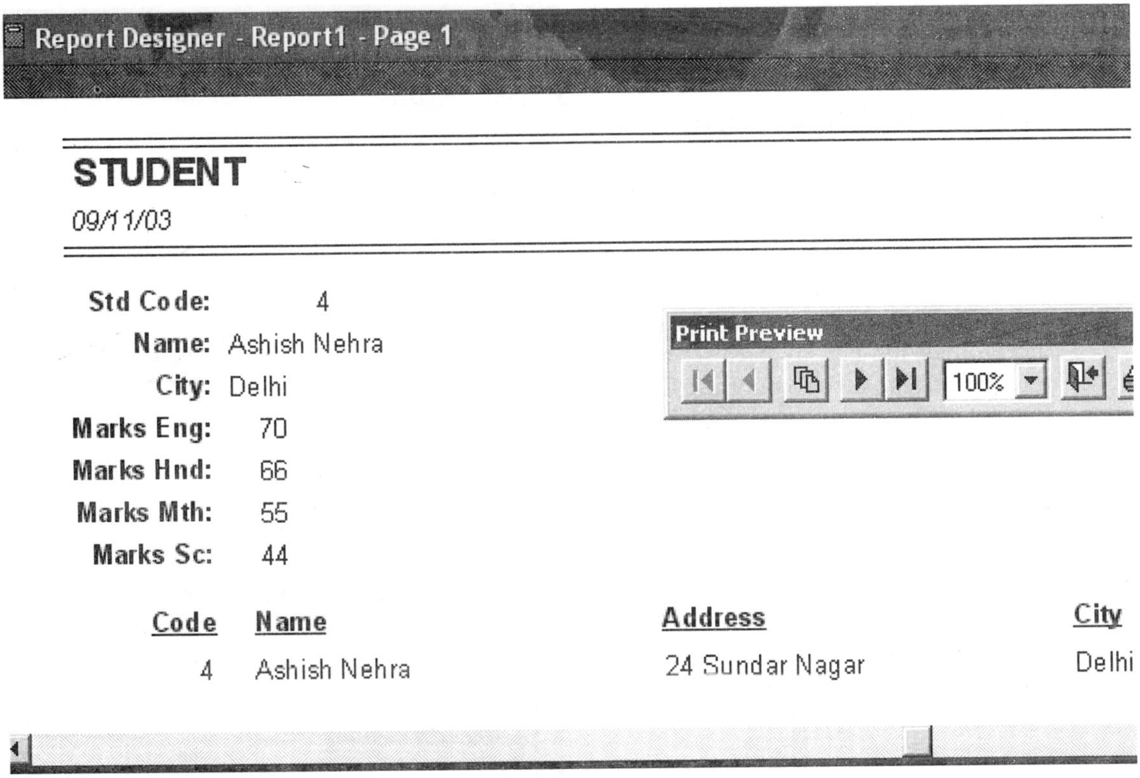

WORKING WITH VIEW WINDOW

This window can be used to open and display tables, to establish temporary relationships and to set work area properties. Let us see how this is done:

1. Click Window menu and choose Data Session. The Data Session window that appears is known as the View window.
2. The Current session: drop down list displays the name of the current data session. The Aliases area displays the view name or table name without the file extension. The Relations area indicates any temporary relationship established between the tables or vies listed in the Aliases box.
3. Click the Open button, to add a table or view to the Aliases list.
4. Click Properties button to see the Work Area Properties dialog box. In this dialog box, you can modify the structure of a table, select index files and fields and define data filters.

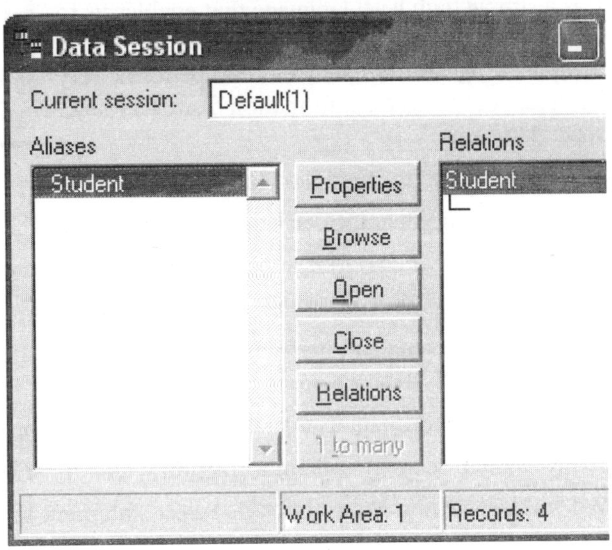

If no tables or views are listed in the Aliases box, an Open dialog box will appear from where you have to open a table or view.

5. Click the Browse button to display the table or view, currently selected, in a Browse window where you can examine, edit and/ or opened data.
6. Click the Relations button to define the relations between tables or views. A Set Index Order dialog box will appear if no index orders has already been set between the two tables. When you click OK, the Expression Builder will appear in which you can set relationship between the tables.
7. Click the One-To-Many button to display the Create One-To-Many Relationships dialog box, where you can establish a one-to-many temporary relationship between child and parent tables. This button gets enabled only when you establish relations between tables by selecting them in the View dialog box and then clicking Relations.
8. Click Close button to remove the selected table or view from the Aliases list.

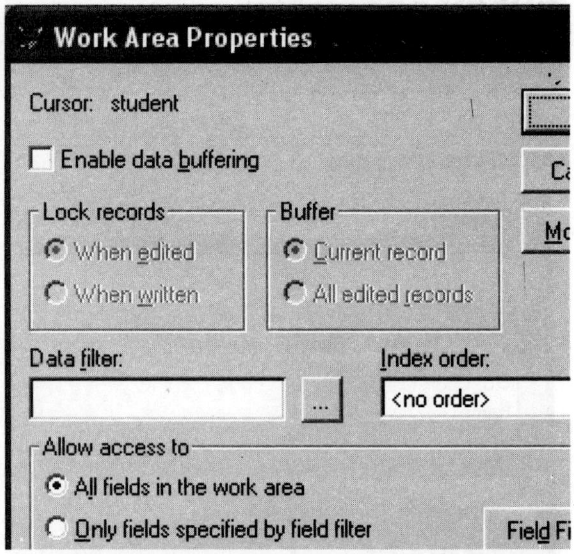

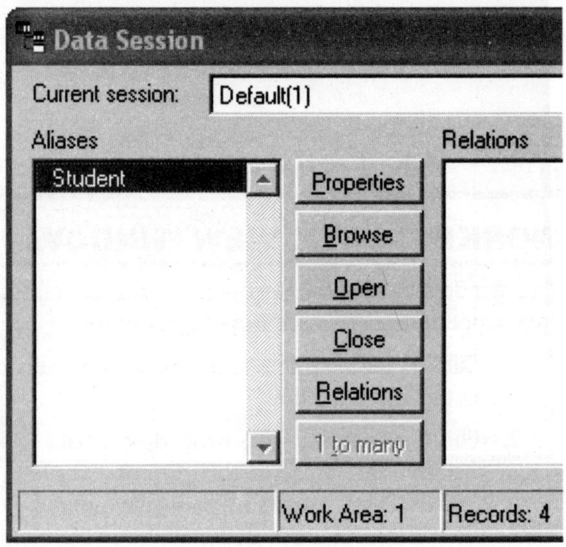

USING QUERIES AND SQL

Let us now read about another programming language called SQL or Structured Query Language. It is a simple high level language that enables us to utilize a database completely and easily. It uses compact, English-like statements and performs very complex jobs to access information from very large sized databases.

SQL can be used for the following purposes:

a. Creating (defining), deleting and modifying table structure.
b. Defining the relationships between two or more tables.
c. Inserting data into tables.
d. Extracting data in meaningful ways, based on the tables' defined relationships, that is accessing or retrieving data.
e. Maintaining data in a database and manipulating the stored values to keep the information current.
f. System security and authorization which must be controlled and maintained.

We will be learning about the SQL Select statement in detail in a later section.

QUERY DESIGNER

You have already worked with the Query Designer in an earlier chapter. In this section, we will learn how to work with multiple tables in Query Designer. The top pane of the Query Designer displays the table in the query. The Query Designer in that figure showed only the "Employee" table. The table is represented by a resizeable window that lists the table's fields. Let us add one more table to the query.

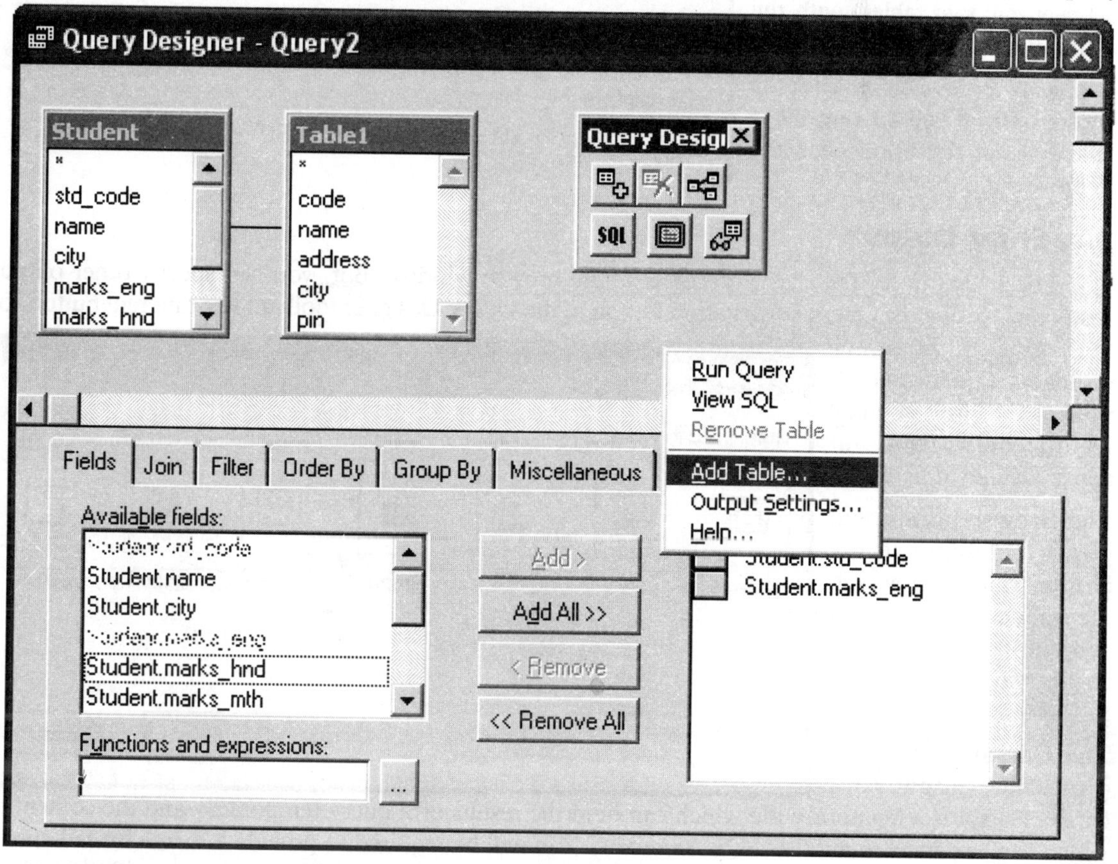

1. Right click the top pane of the designer. Form the menu that appears, select Add Table… In the Add Table or View dialog box that appears, select the table which you want to use and click Add button.
2. A Join Condition dialog box will appear. Select the matching fields from the two tables and specify whether you want Inner, left, Right or Full join. Click OK.
3. You will note that now the top pane of the Query Designer displays two tables. The designer shows join conditions by displaying lines that connect the matching fields between the two tables. You can drag a field from one table to the matching field in the other table to create further join conditions.

The different tab options in the Query Designer window are:

Join

In this tab, you have to specify join type, field name and criteria. For specifying the criteria, you can use

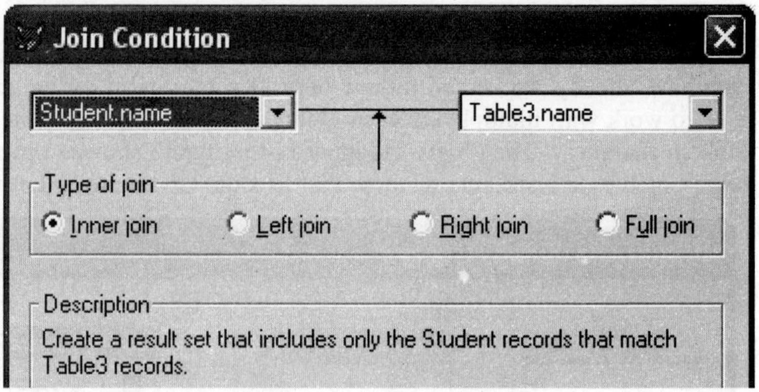

relational operators = (like), == (exactly like), > (more than) and < (less than). These relational operators can be used with the NOT operator to negate the logic. Note, the addition of a new line betwèen the two tables, with the addition of a join condition.

To insert a join condition, click the Insert button and to remove a selected join condition click the Remove button.

Directing Output

The default output for the Query designer is the browse window. But, you can specify other output destinations using the Query Designation button in the Query Designer toolbar (The different buttons of the Query Designer toolbar are identified in figure). The Query Destination window will appear as shown here.

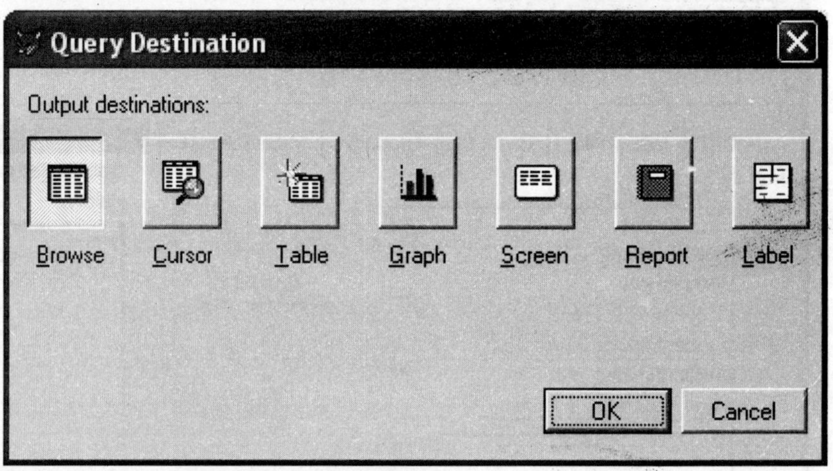

The **Browse** button will direct the output to the browse window. However, the window is read only and one cannot make any changes in the table from the browse window.

The **Cursor** button will direct the output to a cursor. Cursor is a temporary file which can hold the results of a query temporarily and the content of which can be passed to another SQL statement. You will be required to provide a name for the cursor in the Cursor name: text box. You can also choose an existing file by clicking the button with three dots.

The **Table** button will direct the output to a DBF file. You will be required to provide a name for the table in the Table name: text box. You can also choose an existing file by clicking the button with three dots(...). The **Graph** button will connect the output with the Microsoft Graph wizard. It will guide you through the process of creating a rudiment graph. The **Screen** button will connect the output to an input/ edit screen (created in the Forms Designer). The **Report** button will direct the output into a Visual FoxPro report or will create a quick report immediately. The **Label** button will direct the output to a Label Form.

After selecting the output destination, click OK.

Running the Query

To run your query, choose Run Query from the Query menu. This will execute the SQL query you have built and sends the results to the output destination which you have specified. Alternatively, press Ctrl + Q keys to run the query. You can also use the Run button in the standard toolbar to run the query.

SQL Select Command

SQL Select command retrieves data from a table. For example, suppose you want to retrieve all the data stored in student table, then type the following statement, in the command window:

```
SELECT * FROM DEPARTMENT
```

From

It is the keyword in SQL, which must be present in every select query. It is followed by a space and then the name of the table being used as the source of the information. The syntax is:

```
SELECT <COLUMNNAME(S)> FROM <TABLENAME>
```

The Select clause is followed by the column list, and from clause specifies the table from which the columns are to be extracted. To select all the columns in a table, a star (*) is used in place of the column list.

Where

Suppose we want to see only a certain number of rows that contain specific values. For this, we would need to place where clause along with the Select statement. The syntax is:

```
SELECT <COLUMNNAME(S)> FROM <TABLENAME> WHERE <COLUMNNAME> <OPERATOR>
<VALUE>
```

All comparison operators, namely >, <, =, >=, <=, <> (not equals) are supported by SQL. Moreover, SQL also supports Boolean operators NOT, AND and OR. The order of evaluation of different operators can be carried out by using parentheses.

Aggregate Functions

SQL aggregate functions produce a single value for the entire group of table entries. Aggregate or column functions can also be used with the Select command. These functions are sum, avg, max, min and count. These aggregate functions are similar to the Functions and expressions: textbox in the Field tab of Query Designer.

Sum: Sum function calculates the arithmetic sum of all selected values of a given column. For example, to find the Sum of basic salary from the Employee table, we would enter the following query:

```
SELECT SUM(MARKS_ENG) FROM STUDENT
```

The output of the sum of the marks_eng calculated by this command will be shown.

Avg: AVG function calculate the average (mean) of all selected values of a given field. For example, to find the average of marks_eng enter the following query:

```
SELECT AVG (MARKS_ENG) FROM STUDENT
```

Max: Max function calculates the largest of all selected values of a given column. For example, using the student table, the following command displays the maximum marks_eng in the column marks_eng. For this, enter the following query:

```
SELECT MAX (MARKS_ENG) FROM STUDENT
```

Min :MIN function calculates the smallest of all selected values of a given column. For example, using the student table, the following command displays the minimum salary value in the column marks_eng. For this, enter the following query:

```
SELECT MIN (MARKS_ENG) FROM STUDENT
```

Count: This function counts the number of rows in the output table. The function Count with the asterisk (*) counts the number of rows in the resulting table. Count (Distinct) eliminates rows containing duplicate field values before counting them in the output table. For example, to find how many students are there in the student table, type the following query:

```
SELECT COUNT(*) FROM STUDENT
```

Order by

In general, the rows displayed from a query do not have any specific order either ascending or descending. But if you want them to be in ascending or descending order in a particular field, then you can control this order for the selected rows. This is done by adding order by to the Select command. The syntax is as follows:

```
SELECT <COLUMNNAME(S)> FROM <TABLENAME> WHERE <CONDITION)> ORDER BY
<COLUMN TO ORDER> [<ASC/DESC>]
```

Group by

Suppose you want to know the total marks, in each city which are groups in the student table, then the clause GROUP BY will be used. The GROUP BY clause allows you to form groups based on the specific condition. The syntax for using this command is:

```
SELECT <COLOUM>, FUNCTION (<COLUMN>), FUNCTIONS (<COLUMN>) FROM TABLE
GROUP BY <COLUMN>
```

Having

You might not always want or need to see all the sub-groups in a table in a single report. Suppose you want to see the list of only those cities where the total marks are greater than 200. In such a case, you cannot use the aggregate functions, namely SUM, etc., in the WHERE clause. The command for this would be:

```
SELECT CITY, SUM(MARKS_ENG) FROM STUDENT GROUP BY CITY HAVING
SUM(MARKS_ENG + MARKS_HND + MARKS_SC + MARKS_MTH) > 200
```

Extracting Data from Multiple Tables

Using the SQL SELECT command, you can retrieve data from several related tables at the same time. But this is possible only if the tables are related with one other. Join operation is used to combine columns from multiple tables. In a join, tables to be included in the query are specified in the FROM clause, separated by commas. The condition required for specifying the relationship between the tables is given in the WHERE clause. The syntax for SELECT statement where we join two tables is mentioned here:

```
SELECT <COLUMNNAME(S)> FROM <TABLE1>, <TABLE2>, …., <TABLEN> WEHRE
<TABLE1.COLUMN1> = <TABLE2.COLUMN1> AND <TABLE3.COLUMN2> =
<TABLE2.COLUMN4> AND ……. AND <TABLE2.COLUMN3> = TABLEN.COLUMNN>
```

Other SQL Commands

Other than retrieving data, SQL provides commands are used to update the data in a table. This involves commands such as Insert, Update, Delete, etc. SQL can also be used to define security, mechanism or scheme for protecting data in a system from unauthorized access, the commands for such operations are Grant, Revoke, etc.

INSERT INTO command: This command adds (appends) new rows (records) to a table. The syntax of INSERT INTO is

```
INSERT INTO <TABLE NAME> VALUES (<VALUE>, <VALUE>, ....)
```

INSERT INTO can also be used to insert only particular values into a table.

UPDATE command: This command is the SQL verb that changes or modifies data values in a table. The syntax is:

```
UPDATE <TABLENAME> SET <COLUMN NAME = NEW COLUMN VALUE> [WHERE
<CONDITION>]
```

DELETE command: You can remove rows from a table with the command DELETE. This command removes specific rows meeting the condition and not the individual field values.

```
DELETE FROM <TABLENAME> WHERE <CONDITION>
```

GRANT command: SQL is normally used in multiuser environments. The GRANT command is used to permit users access to the database. The syntax for GRANT command is:

```
GRANT <PRIVILEGE_NAME> | ALL ON <OBJECT> TO <USER | PUBLIC> [WITH
GRANT OPTION]
```

Here <privilege_name> specifies the actions such as INSERT, DELETE, UPDATE, SELECT, etc., the user can perform on the <object>. ALL indicates all privileges. <user> specifies the name of the user to whom the privileges have been granted. To grant the privileges to all the users PUBLIC option can be used. <WITH GRANT OPTION> is optional.

REVOKE command: This command is used to cancel database privileges from user(s). The syntax for revoke command is:

```
REVOKE <PRIVILEGE_NAME> | ALL ON <OBJECT> FROM <USER | PUBLIC>
```

Opening a Database

You can open an existing Visual FoxPro database in the same way as you open other files.

1. Click the File menu, and choose Open.
2. In the Open dialog box that appears from the Files of type: drop down list select "Database (*.dbc)".
3. The from the Look in: drop down list, select the folder where the database is located.
4. Your database will get listed in the blank rectangular area. Double click the database.
5. Alternatively, you can also open a database, by entering Open Database <database_name> in the command window.

One can open multiple databases at a time. The names of all the open databases are added to the Database drop down list in the standard toolbar. The currently selected database forms the current active database.

Closing a Database

To close all open databases, type the following command in the command window:

```
CLOSE DATABASES
```

The above command will close all databases and all open tables. There is another command as:

```
CLOSE ALL
```

That will close all open databases, all open tables, form designer, report designer, etc.

Deleting a Database

If you no longer require a database, you can delete it by giving the following command in the command window:

```
DELETE DATABASE <DATABASE_NAME> <DELETE TABLES>
```

All the tables in the database will also get deleted permanently.

Multiple Choice Questions

1. In Relational Database Management System two tables are related upon :
   (a) Primary field (b) Main field
   (c) Secondary field
2. One To Many Form Wizard creates Form using :
   (a) One Table (b) Two Tables
   (c) Two Forms
3. Query in RDBMS can be created using :
   (a) Form (b) Query
   (c) Query Wizard
4. Query can be run from :
   (a) Query menu (b) Form menu
   (c) File menu
5. Function which calculates the average of all selected values of a given field is :
   (a) MAX (b) AVG
   (c) MIN

Descriptive Type Questions

1. What are the advantages of Relational Databases?
2. How are relationships among tables developed?
3. Describe the various type of relationships: One to One, One to Many and Many to Many.
4. How would you create a new relational database using Visual FoxPro?
5. How would you use One-to-Many Report Wizard?
6. How would you run the Query?
7. Describe the following SQL functions: Order By and Group By.

30 Visual FoxPro Utilities

IMPORTING TEXT USING IMPORT WIZARD

Visual FoxPro allows you to import and export data files from various other software into it. To import a file called Progress in a new table, we do the following:

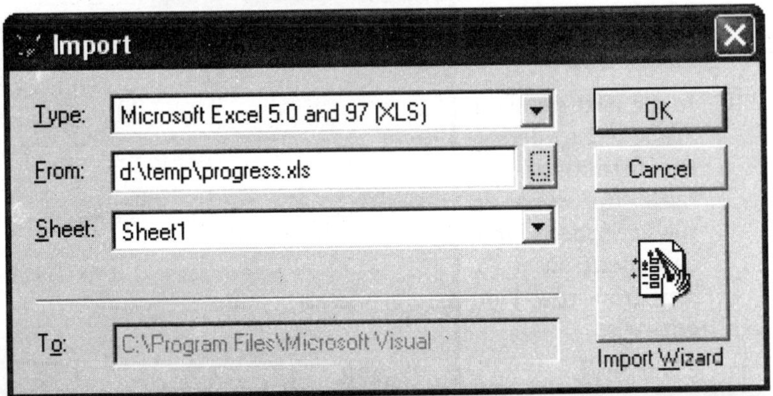

1. Click at Import in the File menu.
2. An import dialog box opens, as shown here.
3. In the Type drop down list, specify the type of file to import. Here I have chosen Microsoft Excel 5.0 and 97(XLS)
4. Click at Import Wizard to start the importing process.
5. In the first step, you have to identify the data. File Type you have already given. You have to locate and tell the system, which file you want to import, i.e., the source file. About the destination, you can have an existing table or create a new table, which would be done for you by the wizard.

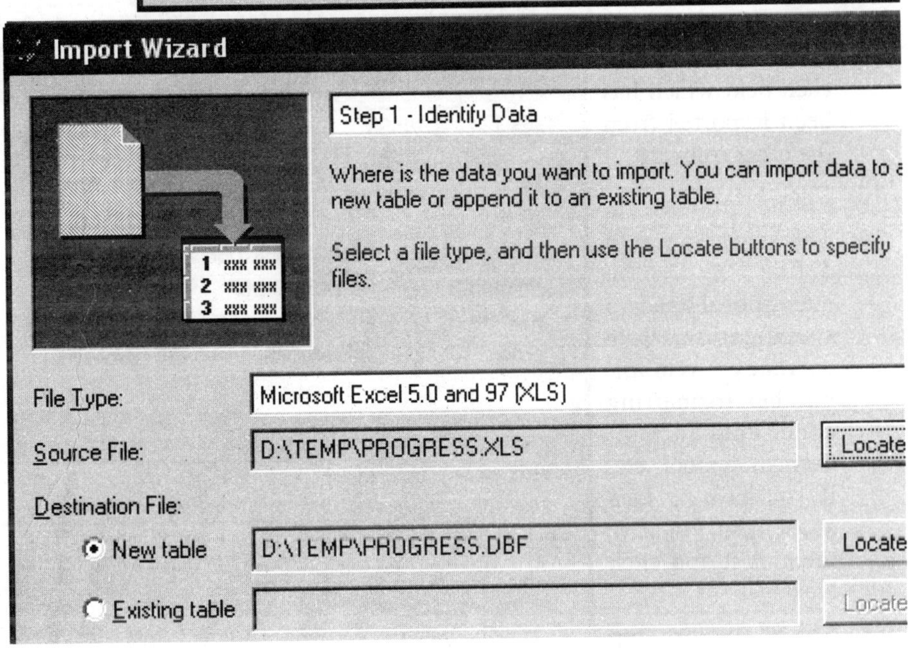

Click Next.

7. Here you can select the database to which you want to add the data.

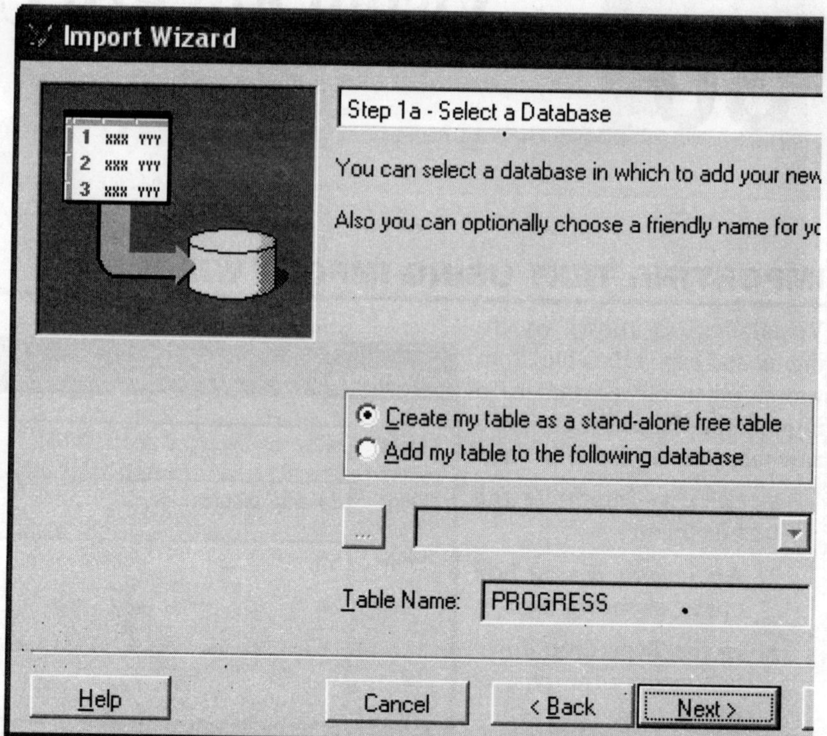

8. If you opt for creating a table as a stand-alone free table, then you would be asked to name it too and save it with a name.
9. Click Next.
10. In the next step you are asked to define the format of the table in terms of rows and sheets. You can mention it to start from row 1 or otherwise.
11. Click Next.
12. Here you can define the width and type of each field which has been imported from the other software.

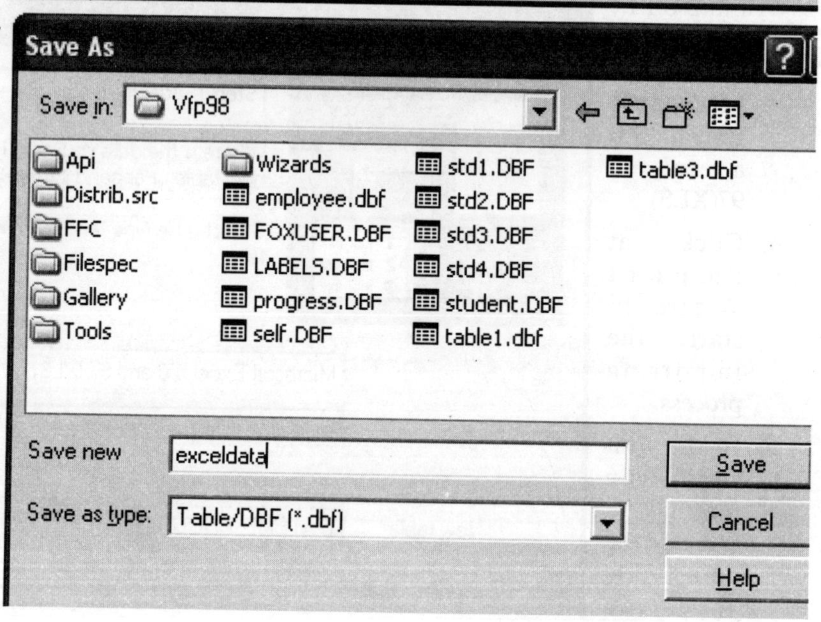

13. Click Next.
14. This step asks you to define the international standard specifications like currency symbol, number formatting code, data format, decimal symbol, etc. If you have no idea about them, just leave them as it and click Next.
15. This is the last step where you have to just click at Finish and the data would start importing.
16. You can see the data in your table by using the Browse command.
17. All the steps and the result in the table are shown on the next pages.

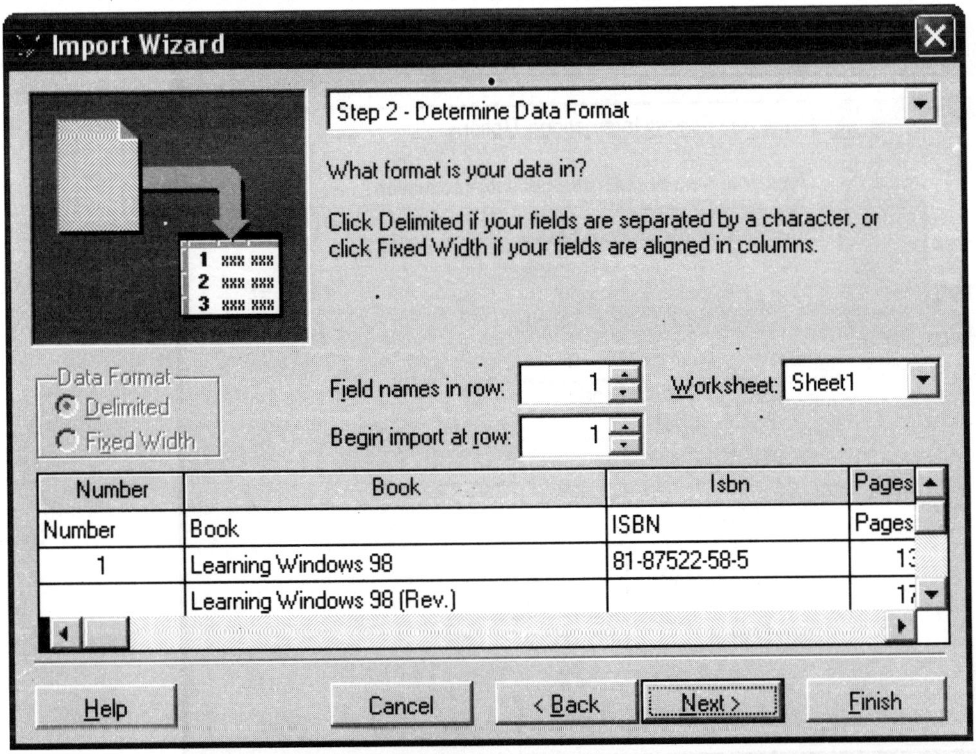
Import Wizard
Step 2 - Determine Data Format
What format is your data in?
Click Delimited if your fields are separated by a character, or click Fixed Width if your fields are aligned in columns.
Data Format
Delimited
Fixed Width
Field names in row: 1
Worksheet: Sheet1
Begin import at row: 1
Number
Book
Isbn
Pages
ISBN
Learning Windows 98
81-87522-58-5
Learning Windows 98 (Rev.)
Help
Cancel
< Back
Next >
Finish

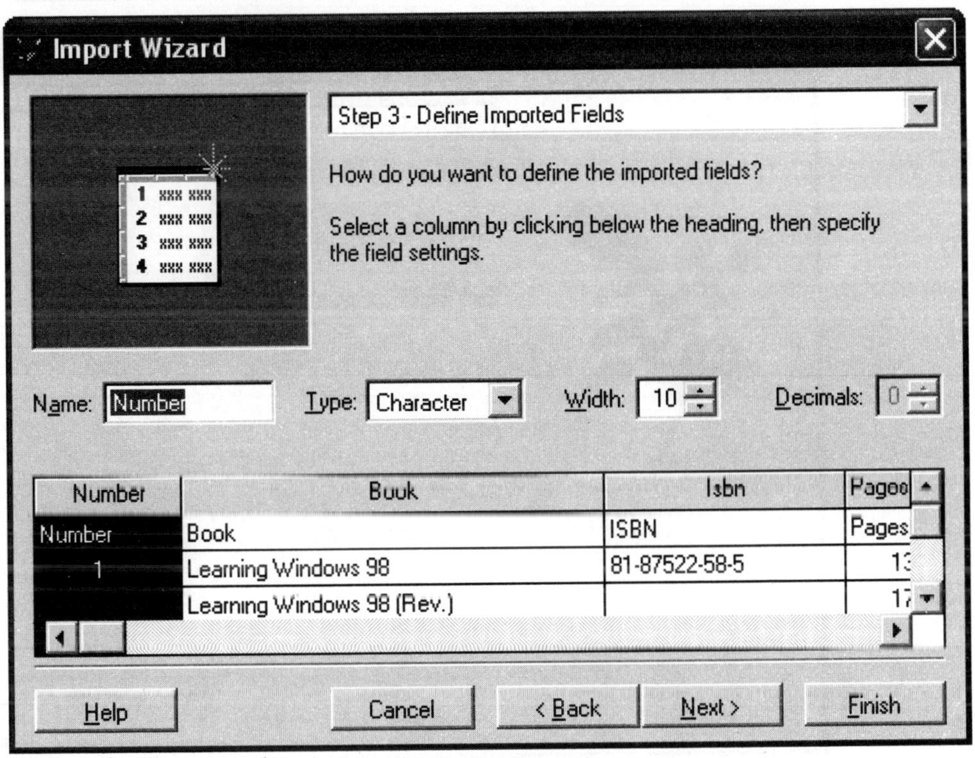
Import Wizard
Step 3 - Define Imported Fields
How do you want to define the imported fields?
Select a column by clicking below the heading, then specify the field settings.
Name: Number
Type: Character
Width: 10
Decimals: 0
Number
Book
Isbn
Pages
ISBN
Learning Windows 98
81-87522-58-5
Learning Windows 98 (Rev.)
Help
Cancel
< Back
Next >
Finish

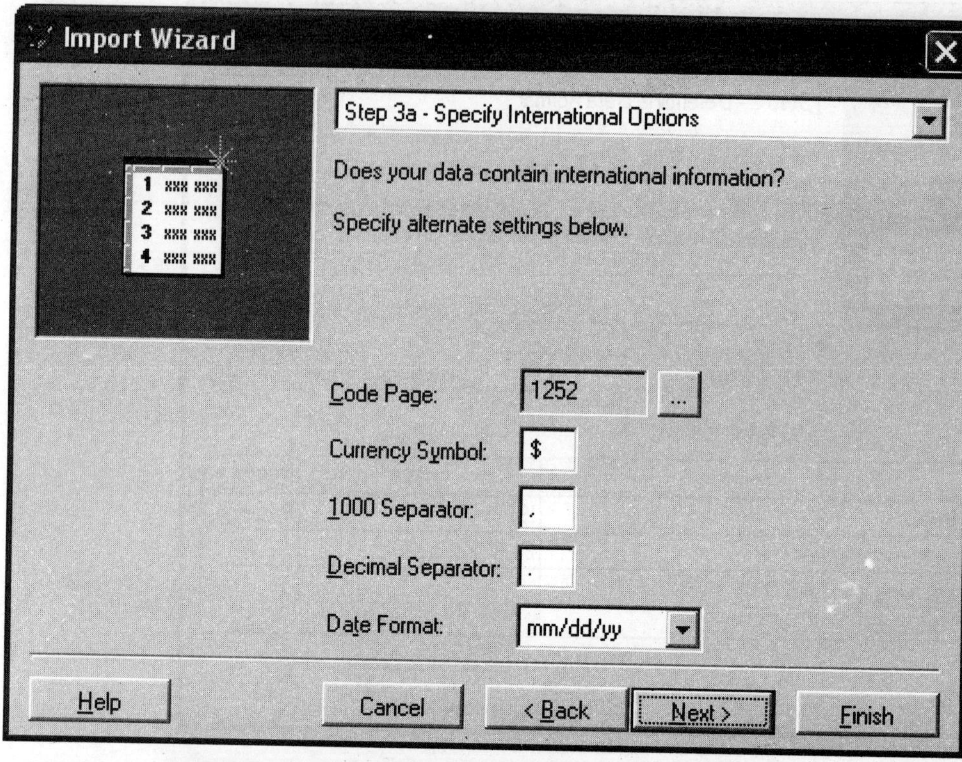
Import Wizard
Step 3a - Specify International Options
Does your data contain international information?
Specify alternate settings below.
Code Page: 1252
Currency Symbol: $
1000 Separator: ,
Decimal Separator: .
Date Format: mm/dd/yy
Help
Cancel
< Back
Next >
Finish

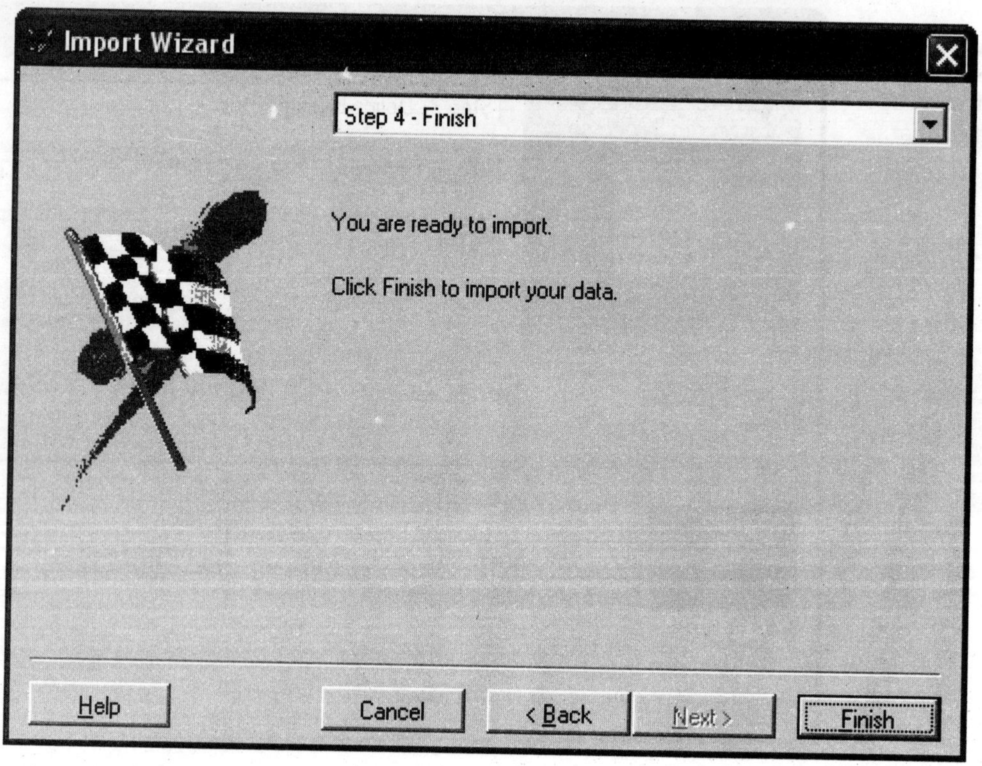
Import Wizard
Step 4 - Finish
You are ready to import.
Click Finish to import your data.
Help
Cancel
< Back
Next >
Finish

Progress

A	B	C	D	E
Number	Book	ISBN	Pages	Delivered on
1	Learning Windows 98	81-87522-58-5	136	1.5.2000
	Learning Windows 98 (Rev.)		176	11.7.2000
2	Learning Word 2000	81-87522-59-3	176	16.5.2000
3	Learning PageMaker 6.5	81-87522-60-7	176	24.5.2000
4	Learning Excel 2000	81-87522-61-5	152	5.6.2000
5	Learning Access 2000	81-87522-64-X	144	26.6.2000
6	Learning CorelDRAW 9	81-87522-62-3	160	12.6.2000
7	Learning PowerPoint 2000	81-87522-63-1	152	19.6.2000
8	Learning Outlook 2000	81-87522-66-6	128	3.7.2000
9	Learning FrontPage 2000	81-87522-65-8	136	10.7.2000
10	Learning MS Office 2000	81-87522-68-2	224	18.7.2000
11	Learning Photoshop 5.5	81-87522-70-4	152	25.7.2000
12	Learning Internet & e-mail	81-87522-73-9	176	16.8.2000
13	Learning Flash 4	81-87522-72-0	136	7.8.2000
14	Learning HTML 4	81-87522-82-8	192	1.11.2000
15	Learning C++	81-87522-81-x	184	20.10.2000
16	Learning DOS 6.0/6.22	81-87522-74-7	168	24.8.2000

Similar to Importing we have the Exporting.

EXPORTING A TABLE

You can export a table to any file format which it defines. Mostly you would be converting the tables to text format for using it in word processors. Let us see how it is done.

1. Click at Export in the File menu.
2. An Export dialog box will be shown you.
3. From the Type drop down list, select the type of text which you want to create. I have selected here the Delimited Text.
4. In To you have to select a file name where the data would go. If not there, you can create a new file and name it too.
5. You can choose a Text delimiter, if you want to. In most of the text for word processing, a comma (,) delimiter is used.

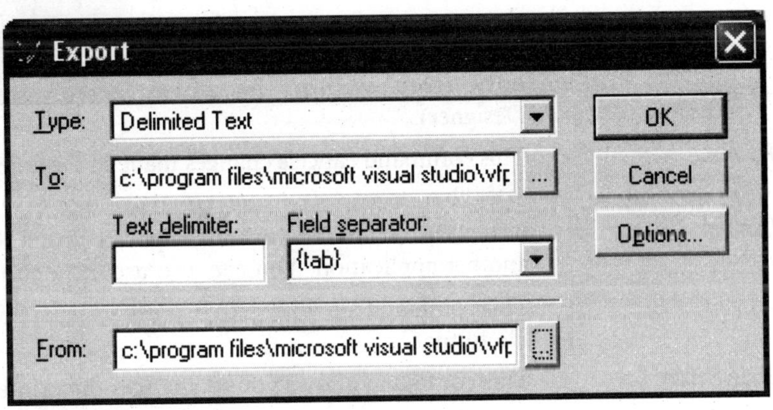

6. Mostly {tab} is used as Field separator.
7. Lastly you have to define the location of the table from where the data is to come.
8. Press Ok to start the process.

Next we study about the various menu commands. So far I don't think we have used more than one-fourth of the commands which are there in Visual FoxPro. To give you a fair idea of the type of commands which are there in the software, I am listing here commands of all menus.

FILE MENU

This menu contains options related to accessing files, etc.

New It opens a dialog box from where you can create new projects, databases, tables, queries, connections, views, remote views, forms, reports, labels, programs, classes, text files, and menus.

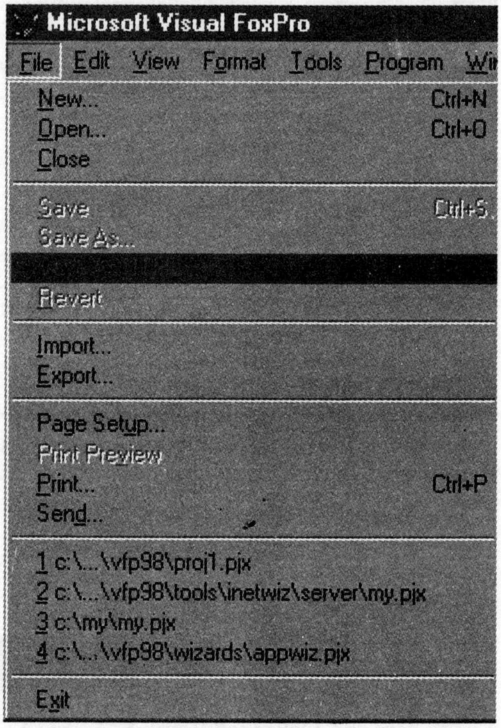

Open It also opens a dialog box, which allows you to open any file type listed above.

Close It closes the active window. If you press Shift and click at this command, then all the active windows will close, making this command as Close All.

Save This command saves the file in the active window with its current name. For a new file that has no name, the option prompts the user to give it a name and then save.

Save As This command allows you to save the current file under a new nâme or overwrite the existing file.

Save As Class This command allows you to save the current form or selected controls as a class definition (active only from within the Form Designer).

Revert This command cancels changes made in the current file during the current editing session.

Import Using this command you can import a Visual FoxPro file or a file formatted by another application. You can also use this option to start the Import Wizard.

Export This command allows you to exports a Visual FoxPro file in another application's file format.

Page Setup This command allows you to changes the printer setting for reports.

Page Preview This command displays pages in a window as they will appear when printed.

Print This command prints the contents of the current window, a file, or Visual FoxPro's Clipboard.

Send This command enables you to send email from the desktop of Visual FoxPro.

<files> It provides quick access to reopen any of the last four opened projects.

Exit It allows you to exits from Visual FoxPro. Choosing this option is the same as typing quit in the Command window.

EDIT MENU

This menu has options for editing programs, forms, and reports, etc.

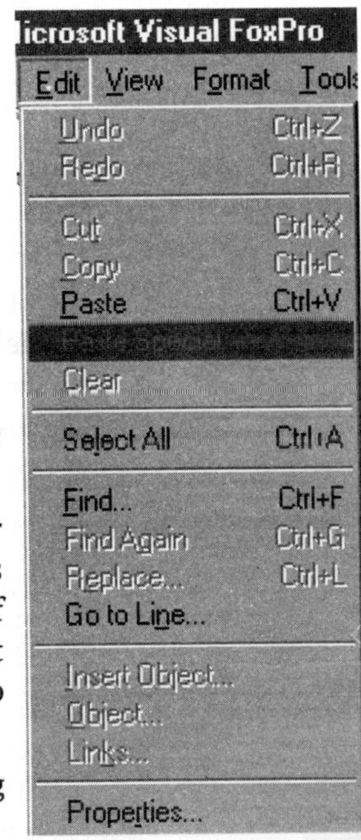

Undo This command allows you to reverse an unlimited number of changes made in the current edit session. Changes made before the last save, even if made during the same session, are not reversible.

Redo You can perform a reversed change again using this command.

Cut This command removes the selected text or object form current document and places it on the Clipboard.

Copy This command makes a copy of the selected text or object and places it on the Clipboard.

Paste This command copies the current contents of the Clipboard to the current insertion point.

Paste Special This command is used to insert OLE objects from other applications into a general files. You can embed objects or merely link them. Visual FoxPro stores a copy of embedded objects in the current object. When an object is linked, FoxPro stores a path and name reference to the original object only.

Clear This command removes selected text without copying it to the Clipboard.

Select All This command selects all objects in the current window. This option is used often in form and report design to move or format all objects at the same time.

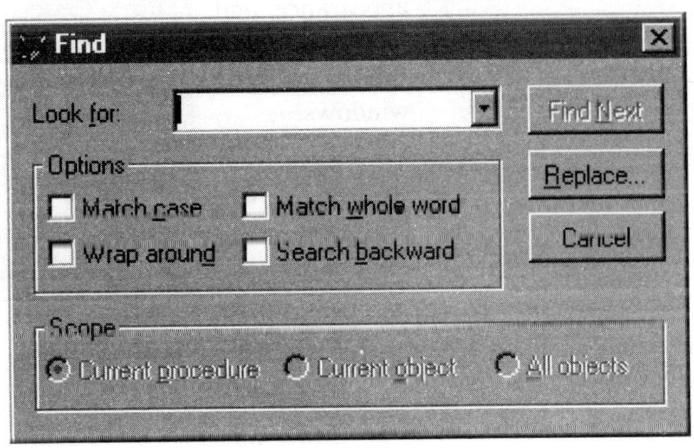

Find This command displays the Find dialog box, which is used to locate text strings in files. Find options include the capability to ignore case, wrap around lines, match entire words, and search forward or backward.

Find Again This command repeats the last Find starting at the current insertion point position rather than the beginning of the document.

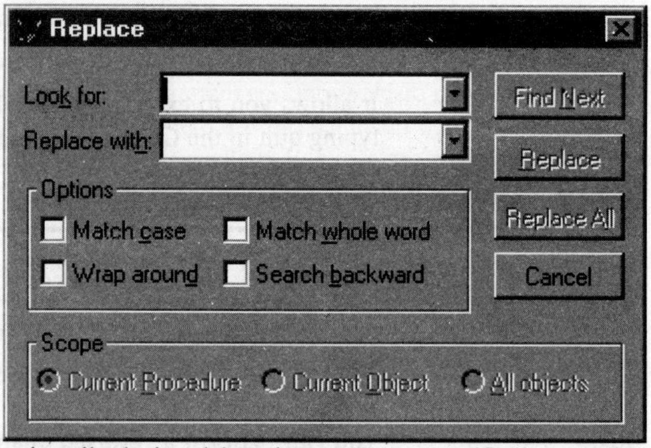

Replace This command displays the Replace dialog box, which is used to locate and replace text strings in files.

Go to Line This command is used primarily during debugging to go to a specific line number in a program file. This option cannot be used when word warp is on.

Insert Objects This command is similar to Paste Special, except that it does not assume that the object already exists and is stored on the Clipboard. The option embeds objects in general type fields. When chosen, Insert Objects opens the other application without exiting Visual FoxPro. After creating the object in the other application, Insert Object returns to Visual FoxPro and inserts the linked or embedded object.

Object This command provides options for editing a selected OLE object.

Links This command opens linked files and enables you to edit the link

Properties This command displays the Edit Properties dialog box, which enables you to affect the behavior, appearance, and save options of the edit windows.

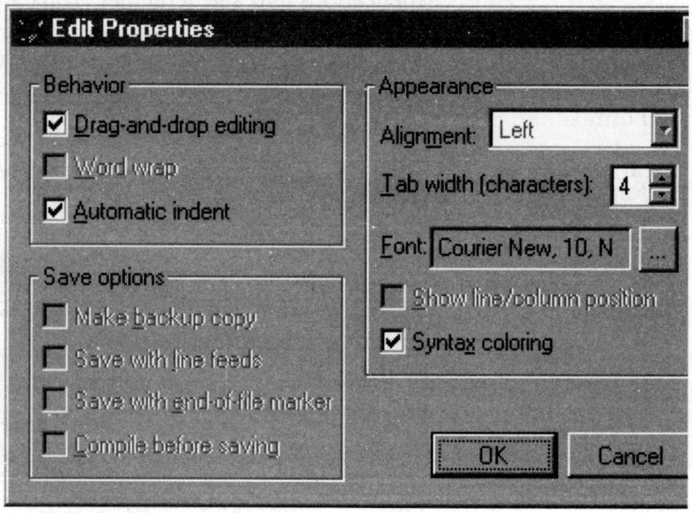

You can also specify the following:

— Alignment of text (usually left for programs)

— Number of spaces in a tab

— Editor font

— Use of syntax coloring (a helpful enhancement)

— Display of the column and row position of the insertion point

VIEW MENU

The view menu displays options that are appropriate for viewing the current table, if one is open. If you are not currently viewing a file, the menu displays a single option (Toolbar) that opens the Toolbar dialog box, which lists the available toolbars used by Visual FoxPro 6.

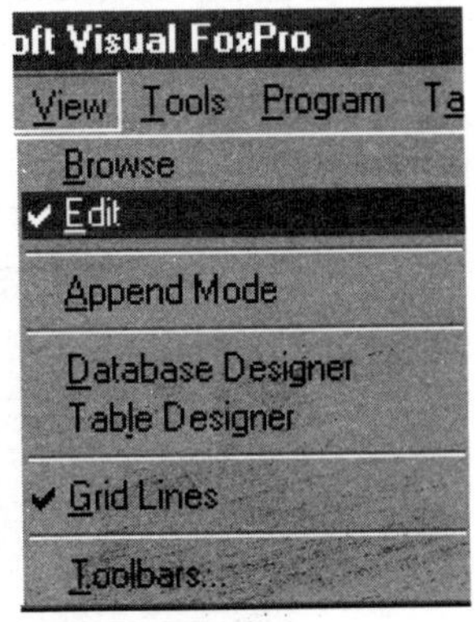

If you are browsing a table or editing a form, menu, or additional options appear as described below:

Edit	This command changes to an Edit layout style for viewing and changing records. The option displays fields vertically, and a horizontal line separates records (if grid lines are active).
Browse	This command changes to a Browse layout style for viewing and changing records. The option displays fields horizontally; rows represent records and columns represent fields.
Append Mode	This command appends a blank record to the end of the table and moves the record pointer to the first field in it.
Design	This command displays the Form, Label, or Report Designer.
Tab Order	This command enables you to set the tab order in forms.
Preview	This command shows a preview of labels or reports onscreen.
Data Environment	This command defines tables and relations used in a form, form set, or report.
Properties	This command displays the Properties dialog box for forms and controls.
Code	This command opens the code windows when you are editing object methods.
Form Controls Toolbar	This command opens the Form Controls toolbar while you are in the Form Designer.
Report Controls Toolbar	To displays the Report Control toolbar, which enables you to add controls to a report, you use this command.
Layout Toolbar	Opens the Layout toolbar, which helps you align controls.
Color Palette Toolbar	Opens the Color Palette toolbar, which enables you to select foreground and background colors for a control.
Report Preview Toolbar	Provides buttons that move between pages of the preview change the zoom factor, print the report, and exit preview mode.
Database Designer	It opens the Database designer, which maintains tables, view, and relationships stored in a database.
Table Designer	It opens the Table Designer, as shown on the next page, which enables you to make structure modifications to associated and free tables and to their indexes.
Grid Lines	This command toggles the display of grid lines on and off.

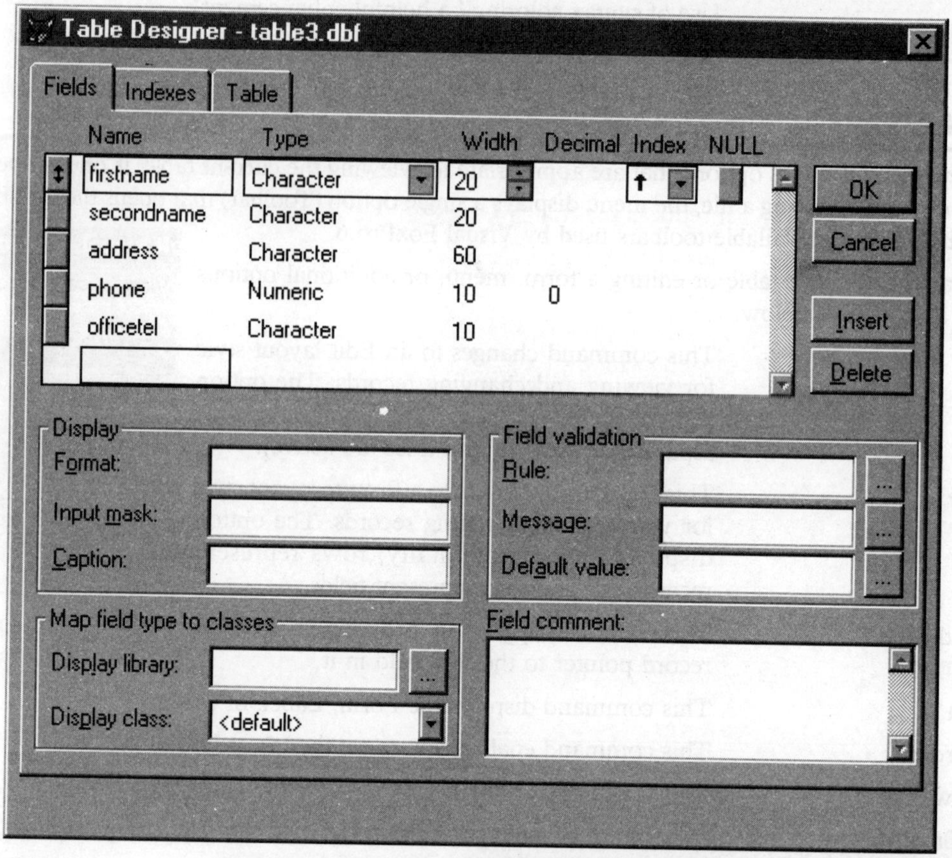

Show Position — This command displays the position, height, and width of the selected object or form in the status bar.

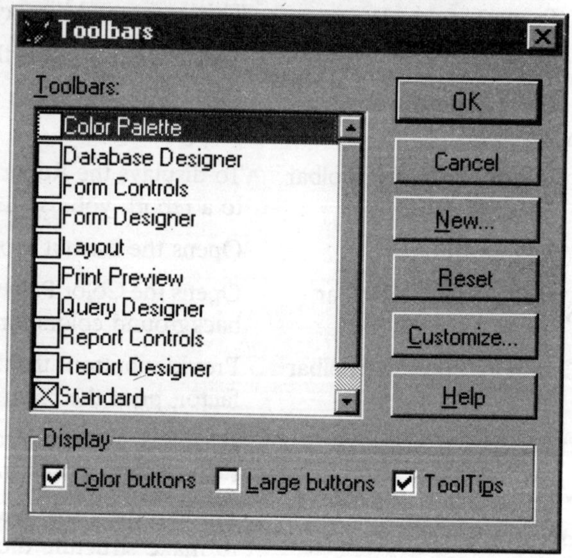

General Options — By using this command you can add code in a menu when you are using the Menu Designer.

Menu Options — This command adds code to specific menu options.

Toolbars — Displays a dialog box, as shown above, that lists every toolbar used by FoxPro, enabling you to customize the buttons in toolbars and to create your own.

FORMAT MENU

This menu normally consists of options that control font characteristics, text indentation, and spacing.

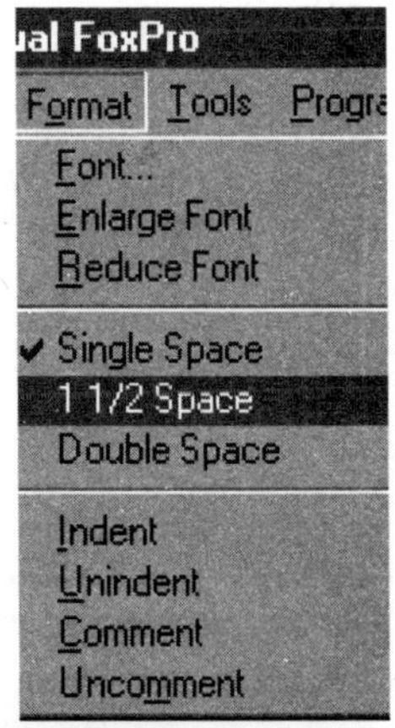

Font	It selects a font and its characteristics.
Enlarge Font	It enlarges the font used in the current window.
Reduce Font	It reduces the font size used in the current window.
Single Space	This command single-spaces the text in the current window.
1½ Space	This command uses 1½-line spacing for the text in the current window.
Double Space	Double-spaces the text in the current window.
Indent	Indents the current or selected lines in the current window.
Unindent	It removes the indent of the current or selected lines in the current window.
Comment	This command comments out selected lines.
Uncomment	It removes comments from the selected lines.
Align	It opens options that align selected objects.
Size	It opens options that size selected objects.
Horizontal Spacing	It provides options that adjust horizontal spacing between selected objects.
Vertical Spacing	It provides options that adjust vertical spacing between selected objects.
Bring to Front	It moves the selected object to the top of the objects in a form.
Sent to Back	It moves the selected object to the back of the objects in a form.
Group	It associates a selected of objects in reports and enables you to work with them as a group.

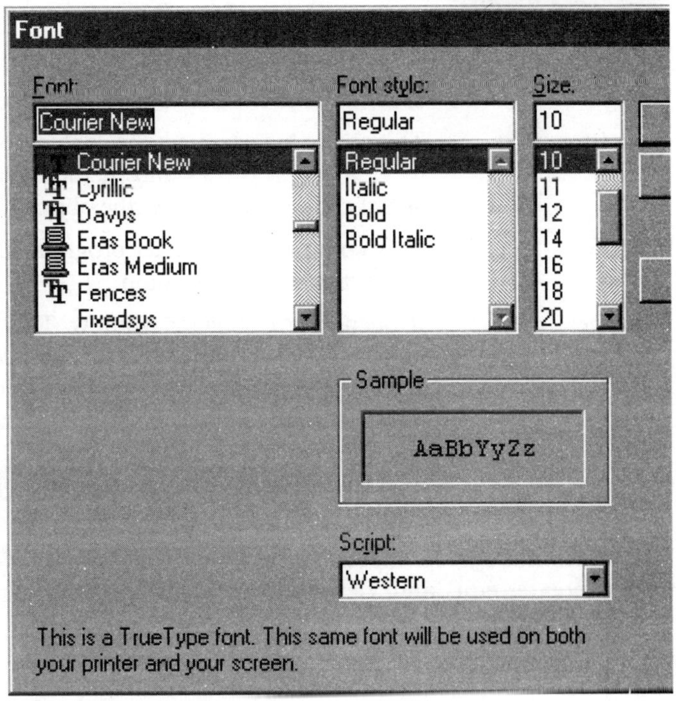

Ungroup
It breaks a group definition into individual objects again.

Snap to Grid
When you are moving objects, repositions and top-left corner to the nearest grid intersection when the mouse button is released.

Set Grid Scale
This command determines how far apart the vertical and horizontal grids are.

Text Alignment
This command aligns text in the selected object.

Fill
This command defines a fill pattern for shapes.

Pen
This command defines a pen thickness and style for shapes.

Mode
This command defines whether the background of an object is opaque or transparent.

TOOL MENU

The Tools menu provides a variety of programmer tools, ranging from wizards to the debugger.

Wizards
As you would see in the next chapter, these wizard are the best to start with the various options of the software.

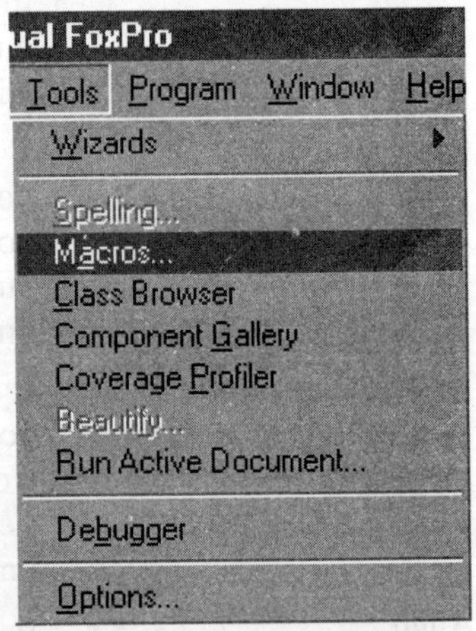

Spelling
It spell-checks text fields and memos.

Macros
It defines and maintains keyboard macros.

Class Browser
This command examines the contents of any class to view its properties and methods or even the actual code used to create the object.

Beautify
This command reformats program files to add indenting and capitalization.

Debugger
It opens the Debugger window. This improved replacement for the Debug and Trace window adds windows for watch variables, locals, call stack, and capability to track events and analyze coverage during testing.

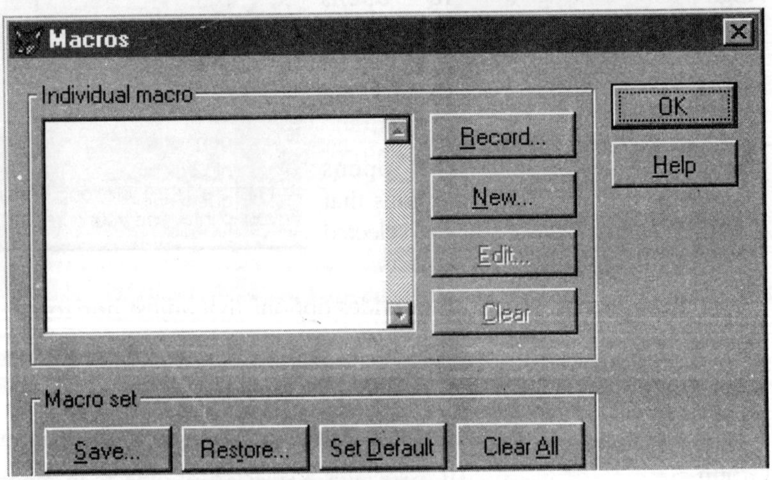

The macro dialog box enables you to create, edit, and view macro definitions. A macro definition consists of a series of Visual FoxPro commands that you can store and execute with a single keystroke. Previously FoxPro provided eight default macro definitions, which are assigned to function keys F2 through F9. Pressing F5, for example, executes the command DISPLAY STRUCTURE, which lists the structure of the current table.

F2	SET	It opens the View window.
F3	LIST	It lists records from the current table; opens the GETFILE window if no table is being used.
F4	DIR	It lists all tables in the current directory.
F5	DISPLAY STRUCTURE	It shows the fields definitions of the current table; opens the STRUCTURE GETFILE window if no database is being used.
F6	DISPLAY STATUS	It shows the table open in each area. If an index is also open. F6 displays its expressing. The key also shows the setting of SET COMMANDS and other system information.
F7	DISPLAY MEMORY	It displays the values stores in all memory variables, including system variables. F7 also shows the definitions of all menus, pads, pop-up lists, and windows.
F8	DISPLAY	It displays the current record; opens the GETFILE window if no table is being used.
F9		It enters append mode for the current table. Opens the GETFILE window if no database is being used.

In addition to these eight macros, you can define your own. In fact, because you can use a variety of key combinations to name macros, you can define more than 250 macros at one time.

PROGRAM MENU

This menu has six options that are related to compiling and running a program.

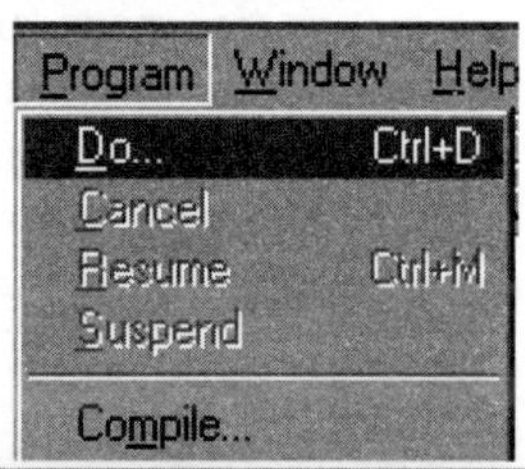

Do	This command runs a program selection from a dialog box.
Cancel	This command cancels the current program.
Resume	This command resumes the current program from a suspended state.
Suspend	It stops the current program form executing but does not remove it from memory.
Compile	This command translates a source file into object code.
Run	This command runs the current program. (The options appears in the menu as DO, followed by the name of the PRG.)

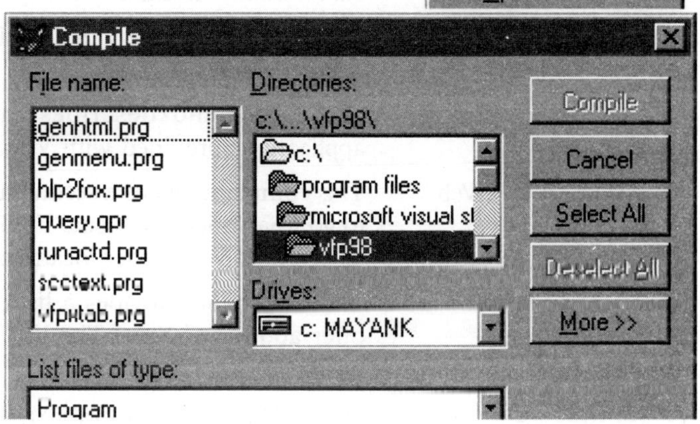

WINDOW MENU

This menu contains options that manage open windows onscreen.

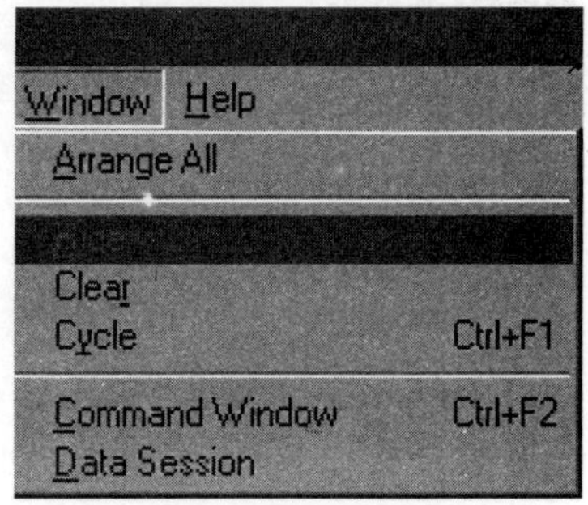

Arrange All — This command arranges open windows as non-overlapping tiles.

Hide — This command hides the active window but does not remove it from memory.

Show All — This command displays all defined windows.

Clear — This command clears text from the application workspace or current output window.

Cycle — This command moves from one open window to the next, making the next window the active one.

Command Window — This command makes the Command window active and brings it to the top, opening it if necessary.

Data Session — This command makes the Data Session window active and brings it to the top, opening it if necessary.

<Window List> — It displays the first nine defined windows. If more than nine windows have been defined, a final option – More Windows – appears. To change focus to any window, simply click its name.

HELP MENU

The first two options on this menu present different ways to access the help file to get information on commands, functions, or features. The third options lists support options that area available from Microsoft. The last option opens the typical copyright screen for the product; it adds additional functionality by providing system information and allowing the user to run other applications from within FoxPro.

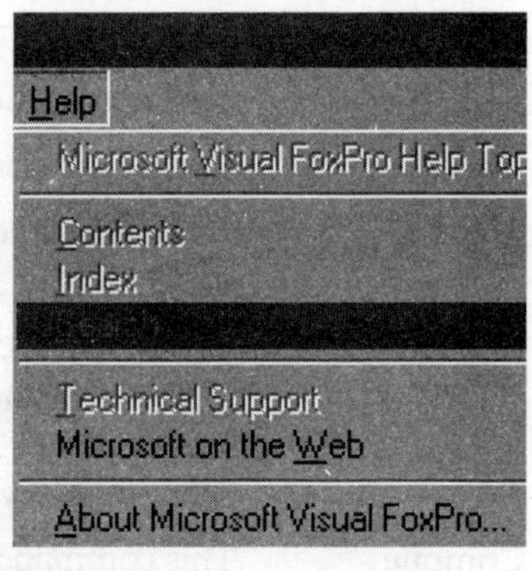

Contents — This command displays help information via an outline format.

Documentation — This command opens the FoxPro online documentation.

Sample Applications — This commend describes the sample applications provided with Visual FoxPro.

Microsoft on the Web — This command opens a second menu with options to use your Web browser to go to a variety of Visual FoxPro pages on the Web, the Microsoft home page, and several other locations.

Technical Support — This command provides a list of available resources from Microsoft that offer additional help. The list includes a section that answers common questions.

About Microsoft Visual FoxPro — This command displays the copyright screen for the product, along with whom it is licensed to, version date, resource filename, default directory, and product ID. Additional features include the capability to list system information and to run other programs.

SPELLING TOOL

It was mentioned briefly while talking about the Tools menu. Let us go into details of it. Using this tool you can spell check the data of your program or of the memo field. Those of you who are familiar with the working of Spell Checker in work processing would find it easier to use since it is very similar. Do the following for spell checking:

1. With the program file or memo field open, click at Spelling in the Tools menu.
2. The spell checking process will start and stop at any wrong spelling.
3. Like in the following case it has stopped at Johars, which I feel is right. But, this is a proper word and is not there in the dictionary of the software, because of which it is given as error.
4. The dialog box shown here has the following options:

Change To	FoxPro usually suggests a word which you can change to. It is the perception of the software, which you may not agree. If you by any chance agree to this, just click at Change. The word would be replaced and the spell checker would move further.
Suggestions	FoxPro would list out a number of similar words out of which you can choose the word which would be the right word according to you. It is not necessary that you would find the correct word here.
Ignore	Like in the case shown here, we know that the word is correct, since it is the name of a person. So you can overrule the system and click at Ignore to accept the word as it is.
Ignore All	Clicking at this would mean that if this word is found again in the remaining text, it would again be ignored.
Change	This button is pressed when you are planning to replace the word.

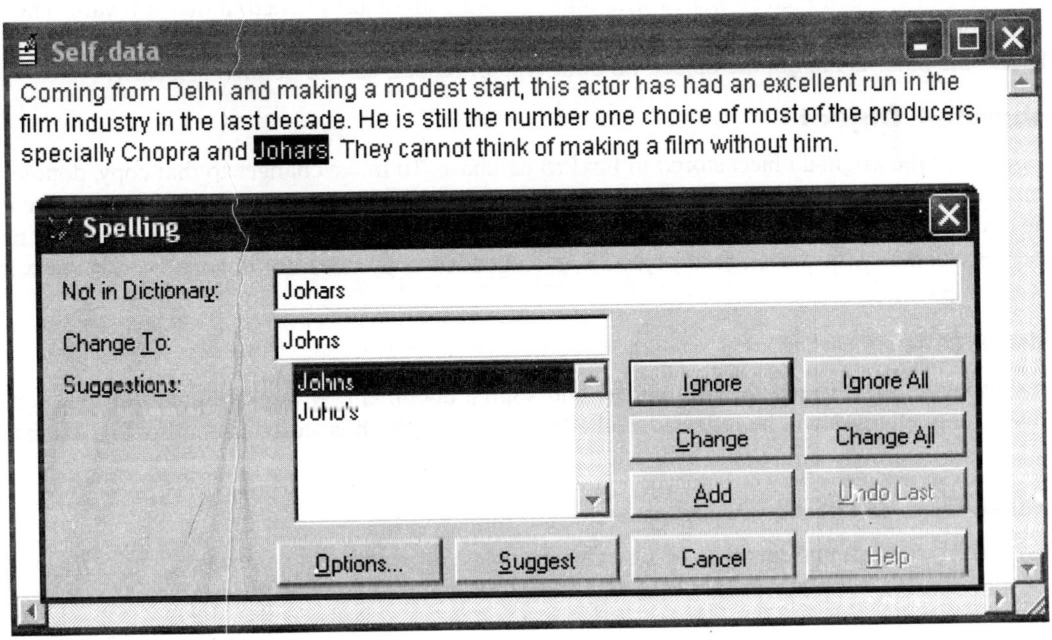

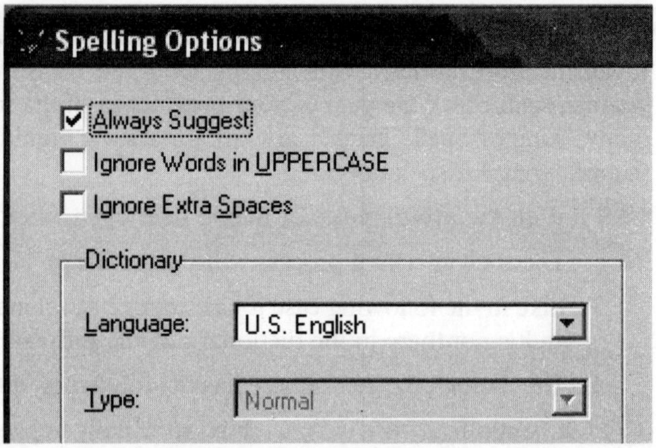

Change All	Pressing this button would mean that all similar words would be changed similarly in the remaining text.
Add	Sometime you feel that you are going to use this particular word many a times and do not want this to be seen as an error everytime. So add this word in the dictionary of the system and the word would be accepted everytime it occurs.
Options	This leads to another dialog box, where you can fix the option for the spell checking. For example, you can opt for always suggesting the other words, Ignoring Extra Spaces, etc. You can also pick up the dictionary to be used.
Suggest	It suggests the word which is similar to the word for your selection.
Cancel	This would stop the spell checking process.

OBJECT EMBEDDING AND LINKING

It is a method by which FoxPro shares with other software an object created in that software. There are two methods by which you can insert an object into a table. One is copying the object and placing it in table and the other is linking the object. So both type of objects can be defined as below:

Embedded Object

It is a copy of the original object stored in FoxPro database. To make changes to that copy, double click the embedded object, FoxPro will launch the source application. However, changes if any, will be made to the embedded copy in FoxPro, and not to the original information. Once the copy is inserted it has no further association with the original object. The embedded copy does not change even if the original object changes

Linked Object

It establishes a link between the destination and source document. If later, original information gets changed, those changes will be reflected in the linked object which is stored in the FoxPro database. A linked object maintains connection between the two documents.

Adding OLE Data to Database

Visual FoxPro support two methods of inserting an object into a field in database.

First method

1. Open the source or its application and copy the object to the clipboard. In this case, I have taken an object of CorelDRAW.
2. Open the database where you want to embed or link the object.
3. Modify the structure of the table to include a field having type as General.
4. Select the record and general field.
5. Open the general field by double clicking on it or by pressing Ctrl + Home.
6. A new window like the memo window comes on screen to accept the picture.
7. From edit menu, click at Paste.
8. Picture would be pasted in the window.
9. Close the window.
10. See how the Gen field is shown having a picture.

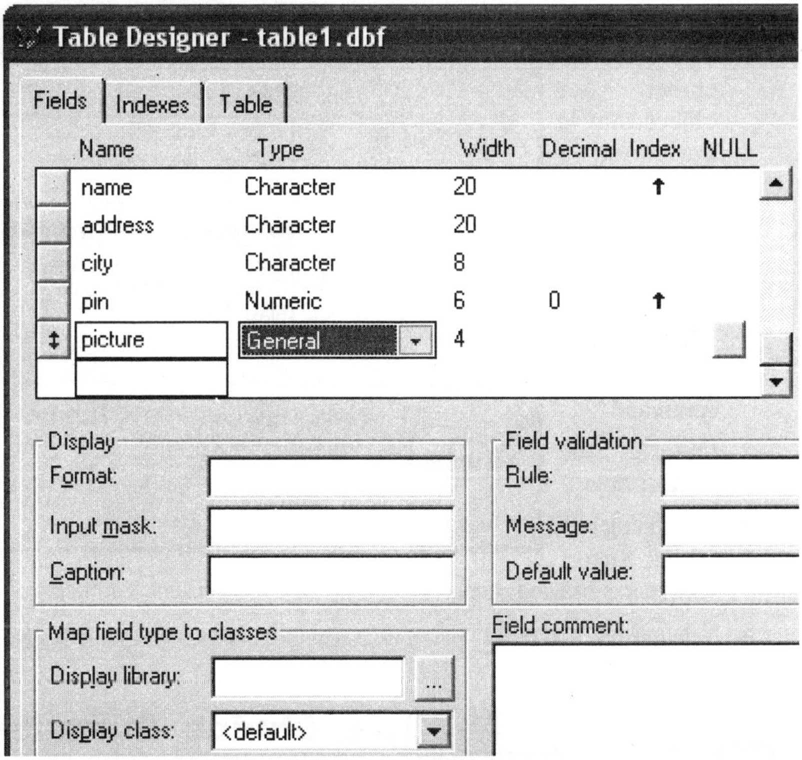

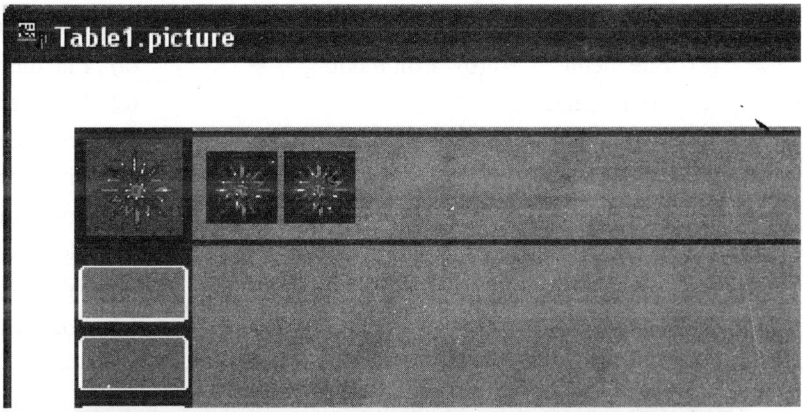

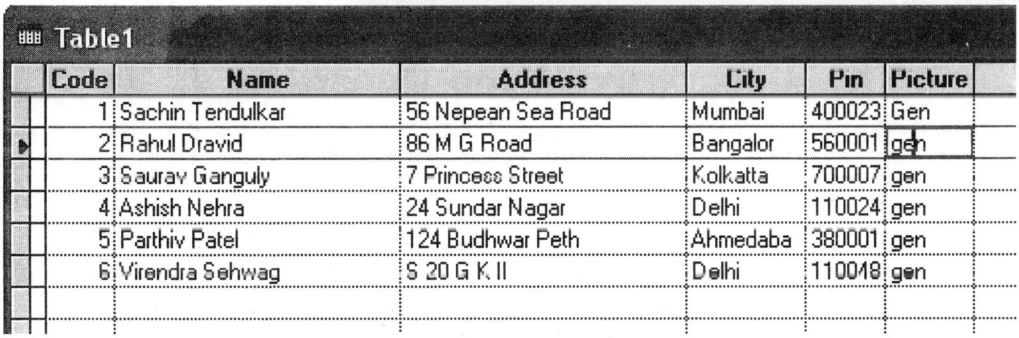

Second Method

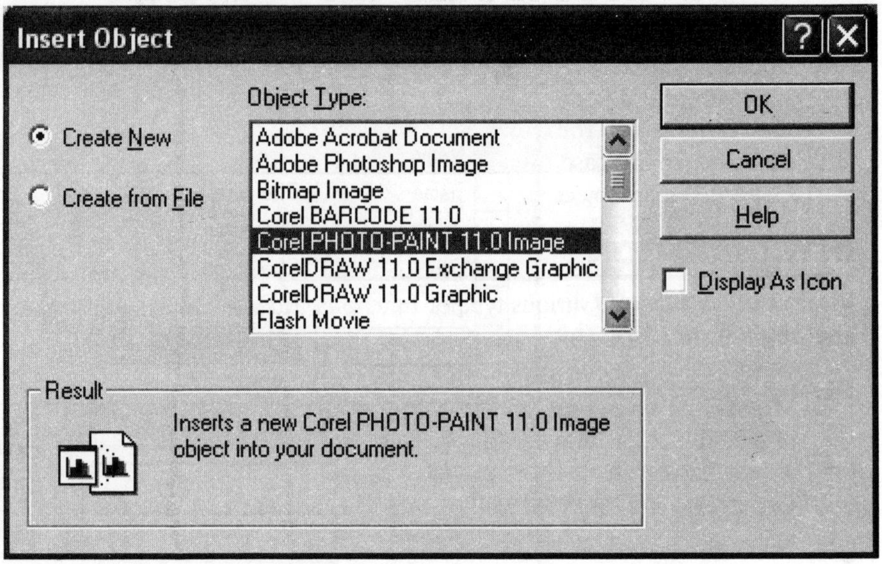

1. You can also embed an object that is not stored in the clipboard, or that has not yet been created, by using the Edit menu and Insert Object command.
2. Open the general field.
3. The dialog box which Insert Object has opened displays a list of all OLE servers. Choose one and create object.
4. When done, exit and FoxPro automatically embeds the entire object file and includes in the general field.

Multiple Choice Questions

1. New file is opened from :
   (a) File menu (b) Edit menu
   (c) Tools menu
2. Using Spell check, you can add a new word to the dictionary :
   (a) Yes (b) No
3. Browse command is available in :
   (a) File menu (b) Edit menu
   (c) View menu
4. Align command is available under :
   (a) Format menu (b) File menu
   (c) Edit menu
5. Replace is part of :
   (a) File menu (b) Edit menu
   (c) Format menu
6. Print command is under :
   (a) File menu (b) Edit menu
   (c) Format menu
7. Double space command is under :
   (a) File menu (b) Edit menu
   (c) Format menu

Descriptive Type Questions

1. Describe the process of importing objects into FoxPro?
2. How would you export a table into other software?
3. What do you understand by Object Linking and Embedding?
4. Write short notes on the commands available under following menus :

File menu	Edit menu
View menu	Format menu
Tool menu	Windows menu
Help menu	

Functions in Visual FoxPro

31

INTRODUCTION

Visual FoxPro supports various type of functions. In this chapter, I list them out alongwith their usages and description.

String Functions

In Visual FoxPro a string is a series of characters and spaces. Using these string functions you can find out the various aspects of these strings. You can even change the form of these strings. Various string functions used in Visual FoxPro are:

$

It returns true (.T.) if a target expression contains a source expression. Its syntax is:

```
SOURCE_EXPRESSION $ TARGET_EXPRESSION
```

For example,

```
? SOURCE_EXPRESSION $ TARGET_EXPRESSION
```

will give the following result if you have "bangia" in source_expression and "ramesh bangia" in target_expression.

```
.T.
```

ACOPY()

This function copies elements from one memory variable array to another location. Its syntax is:

```
ACOPY(SOURCE_ARRAY, TARGET_ARRAY, SOURCE-START, ELEMENTS_TO_COPY,
TARGET_START)
```

ASC()

This function returns the ASCII code equivalent of the leftmost character in a character expression. Its syntax is:

```
ASC(CHARACTER_STRING)
```

For example,

```
? IASC("X")
```

will give the following result,

```
88
```

AT()

This function searches for an occurrence of source_expression in a target_expression. It returns the position where the source expression was found. Its syntax is:

```
AT(SOURCE_EXPRESSION, TARGET_EXPRESSION, NUMBER-OF_OCCURRENCE)
```

For example,

```
? AT(FIND_STR, STRING, 3)
```

will give the following result, if find_str has BBB and string has BBBBBB,

```
3
```

BETWEEN()

This function determiness if an expression lies between two other expressions. It returns a true value (.T.) if the expression is greater than or equal to the lower_limit and less than or equal to the upper_limit. Its syntax is:

```
BETWEEN (SOURCE, LOWER_LIMIT, UPPER_LIMIT)
```

CHR()

This function returns the character whose ASCII code is the same as the value of a numeric expression. Its syntax is:

```
CHR(NUMERIC_EXPRESSION)
```

For example,

```
? CHR(88)
```

will give the following result,

```
X
```

CTOD()

This function converts a character expression to a date expression. Its syntax is:

```
CTOD(CHARACTER_EXPRESSION)
```

DIFFERENCE()

This function returns a relative phonetic difference between two character expressions. Its syntax is:

```
DIFFERENCE(STRING1, STRING2)
```

DTOC()

This function converts a date expression to a character expression. The optional argument returns the date in a form suitable for direct use in INDEXing. This can be particularly useful in combination with the TIME() function to maintain a table in time sequence. Its syntax is:

```
DTOC(DATE_EXPRESSION, 1)
```

For example,

```
? DTOC({09/22/03}, 1)
```

will give the following result,

```
20030922
```

INT()

This function returns the integer portion of a numeric expression. Its syntax is:

```
INT(NUMERIC_EXPRESSION)
```

For example,

```
? INT(-9.4)
```

will give the following result,

```
-9.4
```

ISDIGIT()

This function returns a logical value: true(.T.) if a given character expression begins with a numeric digit; otherwise it returns false (.F.). Its syntax is:

```
ISDIGIT(STRING)
```

For example,

```
? ISDIGIT("65/80 ROHTAK ROAD")
```

will give the following result,

```
.T.
```

ISALPHA()

This function returns true (.T.) if an expression begins with an alpha character. Its syntax is:

```
ISALPHA(EXPRESSION)
```

For example,

```
? ISALPHA("RAMESH")
```

will give the following result,

```
.T.
```

ISLOWER()

This function returns true (.T.) if the first character in a string is a lowercase alpha character. Its syntax is:

```
ISLOWER(STRING)
```

For example,

```
? ISLOWER(RAMESH)
```

will give the following result,

```
.F.
```

ISUPPER()

This function returns true (.T.) if the first character in a string is an uppercase alpha character. Its syntax is:

```
ISUPPER(STRING)
```

For example,

```
? ISUPPER("RAMESH")
```

will give the following result,

```
.T.
```

LEFT()

This function returns a specified number of characters from the left of the string. Its syntax is:

```
LEFT(STRING, NUMBER_OF_CHARACTERS_TO_RETURN)
```

For example,

```
? LEFT("RAMESH BANGIA", 6)
```

will give the following result,

```
RAMESH
```

LEN()

This function returns the length of a character expression. Its syntax is:

```
LEN(CHARACTER_EXPRESSION)
```

For example,

```
? LEN("NAMASTE")
```

will give the following result,

```
7
```

LIKE()

This function compares twwo character expression's pattern and a target expression and returns a true (.T.) or false (.F.). If the target contains the pattern string. Its syntax is:

```
LIKE(PATTERN, TARGET_STRING)
```

For example,

```
? LIKE (PATTERN, TARGET)
```

will give the following result, if target has "Ramesh" and pattern has "Ram".

```
.T.
```

LOWER()

This function returns a specified character expression in lowercase. Its syntax is:

```
LOWER(CHARACTER_EXPRESSION)
```

For example,

```
? LOWER(STRING)
```

will give the following result, if the string has "RAMESH"

```
ramesh
```

LTRIM()

This function returns a character string resulting from removing leading blanks from a character expression.

Its syntax is:

```
LTRIM(CHARACTER_EXPRESSION)
```

For example,

```
? CITY LTRIM(STATE)
```

will give the following result, if city contains "Hyderabad" and state contains AP,

```
HYDERABAD AP
```

PROPER()

This function returns a character expression capitalized as appropriate for proper names. Its syntax is:

```
PROPER(CHARACTER_EXPRESSION)
```

For example,

```
? PROPER(STRING)
```

will give the following result, if the string has "ramesh" in it,

```
Ramesh
```

REPLICATE()

This function returns a character resulting from repeating a character expression to a specified number of times. Its syntax is:

```
REPLICATE(CHARACTER_EXPRESSION, NUMBER_OF_TIMES)
```

For example,

```
? REPLICATE("TEN", 4)
```

will give the following result,

```
TEN TEN TEN TEN
```

RIGHT()

This function returns the rightmost portion of a character string or memory variable. Its syntax is:

```
RIGHT(STRING, NUMBER_OF_CHARACTER_TO_RETURN)
```

For example,

```
? RIGHT("DILIP KUMAR", 5)
```

will give the following result,

```
KUMAR
```

RTRIM()

This function removes trailing blanks from a specified string. Its syntax is:

```
RTRIM(STRING)
```

For example,

```
? RTRIM(STRING)
```

will give the following result, if the string contains, "Delhi   ",

```
DELHI
```

SPACE()

This function returns a character string composed of number of specified blanks. Its syntax is:

```
SPACE(NUMERIC)
```

For example,

```
? STORE SPACE(10) TO BLANK
```

This will store 10 blanks to BLANK.

STR()

This function converts a numeric expression to a character expression. Its syntax is:

```
STR(NUMERIC_EXPRESSION, LENGTH_OF_CHARACTER_STRING, DECIMALS)
```

For example,

```
? STR(789.5678, 8, 3)
```

will give the following result,

```
789.567
```

STRTRAN()

This function returns the given expression with one or more occurrences of an old pattern replaced with a new pattern. Its syntax is:

```
STRTRAN(EXPRESSION, OLD_PATTERN, NEW_PATTERN, NUMBER_OF_REPLACEMENTS,
NUMBER_OF_OCCURRENCES)
```

STUFF()

This function returns a specified number of characters from a given expression. Its syntax is:

```
STUFF(OLD_STRING, LENGTH_OF_CHARACTER, NUMBER_OF_CHARACTERS,
NEW_STRING)
```

For example,

```
? STUFF(OLD_STRING, 7, 0, NEW_STRING)
```

will give the following result, if old_string contains "start end" and "added" is there in new_string.

```
START ADDEDEND
```

SUBSTR()

This function returns a specified number of characters from a given expression. Its syntax is:

```
SUBSTR(EXPRESSION, STARTING_POSITION, NUMBER_OF_CHARACTERS)
```

For example,

```
? SUBSTR(STRING, 1, 5)
```

will give the following result, if string contains Ramesh,

```
RAMES
```

TRANSFORM()

This function allows you to format character strings and numeric variables without the use of the @..SAY command. Its syntax is:

```
TRANSFORM(EXPRESSION,  PICTURE)
```

For example,

```
? TRANSFORM(AMOUNT,'$$$.99')
```

will give the following result, if the amount contains the figure of 99.99

```
99.99
```

TRIM()

This function trims trailing blanks from an expression. TRIM() is identified to the RTRIM() function. Its syntax is:

```
TRIM(CHARACTER_EXPRESSION)
```

For example,

```
? TRIM(CITY)
```

will give the following result, if the city contains, "Mumbai",

```
MUMBAI
```

TYPE()

This function returns character describing the data type of an expression. The values returned include the following:

Value	Description
C	Character string expression
N	Numeric expression
D	Date expression
L	Logical expression
M	Memo expression
U	Undefined type of expression

Its syntax is:

```
TYPE(EXPRESSION)
```

For example,

```
? TYPE("CITY")
```

will give the following result,

```
C
```

For example,

```
? TYPE("NUMBER")
```

will give the following result,

```
N
```

For example,

```
? TYPE("COMPUTER")
```

will give the following result,

```
U
```

For example,

```
? TYPE("DATE()")
```

will give the following result,

```
D
```

UPPER()

This function returns the specified expression in uppercase. Its syntax is:

```
UPPER(STRING)
```

For example,

```
? UPPER("ramesh bangia")
```

will give the following result,

```
RAMESH BANGIA
```

Numeric Functions

These are useful for many mathematical and financial calculations.

ABS()

It returns the absolute value of a numeric expression. Its syntax is:

```
ABS(NUMBER)
```

For example,

```
? ABS(-20)
```

will give the result as

```
20
```

ACOS()

It returns the cosine of a numeric, an angle in radians between 0 and +π (3.141590. The value of the numeric may range between +1 and –1. Its syntax is:

```
ACOS(NUMBER)
```

For example,

```
? ACOS(-1)
```

will give the result as

```
3.14
```

ASIN()

It returns the arc of a numeric value in radians between -π/2 and +π/2. The value of the numeric argument must be between +1 and –1. Its syntax is:

```
ASIN(NUMBER)
```

For example,

```
? ASIN(-20)
```

will give the result as

```
-1.57
```

ATAN()

It returns the arc tangent of a numeric value, an angle in radians between -p/2 and +p/2. The numeric argument can be any value. Its syntax is:

```
ATAN(NUMBER)
```

For example,

```
? ATAN(-1)
```

will give the result as

```
-0.79
```

ATN2()

It returns an arc tangent angle (in radians) for all four quadrants. With the ATN(2) function you specify two arguments, the coordinates, as opposed to specifying the tangent value. The function eliminates errors caused by division by zero. Its syntax is:

```
ATN2(X_COORD, Y_COORD)
```

For example,

```
? ATAN2(1, 0)
```

will give the result as

```
1.57
```

BETWEEN()

The function returns a value of true (.T.) if the first numeric expression is greater than or equal to a second numeric expression and less than or equal to a third numeric expression. Its syntax is:

```
BETWEEN(SOURCE_EXPRESSION, LOWER-LIMIT, UPPER_LIMIT)
```

For example,

```
? BETWEEN(5, 1, 4)
```

will give the result as

```
.F.
```

CEILING()

It returns the nearest integer that is greater than or equal to the numeric argument. It rounds all positive numbers with a decimal portion up to the next highest number and rounds all negative numbers with a decimal portion up to the next number closet to zero. Its syntax is:

```
CEILING (EXPRESSION)
```

For example,

```
? CEILING(10.2)
```

will give the result as

```
11
```

COS()

It returns the cosine of a numeric argument. The result returned by this function ranges between –1 and +1. Its syntax is:

```
COS  (NUMBER)
```

For example,

```
? COS(-1)
```

will give the result as

```
0.54
```

DTOR()

It converts a numeric angle from degrees to radians. You must convert to a decimal angle expressed in degree minute:second format. Its syntax is:

```
DTOR  (NUMERIC_ANGLE)
```

For example,

```
? DTOR(90)
```

will give the result as

```
1.57
```

EXP()

This is the natural exponent (e) operator. Its syntax is:

```
EXP  (NUMBER)
```

For example,

```
? EXP(12)
```

will give the result as

```
162754.79
```

FLOOR()

It returns the nearest integer value that is less than or equal to the numeric argument. This function rounds all positive numbers with a decimal portion down to the next lowest number and rounds all negative numbers with a decimal portion down to the next number farther from zero. Its syntax is:

```
FLOOR(DECIMAL_NUMBER)
```

For example,

```
? FLOOR(10.1)
```

will give the result as

```
10
```

FV()

This is a financial function. It returns the future value of an investiment. You must supply the equal periodic payment, the periodic interest rate, and the number of periods the payments are made. Its syntax is:

```
FV(PAYMENT, INTEREST, PERIOD)
```

For example,

```
? FV(1000, 9.5, 120)
```

will give the result as

```
199080.68
```

INT()

This function evaluates the numeric argument and returns the integer part of the numeric. Its syntax is:

```
INT (DECIMAL_NUMBER)
```

For example,

```
? INT(-1.1)
```

will give the result as

```
1
```

ISDIGIT()

This function returns a true value (.T.) if the first character of a character expression is a digit from 0 to 9. Its syntax is:

```
ISDIGIT (CHARACTER_EXPRESSION)
```

For example,

```
? ISDIGIT(5CHAT)
```

will give the result as

```
.T.
```

LOG()

This is the natural logarithm operator. Its syntax is:

```
LOG (NUMBER)
```

For example,

```
? LOG(10)
```

will give the result as

```
2.30
```

LOG10()

This function returns the common logarithm of the nueric argument. The base for the common logarithm is 10. Its syntax is:

```
LOG10(NUMBER)
```

For example,

```
? LOG10(1)
```

will give the result as

```
0.00
```

MAX()

This function returns the highest value of two numeric expressions. Its syntax is:

```
MAX(NUMERIC_1, NUMERIC_2)
```

For example,

```
? MAX(A, B)
```

will give the following result if A = 11 and B = 15,

```
15
```

MIN()

This function returns the lower value of two numeric expressions. Its syntax is:

```
MIN(NUMERIC_1, NUMERIC_2)
```

For example,

```
? MIN(A, B)
```

will give the following result if A = 11 and B = 15,

```
11
```

MOD()

This function returns the value of the remainder from a division problem. Its syntax is:

```
MOD(NUMBER, DIVISOR)
```

For example,

```
? MOD(25, 5)
```

will give the following result,

```
0
```

PAYMENT()

This function returns the amount of each periodic payment on a loan. You must supply the principal of the loan, the interest rate, and the total number of payments to be made. Its syntax is:

```
PAYMENT (PRINCIPAL, INTEREST, PERIOD)
```

For example,

```
? PAYMENT(PRINCIPAL, INTEREST, PERIOD)
```

will give the following result if Principal = 25000, Interest = 9.5% and for 5 years,

```
525.05
```

PI()

This function returns the numeric constant π(pi). Its syntax is:

```
PI()
```

For example,

```
? PI()
```

will give the following result,

```
3.14
```

PV()

This function returns the present value of an investment. You must supply the equal periodic payment, the periodic interest rate, and the total number of periods the payments are to be made. Its syntax is:

```
PV (PAYMENT, INTEREST, PERIOD)
```

For example,

```
? PV(PRINCIPAL, INTEREST, PERIOD)
```

will give the following result if Principal = 2000, Interest = 9.5% and for 10 years,

```
154562.42
```

RAND()

This function returns aa random number between 0 and 1. Its syntax is:

```
RAND (NUMBER)
```

For example,

```
? RAND (-1)
```

will give the following result,

```
0.55
```

ROUND()

This function rounds a number to a specified number of decimal places. Its syntax is:

```
ROUND(NUMBER, DECIMAL_PLACES)
```

For example,

```
? ROUND(1456.7896, 2)
```

will give the following result,

```
1456.79
```

SIGN()

This function returns a numeric value of 1, –1, or 0 depending on the sign of a numeric expression. If the numeric argument is positive, the function returns 1. If the numeric expression is negative, it returns –1. If the numeric argument is zero, it returns 0. Its syntax is:

```
SIGN(NUMERIC_EXPRESSION)
```

For example,

```
? SIGN(-8)
```

will give the following result,

```
-1
```

SIN()

This function returns the sine of a numeric argument. The value of the argument is an angle measured in radians. The result returned by this function ranges between –1 and 1. Its syntax is:

```
SIN(NUMBER)
```

For example,

```
? SIN(45)
```

will give the following result,

```
0.85
```

SQRT()

This is the square root operator. Its syntax is:

```
SQRT(NUMBER)
```

For example,

```
? SQRT(25)
```

will give the following result,

```
5.00
```

TAN()

This function returns the tangent of a numeric argument. The value of the argument is an angle measured in radians. Its syntax is:

```
TAN(NUMBER)
```

For example,

```
? TAN(45)
```

will give the following result,

```
1.62
```

VAL()

This function returns a numeric value that corresponds to the value of the digits contained in the character string expression. Its syntax is:

```
VAL(CHARACTER_EXPRESSION)
```

For example,

```
? VAL("20G")
```

will give the following result,

```
20.00
```

Logical Functions

In Visual FoxPro you deal with a number of logical functions. They are listed here alongwith their description and example.

BOF()

It finds out whether it is the beginning of the file or not. If it is then a T is returned else F is returned. Its syntax is:

```
BOF(ALIAS)
```

For example,

```
USE TABLE
GOTO TOP
?BOF
```

will give the result as

```
.T.
```

DELETED()

It returns deletion status of one or more records. It returns a logical value such as .T. or .F.. This function supports an optional argument ALIAS which indicates the work area. If you omit the argument, it reutrns the status for the currently selected work area. Its syntax is:

```
DELETED(ALIAS)
```

For example,

```
USE TABLE
DELTE RECORD 2
1 RECORD DELETED
? DELETED
```

will give the result as,

```
.T.
```

EOF()

It is used to determine if the SKIP command moves the record pointer past the last record in a table. If it has, it returns a logical true. The EOF() function supports an optional argument ALIAS which indicates the work area. If you omit the argument, it returns the status for the currently selected work area. Its syntax is:

```
EOF(ALIAS)
```

For example,

```
USE TABLE
GO BOTTOM
? EOF
```

will give the result as,

```
.F.
```

FILE()

It is used to test for the existence of a file. You must explicitly specify any extensions in the filename. Its syntax is:

```
FILE("FILE_NAME")
```

For example,

```
IF  FILE("STUDENT.DBF")
DO  MARKS
```

will run the program marks, if the file is found.

FOUND()

It is used to find a logical true value when it has found the object of the FIND, SEEK, LOCATE, or CONTINUE commands. If it does not find the object, it returns a logical false. The FOUND() function supports an optional argument ALIAS which indicates the work area. If you omit the argement it returns the status for the currently selected work area. Its syntax is:

```
FOUND(ALIAS)
```

For example,

```
USE TABLE
LOCATE FOR CITY = "DELHI"
? FOUND
```

will give the result as,

```
.T.
```

IIF()

It is used in place of an if, else, endif expression. The function checks the logical expression for a logical true or false value. If it is true, it returns the expression. If it is false, it returns the false expression. Its syntax is:

```
IIF(LOGICAL_EXPRESSION,  TRUE_EXPRESSION,  FALSE_EXPRESSION)
```

For example,

```
CHECK = IIF(NUM, A, B)
? CHECK
```

will give the following result if NUM is the numeric expression and A and B contain YES and NO,

```
YES
```

ISALPHA()

If the argument begins with an alphabeticaal character, this function returns a logical true. Its syntax is:

```
ISALPHA(EXPRESSION)
```

For example,

```
? ISALPHA(DETAILS)
```

will give the following result if DETAILS contains TEXT DONE,

```
.T.
```

ISCOLOR()

If you are using a colour display, this function returns a logical true value. Its syntax is:

```
ISCOLOR()
```

ISLOWER()

The function returns a logical true value if the first character in an expression is a lowercase alphabetic character. Its syntax is:

```
ISLOWER(EXPRESSION)
```

For example,

```
? ISLOWER("RAMESH")
```

will give the following result,

```
.F.
```

ISUPPER()

This function returns a logical true value, if the first character in an expression is an uppercase alphabetic basic character. Its syntax is:

```
ISUPPER(EXPRESSION)
```

For example,

```
? ISUPPER("RAMESH")
```

will give the following result,

```
.T.
```

PRINTSTATUS()

This function returns true (.T.) value if the printer or print device is ready to print. It returns false (.F.) if it is not. Its syntax is:

```
PRINTSTATUS()
```

SEEK()

It is used to return the true value if a SEEK was successful. The SEEK() function searches an indexed table for the first occurrence of a record whose index key expression matches a specified expression. If a match is found, it returns a logical true (.T.) value and moves the record pointer to the matching record. If it is not found, it returns a logical false (.F.) value and positions the record pointer at the end of the file. Its syntax is:

```
SEEK(EXPRESSION, ALIAS)
```

Multiple Choice Questions

1. RTRIM() function removes _______ blanks:
   (a) trailing (b) leading
   (c) Workers
2. BETWEEN() function determines if an expression lies between two other :
   (a) strings (b) expressions
   (c) characters
3. ABS() retuns which type of value:
   (a) negative (b) true
   (c) absolute
4. Which type of operator is LOG() ?
   (a) logarithm (b) logic
   (c) logo
5. File() tests for the existence of a :
   (a) Table (b) File
   (c) Document
6. IIF is used for if, else and .
   (a) endif (b) iff
   (c) alsoif

Descriptive Type Questions

1. Describe various type of String functions.
2. Describe Numeric functions.
3. What all Logical functions?

32 Programming and Developing Applications

AN OVERVIEW OF PROGRAMMING

In the earlier chapter we read about the various aspects of programming and the features supported by Visual FoxPro. In this chapter, we will learn more about programming in Visual FoxPro. We know that the programming is based upon commands which are given to the computer to do something. A command file (or program file) created by the programmer in Visual FoxPro contains a group of commands. When required, we can use this file containing group of commands without retyping them. Moreover there are some very powerful control commands such as IF-ELSE-ENDIF, DOWHILE-ENDDO, DO CASE-ENDCASE and FOR-ENDFOR. These can be used in a command file and not in the command window. A command file can be stored on a floppy or hard disk. You record commands in a file because it is more convenient to execute a batch of commands rather than typing every command at the Command window, whenever the program is to be run. Once the commands are saved in a command file, you can execute all such commands as a group.

CREATING COMMAND FILES

For this do the following:

1. Click File menu and choose New... From the New dialog box that appears, choose Program radio button and click on the New file button.
2. A program editor as shown below will appear.
3. Type your program in this editor.
4. After you have entered the commands, invoke File menu and select Save As.. When Visual FoxPro displays the Save As dialog box, type the filename to save the current document.
5. Click save button.

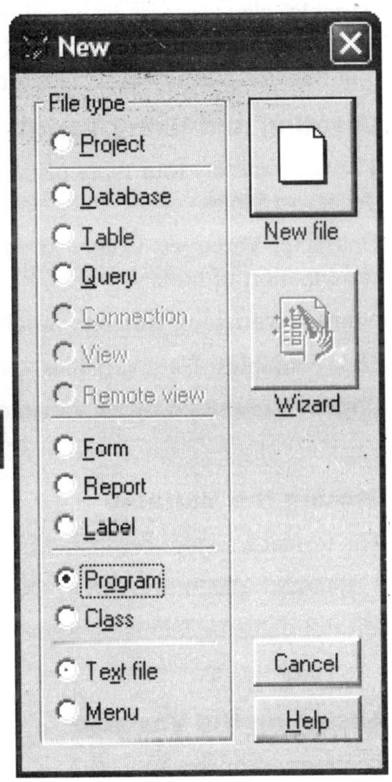

Running the Program

You can run the program by selecting DO from the Program menu and selecting a program from the DO dialog box (which works just like the open dialog box).

If you use the program file without the extension .prg then it is assumed that the program has the extension .prg

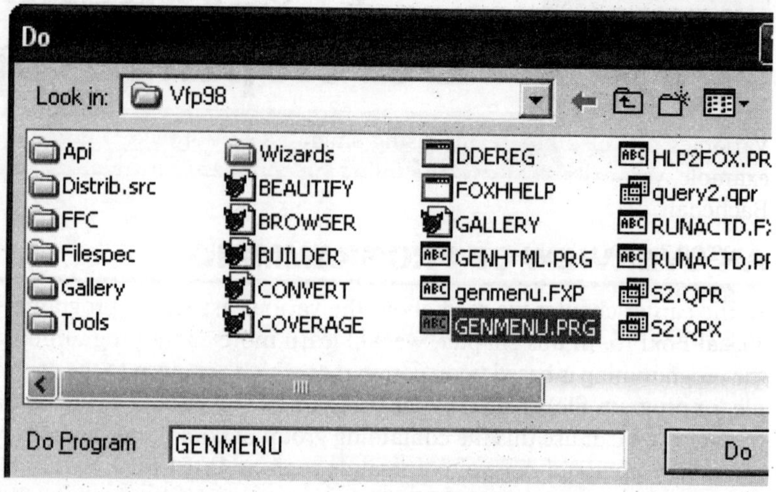

INPUT/OUTPUT

Variables

A variable is a memory location within the computer that is used to store data temporarily. Variables are referred to by their assigned names so that you can refer to the required variable by name and use it in calculations or for some other application. For naming a variable, follow the same rules as are used for naming a field. Variable names must contain only letters, numbers and underscores and must begin with a letter. You cannot use spaces and punctuation marks in variable names. Visual FoxPro is not case sensitive when it comes to variable names. For example WAGE and wage would refer to the same variable.

Variables play very important role in programming by collecting and storing inputs; preserving data from a table record; storing the results of calculations for future use and storing individual items of information that must be globally available throughout an application

Creating and Using Variables

There are mainly four types of variables used in Visual FoxPro. These are character, numeric, data and logical variables.

Character Variables: Character variables store strings of characters, which can be letters, numbers or a combination of both.

Numeric Variables: Numeric variables are used to store numeric values such as whole or decimal numbers.

Data Variables: Data variables store data values written in MM/DD/YY format as (03/25/97).

Logical Variables: Logical variables contain a logical value of T (true) or (false) or Y (yes) or N (no).

Variables can be created in one of the following two ways:

Storing the Variable

The format for store command is;

```
STORE <EXPRESSION> TO <VARIABLE_NAME>
```

For example, the following Store command assigns a numeric value 0 to the variable ZERO:

```
STORE 0 TO ZERO
```

Assigning the Variable

The format for this is:

```
VARIABLE = EXPRESSION
```

For example, the following statement assigns a numeric value 0 to the variable ZERO:

```
ZERO = 0
```

Variables can also be created using single (') or double (") quotation marks or square brackets. For example, you can use any of the following commands to create a variable Mname and store "Amitabh Bachchan" in it

```
STORE 'AMITABH BACHCHAN' TO MNAME
STORE "AMITABH BACHCHAN" TO MNAME
STORE [AMITABH BACHCHAN] TO MNAME
```

The same can be accomplished using the statement like following:

```
MNAME = "AMITABH BACHCHAN"
MNAME = 'AMITABH BACHCHAN'
MNAME = [AMITABH BACHCHAN]
```

A logical variable contains a single true or false value and it can be created with the .T. (TRUE) or the .F. (FALSE) symbol. The following command would assign a logical value True to the variable Test:

```
STORE .T. TO TEST
```

Or

```
TEST = .T.
```

You can store date to variables in Visual FoxPro using various methods. For example, it can be done by surrounding the date value with curly braces as given below:

```
STORE {09/19/03} TO B_DAY
```

Or

```
B_DAY={09/19/03}
```

This would store 01/19/03 in a date variable named B_Day.

Creating Array Variables

You must have read about arrays at various stage of your reading. It is a storage option of storing variables. There are rows and columns in it for storing data. There are one-dimensionald and two-dimensioal arrays. Visual FoxPro lets you create a special type of memory variable. Each items in an array is called an element and the total number of elements is always equal to the number of rows multiplied by the number of columns.

To create an array variable in Visual FoxPro, we use Declare or Dimension statement. The syntax for this is:

```
DECLARE ARRAY NAME [NUMBER OF ROWS[, NUMBER OF COLUMNS]]
```

Or

```
DIMENSION ARRAY NAME [NUMBER OF ROWS[, NUMBER OF COLUMNS]]
```

Number of columns is optional, i.e. you may or may not specify them. If you specify the number of columns you are creating a two-dimensional array and if you specify only the number of rows and not the number of columns, you are creating a one-dimensional array. You can identify elements in the array by the use of subscripts. Note that the subscript in an array always start with 1. To declare an array, we must specify two things: its name and its size. We need not specify the type of data it will hold, as each element can contain a different datatype. For example, you could declare a one-dimensional array containing 31 elements and named MONTH as shown below;

```
DECLARE MONTH[30]
```

Or

```
DECLARE MONTH[30]
```

Or

```
DIMENSION MONTH[30]
```

In the above declaration, 30 refers to the size of the array, i.e., the MONTH memory variable array will have the elements – month(1), month(2), month(3)….. month(30). After you create an array variable, Visual FoxPro makes all its elements as logical variable and stores .F. in them. You can use command:

```
DISPLAY MEMORY LIKE MONTH
```

To enter data in memory variable make use of the command Store. For example:

```
STORE 12 TO MONTH(1)
```

The above example stores a value of 12 in the month(1). You can also store any data such as character, logical, data etc. in any element of the declared array.

Storing Two Dimensional Variable

Visual FoxPro also lets you create two-dimensional array. For example:

```
DIMENSION TEST(3,2)
```

The above statement creates an array memory variable called TEST with the dimension command and you can store values to the array elements with the store or assignment statements. For example:

```
STORE 33 TO TEST(1,1)

STORE "RESULT" TO TEST(2,2)

STORE .F. TO TEST(3,1)
```

Now to view the contents of array variable speed type the following command in the Command window:

```
DISPLAY MEMORY LIKE TEST
```

And press Enter key, you will see the screen as shown in figure.

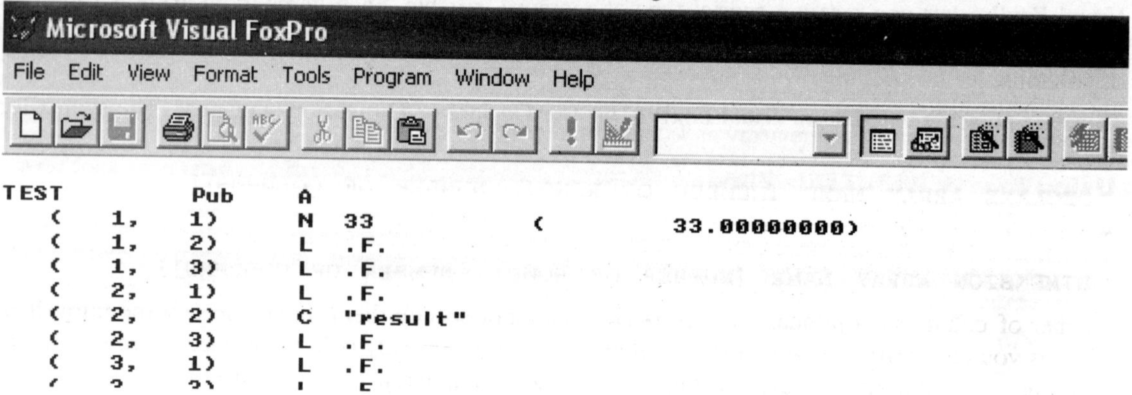

Visual FoxPro allows you to change the size and dimensions of an array. You do this by using the command Dimension in the program. When you need to increase or decrease the number of elements in the array you created, you can increase the size of one-dimensional array or change it to two dimensional array or reduce the size of a two-dimensional array to one dimension. For example:

```
DIMENSION A(3)
STORE 'X' TO A(1)
STORE 'Y' TO A(2)
STORE 'Z' TO A(3)
DISPLAY MEMORY LIKE A
```

This would give you the following result.

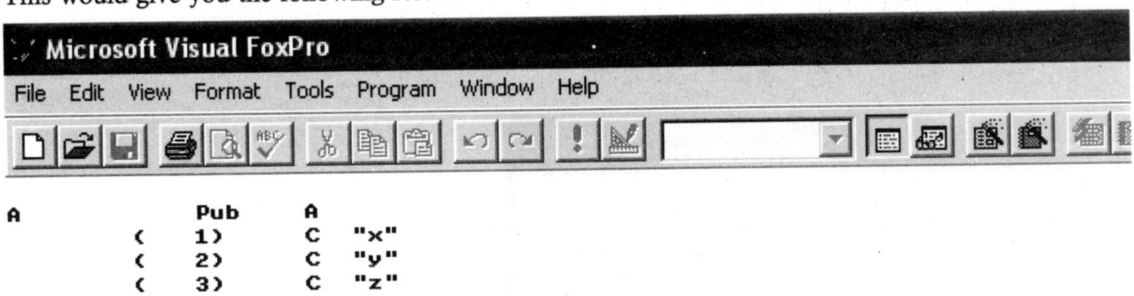

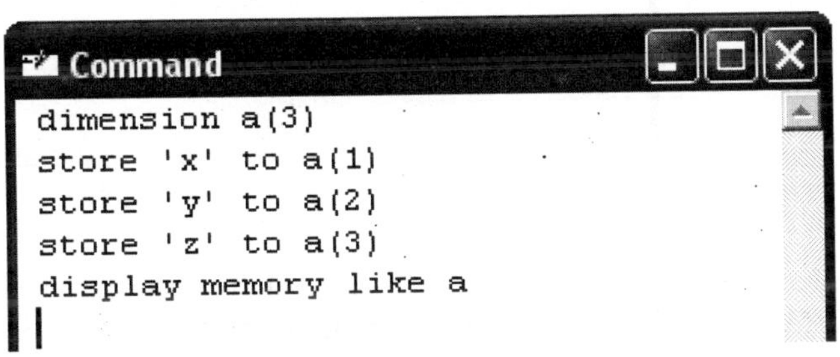

Next we change the dimension to make it a two-dimensional array with the following commands:

```
DIMENSION X(2,3)
DISPLAY MEMORY LIKE X
```

This will show the result as shown on the next page.

When you change from one dimensional array to two dimensional array, Visual FoxPro places data from the elements in the original array into the first row of two-dimensional array. Visual FoxPro initializes the remaining elements in the array as Logical elements and store a logical .F. (False) values.

Using Arrays with Table Files

A common use of array is to move fields to or from a table file. The following Visual FoxPro commands can be used to do so:

a. SCATTER

b. COPY to ARRAY

c. COPY from ARRAY

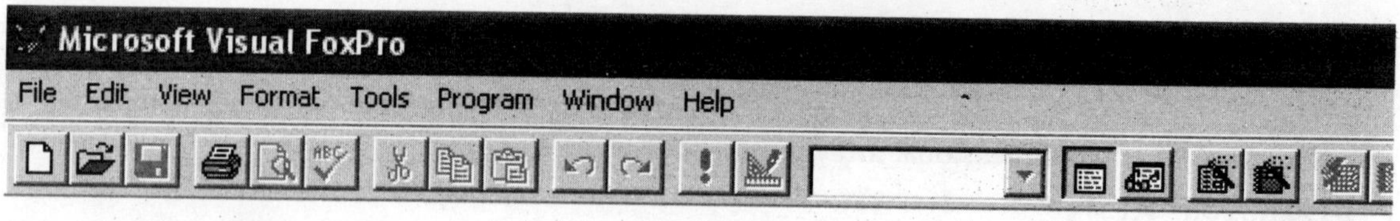


```
A               Pub    A
           (    1)     C    "x"
           (    2)     C    "y"
           (    3)     C    "z"

A               Pub    A
      (    1,   1)     C    "x"
      (    1,   2)     C    "y"
      (    1,   3)     C    "z"
      (    2,   1)     L    .F.
      (    2,   2)     L    .F.
      (    2,   3)     L    .F.
```

Command

```
dimension a(3)
store 'x' to a(1)
store 'y' to a(2)
store 'z' to a(3)
display memory like a
dimension a(2,3)
display memory like a
```

d. GATHER

Using Scatter Command

This command also creates a one-dimensional array. It moves data from the current table record into an array. The fields of the current record are transferred, beginning with the first field of the record, into the corresponding elements of the array. The general form for the command is:

```
SCATTER TO ARRAY
```

For example

```
USE TABLE1
SCATTER TO XYZ
DISPLAY MEMORY LIKE XYZ
```

In the above case the data from the table1 is scattered into an array called zyz. See the result on the next page. If the array xyz does not exist, scatter command automatically creates it.

If you want to transfer selected fields, use the field clause. For example:

```
SCATTER FIELDS NAME, ADDRESS, CITY TO XYZ
```

Above command transfers or copies only name, address and city fields to the array xyz.

Displaying Using '?' Command

The syntax for this is;

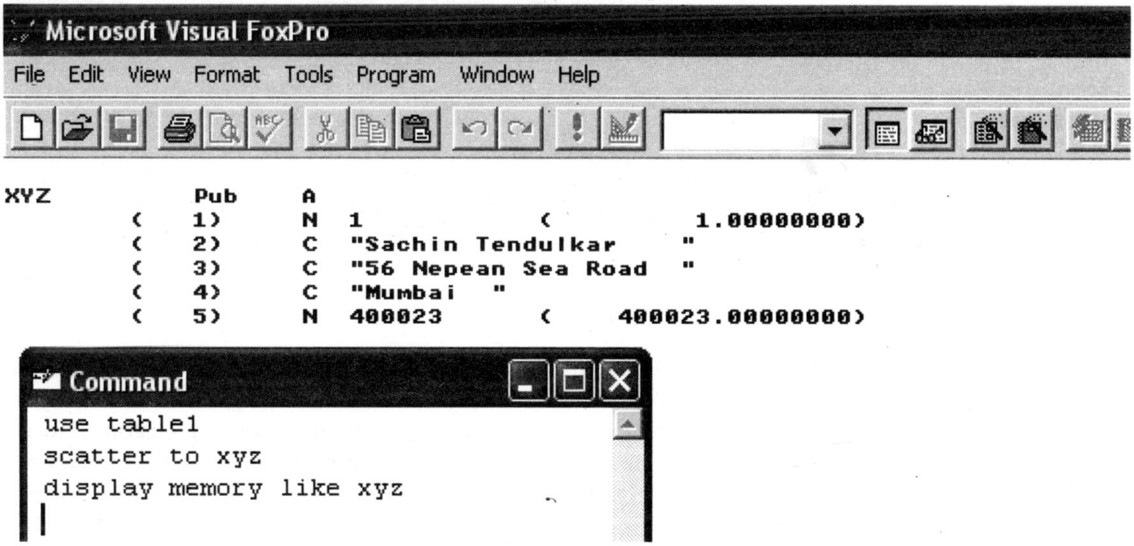


```
? MNAME, ABC, XYZ
```

The ? displays the specific values that had been stored in the memory variables. However, you can use Display memory or List memory commands to show existing memory variable values. Enter the following command to display active memory variable.

```
DISPLAY MEMORY
```

Accepting from User

Variables can be accepted from the user in Visual FoxPro using two commands, mainly, Accept and Input. When you use either Accept or Input commands, you enclose the prompt to be asked in apostrophes (') or double quotes ("). You also need to provide a variable to store the answer to the question. For example, if you type the following commands:

```
ACCEPT "ENTER YOUR NAME:" TO MYNAME
```

You will see the prompt on the screen as shown in figure below.

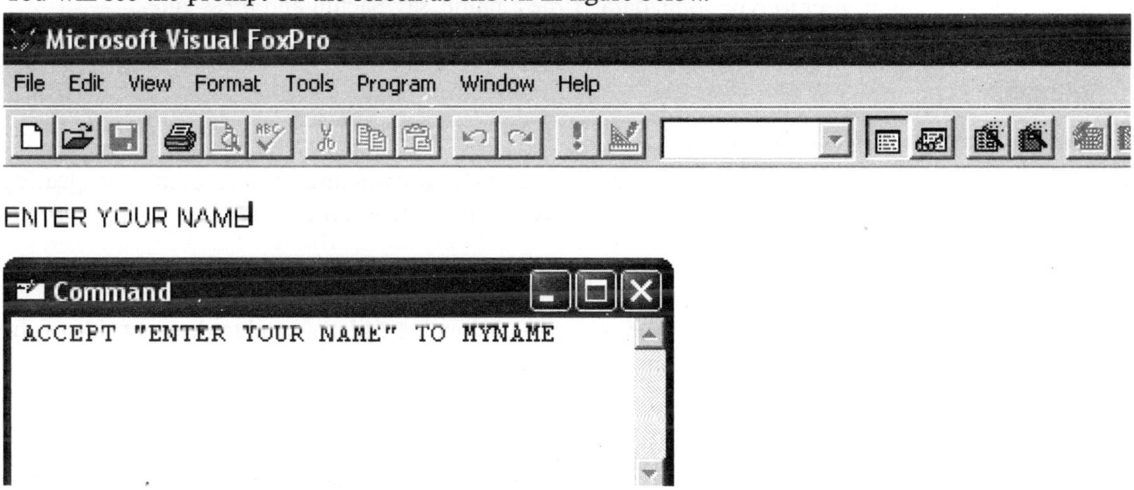

Visual FoxPro will leave the prompt on the screen until you type a name. Type any name and then press Enter. After you press enter, the Command window appears because the program is over. If you now type:

```
?MYNAME
```

you will see the name you typed is displayed on the screen

The input command is very similar to Accept command, but it is used to get numeric values from the user. It shows a prompt for the user and then accepts number from the user through the keyboard. Finally, the number keyed through the keyboard is stored in numeric type variable.

@...Say ...Get Command

You can also use a combination of @, Say, Get and Read commands to prompt the user to enter the values from the keyboard. The @ command allows you to perform many things such as displaying information, inputting data in fields/variables, clearing selected screen and designing custom screens. Most computer terminals have a video screen with 25 rows with 80 columns each. Such a screen can display information in 25 horizontal rows and 80 vertical columns. The rows are numbered from top to bottom (i.e., 0 to 24) and columns are numbered from left to right (i.e., 0 to 79). For example to display:

```
"ENTER YOUR NAME"
```

message in row 3 and column 8, type the following command in command file:

```
MYNAME = SPACE(20)
CLEAR
@ 3,8 SAY "ENTER YOUR NAME" GET MYNAME
READ
```

In the above example the following takes place:

Myname = space(20)	Creates a variable called Myname containing 20 blank spaces
Clear	Clears the screen
@ 3,8 say.....	Displays the message beginning from row 3 and column 8
Read	It puts the cursor into the prompt for the variable Myname and waits for the user to type some data. Type a name, say Sachin and press enter.

To verify that Myname variable now contains the data you typed, enter the command:

```
?MYNAME
```

Clearing Screen with @ Command

You can clear your screen using the @ ...clear statement. This command is very useful for clearing unwanted information from part of the screen before a new information is presented on it. Now use the following command and see the screen.

```
@15,35 CLEAR
```

you will notice that Visual FoxPro has blanked the screen below the 14th row and to the right side of the 34th column. Similarly, use another @..clear command:

```
@10,25 CLEAR
```

and Visual FoxPro blanks more portion of the screen.

Drawing and Clearing Box using @ Command

The @ command can also be used to draw lines and boxes on the screen. Boxes can be drawn with a single or doubleline border. For drawing a box, you need to specify the top-left and bottom-right co-ordinates of the box. First clear the screen with Clear command and then draw two boxes one with single border and the other with double border. For this, type the following in the Command window:

```
@1,5 TO 4,25
@3,30 TO 8,50 DOUBLE
```

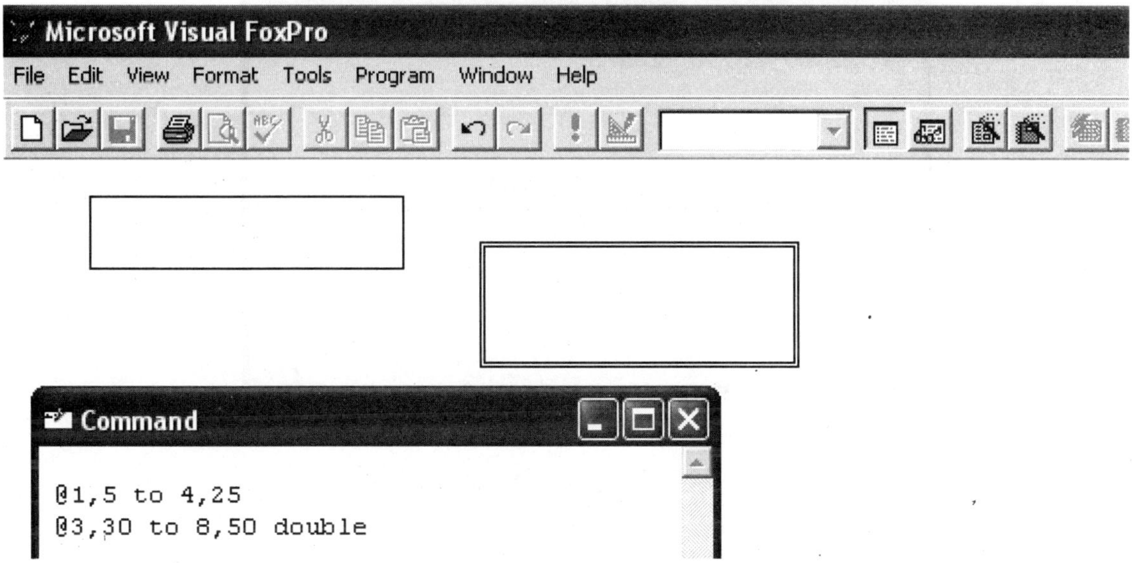

See the result above. Now if you want you can give the command in a specific way, the result would however, remain the same.

```
@2,6 SAY "SINGLE LINED BOX"
@6,32 SAY "DOUBLE LINED BOX"
```

For drawing lines at least one of the variable in the above cases would reamain the same. Look at the following example and you would notice the difference. For example to draw a horizontal line on the screen, type the following in the Command window:

```
@1,5 TO 5,5 DOUBLE
```

similarly, to draw vertical line on the screen, type: the following in the Command window:

```
@20,1 TO 20,10 DOUBLE
```

The result is shown on the next page.

Displaying and Manipulating Information with ?/?? Commands

Both ? and ?? can be used to display data on the screen. The difference between ? and ?? command is that the ? command issues a carriage return before printing the expression list, so it is positioned one line below the previous item displayed. The ?? command does not include a linefeed and carriage return before the display, so the subsequent value is displayed on the current line.

For example, type the following in the Command window:

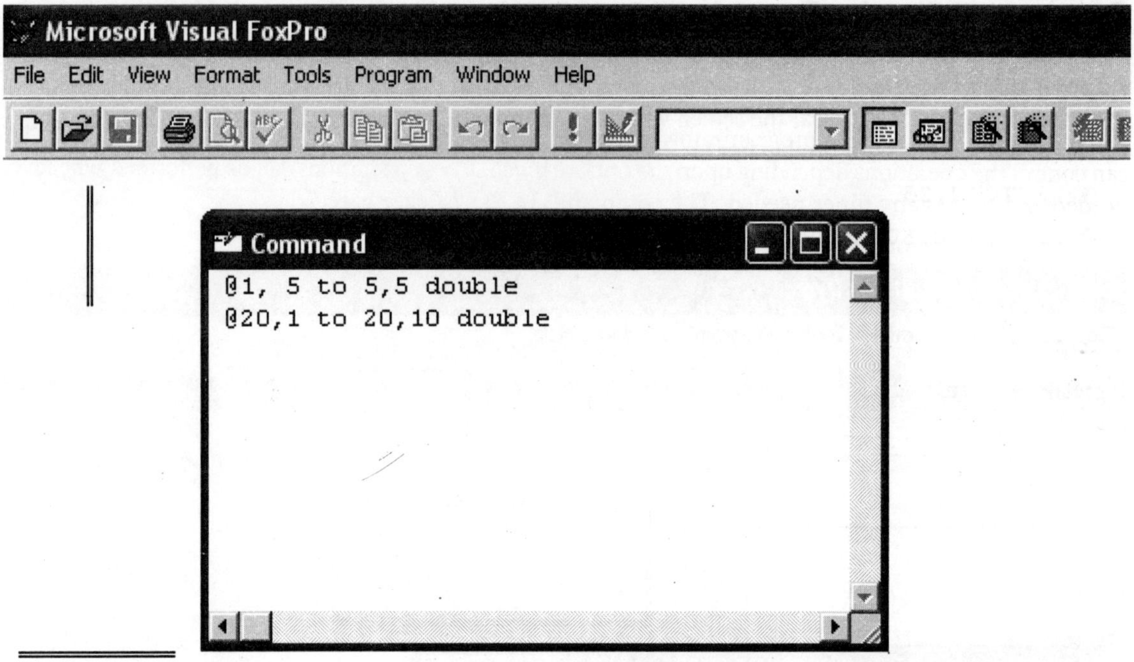


```
? "ENTER NAME:"
?? NAME
? "ENTER SALARY:"
?? SALARY
```

PICTURE CLAUSES

The picture clause restricts entry to specific characters and it validates formats but not values. The following table lists the different picture clause codes.

Symbol	*Meaning*
A	Accepts only alphabetic characters
L	Accepts on Y (yes) or N (no)
N	Accepts letters and digits
X	Accepts any character
9	Accepts only digits or sign
#	Accepts digits, blanks nad sign
!	Converts lowercase letters to uppercase
$	Display currency symbol
.	Specifies decimal point precision
,	Left of the decimal

For example, if you want to get std_code that must begin with an alphabet and has three digits then you can write Picture 'A999'.

CONTROL FLOW

Visual FoxPro like all other programming languages support the various logical commands where you can control the operations depending upon the options given. These operations can be performed whenever needed and how many times needed. The commands in this category are:

Looping statements

Selection Statements

Looping

It means that you do the things again and again. Or for a specified number of times. Visual FoxPro provides three loop commands. These are:

a. Do While...Enddo

b. Scan...Endscan

c. For ...Endfor

Let us first take up Do While ... Enddo

Do while...Enddo

There will be many times when your program will need to perform the same task repeatedly. FoxPro has two commands, DO WHILE and ENDDO, that are used as a matched pair to repeat a series of commands as many times as necessary. The commands that you want to repeat are enclosed between the DO WHILE and the ENDDO commands.

The DO WHILE command always begins the loop, and the ENDDO command normally ends it. The commands inside the loop will continue to execute until the condition that you've specified, as a part of the DO WHILE command, is no longer true. The condition that you specify will determine when the loop should stop; otherwise, the loop could go on indefinitely. The format is

```
DO WHILE CONDITION
   [COMMANDS...]
ENDDO
```

As long as the condition within the DO WHILE command is true, the commands between the DO WHILE and the ENDDO commands are executed. Whenever ENDDO is reached, FoxPro returns to the top of the loop and reevaluates the condition. If the condition is still true, FoxPro executes the commands within the loop again; if the condition is not true, FoxPro jumps to the command following the ENDDO command. If the condition is false when the DO WHILE command is first encountered, none of the commands in the loop will be executed, and the program proceeds to the first command that follows the ENDDO command.

As an example, you could use the DO WHILE and ENDDO commands to create a command file that will print all the names and addresses in the Dayal Videos database, with triple line-spacing between them. Go to the Command window and open a new command file named TRIPLE, by entering

```
MODIFY COMMAND TRIPLE
```

When the FoxPro Editor comes up, enter the following command file:

```
SET TALK OFF
USE MEMBERS
SET PRINT ON
DO WHILE .NOT. EOF()
   ? FIRSTNAME + LASTNAME
   ? ADDRESS
   ? CITY + STATE + " " + PINCODE
   ?
   ?
   ?
   SKIP
ENDDO
? "TRIPLE REPORT COMPLETED."
SET PRINT OFF
EJECT
```

Before you save this command file, take a brief look at its design. After such preliminaries as activating the MEMBERS file and routing the output to the printer, the program begins the DO WHILE loop. The condition for DO WHILE is .NOT. EOF(), which simply means, "As long as the end of the file-EOF()-is NOT reached, continue the DO WHILE loop." The first three statements inside the loop print the name and address from the current record. Next, three question-mark symbols print three blank lines between each pair of records.

The SKIP command moves the pointer down one record, each time the body of the DO WHILE loop is executed. (If this command were absent, the pointer would never reach the end of the file, the condition would never become false, and the program would never leave the loop. It would, in fact, simply continue printing the same record over and over again!)

The ENDDO command is then reached, so FoxPro returns to the DO WHILE statement to re-valuate the condition. If the pointer hasn't reached the end-of-file, the loop is repeated. Once the end-of-file has been reached, FoxPro proceeds past the ENDDO command. The final two commands in the program are executed, and control is returned on the Command window.

Indenting the commands between DO WHILE and ENDDO is a convention that can help you identify the body of the loop. This is especially helpful if you have nested DO WHILE loops-that is, placed a DO WHILE loop within a DO WHILE loop.

After typing the above commands, press Ctrl + S to save the command file to disk, and close the window. Then make sure your printer is on, and enter the command DO TRIPLE. The command file will print the names and addresses on your printer, with three blank lines between each pair.

Scan...Endscan

Another set of commands you may encounter in working with FoxPro programs are the SCAN and ENDSCAN commands. These commands, like DO WHILE and ENDDO, are a matched pair. Also like DO WHILE and ENDDO, the SCAN and ENDSCAN commands let you create a repetitive loop in which operations are performed for a group of records in a database.

The syntax for these commands is

```
SCAN[SCOPE]  [FOR  CONDITION][WHILE  CONDITION]
  [COMMANDS...]
ENDSCAN
```

The SCAN and ENDSCAN commands are simpler alternatives to the DO WHILE and ENDDO commands. If you simply wish to use DO WHILE and ENDDO to perform repetitive processing, you can often use SCAN and ENDSCAN instead, and use slightly fewer lines of programming code.

As an example, perhaps you want to write a program that, using a DO WHILE loop, would print the name and tape limit for every person in the database who has a tape limit of more than three. You could accomplish the task with a program like this:

```
USE MEMBERS
SET PRINT ON
DO WHILE .NOT. EOF()
  IF TAPELIMIT > 3
    ? LASTNAME, FIRSTNAME
    ?? TAPELIMIT
  ENIF
  SKIP
ENDDO
```

By comparison, you could use the SCAN and ENDSCAN commands to accomplish the same task. An example of the program code using SCAN and EDSCAN is shown here;

```
USE MEMBERS
SET PRINT ON
SCAN FOR TAPELIMIT > 3
  ? LASTNAME, FIRSTNAME
  ?? TAPELIMIT
ENDSCAN
```

Because the SCAN command combined the WHILE and IF clauses to specify the condition (a tape limit greater than three), you can use fewer lines of program code to accomplish the same task.

FoxPro automatically skips to the next successive record when it encounters ENDSCAN, unless you are at the end of the file. Once the end of the file is reached, program control drops out of the loop and moves on to the next command. Note that program control may exit from the loop before the end of the file is reached if you include a WHILE clause as a part of the SCAN statement.

If...else...endif

In many command files, FoxPro needs to perform different operations depending on a user's response to an option, a previous calculation or operation, or different values encountered in a database. For example if a program's main menu gives the user a choice of editing or printing a record, the program must be able to check which choice the user makes, and then start the appropriate operation. FoxPro can use the

IF, ELSE, and ENDIF commands to branch to the part of the program where the chosen operation is performed. Much like the DO WHILE-ENDDO loop, the IF and ENDIF commands are used as a matched pair, enclosing a number of commands. The ELSE command is optional, and is used within the body of IF-ENDIF as another decision step. The IF and ENDIF commands can be used to decide between actions in a program.

The format of the command is

```
IF  CONDITION
   [COMMANDS...]
ELSE
   [COMMANDS...]
ENDIF
```

This decision-making command must always start with IF and end with ENDIF. The commands that you place between the IF and ENDIF statements determine exactly what will occur if the condition is true. (Again, indenting the commands within the body of IF-ENDIF makes the flow of the program easier to understand.) The optional ELSE statement can be used to specify an alternate set of commands that will be carried out only if the condition in the IF statement is not true. A good way to build IF and ELSE structures is to write them first in pseudocode, then in the FoxPro command language, and then compare them to make sure your commands specify what you originally intended. For example:

Pseudocode	**FoxPro**
If last name is	IF LASTNAME = "Sharma"
Sharma, then display	? LASTNAME
last name.	ENDIF
If monthly rent is	IF RENTMONTH < 300
less than Rs. 300, then	? "Reasonably priced."
display "Reasonably	ENDIF
priced."	

Using IF and ENDIF alone works fine for making a single decision, but if you wish to add an alternative choice, you need the ELSE statement:

Pseudocode	**FoxPro**
If last name is	IF LASTNAME = "Sharma"
Cook,e then print	?LASTNAME
last name; or lese print	ELSE
"There is no one by that	? "There is no one by
name in this database."	that name in this
	database."
	ENDIF

FoxPro evaluates the condition following the IF command to see if any action should be taken. If no action is necessary (that is, the condition is false), FoxPro looks for an ELSE statement. If it fins one, it executes the commands following the term ELSE; otherwise, control simply passes to the next command after the ENDIF command. In the following example, if SALARY is not 10 then the STORE command will not be executed, and FoxPro will proceed to the command following ENDIF:

```
IF SALARY = 10
  STORE SALARY TO MATCH
ENDIF
```

You can also use multiple IF-ENDIF commands if you need to have the program make more than one decision. Consider this example:

```
? "ENTER 1 TO PRINT MAILING LABELS OR 2 TO EDIT."
INPUT "WHAT IS YOUR CHOICE?" TO CHOICE
IF CHOICE = 1
  DO TRIPLE
ENDIF
IF CHOICE = 2
  DO CHANGES
ENDIF
```

The answer that the user types is stored in a memory variable called CHOICE. One of three things can happen then, depending on whether the user has typed a 1, 2, or something else in response to the question. If CHOICE equals 1, the TRIPLE program is run from disk.

If CHOICE equals 2, then CHANGES program is run. If CHOICE equals neither 1 or 2, then the program proceeds to the next command after the ENDIF command.

Nesting IF-ENDIFs

You can use nested IF-ENDIF statements, which are IF-ENDIF statements placed inside of other IF-ENDIF statements. For the innermost IF-ENDIF statement to be processed, the condition tested by the outermost IF-ENDIF statement must be true.

The following is an example of a nested IF-ENDIF statement:

```
INPUT "DISPLAY REPORT ON (S)CREEN OR (P)RINTER?" TO ANS
IF UPPER (ANS) = "P"
  INPUT "READY PRINTER, PRESS ENTER, OR TYPE C THEN;
  PRESS ENTER TO CANCEL REPORT." TO ANS2
    *USER CANCELED PRINT RUN.
    RETURN
  ENDIF
  REPORT FORM MEMBERS TO PRINT
  EJECT
ENDIF
```

In this example, whether the innermost IF-ENDIF will ever be processed is determined by the response supplied to the outermost IF-ENDIF statement. If the user does not type P for printer, FoxPro skips ahead to the outermost ENDIF statement. If the user does respond with P for printer, FoxPro displays the "Ready printer" message, and the innermost IF-ENDIF tests for the user's response and takes appropriate action.

Tip If you are going to nest IF-ENDIF statements, then indenting your commands will help you keep track of whether you have matching statements (that is, an ENDIF for each IF). It is very important to make sure that nested IFs and ENDIFs match up, or else your program will incorporate serious (and often hard-to-find) errors.

IIF()

Within programs, you may want to make use of the IIF (Immediate IF) function. The syntax for the function is

```
IIF(CONDITION, EXPRESSION1, EXPRESSION2)
```

If the condition specified is true, FoxPro returns the first expression; if the condition is false, FoxPro returns the second expression. As an example, the statement

```
CREDITOK = IIF (INCOME>=15000, "YES", "NO")
```

would, when processed in a program, store a character expression of "YES" to the CREDITOK variable if the amount in INCOME was equal to or greater than 15,000. Otherwise, it would store the character expression "NO". In effect, this statement performs the same task as the following commands:

```
IF INCOME >= 15000
  CREDITOK = "YES"
ELSE
  CREDITOK = "NO"
ENDIF
```

The advantage of the Immediate IF function is that it takes fewer lines of code to accomplish the same task, and it is executed slightly faster.

Using the IF-ENDIF Statement

You can use the IF-ENDIF statement in a command file to search for and display data from a specific record in your database. For example, if you want to find a member named Verma, you can use the ACCEPT and IF-ENDIF commands to search for the record. (This operation can be done faster with SEEK, but for demonstration purposes, a combination of IF and DO WHILE is used here.)

First, let's use pseudocode to outline what needs to be done:

USE MEMBERS database.

ACCEPT the last name.

BEGIN the DO-WHILE loop.

IF the Lastname field = the ACCEPT variable,

PRINT (on the screen) name, address, tape limit, and expiration date.

END the IF test.

SKIP forward one record.

END the DO-WHILE loop.

RETURN to the command window.

Now create a command file by entering

```
MODIFY COMMAND SHOWMEMB
```

When the FoxPro Editor appears in a window, enter the following;

```
*THIS PROGRAM FINDS AND SHOWS DATA IN THE MEMBERS FILE.
USER MEMBERS
SET TALK OFF
CLEAR
*BEGIN LOOP THAT CONTAINS COMMANDS TO DISPLAY RECORD.
ACCEPT "SEARCH FOR WHAT LAST NAME? "TO SNAME
DO WHILE .NOT. EOF()
  IF LASTNAME = SNAME
    ? "LAST NAME IS: "
    ?? LASTNAME
    ? "FIRST NAME IS: "
    ?? FIRSTNAME
    ? "ADDRESS IS: "
    ?? ADDRESS
    ? CITY + STATE + " " + PINCODE
    ?
    ? "TAPE LIMIT IS: "
    ?? TAPELIMIT
    ? "EXPIRATION DATE IS: "
    ?? EXPIREDATE
    ?
  ENDIF
  SKIP
ENDDO
WAIT
RETURN
```

After saving the file with CTRL+S, try running the program by entering DO SHOWMEMB in the Command window. In response to the lastname prompt that appears on the screen, enter Verma, and FoxPro will search the database for the record containing this name. Run the program again, and enter Dayal. You will see the records for both Dayal displayed.

In the search you used the ACCEPT, IF, and ENDIF commands. The ACCEPT command stored the name that you entered into the memory variable SNAME. The IF loop began a decision-making process that stated the condition, "If the memory variable SNAME contains the same name as the Lastname field, then execute the commands that follow the IF command." There is no limit to the number of commands that you can place between IF and ENDIF in the loop. You can also link multiple IF-ENDIF and ELSE commands if multiple choices are needed within a program.

Do Case...Endcase

Your program may need to make more than two or three decisions, based on a single-response. A series of IF-ENDIF statements could do the job, but using more than three IF-ENDIFs to test the value of one field (or memory variable) is unwieldy. There is an easier way: use the CASE statement. With the CASE statement, the IF-ENDIF tests are made into alternative cases of one long conditional statement, and FoxPro then chooses the first case, the second case, or whichever other case matches the user's response.

The CASE statement is framed by a matched pair of terms: DO CASE and ENDCASE. All conditional choices are declared between DO CASE and ENDCASE. The OTHERWISE term functions exactly like the ELSE in an IF-ENDIF statement. The general format is

```
DO CASE
   CASE CONDITION
   [COMMANDS...]
   [CASE CONDITION...]
   [COMMANDS...]
   [OTHERWISE]
   [COMMANDS...]
ENDCASE
```

Whenever FoxPro encounters a DO CASE command, it examines each CASE term until it finds a condition that is true; then it executes the commands below that line, until it encounters either the next CASE term or the ENDCASE term (whichever comes first).

If you want to create a simple menu that offers a choice of displaying a record, printing labels, editing a record, or adding a record, you could write a command file like this:

```
CLEAR
? "1. DISPLAY A MEMBERSHIP RECORD"
?
? "2. PRINT THE MEMBERSHIP DATABASE"
?
? "3. CHANGE A MEMBERSHIP RECORD"
?
INPUT "CHOOSE A SELECTION " TO SELECT
DO CASE
  CASE SELECT = 1
    DO SHOWMEMB
  CASE SELECT = 2
    DO TRIPLE
```

```
  CASE SELECT = 3
    DO EDITMEMB
ENDCASE
```

In this example, the INPUT statement queries the user for selection. When the user's response has been entered, it is stored in the SELECT variable. Then, in the DO CASE series, FoxPro compares the value of the SELECT variable against the test value in each CASE. If it finds a match, it executes the command file named within that CASE statement, and no other CASE statement is evaluated.

If no match is found, FoxPro proceeds to the next statement after the ENDCASE command. Like IF-ENDIF, the DO CASE and ENDCASE commands are used in pairs. You must always end a CASE series with an ENDCASE command. You should use DO CASE to process menu selections if you have more than three choices. For example, if you wanted to offer the same three selections from the last program using IF-ENDIF and ELSE, the command file might look like this:

```
CLEAR
? "1. DISPLAY A MEMBERSHIP RECORD"
?
? "2. PRINT THE MEMBERSHIP DATABASE"
?
? "3. CHANGE A MEMBERSHIP RECORD"
?
INPUT "CHOOSE A SELECTION" TO SELECT
IF SELECT = 1
  DO SHOWMEMB
ENDIF
IF SELECT = 2
  DO TRIPLE
ENDIF
IF SELECT = 3
  DO EDITMEMB
ENDIF
```

Using IF-ENDIF becomes more complex than DO CASE as the number of choices increases.

Let's use a CASE statement to create a main menu for the Dayal Videos database. (Note that FoxPro provides much better and more attractive ways to create menus, but this technique is used here for the sake of simplicity.) In the Command window, enter the statement MODIFY COMMAND MENU1, and when the FoxPro Editor appears, enter the following command file:

```
USE MEMBERS
SET TALK OFF
STORE 0 TO CHOICE
DO WHILE CHOICE <> 5
```

```
CLEAR
* DISPLAY THE MENU.
? " DAYAL VIDOES MEMBERSHIP SYSTEM MENU"
?
? "1. ADD A NEW ENTRY TO THE DATABASE."
? "2. CHANGE AN EXISTING ENTRY."
? "3. PRODUCE THE MEMBERSHIP REPORT."
? "4. DISPLAY DATA REGARDING A PARTICULAR MEMBER."
? "5. EXIT THIS PROGRAM."
INPUT "ENTER SELECTION:" TO CHOICE
DO CASE
  CASE CHOICE=1
    APPEND
  CASE CHOICE=1
    DO EDITMEMB
  CASE CHOICE=3
    REPORT FORM SAMPLE
  CASE CHOICE=4
    DO SHOWMEMB
  CASE CHOICE=5
    CLOSE DATABASES
    SET TALK ON
    RETURN
  ENDCASE
ENDDO
```

The menu offers five choices, and the INPUT command stores the user's response in the CHOICE variable. If FoxPro finds a matching choice, it executes the command or commands that follow that choice.

Save this command file by pressing Ctrl + S, and close the window. When the prompt reappears, enter DO MENU1. Try some of the menu choices on your own to see how the system operates. The simple menu created by the above example does the job, but is not very appealing from a visual standpoint. In the next chapter, you will learn how you can create menus that resemble the menus used by FoxPro.

EXIT AND LOOP COMMAND

The EXIT command can be used within a DO WHILE-ENDDO programming statement; it lets FoxPro exit from the DO WHILE-ENDDO loop to the first command below ENDDO. Note that an EXIT command arbitrarily placed within a DO WHILE loop will prevent FoxPro from ever reaching the commands between the terms EXIT and ENDDO; thus, EXIT makes sense only if it is executed conditionally. For this reason, you will frequently find EXIT commands inside IF-ENDIF and CASE statements. Consider the following example, in a program that lists a name based on a desired address. The same task could be accomplished with a LOCATE command, but to demonstrate the EXIT command, this program uses a DO WHILE loop.

```
USE MEMBERS
SET TALK OFF
GO TOP
ACCEPT "WHAT IS THE ADDRESS- " TO CHOICE
DO WHILE .NOT. EOF()
  IF ADDRESS = CHOICE
    ? LASTNAME, FIRSTNAME
    EXIT
    SKIP
ENDIF
```

If the contents of Address (a field) match CHOICE (a variable), the EXIT command will cause the DO WHILE loop to terminate. Otherwise, the SKIP command below the ENDIF statement will advance the pointer by one record, and the comparison will be repeated. If no match is found at all, control will finally pass out of the loop after the last record is read. Use EXIT commands conservatively: a program that is always jumping out of loops-and around the program, for that matter-is difficult to follow and debug, and is contrary to good program design. Most DO WHILEs that have EXITs can be redesigned to omit them.

CANCEL

The CANCEL command halts execution of a FoxPro command file and returns you to the Command window. It can be useful when you are testing command files. However, using CANCEL in a completed FoxPro program may be unwise. CANCEL simply drops the user into the Command window, and the inexperienced user may not know how to restart the program or exit FoxPro. QUIT is an alternative command, which will exit both the command file and FoxPro, and return the user to the Windows desktop. You can include an option on your command file's mainmenu that invokes the QUIT command.

WAIT

The WAIT command halts execution of a FoxPro program until a key is pressed. WAIT can also display a message or prompt and store the value of the pressed key to a character variable. The normal format of the command is

```
WAIT [PROMPT] [TO MEMORY-VARIABLE]
```

Both prompt and memory-variable are optional. If a prompt is not specified, FoxPro supplies the message "Press any key to continue..." as a default prompt.

As an example, to display a message, halt execution of a program until a key is pressed, and store that key as a variable named ANSWER, you could use the following command:

```
WAIT "ENTER Y TO BEGIN PROCESSING TRANSACTIONS, ANY OTHER KEY TO
CONTINUE:" TO ANSWER
```

You could then use an IF-ELSE-ENDIF structure to test the value of ANSWER and take different actions depending on the result.

ZAP

The ZAP command is a one-step command for erasing all records from a database while leaving the structure of the database intact. Using ZAP is functionally equivalent to entering **DELETE ALL** and then entering **PACK**. However, ZAP operates considerably faster than a DELETE ALL command followed by a PACK command. If you include the ZAP command in a program, you may want to place the SET SAFETY OFF command above it; this tells FoxPro not to ask for confirmation before erasing all records from the database. If so, make sure to SET SAFETY ON again afterwards. Also, since the ZAP command is destructive, be very careful in using it. If the database file which you are ZAPping is anything more important than a temporary scratch database, be sure to make a backup copy of the file before testing the ZAP command.CANCEL

The CANCEL command halts execution of a FoxPro command file and returns you to the Command window. It can be useful when you are testing command files. However, using CANCEL in a completed FoxPro program may be unwise. CANCEL simply drops the user into the Command window, and the inexperienced user may not know how to restart the program or exit FoxPro. QUIT is an alternative command, which will exit both the command file and FoxPro, and return the user to the Windows desktop. You can include an option on your command file's mainmenu that invokes the QUIT command.

PROCEDURES AND PARAMETERS

A procedure is a set of instructions that work as a unit. It is a sequence of Visual FoxPro commands that is functionally equivalent to a program, except that it resides in another program file. You can create procedures in the same way as you create programs, using the Modi Comm command [Visual FoxPro assumes the extension .PRG if you do not include the extension in the file name]. The only difference is that you have to create the procedure by giving the following command:

```
PROCEDURE <PROCEDURE_NAME>
   <COMMANDS>
   [RETURN]
ENDPROC
```

Where procedure_name is the name of the procedure that you create. Procedure name must begin with a letter or underscore(_) and it may contain any combination of letters, numbers and underscores.

The procedure name is followed by a series of Visual FoxPro commands. The return statement is used to return control to the calling program or to another program. The return statement is optional. If you do not write it, the function, by default returns to the calling program when it quits. The endproc statement signifies the end of the procedure.

You can make any number of procedures and functions in a procedure file – a text file that contains only procedures and user-defined functions. Once can also place procedures within the programs that call them. They are placed after the Return command that ends the main portion of the program (sometimes called the mainline routine).

The procedure file is opened with the following command:

```
SET PROCEDURE TO <PROCEDURE_NAME>
```

Once a procedure file is open, you can execute any procedure or function it contains from the Command window.

You can call a procedure located in the same file or in some other file using a simple do command. You can execute a procedure located in any file by naming this file in the Do command, as follows:

```
DO <PROCEDURE NAME> IN <PROGRAM FILE>
```

Visual FoxPro closes any procedure file previously opened before opening a new procedure file. To close a procedure file, without opening another, you can use:

```
SET PROCEDURE TO
```

Or

```
CLOSE PROCEDURE
```

Visual FoxPro does not allow you to edit an open procedure file, although you can open the file in an editing window to view its contents. However, if you begin to edit the text, Visual FoxPro closes the procedure file and displays a message window in the upper-right corner of the screen informing you of this fact. Once the procedure file is closed, you can proceed with the editing session. Remember to reopen the file with a new Set Procedure command after you have made your changes. The Set Procedure command causes Visual FoxPro to recompile the procedure file.

Scope of Variables

A variable's scope specifies the variable makes its value known to other procedures and functions. Visual FoxPro offers two commands, Private and Public that are used to classify variables. These commands let you control the application of variable from one Visual FoxPro command file to another. If you have created a variable in one command file and you need to use it in other command file then you should declare them public. However, if you want the variable you are declaring should be available only to the program that has created the variable and also to programs that are called by that specific program, then declare it as private.

Declaring a variable as public requires two steps:

a. Public <variable_name>

b. declaring the actual variable with the Store command or with an assignment symbol (=).

For example:

```
PUBLIC ABC
ABC = 124.4
```

You can also declare several variable as public by typing a list, such as:

```
PUBLIC X,Y,Z
STORE 'HIM' TO X
STORE 'MOTOR' TO Y
STORE '58.45' TO Z
```

A private variable can be visible to all procedures called by the command file. You do this by not declaring the variable in the Procedure file. For example:

```
* NAME.PRG
PRIVATE NAME
```

```
NAME="RAMESH"
DO NEWNAME
? NAME
RETURN
* PROCEDURE NEWNAME
PROCEDRUE NEWNAME
  ? NAME
RETURN
```

In the above example, the procedure newname displayed "Ramesh" while the main program also displayed "Ramesh". Thus you see that even though you declare the variable Private in the name.prg command file, it is visible to the procedure file newname.

You can use the ALL, LIKE and EXCEPT options with PRIVATE to cover more than one variable at a time. Examples of ALL, LIKE and EXCEPT options with PRIVATE would include:

Command	*Meaning*
PRIVATE ALL	Declares all variables or arrays private
PRIVATE ALL EXCEPT X, Y, Z	Declares variables or arrays private unless they match the list
PRIVATE ALL LIKE M?	Declares variables or arrays Private that match the skeleton.

Passing Parameters

A parameter is a value passed to a function or procedure. A procedure that requires that the calling program should pass parameters to it, must use the command PARAMETER <MEMVAR LIST> as the first command after PROCEDURE <PROCEDURE_NAME>. Enclose the list of parameters in a set of parentheses and separate the parameters with commas. Then, the simplest say of passing the value to a procedure, when you call it, is to use the command Do...with <exp list>. The expressions in the list following Do...with are assigned in order, to the variables in the list following PARAMETER.

The procedure can be run by giving the following command in the Command Window:

```
DO OUTPUT IN MYPROC.PRG WITH 10, "TEN", .T.
```

Note that we have passed a numeric, string and logical value to the procedure. The arguments that appear in procedure definition are formal arguments. For example, suppose we call the "output" procedure as follows:

```
X = 10
Y = "TEN"
Z = .T.
DO OUTPUT IN MYPROC.PRG WITH X, Y, Z
```

Here, x, y and z are the actual or dummy arguments and take the value (a, b, c) from the calling procedure.

Pass by Value

It is a means of passing a variable to a procedure or function. A copy of the value of the variable is created and passed to the called routine. The procedure or function can change the value of this copy but cannot change the value of the argument in the calling procedure.

In pass by value method, the formal argument is a copy of actual argument. To understand it clearly take one real life example. Suppose your English teacher has given you one printed passage with grammatical errors and spelling mistakes on a sheet of paper and wanted you to note down the same passage in your notebook and then do corrections wherever you find any grammatical error or spelling mistake. Here, printed sheet with error represents the actual parameter and your test notebook, where you copied down the passage represents the formal parameter; what ever the changes you made in your notebook would not reflect any change to your teacher's original sheet.

Thus, in pass by value method, the values of actual parameters are passed on to formal parameters and the changes made in the values in the formal parameters are not reflected back into the actual parameters of the calling procedure.

Pass by Reference

If the programmer desires that the changes made to the formal parameter(s) be reflected on the corresponding actual parameter(s) then he/she should use call by reference method for parameter passing. In this method, the calling routine passes the address of the variable to the called routine, which can then use that address to retrieve or modify the variable. When the procedure changes the value of the passed variable, the variable's original value in the calling program is also changed.

In the call by reference method, the actual and formal arguments refer to the same memory location or area. Remember that a reference is an alias, i.e., a different name for a predefined variable. That means the same variable's value can be accessed by one of the two names, i.e., the original variable's name and the reference name. Take again a real life situation to understand this situation. Suppose in your college, all the labs are numbered as 1 for chemistry lab, 2 for physics lab, and 3 for biology lab and 4 for computer lab. Now to refer to any lab you can either say the lab number or call it by its name. For example you can refer to the 'Computer lab' by either giving the original name as 'Computer lab' or by its reference "No. 4 lab".

User-Defined Functions

Apart from the built-in library functions of Visual FoxPro, users can also define and write small programs as functions to do a task relevant to their programs. Such functions are called User-Defined Functions (UDFs). These are procedures that return a value. These functions should be codified by the user, so that such functions can perform the task as desired by the user. Suppose we write a user-defined function to search for a database. If the function finds the database, it returns .T. and otherwise returns .F. The Syntax for using functions is:

```
FUNCTION <FUNCTION_NAME>
COMMANDS
[RETURN [EXPRESSION]]
ENDFUNC
```

The FUNCTION <FUNCTION_NAME> statement designates the beginning of a function in a program and identifies the function by name. This is followed by a series of commands that make up the function. You can include RETURN anywhere in the function to return control to the calling program or to another program and to the calling program or to another program and to define the value to be returned by the user-defined function. If you do not include a RETURN command, an implicit RETURN is automatically executed when the function reaches the last statement. If the RETURN command does not include a return value (or if an implicit return is executed), Visual FoxPro assigns .T. (True) as the return value.

The function ends with the ENDFUNC command. This command is optional. If you do not include this command the function will automatically quit when it encounters another function command or a procedure command or a procedure command or the end of the program file.

Difference in Parameter Passing to Functions and Procedures

By default, Visual FoxPro passes parameters to procedures by reference, which means that only one copy of the variable exists in memory. When you pass a variable to a procedure, the called procedure receives not a specific value, but a reference to this memory location, which the called routine can examine to determine the value of the variable. Because the calling program and the procedure are operating on a single copy of the variable, any changes made to the value of the variable in the procedure are passed back to the calling program.

In contrast, Visual FoxPro passes parameters to user defined functions by value. The UDF (User Defined Function) makes local copies of the all parameters and gives them the values passed by the calling program. Thus, if the UDF changes the values of variables passed as parameters, these changes are local to the function, even if the variables have the same names as variables specified by the calling program. One significant implication of this default behavior is that you do not have to declare as private the variables in the parameters list, in order to protect identically named variables in the calling program. (Other variables defined in the UDF are not given any special treatment and must be declared private if there names might coincide with variables names used in the calling program).

The most likely reason for the difference in the default treatment of parameters in procedures and user defined functions is the context in which you are expected to use these two types of routines. A procedure, like a program, can do anything – open and close databases, manipulate records, perform calculations, display or print data or carry out any other operations that you can describe with the Visual FoxPro programming language. Some of these operations are general, whereas others are tightly linked to the specific requirements of one application. In contrast, a user-defined function receives input from the calling program, processes the input and returns a single value of a particular datatype. You can view all functions as block boxes – the manner in which the return value is calculated should make no difference and any variables required to carry out its calculations should remain hidden. In practice, of course, you can decide whether to write a particular routine as a function or a procedure based primarily on the context in which you intend to call it.

USING THE MENU DESIGNER

In Visual FoxPro, the menu designer is used to create menus, menu items, submenus of menu items, etc. Using menu designer you can design menus for applications. To use the menu designer, do the following:

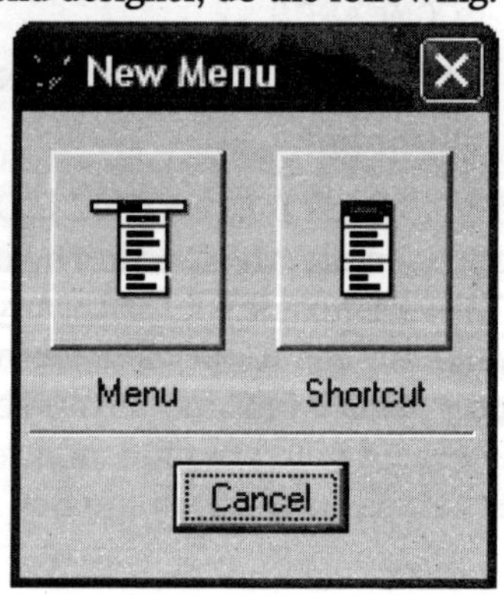

1. Enter the following command in the Command Window;

   ```
   CREATE MENU <MENU-FILE>
   ```

   Menu-file is the filename for the menu table. We have named it as "Test".
2. The menu designer window will open as shown on the next page.
3. Under the Prompt column, specify the menu titles or menu items in your menu system. For example, I have specified the File menu system. I have also chosen Close All, Close, Open, and New.
4. You will notice a double-headed arrow button to the left of the Prompt column. This is known as the Mover Control and it allows

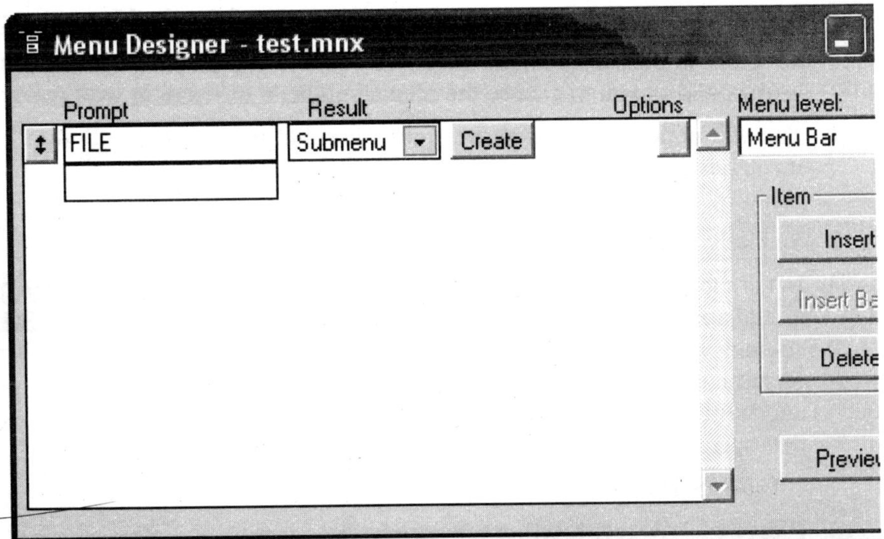

you to arrange the menu items in a certain order. Move this up and down to arrange the menu items.

5. Under the Result column, specify the action that occurs when you choose a menu title or menu item. For example, you can execute a command, open a submenu or run a procedure.

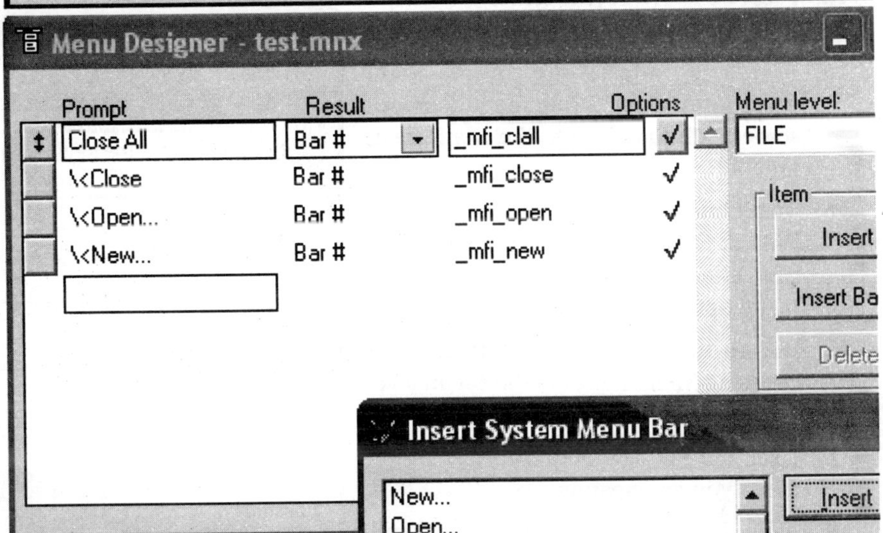

6. For the File and Edit menu items, we have chosen submenu. You will notice that a Create... Button appears to the right of the Result column. Click this button and a sub-menu-designer window appears.

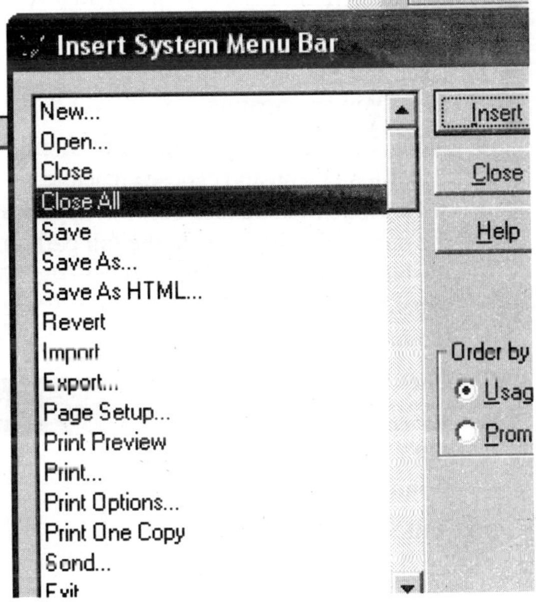

7. Click Insert Bar....Button, to display the Insert System Menu Bar dialog box, which allows you to insert standard Visual FoxPro menu items such as Open, Cut, Copy etc. For the File menu item, we choose New, Open and close menu items. These will work the same way as they work in Visual FoxPro. However you can also change their functions and short-cut keys.

8. Click the Insert Button to insert a new row in the Menu Designer window.

9. Click the Delete button to remove the current row from the Menu Designer window.
10. To return to the main designer, choose Menu Bar from the Menu level: list box. The Menu level: list box allows you to choose the menu, submenu or shortcut with which you want to work.
11. You will notice in the main menu-designer that the Create .... Button associated with the File menu has now changed to Edit... Button. This indicates that you can make changes to the File menu by clicking this button.
12. Similarly, add some standard menu items.
13. In the submenu-designer that appears, let us add a PrintMessage under the Prompt columns and choose procedure from the Result column. Click the Create button and write the following in the window that opens.

    ?"THIS IS TO HELP YOU"

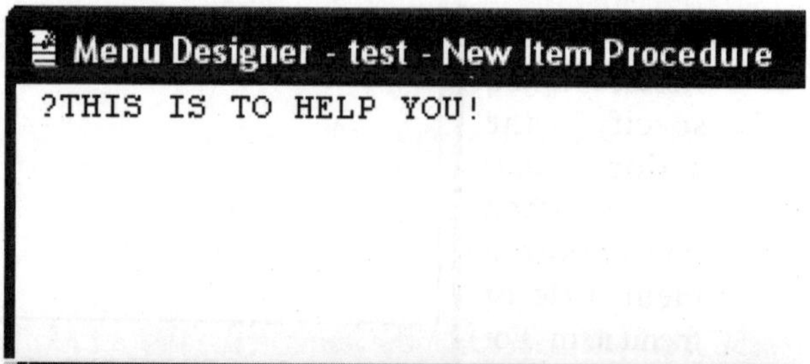

14. Press Ctrl + W keys together to return to Menu Designer.
15. Similarly, add some more string procedures to the String menu item and some math functions to the Math menu item.
16. The Options button will display the Prompt Options dialog box in which you can define keyboard shortcuts and other menu options.

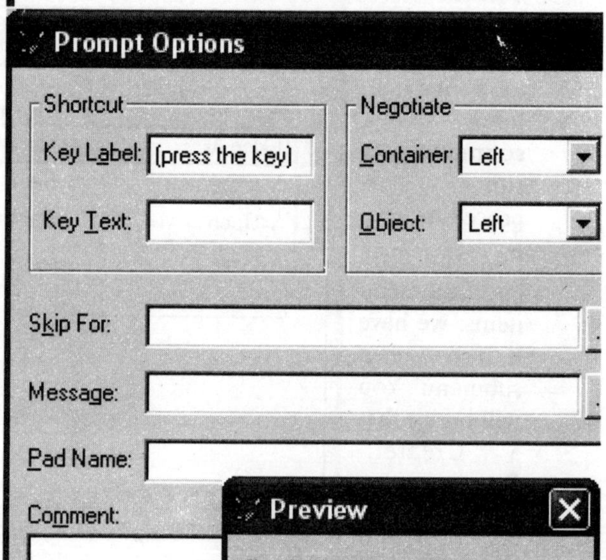

17. Return to the main menu-designer by choosing Menu Bar from the Menu level: list box.
18. Click the Preview button to display the menu you are creating.

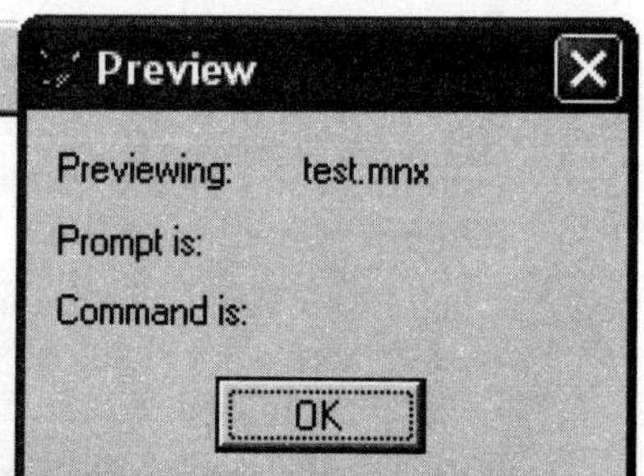

19. After you finish creating your menu, click Menu menu and choose Generate.... A Generate Menu dialog box will appear asking you to specify the output file. Either type the full path and filename or click the button with three dots to locate the file. The output file is usually saved with extension .mpr. For example, the output file for our menu is "test.mpr".
20. Click Generate button.
21. To run the menu, type the following in the Command Window:

```
DO <MENU_NAME>.MPR
```

USING THE PROJECT MANAGER

The Project Manager is used to organize and manage all your files in projects. To open the project manager, do the following:

1. Click File menu and choose new.... In the New dialog box that appears select the Project radio button and click New File button.
2. In the Create dialog box that appears, select the directory of your choice and provide a name for the new Project file. We have provided the name "Proj1". Click Save.

3. The Project Manager window will appear as shown next.
4. When the Project Manager window is active, Visual FoxPro displays the Project menu on the menu bar.
5. You will notice that the items in the Project Manager window are organized in a manner that you can expand or collapse. A plus sign appears to the left of items if there are further items of that type in the project. Once clicked, the plus sign changes to a minus sign, which you click to collapse the expanded list.
6. The project manager window can be docked to the top of your Visual FoxPro. This can be down by either dragging to the menu bar or by double-clicking the title bar of the Project manager window.

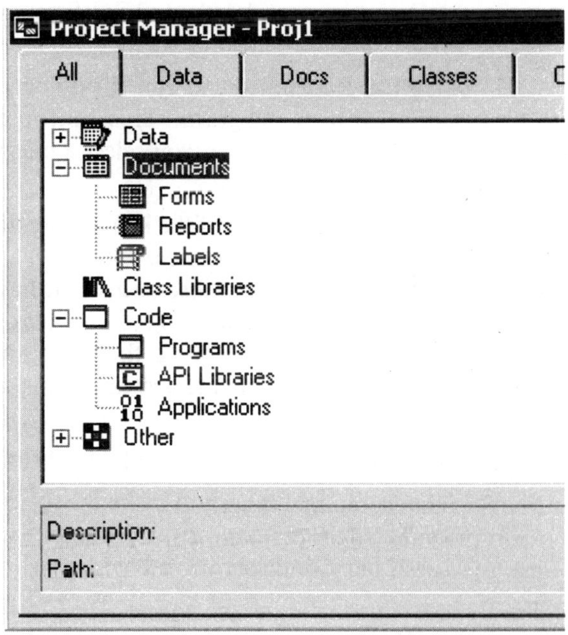

7. When the window is docked click these tabs to display their contents. You can tear off a tab by dragging them away from the menu bar. To replace it, just drag it back to its original position or click the Close box.
8. You may see a list of items in the Project manager window such as tables, Forms, reports, Queries, Labels etc. Clicking the plus (+) sign to the left of an item will display the sub-items. For example, if you click the Forms item, all the forms added to this project will be displayed.
9. Click the Add... Button to add an existing item to the currently selected item.
10. Click the New ... Button to add a new file or object. The new file or object will get added to the currently selected item.
11. Click the Modify button to make any changes to the added item. This button gets enabled only when you select an item.

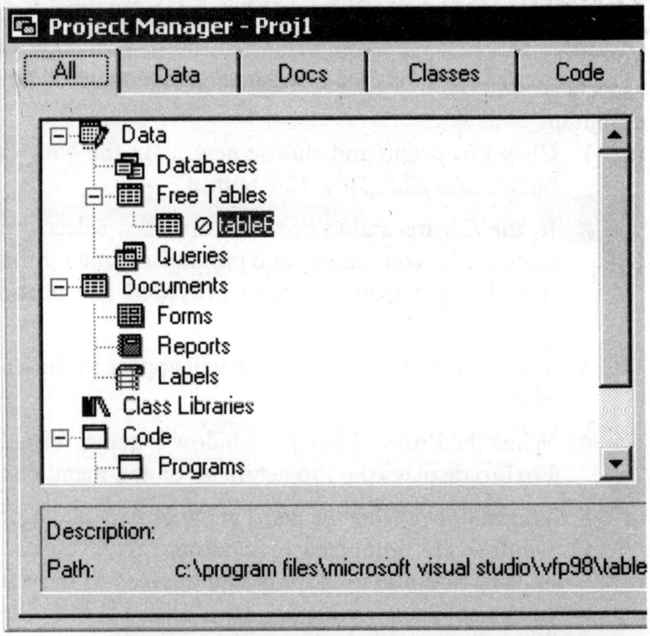

12. Click the Remove... Button to eliminate the selected file or object from the project. A window will appear asking whether you want to just remove the file from the project or you want to delete it from the disk.
13. Click the Build... Button to build a project, application or an executable or OEL server. This is done in the Build Options dialog that appears.
14. Click the Browse button to open a table in the Browse window. This button will appear only when you select a table from the "Free Tables" list.
15. Click the Open button to open a database. This button appears when a database is selected. Once opened, this button changes to Close button.

16. Click the Preview... Button to display the selected report or label in Print Preview mode.
17. Click the Run button to run the selected query, form or program. This button is enabled when you when you select a query, form, menu or program.
18. Icons appear to the left of the item to identify its type. For example, a circle with a slash / appears to the left of those items that have been excluded from the project. An item is excluded by right-clicking the item and choosing Exclude from the context menu that appears.

The same functionalities can also be obtained from the Project menu.

The Set main command is used to make the selected program, menu, query or form as the application's main program. Main program is the program that is initially executed in a compiled application. The main program name is displayed in bold letters in the Project Manager window.

The Refresh option refreshes the project. The Clean Up Project option runs the Pack command to decrease the size of the project (.PJX) file by permanently removing files that have marked for deletion. When you remove a file from a project using the Remove button, the associated record remains in the project's .PJX file but is marked for deletion.

Such files get permanently removed when you choose Clean Up Project from the project menu.

TECHNIQUE OF WRITING EFFICIENT FOXPRO PROGRAMS

You should refer to chapter number 3 for writing good program. This chapter covers in details the various aspects of writing a good program. It also discusses the various other aspects of programming like, designing, coding and flow writing. Data handling, Data input and Data verification is also discussed in it.

Multiple Choice Questions

1. For running a Visual FoxPro program, you use the command :
   (a) Run (b) Do
   (c) Program
2. Date value is stored in the format of :
   (a) DD/MM/YY (b) MM/DD/YY
   (c) YY/DD/MM
3. To move data from table to an array you use the command :
   (a) Move (b) Array
   (c) Scatter
4. Lines and boxes are drawn on the screen using which command :
   (a) Draw (b) @
   (c) Line
5. Program can be restarted after WAIT command by :
   (a) Any key (b) Enter
   (c) Esc
6. For erasing all records and keeping the structure intact, the command is :
   (a) Cancel (b) Wait
   (c) ZAP

Descriptive Type Questions

1. How do you create command files?
2. How do you run the programs?
3. What are the methods of creating arrays?
4. How do you use the @..Say...Get command?
5. Describe the various picture clauses.
6. Which commands form the looping?
7. How would you use Nested if?
8. How is the combination Do while and End do used?
9. How would you use the combination of Scan and Endscan.
10. How is EXIT command used?
11. How is CANCEL command used?
12. What does ZAP command do?
13. What are Procedures?
14. What do you understand by passing parameters?
15. How is menu designer used?
16. What is Project Manager?